Exam 70-240

MCSE

Windows 2000
Accelerated Exam

Exam: 70-240

New Riders

Brian Komar, Editor

MCSE Training Guide (70-240): Windows 2000 Accelerated Exam

International Standard Book Number: 0-7357-0979-3

Library of Congress Catalog Card Number: 00-100514

First Printing: September

05 04 03 02 01   7 6 5 4 3 2 1

Composed in Garamond and MCPdigital by New Riders Publishing

Printed in the United States of America

Trademarks

Warning and Disclaimer

PUBLISHER
David Dwyer

ASSOCIATE PUBLISHER
Al Valvano

ACQUISITIONS EDITOR
Ann Quinn

MANAGING EDITORS
Gina Brown
Sarah Kearns

PRODUCT MARKETING MANAGER
Stephanie Layton

PUBLICITY MANAGER
Susan Petro

DEVELOPMENT EDITORS
Ginny Bess
Lisa Thibault
Chris Zahn

COPY EDITORS
Nancy Albright
Chrissy Andry
Ginny Bess
Suchi Rudra
Elise Walter

TECHNICAL REVIEWERS
John Griffin
David Neilan
Ed Tetz

SOFTWARE DEVELOPMENT SPECIALIST
Michael Hunter

INDEXER
Brad Herriman

PROOFREADER
Debbie Williams

COMPOSITOR
Marcia Deboy

MANUFACTURING COORDINATOR
Chris Moos

COVER DESIGNER
Aren Howell

Contents at a Glance

Table of Contents

6 Implementing, Managing, and Troubleshooting Network Protocols and Services   229

PART II: Installing, Configuring, and Administering Microsoft Windows 2000 Server

8 Installing Windows 2000 Server   327

10 Installing Configuring and Troubleshooting Hardware Devices and Drivers   433

11 Installing Managing, Monitoring, and Optimizing System Performance, Reliability, and Availability   453

13 Installing Configuring and Troubleshooting Windows 2000 Network Connections 547

PART III: Implementing and Administering a Microsoft Windows 2000 Network Infrastructure

23 Configuring DNS for Active Directory   915

PART V: Appendices

About the Editor

Brian Komar is the owner and operator of a small consulting company in Winnipeg, Manitoba specializing in Windows 2000 design consulting and speaking. Brian is currently working with Microsoft Corporation as a contract Program Manager in the Microsoft Official Curriculum team. In addition to developing Microsoft Official Curriculum, Brian speaks at several Microsoft conferences worldwide on topics such as Active Directory design and Windows 2000 security design. Brian can be reached via email at bkomar@home.com.

About the Technical Editors

Edward Tetz graduated from Saint Lawrence College in Cornwall, Ontario with a diploma in Business Administration in 1990. He spent a short time in computer sales, which turned into a computer support position. He has spent the last eight years performing system and LAN support for small and large organizations. In 1994, Edward added training to his repertoire. He is both a Microsoft Certified Trainer and a Microsoft Certified Systems Engineer. He has experience with Apple Macintosh, IBM OS/2, and all Microsoft operating systems. He is currently an Information Technology Coordinator and an Instructor for PBSC Computer Training, delivering certified training in most Microsoft products. Edward has published several certification titles for New Riders.

John Griffin is currently a Senior Internet Developer and Architect at Iomega Corporation. He has worked in the computer industry in one form or another since 1969. Previous employment included contracting work for Sprint Paranet of Houston, TX, systems administration for the Department of Defense, and serving in the United States Navy for nine years. John holds the MCSE, MCNE, MCP+I, and A+ certifications. He lives in Layton, Utah with his wife, Judith, an Australian Shepherd, Maggie. John is an accomplished woodworker and would like to start raising Australian Shepherd puppies, although he hasn't informed Judith that she would like to do this also.

David Neilan is an experienced MCSE who has been working in the computer/network industry for over nine years, the last five dealing primarily with network/Internet security. His experience includes stints at Intergraph, working with graphics systems and networking; and Digital Equipment, working with DEC firewalls and network security. Presently, he is working for Online Business Systems in the areas of LAN/WAN and Internet security. He is designing network infrastructures with Windows 2000 to support secure LAN/WAN connectivity for various companies utilizing the Internet to create secure Virtual Private Networks. David has been a Beta tester for Microsoft products and courses since Windows 3.11 and was an early adopter of Windows 2000.

Acknowledgments

Brian Komar

I would like to thank Ann, Al, Chris, Nancy, and Rob for all the assistance and guidance they have provided in the development of this book. I also to thank the technical editors for their assistance in ensuring that the material within the book is technically accurate. Finally, I want to thank my wife Krista for putting up with the extra hours involved with developing this book over the past few months.

Edward Tetz

I would like to thank my wife, Sharon, and children, Emily and Mackenzie. If not for your love, support, and understanding, I would not be able to find the time or will to write and edit.

xxxii   MCSE TRAINING GUIDE: WINDOWS 2000 ACCELERATED EXAM

Tell Us What You Think!

As the reader of this book, you are the most important critic and commentator. We value your opinion and want to know what we're doing right, what we could do better, what areas you'd like to see us publish in, and any other words of wisdom you're willing to pass our way.

As the Associate Publisher at New Riders Publishing, I welcome your comments. You can fax, email, or write me directly to let me know what you did or didn't like about this book—as well as what we can do to make our books stronger.

Please note that I cannot help you with technical problems related to the topic of this book, and that due to the high volume of mail I receive, I might not be able to reply to every message.

When you write, please be sure to include this book's title and author as well as your name and phone or fax number. I will carefully review your comments and share them with the author and editors who worked on the book.

Fax: 317-581-4663

Email: nrfeedback@newriders.com

Mail: Al Valvano
            Associate Publisher
            Certification
            New Riders Publishing
            201 West 103rd Street
            Indianapolis, IN 46290 USA

How to Use This Book

New Riders Publishing has made an effort in its *Training Guide* series to make the information as accessible as possible for the purpose of learning the certification material. Here, you have an opportunity to view the many instructional features that have been incorporated into the books to achieve that goal.

CHAPTER OPENER

Each chapter begins with a set of features designed to allow you to maximize study time for that material.

List of Objectives: Each chapter begins with a list of the objectives as stated by Microsoft.

Objective Explanations: Immediately following each objective is an explanation of it, providing context that defines it more meaningfully in relation to the exam. Because Microsoft can sometimes be vague in its objectives list, the objective explanations are designed to clarify any vagueness by relying on the authors' test-taking experience.

OBJECTIVES

This chapter will help you prepare for the "Installing Windows 2000 Server" section of the exam by giving you information necessary to make intelligent choices regarding the method of installation and the preparations required for such an installation.

Microsoft provides the following objectives for "Installing Windows 2000 Server":

Perform an attended installation of Windows 2000 Server.

▶ This objective is necessary because someone certified in the use of Windows 2000 Server technology must be able to install a Windows 2000 server as a member server in a Windows 2000 domain. This will include installations from a bootable CD-ROM and from the four-disk set.

Perform an unattended installation of Windows 2000 Server.

• Create unattended answer files by using Setup Manager to automate the installation of Windows 2000 Server.

• Create and configure automated methods for installation of Windows 2000.

▶ This objective is necessary because someone certified in the Windows 2000 Server technology should understand how to automate the installation of member servers in a Windows 2000 domain over a network. This will include creating answer files, as well as deploying installation using these answer files. In addition, it will involve familiarity with the new disk duplication and Remote Installation features of Windows 2000.

CHAPTER 1

Installing Windows 2000 Server

OUTLINE

Chapter Outline: Learning always gets a boost when you can see both the forest and the trees. To give you a visual image of how the topics in a chapter fit together, you will find a chapter outline at the beginning of each chapter. You will also be able to use this for easy reference when looking for a particular topic.

STUDY STRATEGIES

▶ There are many testable items in this long chapter. Remember that Microsoft will incorporate multiple items together into single questions, so make sure you know how these topics are interrelated.

▶ Of course, you should read and understand the concepts in this chapter and go through the review and exam questions at the end.

▶ In order to really understand the topics, you should implement the strategies in the Step by Step examples, and you need to do the exercises. Because of the nature of some of the interoperability sections, you might find it difficult to actually implement the solutions unless you have a number of test machines and access to other operating systems (like NetWare and Macintosh computers). However, you will still find that "going through the motions" will help to make the concepts in this chapter concrete. I suggest that you install the services and go through the configurations until a lack of equipment forces you to stop. Of course, if you can get hold of NetWare servers (regardless of the version) or a Macintosh system or two, you will be able to more fully implement the solutions presented.

▶ Interoperability has always been a big point on the exams—and this is still the case. Make sure you are familiar with the services required to interoperate with NetWare, Macintosh, and UNIX. Specifically for NetWare, be sure that you have an outline in your mind of what steps need to be taken to set up the GateWay for NetWare Service and get it to provide NetWare access to clients. Be sure that you understand

(the software interface) and the print device (the hardware component), you do not even have to have a print device to do the printer module. For the network portions, you will benefit from having a second machine to use as a client with network hub to allow you to connect them (or at the very least a null network cable to directly connect them). You will not be able to implement the encrypted Web connections (using server and client certificates) unless you obtain or create certificates. If you already have certificates then use them; if not, you could use the Windows 2000 Certificate Authority to create them. However, that procedure is not outlined in this chapter.

▶ For the previous points mentioned, make sure that you go through all the configuration properties and that you understand how the configuration is done. Open the Security tab for an NTFS file resource or a printer and fix them, and what their settings do, in your mind.

▶ In the Dfs section, you will be able to implement standalone regardless of your setup. However, domain-based Dfs will require that you have a Windows 2000 domain controller running in Native mode. If you do not have such a machine, then you will be able to implement only part of the Dfs solutions.

▶ Nothing can replace experience. Working through all the modules, understanding their content, and implementing the Step by Steps is a beginning. However, you will greatly benefit from having to work out some of these solutions in an environment where the result is defined but the path to it is not; this will

Study Strategies: Each topic presents its own learning challenge. To support you through this, New Riders has included strategies for how to best approach studying in order to retain the material in the chapter, particularly as it is addressed on the exam.

INSTRUCTIONAL FEATURES WITHIN THE CHAPTER

These books include a large amount and different kinds of information. The many different elements are designed to help you identify information by its purpose and importance to the exam and also to provide you with varied ways to learn the material. You will be able to determine how much attention to devote to certain elements, depending on what your goals are. By becoming familiar with the different presentations of information, you will know what information will be important to you as a test-taker and which information will be important to you as a practitioner.

EXAM TIP

Printer Terminology   Terminology is very important, especially for the exam. Keep in mind that when the exam makes reference to a printer, it is talking about a software interface, not a physical device. The device is called a "print device"; all the software that you install and the icon you see in the Printers window is referred to as a printer. In order to make this clearer, I will often refer to this as the "virtual printer." The term "virtual printer" has been known to show up in Microsoft documentation, but I don't envision it making its way to the exam.

Exam Tip: Exam Tips appear in the margins to provide specific exam-related advice. Such tips may address what material is covered (or not covered) on the exam, how it is covered, mnemonic devices, or particular quirks of that exam.

Warning: In using sophisticated information technology, there is always potential for mistakes or even catastrophes that can occur through improper application of the technology. Warnings appear in the margins to alert you to such potential problems.

---

150   Part I   EXAM PREPARATION

WARNING

Write + Run Access = Trouble   A user that has Write access to a Web site and the ability to run scripts and/or executables could pose a serious security risk to your site. The danger is so great that if this combination is allowed, IIS will display a message informing you of the inherent risks involved. By doing this, you could allow a user to create a damaging script or program, upload it to your site, and then run it.

NOTE

Configuration for Digest Authentication   Two things are required in order for this kind of authentication to work. First, the IIS server must be a member of a domain. Second, each user that needs to authenticate through a browser must have his or her account to store the password using "reversible encryption." To do this, that setting must be enabled in the properties for the user (Account tab), and then the password for the user must be reset.

continued

6. In the Secure Communications dialog box, you can also enable a Certificate Trust List (CTL). A CTL is a list of certifiers you trust. If a client tries to authenticate with a certifier not in the CTL, that certificate will be rejected.

7. When configuration is complete, click OK to exit.

Troubleshooting Web Site Access

Web site access is about two things: access to a running server and security.

Troubleshooting lack of access because of a server not running was covered in the earlier section "Troubleshooting Sharing."

Lack of access because of security issues revolves around all the topics that have been covered in this section. Look for TCP port incompatibilities and fix them if uncovered.

If a user is getting "Access denied" messages, check for authentication methods and underlying NTFS permissions. In addition, check for client certificates and see whether they are required. IP address restrictions may also cause these kinds of messages so check for these, too.

If a user can get to your site but cannot do what is desired (like upload files or execute scripts), check for those permissions and adjust them if necessary.

CONFIGURING AND MAINTAINING PRINTERS

Monitor, configure, troubleshoot, and control access to printers.

Next to accessing data, access to printers is probably the most important need for users. Most often, having a print device physically attached to every person's workstation is impractical, so a

Note: Notes appear in the margins and contain various kinds of useful information, such as tips on the technology or administrative practices, historical background on terms and technologies, or side commentary on industry issues.

Objective Coverage Text: In the text before an exam objective is specifically addressed, you will notice the objective is listed to help call your attention to that particular material.

STEP BY STEP

6.12 Configuring a Server as a First Network DNS on a Windows 2000 Server

1. From the Start menu, choose Programs, Administrative Tools, DNS.

2. In the DNS console, select your server name, open the Action menu, and choose Configure the Server.

3. At the Welcome to the Configure the DNS Server Wizard, click Next.

4. At the Root Server dialog box, choose This Is the First DNS Server on This Network and click Next (see Figure 6.32) .

5. At the Forward Lookup Zone dialog box, choose Yes, Create a Forward Lookup Zone and click Next (see Figure 6.33).

continues

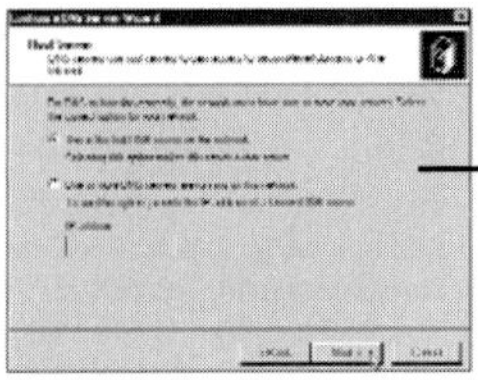

FIGURE 6.32
Create a new zone.

Figure: To improve readability, the figures have been placed in the margins wherever possible so they do not interrupt the main flow of text.

Step by Step: Step by Steps are hands-on tutorial instructions that walk you through a particular task or function relevant to the exam objectives.

---

volume from five 1GB segments of free space, the usable area is (5–1)/5 or 80% of the total hard drive space. That would leave you with 4GB of the original 5GB because 1GB would be used to maintain the fault tolerance.

RAID-5 volumes have moderate write performance (reduced because the parity information must be calculated as the data changes) but excellent read performance because the data is stored on many hard drives, all of which can be accessed independently of one another.

Like striped volumes, RAID-5 volumes cannot be used to hold the System or Boot partition of a Windows 2000 installation.

IN THE FIELD

FAULT TOLERANCE PUTS STRAIN ON YOUR SERVER

All fault-tolerant disk volumes (mirrors and RAID-5) require additional overhead (processor and memory). This is a result of maintenance of the fault-tolerant data as it is being written to the volume. The performance change in your Windows 2000 server may or may not be significant to you or your user community. In a system dedicated to storage of data or retrieval of data, you may see noticeable increases or decreases in system performance when using this fault tolerance method.

In a system in which the primary operation a user performs is queries on a database, the increase in read performance may be significant in terms of throughput. If the system is designed to store data, mirroring may produce disk bottlenecks. You may only know whether these are significant by setting up two identical computers, implementing mirroring on one and not on the other, and then running Performance Monitor on both under simulated load to see the performance differences. For more information on monitoring, see Chapter 4, "Managing, Monitoring, and Optimizing System Performance, Reliability, and Availability."

In the Field Sidebar: These more extensive discussions cover material that perhaps is not directly relevant to the exam, but which is useful as reference material or in everyday practice. In the Field may also provide useful background or contextual information necessary for understanding the larger topic under consideration.

CASE STUDIES

Case Studies are presented throughout the book to provide you with another, more conceptual opportunity to apply the knowledge you are developing. They also reflect the "real-world" experiences of the authors in ways that prepare you not only for the exam but for actual network administration as well. In each Case Study, you will find similar elements: a description of a Scenario, the Essence of the Case, and an extended Analysis section.

CASE STUDY: IN YOUR TOWN INC.

THE ESSENCE OF THE CASE

This case requires that the following results be satisfied:

► Allow Isaiah to connect to head office servers to do administration when he is on the road.

► Secure the communications between his laptop and servers while administration is going on.

SCENARIO

Isaiah is the network administrator for In Your Town Inc. (IYT), a national company with 30 regional offices in the United States and Canada. Although IYT has a number of national locations, it has very few employees and a small IT staff (Isaiah and two technical assistants), which works out of the head office in New Orleans, Louisiana. As a result, Isaiah finds himself traveling a great deal to service servers in different locations (there is at least one Windows 2000 server in each regional office). When he is on the road, Isaiah would like to be able to administer the Windows 2000 servers at the head office from his laptop.

Not only does Isaiah want to be able to do simple administration (like creating new users and checking printer queues), he also wants to be able to start and stop services, start performance monitors, observe running tasks, and restart servers that may have problems.

Essence of the Case: A bulleted list of the key problems or issues that need to be addressed in the Scenario.

Scenario: A few paragraphs describing a situation that professional practitioners in the field might face. A Scenario deals with an issue relating to the objectives covered in the chapter, and it includes the kinds of details that make a difference.

Analysis: This is a lengthy description of the best way to handle the problems listed in the Essence of the Case. In this section, you might find a table summarizing the solutions, a worded example, or both.

CASE STUDY: IN YOUR TOWN INC.

continued

ANALYSIS

Windows 2000 Server has features that will allow Isaiah to satisfy both his accessibility and his security issues. First, he can install the Terminal Services component of Windows 2000 Server and configure it to operate in Administration mode. This, coupled with the installation of the Terminal Services client on his laptop, will enable him to connect remotely to a local session on each server. This feature will work as long as he is inside the firewall. However, on the road, the firewall will prevent direct access to his servers from his laptop. That can be overcome by installing the RRAS services on a server inside the firewall (or by configuring a new server to be an RRAS server). Finally, in order for Isaiah to connect

to the RRAS server, he will need to do three things: configure the RRAS server to accept VPN connections (PPTP), configure his laptop to connect to the RRAS server to establish VPN sessions, and open port 1723 in the firewall to allow the VPN traffic to pass through.

Using this configuration, Isaiah will be able to use any Internet connection to establish a VPN connection, through his firewall to his RRAS server at his head office. Having established that connection, he can then use the Terminal Services client to establish a session with any of his servers, and he will be able to perform secure administration of his servers.

The following table summarizes the solution.

OVERVIEW OF THE REQUIREMENTS AND SOLUTIONS IN THIS CASE STUDY

Requirement	Solution Provided By
Access to server sessions	Installing Terminal Services on servers in Administration mode; installing Terminal Services client on roaming laptop

CHAPTER SUMMARY

Summarized briefly, this chapter covered the following main points.

◆ **Installing, configuring, and updating devices.** This includes the recognition of Plug and Play for most new devices, the presence of the Device Manager, and the ability to manually install and configure non-Plug and Play devices.

◆ **Configuring driver signing options.** This allows you, the administrator, to create a policy on the need for drivers to be signed to ensure validity and to enforce such a policy to keep corrupt or non-verified drivers from being installed.

◆ **Troubleshooting hardware problems.** This is required whenever you encounter problems with drivers. This may be the

KEY TERMS

• user mode

• kernel mode

• driver

• Device Manager

• driver signing

• system log

EXTENSIVE REVIEW AND SELF-TEST OPTIONS

At the end of each chapter, along with some summary elements, you will find a section called "Apply Your Knowledge" that gives you several different methods with which to test your understanding of the material and review what you have learned.

Chapter Summary: Before the Apply Your Knowledge section, you will find a chapter summary that wraps up the chapter and reviews what you should have learned.

Key Terms: A list of key terms appears at the end of each chapter. These are terms that you should be sure you know and are comfortable defining and understanding when you go in to take the exam.

APPLY YOUR KNOWLEDGE

Exercises

4.1   Set Application Priority

In this exercise, you learn how to set application priority at time of invocation and how to reset while it is running. You will also learn how to stop a process using the Task Manager. Note that this exercise will cause your server to stop responding, forcing you to power it off suddenly. Make sure you do not have any critical applications running when you do this exercise.

Estimated Time: 15 minutes

1. The CD-ROM that comes with this book contains a folder called Application Demo. Copy that folder to the hard drive on your Windows 2000 server.

2. From the Start menu, choose Programs, Accessories, Command Prompt.

3. From the Command Prompt, navigate to the location where you copied the Application Demo folder.

4. At the cursor, type **Start /Low Counter.** When it starts running, move the counter dialog box to the bottom of your screen. Note how quickly this program counts, even at low priority.

5. At the cursor, type **Start /Normal Counter.** When it starts running, move the second counter to the bottom of your screen. Note that this counter is counting quickly, but the low priority counter is no longer counting quickly.

6. Right-click the taskbar and choose Task Manager. Make sure that when it comes up, you can still see both counters (see Figure 4.60). Click the Processes tab on the Task Manager.

FIGURE 4.60
You can modify the data shown in the Task Manager by using the View menu.

Review Questions

1. What are the four application execution priorities, and what numeric ranges does each fall into?

2. Name three ways to change the execution priority of an application (whether it's running or not)?

3. What are the two types of logs available in Performance Monitor, and how can you distinguish them from one another?

4. What is the purpose of an alert, and what are three of the actions that can be taken when one happens?

5. What limitation of Windows 2000 Backup should lead you to schedule backups for times when as few people are accessing the server as possible?

6. What are three ways to invoke the Windows

Exercises: These activities provide an opportunity for you to master specific hands-on tasks. Our goal is to increase your proficiency with the product or technology. You must be able to conduct these tasks in order to pass the exam.

Review Questions: These open-ended, short-answer questions allow you to quickly assess your comprehension of what you just read in the chapter. Instead of asking you to choose from a list of options, these questions require you to state the correct answers in your own words. Although you will not experience these kinds of questions on the exam, these questions will indeed test your level of comprehension of key concepts.

APPLY YOUR KNOWLEDGE

Exam Questions

1. Jim is the network administrator for two identical Windows 2000 servers in a high school. They both have SCSI CD-ROM drives, and all data is on NTFS partitions. He has just found one of his servers turned off. When he turns it back on, Jim gets an error that NTOSKRNL.EXE cannot be found and it will not boot. He suspects that a vandal in the school has deleted the file. He does not have the Windows 2000 Server CD-ROM, but he has disks and a CD-ROM writer. How can Jim recover his server?

   A. Boot his server to Safe Mode and then copy the NTOSKRNL.EXE file from the other server using a disk.

   B. Boot his server to the Recovery console using the setup disk set and copy NTOSKRNL.EXE using a disk.

   C. Boot his server to DOS and copy the NTOSKRNL.EXE from the other server using a CD-ROM with the file copied from the other server.

   D. Boot his server to the Recovery console using a secondary boot on the server and copy the NTOSKRNL.EXE using a CD-ROM with the file copied from the other server.

2. Pavel wants to determine whether or not his server is short of memory. Under light load, users get good response. However, as load increases, so does the lack of responsiveness. Which of the following counters will aid him in determining whether memory is the bottleneck in his system? (Choose two.)

   A. Memory\pages/sec

   B. Paging File\% Usage

   C. Processor\Interrupts/sec

   D. Network Segment\% Net Utilization

Answers to Review Questions

1. The four priorities are Idle—sometimes called Low (0–6), Normal (6–11), High (11–15), and Realtime (16–31). For more information, see the section "Maintaining Windows 32-Bit Applications."

2. There are three ways to change the priority of an application. The first way is to start it at a command line (or from a shortcut) using the syntax **Start /priority applicationname**. The second way is to change its priority in the Task Manager while it is running. The third way is to set the foreground boost for all normal applications in the advanced page of the System Properties. For more information, see the section "Maintaining Windows 32-Bit Applications."

3. The two kinds of logs available in Performance Monitor are counter logs and trace logs. They are distinguished by their collection trigger and how much control you have over the information you collect. The collection of data in a counter log is controlled by time interval passing, and you can finely control the kind of data you collect through the application of object counters. The collection of data in a trace log is controlled by events that happen (like user logon), and you have little control over the specific information collected outside of a general category of data. For more information, see the section "Collecting Data Using Performance Monitor."

Exam Questions: These questions reflect the kinds of multiple-choice questions that appear on the Microsoft exams. Use them to become familiar with the exam question formats and to help you determine what you know and what you need to review or study more.

Answers and Explanations: For each of the Review and Exam questions, you will find thorough explanations located at the end of the section.

Suggested Readings and Resources

1. Microsoft Windows 2000 Server Resource Kit: *Microsoft Windows 2000 Server Internetworking Guide* (Microsoft Press)

   • Chapter 2: Routing and Remote Access Service

   • Chapter 3: Unicast IP Routing

   • Chapter 7: Remote Access Server

   • Chapter 8: Internet Authentication Service

   • Chapter 9: Virtual Private Networking

   • Chapter 16: NetBEUI

2. Microsoft Windows 2000 Server Resource Kit: *Microsoft Windows 2000 Server Deployment Planning* Guide (Microsoft Press)

   • Chapter 7: Determining Network Connectivity Strategies

   • Chapter 11: Planning Distributed Security

   • Chapter 7: Windows Internet Name Service

   • Chapter 8: Internet Protocol Security

4. *Microsoft Windows 2000 Professional Resource Kit* (Microsoft Press)

   • Chapter 13: Security

   • Chapter 21: Local and Remote Network Connections

   • Chapter 22: TCP/IP in Windows 2000 Professional

   • Chapter 23: Windows 2000 Professional on Microsoft Networks

   • Chapter 24: Interoperability with NetWare

5. Microsoft Official Curriculum course 1557: *Installing and Configuring Microsoft Windows 2000*

Suggested Readings and Resources: The very last element in every chapter is a list of additional resources you can use if you want to go above and beyond certification-level material or if you need to spend more time on a particular subject that you are having trouble understanding.

Introduction

MCSE Training Guide: Windows 2000 Accelerated Exam is designed for MCSEs certified in the Windows NT 4.0 track who are looking for a simpler path to recertifying as MCSEs under Windows 2000. More specifically, those MCPs or MCSEs who have passed the old 70-067, 70-068, and 70-073 exams can take the Microsoft Windows 2000 Accelerated Exam for MCPs Certified on Microsoft Windows NT 4.0 (70-240) instead of the four core exams ordinarily required for the Windows 2000 track. In other words, the exam measures all the skills measured by the following exams:

◆ Installing, Configuring, and Administering Microsoft Windows 2000 Professional (70-210).

◆ Installing, Configuring, and Administering Microsoft Windows 2000 Server (70-215).

◆ Implementing and Administering a Microsoft Windows 2000 Network Infrastructure (70-216).

◆ Implementing and Administering a Microsoft Windows 2000 Directory Services Infrastructure (70-217).

This book is your one-stop shop. Everything you need to know to pass the exam is in here, and Microsoft has approved it as study material. You do not have to take a class in addition to buying this book to pass the exam. However, depending on your personal study habits or learning style, you may benefit from buying this book *and* taking a few classes.

HOW THIS BOOK HELPS YOU

This book takes you on a self-guided tour of all the areas covered by the Microsoft Windows 2000 Accelerated Exam for MCPs Certified on Microsoft Windows NT 4.0 (70-240) and teaches you the specific skills you will need to achieve your MCSE certification. You will also find helpful hints, tips, real-world examples, and exercises, as well as references to additional study materials. Specifically, this book is set up to help you in the following ways:

◆ **Organization.** The book is organized by individual exam objectives. Every objective you need to know for the Microsoft Windows 2000 Accelerated Exam for MCPs Certified on Microsoft Windows NT 4.0 (70-240) is covered in this book. Although Microsoft has not published specific objectives for this exam, we have followed the objectives for the four core exams. We have also attempted to make the information accessible in the following ways:

• The full list of exam topics and objectives is included in this introduction.

• Each chapter begins with a list of the objectives to be covered.

• Each chapter also begins with an outline that provides you with an overview of the material and the page numbers where particular topics can be found.

- The objectives are repeated where the material most directly relevant to it is covered (unless the whole chapter addresses a single objective).

- Information on where the objectives are covered is also conveniently condensed in the tearcard located on the CD-ROM that comes with this book.

◆ **Instructional features.** This book has been designed to provide you with multiple ways to learn and reinforce the exam material. Some of those helpful methods are described here:

- *Objective Explanations.* As mentioned previously, each chapter begins with a list of the objectives covered in the chapter. In addition, immediately following each objective is an explanation in a context that defines it more meaningfully.

- *Study Strategies.* The beginning of the chapter also includes strategies for how to approach studying and retaining the material in the chapter, particularly as it is addressed on the exam.

- *Exam Tips.* Exam tips appear in the margin to provide specific exam-related advice. Such tips may address what material is covered (or not covered) on the exam, how it is covered, mnemonic devices, or particular quirks of that exam.

- *Review Breaks and Summaries.* Crucial information is summarized at various points in the book in lists or tables. Each chapter ends with a summary as well.

- *Key Terms.* A list of key terms appears at the end of each chapter.

- *Notes.* These appear in the margin and contain a variety of useful information, such as tips on technology or administrative practices, historical background on terms and technologies, or side commentary on industry issues.

- *Warnings.* When using sophisticated information technology, there is always the potential for mistakes or even catastrophes that occur because of improper application of the technology. Warnings appear in the margin to alert you to such potential problems.

- *In the Field.* These more extensive discussions cover material that may not be directly relevant to the exam, but that is useful as reference material or in everyday practice. In the Field may also provide useful background or contextual information necessary for understanding the larger topic under consideration.

- *Step by Steps.* These are hands-on tutorial instructions that walk you through a particular task or function relevant to the exam objectives. The Step by Steps are referred to in the text, but are actually located on the CD-ROM that accompanies this book.

- *Case Studies.* Each chapter concludes with a Case Study. The cases are meant to help you understand the practical applications of the information covered in the chapter.

- *Exercises.* Found on the CD in the "Apply Your Knowledge" folder, exercises are performance-based opportunities for you to learn and assess your knowledge.

◆ **Extensive practice test options.** The book provides numerous opportunities for you to assess your knowledge and practice for the exam. The practice options include the following:

- *Review Questions.* These open-ended questions appear in the "Apply Your Knowledge" section at the end of each chapter. They allow you to quickly assess your comprehension of what you just read in the chapter. Answers to the questions are provided later in a separate section titled "Answers to Review Questions."

- *Exam Questions.* These questions appear in the "Apply Your Knowledge" folder on the CD. Use them to help determine what you know and what you need to review or study further, and to practice with exam-style questions. Answers and explanations for the exam questions are provided in a separate section titled "Answers to Exam Questions."

- *ExamGear.* The special Training Guide version of the *ExamGear* software included on the CD-ROM provides further practice questions.

> **NOTE**
> For a description of the New Riders *ExamGear, Training Guide Edition* software, please see Appendix B, "Using the *ExamGear, Training Guide Edition* Software."

The book includes several other features, such as a section titled "Suggested Readings and Resources" at the end of each chapter that directs you toward further information that could aid you in your exam preparation or your actual work. Appendix B is essentially a manual for the *ExamGear, Training Guide Edition* test simulation software.

For more information about the exam or the certification process, contact Microsoft:

Microsoft Education: 800-636-7544

Internet: `ftp://ftp.microsoft.com/Services/MSEdCert`

World Wide Web: `http://www.microsoft.com/train_cert`

CompuServe Forum: GO MSEDCERT

WHAT THE MICROSOFT WINDOWS 2000 ACCELERATED EXAM FOR MCPS CERTIFIED ON MICROSOFT WINDOWS NT 4.0 (70-240) COVERS

The Microsoft Windows 2000 Accelerated Exam for MCPs Certified on Microsoft Windows NT 4.0 (70-240) covers the Windows 2000 topics represented by the conceptual groupings or units of the test objectives for the four core exams. In the following sections, the objectives are presented by exam and by the units that reflect job skill areas.

Installing, Configuring, and Administering Microsoft Windows 2000 Professional Exam (70-210)

The Installing, Configuring, and Administering Microsoft Windows 2000 Professional Exam (70-210) covers the Windows 2000 Professional topics represented by the conceptual groupings or units of the test objectives. The objectives reflect job skills in the following areas:

◆ Installing Windows 2000 Professional

◆ Implementing and Conducting Administration of Resources

◆ Implementing, Managing, and Troubleshooting Hardware Devices and Drivers

◆ Monitoring and Optimizing System Performance and Reliability

◆ Configuring and Troubleshooting the Desktop Environment

◆ Implementing, Managing, and Troubleshooting Network Protocols and Services

◆ Implementing, Monitoring, and Troubleshooting Security

Before taking the exam, you should be proficient in the job skills represented by the following units, objectives, and subobjectives.

Installing Windows 2000 Professional

Perform an attended installation of Windows 2000 Professional.

Perform an unattended installation of Windows 2000 Professional.

- Install Windows 2000 Professional by using Windows 2000 Server Remote Installation Services (RIS).

- Install Windows 2000 Professional by using the System Preparation Tool.

- Create unattended answer files by using Setup Manager to automate the installation of Windows 2000 Professional.

Upgrade from a previous version of Windows to Windows 2000 Professional.

- Apply update packs to installed software applications.

- Prepare a computer to meet upgrade requirements.

Deploy service packs.

Troubleshoot failed installations.

Implementing and Conducting Administration of Resources

Monitor, manage, and troubleshoot access to files and folders.

- Configure, manage, and troubleshoot file compression.

- Control access to files and folders by using permissions.

- Optimize access to files and folders.

Manage and troubleshoot access to shared folders.

- Create and remove shared folders.

- Control access to shared folders by using permissions.

- Manage and troubleshoot Web server resources.

Connect to local and network print devices.

- Manage printers and print jobs.
- Control access to printers by using permissions.
- Connect to an Internet printer.
- Connect to a local print device.

Configure and manage file systems.

- Convert from one file system to another file system.
- Configure file systems by using NTFS, FAT32, or FAT.

Implementing, Managing, and Troubleshooting Hardware Devices and Drivers

Implement, manage, and troubleshoot disk devices.

- Install, configure, and manage DVD and CD-ROM devices.
- Monitor and configure disks.
- Monitor, configure, and troubleshoot volumes.
- Monitor and configure removable media, such as tape devices.

Implement, manage, and troubleshoot display devices.

- Configure multiple-display support.
- Install, configure, and troubleshoot a video adapter.

Implement, manage, and troubleshoot mobile computer hardware.

- Configure Advanced Power Management (APM).
- Configure and manage card services.

Implement, manage, and troubleshoot input and output (I/O) devices.

- Monitor, configure, and troubleshoot I/O devices, such as printers, scanners, multimedia devices, mouse, keyboard, and smart card reader.
- Monitor, configure, and troubleshoot multimedia hardware, such as cameras.
- Install, configure, and manage modems.
- Install, configure, and manage Infrared Data Association (IrDA) devices.
- Install, configure, and manage wireless devices.
- Install, configure, and manage USB devices.

Update drivers.

Monitor and configure multiple processing units.

Install, configure, and troubleshoot network adapters.

Monitoring and Optimizing System Performance and Reliability

Manage and troubleshoot driver signing.

Configure, manage, and troubleshoot the Task Scheduler.

Manage and troubleshoot the use and synchronization of offline files.

Optimize and troubleshoot performance of the Windows 2000 Professional desktop.

- Optimize and troubleshoot memory performance.
- Optimize and troubleshoot processor utilization.
- Optimize and troubleshoot disk performance.

- Optimize and troubleshoot network performance.
- Optimize and troubleshoot application performance.

Manage hardware profiles.

Recover systems and user data.

- Recover systems and user data by using Windows Backup.
- Troubleshoot system restoration by using Safe Mode.
- Recover systems and user data by using the Recovery Console.

Configuring and Troubleshooting the Desktop Environment

Configure and manage user profiles.

Configure support for multiple languages or multiple locations.

- Enable multiple-language support.
- Configure multiple-language support for users.
- Configure local settings.
- Configure Windows 2000 Professional for multiple locations.

Install applications by using Windows Installer packages.

Configure and troubleshoot desktop settings.

Configure and troubleshoot fax support.

Configure and troubleshoot accessibility services.

Implementing, Managing, and Troubleshooting Network Protocols and Services

Configure and troubleshoot the TCP/IP protocol.

Connect to computers by using dial-up networking.

- Connect to computers by using a virtual private network (VPN) connection.
- Create a dial-up connection to connect to a remote access server.
- Connect to the Internet by using dial-up networking.
- Configure and troubleshoot Internet Connection Sharing.

Connect to shared resources on a Microsoft network.

Implementing, Monitoring, and Troubleshooting Security

Encrypt data on a hard disk by using Encrypting File System (EFS).

Implement, configure, manage, and troubleshoot local Group Policy.

Implement, configure, manage, and troubleshoot local user accounts.

- Implement, configure, manage, and troubleshoot auditing.
- Implement, configure, manage, and troubleshoot account settings.
- Implement, configure, manage, and troubleshoot Account Policy.
- Create and manage local users and groups.
- Implement, configure, manage, and troubleshoot user rights.

Implement, configure, manage, and troubleshoot local user authentication.

- Configure and troubleshoot local user accounts.

- Configure and troubleshoot domain user accounts.

Implement, configure, manage, and troubleshoot a security configuration.

What the Installing, Configuring, and Administering Microsoft Windows 2000 Server Exam (70-215) Covers

The Installing, Configuring, and Administering Microsoft Windows 2000 Server Exam (70-215) covers the Windows 2000 Server topics represented by the conceptual groupings or units of the test objectives. The objectives reflect job skills in the following areas:

- Installing Windows 2000 Server

- Installing, Configuring, and Troubleshooting Access to Resources

- Configuring and Troubleshooting Hardware Devices and Drivers

- Managing, Monitoring, and Optimizing System Performance, Reliability, and Availability

- Managing, Configuring, and Troubleshooting Storage Use

- Configuring and Troubleshooting Windows 2000 Network Connections

- Implementing, Monitoring, and Troubleshooting Security

Before taking the exam, you should be proficient in the job skills represented by the following units, objectives, and subobjectives.

Installing Windows 2000 Server

Perform an attended installation of Windows 2000 Server.

Perform an unattended installation of Windows 2000 Server.

- Create unattended answer files by using Setup Manager to automate the installation of Windows 2000 Server.

- Create and configure automated methods for installation of Windows 2000.

Upgrade a server from Microsoft Windows NT 4.0.

Deploy service packs.

Troubleshoot failed installations.

Installing, Configuring, and Troubleshooting Access to Resources

Install and configure network services for interoperability.

Monitor, configure, troubleshoot, and control access to printers.

Monitor, configure, troubleshoot, and control access to files, folders, and shared folders.

- Configure, manage, and troubleshoot a stand-alone Distributed File System (DFS).

- Configure, manage, and troubleshoot a domain-based Distributed File System (DFS).

- Monitor, configure, troubleshoot, and control local security on files and folders.
- Monitor, configure, troubleshoot, and control access to files and folders in a shared folder.
- Monitor, configure, troubleshoot, and control access to files and folders via Web services.

Monitor, configure, troubleshoot, and control access to Web sites.

Configuring and Troubleshooting Hardware Devices and Drivers

Configure hardware devices.

Configure driver signing options.

Update device drivers.

Troubleshoot problems with hardware.

Managing, Monitoring, and Optimizing System Performance, Reliability, and Availability

Monitor and optimize usage of system resources.

Manage processes.

- Set priorities and start and stop processes.

Optimize disk performance.

Manage and optimize availability of system state data and user data.

Recover systems and user data.

- Recover systems and user data by using Windows Backup.

- Troubleshoot system restoration by using Safe Mode.
- Recover systems and user data by using the Recovery Console.

Managing, Configuring, and Troubleshooting Storage Use

Configure and manage user profiles.

Monitor, configure, and troubleshoot disks and volumes.

Configure data compression.

Monitor and configure disk quotas.

Recover from disk failures.

Configuring and Troubleshooting Windows 2000 Network Connections

Install, configure, and troubleshoot shared access.

Install, configure, and troubleshoot a virtual private network (VPN).

Install, configure, and troubleshoot network protocols.

Install and configure network services.

Configure, monitor, and troubleshoot remote access.

- Configure inbound connections.
- Create a remote access policy.
- Configure a remote access profile.

Install, configure, monitor, and troubleshoot Terminal Services.

- Remotely administer servers by using Terminal Services.
- Configure Terminal Services for application sharing.
- Configure applications for use with Terminal Services.

Configure the properties of a connection.

Install, configure, and troubleshoot network adapters and drivers.

Implementing, Monitoring, and Troubleshooting Security

Encrypt data on a hard disk by using Encrypting File System (EFS).

Implement, configure, manage, and troubleshoot policies in a Windows 2000 environment.

- Implement, configure, manage, and troubleshoot Local Policy in a Windows 2000 environment.
- Implement, configure, manage, and troubleshoot System Policy in a Windows 2000 environment.

Implement, configure, manage, and troubleshoot auditing.

Implement, configure, manage, and troubleshoot local accounts.

Implement, configure, manage, and troubleshoot Account Policy.

Implement, configure, manage, and troubleshoot security by using the Security Configuration Tool Set.

What the Implementing and Administering a Microsoft Windows 2000 Network Infrastructure Exam (70-216) Covers

The Implementing and Administering a Microsoft Windows 2000 Network Infrastructure Exam (70-216) covers the Windows 2000 networking topics represented by the conceptual groupings or units of the test objectives. The objectives reflect job skills in the following areas:

- Installing, Configuring, Managing, Monitoring, and Troubleshooting DNS in a Windows 2000 Network Infrastructure
- Installing, Configuring, Managing, Monitoring, and Troubleshooting DHCP in a Windows 2000 Network Infrastructure
- Configuring, Managing, Monitoring, and Troubleshooting Remote Access in a Windows 2000 Network Infrastructure
- Installing, Configuring, Managing, Monitoring, and Troubleshooting Network Protocols in a Windows 2000 Network Infrastructure
- Installing, Configuring, Managing, Monitoring, and Troubleshooting WINS in a Windows 2000 Network Infrastructure
- Installing, Configuring, Managing, Monitoring, and Troubleshooting IP Routing in a Windows 2000 Network Infrastructure
- Installing, Configuring, and Troubleshooting Network Address Translation (NAT)
- Installing, Configuring, Managing, Monitoring, and Troubleshooting Certificate Services

Before taking the exam, you should be proficient in the job skills represented by the following units, objectives, and subobjectives.

Installing, Configuring, Managing, Monitoring, and Troubleshooting DNS in a Windows 2000 Network Infrastructure

Install, configure, and troubleshoot DNS.

- Install the DNS Server service.
- Configure a root name server.
- Configure zones.
- Configure a caching-only server.
- Configure a DNS client.
- Configure zones for dynamic updates.
- Test the DNS Server service.
- Implement a delegated zone for DNS.
- Manually create DNS resource records.

Manage and monitor DNS.

Installing, Configuring, Managing, Monitoring, and Troubleshooting DHCP in a Windows 2000 Network Infrastructure

Install, configure, and troubleshoot DHCP.

- Install the DHCP server service.
- Create and manage DHCP scopes, superscopes, and multicast scopes.
- Configure DHCP for DNS integration.
- Authorize a DHCP server in Active Directory.

Manage and monitor DHCP.

Configuring, Managing, Monitoring, and Troubleshooting Remote Access in a Windows 2000 Network Infrastructure

Configure and troubleshoot remote access.

- Configure inbound connections.
- Create a remote access policy.
- Configure a remote access profile.
- Configure a virtual private network (VPN).
- Configure multilink connections.
- Configure routing and remote access for DHCP integration.

Manage and monitor remote access.

Configure remote access security.

- Configure authentication protocols.
- Configure encryption protocols.
- Create a remote access policy.

Installing, Configuring, Managing, Monitoring, and Troubleshooting Network Protocols in a Windows 2000 Network Infrastructure

Install, configure, and troubleshoot network protocols.

- Install and configure TCP/IP.
- Install the NWLink protocol.
- Configure network bindings.

Configure TCP/IP packet filters.

Configure and troubleshoot network protocol security.

Manage and monitor network traffic.

Configure and troubleshoot IPSec.

- Enable IPSec.
- Configure IPSec for transport mode.
- Configure IPSec for tunnel mode.
- Customize IPSec policies and rules.
- Manage and monitor IPSec.

Installing, Configuring, Managing, Monitoring, and Troubleshooting WINS in a Windows 2000 Network Infrastructure

Install, configure, and troubleshoot WINS.

Configure WINS replication.

Configure NetBIOS name resolution.

Manage and monitor WINS.

Installing, Configuring, Managing, Monitoring, and Troubleshooting IP Routing in a Windows 2000 Network Infrastructure

Install, configure, and troubleshoot IP routing protocols.

- Update a Windows 2000-based routing table by means of static routes.
- Implement demand-dial routing.

Manage and monitor IP routing.

- Manage and monitor border routing.
- Manage and monitor internal routing.
- Manage and monitor IP routing protocols.

Installing, Configuring, and Troubleshooting Network Address Translation (NAT)

Install Internet Connection Sharing.

Install NAT.

Configure NAT properties.

Configure NAT interfaces.

Installing, Configuring, Managing, Monitoring, and Troubleshooting Certificate Services

Install and configure Certificate Authority (CA).

Create certificates.

Issue certificates.

Revoke certificates.

Remove the Encrypting File System (EFS) recovery keys.

What the Implementing and Administering a Microsoft Windows 2000 Directory Services Infrastructure Exam (70-217) Covers

The Implementing and Administering a Microsoft Windows 2000 Directory Services Infrastructure Exam (70-217) covers the Active Directory topics represented by the conceptual groupings or units of the test objectives. The objectives reflect job skills in the following areas:

- Installing, Configuring, and Troubleshooting Active Directory

- Installing, Configuring, Managing, Monitoring, and Troubleshooting DNS for Active Directory
- Installing, Configuring, Managing, Monitoring, Optimizing, and Troubleshooting Change and Configuration Management
- Managing, Monitoring, and Optimizing the Components of Active Directory
- Configuring, Managing, Monitoring, and Troubleshooting Active Directory Security Solutions

Before taking the exam, you should be proficient in the job skills represented by the following units, objectives, and subobjectives.

Installing, Configuring, and Troubleshooting Active Directory

Install, configure, and troubleshoot the components of Active Directory.

- Install Active Directory.
- Create sites.
- Create subnets.
- Create site links.
- Create site link bridges.
- Create connection objects.
- Create global catalog servers.
- Move server objects between sites.
- Transfer Operations Master roles.
- Verify Active Directory installation.
- Implement an organizational unit (OU) structure.

Back up and restore Active Directory.

- Perform an authoritative restore of Active Directory.
- Recover from a system failure.

Installing, Configuring, Managing, Monitoring, and Troubleshooting DNS for Active Directory

Install, configure, and troubleshoot DNS for Active Directory.

- Integrate an Active Directory DNS with a non-Active Directory DNS.
- Configure zones for dynamic updates.

Manage, monitor, and troubleshoot DNS.

- Manage replication of DNS data.

Installing, Configuring, Managing, Monitoring, Optimizing, and Troubleshooting Change and Configuration Management

Implement and troubleshoot Group Policy.

- Create a Group Policy object (GPO).
- Link an existing GPO.
- Delegate administrative control of Group Policy.
- Modify Group Policy inheritance.
- Filter Group Policy settings by associating security groups to GPOs.
- Modify Group Policy.

Manage and troubleshoot user environments by using Group Policy.

- Control user environments by using Administrative Templates.
- Assign script policies to users and computers.

Manage and troubleshoot software by using Group Policy.

- Deploy software by using Group Policy.
- Maintain software by using Group Policy.
- Configure deployment options.
- Troubleshoot common problems that occur during software deployment.

Manage network configuration by using Group Policy.

Deploy Windows 2000 by using Remote Installation Services (RIS).

- Install an image on a RIS client computer.
- Create a RIS boot disk.
- Configure remote installation options.
- Troubleshoot RIS problems.
- Manage images for performing remote installations.

Configure RIS security.

- Authorize a RIS server.
- Grant computer account creation rights.
- Pre-stage RIS client computers for added security and load balancing.

Managing, Monitoring, and Optimizing the Components of Active Directory

Manage Active Directory objects.

- Move Active Directory objects.
- Publish resources in Active Directory.
- Locate objects in Active Directory.
- Create and manage accounts manually or by scripting.
- Control access to Active Directory objects.
- Delegate administrative control of objects in Active Directory.

Manage Active Directory performance.

- Monitor, maintain, and troubleshoot domain controller performance.
- Monitor, maintain, and troubleshoot Active Directory components.

Manage and troubleshoot Active Directory replication.

- Manage intersite replication.
- Manage intrasite replication.

Configuring, Managing, Monitoring, and Troubleshooting Active Directory Security Solutions

Configure and troubleshoot security in a Directory Services infrastructure.

- Apply security policies by using Group Policy.

- Create, analyze, and modify security configurations by using Security Configuration and Analysis and Security Templates.

- Implement an audit policy.

Monitor and analyze security events.

HARDWARE AND SOFTWARE YOU'LL NEED

As a self-paced study guide, *MCSE Training Guide: Windows 2000 Accelerated Exam* is meant to help you understand concepts that must be refined through hands-on experience. To make the most of your studying, you need to have as much background on and experience with Windows 2000 Server as possible. The best way to do this is to combine studying with work on Windows 2000 Server. This section gives you a description of the minimum computer requirements you need to enjoy a solid practice environment, as follows:

- ◆ Windows 2000 Server software

- ◆ Windows 2000 Professional software

- ◆ A server and a workstation computer on the Microsoft Hardware Compatibility List (the upcoming hardware requirements apply to both)

- ◆ Administrator access to a Windows 2000 Domain Controller (recommended)

- ◆ Pentium 166MHz (or better) processor

- ◆ 2GB (or larger) hard disk

- ◆ VGA (or Super VGA) video adapter and monitor

- ◆ Mouse or equivalent pointing device

- ◆ CD-ROM drive

- ◆ Network Interface Card (NIC)

- ◆ Presence on an existing network, or use of a 3-port (or more) hub to create a test network

- ◆ Internet access with functional browser

- ◆ 64MB of RAM (128MB recommended)

It is fairly easy to obtain access to the necessary computer hardware and software in a corporate business environment. It can be difficult, however, to allocate enough time within the busy workday to complete a self-study program. Most of your study time will occur after normal working hours, away from the everyday interruptions and pressures of your regular job.

ADVICE ON TAKING THE EXAM

Keep this advice in mind as you study:

- ◆ **Read all the material.** Microsoft has been known to include material not expressly specified in the objectives. This book has included additional information not reflected in the objectives in an effort to give you the best possible preparation for the exam—and for the real-world experiences to come.

- ◆ **Do the Step by Steps and complete the exercises in each chapter.** They will help you gain experience using the specified methodology or approach. All Microsoft exams are task- and experienced-based and require you to have experience actually performing the tasks upon which you will be tested.

- ◆ **Use the questions to assess your knowledge.** Don't just read the chapter content; use the questions to find out what you know and what you don't. If you are struggling, study some more, review, and then assess your knowledge again.

◆ **Review the exam objectives.** Develop your own questions and examples for each topic listed. If you can develop and answer several questions for each topic, you should not have difficulty passing the exam.

Remember, the primary object is not to pass the exam—it is to understand the material. If you understand the material, passing the exam should be simple. Knowledge is a pyramid: To build upward, you need a solid foundation. This book and the Microsoft Certified Professional programs are designed to ensure that you have that solid foundation.

Good luck!

NEW RIDERS PUBLISHING

The staff of New Riders Publishing is committed to bringing you the very best in computer reference material. Each New Riders book is the result of months of work by authors and staff who research and refine the information contained within its covers.

As part of this commitment to you, the NRP reader, New Riders invites your input. Please let us know if you enjoy this book, if you have trouble with the information or examples presented, or if you have a suggestion for the next edition.

Please note, however, that New Riders staff cannot serve as a technical resource during your preparation for the Microsoft certification exams or for questions about software- or hardware-related problems. Please refer instead to the documentation that accompanies the Microsoft products or to the applications' Help systems.

If you have a question or comment about any New Riders book, there are several ways to contact New Riders Publishing. We will respond to as many readers as we can. Your name, address, or phone number will never become part of a mailing list or be used for any purpose other than to help us continue to bring you the best books possible. You can write to us at the following address:

New Riders Publishing
Attn: Executive Editor
201 W. 103rd Street
Indianapolis, IN 46290

If you prefer, you can fax New Riders Publishing at
317-581-4663.

You also can send email to New Riders at the following
Internet address:

nrfeedback@newriders.com

NRP is an imprint of Pearson Education. To obtain
a catalog or information, contact us at nrmedia@
newriders.com. To purchase a New Riders book,
call 800-428-5331.

Thank you for selecting *MCSE Training Guide:
Windows 2000 Accelerated Exam.*

Installing, Configuring, and Administering Microsoft Windows 2000 Professional

1 Installing Windows 2000 Professional

2 Implementing and Conducting Administration of Resources

3 Implementing, Managing, and Troubleshooting Hardware Devices and Drivers

4 Monitoring and Optimizing System Performance and Reliability

5 Configuring and Troubleshooting the Desktop Environment

6 Implementing, Managing, and Troubleshooting Network Protocols and Services

7 Implementing, Monitoring, and Troubleshooting Security

This chapter covers topics associated with the Windows 2000 Professional installation component of MCP Exam 70-240, "Microsoft Windows 2000 Accelerated Exam for MCPs Certified on Microsoft Windows NT 4.0." It helps you prepare for the exam by addressing the following exam objectives:

Perform an attended installation of Windows 2000 Professional.

▶ As a system support professional you need to know how to install Windows 2000. No matter how you install Windows 2000, you will find that knowledge of the manual installation process will help you fully understand the installation process and how to troubleshoot a failed installation.

Perform an unattended installation of Windows 2000 Professional:

- **Install Windows 2000 Professional by using Windows 2000 Server Remote Installation Services (RIS).**

- **Install Windows 2000 Professional by using the System Preparation tool.**

- **Create unattended answer files by using Setup Manager to automate the installation of Windows 2000 Professional.**

▶ In most large environments, you want to use the available automated tools to assist in the deployment of Windows 2000.

CHAPTER 1

Installing Windows 2000 Professional

OBJECTIVES

Upgrade from a previous version of Windows to Windows 2000 Professional.

- **Apply update packs to installed software applications.**

- **Prepare a computer to meet upgrade requirements.**

▶ This objective ensures that you understand the issues associated with upgrading existing Windows environments to Windows 2000.

Deploy service packs.

▶ This objective ensures that you understand the role the service pack plays in your environment.

Troubleshoot failed installations.

▶ Anyone installing a product should be able to troubleshoot problems when they pop up, including common installation problems that you may encounter with Windows 2000.

OUTLINE

STUDY STRATEGIES

▶ When studying for this chapter, sit down and install Windows 2000 no less than five times. The more times you see it, the easier it will be to recognize the major phases of the installation process.

▶ After fully exploring attended installations of the Windows 2000 product, you should focus on automating the installation process.

▶ Read about the RIS and RIPrep process, but don't get caught up in the details. For the purpose of this exam, you need to understand only what technology is required to support the RIS process—not details relating to specific services.

INTRODUCTION

Chapter 1 covers the installation of Windows 2000. The chapter starts with an overview of the Windows 2000 product line. During the discussion of the installation, a number of questions are presented so that you will be fully prepared to complete the installation of Windows 2000. Topics include system requirements, disk configurations, file systems, licensing, and workgroup versus domain model. The installation process is also covered in detail so you will be able to identify the steps involved in installing Windows 2000.

Automated installations of Windows 2000 are also covered in this chapter. You explore the use of unattended text files, Remote Installation Services, and the process of imaging a hard drive. At the end of the chapter, you will be able to identify the Windows 2000 technologies that assist in the automated installation of Windows 2000.

The chapter ends with a discussion of the upgrade process for legacy Windows 9x and Windows NT operating systems.

WINDOWS 2000 PRODUCTS

EXAM TIP

What Product Is Right for Your Environment? Expect questions that ask you to identify the right product for a specific environment. To answer these questions, you must understand the platform that each product runs on and what Microsoft intended it to be used for.

Windows 2000 represents the latest version of Microsoft's Windows NT technology. The Windows 2000 product line includes four versions of the product: Windows 2000 Professional, Windows 2000 Server, Windows 2000 Advanced Server, and Windows 2000 Datacenter Server. Table 1.1 outlines the major differences between the different versions.

TABLE 1.1

WINDOWS 2000 PROFESSIONAL/SERVER MINIMUM HARDWARE REQUIREMENTS

Windows 2000 Family	Windows 2000 Professional	Windows 2000 Server	Windows 2000 Advanced Server	Windows 2000 Datacenter Server
Target audience	Business desktops, notebooks	File, print, intranet, networking	Line of business, e-commerce	Large critical applications: OLTP, data warehouses, ASPs, and ISPs
Minimum CPU requirements	Pentium 133MHz (or higher)	Pentium 133MHz (or higher)	Pentium 133MHz (or higher)	TBA
CPUs supported by product	2	4	8	32
Minimum memory	64MB recommended	256MB recommended	256MB recommended	TBA
Maximum memory	4GB	4GB	8GB	64GB
Hard disk	One or more hard disks with a minimum of 2GB on the system partition (with a minimum of 650MB of free space)	One or more hard disks with a minimum of 2GB on the system partition (with a minimum of 1GB of free space)	One or more hard disks with a minimum of 2GB on the system partition (with a minimum of 1GB of free space)	TBA
Clustering	None	None	Two-node fail-over, 32-node network load balancing	Cascading fail-over among four nodes, 32-node network load balancing

BEFORE YOU BEGIN INSTALLATION

After you have determined the version of Windows 2000 you need to install, you must consider a number of options regarding its installation. You need to ensure you have answers to the following before you begin your installation:

◆ Does your system meet the minimum hardware requirements?

◆ Have you determined the optimal disk partition configuration for your system?

◆ Which file system is appropriate for your environment?

◆ Will you install your system in a workgroup or domain?

The following sections provide an overview of these configuration options.

Hardware Requirements

Table 1.1 requires that the following minimum hardware requirements be met prior to installing and operating Windows 2000 Professional:

◆ A Pentium 133MHz processor (or higher)

◆ Minimum 64MB of RAM (more is better)

◆ One or more hard disks with 2GB total disk space on the system drive (there should be at least 650MB of free space)

◆ If working in a network environment, one or more network adapters

◆ A video display adapter and monitor with VGA resolution or higher

◆ A CD-ROM drive, 3.5-inch disk drive, keyboard, and mouse

> **NOTE**
>
> **You Must Plan for Realistic System Requirements!**   These are the recommended *minimum* system requirements. You will find that significantly higher system requirements are typically required in a production environment. After you have chosen an appropriate hardware platform, you need to closely monitor it to ensure you are getting the desired performance.

Disk and Partition Options

Windows 2000 supports two types of disk storage. The first, called *basic storage,* is one you will most likely be familiar with. The second is new to Windows 2000 and is called *dynamic storage.*

Basic storage is similar to disks found in the Windows 95/98 and Windows NT 4.0 environments. Basic storage consists of disks that contain primary partitions and extended partitions with logical drives. You can have up to four primary partitions or up to three primary partitions and one extended partition per physical hard disk.

Dynamic storage consists of a disk that contains volumes instead of partitions. To create a dynamic disk, you must convert a basic disk into a dynamic disk. Dynamic storage offers the following advantages over basic storage:

◆ Volumes can be extended to include noncontiguous space on the available disks.

◆ There is no limit on the number of volumes you can create on a single disk.

◆ Disk configuration information is stored on the disk instead of the Windows Registry. Configuration information is also replicated to all other dynamic disks so that one disk failure will not cause all dynamic storage to become unavailable.

The following issues must be considered if you intend to implement dynamic disks:

◆ Windows 2000 Setup will always leave 1MB of disk space free on a disk when creating a new partition to allow the disk to be converted from a basic disk to a dynamic disk.

◆ When converted to a dynamic disk, a disk cannot be converted back to basic without removing all existing volumes from your disk.

◆ If you want to convert a basic disk into a dynamic disk, you must ensure that a minimum of 1MB of unpartitioned space is available on your basic disk to track dynamic disk configuration information. Windows 2000 Setup always leaves 1MB of disk space unpartitioned when a new partition is created to allow for the conversion process.

◆ Dynamic disks cannot be read by the Windows 9x or Windows NT operating systems. If you are dual-booting to these operating systems, you must continue to use basic disks.

◆ Dynamic disks are not supported on laptop computers.

◆ A hard disk must either be basic or dynamic. You cannot combine the store types on one disk.

◆ To change a disk back to a basic disk from a dynamic disk, you must delete all existing volumes from the dynamic disk. This can result in data loss if backups are not performed.

Managing Partitions on Basic Disks

Basic disks allow for a number of different partition configurations. *Partitions* are areas of a physical hard disk that function as though it were a separate unit. The partitions are limited to four per physical disk.

A *primary partition* is a partition that can contain the files necessary to boot a particular operating system. A primary partition cannot be subpartitioned. There can be up to four primary partitions per physical disk.

A primary partition is needed for a Windows 2000 *system partition.* The system partition is needed to load Windows 2000 (that is, it contains NTLDR, NEDETECT.COM). Only a primary partition can be used for the system partition.

Windows 2000 also uses a *boot partition.* The boot partition contains the actual Windows 2000 operating system files. The system partition can be on the same partition but does not have to be.

You are limited to four primary partitions per physical disk. In some situations, you may require more partitions. To assist in breaking the four-partition limit, you have the ability to create an *extended partition.* Extended partitions are similar to primary partitions because they define areas of space on a physical hard drive.

The main differences between primary partitions and extended partitions are as follows:

◆ There can only be one extended partition per physical hard disk.

◆ Extended partitions need to be divided into logical drives.

◆ The only limit that exists on the number of logical drives is the number of letters in the alphabet.

During installation, the Windows 2000 Setup program examines the hard disk to determine its existing configuration. The Setup program allows you to create new partitions. Microsoft suggests that you create only the partition on which you will install Windows 2000.

Microsoft recommends that you install Windows 2000 on a partition with a minimum of 2GB. As previously mentioned, Windows 2000 Professional requires only 650MB of free disk space. However, the larger partition allows flexibility in the future.

Windows 2000 File Systems

Before you decide which file system to use, you should understand the benefits and limitations of each file system. The following sections provide an overview of the differences between FAT, FAT32, and NTFS file systems.

FAT

File Allocation Table (FAT) is a file system that has been around for a very long time and is currently supported by most operating systems on the market.

The primary benefit of using FAT is that it is supported by Windows NT 3.5x/4.0, Windows 95/98, Windows 3.x, DOS, and other operating systems. It is commonly used on systems that are required to dual-boot between Windows 2000 and one (or more) of the operating systems mentioned previously.

When used under Windows 2000, the FAT file system supports the following additional features:

◆ Long filenames up to 255 characters

◆ Multiple spaces

◆ Multiple periods

◆ Filenames that are not case-sensitive (but that do preserve case)

The FAT file system is a logical choice for systems where dual-boot capabilities are required.

The primary limitations of FAT are as follows:

◆ FAT is inefficient for larger partitions. As files grow in size, they may become fragmented on the disk, causing slower access times. FAT also uses inefficient cluster sizes. If the cluster size is too large, you can end up with lots of wasted space on the partition.

◆ FAT provides no local security. There is no way to prevent a user from accessing a file if the user can log in to the local operating system.

◆ FAT can support only partitions up to 2GB in size.

◆ FAT does not support compression, encryption, remote storage, mount points, or disk quotas under Windows 2000.

FAT32

FAT32 was introduced in the Microsoft product line with Windows 95 OSR 2. The primary difference between FAT and FAT32 is that FAT32 supports a smaller cluster size so it does not have as much of the wasted space associated with larger partitions.

The primary limitations of FAT32 are as follows:

◆ FAT32 has no local security.

◆ FAT32 does not support compression, encryption, remote storage, mount points, or disk quotas under Windows 2000.

◆ FAT32 supports partitions up to 32GB in size.

◆ FAT32 is not supported by all versions of Windows 95 and is not supported by DOS and Windows NT. This can cause a partition to be unavailable if dual-booting to these operating systems.

NTFS

NT File System (NTFS) is the file system of choice on most systems running Windows 2000. NTFS offers the following benefits:

◆ **Support for long filenames.** NTFS supports long filenames up to 255 characters.

◆ **Preservation of case.** NTFS is not case-sensitive, but it does have the capability of preserving case for POSIX compliance.

◆ **Recoverability.** NTFS is a recoverable file system. It uses transaction logging to automatically log all files and directory updates so that in the case of a system failure, the operating system can redo failed operations.

◆ **Security.** NTFS provides folder and file-level security for protecting files.

◆ **Compression.** NTFS supports compression of file and folders to help save disk space.

◆ **Encryption.** NTFS supports file-level encryption. This allows a user the ability to encrypt sensitive files so that no one else can read the files.

◆ **Disk quotas.** NTFS partitions support user-level disk quotas. This gives an administrator the ability to set an upper limit on the amount of space that a user can use on a partition.

◆ **Sparse files.** These are very large files created by applications in such a way that only limited disk space is needed. NTFS allocates disk space only to the portions of a file that are written to.

◆ **Size.** NTFS partitions can support much larger partition sizes than FAT. NTFS can support partitions up to 16 exabytes (EB) in size.

The main limitation of NTFS is that other operating systems do not support it and it has high system overhead.

Licensing Mode

Every installation of Windows 2000 requires a license. When you purchase a copy of Windows 2000, you receive a license for the single instance of the operating system you are installing. You also are required to have a Client Access License (CAL) for all clients that are attaching to your server over the network.

Windows 2000 Servers support two licensing modes: Per Seat and Per Server.

The Per Seat licensing mode requires that a CAL be purchased for each client that will access your server over the network. In environments where clients will be accessing multiple servers, this licensing mode makes sense.

The Per Server licensing mode requires that a license be purchased for each connection to a server. This is the preferred licensing mode in environments where there is a single server and a limited number of clients attached to the network.

The right licensing mode for your environment can be determined by determining the total number of CALs required for each licensing mode:

EXAM TIP

File Systems and the Exam For the exam you should be able to evaluate different scenarios to determine the most appropriate file system.

◆ To determine the number of CALs required for a Per Seat installation, simply count the total number of clients that will be accessing resources over the network.

◆ To determine the number of Per Server licenses required, count the total number of connections required for each server in your environment (clients requesting resources from your server).

Compare the numbers; the mode that requires the smallest number of licenses is preferred for your environment.

When calculating the total number of licenses required, remember that access to the following services does not require CALs:

◆ Anonymous or authenticated access to a computer running Internet Information Server (IIS)

◆ Telnet and File Transfer Protocol (FTP) connections

If you are in doubt, select Per Server. Microsoft allows you to perform a one-time server license conversion from Per Server to Per Seat. Per Seat to Per Server license conversions are not allowed.

Workgroup Versus Domain Models

During the installation of Windows 2000, you must choose the type of network security group you want to belong to. Your choices are between a domain model and a workgroup model.

Workgroup Model

A *workgroup* is a logical grouping of computers created to assist in the organization of equipment. Under the workgroup model, each computer that is part of a workgroup maintains its own security database. To join a workgroup during the installation process, you need to know only the name of the workgroup.

Domain Model

The domain model is similar to the workgroup model because it creates logical groupings of computer equipment. The primary difference between the workgroup and domain models is that the domain model supports a centralized database of security information.

Joining a domain requires that the following be present:

◆ The Domain Name Service (DNS) name of the domain (for example, microsoft.com)

◆ A computer account in the domain for the computer you are installing

◆ A domain controller and DNS server available on the network

> **Windows 2000 Professional in a Windows NT Domain.**   Although the focus of the book is on Windows 2000, a Windows 2000 Professional computer can be configured as a member of a Windows NT domain.
>
> N O T E

INSTALLING WINDOWS 2000 PROFESSIONAL—AN OVERVIEW

After you have planned your Windows 2000 installation, you can start the installation process. This section provides an overview of the installation process and emphasizes the configuration information required during each phase of the installation.

The Windows 2000 installation process is broken into the following steps:

1. Run the Setup program.

2. Complete the Setup Wizard.

3. Install network components.

4. Complete the installation.

Phase 1—Running the Setup Program

To begin the Windows 2000 installation, you need to start your computer and access the Windows 2000 installation files. You have four ways to start the installation process:

◆ Boot the system, load the appropriate drivers to access the CD-ROM, and load the Setup program from the command prompt by executing the WINNT.EXE command or WINNT32.EXE command.

◆ Create a Windows 2000 boot disk using the MAKEBOOT or
MAKEBT32 command (for example, run MAKEBOOT a:, found
in the BOOTDISK directory of the Windows 2000 installation CD, to create a boot disk). Booting from a Windows
2000 boot disk causes the Setup program to run automatically.

◆ If your computer supports booting from the CD-ROM, you
can boot the system from the CD-ROM with the Windows
2000 CD in the drive. This causes the Setup program to run
automatically.

◆ You can also create a network client and attach to the installation files over the network.

The first phase of the installation process is often referred to as the
text-mode portion of the installation. During this portion of the
install, you are asked for the basic installation information to prepare
the installation partition and copy required installation files to the
hard disk.

The text-mode setup process completes the following steps:

1. Setup loads a minimal version of Windows 2000 into memory.

2. The text-mode portion of Setup starts.

3. You are prompted to load third-party RAID/SCSI drivers. To
   load drivers, press F6.

4. The Setup program prompts you to select a boot partition for
   this installation of Windows 2000. Alternatively, you can create a new partition or delete an existing partition at this point.

5. The Setup program prompts you for the file system you would
   like for the partition. If you have selected an existing partition,
   you are asked whether you would like to convert it to NTFS.

6. Setup copies files to the hard disk and saves configuration
   information.

7. Setup restarts the computer and then starts the Graphical User
   Interface (GUI) portion of the installation.

Phase 2—Completing the Setup Wizard

After the text-mode installation has restarted your computer, the GUI-mode installation begins. Many configuration options are specified in this phase.

After the Setup program has installed Windows 2000 security features and detects hardware devices, the Setup Wizard prompts you for the following information:

◆ Regional settings

◆ Name and organization

◆ Product key

◆ Computer name and password for the local Administrator account

◆ Time and date

Phase 3—Installing Networking Components

This phase of the install process guides you through the configuration of the Windows 2000 networking components. During this portion of the installation the following occurs:

1. Setup detects your network adapter(s). If Setup cannot detect your adapter, you need to provide the appropriate drivers on disk. After configuring your network adapter, Windows 2000 attempts to locate a DHCP server on the network.

2. Setup then prompts you to choose to install networking components with typical or custom settings. The typical installation includes the following options:

   • Client for Microsoft Networks

   • File and Print Sharing for Microsoft Networks

   • TCP/IP protocol

3. Setup prompts you to join a workgroup or a domain.

4. Setup installs and configures the Windows 2000 components that you specified.

After installing the networking components, the Setup program moves to the final phase of installation.

Phase 4—Completing the Installation

The final phase of installation completes the following:

◆ Copies remaining file to your system

◆ Applies the configuration you selected

◆ Saves your configuration to the local hard disk

◆ Removes temporary files

◆ Restarts the computer

As soon as system restarts, the Network Identification Wizard runs. This wizard asks whether you are the only user who will be accessing this system, or can other users access it as well. If you indicate that you are the only user, you are assigned administrative privileges on the local machine. The user account is created and set to auto-logon to the Windows 2000 Professional computer.

INSTALLING WINDOWS 2000 PROFESSIONAL MANUALLY

Perform an attended installation of Windows 2000 Professional.

The next two sections focus on how a technician installs Windows 2000 Professional at the computer rather than remotely or through an automated process. Two methods of installation are available: from a CD or from a network.

Installing from a Local CD

Installing from a local CD-ROM is one of the easiest ways of installing Windows 2000. This option makes sense, however, only if you are installing a small number of computers, or a nonstandard configuration, because it is time-consuming.

To install Windows 2000 from the local CD-ROM, you must gain access to the CD by reading the CD from the previous operating system, using the Windows 2000 boot disk set, or booting from the Windows 2000 Professional CD-ROM.

If you booted from a Windows 2000 boot disk or from a Windows 2000 installation CD, the Setup program automatically runs. Alternatively, you will to run the Setup program manually. Depending on the operating system you use to boot the computer, you run either WINNT.EXE or WINNT32.EXE.

If you are using DOS to access your CD-ROM, you will run WINNT.EXE to start the setup process. If you are installing Windows 2000 over Windows 95/98 or Windows NT (either performing an upgrade or new installation), you run WINNT32.EXE to start the setup process.

Both WINNT and WINNT32 support a number of command switches that allow customization of the installation process. Table 1.2 presents the command switches associated with WINNT and WINNT32. To use a switch, type the command followed by a space followed by the switch.

> **EXAM TIP**
>
> **Command Switches and the Exam**
> You need to remember the command switches associated with both the WINNT and WINNT32 Setup programs.

> **EXAM TIP**
>
> **Making Boot Disks**   Windows NT users will notice that the /b option is no longer supported by WINNT or WINNT32. You now run a program called MAKEBOOT or MAKEBT32 from the BOOTDISK directory on the root of the Windows 2000 installation CD.

TABLE 1.2

WINNT AND WINNT32 COMMAND SWITCHES

WINNT Switch	*WINNT32 Switch*	*Description*
/a		Enables accessibility options.
/e:command	/cmd:command	Executes a command before the final phase of setup.
/i:inf_file		Specifies the filename of the setup information file. The default is DOSNET.INF. A setup information file is used to automate the installation.
/r:folder	/copydir:folder	Creates an additional folder under the systemroot that will remain after installation is complete.
/rx:folder	/copysource: folder name	Creates an additional folder within the systemroot. Setup deletes the folder and its files after the installation is complete.
/s:source_path	/s:source_path	Specifies the location of the Windows 2000 installation files.
/t:temp_drive	/tempdrive:drive	Specifies the location where temporary files should be copied during installation.
/u:script_file	/unattend:file	Specifies an unattended text file (this is discussed in greater detail in upcoming sections).
/udf:id, file	/Udf:id, udf_file	Used in conjunction with an unattended text file (this is discussed in greater detail in upcoming sections).
	/cmdcons	Installs the Windows 2000 Recovery Console support files.
	/debug level:file	Creates a debug log at a specified level.
	/syspart:drive	Copies setup startup files to a hard disk and marks the drive as active. Must use the /tempdrive option with this switch.
	/checkupgradeonly	Checks your computer for upgrade compatibility with Windows 2000. Setup creates a report named UPGRADE.TXT for Windows 95 or Windows 98 upgrades. For Windows NT 3.51 or 4.0 upgrades, it saves the report to the file WINNT32.LOG.
	/makelocalsource	Instructs Setup to copy all installation source files to your local hard disk. Use /makelocalsource when installing from a CD to provide installation files when the CD is not available later in the installation.

Installing over a Network

In environments where you are installing a large number of systems, you will find that installing over the network is preferred to local CD-based installations.

To install Windows 2000 over a network, run the setup program from a shared network folder. This process is very similar to the CD-based installation, but has the following additional requirements:

◆ A distribution server with a copy of Windows 2000 installation files must be available.

◆ You must have network client software so that client computers can attach to the distribution server.

◆ Client computers must have an existing partition with 685MB of free disk space (1GB is highly recommended). This partition is required so the installation files can be copied from the distribution server to the client before installation starts.

After you meet these requirements, you will be able to start a networked installation of Windows 2000.

ON THE CD

Step by Step 1.1, "Networked Installation of Windows 2000," walks you through starting a networked installation. See the file **Chapter01-01StepbyStep.pdf** in the CD's **Chapter01\ StepbyStep** directory.

AUTOMATING THE INSTALLATION PROCESS

Perform an unattended installation of Windows 2000 Professional.

Microsoft has greatly improved the tools available to deploy Windows 2000 Professional. Windows 2000 can be installed in three ways: manual installation from CD, imaging, or RIS images.

In most large deployments of Windows 2000, it would be impractical to install each server and workstation using the traditional CD-based installation. Instead, Microsoft has tools that leverage the fact that most systems can be installed using standardized configurations. By using Windows 2000 deployment tools, such as RIS, deployments are automated so that the only user intervention the installations require is to turn the computer on.

Creating Unattended Installation Files

Although the computers on most networks are not identical, they usually have a number of similarities. You can create a script file that will automate the installation process with little or no user intervention.

Files Used for Unattended Installation

Two files are used during an unattended installation. The first file is called an *unattended text file* (sometimes referred to as an *answer file*). This file contains all the information necessary to install Windows 2000. The second file is called a *uniqueness definition file (UDF)* that configures unique aspects for each individual computer.

Most organizations assess the operational requirements of each computer being installed and categorize them into major groupings. An unattended text file is then created for each category of system. A UDF file is also needed so that the unique configuration options for each individual computer, within each category, could be included in the installation process.

Both the answer and UDF files can be created using the Windows 2000 Setup Manager or using a simple text editor. The Setup Manager is part of the Windows 2000 Support Tools and can be installed by running SETUP.EXE from the \Support\tools folder on the Windows 2000 distribution CDs.

The Setup Manager allows you to do the following:

◆ Create answer and UDF files using an easy-to-use graphical interface.

◆ Specify computer-specific or user-specific information.

◆ Include application setup scripts in the answer files.

◆ Create answer file (WINNT.SIF) that can be used if booting from the installation CD.

◆ Automatically create a networked distribution folder for the installation files.

Creating an Unattended Text File

Using an unattended text file allows the administrator to start the installation of Windows 2000 and walk away. The installation process reads the unattended text file and uses the information contained within it to configure the system.

To install Windows 2000 using an unattended text file, use the /u switch after the WINNT or WINNT32 command. The syntax of this command is as follows:

```
WINNT /u:"answer file" /s:"source path where the Windows
➥2000 installation files can be found"
```

or

```
WINNT32 /unattend:"answer file" /s:"source path where the
➥Windows 2000 installation files can be found"
```

The main purpose of the unattended text file is to answer all the prompts that the person performing the installation would manually enter during the installation. You can use the same unattended text file across a number of computers with similar hardware configuration.

> **EXAM TIP**
>
> **Command Syntax Matters**   You are sure to get a question regarding the syntax of the unattended text file. If you can memorize the syntax, these are easy marks.

A sample of the unattended text file can be found on the Windows 2000 CD in the i386 directory. The information found in UNAT-TEND.TXT is categorized into section headings, parameters, and values associated with those parameters. The sample file contains a fraction of the total number of section headings and parameters supported during unattended installations. (For a complete listing see Microsoft Windows 2000 Unattended Setup Parameters Guide: Answer File Parameters for Unattended Installation of Microsoft Windows 2000, Microsoft Corporation, Revision 1.5 April 9, 1999, available at `http://www.microsoft.com/TechNet/win2000/win2ksrv/technote/unattend.asp`.)

As you review this file, note that information is organized in the following format:

```
[Section Heading]
; Comments
; Comments
Parameter = value
```

Here are the file contents:

```
; Microsoft Windows NT Workstation Version 5.0 and
; Windows NT Server Version 5.0
; (c) 1994 - 1998 Microsoft Corporation. All rights
➥reserved.
;
; Sample Unattended Setup Answer File
;
; This file contains information about how to automate the
➥installation
; or upgrade of Windows NT Workstation and Windows NT
➥Server so the
; Setup program runs without requiring user input.
;
; For information on how to use this file, read the
➥appropriate sections
; of the Windows NT 5.0 Resource Kit.

[Unattended]
Unattendmode = FullUnattended
OemPreinstall = NO
```

```
TargetPath = WINNT
Filesystem = LeaveAlone

[UserData]
FullName = "Your User Name"
OrgName = "Your Organization Name"
ComputerName = "COMPUTER_NAME"

[GuiUnattended]
TimeZone = "004"
; Sets the Admin Password to NULL
AdminPassword = *
; Turn AutoLogon on
AutoLogon = Yes

;For Server installs
[LicenseFilePrintData]
AutoMode = "PerServer"
AutoUsers = "0"

[GuiRunOnce]
; List the programs that you want to launch when the
➥machine is logged into for the first time
; "Notepad %WINDIR%\Setuperr.log"

[Display]
BitsPerPel = 4
XResolution = 800
YResolution = 600
VRefresh = 70

[Networking]
; When set to YES, setup will install default networking
➥components. The components to be set are
; TCP/IP, File and Print Sharing, and the Client for
➥Microsoft Networks.
InstallDefaultComponents = YES

[Identification]
JoinWorkgroup = Workgroup
```

Information in the UNATTEND.TXT file is divided into seven
main sections. Table 1.3 provides explanations of the section headings and parameters found in a typical UNATTEND.TXT file.

TABLE 1.3

SECTION HEADINGS AND PARAMETERS IN A TYPICAL UNATTENDED TEXT FILE

Section Heading	Option (Values)	Description
Unattended This section header is used to identify whether an unattended installation is being performed. This section is required in a UNATTEND.TXT file; otherwise, the answer file is ignored.	UnattendMode (Values: GuiAttended | Provide Default | DefaultHide | Read only | FullUnattended)	This parameter defines the unattended mode to be used during GUI-mode Setup. The default value is DefaultHide when the key is not specified. When this key is specified, text-mode Setup is fully automated with or without the necessary answers. GuiAttended specifies that the GUI-mode section of Setup is attended. This mode is useful in preinstallation scenarios in which the OEM or administrator wants to automate only text-mode Setup. ProvideDefault specifies that answers in the answer file are defaults. In this case, Setup displays these default answers to the user, who may change them if desired. DefaultHide specifies that answers in the answer file are defaults. Unlike the ProvideDefault value, Setup does not display the user interface to end users if all the answers relating to a particular wizard page are specified in the answer file. This is the default behavior if unattended mode is not specified. ReadOnly specifies that answers in the answer file are read-only if the wizard pages containing these answers are displayed to the end user. Unlike the DefaultHide parameter, however, the user can specify only new answers on a displayed page. FullUnattended specifies that GUI mode is fully unattended. If a required Setup answer is not specified in the answer file, an error will be generated.
	Repartition (Value: Yes/No)	Specifies whether all partitions on the first drive on the client computer should be deleted and the drive reformatted with the NTFS file system.
	FileSystem (Value: ConvertNTFS/LeaveAlone)	Specifies whether the primary partition should be converted to NTFS or left alone.
	NtUpgrade (Values: Yes/No)	Determines whether a previous version of Windows NT should be upgraded.
	Win9xUpgrade (Values: Yes/No)	Determines whether previous installations of Windows 95 or Windows 98 should be upgraded to Windows 2000 Professional. It is valid only if used in conjunction with WINNT32.EXE.
	TargetPath (Values: * or <path name>)	Determines the installation folder in which Windows 2000 should be installed. <path name> is the user-defined install folder and should not include the drive letter. To specify the target drive, the /tempdrive command-line option to WINNT32.EXE or /t option to WINNT.EXE must be specified.

Section Heading	*Option (Values)*	*Description*
UserData	FullName (Value: <string>)	Specifies the user's full name. If the key is empty or missing, the user is prompted to enter a name.
This section is used to specify user-specific data into the installation process—specifically the users name, organization, and computer name.		
	OrgName (Value: <string>)	Specifies an organization's name. If the OrgName key is empty or missing, the user is prompted to enter an organization name.
	ComputerName (Value: <string>)	Specifies the computer name. If the ComputerName key is empty or missing, the user is prompted to enter a computer name. If the value is *, Setup generates a random computer name based on the organization name specified.
		The computer name specified should contain no more than 64 characters. If more than 64 characters are used for the ComputerName parameter, the computer name is truncated to 64 characters.
	ProductID (Value: <string>)	Specifies the Microsoft Product Identification (Product ID) number.
		This parameter sets the Product ID for all computers installed using this unattended text file to the same value. This could cause issues when calling Microsoft product support.
GuiUnattended	AdminPassword (Value: <password>/*)	Sets up the Administrator account password. If the value is *, Setup sets the Administrator password to NULL.
This section is used to specify settings for the GUI portion of the installation. It can be used to indicate the time zone and to hide the administrator password page.		
	AutoLogon (Value: Yes/No)	This key, if set to Yes, sets up the computer to auto-logon once with the Administrator account. The default behavior is No. The key is not valid on upgrades.
		If you specify an AdminPassword, that password will be used to perform the auto logon process. The password will be deleted from the copy of the answer file left on the computer after the installation is complete.
	AutoLogonCount (Value: <integer>)	Lists the number of times that the computer should automatically log on using the Administrator account and password specified. The value is decremented after each reboot, and the feature is disabled after the specified number of logon attempts is complete. It is useful only when Autologon = Yes.

continues

TABLE 1.3	*continued*

SECTION HEADINGS AND PARAMETERS IN A TYPICAL UNATTENDED TEXT FILE

Section Heading	Option (Values)	Description
	TimeZone (Value: <index>)	Determines the time zone of the computer. If the key is empty, the user is prompted to select a time zone.
	ProfilesDir (Value: <path to profile directory> Default: %systemdrive%\Documents and Settings)	Specifies the location of Windows 2000 profiles. This parameter is valid only on clean installs of Windows 2000 and it is ignored on upgrades.
		The ProfilesDir parameter is useful in scenarios that require new installations to use the same profile directory as Windows NT 4.0. For example, ProfilesDir = %systemroot%\Profiles
		The directory specified must contain an environment variable, such as %systemdrive% or %systemroot%.
	DetachedProgram (Value: <detached program string>)	Used to indicate the path of the custom program that should run concurrently with the Setup program. If the program requires any arguments, the Arguments key must be specified.
	Arguments (Value: <arguments string>)	Indicates that arguments or parameters accompany the custom program that should run concurrently with the Setup program.
LicenseFilePrintData This section is applied only to Windows 2000 Server installations. It enables you to specify the licensing options you want to use for your server (that is, Per Server or Per Seat licensing and the number of licenses).	AutoMode (Values: PERSEAT/PERSERVER)	Determines whether Windows 2000 Server, Windows 2000 Advanced Server, or Windows 2000 Datacenter Server is to be installed in a Per Seat or a Per Server license mode. If AutoMode = PERSERVER, the AutoUsers key must also be specified.
		PERSEAT indicates that a client access license has been purchased for each computer that accesses the server.
		PERSERVER indicates that client access licenses have been purchased for the server to allow a certain number of concurrent connections to the server.
		If AutoMode is empty or missing, the user is prompted to select the license mode.
	AutoUsers (Value: integer)	This key is valid only if AutoMode = PerServer. The integer value indicates the number of client licenses purchased for the server being installed. The minimum value allowed is 5 (less than 5 causes the install to fail).

Section Heading	Option (Values)	Description
GuiRunOnce This section specifies a command you want run when the installation completes for the fist time and the computer is rebooted. This is useful if you want to install additional software on the computer after the operating system is installed.		
Display This section allows you to specify the display settings you want applied to the system.	BitsPerPixel (Value: <valid bits per pixel>)	Specifies the <valid bits per pixel> for the graphics device being installed. For example, a value of 8 (2^8) implies 256 colors; 16 implies 65536 colors.
	Xresolution (Value: <valid x resolution>)	Specifies a <valid x resolution> for the graphics device being installed.
	Yresolution (Value: <valid y resolution>)	Specifies a <valid y resolution> for the graphics device being installed.
	Vrefresh (Value: <valid refresh rate>)	Specifies a <valid refresh rate> for the graphics device being installed. Be very careful with these settings. An improperly configured refresh rate can damage your monitor.
Networking This section is used to specify network settings, such as network adapters, services, and protocols. If this section is not provided, networking will not be installed.	InstallDefaultComponents (Value: Yes | NoDefault: No)	When set to Yes, Setup installs default networking components. The default networking configuration automatically installs the following: TCP/IP on all network adapters; File and Printer Sharing for Microsoft Networks; and Client for Microsoft Networks.

Creating Uniqueness Database Files

UDF files allow you to specify the unique settings associated with each computer in your environment. As shown in the previous section, UDF files can be created using the Setup Manager. You may, however, want to modify your UDF file to include additional configuration settings (above and beyond unique computer names).

UDF files contain two sections. One section of the file, indicated by the [UniqueIds] header, contains a listing of all unique IDs referenced in the file and the sections associated with them. The second part of the file contains the actual sections that are to be used by each computer when it is installed.

When a UDF file is used in conjunction with an answer file, any configuration setting associated with a unique ID is merged with the contents of the answer file.

The following is a listing of a standard UDF file:

```
;SetupMgrTag
[UniqueIds]
    Workstation1=UserData, Network
    Workstation2=UserData
    Workstation3=UserData
    Workstation4=UserData

[Workstation1:UserData]
    ComputerName=Workstation1

[Workstation2:UserData]
    ComputerName=Workstation2

[Workstation3:UserData]
    ComputerName=Workstation3

[Workstation4:UserData]
    ComputerName=Workstation4

[Workstation1:Network]
    JoinDomain="DomainName"
```

Note the top header of this file. This UDF file is set up to configure four computers: Workstation1, Workstation2, Workstation3, and Workstation4. We see this from the [UniqueIds] section of the file. We can also see that Workstation1 will have a UserData and Network configuration stored in this file. Workstation2 through Workstation4 have UserData configurations stored. In this example Workstation1 has a custom network configuration. Workstation2 through Workstation4 receive the network configuration specified in the unattended answer file.

Using the Setup Manager

The Setup Manager is a powerful tool that assists in the creation of unattended answer and UDF files. The utility is part of the Windows 2000 Support Tools and can be installed by running

SETUP.EXE from the \Support\Tools directory on the Windows 2000 installation CDs.

When installed, performing the steps in Step by Step 1.2 run the Setup Manager.

ON THE CD

Step by Step 1.2, "Running the Setup Manager," shows you how to get the Setup Manager up and running. See the file **Chapter01-02StepbyStep.pdf** in the CD's **Chapter01\StepbyStep** directory.

When the Setup Wizard has finished, you will find it has created three files:

- ◆ Answer file NAME.TXT (the unattended answer file)

- ◆ Answer file NAME.UDF (the UDF file)

- ◆ Answer file NAME.BAT (a batch file to start unattended installs)

Remote Installation Services (RIS)

Windows 2000 RIS allows client computers to be installed throughout an enterprise from a central location. This service greatly reduces the effort required to manage the images that are being used throughout your environment because they are stored and managed from a central location.

RIS provides the following benefits:

- ◆ Enables remote installation of Windows 2000 Professional

- ◆ Simplifies server image management

- ◆ Supports recovery of the operating system and computer if a system failure occurs during installation

EXAM TIP

Remember the Syntax of the Files The syntax of the unattended text and UDF files is complex. The code generated by the UNATTEND.BAT file is especially useful if you want to see the correct syntax associated with using the unattended text and UDF files together.

NOTE

RIS Images Although referred to as an image, RIS images are actual copies of the Windows 2000 installation files. When a client is installed using RIS, the client actually runs the native Windows 2000 install process.

RIS requires a Windows 2000 Active Directory infrastructure and has specific server and workstation requirements. The following sections discuss these requirements.

The RIS Process

Remote installation is the process of a RIS client connecting to a server running RIS, and then starting an automated installation of Windows 2000 Professional on a local computer.

RIS Server Requirements

RIS runs on a Windows 2000 Server. RIS must be installed on the computer by running the Setup Wizard from the Add and Remove Programs icon of Control Panel. When installed, the Windows 2000 Remote Installation Services Setup Wizard can be used to configure the RIS server.

The RIS server can be either a domain controller or a member server. The following network services do not have to be installed on the RIS server, but must be available on the network:

- ◆ **DNS server.** RIS uses DNS to resolve the IP addresses of directory servers and client computers on the network.

- ◆ **DHCP server.** RIS clients need to obtain their network configuration from a DHCP server during the initial stages of the RIS installation procedure.

- ◆ **Active Directory.** RIS relies on the Microsoft Active Directory service in Windows 2000 for locating existing client computers and RIS servers.

Remote installation also requires that RIS be installed on a partition that is formatted as NTFS and shared over the network. This partition must not be the boot partition for Windows 2000 (that is, the drive where Windows 2000 Server is installed) and must also be large enough to store the RIS images.

When RIS is installed, it is ready to receive its first image. RIS can be configured to store multiple images on its local hard drive. Although referred to as images (which sometimes implies a single file that represents the contents of a hard drive), the files copied to the RIS server are actual copies of all the source files required to install Windows 2000 Professional.

After the first image is installed, RIS can be authorized to respond to client requests for installation.

RIS Client Requirements

Client computers that support remote installation must have one of the following configurations:

◆ A configuration meeting the Network PC (Net PC) specification

◆ A network adapter card configured to use the Pre-Boot Execution Environment (PXE) boot ROM

◆ A supported network adapter card and a remote installation boot disk

Computers that support one of these configurations can simply be plugged into the network and switched on. When they initialize, they will boot from the network and receive information regarding the location of the RIS server (most machines require the user to press F12 to indicate a network boot). The user is then prompted to logon. When logged on, a listing of the RIS installation images stored on the RIS server is displayed.

> **NOTE**
>
> **Booting from a Network Interface Card** You need to configure your system to boot from the network interface card. On most systems, this is done through the system BIOS.

RIS servers can also be configured so that they respond only to computers that they are explicitly configured to service. This is called *prestaging* a client. During this process, a unique identifier for each workstation, the Media Access Control (MAC) address is used to create a computer object in the Active Directory. The computer is assigned a RIS server and installation image. The client is then given its preconfigured image.

Using Remote Image Preparation Tool (RIPrep)

Remote Installation Preparation (RIPrep) is a utility that allows you to prepare a workstation image that can be loaded on the RIS server. These images include Windows 2000 Professional and any applications you want included in your download image.

Two systems are required to create a RIPrep image. The first system is the source computer (that is, the computer that contains the base operating system and applications), the second is the RIS server.

The steps in setting up the RIPrep source computer are as follows:

1. Install Windows 2000 Professional.

2. Configure Windows 2000 components and settings to ensure that all settings are correct for your environment.

3. Install and configure all applications you want included in your image as the Administrator.

4. When all configurations are complete you should copy the Administrator profile over the Default User profile to ensure that the default user profile is updated to include all settings.

5. Test the source computer to ensure it is configured properly.

When the source computer is ready, you can start the Remote Installation Preparation Wizard by running `\\RIS_SERVER_NAME\reminst\admin\i386\riprep.exe`.

The wizard removes all unique information, such as security identifier (SID) information, computer name, and registry settings from the computer. A RIPrep image is then transferred to a RIS server and an answer file is associated with the newly created image.

Imaging Windows 2000 Professional Installs

Another popular option for installing Windows 2000 is to use third-party imaging tools to create installation images. This differs from a RIS image, because the Windows 2000 Setup program is not being used to install Windows 2000 on the system. Instead, a binary duplicate copy of one computer's hard drive is being transferred to other machines.

There are some issues associated with this type of installation, however. Because the hard disk is being duplicated, each system that is created using the image is an exact duplicate. For this reason, issues arise because computer names and security GUIs are duplicated across the network.

The System Preparation Tool (SYSPREP)

SYSPREP is a utility that gives users the ability to prepare a computer so it can be imaged. Disk duplication software can then be used to take a snapshot of the computer's hard drive so it can be transferred to another machine.

ON THE CD

Step by Step 1.3, "The SYSPREP Process," illustrates the use of the SYSPREP tool. See the file **Chapter01-03StepbyStep.pdf** in the CD's **Chapter01\StepbyStep** directory.

SYSPREP Command Options

To assist in the disk duplication process, the SYSPREP utility supports a number of command options (as shown in Table 1.4).

TABLE 1.4

SYSPREP COMMAND OPTIONS

Option	Description
SYSPREP.INF	A file created with Setup Manager to customize the Mini-Setup routine that runs the first time the target user reboots the computer.
-pnp	The Mini-Setup Wizard detects new or different Plug and Play devices on the destination computer and disables those that were used on the master computer but not found on the destination computer.
-quiet	Suppresses confirmation dialog boxes displayed to the user.
-nosidgen	Informs the Setup program not to generate new SIDs on the reboot.
-reboot	Forces the computer to reboot instead of shutting down.

USING A DUAL-BOOT SYSTEM

Dual-booting is a term used to describe a computer that has more than one operating system installed on it. When the computer starts, a boot manager presents the user a list of the installed operating systems so that the user can choose the OS to be booted.

When dual-booting a system, you need to be aware of incompatibilities that may arise between the different operating systems you are installing. For example, if you dual-boot Windows 95 with Windows 2000 Professional, partitions formatted as NTFS under Windows 2000 Professional are not accessible from Windows 95.

To create a dual-boot system, install Windows 2000 Professional to a different partition than the current OS found on the computer. When the system reboots, the Windows boot manager presents you with a list of available operating systems.

UPGRADING TO WINDOWS 2000 PROFESSIONAL

Upgrade from a previous version of Windows to Windows 2000 Professional.

Windows 2000 offers a number of new technologies that help simplify network management. To take advantage of these features, network clients need to be upgraded to run Windows 2000 Professional. Upgrading clients also allows them to retain their software configurations and user preferences.

The following steps complete the basic upgrade process:

1. Verify the upgrade path.

2. Ensure that hardware requirements are met.

3. Test compatibility with the Windows 2000 Compatibility tool.

The following sections explore this process.

Verifying Upgrade Paths

You can upgrade earlier versions of Windows to Windows 2000. Table 1.5 presents the upgrade path for older Windows operating systems.

TABLE 1.5

WINDOWS 2000 PROFESSIONAL UPGRADE PATHS

Upgrade From:	Upgrade To:
Windows 3.x	Windows 95 or 98 and then upgrade to Windows 2000 Professional
Windows 95 and Windows 98	Windows 2000 Professional
Windows NT Workstation 3.51 or 4.0	Windows 2000 Professional
Windows NT Workstation 3.1 or 3.5	Windows NT Workstation 3.51 or 4.0 and then upgrade to Windows 2000 Professional

> **EXAM TIP**
>
> **Upgrade Paths**   It is critical you remember the upgrade paths that are available to you.

Client Hardware Requirements

Before you attempt to upgrade your system, you should ensure that it meets the same minimum hardware requirements that are required for a new installation, as discussed earlier in this chapter in the section "Hardware Requirements."

Hardware Compatibility

During an upgrade, a hardware compatibility report is generated, listing the hardware components that are not compatible with Windows 2000.

Microsoft recommends that you run the compatibility tools before you start your system upgrades. Knowledge of incompatibilities before you start your upgrades allows you to research new drivers or fixes that have been created for your specific incompatibility.

You can generate a compatibility report using the Windows 2000 compatibility tools in two ways. This first involves running the WINNT32 Setup program with the /checkupgradeonly command switch to check hardware issues.

The second option is to run the CHKUPGRD.EXE utility. This utility can be downloaded from Microsoft (www.microsoft.com/downloads).

Both the WINNT32 /checkupgradeonly and the CHKUPGRD.EXE compatibility tools report the same information: the report documents system hardware and software that is incompatible with Windows 2000 Professional. It also identifies whether you need to obtain upgrades for software that is installed on your system.

Upgrading Compatible Windows 95/98 Clients

For Windows 95/98 clients that do not present any compatibility issues, you can run the Windows 2000 Professional Setup program (WINNT32.EXE) to upgrade them to Windows 2000.

ON THE CD

Step by Step 1.4, "Upgrading Compatible Windows 95/98 Clients to Windows 2000," illustrates the upgrade process. See the file **Chapter01-04StepbyStep.pdf** in the CD's **Chapter01\StepbyStep** directory.

Upgrading Compatible Windows NT Clients

For Windows NT clients that do not present any compatibility issues, you can run the Windows 2000 Professional Setup program (WINNT32.EXE) to upgrade them to Windows 2000.

ON THE CD

Step by Step 1.5, "Upgrading Compatible Windows NT Clients to Windows 2000," leads you through the upgrade process. See the file **Chapter01-05StepbyStep.pdf** in the CD's **Chapter01\ StepbyStep** directory.

NOTE **Compatibility Reports** During the upgrade, the Setup wizard generates a compatibility report. The report is saved as %systemroot%\winnt32.log. If the upgrade fails, this is an excellent place to start your troubleshooting.

Incompatible Systems

Computers that do not meet the compatibility requirements of Windows 2000 can still participate, to a limited degree, in a Windows 2000 network.

Windows NT 3.51 that do not meet the hardware compatibility requirements can still log on to a Windows 2000 network. They cannot, however, use many of the advanced desktop management tools available in Windows 2000.

Windows 95/98 clients and Windows NT 4.0 clients need a Windows 2000 Directory Service client installed on them to access Windows 2000 fault-tolerant distributed file systems, search the Active Directory, and change passwords in the domain. To install the service, follow Step by Step 1.6.

ON THE CD

Step by Step 1.6, "Installing the Windows 9x Directory Services Client," shows you how to install the service. See the file **Chapter01-06StepbyStep.pdf** in the CD's **Chapter01\StepbyStep** directory.

NOTE **DS Client** The Windows NT 4.0 DS Client will be shipped with Windows NT Service Pack 7. The Windows 9x DS Client is available on the Windows 2000 CD in the \Clients\DSClient folder.

SERVICE PACK DEPLOYMENT

Deploy service packs.

When you have Windows 2000 installed and operational on your network, you need to maintain it. The primary tool Microsoft uses to distribute updates to its operating systems is the service pack. Service packs contain more that just bug fixes.

It is in your best interest to monitor the current service packs available at Microsoft's Web site. As new service packs become available, you should thoroughly test the service packs on your systems. It is also important that you read the release notes that ship with the service packs for information relating to compatibility issues and services you may be running on your systems.

After they're tested, service packs can be easily deployed to workstations and servers in your environment through Windows 2000 Group Policy objects or with products, such as Microsoft's System Management Server (SMS).

Service packs can also be applied directly at installation using a process known as *slip streaming*. This involves copying the original installation files from the i386 directory to a network share and then copying the service pack files over the installation files. An install from this network share results in an installation at that service pack level.

TROUBLESHOOTING THE INSTALLATION PROCESS

Troubleshoot failed installations.

The Windows 2000 installation process is relatively simple. However, you may experience a number of common problems. Table 1.6 presents a listing of common setup problems.

TABLE 1.6

COMMON SETUP PROBLEMS

Problem	Solution
Media errors	If your installation CD has been damaged, you will receive media errors. The only solution to this problem is obtaining a new copy of the installation CD.
Nonsupported CD-ROM drive	If the Windows 2000 setup program reports that it cannot find or access the CD-ROM, you may need to replace the CD-ROM unit or perform a network install.
Nonsupported mass storage device	You may experience the situation where the Windows 2000 Setup program cannot access your hard disks. This is usually a problem with the drivers being used to access your hard drives.
Inability to connect to the domain controller	Verify that the domain name is correct and that the domain controller is running. You should also verify that DNS is configured properly and is running.
Failure of Windows 2000 to install or start	Verify the Windows 2000 Compatibility report.

CASE STUDY: ABC COMPANY

ESSENCE OF THE CASE

Here are the essential elements in this case:

▶ Upgrading Windows 95/98/NT 4.0 to Windows 2000

▶ Upgrading Windows NT 3.5 to Windows 2000

▶ Automating the installation of new computers

ABC Company is in the process of installing Windows 2000 Professional on all desktop computers in its organization. Details of its environment are as follows:

- Existing equipment
  - 200 Windows 95 workstations
  - 200 Windows 98 workstations
  - 150 Windows NT 4.0 workstations
  - 50 Windows NT 3.5 workstations

continues

CASE STUDY: ABC COMPANY

continued

- New equipment

    - 100 500MHz Pentium III computers (new purchases) with 64MB of RAM and 6GB hard drives

Existing workstations need to be upgraded to support Windows 2000. New equipment must be installed to support Windows 2000. ABC Company uses a number of in-house applications and the standard MS Office products.

Before a budget approval can proceed on this project, a detailed rollout plan is required for the board of directors. Budgets are tight for this project, and it must be completed using the smallest amount of staff time as possible.

ANALYSIS

The information presented must be broken down into its individual components to fully analyze this scenario.

One of the first challenges for the installation team will be to fully inventory the existing equipment to determine whether it meets the minimum hardware requirements for Windows 2000. Any equipment that does not meet the minimum requirements needs to be upgraded or replaced. From a budget perspective, it is critical that all upgrade/replacement costs are included in the implementation plan.

A standardized method of upgrading each machine should then be developed. Because each machine is currently in production use, you must include procedures to back up all data on the local machines before the upgrade occurs (to limit the possibility of data loss). Windows 95/98 machines can be upgraded directly to Windows 2000. You need to plan for the creation of computer accounts for computers being upgraded from Windows 95/98. Windows NT 3.5 machines need to be upgraded to Windows NT 4.0 and then upgraded to Windows 2000 Professional.

New systems need to have Windows 2000 Professional installed on them. You need to test the fastest method of Installing Windows 2000 Professional (and required applications) on these machines. You should compare the installation technologies outlined in Table 1.7.

TABLE 1.7

INSTALLATION TECHNOLOGIES

Technology	Additional Considerations
RIS	Are Active Directory, DNS, DHCP, and a domain controller available?
Answer files	How many different common configurations are required?
Images	How well does a software image work on the new machines?

CHAPTER SUMMARY

Microsoft provides a number of excellent tools to aid in the installation of Windows 2000. This chapter reviewed the Windows 2000 product line so you can evaluate your business needs to determine the version of Windows 2000 that best meets those needs. This chapter also presented the information you need before you start the installation of the product. Planning is a very important aspect of any installation. You then reviewed the tools available to automate the installation process.

KEY TERMS
- BOOT partition
- Dual-boot
- System partition
- Primary partition
- Extended partition
- Logical drive
- Basic disk
- Dynamic disk
- NT File System (NTFS)
- FAT
- FAT32
- Bootable disk
- Remote Installation Services (RIS)
- Unattended text file
- Answer file
- Uniqueness definition file (UDF)

APPLY YOUR KNOWLEDGE

Review Questions

1. What are the primary differences between Windows 2000 Professional Server, Advanced Server, and Datacenter Server?

2. What are the minimum system requirements for Windows 2000 Professional?

3. What are the advantages/disadvantages of FAT/FAT32 versus NTFS?

4. What utility is used to generate unattended text files and how is it installed?

5. What are the four Phases of the Windows 2000 installation process?

6. What is the difference between a local CD-based installation of Windows 2000 and a networked installation of Windows 2000?

7. What is the primary difference between a SYSPREP and RIPrep installation?

Answers to Review Questions

1. Windows 2000 Server supports quad processors and is designed for workgroup environments. Advanced Server supports up to eight processors and includes cluster support. Datacenter Server supports up to 32 processors and is designed for very large environments. See the section "Windows 2000 Products" for details.

2. The minimum system requirements include a Pentium 133 with 64MB RAM, and 2GB hard drive with 650MB of free space. See the section "Hardware Requirements" for details.

3. One of the primary advantages of FAT is that it is supported by almost every operating system on the market. On the downside, however, it lacks local security and is inefficient on large partitions.

   Windows 95 (OSR2), Windows 98, and Windows 2000 are the only operating systems that support FAT32. Like FAT, FAT32 lacks local security. FAT32 is, however, more efficient than FAT for larger partitions.

   Windows 2000 or Windows NT (with SP3+) are the only operating systems that support the version of NTFS (5.0) that ships with Windows 2000. NTFS offers a number of advantages, such as local security, encryption, and compression. See the section "Windows 2000 File Systems" for details.

4. Setup Manager is used to generate unattended text files. The Setup Manager utility ships with the Windows 2000 Resource Kit and on the Windows 2000 Server CD in the \support\tools folder. See the section "Automating the Installation Process" for details.

APPLY YOUR KNOWLEDGE

5. Phase I is the text mode of the installation. During this phase, you provide information regarding the installation partition, file format, and installation directory. You configure the following in Phase II (the GUI-mode setup): regional settings, name and organization, licensing mode (server only), computer name, and optional components to install. Phase III of the installation involves setting up the network components on your system (network interface cards and so forth). The last phase of the installation copies remaining files to your computer, applies configuration settings, removes temporary files, and restarts the computer. See the section "Installing Windows 2000 Professional—An Overview" for details.

6. To complete a networked-based installation, you must have the installation files copied to a distribution server, client software so you can attach to the distribution server, and a minimum of 685MG of free drive space on the local machine you want to install. See the section "Installing over a Network" for details.

7. RIPREP is used to create images (a copy of setup files and corresponding script files) that work in conjunction with the RIS server. SYSPREP removes unique information from a computer so it can be "imaged" using third-party disk imaging utilities. The key here is that RIPrep works with RIS, and SYSPREP works with third-party disk imaging utilities. See the sections "Using Remote Image Preparation Tool (RIPrep)" and "Imaging Windows 2000 Professional Installs" for details.

ON THE CD

This book's companion CD contains specially designed supplemental material to help you understand how well you know the concepts and skills you learned in this chapter. You'll find related exercises and exam questions and answers. See the file **Chapter01ApplyYourKnowledge.pdf** in the CD's **Chapter01\ApplyYourKnowledge** directory.

Suggested Readings and Resources

The following Web resources are recommended for your further study:

1. Deploying Windows 2000 Professional, available at `http://www.microsoft.com/windows2000/library/planning/client/deploy.asp`.

2. Microsoft Windows 2000 Unattended Setup Parameters Guide: Answer File Parameters for Unattended Installation of Microsoft Windows 2000, Microsoft Corporation, Revision 1.5 April 9, 1999, available at `http://www.microsoft.com/TechNet/win2000/win2ksrv/technote/unattend.asp`.

3. Step-by-Step Guide to a Common Infrastructure for Windows 2000 Server Deployment—Part 1: Installing a Windows 2000 Server as a Domain Controller, available at `http://www.microsoft.com/windows2000/library/planning/server/serversteps.asp`.

4. Step-by-Step Guide to a Common Infrastructure for Windows 2000 Server Deployment—Part 2: Installing a Windows 2000 Professional Workstation and Connecting it to a Domain, available at `http://www.microsoft.com/windows2000/library/planning/server/prosteps.asp`.

5. Step-by-Step Guide to Remote OS Installation, available at `http://www.microsoft.com/windows2000/library/planning/management/remotesteps.asp`.

6. Understanding the Value of IntelliMirror, Remote OS Installation, and Systems Management Server, available at `http://www.microsoft.com/windows2000/guide/server/solutions/valueim.asp`.

This chapter covers the following Microsoft-specified objectives for the "Implementing and Conducting Administration of Resources" section of the exam:

Monitor, manage, and troubleshoot access to files and folders.

- **Configure, manage, and troubleshoot file compression.**

- **Control access to files and folders by using permissions.**

- **Optimize access to files and folders.**

▶ File system resources represent one of the most important services used on networks today. As a network administrator you must learn to balance the ease of network access against security considerations.

Manage and troubleshoot access to shared folders.

- **Create and remove shared folders.**

- **Control access to shared folders by using permissions.**

- **Manage and troubleshoot Web server resources.**

▶ Shared folders allow users to gain access to folders and files remotely. As a network administrator you must gain a full appreciation of shared folders and shared folder security.

Connect to local and network print devices.

- **Manage printers and print jobs.**

- **Control access to printers by using permissions.**

- **Connect to an Internet printer.**

- **Connect to a local print device.**

CHAPTER 2

Implementing and Conducting Administration of Resources

▶ The print environment is another heavily used network service. This objective ensures that, as a network administrator, you understand how to configure and manage the Windows 2000 printer environment. This objective includes print security, printer management, and print job management.

Configure and manage file systems.

- Convert from one file system to another file system.

- Configure file systems by using NTFS, FAT32, or FAT.

▶ The Windows 2000 file system offers network administrators a large number of configuration options. This objective ensures that you understand the implications of using one file system over another, and that you have the skills required to manage the file system you use in your environment.

STUDY STRATEGIES

▶ The key to understanding the objectives for this chapter is your understanding of permissions. *Permissions* give users certain levels of rights to perform specific actions on resources on the network. If you understand how Microsoft applies permissions to the file system (the most complex of the permissions) you will find permissions, when applied to other services, very easy to understand. In short, focus your efforts on NTFS- and share-level permissions. Understanding these permissions makes working with printer permissions easy.

▶ You will need to understand the limitations of FAT and FAT32 with regard to security in the Windows 2000 environment. You also need to thoroughly understand how to manage these file systems.

▶ Printing is a relatively easy section. I suggest you configure a few local printers and play around with them for a couple of hours. I also suggest you focus on the Web-based printer-management utilities.

INTRODUCTION

The primary focus of this chapter is the efficient management
of network resources. Specifically, it takes a detailed look at the
management of the network file and print environments.

The chapter starts with an overview of the challenges that face
network administrators when it comes to the management of network resources. The issues associated with the management of a
network file system are then covered. Specifically, shared folders are
discussed to ensure that you have a thorough understanding of how
shares and share security work. We then look at NTFS security and
how it can be used, in conjunction with share-level security, to
secure a network file system. The second major service, printing, is
then covered. These sections detail how a print environment is configured, secured, and then managed.

MANAGING NETWORK RESOURCES

Networks allow users to share resources. One of the primary goals of
the network administrator is to control access to resources and
ensure that a resource is accessible to authorized users and secured
from unauthorized users. The following section focuses on the tools
available to manage some of the most common networked resources.

In the world of networks a number of different types of networked
resources exist. Some of the most common networked resources
include file systems, printers, and databases. Regardless of the service
you are dealing with, network administrators typically use permissions to control access to resources. Permissions define the level of
access a user has to resources. Depending on the type of resources
you are managing, different sets of permissions will be available to
control different levels of access.

FILE RESOURCES

Monitor, manage, and troubleshoot access to files and folders.

Manage and troubleshoot access to shared folders.

One of the most heavily used network services found in most environments is file system service. Microsoft Windows 2000 allows network administrators to "share" file system resources so that multiple users are accessing a file system remotely over the network. Windows 2000 also provides a secure file system (NTFS) that gives an administrator the ability to secure a file system by giving a user permission to use the resource.

The following sections provide details on managing file system resources. Specifically, the skills required to manage and troubleshoot shared folders and NTFS permissions are presented.

File Shares

To allow remote access to resources you must make them available over the network. After resources are available on the network, users with the appropriate permissions can access resources from computers found on the network. Windows 2000 allows you to control the resources you want to make available over the network.

Sharing a folder in Windows 2000 means you are making a folder within a file system available to users on the network. After you decide which file system resources you want to make available over the network, you will need to share them and set user permissions. Shared folders are created at the folder level for any supported file systems. After a folder is shared, users with permissions to the share (and underlying file system if it is formatted with NTFS) have access to all the files and subfolders beneath it.

Share Permissions

When sharing a folder you must determine the level of access you are going to assign to different users. Remember that managing access to a file system is a delicate balance of allowing access to appropriate resources for authorized users and protecting resources from unauthorized users. To assist in securing shared resources, Windows 2000 supports the following share-level permissions:

◆ **Read.** Allows the user to display files and subfolders within the shared folder and to execute programs.

◆ **Change.** Allows the user all the permissions associated with the Read permission, and also allows him to add files or subfolders to the shared folder. The user is also allowed to append or delete the information from existing files and folders.

◆ **Full Control.** Allows the user all the permissions associated with the Change permission, and also allows him to change the file permissions or file system resources. The user is also allowed to take ownership of file resources (if he or she has the appropriate NTFS permissions).

Multiple Share Permissions

Share-level permissions can be assigned to users and groups. Because of this you may find that some users have multiple permissions assigned to them. For example, if a user is assigned Read permissions to a shared folder and a group that the user is a member of is assigned Change permissions, the effective shared permissions for the user would be Change permissions. When multiple share permissions are assigned, the least restrictive will be the final, effective permission.

The only exception to the preceding rule is if the Deny permission is applied to a user or group. If you are denied permission to a share, this permission will override all other permissions you receive. You will not be given access to the resource.

Creating Shared Folders

Shared folders can be created in two different ways. Step by Step 2.1 shows how to share a local folder from your local hard drive.

ON THE CD

Step by Step 2.1, "Sharing Folders on Local Drives," walks you through sharing local folders. See the file **Chapter02-01StepbyStep.pdf** in the CD's **Chapter02\StepbyStep** directory.

The second method of creating shares can be performed on both local and remote computers. Step by Step 2.2 demonstrates how to create a share using the Computer Management Microsoft snap-in.

ON THE CD

Step by Step 2.2, "Creating Shares Using the Computer Management Snap-in," shows you how to create a share. See the file **Chapter02-02StepbyStep.pdf** in the CD's **Chapter02\StepbyStep** directory.

Connecting to Shared Folders

After shares have been created, users will need to connect to them. Four common methods that can be used to connect to a share are the following:

◆ **Net Use command.** You can use the Net Use command to connect a share. At a command prompt type *NET USE X: \\COMPUTERNAME\SHARE*. *COMPUTERNAME* represents the name of the computer where the share physically resides, SHARE represents the name assigned to the share, and X: represents the local drive letter you can map to the shared location.

◆ **Map a drive using Windows Explorer.** You can map a network drive from the Tools menu of Windows Explorer. This tool allows you to select a local drive letter and assign it to a network share location (either by typing the UNC path to the share or by browsing the network to find the path).

◆ **Browsing My Network Places.** By opening the computer icons found in My Network Places, you are able to see the shares available on each computer.

◆ **Typing a UNC path.** From the Run menu, you can type the UNC path to a share (such as \\COMPUTERNAME\SHARE). This will cause a new window to be launched on your desktop that displays the contents of the share.

Administrative Shared Folders

Depending on the configuration of your computer, some or all of the following special shared folders are automatically created by Windows 2000 for administrative and system use (see Figure 2.1).

◆ **DRIVELETTER$.** A shared folder that allows administrative personnel to connect to the root directory of a drive. Shown as C$, D$, and so on. For a Windows 2000 Professional computer, only members of the Administrators or Backup Operators group can connect to these shared folders.

◆ **ADMIN$.** A resource used by the system during remote administration of a computer. The path of this resource is always the path to the folder where Windows 2000 is installed.

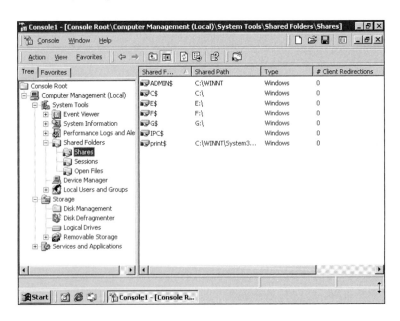

FIGURE 2.1

Windows 2000 default administrative shares.

◆ **IPC$.** A resource used during remote administration of a computer and when viewing a computer's shared resources.

◆ **PRINT$.** This share—used for the remote administration of printers—is formed on any Windows 2000 Professional computer that has a shared printer installed on it.

Web Server Resources

Another method of sharing information with users is through the Windows 2000 Internet Information Server (IIS) and the Internet Explorer (IE). You can make file resources available to users through their browsers by a click of the mouse.

Accessing Information as a Web Page

To share a file system resource through IIS, you will need to access the Web Sharing tab of the property page for the folder (as shown in Figure 2.2). You can access this page by right-clicking the folder you want to share and selecting Properties from the secondary menu.

By selecting the Share This Folder option, you can enter the alias name you want to use to represent the folder on your Web site. For example, if you were to alias a folder as TEST it would be accessible through your browser at HTTP://computer_name/TEST. This allows you to access the information from the Web folder.

Web Folder Functionality

Web Folder Behaviors available in Microsoft Internet Explorer 5.0 allow users to navigate to a folder view. IE 5.0 also includes support for Distributed Authoring and Versioning (DAV) and Web Extender Client (WEC) protocols. *DAV* is a series of extensions to the HyperText Transfer Protocol (HTTP) and defines how basic file functions, such as Copy, Move, Delete, and Create Folder, are performed across HTTP. *WEC* is a Microsoft FrontPage protocol that provides the same sort of functionality as DAV. Both protocols define how to send and retrieve properties on HTTP resources.

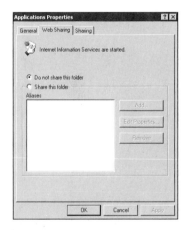

FIGURE 2.2
The Web Sharing tab.

The Web Folder Behaviors enable authors to view sites in a Web folder view, which is similar to the Microsoft Windows Explorer folder view. The DAV and WEC protocols add further capabilities to the Web folder view. Internet Explorer 5.0 and later versions support two Web Folder Behaviors that allow users to browse sites in a Web folder view.

A Web folder view maintains a consistent look and feel between navigating the local file system, a networked drive, and an Internet Web site. Although a Web folder is a part of the file system hierarchy, it does not necessarily represent anything in the file system.

To access a Web folder click Open on the File menu of Internet Explorer 5.0. In the Open dialog box, enter the URL (`HTTP://computer_name/folder_name`) and click the Open as Web Folder option. By selecting the Open as Web Folder option, you will access the folder and acquire the capability to manage its contents as you would any file through Windows Explorer.

NTFS Permissions

Monitor, manage, and troubleshoot access to files and folders.

An optimal configuration for most Windows 2000 systems will include partitions formatted with NTFS. NTFS offers a number of advantages over FAT and FAT32—the most significant being local folder and file security.

To secure folders and files on an NTFS partition, you assign NTFS permissions for each user or group that requires access to the object's Discretionary Access Control List (DACL). The *DACL* contains a listing of all users and groups and their assigned permissions for the object. If a user does not have any permission assigned to her user account, or does not belong to a group with permissions assigned, the user will not be able to access the resource. By default, the Everyone group is given the Full Control permission to all resources on an NTFS partition.

NTFS permissions can be assigned at both the file and folder level. Due to the nature of files and folders, the permissions assigned to files are different from the permissions assigned to folders. Folders are used to organize file resources and act as a container where files can be stored. Files, on the other hand, cannot contain other files. Because folders contain file permissions at the folder level, they give users the ability to create new files or list the files a folder contains. File permissions generally deal with the user's ability to manage the file itself.

NTFS permissions can be assigned to both users and groups. Members of the Administrators group can assign NTFS permissions to files and folders on a system. The owner of a file or folder, and users with Full Control permission, can also assign permissions to a file or folder.

Folder Permissions

You assign folder permissions to control the access that users have to folders and the files contained within those folders. The following permissions can be assigned to a folder:

◆ **Read.** Allows a user to see the files and subfolders in a folder and view folder attributes, ownership, and permissions.

◆ **Write.** Allows a user to create new file and subfolders within the folder, change folder attributes, and view folder ownership and permissions.

◆ **List Folder Contents.** Allows a user to see the names of files and subfolders in the folder.

◆ **Read and Execute.** Gives a user the rights assigned through the Read permission and the List Folder Contents permission. It also gives the user the ability to traverse folders. Traverse folders rights allow a user to reach files and folders located in subdirectories even if the user does not have permission to access portions of the directory path.

◆ **Modify.** Gives a user the ability to delete the folder and perform the actions permitted by the Write and Read and the Read and Execute permissions.

◆ **Full Control.** Allows a user to change permissions, take ownership, delete subfolders and files, and perform the actions granted by all other permissions.

File Permissions

You assign file permissions to control the access that users have to individual files. The standard NTFS file permissions include

- ◆ **Read.** Allows a user to read a file and view file attributes, ownership, and permissions.

- ◆ **Write.** Allows a user to overwrite a file, change file attributes, and view file ownership and permissions.

- ◆ **Read and Execute.** Gives a user the rights required to run applications and perform the actions permitted by the Read permission.

- ◆ **Modify.** Gives a user the ability to modify and delete a file and perform the actions permitted by the Write and Read/and the Read and Execute permissions.

- ◆ **Full Control.** Allows a user to change permissions, take ownership, delete subfolders and files, and perform the actions granted by all other permissions.

Multiple NTFS Permissions

Permissions can be assigned to users and to groups. Because of this, it is possible for a user to be assigned permissions through multiple sources. A user's effective permissions for a resource are the combination of the NTFS permissions that you assign to the individual user account and to all the groups to which the user belongs.

Permissions can be denied. By denying permission to a folder or file, you are denying a specific level of access regardless of the other permissions assigned to a user or group. Even if a user has access permissions to the file or folder as a member of a group, denying permission to the user blocks any other permissions assigned to the user.

When determining a user's effective permissions, you must examine the permissions assigned at the specific resource. Remember that every file and folder on an NTFS partition has a list of permissions assigned to it. For this reason permissions assigned at the file level will override permissions assigned at the folder level.

Permission Inheritance

By default, permissions assigned to a parent folder are inherited by and propagated to the subfolders and files that are contained in the parent folder. This default action, however, can be modified to meet the needs of specific environments. Figure 2.3 shows the folder permissions of a folder. Note the grayed-out permissions; this indicates that these permissions are being inherited from the parent.

You can prevent subfolders and files from inheriting permissions that are assigned to parent folders. By doing so, permission changes made to parent folders will not affect child folders and files.

When you prevent permission inheritance, you must choose to either copy inherited permissions from the parent folder or remove the inherited permissions and retain only the permissions that were explicitly assigned.

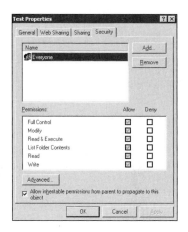

FIGURE 2.3
Folder permissions and inheritance.

Default NTFS Permissions

NTFS-protected resources will have default permissions assigned. The following NTFS permissions are assigned:

◆ For new NTFS partitions, Windows 2000 will assign the Everyone group Full Control permission to the root folder of the partition.

◆ For new folders, the new folder will inherit the permissions assigned to its parent folder.

◆ For any new users or groups added to the DACL for a folder, the users or groups will be assigned Read and Execute, List Folder Contents, and Read permissions.

◆ For new users or groups added to the DACL for a file, the users or groups will be assigned Read and Execute and Read permissions.

Assigning Permissions

Administrators, users with Full Control access, and the owner of a resource can grant permissions to a folder or file. Right-clicking the file or folder you want to manage and selecting Properties can access the Security Property page for an object. Permissions are managed from the Security tab.

NOTE

Owners of a Resource Can Manage Its Permissions Remember that if you own a resource you can manage its permissions. This is a very important concept because administrators always have the ability to take ownership of resources. After you own the resource, you can then manage the permissions on the resource.

On the Security tab, you can manage the permissions assigned users and groups (also known as *security principals*) that require access to the resource. The management can include adding or removing security principals and changing the assigned permissions.

Special Permissions for Files and Folders

Standard permissions consist of a logical group of special permissions. *Special permissions* are the granular permissions that form the default NTFS permissions. They include

- ◆ **Traverse Folder/Execute File.** Allows or denies moving through folders to reach other files or folders, even if the user has no permissions to the folders being traversed. This occurs when applied to a folder. When applied to a file, this permission allows a user to execute the file.

- ◆ **List Folder/Read Data.** Allows or denies viewing filenames and subfolder names within a folder. If applied to a file, this permission allows viewing the contents of the file.

- ◆ **Read Attributes.** Allows or denies viewing the attributes of a file or folder.

- ◆ **Read Extended Attributes.** Allows or denies viewing the extended attributes of a file or folder. Extended attributes are defined by programs and may vary by program.

- ◆ **Create Files/Write Data.** Allows or denies creating files within the folder. If applied to a file, this permission allows or denies making changes to the file and overwriting existing content.

- ◆ **Create Folders/Append Data.** Allows or denies creating folders within the folder. If applied to a file, this permission allows making changes to the end of the file, but not changing, deleting, or overwriting existing data.

- ◆ **Write Attributes.** Allows or denies changing the attributes of a file or folder.

- ◆ **Write Extended Attributes.** Allows or denies changing the extended attributes of a file or folder. Extended attributes are defined by programs and may vary by program.

◆ **Delete Subfolders and Files.** Allows or denies deleting subfolders and files, even if the Delete permission has not been
granted on the subfolder or file.

◆ **Delete.** Allows or denies deleting the file or folder. If you don't
have Delete permission on a file or folder, you can still delete
it if you have been granted Delete Subfolders and Files permission on the parent folder.

◆ **Read Permissions.** Allows or denies reading the permissions
assigned to the file or folder in the file or folder's DACL.

◆ **Change Permissions.** Allows or denies changing permissions
in the DACL of the file or folder.

◆ **Take Ownership.** Allows or denies taking ownership of the
file or folder.

◆ **Synchronize.** Allows or denies different threads to wait on the
handle for the file or folder and synchronize with another
thread that may signal it.

Special permission can be granted to users and groups from the
Advanced button of the Security tab of a file or folder. The
Permission Entry dialog box allows you to add, remove, and
view/edit the special permissions assigned to users and groups.
Figure 2.4 shows the special permissions assigned to the Everyone
group on a folder. (This dialog box is accessed by highlighting a user
and group and clicking the View/Edit button.)

File/Folder Ownership

The owner of a resource can manage the permissions associated with
it. As the administrator of a system, you can always take ownership
of a file or folder and manage its permissions. This is helpful in
instances where a deleted user is the only account with access to a
file or folder.

Step by Step 2.3 shows how to take ownership of a file or folder.

ON THE CD

Step by Step 2.3, "Taking Ownership of a File or Folder," covers
taking ownership of a file or folder. See the file **Chapter02-
03StepbyStep.pdf** in the CD's **Chapter02\StepbyStep** directory.

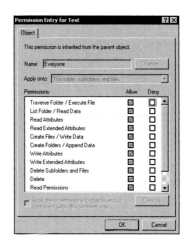

FIGURE 2.4
Special permissions configuration screen.

Ownership can be transferred in two ways:

◆ The current owner can grant the Take Ownership permission to others, allowing those users to take ownership at any time.

◆ An administrator can take ownership of any file on the computer. The administrator cannot transfer ownership to others. This restriction keeps the administrator accountable.

Copying and Moving Folders and Files

You may need to copy or move folders and files in your environment. You will find that copying and moving folders may effect the permissions that are assigned to them.

Copying Folders and Files

When you copy files or folders from one folder to another folder, or from one partition to another, permissions may change. The results you can expect from various copy operations are as follows:

◆ When you copy a folder or file within a single NTFS partition, the copy of the folder or file inherits the permissions of the destination folder.

◆ When you copy a folder or file between NTFS partitions, the copy of the folder or file inherits the permissions of the destination folder.

◆ When you copy a folder or file to a non-NTFS partition, all permissions are lost (because non-NTFS partitions do not support NTFS permissions).

Moving Folders and Files

When you move files or folders from one folder to another folder, or from one partition to another, permissions may change. The results you can expect from various move operations are as follows:

◆ When you move a folder or file within a single NTFS partition, the folder or file retains its original permissions.

◆ When you move a folder or file between NTFS partitions, the folder or file inherits the permissions of the destination folder.

When you move a folder or file between partitions, you create a new version of the resource and therefore, inherits permissions.

◆ When you move a folder or file to a non-NTFS partition, all permissions are lost (because non-NTFS partitions do not support NTFS permissions).

Combining NTFS Permissions and Shared Folders

By combining both shared folder permission and NTFS permissions, you have the greatest level of control and security. To effectively use shared folder and NTFS permissions together, you must understand how they interact with one another.

When users gain access to a shared folder on an NTFS partition, they need shared folder permissions and also the appropriate NTFS permission for each file and folder they access. This requires you to manage two sets of permissions for your environment.

Generally, NTFS permissions are used to secure the resources in your file system. NTFS offers the greatest level of control and can be assigned to resources on an individual basis. You will then pick share points and create shares so that users can access file resources over the network.

Users' effective permissions will be a combination of both the shared folder permissions and NTFS permissions. Unlike individual shared folder and NTFS permissions, however, the effective permissions will be the most restrictive permission of all permissions assigned to the user.

EXAM TIP

Permissions Remember that shared folder permissions and NTFS permissions represent two different security systems within Windows 2000.

NTFS calculates effective permissions by adding all your permissions together (thereby granting you the least restrictive permission). Shared folder permissions are calculated the same way. You have two sets of permissions.

When the two security systems are used in combination, the most restrictive of your effective permissions (from each system) is applied.

Developing an Efficient Directory Structure

Network users will need resources on which to store their work. Where these resources are located is an important aspect of the planning process. A number of decisions will need to be made before users actually start creating documents. The following sections detail user home directories, shared data folders, and application folders.

Home Directories

One of the first things that must be completed is an assessment of the types of information that users will be storing. Home directories are generally considered a location where users can store their own documents. No one else, including the administrator, should have access to these private directories.

When planning the structure of users' home directories, you must decide whether those directories should be on the users' local machine or on the network. Both of these options can work well, depending on your organization's needs. Table 2.1 compares storing users' home directories on local machines versus network servers.

Generally when you are creating home directories on the server, it is best to centralize the directories under one directory (typically called Users). An example of such a structure is shown in Figure 2.5.

TABLE 2.1	

SERVER-BASED HOME DIRECTORIES VERSUS LOCAL HOME DIRECTORIES

Server-Based Directories	*Local Home Directories*
Are centrally located so that a user can access them from any location on the network.	Available only on the local machine. Users cannot retrieve their data if they are away from their computers, unless a share is set up.
Backups of user data are much easier and can be centrally managed.	Backups are much more difficult to manage. Generally, users are left to complete their own backups (something that cannot be counted on). This situation is dangerous; a crashed hard drive will cause all user data to be lost.
Computer policies can be set to limit the amount of space a user has occupied on a server.	If a user stores a lot of information on his local computer, the only person who will notice will be that user.
If the server is down, the users will not have access to their data.	The user has access to his file regardless of whether the network is up or down because his files are stored locally.
Some network bandwidth is consumed due to the over-the-network access of data or files.	No network traffic is generated by users accessing data as it is stored locally.

FIGURE 2.5
User home directory structure.

If your directory structure is on an NTFS formatted partition, you would share out the structure at the Users level and ensure that the NTFS permissions are set to allow users into only their home directories.

Sharing Common-Access Folders

Like users' home directories, which need to have very restricted access controls placed on them, common access or shared data folders will need to be planned carefully. Shared data folders are required on the network so that users or groups of users can exchange data. One of the biggest challenges in planning for shared data folders is to determine who needs to share what and the level of access everyone needs to the information.

Figure 2.6 represents a sample directory structure for a set of common access folders. Note that a top-level directory called Departments was created to act as a share point to the data. Each department (Accounting, Finance, HR, and Sales) has a subdirectory in which to store department-specific data. Each subfolder will have NTFS permissions set so that only members of the specific departments can access their departmental shared folder.

FIGURE 2.6
Shared departmental directory structure.

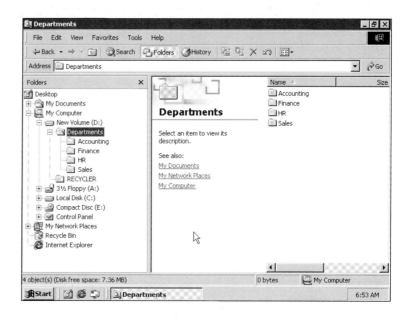

Sharing Application Folders

Another resource you will need to plan for is networked application folders. Shared application folders typically give users access to applications that they will run from a network share point. Another option is to have users run applications locally from their own computer. Table 2.2 shows a comparison of these two options.

TABLE 2.2

NETWORKED APPLICATIONS VERSUS LOCALLY INSTALLED APPLICATIONS

Shared Network Applications	*Locally Installed Applications*
Take up less disk space on the local workstation.	Uses more local disk space.
Easier to upgrade/control.	Upgrades require that staff visit each computer (although this is becoming less of an issue as Group Policy objects and products, such as Microsoft System Management Server can assist in the delivery of applications to the desktop).
More bandwidth is used.	Little network bandwidth is used as applications are stored locally.
If the server is down, users cannot run their applications.	Users can run applications regardless of server status.

As you can see, each method offers advantages, depending on your environment. When setting up shared application resources, consider the following:

◆ Different applications require that users have specific permissions to run over the network.

◆ Many applications require that users have a location available to store their personal preferences or application settings.

◆ Staff will be required to upgrade and maintain application directories.

Based on the preceding considerations, a common approach to application directories is to create a structure similar to the one shown in Figure 2.7.

In this example, you would share at the Applications level and give users and administrators the appropriate NTFS permissions to the underlying applications. If you need to restrict access to specific applications, you would share each application out separately, giving users share-level permissions to only the applications to which they require access.

FIGURE 2.7
Shared application directory structure.

MANAGING FILE RESOURCES

Configure and manage file systems.

As the administrator of a Windows 2000 system, you will need to understand how to manage file resources. The following section provides an overview of the NTFS, FAT, and FAT32 file systems and details common management tasks.

NTFS, FAT32, or FAT

Before you decide which file system to use, you should understand the benefits and limitations of each file system. Changing a volume's existing file system can be time consuming, so choose the file system that best suits your long-term needs. You can convert a FAT or FAT32 volume to an NTFS volume without formatting the volume. To convert from NTFS to FAT or FAT32, you must back up your data and then reformat the volume using the new file system. The following sections provide an overview of the differences among FAT, FAT32, and NTFS file systems.

FAT

File Allocation Table (FAT) is a file system that has been around for a very long time and is currently supported by most operating systems on the market.

The primary benefit of using FAT is that it is supported by Windows NT, Windows 95/98, Windows 3.*x*, and DOS. For this reason, FAT is an exceptional choice for systems that are required to dual boot between Windows 2000 and one (or more) of the previously mentioned operating systems.

The version of FAT supported by Windows 2000 has a number of additional features that are not supported by systems running DOS. When used under Windows 2000, the FAT file system supports the following additional features:

◆ Long filenames up to 255 characters.

◆ Multiple spaces.

◆ Multiple periods.

◆ Filenames are not case sensitive, but do preserve case.

For all the benefits of FAT, it should be recognized that it has a number of major limitations that should make you stop and think before it becomes your file system of choice. These include the following:

◆ FAT is inefficient for larger partitions. As files grow in size, they may become fragmented on the disk and cause slower access times. FAT also uses inefficient cluster sizes (a cluster is the smallest unit of storage on a partition). If the cluster size is too large, you can end up with lots of wasted space on the partition.

◆ The maximum size of a FAT partition is 4GB.

◆ The FAT file system does not support local security, so you cannot prevent a user from accessing a file if the user can log in to the local operating system.

◆ FAT does not support compression, encryption, or disk quotas under Windows 2000.

FAT32

The FAT32 file system is very similar to FAT. FAT32 was introduced in the Microsoft product line with Windows 95 OSR 2. The primary difference between FAT and FAT32 is that FAT32 supports a smaller cluster size, so it does not have as much wasted space associated with larger partitions.

Like FAT, FAT32 supports long filenames, multiple spaces, multiple periods, and preserves case while not being case sensitive.

The primary limitations of FAT32 are as follows:

◆ The FAT32 file system does not support local security, so you cannot prevent a user from accessing a file if the user can log in to the local operating system.

◆ The maximum size of a FAT32 partition is 8TB. (A 32GB limit is imposed by the Windows 2000 format utility if you create the partition on a Windows 2000 system.)

◆ Does not support compression, encryption, and disk quotas under Windows 2000.

◆ FAT32 is not supported by all versions of Windows 95, and is not supported by DOS or Windows NT. If you plan to dual-boot your system, ensure that all operating systems you are using support FAT32.

NTFS

NTFS is the file system of choice on most systems running Windows 2000. NTFS offers the following benefits:

◆ **Support for long filenames.** NTFS supports long filenames up to 255 characters.

◆ **Preservation of case.** NTFS is not case sensitive, but it does have the capability to preserve case for POSIX compliance.

◆ **Recoverability.** NTFS is a recoverable file system. It uses transaction logging to automatically log all files and directory updates in case of a system failure. That way, the operating system can redo failed operations.

◆ **Security.** NTFS provides folder- and file-level security for protecting files.

◆ **Compression.** NTFS supports compression of file and folders to help save disk space.

◆ **Encryption.** NTFS supports file-level encryption. This allows a user the ability to encrypt sensitive files so that no one else can read the files.

◆ **Disk quotas.** NTFS partitions support user-level disk quotas. This gives an administrator the ability to set an upper limit on the amount of space that a user can use on a partition. After users reach their limit, they are not allowed to store any more information on the partition.

◆ **Size.** NTFS partitions can support much larger partition sizes than FAT. NTFS can support partitions up to 16 exabytes in size (equal to 16 billion gigabytes).

WARNING

NTFS 4.0 Versus NTFS 5.0   The version of NTFS used with Windows NT (NTFS 4.0) is different from the version used with Windows 2000 (NTFS 5.0). These two versions of NTFS are not compatible with one another, so you cannot dual-boot a Windows NT 4.0 and Windows 2000 system unless your installation of Windows NT 4.0 is running SP 4 or higher.

The main limitations of NTFS are that other operating systems do not support it, and that it has high system overhead.

File Compression

NTFS compression makes more efficient use of the hard drive space available on your system. If you need more space on your system, you will most likely want to add an additional hard drive. In an emergency, however, you can always compress your existing drives to free up space.

Compression is implemented at the folder or file level on NTFS formatted partitions.

To compress a file or folder within Windows 2000 you can follow Step by Step 2.4.

ON THE CD

Step by Step 2.4, "Compressing a File or Folder," shows you how to compress a file or folder. See the file **Chapter02-04StepbyStep.pdf** in the CD's **Chapter02\StepbyStep** directory.

You can also manage the compression attributes associated with files and folders on your system from the command prompt. The Compact utility allows you to compress files and folders, as well as check the compression statistics.

The syntax for the compact utility is as follows:

```
COMPACT [/C | /U] [/S[:dir]] [/A] [/I] [/F] [/Q] [filename
➥[...]]
```

/C compresses the specified files. Directories will be marked so that files added afterward will be compressed.

/U uncompresses the specified files. Directories will be marked so those files added afterward will not be compressed.

/S performs the specified operation on files in the given directory and all subdirectories. Default "dir" is the current directory.

/A displays files with the hidden or system attributes. These files are omitted by default.

/I continues performing the specified operation even after errors have occurred. By default, Compact stops when an error is encountered.

/F forces the compress operation on all specified files, even those which are already compressed. Already-compressed files are skipped by default.

/Q reports only the most essential information.

filename specifies a pattern, file, or directory.

You may want to use the Compact utility instead of the Property tab of the files or folders, as the Compact command syntax can be included in batch files.

File Encryption

Encrypting File System (EFS) is a system service that allows files and folders to be encrypted. The service is based on public/private key encryption technology and is managed by the Windows 2000 Public Key Infrastructure (PKI) services. Because EFS is an integrated service it is very easy to manage, difficult to break into, and transparent to the user.

A user who has ownership of a file system resource can either encrypt or decrypt the folder or file. If a user who does not own the resource attempts to access the resource, he will receive an access denied message.

The technology is based on a public key structure. Each user has a public and private key. The keys were created in such a way that anything encrypted using the public key can only be decrypted using the private key. As the names suggest, the public key is made available to any resource that requests it. The private key is kept secret and is exposed only to authorized resources.

When the owner of a file encrypts a file system resource, a file encryption key is generated and used to encrypt the file. The file-encryption keys are based on a fast symmetric key designed for bulk encryption. The file-encryption key is then stored with the file (as part of the header of the file), in the data decryption field (DDF) and the data recovery field (DRF). Before the file-encryption keys are stored, they are encrypted by using the public key of the owner—in the case of the DDF keys, and a recovery agent, in the case of the DRF keys. Because the keys are stored with the file, the file can be moved or renamed and it will not impact on the recoverability of the file.

When a file is accessed, EFS detects the access attempt and locates the user's certificate, from the Windows 2000 PKI, and the user's associated private key. The private key is then used to decrypt the DDF to retrieve the file-encryption keys used to encrypt each block of the file. The only key in existence with the capability to decrypt the information is that of the owner of the file. Access to the file is denied to all others, as they do not hold the private key required for decrypting the file-encryption keys.

If the owner's private key is not available for some reason (for example, the user account was deleted), the recovery agent can open the file. The recovery agent decrypts the DRF to unlock the list of file encryption keys. The recovery agent must be configured as part of the security policies of the local computer.

To encrypt a file or folder within Windows 2000, you can complete Step by Step 2.5.

ON THE CD

Step by Step 2.5, "Encrypting a File or Folder," shows you how to encrypt a file or folder. See the file **Chapter02-05StepbyStep.pdf** in the CD's **Chapter02\StepbyStep** directory.

You can also manage the encryption attributes associated with files and folders on your system from the command prompt. The Cipher utility allows you to encrypt files and folders as well as check the encryption statistics.

The syntax for the encryption utility is as follows:

```
CIPHER [/e | /d] [/s:dir] [/i] [/f] [/q] [filename [...]]
```

/e encrypts the specified files or folders. Files added to the folder afterward will be encrypted.

/d decrypts the specified files or folders. Files added to the folder afterward will not be encrypted.

/s:dir performs the specified operation on files in the given directory and all subdirectories.

/i continues performing the specified operation even after errors have occurred. By default, Cipher stops when an error is encountered.

/f forces the encryption or decryption of all specified files. By default, files that have already been encrypted or decrypted are skipped.

/q reports only the most essential information.

filename specifies a pattern, file, or directory.

Converting File Systems

In many instances, you may find that you need to change the format of your partitions. Your options are to reformat the partition or convert it. If you choose to reformat your partition, you will lose all data from the partition. Converting a partition allows you to change your file format without loosing your data. You can only convert from FAT to NTFS or from FAT32 to NTFS. You cannot convert from NTFS to FAT or from NTFS to FAT32.

If Convert cannot lock the drive, it will offer to convert it the next time the computer restarts. Locking the drive requires that the operating system gain exclusive access to all files and folders on the drive (data cannot be in use by other applications) .

```
convert [drive:] /fs:ntfs [/v]
```

drive: specifies the drive to convert to NTFS.

/fs:ntfs specifies that the volume be converted to NTFS.

/v specifies verbose mode. All messages will be displayed during conversion.

> **WARNING**
>
> **Converting to NTFS Could Affect System Performance**   Partitions and volumes that are converted from FAT/FAT32 to NTFS may suffer from performance problems. A chance exists that the Master File Table (MFT) will be fragmented.

PRINT RESOURCES

Connect to local and network print devices.

Printers are a common resource shared by users on the network. As a network administrator, you will need to be able to manage the print environment. Management tasks include setting up printer resources, securing print resources, managing print jobs, and connecting to shared printers over the network. This section reviews each of these management tasks.

The Print Environment

Four primary components make up the Windows 2000 print environment. As a network administrator you should understand these components and how they interact with one another to create the print environment. The components are as follows:

◆ **Printer.** A printer is a software representation of a physical print device. You will find printers configured on computers so that print jobs can be sent to them. When a print job is sent to the printer, it is processed and forwarded to a physical print device.

◆ **Print driver.** A print driver is used to convert print requests into a format understood by the physical print device being used in the environment.

◆ **Print server.** A print server is a computer that receives and processes documents from client computers for processing.

◆ **Print device.** A print device is the physical device that produces the printed output.

The following represents how a print job is processed:

1. A user on a computer generates a print job by issuing a print command from a software application.

2. The print job is sent to a printer configured on the local machine (remember that the printer is a software representation of a physical print device).

3. The printer defines where the printer job will go to reach the physical print device and how the job should be managed during the printing process.

4. From the printer, the print job is sent to a print server for processing.

5. The print server then uses a print driver to format the print job so that the physical print device can process it.

6. After the print driver has converted the print job into a specific printer language, it is forwarded to the physical print device.

7. When the physical print device receives the job, it is printed.

Windows 2000 supports print devices that are either local or networked. As the name implies, local print devices are connected to a local computer. Network print devices are connected to a print server through the network.

Connecting to a Local Print Device

Installing printers in the Windows 2000 environment is accomplished with the aid of the Add Printer Wizard. The Add Printer Wizard is launched by double-clicking the Add Printer icon in the Printers folder of Control Panel. Step by Step 2.6 will walk you through the process of configuring a local printer.

ON THE CD

Step by Step 2.6, "Installing a Local Printer," walks you through setting up a local printer. See the file **Chapter02-06StepbyStep.pdf** in the CD's **Chapter02\StepbyStep** directory.

Sharing a Local Printer

Sharing a local printer allows remote users to access it from across the network. This section describes how to share a local printer.

During the installation of a local printer, the Printer Setup Wizard offers to automatically create a printer share for you. The other method involves viewing the properties of an existing printer object and selecting the Sharing tab. Figure 2.8 shows the Sharing property tab from a local printer object.

From this tab you can configure the share name you would like to use. You can also configure the print drivers associated with the printer. By clicking the Additional Drivers button, you can install additional print drivers.

If you select additional drivers to be installed, then Windows will prompt you for the appropriate disk containing the drivers requested. After drivers are installed, additional types of workstation clients will be able to connect to the share and have the drivers made available to them without user intervention on the client side.

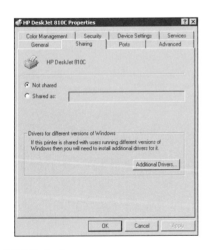

FIGURE 2.8
Sharing property tab for a local printer.

Printers Permissions

In many environments, printers are managed to ensure that only certain groups of users can access specific print devices. Access to the Windows 2000 print environment is managed through printer permissions.

Like file system shares, printer shares allows users to access print resources over the network. Printer shares have three different levels of access that can be granted (see Figure 2.9):

◆ **Print.** Allows a user or group to submit print jobs to a printer.

◆ **Manage Documents.** Allows a user or group to manage documents in the print queue. By default, the Creator Owner group is assigned this permission so that a user can delete or re-order his own print jobs.

◆ **Manage Printers.** Allows a user or group to share a printer, change printer properties, delete a printer, or change printer permissions.

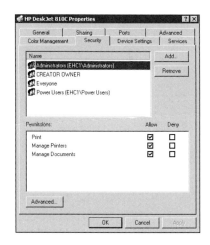

FIGURE 2.9
Printer permissions.

Connecting to a Shared Printer

Connecting to a shared printer allows a user to print to a remote printer over the network. Connecting to a remote printer can be done in a number of different ways. The following section will explore each of these methods.

One of the easiest ways to connect to a remote printer is to run the Add Printer Wizard by double-clicking the Add Printer icon in the Printers folder of Control Panel. If you select to install a network printer, you must provide the UNC name for the printer to which you would like to attach.

You can also access the printer using an HTTP request. In this case, the path to the printer would be `HTTP://SERVER/printer_name`.

You can also connect to a printer by dragging the printer from the Printers folder on the print server and dropping it into your Printers folder, or by right-clicking the icon and then clicking Connect from the secondary menu.

The last option you have for connecting to a printer involves the Net Use command. From the command prompt you can issue the following command to map a local LTP port to a network printer:

```
Net Use LPT1 \\servername\printer name
```

After you have connected to a shared printer over the network, you can use it as if it were attached to your computer.

Managing Printers

After the print environment is set up, you will need to manage the printers. The Windows 2000 print environment is one of the easiest to use and manage. In the following sections you will explore many common printer management tasks.

Assigning Forms to Paper Trays

Many printers support multiple paper trays and paper sizes. You can assign various paper types and sizes to the specific trays installed on your printer. After a form (or paper type/size) has been assigned to a specific tray, a user can select it from within her applications. When the user issues a print command, Windows 2000 automatically routes the print job to the paper tray with the correct form.

Figure 2.10 shows the device settings for an HP LaserJet printer. To assign a form to paper trays complete the following:

1. Open the Properties dialog box to the printer and click the Device Settings tab.

2. From the Form to Tray Assignment option, select a tray and assign a paper size to it (paper sizes are found in the drop-down lists).

FIGURE 2.10
Device Settings tab of printer properties.

Setting Separator Pages

Most printers are able to operate in many different modes (for example, PostScript or PCL [Printer Control Language]). Because different printers are configured to expect different print commands, you should be familiar with different types of separator pages and how they can be specified. A *separator page* is a file that contains the following commands:

◆ Identify each document that is being printed (also referred to as a banner page).

◆ Switch the print device between print modes (if supported by the physical printer). You could use a separator page to specify PostScript or PCL for a printer that is not able to automatically detect the type of print job it is processing.

Windows 2000 ships with four separator page files located in the *systemroot*\system32 directory:

◆ **PCL.SEP.** Prints a page after switching the printer to PCL printing.

◆ **SYSPRINT.SEP.** Prints a page after switching the printer to PostScript printing.

◆ **PSCRIPT.SEP.** Does not print a page after switching the printer to Postscript printing.

◆ **SYSPRTJ.SEP.** A Japanese version of the SYSPRINT.SEP file.

The separator page can be changed from the Advanced tab of a printer property sheet. From the Advanced tab, you can click the Separator Page button and you will be presented with a dialog box prompting you to enter the name and path to a separator file.

Pausing and Restarting Printers

As the administrator of a printer, you may find situations where the printer needs to be taken out of service for a period of time. Printers can be paused (or resumed if currently paused), or all print jobs can be cancelled. This can be accomplished by double-clicking a print object from the Printers folder (found in the Control Panel). A window will open showing all pending print jobs for the printer. From the Printer menu you will find the Pause Printer and Cancel All Documents menu options.

Pausing a printer allows users to continue submitting print jobs to the printer even though the jobs will not print. This is useful in situations where you need to perform simple maintenance on the printer and do not want to disrupt the way users submit print jobs. After the printer is fixed, unpause the printer and print jobs will begin to print.

> **NOTE**
>
> **Restarting the Print Spooler Service**
> In some rare instances, you may find that the Printer Spooler Service of your Windows 2000 system may need to be restarted to get the printing done properly. This service can be restarted from the Computer Management/Service/Print Spooler of the MMC Computer Manager snap-in.

Canceling all documents allows you to quickly clear a print queue that has a large number of documents waiting to print.

Setting Print Priority and Printer Availability

In many environments, managing printers is like being a traffic cop; you must control whose print jobs are printed first. You may, for example, want to ensure that print jobs submitted by the president and her assistant print before all other jobs. To this end, you can install two printers (the software representations of a printer) on a machine and point them to the same physical print device. You would then assign a higher priority to the printer used by the president and her staff.

Figure 2.11 shows where priorities can be set in Printer Properties.

In addition to setting different priorities for a printer, you can also configure options to increase printing performance. These options include

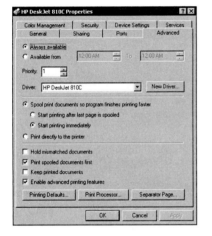

FIGURE 2.11
Printer Properties—Advanced tab.

- ◆ **Setting spool options.** You can choose to either use *spooling* (writing the print job to the hard disk before sending the print job to the print device) or to print directly to the printer. If you choose to enable spooling, you can also select whether to start sending the job to the print device as the job is being spooled or only after the entire document has been spooled.

- ◆ **Prioritizing spooled documents.** You can choose to print fully spooled documents first. This will allow smaller documents to potentially be placed ahead of larger documents in the print queue.

Printer Pooling

In very high-volume print environments, Windows 2000 offers a printer pooling option. Printer pooling allows a single printer to be directed to multiple physical printers.

Figure 2.12 shows the Ports tab of a Printer Properties page.

By checking the Enable Printer Pooling box on the bottom of the page, you are able to select multiple ports from the ports list shown in the figure. As shown in Figure 2.12, this printer will print to LPT1, LPT2, and LPT3, depending on which printer is ready to accept a job when the spooler receives this job.

You will need to ensure that all physical print devices use the same printer driver. It is also recommended that all the printers are located in the same physical area (as users will not know which physical printer will be used to print their job) .

Redirecting Printers

As the printer administrator in your environment, you may find it useful to redirect a printer. For example, if a printer fails and a large number of print jobs are currently spooled (and waiting to print), you can redirect the printer to another print device that uses the same print driver so that the jobs can print without needing to be resubmitted by the users who created them. Step by Step 2.7 demonstrates the process of redirecting a printer.

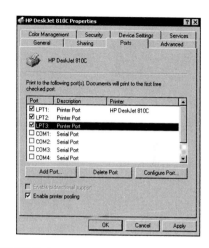

FIGURE 2.12
Printer Properties—Ports tab.

ON THE CD

Step by Step 2.7, "Configuring Printer Redirection," covers redirection of a printer. See the file **Chapter02-07StepbyStep.pdf** in the CD's **Chapter02\StepbyStep** directory.

Managing Print Jobs

In addition to managing the physical printers in your environment, you should become proficient at the management of print jobs. By default, users have the ability to manage their own print jobs. Users assigned the Manage Printers or Manage Documents permissions have the ability to manage all print jobs received at the printer. It is important that you plan for print job management in your environment; jobs will sometimes get stuck in a print queue and hold up printing for everyone.

The next section provides an overview of document-management activities.

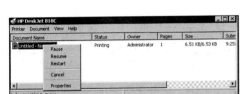

FIGURE 2.13
Print job management options.

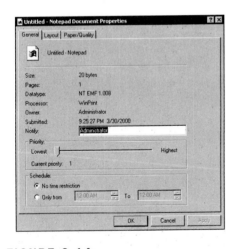

FIGURE 2.14
General tab of a print job.

Pausing, Restarting, and Canceling Print Jobs

By double-clicking a printer icon, you can view the print jobs currently sitting in the print queue. If you have the appropriate permissions you can also manage print jobs.

You have the ability to pause, restart, or cancel jobs. Right-clicking the job you want to manage presents these options to you (as shown in Figure 2.13).

Pausing a print job stops the print job from printing. This will give you the opportunity to correct a problem with the job or allow other print jobs to print first. To resume the job, right-click the paused job and select Resume from the secondary menu.

Restarting a job allows you to restart a print job from the beginning. This is a useful option if a large job starts to print but is disrupted. It allows you to reprint the job without having to regenerate the job.

Canceling a print job causes the job to be removed from the print queue.

Setting Notifications and Priority Print Times

As a user with Manage Printer or Manage Documents permissions, you have the ability to set notification, priority, and printing time for individual print jobs. (As the owner of a print job you can also modify these settings, but only for the print jobs you own.)

Figure 2.14 shows the General tab of a print job. (Double-click a job to access this tab.)

The Notify option allows you to specify a user who should receive a notification when the print job completes. This is a useful option for users who submit jobs but want their assistants to pick them up from the printer.

The Priority option allows a job to be given priority relative to other jobs submitted by the same owner currently in the print queue. The value can range from 1 to 99 (with 99 being the highest priority).

The Schedule option allows you to specify when a specific job will be printed.

Managing Printers Using a Web Browser

Windows 2000 enables you to manage printers from any computer running a Web browser. The Windows 2000 Professional computer, acting as your print server, must have Microsoft's Peer Web Services (PWS) installed.

You can use your browser—you must be using Internet Explorer 4.0 or higher—to manage the printers installed on a remote machine by typing the following URL in the location box of your browser: `HTTP://printer_server_name/printers`. Figure 2.15 shows the resulting Web page that will be loaded.

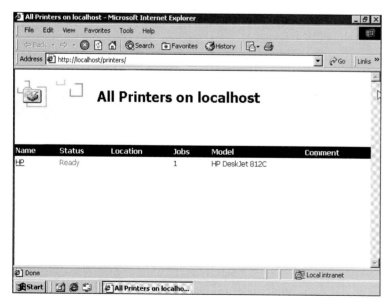

FIGURE 2.15
Web-based printer management screen.

By clicking the name of a printer, you can view the details of the print jobs in the queue for that printer. Figure 2.16 shows the details of a specific printer. Note that on the left side of the Web page you have options that allow you to manage the printer and individual print jobs.

To manage a specific job, click the button beside the job you want to manage. You will find that the only limitation of this interface is that it does not allow you to manage advanced settings (such as notification, print time, or priority).

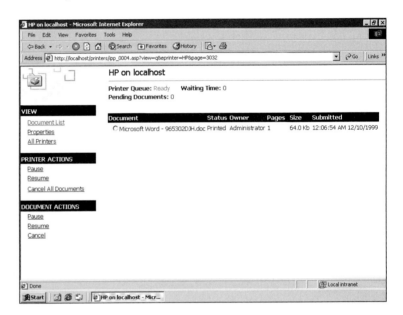

FIGURE 2.16
Web-based printer details screen.

CASE STUDY: ABC COMPANY

ESSENCE OF THE CASE

The essential elements in this case are as follows:

▶ File system security

▶ File system conversion

▶ Efficient directory structures

▶ Shared folder permissions

ABC Company is in the process of installing Windows 2000 Professional on all desktop computers in its organization. You want to ensure that you meet the following criteria with regard to the development of your file system and shared folder access plan.

· All resources must be secured.

· Only members of certain departments can gain access to confidential department data.

A large number of workstations and servers were installed six months earlier as part of the pilot rollout, and have been in operation since. These workstations and servers were configured with FAT32 partitions when they were installed. You need to make sure that data from these machines is not lost.

ANALYSIS

This case revolves around four main issues. The first is that all computers will need to be configured with NTFS. This is the case because NTFS is the only file system supported by Windows 2000 with folder- and file-level security. If security is a prime concern, NTFS is the only file system you can use to protect your equipment.

Second, for the workstations used during the pilot rollout of Windows 2000, you will need to convert the FAT32 partitions to NTFS. It is important that the Convert utility be used to perform the operation, as it is the only utility that will change the file system and allow the data to be preserved.

continues

CASE STUDY: ABC COMPANY

continued

The last two issues revolve around NTFS/shared folder permissions and the directory structure used. It is important the directory structure make sense for the users of the company. To develop the structure, ABC Company will need to fully define all the different users that need to store information on the servers, determine who needs to access the data, and determine what level of access each user needs. The directory structure created should optimize the assignment of permissions so that permissions assigned high in the directory structure do not give too many permissions to users who do not require them.

CHAPTER SUMMARY

Companies install networks so that resources can be shared between users. The challenge facing a network administrator is to ensure that users are given access to the resources they need and nothing more. This chapter presented how to manage, configure, and troubleshoot two of the most heavily used network services (file and print).

In the discussions relating to NTFS permissions, you also looked at the basic skills required to manage an NTFS file system. Specifically, the chapter covered NTFS permissions, compression, encryption, Web folders, and conversion.

The print environment was also covered. In these sections, printer permissions, printer configuration, and print job management were covered.

KEY TERMS

- Folder share
- Printer share
- NTFS permissions
- Printer permissions
- NTFS
- FAT
- FAT32
- Printer
- Print server
- Print driver
- Print device
- HyperText Transport Protocol (HTTP)

APPLY YOUR KNOWLEDGE

Review Questions

1. How are effective NTFS permissions calculated for a user when he receives rights from a number of groups?

2. A user leaves your company and her user account is deleted. You realize that company confidential data is still stored in that user's home directory. When you try to access the folder to retrieve the data (logged in as Administrator), you receive the message Access Denied. How can you fix this problem?

3. What are the default permissions used in the Windows 2000 environment?

4. You move a file from a folder on one partition to a folder on another partition. What permissions will the file have after the move?

5. You move a file from one folder to another folder (on the same partition). What permissions will the file have after the move?

6. You are in a high-volume print environment. What feature of Windows 2000 will you use to help support the large number of print jobs submitted in your environment?

7. What feature of the Windows 2000 environment allows you to remotely manage shared folders?

8. Your printer supports multiple paper trays. When you print, your jobs are put on the incorrect paper. How can you fix this problem?

9. What is the significance of the Deny permission?

10. In NTFS permissions, which permissions take precedence: folder or file level?

Answers to Review Questions

1. Effective NTFS permissions are calculated as the least restrictive permission granted to the user account. For additional information see the section "Multiple NTFS Permissions."

2. Because the user account has been deleted, no users have access to the home folder. When a user account is deleted, all references to the user account's security identifier (SID) are deleted from the operating system. The Administrator is not given access to the directory because the Administrator account does not have permissions to the NTFS folder. To fix this situation, the Administrator will need to take ownership of the folder and give himself permission to access the folder. For additional information, see the section "Assigning Permissions."

3. The default permissions assigned in the Windows 2000 environment are as follows:

   • In new partitions, the Everyone group is given Full Control.

   • New folders or files inherit permissions from their parent folders.

   For additional information see the section "Default NTFS Permissions."

4. The file will inherit the permissions from the parent folder into which it is being moved. When a file is moved between physical partitions, a new copy of the file needs to be created on the target partition. The default NTFS permissions for a file are to inherit permissions from the parent. For additional information see the section "Permission Inheritance."

APPLY YOUR KNOWLEDGE

5. The file will retain its existing permissions. Because you are moving a file within a partition, a new version of the file does not need to be created and therefore it can retain its permissions. For additional information see the section "Copying and Moving Folders and Files."

6. The printer pool option would be best suited for this environment. Printer pooling allows all users in a high-volume print environment to print to the same printer. This printer is configured to send the print jobs to multiple printers. For additional information see the section "Printer Pooling."

7. The Microsoft Management Console with the Computer Management snap-in allows you to manage remote shares. For additional information see the section "Creating Shared Folders."

8. You will need to see how the paper sources have been configured for the printer on your system. This can be accomplished from the Device Setting tab of Printer Properties. For additional information see the section "Managing Printers."

9. The Deny permission will always override permissions that have been granted. For example, a user receives Full Control permissions to a folder from membership in Group1 and also receives Deny Full Control from membership in Group2. Because the user has been granted the Deny permission she is not given access to the resource. For additional information see the section "File Permissions."

10. File-level permissions take precedence over folder permissions. In most environments, however, you will want to make sure you are managing access to your resources at the folder level (the higher up in the folder structure the better). For additional information see the section "NTFS Permissions."

ON THE CD

This book's companion CD contains specially designed supplemental material to help you understand how well you know the concepts and skills you learned in this chapter. You'll find related exercises and exam questions and answers. See the file **Chapter02ApplyYourKnowledge.pdf** in the CD's **Professional\ApplyYourKnowledge** directory.

Suggested Readings and Resources

1. *Microsoft Windows 2000 Network and Operating System Essentials.* Microsoft Official Curriculum (Course 1251).

2. *Microsoft Windows 2000 Administrator's Pocket Consultant.* Microsoft Press, 2000.

3. *Microsoft Windows 2000 Professional Resource Kit.* Microsoft Press, 2000.

4. *MCSE Training Kit—Microsoft Windows 2000 Professional.* Microsoft Press, 2000.

This chapter helps you prepare for the Windows 2000 Professional component of MCP Exam 70-240, "Microsoft Windows 2000 Accelerated Exam for MCPs Certified on Microsoft Windows NT 4.0," by covering the following objectives:

Implement, manage, and troubleshoot disk devices.

▶ Disk technology is constantly evolving in capacity and available features. During the life of your computer you will probably add new functionality to your storage or playback devices. Windows 2000 provides advanced support for new devices, such as logical disk volumes and DVD playback.

Implement, manage, and troubleshoot display devices.

- **Configure multiple-display support.**

- **Install, configure, and troubleshoot a video adapter.**

▶ Windows 2000 provides support for multiple display devices as well as a wide range of video adapters. Being able to utilize these features impacts what you can do with your system.

Implement, manage, and troubleshoot mobile computer hardware.

- **Configure Advanced Power Management (APM).**

- **Configure and manage card services.**

▶ Laptops require configuration to preserve battery length and support PCMCIA devices for network adapters and modems.

Implement, manage, and troubleshoot input and output (I/O) devices.

- **Monitor, configure, and troubleshoot I/O devices, such as printers, scanners, multimedia devices, mouse, keyboard, and smart card reader.**

CHAPTER 3

Implementing, Managing, and Troubleshooting Hardware Devices and Drivers

- **Monitor, configure, and troubleshoot multimedia hardware, such as cameras.**

- **Install, configure, and manage modems.**

- **Install, configure, and manage Infrared Data Association (IrDA) devices.**

- **Install, configure, and manage wireless devices.**

- **Install, configure, and manage Universal Serial Bus (USB) devices.**

▶ A Windows 2000 Professional computer system can have a variety of I/O devices connected to it, including printers, smart cards, cameras, and infrared devices. Being able to manage a wide range of devices is important to getting the most of your computer system.

Update drivers.

▶ Equipment manufacturers are constantly improving the drivers that support their devices. Windows 2000 Professional provides a way to automatically update drivers for devices either from a local source or over the Internet with minimal manual intervention.

Monitor and configure multiple processing units.

▶ If your processing requirements grow as you increasingly use Windows 2000 Professional computer, you can add a processor. The ability to expand your computing power can have a significant impact on the workload your computer can manage.

Install, configure, and troubleshoot network adapters.

▶ If your current computer is not attached to a network, there is a good chance that it soon will be. Additionally, network capacities are constantly improving. Being able to take full advantage of your network connections helps you get the most of your Windows 2000 Professional computer.

▶ Windows 2000 Professional supports more types of devices than any previous version of the OS. In addition to the range of devices supported, configuration is made automatic because of Plug and Play (PnP). You can expect a number of questions that will be presented as scenarios in which the capabilities of these devices are used to solve problems.

▶ You should also expect to see questions dealing with new disk capabilities to provide fault tolerance as well as more options in configuring disk storage.

▶ Greater disk storage capacity creates a need for offline storage capabilities. Expect to see questions on Removable Storage Management (RSM) and the configuration of robotic libraries and Media Pools.

▶ Some new devices that you can expect to see questions on are support for infrared (IrDA) and wireless support, plus support for USB devices.

▶ Windows 2000 Professional can support the usage of an additional processor. You can expect to see some questions that focus on the impact of improving the CPU power of your Windows 2000 Professional computer and the impact that might have on other resources available within your system.

INTRODUCTION

This chapter is mainly concerned with the hardware devices that can tailor the generalized PC into a device that does what you want. The extra pieces of hardware, from DVD devices to additional monitors, can greatly increase the functional value of the computer.

Understanding the configuration options available is key to arriving at solutions to problems likely to be presented in the exam. This chapter examines the disk configurations and removable storage options that can provide solutions to disk storage problems. We will then look at I/O devices, such as multiple displays, wireless I/O, cameras, scanners and printers, and USB devices, to name a few. PnP features are fully supported in Windows 2000 Professional, so we will be looking at that feature as well.

The chapter rounds out with a look at the multiple CPU capability of Windows 2000 Professional and network adapter configurations.

INSTALLING HARDWARE

The Windows 2000 Professional operating system includes many enhancements to simplify device management. Some of these include Advanced Power Management (APM), Advanced Configuration and Power Interface (ACPI), and PnP.

PnP is a combination of hardware and software that enables a computer to recognize and modify its hardware configuration changes with minimal intervention from the user. The hardware device that you are installing must support the PnP initiative to be automatically configured correctly. With PnP, a user can add or remove a device dynamically without manual reconfiguration and without any intricate knowledge of the computer hardware.

When you install a PnP device, Windows 2000 Professional automatically configures the device to allow it to function properly with the other devices already installed in your computer. Windows 2000 Professional assigns system resources to the device, including the following:

◆ Interrupt request (IRQ) number

◆ Direct memory access (DMA) channel

◆ I/O port address

◆ Memory address range

Each resource must be unique or the device does not function properly.

When the device you are installing is not PnP compatible, Windows 2000 Professional has no way of automatically configuring the device settings. You may have to manually configure the device driver or use the manufacturer provided installation program.

You can configure devices using the Add/Remove Hardware applet in the Control Panel or by using the Device Manager, which is located in the Computer Management icon within the Administrative Tools folder in the Control Panel.

PnP can be supported by devices and the drivers that control them. The possible combinations expand to the following four different support scenarios:

◆ Full PnP support is provided when the hardware and the device driver fully support PnP.

◆ If the hardware supports PnP, but the device driver does not, Windows 2000 Professional cannot support PnP and the device is treated as a legacy NT 4.0 device.

◆ If the device driver supports PnP, but the hardware does not, Windows 2000 can provide partial PnP support. In this case, Windows 2000 cannot automatically configure the device drivers, but Plug and Play can manage resource allocations and interface to the power management systems.

◆ Windows 2000 cannot provide support for PnP if neither the device driver nor the hardware supports PnP.

> **WARNING**
>
> **Manually Adjusting Resources** If you must manually configure a non-PnP device, the resources assigned become fixed. This reduces the flexibility that Windows 2000 Professional has for allocating resources to other devices. If too many resources are manually configured, Windows 2000 Professional might not be able to install new PnP devices.

Using the Add/Remove Hardware Wizard

The Add/Remove Hardware Wizard started from the Control Panel is used to initiate automatic hardware installation of both PnP and non-PnP hardware devices. Step by Step 3.1 shows you how to initiate a search for new PnP hardware.

ON THE CD

Step by Step 3.1, "Searching for New Plug and Play Hardware," walks you through searching for new PnP hardware. See the file **Chapter03-01stepbystep.pdf** in the CD's **Chapter03\StepbyStep** directory.

Windows 2000 Professional searches for any new PnP hardware and installs any it finds. In the event that the wizard cannot detect any new hardware, it displays a list of installed hardware from which you choose a device for troubleshooting (see Figure 3.1). The first entry on the hardware list is Add a New Device, which provides the option of installing a new device.

Confirming Hardware Installation

After you have installed new hardware, you can confirm that the device is installed and functioning properly by using the Device Manager.

To start the Device Manager, double-click the System icon in the Control Panel. Select the Hardware tab and click the Device Manager button. A list of installed hardware displays, as shown in Figure 3.2.

FIGURE 3.1
Troubleshooting devices.

FIGURE 3.2
Installed devices listed by the Device Manager.

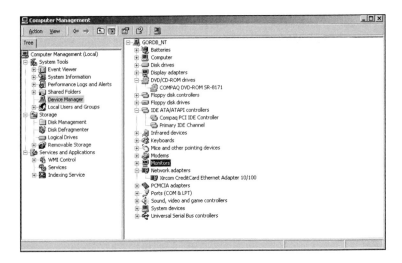

Expanding a device type displays all the specific devices of that type
installed on the computer and the status of each device. Each device
is displayed with one of the following statuses:

◆ **Normal icon.** The device is functioning normally.

◆ **Stop sign.** Windows 2000 Professional has disabled the hardware due to resource conflicts. To correct this, right-click the
device icon, click Properties, and set the resources manually
according to what is available in the system.

◆ **Exclamation point.** The device is not configured correctly or
the device drivers are missing.

Determining Required Resources

When you are manually installing and configuring non-PnP hardware you need to understand the resources the hardware device
expects to use. The manufacturer's product documentation lists the
resources the device requires and you must determine how to fit it
into your existing system. Typically, the following resources must be
configured for hardware devices:

◆ **Interrupts.** Hardware devices use interrupts to indicate to the
processor that attention is needed. Windows 2000 provides
interrupts number 0 through 15 to devices.

◆ **I/O ports.** A device uses these areas of memory to communicate with Windows 2000 Professional. When the processor sees an IRQ request, it checks the I/O port address to retrieve additional information about what the device wants.

◆ **Direct Memory Access (DMA).** These channels allow the hardware device to access memory directly. This allows a device like a floppy drive to write information into memory without interrupting the processor.

◆ **Memory.** Many hardware devices have onboard memory or can reserve system memory for their use. Any reserved memory is not available for any other device or for Windows 2000 Professional.

Determining Available Resources

After you determine what resources your device requires, you can use Device Manager to display the resources available on your computer. By setting the view to Resources by Connection you can view all resources and their availability (see Figure 3.3).

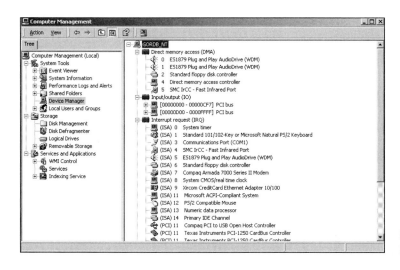

FIGURE 3.3
Hardware resources listed by connection.

Changing Resource Assignments

You might encounter two devices that request the same resources, resulting in a conflict. To change a resource setting, use the Resources tab in the device's Properties information. Step by Step 3.2 describes how to modify a resource setting for a hardware device.

ON THE CD

Step by Step 3.2, "Modifying a Device's Resource Configuration," walks you through how to modify a device's resource configuration. See the file **Chapter03-02StepbyStep.pdf** in the CD's **Chapter03\ StepbyStep** directory.

> **NOTE**
>
> **Changing Resources for Non-PnP Devices** Changing the resources assigned to a non-PnP device might not actually change the resources the device uses. You might have to consult the manufacturer's documentation on what jumpers or software switches to set on the device to conform to the resource assignment you have told Windows 2000 to expect.

At this point you are presented with a screen that allows you to edit the value of the resource you have selected. Saving that new value changes the setting for the resource.

MEDIA DEVICES

Implement, manage, and troubleshoot disk devices.

The following sections address disk and other media devices.

CD-ROM and DVD Devices

Current CD-ROM and DVD devices support PnP and, therefore, should be automatically configured when you install the devices.

Support for the CD-ROM File System (CDFS) is maintained in Windows 2000 Professional for support of legacy applications and is used by RSM in storing CD-ROMs in removable storage libraries. CD-ROM devices support 650MB of storage per platter; and although this was once considered immense, it pales against the emerging standard of DVD, which currently can hold over 26 times as much data (up to 17GB of information) .

DVD used to stand for Digital Versatile Disk. However, now it is recognized by the acronym alone. This line of devices is an enhancement of CD-ROM technology and is quickly replacing that as more multimedia technology is integrated into computer usage.

There are four primary types of DVD storage:

- ◆ **DVD-Video.** This is the actual technology usually referred to as DVD. This is a disk holding a video program, such as a feature film, that can be played back in either a DVD-Video player or a computer with a high-resolution display.

- ◆ **DVD-ROM.** This is the disk technology used to store computer data to be read by a DVD-ROM drive. All DVD devices should be able to read DVD disks, including double-sided, double-layered disks holding up to 17GB of data.

- ◆ **DVD-WO.** This is a variation of DVD-ROM that supports one-time recording capabilities like today's CD-R. The WO stands for Write Once.

- ◆ **DVD-RAM.** This is a variation of DVD-ROM supporting multiple recording capabilities similar to magneto-optical (MO) disks.

Support for DVD in Windows 2000 Professional includes the following:

- ◆ **DVD-ROM driver.** The DVD-ROM industry standard command set is supported by the new Windows Driver Model (WDM) DVD-ROM device driver.

- ◆ **UDF file system.** The Universal Disk Format (UDF) provides support for UDF-formatted DVD disks.

- ◆ **WDM streaming class driver.** This is a driver written to follow the new WDM support. This driver supports MPEG-2 and AC-3 hardware decoders, providing full-motion video and surround-sound capability.

- ◆ **DirectShow.** DirectShow is a replacement for ActiveMovie and supports DVD video and audio streams.

- ◆ **DirectDraw.** The video streams created by DVD devices can overwhelm a PCI bus on a computer. The solution to this is the creation of a dedicated bus to transfer decoded video streams from an MPEG-2 decoder to the display card.

- ◆ **Copyright protection.** DVD provides copyright protection by encrypting key sectors on a disc and then decrypting them prior to decoding.

◆ **Regionalization.** As part of the copyright protection scheme used for DVD, six worldwide regions have been defined by the DVD consortiums. Disks are playable on DVD devices in some or all of the regions according to codes set by the creators of the content.

Monitoring CD-ROM and DVD Devices

Step by Step 3.3 shows you how to view information about the device drivers controlling you CD-ROM and/or DVD devices.

ON THE CD

Step by Step 3.3, "Displaying CD-ROM and DVD Device Information," walks you through displaying CD-ROM and DVD device information. See the file **Chapter03-03StepbyStep.pdf** in the CD's **Chapter03\StepbyStep** directory.

Troubleshooting CD-ROM and DVD Devices

Most of these devices are now PnP compatible and, therefore, not prone to configuration errors. The CD-ROM and DVD devices are not immune to installation problems, however. These errors include the tray door not opening, the usage light not lighting, or the device not showing up on your My Computer display. Loose or badly installed power or data cables often cause these errors. To confirm this, you must physically open the computer case and examine the device connections.

If the power source or data cables are correctly installed, there are other potential problems that can arise. These include

◆ **The device reads data but not audio.** The audio drivers are incorrect or not installed correctly. You must update the device drivers to the latest available from Microsoft (see "Maintaining Updated Drivers" later in this chapter) or the manufacturer.

◆ **The audio drivers are installed but no audio is heard.** The audio cables are installed incorrectly. To check this, you must open the computer case and examine the audio cables from the sound card to the CD-ROM drive. Also verify that external speakers are correctly connected to the sound card.

◆ **The computer plays audio but cannot be read.** The
CD-ROM is faulty.

◆ **The CD-ROM can't be read or play.** Windows 2000
Professional is having difficulty detecting the hardware.
The audio device driver or the hardware might not be PnP
compatible. The next step is to update the device drivers to
the latest available version.

Fixed Disks

Disk Management is a new graphical tool used in Windows 2000
Professional to manage disks and volumes. Disk Management can
be started from within Computer Management or from inside
Administrative Tools in the Control Panel, and can also be configured as an MMC snap-in.

When a new disk has been installed, Disk Management is used to
rescan the drives. Normally you have to power off your computer
hardware to install a new disk drive unless your system has support
for hot-pluggable disk drive bays. When you rescan your disks, Disk
Management scans all attached disks looking for configuration
changes, removable media, CD-ROM drives, basic volumes, file
systems, and drive letters.

Disk storage is now configured as basic or dynamic. The terms basic
disk and dynamic disk are not referring to a different type of disk,
but rather to the way the disk is configured. A disk can be configured as a basic disk and partitioned as you would have done in
Windows NT 4.0 or configured as a dynamic disk and divided into
volumes.

Basic Disk Storage

Basic storage supports partition-oriented disk configurations. A disk
initialized for basic storage is called a *basic disk*. A basic disk can
contain primary partitions, extended partitions, and logical drives.
Basic storage is supported by all versions of Microsoft Windows 3.x
and Microsoft Windows 9x, and on Windows 2000 Professional and
Server.

On a basic disk, a partition is a part of the disk that functions as a physically separate unit. A primary partition is reserved for use by an operating system. An active partition is a primary partition that contains the startup files for the operating system. Any disk can have up to four primary partitions (or three if there is an extended partition). An extended partition is created from free space and can be partitioned into logical drives. Only one extended partition is allowed per physical disk.

Disk Management supports existing mirror and RAID-5 configurations that were created under Windows NT 4.0; however, the creation of these configurations is restricted to dynamic disks only.

Dynamic Storage

Dynamic storage is designed for new volume-oriented disk configurations. A disk initialized for dynamic storage is called a *dynamic disk*. Dynamic disks are physical disks that contain dynamic volumes created using Disk Management. Storage is divided into volumes instead of partitions. A volume consists of a part or parts of one or more physical disks laid out as a simple, spanned, mirrored, striped, or RAID-5 structure. Dynamic disks cannot contain partitions or logical drives and can be accessed only by computers running Windows 2000.

Dynamic disks can be reverted to basic disks using Disk Management; however, there is no procedure to convert dynamic volumes back to partitions. This limitation requires you to remove the volumes contained on a dynamic disk before reverting it to a basic disk.

Whereas basic disks use the partition table located in the Master Boot Record (MBR) to identify the starting and ending of partitions on the physical disk, dynamic disks do not follow the same format. A dynamic disk still has a partition table, but it has only one entry that encompasses the entire disk. This allows the system to see a valid partition table when it is booting. A dynamic disk configuration stores the volume information on the physical disk in a small, 1MB database at the end of the disk.

Each physical disk that has been initialized in a dynamic disk configuration contains a copy of this database replicated among each physical disk in the system. If one of the databases becomes corrupt,

NOTE

Converting Basic to Dynamic For a basic disk to be upgraded to a dynamic configuration, there must be enough available space at the end of the disk for this database. This space is automatically reserved when Disk Management creates partitions or volumes on a disk; however, a disk created by Windows NT 4.0 might not have the room available.

another copy is used and the corrupt one is refreshed with an uncorrupted copy.

In addition, mirrored and RAID-5 configurations are not supported on Windows 2000 Professional (only on Server); however, Windows 2000 Professional can create these configurations on a remote Windows 2000 Server system. Dynamic disk configurations are not supported on portable computers. If you are using Disk Management on a laptop, you will find that the options for converting a basic disk to a dynamic disk are not present.

Disk Management

The Disk Management utility graphically displays disks and volumes and allows a user with Administrative rights to configure disks and volumes.

One of the most basic commands is to rescan the hardware. This allows you to update any hardware information if a new disk has been installed that Disk Management has not detected automatically.

To set up new disks, Disk Management provides wizards to help with the following tasks:

◆ Add disks for basic or dynamic storage

◆ Create primary or extended partitions and logical disk drives (on basic disks only)

◆ Create simple, spanned, striped, mirrored, or RAID-5 volumes (on dynamic disks only)

◆ Format volumes using File Allocation Table (FAT), FAT 32, or Windows NT File System (NTFS) formats

◆ Upgrade disks from basic to dynamic

◆ Mount a local drive at any empty folder on an NTFS-formatted volume

The ability to mount a local drive to a folder rather than using a drive letter is an interesting feature. For example, you might have an NTFS volume that is disk C: and you have a CD-ROM drive

currently known as disk D:. If you create an empty folder at C:\
CD-ROM, Disk Manager can mount the CD-ROM drive at that
folder. Now you can access the information on the CD-ROM from
the C: drive and reuse the D: drive letter for other devices.

Upgrading Basic Disks to Dynamic Disks

When a basic disk has been converted to dynamic, all existing partitions become simple dynamic volumes. This cannot be reversed. Any
existing stripe, mirrored, spanned, or RAID-5 partition becomes the
equivalent volume.

When upgraded, a dynamic disk cannot contain partitions or logical
drives and cannot be accessed by MS-DOS or Windows operating
systems other than Windows 2000.

If the basic disk contains a partition that resides on multiple disks
(such as a spanned volume), all other disks that contain part of the
volume must be upgraded as well. Volumes cannot be created on any
removable media.

System and Boot Partitions

A basic disk that contains the system or active partitions can be
upgraded to dynamic. These partitions become simple system or
active volumes. An existing volume cannot be marked as active.

A basic disk that contains the Boot Partition can also be upgraded
to a dynamic disk. The Boot Partition becomes a simple boot volume. A fresh installation of Windows 2000 Professional cannot be
performed on an existing dynamic volume, but Windows 2000 can
be upgraded on a dynamic boot volume. This limitation results
because the Windows 2000 Professional setup only recognizes
dynamic volumes that contain partition tables. Partition tables only
occur in basic volumes and dynamic volumes that were upgraded
from basic volumes. If you create a new dynamic volume on a
dynamic disk, the new volume will not contain a partition table.

When the disk containing the Boot and System Partitions has been
upgraded to dynamic volumes, you can create a mirror set onto
another disk. If one of the disks in the mirror set fails, you can
restart your computer from the mirrored disk. This requires an entry
in BOOT.INI to reference the mirrored disk.

Troubleshooting Disk Problems

If a disk or volume fails, you naturally want to repair the problem as quickly as possible. Disk Management displays the status of disks or volumes in both the text and graphical view. Each disk or volume displays one of the following statuses:

◆ **Online.** The disk is accessible and has no detected problems.

◆ **Online (errors).** I/O errors have been detected. If the I/O errors are not permanent, you can reactivate the disk to return it to Online status.

◆ **Offline.** The disk is not accessible and may be powered down, disconnected, or corrupt.

◆ **Foreign.** The disk has been moved to this computer from another Windows 2000 system. To set up this disk for use here, use the Import Foreign Disks task.

◆ **Unreadable.** The disk cannot be accessed. It might have experienced hardware failure, corruption, or I/O errors. The 1MB database at the end of the physical disk might also be corrupted.

◆ **Unrecognized.** The disk has a signature that Disk Management does not allow you to use. A disk from a UNIX system displays the Unrecognized status.

◆ **No Media.** No media is in the CD-ROM or removable drive. This disk status changes when you insert the appropriate media into the device.

Volume Sets

Dynamic volumes are new in Windows 2000 and provide new disk storage strategies. There are five types of dynamic volumes:

◆ **Simple volumes.** Exist only on dynamic disks. The by number of volumes that can be created on a disk is limited only the amount of free space available. A simple volume can be extended to other regions on a disk or to other disks. When a simple volume extends to another disk it becomes a spanned volume.

> **NOTE**
>
> **Only on Windows 2000 Server**
> Mirrored and RAID-5 volumes can be created only on systems running Windows 2000 Server. Please refer to Chapter 12, "Managing, Configuring, and Troubleshooting Storage Use," for information on configuring mirrored and RAID-5 volumes.

◆ **Spanned volumes.** Created by combining the 1 to 32 areas of free disk space into one large volume. When the space on one disk is filled up, the system starts writing at the beginning of the next disk. The disks used in a spanned volume can be dissimilar types, such as IDE and SCSI disk devices. A simple volume must use the NTFS file format to be extended into a spanned volume. Spanned volumes are not fault tolerant. If a disk in a spanned volume fails, the data in the entire spanned volume is lost.

◆ **Striped volumes.** A mechanism for combining areas of free space from 2 to 32 disks into one logical volume. Data is written evenly across all disks in the striped volume in 64KB stripes. Striped volumes offer the best performance of all the Windows 2000 Professional disk management strategies but are not fault tolerant. If a disk in a striped volume fails, the data in the entire striped volume is lost.

If a disk or volume fails, it is important to repair the problem as quickly as possible. Disk Management displays the status of disks or volumes in both the list and graphical view. One of the following statuses is displayed for each disk:

◆ **Healthy.** The volume is readable with no detected problems.

◆ **Healthy (at risk).** The volume is currently readable, but I/O errors have been detected on one of the volume's physical disks. Use Reactivate Disk to return the disk to Online status, which returns the volume to Healthy status.

◆ **Initializing.** The volume is being initialized. Only dynamic volumes display the Initializing status.

◆ **Failed.** The volume cannot be started automatically.

Removable Media

Removable Storage Management (RSM) is the interface in Windows 2000 Professional for accessing removable media, including automated devices such as changers, jukeboxes, and libraries. RSM is installed by default to control most types of removable media including CD-ROM, DVD-ROM, MO JAZ, and ZIP drives in both standalone and library configurations.

RSM considers all device changes as a subset of an ideal standard. A given mini-driver tells RSM what functionality the actual changer implements, allowing RSM to treat it appropriately.

Client programs, such as backup applications and Hierarchical Storage Management (HSM) systems, use RSM to access their media. When the media is available, the client applications use standard Windows 2000 API calls to read and write data.

This model provides the following benefits:

- ◆ **A common driver model.** The driver model allows a tape library to be used with any RSM-compatible application. An application written to use RSM can work with any device changer where the manufacturer has provided an RSM mini-driver.

- ◆ **Library sharing.** Multiple applications can now share a common library. Previously, if you wanted to use both a backup application and an HSM application supplied from two different vendors, two device changers were required. When using RSM, both applications can use the same changer.

- ◆ **Offline media.** A backup application does not need to know where the media is. It simply requests the media and RSM loads it or asks the operator to mount it as is required.

- ◆ **Media tracking.** RSM tracks all media that it recognizes in an internal database. Applications can register with RSM, allowing it to recognize its own media. Applications can also use RSM to search the database and load a particular media.

- ◆ **A common interface.** Backup applications that are RSM compatible work the same with a changer or with a standalone drive.

Windows 2000 Professional uses RSM to manage ATAPI CD-ROM changers and to mount and dismount all removable media. This includes disks contained in ATAPI CD-ROM changers that hold several CD-ROMs. This type of device receives only a single letter in Windows 2000.

Media Pools

RSM organizes removable media into media pools. A *media pool* is a logical collection of similar media with similar properties. All RSM media belongs to a media pool, and each media pool holds either tape or disk (but not both). Applications use media pools to gain access to specific types of media from a library.

RSM supports the following classes of media pools:

- ◆ **Unrecognized media pools.** Unrecognized media pools contain new (blank) media. This should be immediately moved from the unrecognized media pool to the free media pool so it can be used by applications.

- ◆ **Import media pools.** Import media pools contain media the RSM recognizes but has not cataloged in the RSM database. Media can be moved from import media pools to free or application media pools for reuse.

- ◆ **Free media pools.** Free media pools contain media that is not currently allocated by an application and contains no current data. Media pools should be configured to draw from the free media pool when there is nothing available for a particular application.

- ◆ **Application media pools.** Application media pools are created and used by data management applications. Media in an application pool is controlled by the management application or by the administrator. An application can use more than one media pool and more than one application can share a media pool.

Library Types

Each media in RSM belongs to a library, and there are two types of libraries:

- ◆ **Robotic libraries.** Automated units (such as jukeboxes) that hold multiple tapes or disks and can have multiple drives.

◆ **Standalone libraries.** Single-slot CD-ROM or tape devices that hold a single piece of media.

RSM can also track offline media that is cataloged but not currently in a library. This media can be physically located offsite to support disaster recovery plans.

Media Resources

Before RSM can be set up and used, there must be removable media resources to manage. There are three types of removable media supported by RSM:

◆ **Tape.** The two major tape technologies in use today are Digital AudioTape (DAT) and Digital Linear Tape (DLT).

◆ **Read-Only Optical Disk.** Read-only optical media includes CD-ROM and DVD-ROM discs. These are written by the manufacturer and cannot be overwritten or erased. This type of media is most useful as reference material or licensed software programs.

◆ **Writeable Optical Discs.** Writeable optical media includes MO devices, Phase Change (PC), Write Once Read Many (WORM), CD-Recordable (CD-R), and DVD-Recordable (DVD-R) discs. MO and PC media can be erased and over-written, while WORM, CD-R, and DVD-R discs can only be written to once.

Operator Requests

An *operator request* is a message that requests a specific task. Operator requests are generated when offline media has been requested or an application has requested media and none is available An operator request is also be generated if a fault occurs in one of the libraries or a drive needs cleaning and no cleaner cartridges are available.

Troubleshooting RSM

Problems can occur when using RSM in either standalone configurations or with robotic libraries. To prevent problems, follow the guidelines in this list:

◆ Verify that the library is supported by Windows 2000. A good place to check is the Hardware Compatibility List (HCL) on the Microsoft Web site (www.microsoft.com/hcl).

◆ Verify that the library is properly connected. If the library uses a SCSI connection, make sure that there are no SCSI ID conflicts with other devices in the computer and verify that all cables are installed and terminated properly and do not exceed the maximum length allowed.

◆ Use Device Manager to ensure that Windows 2000 has recognized the library and associated drives and has configured the device drivers correctly.

◆ If Removable Storage still cannot automatically configure the library correctly, it needs to be manually configured.

◆ If the library is configured correctly but begins malfunctioning, look at the Windows 2000 system event log. Many problems can be caused by device errors.

DISPLAY DEVICES

Implement, manage, and troubleshoot display devices.

Windows 2000 Professional adds support for up to nine display adapters. This allows the desktop to extend to nine monitors supporting large graphical drawings (such as those produced by CAD systems). There are some important considerations to make if setting up a multiple display system.

Multiple Display Support

Multiple display support requires that all video adapters must be Peripheral Component Interconnect (PCI) or Accelerated Graphics Port (AGP) devices.

If the video adapter built in to the motherboard is to be used as a secondary screen in a multiple display, it must be compatible with those requirements. To use the built-in video adapter, you must completely install Windows 2000 Professional before adding any other adapters. By default, Windows 2000 Professional disables an onboard video adapter if an additional adapter is installed. You can only use the built-in video adapter if you can later enable the built-in video adapter.

One final consideration is to remember that the primary video adapter cannot be turned off. Because the multiple-display configuration uses the primary as the "anchor point" of the extended desktop, any system that shuts down the primary video adapter does not support multiple displays. Laptops that are placed in docking stations usually do just that, and do not function correctly in this configuration.

The Virtual Desktop

Windows 2000 Professional creates a virtual desktop when configuring multiple displays and uses this to determine the relationship of the displays to each other. The virtual desktop sets the coordinates of the top-left corner of the primary screen as (0,0). Additional screens are configured to exactly touch each other on the virtual desktop, allowing the mouse to move seamlessly from screen to screen; there are no spots not covered by a display.

The position of the displays on the virtual desktop can be viewed by clicking the Display icon in the Control Panel. Select the Settings tab in the Control Panel to show the screen layout. Display positions are changed by dragging the icon representing the screen to its new location. There is also a check box to indicate which screen (and, therefore, video adapter) is going to be the primary monitor.

Configuring Multiple Display Adapters

When the secondary adapter(s) are installed, the virtual desktop must be configured as outlined in Step by Step 3.4.

ON THE CD

Step by Step 3.4, "Configuring Two Displays," walks you through configuring two displays. See the file **Chapter03-04StepbyStep.pdf** in the CD's **Chapter03\StepbyStep** directory.

This procedure is very similar to the one you would follow when configuring your display. In the case of multiple monitors, you must first choose the monitor you are configuring and then provide the same configuration for all the monitors in the system.

Troubleshooting Multiple Displays

Problems with multiple displays usually relate to the video adapter not initializing properly or not being supported as a secondary display. Typical problems faced in this scenario include

◆ **No output on a secondary display.** Confirm that the device is activated in the Display Properties dialog box, the correct video driver is installed, or that the secondary display was initialized when the computer restarted. You might have to physically switch the order of the adapters in the PCI slots.

◆ **The Extend My Windows Desktop check box is unavailable.** Confirm that the secondary display is highlighted in the Display Properties onto This Monitor dialog box and that the secondary display adapter is supported and/or detected.

◆ **There are problems displaying an application on a multi-display configuration.** Run the application on the primary display rather than on a secondary display, run the application on a window that spans more than one screen, run the application full screen rather than in the windows, or disable the secondary display and attempt to run the program again.

Video Adapters

Most computers are designed with a video adapter built in to the motherboard, and generally this device works best with most applications. With some new games, however, additional hardware acceleration is needed to power the effects.

Video adapters now support the PnP standard and are detected and installed by Windows 2000 Professional either during setup or when you reboot your computer after installing the device. In the event that PnP cannot detect the card directly, you can use Step by Step 3.5 to install the new device.

ON THE CD

Step by Step 3.5, "Installing a New Video Adapter," walks you through installing a new video adapter. See the file **Chapter03-05StepbyStep.pdf** in the CD's **Chapter03\StepbyStep** directory.

When the new video adapter is installed, you can change the characteristics of your screen using the Display applet in the Control Panel. Figure 3.4 shows the Settings screen from the Display applet in Control Panel. From this point, you can vary the color depth and the screen resolution.

MOBILE COMPUTING

Implement, manage, and troubleshoot mobile computer hardware.

Being mobile with your computer is becoming the rule rather than the exception. Within corporations, a significant number of desktop systems are laptops in docking stations. Support for these devices requires special consideration compared to stationary desktop systems. Chiefly, this includes power management and support for PCMCIA cards.

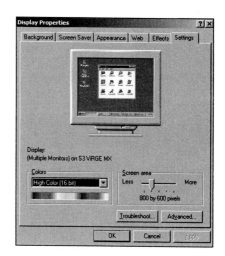

FIGURE 3.4
Display settings.

Power Management

Advanced Power Management (APM) is the legacy power-management scheme based on a BIOS approach that was first supported in Windows 95. Most of the interesting features of APM are located in the machine-specific BIOS rather than the Windows 2000 Professional operating system.

APM has been superseded by the Advanced Configuration and Power Interface (ACPI) standard. This is a more robust scheme for power management and system configuration supported in Windows 98 and Windows 2000 Professional.

When to Use APM

If the laptop has a supported ACPI BIOS, ACPI should be used for power management. Some functions, such as timed wakeups, are only available using ACPI under Windows 2000 Professional.

APM should not be used if the BIOS has been identified as incompatible with APM or if the BIOS is not compliant with the APM standard. This results in an unstable system with the potential for data loss.

APM can be used when there is no ACPI BIOS or when the ACPI BIOS is not compliant or not implemented properly. However, APM might not work any better.

During installation, Windows 2000 Professional setup procedures use values in the BIOSINFO.INF file (supplied on the Windows 2000 Professional CD-ROM) to determine whether the system is on the AutoEnable APM list or the Disable APM list.

If the system is on the AutoEnable list, Setup automatically installs APM support. If the system is on the Disable APM list, Setup does not install or enable APM support. It might still be necessary to disable the APM BIOS settings using the computer's BIOS setup routines.

If the system is not found on either list, the system is considered neutral. In this case, Setup installs APM support but leaves it disabled. You can enable APM support by double-clicking the Power icon in the Control Panel and selecting the APM tab.

You can determine whether APM support is configured for your system by clicking Start and then selecting Shutdown. If APM support is running, the Stand-By entry appears in the list of choices.

Troubleshooting APM in Windows 2000 Professional

The following are items you should consider when using APM support in Windows 2000 Professional.

- ◆ **APM and multiprocessors.** Ensure that APM is turned off in the BIOS on multiprocessor systems. If possible, use ACPI, which is supported with multiprocessor systems.

◆ **Desktop system.** APM support should be disabled on all desktop systems. The APM BIOS cannot correctly save most of the video displays on desktop systems, resulting in a vanished display after a Suspend and Resume.

◆ **Incompatible systems.** If APM support has been enabled on a system in the Disable APM list, use the Power applet in the Control Panel to disable APM support. Reboot the system in Safe mode (F8) and delete the NTAPM.SYS file from `\WINNT\System32\drivers`.

◆ **Additional video adapter.** Using a video adapter other than the one included with the computer changes the system's APM configuration. If the adapter is not detected by the APM BIOS, Suspend does not function properly.

◆ **Screen blanking.** If the video timeout is set in the BIOS and the screen blanks, moving a mouse wakes the system; however, an external USB mouse does not. To work around this, disable the BIOS timeout and use the blank screen saver.

◆ **APM BIOS timeouts.** The BIOS should be configured to allow the Windows 2000 Professional operating system to blank the screen, and turn off the disk, and so on. If APM is used to control these functions, the system does not always restore correctly on wake-up. BIOS timeouts should be set to none or for as long as possible.

Card Services

Windows 2000 Professional supports the connection of credit card–sized add-on devices through its card services.

Windows 2000 Professional supports PC Card socket controllers, 16-bit PC I/O cards (sometimes referred to as PCMCIA cards), and the newer 32-bit cards. Although PCMCIA cards were originally intended only as memory cards, the currently available cards are also used for many I/O devices such as modems and network adapters. Windows 2000 Professional also supports power management and PnP for PCMCIA cards.

Stop the Device First It is important to use the Add/Remove Hardware Wizard or the Eject Device taskbar icon to stop a PC Card device that you are about to unplug or eject. Doing so prevents data loss or other serious malfunction of the device.

Step by Step 3.6 shows you the proper way to unplug a PC Card.

ON THE CD

Step by Step 3.6, "Unplugging or Ejecting a PC Card," walks you through unplugging and ejecting a PC card. See the file **Chapter03-06StepbyStep.pdf** in the CD's **Chapter03\StepbyStep** directory.

INPUT AND OUTPUT (I/O) DEVICES

Implement, manage, and troubleshoot input and output (I/O) devices.

Since their introduction, personal computers have always been generalized in design. Additional functionality and personalization features were provided by manufacturers of add-on cards and adapters. With many different manufacturers all providing different approaches to installing and configuring their devices, using PC add-ons was often confusing and contradictory.

Windows 2000 Professional supports the PnP standard, and most new devices use this to standardize their installation steps.

Configuring Input and Output Devices

Devices such as printers, image-capturing devices, multimedia, pointing and input devices, and now smart cards form a class of device that works more at the Human Machine interface than other devices. This means that there are more features combined into these devices, giving them more than a single-purpose device.

Printers

The printing system is modular and works hand-in-hand with other systems to provide printing services. When a printer is a local printer and a print job is specified by an application, data is sent to the Graphics Device Interface (GDI). The GDI calls the printer driver for print device information useful in rendering the print job into the printer language of the print device. The *GDI* is, therefore, the main interface between the application and the printing system. The print job is passed to the spooler and is written to disk as a temporary file so it can survive a power outage or system shutdown. Print jobs can be spooled in either the RAW or Enhanced Meta File (EMF) printer language. Figure 3.5 shows the layout of the components of the Windows 2000 Professional printing subsystem.

The client side of the print spooler is WINSPOOL.DRV, and that driver makes an RPC call to the SPOOLSV.EXE server side of the spooler. This split-in functionality is what allows print devices to be local to your computer or remotely installed on a print server and still function the same way. Clients for spoolsv.exe include WINSPOOL.DRV for handling locally created print jobs and WIN32SPL.DLL for print jobs created on remote machines.

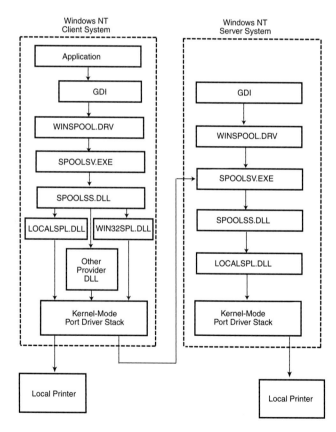

FIGURE 3.5
Components of the Windows printing subsystem.

If the printer is located on a different Windows 2000 or Windows NT Server, the network provider WIN32SPL.DLL is used. This module uses RPC calls to redirect the print jobs from the client's computer to the server's SPOOLSV.EXE PROCESS. When there, the server's local print provider handles the print job.

You generally install printers using the Add Printer Wizard found in the Printers folder in Control Panel. After you step through the wizard, you have created a local printer with the name you provided. You can manipulate printers by performing the following actions:

◆ Double-click the printer to see any spooled jobs, provided you have the privilege to do so.

◆ Right-click the printer to view a shortcut menu from which you can delete a printer that no longer exists or use the Default Printer command.

◆ Right-click a printer and select the Properties command from the shortcut menu to access the Printer Properties and control any number of settings.

Using a Basic Error Checklist

Any number of things can go wrong when you attempt to print to a printer. In many cases, Windows 2000 Professional alerts you to an error and in some cases actually tells you what the error type is.

If your print job spools but does not print, try the following:

◆ Check that the printer is turned on and all the connections are secure.

◆ Check that the paper tray is full and no paper is jammed inside the printer.

◆ Verify that the printer is operational. If the printer is a shared resource and other users can print, the problem is not with the printer or the print server.

◆ Verify that the printer does not have any outstanding error conditions set.

◆ If there is a job currently printing that is hung up, you can delete it by pausing the printer and deleting the stopped print job. Restarting the printer allows other spooled jobs to complete.

If none of these solutions seems to work, try the following:

◆ Verify that the printer is using the correct printer driver. If the printer is a shared resource and other users have operating systems other than Windows 2000 Professional, make sure that you install all the necessary drivers.

◆ Verify that the printer you attempted to print to is either the default printer for your system, or the printer you selected from your application.

◆ Verify that you can access the printer you are attempting to use. If the status appears at Opening or Unable to Connect, there could be a permissions problem.

◆ Verify that there is enough hard disk space to create the temporary spool file.

◆ Try printing a smaller page of text from Notepad. This often confirms that the print problem is application specific.

◆ Print to a file and copy the file to the printer port being used either locally or on the printer server. If you can print in this manner, there could be a spooler or data-transmission error.

◆ Obtain the latest print drivers for the printer. You can obtain print drivers from the Windows 2000 Professional distribution disks, the setup disks that come with the printer, the printer manufacturer's Web site, or the Microsoft Web site.

Scanners

Scanners are added by using the Scanners and Cameras Wizard found in the Control Panel. Only administrators of the local computer can add scanners to a Windows 2000 Professional computer.

After installing the scanner and connecting any cables required to your Windows 2000 Professional computer, you can use Step by Step 3.7 to install a scanner.

ON THE CD

Step by Step 3.7, "Installing a Scanner," walks you through scanner installation. See the file **Chapter03-07StepbyStep.pdf** in the CD's **Chapter03\StepbyStep** directory.

Keyboards

Keyboards can be built in, connected with a specific device port, or operate as a USB device connected directly or via a USB hub.

Windows 2000 Professional detects a new keyboard if it is PnP compatible. If it is not, you have to use the Add/Remove Hardware Wizard and use the manufacturer's setup disks to install the device manually.

When the keyboard is installed, you can change the characteristics of the device, such as the keyboard repeat rate, to meet your personal requirements.

The Accessibility Options applet in the Control Panel also provides a number of ways to customize how your keyboard functions. These include

◆ **StickyKeys.** This option allows you to press a modifier key such as Ctrl, Alt, Shift, or the Windows Logo key and have it remain in effect until a non-modifier key is pressed.

◆ **FilterKeys.** This option allows you to ignore brief or repeated keystrokes.

◆ **ToggleKeys.** This option emits a sound when locking keys are pressed.

Mouse

Like keyboards, the mouse can be directly connected to a mouse port, built in to the keyboard as a piezoelectric control, or connected to the serial port or device on a USB port or hub.

After the mouse has been installed, you can adjust the characteristics of its action by changing the configuration on the Properties page of the Mouse applet in the Control Panel.

Using the Mouse applet you can select the mouse to be left handed or right handed, select double- or single-click to select objects, and set the speed at which a double-click is recognized.

You can also have the mouse pointer jump to the default dialog box or button, thereby requiring fewer mouse movements to make a selection. You can configure the mouse pointer to accelerate if you move the mouse faster. This results in the mouse pointer moving a longer distance with a quick mouse movement than it would if you moved the mouse over the same distance but at a slower rate.

Multimedia

Categories of multimedia devices in Windows 2000 Professional include audio, video, and MIDI. In addition, the Microsoft Media Player can use the Web to access music files and radio stations that broadcast programming. The CD Player can be used to control the playback of music CDs from the system CD-ROM drive.

The Sounds and Multimedia applet provides a mechanism to control the sounds used for specific events within Windows 2000 and many of its installed services (such as Netmeeting, MSN messaging, or Active Sync). You can also customize the sounds used for these events and save the configuration as a sound scheme.

Smart Cards

Smart cards are programmable computing devices that are usually credit card sized. Applications and data can be downloaded onto these cards for a variety of uses including authentication, certificate storage, record keeping, and so on.

Although the processor included in the card can give it great capability, a smart card is not a standalone computer. It must be connected to other computers to be useful. Smart cards today have an 8-bit microcontroller with 16KB or more of memory.

In the Windows 2000 operating system, smart cards and certificate-based logon are fully supported. In this architecture, the smart card contains the certificate and associated private key. When you are logging on to your Windows 2000 Professional computer, a challenge is sent to the smart card. The smart card signs the challenge with the private key and the result, along with the certificate are submitted to the authentication service. The authentication service verifies the signature and permits or denies the logon request.

To communicate with its host computer, a smart card must be placed in a smart card reader. Step by Step 3.8 describes how to connect a smart card reader to your Windows 2000 Professional computer.

ON THE CD

Step by Step 3.8, "Installing a Smart Card Reader," walks you through smart card installation. See the file **Chapter03-08StepbyStep.pdf** in the CD's **Chapter03\StepbyStep** directory.

Cameras

Cameras are added by using the Scanners and Cameras Wizard found in the Control Panel. After installing the camera and connecting any cables required to your Windows 2000 Professional computer, you can follow Step by Step 3.9 to install a camera.

ON THE CD

Step by Step 3.9, "Installing a Camera," walks you through camera installation. See the file **Chapter03-09StepbyStep.pdf** in the CD's **Chapter03\StepbyStep** directory.

Modems

Windows 2000 Professional supports many different brands of modems. To check whether the modem you are installing is supported, you can review the HCL at `http://www.microsoft.com/hcl`.

Modems are most commonly used to dial up remote systems or Internet service providers using speeds up to 56Kb over analog phone lines. Modems from different manufacturers achieve high-speed transmission by using a variety of techniques (some of which are proprietary to that company). Compatibility problems between these different methods can cause your modem to drop to a lower speed in search of a compatible transmission technique.

Step by Step 3.10 shows how to install a new modem on your Windows 2000 Professional computer.

> **ON THE CD**
>
> Step by Step 3.10, "Installing a Modem," walks you through modem installation. See the file **Chapter03-10StepbyStep.pdf** in the CD's **Chapter03\StepbyStep** directory.

If you run into problems installing a modem, you can try the following troubleshooting steps to get the modem functioning:

◆ **Turn on external modems.** PnP-compliant devices might not be detected correctly if they are not powered on.

◆ **Check the manufacturer's Web site.** The modem manufacturer might have new installation files (INF files) available online.

◆ **Use diagnostics.** By selecting your new modem, clicking Properties, and selecting the Diagnostics tab, you can query the modem and view log files.

◆ **Check hardware settings.** Typical settings for a modem are 8 data bits, no parity, and 1 stop bit. An alternate (and older) configuration is 7 bits, even parity, and 1 stop bit.

◆ **Use the Add/Remove Hardware Wizard.** If you install an internal modem card or PCMCIA modem card that is not PnP compatible, you might need to configure its internal COM port using the Add/Remove Hardware Wizard in the Control Panel.

Infrared Data Association (IrDA) Devices

Windows 2000 Professional supports the IrDA protocols enabling data transfer over infrared connections. The Windows 2000 Professional PnP architecture automatically detects and installs the IrDA components for computers with built-in IrDA hardware. For computers that do not have built-in infrared ports, you can attach a serial IrDA device to a COM port or connect one using a USB port or hub.

Most laptops now ship with IrDA ports that provide either 115Kbps or 4Mbps transmission speeds.

The most common implementation of the infrared ports on portable computers is the *Serial IrDA* (SIR) standard. This is a half-duplex system with a maximum transmission speed of 115Kbps and adjusts to accommodate lower-speed devices. This standard provides short-range infrared asynchronous serial connections with 8 bits of data, no parity, and 1 stop bit.

There is a high-speed extension (FIR) that supports half-duplex connections at 4Mbps. This standard is commonly installed on new devices and can communicate with existing lower-speed devices. In a device that is half duplex, communications cannot go in both directions at once. Access to the line is signaled and control of the communications link flips back and forth between one device and the other. This turnaround does take some time to happen, so if many small messages are being sent, full duplex (even at a slower speed) might be more efficient. The high-speed half-duplex connections are best for devices that are transmitting data in bulk (such as cameras or scanners).

Installing Infrared Devices

Most internal IrDA devices are installed automatically by Windows 2000 Professional Setup or when you reboot your computer after adding an IrDA device.

Step by Step 3.11 shows you how to install a new infrared serial transceiver.

ON THE CD

Step by Step 3.11, "Installing an Infrared Device," walks you through infrared device installation. See the file **Chapter03-11StepbyStep.pdf** in the CD's **Chapter03\StepbyStep** directory.

Wireless Devices

The Wireless Link file transfer program, infrared printing functions, and image transfer capability are installed by default with your Windows 2000 Professional operating system. In addition, IrDA supports Winsock API calls to support programs created by other software and hardware manufacturers. The Winsock API calls can be used to provide infrared connections to printers, modems, pagers, PDAs, electronic cameras, cell phones, and handheld computers.

In addition to sending or printing files, you can also set up network connections between two computers using the infrared port. This capability can be used to set up shared drives and work with files and folders from your laptop to a host computer.

If your computer comes with an infrared port or you have installed an infrared transceiver, Windows 2000 Professional includes an infrared port as a local port in the Add Printers Wizard dialog box. If you associate a printer with this port, Windows 2000 Professional uses the IrDA port (using a protocol called IrLPT) to transmit output to the printer. Figure 3.6 shows the point in the Add Printer Wizard dialog box where the infrared printer port can be selected.

FIGURE 3.6
The infrared port is available for printing.

Linking Infrared Devices

Infrared links are established between two infrared devices. In any link, one device is considered to be primary and one secondary. This role is determined dynamically when the link is established and continues until the link is broken. Normally, any station can assume any role, so data transfer can be initiated from ether side.

When communications are initially established, the commanding station sends out a connection request at 9600bps. The responding station assumes the secondary role and returns information listing its capabilities. Both the primary and secondary stations then change the connection rate and link parameters to the common set established by this initial negotiation. With the connection established, data transfer is put under the control of the primary device.

A single IrDA device cannot link to more than one other IrDA device at a time. You can, however, install multiple IrDA devices to COM ports or USB hubs to provide simultaneous links to multiple remote devices. For example, you connect a desktop computer to a notebook and a digital camera simultaneously using two IrDA transceivers.

The Winsock API does support multiple simultaneous connections over a single IrDA device. This allows different programs to use the infrared device to perform many tasks with the remote device. For example, your laptop can connect to a desktop device, share files, synchronize offline folders, and send and receive mail. Different programs on the laptop control each task; however, they all use the single connection over an IrDA device.

Printing to an Infrared Printer

Printing to an infrared-connected printer is much the same as printing to a locally connected printer. After you establish an infrared connection to the printer, Windows 2000 Professional automatically installs the printer onto your system. You might need to install the printer manually using the Add Printer Wizard if PnP does not detect or install the new printer, or if you have installed the infrared transceiver to the COM port.

Infrared Network Connections

If your computer has a built-in infrared port or you have installed an infrared transceiver, you can create a direct connection to another computer using the infrared port. When Windows 2000 Professional detects an infrared port, it includes that information as an available connection using Network and Dial-Up Connections. This enables you to map shared drives on your network (through a host computer) to your laptop.

To connect two computers using the infrared port, you must first create an infrared network connection on both computers. When you use the Network and Dial-Up Connections Wizard to create a network connection, you specify a local connection using the infrared port.

Step by Step 3.12 can be used to create an infrared network connection.

ON THE CD

Step by Step 3.12, "Creating an Infrared Network Connection," walks you through infrared network connection creation. See the file **Chapter03-12StepbyStep.pdf** in the CD's **Chapter03\StepbyStep** directory.

N O T E

Establish a Connection   Before printing to the infrared-attached printer, you must always establish a connection first. You do that by aligning the IR "eyes" until the InfraRed connection icon appears in the taskbar.

Universal Serial Bus Devices

The *Universal Serial Bus* (USB) is an external-polled serial bus deployed in a star topology that allows you to connect high-speed, low-latency devices to your computer. The USB protocol runs at 1 to 12Mbps and supports PnP and power management. USB devices are hot-pluggable to allow you to add or change devices without restarting your Windows 2000 Professional computer. The higher speed and polling rate that USB performs provides better support for games, and the higher bandwidth provides better support for multimedia devices.

USB is a token-based protocol that Windows 2000 Professional polls to detect changes to the number and type of devices connected. A computer equipped with a USB port can support up to 127 devices attached simultaneously. This means you can have a scanner, printer, camera, mouse, keyboard, game controller, and speakers running simultaneously. Connecting this many devices to the USB port is accomplished using a USB hub or set of USB hubs.

Hubs can be self-powered with an external power source or they can be bus-powered and get their power from the bus itself. The USB definition allows for a total of five tiers (that is, hubs attached to hubs) in a USB network. With the Windows 2000 Professional computer acting as the USB host, that leaves a total of four tiers (or network segments) for actual devices.

Figure 3.7 is a representation of the way that USB connections are depicted.

There are a few restrictions on using a multitiered architecture. The following is a list of restrictions:

◆ Bus-powered hubs cannot be plugged into bus-powered hubs if a device is connected after the second hub that uses the full bandwidth of 12Mbps.

◆ Bus-powered hubs cannot have more than four downstream ports.

◆ Bus-powered hubs cannot support bus-powered devices that use more than 100 milliamps. Bus powered hubs can, however, support self-powered devices.

◆ The hub cascade depth including the host computer cannot exceed five tiers.

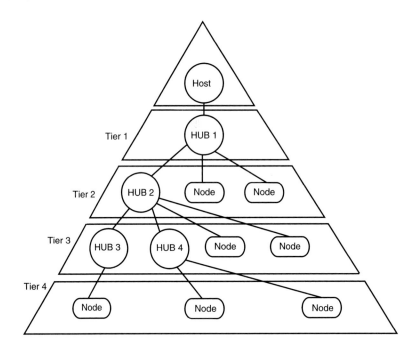

FIGURE 3.7
USB architecture.

Configuring Accessibility Options

If you have a motion-related disability, you can use Windows 2000
Professional to configure the keyboard and mouse to provide a more
comfortable environment. The Keyboard applet in Control Panel
contains configurations for people who use alternate keyboard lay-
outs or type with one hand. The Mouse applet in Control Panel can
be used to configure the mouse for left- or right-handed usage and
to vary the double-click speed or acceleration of the pointer.

On Screen Keyboard

The On Screen Keyboard is a utility that displays a virtual keyboard
on the display screen and allows you to type in data using a pointing
device such as a mouse or joystick. This is intended to provide a
minimum level of functionality to uses with mobility impairments.

The On Screen Keyboard is started by clicking on Start, selecting
Programs, Accessories, Accessibility, and clicking the On Screen

Keyboard menu item. Within the On Screen Keyboard, there are three modes for typing:

◆ **Clicking mode.** You click the onscreen keys to type in text.

◆ **Scanning mode.** The On Screen Keyboards continually scan the keyboard and highlight areas where you can type by pressing a hot key or using a joystick.

◆ **Hover mode.** You use a mouse or joystick to point to a key for a predefined period of time, and the selected character is automatically typed.

MouseKeys

Through the Accessibility Options applet in the Control Panel and by selecting the Mouse tab, you can enable MouseKeys. This allows the numeric keyboard to move the cursor and provides for left- and right-clicking plus dragging and dropping. To perform these actions, try one of the following:

◆ To click, press 5 on your numeric keypad.

◆ To double-click, press the plus sign (+) on your numeric keypad.

◆ To right-click, press the minus sign (-) on your numeric keypad, and then press 5 to click, or press the plus sign (+) to double-click.

◆ To click as if you were using both mouse buttons at once, press the asterisk (*) on your numeric keypad, and then press 5 to click or use the plus sign (+) to double-click.

◆ To switch back to standard clicking, press slash (/) on your numeric keypad.

The mouse is also used in an additional accessibility option called Magnifier. This is a utility that makes the screen more readable if you have low vision. Magnifier creates a separate window that displays a magnified portion of your screen. The Magnifier tracks the mouse pointer as it moves on the screen, follows the keyboard focus, and follows text editing. Magnifier also provides the following functionality:

◆ You can change the magnification level.

◆ You can change the size of the magnification windows.

◆ You can change the position of the magnification windows on your desktop.

◆ You can invert the screen colors.

◆ You can set the contrast high.

MAINTAINING UPDATED DRIVERS

Updating drivers.

Windows 2000 Professional provides a mechanism to automatically update device drives on you computer. If you are logged on as a member of the Administrators group, you can run Step by Step 3.13 to update a single device driver.

ON THE CD

Step by Step 3.13, "Updating a Device Driver," walks you through updating a device driver. See the file **Chapter03-13StepbyStep.pdf** in the CD's **Chapter03\StepbyStep** directory.

Windows 2000 Professional provides an additional mechanism for updating all device drivers and software at once, rather than by individually addressing each device on your computer.

When using Windows Update, the hardware IDs for the devices installed are compared to what the Microsoft Web site has to offer. If an exact match is made, the new driver is downloaded and installed. If an update to an existing driver is found, the new software components are listed in the Web site and a download button loads the updated drivers onto your Windows 2000 Professional computer into a temporary directory for installation.

Step by Step 3.14 will update all the device drivers on your computer.

ON THE CD

Step by Step 3.14, "Using Windows Update," walks you through using Windows Update. See the file **Chapter03-14StepbyStep.pdf** in the CD's **Chapter03\StepbyStep** directory.

MULTIPLE PROCESSOR MACHINES

Monitor and configure multiple processing units.

Windows 2000 Professional is designed to run uniformly on uniprocessors and symmetric multiprocessor platforms.

Windows 2000 Professional supports the addition of a second CPU. Support for multiprocessors has the following conditions:

◆ Both CPUs are identical and either have identical coprocessors or no coprocessors.

◆ Both CPUs can share memory and have uniform access to memory.

◆ Both CPUs can access memory, process interrupts, and access I/O devices.

Although the Windows 2000 Professional operating system has been designed for both uniprocessor and multiprocessor operations, if you originally installed Windows 2000 Professional on a computer with a single CPU, the HAL must be updated to use the additional CPU. Step by Step 3.15 outlines the procedure to install support for multiple CPUs.

ON THE CD

Step by Step 3.15, "Supporting Multiple CPUs," walks you through multiple CPU support. See the file **Chapter03-15StepbyStep.pdf** in the CD's **Chapter03\StepbyStep** directory.

Monitoring Multiple CPUs

Scaling is the process of adding processors to your system to achieve greater throughput. CPU-intensive applications such as database servers, Web servers, and file and print servers benefit from multiple CPUs. Applications such as scientific, financial, or CAD systems might also demand the power of multiple CPUs.

You can monitor the activity of your multiprocessor system by using the Performance Monitor counters and charts. The following factors are important when looking at the performance of multiple CPUs:

- ◆ **Processor utilization and queue length.** Your workload might be structured such that one CPU is overloaded.

- ◆ **Processor data.** Context switches and interrupts, for example, can provide information on the workload your system is handling.

- ◆ **Resource utilization information.** Disk, memory, and network components, for example, might indicate that your system requires an increase in the capacity of these resources.

Impact on Resources

Increasing the performance power of your computer places additional strain on system resources. For example, sharing resources increases memory latency. A multiprocessor system needs to lock out shared data to ensure data integrity, and locked shared data may result in contention for shared data structures. The synchronization mechanism used to lock shared structures increases the processor code path. As a rule of thumb, it is be necessary to increase other resources when adding additional processor resources.

Memory

It is recommended that you scale the amount of memory with the number of CPUs. For example, if your uniprocessor system required 64MB of memory, a dual-processor system requires 128MB of memory.

Disk and Networking

When adding processors to your system, it is generally necessary to increase the disk capacity and network capacity. This can mean replacing your disks with disks of higher rotational speed or by striping or mirroring some data disks. Networking components can be upgraded to intelligent interrupt pooling adapters that reduce the processor workload. The following Performance Monitor objects should be used when monitoring a system with multiple CPUs:

◆ **Process: Thread Counter.** Shows the instantaneous value, not the average. You need to monitor this counter at various times to get an accurate picture of activity.

◆ **Processor:% DPC Time.** Determines how much time the processor spends processing *Deferred Procedure Calls* (DPCs). DPCs originate when the processor performs tasks requiring immediate attention (such as answering an interrupt request), and then defers the remainder of the task to be handled at lower priority. DPCs represent further processing of client requests.

◆ **Processor:% Interrupt Time.** Determines how much time the processor spends processing interrupts. If processor time is more than 90 percent and this value is greater than 15 percent, the processor is probably overloaded with interrupts.

◆ **Processor:DPCs Queued/Sec.** Monitors the rate at which DPCs are queued on a particular processor.

◆ **Processor:Interrupts/Sec.** Reflects the rate at which the processor is handling interrupts.

◆ **Thread:% Processor Time.** Monitors processor time usage by specific thread instances on the system.

NETWORK ADAPTERS

Install, configure, and troubleshoot network adapters.

If you install a new network adapter in your computer, the next time you start Windows 2000 Professional, a new local area connection icon appears in the Network and Dial-Up Connections folder. PnP functionality finds the network adapter and creates a local area connection for it. By default, the local area connection is always activated. If your computer has more than one network adapter, a local area connection icon is displayed for each adapter in the Network and Dial-Up Connections folder.

The new network adapter is linked into the operating system by using bindings. Windows 2000 Professional divides networks into several layers, each acting independently of the other. The bottom layer is the network adapter card and driver.

A *binding* is the process that links the network components on different layers. A component in a layer can be linked to multiple components in the layer just above or below. Figure 3.8 shows an example of the network architecture and how bindings connect different components in different layers.

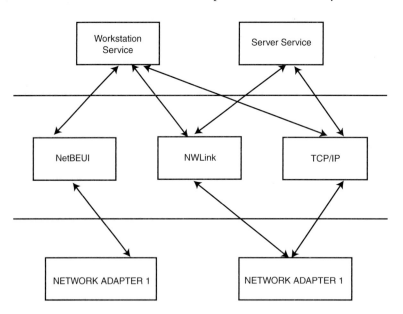

FIGURE 3.8
Network bindings.

In this example, the Workstation service is bound to all possible protocols; however, the Server service is only bound to the routable protocols (NWLink and TCP/IP). When configuring a network card, you assign protocols to it. The order in which these protocols are assigned can significantly improve the response you get from your network. If you have NWLink and TCP/IP traffic on your network, but your computer usually uses TCP/IP, moving that binding to the top of the list provides better response overall. If you are connecting to a server, the server does not need to have the protocols ordered, just the Windows 2000 Professional workstation.

Step by Step 3.16 shows you how to modify the network binding order.

ON THE CD

Step by Step 3.16, "Modifying the Network Binding Order," walks you through network binding order modification. See the file **Chapter03-16StepbyStep.pdf** in the CD's **Chapter03\StepbyStep** directory.

Installing a Network Adapter

In addition to checking the connection into the operating system, you can also view and change the characteristics of a network card itself from the Device Manager screen.

Step by Step 3.17 shows you how to view and modify network adapter options.

ON THE CD

Step by Step 3.17, "Modifying Network Adapter Options," walks you through network adapter option modification. See the file **Chapter03-17StepbyStep.pdf** in the CD's **Chapter03\StepbyStep** directory.

If you disconnect your local area connection, the connection is not automatically activated. Because your hardware profile saves this setting, it can accommodate your requirement for differing devices at different locations. By selecting the Advanced tab in Network and Dial-Up Connections and clicking on Advanced Settings, you can modify the order in which adapters are used by a connection and the associated clients, services, and protocols for the adapter.

Managing Network Adapters

You can eliminate possible confusion with multiple network adapters by renaming each local area connection to reflect the network it is connected to.

You must enable the network clients, services, and protocols that are required for your local area connections. When you do so, the client, service, or protocol is enabled in all other network and dial-up connections automatically.

You can create multiple dial-up, VPN, or direct connections by creating new ones with the wizard or by copying them in the Network and Dial-Up Connections folder. After you copy the connections, you can rename them and modify the connections settings.

CASE STUDY: THE AMARANTH ENGINEERING COMPANY

ESSENCE OF THE CASE

The following points summarize the essence of the case study:

▶ The back-end database has all the important files on one disk.

▶ The disk failed with no recent backup.

▶ Recovery to the previous night required the next day's data to be re-entered.

SCENARIO

Although you work at an engineering company, your responsibility is to oversee the computer systems that support the company's works. In this case, you are analyzing the recent events of the company's accounting system. The company uses a commercial accounting system that uses a single server for a back-end database. This was installed over a year ago and has been working well. However, the database was installed with all the default settings and a single large database file holding indexes and data was created. The transaction log files are also held on this main disk and full backups are done each night. The incident you are reviewing involves a disk failure on the database disk late one afternoon last week. The disk was replaced but the database needed to be recovered from the previous backup. No transaction logs are available to apply and the entire day's work needs to be re-entered. Your task is to prevent this from happening again.

ANALYSIS

This situation is quite a common one. An application system (in this case an accounting application) uses a back-end database to store data and produce invoices and reports. When all this is set up, there is a tendency to not revisit the initial configuration again until there is a problem.

Having the database tables and indexes on one disk is generally considered a potential disk performance bottleneck; however, the real problem

continues

CASE STUDY: THE AMARANTH ENGINEERING COMPANY

continued

comes when the previous night's backup is restored to disk. There are no transaction logs left to apply to the database to bring it up to the current time. With the database recovered to the previous night, all the day's transactions are lost.

The solution to this problem lies in using the disk management features of Windows 2000 Professional to create a fault-tolerant disk structure on the Windows 2000 Server to house the database and transaction logs. First, transaction logs should always be separated from the database tables because they are written sequentially and the database is accessed randomly. Because the transaction logs are usually only written and not read, they are best on mirrored volumes that are not striped. Striping divides the data across multiple spindles so that reading can proceed in a parallel fashion. If you are only writing to a file, this is not important.

The database tables, however, are read and written randomly. In an accounting application, it might seem that you are entering a great deal of data, but almost every field must be validated against existing data (customer name, address, existing invoice number, and so on); therefore, the database is read from much more than it is written to. Because of this, the database tables should be striped (to allow parallel reads) but configured as a striped mirror or RAID-5 structure to provide redundancy.

The combination of separating the transaction logs onto a mirrored set of disks, and the database files to a mirrored striped set of disks or a RAID-5 structure, reduces your system's vulnerability to single device failures in the future.

CHAPTER SUMMARY

This chapter focused on devices and drivers that you can add to your computer to customize it for your needs.

First, the Windows 2000 Professional implementation of PnP was discussed along with resources available in Windows 2000 Professional and ways of assigning them to devices. The new dynamic disk structures available were discussed along with CD-ROM technology and removable storage.

Second, the new Windows 2000 Professional feature allowing multiple video displays was discussed, along with the procedures for configuring your virtual desktop.

Third, to support mobile computing, the card services and APM/ACPI features of Windows 2000 Professional were discussed along with problems associated with these devices.

Fourth, the general I/O devices available for both the desktop and laptop computer were discussed. This includes keyboards, the mouse, printers, scanners, and cameras.

Fifth, the procedures for automatically updating device drivers on Windows 2000 Professional were discussed, along with the procedure for installing multiple CPUs into your computer and the performance characteristics you should measure when you do this.

Finally, the installation and troubleshooting of network adapters was discussed.

KEY TERMS

- Plug and Play
- Dynamic disks
- Simple volumes
- Spanned
- Striped
- RAID-5
- Mirrored
- Media pools
- Libraries
- Advanced Power Management (APM)
- Advanced Configuration and Power Interface (ACPI)
- IrDA devices
- USB devices

APPLY YOUR KNOWLEDGE

Review Questions

1. You change the resources your non-PnP video adapter uses in Device Manager, and the system does not boot correctly. What is wrong?

2. Your application currently uses logical disks on which to store some of its data. The application needs to reference these logical devices using drive letters. You have converted your system to use dynamic disks and would like to organize these files into a subdirectory. Will your application be able to read its data? Why or why not?

3. What devices does RSM manage on a typical desktop computer?

4. You have a laptop that you have configured with multiple display adapters while it is in its docking bay. When you boot your laptop, the multiple displays do not work correctly. Why?

5. When you installed Windows 2000 Professional you notice that APM was not enabled. After you enable APM, your system does not boot correctly. What is the reason?

6. You install a new high-speed modem that the salesman said would run at 56Kb. When you dial up to your Internet service provider, you find you can't get as much speed as you expected. What is the reason?

7. You have just purchased a new desktop computer that has Windows 2000 Professional already installed on it. You want to ensure that the latest device drivers available are installed and the drivers are all signed. What is your most efficient course of action?

8. You are using Performance Monitoring to display how busy your computer is. You note that the CPU is at 100% utilized for extended periods of time. What other performance variable should you chart to help you decide if adding an additional CPU would help the throughput of your system?

9. Your business has a network that uses both IPX and IP for data communications, but your Windows 2000 Professional computer uses IP almost exclusively. How should you configure your network connections to reflect this usage?

Answers to Review Questions

1. Non-PnP devices are not detected by Windows 2000 Professional and therefore their requirements as far as the Device Manager is concerned are unknown. By manually configuring the resources used, you have told Windows 2000 Professional which resources to reserve for your device. You now need to reconfigure the device by using the manufacturer-supplied configuration program or by manually selecting onboard switches or jumpers. See "Installing Hardware."

2. Dynamic disks can be accessed by using an assigned drive letter as well as by using a path. If, however, you are going to reorganize your files into subdirectories, then your only access is via the path. Your application that expects to use drive letters will not be able to access its data. See "Fixed Disks."

APPLY YOUR KNOWLEDGE

3. RSM manages all devices that can be removed or replaced with other media. This includes tape drives, CD-ROM and DVD-ROM drives, and JAZ and ZIP drives. RSM can handle any removable device except A: and B:. See "Removable Media."

4. One of the rules for using multiple displays on your Windows 2000 Professional computer is that the primary display cannot be turned off. When you insert a laptop into its docking station, the display is usually disabled. This prevents the multiple display system from functioning. See "Troubleshooting Multiple Displays."

5. If APM was installed but not enabled, Windows 2000 Professional has not found your system in its list of systems on which APM is unsafe to run. It also has not found your system in its list of APM safe systems. Thus, it considers your system to be APM neutral. When you enabled APM, you discovered that your system should have been placed on the APM unsafe list since it has destabilized your computer. See "When to Use APM."

6. Modems get their speed from various compression techniques. The faster the modem, the more elaborate the compression techniques. Unfortunately, these methods are not always compatible and, when connecting to an ISP, your system has negotiated a lower speed to where both devices agree on the compression methods being used. See "Modems."

7. The most efficient way to ensure that you have the latest device drivers installed on your system and that these drivers have been signed is to use the Windows Update option directly from the Start menu. This canvasses the Microsoft Web site for the latest signed version of drivers for your system and allows you to download them for installation. See "Maintaining Updated Drivers."

8. The other variable to chart would be the Processor Queue Length. A busy processor may be handling the workload very efficiently, or it could be overwhelmed by the workload. In that case, the backlog of work waiting to be done by the CPU would be building. This situation is identified by the processor queue length or by the number of tasks that are ready to execute if there are enough CPU resources available. See "Monitoring Multiple CPUs."

9. The priority of the protocols used by your Windows 2000 Professional computer is reflected in the binding order. By moving TCP/IP to the top of the list and lowering IPX below it, you can significantly improve the response you get from your network. See "Managing Network Adapters."

ON THE CD

This book's companion CD contains specially designed supplemental material to help you understand how well you know the concepts and skills you learned in this chapter. You'll find related exercises, review questions and answers, and exam questions and answers. See the file **Chapter03ApplyYourKnowledge.pdf** in the CD's **Chapter03\ApplyYourKnowledge** directory.

Suggested Readings and Resources

1. *MCSE Training Kit: Upgrading to Windows 2000.* Microsoft Press, 2000.

2. *Microsoft Windows 2000 Professional: Step by Step.* Microsoft Press, 2000.

3. Joyce, Jerry, and Marianne Moon. *Microsoft Windows 2000 Professional at a Glance.* Microsoft Press, 2000.

This chapter helps you prepare for the Windows 2000 Professional component of MCP Exam 70-240, "Microsoft Windows 2000 Accelerated Exam for MCPs Certified on Microsoft Windows NT 4.0," by covering the following exam objectives:

Manage and troubleshoot driver signing.

▶ One of the areas in earlier versions of Windows that has caused support problems deals with device drivers. To that end, Microsoft has developed a rigorous driver testing program to ensure that device drivers function correctly.

Configure, manage, and troubleshoot the Task Scheduler.

▶ The Windows 2000 Task Scheduler can be used to schedule programs and batch files to run at regular intervals or specific times. You can also have the Task Scheduler execute programs or scripts when certain operating system events occur.

Manage and troubleshoot the use and synchronization of offline files.

▶ The increase in the use of laptop computers indicates the need for access to information when you are traveling and without a network connection. With offline folders, you can continue to access network files and programs when you are not connected to the network and automatically synchronize the changes the next time you reconnect to your network.

CHAPTER 4

Monitoring and Optimizing System Performance and Reliability

Optimize and troubleshoot performance of the Windows 2000 Professional desktop:

- **Optimize and troubleshoot memory performance.**
- **Optimize and troubleshoot processor utilization.**
- **Optimize and troubleshoot disk performance.**
- **Optimize and troubleshoot network performance.**
- **Optimize and troubleshoot application performance.**

▶ Monitoring disk performance, memory usage, application assigned resources, and network activity can enhance the performance of your system.

Manage hardware profiles.

▶ Hardware profiles allow you to tailor the devices that start up when you power on your computer based on the configuration you have available. This is particularly useful when your system is a laptop and may have a docked configuration that includes other external devices and network adapters.

Recover systems and user data:

- **Recover systems and user data by using Windows Backup.**
- **Troubleshoot system restoration by using Safe Mode.**
- **Recover systems and user data by using the Recovery Console.**

▶ The ultimate goal of backing up your system and data files is the recovery of all your data in the event of a hardware or software failure. Being able to recover your system, regardless of the type and extent of the failure, significantly improves the reliability of your computer.

STUDY STRATEGIES

▶ You can expect a number of questions related to maintaining or increasing the performance of the disk, memory, and network subsystems of your Windows 2000 Professional computer. Many of these will be in scenario format, where the causes of a performance problem will be related to more than one factor. The author's suggestion is to first understand the important counters maintained within the performance monitoring system and be able to relate changes in those counters to events happening in the computer. After you have a solid understanding of the theory presented here, you should work with your Windows 2000 Professional system to see firsthand the impact of varying the availability of resources on system response.

▶ You should also expect scenario questions on both recovering a system using some options from the safe boot menu (the Recovery Console and using the Last Known Good configuration) and saving and restoring data using backup. In the latter, you can expect questions regarding instances in which the backup method is not wisely chosen and can be optimized to better suit the users' needs. Understanding the options available and the impact that one style of backup has over another regarding the availability of your computer system in the event of a failure allows you to address this type of exam question well.

INTRODUCTION

This chapter is mainly concerned with the performance and reliability of your computer. The techniques available in Windows 2000 range from digitally signing device drivers and operating system files to running a command-based Recovery Console in the event the system will not even boot.

To make the most of the hardware you have available, you need to take steps to optimize its use and to prevent the operating system from being modified without your consent. Finally, you need to be able to recover the system in the case of a catastrophic failure.

MANAGING AND TROUBLESHOOTING DRIVER SIGNING

Manage and troubleshoot driver signing.

A new feature in Windows 2000 Professional offers you the ability to digitally sign both drivers and operating system files. This is the assurance that a particular file has met a certain level of testing and that the file has not been overwritten by the installation program of another application. The application of driver signing is governed by a policy set using the System program in the Control Panel.

Digitally Signing a File

Digitally signing a file is the process by which you can guarantee that a particular file comes from the source that it claims to. Because any file can be signed, it is necessary to be able to handle all formats of files, including binary files. A technique called Catalog File signing is used to provide digital signing information about files without modifying the file itself.

In Catalog File signing, a CAT file is created for each driver or operating system file that is being signed. The CAT file includes a hash of the binary file. A hash is the result of a mathematical operation on some data (in this case, the binary file) that is sensitive to any changes made in the source data. Any change to the binary file can be detected because the hash procedure will produce a different value. A certificate from the publisher along with a Microsoft digital signature is included in the catalog file to complete the signing process.

The relationship between the catalog file and the driver binary is contained in the information file (.INF) that is maintained by the system after the driver is installed.

The Windows 2000 Professional system provides you with three choices when installing a new device driver (see Figure 4.1).

The first is to disable signature checking and install all new device drivers regardless of the file signature. The second choice is to check for driver signatures before installing them and display a warning if the signature verification fails. The third choice is to check for driver signatures and block any installation if the signature verification fails.

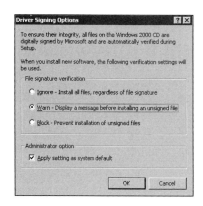

FIGURE 4.1
The Driver Signing Options screen.

ON THE CD

Step by Step 4.1, "Configuring Driver Signing," shows how to configure driver signing. See the file **Chapter04-01StepbyStep.pdf** in the CD's **Chapter04\StepbyStep** directory.

System File Checker

System File Checker (SFC.EXE) is a command-line utility (S) that an Administrator can run to scan and verify the versions of all protected system files. SFC.EXE will discover that a protected file has been overwritten and replace it with the correct version of the file from the %systemroot%\system32\dllcache folder.

The command to start System File Checker is

```
sfc [/scannow] [/scanonce] [/scanboot] [/cancel] [/quiet]
➡[/enable] [/purgecache] [/cachesize=x]
```

System File Checker parameters are outlined in Table 4.1.

TABLE 4.1	

SYSTEM FILE CHECKER PARAMETERS

Parameter	Action
Scannow	Scans all protected files immediately
Scanonce	Scans all protected system files once at the next boot
Scanboot	Scans all protected system files every time the computer is rebooted
Cancel	Cancels all pending scans
Quiet	Replaces all altered system files without prompting the user
Enable	Turns prompting back on
Purgecache	Purges the file cache and rescans all protected files immediately
Cachesize=x	Sets the cache size (in MB)

CONFIGURING, MANAGING, AND TROUBLESHOOTING THE TASK SCHEDULER

Configure, manage, and troubleshoot the Task Scheduler.

The Task Scheduler is a graphical utility that allows you to schedule programs or batch files to run at specific times or when specific events occur. Tasks scheduled are saved as files (with a .JOB extension) in the Winnt\Tasks folder.

Task Scheduler and the AT Command

Earlier versions of Windows provided the AT command to schedule programs or scripts to run at specific times. Windows 2000 introduces the Task Scheduler to enhance this scheduling capability.

The Task Scheduler is not the same as the AT command. However, they share many common characteristics. When a task is scheduled by AT, an entry for it appears in the Task Scheduler task window.

With the Task Scheduler, you can specify the user account to run a task.

Creating a Scheduled Task

When you open the Scheduled Tasks folder from the Control Panel and double-click Add Scheduled Task, you start a wizard that creates the job file representing the task to run (see Figure 4.2). The file contains userid and password information to allow the job to be copied from one machine to another.

The wizard allows you to customize the following information:

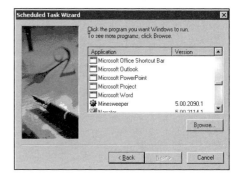

FIGURE 4.2
Selecting programs to run with the Scheduled Task Wizard.

◆ **Program to Run.** The application or batch file the Task Scheduler will execute.

◆ **Task Name.** The name of the task that will appear in the Task Scheduler listing.

◆ **Frequency.** How often the task will execute. Options include daily, weekly, monthly, only once, when the computer starts, or when a user logs on.

◆ **Time and Date.** The start time and date the program will run.

◆ **User Name and Password.** The credentials that will be used to execute the scheduled task.

◆ **Advanced Properties.** This option allows the individual property pages to be edited after the Scheduled Task Wizard has completed.

ON THE CD

Step by Step 4.2, "Creating a Scheduled Task," outlines the actual configuration of a Scheduled Task. See the file **Chapter04-02StepbyStep.pdf** in the CD's **Chapter04\Stepby Step** directory.

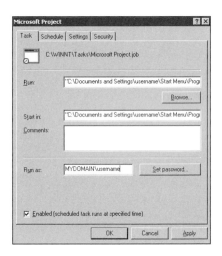

FIGURE 4.3
Properties of a sample job in Scheduled Tasks.

NOTE   **Support for Offline Files**   Computers running Windows 95, Windows 98, and Windows NT 4.0 support offline files. Offline files are not supported for computers running Novell NetWare.

After you complete the Step by Step, there is a file in the Winnt\ Tasks folder with a .JOB extension that represents the task you just created. Right-clicking the task icon and selecting the Properties menu item displays the parameters used to run this job (see Figure 4.3).

MANAGING AND TROUBLESHOOTING THE USE AND SYNCHRONIZATION OF OFFLINE FILES

Manage and troubleshoot the use and synchronization of offline files.

Network connections are becoming more common and it is often assumed that your computer always has network access. Offline folders allow you to access files and folders when you are *not* connected to the network. Using offline files, you can navigate the shared folders and files as if you are connected to the network.

Offline Files and Mobile Users

If you travel frequently and use your laptop for most of your work, offline files provide a way to ensure that changes you make when offline will be synchronized when you reconnect to the network.

When you undock your laptop, the shared network files that were configured as available offline remain just as they were when you were connected. You continue to work with them normally with the same access permission as the original network files.

Selecting Items to Be Available Offline

The first step is to enable your Windows 2000 Professional computer to use offline files. Click Open My Computer on your desktop and select Folder Options from the Tools drop-down menu. Selecting the Offline Files tab allows you to set synchronization events and enable offline file use.

When offline files have been enabled, you can perform Step by Step 4.3 to indicate which folders or files can be accessed when your computer is disconnected from the network.

ON THE CD

Step by Step 4.3, "Selecting a Folder for Offline Access," covers offline files. See the file **Chapter04-03StepbyStep.pdf** in the CD's **Chapter04\StepbyStep** directory.

Synchronizing

When you reconnect to the network (that is, dock your portable computer), changes that you have made to an offline file are synchronized back to its original network file. If someone else has made changes to the same file, you have the option of saving your version of the file, keeping the other version, or saving them both by providing a different filename for your version of the file.

Synchronization can be started manually or by using the Synchronization Manager when you want to control what files are synchronized and when it occurs. Step by Step 4.4 shows how to manage synchronization with the Synchronization Manager.

ON THE CD

Step by Step 4.4, "Using the Synchronization Manager," shows you how to manage synchronization. See the file **Chapter04-04StepbyStep.pdf** in the CD's **Chapter04\StepbyStep** directory.

NOTE

Managing Synchronization   When using offline files, you should always synchronize at logon. This ensures that changes made on your computer are synchronized with changes made to the network files while you were disconnected.

OPTIMIZING AND TROUBLESHOOTING PERFORMANCE OF THE WINDOWS 2000 PROFESSIONAL DESKTOP

Optimize and troubleshoot performance of the Windows 2000 Professional desktop.

Windows 2000 Professional defines performance data in terms of objects, counters, and instances. An object is any resource, application, or service that you can measure.

Each object has counters that are used to measure various aspects of performance, such as transfer rates for disks, packet transmit rates for networks, or memory and processor time consumed by applications or services.

The tool used to display performance statistics is the Performance Monitor. The Performance Monitor provides a graphical interface to the counters maintained by the operating system and provides ways to capture or log the output or to display it graphically on the screen.

In general, performance monitoring addresses how the operating system and any applications or services use the resources of the system. The four most common areas analyzed are memory, processors, disk usage, and network components.

Optimizing and Troubleshooting Memory Performance

Memory availability is one of the most important factors in managing the performance of Windows 2000 Professional. Windows 2000 supports the use of virtual memory. That is, the actual amount of physical memory in the computer is supplemented by using a portion of the computer's disk space, known as a *paging file*, to supplement the memory.

Windows 2000 creates one paging file (PAGEFILE.SYS) on the same hard drive as the operating system. The default size is the amount of physical memory plus 12MB. If the paging file is too small, you exhaust the amount of virtual memory available for applications. If the amount of physical memory is too low, it generates excessive activity on the paging file disk, slowing response time for the system.

Although Windows 2000 limits the size of each paging file to 4GB, you can supply more virtual memory to applications by spreading paging files across multiple disks. Creating multiple paging files on a single volume provides more space but does not improve performance. For computers with more than 4GB of RAM, Microsoft recommends that a 2GB page file be implemented.

> **NOTE**
>
> **Placing the Paging File** To optimize performance of the paging file, move the paging from the boot partition to a different physical volume.

Diagnosing Memory Shortages

Your Windows 2000 Professional computer can develop memory shortages if processes demand much more memory than what is available or the applications you are running leak memory. To identify a memory shortage situation, watch the following counters:

- ◆ **Memory: Available Bytes.** The amount of physical memory available to processes. This should not drop below 5MB.

- ◆ **Memory: Committed Bytes.** The amount of memory (virtual and physical) committed to running processes. This should not be greater than the amount of physical memory installed.

- ◆ **Memory: Page Faults/Sec.** The overall rate of occurrence where memory required is located on the paging file or elsewhere in memory.

- ◆ **Memory: Pages/Sec.** The number of pages read from or written to disk to resolve hard page faults. High values can indicate a shortage of physical memory.

Resolving Memory Bottlenecks

Adding memory to a computer is an easy solution, but it is not always cost-effective. Prior to purchasing more memory, you can try some of the following:

- ◆ Correct any applications that may have memory leaks.

- ◆ Increase the size of the paging file by creating multiple paging files on different physical disks to increase performance. Striped volumes can also be used to spread the work of accessing the paging file over many disks.

◆ Check for available space on the disk with the paging file(s). Low disk space can manifest itself as memory problems.

◆ Remove unused protocols and drivers. Idle protocols still use space from both paged and nonpaged memory.

Optimizing and Troubleshooting Processor Performance

The processor on a Windows 2000 Professional computer can become a bottleneck if the processor is unable to handle the tasks assigned to it in a timely manner. A processor bottleneck occurs when the processor is so busy that it cannot respond to an application that is requesting time. High activity might indicate that a processor is either handling the work adequately or it is a bottleneck and slowing down the system. Looking for a sustained processor queue is a better indicator of a bottlenecked processor.

Diagnosing Processor Bottlenecks

A busy processor might be efficiently handling all the work on your computer, or it might be overwhelmed. The following counters provide an indication of the workload on your Windows 2000 Professional computer:

◆ **System: Interrupts/Sec.** The average rate per second at which the processor handles interrupts. A high rate can suggest an overworked processor.

◆ **System: Processor Queue Length.** The number of threads that are in the processor queue. A value greater than 2 can indicate an underpowered processor. Figure 4.4 shows the effects of a busy processor on the Processor Queue Length counter.

◆ **Processor: % Processor Time.** The percentage of time the processor was busy during the sampling interval. Sustained rates greater than 80% indicate an overworked processor.

◆ **Process: % Processor Time.** The percentage of time a specific process was busy during the sampling interval. Sustained rates greater than 80% indicate that a specific process is overworking the processor.

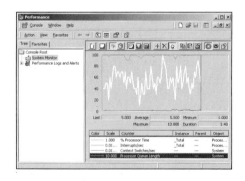

FIGURE 4.4
Processor Queue Length on a busy system.

Resolving Processor Bottlenecks

The key to resolving processor bottlenecks is to identify what processes on the computer are overusing the processor. Do not be frightened by spikes in processor use; *persistently* high values indicate a problem.

When you have identified that your processor is overloaded and that it is the cause of your computers performance problem, the key is to investigate whether there is a single process that is monopolizing your CPU or it is being consumed by running many processes. You can display the percentage of the processor time that each process is consuming by using the procedure outlined in Step by Step 4.5.

ON THE CD

Step by Step 4.5, "Process Use of the CPU," shows you how to display the percentage of the processor time being used by a process. See the file **Chapter04-05StepbyStep.pdf** in the CD's **Chapter04\StepbyStep** directory.

If a single process is monopolizing the processor, the chart for that process will be higher than the rest. If the cause of your processor performance problems is a specific application, your options include moving it to a different computer (perhaps running it on a larger Windows 2000 Server system or running it at times when you are not trying to use the Windows 2000 Professional computer at the same time.)

If you determine that you do have a processor bottleneck, some of the following steps might shorten the processor queue and reduce the burden on your processor:

◆ Resolve memory bottlenecks that might be consuming the processor. Memory bottlenecks are far more common than processor bottlenecks and severely degrade processor performance.

◆ Upgrade your network or disk adapters to intelligent, 32-bit, adapters. Intelligent adapters provide better overall system performance because they allow interrupts to be processed on the adapter itself, relieving the processor of this work.

◆ Try to obtain adapters that have optimization features, such as interrupt moderation, and features for networking, such as card-based TCP/IP checksum support.

◆ Upgrade to a faster processor. A faster processor improves response time and throughput for any type of workload.

◆ Add another processor. If the process you are running has multiple, active threads that are processor-intensive, it is a prime candidate for a multiprocessor computer.

Examining and Tuning Disk Performance

The disk system handles the storage of programs and data as well as the movement of these between disk and memory. Because disk transfers run many hundreds of times slower than memory transfers, the overall influence of disk problems on your system will be great.

Diagnosing Disk Bottlenecks

There are many factors that you need to consider in determining whether the disk system is impacting the performance of your Windows 2000 Professional computer. The level of use, the rate of throughput, and the development of a queue are all important factors. Windows 2000 Professional includes counters that monitor the activity of physical disks. The PhysicalDisk object provides counters that report physical disk activity; the LogicalDisk object provides counters that report statistics for logical disks and storage volumes.

The same counters can be investigated for both physical disks and logical disks. The decision of which object to select depends on whether you are focusing on total disk usage (PhysicalDisk) or looking at usage on a specific partition (LogicalDisk). The following counters can be used to determine a disk bottleneck:

◆ **Avg. Disk Bytes/Transfer.** Measures the size of I/O operations. If disk accesses are efficient, larger amounts of data will be transferred.

WARNING

Is It Really a Disk Bottleneck?
When analyzing a potential disk bottleneck, always include counters to diagnose memory bottlenecks. A common symptom of a memory shortage is excess paging. This could lead to the diagnosis that the disk subsystem is inadequate, instead of the need for more memory.

NOTE

Automatic Versus Manual The Windows 2000 Professional operating system automatically enables PhysicalDisk counters. However, you must manually enable the LogicalDisk counters using the command diskperf -yv and then restarting the system.

◆ **Avg. Disk Queue Length.** Total number of requests waiting as well as the requests in service. If there are more that two requests continually waiting, the disk might be a bottleneck.

◆ **Disk Bytes/Sec.** The rate at which data is being transferred to or from the disk. This is the primary measure of disk throughput.

◆ **% Disk Time.** The percentage of time the selected disk drive is busy reading or writing. This counter can span more than one sample period and therefore overstate the disk utilization.

◆ **% Disk Write Time.** The percentage of time the selected drive was busy servicing write requests.

◆ **% Disk Read Time.** The percentage of time the selected drive was busy servicing read requests.

Resolving Disk Bottlenecks

A disk bottleneck may cause the entire system to slow. If you have determined that disk availability or capacity is responsible for your performance problem, you should consider taking one or more of the following actions:

◆ Add an additional disk if you can move some files to it, if you can create a striped volume, or if you are out of space. For disk space problems only, you can consider compressing the disk if your processor has enough power to handle the compression activity.

◆ Add memory if the disk activity you have measured is related to the paging file.

◆ Defragment the disk. A fragmented hard drive can greatly reduce the performance of reading and writing to files.

◆ Use stripe sets to spread the I/O requests across a number of disks simultaneously. If your applications are read-intensive and require fault tolerance, consider a hardware-level Raid 5 volume. Use mirrored volumes for fault tolerance and good overall I/O performance. If you can live without fault tolerance, a stripe set will provide fast reading and writing and, usually, higher storage capacity.

◆ If there is no throughput improvement seen with additional disk capacity or the addition of a stripe set, the bottleneck could be caused by contention between disks for the disk adapter. You should consider adding an adapter to distribute the load.

◆ Distribute the workload across multiple drives. For example, a database application may have the transaction logs on separate disks from the data. Writing to a transaction log is sequential and performs better on a physical disk than the random operations against the data, which perform better on striped volumes.

◆ Limit the use of file compression or encryption. These features add overhead to disk I/O and should be used only if performance is not critical.

◆ When purchasing disk systems, use the most intelligent and efficient components available. Upgrading to faster controllers with wider bandwidth access generally improves throughput.

Monitoring Network Performance

Most workstations now require some communications over a network. The behavior of the network components of your Windows 2000 Professional computer has a direct impact on the performance your system can deliver.

Windows 2000 Professional provides two mechanisms for monitoring network performance: Performance Monitor network objects and the Network Monitor. The Performance Monitor network counters track resource use and throughput, and the Network Monitor tracks packets in and out of a network adapter.

Determining Network Bottlenecks

The best approach for understanding the performance characteristics of your Windows 2000 Professional computer is to look at the network performance objects from the Physical layer to the Application layer. The following counters can be used to detect network bottlenecks:

◆ **Network Interface: Output Queue Length.** The length of the output packet queue. Queue lengths of 2 or more means the adapter cannot keep pace with server requests.

◆ **Network Interface: Packets Outbound Discarded.** The number of packets discarded even though there were no errors. If this number is incrementing continuously, it might indicate the network is so busy that the network buffers cannot keep up with the outbound flow of packets.

◆ **Network Interface: Bytes Total/Sec.** The rate at which data is sent and received by the adapter.

◆ **Network Segment: % Network Utilization.** The percentage of network bandwidth used for the local segment. A low value is preferred. For a TCP/IP network, this value should not exceed 30%. If the value is above 40%, collisions can cause performance problems.

◆ *Protocol*: **Bytes/Sec.** The total number of bytes sent in one second using the selected protocol.

Resolving Network Bottlenecks

An overloaded processor, an overloaded network, or a problem on the network itself typically cause network bottlenecks. Some of the approaches you can take to resolving network bottlenecks include the following:

◆ Use adapters with the highest bandwidth available for the best performance.

◆ Remove unused network adapters to reduce overhead.

◆ Reduce the number of protocols in use on the network.

◆ Use network adapters that support interrupt moderation to improve performance.

◆ Modify the protocol binding order on your Windows 2000 Professional computer to reflect the amount of use each protocols gets. If TCP/IP is the protocol used most often, it should be first in the binding order.

> **NOTE**
>
> **Protocol Counters** There are also individual Network Protocol objects (TCP, UDP, NWLink, and so forth) that can produce analysis of specific protocols in use on the network.

MANAGING HARDWARE PROFILES

Manage hardware profiles.

Hardware profiles tell your Windows 2000 Professional computer which devices to start and what setting to use for each device.

When you first install Windows 2000 Professional, a hardware profile called Profile 1 (or for laptops, Docked Profile or Undocked Profile) is created. By default, this profile contains every device that is installed on your computer at the time you install Windows 2000 Professional.

Hardware profiles are useful if you have a portable computer and use it in a variety of locations. Most people who have laptops use them in locations other than where the docking station is (at home or in the office). Because of that, network adapters, CD-ROM devices, and perhaps floppy disk drives that are part of the docking station are not available when you are staying in a hotel. Hardware profiles allow you to maintain different configurations of available peripherals.

An Administrator of the local computer can create hardware profiles from the System applet in the Control Panel using Step by Step 4.6.

ON THE CD

Step by Step 4.6, "Creating a Hardware Profile," illustrates the creation of hardware profiles. See the file **Chapter04-06StepbyStep.pdf** in the CD's **Chapter04\StepbyStep** directory.

If there is more than one hardware profile, you can designate one as the default that will be loaded when you start your Windows 2000 Professional computer (assuming you don't make a choice manually). When you create a hardware profile, you can use Device Manager to enable or disable devices in the profile by following Step by Step 4.7.

ON THE CD

Step by Step 4.7, "Changing Devices in a Profile," walks you through enabling or disabling devices in a profile. See the file **Chapter04-07StepbyStep.pdf** in the CD's **Chapter04\StepbyStep** directory.

RECOVERING SYSTEM AND USER DATA

Recover systems and user data.

This section addresses the recovery of system and user data through the use of Windows Backup, Safe Mode, and Recovery Console.

Recovering System and User Data by Using Windows Backup

Information is the most important resource on your computer. Programs and services can often be easily reinstalled in the event of a hardware problem. However, the data is often irreplaceable. The best mechanism to back up your Windows 2000 Professional computer is to copy important data using the Windows 2000 Backup utility. Windows 2000 Backup now supports backup to devices other than tape drives, although tape drives still remain the most common backup devices.

Backing up your computer to tape is safer than making copies to disk, and it allows you to keep versions of your data over time. The capability of keeping backup copies for an extended period of time (for example, a 12-week rotation of tapes) can be used to provide protection against virus infections (you can retrieve a file from an earlier time) or from problems that may occur but not be fatal until later.

When you are creating your backup policy you must consider the following issues:

◆ How often should a backup be done?

◆ What type of backup is the most appropriate?

◆ How long should backup tapes be stored?

◆ How long will the recovery of lost data take?

An occasional reassessment of risk helps keep your backup policy relevant and minimize your exposure to loss.

Backup Types

There are five types of backups available through the Windows 2000 Backup utility:

◆ A *normal backup* copies all selected files and marks each as being backed up. If your files do not change frequently, the backups are redundant.

◆ A *copy backup* copies all the selected files but does not mark them as backed up.

◆ An *incremental backup* copies only those files created or changed since the last normal or incremental backup. It marks the files as having been backed up. This uses the least amount of tape storage and takes the least amount of time. Although an incremental backup takes less time to perform, a restore will take more time as the previous full backup and each of the incremental backups must be restored in order.

◆ A *differential backup* copies those files created or changed since the last normal backup. It does not mark the files as having been backed up. If most of your backed-up files change every day, this begins to resemble a normal backup. A differential backup takes less time to restore because only the previous full backup and the most recent differential backup must be restored.

◆ A *daily backup* copies those files that have been modified the day the daily backup is performed. The files are not marked as backed up.

Backing Up Your Data

Windows 2000 Professional provides two ways to create backup jobs using the Windows Backup utility: a wizard to walk you through the steps involved and a graphical interface to allow you to define the backup job manually.

To define the files to back up and the tape drive to write to, use the procedure outlined in Step by Step 4.8.

WARNING

Always Include the System State
The System State information ensures that the registry, the COM+ database, and all essential Windows 2000 System files are included in the backup set.

ON THE CD

Step by Step 4.8, "Creating an Example Backup Job," shows you how to set up a backup job. See the file **Chapter04-08StepbyStep.pdf** in the CD's **Chapter04\StepbyStep** directory.

When you finish creating this job, you will find that the Windows Backup utility has created a job that you can now review using the Task Scheduler.

Restoring Your Data

When you want to recover some or all of the files stored during a backup job, you must select the backup set to restore from and then the specific files (or all files) to restore. The backup catalogs are stored by the name of the media (see Figure 4.5). You can also restore the files to their original location or to an alternate location if you want to copy the recovered files by hand.

Step by Step 4.9 presents an example of restoring some selected files from a previous backup.

ON THE CD

Step by Step 4.9, "Restoring Files from a Normal Backup," illustrates restoring selected file from a previous backup. See the file **Chapter04-09StepbyStep.pdf** in the CD's **Chapter04\Step by Step** directory.

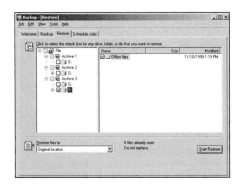

FIGURE 4.5
Backup catalogs are stored by media name.

Creating an Emergency Repair Disk

The Backup tool also provides a mechanism to create an Emergency Repair Disk (ERD). The wizard for this is started from the main backup screen and requires a blank 1.44MB floppy disk. Choosing to also back up the Registry saves the current registry files in a folder within the *systemroot\repair* directory. This is useful if you need to recover your system in the event of a hard disk failure. The emergency repair process relies on information that is saved in the *systemroot\repair* folder.

To create or update the ERD, follow the process in Step by Step 4.10.

ON THE CD

Step by Step 4.10, "Creating an Emergency Repair Disk (ERD)," shows you how to create or update the ERD. See the file **Chapter04-10StepbyStep.pdf** in the CD's **Chapter04\StepbyStep** directory.

To restore your settings from the Emergency Repair Disk, you need the Windows 2000 Professional CD or the Windows 2000 Professional setup disks.

ON THE CD

Step by Step 4.11, "Restoring Your System Using the ERD," shows you how to restore your settings from the ERD. See the file **Chapter04-11StepbyStep.pdf** in the CD's **Chapter04\StepbyStep** directory.

Troubleshooting System Restoration Using Safe Mode

If you reboot your Windows 2000 Professional computer and it fails before Windows 2000 is started, you could have a problem somewhere in the boot process. The key to solving this type of problem is to understand the sequence of events that occur in the computer as it is starting up. Windows 2000 shows you various boot sequence errors, the meaning of which should help you diagnose the problem with your system. You can also diagnose problems in the BOOT.INI file, apply your Emergency Repair Disk to fix your system, and have Windows 2000 automatically attempt to repair the process.

A boot error is a very obvious problem. When you can't start your computer system, you know you have a problem. It's also the kind of problem that forces you to stop what you are doing and fix it before you go on.

The Boot Process

The boot process occurs in stages. The first stage is *preboot* in which the system is checked and the boot information located.

Preboot

The computer runs a power-on self test (POST) to determine the amount of memory and what hardware components are present. The hardware devices are enumerated and configured during pre-boot. Failure at this stage represents a hardware concern and is not really a boot sequence error.

If all the hardware components are present and working, the computer BIOS locates the boot device and loads the Master Boot Record (MBR) into memory and executes it. The MBR scans the partition table to locate the active partition and loads the boot sector from the active partition into memory and executes it.

The computer finds and loads the file NTLDR from the active partition. NTLDR is a hidden system file located in the root folder of your system partition.

Initial Boot Phase

When NTLDR is executing, it does the following:

◆ Switches the processor from real mode into a 32-bit flat memory mode that NTLDR requires to complete its function.

◆ Starts the appropriate minifile system drivers, which are built into NTLDR to find and load Windows 2000 from different file system formats—File Allocation Table (FAT) or Windows NT File System (NTFS).

NOTE

Dual Boot Systems   If you select another operating system, such as Microsoft Windows 98, NTLDR loads and executes BOOTSECT.DOS. This is a copy of the boot sector that was on the system partition at the time that Windows 2000 Professional was installed, and executing it begins the boot process for the selected operating system.

NOTE

Debugging the Boot Process   When you enter the /SOS switch in the BOOT.INI file, Windows 2000 Professional lists the drivers' name on the screen as the system starts up.

NOTE

Loading the Device Drivers   A *control set* contains configuration data used to control the system, such as a list of the device drivers and services to load and start.

NOTE

Specifying Driver Order   The value of the LIST entry specified in the HKEY_LOCAL_MACHINE\SYSTEM\CurrentContr olSet\Control\ServiceGroupOrder subkey defines the order in which NTLDR loads the device drivers.

◆ Displays the Boot Loader Operating System Selection menu from the BOOT.INI file. This provides you with a selection of the operating system to use. If you do not select an entry before the timer reaches zero, NTLDR loads the operating system specified by the default parameter in BOOT.INI.

◆ After you select the operating system, a hardware detection routine is initiated. For Windows 2000, this is NTDETECT.COM and NTOSKRNL.EXE.

NTDETECT.COM collects a list of the hardware components currently installed and returns this list to NTLDR for inclusion in the Registry under HKEY_LOCAL_MACHINE/HARDWARE.

Configuration Selection

After NTLDR starts loading Windows 2000 and collects hardware information, OS Loader presents you with the option of selecting a hardware profile to use. If you do not press the spacebar, or if there is only a single hardware profile, NTLDR loads Windows 2000 Professional using the default hardware profile configuration.

Kernel Load Phase

After the configuration has been selected, the Windows kernel (NTOSKRNL.EXE) loads and initializes. NTOSKRNL.EXE also loads and initializes device drivers and services. During this phase of the boot procedure, the screen clears and a bar graph appears at the bottom of the screen.

During the kernel load phase, NTLDR performs the following:

◆ Loads NTOSKRNL.EXE but does not initialize it.

◆ Loads the hardware abstraction layer file (HAL.DLL).

◆ Loads the HKEY_LOCAL_MACHINE\SYSTEM Registry key from %systemroot%\System32\Config\System.

◆ Selects a configuration. The first hardware profile is highlighted by default. If you have created other hardware profiles, use the down-arrow key to select the one that you want to use.

◆ Selects the control set it will use to initialize the computer.

◆ Loads the low-level hardware device drivers (for example, hard disk device drivers).

NTLDR now initializes the kernel and passes control to it. The kernel uses the data collected during hardware detection to create the HKEY_LOCAL_MACHINE\HARDWARE key. This key contains information about the hardware components and interrupts used.

When the kernel load phase is complete, the kernel initializes, and then NTLDR passes control to the kernel. At this point, the system displays a graphical screen with a status bar indicating load status.

The kernel initializes the low-level device drivers that were loaded during the kernel load phase. If an error occurs while loading or initializing a device driver, the boot process might

◆ Ignore the error and proceed without issuing an error message.

◆ Display an error message and proceed.

◆ Restart using the LastKnownGood control set or ignore the error if the LastKnownGood control set is causing the error.

◆ Restart using the LastKnownGood control set or halt if the LastKnownGood control set is causing the error.

Advanced Boot Options

Pressing F8 during the operating system selection phase displays a screen with advanced options for booting Windows 2000. These include the following:

◆ **Safe Mode.** Loads only the basic devices and drivers required to start the system, including base video, mouse, keyboard, mass storage, and the default set of system services.

◆ **Safe Mode with Networking.** Performs Safe Mode with the drivers and services necessary for networking.

◆ **Safe Mode with Command Prompt.** Launches a command prompt rather than the graphical Explorer interface.

◆ **Enable Boot Logging.** Logs the loading and initialization of drivers and services.

◆ **Enable VGA Mode.** Restricts the startup to use only base video.

◆ **Last Known Good Configuration.** Uses the configuration that was used for the previous boot; Last Known Good is written when a user logs onto the computer.

◆ **Debugging Mode.** Enables kernel debugging options.

◆ **Directory Services Restore Mode.** Allows the restoration of Active Directory (only on domain controllers).

Understanding the BOOT.INI File

The BOOT.INI file includes two sections, BOOT LOADER and OPERATING SYSTEMS, that contain information NTLDR uses to create the Boot Loader Operating System Selection menu.

During installation, Windows 2000 generates the BOOT.INI file, which contains Advanced RISC Computing (ARC) paths pointing to the computer's boot partition. The following is an example of an ARC path:

```
multi(0)disk(0)rdisk(1)partition(2)
```

The four fields in an ARC path are

◆ **multi(*x*) or scsi(*x*).** This field indicates the adapter or disk controller. Use *scsi* to indicate a SCSI controller on which SCSI BIOS is not enabled. For all other adapter/disk controllers, use *multi*, including SCSI disk controllers with the BIOS enabled. The *x* field represents the number indicating the load order of the hardware adapter and starts with (0).

◆ **disk(x).** This field indicates the SCSI ID of the adapter. For multi(x) disks, the value is always set to 0.

◆ **Rdisk(*x*).** This field indicates disk number. This is not used with SCSI controllers.

◆ **Partition(*x*).** This field indicates the partition where Windows 2000 is installed. Partition numbers start with (1).

You can add a variety of switches to the entries in the [operating systems] section of the BOOT.INI file to provide additional functionality

◆ /basevideo boots the computer using the standard VGA video driver.

◆ /baudrate=n sets the baudrate for debugging sessions.

◆ /crashdebug enters debug mode only after a fatal system error.

◆ `/debug` allows debug mode to be invoked at any time.

◆ `/debugport=comx` defines the serial port to use for debugging purposes.

◆ `/maxmem:x` limits the amount of RAM that Windows 2000 uses.

◆ `/nodebug` prevents debug mode from being invoked.

◆ `/noserialmice=comx` prevents serial mouse detection on the indicated serial port.

◆ `/sos` displays driver names as they are loaded.

Last Known Good Configuration

Windows 2000 Professional keeps track of the configuration used for the last successful boot sequence. This configuration is stored in a registry key known as the *clone set*. A boot sequence is considered successful when the first user successfully logs on to the computer. At this time, the clone set is copied to the Last Known Good key.

Actual configuration information is controlled by values in the `HKEY_LOCAL_MACHINE\SYSTEM\Select` key. This key contains the following values:

◆ **Current.** This value identifies which control set is the CurrentControlSet.

◆ **Default.** This value identifies the control set to use the next time Windows 2000 starts (unless you choose Last Known Good configuration during the boot process).

◆ **Failed.** This value identifies the control set that was the cause of a boot failure the last time the computer started.

◆ **LastKnownGood.** This value identifies the control set that was used the last time Windows 2000 was started successfully. After a successful logon, the Clone control set is copied to the LastKnownGood control set.

The Last Known Good configuration is useful for troubleshooting boot failures because of newly installed drivers or services. Remember that if you do successfully log on to the Windows 2000 Professional workstation, you have now overwritten the previous Last Known Good configuration.

Saving and Restoring System State Data

The Backup utility can save and restore system state data. For Windows 2000 Professional, system state data refers to the registry, the COM+ Class Registration database, and boot files. When you choose to back up system state data, all system state data is saved (it is not possible to save components of the system state data).

If you use Backup to restore the saved system state data, it erases the system state data currently on your computer and replaces it with the system state data that you are restoring. This method saves Registry data on a regular basis to have a recent copy available for restoration in the event of corruption or loss of the Registry information.

Using the Windows 2000 Recovery Console

If your computer will not start due to a corrupted or missing file, you can use the Windows 2000 Recovery Console to gain access to the disk without starting Windows 2000. This provides you with a command prompt from which you can perform limited administrative tasks. The following are some of the tasks you can perform from the Recovery Console:

◆ Start and stop services.

◆ Copy data from a floppy disk or a CD.

◆ Read or write data on a local drive.

◆ Format a disk drive.

◆ Repair the boot sector or boot record.

The Recovery Console has some limitations:

◆ You cannot copy files from the hard drive to a floppy.

◆ You need to identify yourself by logging in as the Administrator. If the Security Accounts Manager (SAM) hive is corrupt or missing, you will not be able to use the Recovery Console.

Configuring the Windows 2000 Recovery Console

To use the Recovery Console, you must first install it from the Windows 2000 CD. The installation wizard creates all the files necessary and modifies BOOT.INI to provide an additional boot menu item that will allow you to select the Recovery Console while starting your system.

Installing the Recovery Console

The Recovery Console Wizard is started with the command

```
CD:\i386\WINNT32 /cmdcons
```

where CD: refers to the drive letter of your CD-ROM.

Using the Recovery Console

Step by Step 4.12 can be used to start your computer with the Windows 2000 Recovery Console.

ON THE CD

Step by Step 4.12, "Starting the Windows 2000 Recovery Console," shows you how to start your computer from the Windows 2000 Recovery Console. See the file **Chapter04-012StepbyStep.pdf** in the CD's **Chapter04\StepbyStep** directory.

The Windows 2000 Recovery Console gives you a command prompt in the %windir% directory, usually c:\Winnt. The following commands are available when running the Windows 2000 Recovery Console:

◆ Disable *xxx* disables the indicated service or driver.

◆ Enable *xxx* enables the indicated service or driver.

◆ Diskpart adds or deletes a disk partition.

◆ Fixboot [x:] replaces the Windows 2000 boot sector in the system partition or indicated drive letter (x:).

◆ FixMBR repairs the master boot record of the system partition.

◆ Listsvc lists all services and their start state.

◆ logon lists the available Windows 2000 installations and requests the administrative password for the selected installation.

◆ map [arc] lists all installed drives; the [arc] option lists them as ARC paths, rather than device maps.

◆ systemroot sets the current directory as the systemroot.

The Windows 2000 Recovery Console also supports a number of DOS commands, such as Attrib, Cd, Cls, Copy, Delete, Dir, Extract, Format, Md, More, Rd, Rename, and Type.

Troubleshooting Stop Errors

If a Stop error screen appears, it could be a transient problem that will not reoccur if you restart, or it could signify a more serious or permanent error occurring in your computer. If the Stop screen reoccurs, use the following steps to identify the problem:

1. Verify that any recently installed hardware or software is properly installed.

2. Disable or remove any newly installed hardware (RAM, network adapters, modems, and so forth), drivers, or software.

3. If you can start Windows 2000, check the Event Viewer for additional error messages that might help identify the cause of your problem.

4. If you cannot start Windows 2000, try to start the computer in Safe mode. From here, you should be able to disable or remove any added drivers or programs.

5. Verify that you have the latest drivers for any hardware devices and that you have the most recent system BIOS.

6. Disable any BIOS memory options, such as caching or shadowing.

7. Check for viruses on your computer, using a recent version of your virus-protection software.

8. Verify that all the hardware and drivers installed in your computer are on the Microsoft Hardware Compatibility List (HCL) for Windows 2000.

9. Run any system diagnostic programs that were included when you purchased the computer—memory checks are especially important.

10. Revert to the Last Known Good configuration.

CASE STUDY: PERFORMANCE PROBLEMS WITH A NEW PROCESS

ESSENCE OF THE CASE

The following points summarize the essence of the case study:

▶ The system has just had a new application installed.

▶ The application runs continually as a service to local and remote users.

▶ After a number of days of continual running, the system performance degrades.

▶ Rebooting the system temporarily resolves the problem. However, it eventually returns.

▶ Available memory is consumed and paging activity increases.

SCENARIO

You have installed a new locally developed service program. This service runs in the background continually. You and a number of remote users who are accessing data on your system use it. When you first install it, you run the Performance Monitor on your system to establish a baseline of performance during normal working conditions. A few days later, your system becomes sluggish and noticeably slower in all functions. You reboot your system and it appears to be working normally again. A few days later, the same performance problems occur again. You run the Performance Monitor and discover that the amount of available memory has dropped to almost zero and the paging file is active.

ANALYSIS

When dealing with performance problems, remember that almost everything is interrelated with everything else. Memory problems can cause disk activity, which can manifest itself as a processor bottleneck. In this case, because the problem was apparently solved when the system was restarted, the problem is likely related to consumption of a resource rather than an elevated rate of activity. When the problem occurred again days later, the Performance Monitor showed a higher than expected paging activity and almost no available memory. That combination would normally indicate a system that is underconfigured in memory for the process running. Because this situation did not exist when the new application was brought on line, the conclusion is that the new background service

CASE STUDY: PERFORMANCE PROBLEMS WITH A NEW PROCESS

leaks memory. In this situation, memory acquired by the service during normal processing is not returned to the system. Over time, the amount of working memory assigned to the service would exceed the amount available and the Windows

2000 Professional operating system would begin to page to meet the needs of its normal workload. The recommendation would be to send the new service back to the developers for analysis.

CHAPTER SUMMARY

This chapter focused on actions you can take and procedures you can use to increase the reliability and performance of your Windows 2000 Professional computer system. Knowing how your system functions and the workload under which you normally expect to see it perform is vital to being able to recover your data in the event that something catastrophic occurs. Planning how to recover your system is not a task that can occur after the problem happens.

First, this chapter covered the processes built into Windows 2000 Professional to assist in protecting your currently well-running system from being corrupted by the addition of an incompatible driver or a driver not certified as working with Windows 2000 Professional.

Next, you explored additional built-in processes to assist in running daily or routine tasks using the Task Scheduler. Additionally, offline folders and synchronization were shown to allow mobile users to function off the network as well as they could when on the network and to allow them to reintegrate changes made when reconnected.

The third topic of performance monitoring was discussed from the point of view of memory use, processor resource use, and network and disk activity, as well as how all those factors combine to influence how user applications run.

Finally, you looked at the topics of backup and restore, booting options available when problems arise during startup, and the added functionality of the Recovery Console.

KEY TERMS
- Performance Monitor
- Hardware profiles
- Task Scheduler
- Offline folders
- Synchronization
- Performance counter
- Last Known Good configuration
- Recovery Console

APPLY YOUR KNOWLEDGE

Review Questions

1. Where is the digital signature kept for a signed device driver?

2. How do you run a job under administrative rights with the Task Scheduler?

3. If memory is in short supply, what does the Windows 2000 Professional operating system rely on?

4. What is the best indicator to look at when judging a process to be overloaded?

5. How do you enable logical disk counters?

6. If you have copied Profile 1 to a new hardware profile, how do you disable devices you don't want to load?

7. If you want to reload some files by using only two sets of backup tapes, what backup method should you use?

8. If you load a new device driver and your Windows 2000 Professional computer will not boot, what safe boot option should you use to recover?

Answers to Review Questions

1. Digital signing is not strictly limited to device drivers and can be applied to any type of file. The file itself cannot be modified (because each type would require a separate mechanism to accommodate the signature information). The digital signatures are kept in an associated file with a .CAT extension. The link between the .CAT file and the device driver is in the .INF file for the driver. See the section "Managing and Troubleshooting Driver Signing."

2. Part of the information required by the Task Scheduler's Add a New Task Wizard is the inclusion of a domain/userid and password to run the job under. This allows the user to schedule a job with a userid that has privileges other than the one currently logged in. See "Configuring, Managing, and Troubleshooting the Task Scheduler."

3. The Windows 2000 Professional operating system uses the paging file as the extension to physical memory. It is used as a backup to allocated virtual memory and to provide a place to contain memory dumps of the system in case of a failure. The paging file is normally 12MB larger than physical memory, but that can vary depending on the processes run on the system. The paging file can be moved, added to, or split across a number of disks and controllers to increase performance. See "Optimizing and Troubleshooting Memory Performance."

4. The best indicators are those that show that a queue is forming to access the resource. This is true for other resources (such as disk and network interfaces) as well. If there is a process-bound task running, the Windows 2000 Professional operating system allocates all of it to that task. The CPU appears to be 100% busy. It is not a bottleneck until some other task needs it, but the processor is not available because it is being monopolized or is busy doing other administrative tasks, such as paging or seeking disk sectors. See "Optimizing and Troubleshooting Processor Performance."

5. Normally, Windows 2000 Professional enables physical disk counters when it starts. This can be verified by running the diskperf command, which shows the status of both physical and logical disk

APPLY YOUR KNOWLEDGE

counters. To enable the logical disk counter, the command is `diskperf -yv`. After the system is restarted, the logical counters are available. See "Examining and Tuning Disk Performance."

6. The process to modify a hardware profile is to reboot the system under that hardware profile and then, by using an account with administrative privileges on the local computer, start the system application from the Control Panel, access the Device Manager, and disable those devices that are not needed. By copying the original hardware profile, you start with all the devices you have configured on your computer. See "Managing Hardware Profiles."

7. Planning your backup strategy is important and, of course, dependent on how you want to perform any recover actions. By performing a mix of normal and differential backups, you ensure that any recovery from failure will require no more than two backup sets to be restored to restore all data. The timing between normal backups depends on how long you want to maintain those tapes and also how much the system is changing. If the number of files chosen by the differential backup becomes a significant portion of the normal backup, the differential backup becomes wasteful of both time and tape resources. See "Recovering System and User Data by Using Windows Backup."

8. The best option is to reboot your computer and press F8 during the boot process to access the Last Known Good configuration. When a change is made to the registry to include a new driver, that change is not made permanent until after a successful reboot. If you have problems getting past that point, you still have the last working copy of the registry to fall back on. Rebooting with the Last Known Good option throws the changes away and reverts to a working environment. See "Troubleshooting System Restoration by Using Safe Mode."

ON THE CD

This book's companion CD contains specially designed supplemental material to help you understand how well you know the concepts and skills you learned in this chapter. You'll find related exercises and exam questions and answers. See the file **Chapter04ApplyYourKnowledge.pdf** in the CD's **Chapter04\ ApplyYourKnowledge** directory.

Suggested Readings and Resources

1. Joyce, Jerry, and Marianne Moon. *Microsoft Windows 2000 Professional at a Glance.* Microsoft Press, 2000.

2. Stanek, William R. *Microsoft Windows 2000 Administrator's Pocket Consultant.* Microsoft Press, 2000.

3. *Microsoft Windows 2000 Professional Step by Step.* Microsoft Press, 2000.

This chapter will help you prepare for the "Configuring and Troubleshooting the Desktop Environment" section of the exam.

Configure and manage user profiles.

▶ All users logging on to a local computer running Windows 2000 or a Windows 2000 domain receive a user profile. The two types of user profiles are local and roaming. As the administrator, you can specify the type of user profile that the user receives and whether the user is able to make changes to the profile that persist after the user logs off.

Configure support for multiple languages or multiple locations.

- **Enable multiple-language support.**
- **Configure multiple-language support for users.**
- **Configure local settings.**
- **Configure Windows 2000 Professional for multiple locations.**

▶ In multinational organizations it is common to see the use of different versions (linguistically) of the Windows 2000 operating system in different countries. To accommodate users that travel between countries it may be necessary to enable and configure different regional settings that allow a user to easily switch between languages.

Install applications via Windows Installer packages.

▶ The Windows Installer service is a component of the Intellimirror Management Technologies. Intellimirror can be broken into three core areas: User Data Management, User Settings Management, and Sofware Installation and Maintenance. The Windows Installer service falls

CHAPTER 5

Configuring and Troubleshooting the Desktop Environmewnt

within the Software Installation and Maintenance component of Intellimirror. Two goals of Intellimirror and, subsequently, the Windows Installer service are to reduce total cost of ownership and provide all users with a truly roaming desktop wherein a user's desktop area and applications are always available. It achieves this lofty goal through a new file type known as an .MSI file that allows applications to be rolled out to users and computers through application packages. The cost reduction is achieved through rollout benefits and through application self-repair features that we will examine.

Configure and troubleshoot desktop settings.

▶ A user's desktop settings are the personal settings that a user is sometimes able to configure himself to personalize his computer's desktop. Users tend to like to create work environments that are comfortable to them. We will look at how a user can configure their personal local profile to include their desired desktop settings. Unfortunately, not all jobs can offer the ability to customize the work environment. We will look at ways to limit or entirely remove the ability of the user to make changes to their profile by using roaming mandatory profiles.

Configure and troubleshoot fax support.

▶ Fax support has been incorporated into Windows 2000 to provide organizations with the ability to send, receive, and store faxes for users in your network. We will look at the steps involved in setting up fax support and troubleshooting some of the more common fax problems.

Configure and troubleshoot accessibility services.

▶ In today's work environment, most individuals are required to work at a computer in some capacity throughout the day. To allow individuals with special needs to interact more effectively, Microsoft has improved upon the accessibility features in Windows 2000. We will examine the configuration of these services for our users and troubleshoot some common problems.

STUDY STRATEGIES

▶ The concept of local and roaming profiles has not changed for Windows 2000 Professional. You need to understand how to configure both local and roaming profiles as well as personal and mandatory profiles.

▶ Know how to analyze and configure a local security policy through the Security Configuration and Analysis snap-in.

▶ Know how to set up and configure a local Group Policy and the order in which multiple policies get applied.

▶ Have an understanding of the types of IPSec policies available and what each one does.

▶ Make sure you are comfortable with the theory and application of the Windows Installer service in Windows 2000 Professional and the available options for software installation.

▶ Know the available Internet Explorer options that allow you to configure your Internet settings in Windows 2000 Professional.

INTRODUCTION

In this chapter we will explore how to configure and troubleshoot the Windows 2000 desktop environment. Knowing how to configure the Windows 2000 desktop environment is critical for systems administrators; this skill will be a key component of their management responsibilities. We will cover creation and configuration of local and roaming profiles, use of Windows Installer, and configuration of desktop and Internet options.

CONFIGURING USER PROFILES

Configure and manage user profiles.

User profiles define a specific user's desktop settings, printer and drive mappings, background color, wallpaper, and display options. A user's personal profile defines their own unique settings on the computer. The way in which you set up your office can be correlated to your user profile. Local user profiles are stored on one computer—the computer that the profile was originally created. The path to this profile is %systemdrive%\Documents and Settings\Username, where *Username* is the user's logon name and is known as the local user profile.

In this directory, a series of subdirectories exist, as shown in Figure 5.1 for the user fsmith.

As you can see, some of the subdirectories appear shaded, which denotes a hidden directory. To see these directories, you must change your view settings in Windows Explorer to Show All Files. In addition to the directories in each user's profile folder is a file called NTUSER.DAT. When a user logs on, the configuration settings in their profile directory and the settings in the NTUSER.DAT file are loaded. The user's profile settings found within the user's directory are used to make changes to the desktop and the contents of the NTUSER.DAT are loaded into the HKEY_CURRENT_USER portion of the Registry. It is the NTUSER.DAT file that is used to maintain the user's environment preferences during their logon session. The following settings are stored in the NTUSER.DAT file:

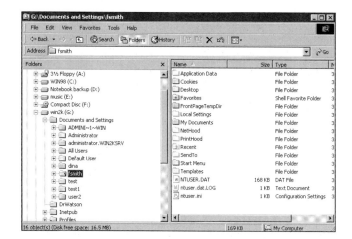

FIGURE 5.1
Local profile directory structure.

◆ **Windows Explorer.** Any persistent connections and user-defined Windows Explorer settings.

◆ **Taskbar.** Taskbar settings, personal program group settings, and program item properties.

◆ **Printer settings.** All the user's network printer settings.

◆ **Control Panel.** Any user settings made in Control Panel.

◆ **Accessories.** All Windows 2000 application settings for applications, such as Notepad, Paint, Calculator, Clock, and Hyperterminal.

◆ **Help favorites.** Any user-defined Help favorites.

The following settings are stored in the user's profile directory:

◆ **Application data.** Contains application-specific data. Content is determined by the software vendors.

◆ **Cookies.** User preferences and information, most commonly used on the Web to track site visits and areas of interest.

◆ **Desktop.** The desktop layout and content, including program shortcuts, files, and folders.

◆ **Favorites.** Shortcuts to your favorite sites on the Internet or intranet.

◆ **Local settings.** Application data, temporary files, and your history of sites on the Web you have recently visited.

◆ **My Documents.** The default location where you store your data.

◆ **My Pictures.** A subdirectory of My Documents created to save your personal pictures.

◆ **NetHood.** Shortcuts contained in My Network Places.

◆ **PrintHood.** Printer shortcuts.

◆ **Recent.** Shortcuts to your most recently accessed documents.

◆ **SendTo.** Contents of SendTo menu. Applications or storage locations to which to send a document (such as Notepad, 3 1/2-inch Floppy, Mail Recipient, and so on).

◆ **Start menu.** User's personal Start menu configuration. All common Start menu shortcuts are found in the All Users profile directory in C:\Documents and Settings\All Users.

◆ **Templates.** User templates.

Two types of profiles exist in Windows 2000: local and roaming. Each of these types can be further divided into two subtypes, known as either personal or mandatory.

Local User Profiles

A local user profile is created automatically when a user logs on to a computer running Windows 2000 and are stored locally on that machine. This makes the local user profile available to the user only when logging on to that same machine. A local user profile is configurable by the user and the changes made to that profile get saved when the user logs off the computer.

Every user who logs on locally to a computer running Windows 2000 Professional receives a local user profile. Two default profile folders are used in the creation of all new local user profiles and are installed with Windows 2000. These two default profile folders are known as the Default User profile and the All Users profile.

EXAM TIP

Local Mandatory Profiles
Although the creation of local mandatory profiles is possible, their use is very limited and therefore should not be a focus on the exam.

The Default Users profile acts as a template for all local user profiles. The contents of the Default User profile are copied to a folder named after the username of the user logging on. Every user's initial local profile begins as a copy of the Default User profile. This copy gets stored on the local machine in the path C:\Documents and Settings*Username*.

The All Users profile contains settings that apply to every user logging on locally to the computer. These settings are merged with the user's own profile settings. An example of the types of settings contained in the All Users profile are program shortcuts that appear on every user's Start menu. These shortcuts for tools or applications, such as Solitare, Calculator, or Paint, are stored in the All Users profile. This prevents the same set of shortcuts being duplicated for each user.

Step by Step 5.1 demonstrates the automatic creation of a local user profile.

NOTE **Location of Local Profiles** The local profiles location may vary, depending on how Windows 2000 was installed. If you upgraded to Windows 2000 from Windows NT Workstation 4.0, local profiles will still be located in their NT 4.0 location (%windir%\profiles*Username*). If a clean installation of Windows 2000 Professional was performed, the local profiles will be stored in the path C:\Documents and Settings*Username*.

ON THE CD

Step by Step 5.1, "Creating a Local Profile," walks you through the creation of a local profile. See the file **Chapter05-01StepbyStep. pdf** in the CD's **Chapter05\StepbyStep** directory.

Now we know how local user profiles are created and where they are stored when a user logs on locally to a computer running Windows 2000 Professional. Unfortunately, having a local profile on one computer doesn't help us if we want to log on to another computer. To solve this dilemma we need to configure the second type of user profile: a roaming profile.

Roaming User Profiles

A roaming user profile is very similar to a local user profile; the difference is that a roaming user profile can be accessed from any computer on the network. If changes to the profile are permitted, they are saved to a network location as opposed to the local hard disk when the user logs off, and are applied again when the user logs back on by accessing the network location.

To configure a roaming user profile, you must edit the user's properties and enter the path to the network share that contains the user's profile. Step by Step 5.2 demonstrates how to enable a roaming user profile.

ON THE CD

Step by Step 5.2, "Creating a Roaming User Profile," walks you through the creation of a roaming user profile. See the file **Chapter05-02StepbyStep.pdf** in the CD's **Chapter05\StepbyStep** directory.

Personal User Profiles

The recommended approach for implementing roaming profiles would be to configure a domain environment and create user accounts in the domain. You would then create a network-based share for each user and configure the profile path of each user account to point to the shared network location. Step by Step 5.3 walks through an alternate method of changing a user's profile from local to roaming that involves using the User Profiles tab in the System applet in Control Panel.

ON THE CD

Step by Step 5.3, "Changing a Local User Profile to a Roaming User Profile Through the System Applet in Control Panel," walks you through changing a local user profile to a roaming one. See the file **Chapter05-03StepbyStep.pdf** in the CD's **Chapter05\StepbyStep** directory.

Mandatory User Profiles

A mandatory user profile can be configured to be either local or roaming. A roaming mandatory user profile travels with the user regardless of the computer the user is logging on to. Any changes that the user makes during their logon session do not get saved when they log off. Mandatory roaming user profiles are useful in environments where you want a group of users to use a common profile regardless of the computer they log on to.

To accomplish this, you could create a mandatory roaming user profile and configure each of the accounts to use that profile.

Think of a mandatory profile as a hotel room. While you are checked into the hotel, you can hang your own pictures on the wall and change the layout of the room, but when you check out the staff will change everything back to the way it was when you originally checked in. In this case, the changes you made do not persist after you check out or log off in the case of a mandatory profile.

Creating a roaming mandatory user profile is not very different from creating a roaming personal user profile except we must ensure that any changes the user makes to the profile are not saved. The key to not allowing the user to maintain changes is to rename the NTUSER.DAT file to NTUSER.MAN. The NTUSER.DAT file can be found in the user's profile folder and renamed from there.

Step by Step 5.4 walks you through the process of changing user2's roaming personal profile to a roaming mandatory profile.

ON THE CD

Step by Step 5.4, "Changing a Roaming Personal User Profile to a Roaming Mandatory User Profile," walks you through changing a roaming user profile to a roaming mandatory one. See the file **Chapter05-04StepbyStep.pdf** in the CD's **Chapter01\StepbyStep** directory.

Before we move on, we should discuss one of the potential troubleshooting issues with mandatory profiles that might arise. When configuring a roaming mandatory profile, the user's properties must be changed to indicate the network share in which the profile is located. This folder should not include an extension (such as \\ *computername**profiles*\Bill.man) because this will prevent the user from logging on.

CONFIGURING THE DESKTOP ENVIRONMENT

Configure and troubleshoot desktop settings.

Understanding that not all users are the same is the first step in configuring the desktop environment. Some of the users that we as administrators are responsible for supporting have special needs. The Windows 2000 operating system offers us a number of options to address the needs of our users.

In this section, we will look at the available regional and accessibility options in Windows 2000 Professional.

Configuring Regional Options

Configure support for multiple languages or multiple locations.

Windows 2000 offers users the ability to switch between various regional settings to change the display format of numerical data or the keyboard layout.

The Regional Options applet in Control Panel allows you to switch between units of measurement, or the way the time, date, currency amounts, and numbers with decimals or fractions are displayed to the user. It also allows you to add in the support for multiple input locals so that a user visiting a United States office from your Paris office could switch to the French keyboard layout from the current default US keyboard layout. Step by Step 5.5 walks you through the set up of multiple input locales in the Regional Options utility.

ON THE CD

Step by Step 5.5, "Configuring Multiple Input Locales," walks you through the configuration of multiple input locales. See the file **Chapter05-05StepbyStep.pdf** in the CD's **Chapter05\StepbyStep** directory.

Another potential need in multinational organizations is to switch between languages and language settings on the desktop. The Windows 2000 operating system comes in a number of localized versions that are language specific, as well as a language-independent version that allows you to install multiple languages. To take advantage of the different input locales that were discussed earlier it may be necessary to install additional languages first. Step by Step 5.6 looks at how to install multiple languages.

ON THE CD

Step by Step 5.6, "Installing Multiple Languages," walks you through multiple language installation. See the file **Chapter05-06StepbyStep.pdf** in the CD's **Chapter05\StepbyStep** directory.

Configuring Accessibility Options

Configure and troubleshoot accessibility services.

Accessibility options can be configured within Windows 2000 to assist users with special needs or disabilities and to help those users to more effectively interact with the operating system. The following accessibility options are available in Windows 2000:

◆ **StickyKeys.** Allows you to press key sequences, such as Ctrl, Alt + Del individually in sequential order instead of all at once for users with limited hand dexterity.

◆ **FilterKeys.** Alerts Windows 2000 to ignore brief or repeated keystrokes.

◆ **ToggleKeys.** Allows you to configure sounds for certain locking keys, such as Caps Lock, Num Lock, and Scroll Lock.

◆ **SoundSentry.** Provides visual warnings when your system makes a sound for the hearing impaired.

◆ **ShowSounds.** Displays captions for speech and sound made by your applications.

◆ **High Contrast.** Configures Windows 2000 to use colors and fonts designed for easier reading.

◆ **MouseKeys.** Allows the mouse pointer to be controlled by the numeric keypad.

◆ **SerialKey Devices.** Allows support for serial key devices.

Using Control Panel is not the only way to enable the accessibility options; they can also be enabled by a hotkey. Holding down the right Shift key for more than eight seconds will prompt you with the FilterKeys dialog box, which contains a Settings button that opens up the Accessibility Options applet. Step by Step 5.7 walks through how to configure and enable FilterKeys.

ON THE CD

Step by Step 5.7, "Configuring and Enabling FilterKeys Options," walks you through starting the FilterKeys options. See the file **Chapter05-07StepbyStep.pdf** in the CD's **Chapter05\StepbyStep** directory.

In addition to the accessibility options enabled through Control Panel, Windows 2000 also ships with accessibility programs. The accessibility programs can be found in the Accessories area on the Start menu. These programs include

◆ **Magnifier.** Allows a portion of the screen to be magnified for easier viewing.

◆ **Narrator.** Reads the contents of the screen aloud, assisting people with limited vision or a vision impairment.

◆ **On-Screen Keyboard.** Allows users the capability to type on-screen with a pointing device.

◆ **Utility Manager.** Enables administrative users to define the startup properties of accessibility programs and to start and stop individual accessibility programs.

The accessibility options included with Windows 2000 are not all encompassing; many users with special needs will require additional applications that address their special requirements. To find out about more about available accessibility programs, visit the Microsoft Accessibility section of the Microsoft Web site at http://www.microsoft.com/enable.

INSTALLING AND CONFIGURING APPLICATIONS

Install applications via Windows Installer packages.

The ongoing management and administration involved with desktop applications is generally one of the highest contributors to the cost of ownership of desktop computers. Microsoft has realized this and integrated technologies into the Windows 2000 operating system to reduce these associated costs.

The Windows 2000 operating system offers a number of options to install and configure applications on computers running Windows 2000 Professional. One of the options available to install applications is the Add/Remove Programs utility in Control Panel. Another option that is new to Windows 2000 is the Windows Installer service. The Windows Installer service allows application packages to be assigned or published to users or computers running Windows 2000 Professional and offers some additional features that help to reduce the total cost of ownership.

The first step in managing applications in the Windows 2000 environment is to ensure that the application is supported. Microsoft has established an online Directory of Windows 2000 Applications that classifies applications into the four following categories:

◆ **Certified.** The highest level of certification. Applications have been tested by both the Independent Software Vendor (ISV) and VeriTest, and meet all standards.

◆ **Ready.** The ISV has approved the application as compatible for Windows 2000 and provides product support for the application.

◆ **Planned.** The ISV has committed to providing a Windows 2000-compatible version at the Ready or Certified levels at some later point in time.

◆ **Caution.** Before upgrading to Windows 2000 Professional, read the important information about the application.

The online directory can be found on the Web at http://www.microsoft.com/windows2000/upgrade/compat/search/CompatApps.asp.

After you have identified that the application you are about to install is supported, you can proceed by following the setup instructs that come with the application, or by using Add/Remove Programs in Control Panel.

Add/Remove Programs

The Add/Remove Programs utility found in Control Panel in Windows 2000 uses the Windows Installer service to simplify the installation, removal, configuration, and repair of applications.

The Windows Installer Service is a client-side service that is included with Windows 2000 Professional. The Windows Installer service manages the installation of applications and their associated system files, including .DLLs, so that the applications can be efficiently removed if that need arises. Step by Step 5.8 walks through the process of removing an installed application.

ON THE CD

Step by Step 5.8, "Removing an Installed Application Through Add/Remove Programs," walks you through removing an installed application. See the file **Chapter05-08StepbyStep.pdf** in the CD's **Chapter05\StepbyStep** directory.

Add/Remove Programs has been enhanced in Windows 2000 and now includes three sections as shown in Figure 5.2.

The Change or Remove Programs section lists all your currently installed programs, listed by name, and indicates their respective size. By clicking one of the installed applications, as is shown in Figure 5.2, you receive more information about the application and are able to change or remove it. Other very useful information from an administrative perspective includes the date when the application was last used. This can be helpful when deciding on an application to remove if disk space is filling up.

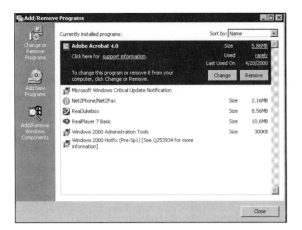

FIGURE 5.2
Add/Remove Programs applet.

Additionally, if you want to sort the installed applications by size or last used, you can use the Sort By option at the top-left corner of the Add/Remove Programs dialog box.

The second section is Add New Programs, which allows you to install an application from floppy disk, CD, the hard drive, or across the network. It also allows you to activate a Windows Update. Windows Update is a Web extension to the operating system that allows you to connect to the Microsoft Web site and download critical or optional updates, fixes, and device drivers. Clicking the Windows Update button launches Internet Explorer and takes you to `http://windowsupdate.microsoft.com`. Step by Step 5.9 demonstrates how to perform a Windows Update.

ON THE CD

Step by Step 5.9, "Performing a Windows Update," walks you through performing a Windows update. See the file **Chapter05-09StepbyStep.pdf** in the CD's **Chapter05\StepbyStep** directory.

The third section to Add/Remove Programs is Add/Remove Windows Components. This is where new or additional services and accessories, such as games, are added or removed.

Windows Installer

The Windows Installer service does not exist in isolation. With the introduction of the Windows Installer service comes Windows Installer files, which end with the extensions .MSI and .MST. All applications and service packs released from Microsoft will now be released with Windows Installer files. Windows 2000 also comes with an application called WinInstall LE that allows for the creation of Windows Installer package files if an application does not come with one. A Windows Installer file is an alternative or a replacement to your applications SETUP.EXE or INSTALL.EXE files and offers some enhanced functionality.

An example of a Windows Installer file can be found in the *system-root*\System32 directory and is called ADMINPAK.MSI. This Windows Installer file gets added to the system32 directory during the installation of Windows 2000 Professional and is used to install the Windows 2000 Administrative Tools. Some of the functionality provided by Windows Installer files can be seen by right-clicking the file to bring up the Context menu seen in Figure 5.3.

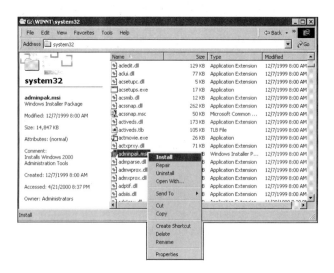

FIGURE 5.3
Context menu of an .MSI
(Windows Installer) file.

The Context menu includes a number of choices, including Install, Repair, and Uninstall. These options do not require a great deal of additional explanation except to note that total cost of ownership can be greatly reduced by their use.

Support for the Windows Installer service and Windows Installer files can also be incorporated into Windows 9x and Windows NT 4.0 by downloading and installing the self-extracting executable from the Microsoft site at `http://msdn.microsoft.com/downloads /sdks/platform/WinInst.asp`.

In a corporate environment with an Active Directory infrastructure, it is possible to roll out software through Windows Installer packages to either users or computers. Windows Installer packages can be either assigned or published. The configuration of Group Policy is broken into two different configurations much like System Policy in NT 4.0: User Configuration and Computer Configuration. The creation of the Windows Installer packages, although important, will not be a focus of this exam, but an understanding of how the packages could affect the Windows 2000 Professional desktop environment is important, so that is where we will focus our attention.

Assigning Windows Installer Packages

A Windows Installer package file can be assigned to either a user or a computer. When a package is assigned to a user, the application's shortcuts will be created on the Start menu and the desktop the next time the user logs on. The application is not installed at logon—only the shortcuts are created and the file associations made within the Registry. The application is installed the first time the user starts the application via the shortcuts, or by double-clicking a file with an extension associated with the assigned application.

A Windows Installer package can also be assigned to a computer. Assigning a package to a computer launches the installation of the application the next time the computer is turned on. This is a useful approach if the assigned application is required by all users of that computer. This ensures that the application is available to all users of the computer and is not tied to a specific user.

The assignment of applications through Windows Installer packages has an additional benefit: resilience through self-repair. If a system file or executable is accidentally or maliciously deleted, but was

WARNING

Planning and Testing when Using Windows Installer Caution and testing should be the rule of thumb with Windows Installer files and the Windows Installer service. Although it is not well documented, Windows Installer files that were installed manually have been known to be resilient in some cases. It appears that the MSI installs remember the original installation location and try to go back to that location for self-repair. Oftentimes, the location will no longer contain the installation files, particularly in the case of a CD drive where the CD has been removed, but the point is that it does seem to try. Planning and testing the use of Windows Installer files is highly recommended.

originally assigned to either a user or computer, it will repair itself the next time it is started. The application will use the Windows Installer service to reconnect to the original distribution point and copy the required files back to the computer running Windows 2000 Professional and re-install them. Following that, the application will launch and a technical support call will be averted.

Publishing Windows Installer Packages

Windows Installer packages can also be published, but the publishing support is limited to users only. Publishing a Windows Installer package to a user makes that application available through Add/Remove Programs the next time the user logs on. The application can be installed in one of two ways when it is published to a user. The first way involves the user installing the application through Add/Remove Programs. The second way is through document invocation. By double-clicking a file with an extension that is associated with the published application, the installation will begin.

Windows Installer packages cannot be published to a computer. The reason for this is that a computer will never invoke an application nor will a computer ever know to install an application through Add/Remove Programs.

One of the key differences between publishing and assigning Windows Installer packages is that published packages are not resilient. If a published package is accidentally deleted, it will not automatically install or repair itself.

Publishing ZAP Files

An alternative to publishing Windows Installer files is to use .ZAP files. A .ZAP file is a text file that can be read and used to execute software installation. These files come with some restrictions and offer a lot less functionality than Windows Installer files, so it should be stressed that the use of Windows Installer files is recommended whenever possible.

The limitations of .ZAP files include the following:

◆ .ZAP files can only be published. They cannot be assigned to users or computers.

◆ .ZAP files offer no resiliency and do not attempt to repair themselves if files are deleted or become corrupted.

◆ The majority of .ZAP files will require user intervention during the installation.

◆ .ZAP files do not have the ability to install with elevated privileges, which means that users must have the capability to install software on their local computers.

Any text editor can be used to create a .ZAP file. Each file has two primary sections: the Application section and the File Extensions section.

The Application section includes information that will be displayed to users in the Add/Remove Programs and must include two tags: FriendlyName and SetupCommand. The Application section is mandatory.

The FriendlyName tag is the name that will be used in Add/Remove Programs.

The SetupCommand tag is the name of the executable or command to install the application. The path to this command should be relative to the .ZAP file itself, meaning that if the Setup command is in the same folder as the .ZAP file only the name of the Setup file needs to be entered.

The second section of the .ZAP file is the File Extensions section. This section is used to associate the application with file extensions saved in Active Directory. This section is optional. A sample .ZAP file looks something like the following:

```
[Application]
FriendlyName = Microsoft Office 2000
SetupCommand = SETUP.EXE /unattend
[Ext]
DOC=
DOT=
```

SECURING THE DESKTOP USING SECURITY POLICIES

Security policies are a means of enforcing security in a corporate network. A security policy should define your corporate computer usage policy and prevent inappropriate access. Security policies can also be used to prevent users from damaging a computer's configuration or limit a particular user's or group's access to specific computers or applications running on those computers. The use of security templates is the most efficient way to implement security policies. A security template contains configurable security settings and is saved as a text file.

Security settings can be applied through either a local security policy on each individual computer or through a Group Policy in a domain, which could be configured to apply to all computers in the domain. The application of security policy at the domain level via a Group Policy is beyond the scope of this section of the book. Chapter 27, "Using Group Policy to Manage Users," discusses the use of Group Policy to manage users. Here, we will endeavor to explain the use of local security policy settings applied to a single computer.

Before we look at the different available local security options, it should be made clear that if both local security and domain security policies exist for the same computer, the local security policy will be overwritten by the domain policy. The order in which security policy is applied is local policy first followed by site, domain, and organizational unit policies. Figure 5.4 is a snapshot of the Local Security Policy snap-in and illustrates this concept. Looking at the Local Security Policy snap-in, you will notice that the settings in the right frame are divided into two categories: local settings and effective settings. What is important to understand is that the effective settings could be different from the local settings if both a local and domain security policy exist. The local security policy will be applied first, but the domain policy will overwrite the local policy because it takes precedence.

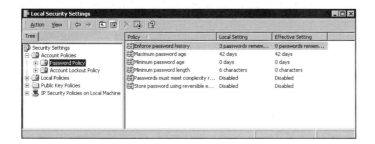

FIGURE 5.4
Local Security Settings screen.

Implementing Security on a Local Computer

Security can be set on a local computer using Administrative Tools, Local Security Policy. Available security settings include

- ◆ **Account policy.** Used to set password and account policies.

- ◆ **Local policy.** Used to configure auditing, user rights, and security options.

- ◆ **Public Key policy.** Used to configure data recovery agents, domain roots, and trusted certificate authorities.

- ◆ **IPSec policy.** Used to configure and assign IP Security on a computer.

Security settings can be individually defined for each computer in your workgroup, but this would not be the most efficient use of your administrative time. If your goal is to configure all workstations in the workgroup with the same security settings, it would be much more efficient to use security templates. Windows 2000 comes with a set of predefined templates, which are defined in Table 5.1. Any of the predefined templates can be imported and applied to a local computer or they can be modified to meet your own unique requirements and then applied to the local computer.

TABLE 5.1

SECURITY TEMPLATES

Template Name	Definition
BASICWK.INF	Default workstation security template.
BASICV.INF	Default server security template.
BASICDC.INF	Default domain controller security template.
COMPATWS.INF	Compatible workstation or server; provides a higher level of security than the basic templates but still ensures that all applications will run.
SECUREWS.INF	Secure workstation or server; provides increased security but does not guarantee that all applications will function.
SECUREDC.INF	Secure domain controller; provides increased security for domain controllers but does not guarantee that all applications will function.
HISECWS.INF	Highly secure workstation or server; enforces the maximum security regardless of the functionality of applications.
HISECDC.INF	Highly secure domain controller; enforces the maximum security regardless of the functionality of applications.

These predefined security templates are stored in the path
`Winnt\security\templates`. Step by Step 5.10 walks through the
steps involved in setting up a password policy on a local computer
running Windows 2000 Professional.

ON THE CD

Step by Step 5.10, "Setting Up a Local Account Security
Policy," walks you through setting up a local account security
policy. See the file **Chapter05-10StepbyStep.pdf** in the CD's
Chapter05\ StepbyStep directory.

Step by Step 5.11 shows you how to compare your computer's local
security configuration to that of a predefined template by using
Security Configuration and Analysis. This is useful in determining
how secure your computer is compared to the predefined template.

After you analyze the differences you can decide whether to import the predefined security template into the local workstation to increase or decrease the existing level of security.

ON THE CD

Step by Step 5.11, "Comparing Your Local Computer's Security Against a Predefined Template," walks you through comparing your local computer's security against a template. See the file **Chapter05-11StepbyStep.pdf** in the CD's **Chapter05\StepbyStep** directory.

Step by Step 5.12 covers how to configure the local computer with the policy in the predefined template and overwrite all existing local settings.

ON THE CD

Step by Step 5.12, "Apply a Security Template to the Local Computer," walks you through applying a security template to the local computer. See the file **Chapter05-12StepbyStep.pdf** in the CD's **Chapter05\StepbyStep** directory.

IP Security Policy

IP Security is new to Windows 2000 and deserves a look at the types of IP Security policies that can be set. The three following IPSec policies are included by default:

◆ **Client (Respond Only).** Allows for IPSec negotiations with other computers requesting IPSec. Only the requested protocol and port traffic is secured.

◆ **Secure Server (Require Security).** Requires that secure communications be used at all times.

◆ **Server (Request Security).** The computer will always attempt to secure communications, but will accept unsecured communications if IPSec negotiations fail.

Internet Protocol Security (IPSec) allows computers to authenticate and encrypt data for transmission between other computers in a network. Currently, Windows 2000 is the only Microsoft operating system to support IPSec. To learn more about IPSec, read the whitepaper available at www.microsoft.com/windows2000/library/howitworks/security/ip_security.asp, or read RFC 2401, which can be found at http://www.ietf.org/rfc/rfc2401.txt.

Implementing Local Group Policy

Local Group Policy is another way to enforce security settings on a local computer. Every computer running Windows 2000 has one local Group Policy object. Again, like local security policy, a local Group Policy will be overwritten by site, domain, or organizational unit Group Policy objects. Therefore, use of local Group Policy will be minimal in a domain environment.

Local Group Policy objects are stored in the path Winnt\System32\GroupPolicy and can be edited with GPEDIT.MSC, also known as the Group Policy snap-in. The Group Policy snap-in is not one of the default administrative tools. Step by Step 5.13 walks through the process of adding the Group Policy snap-in to a new Microsoft Management console.

ON THE CD

Step by Step 5.13, "Adding the Group Policy Snap-in to a New Microsoft Management Console," walks you through adding the Group Policy snap-in to a new Management console. See the file **Chapter05-13StepbyStep.pdf** in the CD's **Chapter05\StepbyStep** directory.

When you complete Step by Step 5.13, you should have the Group Policy window on the screen, which should look similar to Figure 5.5.

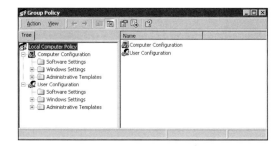

FIGURE 5.5
Group Policy screen.

Group Policy replaces system policy in Windows 2000 as a means of establishing a set of rules in your environment. Like system policy in Windows NT 4.0, Group Policy is divided into two configurations: computer configuration and user configuration.

Computer configuration settings set through local Group Policy will apply to the local computer. User configuration settings set through local Group Policy will apply to the local user logging on to the computer. Both user and computer configurations are subdivided into three sections: software settings, Windows settings, and administrative templates.

Software settings are not configurable through local Group Policy.

The Windows settings found within the computer configuration section are identical to the settings we examined earlier in the Local Security Settings snap-in with the exception of the scripts settings for Startup and Shutdown scripts. The Windows settings found within the user configuration are unique to this snap-in.

The administrative templates section of both user and computer configurations have some similarities between them and allow you to define a set of rules or restrictions on either a user or computer basis. Step by Step 5.14 walks you through the creation of a local Group Policy used to disable the Control Panel. For this Step-by-Step tutorial, you will need to have completed Step by Step 5.13, which created the Group Policy snap-in.

ON THE CD

Step by Step 5.14, "Disabling the Control Panel Through a Local Group Policy," walks you through disabling the Control Panel through a local group policy. See the file **Chapter05-14StepbyStep. pdf** in the CD's **Chapter05\StepbyStep** directory.

The list of settings available for configuration in the Group Policy snap-in is quite exhaustive; because the individual settings will probably not be a focus of the exam, they will not be covered here individually. However, one of the nice features of Group Policy that will help to define the individual settings is the Explain tab and Help button. To find out more about a specific policy in Windows 2000, double-click that policy setting and its dialog box will appear, similar to the Explanation dialog box shown in Figure 5.6.

On the Explain tab, you will find an explanation of the policy setting to help you decide whether you want to use it. Some policy settings do not come with an Explain tab but rather offer a Help button to provide an explanation of what the setting is meant to do.

Sources for information on Group Policy settings include the Explain tab for individual Group Policy settings, the Group Policy help file (GP.CHM) in the Microsoft Windows 2000 Server documentation, and the Windows 2000 Group Policy whitepaper available at the Microsoft Web site at `http://www.microsoft.com /windows2000/library/planning/management/groupsteps.asp`.

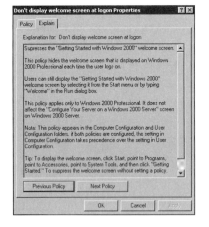

FIGURE 5.6
Explain tab for Group Policy settings.

CONFIGURING FAX SUPPORT

Configure and troubleshoot fax support.

Windows 2000 ships with built-in fax support that allows you the ability to fax a document as easily as you could print the document and receive incoming faxes. Single-user fax support is integrated into Windows 2000 and configured in the Printers dialog box as shown in Figure 5.7.

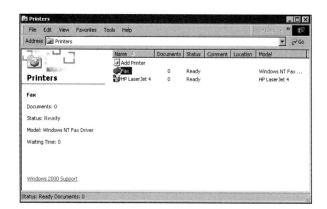

FIGURE 5.7
The Printers screen.

Installing fax support is a two-step process; if your hardware is Plug and Play, both steps could be performed automatically by the operating system.

As with any hardware installation, the first step is to install the physical device after confirming that it is included on the Hardware Compatibility List. The second step is to configure the device within the Printers dialog box and through the Fax Service Management tool.

Fax support in Windows 2000 is single user because an installed fax device does not support sharing with other network users.

Fax Service Management is the tool that is installed when a fax device is added to the computer. The Fax Service Management tool can be found in Start, Programs, Accessories, Communications, Fax or can be launched from the Advanced Options tab from the Fax icon in Control Panel.

The Fax icon in Control Panel consists of four tabs that allow you to accomplish a number of administrative tasks:

◆ **User Information.** Allows for the configuration information that will appear on a fax cover page.

◆ **Cover Pages.** Allows you to add and manage multiple cover pages.

◆ **Status Monitor.** Offers configuration options for notification and the enabling of manual answer for the first device.

◆ **Advanced Options.** Provides access to Fax Service Management, Help, and Adding a Fax Printer.

The Fax Service Management tool allows for a number of device-specific settings to be configured, including the options to send and receive. The receive options include the capability to print to a print device, save in a folder, or send to a local email inbox. The option to receive is not enabled by default. Logging of Initialization/Termination, Outbound, Inbound, and Unknown can also be configured within Fax Service Management.

Step by Step 5.15 assumes that you already have a fax device installed on your computer. Based on this assumption, this tutorial walks you through the steps involved in setting up a fax device to receive incoming faxes on a shared voice/data line, similar to a home-based business setup.

ON THE CD

Step by Step 5.15, "Setting Up a Fax Device to Receive Incoming Faxes," walks you through setting up a fax device. See the file **Chapter05-15StepbyStep.pdf** in the CD's **Chapter05\StepbyStep** directory.

Step by Step 5.16 walks you through the process of viewing and printing a received fax.

ON THE CD

Step by Step 5.16, "Viewing and Printing a Received Fax," walks you through viewing and printing a fax. See the file **Chapter05-16StepbyStep.pdf** in the CD's **Chapter05\StepbyStep** directory.

The reasons why faxing might not function properly are numerous. Troubleshooting should be approached very methodically in all instances where it is required. The first spot to check when faxing problems occur, is that a fax device is installed. Without a hardware fax device installed on the computer, none of the previously discussed fax options will be available.

If faxes are not being sent, check that the user sending the fax has the required permissions. Fax permissions can be viewed by right-clicking the Fax icon found in Start, Settings, Printers, and selecting Properties from the Context menu. In the Fax Properties dialog box, select the Security tab to display the permissions for the fax. Also ensure that the fax device has not been configured to fax only during specific times of the day.

If faxes are not being received, ensure that the feature to Enable Receive has been enabled. If the fax server is connected to a dedicated line for faxing, ensure that the feature to Enable Manual Answer for the First Device is *not* selected; otherwise, someone will have to physically answer the call.

A number of possible scenarios could be preventing a fax device from working properly. Use your common sense and the process of elimination to troubleshoot the problem.

CONFIGURING INTERNET OPTIONS

The configuration of Internet options is becoming increasingly important as more and more companies have integrated Internet access into their network architecture. We look at some of the settings that can be configured for Internet Explorer, which can simplify administration and streamline Internet access.

One of the most basic of choices that we can configure for individual users is the default home page. The default home page is defined in the properties of Internet Explorer but can also be assigned through a Group Policy. Step by Step 5.17 walks through the steps of setting up the default home page individually.

ON THE CD

Step by Step 5.17, "Setting the Default Home Page," walks you through starting a networked installation. See the file **Chapter05-17StepbyStep.pdf** in the CD's **Chapter05\StepbyStep** directory.

The location and size of temporary Internet files is also an important setting to govern, particularly if the amount of available disk space on a client computer is limited. Step by Step 5.18 walks through how to set the size and location of temporary Internet files.

ON THE CD

Step by Step 5.18, "Setting the Size and Location of Temporary Internet Files," walks you through setting temporary Internet files' size and location. See the file **Chapter05-18StepbyStep.pdf** in the CD's **Chapter05\StepbyStep** directory.

Proxy settings can also be set within the properties of Internet Explorer for users that access the Internet through a proxy server. Internet Explorer can be set up to automatically detect settings, use an automatic configuration script, or use a static proxy server address. The benefit of the automatic configuration script is that a number of settings can be provided through the automatic configuration script as opposed to a simple proxy address. The automatic configuration script also centralizes administration by allowing the administrator to create one script for all users; by directing users to that script, all users are identically configured.

Step by Step 5.19 addresses the process of configuring proxy settings.

ON THE CD

Step by Step 5.19, "Configuring Proxy Settings," walks you through proxy setting configuration. See the file **Chapter05-19StepbyStep. pdf** in the CD's **Chapter05\StepbyStep** directory.

Many companies have, or are beginning to establish, a set of Internet user guidelines that restrict users to viewing only certain material or surfing only to specific sites using the corporation's Internet access.

Internet Explorer offers the capability to control security through authenticode publishers, security zones, and content ratings.

Authenticode publishers allow you to restruct ActiveX controls from being downloaded to a client computer. You can restrict downloads to only signed software and choose whether to warn or block unsigned controls from being downloaded to a client computer.

Security zones enable you to assign specific Web sites to specific security zones. The five defaults to choose from are as follows:

◆ **Internet.** Contains all Internet sites.

◆ **Local Intranet.** Used for computers connected to the local intranet.

◆ **Trusted Sites.** Allows for the assignment of sites you trust for download of content.

◆ **Restricted Sites.** Allows for the assignment of sites you do *not* trust.

◆ **My Computer.** Contains the files on the local computer; configurable only through the Internet Explorer Administration Kit or from Group Policy.

Adding sites to which you are interested in preventing access can be accomplished by adding those particular sites to the Restricted Sites zone. Step by Step 5.20 details the process of adding sites to the Restricted Sites zone.

ON THE CD

Step by Step 5.20, "Configuring a Restricted Zone," walks you through restricted zone configuration. See the file **Chapter05-20StepbyStep.pdf** in the CD's **Chapter05\StepbyStep** directory.

Finally, content ratings can be implemented to prevent access to Web sites with objectionable content. By defining content ratings, only rated sites can be accessed by users of the network. If a Web site is either unrated or rated at a restricted level, access to the Web site will be prevented by Internet Explorer.

CHAPTER SUMMARY

KEY TERMS

- Accessibility options
- Group Policy
- Local profile
- Roaming profile
- Mandatory profile
- Windows Installer
- IP Security

Summarized briefly, this chapter covered the following main points.

◆ **Understanding profiles.** This section defined the two types of profiles (local and roaming) and the differences between personal and mandatory profiles.

◆ **Understanding the Windows Installer service.** This new service in Windows 2000 helps to reduce the total cost of ownership through both application self-repair and making applications available to users from any Windows 2000 computer they log on to.

◆ **Configuring the desktop.** We broke this section into local security policy and local Group Policy and examined the similarities and differences between the two. We also discussed the application of local policy and the order in which it is applied—first. In addition to security, we also looked at setting up and configuring both fax and accessibility options to meet the needs of our user community.

◆ **Configuring Internet options.** This section looked at the options available to us in Internet Explorer and how to configure the home page, proxy settings, temporary Internet file size, and location and the setting of security zones.

APPLY YOUR KNOWLEDGE

Review Questions

1. What are the two different types of user profiles?

2. What feature allows Windows Installer to dynamically install applications?

3. What are the two sections of a .ZAP file?

4. What is the purpose of accessibility options?

Answers to Review Questions

1. The two different types of user profiles are local and roaming. Local and roaming profiles can be further divided into either personal (which allow the users changes to be saved) and mandatory (which do not save the user's changes). See the section "Configuring User Profiles."

2. Advertising an application allows it to be installed automatically and with elevated privileges by the Windows Installer service. An application can be assigned to either a user or a computer. Assigning an application to a user creates the program shortcuts and file associations in the Registry but does not install the application until it is invoked.

Assigning an application to a computer forces the install to take place at the next reboot. See the section "Assigning Windows Installer Packages."

3. The two sections of a .ZAP file are the Application section and the File Extensions section. The Application section is mandatory within a .ZAP file, but the File Extensions section is not. See the section "Publishing ZAP Files."

4. The purpose of accessibility options is to make Windows 2000 Professional usable to a wider audience. In addition to the accessibility features included with the operating system, a number of additional add-on programs and products exist to assist people with disabilities. See the section "Configuring Accessibility Options."

ON THE CD

This book's companion CD contains specially designed supplemental material to help you understand how well you know the concepts and skills you learned in this chapter. You'll find related exercises and exam questions and answers. See the file **Chapter05ApplyYourKnowledge.pdf** in the CD's **Chapter05\ApplyYourKnowledge** directory.

Suggested Readings and Resources

1. Web sites
   - http://www.microsoft.com/windows2000/professional/
   - http://www.microsoft.com/train_cert/
   - http://activewin.com/win2000/
   - http://www.microsoft.com/enable (Accessibility section)
   - http://www.microsoft.com/windows/professional/deploy/compatible/default.asp (Hardware and Software Compatibility List)
   - http://windowsupdate.microsoft.com/ (Windows Update)
   - http://www.microsoft.com/windows2000/library/howitworks/security/ip_security.asp
   - http://www.ietf.org/rfc/rfc2401.txt

2. MOC 1560B *Updating Support Skills from Microsoft Windows NT to Microsoft Windows 2000.*

3. MOC 2152A *Supporting Microsoft Windows 2000 Professional.*

4. *Windows 2000 Group Policy Technical Paper,* Version 2.0 (May 1999).

5. *Microsoft Windows 2000 Professional Support and Management Improvements* whitepaper.

This chapter helps you prepare for the Windows 2000 Professional component of MCP Exam 70-240, "Microsoft Windows 2000 Accelerated Exam for MCPs Certified on Microsoft Windows NT 4.0," by covering the following objectives:

Configure and troubleshoot the TCP/IP protocol.

▶ To effectively access network resources, you must understand how to install and configure the TCP/IP client and use the services available on TCP/IP networks.

Connect to computers by using dial-up networking:

- **Connect to computers by using a virtual private network (VPN) connection.**

- **Create a dial-up connection to connect to a remote access server.**

- **Connect to the Internet by using dial-up networking.**

- **Configure and troubleshoot Internet Connection Sharing.**

▶ Connectivity between LANs where a persistent connection is not needed can be provided by dial-up network connections. To accomplish this, you must be able to install and configure dial-up components in various configurations.

Connect to shared resources on a Microsoft network.

▶ The availability of networking technology means resources need not be centralized in a few large servers. File shares and printers can be distributed across the entire network, and applications can involve many remote computers as system components.

CHAPTER 6

Implementing, Managing, and Troubleshooting Network Protocols and Services

INTRODUCTION

A *local area network* (LAN) is a collection of computers in a specific area that are connected by a high-speed communications network. This can range from just two computers to hundreds or thousands. LANs in geographically separate areas can be connected in a wide area network (WAN). Generally, the speed at which computers connect within a LAN is greater than what is available between LANs (across the WAN).

THE WINDOWS 2000 PROFESSIONAL NETWORKING MODEL

Before reviewing how to configure the networking components of Windows 2000 Professional, it is important to examine the underlying components that make up the network architecture. These components are put together as layers from interfacing with an application program down to interfacing with the physical connection to the network. Each layer interacts only with the layers directly above and directly below through a well-defined interface. Knowing the actual layers helps you understand how the Windows 2000 network architecture works.

All the networking components in Windows 2000 Professional are built in to the operating system, although some of them are not automatically installed. Any Windows 2000 computer can participate as the following:

◆ A client or a server in a distributed application environment

◆ A client in a peer-to-peer networking environment

The built-in networking components allow Windows 2000 Professional systems to share printers, files, and applications with other networked computers.

WINDOWS 2000 NETWORKING VERSUS THE OSI REFERENCE MODEL

The Open Systems Interconnection (OSI) model is one system that can help you understand the networking architecture used in Windows 2000 Professional. The *OSI model* was developed by the International Standards Organization (ISO) and is a layered model that defines how computers participating in a network communicate and how the network data is exchanged between layers from the application to the network media.

The OSI model divides the network protocol stack into seven layers to which software systems must adhere to communicate over the network. In the case of Windows 2000, the system does not implement each layer separately; however, the result complies with the overall OSI model. Figure 6.1 compares the Windows 2000 network architecture with the OSI network model.

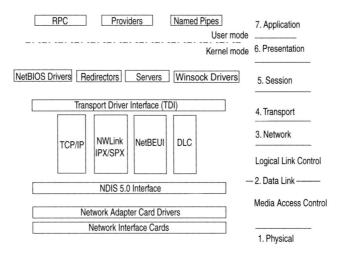

FIGURE 6.1
Windows 2000 networking architecture versus the OSI model.

NDIS-Compatible Network Adapter Card Drivers

The bottom layers of the Windows 2000 network architecture include the network adapter card driver and the network interface card (NIC). These must be 32 bit and compliant with Network Device Interface Specification (NDIS) 3.0, 4.0, or 5.0. The mechanism that NDIS uses to bridge these two layers is the *miniport driver specification.* The miniport drivers directly access the network adapters while providing common code where possible. This allows hardware vendors to create drivers that can call the underlying NDIS drivers, rather than code the functionality into their drivers.

NDIS 5.0

NDIS 5.0 extends the previous versions of NDIS that define the interaction of network protocols and network card adapters. NDIS allows multiple protocols and multiple network adapters to exist within a computer.

If you have more than one network adapter in your computer, each adapter card's protocol stack can be configured individually. The only limit on the number of network adapter cards you can install is the capacity of your computer hardware.

Windows 2000 Professional and NDIS 5.0 provide the following new features in addition to those of the NDIS 4.0 specification:

◆ **Power management and network wake-up.** NDIS power management can power down network adapters at the request of the user or the system or when a network cable is disconnected.

◆ **NDIS Plug and Play.** Installs, loads, and binds miniports when a new adapter card is introduced.

◆ **Support for Web-Based Enterprise Management (WBEM) and Windows Management Instrumentation (WMI).** Supplies device information to management services. WMI is used by management applications (such as SMS) to query and set device status and retrieve configuration information directly from hardware devices.

◆ **Task offload.** Available if the network adapter card has the capability of supporting checksums and forwarding. This results in performance gains for processes such as IPSec encryption.

◆ **Support for Quality of Service (QoS) and connection-oriented media, such as ATM and ISDN.** These improvements extend the functionality of Windows 2000 Professional even further.

Most of the new features in NDIS 5.0 are accessible only by using the miniport driver model and are therefore not supported for MAC drivers or older miniport drivers.

> **N O T E**
>
> **Backward Compatibility** Windows 2000 Professional can also use drivers written to be compliant with the NDIS 3.0 and 4.0 specifications that were used by Windows NT 3.x and Windows 4.0.

Network Protocols

The network protocols referred to in Figure 6.1 control the communications between computers on the network. Different network protocols provide varying communications services and capabilities.

TCP/IP

Transmission Control Protocol/Internet Protocol (TCP/IP) is the default protocol for Windows 2000 Professional and is an industry standard suite of protocols available for WANs and the Internet. Microsoft's implementation of TCP/IP provides a number of standard features, including the following:

◆ Capability of binding to multiple network adapters with different media types

◆ Logical and physical multihoming

◆ Internal IP routing capability

◆ Internet Group Management Protocol (IGMP) version 2 (IP Multicasting)

◆ Duplicate IP address detection

◆ Multiple default gateways

◆ Dead gateway detection

◆ Automatic Path Maximum Transmission Unit (PMTU) discovery

◆ IP Security (IPSec)

◆ Quality of Service (QoS)

◆ Virtual private networks (VPNs)

In addition, Windows 2000 includes the following performance enhancements:

◆ **Internet Router Discovery Protocol (IRDP).** Hosts can dynamically discover routers on their subnet and can automatically switch to a backup router if the primary router fails or the network administrators change router preferences.

◆ **TCP scalable window sizes.** The Windows 2000 TCP/IP stack will tune itself and use a larger default window size than earlier versions if sending and receiving computers can support a larger TCP window size.

◆ **Selective acknowledgments (SACK).** SACK allows the receiver to use the ACK number to acknowledge the left edge of the receive window, but it can also acknowledge other blocks of received data individually. This results in increased performance.

◆ **TCP fast retransmit.** When a receiver that supports fast retransmit receives data with a sequence number beyond the current expected one, it is likely that some data was dropped. To help make the sender aware of this event, the receiver immediately sends an ACK, with the ACK number set to the sequence number that it was expecting. The sender will determine that the sequence number in the ACK packet is earlier than the current sequence number being sent and immediately resend the segment that the receiver is expecting to fill in the gap in the data.

NWLink IPX/SPX-Compatible Transport

NWLink is an NDIS-compliant, native 32-bit implementation of Novell's IPX/SPX protocol. NWLink supports two networking Application Programming Interfaces (APIs): NetBIOS and Windows

Sockets. These APIs allow communication among computers running Windows 2000 and among computers running Windows 2000 and NetWare servers.

The NWLink transport driver is an implementation of the lower-level NetWare protocols, which include IPX, SPX, Routing Information Protocol over IPX (RIPX), and NetBIOS over IPX (NBIPX). IPX controls addressing and routing of packets of data within and between networks. SPX provides reliable delivery through sequencing and acknowledgments. NWLink provides NetBIOS compatibility with NetBIOS layer over IPX.

Table 6.1 shows the interoperability that exists between Windows 2000 and NetWare.

TABLE 6.1

WINDOWS 2000 INTEROPERABILITY WITH NETWARE

Platform	Running	Can Connect To
Windows 2000	NWLink	Client/server application running on a NetWare server
Windows 2000	NWLink and Client Services for Netware	NetWare servers for file and print services
NetWare Client	IPX with NetBIOS, named pipes, or Windows Sockets	Computers running Windows 2000 (with NWLink) running IPX-aware applications (such as SQL Server)
NetWare Client	IPX	Computers running Windows 2000 Server with NWLink and File and Print Services for NetWare (FPNW)

NetBIOS Extended User Interface (NetBEUI)

NetBEUI is a simple nonroutable protocol designed for peer-to-peer networks that takes little memory overhead. All hosts are considered to be on the same logical network, and all resources are considered to be local. Other machines on the network are located via their NetBIOS computer name. This name is resolved to a MAC address mapping via the use of broadcast messages. Without the added complexity of other protocols, more of the packet is used to transport data, making NetBEUI faster than TCP/IP and IPX/SPX in a small network (fewer than 50 computers).

Transport Driver Interface

The *Transport Driver Interface* (TDI) is a common interface that drivers (such as the Windows 2000 Server and redirector) use to communicate with the various network transport protocols, allowing services to remain independent of transport protocols. Unlike NDIS, there is no driver for TDI. It is just a specification for passing messages between two layers in the network architecture.

Network Application Programming Interfaces

An *API* is a set of routines that an application program uses to request and carry out lower-level services performed by the operating system. Windows 2000 network APIs include

- **Winsock API.** A protocol-independent implementation of the widely used Sockets API that allows Windows-based applications to access the transport protocols.

- **NetBIOS API.** A standard application programming interface used for developing client/server applications.

- **Telephony API (TAPI).** An API that supports both speech and data transmission and allows a variety of terminals. Commonly used by applications that provide support for call management, call conferencing, call waiting, and voice mail.

- **Messaging API (MAPI).** An API that allows developers to write messaging applications and back-end services that can be connected in a distributed computing environment.

- **WNet API.** An API that provides Windows networking (Wnet) capabilities that extend networking functionality to applications while remaining independent of the network over which they communicate.

Interprocess Communication

Interprocess Communication (IPC) allows bidirectional communication between clients and multiuser servers working on different computer systems. IPCs can be used as an intertask communication system on a local computer, as well as between a local computer and a remote one.

Applications that split processing between one or more networked computers are referred to as *distributed* applications. A client/server application uses distributed processing, in which processing is divided between a workstation (the client) and a more powerful server. The client portion is sometimes referred to as the *front end* and the server portion is referred to as the *back end*.

Multitier applications (often called three-tier) are an extension of the basic client/server model with an additional application-specific component between the client and the back-end server. It is common for this type of application to be split between a user interface on the client, the application code or business rules in the middle tier, and data services interacting with a large shared database server on the back end.

There are a number of ways in which the Windows 2000 operating system implements IPC mechanisms:

◆ **Distributed Component Object Model (DCOM).** Allows components to be efficiently invoked on multiple computers so that the application can take advantage of the most optimal resources on the network while remaining transparent to the user.

◆ **Remote Procedure Call (RPC).** A mechanism that allows communication between a client and server by using other IPC mechanisms such as named pipes, NetBIOS, or Winsock to establish communications between the client and the server with the program logic and related procedure code existing on different computers.

◆ **Named pipes.** Provides connection-oriented messaging by using a portion of memory called a pipe. A pipe connects two processes so that the output of one process is used as the input to the other. The Windows 2000 operating system provides special APIs that increase security for named pipes called impersonation. With impersonation, the server can change its security identity to that of the client at the other end of the message to ensure that security is applied at the level of the connecting client.

◆ **Common Internet File System (CIFS).** The standard way that computer users share files across corporate intranets and the Internet. It is an enhancement to the cross-platform Server Message Block (SMB) protocol that defines a series of commands used to pass information between networked computers.

Basic Network Services

Network services support application programs and provide the components and APIs necessary to access files on networked computers.

Server Service

The Server service is located above the TDI and is implemented as a file-system driver. The CIFS Server service interacts directly with other file-system drivers to satisfy I/O requests, such as reading or writing to a file. When the Server service receives a request from a remote computer asking to read a file that resides on the local hard drive, the following steps occur:

1. The low-level network drivers receive the request and pass it to the server driver.

2. The Server service passes the request to the appropriate local file-system driver.

3. The local file-system driver calls lower-level, disk-device drivers to access the file.

4. The data is passed back to the local file-system driver.

5. The local file-system driver passes the data back to the Server service.

6. The Server service passes the data to the lower-level network drivers for transmission back to the remote computer.

The Server service is composed of two parts. SERVICES.EXE is the Service Control Manager where all services start. SRV.SYS is a file-system driver that handles the interaction with the lower levels of the protocol stack and directly interacts with various file system devices to satisfy command requests, such as file read and write.

Workstation Service

All user requests from the Multiple Uniform Naming Convention Provider (Multi-UNC Provider) go through the Workstation service. This service consists of two components: the user interface, which resides in SERVICES.EXE in Windows 2000, and the redirector (MRXSMB.SYS), which is a file-system driver that interacts with the lower-level network drivers by means of the TDI interface.

The Workstation service receives the user request and passes it to the kernel redirector.

Windows 2000 Redirectors

The *redirector* is a component that resides above TDI and is the mechanism through which one computer gains access to another computer. The Windows 2000 operating system redirector allows connection to Windows 9x, Windows for Workgroups, LAN Manager, LAN Server, and other CIFS servers. The redirector communicates to the protocols using the TDI specifications.

The redirector is implemented as a Windows 2000 file-system driver. This provides several benefits:

◆ It allows applications to call a single API (the Windows 2000 I/O API) to access files on local or remote computers.

◆ It runs in kernel mode and can directly call other drivers and other kernel-mode components, such as cache manager.

◆ It can be dynamically loaded and unloaded, like any other file-system driver.

◆ It can easily coexist with other redirectors.

Interoperating with Other Networks

Besides allowing connections to Windows 9x, peer-to-peer networks, LAN Manager, LAN Server, and MS-Net servers, the Windows 2000 redirector can coexist with redirectors for other networks, such as Novell NetWare and UNIX networks.

Providers and the Provider-Interface Layer

For each additional type of network, such as NetWare or UNIX, you must install a provider. The provider is the component that allows a computer running Windows 2000 Professional to communicate with the lower levels of the network.

Client Services for NetWare is included with Windows 2000 Professional and allows the computer to connect as a client to the NetWare network.

Network Resource Access

Applications have a unified interface for accessing network resources, independent of any redirectors installed on the system. Access to resources is provided through the Multi-UNC Provider and the Multi-Provider Router (MPR).

Multiple Universal Naming Convention Provider

When applications make I/O calls containing Uniform Naming Convention (UNC) names, these requests are passed to the UNC Multi-UNC Provider. The Multi-UNC Provider is implemented as a driver, unlike the TDI, which is only a specification defining the way one network layer talks to another.

The Multi-UNC Provider allows multiple redirectors to coexist in the computer. However, if there are multiple redirectors present, there must be a means of deciding which one to use. One of the Multi-UNC Provider's functions, then, is to act as an arbitrator to decide the most appropriate redirector to use.

Universal Naming Convention Names

UNC is a naming convention for describing network servers and the share points on those servers. A typical UNC name appears as follows:

```
\\server\share\subdirectory\filename
```

Only the server and share component of a UNC are required to be present with each command. For example, the following command can be used to obtain a directory of the root of a specified share:

```
dir \\server_name\share_name
```

I/O requests from applications that contain UNC names are received by the I/O manager, which passes the requests to the Multi-UNC Provider. If the Multi-UNC Provider has not seen the UNC name during the previous 15 minutes (approximately), the Multi-UNC Provider sends the name to each of the UNC providers registered with it.

When the Multi-UNC Provider receives a request containing a UNC name, it checks with each redirector to find which one can process the request.

Multi-Provider Router

Not all programs use UNC names in their I/O requests. Some applications use *Wnet APIs*, which are the Win32 network APIs. The MPR supports these applications.

MPR is similar to Multi-UNC Provider. MPR receives Wnet commands, determines the appropriate redirector, and passes the command to that redirector.

ADDING AND CONFIGURING THE NETWORK COMPONENTS OF WINDOWS 2000

You can configure all your network components when you first install Windows 2000 Professional. Changes to the network configuration include the following:

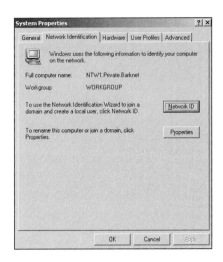

FIGURE 6.2
Network Identification tab in the System applet.

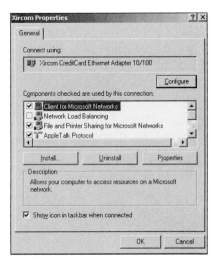

FIGURE 6.3
Viewing a network connection's properties.

> **NOTE**
>
> **Adding Computer Accounts** By
> default, all domain users can add up
> to a maximum of 10 machine
> accounts to a domain.

◆ Network identification properties

◆ Network connection properties

Identification Options

Network identification properties are changed using the System
applet in the Control Panel (see Figure 6.2).

Properties that can be changed in the System applet include the
computer name and the workgroup or domain information. When
changing the domain name, a computer account must preexist in
the domain, or the user performing the configuration change must
provide credentials that have the user right to add computer
accounts to the domain.

Network Connection Properties

Network connection properties are configured in the properties
of individual network connections in Network and Dial-Up
Connections from the Start menu, or from the Control Panel (see
Figure 6.3). This is performed on a connection-by-connection basis.

Additional protocols, services, or clients can be installed for an
interface by clicking the Install button in the network connection's
Properties dialog box.

Additionally, advanced options can also be configured.

Protocol Options

Additional protocols can be installed by selecting Protocol in the Select Network Component Type dialog box and clicking the Add button (see Figure 6.4). The following protocols can be added to a Windows 2000 Professional installation:

FIGURE 6.4
Selecting network components.

- ◆ **Internet Protocol (TCP/IP).** This is the default protocol for Windows 2000 Professional. It is required for Internet connectivity.

- ◆ **NWLink IPX/SPX/NetBIOS Compatible Transport Protocol.** This is Microsoft's implementation of NetWare's IPX/SPX protocol.

- ◆ **NetBEUI Protocol.** This nonroutable protocol is used to connect a small number of Microsoft-based computers.

- ◆ **DLC Protocol.** This protocol allows communication with IBM mainframes and HP printers attached directly to the network.

- ◆ **AppleTalk Protocol.** This protocol allows other computers to communicate with your computer and printers via the AppleTalk protocol.

- ◆ **Network Monitor Driver.** This driver allows the Network Monitoring system (NetMon) to acquire packets from the network.

Service Options

Selecting the Service entry and clicking the Add button shows the additional services available to install on your computer These additional services include

- ◆ **File and Printer Sharing for Microsoft Networks.** This allows other computers to access resources on your computer.

- ◆ **SAP Agent.** This is a NetWare service that advertises servers and addresses on a network.

- ◆ **QoS Packet.** The QoS service provides network traffic control, rate control, and prioritization.

Client Options

Selecting the Client entry and clicking the Add button shows the
clients available to install on your computer. The following network
clients can be added to a Windows 2000 Professional workstation:

- ◆ **Client for Microsoft Network.** Allows your computer to
  communicate on Microsoft networks.

- ◆ **Client Service for NetWare.** Allows your computer to access
  resources on NetWare networks.

Advanced Options

The advanced options provide you a place to improve the performance of your computer on networks that contain more than one
protocol.

Two options are available from the Network and Dial-Up
Communications applet in the Control Panel. Select the Advanced
tab from the menu bar and Advanced Settings within the drop-
down list.

Provider Order

This tab allows you to choose the order in which network providers
(such as Microsoft networks and NetWare networks) are accessed.

If your network connection accesses both Microsoft and NetWare
networks using both IPX/SPX and TCP/IP, but your primary interface is the Microsoft Network, move the Microsoft Windows
Network to the top for best performance.

Adapters and Bindings

The Bindings tab allows you to choose the order in which protocols
(such as IPX/SPX and TCP/IP) are accessed.

Setting the order of the protocols on a server therefore does not
enhance performance, whereas changing the order of the protocols
on your Windows 2000 Professional client will impact performance.

NOTE

Unnecessary Protocols For maximum performance, remove any unnecessary protocols and always make
sure that your most frequently used
protocol is configured to be the first
one accessed.

CONFIGURING THE TCP/IP PROTOCOL

Configure and troubleshoot the TCP/IP protocol.

TCP/IP is the default protocol for Windows 2000 Professional and is supported by most common operating systems. When you manually configure a computer with a TCP/IP network adapter, you must enter the appropriate settings for connectivity with your network.

IP Addressing

IP addresses are 32-bit integers that are usually depicted as four 8-bit numbers that uniquely identify each host on a network. The smallest integer number that can be represented with 8 bits then is 0 0 0 0 0 0 0 0 (2^0–1), or 0. The largest integer that can be represented by 8 bits is 1 1 1 1 1 1 1 1 (2^8–1), or 255. Because of this, you will always see IP addresses as four numbers ranging from 0 to 255 separated by dots. This can be referred to in dotted-decimal format and is expressed as $w.x.y.z$—for example, 192.168.10.4.

This addressing scheme is again broken down into two halves: a network ID (also known as the network address) and the host ID (also known as the host address). The network ID must be unique in the Internet or intranet, and the host ID must be unique to the network ID. The network portion of the $w.x.y.z$ notation is separated from the host through the use of the subnet mask.

TCP/IP addresses can be broken into five different classes of addresses. These classes define which bits are used for the network ID and which bits are used for the host ID in an IP address. Microsoft clients support IP addresses from the Class A, Class B, and Class C address ranges. Table 6.2 indicates how the three classes supported by Microsoft TCP/IP divide network IDs and host IDs.

TABLE 6.2

CLASS ADDRESS RANGES

Class	Network ID	Network Portion	Host Portion	Number of Networks	Number of Hosts
A	1–126	w.	x.y.z	126	16,777,214
B	128–191	w.x	y.z	16,384	65,534
C	192–223	w.x.y	z	2,097,152	254

Subnet Mask

NOTE

Hosts Need a Subnet Mask   Each host on a TCP/IP network requires a subnet mask even if it is on a single-segment network. Although the subnet mask is expressed in dotted-decimal notation, a subnet mask is not an IP address.

After an IP address from a particular class has been decided upon, it is possible to divide it into smaller segments to better use the addresses available. A *subnet mask* (also known as an address mask) is defined as a 32-bit value that is used to distinguish the network ID from the host ID in an IP address. The bits of the subnet mask are defined as follows:

◆ All bits that correspond to the network ID are set to 1.

◆ All bits that correspond to the host ID are set to 0.

Table 6.3 lists the default subnet masks using dotted-decimal notation.

TABLE 6.3

DEFAULT SUBNET MASKS

Address Class	Bits for Subnet Mask	Subnet Mask
Class A	11111111 00000000 00000000 00000000	255.0.0.0
Class B	11111111 11111111 00000000 00000000	255.255.0.0
Class C	11111111 11111111 11111111 00000000	255.255.255.0

Default Gateway (Router)

This optional setting is the IP address of the router for this subnet segment. Routers are used to direct packets destined for segments outside the local one to the correct segment or to another router that can complete the connection. If this address is left blank, this computer will be able to communicate only with other computers on the same network segment.

Windows Internet Name Service (WINS)

Computers may use IP addresses to identify one another, but users generally prefer to use computer NetBIOS names. A Windows Internet Name Service (WINS) server is used to resolve NetBIOS names to IP addresses. WINS provides a dynamic database that maintains mappings of computer names to IP addresses.

> **NOTE**
> **The Dynamic Nature of WINS** WINS eliminates the need for an LMHOSTS file, which is a static alternative to WINS. Maintaining an LMHOSTS file requires much more administrative overhead than using WINS.

Domain Network Systems (DNS) Server Address

The DNS server address is used to resolve fully qualified domain names (FQDNs) to IP addresses. Under Windows 2000, DNS supports dynamic update as defined in RFC 2136. This allows DNS clients to dynamically update their IP address information to the DNS server.

The IPCONFIG command can be used to display information recently obtained from the DNS service using the following options:

◆ /displaydns displays the contents of the DNS client resolver cache. This cache contains all DNS resource records recently resolved by the client computer.

◆ /flushdns flushes and resets the DNS resolver cache.

◆ /registerdns forces the TCP/IP client to register its host and reverse lookup resource records with a DNS server that supports DNS dynamic updates.

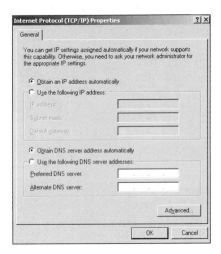

FIGURE 6.5
Specifying that TCP/IP configuration comes from a DHCP server.

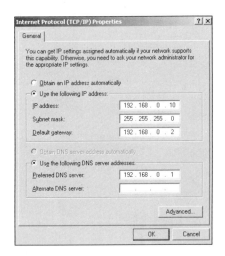

FIGURE 6.6
Manual configuration of a TCP/IP host.

ASSIGNING IP ADDRESSES TO CLIENTS

IP addresses can be assigned to TCP/IP clients using either Dynamic Host Configuration Protocol (DHCP) or by manually configuring TCP/IP options individually for each client on the network.

Using DHCP

One way to avoid the possible problems of administrative overhead and incorrect settings for the TCP/IP protocol (which are usually caused by manual configurations) is to set up your clients to receive their TCP/IP configuration information automatically through a DHCP server.

To configure a computer as a DHCP client, all you must do is specify an IP address automatically in the Internet Protocol, TCP/IP, Properties box (see Figure 6.5). Exercise 6.2 in the Chapter06ApplyYourKnowledge.pdf on the CD contains complete instructions.

IPCONFIG can be used to determine IP configuration information that has been assigned by a DHCP server using the following options:

◆ /all displays the current TCP/IP configuration for all network connections.

◆ /release releases any DHCP-assigned IP addresses and their configuration.

◆ /renew forces a renewal of any DHCP-leased IP addresses and their configuration information.

Manually Configuring TCP/IP

You can manually configure your TCP/IP settings by entering the required values into the TCP/IP Properties sheet (see Figure 6.6). For complete details, see Exercise 6.1 in the file Chapter06ApplyYourKnowledge.pdf on the CD.

CONNECTING TO COMPUTERS BY USING DIAL-UP NETWORKING

Connect to computers by using dial-up networking.

Dial-up networking enables you to extend your network to unlimited locations. After a client connects to a Remote Access Server (RAS), it is registered into the local network and can take advantage of the same network services and data as if they were locally connected to the local network. The only difference is that network performance will be slower than when locally connected to the network.

Line Protocols

The network transport protocols (TCP/IP, NWLink, and NetBEUI) were designed for the characteristics of LANs. To make the network transport protocols function properly over phone-based connections, it is necessary to encapsulate them in one of the two supported line protocols in Windows 2000 Professional: SLIP and PPP.

Serial Line Internet Protocol (SLIP)

SLIP is an industry-standard line protocol that supports TCP/IP connections made over serial lines. SLIP implementations have several limitations:

◆ SLIP supports TCP/IP only and does not support other protocols, such as IPX or NetBEUI.

◆ SLIP requires that both computers understand the other's IP address for routing purposes. SLIP provides no mechanism for hosts to communicate addressing information over a SLIP connection, and there is not support for DHCP.

◆ SLIP has no error detection, so noisy phone lines will corrupt packets in transit.

◆ SLIP does not support any encryption and therefore passwords are sent as clear text.

◆ Due to clear-text transmissions, SLIP is supported only for client purposes. You cannot configure a Windows 2000 computer to accept SLIP connections.

◆ It is usually necessary to include some scripting or manual intervention to log on to a SLIP server.

Point-to-Point Protocol (PPP)

The limitations of SLIP prompted the development of Point-to-Point Protocol. Some of the advantages of PPP include the following:

◆ PPP supports TCP/IP, IPX, NetBEUI, and other protocols.

◆ PPP supports both static IP addresses and DHCP.

◆ PPP supports encrypted authentication.

◆ Scripting and other manual interventions are not required for the logon process.

◆ PPP supports multilink connections, which allows you to combine multiple physical links into one logical connection.

◆ Multiple links can also be allocated only as they are required, thereby eliminating excess bandwidth.

Virtual Private Networks (VPNs)

VPN allows the computers in one network to connect to the computers in another network by the use of a tunnel through the Internet or other public network. A VPN connection allows you to connect to a server on your corporate network from home or when traveling using the routing facilities of the Internet. The connection appears to be a private point-to-point network connection between your computer and the corporate server.

Additionally, VPNs can be used to connect remote office LANs to the corporate LAN or to other remote LANs to share resources and information using direct connect of dial-up access.

The basic functions managed by VPNs are the following:

◆ **User authentication.** Verify the user's identity and restrict VPN access to authorized users only.

◆ **Address management.** Assign the client's address on the private net and ensure that private addresses are kept private.

◆ **Data encryption.** Data carried on the public network must be unreadable to unauthorized clients on the network.

◆ **Key management.** Encryption keys must be refreshed for both the client and the server.

◆ **Multiprotocol support.** The most common protocols used in the public network are supported.

Windows 2000 Professional provides two encapsulation methods for creating VPN connections.

Point-to-Point Tunneling Protocol (PPTP)

This protocol enables the secure transfer of data from your computer to a remote computer on TCP/IP networks. PPTP *tunnels,* or encapsulates, IP, IPX, or NetBEUI protocols inside of PPP datagrams. PPTP can work over dedicated Internet connections or over dial-up connections; however, it does require IP connectivity between your computer and the server to which it is authenticating before the tunnel can be established.

In PPTP, a PPP frame is wrapped with a Generic Routing Encapsulation (GRE) header and an IP header. In the IP header is the source and destination IP address that corresponds to the VPN client and VPN server.

Figure 6.7 shows the PPTP encapsulation of a PPP payload.

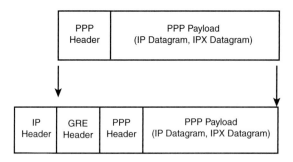

FIGURE 6.7
PPTP encapsulation of an encrypted datagram.

The PPP frame is encrypted with Microsoft Point-to-Point Encryption (MPPE) by using encryption keys generated from the MS-CHAP or EAP-TLS authentication process.

Layer 2 Tunneling Protocol (L2TP) over IPSec

L2TP is an Internet tunneling protocol with roughly the same functionality as PPTP. The Windows 2000 implementation of L2TP is designed to run natively over IP networks.

Encapsulation for L2TP consists of two layers:

◆ A PPP frame (containing an IP datagram or an IPX datagram) is wrapped with an L2TP header and a UDP header.

◆ The resulting L2TP message is then wrapped with an IPSec Encapsulating Security Payload (ESP) header and trailer, an IPSec Authentication trailer that provides message integrity and authentication, and a final IP header. In the IP header are the source and destination IP addresses that correspond to the VPN client and VPN server.

Figure 6.8 shows the L2TP encapsulation of a PPP payload.

The L2TP message is encrypted with IPSec encryption mechanisms by using encryption keys generated from the IPSec authentication process. The portion of the packet from the UDP header to the IPSec ESP Trailer inclusive is encrypted by IPSec.

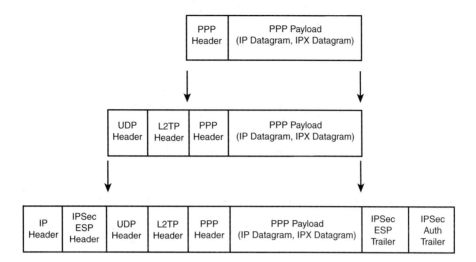

FIGURE 6.8
L2TP encapsulation of an encrypted PPP payload.

Internet Connection Sharing

With the Internet Connection Sharing (ICS) feature of Network and Dial-Up Connections, you can use Windows 2000 to connect your home network or small office network to the Internet.

A computer with ICS needs two connections: one to the internal LAN and one to the Internet. ICS is enabled on the interface connected to the Internet. This shared connection allows your internal network to receive its addresses using DHCP, provides a DNS service to resolve names, and provides a gateway service to access computer systems outside your home network.

The DHCP allocator provides IP addresses and gateway configurations to all computers on the local network that require an Internet connection.

All internal clients send their DNS requests to the ICS server. The DNS requests are then sent to the Internet for resolution using a DNS proxy service.

The network address translation (NAT) service within ICS assigns the computer hosting the ICS service the IP address 192.168.0.1/24, and the DHCP allocator issues addresses to clients for that subnet.

When the NAT receives an outgoing packet, the packet has the source IP address changed to the IP address of the external network interface. The source port also is changed to a unique value to allow the returned packet to be returned to the correct host. All mapping is stored in a NAT table.

When the NAT receives an incoming packet, the NAT modifies the destination IP address and port number based on the previous connection information stored in the NAT table, and it checks the packet's internal tables to see whether there is already a mapping. If there is a mapping, it will be used; if not, a new one is created.

NOTE

Role. You must be a member of the Administrators group to configure Internet Connection Sharing.

Internet Connection Sharing Settings

When you enable Internet Connection Sharing, certain protocols, services, interfaces, and routes are configured automatically. Table 6.4 describes the settings used when Internet Connection Sharing is enabled.

TABLE 6.4

INTERNET CONNECTION SHARING SETTINGS

Configured Item	Action
IP address 192.168.0.1	Configured with a subnet mask of 255.255.255.0 on the LAN adapter that is connected to the small office or home office network
Autodial feature	Enabled
Static default IP route	Created when the dial-up connection is established
Internet Connection Sharing service	Started
DHCP allocator	Enabled with the default range of 192.168.0.2 to 192.168.0.254 and a subnet mask of 255.255.255.0
DNS proxy	Enabled

Internet Connection Sharing for Applications

If you have applications that interact with services on the Internet (usually games), you need to configure the application in the Internet Connection Sharing service. In addition, if you want to provide services to users on the Internet (for example, you are hosting a Web site), you must configure the Web server service.

ON THE CD

Step by Step 6.1, "Configuring Internet Connection Sharing for Applications and Services," shows you how to configure Internet Connection Sharing. See the file **Chapter06-01StepbyStep.pdf** in the CD's **Chapter06\StepbyStep** directory.

INSTALLING A DIAL-UP NETWORKING CONNECTION

The Network Connection Wizard for installing a dial-up networking connection is started when you double-click the Make New Connection icon in the Network and Dial-Up Connections Control Panel applet. The wizard automatically creates outgoing connections to other networks or incoming connections from remote computers.

The wizard allows the creation of five types of connections (see Figure 6.9), and these are discussed in the following sections.

Dial-Up to Private Network

Dial-Up to Private Network is used to connect to a RAS server on a private network (such as a RAS server connected to a corporate network), using either modem connections or X.25 connections.

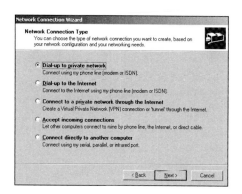

FIGURE 6.9
Dial-up connection types available.

Dial-Up to the Internet

Dial-Up to the Internet is used to connect to an Internet service provider (ISP). Configuration options include the following:

◆ Phone number of the ISP to connect to

◆ PPP/SLIP/C-SLIP connectivity

◆ Logon scripts if required by the ISP

◆ IP addressing configured or supplied by the ISP

◆ DNS addresses

◆ User ID and password

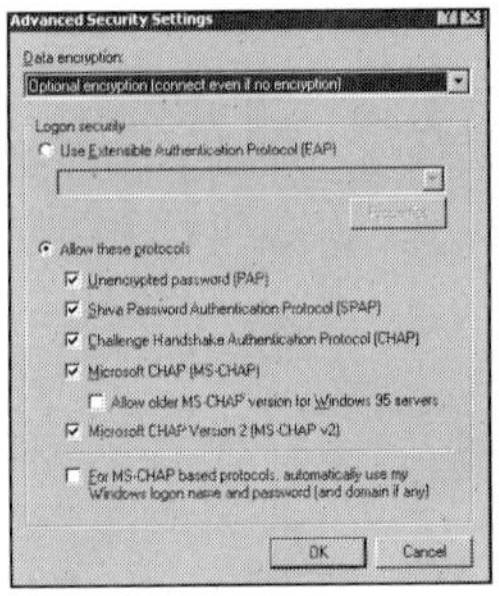

FIGURE 6.10
Encrypted authentication options.

Security is a major consideration when connecting to a public network. As shown in Figure 6.10, you can choose from several different security settings, including the following:

◆ **Password Authentication Protocol (PAP).** This uses clear-text passwords and is the least sophisticated authentication protocol.

◆ **Challenge Handshake Authentication Protocol (CHAP).** This uses a secure encryption authentication technique based on Message Digest 5 (MD5) encryption. CHAP uses challenge-response with one-way MD5 hashing on the response. In this way, you can prove to the server that you know your password without actually sending the password over the network.

◆ **Microsoft Challenge Handshake Authentication Protocol (MS-CHAP).** This is a variation on CHAP authentication that does not require the use of clear text or reversibly encrypted passwords.

◆ **Shiva Password Authentication Protocol (SPAP).** This allows Shiva clients to dial in to computers running Windows 2000 Server.

◆ **Extensible Authentication Protocol (EAP).** This is an extension to PPP that provides a standard method for supporting additional authentication methods, such as smart cards and certificates.

Connect to a Private Network Through the Internet

Connect to a Private Network Through the Internet provides for a secure VPN connection over the public Internet. This type of network connection allows you to select a dial-up connection to establish first; or, if you already have a persistent connection to the Internet through a LAN connection (for example, a cable modem), the VPN can be established using the local connection. The remote VPN server computer's name or IP address is added to complete the configuration.

The type of connection (PPTP or L2TP) is defined by the RAS server to which the client connects. In any case, the connection and security are negotiated automatically.

Accept Incoming Connections

Accept Incoming Connections allows you to configure your Windows 2000 computer to accept connections from phone lines, from the Internet, or via direct cable. Configuration options include the following:

◆ The device (modem or serial port) to answer

◆ Whether to allow VPN connections

◆ Users allowed to connect to your computer

◆ Network components available to incoming users

Connect Directly to Another Computer

Connect Directly to Another Computer allows you to configure your Windows 2000 computer with a direct connection to another computer. The configuration options include the following:

◆ Whether to be the host of the connection or a guest on another computer

◆ The port to use (infrared, direct connection, or a COM port)

◆ Users allowed to connect to your computer

CONNECTING TO SHARED RESOURCES ON A MICROSOFT NETWORK

Connect to shared resources on a Microsoft network.

Windows 2000 provides different methods to work with network resources and to determine what network resources are available.

Browsing

Users on a Windows 2000 network often need to know what domains and computers are accessible from their local computer. The Windows 2000 Browser service maintains a list (called the *browse list*) of all available domains and servers. This list can be viewed using Windows 200 Explorer and is provided by a browser in the local computer's domain.

The Windows 2000 browser system consists of a Master Browser, Backup Browsers, and Browser Clients. The computer that is the Master Browser maintains the browse list and sends copies to the Backup Browsers every 15 minutes. When a Browser Client needs information, it obtains the current browse list by remotely sending a request to either the Master Browser or a Backup Browser.

Browsing Other Domains

Users need to be able to retrieve lists of servers within their domain and also a list of other workgroups and domains. Upon becoming a Master Browser, each Master Browser in each domain broadcasts an announcement every minute for the first 5 minutes and once every 15 minutes thereafter. If a domain has not announced itself for a period equaling 45 minutes, it is removed from the master browse list.

Browsing a Wide Area Network

With domains that are split across routers, each network segment functions as an independent browsing entity with its own Master Browser and Backup Browsers. Therefore, browser elections occur within each network segment.

Domain Master Browsers are responsible for spanning the network segments to collect computer name information for maintaining a domain-wide browse list of available computers in the domain.

Universal Naming Convention

The UNC was introduced earlier in this chapter as a network provider service. This is a standardized way of specifying a share name on a specific computer. The share name can refer to folders or printers. The UNC path takes the form of `\\server\share`.

You can also use UNC paths to refer to network printers. For example, `\\ACCTSERSVER\ACCTPRINT` refers to the printer named ACCTPRINT on the server named ACCTSERVER.

My Network Places

The My Network Places icon can be used to browse recently used network resources or a view of the entire network. The entire network includes each network provider available on your network (perhaps NetWare networks as well as Microsoft Networks) and the Directory.

The network providers show the servers available under the network provider, and the Directory shows the objects within Active Directory that the user has permission to view.

The NET VIEW Command

You can also access the list of computers in your workgroup by using the NET VIEW command. A sample listing looks like this:

```
C:\Net View
Server Name          Remark — — — — — — — — — — — — — —
\\TEST1
\\TEST2
\\NTW1
The command completed successfully.
```

NOTE

New Feature Alert   You are now
able to set artificial root paths for
shared folders by including the full
path to where you want the root to be
established. For example, if you want
h:\
to be the home directory for the user
bkomar, you can use this command:

        net use h: \\server\users\
        bkomar

The NET USE Command

You can assign network resources to drive letters from the command
prompt or from the Tools menu from Windows Explorer. To connect drive letter X: to a share called GoodStuff on a server named
SERVER1, for example, you type the following command at the
command prompt:

    C:\Net Use X: \\SERVER1\GoodStuff

You can also use the Net Use command to connect clients to network printers. If you want to connect port LPT1: to a network
printer named HP5 on a server named SERVER1, use the following
command:

    Net Use LPT1: \\SERVER1\HP5

To disconnect the network resources for these two, use the following
two commands:

    Net Use X: /d
    Net Use LPT1: /d

TROUBLESHOOTING TCP/IP CONNECTIONS

The best approach for troubleshooting network connections is to
work from the bottom up, eliminating configuration issues first
before checking basic connectivity and then advancing to higher
functions and services.

Configuration Errors

The first thing to check when troubleshooting TCP/IP networking
connections is the local TCP/IP configuration.

Use the Ipconfig /all command to get a detailed listing of the host
computer configuration information, including the IP address,
subnet mask, and the default gateway.

Typical problems found in the configuration include

◆ **Duplicate IP addresses exist.** Windows 2000 will display
a dialog box and record an entry to the Event Viewer if a
duplicate IP address is found on the network.

◆ **Media state is set to Cable Disconnected.** A physical network problem is preventing connectivity.

◆ **Address assigned from the 169.254.y.z network range.** A
DHCP server was unavailable to assign an IP address to the
client.

Troubleshooting TCP/IP Configuration Errors

If your client has correctly been assigned an IP address, yet connectivity is not working, the following tools can be used to troubleshoot
connectivity problems.

Packet Internet Groper (PING)

PING is a tool that helps verify connectivity at the IP level. The
PING command sends an ICMP echo request to the target hostname or IP address.

The best process to follow when using PING to detect network
problems is to use IP addresses only (so as not to confuse name-
resolution errors with network errors) and to ping progressively
more remote computers.

The following order should be used when diagnosing connectivity
problems:

1. Ping 127.0.0.1, the loopback address. This verifies that
TCP/IP is correctly installed on the local computer.

2. Ping the IP address configured for the local computer. This
ensures that the correct address is bound to the NIC.

3. Ping the IP address of the default gateway. This ensures that local network communication is working.

4. Ping the IP address of a host on a remote network. This verifies that routing is functioning correctly to and from the network segment.

Trace Route (Tracert)

The Tracert diagnostic utility determines the route taken to a destination by sending Internet Control Message Protocol (ICMP) echo packets with varying IP Time-to-Live (TTL) values to the destination. Each router that is crossed between the source computer and the destination IP address is displayed on the screen.

If Tracert cannot record the path the packet takes in returning, the remote computer might be off the network, behind a firewall, or behind a router that filters ICMP packets.

Address Resolution Protocol (ARP)

All TCP/IP communications ultimately result in one network interface communicating with another network interface. The network interfaces are uniquely identified by the Media Access Control (MAC) address.

When communications with a client are performed, ARP caches the MAC address of the network interface associated with the destination IP address, using the following rules:

◆ If the destination IP address is on the local subnet, the MAC address ARP cache will contain the actual MAC address of the destination network interface.

◆ If the destination IP address is on a remote subnet, ARP will add the MAC address of the default gateway to the ARP cache.

The command Arp –a can be used to display the current cache of IP addresses and the MAC addresses associated with them:

```
Arp -a
Interface: 157.57.18.16 on Interface 0x1000003
  Internet Address      Physical Address      Type
  157.57.18.1           00-d0-ba-09-9c-d6     dynamic
  157.57.18.26          00-a0-c9-96-03-7f     dynamic
```

Route

The Route command can be used to display the routing table for
the local computer. The entries in the routing table enable TCP/IP
to determine which gateway to send outgoing traffic through. The
routing table has many entries for individual routes, each one
consisting of a destination, network mask, gateway interface, and
hop count (metric) .

The structure of the Route command line is as follows:

```
ROUTE [-F] [-P] [COMMAND [destination] [MASK subnetmask]
[gateway] [METRIC costmetric]]
```

where

◆ -F clears the routing tables of all gateway entries.

◆ -P adds persistent entries to the routing table.

◆ COMMAND indicates the following command-line arguments for
Route:

  • PRINT prints a route.

  • ADD adds a route.

  • DELETE deletes a route.

  • CHANGE modifies an existing route.

◆ destination specifies the IP network address that the route is
defined for.

◆ MASK subnetmask specifies a subnet mask to be associated with
this route entry.

◆ gateway specifies the gateway to be used for the routing entry.

◆ METRIC costmetric assigns an integer cost metric (ranging
from 1 to 9999) to be used in calculating the fastest, most
reliable, and/or least expensive routes.

Resolving Logical Names to IP Addresses

The process for two computers to communicate using TCP/IP involves four steps:

1. Resolve the hostname or NetBIOS name to an IP address.

2. Use the IP address and the routing table to determine the interface to use and the forwarding IP address.

3. Use ARP to resolve the forwarding IP address to a MAC address.

4. Use the MAC address to send the IP datagram.

If the computer to be reached is a hostname or a NetBIOS name, the name must be resolved to an IP address before any data can be sent. Hostnames and NetBIOS names are resolved in different ways.

Resolving a NetBIOS Name to an IP Address

Resolving a NetBIOS name means successfully mapping a 16-byte NetBIOS name to an IP address. The File and Printer Sharing for Microsoft Networks service in Windows 2000 Professional uses NetBIOS name resolution. When your computer starts, the Server service registers a unique NetBIOS name based on the name of your computer (padded out to 15 characters if it is shorter than that) with 0×20 as the 16th character.

When you attempt to make a file-sharing connection to a computer running Windows 2000 by name, the File and Printer Sharing for Microsoft Networks service on the file server you specify corresponds to a specific NetBIOS name. For example, when you attempt to connect to a computer called COMMONSERVER, the NetBIOS name corresponding to the File and Printer Sharing for Microsoft Networks service on that computer is as follows:

```
COMMONSERVER    [20]
```

Note that the name of the server is padded out to 15 characters.

To actually use the file server, its IP address must be established.

The exact mechanism by which NetBIOS names are resolved to IP addresses depends on the NetBIOS node type that is configured for the node. Supported NetBIOS node types include

◆ **B-node.** A broadcast-node client uses broadcasts for name registration and resolution.

◆ **P-node.** A peer-node client uses a NetBIOS Name Server (NBNS), such as WINS, for name registration and resolution.

◆ **M-node.** A mixed-node client uses broadcasts for name registration. For name resolution, it tries broadcasts first, but switches to p-node if it receives no answer.

◆ **H-node.** A hybrid-node client uses an NBNS for both registration and resolution. However, if an NBNS cannot be located, it switches to b-node. It continues to poll for the name server and switches back to p-node when one becomes available.

NetBIOS names are resolved to an IP address by the NetBIOS session service through the following sequence if the client is set to be an h-node client:

◆ Consults the NetBIOS cache

◆ Queries a WINS server if it is configured

◆ Broadcasts a request for the computer to identify itself

◆ Consults the LMHOSTS file directly for an address assigned to the computer name

If these methods fail, a Windows 2000 client then uses the following methods to attempt to resolve the NetBIOS name:

◆ Query the HOSTS file.

◆ Query the DNS server if it is configured.

Troubleshooting NetBIOS Name Resolution Problems

The following commands and configurations can be used to diagnose NetBIOS name resolution problems:

◆ NBTStat can display the registered NETBIOS names for the local computer, the registered NetBIOS names for a remote computer, and the current contents of the NetBIOS name cache.

◆ NET USE can be used to map network drivers to UNC names. If the command succeeds, the NetBIOS name was successfully translated to an IP address.

◆ The LMHOSTS file is scanned from the top down. If there is more than one address listed for the same hostname, TCP/IP uses the first value it encounters. Verify the contents of the LMHOSTS file located in the *systemroot*\system32\drivers\ etc folder.

◆ Verify WINS configuration to ensure that the TCP/IP configuration points to the correct WINS server, as shown in Step by Step 6.2.

ON THE CD

Step by Step 6.2, "Examining Your WINS Configuration," walks you through verification of the correct WINS server. See the file **Chapter06-02StepbyStep.pdf** in the CD's **Chapter06\StepbyStep** directory.

Resolving a Hostname to an IP Address

Hostnames are resolved to an IP address using the DNS system. The *DNS system* is a worldwide distributed database that replaces the HOSTS file with a hierarchical domain name system that maps names to IP addresses.

If you were trying to contact a computer with the name testcomp.microsoft.com, the following steps would be performed in resolving this hostname

1. The local HOSTS file is queried for the testcomp.Microsoft. com entry.

2. The client contacts the DNS name server with a recursive query for testcomp.microsoft.com. The server must now return the answer or an error message.

3. The DNS name server checks its cache and zone files for the answer, but doesn't find it. It contacts a server at the root of the Internet (a root DNS server) with an iterative query for `testcomp.microsoft.com`.

4. The root server doesn't know the answer, so it responds with a referral to an authoritative server in the `.com` domain.

5. The DNS name server contacts a server in the `.com` domain with an iterative query for `testcomp.microsoft.com`.

6. The server in the `.com` domain does not know the exact answer, so it responds with a referral to an authoritative server in the `microsoft.com` domain.

7. The DNS name server contacts the server in the `microsoft.com` domain with an iterative query for `testcomp.microsoft.com`.

8. The server in the `microsoft.com` domain does know the answer. It responds with the correct IP address to the preferred client's DNS server.

9. The DNS name server responds to the client query with the IP address for `testcomp.microsoft.com`.

Troubleshooting Hostname Resolution Problems

The following commands can be used to diagnose hostname resolution problems:

◆ NSLOOKUP can be used to diagnose hostname resolution problems by querying the configured DNS server for specific hostnames.

◆ NETDIAG (found in the Windows 2000 Resource Kit) ensures that communications are working correctly with the client's configured DNS server. It also verifies that network connectivity is functioning correctly.

◆ The HOSTS file could have incorrect entries due to typographical errors. Verify the contents of the HOSTS file to ensure that this is not the case. You can find the HOSTS file in the `%systemroot%\system32\drivers\etc` folder.

Step by Step 6.3 shows the methodology used to check hostname resolution problems.

ON THE CD

Step by Step 6.3, "Checking the Hostname Resolution Configuration," illustrates checking of hostname resolution problems. See the file **Chapter06-03StepbyStep.pdf** in the CD's **Chapter06\StepbyStep** directory.

Additional Troubleshooting Tools

There are also some Windows 2000 tools that can be used to aid in TCP/IP network troubleshooting:

◆ Microsoft SNMP service provides statistical information to SNMP management systems.

◆ Event Viewer tracks errors and events.

◆ Microsoft Network Monitor performs in-depth network traces. The full version is part of the Systems Management Server (SMS) product, and a limited version is included with Windows 2000 Server.

◆ Performance Monitor analyzes TCP/IP network performance.

◆ Registry editors REGEDIT.EXE and REGEDT32.EXE allow viewing and editing of Registry parameters.

CASE STUDY: HOME OFFICE

ESSENCE OF THE CASE

▶ There is an internal TCP/IP network.

▶ There is a Windows 2000 Server sharing a connection with the Internet.

▶ There is a VPN connection to a corporate server.

▶ Access to hosts on the Internet is failing.

SCENARIO

Like everyone else, you work too much and have set up an office in your home. There is a TCP/IP network internal to your house that connects all the PCs and laptops you have to make one network. You are running Windows 2000 Server on one of the systems, which acts as a gateway, and it is sharing a connection to the Internet through a local cable company. Your laptop is running Windows 2000 Professional with TCP/IP configured by DHCP. You normally connect to your company VPN server via the cable modem and from there, to the Internet in general. Today, you find that you cannot access your favorite search engine Web page.

ANALYSIS

There are a number of network interfaces that are being used in this case study. The first is the TCP/IP configuration of the Windows 2000 Professional computer that is trying to access the search engine home page. The TCP/IP configuration for this computer will be DHCP-enabled and point to the internal domain hosted by the Windows 2000 Server system. The Ipconfig /all display should show a DHCP enabled connection with the IP address in the range 192.168.0.x (the default address assigned by the server) with a gateway address that points to the Windows 2000 Server computer. In addition, the domain name should be the domain that was set up when the Windows 2000 Server was installed. If any of these values are missing or incorrect, the following commands refresh the configuration:

```
Ipconfig /release
Ipconfig /renew
```

continues

CASE STUDY: HOME OFFICE

continued

The second network interface is on the Windows 2000 Server. This system has two network adapters: one on the inside network and one on the outside. When this system was installed, that distinction was made and Connection Sharing was enabled on the outside connection. The Ipconfig /all display should show two connections: an inside connection that has a static IP address (usually 192.168.0.1) and an outside address that is usually configured as DHCP-supplied. The local cable company would normally supply the outside address when the cable modem became active on its network. As with the Windows 2000 Professional system, the following commands refresh the configuration provided by the cable company (if using automatic TCP/IP configuration):

```
Ipconfig /release
Ipconfig /renew
```

The third network interface is the VPN connection between the Windows 2000 Professional computer and the VPN server in your corporation. That connection is established on the Windows 2000 Professional machine through the gateway server (the gateway server does not need a connection itself). This appears as a new network entry on your Windows 2000 Professional computer with an IP address from your corporate network. In addition, DNS and WINS entries are assigned from your corporate network and they should be displayed by the Ipconfig /all command.

The first thing to try after reviewing all the configurations is pinging your gateway. From the Windows 2000 Professional computer, that would be the Windows 2000 Server system. If that works, try to ping an outside host (such as your search engine home page) from the Windows 2000 Server. If that works, but it does not work from the Windows 2000 Professional computer, the problem is in the Connection Sharing setup. Removing the configuration and reinstalling it on the server will correct any problem.

The next thing to try is tracing the route that packets take to a known outside host (the search engine home page again). From the Windows 2000 Professional computer enter the following command, where <host name> is the search engine hostname:

```
Tracert <host name>
```

Tracert traces the hops (routers) that a packet must take to get to the destination. If it gets to the destination, your problems are solved. If it can't display a router name and shows only IP addresses, the problem is in the DNS servers provided by your cable company. If you get to your corporate network routers (as identified by the IP address ranges) but you don't get from there to the destination, the problem is in your corporate DNS servers or gateway or the configuration provided when you logged in to the VPN server. Logging out and logging back in refreshes this configuration and solves the problem. If the problem persists, the error is likely on your corporate network and a call to tech support is in order.

CHAPTER SUMMARY

This chapter discussed the main topics of implementing, managing, and troubleshooting network protocols and services.

The essence of these topics is to understand the components of networking with emphasis on TCP/IP and the role that each component plays in successfully connecting to a network. In addition, the chapter also highlighted two other points not addressed by the objectives, but which you may be tested on:

◆ Access to IPX/SPX and NetBEUI protocols to access legacy applications

◆ The steps taken to perform name resolution in TCP/IP (primarily to help you analyze the problem occurring when all you have to work with is a null response)

Also covered were the various configurations available for accessing outside networks, including multilink, access to private RAS servers, connections to the Internet, and VPN connections through the Internet to secure servers on your corporate network.

KEY TERMS
- TCP/IP
- IPX/SPX
- NetBEUI
- DNS
- WINS
- DHCP
- VPN
- IPSec
- UNC

APPLY YOUR KNOWLEDGE

Review Questions

1. You have two networks that use the NetBEUI protocol. You connect the two networks with a router, but the computers on the different networks can't connect to one another. What is wrong?

2. You have installed NWLink IPX/SPX Compatible Transport protocol on your computer, but you can't establish a session with the NetWare file server. What other component do you need to install?

3. What command should you use to redirect port LPT1: to a printer named HP5 on a server named PRINTSERVE?

4. When do you need to install a default gateway on a computer configured with TCP/IP?

5. You have a computer configured for IPX and you can't make a connection to a UNIX computer running SLIP. What is the problem?

6. You have an older network adapter card that had drivers only for Windows for Workgroups. Can you use it with Windows 2000 Professional?

7. What are network bindings?

8. How many network adapter cards can you put into a single Windows 2000 Professional computer?

9. You have manually configured a TCP/IP connection with a subnet mask of 255.255.255.252 but find that you can't connect to any other computers on your network. What is the problem?

Review Answers

1. NetBEUI is not normally supported by routers. Either configure your router to support NetBEUI or switch your network protocol to IPX or TCP/IP. See "NetBIOS Extended User Interface (NetBEUI)."

2. NWLink is not sufficient to access file shares and print services on a NetWare server. You must also install CSNW. See "NWLink IPX/SPXs Compatible Transport."

3. Use the command Net Use LPT1:\\PRINTSERVE\HP5. See "The NET USE Command."

4. You need to install a default gateway when your TCP/IP-configured computer needs to communicate with a computer located on a different physical network or subnetwork. See "Default Gateway (Router)."

5. SLIP does not support IPX or NetBEUI. SLIP stands for Serial Line Internet Protocol and supports only encapsulating TCP/IP. See "Serial Line Internet Protocol (SLIP)."

6. Windows 2000 Professional does not support any 16-bit devices. You must use a device driver written to support Windows NT or Windows 2000. See "NDIS-Compatible Network Adapter Card Drivers."

7. Network binding is the association of a network adapter card to a protocol being used. See "NDIS 5.0."

8. Windows 2000 Professional supports an unlimited number of network adapters. The number of network adapter cards that you can install in your computer, however, will be the limiting factor. See "NDIS 5.0."

APPLY YOUR KNOWLEDGE

9. The subnet specified has only two nodes on it. With such a restricted subnet, every address other than the one remaining address on your subnet would be considered remote. The other local address must therefore be a router if you are to communicate with any remote systems at all. This configuration is usually used for router connections; however, it is not very useful when connecting computers. See "Subnet Mask."

ON THE CD

This book's companion CD contains specially designed supplemental material to help you understand how well you know the concepts and skills you learned in this chapter. You'll find related exercises and exam questions and answers. See the file **Chapter06ApplyYourKnowledge.pdf** in the CD's **Chapter06\ApplyYourKnowledge** directory.

Suggested Readings and Resources

1. Lee, Thomas, and Joseph Davies. *Microsoft Windows 2000 TCP/IP Protocol and Services Technical Reference.* Microsoft Press, 2000.

2. Stanek, William R. *Microsoft Windows 2000 Administrator's Pocket Consultant.* Microsoft Press, 2000.

3. Joyce, Jerry, and Marianne Moon. *Microsoft Windows 2000 Professional at a Glance.* Microsoft Press, 2000.

4. *Optimize Network Traffic (Notes from the Field).* Microsoft Press, 2000.

This chapter covers topics associated with Windows 2000 security. It helps you prepare for the exam by addressing the following exam objectives:

Encrypt data on a hard disk by using Encrypting File System (EFS).

▶ Encrypting File System is a new service supported in the Windows 2000 environment. It is important that network administrators understand how EFS can be used to secure file resources. It is also important that administrators understand how encrypted files can be recovered if a user is not available to decrypt the file.

Implement, configure, manage, and troubleshoot local Group Policy.

▶ Group Policy is a very powerful tool built in to Windows 2000. Group Policy gives an administrator the ability to secure a computer's local settings.

Implement, configure, manage, and troubleshoot local user accounts.

- **Implement, configure, manage, and troubleshoot auditing.**

- **Implement, configure, manage, and troubleshoot account settings.**

- **Implement, configure, manage, and troubleshoot account policy.**

- **Create and manage local users and groups.**

- **Implement, configure, manage, and troubleshoot user rights.**

▶ The efficient management of user accounts is critical to the overall management of a network. Administrators must understand the tools that are available to them to manage user accounts in the Windows 2000 environment.

CHAPTER 7

Implementing, Monitoring, and Troubleshooting Security

Implement, configure, manage, and troubleshoot local user authentication.

- **Configure and troubleshoot local user accounts.**

- **Configure and troubleshoot domain user accounts.**

▶ Administrators must be able to distinguish between local and domain-based users. They also must understand how to manage each type of account.

Implement, configure, manage, and troubleshoot a security configuration.

▶ A new tool introduced to the Windows 2000 environment is the security template. Administrators will find that security templates are a powerful feature of Windows 2000 that can make the overall administration of computers in their environment easier.

STUDY STRATEGIES

▶ This chapter presents a number of concepts related to securing your environment. As you read this chapter, it is important that you remember that securing your environment is a process of setting up many different features and services. Each feature/service works in conjunction with the others to provide a secure environment.

▶ As you review the material in this chapter, always try to distinguish whether the topic is related to the workgroup or domain environment.

INTRODUCTION

This chapter provides an overview of Windows 2000 security. The chapter presents a number of different topics that relate to securing your environment. These include user and group management, local Group Policy, local account policy, monitoring security events, Windows 2000 security events, and the Encrypting File System.

USER AND GROUP MANAGEMENT

Implement, configure, manage, and troubleshoot local user authentication.

User accounts are used to represent people in your network environment. A user account contains information about a person who can gain access to your network. Information stored in a user account includes the user's name and password, as well as other information that describes the configuration of the user. Users accounts are used to grant (or deny) access to resources. Through user accounts, you can control how a user gains access to a resource.

Windows 2000 supports two user account models: the workgroup model and the domain model. The following sections provide a brief overview of these models.

The Workgroup Model

Under the workgroup model, each computer in your environment is responsible for the management of its own local account database. Local user accounts contain information that defines users for the local computer. With a local user account, a user can log on to the local computer and gain access to local resources. To gain access to resources on another computer, a user must use an account on the other computer.

The workgroup model is meant for small environments. This model has a very high administrative cost, as user accounts must be managed on each computer in your environment. If you change the password on one computer, you also need to change the password on the remaining computers. The workgroup model is very simple to implement, however, and does not require specialized computers to manage a shared account database. The workgroup model is also useful for temporary environments.

The Domain Model

Under the domain model, a centralized database of user accounts is managed for a grouping (or domain) of computers. Domain user accounts contain information that defines users within the domain.

In Windows 2000, all user account information for the domain is stored in the Active Directory database. Active Directory is stored on a special computer called a domain controller. With a single domain user account, a user can log on to the network and gain access to resources on any computer in the Active Directory environment provided they have the correct permissions. The primary benefit of the domain model is that account management is simplified, as each user in your environment will have only a single user account defined. This model, however, is much more complex to set up, design, and configure.

The basic building blocks of the Active Directory are domains. Active Directory organizes domains into a hierarchical structure, based on Domain Name Service (DNS) naming conventions.

The primary characteristic of an Active Directory tree is that the domain names used fall with a contiguous DNS namespace (for example, a parent/child relationship is created between domains, based on a contiguous namespace). Figure 7.1 shows a sample of an Active Directory tree.

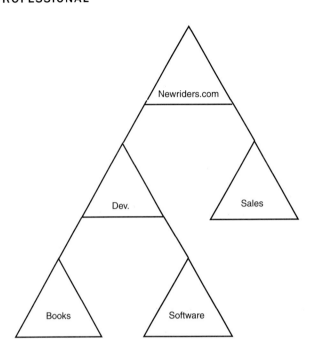

FIGURE 7.1
Sample Active Directory tree.

Active Directory also enables the creation of forests. A *forest* is a collection of domains that do not share a common DNS namespace. Figure 7.2 shows a sample of an Active Directory forest.

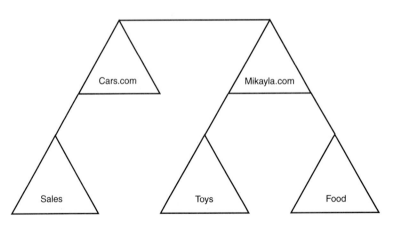

FIGURE 7.2
Sample Active Directory forest.

All domains within an Active Directory tree or forest share the following three things in common:

◆ **Database schema.** The database schema defines the database objects and the attributes that can be stored about each object.

◆ **Two-way transitive trust relationships.** Two-way transitive trusts enable users from any domain to access resources in any other domain.

◆ **A Global Catalog (GC).** The GC is a service that runs on selected domain controllers within the Active Directory forest. The GC contains a partial replica of every object in the forest.

Active Directory is a very powerful tool that can be used to manage your environment. The directory database in Active Directory can be modified to support new classes of objects and attributes. In the future we will see new Active Directory–aware applications (MS Exchange 2000, for example) that can access the data stored in Active Directory. The benefits of this environment are significant, as all data is stored in one secure and manageable location.

Accounts and Security Identifiers

Every account with Windows 2000 that can be assigned permission to a resource is considered a *Security Principal* within Windows 2000. A unique security identifier, or SID, identifies Security Principals on the network. This is a very important concept, as a SID is unique to each Security Principal and will never be modified for the life of the account (unless it is migrated to another domain). In addition, SIDs are never reused when new objects are created. If an account is deleted, all references to the object's SID are removed from the network.

Renaming a user account enables an account to receive a new name and retain its security assignments and group membership (as the SID is not changed). Instead of creating a new user account for the replacement staff members, you can rename the old staff member's account so that the new staff member can use it.

User Accounts

As a network administrator in the Windows 2000 environment, you need to learn the skills required to manage users and groups.

Windows 2000 automatically creates two user accounts, called built-in accounts, when it is installed. The *Administrator account* is the account that is used to manage the configuration of the computer and users stored on the computer. You can rename the Administrator account, but it cannot be deleted. *Guest* is the second built-in account created when Windows 2000 is installed. The Guest account can be used to grant occasional users access to resources. The Guest account is disabled by default.

Regardless of whether you are managing a workgroup or domain environment, you need to plan for user accounts. Details to consider include the following:

◆ **Naming conventions.** Domain user accounts must be unique to the domain. Local user accounts must be unique to the local machine. You must develop a naming convention that will accommodate duplicate employee names. Logon names can contain up to 20 characters of uppercase or lowercase characters. Windows recognizes any alphanumeric character except for "/ \ [ ] ; : || = . + * ? < >.

◆ **Secure passwords.** All local and domain user accounts should have a password assigned. You must determine whether the Administrator or the users will control password changes. A policy should be established that defines password standards. For example, password rules can be set that passwords must include combinations of uppercase letters, lowercase letters, numbers, and punctuation.

Creating Local User Accounts

Local user accounts are typically associated with the workgroup model previously discussed. Local user accounts can be used to access the computer on which the account physically resides and resources on the local machine. Local user accounts are limited to local resources.

NOTE

Users and Passwords Applet If you are working with Windows 2000 Professional systems configured as part of a workgroup, you also can use the Users and Passwords applet to create user accounts. The applet is found under Control Panel.

Local user accounts are managed from the Computer Management Microsoft Console (MMC) snap-in. Step by Step 7.1 demonstrates how to view the Computer Management snap-in from a custom MMC and how to create a new local user account.

ON THE CD

Step by Step 7.1, "Creating Local User Accounts by Using the Computer Management Snap-in," demonstrates how to view the Computer Management snap-in from a custom MMC and how to create a new local user account. See the file **Chapter07-01StepbyStep.pdf** in the CD's **Chapter07\StepbyStep** directory.

Every user in your environment should have his or her own user account. For security reasons, users should not share user accounts. You also should ensure that users protect their passwords. Users need to understand that passwords protect their identities on the network. If system administrators cannot rely on users to protect their passwords, many audit and security functions on the network are defeated.

In some special instances, groups of users might share user accounts. For example, your company might have a large team of users acting as order desk representatives who require the same access to network resources. If users do share the same account, you should ensure that the User Cannot Change Password option is set for the account. This limits an individual's ability to change the password and lock out all other users.

Network administrators also should ensure that users change their passwords often. This can be accomplished through group and local policies. Again, it is important that users understand the importance of their passwords.

After the user account is created, you might need to manage the account. Common management tasks performed from the Computer Management snap-in include the following:

◆ **Resetting passwords.** Passwords can be reset for a user account by right-clicking the user account and selecting Set Password from the secondary menu.

NOTE **User Accounts and Windows 2000 Server**   You will find that user accounts created on a Windows 2000 domain controller will not be able to log on locally at the domain controller by default. Users need the user right called Log on Locally to enable them to log on to a system from the console.

◆ **Renaming accounts.** Accounts can be renamed so that group memberships and security assignments remain. This is done by right-clicking the user account and selecting Rename from the secondary menu.

◆ **Deleting accounts.** Deleting a user account will permanently remove the account from the system. An account is deleted by right-clicking the user account and selecting Delete from the secondary menu.

◆ **Enabling accounts.** If an account has been previously disabled, you can enable the account by double-clicking the user account and clearing the Account Is Disabled check box from the user account property pages.

◆ **Unlocking accounts.** If an account is locked due to incorrect password entry, the Account is Locked Out check box can be cleared to unlock the user account. Always verify that it was the user supplying the incorrect passwords, in case an attacker is attempting to compromise an account.

◆ **Changing group membership.** Groups are used to simplify resource access (groups will be discussed in greater detail later in this chapter). The Member Of tab enables you to manage the group membership of a user account. From this tab, you can click the Add or Remove buttons to modify group membership.

◆ **Modifying profile paths.** The user profile path is used to configure roaming profiles. This allows a user to logon at multiple computers and maintain a single desktop and user settings preferences.

◆ **Modifying user home directory paths.** The user's home directory is used to store personal data that only the user can access on the network. When setting up a user's home directory you can use the UNC path \\servername\sharename\ %username%, where %username% will be replaced with the user's account name.

Creating Domain User Accounts

Domain user accounts are very similar to local user accounts. The primary difference between a local user account and a domain user account is that a domain account can be used to gain access to resources throughout a domain or within an Active Directory environment.

Domain user accounts are created and managed through the Active Directory User and Computers snap-in of the MMC. Step by Step 7.2 demonstrates how to view the Active Directory Users and Computers snap-in from a custom MMC and create a new domain user account.

ON THE CD

Step by Step 7.2, "Creating Domain User Accounts by Using the Active Directory Users and Computers Snap-in," demonstrates how to view the Active Directory Users and Computers snap-in from a custom MMC and create a new domain user account. See the file **Chapter07-02StepbyStep.pdf** in the CD's **Chapter07\StepbyStep** directory.

Managing a domain account in Active Directory Users and Computers is similar to managing local account in Computer Management. The only difference is the actual tabs where the changes are implemented when using Active Directory Users and Computers (see Figure 7.3). A list of each of the tabs follows:

◆ **General.** Contains the user's name, description, office location, telephone number, email address, web page, and telephone number(s).

◆ **Address.** Contains the user's street address, post office box, city, state, postal code, and country.

◆ **Account.** Manage a user's logon name, password settings, the hours during which the user can log on, the computers from which the user can log on, and an expiration date if the user account is for a temporary employee.

◆ **Profile.** Enables you to configure the user profile path, logon script, and home folder location.

◆ **Telephones.** Contains telephone numbers (home, office, pager, and so on).

◆ **Organization.** Contains the user's title, department, company, manager, and direct reports.

NOTE **Administration Snap-ins** Many administration snap-ins are available only if you install the services that they manage. To manage domain user accounts from a Windows 2000 Professional system, you need to install the Windows 2000 administration pack. This is found in the i386 directory of the Windows 2000 Server CD in the file named ADMINPAK.MSI.

NOTE **Logon Hours** A security policy can be configured to automatically log users off when logon hours expire. This option is set through a local or group policy.

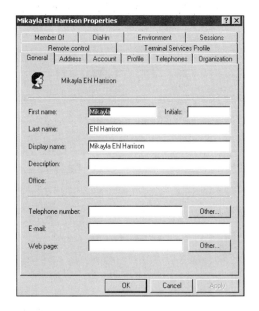

FIGURE 7.3
Domain user account Properties dialog box.

◆ **Remote Control.** If Terminal Services are installed, you can enable whether a user must agree to remote control of the Terminal Services session or automatic control can be performed, and whether the user is notified that their session is being remote controlled.

◆ **Terminal Services Profile.** If Terminal Services are installed, you can enable an account for Terminal Services and configure separate profile and home directories when connected to Terminal Services.

◆ **Member Of.** Enables you to manage the group membership of a user account.

◆ **Dial-in.** Enables you to control how the remote access privilege is granted to a user, set call-back options for security, and set dial-up options such as caller-ID, static IP address requests, and IP routing information.

◆ **Environment.** If Terminal Services are installed, you can configure an alternate shell program and set whether a Terminal Services user can use local drives and printers during a Terminal Services session.

◆ **Sessions.** If Terminal Services are installed, you can set defaults for sessions. This includes session timeout values, limits for the number of simultaneous sessions, and whether you can reconnect to a session from a different client computer.

Groups

Groups are used to simplify the overall management of accounts in your environment. In most environments, users can be grouped into categories of user accounts (accountants, sales people, and so on). These categories of user accounts generally define common access needs for groups of users in your environment. To assist in the management of access needs for these users, Windows 2000 supports the creation of groups within its account database. Group objects can then be granted access to resources. Being a member of a group automatically grants you the same rights as the group object. If you have memberships in multiple groups, the rights associated with each group will be combined (how your effective rights are calculated depends on the type of rights being combined). Depending on the type of group, you can also make one group a member of another group.

Group Types

In the Windows 2000 domain environment, different types of groups are supported. The group type determines the tasks that you manage with the group.

The first group type is called a security group. Security groups are used to organize user accounts so that the group of users can be given permission to the resource.

The second group type is called a distribution group. Distribution groups are used to organize users into groups for non-security related purposes. For example, if a group of users needs to have email messages sent to them, a distribution group is appropriate.

The main difference between a security group and a distribution group is that membership in a distribution group is not added to a user's access token when he or she logs on to the network. The goal of distribution groups is to make the logon token of users as small (and efficient) as possible.

Distribution groups do not exist on a member server or workstations. Groups created on these machines are security groups by default.

Group Scope

The scope of a group controls where a group can be used within your environment. Specifically group scope defines the following characteristics of a group:

◆ The domains in which you can use the group to grant permissions

◆ The domains from which you can add members to the group

◆ The domains in which you can nest the groups within other groups

NOTE

Groups in Mixed Mode Versus Native Mode Active Directory domains can be configured to support a mixed mode or native mode. In mixed mode, domains can emulate a Windows NT environment so you can synchronize the directory database with legacy Windows NT Backup domain controllers. Native-mode domains support only Windows 2000–based domain controls. In native mode, however, Windows 2000 supports new groups (domain local and universal groups) and supports greater nesting of groups. The following section assumes that you are working in a Windows 2000 domain environment configured in native mode.

Global Groups

Global groups are used to organize users who share similar network access requirements. The characteristics of global groups include the following:

- Global groups can be used in any domain in the forest.

- Global groups can contain only user accounts and global groups from the domain in which you create the global group.

- You can add global groups to another global group within the same domain or to universal groups and domain local groups in the same domain or other domains.

Domain Local Groups

Domain local groups are used to assign permissions to resources in Discretionary Access Control Lists (DACLs). The characteristics of Domain Local groups include the following:

- Domain local groups are used to assign permissions to gain access to resources that are located in the same domain in which you create the domain local group.

- Domain local groups can contain user accounts, universal groups, and global groups, from any domain.

- Domain local groups can be nested in other domain local groups in the same domain.

- Domain local groups can be used on any Windows 2000–based computer that is a member of the domain where the domain local group is defined.

NOTE

Use Domain Local Groups in a Domain Environment Microsoft does not recommend using local groups if you are in a domain environment. You should use Domain local groups instead. Domain local groups enable centralized management of the group (for example, its membership); therefore, you should limit the use of local groups to systems in a workgroup environment.

Local Groups

Local groups are defined on Windows 2000 Professional computers and Windows 2000 Server computers that are not domain controllers. They have the same properties as domain local groups with one major exception—local groups can only be used at the computer where the local group is defined. They must be defined at multiple computers if they are required for use at multiple computers.

Universal Groups

Universal groups are used to assign permissions to resources in multiple domains, rather than define domain local groups in each domain where the group is required. The characteristics of universal groups include the following:

◆ Universal groups can be used within any native-mode domain in the forest.

◆ Universal groups can contain user accounts, universal groups, and global groups from any domain in the forest.

◆ Universal groups can be members of any domain local group or universal group in the forest.

◆ The membership of a universal group is maintained in the domain where the universal group is created and in the global catalog.

NOTE   **Changing Groups**   After you create your groups, you can convert them if necessary. The trick to converting groups is to evaluate whether the target group you want to convert to supports the current members of your group. To convert a group's type, you need to access the properties of the group and change the type from the General tab.

Implementation Strategies

When determining your approach to groups, the following strategy will simplify things:

1. Organize users based on administrative needs, such as job responsibilities. Create a global group for each grouping of users. Add the users to the appropriate global group(s).

2. Identify the resources to which users need to gain access. Create a domain local group for each resource. Assign the appropriate permission to each domain local group.

3. Make all global groups that require access to a resource a member of the appropriate domain local group.

4. If a resource is spread over a number of domains, consider using a universal group. Follow steps 1 through 3, but instead of making the global group a member of the domain local group, make it a member of a universal group. Then make the universal group a member of the domain local groups with permission to the resources.

EXAM TIP

Remember the AGDLP Strategy for Groups Expect questions regarding the use of groups in the Windows 2000 environment.

NOTE

Universal Group Membership Do not make users members of a universal group directly. Membership in universal groups is tracked in the Active Directory global catalog server(s). Assigning membership directly to users can generate excess Active Directory replication traffic.

Microsoft uses the abbreviation A-G-DL-P to describe the Windows 2000 group strategy. The abbreviation stands for accounts (A) should be organized into global (G) groups, global groups are placed in domain local (DL) groups, and domain local groups are given permission (P) to resources.

Creating Local Groups

Local groups are managed from the Computer Management Microsoft Management Console (MMC) snap-in.

ON THE CD

Step by Step 7.3, "Creating Local Groups by Using the Computer Management Snap-in," demonstrates how to view the Computer Management snap-in from a custom MMC and create a new local group. See the file **Chapter07-03StepbyStep.pdf** in the CD's **Chapter07\StepbyStep** directory.

You can rename and delete a group by right-clicking it and selecting the appropriate option from the secondary menu. If you rename a group, the name of the group is changed and the security assignments (such as the permissions assigned to it) will be retained. If you delete a group, all references to it will be deleted and its security assignments will be lost (the objects that represent the members of the group will not be deleted).

Creating Domain Local, Global, and Universal Groups

Domain groups are very similar to local groups. The primary difference between a local group and a domain group is that a domain group can be used to gain access to resources throughout a domain environment.

Domain groups are created and managed through the Active Directory User and Computers snap-in of the MMC. Step by Step 7.4 demonstrates how to view the Active Directory Users and Computers snap-in and create a new domain group account.

Step by Step 7.4, "Creating Group Account by Using the Active Directory Users and Computers Snap-in," illustrates how to view the Active Directory Users and Computers snap-in. See the file **Chapter07-04StepbyStep.pdf** in the CD's **Chapter07\StepbyStep** directory.

To manage groups after they have been created, right-click the group and select Properties from the secondary menu. From the Members and Member Of tabs, you can manage who is a member of the group and what groups the group is a member of.

As with local groups, renaming a group retains its security assignments on the network, while deleting a group results in the group being removed from all DACLs.

Built-in Groups

Windows 2000 has a number of built-in groups. These groups provide a powerful tool for the management of resources on the local system/domain. Membership in one (or more) of these groups gives users rights to access (and manage) the local operating system, depending on the group. Each group is, by default, assigned a useful collection of rights and privileges.

User rights are rules that determine the actions a user can perform on a computer (user rights are discussed in detail in later sections). In addition, user rights control whether a user can log on to a computer directly (locally) or over the network, add users to local groups, delete users, and so on. Built-in groups have sets of user rights already assigned. Users who are subsequently added to a group are automatically granted all user rights assigned to the group account. User rights are managed by using Group Policy.

To gain an understanding of how groups and user rights relate, the following section provides a review of the privileges that have been assigned to each built-in group. We will then look at where the built-in groups receive their default configuration.

Built-in Local Groups

Built-in local groups are used to manage Windows 2000 Professional workstation and Windows 2000 Servers (configured as a member server). The built-in local groups added during installation are as follows:

◆ **Administrators.** Membership in the Administrators groups enables a user to manage all aspects of the local operating system. Administrator access to the system should be limited to individuals who perform the following types of tasks:

   • Install the operating system and components such as hardware drivers, system services, and so on

   • Install service packs and Windows packs

   • Upgrade the operating system

   • Repair the operating system

   • Configure critical operating system parameters such as password policy, access control, audit policy, kernel-mode driver configuration, and so on

◆ **Backup Operators.** Members of this group can back up and restore all files on a hard drive, regardless of permissions, ownership, encryption settings, or audit settings.

◆ **Guests.** The Guests group is used to give someone limited access to resources on the system. The Guest account is automatically added to this group. The Guest account can be removed from the Guests group if you want.

◆ **Power Users.** Members of the Power Users group have more permission than members of the Users group and less permission than members of the Administrators group. For example, a member of the Power Users group can create a new user account, but cannot modify the membership of the Administrators group.

Members of the Power Users group can perform the following tasks:

   • Install and remove applications that can be run by all users (except for the software that can be removed only by an administrator)

NOTE

Two Additional Guest Accounts Two additional Guest accounts are added if you have installed the Internet Information Server (IIS) on your system (ISUR_computername and IWAM_computername). These accounts are used to support anonymous access to the IIS content.

- Customize system-wide resources including printers, date/time, power options, and other Control Panel resources

- Share resources on the local system

◆ **Replicator.** The Replicator group is a group used by Windows NT 4.0 backup domain controllers when they replicate the NETLOGON share from the Windows 2000 Primary domain controller emulator in a mixed-mode domain.

◆ **Users.** The Users group provides the user with all of the necessary rights to run the computer as an end user. By default, all users (with the exception of the built-in Administrator and Guest accounts) created on the local system are made members of the Users group. Members of the Users group are only able to access files that they have permission to use. For this reason, users are not able to see one another's files and folders.

Built-in Domain Local Groups

Built-in domain local groups are used to provide users with rights and permissions to perform tasks on domain controllers in a domain environment. The built-in local groups added during installation are as follows:

◆ **Account Operators.** Members of the Account Operators group can create, delete, and modify user accounts and groups. Members cannot modify the Administrators group, Server Operators, Printer Operators, or Account Operators groups.

◆ **Server Operators.** Members of the Server Operators group can manage disk resources, back up and restore file system resources, manage file system resources, and manage system services and software.

◆ **Print Operators.** Members of the Print Operators group can manage print resources. Members of this group also have the ability to add and remove printers.

◆ **Administrators.** Provides the same rights as the Backup Operators on Windows 2000 Professional computer, but on a domain level.

◆ **Backup Operators.** Provides the same rights as the Backup Operators on Windows 2000 Professional computer, but on a domain level.

◆ **Replicator.** Provides the same rights as the Backup Operators on Windows 2000 Professional computer, but on a domain level.

◆ **Pre-Windows 2000 Compatible Access.** Windows 2000 does not enable accounts logged on with anonymous access to view group membership, whereas Windows NT 4.0 did enable such operations. For compatibility reasons, you might want to add the Everyone group to the Pre-Windows 2000 Compatible Access group to support legacy Windows NT resources in your environment. By adding the Everyone group to this group, you weaken the Windows 2000 security configuration, so legacy Windows NT resources can view group information before users are authenticated.

◆ **Guests.** Provides the same rights as the Backup Operators on Windows 2000 Professional computer, but on a domain level.

◆ **Users.** Provides the same rights as the Backup Operators on Windows 2000 Professional computer, but on a domain level.

N O T E

Pre-Windows 2000 Compatible Access The Active Directory Installation Wizard offers you the opportunity to weaken dial-in permissions during install. Selecting this option will add the Everyone group to the Pre-Windows 2000 Compatible Access group.

Built-in Global Groups

Built-in global groups are used to provide users with rights and permissions to perform tasks on domain controllers in the domain environment. By default, Windows 2000 automatically adds members to some built-in global groups. This enables Windows 2000 to control the default administrative structure used to manage the Windows 2000 environment. Membership in these groups should be managed very carefully.

Four built-in Global groups added during installation are as follows:

◆ **Domain Users.** Windows 2000 automatically adds the Domain Users global group to the Users domain local group. Windows 2000 also adds each newly created domain user account to the domain users group when they are created. The Administrator account is the default member of this global group.

◆ **Domain Admins.** Windows 2000 automatically adds the Domain Admins global group to the Administrators domain local group so that the domain administrator can manage all local systems in the domain. This group is also added to the local Administrators group of all computers that are part of the domain. This gives the Domain Admins the capability to manage systems anywhere in the domain.

◆ **Domain Guests.** Windows 2000 automatically adds the Domain Guests global group to the Guests domain local group. By default, the Guest account is a member.

◆ **Enterprise Admins.** You can add user accounts to the Enterprise Admin global group that requires administrator control over the entire network. Windows 2000 automatically adds the Enterprise Admin group to the Domain Admin global group for all domains in the enterprise. The Enterprise Admins group is converted to a universal group when the forest root domain is converted to native mode.

> **NOTE**
>
> **Built-in Global Groups** There are a number of additional built-in global groups in the Windows 2000 environment (for example, Cert Publishers, DnsAdmins, DnsUpdateProxy, Domain Computers, Domain Controllers, Schema Administrators, RAS, and IAS Servers). Each of these groups is used to manage access to a specific set of services and are beyond the scope of this book.

Special Groups

Windows 2000 supports a number of built-in groups that can be used for a variety of purposes. You cannot change the membership of these groups; the assignment happens as an internal part of Windows 2000.

◆ **Everyone.** Includes all current network users, including guests and users from other domains. Any user that connects to your network is a member of the Everyone group.

◆ **Authenticated Users.** Includes all users with valid user accounts on the computer or Active Directory. Use the Authenticated User group instead of the Everyone group to prevent anonymous access to a resource.

◆ **Creator Owner.** Represent the user account that either created or took ownership of a resource.

◆ **Interactive.** Includes all users currently logged on locally at a particular computer. This group is used to restrict resource access to users physically logged on at a computer.

> **WARNING**
>
> **Use Authenticated Users When Granting Permissions** The default permissions used in Windows 2000 are that the Everyone group is given Full Control to resources. This assignment should be changed to the Authenticated Users group as soon as resources are created.

◆ **Network.** Includes users currently accessing a given resource over the network (as opposed to users who access a resource by logging on locally to the computer on which the resource resides). Whenever users access a given resource over the network, Windows 2000 automatically adds them to the Network group.

User Rights

In the previous section, you read about the rights that each of the built-in groups has on a Windows 2000 Professional computer. These groups receive their rights from a set of local user rights. Local user rights can be modified if necessary.

You can view the current configuration of your system's local user rights from the Microsoft Management Console snap-in called Local Computer Policy.

ON THE CD

Step by Step 7.5, "Viewing the Local Computer Policy Settings," provides details on how to view the Local Computer Policy settings. See the file **Chapter07-05StepbyStep.pdf** in the CD's **Chapter07\ StepbyStep** directory.

WARNING

Windows 2000 Server Versus Professional By default, the Users and Guests groups have the capability to log on to Windows 2000 Professional and Windows 2000 Server (configured as standalone or member servers). This could be a potential security risk, as anyone with a valid user account can log on to your server(s).

To see the rights assignments for each policy, double-click the policy. Table 7.1 provides a description of the most commonly used default user rights assigned to the built-in Windows 2000 groups on Windows 2000 Professional (see Figure 7.4).

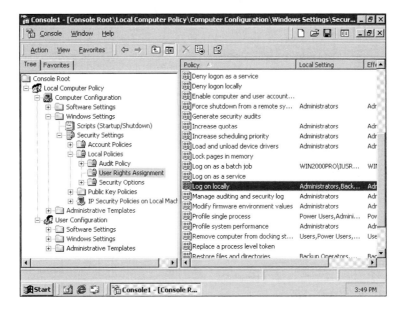

FIGURE 7.4
Viewing a specific user right.

When determining what group to add a particular user account to, remember the default assignments. If a group exists that has the rights required by a user, add them to that group. If a group does not exist with the appropriate privileges, create a new one. Be careful when assigning group membership; do not use groups with too many rights, and only give users the rights they need to get the job done (no more, no less).

TABLE 7.1

WINDOWS 2000 PROFESSIONAL USER RIGHTS

User Right	Description	Granted To
Access this computer from the network	Having this user right enables you to access resources from the computer over the network (for example, attach to a network share being hosted from computer). Having this right does not give you the ability to access resources that your user account has not been given permission to use.	Everyone, User, Power Users, Backup Operators, Administrators
Back up files and directories	This user right enables users to back up file system resources regardless of permissions held by the user. Most users can only back up files that they have permission to use or own. This does not lend itself to the centralized management of backups.	Backup Operators, Administrator
Bypass traverse checking	This right enables a user to access a file resource deep in a directory structure even if the user does not have permission to the file's parent directory.	Everyone, User, Power Users, Backup Operators, Administrators
Change the system time	This user right enables a user to change system time.	Power Users, Administrators
Create a pagefile	The user right enables a user to configure the virtual memory management of a system.	Administrators
Deny access to this computer from the network	This user right (or lack of a right, in this case) restricts a user from accessing this computer over the network regardless of group membership. For example, the Joe user account has been granted the right to access this computer from the network through his membership in the Users group. If we wanted to override Joe's ability to access this computer from the network, we could explicitly restrict Joe from doing so by granting him this user right.	
Deny logon locally	This user right explicitly restricts a user from logging on to a system from the local console.	
Force shutdown from a remote system	This user right enables a user to remotely shut down a system by using a remote shutdown utility. (You can find the shutdown utility in the Windows 2000 Resource Kit.)	Administrators

User Right	*Description*	*Granted To*
Increase quotas	This user right enables users to modify quota settings for NTFS formatted partitions.	Administrators
Increase scheduling priority	This user right enables you to reschedule jobs that have been submitted to the scheduling service.	Administrators
Load and unload drivers	This user right enables you to load and unload device drivers.	Administrators
Log on locally	This user right enables you to log on at the computer from the local computer console.	Guest, Users, Power Users, Backup Operators, Administrators
Manage auditing and security	This user right enables a user to specify what type of resource access will be audited.	Administrators
Remove computer from docking station	This user right enables a user to undock a laptop from its docking station.	Users, Power Users, Administrators
Restore files and directories	This user right enables users to restore a backup of a file system of permissions held by the user.	Backup Operators, Administrators
Shut down the system	This user right enables a user to shut down the local system.	Users, Power Users, Backup Operators, Administrators
Take ownership of files of other objects	This user right enables a user to take ownership of files, directories, printers, and other objects on the computer. This right supersedes permissions protecting objects.	Administrators

Windows 2000 also has built-in user capabilities. You cannot modify these built-in rights. The only way to give a user one of these rights is to put that user in a group that has the capability. If you want to give a user rights to create and manage user accounts, for example, you must put that user into either the Power Users or Administrators groups.

Table 7.2 lists the built-in capabilities on a Windows 2000 Professional computer.

TABLE 7.2

WINDOWS 2000 BUILT-IN USER CAPABILITIES

Right	Admin	Power Users	Users	Guests	Everyone	Backup Operators
Create and manage user accounts	X	X				
Create and manage Local groups	X	X				
Lock the workstation	X	X	X	X	X	X
Override the lock of a workstation	X					
Format a hard drive	X					
Share and stop sharing directories	X	X				
Share and stop sharing printers	X	X				

LOCAL GROUP POLICY

Implement, configure, manage, and troubleshoot local Group Policy.

After you develop an effective user and group management strategy, you need to consider the management of the computers in your environment. Specifically we are concerned with how a user (or group of users) can interact with the computer (for example, reconfigure the computer).

Group Policy is a new set of technologies included with the Windows 2000 products. Group Policy is primarily used to manage the user and computer environment through Active Directory. A complete discussion of Group Policy is beyond the scope of this book, but we will look at local Group Policy and how it relates to Windows 2000 Professional.

Each computer running Windows 2000 has a local Group Policy object associated with it. Using this object, Group Policy settings can be stored on individual computers whether or not they are part of an Active Directory environment or a networked environment.

Local Group Policy objects enable you to control the following components:

♦ **Administrative templates.** Registry-based settings that control access to various system settings

♦ **Software settings.** Enables software to be assigned to users and computers so that it is available to users when they need it

♦ **Security settings.** Security settings for computers and users

♦ **Scripts.** User Logon/Logoff, Computer Startup/Shutdown scripts

♦ **Folder redirection.** Enables data directories (usually part of a user's profile) to be placed on networked drives instead of the local computer

> N O T E
>
> **Local Policy Versus Domain-Level Group Policy** Because Group Policy objects associated with sites, domains, or organizational units can overwrite its settings, the local Group Policy object is the least influential one in an Active Directory environment. This discussion focuses on using local policy in a workgroup environment.

LOCAL ACCOUNT POLICY

Implement, configure, manage, and troubleshoot local user accounts.

Account policies give administrators the ability to control how user passwords and lockouts are configured.

The following section provides details on password policy settings and account lockout policy settings.

Password Policies

Password policies enable you to manage the properties of a user's password. These properties include the following:

♦ **Enforce Password History.** Indicates how many previous unique passwords a user must use before he can reuse a previous password. Windows 2000 can track the history for your previous 24 passwords.

♦ **Maximum Password Age.** Specifies the maximum age of a user password. Users are forced to change their password when the maximum age is set. The maximum value you can enter is 999 days.

◆ **Minimum Password Age.** Specifies the minimum age of a user password. Users are not allowed to change their passwords unless the minimum password age has passed.

◆ **Minimum Password Length.** Specifies the minimum length for a user's password. The value can be set between 0 and 14 characters.

◆ **Password Must Meet Complexity Requirements.** This requires users to use passwords that are at least six characters long and contain three of the following four classes: uppercase letters (A, B, C), lowercase letters (a,b,c), numbers (1,2,3), and punctuation symbols (%,^,&). Additionally, passwords may not contain the user's user account name or any part of the user's full name.

◆ **Store Password Using Reversible Encryption.** Stores user passwords in encrypted, clear-text format. This setting is used to support digest authentication for Web sites.

◆ **User Must Log On to Change Password.** Specifies that users must be logged on to the system to change their passwords. If users let their passwords expire, they will not be able to log on and will need the assistance of an administrator to reset their passwords.

Account Lockout Policy

Account Lockout policy determines how the system should react when a user account experiences a series of failed user logon attempts for a specific user account. You should ensure that you use Account Lockout policy settings appropriately for your environment. You should ensure that you are using the auditing functions of Windows 2000 to detect invalid logon attempts. Account lockouts will go unnoticed in many environments in which the user account is enabled after the account lockout duration has passed. The following Account Lockout policy settings can be applied:

◆ **Account Lockout Duration.** Sets the duration that an account is locked out for. Can be set between 1 and 99,999 minutes.

◆ **Account Lockout Threshold.** Specifies the number of times you can use an incorrect password before your account lockout is triggered. This setting can be configured between 1 and 999 invalid logon attempts.

◆ **Reset Account Lockout Counter After.** Specifies the number of minutes between resets of the account lockout counter. This setting can be configured between 1 and 99,999 minutes.

MONITORING SECURITY EVENTS

As a network administrator, you might find that monitoring the activities of users, Windows 2000 system events, and application events is a powerful method of ensuring that your systems are secure and running properly. Windows 2000 enables you to monitor most events on a system. Events are user actions that are recorded, based on an audit policy, other significant occurrences in Windows 2000, or an application running on the system. Administrators need to monitor these events to track security, system performance, and application errors.

Events are recorded in event logs. You can view and analyze event logs to determine whether or not security breaches are occurring or system services are failing or to determine the nature of application errors. This section provides an overview of the Event Viewer, audit policies, the security log, categories of security events, object access events, and analyzing security events.

Event Logs and the Event Viewer

The Event Viewer is a tool that enables you to view three different logs that are stored by Windows 2000. The Event Viewer can be used to view the following logs:

◆ **System log.** The system log contains events logged by the Windows 2000 system components, such as drivers or other system components that failed to load during startup. Windows 2000 predetermines the event types logged by system components.

◆ **Application log.** The application log contains events logged by applications or programs. For example, a database program might record a file error in the application log. The program developer decides which events to record. Many Windows 2000 services (such as DHCP, File Replication Services, and so on) use the application log.

◆ **Security log.** The security log, if configured to do so, records security events, such as valid and invalid logon attempts. Events that are related to resource use such as creating, opening, or deleting files also can be logged. An administrator can specify what events are recorded in the security log policy.

ON THE CD

Step by Step 7.6, "Adding the Computer Management Snap-in to the Microsoft Management Console," shows you how to add the snap-in associated with the Event Viewer. See the file **Chapter07-06StepbyStep.pdf** in the CD's **Chapter07\StepbyStep** directory.

By selecting the log type in the node pane (the left pane) of the MMC, the corresponding log data is displayed in the results pane (the right pane). Figure 7.5 shows the system log being displayed.

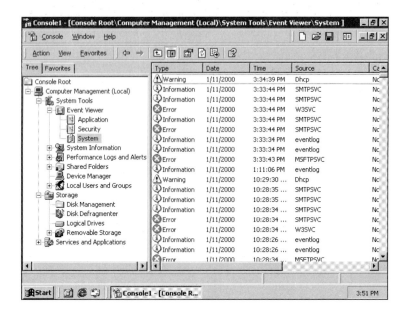

FIGURE 7.5
The Microsoft Windows 2000 Event Viewer.

The data being displayed can be sorted by selecting a column heading. You also have the ability to filter the results log entries being presented as shown in Figure 7.6.

You also can set the columns of data being presented by selecting Choose Columns from the View menu. This option includes the following:

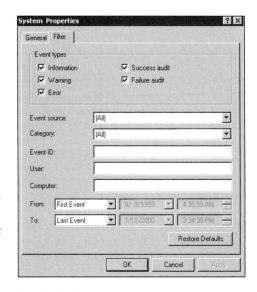

FIGURE 7.6
Microsoft Windows 2000 Event Viewer filter options.

◆ **Type.** The event viewer can track five types of events: Errors, Warnings, Information, Successes, and Failures. Errors show a significant problem such as a service failure. Warnings indicate an event that could cause problems in the future, such as when disk space is low on a local drive. Information events describe a successful operation, such as the event log starting during the boot sequence. Success audit events, only available in the security log, indicate that the audited event occurred successfully, such as successfully logging on to a computer. Failure audits indicate that the audited event failed, such as a user logging on with the incorrect password.

◆ **Date.** The date of the event.

◆ **Time.** The time at which the event occurred.

◆ **Source.** The source (typically a service or process) that reported the event to the Event Viewer.

◆ **Category.** The subsystem that reported the event. For example, any events related to disk quotas would be reported in the application log as a "Disk" category event.

◆ **Event ID.** A numeric code that can be used to obtain information from Microsoft regarding the event being logged. You can search Microsoft's Web site for the Event ID or Microsoft TechNet for details on each code.

◆ **User.** The user account associated with the event.

◆ **Computer.** The computer at which the event occurred.

Audit Policies

An *audit policy* defines the categories of user activities that Windows 2000 records in the security logs on each computer. Audit policies are set up to track authorized and unauthorized access to resources.

By default, auditing is not enabled. Before your organization enables auditing, you must define exactly what needs to be audited and why you want it to be audited. Auditing can slow down system performance.

Categories of Security Events

Security events are divided into categories. This enables the system administrator to configure audit policies to specific categories of events (based on your organization's auditing and security plan). When viewing the event logs, you can search for specific categories of events. The categories of security events that can be audited include the following:

◆ **Account logon.** Logs an event each time a user succeeds or fails in an attempt to log on. Specific events logged include logon failures for unknown user accounts, time restriction violations, user account has expired, user does not have the right to log on locally, account password has expired, and account is locked out.

◆ **Logon events.** Logs an event for logon events that are occurring over the network or generated by service startup.

◆ **Account management.** Logs an event each time an account is managed. This is a useful function if you are concerned about changes being made to user accounts in your environment.

◆ **Directory service.** Logs an event each time an event occurs within the Active Directory services—for example, successful or failed replication events.

◆ **Policy change.** Logs an event each time a policy is successfully or unsuccessfully changed in your environment.

◆ **Process tracking.** Logs an event for each program or process that a user launches while accessing a system. Administrators can use this information to track the details of a user's activities while accessing a system.

◆ **Object access.** Logs an event each time a user attempts to access a resource (such as a printer, folder on an NTFS partition, and so on). These events provide a very effective way of monitoring access to sensitive data on your network.

◆ **Privilege use.** Logs an event each time a user attempts, successfully or unsuccessfully, to use special privileges, such as changing system time. These events enable you to closely monitor the activities of the administrators in your environment.

◆ **System event.** Logs a designated system event such as when a user restarts or shuts down a computer.

Auditing can be enabled for either success or failure of specific events. You need to decide what you want to use your log information for; to determine whether logging successes or failures is most appropriate. For example, if you decide to audit account logons, you need to look at what the information will be used for. Your network security group will most likely be interested in logging failed logon events. (It can provide signs that someone is trying to log on with an account for which he or she does not have a correct password.) This same security group also might be interested in logging successful logons to determine whether users are accessing workstations in areas of the network that they should not be using.

Audit policies can be defined through Group Policy (either at the domain or computer level). Enabling auditing for Account Logon, Privilege Use, or System Events will automatically enable auditing of those events. Auditing of Object Access requires levels of configuration. The following section will review the configuration of Object Access audit policies.

An audit policy can be configured to monitor access to objects such as files and folders, printers, and other objects. The audit policy defines what events will be entered in the event log. Table 7.3 presents a listing of the objects that can be audited and the type of events that can be audited for each.

TABLE 7.3	
AUDITING OBJECT ACCESS	
Object	*Activities That Can Be Audited*
File and folders (files and folders can be audited only in an NTFS partition)	Displaying the contents of a file or folder
	Changing the contents of a file or folder
	Adding data to a file
	Deleting a file or folder in a folder
	Changing permissions for a file or folder
Printers	Changing printer settings, pausing a printer, sharing a printer, or removing a printer
	Changing job settings; pausing, restarting, or deleting documents
	Changing printer properties
Objects in the Active Directory	Viewing audited objects
	Creating objects within an audited container
	Deleting objects within an audited container (or an audited object)
	Changing the permissions for the audited object

Setting Up Auditing

Setting up auditing is a two-step process. Step 1 involves enabling auditing for the local policy of the computer (or domain). Step 2 requires you to configure auditing for each resource that you want to monitor.

To enable auditing for the local security policy, you need to access the computer's local policy.

ON THE CD

Step by Step 7.7, "Enabling Auditing for a Computer," provides details for enabling object auditing. See the file **Chapter07-07StepbyStep.pdf** in the CD's **Chapter07\StepbyStep** directory.

Windows 2000 Security Configurations

Implement, configure, manage, and troubleshoot a security configuration.

Windows 2000 supports the management of computers through security templates. Security templates are provided for common security scenarios. These can be assigned directly to a computer as is or modified to suit unique security requirements.

The predefined security templates are as follows:

- ◆ Default workstation (DEFLTWK.INF)
- ◆ Default server (DEFLTSV.INF)
- ◆ Default domain controller (DEFLTDC.INF)
- ◆ Basic workstation (BASICWK.INF)
- ◆ Basic server (BASICSV.INF)
- ◆ Basic domain controller (BASICDC.INF)
- ◆ Compatible workstation or server (COMPATWS.INF)
- ◆ Secure workstation or server (SECUREWS.INF)
- ◆ Secure domain controller (SECUREDC.INF)
- ◆ Highly secure workstation or server (HISECWS.INF)
- ◆ Highly secure domain controller (HISECDC.INF)

By default, these templates are stored in the `\systemroot\security\templates` folder.

By default, Windows 2000 applies security templates to new installations of Windows 2000. The default templates are used to secure Windows.

If Windows 2000 is installed on a computer with FAT or FAT32 partitions, you should be aware that security configuration templates cannot be fully applied.

The following section looks at some of the security templates in more detail.

> **WARNING**
>
> **Security Templates and the Upgrade Process** Windows 2000 default security settings are not applied to upgrade installations of Windows 2000. Once the upgrade is completed, you can apply the basic templates to modify the security settings to match the Windows 2000 default security settings.

Default Security Templates

The default security templates (DEFLTWK.INF, DEFLTSV.INF and DEFLTDC.INF) apply the Windows 2000 default security settings during a fresh install of the operating system. These security templates are not used during an upgrade from Windows NT 4.0 to Windows 2000, but are used when upgrading from Windows 9x to Windows 2000 Professional.

Basic and Advanced Security Templates

The basic configuration (BASICWK.INF, BASICSV.INF, BASICDC.INF) templates are provided to assist you if you apply an inappropriate security configuration to your system. The basic configuration applies the Windows 2000 default security settings to all security areas except for sections covering user rights. User rights are not modified in the basic templates because application setup programs commonly modify user rights.

Compatible (COMPAT*.INF)

Windows 2000 and Windows NT use different security settings to support applications running on them. Windows 2000 provides a more structured environment for the installation of applications. Windows 2000 applications (that is, applications that use the Windows Installer service to install) are fully managed during installation, and users do not require elevated privileges as the application is installed in the security context of the Installer service.

If you require compatibility with non-Windows 2000 applications in your environment, you might need to apply the compatible template. Under this template all users that are authenticated by Windows 2000 are automatically elevated to have the permissions associated with the Power Users group. This enables applications to access system files and registry keys that are required to operate properly.

Secure (SECURE*.INF)

The secure templates define a secure network communications environment for Windows 2000. The security areas are set to protect network traffic and protocols used between computers running Windows 2000. Computers configured with this template will attempt to enforce strong security measures but will fall back to less secure methods if clients cannot comply. This still allows the ability to communicate with Windows NT and Windows 9x systems.

Highly Secure (HISEC*.INF)

The highly secure templates define a secure network communications environment for Windows 2000. The security areas are set to protect network traffic and protocols used between computers running Windows 2000. Computers configured with this template can communicate only with other Windows 2000 machines. This limits their capability to communicate with Windows NT and Windows 9x systems.

Configure System Security

The Security Templates snap-in enables you to manage security templates from the Microsoft Management Console.

ON THE CD

Step by Step 7.8, "Creating Security Templates," demonstrates how to create security templates. See the file **Chapter07-08StepbyStep.pdf** in the CD's **Chapter07\StepbyStep** directory.

After you create a security template for your environment, you need to apply it to your computer. When you apply a template to existing security settings, the settings in the template are merged into the computer's security settings.

ON THE CD

Step by Step 7.9, "Applying Security Templates," shows you how to apply security templates. See the file **Chapter07-09StepbyStep.pdf** in the CD's **Chapter07\StepbyStep** directory.

From the Group Policy snap-in, you are also able to export the security template for your system.

ON THE CD

Step by Step 7.10, "Exporting Security Templates," gives you the procedures for exporting security templates. See the file **Chapter07-10StepbyStep.pdf** in the CD's **Chapter07\StepbyStep** directory.

Validating a Security Configuration

The state of the operating system and applications on a computer is dynamic. For example, security levels might be required to change temporarily to enable immediate resolution of an administration or network issue; this change can often remain. This means that a computer might not meet the requirements for enterprise security any longer.

Regular analysis enables an administrator to track and ensure an adequate level of security on each computer. Analysis is provided at a detailed level; information about all system aspects related to security is provided in the results. This enables an administrator to tune the security levels and, most importantly, to detect any security flaws that might open up in the system over time.

Security configuration and analysis enables quick review of security analysis results. Recommendations are presented alongside current system settings, and icons or remarks are used to highlight any areas where the current settings do not match the proposed level of security. Security configuration and analysis also offer the ability to resolve any discrepancies revealed by an analysis.

If frequent analyses of a large number of computers are required, as in a domain-based infrastructure, the SECEDIT.EXE command-line tool may be used as a method of batch analysis. Analysis results still must be viewed, however, with security configuration and analysis.

Step by Step 7.11 provides details on how to use the Security Configuration and Analysis tool to compare the security configuration of a computer against a security template.

ON THE CD

Step by Step 7.11, "Security Configuration and Analysis," shows you how to use the Security and Analysis tool to compare the security configuration of a computer against a security template. See the file **Chapter07-11StepbyStep.pdf** in the CD's **Chapter07\ StepbyStep** directory.

After completing the analysis, you can perform a number of tasks, including the following:

◆ Eliminate discrepancies by configuring the settings in the database to match the current computer settings. To configure the database settings, double-click the setting in the detail pane of the MMC.

◆ Import another template file. This enables you to add additional security templates to the analysis.

◆ Export the current database setting to a template file. To export the template file, right-click Security Configuration and Analysis and then click Export Template.

ENCRYPTING FILE SYSTEM (EFS)

Encrypt data on a hard disk by using Encrypting File System (EFS).

Encrypting File System (EFS) is a system service that enables users to encrypt file system resources that they have access to (you need a minimum of modify permissions). The service is based on public/private encryption technology and is managed by the Windows 2000 Public Key Infrastructure (PKI) services. Because EFS is an integrated service, it is very easy to manage, difficult to break into, and transparent to the user.

Once a file is encrypted, only the user who encrypted it (and a special account called recovery agent) can decrypt the file. If a user other than the recovery agent or the user who encrypted the file tries to use the resource, he or she will receive an access denied message.

The technology is set up on a public key–based structure. Each user has a public and private key. The keys were created in such a way that anything encrypted with the public key can be decrypted only by using the matching private key. As the names suggest, the public key is made available to any resource that requests it. The private key is kept secret and never exposed to unauthorized resources.

When the owner of a file encrypts a file system resource, a file encryption key is generated and used to encrypt the file. The file encryption keys are based on a fast symmetric key designed for bulk encryption. The file is encrypted in blocks with a different key for each block. All the file encryption keys are then stored with the file in field headers known as the Data Decryption Field (DDF) and the Data Recovery Field (DRF). Before the file encryption keys are stored, they are encrypted by using the public key of the owner, in the case of the DDF keys, and a recovery agent, in the case of the DRF keys. Because the keys are stored with the file, the file can be moved or renamed without impacting the recoverability of the file.

When a file is accessed, EFS detects the access attempt and locates the user's certificate from the Windows 2000 PKI and the user's associated private key. The private key is then used to decrypt the DDF to retrieve the file encryption keys used to encrypt each block of the file. The only key in existence with the capability to decrypt the information is the user who encrypted the file. Access to the file is denied to everyone else, as they do not hold the private key required for decrypting the file encryption keys.

If the owner's private key is not available for some reason (for example, the user account was deleted), the recovery agent can open the file. The recovery agent decrypts the DRF to unlock the list of file encryption keys. The recovery agent must be configured as part of the security policies of the local computer.

Step by Step 7.12 provides details for encrypting a file or folder within Windows 2000.

ON THE CD

Step by Step 7.12, "Encrypting Files and Folders," illustrates how to encrypt files and folders. See the file **Chapter07-12StepbyStep.pdf** in the CD's **Chapter07\StepbyStep** directory.

WARNING

Manage the Recovery Agent Properly The recovery agent can be configured through local policies (or Group Policy objects in the domain environment). If you change the recovery agent, you might not be able to recover encrypted files that were encrypted prior to the change.

You also can manage the encryption attributes associated with files and folders on your system from the command prompt. The Cipher utility enables you to encrypt files and folders as well as check the compression statistics.

The syntax for the encryption utility is as follows:

```
CIPHER [/e| /d] [/s:dir] [/i] [/f] [/q] [filename [...]]
```
Where:

- ◆ /e encrypts the specified files or folders. Files added to the folder afterward will be encrypted.

- ◆ /d decrypts the specified files or folders. Files added to the folder afterward will not be encrypted.

- ◆ /s:dir performs the specified operation on files in the given directory and all subdirectories.

- ◆ /i continues performing the specified operation even after errors have occurred. By default, Cipher stops when an error is encountered.

- ◆ /f forces the encryption or decryption of all specified files. By default, files that have already been encrypted or decrypted are skipped. This option forces files to be re-encrypted, even if they are currently encrypted. This would be important if a new recovery agent has been configured for your system, as the file(s) would be re-encrypted with a new key.

- ◆ /q reports only the most essential information.

- ◆ filename specifies a pattern, file, or directory.

Step by Step 7.13 demonstrates how to use EFS.

ON THE CD

Step by Step 7.13, "Using EFS," demonstrates how to use EFS. See the file **Chapter07-13StepbyStep.pdf** in the CD's **Chapter07\ StepbyStep** directory.

CASE STUDY: ABC COMPANY

ESSENCE OF THE CASE

The essential elements in this case are as follows:

▶ Group strategy in a multi domain environment

▶ Account policies

▶ Security template development

▶ Audit policies

▶ Company policies for EFS

ABC Company is in the process of developing a network design for their Canadian operation. ABC Company has nine offices spread across Canada and employs a staff of 5,000. They are currently running a mix of Novell and Windows NT 3.51/4.0. The company is very concerned with the rising cost of managing their networked resources. The company has decided on a multiple-domain design based on the legal organization of their company (that is, one division in their company partners with a company in Europe and, therefore, requires lower levels of encrypting technology). Your job is to develop a complete security strategy plan for this company.

ANALYSIS

ABC Company is undertaking a major reworking of their network. This case focuses on security. To secure your environment, you need to manage your groups, account policies, security templates, and audit policies correctly.

Because we are dealing with a multidomain environment, you need to develop a strategy for the management of groups. You should use global groups to organize users in each domain. You then need to evaluate the resources to determine which staff employees need access. You will then create domain local groups and give these groups permission to the resources users need. Global groups are then placed in the domain local groups.

After you organize your users and groups, you should evaluate password policies. Does your company require complex passwords? What is

---

CASE STUDY: ABC COMPANY

the minimum length of passwords? How long can a user use a password before he or she must change it?

Now that the user accounts are protected, you will want to develop a strategy for securing individual systems. One of the most effective ways of doing this is through a security template and by auditing access to resources.

Remember that each of the above features of Windows 2000 work together to secure your environment. Think of them as lines of defense. If one line fails, another is there to protect your resources.

CHAPTER SUMMARY

In this chapter, we explored the tools built in to Windows 2000 to secure the networked environment. The chapter started with an overview of the user account. User accounts are a very important aspect of network security, as they are your first line of defense against intruders. If your user accounts are not managed properly, it is impossible to secure the network. In the discussion of user accounts, we also reviewed the differences between a workgroup and a domain environment. Next, groups were covered in detail. Groups are a very powerful tool that can ease management and, if used properly, make implementing a secure environment easier. With a

KEY TERMS
- Workgroup
- Domain
- Active Directory
- User Account
- Group
- Security groups
- Distribution groups
- Local groups
- Domain local groups

CHAPTER SUMMARY

KEY TERMS

- Global group
- Universal group
- Built-in group
- Local group policy
- Account policy
- Auditing
- Event logs
- Security template
- Encrypting File System

full understanding of users and groups, we then looked at local policies and account policies. Policies are tools that we can use to secure user accounts and computers.

Monitoring security events was also described, as well as the process of defining an audit policy. Security templates and the Encrypting File System were also discussed.

APPLY YOUR KNOWLEDGE

Review Questions

1. What utilities are used to create users and groups in a workgroup environment?

2. What utilities are used to create users and groups in a domain environment?

3. What is Microsoft's preferred strategy for groups in a domain environment?

4. What are the differences between a global group and a universal group?

5. When is it more appropriate to use a global group over a universal group?

6. What are the differences between a workgroup and a domain environment?

7. You want to stop hackers from trying to guess passwords in your environment; what feature of Windows 2000 should you use?

8. How does the Encrypting File System work and why would you want to use it?

9. What are local policies used for?

10. What is the SECEDIT.EXE utility used for?

11. What are user rights and how do they relate to built-in groups?

12. What types of events can be audited?

Answers to Review Questions

1. The Computer Management snap-in is used to manage users and groups in a workgroup environment—in the Computer Management snap-in, there is a node called Local Users and Groups. See the section "Creating Local User Accounts."

2. The Active Directory Users and Computer snap-in is used to manage users and groups in a domain environment. See the section "Creating Domain User Accounts."

3. Microsoft's preferred strategy is for accounts to be placed in global groups. The global groups are then placed in domain local groups. The domain local groups are then given permission to access resources. See the section "Groups."

4. Global groups can be used to assign permission to resources that are located in any domain. Membership in a global group is limited to user accounts and global groups from the domain in which the global group resides. You can add global groups to another global group within the same domain, or to universal groups and domain local groups in other domains.

APPLY YOUR KNOWLEDGE

Universal groups can be used to assign permissions to resources that are located in any domain. You can add user accounts, universal groups, and global groups from any domain to its membership list. You can add a universal group to domain local or u niversal groups in any domain. See the section "Groups."

5. Global groups are used to organize user accounts within a domain. Global groups are then placed in the domain local groups to gain access to resources. Universal groups are used to grant access to resources that reside in multiple domains. You should not use universal groups to organize user accounts (it can impact replication traffic). Instead, if you have resources that reside in multiple domains, place global groups from each domain in a universal group and then make the universal group a member of a Domain Local group. See the section "Groups."

6. Under the workgroup model, each computer in your environment is responsible for the management of its own local account database. The workgroup model is meant for small environments. This model has a very high administrative cost, as user accounts must be managed on each computer in your environment. The workgroup model is very simple to implement and does not require that specialized computers manage a shared account database.

   Under the domain model, a centralized database of user accounts is managed for a grouping (or domain) of computers. Domain user accounts contain information that defines users within the domain. In Windows 2000, all user account information for the domain is stored in the Active Directory database. Active Directory is stored on a special computer called a domain controller. With a single domain user account, a user can log on to the domain and gain access to resources on any computer in the domain. The primary benefit of the domain model is that account management is simplified, as each user in your environment will have only a single user account defined. This model, however, is much more complex to set up, design, and configure. See the sections "The Domain Model" and "The Workgroup Model."

7. The local policy of a computer contains settings related to account policies. Under account policies you can configure an account lockout policy. These settings enable you to specify the total number of failed password attempts a user can have within a given period of time. If the number of failed password attempts is exceeded, the user account is locked. You also should consider auditing failed logons. See the sections "Local Group Policy" and "Audit Policies."

8. The Encrypting File System (EFS) enables a user to encrypt the contents of a file so that only that user (and a recovery agent) can access the file. This is helpful in environments in which users work with very sensitive data.

   When a user encrypts a file, a session key is generated. This session key is used to encrypt the file. The session key is then encrypted by using the user's public key. The encrypted session key is then saved with the file. A version of the key encrypted by a recovery agent is also saved with the file so that it can be recovered if the user account (and corresponding private key required to retrieve the session key) is unavailable.

When a user attempts to open the file, the system will detect that it is encrypted and use the user's private key to decrypt the session key stored with the file. The session key is then used to decrypt the file. See the section "Encrypting File System (EFS)."

9. Local Group Policy objects enable you to control the following components:

- **Administrative templates.** Registry-based setting that controls access to various system settings.

- **Software settings.** Enables software to be assigned to users and computers so that it is available to users when they need it.

- **Security settings.** Security settings for computers and users.

- **Scripts.** User Logon/Logoff, Computer Startup/Shutdown scripts.

- **Folder redirection.** Enables data directories (usually part of a user's profile) to be placed on networked drives instead of the local computer.

See the section "Local Group Policy."

10. The SECEDIT.EXE command-line tool, when called from a batch file or automatic task scheduler, can be used to automatically create and apply templates and analyze system security. It can also be run dynamically from a command line.

This tool is useful when you have multiple computers on which security must be analyzed or configured, and you need to perform these tasks during off-hours. See the section "Windows 2000 Security Configurations."

11. User rights are specific permissions that can be assigned to users and groups. These permissions give users or groups the ability to manage various aspects of a system. Built-in groups relate to user rights because built-in groups get their rights from being assigned, by default, useful combinations of user rights. See the section "User Rights."

12. The following events can be audited:

- **Account logon.** Logs an event each time a user attempts to log on.

- **Logon events.** Logs an event for logon events that are occurring over the network or generated by service startup (for example, an interactive logon or a service such as SQL starting).

- **Account management.** Logs an event each time an account is managed. This is a useful function if you are concerned about changes being made to user accounts in your environment.

- **Directory service.** Logs an event each time an event occurs within the Active Directory services (for example, successful or failed replication events).

- **Policy change.** Logs an event each time a policy is successfully or unsuccessfully changed in your environment.

APPLY YOUR KNOWLEDGE

- **Process tracking.** Logs an event for each program or process that a user launches while accessing a system. This information can be used by administrators to track the details of a user's activities while accessing a system.

- **Object access.** Logs an event each time a user attempts to access a resource, such as a printer, shared folder, and so on.

- **Privilege use.** Logs an event each time a user attempts, successfully or unsuccessfully, to use special privileges such as changing system time.

- **System event.** Logs designated system events. Windows 2000 may log system events when a user restarts or shuts down a computer.

Suggested Readings and Resources

1. *Active Directory Overview*, White Paper. Microsoft Corporation, 2000. Available from `www.microsoft.com`.

2. *MS 2151—Supporting Windows 2000 Professional.* Microsoft Official Curriculum, Microsoft Corporation, 2000.

PART

II

INSTALLING, CONFIGURING, AND ADMINISTERING MICROSOFT WINDOWS 2000 SERVER

This chapter helps you prepare for the "Installing Windows 2000 Server" section of the Microsoft Windows 2000 Accelerated Exam for MCPs Certified on Microsoft Windows NT 4.0 exam by giving you information necessary to make intelligent choices regarding the method of installation and the preparations required to do such an installation.

This chapter covers the following Microsoft-specified objectives:

Perform an attended installation of Windows 2000 Server.

▶ Someone certified in the use of Windows 2000 Server technology must be able to install a Windows 2000 Server as a member server of a Windows 2000 domain. This includes both installations from a bootable CD-ROM and from the four-disk set.

Perform an unattended installation of Windows 2000 Server.

▶ Create unattended answer files by using Setup Manager to automate the installation of Windows 2000 Server.

▶ Create and configure automated methods for installation of Windows 2000.

▶ Someone certified in the Windows 2000 Server technology should understand how to automate the installation of servers as members of a Windows 2000 domain over a network. This includes the creation of answer files to be used during a Windows 2000 Server installation. It also involves familiarity with the new disk duplication and remote installation features of Windows 2000.

CHAPTER 8

Installing Windows 2000 Server

Upgrade a server from Microsoft Windows NT 4.0.

▶ Someone certified in the Windows 2000 Server technology should understand how to upgrade a current Windows NT 4.0 Server to a Windows 2000 Server. This includes both the preparation and the implementation of an upgrade.

Deploy service packs.

▶ Someone certified in the Windows 2000 Server technology should understand how to apply incremental upgrades and software fixes through the use of service packs periodically released by Microsoft.

Troubleshoot failed installations.

▶ Someone certified in Windows 2000 Server technology should understand how to diagnose installation problems and recover from installation failures.

STUDY STRATEGIES

▶ The topic of installation has had its fair share of the focus in previous Microsoft certification exams. This exam will be no different. In addition to being able to answer the standard questions about manual installation, be prepared for questions on the new features that Windows 2000 Server has that previous versions of Windows NT did not. That means that you should be prepared for questions on Setup Manager, the System Preparation Tool (SYSPREP), and Remote Installation Services (RIS). In addition, you should know the pitfalls of upgrading a Windows NT 4.0 Server to Windows 2000 Server so that if scenario questions come up about it you are prepared. In addition, you also need to be aware of the new service pack technology so that you can correctly answer questions about slip streaming and the benefits that it brings.

▶ Preparation for this section requires hands-on experience. You should try as many installation options as you have time and equipment for. Start by reading and understanding the content of this chapter. Then, do the exercises and questions in the Apply Your Knowledge section. Finally, go back through the Step by Steps and work through them, especially those where there were no exercises that covered that material. It is only though practice and repetition that you will be able to answer the many question forms (from straight informational to scenario-based) that you will see on this exam.

Introduction

It is probably redundant or obvious to say that a good installation is essential to the proper operation of your Windows 2000 Server. If you do not install properly, you will spend a lot of time subsequent to installation in fixing your configuration. Moreover, the more installations you do, the more efficient you will want the process to be. As a result, this chapter deals with a wide variety of attended and unattended installation methods. You will consider the pros and cons of the methods to ensure that you are doing the right thing at the right time.

Windows 2000 Server and the 70-215 Exam

The prelude to the published exam objectives states that the 70-215 exam covers areas of Windows 2000 Server functionality as it relates to your ability to "implement, administer, and troubleshoot Windows 2000 Server as a member server of a domain in an Active Directory environment." As a result, this text presupposes that you are operating in an environment in which you have already set up (or have available) a Windows 2000 domain controller. In addition, no attempt is made to explain Active Directory, except where it is imperative to the understanding of a member server concept (that is for another text and other exams).

A *member server* is a Windows 2000 Server that functions in a domain but does not hold a copy of the Active Directory database. As a result, it does not validate domain logon, but it might validate logon to the local machine's account database. Member servers require the presence of a domain controller to create a computer account to enable them to join a domain. Member servers generally perform functions, such as file and print services, application services (such as running an email server), and Web services (such as being a Web server). All these are discussed in other chapters.

The exam focuses on five main areas of installation: attended installations, unattended installations, upgrades from Windows NT 4.0, incremental installations of service packs, and troubleshooting installation. Each of these topics is covered in detail in the following sections.

PREPARING FOR INSTALLATION

There are a number of factors you need to take into consideration when installing Windows 2000 Server (either as a fresh install or as an upgrade): hardware compatibility, software compatibility, disk and partition sizing, and current operating system upgradability. Each of these factors must be considered and dealt with before you attempt to do an installation of Windows 2000 Server.

Hardware Compatibility

Windows 2000 has very strict hardware requirements. If you do not meet them, at best, some of your components will not function properly and, at worst, the operating system will not install at all. Two criteria are required to install and operate Windows 2000 Server:

◆ The components must meet the minimum requirements for installation (see Table 8.1).

◆ The components must be on the Hardware Compatibility List.

Minimum Hardware Requirements

The minimum hardware requirements refer to the processor type and speed, the amount of disk space, and the amount of memory available. In the past, Microsoft published minimum installation requirements—that is, the minimum hardware required to install the operating systems. However, the published minimums now reflect the minimum hardware required to run servers in specific configurations. As a result, you may be able to install Windows

2000 Server with less than the minimum requirements, but these servers will not function effectively in a production environment. Table 8.1 outlines those minimum requirements.

<table>
<tr><td colspan="2">**TABLE 8.1**</td></tr>
<tr><td colspan="2">**MINIMUM REQUIREMENTS FOR WINDOWS 2000 SERVER OPERATING SYSTEM INSTALLATION**</td></tr>
<tr><td>*Component*</td><td>*Published Minimums*</td></tr>
<tr><td>Processor</td><td>Pentium 133 (also see the Note on this page)</td></tr>
<tr><td>RAM</td><td>256MB</td></tr>
<tr><td>Free disk space</td><td>1GB on a single partition*</td></tr>
</table>

NOTE

Alpha Chips Compaq is no longer supporting Windows 2000 on the Alpha chip.

* This disk space must be contiguous on a single partition. Please see the updated minimum requirements as posted at `http://www.microsoft.com/windows2000/guide/platform/overview/default.asp`.

It should be noted that the minimum hardware requirements have increased considerably since Windows NT 4.0 and if you were running your Windows NT 4.0 machine at, or near, the minimum hardware requirements, you need to upgrade your hardware prior to upgrading to Windows 2000 Server.

The Hardware Compatibility List (HCL)

The *HCL* is Microsoft's published list of hardware components that have been fully tested with Windows 2000. Items that are listed in the HCL are guaranteed to function (at least to a bare minimum) with Windows 2000. If you want to ensure that all your hardware will function properly under Windows 2000, you should consult the current version of the HCL, which can be found on the Internet at `http://www.microsoft.com/hcl`.

It should be noted that although many products will be on the HCL (which means that they have been tested and found to function with Windows 2000), not everything is. If the manufacturer has a driver available for the device that has been created for Windows 2000, it should function. However, any problems with the driver should be addressed to the manufacturer, not Microsoft.

Software Compatibility

In addition to ensuring that your hardware is Windows 2000 compatible, you should also ensure that your software is Windows 2000 compatible. This software compatibility extends not only to the installation and operation of the Windows 2000 operating system but also to applications that formerly operated under DOS, Windows 9x, or Windows NT 4.0. The fact is, some software will no longer function (or function properly) under Windows 2000.

Microsoft has created the Windows 2000 logo program to certify software as Windows 2000 compliant. This program defines how programs must interact with the operating system to gain logo acceptance.

To check your software, you can do two things. First, you can consult the software compatibility Web site at `http://www.`
`microsoft.com/windows/professional/deploy/compatible/`
`default.asp`. This Web site allows you to search for your software products based on manufacturer, product name, category, or key word(s). Having searched, a list will be returned indicating the status of that software. The possible statuses are Certified (tested by the vendor and by an independent firm to ensure that it functions correctly under Windows 2000), Ready (tested by only the vendor), and Planned (a version that is Windows 2000 compatible is in the works). Any software that is not listed has not been verified through the Microsoft-sanctioned channels.

If you do not find your software product on the Web site mentioned, do not be dismayed (at least not yet), because the second step is to contact the software vendor or to test it yourself. Of course, if you are using software that was developed in-house, you have to get your developers to test it thoroughly on Windows 2000 before you release it to your users.

Disk Size and Partitions

To install Windows 2000 Server on your computer, you have to have disk space—and a reasonable amount of it, too. To install Windows 2000 Server, 685MB of free disk space is required, and 1GB is recommended (as shown in Table 8.1). That free space

needs to be on a single partition, so two 500MB partitions will not
do. If this is a typical Windows 2000 installation, you will want to
install the operating system on your active partition (usually the C:
drive), but you do not have to. If you plan to dual-boot your
Windows 2000 Server with another operating system, you will
want to install Windows 2000 on another partition. If you do this,
Microsoft is going to use different terms to describe the partition
that your computer starts up from and the one on which the
Windows 2000 operating system files are found.

Microsoft uses the term *System Partition* to describe the partition
that is active—that is, the one from which your computer's BIOS
wants to begin the boot process. This partition is usually, but not
always, the C: drive. This partition contains the Master Boot Record
and system files that allow Windows 2000 to take control of the
boot process.

Microsoft uses the term *Boot Partition* to describe the partition
where the Windows 2000 operating system files are held. These files
are commonly found in a folder called WINNT. These are files that
Windows 2000 uses to complete the startup process and to run
Windows 2000 when it is started.

In most cases, it is recommended that you install Windows 2000 on
the same partition as you are booting from (the Active Partition).
This means that the Boot and System Partitions are in the same
location, the System/Boot Partition.

When you have found a partition to install on, you may want to
format it. You don't have to format it in advance, because the install
process has a utility to both create new partitions and to format
them. If you do choose to preformat the partition, you have the
following format choices: NTFS, FAT16, and FAT32. These format
types are discussed in detail in Chapter 2, "Implementing and
Conducting Administration of Resources." To summarize, NTFS
is a proprietary file format used only by Windows NT and Windows
2000, FAT16 is a universal file format that is used in most operating
systems, and FAT32 is an enhanced version of FAT16 that is
supported by Windows 95 (OSR2) and Windows 98, in addition
to all versions of Windows 2000.

Current Operating System Upgradability

If you want to upgrade a machine running another operating system to Windows 2000, you have a number of paths. The working definition for upgrade is "the ability to install a new operating system without having to completely reconfigure the resulting system and without having to reinstall the software." Upgrade to Windows 2000 Server can be done directly from Windows NT 4.0 Server and from Windows 3.51 Server. Because of the new fluidity of domain controller roles, the current role of the server is not significant.

In the case of other operating systems (such as DOS, for example), you have to choose whether to remove (or install over) the existing operating system or to dual-boot with it. *Dual-booting* means that you choose which operating system you will boot from at system startup and that all software has to be installed once for each operating system.

When the preceding steps have been taken, you are ready to install Windows 2000 Server on your computer.

> **EXAM TIP**
>
> **Can I Upgrade from Windows NT 4.0 Workstation to Windows 2000 Server?** In a word, NO! You can upgrade to Windows 2000 Server only from Windows NT 4.0 Server or Windows NT 3.51 Server. The Windows NT Workstation clients can be upgraded only to Windows 2000 Professional.

ATTENDED INSTALLATIONS OF WINDOWS 2000 SERVER

Perform an attended installation of Windows 2000 Server.

Attended installations of Windows 2000 Server are very common, and, as a result, are the first installation topic covered in the objectives. When Microsoft says *attended,* it is pointing to any installation where all the questions of configuration are answered by the person performing the installation. This is as opposed to an unattended installation where the answers are provided by a script that has been created ahead of time. There are four ways of performing an attended installation:

◆ Booting to a CD-ROM and thereby invoking the Setup routine

◆ Booting to a current operating system with CD-ROM support and manually invoking the Setup routine

◆ Booting with a set of four Setup disks and then providing the CD-ROM when prompted.

◆ Booting to a network-aware operating system and invoking Setup over the network.

In the final analysis, all these methods end up the same—only the way they start is different.

Installing by Booting to a CD-ROM

If you have a computer whose BIOS supports booting from a CD-ROM, you can set up Windows 2000 Server without installing an operating system on your hard drive and without requiring network support. To do so, configure your computer to boot to the CD-ROM in the BIOS and then follow the instructions in Step by Step 8.1.

ON THE CD

Step by Step 8.1, "Installing Windows 2000 from a Bootable CD-ROM," walks you through this form of installation. See the file **Chapter08-01StepbyStep.pdf** in the CD's **Chapter08\StepbyStep** directory.

Installing by Manually Invoking Setup from a CD-ROM or a Network Share

If you have a 32-bit Microsoft operating system installed on the target computer that will read from the CD-ROM, you can run SETUP.EXE. If CD-ROM autorun is enabled on your system, inserting the Windows 2000 Server CD-ROM into the drive also invokes SETUP.EXE. Alternatively, you can also invoke the program WINNT32.EXE, which is found on the CD-ROM in the i386 folder. In addition, if you have network connectivity, you can connect to a share point on another computer that has the Windows 2000 Server files on it and run SETUP.EXE or WINNT32.EXE from there. After you have begun the Setup process, it progresses exactly as in Step by Step 8.1.

Installing by Manually Invoking WINNT from a CD-ROM or a Network Share

If you have MS-DOS or Windows 3.x installed on the target computer, you have two choices. If you have a CD-ROM drive in that machine and the appropriate drivers to access it from DOS, you can use a program called WINNT to begin the installation. If you do not have access to a local CD-ROM but you have a networking client installed on the target machine, you can connect to a network share where the Windows 2000 Server CD has been copied and use the WINNT program to begin the installation. This procedure is outlined in Step by Step 8.2.

ON THE CD

Step by Step 8.2, "Installing Windows 2000 from DOS Using a CD-ROM," shows you how to install the operating system using this method. See the file **Chapter08-02StepbyStep.pdf** in the CD's **Chapter08\StepbyStep** directory.

Installing by Using Setup Disks and a CD-ROM

If you have a machine with no current operating system and a BIOS that does not support booting from a CD-ROM, you are forced to use this method. Setup disks are a set of four disks that form a minimal install of Windows 2000 (the closest thing you have to booting Windows 2000 from disk). Having made the disks, you boot from the first one and progress through all four, at which point you are prompted to insert the CD-ROM in the CD-ROM drive and the installation will continue using that medium.

The disks are created using either the program MAKEBOOT.EXE or MAKEBT32.EXE, which are both found in the BOOTDISK folder on your Windows 2000 Server CD-ROM. Both programs do the same thing; however, the "32" version is designed to be run under 32-bit operating systems, whereas the other is designed to be run under 16-bit operating systems, such as DOS and Windows 3.1.

Step by Step 8.3 walks you through the creation of the Setup disks.

NOTE **For Windows NT 4.0 Users**   Under Windows NT 4.0, you created a three-disk set by using the command WINNT /ox (or WINNT32 /ox if you were doing it from an existing NT machine). This switch no longer exists under Windows 2000, and you must create the set (which is now four disks) using one of the executables mentioned previously.

> **ON THE CD**
>
> ---
>
> Step by Step 8.3, "Creating a Setup Disk Set," walks you through
> the creation of the disks. See the file **Chapter08-03StepbyStep.pdf**
> in the CD's **Chapter08\StepbyStep** directory.
>
> ---

After you have a set of Setup disks, you can begin the process of
installing Windows 2000 Server. Step by Step 8.4 outlines the
process up to the final GUI setup.

> **ON THE CD**
>
> ---
>
> Step by Step 8.4, "Installing Windows 2000 with Setup Disks,"
> shows you how to intall Windows using Setup disks. See the file
> **Chapter08-04StepbyStep.pdf** in the CD's **Chapter08\StepbyStep**
> directory.
>
> ---

Although attended installations are common, there may be times
when a number of similar servers need to be installed. To do that,
the configuration of unattended installations is preferable. The next
section deals with that method of installation.

UNATTENDED INSTALLATIONS OF WINDOWS 2000 SERVER

Perform an unattended installation of Windows 2000 Server.

Unattended installation methods allow installation of Windows
2000 Server to be done with little or no user intervention. They are
very beneficial when a number of similar servers need to be installed.
When configured properly, unattended installations can be completely hands-off after the installation has begun.

There are three main methods of unattended installation: installation from scripts, installation using disk images and third-party
distribution software, and installation using Remote Installation
Services (RIS). All three are covered on the exam, but only script

installation is covered in detail. As a result, you will look in depth at the configuration and deployment of script-based installation. This chapter gives an overview and some basic configuration tips in the other two areas but does not cover them in detail, because the exam does not do so.

Script-Based Unattended Installation

The premise of the script-based installation is that you create a scenario where the installation progresses is like a normal attended installation, except where a user would normally answer questions you have a text file that provides the answers.

The basic components of a script-based installation are as follows:

◆ The i386 directory from the Windows 2000 CD-ROM copied into a server-based folder and shared (unattended installations are almost exclusively network based)

◆ The WINNT.EXE or WINNT32.EXE programs (WINNT is for DOS-based installations, whereas WINNT32 is used for installations from 32-bit Windows operating systems)

◆ An answer file providing the generic answers to setup questions, typically a file with a TXT extension (although the extension does not matter)

◆ A uniqueness definition file (UDF extension) that provides the answers to computer-specific questions that change from machine to machine (for example, the computer name)

◆ A batch file or command line that invokes the unattended installation

Although you can create the answer file using any text editor, to make it simple to create and to ensure that you do not leave out crucial information, a wizard is available to aid you.

Using the Setup Manager to Create Unattended Answer Files

The Setup Manager is part of the Windows 2000 Support Tools that can be found in the \Support\Tools folder on the Windows 2000 CD-ROM. It is contained in a file called DEPLOY.CAB and must be extracted from that CAB file before it will operate. Step by Step 8.5 runs you through the extraction of the Setup Manager.

ON THE CD

Step by Step 8.5, "Extracting the Setup Manager," covers the extraction of the Setup Manager. See the file **Chapter08-05StepbyStep.pdf** in the CD's **Chapter08\StepbyStep** directory.

After the Setup Manager is extracted and accessible, you can then use it to create an answer file by answering a series of questions presented by the Setup Manager Wizard. Creating an answer file is presented in Step by Step 8.6.

ON THE CD

Step by Step 8.6, "Creating an Answer File to Install Windows 2000 Server with the Setup Manager," shows you how to set up an answer file. See the file **Chapter08-06StepbyStep.pdf** in the CD's **Chapter08\StepbyStep** directory.

A sample answer file (ANSWER.TXT), which could have been created using a text editor, looks like the following:

```
;SetupMgrTag
[Unattended]
    UnattendMode=FullUnattended
    OemPreinstall=Yes

[GuiUnattended]
    AdminPassword=PASSWORD
    TimeZone=20

[UserData]
    ProductID=111111-111111-111111-111111-111111
    FullName="Robert Deupree"
    OrgName="Rockflower"
```

```
[Display]

[LicenseFilePrintData]
    AutoMode=PerServer
    AutoUsers=100

[TapiLocation]

[RegionalSettings]

[MassStorageDrivers]

[OEMBootFiles]

[OEM_Ads]

[SetupMgr]
    ComputerName0= YODA
    ComputerName1= R2D2
    ComputerName2= C3P0
    DistFolder=E:\W2Kserver
DistShare=W2KS

[Identification]
    JoinDomain=NWTRADERS
    CreateComputerAccountInDomain=Yes
    DomainAdmin=ADMINISTRATOR
    DomainAdminPassword=password

[Networking]
    InstallDefaultComponents=Yes
```

You will notice in the preceding file that the sections, headed by titles in square brackets ([]), roughly correspond to the screens where you filled in answers in the wizard.

A .UDF file was also created, because a number of computer names were entered in the wizard. The UDF file will look something like this:

```
;SetupMgrTag
[UniqueIds]
    YODA=UserData
    R2D2=UserData
    C3P0=UserData

[YODA:UserData]
    ComputerName= YODA
```

```
[R2D2:UserData]
    ComputerName= R2D2

[C3P0:UserData]
    ComputerName= C3P0
```

The structure of the UDF file begins with a set of computer names under the heading [Uniqueids]. Following is a section for each computer with the heading [computername:UserData] and under it the unique variable name (for example, ComputerName) and the value associated with that value. By using a combination of a single answer file with a single UDF file you can avoid having to create an answer file for every machine you are going to install.

Now that the answer files are created, your task is simply to invoke the Setup routine, indicating the answer files to use. That is the first topic in the next section.

Installing Windows 2000 Server Using Answer and Uniqueness Files

Unlike the attended forms of installation, unattended installs do not use the SETUP.EXE program. Instead, they use a program called WINNT.EXE. Actually, there are two forms of that program: WINNT.EXE, which installs from DOS-based operating systems, such as MS-DOS and Windows 3.x; and WINNT32.EXE, which installs from 32-bit operating systems, such as Windows 9x and Windows NT.

Although WINNT/WINNT32 can be used for attended installations, its forte is in providing command-line syntax for unattended installs. It does this by providing a number of switches that control how the install is to progress and allows you, among other things, to dictate the name and location of the answer and UDF files. Table 8.2 outlines the switches for WINNT and WINNT32 and their functions.

NOTE

WINNT32 Used for All 32-Bit OS
It is important to note that whereas under Windows NT 4.0, WINNT32 could be used for installs onto other Windows NT systems, now the functionality has been extended to all 32-bit operating systems. That means that whereas before you had to use WINNT for Windows 95 installs, now you use WINNT32.

```
TABLE 8.2
```

SWITCHES FOR WINNT AND WINNT32

WINNT	WINNT32	Function
/a	N/A	Enable accessibility options.
/e:command	/cmd:command	Execute a command before the final phase of Setup.
/i:inf_file	N/A	Specify the name of the Setup information file.
/r:folder	/copydir:folder	Specify optional folder to be installed in the system root directory.
/rx:folder	/copysource:folder	Specify optional folder to be copied for use by installation and then deleted when install is done.
/s:path	/s:path	Specify the location of the installation files for Windows 2000 server.
/t:drive	/tempdrive:drive	Specify the location that the temporary installation files can be copied to and the location that Windows 2000 will be installed to (this becomes the Boot Partition).
/u:file	/unattend:[num]:[file]	Specify the location of the answer file for unattended installations and the number of seconds to wait between copying the files and restarting the computer.
/udf:file	/udf:id,file	Specify the location of the uniqueness definition file for unattended installations. ID is the identifier within the UDF that defines the unique installation options for this computer.
N/A	/cmdcons	Specify that files required for command-line repair console be installed.
N/A	/debug level:file	Create a log file when conditions of certain severity occur during install. By default, level is 2 (warning).
N/A	/syspart:drive	Copy files to a hard drive and mark it as active. Used to begin installation to a hard drive that will then be relocated to another machine (its permanent home).
N/A	/checkupgradeonly	Check your computer to see whether it is upgradable to Windows 2000. This option does not actually perform an installation but, instead, creates a log file (WINNT32.LOG for NT and UPGRADE.TXT for Windows 9x) indicating the results of an upgrade.

An example is in order. If you want to create a batch file for the installation of a server called R2D2 from the answer file and UDF files shown previously it would look like this:

```
net use q: \\yoda\w2ks
net use r: \\yoda\answers

q:\winnt /s:q: /u:r:\answer.txt /udf:r2d2,r:\answer.udf
```

This code supposes that the installation is being done from a machine that is running MS-DOS and that has network connectivity.

Although creating unattended installations using scripts is a very popular method, many people have found that other methods can be quicker and more efficient. The next section deals with disk duplication as an installation technique.

Unattended Installations Using Disk Duplication

Disk duplication, the process by which the entire hard drive of one machine is duplicated to the hard drive of another is not new. People have been doing it in one form or another for years, using third-party products such as Ghost (now owned by Symantec Corporation). Configuring a machine completely, right down to all the application software, then copying the disk and transferring it to a target machine is very appealing.

The disk duplication process formalizes the steps for creating a duplicate of a hard drive and allows automated Setup using the SYSPREP.EXE program. SYSPREP, like the Setup Manager, is a tool contained in the DEPLOY.CAB file (located in the \support\tools folder on the CD-ROM). It is recommended that you extract the SYSPREP files from this CAB file into a folder called Sysprep, as outlined in Step by Step 8.7.

ON THE CD

Step by Step 8.7, "Extracting and Making Available the SYSPREP Utility," shows you how to set up the SYSPREP program. See the file **Chapter08-07StepbyStep.pdf** in the CD's **Chapter08\StepbyStep** directory.

Having extracted the SYSPREP tool, you can now use it to duplicate a disk. In Step by Step 8.8, which describes this process, the
master computer is the machine that you are using as a model for
your disk duplicates.

ON THE CD

Step by Step 8.8, "Duplicating a Disk with SYSPREP.EXE," covers
the use of SYSPREP. See the file **Chapter08-08StepbyStep.pdf** in
the CD's **Chapter08\StepbyStep** directory.

When the image has been transferred to a target machine, that
machine is restarted and is configured through a minimum of questions to the user. One of the problems in disk duplication in the
past has been the information on the target machine that needed to
be different from the source machine (such as security identifiers,
SIDs, and computer names). SYSPREP takes care of that by running a mini-Setup wizard after the target machine is restarted.

If you want to completely automate the process, you can have
SYSPREP create a SYSPREP.INF file that provides answers to the
Setup routine that runs when the target machine is started after the
disk image has been placed on it. This INF file can make the installation completely automated (which is why this discussion falls
under the topic of unattended installations).

Using SYSPREP.EXE

The role of SYSPREP.EXE is to prepare a disk for duplication.
When prepared, a third-party tool can be used to copy the
duplicated drive onto other machines. SYSPREP.EXE, run from the
Tools Management Console or from a command line, configures the
disk image so that SIDs, and other unique information, are removed
and ready to be re-created on the target machine. This ensures that
no conflicts arise in interaction with other machines that have the
same SID.

There are some additional parameters for SYSPREP.EXE that allow
you to control how it operates from a command line. Table 8.3
outlines their use.

TABLE 8.3

SWITCHES FOR SYSPREP.EXE

Switch	Function
-quiet	Run the target computer's Setup with no user interaction.
-pnp	Force the detection of Plug and Play resources on the destination computer. This ensures that any Plug and Play devices on the target computer are detected rather than simply configuring for the devices on the source computer.
-reboot	Restart the configuration computer when SYSPREP is complete rather than simply shutting it down. This invokes the Setup program on the configuration computer and is used only when you want to check that the Setup program is going to function properly.
-nosidgen	Prevent the regeneration of SIDs on the target computer. This is useful when you are transferring the contents of one machine to another for the purpose of decommissioning the original. The new machine then becomes an exact duplicate of the first.

If you want to completely automate the installation, you will create a SYSPREP.INF FILE (which takes the same form as a script-based answer file) and place it into a SYSPREP folder on the C: drive of your configuration computer. When the Setup program runs on the target computer, it checks for this file and uses it if present.

Unattended Installations Using Remote Installation Services

Given the proper network configuration, remote installation of Windows 2000 is possible. Although this is an interesting topic, it must be stated at the outset that this feature will not install Windows 2000 Server, only Windows 2000 Professional. As such, it is not strictly an unattended Windows 2000 method. Having said that, the Remote Installation Services are a part of the automation of Windows 2000 installations and, as a result, may find its way onto the exam.

Remote Installation Services is a way to take control of another machine for the purpose of installing Windows 2000 Professional on it. It has advantages over other methods because you can oversee the installation while not having to be at the site of the target computer. To use this service, you run the Remote Installation Services Setup Wizard. But first, you have to ensure that your network is capable of doing remote installation.

Preparing for Remote Installation

To use the Remote Installation Services, your clients must be able to support remote installation. In addition to the standard requirements for the installation of Windows 2000 Professional (Pentium 166, 32MB of RAM, and 800MB of free disk space), they also must have certain networking capabilities. One of the following three criteria must be met:

◆ Meet the current Network PC (Net PC) specification. This specification is the definition for what is commonly termed a "thin client." Machines of this sort generally are without floppy or CD-ROM drives and must be managed from an external source. A machine such as this must have the network adapter set as its primary boot device in the system BIOS. In addition, for the installation to progress properly, the user account that is used to perform the installation must be granted the Log On as a Batch Job in the domain policies. Finally, users must have the ability to create computer accounts in the domain that the Windows 2000 Professional installation is joining.

◆ Have a network card with a Pre-Boot Execution Environment (PXE) boot ROM and a BIOS set to allow starting from the PXE boot ROM. PXE is a network card technology that allows the card to interact with the network before an actual operating system boot has been accomplished. This allows the card to obtain a TCP/IP address and be communicated to from the outside—in our case, for the purpose of having Windows 2000 Professional installed on it. The requirements for this are that the card have a PXE boot ROM integrated into it, that the computer's BIOS be set to start from the network card, and that the user permissions be set as for the Net PC described previously.

◆ Have a Remote Boot Disk available for the target machine. If the target machine is not Net PC–compliant and it does not have a PXE boot ROM on its network card, you can create a remote installation boot disk. This allows you to take control of the machine for the purpose of installing Windows 2000 Professional. You can create such a disk by running the RBFG.EXE program (found in the `\RemoteInstall\Admin` folder) on the RIS server. The user permissions for the target machine must be as for a Net PC machine.

Having met one of these network criteria, you can then create a RIS server by running the RIS Setup Wizard. This is exemplified in Step by Step 8.9.

ON THE CD

Step by Step 8.9, "Creating a RIS Server," shows you how to establish a RIS server. See the file **Chapter08-09StepbyStep.pdf** in the CD's **Chapter08\StepbyStep** directory.

Configuration for many machines will be via BIOS settings. However, if your computer does not conform to the Net PC or the PXE standards, you have to create a Remote Boot Disk. Step by Step 8.10 outlines that procedure.

ON THE CD

Step by Step 8.10, "Creating a Remote Boot Disk," covers creation of a Remote Boot Disk. See the file **Chapter08-10StepbyStep.pdf** in the CD's **Chapter08\StepbyStep** directory.

From the client side, the machine boots, seeks out the RIS server, and downloads the list of images that can be chosen from. Then installation begins.

UPGRADING A WINDOWS NT 4.0 SERVER TO WINDOWS 2000

Upgrade a server from Microsoft Windows NT 4.0.

In the early stages of the deployment of Windows 2000 worldwide, the scenario of upgrade from Windows NT 4.0 to Windows 2000 arises frequently. Fortunately, the upgrade of a Windows NT 4.0 Server to a Windows 2000 Server is very straightforward. Moreover, unlike the upgrade of domain controllers, you do not have to worry about when in the total domain upgrade you upgrade your Windows NT 4.0 Servers. A Windows 2000 server can reside comfortably in a workgroup, a Windows NT 4.0 domain, or a Windows 2000 domain.

There are two main ways of upgrading a Windows NT 4.0 Server to Windows 2000: You can use the Setup program from a network share or from a local CD-ROM (attended), or you can use the WINNT32 program from a network share (unattended). Step by Step 8.11 illustrates an attended upgrade.

ON THE CD

Step by Step 8.11, "Installing an Attended Upgrade of an NT 4.0 Member Server to Windows 2000," shows you how to conduct an attended upgrade. See the file **Chapter08-11StepbyStep.pdf** in the CD's **Chapter08\StepbyStep** directory.

Unattended upgrades can be done using WINNT32.EXE from a network share. You have two main options when installing. First, you can use an answer file and a UDF just as you would with a regular unattended installation. In this case, you can use the same wizard to help you create these files (refer to Step by Step 8.6). Second, you could use WINNT32.EXE with the /unattend switch. This switch indicates that the installation is to progress without user input and that the answers to the Setup questions are to be provided by looking at (and duplicating) the current Windows NT 4.0 configuration. For simple upgrades, this is the easiest method.

DEPLOYING SERVICE PACKS

Deploy service packs.

Microsoft's vision of the future of software upgrades revolves around service packs. A *service pack* is an executable that provides the replacement of one set of files with another. In the case of an operating system (such as Windows NT 4.0), service packs have been a way to distribute bug fixes and fixes to security holes. With Windows 2000, Microsoft's plan is to release service packs on a regular schedule to fix bugs or security flaws. This plan is designed to keep the size of service packs to a manageable level.

In many regards, Windows 2000 service packs are not very different from Windows NT 4.0 service packs. When they are released, the intent is for you to install the service pack on all your Windows 2000 computers to implement any fixes included in them. However, one significant improvement has been made in the application of service packs: the concept of slip streaming.

To understand slip streaming, a digression into service packs on Windows NT 4.0 is required. Under Windows NT 4.0, if you installed a service pack, you had to ensure that, if you made modifications to the operating system that involved reading files from the distribution CD or a network share, you subsequently reinstalled the latest service pack. This was because the files found on the distribution CD or in the network share were pre–service pack versions, and reapplication was necessary to ensure that all components of the operating system were up to the current service pack.

With slip streaming, this is unnecessary. Changes from the service pack can be applied to the source files found on a local folder or network share by copying the service pack files over the existing files. This means that subsequent access to those files result in obtaining the fixed versions of those files, not the old ones. This saves time because it means that the service packs have to be applied only once to any machine (provided that it uses a network share as its installation source) and not multiple times as services (and other operating system components) are installed. In addition, this also means that new installations done over the network will also automatically be up to date with the current service pack.

It must be noted that slip streaming does not remove the need for each machine to have the service pack installed on it. It does remove the need to install the service pack on fresh Windows 2000 installations and the need to install the service pack after making operating system changes.

As of this writing, there were no service packs to install, so all that can be concretely demonstrated is service packs in Windows NT 4.0. However, that knowledge can be applied to service packs under Windows 2000.

In the standard service pack installation, two major things happen. First, the files that are going to be replaced are copied into a backup directory so that the installation can be reversed if necessary. Although this is an optional process prompted for by the service pack installation routine, it is always recommended that you use it. Second, the service pack replaces the operating system files that it finds installed on the target system with the new versions of those files.

The recommended procedure for the installation of a service pack is outlined in Step by Step 8.12.

ON THE CD

Step by Step 8.12, "Installing a Service Pack," lists the basic steps involved in applying a Service Pack. See the file **Chapter08-12StepbyStep.pdf** in the CD's **Chapter08\StepbyStep** directory.

TROUBLESHOOTING FAILED INSTALLATIONS

Troubleshoot failed installations.

Unfortunately, sometimes installations of Windows 2000 Server fail. There are a variety of factors that might cause such a thing to happen. As a system administrator, you need to know as much about the causes for failure as you can to ensure that you can quickly recover from such a failure.

Most problems with installation are caused by an installer not following the correct procedures. Granted, there are some cases when the failure is caused by faulty media. However, those are the exception, not the rule. In general, if you follow the procedures outlined to this point in the chapter, you will have successful installations.

If there is any question about any of your hardware or software being Windows 2000 compatible, it is recommended that you run the upgrade check tool, which is part of the WINNT32 program. Executing WINNT32 /checkupgradeonly from the Windows 2000 Server CD-ROM generates a report telling you about possible issues. This report details hardware that may not work without new drivers and software that is not Windows 2000 compatible, that may not be Windows 2000 compatible, or that needs to be reinstalled after upgrade. It also identifies system settings that will not function the way they used to or that will be disabled by the Setup routine. If you have many servers, you are well advised to run the upgrade check on a representative sample of your servers so you can anticipate problems and, using hardware and/or software upgrades, preempt them.

The following are the reasons for failure that arise most frequently:

◆ **Minimum Hardware Requirements not met.** Windows 2000 Server has minimum hardware requirements that must be met for installation to complete. If the processor is too slow, there is not sufficient RAM, or the amount of free disk space is insufficient, you have to upgrade your server before installation can continue. This may be the case even when you are upgrading from Windows NT 4.0 because of the increased minimums in these areas.

◆ **Hardware not on the HCL.** If hardware is not on the HCL, it may not be detected and installed properly. If the hardware is a network card, you may not be able to contact a domain controller or network server and the installation may fail. Check the Microsoft HCL Web site and run the upgrade check to see whether there are going to be any HCL problems.

◆ **Media errors.** If there seems to be a problem with the Windows 2000 Server Installation CD-ROM, contact your software
vendor to request a replacement.

◆ **Failure of dependency service to start.** At installation, this error is most often caused by an improperly configured network adapter. Make sure that the hardware is detected properly and manually change properties if required.

◆ **Inability to connect to the domain controller.** If you are joining a domain, you have to contact a domain controller to create or check for a computer account. Ensure that the correct name has been given for the domain, that the provided credentials can create computer accounts in the domain, and that a domain controller can be contacted from your location.

◆ **Automated Installation fails.** Check the parameters you specified for the installation. If you specified incorrect information or if you manually created or modified the answer file or UDF file, you may have introduced errors.

◆ **RIS installation fails.** Check that you have correctly configured the RIS server and that its services have started. Check that the client meets the client criteria. Ensure that the network is functioning properly.

CASE STUDY: WHIPPETS AND WIDGETS

ESSENCE OF THE CASE

This case requires that the following results be achieved:

▶ Configure 15 identical Windows 2000 Servers.

▶ Make the configuration of these servers as simple as possible and as quick as possible.

▶ Find a way to save the configuration to allow similar installations to be performed in the future.

SCENARIO

Whippets and Widgets is a dog breeding and metal fabrication company (built out of the dreams of the founders, Edna and Rodger Coombs). In business for 30 years, they have created 15 small offices in the towns surrounding Kalamazoo, Michigan, their head office location. Edna hired Arnold last year to take over their network, which had grown too complex for Rodger, a career dog breeder and computer hacker, to manage on his own. The current network infrastructure is one where a domain controller at the head office is used to authenticate logon for all the Windows 95 and 98 users in the branch offices.

Arnold realizes that the idea of logging on over a WAN is not very good but he has been given another job: to install a file and print servers at each of the 15 branch locations. Because he will have free rein to purchase the new equipment, he has decided to purchase identical machines for each location. His problem is that he needs an effective way of installing each machine without the tedium of manually doing the configuration for each. He would also like a way to be able to configure any number of additional machines with the same configuration should the need arise.

ANALYSIS

Given Arnold's problem, it is obvious that he needs some kind of automated installation solution. The tedium of installing 15 machines manually would probably bore him to death, not to mention take up a lot of his time. In addition, a manual installation would have to

CASE STUDY: WHIPPETS AND WIDGETS

be documented for it to be repeated in the future. If he could create an unattended installation, he could ensure that the servers are installed while he performs some other task. In addition, the configuration of an unattended installation also ensures that he can use that configuration in the future on any new machines that he purchases.

Given that he wants to set up an unattended installation, he must then look at the different methods available. Although a RIS solution is possible, it typically needs specialized configuration and perhaps specialized hardware that will not have any lasting benefit. As a result, he is best off looking at a scripted installation from a network share (using unattended answer files and a uniqueness definition file) or a solution that uses disk duplication (through the SYSPREP program and a third-party imaging program, such as Norton's Ghost) to distribute disk images to the destination machines.

Both of these solutions are acceptable and, as a result, a combination of the two is probably the best way to go. Because the machines are all identical, they are perfect candidates for the use of SYSPREP and disk duplication. However, if Arnold purchases new equipment in the future that is not identical, the master disk created here will probably not work. If, however, he creates a scripted installation (which makes use of Plug and Play to detect hardware), he can ensure

that the master computer used to create the disk for duplication is identical to the current master. In this way, every time he purchases new hardware (which is different from the current standard) he can simply use the script to install and then create a new master for that series of machines.

Table 8.4 summarizes the solution.

TABLE 8.4

REQUIREMENTS AND SOLUTIONS IN THE WHIPPETS AND WIDGETS CASE STUDY

Requirement	Solution Provided By
Configure 15 identical servers.	Unattended installation using answer files to configure the master, and disk duplication to configure the additional machines.
Make the configuration simple and quick.	Disk duplication to configure multiple identical machines.
Save the configuration for future use.	Unattended installation using answer files to configure a new master, and disk duplication to configure additional machines matching the hardware profile.

CHAPTER SUMMARY

KEY TERMS

- Member server
- HCL
- System Partition
- Boot Partition
- Attended installation
- Unattended installation
- Computer account
- WINNT
- WINNT32
- MAKEBOOT
- MAKEBT32
- Setup disks
- Unattended answer file
- Uniqueness definition file (UDF)
- Setup Manager
- SYSPREP
- Remote Installation Services (RIS)
- Remote Boot Disk
- Service pack
- Slip streaming

This chapter discussed the main installation topics you will encounter on the Windows 2000 Server exam. These included attended and unattended installations, upgrades from Windows NT 4.0, service pack deployment, and installation troubleshooting.

Each of these is important, both from an exam perspective (you must know them to pass) and from the perspective of the system administrators or technicians who are going to install Window 2000.

For one-time (or unique) installations, knowledge of attended installations is required. You have to be able to start the installation given a number of machine-specific circumstances, and you have to be able to answer the questions asked by the Setup program.

For multiple installations on similar platforms, unattended installations will make your life much easier. By setting up and deploying unattended installations, you can save time, make yourself more productive, and avoid redundant, repetitive work.

If you are migrating from an existing Windows NT 4.0 implementation, you need to understand the implications of upgrading and the mechanics of the upgrade process. This will help you avoid some painful mistakes in the process.

As Windows 2000 matures, you also need to be able to install service packs. It will become part of regular server maintenance.

Finally, you have to be able to troubleshoot in case your installation fails. This means understanding how things should function when everything is okay, but also means being able to adapt to things going wrong and quickly diagnose and repair problems.

APPLY YOUR KNOWLEDGE

Review Questions

1. What three methods can be used to begin Windows 2000 Server Setup and under what circumstances are they used?

2. Which program is used to aid you in creating automated Setup scripts and where is it found?

3. What is the purpose of a service pack and where would you get the latest one?

4. What are the minimum hardware requirements (processor, RAM, and free disk space) for the installation of Windows 2000 Server?

5. What are the three unattended installation methods discussed in this chapter and how do they work? (Provide a general overview.)

6. What does the term *member server* mean and what is required on your network to configure one?

Answers to Review Questions

1. The three programs used for starting a Server setup are Setup, WINNT, and WINNT32. Setup is used when doing an attended install on a Windows 32-bit platform; it can be invoked manually or by the AUTORUN.INF file when the CD is inserted in the drive. WINNT is used to do an attended or an unattended install from a 16-bit platform (like Windows 3.1 or DOS). WINNT32 is used to do an unattended install from a Windows 32-bit platform. For more information, see the sections "Attended Installations of Windows 2000 Server" and "Script-Based Unattended Installation."

2. The program for aiding in the creation of installation scripts is called the Setup Manager and it is found on the Windows 2000 Serve CD-ROM in the path \Support\Tools\deploy.cab. To use it, you must extract the EXE file and the associated DLL to a folder on your hard drive.. With a wizard, you can use Setup Manager to create both answer files and UDF files. For more information, see the section "Using the Setup Manager to Create Unattended Answer Files."

3. Service packs are designed to allow incremental upgrades to a piece of software—in this case, to the Windows 2000 operating system. Service packs distribute bug fixes and security patches.. Service packs can be obtained from the Microsoft Web site or from other distribution media, such as TechNet and MSDN. For more information, see the section "Deploying Service Packs."

4. The minimum hardware requirements for the installation of Windows 2000 Server are: RAM = 256MB; Processor = 166MHz Pentium; and free disk space = 1GB. Being minimums, these require upgrading as the number of clients and the complexity of processing on a server increases. For more information, see the section "Minimum Hardware Requirements."

5. The three unattended installation methods described are scripted installations using answer files and uniqueness files, disk duplication using SYSPREP and disk imaging software, and remote installation by booting to a network location. Scripted installations used answer files and uniqueness definition files to define responses to the installation prompts. In essence, this is a regular installation, with the answers being provided by a file rather than by a user. Disk duplication

APPLY YOUR KNOWLEDGE

relies on the SYSPREP program to prepare a machine to have its disk duplicated by a third-party program (such as Norton's Ghost) and that disk image placed into a network share or onto a CD-ROM. After the image has been created, it is copied onto a destination machine as an image that requires only that a mini-Setup wizard be run to complete configuration. Finally, remote installation requires a RIS server and client machines that are capable of booting to a network location. Often these are thin clients without floppy drives or CD-ROMS. The client connects to a network location and the installation progresses from there rather than from a local machine. For more information, see the section "Unattended Installations of Windows 2000 Server."

6. A member server is a Windows 2000 Server machine that is configured to participate as a part of a domain, but which lacks Active Directory

and therefore does not validate domain logon. Member servers typically provide one or more of the following services on a network: print services, file services, application services, or Web services. To configure a member server, you must have a domain defined, and that requires a machine configured as a domain controller (running Active Directory). For more information, see the section "Windows 2000 Server and the 70-215 Exam."

ON THE CD

This book's companion CD contains specially designed supplemental material to help you understand how well you know the concepts and skills you learned in this chapter. You'll find related exercises and exam questions and answers. See the file **Chapter08ApplyYourKnowledge.pdf** in the CD's **Server\ApplyYourKnowledge** directory.

Suggested Readings and Resources

1. *Windows 2000 Deployment Guide,* available on the Internet at `http://www.microsoft.com/windows2000/library/resources/reskit/dpg/default.asp`. Reference any installation and deployment chapters. This is probably the best source anywhere on Windows 2000 topics.

2. Windows 2000 Server Resource Kit: *Microsoft Windows 2000 Server Deployment Planning Guide.* Microsoft Press, 2000.

   - Part 4: Windows 2000 Upgrade and Installation

3. *Microsoft Windows 2000 Professional Resource Kit.* Microsoft Press, 2000.

   - Chapter 5: Customizing and Automating Installations

4. Microsoft Official Curriculum course 1557: *Installing and Configuring Microsoft Windows 2000.*

   - Module 2: Installing Microsoft Windows 2000
   - Module 16: Upgrading a Network to Windows 2000

5. Microsoft Official Curriculum course 1567: *Preinstalling and Deploying Microsoft Windows 2000 Professional.*

   - Module 2: Automating an Installation of Windows 2000 Professional
   - Module 4: Creating and Deploying an Image of Windows 2000 Professional

6. Microsoft Official Curriculum course 2152: *Supporting Microsoft Windows 2000 Professional and Server.*

   - Module 1: Installing or Upgrading to Windows 2000
   - Module 11: Maintaining the Windows 2000 Environment
   - Module 16: Implementing Windows 2000 Servers and Clients

Microsoft provides the following objectives for "Installing, Configuring, and Troubleshooting Access to Resources" within MCP Exam 70-240: Microsoft Windows 2000 Accelerated Exam for MCPs Certified on Microsoft Windows NT 4.0:

Install and configure network services for interoperability.

▶ This objective is necessary because someone certified in the use of Windows 2000 Server technology must be able to configure such a server to operate in an environment where Windows 2000 is not the only network operating system. Access to printers and data must be configured so all clients can access the resources (if security considerations do not make that inappropriate). Primary interoperation is with Novell NetWare clients and servers but also extended to UNIX and Macintosh clients.

Monitor, configure, troubleshoot, and control access to printers.

▶ This objective is necessary because someone certified in the use of Windows 2000 Server technology must understand how to grant and deny access to printers. In addition, one must be able to monitor and perform routine maintenance and troubleshoot problems with access and performance relating to printers.

Monitor, configure, troubleshoot, and control access to files, folders, and shared folders.

- **Configure, manage, and troubleshoot a standalone Distributed file system (Dfs).**

- **Configure, manage, and troubleshoot a domain-based Distributed file system (Dfs).**

- **Monitor, configure, troubleshoot, and control local security on files and folders.**

CHAPTER 9

Installing, Configuring, and Troubleshooting Access to Resources

- **Monitor, configure, troubleshoot, and control access to files and folders in a shared folder.**

- **Monitor, configure, troubleshoot, and control access to files and folders via Web services.**

▶ This objective is necessary because someone certified in the use of Windows 2000 Server technology must understand methods for providing access to data resources. In addition, one must be able to control access to those resources and to troubleshoot problems that might prevent access to resources.

Monitor, configure, troubleshoot, and control access to Web sites.

▶ This objective is necessary because someone certified in the use of Window 2000 Server technology must be able to configure a Web server using Internet Information Server (IIS) and to control access to it. In addition, one must be able to troubleshoot problems relating to too much or too little access.

▶ This chapter contains many testable items. Remember that Microsoft incorporates multiple items together into single questions, so make certain you know how these topics are interrelated.

▶ You should read and understand the concepts in the chapter and go over the review and answer the exam questions at the end.

▶ To understand the topics thoroughly, you should implement the strategies in the Step by Step examples. Because of the nature of some of the interoperability sections, you might find it difficult to actually implement the solutions unless you have a number of test machines and access to other operating systems (such as NetWare and Macintosh computers). I suggest you install the services and go through the configurations until a lack of equipment forces you to stop.

▶ Interoperability has always been a focal point on the exams. Make sure you are familiar with the services required to interoperate with NetWare, Macintosh, and UNIX. Specifically for NetWare, be certain you have an outline in your mind of which steps need to be taken to set up the Gateway Service for NetWare Service (GSNW) and to get it to provide NetWare access to clients. Be sure you understand which protocols are required as well as where they are required.

▶ Sharing, Windows NT File System (NTFS) security, printing, and Web implementation can all be configured, even if you have only one machine. Because there is a logical distinction between the printer (the software interface) and the print device (the hardware component), you do not have to have a print device to do the printer module. For the network portions, you can benefit from having a second machine to use as a client with a network hub to enable you to connect them. You cannot implement the encrypted Web connections (using server and client certificates) unless you obtain or create certificates. If you already have certificates, use them; if not, you can use the Windows 2000 Certificate Services to create them.

▶ In the Dfs section, you can implement standalone regardless of your setup; however, domain-based Dfs requires that you have a Windows 2000 domain controller running in native mode. If you do not have such a machine, you can implement only part of the Dfs solutions.

INTRODUCTION

This chapter helps you prepare for the "Installing, Configuring, and Troubleshooting Access to Resources" section of the exam. Because many Windows 2000 standalone servers are used for file and print servers, it is essential that you thoroughly understand the many ways to provide access to resources, as well as ways to secure those resources. In this case, the resources are data and printers. As indicated in the exam objectives, your understanding of a wide variety of access methods is expected.

LOCAL GROUPS AND USERS

To understand the topic of access to network resources, you must first have an understanding of groups. Part of making a resource available on the network is controlling access to it. This is done through a Discretionary Access Control List (DACL), which is part of the sharing properties.

Instead of assigning permissions directly to the user accounts that require access to a share, you can create a single group, which can be assigned permissions. Call it by some meaningful name, such as Accounting, and then populate membership of this group with the people in the accounting department. Next, place the group in the DACL of each of the shared folders. Access for each individual user is granted based on the group's access level. Not only is this an easier way to populate the DACL of each folder (one entry rather than a separate entry for each member of the group), but it is easier also to change access. A change in the accounting department means only one change to the group. That change is then reflected in all the DACLs of which the group is a member.

Local groups are used to control access to resources on specific machines such as data folders and printers. On a Windows 2000 Server, the local groups are part of the local security model for the machine.

Three other group types are universal groups, global groups, and domain local groups, which are found exclusively on domain controllers. *Universal groups* can consist of user accounts, computer accounts, global groups, or other universal groups from any domain in an Active Directory forest. *Global groups* can contain other global groups or users from the domain in which they are created and can be added to any universal groups or domain local groups in the forest. *Domain local groups* can contain global groups, universal groups, or user accounts and computer accounts from the forest. Domain local groups are used to grant access only to the resources of the domain in which they exist. The purpose of each of these group types is to provide convenient mechanisms to apply user permissions to access resources. Using groups is always recommended over using individual user or computer accounts.

This discussion of local users and groups is important because when it comes to security, local means everything. If a server is a member of a workgroup, it is an authority unto itself. Users log on locally to the machine, and it validates those logons locally in its own security database. These are called *local users*. If you want to group together users for administrative ease, you can create local groups, local to a certain machine. Finally, you can then give access permission to a resource at the local machine level. In the end, the local machine controls all access to the resources it holds.

Even when a Windows 2000 Server joins a domain, it is still king of all it contains. By joining a domain, however, it gives some of its control away because the administrators for the domain (called *Domain Admins* in Active Directory) are added to the server's local Administrators group. The administrators of the domain can then administer the server itself.

Typically, when access is given to resources on a server (for example, one that has joined a domain and has access to groups and users in Active Directory), the following pattern is followed:

1. Domain users can be added to universal, global, or domain local groups in Active Directory. This enables Domain Administrators to group domain users together for domain-wide purposes.

2. Local groups are created on each server for the purpose of granting access to resources located on the server. In addition, if a server is a member of a domain, the domain local groups created in its domain also can be used to control access to resources on the server.

3. Local users, global groups, and universal groups can then be used to populate the local groups on the server. The population of domain local groups is similar to that of local groups except that you cannot use local users from a specific server to populate them. Local users are created only when there is no good reason to create a user who has access to resources across the whole domain but who only needs access to resources on a local machine. These cases are rare, but they do exist.

4. Permissions are then granted to access resources by adding local groups to the DACLs of the local resources.

In general, the pattern of group memberships and permissions is as follows:

domain accounts ➠ global groups ➠ domain local groups ➠ permission to access resources

Universal groups can be used in cases in which you want to group users from multiple domains but do not want to perform multiple assignments of the same global groups in domain local groups in each domain. Instead, create a single universal group and populate the universal group with global groups from each domain. The single universal group can then be made a member of each domain local group.

Global groups also can be made members of domain local groups directly. Universal groups are optional and can only be used when a domain is in native mode. Alternatively, if you use local accounts, they would be added to local groups on the server and would be used to grant access to resources.

To put this methodology to use, you need to know how to manage local groups and users.

Managing Local Groups

Managing local groups consists of the following activities: creating local groups, modifying group memberships, renaming groups, and deleting local groups.

Creating and maintaining local groups is done in the Computer Management console on a server. The following Step by Step leads you through the process of creating a local group.

ON THE CD

Step by Step 9.1, "Creating a Local Group on a Server," leads you through the upgrade process. See the file **Chapter09-01StepbyStep.pdf** in the CD's **Chapter09\StepbyStep** directory.

You might want to modify the members of a group after it has been created. To do so, follow Step by Step 9.2.

ON THE CD

Step by Step 9.2, "Modifying the Membership of a Local Group on a Member Server," leads you through the upgrade process. See the file **Chapter09-02StepbyStep.pdf** in the CD's **Chapter09\ StepbyStep** directory.

You also can rename any group in the group listing. When you do that, the group name is changed everywhere it appears. Step by Step 9.3 addresses renaming.

ON THE CD

Step by Step 9.3, "Changing the Name of a Local Group on a Member Server," leads you through the upgrade process. See the file **Chapter09-03StepbyStep.pdf** in the CD's **Chapter09\ StepbyStep** directory.

Deleting a group is another action taken within group maintenance. You should be very careful when deciding whether to delete a group, however, because when you delete a group, it is removed from the DACLs of all the resources it was added to. Renaming a group might be all you really need to do; but if you do need to remove a group, it is a simple process, as shown in Step by Step 9.4.

ON THE CD

Step by Step 9.4, "Deleting a Local Group on a Member Server," leads you through the upgrade process. See the file **Chapter09-04StepbyStep.pdf** in the CD's **Chapter09\StepbyStep** directory.

Managing Local Users

A local user on a Windows 2000 member server is one who exists only on that machine and does not exist in the domain's Active Directory. Local users are generally created only when you need to give access to resources to someone who does not log on to your domain. There is one local account that is always available—the Administrator for the computer. This account is created when the operating system is installed, and it cannot be deleted. This account may be used when you need to log on to the local machine to do maintenance, and a domain logon is not possible.

Local users can be given all rights that domain users can be given. The real difference is that they exist only within the context of the local server. As with local group maintenance, local account maintenance consists of the following tasks: creating a new account, renaming an account, and deleting an account. Local account maintenance is done in the Computer Management console. Follow Step by Step 9.5 to create a local account on a server.

ON THE CD

Step by Step 9.5, "Creating a Local Account on a Member Server," leads you through the upgrade process. See the file **Chapter09-05StepbyStep.pdf** in the CD's **Chapter09\StepbyStep** directory.

Renaming a local account is another task that you might have to perform. Step by Step 9.6 walks you through this process.

ON THE CD

Step by Step 9.6, "Renaming a Local Account," leads you through the upgrade process. See the file **Chapter09-06StepbyStep.pdf** in the CD's **Chapter09\StepbyStep** directory.

Deleting users is a task you should undertake only with much forethought. When a user account is created, it is assigned a *security identifier* (SID). This SID is unique, and it is what identifies a specific user account. When the account is deleted, the SID is removed from the system as well. Even if you create a new user with the same username, the SID is different, and the new user must be added to groups and DACLs all over again. It is recommended that if a user account is no longer needed because the owner has left the company, you should disable it for a time. The account remains available and can be renamed when a new user takes over the vacated position. Then you can simply rename the account and change its properties to reflect the new user.

Step by Step 9.7 outlines how to delete a user account.

ON THE CD

Step by Step 9.7, "Deleting a Local User Account," leads you through the upgrade process. See the file **Chapter09-07StepbyStep.pdf** in the CD's **Chapter09\StepbyStep** directory.

GIVING AND CONTROLLING DATA ACCESS

Monitor, configure, troubleshoot, and control access to files, folders, and shared folders.

The primary function of a file server is to provide centralized access to data over the network, which is then accessible to anyone who has physical access to your network. Moreover, as if the risks from internal people getting unapproved access to data were not enough, the Web server providing access to the entire computerized population of the world adds considerably to security issues. This section covers data access, starting from the simplest scenario, sharing data, and then moving to more complex scenarios that must be configured and administered. It begins with the start of most network access: sharing folders from the server.

Configuring and Controlling Shared Access

The genesis of the network came from a desire to enable a number of people to exchange information via computers. A network allows for the rapid, electronic exchange of data through its infrastructure, and the file server provides a centralized storage location for that information. Data is stored in folders, but in order to provide network access to those folders, they need to be shared.

Preparing to Share

On a Windows 2000 Server, sharing information requires the following:

◆ The Server service must be running.

◆ The data must be present on the server.

◆ The container in which the data is held must be shared. (The container can be a hard drive, a floppy drive, a CD-ROM, or a folder).

The *Server service* is the software component that allows the server computer to be contacted from other network machines and allows the server computer to respond to requests. The Server service is set to start automatically by default; and if it is not running, chances are the network card has failed.

To check the condition of the Server service and to stop and start it if necessary, follow Step by Step 9.8.

ON THE CD

Step by Step 9.8, "Starting and Stopping the Server Service," leads you through the upgrade process. See the file **Chapter09-08StepbyStep.pdf** in the CD's **Chapter09\StepbyStep** directory.

Setting Up and Maintaining Sharing

In order to share folders on a Windows 2000 Server, a user must be a member of either the Administrators or the Power Users group on the local machine, which are both are built-in groups that have certain rights on the machine. One of the rights given to these groups is the ability to share folders. The Administrators, Server Operators, Enterprise Admins, and Power Users groups can share folders by default.

When a folder is shared, access to it over the network is controlled by a DACL that contains a list of users or groups and details the access permissions they have on the network. It should be noted that share-level permissions control access only over the network. If a user is able to log on to a server locally, the share permissions have no effect on that user.

Three levels of access can be given to a DACL entry (person or group): Full Control, Change, and Read. *Full Control* means a user can do anything to the files in the folder, including looking at and changing the content, deleting the files, or changing NTFS permissions within the shared folder. *Change* enables the user or group to modify all files but does not allow permissions to be modified over the network. *Read* enables the user to view the contents of a folder and to open each file in read-only mode. It also allows files to be copied from the shared folder to another location but does not allow files to be copied into the folder nor removed from it.

The administrator can assign each user or group in the DACL different permissions. By default, the Everyone group is given Full Control access. This means what its name implies: Everyone has full access to the files in the folder.

In Step by Step 9.9, you see that permissions enable you to give or remove a specific access level. For example, you can give a group explicit Read access. Anyone who is not a member of a group specified in the DACL, has an implicit No Access to the folder.

ON THE CD

Step by Step 9.9, "Sharing a Folder from a Member Server," leads you through the upgrade process. See the file **Chapter09-09StepbyStep.pdf** in the CD's **Chapter09\StepbyStep** directory.

Permissions granted in the DACL are cumulative (with one exception, which is discussed shortly). If you are listed explicitly as a member of one or more groups, you receive the combination of all the permissions given to you. For example, if you are listed as having Read access and you are in a group that is given Change access, you

receive Change access. The exception to this rule occurs when either
your explicit listing or your group memberships prevent access; then
you will have access taken away. Because permissions always err on
the side of caution, deny permissions always takes precedence over
allow permissions.

In addition, DACLs enable you to explicitly deny access to a certain
resource. Explicit denial always takes precedence over any permissions allowed. This can be used where a single member of an
existing group should not have the same access as the remaining
members of the group. By explicitly denying the user access, all
members of the group have access to the file except that single user.

Troubleshooting Sharing

Problems with share permissions are difficult to diagnose. First see
whether a user is supposed to be able to do what he or she is
attempting. Then you need to verify that the combined permissions
do not prevent some action. For example, if a group is given Change
permission but a user has had Change permission explicitly denied,
the user cannot change data.

Another issue that can affect share permissions is network availability. If the network is down, shared folders become inaccessible. In
Windows 2000, an icon will appear in the system tray (near the
clock), showing a network connection with a red X through it, indicating a loss of network connectivity.

Users having too much access to data is the most problematic issue
regarding shared folders. It is easy to rectify insufficient access by
simply apologizing and correcting the user's access level. However, if
someone gets *too much* access, the data might be deleted, or sensitive
information might fall into the wrong hands.

One risk that you face when creating shared folders is to create
shared folders within existing shared folders. There exists the possibility that a user can access a resource with elevated privileges by
connecting to the resource by using a different share.

In the directory structure shown in Figure 9.1, you can see that the
folder called Pictures is shared, as are its subfolders, Public Pictures
and Secret Pictures. The structure's form is apparent because you can
see the view of it on the disk. If Pictures were shared with Read
access to the Everyone group, you could look at the structure and

know that access to the Just Pictures folder would be Read when someone accessed it over the network. However, if I also told you that access to the Secret Pictures folder was Full Access, how would that be affected by the access level of Read given to the parent folder? The answer to that depends on how a user accesses the data.

As you can see in Figure 9.2, when a user looks through a browser list for the folders shared from a specific server, the list is flat; there is no notion or representation of the on-disk hierarchy. If a user happens to access the data through the Pictures share, he or she receives only Read access to any folder inside it. However, if a user accesses the Secret Pictures share, he or she gets get Full Control, despite the fact that if he or she accessed the same data though the Pictures share he or she would have only Read access.

An administrator must take special care to ensure that access at one level does not counteract the access given at another.

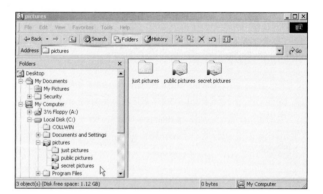

FIGURE 9.1
Knowledge of the file structure does not always help you know which access users have to the data.

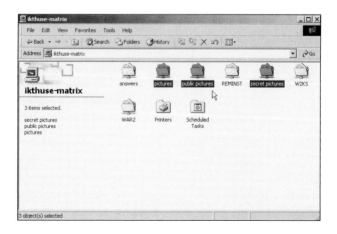

FIGURE 9.2
To a user browsing the shares, the on-disk tree structure is not apparent; everything looks flat.

Configuring and Controlling Local Access

In the previous section, you learned about the ability to control access to data via the network. In utilizing share permissions, there is no way to apply different permissions to files located within a shared folder. In addition, shared permissions have no affect when a user accesses the files locally at the server.

The NTFS File System

The answer to these problems is found in the NTFS file system and the properties inherent in it. *NTFS* is a proprietary file structure available on Windows 2000 computers. One of the features of the NTFS file system is the ability to locally secure files and folders.

For security reasons, format all drives on your Windows 2000 Server with NTFS to locally secure files and folders. If you simply reformat all the drives, your data will be lost, or at best you will have to recover from a backup. Moreover, if you are dealing with your System Partition or Boot Partition, reformatting means reinstalling your operating system. You can change your file system from FAT/FAT32 to NTFS, however, through the CONVERT function.

The CONVERT function is a one-time, one-way conversion from FAT or FAT32 to NTFS. There are no adverse effects from converting, and all existing data is maintained after the conversion is complete.

Step by Step 9.10 outlines the conversion process.

ON THE CD

Step by Step 9.10, "Converting a Partition from FAT/FAT32 to NTFS," leads you through the upgrade process. See the file **Chapter09-10StepbyStep.pdf** in the CD's **Chapter09\StepbyStep** directory.

> **NOTE**
>
> **Windows NT 4.0 Service Pack (SP) 4 Provides Limited Interoperability with NTFS Version 5** Windows NT 4.0 with SP 4 introduced an NTFS driver, which allows Read and limited interoperability with NTFS v5. If a machine is configured to dual boot between NT 4.0 and Windows 2000, it is imperative that the NT 4.0 machine be at SP4 or higher in order to access any of the data on an NTFS v5 partition.

Defining NTFS File and Folder Permissions

You set up and maintain local file and folder security in much the same way you do shared security, with the following differences:

◆ NTFS permissions can be applied to both folders and files.

◆ Any subfolders automatically inherit NTFS permissions.

◆ NTFS permissions are more specific than share permissions.

The following permissions can be assigned to NTFS-protected folders and files:

◆ **Traverse Folder/Execute File.** Allows or denies users the ability to pass through or traverse a folder they do not have access to in order to get to a folder or file they have access to.

◆ **List Folder/Read Data.** Allows or denies a user to list the contents of a folder that it is applied to. When applied to a file, it allows or denies the ability to open the file for reading.

◆ **Read Attributes.** Allows or denies the ability to look at file or folder attributes (such as system, archive, or read-only).

◆ **Read Extended Attributes.** Allows or denies the ability to look at special file or folder attributes, such as file encryption or compression.

◆ **Create Files/Write Data.** Allows or denies the ability to create new files (when applied to a folder) or to edit files (when applied to a file).

◆ **Create Folders/Append Data.** Allows or denies the ability to create new folders in a folder (when applied to a folder) or to append data to a file without changing existing data in that file (when applied to a file).

◆ **Write Attributes.** Allows or denies the ability to modify file or folder attributes (such as system, archive, or read-only).

◆ **Write Extended Attributes.** Allows or denies the ability to modify special file or folder attributes such as file encryption or file compression.

◆ **Delete Subfolders and Files.** Allows or denies the ability to delete subfolders and files from a folder. This applies even if explicit delete permission is denied to the child folders or files.

◆ **Delete.** Allows or denies the ability to delete the folder or file to which it is applied.

◆ **Read Permissions.** Allows or denies the ability to look at the permissions applied to a file or a folder.

◆ **Change Permissions.** Allows or denies the ability to modify the permissions applied to a file or a folder.

◆ **Take Ownership.** Allows or denies the ability to become the owner of a file or a folder. If you have ownership of a file or a folder, you can always change permissions, regardless of any other permissions set on a file or folder.

To simplify NTFS permission assignments, default permission combinations are defined within Windows 2000. These default groupings separate these permissions into more manageable units. The basic folder permissions are shown in Table 9.1.

TABLE 9.1

BASIC LOCAL (NTFS) SECURITY PERMISSIONS FOR FOLDERS

Special Permission	Full Control	Modify	Read & Execute	List Folder Contents	Read	Write
Traverse Folder/ Execute File	X	X	X	X		
List Folder/ Read Data	X	X	X	X	X	
Read Attributes	X	X	X	X	X	
Read Extended Attributes	X	X	X	X	X	
Create Files/ Write Data	X	X				X
Create Folders/ Append Data	X	X				X
Write Attributes	X	X				X
Write Extended Attributes	X	X				X
Delete Subfolders and Files	X					
Delete	X	X				
Read Permissions	X	X	X	X	X	X
Change Permissions	X					
Take Ownership	X					

Basic NTFS permission combinations also exist, which can be applied directly to files. Table 9.2 outlines the basic NTFS permissions that can be applied to files on an NTFS partition.

TABLE 9.2

BASIC LOCAL (NTFS) SECURITY PERMISSIONS FOR FILES

Special Permission	Full Control	Modify	Read & Execute	List Folder Contents	Read	Write
Traverse Folder/ Execute File	X	X	X			
List Folder/ Read Data	X	X	X			
Read Attributes	X	X	X	X		
Read Extended Attributes	X	X	X	X		
Create Files/ Write Data	X	X				X
Create Folders/ Append Data	X	X				X
Write Attributes	X	X				X
Write Extended Attributes	X	X				X
Delete Subfolders and Files	X					
Delete	X	X				
Read Permissions	X	X	X	X	X	
Change Permissions	X					
Take Ownership	X					
Synchronize	X	X	X	X	X	

Applying NTFS Permissions

Applying file or folder permissions is much the same as applying
share permissions. The major difference is that when you apply a
specific permission, it is cascaded down to all the files and folders in
the hierarchy by default, beginning with the folder you are applying
it to. In addition, when you create a new file or folder in an existing
folder, this new object inherits the security properties of its parent
container by default.

Unless you explicitly break the connection between the parent container and a child object, you are not allowed to modify the permissions on the child; the permissions remain grayed-out. If you remove the ability for a child object to inherit permissions, you can choose either copy or remove the permissions that were inherited from the parent folder.

It also should be noted that every file and folder on an NTFS partition has local security applied to it. By default, the Everyone group has Full Control locally. The following Step by Step walks you through modifying NTFS permissions.

ON THE CD

Step by Step 9.11, "Modifying File or Folder Local Permissions," leads you through the upgrade process. See the file **Chapter09-11StepbyStep.pdf** in the CD's **Chapter09\StepbyStep** directory.

Although local security resolves a number of security issues, it introduces a problem that only it can resolve. That is the problem of a file or folder being secured by its owner for only that person's access and then that person leaving the company.

Taking ownership is one way to take back the control of locally secured files. By default, an administrator has the ability to take ownership of any file or folder on his or her server. All other users must be specifically assigned the Take Ownership permission in order to take ownership of a file or folder. Step by Step 9.12 shows you how to take ownership of a file or folder.

ON THE CD

Step by Step 9.12, "Taking Ownership of a File or Folder," leads you through the upgrade process. See the file **Chapter09-12StepbyStep.pdf** in the CD's **Chapter09\StepbyStep** directory.

Troubleshooting Local File Security

Troubleshooting local file security is a fairly simple matter. Because you are dealing with individual users accessing local objects, if the file exists, lack of access or too much access are caused by permission problems. To rectify such problems, log on as an Administrator, check to see what the current permissions on the object are and repair them if necessary.

When Local File Security Interacts with Shared Folder Security

Local security applies across the board to all accesses to a file, whether over the network or locally. The question is, how do local (NTFS) permissions interact with share (network) permissions? The answer is that the most restrictive of the permissions always apply. Therefore, if your share security permissions are Full Control but your local permissions are Read, you cannot get more than Read access to the data. The same holds true if share security permissions are Read but your local permissions are Full Control; again, you cannot get more than Read access to the data.

Although this sounds confusing, it really makes things simpler. If you want to ensure that permissions act the same for a user whether he or she is accessing data locally or over the network, you can do the following:

◆ Set all the share permissions to Authenticated Users with Change permissions and Administrators with Full Control.

◆ Ensure that the host partition is formatted (or converted to) NTFS.

◆ Apply local permissions restricting users to appropriate levels.

This ensures that share permissions do not interfere with users' ability to access data, and it makes your job as an administrator that much easier because you do not have to deal with two sets of permissions and circumstances.

The Distributed File System (Dfs)

If you have many file servers in your organization and many shares on each one, you might run up against the problem of users being confused about where to go to get what. As soon as you distribute the location of your shares, you invite problems with users locating them.

The Dfs included with the Windows 2000 Server operating system enables you to collect in a tree a number of share points. This collection makes it appear to a user browsing a server that all data is located under a certain tree structure when, in fact, the data remains scattered all over your network on different file servers. As indicated in Figure 9.3, although the shared folders are on Servers 2 and 3, it appears as though they are on Server 1, thanks to Dfs.

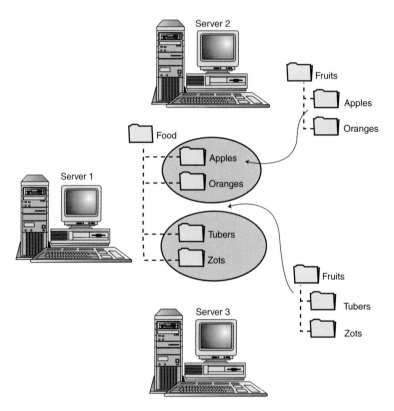

FIGURE 9.3
Dfs creates a tree structure.

Dfs depends on the share permissions and NTFS permissions set at the actual file servers where the data exists. In fact, there is no security configuration available within Dfs; it is all controlled from the remote location.

A Dfs root can be accessed only by a client operating system that understands Dfs. Such operating systems include Windows 2000 (all versions), Windows NT 4.0 (all versions), and Windows 98. Windows 95 can be Dfs enabled by installing the Directory Services Client. This client software is available on the Windows 2000 Server CD-ROM in the path `Clients\Win9x`.

All Dfs requires is the Dfs service installed on one or more servers, a configured Dfs root, and the configuration of DFS child nodes that link remote shares to the DFS root.

In this section, you are introduced to two methods of administering a Dfs: locally on a server and in a domain-wide structure in Active Directory.

Standalone Dfs

In a standalone Dfs structure, the administration of Dfs is controlled at a server with no redundancy built in to it. If the main Dfs server goes down, there is no way to get to the data that has been collected under its Dfs root.

The first step in the configuration process is to install the Dfs root on a server. For a standalone Dfs, this is done as outlined in Step by Step 9.13.

ON THE CD

Step by Step 9.13, "Installing a Standalone Dfs Root," leads you through the upgrade process. See the file **Chapter09-13StepbyStep.pdf** in the CD's **Chapter09\StepbyStep** directory.

After a Dfs root has been established, you need to maintain it. Maintenance of a standalone Dfs root consists of three tasks: adding Dfs links, removing Dfs links, and disabling Dfs links.

You add a new Dfs link when the Dfs tree needs to be expanded through the addition of a new link. Step by Step 9.14 walks you through adding a Dfs link to a Dfs root.

> **ON THE CD**
>
> ---
>
> Step by Step 9.14, "Adding Dfs Links to a Dfs Root," leads you through the upgrade process. See the file **Chapter09-14StepbyStep.pdf** in the CD's **Chapter09\StepbyStep** directory.
>
> ---

Removing a node is necessary when you *permanently* no longer need that node. Step by Step 9.15 outlines that process.

> **ON THE CD**
>
> ---
>
> Step by Step 9.15, "Removing a Dfs Link from an Existing Dfs Root," leads you through the upgrade process. See the file **Chapter09-15StepbyStep.pdf** in the CD's **Chapter09\StepbyStep** directory.
>
> ---

NOTE

Disabled Links Are Still Visible to Clients Even if a Dfs link is disabled, it still appears to the user when the Dfs root is opened. However, after the user tries to access it, an error message appears, informing the user that the network location is inaccessible.

You disable a Dfs link when you want to temporarily prevent a certain node from being accessed from within the Dfs tree. For example, you may want to disable a Dfs link when a server is down for maintenance. Step by Step 9.16 shows you that procedure.

> **ON THE CD**
>
> ---
>
> Step by Step 9.16, "Disabling and Enabling a Dfs Link in a Dfs Root," leads you through the upgrade process. See the file **Chapter09-16StepbyStep.pdf** in the CD's **Chapter09\StepbyStep** directory.
>
> ---

Troubleshooting access problems with standalone Dfs has to do primarily with configuring the Dfs properly. You must first ensure that the computers and shares you are linking to are set up and are accessible to the Dfs root. In addition, the share security needs to be set up so that users can access the right information. Because a standalone Dfs is not fault tolerant, making certain the Dfs root is always up is a major consideration in troubleshooting resource access. Finally, if some clients connect and others do not, the client software is probably to blame. Remember that Windows 9x clients require that the DS Client software be installed to access Dfs shares.

Domain-Based Dfs (Fault-Tolerant Dfs)

Although standalone Dfs works well in a small environment, when the number of clients you are serving increases, the need to have the Dfs root available on a consistent basis increases. Standalone Dfs has a weakness: If the Dfs root server goes down, the entire tree becomes inaccessible. By using Active Directory to store the Dfs structure and by providing redundant locations to child nodes, you can ensure that your Dfs tree is available if your Dfs server goes down.

As its name implies, domain-based Dfs requires that the server hosting the Dfs root be part of a Windows 2000 domain. This is required because the Dfs information is stored in Active Directory, and only a domain controller has a copy of Active Directory.

The steps for creating a domain-based (fault-tolerant) Dfs root are listed here.

1. Share folders on one or more servers.

2. Create a fault-tolerant Dfs root using the Dfs Manager on a member server.

3. Add links to remote child nodes.

4. Add a second (or more) Dfs root server as a replica of the first.

5. Add replicas of the shared folders (if desired).

Creating a domain-based Dfs root is almost the same as creating a standalone version, as illustrated in Step by Step 9.17.

ON THE CD

Step by Step 9.17, "Creating a Domain-Based Dfs Root," leads you through the upgrade process. See the file **Chapter09-17StepbyStep.pdf** in the CD's **Chapter09\StepbyStep** directory.

To add, remove, or disable child nodes in the domain-based Dfs structure, refer to Step by Steps 9.14, 9.15, and 9.16. The procedures are the same whether the Dfs is domain based or standalone.

Simply storing the Dfs root information in Active Directory does not make it fault tolerant. You also must set up replicas of the Dfs structure on one or more servers to enable fail-over. By setting up root replicas, you can be certain that a user trying to access the Dfs root when the Dfs root server is down will be automatically (and transparently) redirected to another location for the tree information. Step by Step 9.18 walks you through the process of setting up root replicas.

ON THE CD

Step by Step 9.18, "Creating and Enabling a Dfs Root Replica," leads you through the upgrade process. See the file **Chapter09-18StepbyStep.pdf** in the CD's **Chapter09\StepbyStep** directory.

At this point, fault tolerance is set up, but it is not enabled. To enable it, you must configure a replication policy to define how the fault-tolerant roots obtain information about the main root. This is outlined in Step by Step 9.19. Note that for automatic replication to work properly, the file system on the Dfs roots must be NTFS.

ON THE CD

Step by Step 9.19, "Enabling Dfs Root Replication," leads you through the upgrade process. See the file **Chapter09-19StepbyStep.pdf** in the CD's **Chapter09\StepbyStep** directory.

The Dfs Manager also enables you to configure replication of shared folders. This ensures that if a host server is not available, another replica of the same data is provided automatically to the user. Therefore, if a user clicks on a folder inside the Dfs tree, and the server hosting that folder is not available, Active Directory is searched. If a replica of that folder has been configured, it is presented to the user automatically. Step by Step 9.20 walks you through configuring folder replication in a domain-based Dfs.

ON THE CD

Step by Step 9.20, "Configuring Folder Replication in a Domain-Based Dfs," leads you through the upgrade process. See the file **Chapter09-20StepbyStep.pdf** in the CD's **Chapter09\StepbyStep** directory.

Replication can make Dfs completely redundant, which makes data accessible to users on a continuous basis.

Troubleshooting domain-based Dfs is much like troubleshooting standalone Dfs. You must confirm that the links you have established are accessible by the root Dfs server; however, you also must ensure that Active Directory is accessible so that Dfs information can be obtained. Some troubleshooting problems incurred with standalone Dfs can be avoided in domain-based Dfs simply by making certain that redundancy has been configured.

Configuring and Controlling File Access via Web Services

In addition to sharing files over the network using regular share-level security, if you choose to install IIS on your server, you also can share folders to Web browser clients. Web sharing provides access to browser users, but it does not share the folder over your internal network. If you want a folder to be shared over the network as well as Web shared, you must share it twice.

Preparing for Web Sharing

Web sharing requires two things. First, you must be running IIS, specifically the WWW service on your server. The default installation of Windows 2000 Server actually includes IIS, so it might already be configured on your server. If it is not, you need to install it. Second, you must have Administrator or Power User access to your server. Step by Step 9.21 outlines the installation process for IIS.

> **ON THE CD**
>
> Step by Step 9.21, "Installing IIS on a Windows 2000 Member Server," leads you through the upgrade process. See the file **Chapter09-21StepbyStep.pdf** in the CD's **Chapter09\StepbyStep** directory.

This installation process modifies your server in two ways. First, it creates a folder called Inetpub on your hard drive (generally on the Boot Partition). Second, it creates two local user accounts, one called IUSR_*servername* (for granting anonymous access to browser clients) and another called IWAM_*servername* (the account that IIS uses internally to start out of process applications). Any unauthenticated user who connects to your Web server uses the name IUSR_*servername* and has whatever access has been given to that account.

After IIS has been installed, a new tab appears in the Properties dialog box for your folders, called Web Sharing.

Setting Up and Maintaining Web Sharing

Web folders can be made accessible to any of the Web sites you have configured on your server; you are not restricted to only the default site. These folders appear on your Web site and are accessible when a user types in addresses similar in format to the following:

```
http://servername/webfolderalias
```

Step by Step 9.22 describes the mechanics of sharing a folder via IIS.

> **ON THE CD**
>
> Step by Step 9.22, "Sharing a Folder via Web Services (IIS)," leads you through the upgrade process. See the file **Chapter09-22StepbyStep.pdf** in the CD's **Chapter09\StepbyStep** directory.

To modify or stop Web sharing, you can return to the folder's properties and add a new alias, remove an existing alias, or stop sharing altogether. If you stop sharing, all the aliases for the folder are removed, and you must re-create them if you change your mind.

Web Sharing in Its Context

Similar to shared folder permissions, Web sharing interacts with local security. If Web sharing is configured for a folder that is on an NTFS partition, the more restrictive of the two permissions is effective for a Web browser client connecting to the folder. In addition to NTFS security, you also need to know that the security is on the entire Web site you are sharing under. Any browser client trying to get to a Web share must pass through the Web-site security before it gets to that share. If the site is secured so that only Read access is allowed, even if Write access is given to the Web share, that access is not effective for the browser client trying to gain access to the data.

Troubleshooting Web Sharing

A number of things can go wrong with Web sharing, such as the following:

◆ If the Web sharing tab does not appear in the Properties dialog box for a folder, this can be due to IIS Services not being installed. To solve this, install IIS on your Windows 2000 Server.

◆ Only Administrators and Power Users can create Web shares.

◆ Permissions are configured incorrectly for Web sharing, the Web site, or NTFS permissions. Incorrect permissions can result in non-access or in the worse case, excessive privileges assigned to a visiting user.

◆ The Web service is not running. This prevents the Web folder from being accessible. If the Web service is not running, you can start it by following Step by Step 9.23.

◆ If the Web service is running, the problem might be that the Web *site* is not running. To start it, you need to open the IIS Services Manager Console. Step by Step 9.24 leads you through the process of starting a Web site.

ON THE CD

Step by Step 9.23, "Starting the World Wide Web Publishing Service," leads you through the upgrade process. See the file **Chapter09-23StepbyStep.pdf** in the CD's **Chapter09\StepbyStep** directory.

ON THE CD

Step by Step 9.24, "Starting a Web Site," leads you through the upgrade process. See the file **Chapter09-24StepbyStep.pdf** in the CD's **Chapter09\StepbyStep** directory.

CONTROLLING ACCESS TO WEB SITES

Monitor, configure, troubleshoot, and control access to Web sites.

Web sites are made available through the Web service component of Internet Information Services. Because these Web sites contain data, they need to be secured.

Any security measure you want to place on your Web site(s) can be done through the Internet Services Manager.

The following list outlines ways in which you can control access to your Web site:

◆ Changing the Transmission Control Protocol (TCP) port

◆ Changing access permissions

◆ Changing execute permissions for scripts and programs

◆ Changing authentication methods

◆ Adding Internet Protocol (IP) address and domain name restrictions

◆ Adding server certificates for Secure Socket Layer (SSL) transmissions

◆ Authenticating users with client certificates

Changing the TCP Port

You can hide your Web site from most casual users by choosing any TCP port other than the default TCP port 80. Of course, this is not very robust security because if someone knows which port you are running on, that person can to return to your site. For example, if your site is www.mydata.com and you are using TCP port 8080, a browser client could access your site by typing the URL, http://www.mydata.com:8080.

Step by Step 9.25 demonstrates how to determine and change a Web site's TCP port.

ON THE CD

Step by Step 9.25, "Discovering and Changing a Web Server's TCP Port," leads you through the upgrade process. See the file **Chapter09-25StepbyStep.pdf** in the CD's **Chapter09\StepbyStep** directory.

Changing Access Permissions

There are four access rights (see Figure 9.4) you can control for the entire site: Script Source Access (enabling users to see source code behind an HTML page being viewed), Read access (enabling users to view content of Web pages), Write access (enabling users to upload content to a Web site or modify existing content), and Directory Browsing access (enabling users to see all files within a Web site's folder).

Enabling Script Source Access enables users to see source code behind the HTML page being viewed. Read access enables users to view content of Web pages and is required to create a Web site. Write access enables users to upload content to a Web site or modify existing content. Directory Browsing access enables users to see all files within a Web site's folder, rather than auto loading the configured default Web page for IIS.

Step by Step 9.26 shows how to adjust a site's access permissions.

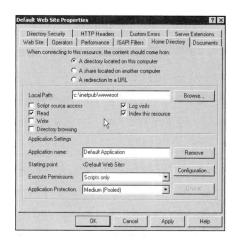

FIGURE 9.4
Web access rights can be used to restrict the file-level permissions on a site.

ON THE CD

Step by Step 9.26, "Changing Site Access Permissions," leads you through the upgrade process. See the file **Chapter09-26StepbyStep.pdf** in the CD's **Chapter09\StepbyStep** directory.

Changing Execute Permissions for Scripts and Programs

Execute permissions define which kind of scripts or executables a browser client can invoke on your site. The execute permissions include None, Scripts Only, and Scripts and Executables. If you have Active Server Pages (ASPs), you must enable Scripts Only to allow the ASP to formulate the desired Web page.

Step by Step 9.27 demonstrates how to change a site's execute permissions.

ON THE CD

Step by Step 9.27, "Changing Site Execute Permissions," leads you through the upgrade process. See the file **Chapter09-27StepbyStep.pdf** in the CD's **Chapter09\StepbyStep** directory.

WARNING

Write + Run Access = Trouble   A user who has Write access to a Web site and the ability to run scripts and/or executables can pose a serious security risk to your site. With Write access, a user could create a damaging script or program, upload it to your site, and then run it.

Changing Authentication Methods

Authentication for a Web site can be set to anonymous or authenticated access. Anonymous access authenticates the connecting user with the IUSR_*servername* account for resource access. If you enable authenticated access, you can force clients to provide credentials to access a Web site. There are three levels: basic authentication, digest authentication for Windows domain servers, and Integrated Windows authentication.

◆ **Basic authentication.** Basic authentication is the least secure but most accessible across a variety of browsers. This kind of authentication sends all logon information in clear text, which makes it susceptible to interception by a network sniffer.

Although sending passwords in clear text is a security risk, this can be overcome by using server certificates and SSL (covered later).

◆ **Digest authentication**. This form of authentication uses a hashing algorithm to encrypt data sent between the browser and the server. This hashing algorithm is classed as *one-way* in that it can be used to encrypt but not decrypt the data. This type of authentication works only on browsers that support the HTTP 1.1 standard and can respond to the requests the IIS server is making. Some consider digest authentication a security risk in that the password must be stored using *reversible encryption* on a domain controller.

◆ **Integrated Windows authentication (IWA)**. This form of authentication (formerly called NTLM or Windows NT Challenge-response authentication), uses special encryption protocols to secure the authentication process. Unlike the other two authentication methods, IWA does not initially prompt for a username and password. Instead, it uses the current user's access token for authentication. If the user is granted access, he or she may never know that any restrictions are in place on the site. If the user does not authenticate or a Windows logon name cannot be determined, the browser displays a logon dialog box. The disadvantage with IWA is that it works only on Internet Explorer 2.x or later.

Step by Step 9.28 demonstrates changing the kind of user authentication required by your Web server.

ON THE CD

Step by Step 9.28, "Changing Site Authentication Methods," leads you through the upgrade process. See the file **Chapter09-28StepbyStep.pdf** in the CD's **Chapter09\StepbyStep** directory.

NOTE

Configuration for Digest Authentication Two things are required in order for this kind of authentication to work. First, the IIS server must be a member of a domain. Second, each user who needs to authenticate through a browser must have his or her account store the password using "reversible encryption." To do this, that setting (in the Account tab) must be enabled in the properties for the user, and then the password for the user must be reset.

NOTE

Multiple Authentication Methods If you choose more than one authentication method, after attempting anonymous access, IIS attempts to authenticate using the most secure method (Integrated Windows) first. Then it tries less secure methods until all avenues of authentication have been exhausted.

Controlling Web Site Access Through IP Address and Domain Name Restrictions

You can control the access people have to your Web site based on a client's IP address or the client computer's domain name. By using IP address and domain-name restrictions, you can ensure that even if someone obtains a valid username and password, that person can still be prevented from accessing data.

When you restrict based on IP addresses or domain names, you can configure single IP addresses, multiple addresses based on a network ID and a subnet mask, or addresses falling into a certain domain. If you choose to restrict based on domain, your IIS server has to do a reverse lookup on each IP address that traffic comes from. This is very time and resource intensive and might not yield accurate results. Caution should be exercised when choosing this method.

Disallowing access using this method takes precedence over all other access a user might have been given to the Web site.

This method for changing site address and name restrictions is covered in Step by Step 9.29.

ON THE CD

Step by Step 9.29, "Changing Site IP Address and Domain Name Restrictions," leads you through the upgrade process. See the file **Chapter09-29StepbyStep.pdf** in the CD's **Chapter09\StepbyStep** directory.

Securing Web Access Using Server Certificates and SSL

Implementing server Certificates is a final way of securing Web access and authenticating users. The idea of the certificate as it applies to Web transactions is that an entity (server or client) proves its identity to another by possessing a certificate.

A server certificate issued to a Web server identifies it as a particular entity and is verified by a Certification Authority (CA). When a Web browser connects to the Web server, the Web browser must trust the issuing CA to verify the server certificate. For example, if the issuing CA is Verisign, the Web browser must trust Verisign to make assertions about servers. After the browser and the Web server have verified that the server is what it says it is, a security negotiation takes place, thus enabling encrypted transmissions to ensue.

The use of server certificates enables encryption of Web transmissions by way of SSL, which is an encryption methodology that relies on a server certificate to establish server identity and forms the basis for encryption. Under this system, clear-text authentication is no longer a security hazard because the clear-text password is being encrypted by the SSL connection and is therefore no longer clear text. This allows for not only the secure transmission of passwords but also for secure transmission of other confidential information (such as credit card numbers on an e-commerce site). In addition, SSL transmissions can pass through firewalls, providing that TCP port 443 is open.

Step by Step 9.30 demonstrates the process of adding a server certificate to a Web site.

ON THE CD

Step by Step 9.30, "Adding a Server Certificate to a Web Site," leads you through the upgrade process. See the file **Chapter09-30StepbyStep.pdf** in the CD's **Chapter09\StepbyStep** directory.

After the server certificate has been added to your site, you must configure your server for certificate authentication. Step by Step 9.31 explains how to do this.

ON THE CD

Step by Step 9.31, "Configuring Secure Communications on a Web Site," leads you through the upgrade process. See the file **Chapter09-31StepbyStep.pdf** in the CD's **Chapter09\StepbyStep** directory.

Enabling Client Authentication Using Client Certificates

Client certificates are an alternate form of authentication to the ones described in the previous sections. What sets this form of authentication apart from the others is that no passwords are required by the client when a browser connects to a site requiring authenticated access. Instead, the browser sends certificate information the Web server has mapped to a specific user account. Using this method, any browser can be used to connect to a site requiring authentication, without having to allow clear-text passwords and without requiring the user to actually log on using a username and password.

This identification is made possible by incorporating the client certificate into the Web browser and then exporting it to the IIS server. The certificate is then mapped to an account recognized by the IIS server and, when the certificate is seen in the future, it is recognized as being verification of a specific user. From that point on, all permissions that apply to the user are applied to the holder of the certificate. Certificates can be mapped on a one-to-one basis, each mapped to a unique user account, or a group of certificates can be mapped to a single account that has access to a Web site or set of data.

The steps for configuring authentication using client certificates are straightforward.

First, the server must have a certificate installed to enable SSL encryption.

Next, your clients must have a certificate installed on their browser. Like server certificates, these certificates need to be authenticated by a trusted source. If the browsers are connecting to an intranet, you could use Certificate Services to generate a root certifier and client certificates. If the connection is to an Internet site, the clients will most likely use a third-party certificate vendor such as Verisign.

Finally, once certificates are installed, they need to be exported to the Web server and mapped to user accounts. Once the mapping has occurred, the server can authenticate the client as being a particular

> **NOTE**
>
> **The Role of Certificate Services**
> Certificate Services allows an organization to deploy and manage certificates used for deploying a Public Key Infrastructure. These certificates can be used for user authentication, Web server security and EFS security, and many other tasks. Certificate Services allows you to deploy certificates without using a third-party certificate vendor.

user simply by being shown the client certificate. When the user is authenticated, access to resources is the same as that of any other authenticated user.

Step by Step 9.32 shows how to enable client certificates for authentication.

ON THE CD

Step by Step 9.32, "Configuring a Web Server to Accept Client Certificates for Authentication," leads you through the upgrade process. See the file **Chapter09-32StepbyStep.pdf** in the CD's **Chapter09\StepbyStep** directory.

CONFIGURING AND MAINTAINING PRINTERS

Monitor, configure, troubleshoot, and control access to printers.

Next to accessing data, accessing printers is probably the most important need for users. Most often, having a print device physically attached to every person's workstation is impractical, so a shared solution is desired. Windows 2000 Server provides the capability to host one or more print devices and to make them accessible to users.

Before concentrating on the mechanics of setting up printers and administering them, first look into the processes and terminology.

The Printing Process

You will rarely print from an application running directly on your Windows 2000 Server. Instead, from a client computer, you will print to a printer that is shared on a Windows 2000 Server. The act of sharing a printer on a Windows 2000 Server denotes that server as a print server.

The process of printing can be broken down into discrete steps:

1. The client application requests to print to a printer defined on the network.

2. If the client operating system is Microsoft 32 bit, the following things happen locally on the client:

   • A local printer driver formats the request and sends it to a local spooler. If the client operating system is Windows NT or Windows 2000, the client also contacts the print server to ensure that it has the most recent version of the printer driver; if it does not, that server's version of the printer driver is downloaded to the client. Windows 9x clients do not check for updated drivers.

   • A Remote Procedure Call is used to contact the print server and to transfer the print job to the server. If the print server cannot be contacted, the print job is held in the local spooler until the print server can be contacted.

3. If the client operating system is not Microsoft 32 bit (or if it is configured to send only RAW), a local printer driver formats it into a RAW (printable) format and sends it to the print server.

4. When the print server receives the job, if it is in RAW format, it is written directly to disk in the spooler file in preparation to be sent to the print device. If it is not in RAW format, the print job may be modified to include separator pages and to print in duplex modes. This happens in the spooler file.

5. When the job reaches the top of the print queue, the job is sent to the print device, converted into a bitmap format, and printed.

A *printer driver* is a piece of software responsible for communicating specific commands to a print device. Each driver is a little different because each print device is different.

A *spooler* is a file on a hard drive, which is the location that a client or a server uses to store print jobs that are pending.

The *print queue* is the list of jobs stored on the spooler; this queue can be observed through the Print Manager.

EXAM TIP

Printer Terminology Terminology is very important, especially for the exam. Keep in mind that when the exam makes reference to a printer, it is talking about a software interface, not a physical device. The device is called a *print device*; all the software you install and the icon you see in the Printers window is referred to as a printer.

As you can see from the previous points, Microsoft 32-bit operating systems maintain their own spoolers and keep their own copies of the printer drivers. In this way, the client can ensure that most of the work is done in the printing processes before the job gets sent to the print server. It also ensures that jobs can "print" even if the printer cannot be contacted at the time the job is submitted. In that case, the job simply sits on the local spooler until the print server can be contacted.

On non-32-bit clients (such as Windows 3.11, or DOS clients), the print job is completely formatted at the client and sent to the server. There is no spooler on the client, and if the print server cannot be contacted, the print process fails at the client side.

Configuring the Print Server

The *print server* is the collection of software routines that provides print capabilities either locally or over a network. It is configured from the Printers folder, which is accessible via Start, Settings, Printers. After the Printers folder has been opened, you can get to the properties of the print server by choosing File, Server Properties.

The properties of the print server configuration dialog box are divided into four tabs: Forms, Ports, Drivers, and Advanced (see Figure 9.5).

The Forms Tab

The Forms tab is used to create new form (paper size and format) configurations. All forms defined here are available to any printers hosted by the print server.

A number of forms are predefined, and you cannot modify or delete them. In addition, if you have a need to define a form that is not present, you can create custom forms.

The advantage of forms is that they can be assigned to different paper trays on your printer (if you have more than one) and can be used to ensure that a user printing from an application will always print on the correct size paper.

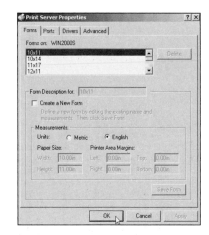

FIGURE 9.5
The Print Server Properties dialog box is used to set print server default settings.

The Ports Tab

From the Ports tab, you define output locations for print jobs. When you define a printer on your server, it must direct the print jobs to a location, such as a data pipe. When information goes into the pipe, it is assumed that there is a print device at the other end.

A number of ports come predefined in Windows 2000 Server. Not all of these ports actually define physical connections; these are defined by default, and it is up to you to configure the ones that will actually be used.

This is the place where you can create your own ports and configure them. You might create new ports when you want to have the print server send print jobs to network-connected printers. With no additional services installed on your Windows 2000 Server, you have two port types available: Local and Standard TCP/IP. (Other port types might show up if you have specific print services installed.)

A local port defines a connection to a printer that is physically connected to your server (such as on a parallel port), a test connection, an infrared connection (accessible through a Universal Naming Convention, or UNC, name), or a local file.

When you define a new local port, you are prompted for the name of the port. The answer you give determines where the print output will be directed. The following list outlines the possible answers and what they indicate:

◆ **A filename (such as C:\PRINTOUT\JOB.TXT).** This defines a file the jobs are redirected to. Each subsequent print job overwrites the previous.

◆ **The UNC name of a printer defined on another computer (such as \\server1\hpprinter).** This will redirect the output to a shared printer or another print server. This is often used when a print device goes down and you want to redirect all print jobs to an alternate printer without reconfiguring all clients.

◆ **The word NUL.** Jobs sent to the null port will be immediately deleted. This port type is used to test whether a client can print without having to waste paper or to queue up in front of other print jobs.

◆ **The word IR.** This defines a connection to an infrared port to allow you to print to infrared-capable printers.

Step by Step 9.33 demonstrates how to add a new local port to a Windows 2000 computer.

ON THE CD

Step by Step 9.33, "Adding a New Local Port," leads you through the upgrade process. See the file **Chapter09-33StepbyStep.pdf** in the CD's **Chapter09\StepbyStep** directory.

A Standard TCP/IP port is used to connect directly to a network printer that supports TCP/IP communication. This kind of printer has a network card in it and acts much like a regular computer on the network. When you configure a standard TCP/IP port, you define the connection via the TCP/IP address of the printer, and requests to print on this printer are redirected to its TCP/IP address. The configuration of such a port generally varies depending on the printer type. Some print devices have special software you can install on your print server that gives you a console from which to do administration. If you use the standard Windows 2000 TCP/IP port configuration, you will need to know the TCP/IP address of the print device (however that is determined).

Step by Step 9.34 walks you through the configuration of a standard TCP/IP port.

ON THE CD

Step by Step 9.34, "Configuring a Standard TCP/IP Port," leads you through the upgrade process. See the file **Chapter09-34StepbyStep.pdf** in the CD's **Chapter09\StepbyStep** directory.

After ports have been configured, you can then install printers to print to them.

The Drivers Tab

Drivers are the software components responsible for converting high-level requests for printing into commands the processor can execute. These commands are specific to the print device, the operating system requesting a print service, and the processor in the computer requesting the print service.

After you install a printer on your Windows 2000 Server, the driver for your print device that is specific to an Intel-based Windows 2000 Server is installed on your print server. The driver for this installation is obtained from the DRIVERS.BIN file local on your Windows 2000 computer. However, there are reasons for installing more drivers. As already indicated, when a 32-bit client configures connectivity to a network printer, the first check made is to see if the driver is available from the print server. If it is not, the client is prompted to produce the driver (usually from a CD-ROM). You can make certain that the most up-to-date drivers are available to your clients by installing the hardware and software platform-specific drivers on your print server.

Step by Step 9.35 outlines the procedure for installing a printer driver on a Windows 2000 Server.

ON THE CD

Step by Step 9.35, "Installing a Printer Driver," leads you through the upgrade process. See the file **Chapter09-35StepbyStep.pdf** in the CD's **Chapter09\StepbyStep** directory.

In addition to adding a new driver, you may need to update a driver. When new versions of the drivers are created, it is a good practice to update your drivers with the new versions. For Windows 9.x clients, updating a driver requires actually installing the new driver manually on the computers. For Windows 2000 and NT clients, the new drivers will be automatically downloaded during the printing process.

A walk-through of the procedure for updating printer drivers is shown in Step by Step 9.36

ON THE CD

Step by Step 9.36, "Updating a Printer Driver," leads you through the upgrade process. See the file **Chapter09-36StepbyStep.pdf** in the CD's **Chapter09\StepbyStep** directory.

If you find that a driver is no longer required, it is good to remove it from your print server. This is especially helpful when you upgrade your printing hardware, and the drivers installed are for printers no longer accessible from the print server. Removing a driver is covered in the Step by Step 9.37.

FIGURE 9.6
The Advanced tab.

ON THE CD

Step by Step 9.37, "Removing Printer Drivers," leads you through the upgrade process. See the file **Chapter09-37StepbyStep.pdf** in the CD's **Chapter09\StepbyStep** directory.

The Advanced Tab

The Advanced tab (see Figure 9.6) allows you to set global defaults, including the following:

◆ **Spooler file location.** This option allows you to move the spooler file from the default drive if the drive is running out of space. If the spooler file is located on a drive with insufficient disk space, this can lead to failure of print jobs.

◆ **Logging options.** You can set whether to log printer errors, warning, and information events. This will place printing events into the print server's system log.

◆ **Error notification.** The print server can be configured to beep when a print error occurs.

◆ **Print notification.** The print server can be configured to send print notification either to the user who sent the print job or to the computer from which the print job originated. The notification will be sent using the Windows 2000 Messenger service to the user or computer based on the print server configuration.

When the print server has been configured, you can begin installing printers on your server.

Installing a Local Printer on a Windows 2000 Server

The underlying assumption of the printer server is that one or more local print devices will be accessible from printers installed on a Windows 2000 Server. From those printers, you can configure availability and access to the print devices. This section will examine the installation of printers and their configuration.

The addition and configuration of printers is done through the Printers folder. This folder can be accessed from the Control Panel by choosing Start, Settings, Printers, or from the Printers share on the server. (This share allows you to access the Printers folder even when you do not have local access to the server.)

You have been exposed to this folder previously; it is from here you configured the print server itself. From this folder, you also can add new printers (local and network), share printers for client access, and remove printers. Step by Step 9.38 walks you through installing a local printer.

ON THE CD

Step by Step 9.38, "Installing a Local Printer," leads you through the upgrade process. See the file **Chapter09-38StepbyStep.pdf** in the CD's **Chapter09\StepbyStep** directory.

> NOTE
>
> **Different Properties for Different Printers** The property sheets that appear in Figure 9.7 are the default tabs for a simple print device. Some print devices have more complex configurations, so you can expect to see some additions to the configuration pages. The tabs discussed in this section should always be present, however.

It is important to note at this point that many printers can be configured for a single print device. As you move to the configuration section, I will point out why this is advantageous in many circumstances.

Configuring a Local Printer on a Windows 2000 Server

After you have added a printer to the Printers window, you can configure it. To do so, access the printer's Properties dialog box by right-clicking the printer you want to configure and choosing Properties from the menu that appears.

As you can see from Figure 9.7, the printer's Properties dialog box is divided into six tabs: General, Sharing, Ports, Advanced, Security, and Device Settings. This section covers all the tabs except Sharing; it will be covered in a later section.

The General Tab

The General tab is used to configure the printer's name, fill in information about its location, and make general comments. In addition, this tab also shows a summary of the features present on the printer.

The two buttons at the bottom of the page are Printing Preferences and Print Test Page. Clicking the Print Test Page button sends a test job for printing. This is used to confirm connectivity and configuration. The Printing Preferences button enables you to set the default print specifications for jobs sent to the printer without indicating any special settings.

The Special Settings button brings up a Preferences dialog box. On it, you can set paper orientation, page order, and the number of document pages to print per piece of paper. You also can set advanced settings such as the print resolution—dots per inch (dpi)—and any advanced features that might be supported by the print device.

The Ports Tab

The Ports tab has the same configuration as the Ports tab that is accessible from the Server Properties dialog box, except for the check box labeled Enable Printer Pooling (see Figure 9.8).

Printer pooling is the ability to have two or more print devices accessible from a single printer and will send a print job to whichever print device is free at the time the job is received at the print server. Because there is only one queue (line), all jobs will be serviced in the order they went into the queue.

To make printer pooling work effectively, a number of guidelines must be followed:

◆ The print devices must be the same or, at the very least, they must use the same print drivers.

◆ The print devices must all be accessible from ports on a single print server.

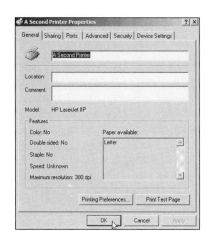

FIGURE 9.7
All printer properties can be accessed from the printer's Properties dialog box.

FIGURE 9.8
This property sheet is almost identical to the Ports sheet in the print server properties.

◆ You must locate the print devices in close physical proximity.
It is important that the people who are printing are able to
find their print jobs because there is no way to determine
which print device the job is sent to, except through visual
inspection.

Step by Step 9.39 describes how to set up a printer pool.

ON THE CD

Step by Step 9.39, "Configuring a Printer Pool," leads you through
the upgrade process. See the file **Chapter09-39StepbyStep.pdf** in
the CD's **Chapter09\StepbyStep** directory.

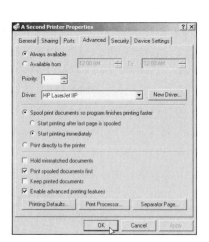

FIGURE 9.9
Users and groups can be added, and permissions can be given to each.

The Advanced Tab

The Advanced tab (see Figure 9.9) allows you to configure a number
of miscellaneous advanced functions of the printer, as follows:

◆ **Printer availability.** You can configure a printer to be available
at all times or to be available for only a specific range of hours.
When a print job is sent to a printer that is not available at
that time, the job is held in the queue until the printer
becomes available, and then the job will begin to print. This is
commonly used to defer large print jobs until after the workday has ended.

◆ **Printer priority.** The priority sets the default importance of
documents being printed from a specific printer to a certain
print device. The priority of a specific print device can be set
anywhere from 1 to 99, with 1 being highest priority. This is
used to allow specific groups to have their print jobs take priority over other groups. This is done by creating two printers
that print to the same physical print device. The specific
groups that require higher access to the printer will send print
jobs to the printer with the higher priority.

◆ **Printer driver.** This option allows you to change the current
print driver used by the printer. This is changed if the actual
print device has been changed, while the original printer is
maintained.

◆ **Spooling options.** This option sets how the printer will manage spooled documents. If you choose to enable spooling by selecting Spool Print Documents So Program Finishes Printing Faster, you can either begin to print the print job immediately as it begins to spool, or you can wait until the entire document has been spooled before it begins to print. If you select to Print Spooled Documents first, a large document must be completely spooled to the printer before it is sent to the print device. This will allow smaller jobs to bypass the larger job in the print queue.

◆ **Mismatched documents.** This option allows the spooler to verify that printer accepts the document's format. If this check box is selected, mismatched documents will be held in the queue; otherwise, they will be discarded.

◆ **Keep Printed documents.** This option enables you to hold copies of documents in the queue after they have printed, rather than deleting them.

◆ **Printing defaults.** This option enables you to set the printing defaults.

◆ **Print processor.** This option enables you to set how print jobs are rendered by the print driver.

◆ **Separator page.** This option allocates a page to be printed between each print job. The separator page identifies certain characteristics of the document being printed, such as the owner. By clicking the Separator Page button, you can browse to a separator page file on your hard drive. The page you choose or create must be selected based on the class of printer you are using (PCL, Postscript, and so on) If no file is specified, no separator page will be printed.

The Security Tab

Security on printers is very much like local file security through NTFS permissions on files; it applies whether you are accessing a printer locally (logged on to the server) or remotely (over the network). In fact only one set of permissions exists for printers, which makes printer security easier to manage.

The basic security model has three levels, with a few more granular modifications that can be adjusted through advanced settings. These levels are as follows:

◆ **Print.** This permission gives users the ability to send print jobs to the printer.

◆ **Manage Printers.** This option gives all rights of Print and Manage Documents but also provides the ability to modify the properties of the printer itself (including changing the DACL for the printer) and to take ownership of the printer.

◆ **Manage Documents.** This permission gives the assigned user or group the ability to manipulate documents in the print queue, including adjusting documents' properties and deleting them from the queue.

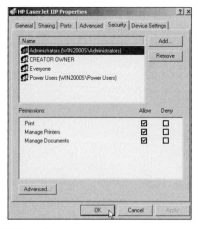

FIGURE 9.10

Users and groups can be added, and permissions can be given to each.

Figure 9.10 shows the default security configuration for a newly installed printer. Listed are the Administrators of the print server, Power Users of the print server, the CREATOR OWNER of the print jobs, and the Everyone group. Both the Administrators and the Power Users have all three permissions. These groups will be able to print to the printer, manage all the documents, and change the ACL of the printer. The CREATOR OWNER (the person who created the specific print job being manipulated) has Manage Document permission. In addition, CREATOR OWNER also gets all the permissions the Everyone group gets (Print permissions).

Like NTFS permissions and shared access permissions, the effective printer permission is the combination of all the permissions granted. Therefore, although the CREATOR OWNER has only explicitly been given Manage Documents permission, because she is a member of the Everyone group, she also has Print permission. Also like NTFS and shared access permissions, explicit denial of a permission takes precedence over explicit allowance.

Step by Step 9.40 demonstrates the procedure for changing printer security settings.

Step by Step 9.40, "Changing Security Settings on a Printer," leads you through the upgrade process. See the file **Chapter09-40StepbyStep.pdf** in the CD's **Chapter09\StepbyStep** directory.

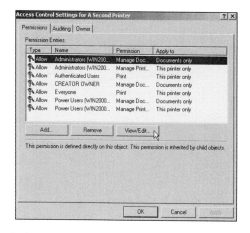

FIGURE 9.11
Special permissions allow more granular control over printer access.

As with NTFS security, advanced settings also can be applied to printer security. From the Security property sheet, you can click the Advanced button to access those properties (see Figure 9.11).

Advanced permissions break down the permissions set on the Security property sheet into their component parts. You can modify the permissions for a specific user or group by adding that user to the list and then clicking the View/Edit button.

As you can see in Figure 9.12, the advanced permissions add to the basic permissions set on the Security tab. Added to the basic permissions are Read Permissions, Change Permissions, and Take Ownership. Read Permissions allow a user to view the current security configuration of a printer. Change Permissions enables a user to modify permissions for a printer. Take Ownership enables a user to become the owner of a printer. By default, the owner of a printer has the ability to change permissions.

To take ownership of a printer a user must have the advanced permission, Take Ownership. Even if he or she has no other permissions, that user can still access the Security property sheet and modify ownership. Taking ownership of a printer is outlined in Step by Step 9.41.

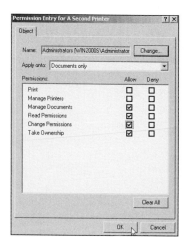

FIGURE 9.12
Special permissions can be explicitly given or denied.

Step by Step 9.41, "Taking Ownership of a Printer," leads you through the upgrade process. See the file **Chapter09-41StepbyStep.pdf** in the CD's **Chapter09\StepbyStep** directory.

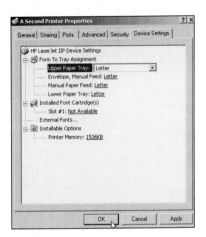

FIGURE 9.13
The Device Settings tab.

The Device Settings Tab

The Device Settings tab (see Figure 9.13) has contents specific to the particular printer model being configured. Generally, there will be options for assigning specific forms to paper trays, configuring installed font cartridges, and configuring other installable options.

Sharing a Printer on a Windows 2000 Server

Printers are only available to network users by sharing the printers on a Windows 2000 Server. Sharing can be configured while you install a printer or after the fact. Step by Step 9.42 describes how to configure sharing for a printer you have already installed.

ON THE CD

Step by Step 9.42, "Sharing a Printer," leads you through the upgrade process. See the file **Chapter09-42StepbyStep.pdf** in the CD's **Chapter09\StepbyStep** directory.

All security for the printer is defined when the printer is shared. Separate NTFS permissions do not apply for shared printers.

Maintaining Documents on a Windows 2000 Print Server

After printers have been configured, they will operate without much intervention (other than having paper and toner added). However, there are times when the printer and the documents in the queue must be managed. This management includes pausing a printer for maintenance, redirecting documents when a printer stops functioning, removing documents from the print queue, and changing the properties of documents in the print queue.

All ongoing printer maintenance is handled from the print queue for that printer. Double-click the printer for which you want to see the print queue, and a dialog box opens, showing the queue.

Many features of the print queue are accessible from the menus. The Printer menu enables you to change access and configuration for the printer; the Document menu enables you to change access and configuration for documents. To manipulate the printer, you must have Manage Printer permissions for the printer. To manipulate all the documents, you must have Manage Documents permissions for the printer. Anyone can manipulate his or her own documents because the CREATOR OWNER account is assigned Manage Documents permission.

In the event you need to temporarily stop a printer from sending print jobs to a print device, you can select the Pause Printing option in the Printer menu. You might do this, for example, if you see that print jobs are being printed on letterhead by mistake and want to suspend printing so you can change paper.

In the event that all jobs need to be removed, you can select Cancel All Documents from the Printer menu. This will delete all documents from the queue.

Whereas the printer properties enable you to adjust options for all the documents being printed, the Document menu enables you to adjust properties for documents one at a time. The Document menu enables you to pause, resume, or restart a document's printing (something that is very handy in the case of a paper jam). From the Document menu, you also can access the Document Properties dialog box. Finally, the Document menu enables you to cancel (delete) a document.

The Properties dialog box has three property sheets: General, Layout, and Paper/Quality. Of the three, only the General property sheet has properties that can actually be changed; the other two have read-only attributes.

On the General property sheet, you can change the person who is notified when the job is complete, the priority for the current document, and the time at which the document is printed (see Figure 9.14).

FIGURE 9.14
Document properties can be set to override the default printer settings.

Although these properties may be adjusted by the owner of the document, the priority will affect only documents that belong to the same owner by default. Only if the person changing priorities has been explicitly assigned the Manage Documents permission can he or she change the order of other user's documents.

Managing a Windows 2000 Printer from a Browser

If you have IIS installed on your Windows 2000 Server, you can manage the print queue of any shared printer from a browser. From a browser window, you can pause and resume a printer; view, pause, resume, and cancel documents; and view the properties of your printers. These capabilities are explored in Step by Step 9.43.

ON THE CD

Step by Step 9.43, "Managing a Windows 2000 Printer from a Browser," leads you through the upgrade process. See the file **Chapter09-43StepbyStep.pdf** in the CD's **Chapter09\StepbyStep** directory.

Auditing a Windows 2000 Printer

Suppose you want to track access to a specific printer so you can determine who modifies permissions or who tries to access a printer and fails because of access restrictions. Auditing writes entries to the security log, and you can access it at your convenience.

Auditing can watch for both success and failure of a specific type of access. Usually, you will want to audit only failures because they are the ones that will help you spot unauthorized people trying to access your printers.

Setting up auditing is a two-step process. First you configure your server to watch for audit events, and then you configure your printer to generate audit events for certain access types. Step by Step 9.44 walks through this process.

ON THE CD

Step by Step 9.44, "Configuring Auditing on a Windows 2000 Server," leads you through the upgrade process. See the file **Chapter09-44StepbyStep.pdf** in the CD's **Chapter09\StepbyStep** directory.

After you configure your server to watch for audit events, you must set up your printer(s) to define which events will trigger recording audit information. This is covered in Step by Step 9.45.

ON THE CD

Step by Step 9.45, "Configuring Auditing for a Windows 2000 Printer," leads you through the upgrade process. See the file **Chapter09-45StepbyStep.pdf** in the CD's **Chapter09\StepbyStep** directory.

After auditing is configured and your server is collecting information, you need to check the logs to see whether events are being generated. These events will be logged in the security log, which is accessible from the Event Viewer console. Step by Step 9.46 shows you how to examine the security log.

ON THE CD

Step by Step 9.46, "Examining the Security Log," leads you through the upgrade process. See the file **Chapter09-46StepbyStep.pdf** in the CD's **Chapter09\StepbyStep** directory.

Non-Windows Operating System Interoperability

Install and configure network services for interoperability.

In many network environments, Windows is not the only operating system in use. In those cases, some level of interoperability must be attained between Windows 2000 and the other operating system in order to share information. Windows 2000 Server provides a number of services that allow for interoperation with network operating systems such as NetWare, AppleTalk, and UNIX.

Interoperation with Novell NetWare

Microsoft has invested many years of research and development into creating tools to interoperate with NetWare as well as to migrate from NetWare. This discussion focuses primarily on the tools that come with Windows 2000 Server, but for the sake of well-rounded knowledge and because other issues may crop up on the exam, the discussion touches briefly on some of the add-ons.

Installing and Configuring the NWLink Protocol

Although TCP/IP is available for NetWare and is becoming popular, especially on NetWare 5 servers, the proprietary IPX/SPX protocol suite is still the mainstay of NetWare network communications. As a result, in order to have any level of interoperability with NetWare servers, a compatible protocol must be installed on Windows 2000 Server machines. Microsoft's implementation of the IPX/SPX protocol is called NWLink IPX/SPX/NetBIOS Compatible Transport Protocol, and it is fully compatible with IPX/SPX, thus ensuring baseline communication with NetWare servers.

With NWLink installed on a Windows 2000 computer, you are able to connect to client/server applications running on NetWare servers. This is apart from any functionality gained by installing additional services.

To install NWLink, follow the steps in Step by Step 9.47.

ON THE CD

Step by Step 9.47, "Installing the NWLink Protocol," leads you through the upgrade process. See the file **Chapter09-47StepbyStep.pdf** in the CD's **Chapter09\StepbyStep** directory.

After installing NWLink, you might need to configure it, depending on how many different kinds of NetWare servers you have in your environment. Different versions of NetWare (and NetWare servers using different network types—for example, Ethernet versus Token Ring) use different frame types (think of this as a dialect of IPX/SPX). These frame types are not compatible with one another.

If you have only one frame type, NWLink will detect it and auto-matically configure itself. If there is more than one frame type (your NetWare administrator will be able to tell you this), you will have to manually configure the frame types. If you do not, only one frame type will be used, and the others will be ignored. (The frame type used will be either 802.2 or the first one detected if 802.2 is not detected on your network.)

To manually configure frame types for NWLink, follow Step by Step 9.48.

ON THE CD

Step by Step 9.48, "Manually Configuring NWLink Frame Types," leads you through the upgrade process. See the file **Chapter09-48StepbyStep.pdf** in the CD's **Chapter09\StepbyStep** directory.

Although the NWLink protocol gives you basic connectivity to a NetWare server, it is often insufficient for interoperation with a NetWare environment. The Gateway Service for NetWare (GSNW) provides further connectivity.

Installing and Configuring the Gateway Service for NetWare (GSNW)

GSNW provides two connectivity services for Windows 2000 Servers. First, it provides connectivity to a NetWare server's printers and files through the installation of a NetWare Client for Windows 2000. (This is the same client that is installed on Windows 2000 Professional when Client Services for NetWare is installed.) The client service allows a Windows 2000 Server to log in to a NetWare server and access files and printers based on the permissions assigned to the account used to connect to the NetWare server.

Although the client portion of GSNW is useful, the Gateway Service allows other Microsoft clients to connect to NetWare resources without loading NetWare client software.

After GSNW has been configured, it can be used to provide folders on a Windows 2000 Server that can be accessed by anyone with access to the Windows 2000 Server. These folders are really connec-tions to folders on a NetWare 3.x or 4.x server. (Note that 5.x is supported with this service only if IPX/SPX has been installed on it because GSNW will not work over TCP/IP, which is the default protocol for NetWare 5.x.) A Microsoft client sees a regular share on a Windows 2000 Server, but access to that share causes the Windows 2000 Server to retrieve information from the corresponding NetWare server.

The advantage of using the GSNW is that you do not have to configure NWLink and a NetWare client on those machines. In addition, they do not need to authenticate with the NetWare server. All your Microsoft clients can continue to operate the way they used to except they now have access to some additional shared folders on a Windows 2000 Server.

Because GSNW is a gateway, you must ensure that clients are using it only periodically. If people need frequent access to large amounts of data on a NetWare server, you might be better off to configure the client to directly access the NetWare server than to go through the gateway.

To set up a gateway, you must perform three basic steps:

1. Configure the NetWare server.

2. Install GSNW.

3. Configure GSNW.

The following must be done on a NetWare server to prepare it for access by a Windows 2000 Server running GSNW:

1. Designate an existing account as a gateway account or create one or more accounts for that purpose.

2. Create a group called NTGATEWAY and populate it with the account(s) you identified or created in step 1.

3. Grant the NTGATEWAY group the minimum permissions required to access the resources that need to be available to clients connecting through the Windows 2000 Server running GSNW.

Step by Step 9.49 will guide you through installing GSNW on a Windows 2000 Server machine.

ON THE CD

Step by Step 9.49, "Installing GSNW on a Windows 2000 Server," leads you through the upgrade process. See the file **Chapter09-49StepbyStep.pdf** in the CD's **Chapter09\StepbyStep** directory.

After installing GSNW, you must configure it. You do this by creating shares on your server that map to file resources on the NetWare server. You also can configure security on those shares at the same time using share-level security, as you would on shared folders that are actually on your server.

Step by Step 9.50 demonstrates how to configure GSNW.

ON THE CD

Step by Step 9.50, "Configuring Gateway Services for NetWare," leads you through the upgrade process. See the file **Chapter09-50StepbyStep.pdf** in the CD's **Chapter09\StepbyStep** directory.

The list of shares from a client on the server, configured in the preceding steps, appears like that shown in Figure 9.15. Note the presence of the share called System, which is a gateway share to the SYS:System folder on the NetWare server.

NOTE

Most Restrictive Rights Apply You cannot give more share-level permission to the gateway shares than the Gateway account has been given to the NetWare shares. For example, suppose that on the NetWare server, your Gateway account has been given only Read access. You can configure Full Access from the gateway share, but the effective permission to the resource will be Read.

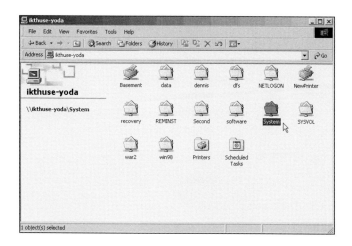

FIGURE 9.15
The shares listed when you browse a server running GSNW include the shares that are redirected to the NetWare server.

As we have seen, through GSNW, Microsoft clients can be configured to obtain occasional access to NetWare servers. However, you might have NetWare clients who want access to Windows 2000 files and printers. To provide this access, you must install File and Print Services for NetWare (FPNW).

File and Print Services for NetWare (FPNW)

FPNW provide, NetWare clients running IPX access to Windows 2000 resources hosted on a Windows 2000 Server. This tool is not provided with Windows 2000 Server; it must be purchased separately. It is ideal for environments in which Windows 2000 is in the minority, but your clients need access to its resources.

Like GSNW, FPNW functions using only NWLink. Therefore, any NetWare client attempting to use FPNW must be running IPX/SPX, not TCP/IP.

Because this is an add-on to Windows 2000, the exam will not ask any questions about it except for those that require you to show a basic understanding of the function of the product. You will not be required to know how to install or configure it.

Interoperation with Apple Macintosh

Although Apple Macintosh does not hold an overwhelming share of the personal computer market, it is still supported in many organizations. Because of its strengths in desktop publishing and graphic manipulation, it has earned itself a place in a niche market of the computer industry. As a result, many companies with Windows 2000 Servers also have one or more Apple Macintosh computers. For this reason Microsoft continues to support three tools for Macintosh interoperability under Windows 2000:

◆ File Server for Macintosh

◆ Print Server for Macintosh

◆ The AppleTalk protocol

Installing and Configuring the AppleTalk Protocol

The AppleTalk protocol is the proprietary Macintosh protocol designed to allow Macintosh computers to communicate in their own workgroups. To provide interoperability with Macintosh machines, AppleTalk is required.

Step by Step 9.51 outlines the procedure for installing the AppleTalk protocol.

NOTE **The Protocol and the Services** The AppleTalk protocol does no good without the accompanying services. Moreover, if you install the accompanying services, AppleTalk will be installed automatically as part of the process.

ON THE CD

Step by Step 9.51, "Installing the AppleTalk Protocol," leads you through the upgrade process. See the file **Chapter09-51StepbyStep.pdf** in the CD's **Chapter09\StepbyStep** directory.

After the protocol has been installed, you might need to configure it. Macintosh machines divide themselves up locally through the use of zones (such as Windows workgroups). To make a computer part of a zone, its AppleTalk protocol must be configured to participate in the zone of choice, as demonstrated in Step by Step 9.52.

ON THE CD

Step by Step 9.52, "Configuring AppleTalk Zones," leads you through the upgrade process. See the file **Chapter09-52StepbyStep.pdf** in the CD's **Chapter09\StepbyStep** directory.

Installing and Configuring the File Server for Macintosh

The File Server for Macintosh allows your Windows 2000 computer running AppleTalk to act as a file server for Macintosh computers. In order to act as a Macintosh file server, your Windows 2000 Server must have NTFS volumes available on which to create a Macintosh-accessible volume.

Step by Step 9.53 identifies the process for installing a file server for Macintosh.

ON THE CD

Step by Step 9.53, "Installing File Server for Macintosh," leads you through the upgrade process. See the file **Chapter09-53StepbyStep.pdf** in the CD's **Chapter09\StepbyStep** directory.

After installing the File Services for Macintosh, you must create a Macintosh accessible volume. Step by Step 9.54 guides you through this process.

ON THE CD

Step by Step 9.54, "Creating a Macintosh Accessible Volume," leads you through the upgrade process. See the file **Chapter09-54StepbyStep.pdf** in the CD's **Chapter09\StepbyStep** directory.

After you create a Mac-accessible volume, you also will need to secure it. Step by Step 9.55 shows you how to do this.

ON THE CD

Step by Step 9.55, "Securing a Macintosh Accessible Volume," leads you through the upgrade process. See the file **Chapter09-55StepbyStep.pdf** in the CD's **Chapter09\StepbyStep** directory.

As this section comes to a close, there are some things worth mentioning. First, when a Macintosh-accessible volume is created, Windows users can access the volume by using regular network share access. To Windows users, these volumes appear as shares, and data can be shared between Windows and Macintosh clients.

Second, in order for a Macintosh client to access data on a Windows 2000 Server, it must authenticate with the Windows 2000 Server. It is advisable to install Microsoft's User Authentication Manager (UAM) on your Macintosh clients. This UAM is present on your server in a folder called Microsoft UAM Volume, which is installed when you install the File Services for Macintosh. The reason for installing this UAM rather than leaving the Macintosh one in place is that the Macintosh UAM allows account and password information to be saved (bad security) and transmits the credentials in clear text (even worse security). The UAM presents a Windows dialog box where the Mac user fills in his name and password.

Finally, although it was mentioned that AppleTalk must be installed in order to use the Macintosh services, if it is not installed before the services are installed, it will be installed automatically as part of the installation of either of the Macintosh services.

Installing and Configuring the Print Server for Macintosh

Print Server for Macintosh provides for two functions on a network: 1) the ability for Macintosh clients to print to printers controlled by Windows 2000 print servers and 2) the ability for Windows clients to connect to Macintosh printers through a Windows 2000 print server.

To configure this functionality, you must install the AppleTalk protocol and the Print Server for Macintosh following Step by Step 9.56.

ON THE CD

Step by Step 9.56, "Installing Print Server for Macintosh," leads you through the upgrade process. See the file **Chapter09-56StepbyStep.pdf** in the CD's **Chapter09\StepbyStep** directory.

After Print Services for Macintosh is installed, you can then install a local Macintosh print device or connect to a shared Macintosh printer. While installing a local Macintosh print device, you can create a new port for that device with the type set as AppleTalk Printing Devices.

Interoperation with UNIX

UNIX has many variations (not the least of which is Linux) that are used in the corporate network. As a result, Microsoft is actively developing interoperability tools for UNIX.

Because many of the TCP/IP-based tools in Windows 2000 were modeled after tools that were originally part of UNIX systems, interoperability through that protocol was a natural path to take. Interoperability with UNIX consists of the use of the following Windows 2000 components: the TCP/IP protocol, Print Services for UNIX, and Microsoft Windows Services for UNIX 2.0.

Installing and Configuring Print Services for UNIX

After you install Print Services for UNIX, Windows 2000 Servers can connect to printers hosted by UNIX computers as well as allow UNIX clients to connect to printers hosted on the local Windows 2000 Server.

UNIX machines support a variety of print utilities. Some of the supported ones under the Print Services for UNIX are line printer remote (LPR), which allows a client to send print jobs to a remote printer; line printer daemon (LPD), which allows a UNIX server to receive print job requests (and print them); and line printer queue (LPQ), which enables an administrator to review the items in an LPD print queue. The Print Services for UNIX provide all these utilities running on a Windows 2000 Server. This means that with Print Services for UNIX running on your Windows 2000 Server, you are able to create a local printer (which you can share to your Windows clients) that connects through the local LPR service (LPRMON) to a UNIX printer hosted on a UNIX computer running an LPD. In addition, through the local LPD service (LPDSVC), a UNIX client running an LPR service would be able to connect to a printer configured locally on a Windows 2000 Server.

To start either of these services, you must first install them. Step by Step 9.57 leads you through that process.

ON THE CD

Step by Step 9.57, "Installing the Print Services for UNIX," leads you through the upgrade process. See the file **Chapter09-57StepbyStep.pdf** in the CD's **Chapter09\StepbyStep** directory.

When the print services have been installed, you can add an LPR port on your server to redirect print jobs to an LPD service hosted on a UNIX computer or have UNIX clients submit print jobs to your LPD service. All jobs submitted to it are forwarded to a spooler on the UNIX server. In addition, UNIX clients can connect to the IP address of the Windows 2000 UNIX print server and then to the specific queue.

In addition to the standard print services, there are also file services that allow your Windows clients to connect to data hosted on a UNIX server, much like GSNW allows clients to connect to data on NetWare servers.

Services for UNIX

Services for UNIX (an additional utility that can be purchased from Microsoft) gives you some additional interoperability options. This package provides you with Client Services for UNIX, Gateway Services for UNIX, Directory Synchronization for UNIX, and many other helpful utilities. These function in much the same way as the NetWare services described in the previous sections.

CASE STUDY: WORDS, WORDS, WORDS

ESSENCE OF THE CASE

This case requires that the following end results be satisfied:

▶ The production printers should be configured so that the most efficient use can be made of all of them at all times.

▶ The administrative printer should be configured so that non-administrative personnel cannot direct print jobs to it.

▶ Areas on the servers that can hold confidential documents should have restricted access, so that only certain people can get any access to the files at all.

SCENARIO

Words, Words, Words Inc. is a publishing company whose primary business is to reprint classic works of literature. As a result, much of what they produce is stored in digital form on servers. They have a local area network with five Windows 2000 Servers performing print and file services. They have called you in to resolve two problems.

The first problem relates to five high-speed printers they purchased last year. Four of these printers were purchased for the document-processing departments and are used to print draft copies of books they are reformatting for print. All four are located centrally in the building and are readily accessible by all departments. The fifth printer is used by the Accounting and Human Resources departments to print administrative documents and reports. The four production departments cooperate quite well, and because the various production schedules are not the same, when one printer is not being heavily utilized by one department, people from another will redirect their print jobs to that printer. The problem is that only some of the production employees understand how to redirect print jobs (most of them just click the Print button), and those who do sometimes accidentally send large jobs to the administration printer. You have been asked to resolve the problems related to redirecting jobs from printer to printer and to prevent jobs from being sent to the administrative printer by unauthorized users.

CASE STUDY: WORDS, WORDS, WORDS

The second issue has to do with confidential information that is held on some of the print servers. Although most of the documents are accessible by everyone, some are confidential, and access to those needs to be restricted. Company managers understand that you can prevent remote access to files by not sharing them, but they want security against access by some of the people who can get local access to the servers. Some users who perform delegated administrative duties (but who are not full-blown administrators) have rights to log on to the servers, and they have been caught browsing through confidential information. The company wants to put an end to this.

ANALYSIS

In this case, analysis and solutions will fall into two categories—printer security/configuration and local file security. You are dealing with four departments with four identical printers. Moreover, these departments already have a good cooperative relationship. These printers were all purchased at the same time and, therefore, are probably all the same. As a result, printer pooling is a good solution to the problem of different usage patterns. By placing all the print devices in the same place and then implementing printer pooling, you can ensure that each device is used the same amount and that

jobs will always go to the print device that is currently free. With this solution in place, users will no longer have to decide where their jobs are to be sent because sending it to the default printer (which is now the printer pool) will cause the job to be printed on one of four print devices, which are all located together.

The second problem is one of restricted access to the administrative print device. You can easily solve this problem by removing the default print access from the printer (Everyone: Print) and replacing it with Print access for a local server group that includes only members of the Human Resources and Accounting departments. Doing this will ensure that even if other employees try to direct jobs to this print device, they will fail to print.

The third problem involves the configuration of local security on certain files or folders on the servers. For this to be possible, NTFS partitions must be present. If they are not, you will first need to convert the FAT volumes to NTFS. You can then modify the DACLs of the files or folders to remove the Everyone group from having Full Control and add a group (or groups) representing the people who should have access to the data. This ensures that whether or not the folders are ever shared, only the correct people will have access to the files and folders.

continues

CASE STUDY: WORDS, WORDS, WORDS

continued

The following table summarizes the solution.

TABLE 9.3

OVERVIEW OF THE REQUIREMENTS AND SOLUTIONS IN THIS CASE STUDY

Requirement	Solution Provided By
Access to a number of print devices	Moving the print devices into physical proximity and configuring a printer pool on the server
Secure the administration printer	Creating a local group representing all the people who should have access to the print device and modifying the print device's DACL to allow Print access to only people in that group
Secure files and folders on the servers	Converting partitions to NTFS and using local groups and file/folder DACLs to restrict access to only group members

CHAPTER SUMMARY

Summarized briefly, this chapter covered the following main points:

◆ **Making files available on a Windows 2000 Server.** This includes sharing folders using network shares and sharing folders using IIS Web sharing. It also includes using Dfs to make shares on other servers available at a central Windows 2000 file server.

◆ *S*ecuring files on a Windows 2000 Server. This includes implementing security on network shares, local security using NTFS permissions, and security on Web sites using a variety of methods.

◆ **Managing and configuring printers on a Windows 2000 Server.** This includes installing printers and configuring availability (including sharing and securing). It also includes configuring printer pools, available times, and priorities, as well as managing printers both locally and from a Web browser.

KEY TERMS

- Discretionary Access Control List (DACL)
- Local group
- Local user account
- Security identifier (SID)
- NTFS permissions
- Local file access
- CONVERT
- Ownership
- Distributed file system (Dfs)
- Fault-tolerant Dfs
- Web sharing
- Internet Information Services (IIS)
- TCP port
- Anonymous access
- Basic authentication
- Digest authentication
- Integrated Windows authentication
- Secure Sockets Layer (SSL)

CHAPTER SUMMARY

- Printer

- Print device

- Spooler

- Printer driver

- Printer pooling

- NWLink

- Gateway Services for NetWare (GSNW)

- AppleTalk

- Macintosh-accessible volume

♦ **Configuring interoperability with non-Windows operating systems.** This includes ensuring interoperability with NetWare, UNIX, and Macintosh computers. It includes configuring access to non-Windows resources from Windows clients through gateways. In addition, it includes making Windows 2000 resources available to non-Windows clients through file and print services for NetWare, UNIX, and Macintosh.

Configuring proper access to resources is a very important part of an administrator's job, so you can expect a number of questions in these areas. Because data and printer availability are often the most critical part of what users need, this information must be well understood by any Windows 2000 administrator.

APPLY YOUR KNOWLEDGE

Review Questions

1. What is the default authentication method for an IIS server, and what changes are made to your Windows 2000 security to allow this access?

2. What do you need to do to your servers to enable local security on files and folders?

3. If you have share-level permissions enabled on a folder and NTFS permissions enabled on the same folder, what are the effective permissions to the folder over the network? What are the effective local permissions?

4. If you want to enable Web sharing of a folder, what must be present on the computer on which you are working?

5. What is the difference between a standalone Dfs and a domain-based Dfs?

6. What is GSNW, and how does it allow for simplification of administration?

7. How is a print device distinguished from a printer?

Answers to Review Questions

1. By default, an IIS server is configured to enable anonymous users to access the Web site without being prompted for a password in the event that NTFS security does not prevent it; otherwise, Integrated Windows authentication is used. To facilitate the identification of anonymous users, a special local account is created called IUSR_*SERVERNAME*. Any user connecting to the server is automatically assigned the rights this user has to the Web site. For more information, see the section "Controlling Access to Web Sites."

2. To enable local security, you must host your folders and files on NTFS partitions and set the DACLs on resources to be secured. If your partitions are FAT, you can convert to NTFS without data loss by using the convert command. For more information, see the section "The NTFS File System."

3. When both share-level and local permissions are applied to a folder, the effective permissions when accessing over the network are the more restrictive of the two sets of permissions. When accessing locally, the NTFS permissions are all that apply. For more information, see the section "When Local File Security Interacts with Shared Folder Security."

4. To enable Web sharing of a folder, you must have a way to publish it to the Web. This requires that IIS be installed on the machine you want to Web share on, and directory browsing must be enabled in the IIS configuration For more information, see the section "Preparing for Web Sharing."

5. The essential difference between a standalone Dfs and a domain-based Dfs is that the root servers in a domain-based Dfs are published to Active Directory. This enables redundant copies of the root to be configured, thus ensuring that if the root server goes down, clients will be automatically directed to a functioning root when they try to connect. For more information, see the section "The Distributed File System (Dfs)."

APPLY YOUR KNOWLEDGE

6. The GSNW (Gateway [and Client] Service for NetWare) allows occasional access of NetWare file resources by Windows clients through a Windows 2000 Server. The GSNW makes administration simpler by ensuring that client systems do not need to be reconfigured to allow access to NetWare resources. If the user can connect to the Windows 2000 Server, the user has access to the NetWare resources. For more information, see the section "Installing and Configuring the Gateway Service for NetWare (GSNW)."

7. A print device is the physical machine that paper spews out of, whereas a printer is a software interface that is configured to allow control of the device. For more information, see the section "The Printing Process."

ON THE CD

This book's companion CD contains specially designed supplemental material to help you understand how well you understand the concepts and skills you learned in this chapter. You'll find related exercises and exam questions and answers. See the file **Chapter09ApplyYourKnowledge.pdf** in the CD's **Chapter09\ApplyYourKnowledge** directory.

Suggested Readings and Resources

1. Microsoft Windows 2000 Server Resource Kit: *Microsoft Windows 2000 Server Internetworking Guide* (Microsoft Press).

   - Chapter 11: Services for UNIX
   - Chapter 12: Interoperability with NetWare
   - Chapter 13: Services for Macintosh

2. Microsoft Windows 2000 Server Resource Kit: *Microsoft Windows 2000 Server Deployment Planning* Guide (Microsoft Press).

   - Chapter 22: Defining a Client Connectivity Strategy

3. Microsoft Windows 2000 Server: *Operations Guide* (Microsoft Press).

   - Chapter 4: Network Printing

4. Microsoft Internet Information Services 5.0: *Resource Guide* (Microsoft Press).

   - Chapter 9: Security

5. *Microsoft Windows 2000 Professional Resource Kit* (Microsoft Press).

   - Chapter 14: Printing
   - Chapter 24: Interoperability with NetWare
   - Chapter 25: Interoperability with UNIX

6. Microsoft Official Curriculum course 1556: *Administering Microsoft Windows 2000.*

   - Module 6: Administering Printer Resources

7. Microsoft Official Curriculum course 1557: *Installing and Configuring Microsoft Windows 2000*

   - Module 5: Configuring Network Protocols
   - Module 11: Installing and Configuring Printers
   - Module 13: Installing and Configuring Web Services

8. Microsoft Official Curriculum course 2152: *Supporting Microsoft Windows 2000 Professional and Server.*

   - Module 3: Connecting Windows 2000 Clients to Networks and the Internet
   - Module 7: Managing Data by Using NTFS
   - Module 8: Providing Network Access to File Resources
   - Module 9: Configuring Printing

9. Microsoft Official Curriculum course 2153: *Supporting a Microsoft Windows 2000 Network Infrastructure.*

   - Module 11: Configuring a Web Server
   - Module 16: Configuring Network Connectivity Between Microsoft Windows 2000 and Other Operating Systems

10. Web Sites.

    - www.microsoft.com/windows2000
    - www.microsoft.com/train_cert

Microsoft provides the following objectives for "Configuring and Troubleshooting Hardware Devices and Drivers":

Configure hardware devices.

▶ This objective is necessary because someone certified in the use of Windows 2000 Server technology must understand the methods for configuring the hardware in a Windows 2000 Server computer. This includes tuning the hardware devices for optimal performance.

Configure driver signing options.

▶ This objective is necessary because someone certified in the use of Windows 2000 Server technology must understand the implications of driver signing. This includes understanding how driver signing can increase system reliability, protect a server against corrupted and/or virus-stricken device drivers, and ensure that fraudulent drivers are not loaded by mistake.

Update device drivers.

▶ This objective is necessary because someone certified in the use of Windows 2000 technology must be able to update the device drivers. This includes knowing where to obtain new drivers, what the procedures are for updating them, and what the implications are of upgrading or not upgrading these drivers.

Troubleshoot problems with hardware.

▶ This objective is necessary because someone certified in the use of Windows 2000 Server technology must be able to effectively troubleshoot problems with hardware. This includes detecting and solving problems using system tools, logic, intuition, and past experience.

CHAPTER 10

Configuring and Troubleshooting Hardware Devices and Drivers

OUTLINE

STUDY STRATEGIES

▶ Although this is one of the shorter chapters in this book, it contains a fair share of testable Windows 2000 features. When you go through this material, make sure that you have a good knowledge of Plug and Play (PNP), driver signing, and the Hardware Compatibility List. Any of these are possible topics for exam questions.

▶ To prepare for the questions that may arise from the objectives, you should, of course, study the conceptual material presented in the chapter. In addition, you should also do the Step by Steps and Exercises, which will introduce you to most of this material in a hands-on fashion.

▶ Finally, and probably most importantly, you should try to gain experience with the installation and configuration of as many hardware devices as possible in Windows 2000 Servers. This may include (but should not be limited to) video cards, sound cards, modems, and network cards. Try to find some legacy hardware so that you can experience the challenge (and sometimes the frustration) of manually installing and configuring drivers for hardware that is not configured automatically by the Plug and Play (PNP) manager.

INTRODUCTION

This chapter will help you prepare for the "Configuring and Troubleshooting Hardware Devices and Drivers" section of Microsoft's Exam 70–215. Every Windows 2000 Server has hardware. Drivers are the software that allows Windows 2000 Server to talk to the physical devices.

This chapter will provide you with an overview of drivers, their place in the Windows 2000 architecture, and the new signing options that guarantee driver authenticity and reliability.

HARDWARE AND DRIVERS IN WINDOWS 2000

To understand what drivers are and how they function, you must have a grasp of how a Windows 2000 Server is constructed. Figure 10.1 shows the architectural components of Windows 2000.

The Windows 2000 operating system is divided into two major operating environments called modes. *User mode* is where all user interaction happens; this includes logon and the Win32 subsystem, in which 32-bit programs are run (see Chapter 11, "Managing, Monitoring, and Optimizing System Performance, Reliability, and Availability"). The other mode is called *kernel mode.* All essential processes run in kernel mode. Processes in the kernel mode are protected from direct user interaction, ensuring that you (and your software) have very limited ability to cause system crashes or to compromise security.

The kernel mode consists of a number of components, including the Windows 2000 Executive. The Windows 2000 Executive has a number of processes that control internal system functions. These processes include the GUI manager, the virtual memory manager, and the device drivers.

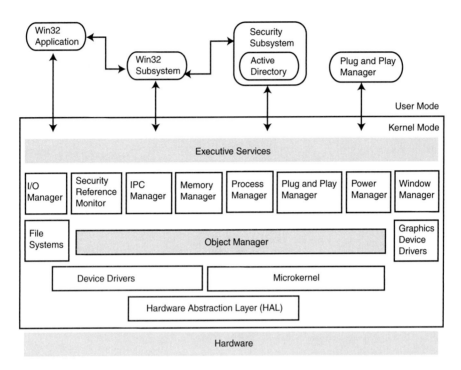

FIGURE 10.1
The Windows 2000 architecture is divided into
user mode and kernel mode.

To make access to hardware by processes in user mode as simple as
possible, a set of hardware interfaces (drivers) have been established,
which reside in kernel mode. A driver creates a standard program-
mer interface for directing output from and receiving input into a
program. Programmers do not want to have to write a separate program (or subroutine) for every possible video card that might be
installed in a system running their software. So, they simply ask for
things to be displayed in a generic way. The device drivers convert
those generic requests into specific requests to the hardware that they
are configured to support.

Because so much is riding on the correct functioning of the interface
between the user mode and the hardware, it is essential that drivers
work properly with Windows 2000 and with the devices they are
designed to interface with. Microsoft has created standards that

define what the generic interface to the user mode should look like. Standards also define how the driver should be positioned (and function) within the kernel mode processes.

One particular new feature in the Windows 2000 operating system is called Plug and Play. The addition of a Plug and Play manager (with a component in both the user mode and the kernel mode) makes it much easier to configure hardware devices. Now many devices will be automatically detected, and the drivers will be installed for you.

CONFIGURING HARDWARE DEVICES

Configure hardware devices.

The ability to configure your server hardware properly is essential to a smooth-running operating system. Windows 2000 makes the configuration of hardware devices much easier through the implementation of the Plug and Play manager, which ensures PNP devices are automatically detected and that their drivers are installed. Even devices that are not Plug and Play may still be located by Windows 2000. These drivers must be manually configured. Of course, despite all these new features, you will still need to do your homework before trying to install a new device. All devices must be on the Windows 2000 Hardware Compatibility List (HCL) or have a driver supplied by a third-party vendor. You can go to `http://www.microsoft.com/windows2000/upgrade/compat/search /devices.asp` to search for your device compatibility using an online tool. You can also go to `http://www.microsoft.com/hcl` for a current version of the Windows 2000 HCL.

Even with the new features, you still need to manually configure some hardware. In some cases, your server may not have sufficient IRQs (or resources) for all your devices. You might have to manually disable one device to enable another. Finally, you might want to have some devices accessible under certain circumstances and not under others. For those situations, you might find that a hardware profile or two is helpful (these will be discussed in a later section).

Viewing Installed Devices

You can view and change the properties of devices and drivers installed on your Windows 2000 Server through the Computer Management console (see Figure 10.2).

Among other things, this console allows you to access two tools: the Device Manager and System Information. The Device Manager allows you to view, add, and configure hardware devices. System Information allows you to access a variety of reports showing the allocation of system resources to specific devices and software.

System Information allows you to see information on IRQs, memory locations for devices, and hardware and software components on your system. All of these reports are read-only, so they are good only for reporting purposes. Figure 10.3 shows a System Information report.

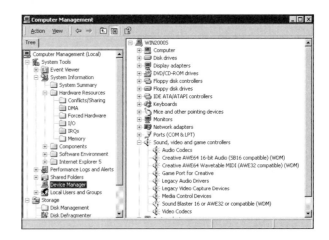

FIGURE 10.2

The Computer Management console with System Information expanded and the Device Manager selected.

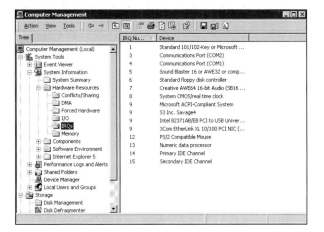

FIGURE 10.3
The System Information section of the Computer Management console is shown here with the IRQ report displayed.

The other area of interest is the Device Manager (refer to Figure 10.2). The Device Manager allows you to see the categories of devices installed on your server and the specific devices that have been installed or detected. You can also tell from the Device Manager if all the devices are functioning properly. If a device is not functioning correctly, the device name will have a yellow exclamation mark on it indicating a problem with the device. The problem might be that the drivers could not be found or that the device could not be started for some reason. Figure 10.4 shows the Device Manager screen for a Windows 2000 computer in which a sound card has been configured improperly, thus preventing it from starting correctly.

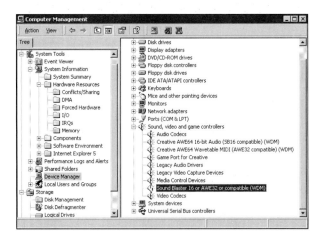

FIGURE 10.4
Devices with problems are identified with a yellow-circled exclamation mark.

From the Device Manager, you can also see the specific properties of a device and, for some properties, change them. Double-click the device's name, and the properties for the device appear in a Properties dialog box. The Properties dialog box frequently consists of four tabs: General, Advanced, Driver, and Resources (see Figure 10.5). This is not universal, however, because some devices have more or fewer configuration options.

The common tabs for device drivers include

FIGURE 10.5
In this Properties dialog box for a network card, the General tab shows information about the device, including its status.

◆ **General tab.** Shows information about the device including the device name, its type, and its manufacturer. This tab allows you to invoke the device troubleshooter and to disable or enable the device.

◆ **Advanced tab.** This tab allows you to set specific properties for the device that are not available on the other tabs. These properties will differ from device to device or might not be present at all.

◆ **Driver tab.** This tab gives you information about the device and allows you to configure the driver software installed for the device. This tab allows you to update or uninstall the current drive.

◆ **Resources tab.** This tab shows you the resources being used by the device, including the IRQ and memory address. It also shows you if the settings for this device are conflicting with those for another device and allows you to change the resource settings to remove the conflict.

Configuring a Hardware Device

Windows 2000 Server fully supports Plug and Play technology. Most of your hardware should be automatically detected and configured, and your drivers should be installed. As a result, the need to manually configure a new device occurs much less frequently than it did in Windows NT 4.0.

Installing a new device begins when your server is prompted to begin a hardware scan. This normally is initiated at startup, but it can also be initiated manually. Step by Step 10.1 walks you through initiating a hardware scan.

ON THE CD

Step by Step 10.1, "Initiating a Hardware Scan," walks you through initiating a hardware scan. See the file **Chapter10-01StepbyStep. pdf** in the CD's **Chapter10\StepbyStep** directory.

Many legacy devices will not be detected by a hardware scan. Therefore, those devices must be configured manually. This configuration cannot be done from the Device Manager. The Device Manager will allow you to configure only devices that have already been installed.

To manually install and configure a device, you must bring up the System Properties dialog box. This dialog box contains general information about your system, as well as specific configuration options dealing with hardware (see Figure 10.6).

Step by Step 10.2 walks you through the manual installation of a hardware device.

ON THE CD

Step by Step 10.2, "Manually Installing a Hardware Device," walks you through hardware device manual installation. See the file **Chapter10-02StepbyStep.pdf** in the CD's **Chapter10\StepbyStep** directory.

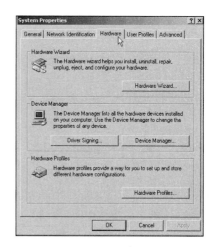

FIGURE 10.6
The Hardware tab of the System Properties dialog box is where you begin to install new non-Plug and Play hardware.

Creating Hardware Profiles

Hardware profiles are configuration groupings that define which hardware devices are to be started under certain circumstances. Hardware profiles are commonly used on laptop computers using Windows 2000 where the laptop may be docked or undocked from a docking station.

The idea of the hardware profile is simple. Under certain circumstances you do not want certain hardware devices to start, but you do not want to go through the work of physically adding and removing the devices.

After multiple hardware profiles have been created, you will be prompted to choose one at system startup. You can configure which profile is the default and how long the system will wait before defaulting to that profile.

Hardware profiles can be configured from the Device Manager. Each device can be associated with one or more hardware profiles. The actual hardware profiles are identified by name. When a profile is created, each device is, by default, started in conjunction with that profile. At that point, you can disable certain devices for certain profiles. Step by Step 10.3 shows how to create a hardware profile in Windows 2000.

ON THE CD

Step by Step 10.3, "Creating a Hardware Profile," walks you through hardware profile creation. See the file **Chapter10-03StepbyStep.pdf** in the CD's **Chapter10\StepbyStep** directory.

If you don't want specific devices to start for a specific hardware profile, you have to manually configure to exclude the device using Step by Step 10.4.

ON THE CD

Step by Step 10.4, "Configuring a Hardware Profile," walks you through hardware profile configuration. See the file **Chapter10-04StepbyStep.pdf** in the CD's **Chapter10\StepbyStep** directory.

CONFIGURING DRIVER SIGNING OPTIONS

Configure driver signing options.

Drivers are the crux of communication between your applications/ operating system and your hardware. It is essential that they function properly. To this end, Microsoft has implemented driver signing in Windows 2000. The concept is straightforward. Each driver that Microsoft creates or verifies is digitally signed by them. As a result, that driver is guaranteed to work with Windows 2000 and is verified to be free of corruption.

As new drivers are created by hardware vendors, they will be signed by Microsoft (or other trusted sources) and released. This section describes how to configure your system to watch for signed drivers and to respond appropriately when unsigned drivers are detected.

As a system administrator, you can implement a local security policy that checks for signatures on your drivers. You have three choices when it comes to signatures (see Figure 10.7).

◆ **Ignore.** You can ignore signatures and enable the installation of drivers without checking them.

◆ **Warn.** You can have the system check signatures on drivers when they are installed and warn you if they are not signed (this is the Windows 2000 default).

◆ **Block.** You can block the installation of unsigned drivers to ensure that your system is free of unsigned and possibly corrupt drivers.

Making the desired driver signing setting the system default can ensure an administrator's desired setting. Be careful, if you set the driver signing setting to block, you may not be able to use certain pieces of hardware. Some might argue that this is the price you have to pay for the increased peace of mind, but that is sometimes debatable. The following Step by Step outlines how to configure driver signing options.

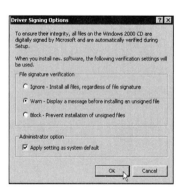

FIGURE 10.7
You can choose to verify digital signatures before a driver is installed.

<table>
<tr><td>**ON THE CD**</td></tr>
</table>

Step by Step 10.5, "Configuring Driver Signing Options," walks you through driver signing option configuration. See the file **Chapter10-05StepbyStep.pdf** in the CD's **Chapter10\StepbyStep** directory.

To summarize, driver signing ensures that device drivers will function—and function well. Windows 2000 has configuration options to protect you against unsigned drivers (or at least to warn you before you install one).

UPDATING DEVICE DRIVERS

Update device drivers.

Like any software, drivers are never static. As the underlying operating system changes and improvements are made to hardware, the drivers change. In addition, some drivers are discovered to have bugs and are then fixed. Therefore, you might find that drivers need to be updated occasionally. These updates might come from Microsoft or from the hardware vendor. They might come to you on floppy disk, CD-ROM, or they might be downloadable from the Internet. Whatever their source, updating them generally provides more stability in the operation of your hardware devices.

You can update drivers from the Device Manager. The process for updating a driver is covered in Step by Step 10.6.

<table>
<tr><td>**ON THE CD**</td></tr>
</table>

Step by Step 10.6, "Updating a Device Driver," walks you through device driver updating. See the file **Chapter10-06StepbyStep.pdf** in the CD's **Chapter10\StepbyStep** directory.

TROUBLESHOOTING HARDWARE PROBLEMS

Troubleshoot hardware problems.

Trouble with hardware comes from a number of sources. The device might be installed improperly or be faulty. If the device is not Plug and Play compliant, it might have been configured improperly. If a device is Plug and Play compliant, an incorrect driver might have been manually installed for that device or someone might have tried to manually configure it when it would have been better to let autoconfiguration do so.

The two main sources for troubleshooting hardware problems are the system log in the Event Viewer and the Device Manager.

Troubleshooting Using the System Log

Problems that stem from a device not starting will sometimes cause a message to be displayed on startup telling you that a service failed to start (see Figure 10.8). This is especially true when the failure is in the network card, because that device's starting is the precursor to the starting of all the networking services. These messages will have corresponding entries in the system log describing the nature of the problem.

FIGURE 10.8
A warning message like this is often the first sign that something is wrong.

To solve problems of this kind, you need to be able to find and interpret log entries. Step by Step 10.7 describes this process.

> **ON THE CD**
>
> Step by Step 10.7, "Opening the System Log," walks you through opening the system log. See the file **Chapter10-07StepbyStep.pdf** in the CD's **Chapter10\StepbyStep** directory.

System log entries come in three levels of severity. A fatal error, represented by a red circle with an X in it, exists when a driver or service fails. A warning, represented by a yield sign logo with an

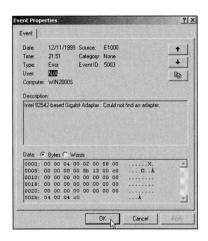

FIGURE 10.9
Log entries are sometimes obscure, but they generally have a nugget of information that is useful to the average administrator.

exclamation mark in it, indicates a problem that may have serious ramifications, but they do not necessarily indicate that a problem must be corrected. Informational entries, represented by a blue circle with an "I" in it, indicate that something happened successfully.

Figure 10.9 shows a typical log entry. Much of it is obscure, but in this case, what is clear is that something is wrong with the network adapter. This should be enough to suggest that the next likely source of troubleshooting information should be the Device Manager.

Troubleshooting Using the Device Manager

When you know which device is causing your problem, the Device Manager is the place to go. It shows you all the devices you have installed, as well as the status of each.

As you can see in Figure 10.10, a yellow circle with an exclamation mark in it is displayed over the name of the device that is not functioning properly. Any device that is not functioning will be identified in that way.

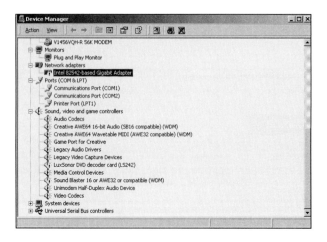

FIGURE 10.10
The network adapter is not functioning properly.

In this case, you can see that in addition to some other faulty devices, the network adapter is not functioning properly. You can double-click it to see its properties (see Figure 10.11) and diagnose the problem.

The properties can tell you a number of things. The General property tab will tell you the status of the device. From here, you can also invoke the Troubleshooter, which will lead you through a text-based analysis of the problem with your device. The Driver property tab will tell you if the driver is signed by Microsoft and, therefore, whether it is certified to function properly. The Resources property tab will tell you if there are memory or IRQ conflicts with other devices. Step by Step 10.8 shows you how to examine a device's properties.

FIGURE 10.11
The device status might tell you what the problem is with the device.

ON THE CD

Step by Step 10.8, "Opening a Device's Properties," walks you through opening a devices properties. See the file **Chapter10-08StepbyStep.pdf** in the CD's **Chapter10\StepbyStep** directory.

A major problem with devices is misconfiguration or malfunction. In many cases, reinstalling or updating the driver can fix the problem. In other cases, you might have to replace the device. This is often the solution when no reconfiguration has been done to a system that used to work but no longer functions.

Troubleshooting skills are essential for maintaining any Windows 2000 computer. The ability to use the event logs and the Device Manager is essential in these skills. However, do not discount instinct and experience as you troubleshoot; and do not be afraid to ask someone with more experience than you for help.

CASE STUDY: GOTHIC CLOTHIERS

ESSENCE OF THE CASE

This case requires that the following end results be satisfied:

▶ You need to ensure that the drivers installed are safe for the system and will function properly.

▶ You need to ensure that Wanda can continue to do her other duties (including, in some cases, installing drivers).

SCENARIO

Gothic Clothiers is a small garment manufacturing company with 30 employees. Boris is the de facto network administrator, mainly because no one else knows as much about computers as Boris. A consultant came into the plant and set up a small LAN with 5 Windows 98 workstations and a Windows 2000 file-and-print server to store their documents. Lately, one of the other employees, Wanda, has been experimenting with the server and has added a new video card and a modem. Although Boris would like to take Wanda's privileges away, she has Power User status because she needs to do server maintenance. It is not what she is doing that bothers Boris, but the lack of concern that she has about the possible ramifications. He heard of another company whose server was devastated by a virus introduced through a driver downloaded from the Internet. Boris wants to make sure that this will not happen to his server. He calls you to get your advice on how to solve his dilemma.

ANALYSIS

The issue here is being able to control the installation of bad drivers, while at the same time ensuring that Wanda can still perform her other duties. This means that you cannot simply take away her rights as a Power User. Of course, education in matters of downloading and installing drivers on a public server is necessary, but Boris needs to put driver signing into place to eliminate the possibility that invalid drivers can be installed. In addition, he needs to configure this driver signing to be the system default to ensure

CASE STUDY: GOTHIC CLOTHIERS

that Wanda cannot simply remove the requirement for driver signing. By blocking all unsigned drivers from being installed, Boris can ensure that the server is safe from corruption and malfunction. This will probably necessitate paying a little more for components that have

signed drivers. Although most hardware will have drivers that are signed by Microsoft, the expense is worth it for the safety that is required in this case.

The following table summarizes the solution.

OVERVIEW OF THE REQUIREMENTS AND SOLUTIONS IN THIS CASE STUDY

Requirement	Solution Provided By
Wanda maintains her capability to perform tasks, including new hardware.	Maintaining Wanda's Power User status.
No one can install unsigned drivers.	Implement driver signing to block all unsigned drivers.
	Set this as the default Windows 2000 setting to ensure that no users can go in and change the driver signing options.

CHAPTER SUMMARY

Summarized briefly, this chapter covered the following main points.

- ◆ **Installing, configuring, and updating devices.** This includes the recognition of Plug and Play for most new devices, the presence of the Device Manager, and the ability to manually install and configure non-Plug and Play devices.

- ◆ **Configuring driver signing options.** This allows you, the administrator, to create a policy on the need for drivers to be signed to ensure validity and to enforce such a policy to keep corrupt or non-verified drivers from being installed.

- ◆ **Troubleshooting hardware problems.** This is required whenever you encounter problems with drivers. This may be the result of drivers that have been manually misconfigured, drivers for legacy hardware that require configuration, or hardware that has malfunctioned.

KEY TERMS

- User mode
- Kernel mode
- Driver
- Device Manager
- Driver signing
- System log

APPLY YOUR KNOWLEDGE

Review Questions

1. What major change has been made to the Windows 2000 architecture to make installation and configuration of drivers easier?

2. What are the implications of using each of the three levels of driver signing?

3. What utility shows you the Event Viewer, the System Information, and the Device Manager in one place?

4. Under what circumstances will you have to manually install and configure a hardware driver?

5. What indispensable source of information can be used to determine whether hardware is certified for use with Windows 2000? Where can you obtain this information?

6. Under what circumstances will you update a device driver? What are the possible benefits of doing so?

Answers to Review Questions

1. The new addition is the Plug and Play manager, which allows full support for Plug and Play devices. For more information, see the section "Hardware and Drivers in Windows 2000."

2. The three levels of driver signing are Ignore, Warn, and Block. Ignore means that no warning will be issued when an unsigned driver is installed, which could allow the installation of corrupt or unstable drivers. Warn means that when an unsigned driver is installed, a warning will be issued, but the user will be able to continue with the installation or abort it. Block

means that no unsigned drivers can be installed on the system. A warning will be issued, but no possibility for override will be possible. For more information, see the section "Configuring Driver Signing Options."

3. The utility that allows for all the main system configuration utilities to be displayed in one place is the Computer Management console. For more information, see the section "Viewing Installed Devices."

4. Most hardware will be installed and configured by the Plug and Play manager. The only time you will have to manually configure is for legacy devices that are not Plug and Play. For more information, see the section "Configuring a Hardware Device."

5. A certified hardware list is available in the Hardware Compatibility List (HCL). This list is available both on the Internet (http://www.microsoft.com/hcl) and on the Windows 2000 Server CD (HCL.TXT). For more information, see the section "Configuring Hardware Devices."

6. Devices drivers should be updated whenever a new version becomes available (provided that it has been thoroughly tested by the manufacturer and, if possible, signed by Microsoft). Updates to device drivers often fix possible bugs in the software and increase reliability, functionality, and speed. As a result, the benefits are more stable access to hardware and a more reliable Windows 2000 Server. For more information, see the section "Updating Device Drivers."

APPLY YOUR KNOWLEDGE

ON THE CD

This book's companion CD contains specially designed supplemental material to help you understand how well you know the concepts and skills you learned in this chapter. You'll find related exercises, review questions and answers, and exam questions and answers. See the file **Chapter10ApplyYourKnowledge.pdf** in the CD's **Chapter10\ApplyYourKnowledge** directory.

Suggested Readings and Resources

1. Windows 2000 Server Resource Kit: *Microsoft Windows 2000 Server Operations Guide.* Microsoft Press, 2000.

   • Chapter 14: Troubleshooting Strategies

2. *Microsoft Windows 2000 Professional Resource Kit.* Microsoft Press, 2000.

   • Chapter 6: Setup and Startup

   • Chapter 19: Device Management

3. Microsoft Official Curriculum course 2152: Supporting Microsoft Windows 2000 Professional and Server.

   • Module 2: Configuring the Windows 2000 Environment

   • Module 11: Maintaining the Windows 2000 Environment

4. Web Sites

   • www.microsoft.com/windows2000

   • www.microsoft.com/train_cert

This chapter will help you prepare for the "Managing, Monitoring, and Optimizing System Performance, Reliability, and Availability" section of the Server portion of the Accelerated exam.

Microsoft provides the following objectives for the "Managing, Monitoring, and Optimizing System Performance, Reliability, and Availability" section:

Monitor and optimize usage of system resources.

▶ You must be able to use Performance Monitor to effectively monitor the use of the server and be able to adjust hardware and system usage to maximize performance.

Manage processes.

- **Set priorities and start and stop processes**

▶ You must understand how to adjust the priority of processes and how to start and stop them through the Task Manager.

Optimize disk performance.

▶ You must be able to monitor how hard drives are being used by users and the system and be able to configure them for optimal performance.

Manage and optimize availability of system state data and user data.

▶ You must be able to use backup strategies effectively to ensure that both system and user data is available at all times.

CHAPTER 11

Managing, Monitoring, and Optimizing System Performance, Reliability, and Availability

OBJECTIVES

Recover systems and user data.

- **Recover systems and user data by using Windows Backup.**

- **Troubleshoot system restoration by using Safe mode.**

- **Recover systems and user data by using the Recovery Console.**

▶ When disaster strikes, you must be able to recover from system failure. This failure might come in the form of catastrophic disk or system failure or temporary failure resulting from incorrect configuration.

OUTLINE

STUDY STRATEGIES

▶ As in other chapters, this study strategy begins by pointing out that features in the Windows 2000 operating system that were not present in Windows NT are prime targets for exam questions. This chapter covers two new features: Recovery Console and Safe mode. The Recovery Console is by far the more significant of the two.

▶ As it pertains to the other objectives, here are some tips: Understand application priority, and, specifically, how to change foreground boost. Also, understand how to change application priority, both at the time an application begins and while it is running (using the Task Manager).

▶ Understand how the Performance Console is set up and what the component parts are. Know how to create a System Monitor, how to create counter and trace logs, and how to configure alerts. Know specifically the main counters involved in the processor, memory, network, and disk (physical and logical), as outlined in this chapter.

▶ As it pertains to system recovery, know the various mechanisms for saving system information and when each would be used. Know the limitations of Last Known Good configuration and the Emergency Repair Disk. In addition, know how to save this information using Windows 2000 Backup, because that has always been a popular question.

▶ As it pertains to data backup and recovery, know how Windows Backup and Restore work, how to invoke them, and how the scheduler works.

▶ As usual, you should know the content of this chapter and work through the exercises and questions at the end. These have been designed to reinforce important concepts, so you should at least have a good look at them. In addition, going through the Step by Steps on the CD as you read the chapter will help reinforce the concepts presented.

INTRODUCTION

The purpose of a standalone server is to provide services as diverse as printing, data storage, application hosting, and Web services. These things have in common a requirement for availability and performance. A file server that is capable of storing all the corporate data is not much use if its hard drive has just crashed and you cannot recover the information.

This chapter covers three main topics: controlling program execution and priority, monitoring and optimizing system performance, and recovery from failure.

MAINTAINING WINDOWS 32-BIT APPLICATIONS

Manage processes.

The execution of applications is very important on a Windows 2000 Server, especially if its primary role is that of Applications server. An Applications server is one dedicated to providing services in the form of applications execution, such as an Exchange server providing mail services or a SQL Server providing database management.

In this section, you also see the priority levels that can be assigned to a process and how they can be assigned at the time the process is started. The section also discusses the idea of providing extra processing cycles that can be given automatically to a foreground application. Finally, the Task Manager utilities for changing priorities and starting and stopping processes are covered.

Windows 2000 allows multiple processes to run at once through the use of *multitasking*, which means that more than one process appears to execute at one time. This is made possible by fast processors and a specific kind of multitasking called *preemptive multitasking*.

Preemptive multitasking lets the operating system control which processes (or threads) get access to the processor and for how long. This determination is made through the assignment of priorities to each process. The higher the priority that is assigned to a process, the longer (and more frequent) its processor access is. Windows 2000 ensures that a process's priority is adjusted from its base prior-

ity enough to get access to the processor, even if it is only infrequently, for low-priority processes.

Windows 2000 is also capable of using multiple processors. This
completely depends, of course, on having multiple processors
installed on the motherboard. Windows 2000 Server supports up to
four processors. The multiprocessor capabilities use a system called
symmetric multiprocessing. Symmetric multiprocessing systems allocate processor time from any available (or the least busy) processor.
This is as opposed to asymmetric processor systems in which one
processor (the master) is responsible for switching between tasks,
regardless of how busy (or idle) that processor is at any given time.

Although it happens infrequently on any Windows 2000 computer,
you have the capability of modifying the base priority at which an
application runs. Process priorities, which can be set either manually
(at startup or during execution) or through the application itself, are
given a numbered priority between 0 and 31.

Figure 11.1 illustrates how processes are divided into four categories:
Idle, Normal, High, and Real-Time. As you can see, Idle ranges
from 0 to 6, Normal from 6 to 11, High from 11 to 15, and
Real-Time from 16 to 31. In Figure 11.1, the Normal priorities
are identified above the priority line.

Priorities can be manually assigned to processes for the purpose
of making them more or less likely to consume the processor. In
addition, the effective priority of an application can change, simply
based on whether the window in which it is running is in the
foreground.

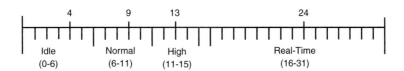

FIGURE 11.1
All application priorities fall on the
scale between 0 and 31.

Controlling Normal Priority Applications

Windows 2000 can be configured to put higher priority on processes that are running in the foreground than those that are running in the background; this is called a *priority boost*. This is very reasonable when the applications you are running interact with a user. However, this is not so desirable when the background process is not sitting idle and waiting for user input, but is actively doing some processing.

Windows 2000 Server can be configured either to treat all Normal-priority applications the same, whether they're in the foreground or the background, or to boost the priority of foreground applications by two.

By default, Windows 2000 Server does not boost foreground applications as Windows 2000 Professional does. This is because on a server, most of the processes running run in the background with no user interaction. If you want to configure your Windows 2000 Server to boost the priority of foreground applications (or to return it to the default), follow Step by Step 11.1.

ON THE CD

Step by Step 11.1, "Configuring Normal Priority Boost," demonstrates how to configure your Windows 2000 Server to boost the priority of foreground applications. See the file **Chapter11-01StepbyStep.pdf** in the CD's **Chapter11\StepbyStep** directory.

Most applications run just fine at Normal priority. Sometimes you want to relegate a process to a low (Idle) priority or to a High priority. Microsoft recommends that you not run applications at Real-Time priority unless they were specifically designed as real-time applications. You must be an Administrator to run a process at Real-Time priority.

Assigning Priorities at Runtime

To invoke an application with a priority other than Normal, use the following syntax from the Run command, in a command prompt, or in the shortcut associated with the application:

```
start /priority APPLICATION.EXE
```

In this syntax, /*priority* represents one of the following options: /low, /normal, /high, or /realtime. For example, if you wanted to start Word at Low priority, you use the command start /low WINWORD.EXE.

In addition to being able to start a process with a certain priority, you can also adjust the priority while a process is running. This is done in the Task Manager. When you adjust the priority, you are presented with a list of options. Table 11.1 provides numeric interpretations of the various priority names.

TABLE 11.1

PRIORITY NAMES AND THEIR VALUES

Priority	Numeric Value
Realtime	24
High	13
AboveNormal	10
Normal	9
BelowNormal	8
AboveNormal	8
Normal	7
BelowNormal	6
Low	4

Step by Step 11.2 describes how to adjust a process's priority while it is running.

ON THE CD

Step by Step 11.2, "Adjusting a Process's Priority," explains how to adjust a process's priority while it is running. See the file **Chapter11-02StepbyStep.pdf** in the CD's **Chapter11\StepbyStep** directory.

Stopping and Starting Processes with the Task Manager

The Task Manager can be used to perform the following tasks:

◆ **Stop running processes.** The Task Manager can be used to stop individual *processes* (threads of execution). An application may actually have several processes associated with it. When an application hangs, you can try to close the application; or you can use the Task Manager to stop the hung application by opening the Task Manager, going to the application's tab, and stopping the application from there. This is not always completely successful. Some applications leave residual processes running even after the application stops. In such cases, you might need to manually end the process in order to clean up your system and allow applications and processes to run again. Step by Step 11.3 demonstrates how to end a process using the Task Manager.

> **WARNING**
>
> **Exercise Caution When Stopping Processes**   Although Microsoft wants you to know how to stop processes using the Task Manager, you must be *very* careful when actually doing so. You could stop a process that is vital to the proper functioning of the operating system and cause a server crash. You should never stop a process unless you are sure that you know and understand the ramifications of your action.

ON THE CD

Step by Step 11.3, "Ending a Process Using the Task Manager," demonstrates how to end a process using the Task Manager. See the file **Chapter11-03StepbyStep.pdf** in the CD's **Chapter11\StepbyStep** directory.

◆ **Start a new process.** You can start processes either by typing a command or by browsing for an application file. Just as in the Run dialog box, however, you must know the name of the process you want to start. Step by Step 11.4 shows you how to start a new process using the Task Manager.

ON THE CD

Step by Step 11.4, "Starting a New Process Using the Task Manager," shows you how to start a new process using the Task Manager. See the file **Chapter11-04StepbyStep.pdf** in the CD's **Chapter11\StepbyStep** directory.

MONITORING AND OPTIMIZING SYSTEM RESOURCE USE

Monitor and optimize usage of system resources.

Optimize disk performance.

This section covers topics related to the assessment of server performance. It includes a variety of monitoring and logging utilities found in the Performance Console. In addition, it discusses some tips on how to tune your server before problems occur and what devices should be monitored when they do.

Periodic monitoring of your Windows 2000 Server is important to the process of optimization. By gathering current information and comparing it against established norms for your systems (a *baseline*), you can detect bottlenecks and identify those system components that are slowing down server performance and fix them before they become a problem to your users.

A baseline is an established norm for the operation of your server as determined by normal load. This baseline can then be used as a basis of comparison for future performance to see whether repairable problems exist. As the configuration of your server changes (when, for example, a processor is added or RAM is added), new baselines are established to reflect the new expected performance.

It is imperative that a baseline be established before problems begin to occur. If users are already beginning to complain, "The network is slow," it is too late to establish a baseline, because the statistics gathered include whatever performance factors are contributing to the dissatisfaction.

The Performance Monitor allows you to watch various facets of your system. Whether you are looking for real-time graphical views or a log that you can peruse at your convenience, the Performance Monitor can provide the kind of data you need to evaluate performance and recommend system modification if necessary.

Collecting Data Using Performance Monitor

Monitoring performance begins with the collection of data. Methods available for collecting data are the System Monitor, counter logs, trace logs, and alerts.

Using the System Monitor

The System Monitor enables you to view statistical data, either live or from a saved log. You can view the data in three formats: graph, histogram, or report. Graph data is displayed as a line graph. Histograms are displayed as bar graphs. Reports are text based and show the current numeric information available from the statistics.

The basic use of the System Monitor is straightforward. You decide which object, instance, or counter combinations you want to display and then configure the monitor accordingly.

Figure 11.2 shows a typical Add Counter dialog box, which allows you to collect statistics from either the local machine or a remote machine. After you select where you will collect statistics from, you then designate the performance objects to be monitored.

Under each performance object, is a list of specific counters that you will record. Each object has its own set of counters from which you can choose. Counters allow you to move from the abstract concept of an object to the concrete events that reflect that object's activity. For example, if you choose to monitor the processor, you can watch for the average processor time and how much time the processor spent doing non-idle activity.

If a counter has multiple instances, you can watch each instance individually or watch them as a collective unit by selecting the _Total instance.

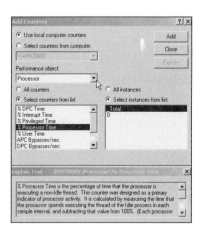

FIGURE 11.2
Adding a Processor counter in the Add Counters dialog box.

ON THE CD

Step by Step 11.5, "Adding a Counter to the System Monitor," shows you how to add a counter to the System Monitor. See the file **Chapter11-05StepbyStep.pdf** in the CD's **Chapter11\ StepbyStep** directory.

You can make a number of modifications to the System Monitor to improve how it functions in your environment by right-clicking the graph and choosing Properties from the menu that appears (see Figure 11.3).

The following tabs open the System Monitor property pages:

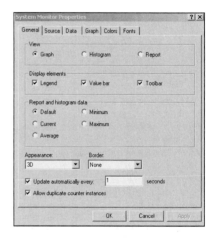

FIGURE 11.3
The System Monitor Properties dialog box.

◆ **General tab.** This tab allows you to change such features as the view, what elements are displayed, appearance, and how frequently the display is updated. The three views are Graph, Histogram, and Report. Graph view displays a line graph, Histogram displays a bar graph, and Report displays text. If Histogram or Report is selected as the view, you can specify what value will actually be displayed for reports and histograms.

◆ **Source tab.** This tab allows you to indicate the source of the data. You can either use current activity based on the time interval specified on the General property sheet or display previously logged data from a file. If you choose to get logged data, you can also specify the time slice that you want to examine. Logged data may span many days or weeks.

◆ **Data tab.** This tab displays the counters that are currently active for your monitor and allows you to add or remove counters. You can also change display properties for each object. This includes the scale, color, width, and style of the lines displayed in the graph view.

◆ **Graph tab.** This tab allows you to customize the view of your graph display, including titles, grids, and vertical scale settings.

◆ **Colors tab.** This tab allows you to modify the colors that are used to highlight the data displayed on the graph.

◆ **Fonts tab.** This tab allows you to modify the font faces, sizes, and styles. Any change you make here modifies all text on the graph.

Using Counter Logs

Although the System Monitor is useful for immediate analysis of a performance problem, it is not very useful as a real-time tool for bottleneck analysis. In order to get a good picture of the way resources are used on your server, you need to be able to examine data collected over a long period of time. To determine system performance and the need for upgrades, you should collect data over a long period of time. This precludes using the System Monitor in real-time mode; you would have to sit in front of the console for long periods of time recording the current statistical results.

A solution is to use *counter logs*. A counter log takes the same information that is captured by the System Monitor, and, instead of displaying it in a graph, records it in a file. After the log has been created, you can use the System Monitor in a static mode to look at the data collected by the log.

One of the advantages of logging is that it can be configured to automatically start and stop itself at specific times and on specific days so that an administrator does not have to be present to start and stop the logging.

Logging does not create much system overhead, but you need to be careful of how much data you collect and where you store the collected data. It is recommended that when you log, you create a partition that contains nothing but log data.

When you create a log, you are presented with a dialog box with three property sheets (see Figure 11.4):

◆ **General tab.** This tab allows you to configure the log with the counters you want to track and the interval at which you want to collect information. The rule of thumb setting the interval is the longer you are going to log, the larger the interval should be to prevent your log file from getting too large.

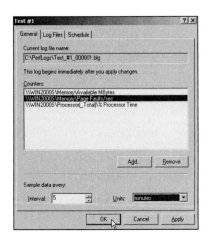

FIGURE 11.4
A log file properties dialog box.

◆ **Log Files tab.** This tab allows you to specify the filename and path for the log. You can have the logs uniquely identified using a suffix of a number (nnnnnn) or a date in any one of six formats. In addition, you can define the format of the log content: comma-delimited text file (CSV), tab-delimited text file (TSV), binary file, or binary circular file (the log file overwrites itself from the beginning when it reaches its maximum size). When you choose a format, you can also set a maximum size for the log file.

◆ **Schedule tab.** This tab allows you to configure the start and stop time for automatic logging or to manually start and stop the logging process. When the log file is full, you can choose to begin a new log file and/or execute a command to do some post-logging processing.

Step by Step 11.6 shows you how to create a counter log.

ON THE CD

Step by Step 11.6, "Creating a Counter Log," demonstrates how you create a counter log. See the file **Chapter11-06StepbyStep.pdf** in the CD's **Chapter11\StepbyStep** directory.

If you configure your log to start manually, you have to start it before logging will begin. A stopped log is marked with a red icon next to the log definition name. A green icon indicates that the log is active or is waiting for its scheduled time to start.

Step by Step 11.7 shows how to start a log manually.

ON THE CD

Step by Step 11.7, "Manually Starting a Log," shows you how to manually start a log. See the file **Chapter11-07StepbyStep.pdf** in the CD's **Chapter11\StepbyStep** directory.

After a log has been created, you can analyze it in a number of ways. You can open binary formats in the System Monitor. Microsoft Excel recognizes and opens files in CSV or TSV format.

Opening a binary file using the System Monitor is much the same as creating a real-time graph. The exception in this case is that the data is static, and you cannot add counters to the view that are not contained in the log. Step by Step 11.8 describes the process for opening a log file using the System Monitor.

ON THE CD

Step by Step 11.8, "Opening a Log File with System Monitor," describes the process for opening a log file using the System Monitor. See the file **Chapter11-08StepbyStep.pdf** in the CD's **Chapter11\StepbyStep** directory.

You can create a similar graph by importing a CSV text file into a spreadsheet (such as Microsoft Excel). When you import the CSV text file, the results come in as headers with numeric data. You can then graph the results by hand. The advantage of this method over the System Monitor is that these results can be pasted into word processors. Step by Step 11.9 shows you how to analyze log data in Microsoft Excel.

ON THE CD

Step by Step 11.9, "Analyzing Log Data in Microsoft Excel," shows you how to analyze log data in Microsoft Excel. See the file **Chapter11-09StepbyStep.pdf** in the CD's **Chapter11\StepbyStep** directory.

Creating Trace Logs

The difference between a trace log and a counter log is the trigger that causes data collection. With a counter log, the trigger of data collection is a time interval. If you set the time interval to 10 seconds, you get data every 10 seconds, whether or not there is any change to the data from the last interval. With a trace log, the trigger of data collection is the occurrence of an event. For example, if you want to track user login, you can set the Local Security Administrator to watch for the event. When a user login occurs, the trace process collects the data.

The options for a trace log are much the same as those for a counter log, with some subtle differences (see Figure 11.5):

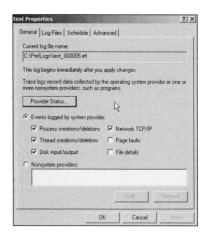

◆ **General tab.** This tab allows you to configure the trace provider, as well as the event types to watch for and log. A trace provider is a piece of software that can be either provided in the operating system, as the system provider is, or an additional utility created to watch for certain event types. Three providers are included with Windows 2000 Server—the Windows 2000 Kernel Trace Provider (system provider) that allows you to watch for processes and threads being created or destroyed, disk input or output, network traffic, memory page faults, and file I/O (reads and writes); the Active Directory: NetLogon Provider (which tracks user logon events at the domain level); and the Local Security Authority (which tracks user logon events at the local SAM level).

FIGURE 11.5
The trace log Properties dialog box.

◆ **Log Files tab.** This allows you to configure log file information. The major difference from counter logs is the file formats for the trace logs. Trace log files can be only a sequential trace file or circular trace file. The format of the trace log files is proprietary to the trace log. No utilities are provided with Windows 2000 for reading the ETL files created by the log.

◆ **Schedule tab.** This tab is configured the same as the Schedule tab for counter logs.

◆ **Advanced tab.** This tab allows you to configure memory buffer number and size. These memory buffers are where the event data is initially captured before being written to the log file.

Creating Alerts

It is probable that, over the long term, you won't want logging enabled all the time. However, that will necessitate that you check the system periodically to ensure that it is working efficiently and that potential problems are not sneaking up on you. Alerts are used to watch certain objects reaching or crossing predefined thresholds. For example, if you decide that disk use greater than 80% is a serious condition, you can configure an alert to watch for disk use crossing this threshold. When this threshold is reached, an action that you configure will occur.

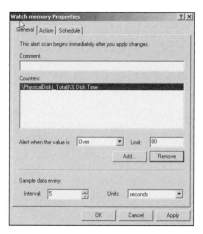

FIGURE 11.6
The Watch Memory Properties dialog box.

The Watch memory Properties dialog box consists of three tabs—General, Action, and Schedule (see Figure 11.6):

◆ **General tab.** This tab allows you to configure multiple counters and the thresholds for each. In addition, you can configure the polling interval. It is important to note that if you create more than one counter, an alert is generated if any of the thresholds are crossed. In addition, if a condition is present for 20 polling intervals in a row, 20 alerts will be generated.

◆ **Action tab.** This tab allows you to configure what happens in response to an alert. The default response is to write a message to the application log in the Event Viewer console. Alternatively, you can have a message sent to a specific computer in the form of a pop-up window or have the Performance Monitor trigger a specific counter log. Finally, you can also have a program of your choice run.

◆ **Schedule tab.** The schedule settings are identical to those set for counter and trace logs.

Optimizing System Resource Availability

Now that you have seen how to collect statistical data, you need to understand how to use it. Your Windows 2000 Server is a dynamically changing entity that has weaknesses in some areas. A server that appears to have a disk problem, thrashing every time a user tries to read something, may, in fact, have too little RAM. Unless you have an understanding of how the major subsystems interact, you will not be able to effectively optimize your server.

Although there are dozens of objects and 10 times that number of counters to sift through, four primary subsystems interact to make a server appear either fast or slow. These subsystems are disk, memory, processor, and network. Of course, other objects are important, but these four form the core of server performance. The performance of these four subsystems affects all other objects.

Changing the System to Increase Performance

Even before you begin to monitor your system to increase performance, there are some things that you can do proactively. In fact, even if you do not experience a lack of performance in any area, performing some basic tasks ensures that it will be longer until you do experience problems than if these were left undone.

Three major areas of system cleanup and tuning are identified here: removing unneeded components, tuning the paging file, and tuning the Server service.

Removing Unnecessary Software Components

Removing unnecessary software components—devices, protocols, and services—can lead to performance increases. Unnecessary components are those that were loaded for some reason in the past, but they no longer have a use. Perhaps you have a device installed that you no longer use. If that device was installed manually, the driver may still load into memory when your server starts. You can use the Device Manager to be ensured that the driver is no longer installed.

Network protocols are another software component that may have become unnecessary. If you used to have a NetWare server that you communicated with, you might still have NWLink installed. If you no longer require NWLink, consider uninstalling the protocol. Unused protocols not only use more system memory, but they also increase the network traffic that your communications generate.

Finally, you should look at unnecessary services. For example, Windows 2000 Server installs IIS by default. If you are not using any of the Web-related services, you should uninstall IIS.

Tuning the Size and Location of the Paging File

The next system configuration setting that might impact performance is the size and location of the paging file. The *paging file* is the disk location facilitating Windows 2000's virtual memory model. In that model, RAM is simulated through a swapping process that moves information from physical memory into virtual memory residing in a file on the hard drive.

If this file is too small or if it resides on a disk with a lot of activity, you could get a reduction in server performance. The paging file starts at a certain size and is configured to expand as memory needs increase. Every time the paging file expands, it takes system resources to resize the file. One recommendation is that you watch your server under typical load and then note the size of the paging file. If the paging file is larger than the minimum size, you should change the settings to make sure the paging file starts out at that size. This uses up a bit more disk space, but you increase the efficiency of the server. Step by Step 11.10 identifies the steps for resizing a paging file.

ON THE CD

Step by Step 11.10, "Resizing the Paging File," identifies the steps for resizing a paging file. See the file **Chapter11-10StepbyStep.pdf in the CD's Chapter11\StepbyStep** directory.

> **WARNING**
>
> **Moving the Page File** If you choose to move your paging file, make sure you do not move it to another logical drive on the same physical disk; move the paging file to a separate physical disk or disk array.

In addition to changing the size of the paging file, you might think about moving the paging file from its default location. The default location for the paging file is the Boot Partition. This tends to be a fairly active partition, so you might benefit from moving the paging file to another location.

If you need to relocate your paging file, Step by Step 11.11 shows you the process.

ON THE CD

Step by Step 11.11, "Relocating the Paging File," shows you how to relocate your paging file. See the file **Chapter11-11StepbyStep.pdf** in the CD's **Chapter11\StepbyStep** directory.

Tuning the Server Service

The final system configuration option you need to look at is the configuration of the Server service. The Server service is responsible for responding to all incoming network requests for file, print, and named pipe sharing. Without the Server service running, no inbound connections for sharing files and printers is possible. The Server service can be configured to optimize performance for the role that the actual server plays.

The Server service can be configured to perform optimally in a file and print sharing environment. The Server service can also be configured to perform optimally in an application-serving environment, such as an Exchange server or SQL Server. When you open the Server Optimization dialog box, four settings are presented:

◆ **Minimize Memory Used.** This setting is more applicable to Windows 2000 Professional where resources are not commonly shared with other workstations on the network.

◆ **Balance.** This setting balances caching performance for both file sharing and network applications. This is often used when a Windows 2000 Server is configured with multiple purposes. For example, hosting shared data files and running SQL Server.

◆ **Maximize Data Throughput for File Sharing.** This setting optimizes the memory caching by having Windows 2000 control the system cache.

◆ **Maximize Data Throughput for Network Applications.** This setting configures the memory cache maintained by the application (such as Microsoft SQL Server) rather than the system cache. This makes sense because it is the application that is processing the data and data requests and is in the best position to cache data and process it.

Step by Step 11.12 outlines how to change the properties for the Server service.

ON THE CD

Step by Step 11.12, "Tuning the Server Service," outlines how to change the properties for the Server service. See the file **Chapter11-12StepbyStep.pdf** in the CD's **Chapter11\StepbyStep** directory.

Using Performance Monitor to Discover Bottlenecks and Optimize Resource Utilization

Every chain, regardless of its strength, has its weakest link. When pulled hard enough, some point will give before all the others. Your server is like a chain. When it's under stress, some component will not be able to keep up with the others. This results in a degradation of overall performance. The weak link in the server is referred to as a *bottleneck* because it is the component that slows everything else down. As an administrator responsible for ensuring efficient operation of your Windows 2000 Server, you need to answer the following two questions:

◆ What is the component causing the bottleneck?

◆ Is the stress on the server typical enough that action is warranted either now or in the future?

As was mentioned previously, under normal operation, only four system components affect system performance—memory, processor, disk, and network card. Therefore, you need to monitor the counters that will tell you the most about how those four components affect system performance so you can determine the answer to the two diagnostic questions.

The biggest problem in monitoring is not the collection of data; it is the interpretation of the data. Not only is it difficult to determine what a specific value for a particular counter means when taken in isolation, it is also difficult to determine what it means in the context of other counters. No subsystem (disk, network, processor, memory) exists in isolation. As a result, weaknesses in one might show up as weaknesses in another. Unless you take them all into consideration, you might end up adding another processor when all you needed was more RAM.

Understanding how the subsystems interact is important to understanding the significance of the counter values that are recorded. For example, if you detect that your processor is constantly running at 90%, you may be tempted to go out and purchase either a faster processor or an additional processor if the motherboard supports multiple processors. However, it is important to look at memory and disk use. If you do not have enough memory, the processor has to swap pages to the disk frequently. This results in high memory use, high disk use, and higher processor use. By purchasing more RAM, you could alleviate all those problems.

That one example illustrates how no one piece of information is enough to analyze your performance problems or your solution. You must monitor the server as a whole unit by putting together the counters from a variety of objects. Only then can you see the big picture and solve problems that may arise.

The recommended method of monitoring is to use a counter log. This helps you eliminate questions of whether the stress on the server is typical. If you log over a period of a week or a month and you consistently see a certain component under excessive load, you can be sure the stress is typical.

By default, counters are available to monitor the physical disk object. Although these counters are generally sufficient for monitoring disk performance, in some rare cases you may also want to monitor the performance of logical partitions. To modify the disk counters available, you need to use the diskperf command. Following is the basic syntax of diskperf:

```
diskperf -switch
```

where

- ◆ *No switch* identifies the current status of disk counters.

- ◆ -y enables all disk counters (both logical and physical) at next restart.

- ◆ -yd enables physical disk counters at next restart (this is the default).

- ◆ -yv enables logical disk counters at next restart.

- ◆ -n disables all disk counters at next restart.

- ◆ -nd disables physical disk counters at next restart.

- ◆ -nv disables logical disk counters at next restart.

NOTE **Windows 2000 Disk Counters Differ from Those in NT 4.0** Windows NT 4.0 users are aware that no disk counters were initialized on startup. With Windows 2000, physical disk counters are initialized on startup, but not the logical counters.

You can monitor two kinds of network counters when analyzing network performance: network interface counters and network segment counters. *Network interface counters* trace actual information passing in and out of the network interface card being monitored. These counters are useful only when monitoring the network performance as it relates to the specific card in question. On the other hand, *network segment counters* allow you to monitor the performance of the entire physical network segment the card is attached to. This is useful for monitoring network bandwidth use. However, in order to monitor this, you must install the full version of Network Monitor and the corresponding Network Monitor driver.

Unfortunately, this Network Monitor does not ship with Windows 2000. Instead of the full version, you get a simplified version. The full Network Monitor allows you to scan the entire network segment your machine is sitting on and pick up packets and traffic information, regardless of the source or destination. The Windows 2000 Network Monitor allows you to observe only network traffic for which your computer is the source or the destination. The result is that it cannot give you statistics on the network segment.

The full Network Monitor is available with the BackOffice product called Systems Management Server (version 2.0 at the time of this printing) .

If you can get the full version of Network Monitor, Step by Step 11.13 shows you how to install it.

ON THE CD

Step by Step 11.13, "Installing Network Monitor 2.0 and Network Monitor Drivers v.2 to Enable Network Segment Counters," walks you through the installation of Network Monitor. See the file **Chapter11-13StepbyStep.pdf** in the CD's **Chapter11\StepbyStep** directory.

As was indicated at the beginning of the section titled "Monitoring and Optimizing System Resource Use," baselines need to be established long before you begin to encounter problems. When you have all your counters enabled, creating a baseline is the next step in the process of monitoring.

To establish a baseline, you pick a time or duration of time that represents typical user interaction with the server. Then you create a log of important counters for the duration you have decided on. These counters are described in the next section. The log you create should be stored in a safe place to ensure that you can refer to it in the future. Every time you do a major hardware upgrade (such as increasing RAM or adding a processor), you should create a new baseline and delete the old one.

Which actual counters you want to monitor are based on the particular applications running on your server and the requirements you have for the server. Although some recommendations are given in Table 11.2, you may want to watch other objects as well if you have specific applications installed. In addition, and as a point of clarification to the table, the second column provides an indication as to whether the counter is used to simply watch the component in question (usage), or whether that counter is used to determine whether the component is a performance bottleneck.

TABLE 11.2

COUNTERS TO MONITOR

Component	Monitoring	Recommended Counters
Disk	Usage	Physical Disk\Disk Reads/sec
		Physical Disk\Disk Writes/sec
		Logical Disk\% Free Space
		Logical Disk\% Disk Time
		Logical Disk\% Idle Time
Disk	Bottlenecks	Physical Disk\Avg. Disk Queue Length (all instances)
Memory	Usage	Memory\Available Bytes
		Memory\Cache Bytes
	Bottlenecks	Memory\Pages/sec
		Memory\Page reads/sec
		Memory\Transition Faults/sec
		Memory\Pool Paged Bytes
		Memory\Pool Nonpaged Bytes
		Paging File\% Usage (all instances)
		Cache\Data Map Hits %
		Server\Pool Paged Bytes
		Server\Pool Nonpaged Bytes
Network	Usage	Network Segment\% Net Utilization
Network	Throughput	Network Interface\Bytes total/sec
		Network Interface\Packets/sec
		Server\Bytes Total/sec
Processor	Usage	Processor\% Processor Time (all instances)
	Bottlenecks	System\Processor Queue Length (all instances)
		Processor\Interrupts/sec

The following are descriptions of some of the counters in Table 11.2:

◆ **Physical Disk\Disk Reads/Sec.** How many disk reads occur per second.

◆ **Physical Disk\Disk Writes/Sec.** How many disk writes occur per second.

◆ **Logical Disk\% Free Space.** The ratio of free space total disk space on a logical drive. To prevent excessive fragmentation, the value here should not be allowed to drop below 10%.

◆ **Physical Disk\% Disk Time.** The ratio of busy time to the total elapsed time. This represents the percentage the physical disk is servicing read or write requests. If one drive is being used more than another, it might be time to balance the content between the drives.

◆ **Physical Disk\Avg. Disk Queue Length.** The average number of read and write requests that are waiting in queue for a physical disk. Optimally, this number should be no more than 2 because a larger number means the disk is a bottleneck.

◆ **Memory\Available Bytes.** The total amount of physical memory available to processes running on the computer. This number's significance varies as the amount of memory in the computer varies, but if this number is less than 4MB, you generally have a memory deficiency.

◆ **Memory\Cache Bytes.** The amount of cache memory available to processes running on the computer.

◆ **Memory\Pages/Sec.** The number of hard page faults occurring per second. A hard page fault occurs when data or code is not in memory and must be retrieved from the hard drive. A bottleneck in memory is likely when this number is 20 or greater.

◆ **Memory\Page reads/Sec.** The number of times the disk needed to be read to resolve a hard page fault. Unlike Memory\Pages/sec, this counter is not an indicator of the quantity of data being retrieved but rather the number of times the disk had to be consulted.

◆ **Memory\Transition Faults/Sec.** The number of times page faults were recovered by locating the material somewhere else in memory than where it originally was marked to be. This is usually caused by modifications to the data. Transition faults can be tolerated in large numbers because their resolution does not require disk access.

◆ **Memory\Pool Paged Bytes.** The number of bytes of memory taken up by system tasks that can be swapped out to disk if needed. If the number of Pool Paged Bytes is large, it may indicate a large number of system processes. If this number is a significant percentage of total memory, you may need to increase RAM to allow these tasks to remain in RAM instead of being swapped out.

◆ **Memory\Pool Nonpaged Bytes.** The number of bytes of memory taken up by system tasks that cannot be swapped out to disk. This figure can indicate a bottleneck in memory, especially if the figure is a significant percentage of the total amount of RAM.

◆ **Paging File\% Usage.** The ratio of the amount of the paging file being used to the total size of the paging file. A high number is desired here because it indicates that the paging file is sized correctly for the system.

◆ **Cache\Data Map Hits %.** The ratio of positive hits to memory for data trying to be retrieved. A small number indicates that a large percentage of the time, data had to be recovered from the disk rather than from memory indicating a shortage of memory.

◆ **Server\Pool Paged Bytes.** Indicates the amount of paged memory that is being consumed by the Server service. This is an indication of the amount of memory being used by network requests, and in conjunction with Memory\Pool Paged Bytes, it can be an indication of where the majority of a memory bottleneck is located.

◆ **Server\Pool Nonpaged Bytes.** Indicates the amount of memory being consumed by the Server service that cannot be paged. In conjunction with Memory\Pool Nonpaged Bytes, this can show how much permanent memory is allocated to processes and can be an indication of memory bottlenecks.

◆ **Network Interface\Bytes Total/Sec.** This is an indication of the total throughput of the network interface. It can be used for general capacity planning and does not necessarily indicate a network bottleneck.

◆ **Server\Bytes Total/Sec.** The number of bytes the Server service is sending to and receiving from the network. This is a general indication of how busy the Server service is.

◆ **Processor\% Processor Time.** The amount of time the processor spends executing non-idle threads. This is an indication of how busy the processor is. The processor for a single-processor system should not exceed 75% capacity for a significant period of time. High processor use may be an indication of processor bottlenecks, but it could also indicate lack of memory.

◆ **System\Processor Queue Length.** The number of processes that are ready but waiting to be serviced by the processor(s). There is a single queue for all processors, even in a multi-processor environment. A sustained queue of more than 2 generally indicates processor congestion.

◆ **Processor\Interrupts/Sec.** The number of hardware requests the processor is servicing per second. This is not necessarily an indicator of system health, but when compared against the baseline, it can help determine hardware problems. Hardware problems are often identified by the increased number of interrupts that are recorded in the Performance Monitor logs.

All this information shows that monitoring is not a strict science. You should watch for indicators and specific counters should be monitored. But in the end, your experience and intuition will tell you as much about what a specific counter means as specific numeric comparisons do.

MAINTAINING SYSTEM RECOVERY INFORMATION

Manage and optimize availability of system state data and user data.

Making your Windows 2000 Server run efficiently is only part of your task as a server administrator. In the back of every administrator's mind is the inevitability of data loss, either through user error or through catastrophic hardware failure. The systems you put in place to recover from these situations may well make or break your standing as an administrator.

A number of available tools enable you to recover your system and your data in the case of loss. Of course, recovery presupposes that you use the tools, and this section discusses about how to do just that. The next section deals with the actual recovery processes themselves.

The list that follows identifies the tools available and what kinds of loss each allows you to recover from:

◆ **Last Known Good configuration.** This allows you to recover from configuration changes that affect Registry settings for devices (such as installing an incorrect video driver or configuring it incorrectly). This tool has only a limited window of effectiveness; when you successfully log on locally to a Windows 2000 computer, this no longer functions.

◆ **Emergency Repair Disk.** This enables you to recover from Registry settings that render your system inoperable. This might be misconfiguration that could not be caught with the Last Known Good configuration or other Registry changes.

◆ **Windows 2000 Backup.** This is useful for recovering other Registry settings as well as user data. This option allows the widest breadth of recovery but also takes the most time.

Each of these tools is covered in this section. How to use them to recover your system is covered in the following section.

System state, simply put, is the current configuration of your Windows 2000 Server. *Current configuration* refers to any information required to bring the operating system from a newly installed state to the configuration that it currently is in. System state does not include the installation of applications, nor does it include user data; those need to be dealt with through backups of file data.

Before looking into the ways that system information and data can be saved, let's digress into the kinds of failure you are protecting against. Data on your Windows 2000 server can become corrupt and nonfunctional in many ways.

Saving System State with Last Known Good Configuration

The first mechanism for saving system state data is the easiest to use, because Windows 2000 automatically does it for you. All the current information about system configuration is stored in a Registry location called the *current control set*. The current control set defines your hardware configuration, the protocols installed, the drivers installed, and other configurations in those categories. Each time you successfully log in to your Windows 2000 Server (that is, when, as a user, you complete the name and password dialog box locally on the server), the current configuration is written into the backup configuration known as the Last Known Good configuration.

In the event that you make a change you regret, you can invoke the Last Known Good configuration to recover the backup control set. The *backup control set* allows you to reset your machine's configuration to the last good configuration.

Although it's useful, Last Known Good configuration has a number of limitations, not the least of which is that the "system backup" is overwritten every time you log in to the system. Further, Last Known Good configuration does not save a number of pieces of useful information, including system files used to load Windows 2000, the boot sector, and the startup environment (which partition to boot each operating system from in a multioperating system configuration).

Saving System State with Emergency Repair Directory and Disks

Another mechanism for saving system state data is the emergency repair directory and disks. The emergency repair information is stored in a folder in the path %systemroot%\repair. %systemroot% is the location of your Windows 2000 operating system files, usually WINNT. Repair information is automatically written into the repair folder when the system is installed.

If you choose, you can create a backup of the Registry into the repair folder. This backup information can be used to restore your Registry if it becomes corrupt, but is unavailable in the case of a hard drive failure of the hard drive where the repair directory is located. As a precaution, always store the recovery information to an Emergency Repair Disk (ERD).

The ERD can be used to facilitate some system repairs on your Windows 2000 Server. Essentially, the disk can be used to repair startup problems, such as when essential startup files are not present and your Server refuses to boot.

Step by Step 11.14 shows how to create an ERD.

ON THE CD

Step by Step 11.14, "Creating an ERD," shows you how to create an Emergency Repair Disk. See the file **Chapter11-14StepbyStep. pdf** in the CD's **Chapter11\StepbyStep** directory.

Instructions on how to repair your system with an ERD is provided in the upcoming section "Saving System State with Emergency Repair Directory and Disks."

Saving System State and User Data with Windows 2000 Backup

The most robust method of saving both system state and user data is to use Windows 2000 Backup. Windows 2000 Backup allows full backup of all system state information at the click of a check box, as well as the scheduling of backup times and dates.

You must ensure that you regularly back up your Windows 2000 servers. The ability to recover from catastrophic failure or user error depends on your backups being up-to-date and secure from theft and physical damage.

The next two sections provide a discussion of backup in general and a discussion of backup using Windows 2000 Backup.

NOTE **How Do Backups Determine Which Files to Include in the Backup Set?** On a Windows 2000 Server, each file has an archive bit that identifies whether that particular file has been backed up. If the archive bit is set to False, the file has not been modified since the last backup occurred. If the archive bit is set to True, the file has either been modified or created since the last backup occurred. The backup types are differentiated by how they respond to the archive bit and how they modify the archive bit.

Elementary Backup Theory

The theory of backups has not changed since the backup was invented. Regardless of the backup software you choose, the main features remain the same. The five backup types or five ways to determine what should be backed up and how this affects further backups are as follows:

◆ **Normal backups.** Sometimes called full backups, these save all files regardless of the state of the archive bit. While saving the files, normal backups set the archive bit to False to indicate that the files have been backed up.

◆ **Incremental backups.** These check the current status of the archive bit before backing up data. If the archive bit is False, an incremental backup skips the file because it has been backed up. If the archive bit is True, an incremental backup saves the file and sets its archive bit to False.

◆ **Differential backups.** These backups also check the current status of the archive bit before backing up data. As with an incremental backup, if the archive bit is False, a differential skips the file, and if the archive bit is True, the differential backup saves the file. However, it leaves the archive bit set to True after backing up the file. This means that two differentials in a row will both back up the same changed file, because the first backup will not set the archive bit to tell the second to skip the file.

◆ **Copy backups.** These are like normal backups because they back up all data regardless of the state of the archive bit. However, they do not set the archive bits to True after backing up the data.

◆ **Timeframe backups.** Like copy backups, timeframe backups back up all data regardless of the state of the archive bit, but they also look at the date a file was changed. As an example, daily backups back up only those files modified on a specific day.

General backup theory indicates that the three types of ongoing backup strategies are normal only, normal/incremental, and normal/differential. The decision to use one over the other is determined by a number of factors.

A normal only backup strategy can be chosen if you have the time to do a complete backup of all your systems every day. Using a normal only strategy ensures that all your data is backed up at the end of every day. This means recovery requires that only the last backup set be available. Unfortunately, time is often a factor. In some cases, the amount of time available to do backups is exceeded by the amount of time it would take to do a normal backup every day. In these cases, the next decision is to determine whether to reduce the time to complete the backup or to reduce the time required recovering from a failure.

If you choose to reduce the time to complete the backup, you probably want to choose a normal/incremental strategy. These strategies make backup faster, because you back up only data that has changed since the last incremental (or normal) backup. However, this strategy results in a slower recovery because there are more tapes to apply.

If you choose to reduce the time required recovering from a failure, a normal/differential strategy can be used. This strategy makes backup slower because each day's backup is saving all data that has changed since the last normal backup. However, recovery is faster than normal/incremental, because to recover to any specific day, you have to apply only the last differential tape after restoring the normal backup.

No matter what backup solution is selected, each day's backup should be performed on a separate tape. This ensures that the same tape does not stay in the tape drive for a whole week, which would increase the likelihood that an environmental disaster (such as a fire) or a tape drive failure would destroy the tape. You will eventually reuse the tapes, so ensure that you have a sufficient number of tapes to meet your backup requirements.

For example, if you implemented a normal/incremental strategy for backup, you could use the following tape rotation:

◆ On alternate Fridays, you could reuse the same tape that is being used for the normal backup, but not on successive Fridays. This ensures that if a failure occurs in the middle of a normal backup, the previous normal backup has not been destroyed.

◆ Eight incremental tapes could be implemented so that an incremental tape is not reused until two full backups have been completed.

◆ All tapes should be stored in a physically and environmentally secure environment as soon as possible after the backup is complete. Servers sometimes fail because of environmental factors such as water or fire damage. If the backup is in the same place as the server, it will be destroyed, too.

◆ Periodically, a normal backup tape should be stored offsite to ensure that a natural disaster such as fire will not destroy a backup tape. Many companies store a normal backup tape from each month offsite to ensure that recoverability requirements are met.

Backing Up System State and User Data Using Windows 2000 Backup

Now that you understand generic backup theory, you're ready to move to the specific implementation that you find in Windows 2000 Server. Windows 2000 Backup is really a pared-down version of BackupExec, a product supplied to Microsoft by Veritas Inc.

Under Windows 2000, backup can be invoked in three ways. You can configure a backup with the GUI and start it immediately. You can schedule it to start at another time as either a single job or a repeating one. You can configure a backup to start from a command line. In the first two cases, a wizard walks you through the configuration. All three methods allow you to back up the data to either a file or a tape drive.

Windows 2000 Backup allows you to back up files from either the local computer or remote computers, provided that you have access to the files you want to back up on the remote computer. The limitation of backing up a computer remotely is that system state information cannot be saved.

To perform a backup, you must have read access to the files or the user right of Backup and Restore Files, which is granted by default to Administrators and Backup Operators.

Special permissions are granted the Administrators and Backup Operators groups to access all files for the purposes of doing backups. Even if members of these groups cannot access the data as users, they will be able to back it up.

Before beginning a backup, you need to set the general backup options. These allow you to configure defaults, system responses, logging sensitivity, and files to be excluded from backups. When you bring up the backup options, you are presented with five property tabs that define these options: General, Restore, Backup Type, Backup Log, and Exclude Files.

The General property tab lets you configure some default properties, as well as some alert messages that have to do with removable storage (see Figure 11.7).

The list that follows describes the options on the General property sheet:

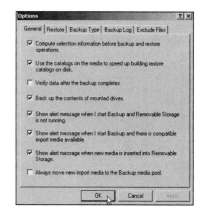

FIGURE 11.7
The General property tab.

◆ **Compute Selection Information Before Backup and Restore Operations.** This option shows the number of files and bytes that will be backed up or restored, given the current selections.

◆ **Use the Catalogs on the Media to Speed Up Building Restore Catalogs on Disk.** This option indicates that when you restore data from a backup, the catalog built at backup time should be used. This catalog tracks the files and paths that were backed up and should be used to display what can be restored.

◆ **Verify Data After the Backup Completes.** This option indicates that, by default, data on the backup should be checked against the content of the hard drive files before the backup is deemed to be complete. It is recommended that you do this at least once a week during a normal backup. Verification is a piece of insurance that will make your backups work when you need them.

◆ **Back Up the Contents of Mounted Drives.** This option indicates that mounted drives should be backed up when the drive they are mounted to is backed up. A mounted drive is a drive that is accessed from a folder defined on another drive. For example, you could mount the CD-ROM drive (D:) into the folder CDROM on the C: drive. If you select this check box, the content of the mounted drive will be backed up when the parent drive is backed up. Otherwise, only the path to the mounted drive will be backed up, not the data.

◆ **Show Alert Message When I Start Backup and Removable Storage Is Not Running.** This option indicates that a message should be displayed if the Removable Storage service is not running when backup is started. If you use tape drives, this should be checked.

◆ **Show Alert Message When I Start Backup and There Is Compatible Import Media Available.** This option indicates that a message should be displayed if import media is available to use for the backup. Import media is used with removable storage and is an indication that media, such as a tape that's used on another computer, has been inserted into the tape drive.

◆ **Show Alert Message When New Media Is Inserted into Removable Storage.** This option indicates that you should be informed when new media is available. If you do disk-based backups, it is not necessary to select this check box.

◆ **Always Move New Import Media to the Backup Media Pool.** This option indicates that any import media should be made available to the backup program. If you do disk-based backups, it is not necessary to select this check box.

The Restore property tab contains options with which you define the defaults for restoring system state data and user data from backup. You can define the action taken when a file that is being restored from backup is also present on the hard drive. You can choose never to restore, always to restore, or to restore only if the file in the backup set is newer than the one found on the hard drive.

The Backup Type property tab sets the default backup type. If you do not choose the backup type from the advanced properties, the type of backup indicated here will be implemented.

The Backup Log property tab defines the amount of detail the log file should contain. When you do a backup, the default is to create a log that tracks what happened during the backup. You can choose to log the name and path of each file backed up or skipped (making a large log), or you can choose to log only key operations (such as the backup starting and open files being skipped). You can also choose not to log at all.

The Exclude Files property tab lets you define the files that are never backed up. This list can be configured for all users, as well as for the user who is doing the backup. The kinds of files that are excluded by default include the paging file and temporary Internet files.

Now that you know all the backup options, Step by Step 11.15 shows you how to change them.

ON THE CD

Step by Step 11.15, "Changing Backup Options," shows you how to change backup options. See the file **Chapter11-15StepbyStep.pdf** in the CD's **Chapter11\StepbyStep** directory.

When the backup options have been set, it is time to do a backup. Step by Step 11.16 demonstrates how to configure a backup using the Backup Wizard.

ON THE CD

Step by Step 11.16, "Backing Up Data Using the Backup Wizard," demonstrates how to configure a backup using the Backup Wizard. See the file **Chapter11-16StepbyStep.pdf** in the CD's **Chapter11\StepbyStep** directory.

> **NOTE**
>
> **Windows 2000 Backup Does Not Back Up Open Files**   Like many other backup programs, Windows 2000 Backup does not back up open files. This means you might have to stop some running processes in order to ensure that files accessed by them will be backed up. Files that are open when the backup process gets to them will be skipped, and that fact will be noted in the backup log.

One of the strengths of Windows 2000 Backup is the ability to schedule backups for times of low system usage. An administrator does not need to be present during the backup as long as the correct tape or tapes are mounted.

Scheduling a Backup Using the Backup Wizard

Scheduled backups can be created using the advanced features of the Backup Wizard. However, you can also invoke the scheduled Backup Wizard from the Schedule Jobs page of the Backup dialog box.

This page allows you to scan through a calendar and see which backups are scheduled to run. By double-clicking a date, you begin the scheduled Backup Wizard. Essentially, the Scheduled Jobs Wizard is the same as the Backup Wizard except that the advanced options are automatically presented to you. It is expected that you are going to create a scheduled backup rather than an immediate one.

Step by Step 11.17 shows you how to use the Scheduled Jobs Wizard.

ON THE CD

Step by Step 11.17, "Scheduling Jobs for Backup Using the Wizard," demonstrates how to use the Scheduled Jobs Wizard. See the file **Chapter11-17StepbyStep.pdf** in the CD's **Chapter11\ StepbyStep** directory.

When you finish scheduling a backup, an icon appears on the calendar in every location where a backup is scheduled to occur. A letter also appears beside the icon to indicate what kind of backup is scheduled to be performed on that date. The detail of the job can be viewed by double-clicking the icon.

Configuring a Backup with a Command Line

The final method for invoking a backup is through a command line. A backup of any sort can be invoked using the NTBACKUP.EXE program and a set of command-line parameters that define how the backup is to progress.

The primary reasons for using the command-line version of NTBACKUP is that you might need to perform a backup as one of a series of scheduled tasks, or you might need for some sort of processing to precede the backup. In these cases, you could configure a batch file with a command-line backup and then have other commands execute from the same batch file. This batch file could be scheduled using the Windows 2000 Scheduler, found under Start, Programs, Accessories, System Tools, Scheduled Tasks.

Because the command-line parameters can get very complex and most of them will not be included on the exam, here is an example of how to use the parameters to create a normal backup. Then you

will look at an explanation of each component used in the following
command line:

```
Ntbackup backup "c:\backups\full backup.bks" /m normal /j
"Server Backup—Dec 31/99" /t "Normal Backup Tape" /d
"Server Backup" /v:yes /r:no /l:s /rs:no /hc:on
```

This command line reads as follows:

Back up the set of files defines the `"c:\backups\full backup.bks"`
backup set file. Do a `normal` backup. In the log, call the set `"Server
Backup-Dec 31/99"`. Get a tape from the pool defined as the backup
media. The name of the tape is to be set to `"Normal Backup Tape"`
and the label for the backup set is `"Server Backup"`. Verify the
backup after it is complete, do not restrict the tape to just the owner
or an administrator, do not back up the removable storage database,
and turn hardware compression on.

The following command gives the full syntax of the command-line
backup and provides a brief description of each:

```
ntbackup backup [systemstate] "bks file name" /J {"job
name"} [/P {"pool name"}] [/G {"guid name"}] [/T { "tape
name"}] [/N {"media name"}] [/F {"file name"}] [/D {"set
description"}] [/DS {"server name"}] [/IS {"server name"}]
[/A] [/V:{yes|no}] [/R:{yes|no}] [/L:{f|s|n}] [/M {backup
type}] [/RS:{yes|no}] [/HC:{on|off}] [/UM]
```

where

- ◆ `systemstate` specifies that you want to back up the system
  state data. This parameter forces the backup type to be normal
  or copy.

- ◆ `bks file name` specifies the name of the backup selection file
  (BKS file) to be used for this backup operation. A backup
  selection file contains information on the files and folders you
  have selected for backup. This switch can also be replaced by
  the path to the files you want to back up (for example,
  `c:\data or \\server\pictures`).

- ◆ `/J {"job name"}` specifies the job name to be used in the log
  file. The job name usually describes the files and folders you
  are backing up in the current backup job, as well as the date
  and time you backed up the files.

- ◆ `/P {"pool name"}` specifies the media pool from which you
  want to use media. This is usually a subpool of the Backup
  media pool, such as 4mm DDS.

◆ /G {"*guid name*"} specifies the tape you want to write to by its Globally Unique Identifier (GUID). The backup overwrites or appends to this tape.

◆ /T {"*tape name*"} specifies the tape you want to write to by its name. The backup overwrites or appends to this tape.

◆ /N {"*media name*"} specifies the new tape name.

◆ /F {"*file name*"} provides the logical disk path and filename.

◆ /D {"*set description*"} specifies a label for each backup set.

◆ /DS {"*server name*"} backs up the directory service file for the specified Microsoft Exchange Server.

◆ /IS {"*server name*"} backs up the Information Store file for the specified Microsoft Exchange Server.

◆ /A appends the current backup set to a previous backup set on the tape.

◆ /V:{yes|no} verifies the data after the backup is complete.

◆ /R:{yes|no} restricts access to this tape to the owner or members of the Administrators group.

◆ /L:{f|s|n} specifies the type of log file: f = full, s = summary, n = none.

◆ /M {*backup type*} specifies the backup type to be normal, copy, differential, incremental, or daily.

◆ /RS:{yes|no} backs up the removable storage database.

◆ /HC:{on|off} uses hardware compression, if available, on the tape drive.

◆ /UM finds the first available media, formats it, and uses it for the current backup operation. When you use the /UM switch, Backup searches the following media pools for available media: Free pool, Import pool, Unrecognized pool, and Backup pool. When available media is found, the search stops, and the media is formatted and used without prompting you for input. This command should only be used if you have a standalone tape device.

A backup selection file contains the specific files that are to be included in a backup set. Step by Step 11.18 shows you how to create a backup selection file.

ON THE CD

Step by Step 11.18, "Creating a Backup Selection File (BKS)," demonstrates how to create a backup selection file. See the file **Chapter11-18StepbyStep.pdf** in the CD's **Chapter11\StepbyStep** directory.

SERVER, SYSTEM STATE, AND USER DATA RECOVERY

Recover systems and user data.

If you are very fortunate, you will never have to recover any lost data or restore a server after a crash. In that case, the backups and repair disks you learned about in the previous sections are like insurance you will never use.

However, chances are unlikely that you will be so fortunate. If nothing else, you will encounter an end user who has accidentally deleted a file and needs you to restore it. There's a good chance that a catastrophic accident will happen while you are an administrator, and you will need to recover from it. At that point, all the talk about saving data becomes practical and not simply theoretical; you had better hope that you've implemented a good strategy for saving system data.

Just as there are a number of ways to save data, there are also a number of ways to recover lost data.

Recovering System State with Last Known Good Configuration

As was mentioned in the section "Saving System State with Last Known Good Configuration," the Last Known Good configuration is automatically saved whenever a user successfully logs on locally to the system. This state represents the last configuration settings that were able to support logon.

If you make a change to your system and want to be able to back out of it, you can do so at restart by invoking the Last Known Good configuration. However, one of the problems is that you might not know anything is wrong until you log on again. One of the major indicators of poor configuration is that the Service Control Manager issues a message that a service failed to start. The problem with this warning is that, if you log in quickly, the message does not appear until after you have logged on and replaced the previous Last Know Good configuration.

One recommendation is that if you make changes to your system and then restart, wait a minute or two at the logon dialog box to see whether the Service Control Manager issues a message. Step by Step 11.19 shows you how to invoke the Last Known Good configuration.

ON THE CD

Step by Step 11.19, "Invoking Last Know Good Configuration," shows you how to invoke the Last Know Good configuration. See the file **Chapter11-19StepbyStep.pdf** in the CD's **Chapter11\StepbyStep** directory.

Recovering System State with Emergency Repair Information

The emergency repair folder and disk can be used to recover a variety of system files and configuration settings. It can be used to recover the Registry if it becomes corrupted. It can also be used to recover system files if they are accidentally deleted.

In order to recover, you must provide the Windows 2000 Server CD-ROM and the Emergency Repair Disk. If you computer does not support booting from the CD-ROM, the Windows 2000 startup disks can be used to start the computer.

Step by Step 11.20 demonstrates how to recover a lost system state using the emergency recovery process.

ON THE CD

Step by Step 11.20, "Recovering System State Using the Emergency Repair Process," demonstrates how to recover a lost system state using the emergency recovery process. See the file **Chapter11-20StepbyStep.pdf** in the CD's **Chapter11\StepbyStep** directory.

Recovering Systems with the Recovery Console

The Recovery Console is a powerful text-based boot alternative for Windows 2000 Server. If your system becomes so corrupt that it will not boot and no other repair process will help, you can boot to the Recovery Console and copy files to or from your server. In addition, you can disable services if a service that you have installed causes problems with booting.

Two ways to boot to the Recovery Console are using the Setup disks or configuring the Recovery Console as a secondary boot in the boot menu and choosing it at system startup.

Because the Recovery Console is so powerful, when it starts you must log on as the Administrator. Step by Step 11.21 shows how to boot to this console.

ON THE CD

Step by Step 11.21, "Booting to the Recovery Console with Setup Disks," explains how to boot to this console. See the file **Chapter11-21StepbyStep.pdf** in the CD's **Chapter11\StepbyStep** directory.

To make booting to the Recovery Console more convenient, you can make it a boot item on the Windows 2000 boot menu. Step by Step 11.22 shows you how to install Recovery Console as a boot item.

ON THE CD

Step by Step 11.22, "Installing the Recovery Console as a Boot Item," walks you through the installation of Recovery Console as a boot item. See the file **Chapter11-22StepbyStep.pdf** in the CD's **Chapter11\StepbyStep** directory.

Troubleshooting with Safe Mode

Until Windows 2000, Safe mode was available only in Windows 9x operating systems. Safe mode allows you to boot an operating system with a minimal set of generic drivers and allows you to make changes to configurations that normally would prevent your system from starting. For example, if you changed your video driver to an incorrect drive, Safe mode would allow you to restart and use a generic setting for your video that will allow you to repair your system.

When you boot with advanced options, you are presented with three Safe mode choices: Safe Mode, Safe Mode with Networking, and Safe Mode with Command Prompt. Choosing Safe Mode starts Windows 2000 using only basic files and drivers. Choosing Safe Mode with Networking adds networking capabilities to the basic Safe mode. Choosing Safe Mode with Command Prompt starts Windows 2000 in a text mode instead of a GUI mode. You have to restart your computer to exit from the text mode.

Step by Step 11.23 illustrates how to boot to Safe mode.

ON THE CD

Step by Step 11.23, "Booting to Safe Mode," illustrates how to boot to Safe Mode. See the file **Chapter11-23StepbyStep.pdf** in the CD's **Chapter11\StepbyStep** directory.

Recovering System State and User Data with Windows 2000 Backup

Most Windows 2000 Server implementations require that data be restored from backup at some point. Assuming that you have been using good backup methods, you should be able to quickly recover from any incident, whether it is a hard drive failure or a user deletion error.

The number of options for recovery of information are greatly reduced compared to options for saving information. In a simple recovery, you can indicate what needs to be restored and from what tape or file. Advanced options allow you to configure recovery in three ways:

◆ **Location of recovered files.** You can recover data to its original location or to an alternate location. In addition, you can choose to maintain the previous folder structure or to restore to a single folder.

◆ **Overwrite policy for existing files.** You can choose to never overwrite existing data, to overwrite only older versions of the file, or to always overwrite existing data.

◆ **Set additional options.** Three additional options can be set. These include deciding whether to recover security information (including NTFS permissions, auditing settings, and ownership settings), recover the removable storage database (this tracks all removable storage media in use), or recover mounted volumes.

Step by Step 11.24 shows you how to recover information stored on backup tapes or files.

> NOTE
>
> **You Can Restore from GUI Only**
> Using the GUI program is the only way to restore data using Windows 2000 Backup. There is no command-line interface, nor can it be scheduled.

ON THE CD

Step by Step 11.24, "Recovering Data from Backup Tapes or Files," shows you how to recover information stored on backup tapes of files. See the file **Chapter11-24StepbyStep.pdf** in the CD's **Chapter11\StepbyStep** directory.

CASE STUDY: WEBCRAZY CONSULTING

ESSENCE OF THE CASE

This case requires that the following results be satisfied:

▶ Devise a way to back up all Emilio's critical data.

▶ Make sure the backup strategy allows storage on a single tape drive. Emilio does not want to buy more hardware.

▶ Make sure a clear schedule is devised that will provide for the most up-to-date backups with the least amount of inconvenience to Emilio.

SCENARIO

Emilio is the sole proprietor of a small home-based Internet consulting company called WebCrazy. He has a dedicated Internet connection, and he hosts his own Web page and those of some of his clients on a Web server running Windows 2000 Server, which is located in his basement. In addition, he has three other computers on a LAN in a workgroup configuration. Of these, one is a laptop on which he does most of his development; it runs Windows 2000 Professional. One computer is a test machine that he frequently formats and reinstalls. The other computer is one his family uses; it runs Windows 98.

Emilio knows that being able to recover data in the event of a hard drive crash is essential. Therefore, he purchased a 4mm DAT drive for his server. What he is unsure of is how to back up all the data on his server, laptop, and family machines from a single location—if that is possible at all. He also wants to know the recommended frequency for his backups and how many tapes he needs. He has called you to look over his network and advise him on a strategy.

ANALYSIS

Given the capabilities of Windows 2000 Backup and Emilio's network configuration, it is possible to fulfill all his backup needs with a minimum of hardware purchase. Emilio will have to buy only tapes. The backup can also be configured with a minimum of interaction between Emilio and the system. However, he will have to change tapes occasionally.

CASE STUDY: WEBCRAZY CONSULTING

All Emilio's data can be accessed from a central location if the proper accounts have been created. In the case of the Windows 98 computer, the proper folder sharing must be put into place. It is recommended that Emilio create user accounts on both the server and the laptop that have the same name and password and that are in the Administrators group of the respective machines. In addition, on the Windows 98 computer, he should share the root of each hard drive (if there is more than one). This ensures that all data of all computers can be accessed from the server.

Because all the data is accessible from the server, Emilio can perform centralized backups from the server onto the DAT drive installed in it. By using Windows 2000 Backup, he can connect to the administrative shares on the laptop (C$, D$, and so on.). Emilio is an administrator on the laptop and the drives of the Windows 98 computer through the shares. This allows him to back up all network data on a single tape.

Finally, you will recommend a backup procedure that includes scheduling incremental backups Saturday though Thursday nights and normal backups on Friday nights. Using a rotating tape system in which normal backups use two tapes (rotated each week), and incremental backups use two more tapes (with all incrementals from one week on a single tape), Emilio needs only four DAT tapes to ensure that all his data is safe. In addition, using this procedure, he also ensures that he can go back to the previous week to recover data that might be accidentally deleted.

This table summarizes the solution.

OVERVIEW OF THE REQUIREMENTS AND SOLUTIONS IN THIS CASE STUDY

Requirement	Solution Provided By
Emilio's critical data must be backed up.	Using administrative shares on Windows 2000 and network shares on Windows 98 provides access to all network data from the server.
Data must be saved at a central point.	Running Windows 2000 Backup on the server (from which we have access to all network data) is possible using the DAT drive Emilio already has.
Schedule needs to be automated.	Using the scheduling features of Windows 2000 Backup, all Emilio has to do is make sure the correct tape is present in the tape drive at the end of every day. (It would have to be changed on Friday and Saturday of each week.)

CHAPTER SUMMARY

KEY TERMS

- Applications server
- Preemptive multitasking
- Idle priority
- Normal priority
- High priority
- Real-time priority
- Task Manager
- Performance Monitor
- System Monitor
- Counter log
- Trace log
- Alert
- Counter
- Object
- Instance
- DISKPERF.EXE
- Graph view

This chapter outlined the main points for saving system configuration and data, with an eye toward being able to restore those configurations and data should the need arise. Summarized briefly, this chapter covered the following main points:

◆ **Managing processes.** This includes setting application priorities through foreground boost and priority switches at runtime and through the Task Manager. This also includes starting and stopping processes through the Task Manager.

◆ **Monitoring and optimizing use of system resources.** This includes the use of Performance Monitor (System Monitor, counter logs, trace logs, and alerts) to gather information. In addition, it includes using the data gathered from Performance Monitor to isolate bottlenecks and improve performance.

CHAPTER SUMMARY

◆ **Saving system state and user data**. This includes using the Last Known Good configuration, emergency repair folder and disks, and Windows 2000 Backup to save critical system and user data.

◆ **Recovering system state and user data**. This includes using the Last Know Good configuration, emergency repair folder and disks, Recovery Console, Safe Mode, and Windows 2000 Backup to recover critical data that has been saved.

KEY TERMS

- Histogram view
- Report view
- Trace provider
- Bottleneck
- Baseline
- Last Known Good configuration
- Emergency Repair Disk (ERD)
- Normal backup
- Incremental backup
- Differential backup
- Copy backup
- Daily backup
- NTBACKUP.EXE
- Backup selection file
- Recovery Console
- Safe mode

APPLY YOUR KNOWLEDGE

Review Questions

1. What are the four application execution priorities, and what numeric ranges does each fall into?

2. Name three ways to change the execution priority of an application (whether it's running or not).

3. What are the two types of logs available in Performance Monitor, and how can you distinguish them from one another?

4. What is the purpose of an alert, and what are three of the actions that can be taken when one happens?

5. What limitation of Windows 2000 Backup should lead you to schedule backups for times when as few people are accessing the server as possible?

6. What are three ways to invoke the Windows 2000 Backup process?

7. How does the Recovery Console differ from Safe Mode with Command Prompt?

8. What do you need to perform an emergency repair?

Answers to Review Questions

1. The four priorities are Idle—sometimes called Low (0–6), Normal (6–11), High (11–15), and Real-Time (16–31). For more information, see the section "Maintaining Windows 32-Bit Applications."

2. The priority of an application can be changed in three ways. The first way is to start it at a command line (or from a shortcut), using the syntax Start /priority applicationname. The second way is to change its priority in the Task Manager while it is running. The third way is to set the foreground boost for all Normal applications in the advanced page of the System Properties. For more information, see the section "Maintaining Windows 32-Bit Applications."

3. The two kinds of logs available in Performance Monitor are counter logs and trace logs. They are distinguished by their collection trigger and how much control you have over the information you collect. The collection of data in a counter log is controlled by time interval passing, and you can finely control the kind of data you collect through the application of object counters. The collection of data in a trace log is controlled by events that happen (such as user logon), and you have little control over the specific information collected outside a general category of data. For more information, see the section "Collecting Data Using Performance Monitor."

4. The purpose of an alert is to have Performance Monitor tell you when a critical situation happens so you don't have to check for it periodically. When an alert is triggered, you can have Performance Monitor take one of the following actions: create an application log entry, send a network message, start a counter log, or run a program. For more information, see the section "Creating Trace Logs."

5. The major drawback of Windows 2000 Backup is its inability to back up open files. That means that files that are open by system processes or by users when the backup process comes to them

APPLY YOUR KNOWLEDGE

will be skipped over. Therefore, you should have as few people interacting with server data as possible when a backup is in progress. For more information, see the section "Saving System State and User Data with Windows 2000 Backup."

6. You invoke the Windows 2000 Backup process three ways: immediately through the GUI, on schedule through the GUI, and immediately through the NTBACKUP program at a command line. For more information, see the section "Saving System State and User Data with Windows 2000 Backup."

7. The Recovery Console differs from Safe Mode with Command Prompt primarily because it is a separate boot from the regular Windows 2000 Server boot process. Safe mode requires that the server still be bootable in order for you to use it to effect changes. Recovery Console can be used even if your Windows 2000 Server is not bootable through normal means. In addition, Recovery Console offers only a limited set of commands, whereas Safe mode provides the full set of command-line commands. For more information, see the sections "Recovering Systems with the Recovery Console" and "Troubleshooting with Safe Mode."

8. To perform an emergency repair, you must have the four-disk startup set. In addition, it is helpful (but not necessarily required) to have the Windows 2000 Server CD-ROM and an Emergency Repair Disk. If your system is capable of booting from its CD-ROM drive, you could do without the four-disk set and simply boot to the Windows 2000 Server CD. For more information, see the section "Recovering System State with Emergency Repair Information."

ON THE CD

This book's companion CD contains specially designed supplemental material to help you understand how well you know the concepts and skills you learned in this chapter. You'll find related exercises, review questions and answers, and exam questions and answers. See the file **Chapter11ApplyYourKnowledge.pdf** in the CD's **Chapter11\ApplyYourKnowledge** directory.

Suggested Readings and Resources

1. Microsoft Windows 2000 Server Resource Kit: *Microsoft Windows 2000 Server Operations Guide.* Microsoft Press, 2000.

   - Part 2 (Chapters 5–10): Performance Monitoring
   - Part 3 (Chapters 11–13): System Recovery

2. *Microsoft Windows 2000 Professional Resource Kit.* Microsoft Press, 2000.

   - Chapter 18: Removable Storage and Backup
   - Part 6 (Chapters 27–30): Performance Monitoring

3. Microsoft Official Curriculum course 1560: *Updating Support Skills from Microsoft Windows NT 4.0 to Microsoft Windows 2000.*

   - Module 16: Implementing Disaster Protection

4. Microsoft Official Curriculum course 2152: *Supporting Microsoft Windows 2000 Professional and Server.*

   - Module 12: Monitoring and Optimizing Performance in Windows 2000
   - Module 13: Implementing Disaster Protection

5. Web Sites

   - www.microsoft.com/windows2000
   - www.microsoft.com/train_cert

This chapter will help you prepare for the "Managing, Configuring, and Troubleshooting Storage Use" section of the exam.

Microsoft provides the following objectives for "Managing, Configuring, and Troubleshooting Storage Use":

Configure and manage user profiles.

▶ Someone certified in the use of Windows 2000 Server technology must understand how to create and manage local, roaming, and mandatory profiles.

Monitor, configure, and troubleshoot disks and volumes.

▶ Someone certified in the use of Windows 2000 Server technology must understand both basic and dynamic disks. In addition, an understanding of the different partitions and volumes is necessary, as well as an understanding of the scenarios in which to use them.

Configure data compression.

▶ Someone certified in the use of Windows 2000 Server technology must understand how NTFS volumes can support file compression. An understanding of how to apply compression and the implications of compressing a disk and folder is also necessary.

CHAPTER 12

Managing, Configuring, and Troubleshooting Storage Use

Monitor and configure disk quotas.

▶ Someone certified in the use of Windows 2000 member server technology must understand how to control the amount of disk space users consume through the use of disk quotas.

Recover from disk failures.

▶ Someone certified in the use of Windows 2000 member server technology must understand the various methods for recovering from disk failures with a minimum loss of data.

STUDY STRATEGIES

▶ As it pertains to profiles, you need to understand the types of profiles and their function. You need to understand the implications of using local versus roaming profiles and how each is configured. In addition, you need to know how mandatory profiles can be configured and when you would want to use them. Finally, you need to understand how to configure user accounts to use profiles.

▶ The exam questions regarding disks are almost exclusively directed toward dynamic disks, the preferred disk type in Windows 2000. Be sure that you understand what the dynamic types are, how they are created, and what their properties are. In addition, you need to know their strengths and their limitations. You should also understand the concept of mounting volumes inside NTFS folders. Finally, you need to understand the recovery techniques for mirror volume and RAID-5 volume failures.

▶ Data compression is not new to Windows 2000, but there is bound to be a question dealing with it. Make sure you know how to turn it on at the volume, folder, and file level and the implications of turning it on for each.

▶ Disk quotas are new, so you can expect one or two questions dealing with them. Understand the implications of imposing quotas and whom they apply to. In addition, know how to remove them if that becomes necessary.

▶ As with the other chapters, going through the material in this chapter is the beginning of understanding it. Then you should do the exercises and the Step by Step examples and attempt to implement them. You need to do these things to understand the concepts. Having a server with a hard drive on which you can create, format, and delete partitions is essential to being able to apply and understand these concepts.

INTRODUCTION

Many Windows 2000 standalone servers function wholly or in part as data repositories (file servers). Many administrative tasks are required to manage this data. This includes creating volumes and partitions for storing this data, setting quotas to prevent individual users from consuming all the available disk space, and recovering from disk failures. This chapter deals with the theory and tasks required to maintain data on Windows 2000 Servers.

CREATING AND MAINTAINING USER PROFILES

Configure and manage user profiles.

The idea that each user on a local area network has a single computer that only he or she logs on from is foreign to most network environments. The concept behind the user profile is that separate user settings are stored for each person, and that a user can maintain his or her desktop settings without affecting other people who use the same computer.

Windows 2000 provides for three kinds of user profiles; local, roaming, and mandatory. The following sections provide details on each kind of user profile.

Local User Profiles

Local profiles are stored on a specific computer and are available only from that computer. They are created automatically for each user who logs on and will retain desktop settings for each user from session to session.

Settings that are stored in a user profile include application data, cookies, desktop, favorites, temporary data locations, the My Documents folder, network shortcuts, printers, recent documents, the Send-to menu items, personal Start menu shortcuts, user templates, and the HKEY_CURRENT_USER Registry subkey.

The local user profile for a user is created in the following way. The first time a user logs on to a Windows 2000 computer, the default profile is copied into a profile with his or her username associated with it. Then the All Users profile is consulted to determine what items are also to be applied to this user in addition to his or her own personal profile.

Local user profiles are stored in the Documents and Settings folder on the System Partition.

Roaming User Profiles

Roaming user profiles perform the same function as local user profiles. The difference is that whereas local user profiles are always accessed locally on the machine a user is logging in on, roaming profiles are accessed over the network from a central location. This allows the same profile to be accessed from anywhere on the network.

The creation of a roaming profile always follows the same basic steps:

1. Configure a shared folder on a server to hold the roaming profiles.

2. Create a folder within the shared folder for each user who is going to be roaming. The name of the folder should be the user's logon name.

3. Copy an existing profile into the folder for each user. (If you do not do this, a profile will be created for the user using the default and All Users profiles of the machine being used.)

4. Configure the user's account to point to the roaming location.

If the user is being converted from a local profile to a roaming profile, copy that local profile to the user's roaming location.

> NOTE
>
> **Default Is Static; All Users Is Dynamic** The copying of the default user profile is a one-time-only task. If the default user profile is changed, it does not retroactively modify user profiles. On the other hand, the All Users profile is completely dynamic. Any modifications made to it immediately result in changes to the current user's environment and affect all users who subsequently log on.

ON THE CD

Step by Step 12.1, "Copying a Local Profile to a Roaming Location," illustrates how to copy a local profile to a roaming location. See the file **Chapter12-01StepbyStep.pdf** in the CD's **Chapter12\StepbyStep** directory.

After you create the roaming profile, you must change the user account to point to that profile. This is slightly different depending on whether you are configuring roaming profiles for local users or domain users.

ON THE CD

Step by Step 12.2, "Configuring a Roaming Profile for a Local User Account," shows how to configure roaming profiles for a local user account. See the file **Chapter12-02StepbyStep.pdf** in the CD's **Chapter12\StepbyStep** directory.

ON THE CD

Step by Step 12.3, "Configuring a Roaming Profile for an Active Directory User Account," demonstrates the process for configuring a roaming profile for Active Directory user accounts. See the file **Chapter12-03StepbyStep.pdf** in the CD's **Chapter12\StepbyStep** directory.

Mandatory User Profiles

There are some cases in which a user's profile should not be changed by a user. For times when company politics or procedures require that a user's desktop remain constant, a mandatory profile can be created.

Mandatory profiles are a special subclass of roaming profiles. There are two primary differences between a mandatory profile and a roaming profile. Mandatory profiles are read-only and can be used by more than one user. In fact, if you group your users into functional groups, each functional group may require a different desktop, and you could be forced to create a mandatory profile for each group.

The creation of a mandatory profile always follows the same basic steps:

1. Configure a shared folder on a server to hold the mandatory profile.

2. Create a folder within the shared folder for each mandatory profile.

3. Copy an existing profile into the folder.

4. Rename the NTUSER.DAT file to NTUSER.MAN.

5. Configure each user's account with the mandatory profile location.

One component of the profile is the HKEY_CURRENT_USER Registry subtree. This set of Registry settings is represented on your hard drive by a file called NTUSER.DAT. This file is stored in each user's profile, and it defines the Registry settings for the user.

To make this file read-only, simply change the extension from DAT to MAN, thereby making the file NTUSER.MAN. When the user logs out, the NTUSER.MAN file will not be updated, so the settings will not be changed.

ON THE CD

Step by Step 12.4, "Creating a Mandatory Profile," shows you how to create a mandatory profile. See the file **Chapter12-04StepbyStep.pdf** in the CD's **Chapter12\StepbyStep** directory.

The procedure for pointing a user to a mandatory profile is the same as pointing to a roaming profile.

CONFIGURING DISKS AND VOLUMES

Monitor, configure, and troubleshoot disks and volumes.

Before you can install and run a Windows 2000 Server, you must begin configuring storage locations on your hard drives.

System and Boot Partitions

Two important terms you will hear (and probably be tested on) with reference to Windows 2000 Server are System Partition and Boot Partition.

> **NOTE**
>
> **When Does a Mandatory Profile Take Effect?**   A mandatory profile comes into effect only when it is initially downloaded from a network share. If the network share is unavailable after the mandatory profile is created, the user logs on using his or her local profile. After the mandatory profile has been downloaded, the user is no longer able to use the local profile.

> **NOTE**
>
> **An Alternative Method to Implement Mandatory Profiles**   As an alternative to renaming the NTUSER.DAT file to NTUSER.MAN, you can also rename the profile directory to have the MAN extension. For example, by placing the profile in \\server\profiles\ BKOMAR.MAN, you also implement mandatory user profiles.

The *System Partition* is the partition that tells a computer where to begin the operating system boot. The System Partition is also referred to as the Active Partition. On the System Partition, there is a small amount of boot code that looks further to some special files Windows 2000 uses to start the operating system. These files are BOOT.INI, NTDETECT.COM, and NTLDR. If the System or Boot Partitions are stored on a SCSI disk and the SCSI disk controller does not have the BIOS enabled, the file NTBOOTDD.SYS will also be located in the System Partition.

The WINNT folder and actual operating system files are located on the Boot Partition.

The distinction between the System Partition and the Boot Partition is sometimes purely definitional. They are spoken of separately to distinguish the function of each group of files in starting and running Windows 2000. However, if your server has a single partition, both the System Partition and the Boot Partition refer to the same disk partition.

ARC Paths and Volumes/Partitions

The BOOT.INI file, located on the System Partition, contains the path to the Windows 2000 files (the Boot Partition). To accurately define the location of these files, Windows 2000 uses a convention called Advanced RISC Computing (ARC) paths. *ARC standards* are conventions adopted by a variety of vendors that allow a piece of hardware to be defined by physical characteristics instead of by labels provided in the user interface of an operating system.

The BOOT.INI file, in its simplest form, defines the location of a single operating system's boot files on a computer. When more than one operating system is available, at system startup you are presented with a menu that allows you to choose the operating system you want to start.

Following is a sample BOOT.INI file:

```
[boot loader]
timeout=20
default=multi(0)disk(0)rdisk(0)partition(1)\WINNT
[operating systems]
multi(0)disk(0)rdisk(0)partition(1)\WINNT="Microsoft
Windows 2000 Server" /fastdetect
```

In the preceding example, the line beginning `timeout=` defines the length of time the system will wait before booting the default operating system. In the case of a single operating system to boot (like this example), the system starts Windows 2000 Server immediately; the 20-second delay is invoked only if there is more than one operating system to choose from.

The next line, `default=`, defines the location of the default operating system; that definition is an ARC path to the WINNT folder. This line should correspond to an entry listed beneath the `[operating systems]` label.

The entries under the label `[operating systems]` define the operating systems that are bootable from this BOOT.INI file. For Windows 2000 Servers in production environments, the only other option you might see here is a boot to the Recovery Console. Otherwise, a single entry is all you should see.

The ARC specification for volumes and partitions (ARC path) defines physical location based on four parameters: the disk controller, the physical hard drive on the controller, the partition on the physical hard drive, and the folder on the partition.

The full syntax for an ARC path can consist of one of two sets of parameters:

```
multi(0)disk(0)rdisk(0)partition(1)\Ospath
```

or

```
scsi(0)disk(0)rdisk(0)partition(1)\Ospath
```

The first one is far more common than the second, but you might encounter either.

In an ARC path, the first parameter (`multi` or `scsi`) defines the type of controller to which the hard drive is attached. `multi` indicates that the controller is either non-SCSI (IDE, EIDE, and so on) or is SCSI with the BIOS enabled. Most PC-based controllers fall into this category. `scsi` indicates that the controller is SCSI with the BIOS disabled. This parameter's numbering scheme begins with 0, so the first controller is either `multi(0)` or `scsi(0)`.

The second ARC parameter is the number of the hard drive. This parameter consists of the pair of values `disk(x)rdisk(y)`. In this pair, only one value (either x or y) is significant. Which one is significant depends on the controller type. If the controller is `multi`, the disk parameter to watch is `rdisk`. Conversely, if the controller is `scsi`, the disk parameter to watch is `disk`. Regardless of the controller type, both elements of the parameter pair must be present. Like the controller number, disk numbers begin with `0`; the first disk on a controller is numbered `0`.

The third ARC parameter is `partition(z)`. This defines the physical partition number of the volume that you want the path to point to. Unlike for the controller and drive, the numbering for partition begins at `1`.

The final parameter is the folder on the partition to which you want to point.

The numbers for controllers depend on the physical position in which they are installed in the computer. The numbers for hard drives are determined by their physical location on the cable attached to the controller. These two numbering systems are fixed unless you physically move components around in the computer.

Only volumes or partitions with true ARC paths can be the location of the System or Boot Partition for Windows 2000 operating systems. Moreover, the only volumes or partitions with true ARC paths must have at one time been a primary or logical partition on a basic disk.

The exam does not deal with multiple boot scenarios because the idea of bringing a production server offline to boot another operating system is not reasonable. Moreover, the introduction of dynamic disks (to be covered in the upcoming section "The Dynamic Disk") makes the ARC path specification less useful as well for more than two partitions on each drive.

EXAM TIP

Determining ARC Paths If you have problems booting because the ARC path is incorrect, you can boot to the Recovery Console and issue a MAP ARC command to find out what the arc path is for your bootable partition.

The Basic Disk

The disk structure known as the *basic disk* is the industry standard for disk configuration across all PC operating systems, whether you are working with OS/2, Windows 9x, or DOS; all support basic disk structures.

Because it is often useful to divide your disks into distinct logical units, basic disks support subdivision into two major types (or partitions):

◆ **Primary partition.** A primary partition can be designated as an Active Partition (indicating that it can be made bootable). As a result, every machine must have at least one primary partition. On most machines, this would be the C: drive. A basic disk supports up to four primary partitions.

◆ **Extended partition.** On a single hard drive, you can have only one extended partition. Within the extended partition, you can create an unlimited number of logical drives (subject to the letters of the alphabet).

Because of the limitation that you can have a total of only four partitions on a hard drive, you can combine partitions in only a limited number of combinations.

Using the basic disk structure, a physical disk can consist of up to four primary partitions or up to three primary partitions with one extended partition. An extended partition can be subdivided into an unlimited number of logical drives (theoretically).

If, however, you want to introduce fault tolerance into your disk system (which enables you to easily recover from disk failure), you need to consider another disk type—the dynamic disk.

The Dynamic Disk

The term *dynamic disk* is new for Windows 2000, but the kinds of utilities available as a result are not new and have been available since the early days of Windows NT. A dynamic disk consists of a single partition that is identified as dynamic (either when it's created or when it's converted from basic) and then subdivided into volumes. This can be done before or after a basic disk has been subdivided into partitions. The conversion program takes care of amalgamating the existing partitions and creating volumes out of them. A dynamic disk is a proprietary structure that is readable only by Windows 2000. Therefore, any data held on a dynamic disk cannot be read by other locally booting operating systems.

Within a dynamic disk, the following volume types can be created: simple, spanned, mirrored, striped, and RAID-5. Each of these has its advantages and disadvantages, which the following discussions look at in depth.

The Simple Volume

A *simple volume* is the most straightforward of the volume types. It is one or more segments of free space coming from a single hard drive with a letter identifying it. A simple volume is not fault-tolerant because it is only a single entity and has no redundancy built in to it.

A simple volume that was converted from a primary or logical partition on a basic disk has special properties. It is, in fact, the only partition type that can be home to the System or Boot Partition of a Windows 2000 Server implementation. If you create a simple volume from scratch, it does not have a true ARC path and, therefore, cannot be booted from.

The Spanned Volume

A *spanned volume* is one that consists of fragments of disk space from between 2 and 32 different hard drives. These fragments of disk space are treated as a single drive and have a single letter associated with them. The fragments that are joined together do not have to be the same size. When the volume is filled, each piece is filled in turn before the space on the next is used. Spanned volumes are not fault tolerant and, in fact, if any of the pieces are removed or corrupted, all the information is lost.

Planning is important when you're thinking about spanned volumes. If you begin with a basic disk and format it using partitions (primary, extended, and logical), you can convert those partitions to simple volumes. However, once converted, these volumes can never become spanned volumes. For you to create a spanned volume, your volume must have been created as a simple volume, never as a basic disk partition that was converted to a simple volume.

The Mirrored Volume

A *mirrored volume* (also referred to as *RAID 1*) consists of two areas of disk space on two separate hard drives. These two segments of space, like the spanned volume, are treated as a single drive and have a single drive letter associated with them. Both pieces need to be the same size in a mirrored volume (but these pieces do not have to be taken from hard drives of the same size). However, unlike the spanned volume, the total amount of storage space is not the accumulation of the two segments but the size of only one.

The basic function of mirroring is to provide redundancy and fault tolerance by writing the same information to two separate locations. This ensures that if either of the hard drives experiences a failure, there is always another copy of all the data available to recover from. In addition, mirroring also provides improved read capabilities because either disk could be accessed for information, and both could be concurrently accessed for different information, thus improving a disk's read throughput.

Any information can be stored on a mirrored volume, including the Boot and System Partitions. One variation of the mirrored volume is referred to as a *duplexed mirror*. The only difference between a mirrored volume and a duplexed mirror is that each disk in a duplexed mirror is controlled by different disk controllers.

The Striped Volume

Striped volumes (also referred to as *RAID 0*), like spanned volumes, consist of between 2 and 32 chunks of free space joined together. The difference is that while a spanned volume can consist of free space from a single hard drive, striped volumes must have free space from multiple hard drives. In addition, whereas the free space in spanned volumes does not need to be the same size, the pieces in a striped volume do. The reason for that comes down to the way in which the information is written to a striped volume. In a spanned volume, the information is written into one piece of free space at a time. The next segment of the spanned volume is not populated until the previous segment is full. In a striped volume, data is written to the volume in 64KB blocks across each segment of the volume. In this way, the stripes that are created span the volumes and results in faster disk input/output than with volume sets or disk mirrors. Like the spanned volume, the removal of any of the free space causes all the data in the volume to be lost. Therefore, this kind of volume is not fault tolerant.

Like the spanned volume, a striped volume cannot hold the System or Boot Partition of a Windows 2000 system.

The RAID-5 Volume

RAID-5 is a term that originally came from the hardware industry. The term *RAID* is an acronym for Redundant Array of Inexpensive Disks and was originally strictly implemented with hardware (multiple hard drives that functioned as one unit). RAID-5 is the implementation of a stripe set with parity to provide redundancy and recoverability in the case of a hard disk crash. The RAID-5 volume is the Windows 2000 implementation of stripe sets with parity and provides fault tolerance in systems where hardware RAID arrays are cost prohibitive or in other ways not desired.

RAID-5 volumes have all the features of the striped volume except that they require at least 3 hard drives (and as many as 32). Setting them apart is the presence of parity information written as part of each stripe. This parity information ensures that if a single hard drive is lost, the data on the missing drive can be determined from the remaining drives in the RAID-5 volume. While the drive is missing, performance is greatly reduced because of the calculations required to rebuild the missing drive from the existing data plus the parity. However, when repaired, the volume operates as though no problem ever occurred.

The one drawback of the RAID-5 volume is the loss of some of the data area to this parity information. If x represents the total number of hard drives across which the RAID-5 volume is implemented, the total amount of usable space can be calculated with the following formula: $(x-1)/x$. For example, if you create a RAID-5 volume from five 1GB segments of free space, the usable area is $(5-1)/5$ or 80% of the total hard drive space. That leaves you with 4GB of the original 5GB because 1GB is used to maintain the fault tolerance.

RAID-5 volumes have moderate write performance (reduced because the parity information must be calculated as the data changes) but excellent read performance, because the data is stored on many hard drives, all of which can be accessed independently of one another.

Like striped volumes, RAID-5 volumes cannot be used to hold the System or Boot Partition of a Windows 2000 installation.

Table 12.1 summarizes the characteristics of the partition and volume types described in the previous sections.

TABLE 12.1

PARTITIONS AND VOLUMES IN SUMMARY

	Basic		Dynamic				
Characteristic	Primary Partition	Extended Partition	Simple Volume	Spanned Volume	Mirrored Volume	Striped Volume	RAID-5 Volume
System Partition	Yes	No	Yes	No	Yes	No	No
Boot Partition	Yes	Yes	Yes	No	Yes	No	No
Fault tolerant	No	No	No	No	Yes	No	Yes
Space utilization	100%	100%	100%	100%	50%	100%	$(n/1)/n*100\%$
Drives required	1	1	1	2	2	2	3
Number of pieces that make it up	1	1	1–32	2–32	2	2–32	3–32
Must pieces be on different drives?	N/A	N/A	No	Yes	Yes	Yes	Yes
Formats supported	All	All	All	All	All	All	All
Accessible locally by non-2000 OS if FAT?	Yes	Yes	No	No	No	No	No
Read performance	Avg	Avg	Avg	Avg	Up	Up	Up
Write performance	Avg	Avg	Avg	Avg	Down	Up	Down

Choosing a Format for Partitions and Volumes

All drives must be formatted before information can be placed on them. Windows 2000 supports three kinds of file systems with which you can format drives: FAT, FAT32, and NTFS.

> **NOTE**
>
> **You Cannot Format Compact Disks!** In addition, Windows 2000 also supports CDFS for CD-ROMs, but you don't format drives with that file system.

File Allocation Table (FAT)

FAT was the original DOS file format. It continues to be very popular for Windows and non-Windows operating systems alike. FAT uses a linked-list format to chain together files. A table contains pointers to the beginning of each list, and files are located through lookup to the table and navigation of the links that result.

The FAT system supports long filenames and preserves case (although it does not recognise case sensitivity), but does not support local file security.

File Allocation Table Version 2 (FAT32)

FAT32 is simply an updated version of FAT that was implemented in Windows 95 OSR2, in Windows 98, and now in Windows 2000. Under FAT32, disk space is used more efficiently (the allocation units are smaller), which allows more information to be stored on hard drives. In addition, FAT32 also allows Windows 9x machines to create and use partitions larger than 2GB (something that was not possible under FAT).

As with FAT, FAT32 supports long filenames, preserves case, but does not support local security.

New Technology File System (NTFS)

NTFS is a proprietary file system that was introduced in the early days of Windows NT. It is readable by Windows NT and Windows 2000 only. This means that in any multiboot system, the non–Windows NT or non–Windows 2000 operating system will not be able to read from a partition or volume formatted with NTFS. Windows 2000 implements NTFS version 5 (NTFS v.5) that introduces the following features:

◆ **Local file security.** NTFS allows local security of files. This affects any users logged on locally to a Windows 2000 workstation.

NOTE

Planning for Dual-Boot Systems   FAT and FAT32 are recommended as file formats only if you are planning to install more than one operating system on your Windows 2000 machine. If, for example, you want to dual-boot Windows 2000 Server with Windows 98, you should format the Active Partition with FAT32.

◆ **File compression.** Built-in compression can be implemented at the directory and file levels. This compression is intrinsic to the file system and does not need to be installed. It provides on-the-fly compression and decompression with little loss of performance.

◆ **Larger volume sizes.** NTFS is more efficient at file storage than FAT. NTFS can theoretically be configured for partitions and volumes up to 16 exabytes (16EB).

◆ **Sector sparing.** If a sector fails on an NTFS partition of a SCSI hard drive, NTFS tries to write the data to a good sector (if the data is still in memory) and map out the bad sector so that it is not reused.

◆ **Disk quotas.** One other new feature of NTFS under Windows 2000 is the capability of implementing disk quotas. This prevents users from using more than a specific amount of disk space on a volume.

◆ **File encryption.** File encryption is available using NTFS in Windows 2000 and allows files to be secured in such a way as to allow only the user who encrypted the file and a configured recovery agent to access those files.

Table 12.2 shows a comparison in features between FAT, FAT32, and NTFS v.5 (the version available with Windows 2000).

> **NOTE**
>
> **NTFS Partitions Are Automatically Converted to NTFS v.5** If you upgrade a computer from Windows NT (SP3 or greater), all NTFS partitions are automatically converted to NTFS v.5.

The Disk Manager

Partitions and volumes are more than theory. Of course, you need a tool to be able to create and manage partitions and volumes. That tool is the Disk Manager, and it is a subcomponent of the Computer Management console.

ON THE CD

Step by Step 12.5, "Starting the Disk Manager," shows you how to start the Disk Manager. See the file **Chapter12-05StepbyStep.pdf** in the CD's **Chapter12\StepbyStep** directory.

TABLE 12.2

A COMPARISON BETWEEN FAT, FAT32, AND NTFS

Feature	FAT	FAT32	NTFS (v. 5)
Maximum filename length	255	255	255
8.3 filename compatibility	Yes	Yes	Yes
Maximum file size	4GB	2TB	16EB
Maximum partition size	4GB	2TB	16EB
Recommended volume size	<500MB	512MB–32GB	>500MB
Directory structure	Linkedlist	Linkedlist	B-tree
Intrinsic local security	No	No	Yes
Intrinsic local encryption	No	No	Yes
Intrinsic compression	No	No	Yes
Supports disk quotas	No	No	Yes
Transaction tracking	No	No	Yes
Hot fixing	No	No	Yes
Overhead	1MB	1MB	4.5–10MB
Locally accessible MS-DOS	Yes	No	No
Locally accessible Win 95 OSR2	Yes	Yes	No
Locally accessible Win 98	Yes	Yes	No
Locally accessible Windows 2000	Yes	Yes	Yes
Locally accessible Windows NT 4.0	Yes	No	Limited
Locally accessible Windows NT 3.5x	Yes	No	No
Case-sensitive filenames	No	No	POSIX only
Case-preserving filenames	Yes	Yes	Yes
Fragmentation level	High	High	Low
Used on floppy disk	Yes	No	No

Maintaining Partitions on Basic Disks

If you choose to keep your disks as basic, you will be able to maintain the logical drives as partitions. Partition maintenance involves the following tasks:

◆ **Creating a primary partition.** Primary partitions can be created using any free space on a disk, as long as that free space is not contained in an extended partition and as long as there are not already four primary partitions. A primary partition is created when you want to configure a partition to contain the System Partition.

ON THE CD

Step by Step 12.6, "Creating a Primary Partition on a Basic Disk," demonstrates how to create primary partitions on basic disks. See the file **Chapter12-06StepbyStep.pdf** in the CD's **Chapter12\ StepbyStep** directory.

◆ **Creating an extended partition.** Extended partitions can be created on a basic disk when you want to create more than four partitions. An extended partition does nothing in itself, but it can be the container for a number of logical partitions (drives).

ON THE CD

Step by Step 12.7, "Creating an Extended Partition on a Basic Disk," demonstrates how to create an extended partition on a basic disk. See the file **Chapter12-07StepbyStep.pdf** in the CD's **Chapter12\StepbyStep** directory.

◆ **Creating a logical partition.** Within an extended partition, you must create one or more logical partitions to use the disk space.

ON THE CD

Step by Step 12.8, "Creating a Logical Partition in an Extended Partition," illustrates the process of establishing a logical partition. See the file **Chapter12-08StepbyStep.pdf** in the CD's **Chapter12\StepbyStep** directory.

◆ **Deleting a partition.** Deleting a partition is an easy process, but can result in the loss of all data stored on the partition. Ensure that all data is backed up on a partition before attempting to delete the partition. To delete a partition, right-click the partition and choose Delete from the menu that appears. When you're asked to confirm the deletion, click Yes.

◆ **Formatting a partition.** As mentioned earlier, partitions can be formatted using either the FAT, FAT32, or NTFS file systems. To delete a partition, right-click the partition and choose Format from the menu that appears. In the dialog box that appears, select the file system you want to use and then click OK.

◆ **Changing the drive letter.** Drive letters can be changed for any partitions except the System and Boot Partitions. You cannot change the drive letter for the System or Boot Partitions, because some programs store the assigned drive letters in the Registry.

> **WARNING**
>
> **Formatting Destroys All Information on an Existing Partition** If you want to convert a FAT or FAT32 partition to NTFS, use the CONVERT command. You cannot easily convert from NTFS to FAT or FAT32. If you want to convert from NTFS to FAT or FAT32, you must back up the data, delete the existing partition, format the partition using FAT or FAT32, and restore the original data from the backup.

ON THE CD

Step by Step 12.9, "Changing a Drive Letter," walks you through the process of changing a drive letter. See the file **Chapter12-09StepbyStep.pdf** in the CD's **Chapter12\StepbyStep** directory.

◆ **Marking a primary partition as active.** The Active Partition is the one your computer's BIOS will try to boot from. Therefore, you need to be careful when changing the Active Partition because it could render your server unable to boot.

ON THE CD

Step by Step 12.10, "Marking a Primary Partition as Active," demonstrates how to mark a primary partition as an Active Partition. See the file **Chapter12-10StepbyStep.pdf** in the CD's **Chapter12\StepbyStep** directory.

Maintaining Volumes on Dynamic Disks

At server installation, all disks are basic. To take advantage of any of the features of dynamic disks, you have to convert from basic to dynamic.

ON THE CD

Step by Step 12.11, "Upgrading a Basic Disk to Dynamic," shows you how to upgrade a basic disk to a dynamic disk using Disk Manager. See the file **Chapter12-11StepbyStep.pdf** in the CD's **Chapter12\StepbyStep** directory.

When a disk is converted from a basic disk to a dynamic disk, you will then be able to perform the following tasks:

◆ **Create a new simple volume.** New volumes can be created to be any size you want (subject to the size of the dynamic disk). Unlike basic disks, you can expand a new volume to a spanned volume without losing data.

ON THE CD

Step by Step 12.12, "Creating a Simple Volume," demonstrates how to create a simple volume. See the file **Chapter12-12StepbyStep.pdf** in the CD's **Chapter12\StepbyStep** directory.

◆ **Create a new spanned volume.** Spanned volumes are single volumes that contain between 2 and 32 pieces of free space from one or more physical disks. You must exercise caution with spanned volumes because they are not fault tolerant; losing one piece causes all the data in the volume to be lost. Windows 2000 offers two ways to create a spanned volume.

ON THE CD

Step by Step 12.13, "Creating a Spanned Volume from Free Space," shows you how to create a spanned volume from free space. See the file **Chapter12-13StepbyStep.pdf** in the CD's **Chapter12\StepbyStep** directory.

ON THE CD

Step by Step 12.14, "Expanding a Simple Volume to Create a Spanned Volume," demonstrates how to expand a simple volume to create spanned volumes. See the file **Chapter12-14StepbyStep.pdf** in the CD's **Chapter12\StepbyStep** directory.

◆ **Create a new mirrored volume.** A mirrored volume provides fault tolerance by creating two exact duplicates of the same data on two different drives. To create a mirror volume, you must have two physical drives with equal free space. The largest mirror you can create is equal to the smallest piece of free space provided.

ON THE CD

Step by Step 12.15, "Creating a Mirrored Volume from Free Space," shows you how to create a mirrored volume from free space. See the file **Chapter12-15StepbyStep.pdf** in the CD's **Chapter12\StepbyStep** directory.

ON THE CD

Step by Step 12.16, "Creating a Mirrored Volume from an Existing Simple Volume," shows you how to create a mirrored volume from an existing simple volume. See the file **Chapter12-16StepbyStep.pdf** in the CD's **Chapter12\StepbyStep** directory.

◆ **Create a new striped volume.** Striped volumes combine between 2 and 32 pieces of free space on separate physical disks. As with spanned volumes, the loss of one of the pieces of free space causes the loss of all the data. Striped volumes are not fault tolerant; therefore, as with spanned volumes, you must make sure they are backed up regularly.

ON THE CD

Step by Step 12.17, "Creating a Striped Volume," demonstrates the process for creating striped volumes. See the file **Chapter12-17StepbyStep.pdf** in the CD's **Chapter12\StepbyStep** directory.

◆ **Create a new RAID-5 volume.** RAID-5 volumes provide fault tolerance by storing parity information that allows the removal of one drive of the volume with continued operation. A RAID-5 volume requires at least 3 and as many as 32 physical drives.

ON THE CD

Step by Step 12.18, "Creating a RAID-5 Volume," shows you how to create a RAID-5 volume. See the file **Chapter12-18StepbyStep.pdf** in the CD's **Chapter12\StepbyStep** directory.

> **NOTE**
>
> **Some Tasks Are the Same!**   All the maintenance tasks that you can perform on a partition, you can also perform on a volume. This includes formatting, changing the drive letter, and deleting. The same procedures are used whether the disk is a basic disk or a dynamic disk.

Mounting Partitions and Volumes in NTFS Folders

A new feature in Windows 2000 offers you the ability to mount volumes and partitions in NTFS folders. This allows you to reference a partition or volume by a folder name instead of a letter name. For example, you could create a folder called Data on the C: drive and then mount a 10GB simple volume into that folder. This would effectively increase the size of the C: drive and make all that space available in the path `C:\Data`. Mounting can also be used to increase space in commonly used folders without having to reformat drives and reinstall applications. Mounting also removes the alphabetic limit on the number of partitions that you can install in Windows 2000.

ON THE CD

Step by Step 12.19, "Mounting a Volume or Partition in an NTFS Folder," demonstrates how to mount a volume or partition into an NTFS folder. See the file **Chapter12-19StepbyStep.pdf** in the CD's **Chapter12\StepbyStep** directory.

Troubleshooting Problems with Disks and Volumes

There are not many problems that can arise with disks. Outside of the problems that arise when disks fail, you should not see very many problems. The following list contains some of the problems that may arise with disks and how you can remedy them:

◆ **When you boot to another operating system, the hard drive is not available.** Either the file format being used on a Windows 2000 volume is not readable by the other operating system, or a dynamic volume is being used in Windows 2000, and it cannot be read by the other operating system. If you are booting between operating systems, the volume must use the FAT or FAT32 format.

◆ **When you boot, the System Partition cannot be located.** This problem usually indicates that your BOOT.INI has been modified or disk configuration has changed, and the BOOT.INI points to a partition that does not exist. You can repair this problem by booting to the Recovery Console (see Chapter 11, "Managing, Monitoring, and Optimizing System Performance, Reliability, and Availability") and replacing the BOOT.INI file or by booting from a boot disk with a correct ARC path.

◆ **Data access to a RAID-5 volume is unusually slow.** This generally indicates that one of the partitions in the volume is no longer functioning. This problem can be repaired by replacing the faulty drive with a new one and then rebuilding the volume (see the section "Recovering from a RAID-5 Volume Failure," later in this chapter).

◆ **You are unable to install an additional copy of Windows 2000 on a dynamic disk.** This usually results from one of two conditions: The dynamic disk type you are trying to install on cannot hold the Boot Partition of Windows 2000; or the dynamic disk is not accessible via an ARC path. In the first case, there are enforced prohibitions against installing Windows 2000 on spanned, striped, or (software-based) RAID-5 volumes. As a result, these will not show up in the list of available partitions in the text mode of Windows 2000 installation.

The second case is more abstract in its cause and is a result of a limitation of ARC paths as they relate to dynamic disks. To boot to a copy of Windows 2000 on your hard drive, the BOOT.INI file must be able to point to the partition on which Windows 2000 is installed. The problem is that only partitions created on basic disks are listed in the partition table on the hard drive; dynamic disks are not. Therefore, dynamic disks do not technically have ARC numbers. As a result, you will not be able to see dynamic volumes in the text mode of the installation program unless those volumes were present before the disk was upgraded.

CONFIGURING DATA COMPRESSION

Configure data compression.

If a volume is formatted with the NTFS file system, it has a number of features that are not available on FAT or FAT32 volumes. One of those features is built-in compression.

Compression on an NTFS volume is drastically different from the compression you find employed in Windows 9x or products such as PKZIP or WINZIP. NTFS compression does not have the limitations of either hosted compressed drives (as in Windows 9x) or static compression (as in PKZIP or WINZIP). On an NTFS volume, as much or as little of the drive can be compressed at any time. In addition, because compression is a property and not a new storage format, you do not need to apply an external process to the files to access them; you simply access them as you do any noncompressed file. Conversely, when you compress a folder or a disk, any new files placed into it are automatically compressed.

Compressing Objects Using the GUI Interface

Compressing a volume, folder, or file is as simple as ensuring that it is on an NTFS volume and setting the compressed attribute. If you compress a volume or a folder, you have the option of cascading the compression down the tree to the lowest-level files contained in it.

ON THE CD

Step by Step 12.20, "Compressing an NTFS Volume," illustrates how to compress an NTFS volume. See the file **Chapter12-20StepbyStep.pdf** in the CD's **Chapter12\StepbyStep** directory.

ON THE CD

Step by Step 12.21, "Compressing a Folder on an NTFS Volume," shows you how to compress a folder on an NTFS volume. See the file **Chapter12-21StepbyStep.pdf** in the CD's **Chapter12\StepbyStep** directory.

ON THE CD

Step by Step 12.22, "Compressing a File on an NTFS Volume," shows you how to compress a file on an NTFS volume. See the file **Chapter12-22StepbyStep.pdf** in the CD's **Chapter12\StepbyStep** directory.

Uncompressing an object is as simple as deselecting the check box in the Advanced Properties dialog box for any object.

Changing Views to Identify Compressed Objects

By default, when files and folders are compressed they do not look different from those that have not been compressed. However, this can lead to confusion when it comes to determining what is compressed and what is not. You can set a View property that displays all compressed files and folders with blue text. The color is not configurable, only its presence or absence.

ON THE CD

Step by Step 12.23, "Changing the View Properties to Identify Compressed Objects," demonstrates how to change the View properties to identify compressed objects. See the file **Chapter12-23StepbyStep.pdf** in the CD's **Chapter12\StepbyStep** directory.

Compressing Files Using the Command-Line Utility

Windows 2000 offers an alternative method of compressing files. That is to use the command-line application called COMPACT. EXE. For most applications, you will find it most convenient to use the GUI to compress items. However, some useful features are available only when you use the command-line method. For example, if you want to compress only those files whose extension is .DOC or .BMP, you can do that with COMPACT. Also,

COMPACT allows you to force compaction of files that Windows
2000 thinks are compacted but that really have not been because
an error prevented them from being compacted completely.

The basic syntax of the COMPACT program is as follows:

```
COMPACT [/c or /u] [/s[:dir]] [/a] [/q] [/i] [/f]
➥[filename(s)]
```

where

- ◆ none displays the compression state of the current folder.

- ◆ /c compresses the specified folder or file.

- ◆ /u uncompresses the specified folder or file.

- ◆ /s:dir applies the compression or uncompression to the folder
  specified by dir (or, if dir is missing, applies to the current
  folder).

- ◆ /a displays hidden or system files.

- ◆ /q suppresses detailed progress information.

- ◆ /I ignores errors during compression.

- ◆ /f forces compression or uncompression even if the attributes
  indicate that the object(s) to be acted on are already in that
  state.

- ◆ filename indicates the file or folder to compress. Many files or
  folders can be listed with spaces between them, and wildcards
  can be used.

How Compression Is Applied to New Files in a Folder

Because compression can be added at the container (folder or
volume) level, it needs to be made clear what happens to a file or
folder when it is created in or moved into a container. Five rules
govern how compression attributes are applied when something
arrives in a container:

◆ Any object that is created inside a container gets the compression attribute of its direct container. If a new text document is created in a folder with its compression attribute set, the document will also have its compression attribute set.

◆ Any object that is copied into a container gets the compression attribute of its direct container. If a folder is copied into a folder for which the compression attribute is set, that folder will also have its compression attribute set. Additionally, if a folder is moved into a compressed folder, all files and folders inside the folder retain their noncompressed attribute settings.

◆ Any object that is moved into a container from another volume gets the compression attribute of its direct container (moving from one volume to another really consists of a copy operation followed by a delete operation).

◆ Any object that is moved into a container from the same volume retains its compression attribute.

◆ Any object that is moved from an NTFS volume onto a FAT volume loses its compression attribute and will no longer be compressed.

MONITORING AND CONFIGURING DISK QUOTAS

Monitor and configure disk quotas.

Trying to monitor and control the amount of disk space users consume on server drives has always been a source of frustration for administrators. Even when the location is used strictly for work-related files, the amount of "essential" information grows every day, and it seems as though it will never end.

Disk quotas are a new feature in Windows 2000 that are designed to solve your storage and monitoring problems. Not only do they let you set storage boundaries, they also inform users when they have reached those boundaries.

Quotas are set at the volume (or partition) level. To implement them, the volume must be formatted using the NTFS file format. Quotas are set for individuals and not for groups (the Adminis-trators group being the one exception to this rule).

When creating quotas for a specific volume, you can set parameters for disk space usage, decide whether crossing those bounds results in a warning or a refusal to allocate space, and determine the default parameters for new users being added to the quota list.

By default, quotas are disabled for all volumes. However, after you enable quotas, the defaults are applied to every person who owns files on the hard drive. If you are the creator/owner of a file, its space is credited to you. You can then set specific users to whose quota is allowed to deviate from the defaults by adding them to the quota list and setting specific quota limits for them. Each user can be config-ured with different quota settings, so not everyone has to be treated the same. The only users who are exempt from quotas are the mem-bers of the built-in local Administrators group. The most that can be applied to them is a warning level at which an entry will be logged in the system log; they will never be denied disk space, regardless of the quotas applied to others.

FIGURE 12.1
By enabling quota management, you can control the amount of disk space selected users are allowed to consume.

The Properties dialog box of each NTFS volume has a tab labeled Quota, which contains the quota information for that volume. By enabling quota management, you have access to all the default quota management settings and the specific quota settings for each user via the Quota Entries button (see Figure 12.1) .

The second check box, Deny Disk Space to Users Exceeding Quota Limit, ensures that users who exceed their quota will have that fact logged, any further disk space requests will be refused, and a message indicating a lack of free space on the volume will be displayed.

Under the heading Select the Default Quota Limit for New Users on This Volume, you can define the default disk usage limits that will be set for all users by default, whether they are in the quota list or not. Either limits are set to Do Not Limit Disk Usage, or you can set the space limit and the warning level limit. Both of these can be set to a number of kilobytes (KB), megabytes (MB), gigabytes (GB), terabytes (TB), petabytes (PB), or exabytes (EB). These limits do not define what users will get; they simply define the defaults for new users added to the quota list. If a user is not in the list, the default

NOTE

Compression Won't Help! All quota values are based on the uncom-pressed size of the data stored on a volume. User cannot exceed their quota limits by implementing compression on their data.

quota will be applied when they save their first file to the disk. If a user is added to the list, you can change the actual figures to deviate from the default.

Under the heading Select the Quota Logging Options for This Volume, you can specify whether an event is logged when a user hits his or her quota and/or warning level.

From this page, you also can progress to actually adding people to the quota list. You do so by clicking the Quota Entries button.

ON THE CD

Step by Step 12.24, "Enabling Disk Quota Management," shows you how to enable disk quota management. See the file **Chapter12-24StepbyStep.pdf** in the CD's **Chapter12\StepbyStep** directory.

After quota management has been enabled, Windows 2000 goes through a cataloging process that tabulates how much space each user is currently using.

ON THE CD

Step by Step 12.25, "Adding Users to the Quota List," shows you how to add users to the quota list. See the file **Chapter12-25StepbyStep.pdf** in the CD's **Chapter12\StepbyStep** directory.

After you create quota entries, you can maintain them by returning to the Quota Manager and double-clicking the entry you want to modify. From there, you can change the quota for a specific user. You can also delete a user from the quota list, providing that the user is not currently using disk resources.

In Figure 12.2, you can see that beside each entry is a status that indicates whether a user is below the warning threshold (a green arrow), at the warning threshold but below the quota limit (a yellow triangle with an exclamation mark in it), or at or above the quota limit (a red circle with an exclamation mark in it).

FIGURE 12.2

The status icon indicates the current level of disk usage for each listed user.

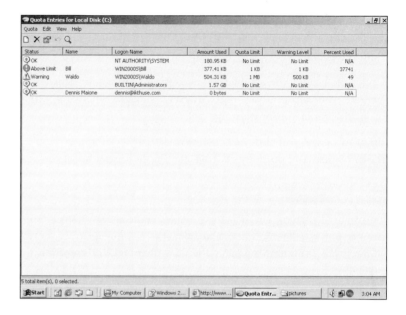

RECOVERING FROM DISK FAILURES

Recover from disk failures.

Hard drives are physical devices, and eventually every hard drive will fail. Either the heads will contact the drive surface and damage it, or the bearings will seize, locking the disk drive up. Whatever the cause, eventually something will happen to make your drives fail. When that happens, knowing about your recovery options will enable you to get your server running again in short order (if it has to come down at all).

This section covers a variety of recovery techniques. Each of them relies on your forethought in preparing your system for the inevitability of a crash.

Recovering Using a Windows 2000 Boot Disk

Earlier in this chapter, you were introduced to the distinction between the System Partition and the Boot Partition. You can use this distinction to allow you to recover from hard drive failure.

Although Windows 2000 cannot technically be booted from a floppy disk because of the size of the operating system and the limitation of the size of a floppy, you can initiate boot from a floppy disk. If you recall the discussion of System and Boot Partitions, you will remember that the System Partition contains the files required to begin the boot process and to direct system start to the correct Boot Partition. The files required to perform that service can be copied onto a floppy disk that was formatted under Windows 2000, which can then serve as the System Partition.

The following essential files need to be copied onto a boot floppy: BOOT.INI, NTLDR, and NTDETECT.COM. Two other files may be needed to provide functionality. If you are using SCSI drives and they have the SCSI BIOS disabled, you must include a special driver called NTBOOTDD.SYS that is placed on the System Partition. If this file exists, it must be copied onto the boot floppy. This file is actually the driver for the SCSI controller and will be a different file for different controller types. So you need to copy it from a machine with the same SCSI adapter card.

ON THE CD

Step by Step 12.26, "Creating a Windows 2000 Boot Disk," walks you through the process of creating a Windows 2000 boot disk. See the file **Chapter12-26StepbyStep.pdf** in the CD's **Chapter12\StepbyStep** directory.

You can (and should) test this disk by placing it in the floppy drive and restarting your server. To really test it, you can rename NTLDR on your hard drive and boot the disk again.

This disk will come in handy in a number of situations. If your System Partition fails, you can still boot to the Boot Partition and operate your server. Second, if your system files become corrupt or are deleted, you can boot to the disk and copy the files back onto your hard drive. Third, if a mirror volume fails, you can use the disk to point to an alternate drive by adjusting the ARC path in the BOOT.INI file.

Recovering Using Windows 2000 Backup

Windows 2000 Backup can be used as a source of recovery information, providing that the backups have been done and that they are current. Because Windows 2000 Backup does not back up at the sector level, it cannot be used by itself to recover a Windows 2000 system. Instead, you have to rebuild the server by installing from a network share or CD-ROM and then applying the backup to it.

Recovering from a Mirror Volume Failure

Mirror volumes are fault tolerant: If one of the drives that make up the set fails, the other will continue to operate. Because of the nature of the volume, users are unaware that anything has happened.

Two scenarios exist in the configuration of a mirror volume that require two different approaches to recovery: mirror volumes that contain the System and/or Boot Partitions, and mirror volumes that do not.

Recovering from a Mirrored System or Boot Partition Failure

If a mirror volume that fails contains the System or Boot Partition, possible restart problems exist if the failed drive is the first one (see Figure 12.3 for two scenarios).

The BIOS of your computer looks to a specific physical drive to begin the startup process. If the System Partition is on a mirror volume, and if the first volume of the set no longer exists, it will be impossible to start your server from the good component of the volume. Secondly, the BOOT.INI file points to a specific physical location for the Windows 2000 system folder (usually WINNT). If the physical location of the Boot Partition is defined as being on the hard drive that no longer functions, again, your server will not start.

Both of these scenarios can be accounted for if you take the right steps to correct them.

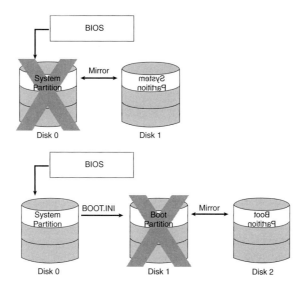

FIGURE 12.3
Special preparations must be made to recover from a mirror set failure that involves the System or Boot Partition.

In the first scenario in Figure 12.3, an alternate System Partition is required to initialize Windows 2000. This can be provided via a boot disk. The boot disk contains a BOOT.INI file. To boot from it, make sure the BOOT.INI file defines the correct ARC path to the Boot Partition that is functioning normally.

In the second scenario, the boot process will begin properly. However, system startup does not happen because the BOOT.INI file on the System Partition points to a physical location that no longer exists. To start Windows 2000 properly, you need to either correct the BOOT.INI file on the hard drive or modify the BOOT.INI file on your boot disk to point to the correct Boot Partition.

When you are set to boot Windows 2000 properly again, you can replace the failed hard drive and follow the mirror repair process outlined in the next section.

Recovering from a Mirrored Data Volume Failure

Recovering a mirror volume that has failed is a relatively easy process if you do not have to deal with booting. A mirror can easily be regenerated after the failed drive has been replaced and your Windows 2000 Server is restarted.

To repair a damaged mirror, you must first remove the mirror (isolating the functioning volume) and then re-establish the mirror to an alternate drive (a new one that replaced the failed drive or the equivalent free space on an existing drive) .

ON THE CD

Step by Step 12.27, "Regenerating a Mirror Volume," illustrates how to regenerate a mirror volume. See the file **Chapter12-27StepbyStep.pdf** in the CD's **Chapter12\StepbyStep** directory.

Recovering from a RAID-5 Volume Failure

RAID-5 volumes have redundancy built in to their structure. As a result, a RAID-5 volume tolerates the failure of a single hard drive in the RAID-5 set without a loss of data. As with a mirror volume, repairs can be made to the volume that will restore it to full functionality.

To recover a RAID-5 volume when one hard drive fails, you must replace the drive and then manually invoke a RAID-5 volume regeneration. This replaces the data on the new drive with the data generated from the existing data and the parity information. This regeneration process may take a long time and is influenced by a number of factors, including how much data was on the drive and the total number of drives in the volume. First, you have to shut down the server and replace the defective drive. The only exception is when hot swappable disks are installed. In this case, you can use disk management to rescan the drives to detect the replaced drives.

ON THE CD

Step by Step 12.28, "Regenerating a RAID-5 Volume," demonstrates how to regenerate the RAID-5 volume. See the file **Chapter12-28StepbyStep.pdf** in the CD's **Chapter12\StepbyStep** directory.

CASE STUDY: ROAMING PROFILES AND DISK QUOTAS

ESSENCE OF THE CASE

This case requires that the following results be satisfied:

▶ Devise a way to ensure that users' desktops and settings follow them as they move from computer to computer.

▶ Place a cap on the amount of server storage space for each user.

▶ Separate the storage areas for users from different departments to eliminate the possibility that files of one department encroach on the available space for another.

SCENARIO

Claudio is the administrator of a Windows 2000 network. He manages five Windows 2000 Servers, one of which functions as a file server for three departments. Lately, he is faced with two separate problems. First, a research library was just put into the building. It has two computers running Windows 2000 Professional, and users can log on to them while they are doing research. They are automatically connected to a home directory on the server where the users can create documents based on their research findings. However, the users are finding that, when they move from the computers in their offices to the research computers, they have to reset their desktops, and if they create a shortcut on their office computers, they have to create the same shortcut on the research machines. The users are asking for a solution to this problem.

The second issue is one that the users are not presently complaining about, but that is becoming a problem for Claudio. The users' home folders are stored on the file server. He periodically checks storage use and finds that some users are consuming a disproportionate amount of hard drive space on the server.

continues

CASE STUDY: ROAMING PROFILES AND DISK QUOTAS

continued

In addition, this space usage is increasing dramatically over time. When he investigates, he finds that many users are downloading quite a large quantity of game demos and pictures, and these items are creating most of the storage consumption.

Claudio wants to be able to provide for the ongoing storage needs of the users while enforcing an upper limit on the amount of space any one user can consume. He also wants to be able to separate each department so that if the users in one department consume the maximum amount of space, that will not overrun the free space available to the users in another department. He currently has two hard drives with capacities of 10GB and 20GB, and he would like to allocate 10GB to each department.

You have been called in to analyze this situation and make recommendations.

ANALYSIS

Windows 2000 Server has features that will allow Claudio to solve all his current problems. He can begin by creating a Profiles folder and sharing it on the server. He can then copy user profiles into this folder. Then when he configures the user accounts of each of the users to point to that shared location, any changes users make to their desktops from any of the locations will follow them from computer to computer.

The problem of storage will take a bit more work. First, Claudio needs to isolate the storage locations of each department. He can do this by dividing the larger drive into two 10GB simple volumes. Then he can convert the three volumes to NTFS (if they are not already using that file system). He will then need to configure the user accounts to point to the new locations when users log into the network and secure the contents of the volumes so that only users from a specific department are allowed to access that volume.

The final issue can be solved by using disk quotas. For each of the volumes, he can configure quotas for the departmental users authorized to access that volume. At first, he will probably want to allocate the same amount of storage to each user. However, as time goes on, he may find that some users need more storage space than others, and the quotas can be modified accordingly.

Finally, Claudio needs to educate the users about the use of server space to store personal data. The quotas will help to reinforce the finite nature of storage space and the need to store only essential company data in home folders. He will also need to inform users of the implementation of quotas to prevent (or at least reduce) the users' surprise when they run out of space.

The following table summarizes the solution.

CASE STUDY: ROAMING PROFILES AND DISK QUOTAS

OVERVIEW OF THE REQUIREMENTS AND SOLUTIONS IN THIS CASE STUDY

Requirement	Solution Provided By
Consistent user desktop	Implement roaming user profiles in a shared folder on the server and configure user accounts to use them.
Storage space cap per user	Configure disk quotas on each volume for the users who will be accessing storage locations on it.
Separate departmental storage	Configure three 10GB simple volumes with NTFS and secure each against write access by the other departments.

CHAPTER SUMMARY

Summarized briefly, this chapter covered the following main points:

◆ **Creating and managing user profiles.** This includes recognizing local profiles and creating roaming and mandatory profiles stored on a Windows 2000 Server.

◆ **Creating partitions and volumes.** This includes differentiating primary, extended, and logical partitions on basic disks from the volumes created on dynamic disks. This also includes understanding the different volume types (simple, spanned, striped, mirrored, and RAID-5) and their recommended uses.

◆ **Configuring data compression.** This includes configuring compression for disks, folders, and files. This also includes knowing the implications of moving an object into (or creating an object in) a container for which the compression attribute is set.

KEY TERMS

• Local profile

• Roaming profile

• Mandatory profile

• Default user profile

• All Users profile

• NTUSER.DAT

• NTUSER.MAN

• System Partition

• Boot Partition

• BOOT.INI

• ARC path

• Basic disk

• Primary partition

• Extended partition

CHAPTER SUMMARY

KEY TERMS

- Logical disk
- Dynamic disk
- Simple volume
- Spanned volume
- Mirrored volume
- Striped volume
- RAID-5 volume
- NTFS
- FAT
- FAT32
- COMPACT.EXE
- Disk quota
- Quota limit
- Quota warning threshold
- Boot disk

◆ **Creating and maintaining disk quotas.** This includes activating disk quotas and enforcing quotas for selected users.

◆ **Recovering from failed disks.** This includes recovering both fault-tolerant (mirror and RAID-5) as well as non–fault-tolerant volumes.

APPLY YOUR KNOWLEDGE	

Review Questions

1. What are the three profile types, and how are they distinguished from each other?

2. What is the difference between a basic and a dynamic disk in Windows 2000?

3. What are the five volume types available on a dynamic disk? How are they defined? Which are fault tolerant, and how is their fault tolerance accomplished?

4. What is a disk quota and how is it enforced?

5. What are two methods for compressing a single file?

6. What is the process for recovering from a failed disk in a mirrored volume that does not contain the System or Boot Partition?

7. What is a boot disk and how do you create one?

Answers to Review Questions

1. The three profile types are local, roaming, and mandatory. Local profiles are created automatically when any user logs on to a Windows 2000 Server. They are local to the machine onto which you are logging on and are not available anywhere else. Roaming profiles are pointed to from the properties of a user's account. These profiles are located centrally in a shared location and, therefore, are accessible from anywhere on the network. As a result, desktop settings are available from any machine a user logs on to. Mandatory profiles are roaming profiles (with the same characteristics and configuration) but are read-only. This means that when changes are made to the

desktop, they are not carried from session to session. For more information, see the section "Creating and Maintaining User Profiles."

2. The difference between a basic and a dynamic disk is that dynamic disks support volumes and can, therefore, be configured with simple, spanned, mirrored, striped, or RAID-5 volumes. Basic disks support only primary partitions and logical drives and will not, therefore, support fault-tolerant configurations (except where they already existed in a version of NT that was upgraded) or expandable volumes. For more information, see the sections "The Basic Disk" and "The Dynamic Disk."

3. The five volume types are simple, spanned, mirrored, striped, and RAID-5. Simple volumes allow for a single non–fault-tolerant drive to be created from one or more blocks of free space on a single disk. Spanned volumes allow for a single non–fault-tolerant drive to be created from one or more (possible unequally sized) blocks of free space on more than one disk. Mirrored volumes allow for a single fault-tolerant drive to be created from two equal-sized blocks of free space on two disks. Striped volumes allow for a single non–fault-tolerant drive to be created from one or more equal-sized blocks of free space on more than one disk. RAID-5 volumes allow for a single fault-tolerant drive to be created from three or more equal-sized blocks of free space on three or more disks. For more information, see the section "The Dynamic Disk."

4. Disk quotas are thresholds established on NTFS partitions that define the amount of disk space a user can consume. Total amount of storage attributed to a user is determined by the files of which

APPLY YOUR KNOWLEDGE

a user is the owner. For more information, see the section "Monitoring and Configuring Disk Quotas."

5. A single file can be compressed by setting its advanced attribute Compress Contents to Save Disk Space. In addition, a single file can also be compressed with the COMPACT command from a command line, specifying the path to the file to be compressed. For more information, see the section "Configuring Data Compression."

6. To recover a mirror volume when one disk fails, do the following: shut down the server; replace the faulty drive; restart the server; in Disk Manager, remove the mirror; and in Disk Manager, add a mirror to the functioning mirror volume and point it to the new disk for free space. For more information, see the section "Recovering from a Mirrored Data Volume Failure."

7. A boot disk is a disk that replaces the System Partition for the purposes of booting a Windows 2000 Server. You create a boot disk by formatting a disk under Windows 2000 and then copying the following files onto it: NTLDR, NTDETECT.COM, BOOT.INI, NTBOOTDD.SYS (optional), and BOOTSECT.DOS (optional). For more information, see the section "Recovering Using a Windows 2000 Boot Disk."

ON THE CD

This book's companion CD contains specially designed supplemental material to help you understand how well you know the concepts and skills you learned in this chapter. You'll find related exercises and exam questions and answers. See the file **Chapter12ApplyYourKnowledge.pdf** in the CD's **Chapter12\ApplyYourKnowledge** directory.

Suggested Readings and Resources

1. Microsoft Windows 2000 Server Resource Kit: *Microsoft Windows 2000 Server Deployment Planning Guide.* Microsoft Press, 2000.

    • Chapter 19: Determining Windows 2000 Storage Management Strategies

2. Microsoft Windows 2000 Server: *Operations Guide.* Microsoft Press, 2000.

    • Chapter 1: Disk Concepts and Troubleshooting

    • Chapter 2: Data Storage and Management

    • Chapter 3: File Systems

3. *Microsoft Windows 2000 Professional Resource Kit.* Microsoft Press, 2000.

    • Chapter 17: File Systems

    • Chapter 32: Disk Concepts and Troubleshooting

4. Microsoft Official Curriculum course 1556: *Administering Microsoft Windows 2000.*

    • Module 4: Administering File Resources

    • Module 7: Managing Data Storage

5. Microsoft Official Curriculum course 1557: *Installing and Configuring Microsoft Windows 2000.*

    • Module 4: Configuring Disks and Partitions

    • Module 10: Configuring File Resources

6. Microsoft Official Curriculum course 1560: *Updating Support Skills from Microsoft Windows NT 4.0 to Microsoft Windows 2000.*

    • Module 14: Managing File Resources

    • Module 15: Performing Disk Management

7. Microsoft Official Curriculum course 2152: *Supporting Microsoft Windows 2000 Professional and Server.*

    • Module 6: Configuring and Managing Disks and Partitions

    • Module 7: Managing Data by Using NTFS

8. Web Sites

    • www.microsoft.com/windows2000

    • www.microsoft.com/train_cert

This chapter helps you prepare for the "Configuring and Troubleshooting Windows 2000 Network Connections" unit of the exam.

Microsoft provides the following objectives for "Configuring and Troubleshooting Windows 2000 Network Connections":

Install, configure, and troubleshoot shared access.

▶ You must understand how to configure Internet Connection Sharing, as well as how to use the NAT protocol to distribute access to a single Internet connection to a number of users.

Install, configure, and troubleshoot a virtual private network (VPN).

▶ You must understand how to configure remote access to a Windows 2000 LAN through a public Internet connection and a virtual private network. This includes both allowing access by way of PPP, and securing that access through the use of the PPTP and L2TP tunneling protocols.

Install, configure, and troubleshoot network protocols.

▶ You must understand the most commonly used protocols. This includes understanding how NetBEUI, NWLink, and TCP/IP are installed and configured, and under what circumstances they are commonly used.

Install and configure network services.

▶ You must understand how to install and maintain network services. This includes installing and configuring the Dynamic Host Configuration Protocol (DHCP) service for automatic TCP/IP configuration in clients. In addition, it also includes name resolution services, such as Domain Name Service (DNS) and Windows Internet Name Service (WINS).

C H A P T E R 13

Configuring and Troubleshooting Windows 2000 Network Connections

Configure, monitor, and troubleshoot remote access:

- **Configure inbound connections.**
- **Create a remote access policy.**
- **Configure a remote access profile.**

▶ You must understand the various ways of implementing remote access via a dial-up connection.

Install, configure, monitor, and troubleshoot Terminal Services:

- **Remotely administer servers by using Terminal Services.**
- **Configure Terminal Services for application sharing.**
- **Configure applications for use with Terminal Services.**

▶ You must understand how to configure the server side of a Terminal Services–based network. This includes the installation of a Terminal Services server to host applications and facilitate remote administration. In addition, it also includes an understanding of Terminal Services Client installation.

Configure the properties of a connection.

▶ You must understand how to create connections through the network properties. These include not only network connections, but also connections for dial-up access.

Install, configure, and troubleshoot network adapters and drivers.

▶ You must understand how to install and maintain the drivers for network adapters.

▶ This chapter is full of content that could be prime test material on the Windows 2000 exam. Because networking and its services are so important to the successful operation of a Windows 2000 Server, you can expect the content of this chapter to play a major role on the exam.

▶ This chapter provides you with a lot of information; much of it is background that you need to understand to implement the solutions described. However, you will not be tested on many of these components. Be sure you know what the protocols are and what their characteristics are so you will be able to weed the irrelevant information from the relevant information on exam questions.

▶ Much of the content of this chapter deals with TCP/IP and the services that can be installed to support it. You should know the installation and implementation of DHCP in detail.

▶ Connection Sharing and the NAT protocol are new for Windows 2000, so they are bound to find their way onto the exam. Expect a question or two on their configuration and use.

▶ Remote access has always been a major point on the server exams; expect the Windows 2000 Server exam to be no different. Make sure you understand and can implement PPP servers and connections. In addition, understand the uses for PPTP and L2TP—how they are similar and how they are different.

▶ Terminal Services is a likely target for exam questions. Understand application and remote administration modes and how they are configured. In addition, understand the limitations and licensing requirements of each. It would be good to know the list of Windows clients that can be configured as Terminal Services Clients and how to configure them.

▶ As is usual for the study strategies, you are encouraged to know the content of this chapter, to do the labs and Step by Steps on the accompanying CD, and to test your knowledge with the review questions. Furthermore, creating a test lab with two or three networked computers will be helpful by allowing you to try test scenarios that might be beyond the direct scope of the book but will reinforce the concepts covered in this chapter.

INTRODUCTION

Windows 2000 Server is about networking. From the underlying architecture, to network cards and drivers, to network support services, all the communication features are required knowledge. From there, you also have to know the different features for supporting client access. These include Internet Connection Sharing, virtual private networks, Remote Access Services, and Terminal Services.

INSTALLING AND CONFIGURING NETWORK ADAPTERS AND DRIVERS

Install, configure, and troubleshoot network adapters and drivers.

Like other hardware devices, many new network cards are Plug and Play–compatible, so whether you have one or five cards installed, they should be detected by Windows 2000 and their drivers installed. Like other hardware, network cards have device drivers that allow Windows 2000 Server and the applications that run on it to communicate with the hardware.

CONFIGURING CONNECTIONS

Configure the properties of a connection.

Connections are what Windows 2000 uses to create all its network communication. When a network card is installed in a Windows 2000 Server, a connection is created to allow communication on that card. From the connection, network protocols are installed, as are interfaces to other networks, such as NetWare.

In addition to LAN connections, which are created automatically, there are other kinds of connections (such as those for modems) that must be created manually.

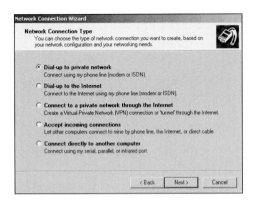

FIGURE 13.1

Five types of connections can be configured from the Network Connection Wizard.

Creating a New Connection

The Connections dialog box can be accessed from the properties of the My Network Places icon, which is on your desktop. When a new network adapter is installed in your server, a new connection icon automatically appears in this dialog box.

In addition to LAN connections, you can also manually create connections of other types. When you double-click the Make New Connection icon in the Connections dialog box, a wizard appears that allows you to create a new connection from the dialog box displayed in Figure 13.1.

The following types of connections can be created:

◆ **Dial-up connection to a private network.** Allows you to establish a connection to a remote network using a modem, X-25, or ISDN connection. Each connection will have different dialing characteristics (such as phone numbers). This connection type is created via the radio button labeled Dial-Up to Private Network.

◆ **Dial-up connection to the Internet.** Allows you to establish a connection to the Internet using a modem, X-25, or ISDN connection. Each connection will have different dialing characteristics (such as phone numbers) and will appear as a separate connection listing. This connection type is created via the radio button labeled Dial-Up to the Internet.

◆ **VPN connection.** Allows you to establish a secure connection on a public network. VPNs use an already existing connection to piggyback secure transmissions. As such, they require either a dial-up or a LAN connection. This connection type is created via the radio button labeled Connect to a Private Network Through the Internet.

◆ **Incoming connection.** Allows a Windows 2000 standalone server to be the host for an incoming connection. After you create such a connection, other computers will be able to connect to your computer using a modem or other connection mechanism, and you will host their sessions. This connection type is created via the radio button labeled Accept Incoming Connections. This method is not available to Windows 2000 Servers that are member servers or domain controllers. Instead, you use routing and remote access to fill that need.

◆ **Direct connection.** Allows you to establish a connection from one computer to another without using a network interface card or cable. This can be done to allow connectivity between devices in close proximity on a temporary basis. You can use the serial or parallel ports on two computers to establish this connection. In addition, you can also use infrared ports to connect directly. This connection type is created via the radio button labeled Connect Directly to Another Computer.

Configuring a Connection in Windows 2000

A network connection can be configured after initial creation. Network connections can be modified by configuring advanced settings, installing optional networking components, or modifying the properties of the network connection.

The Advanced Settings Dialog Box

To access the Advanced Settings dialog box, you choose the menu command Advanced, Advanced Settings in the Network and Dial-Up Connections dialog box. From the Advanced Settings dialog box, you can configure network adapter preference, protocol binding order, and network provider order.

If multiple network connections exist for a computer, the network connections must be prioritized so that one network connection is preferred over another network connection when accessing resources. In Figure 13.2, the network connections are ordered so that network services will first attempt connections using the Local Area Connection before attempting the connection using Remote Access connections.

For each individual network connection, you can configure a preference for protocol use. By default, a defined network connection will be able to use all protocols installed on a computer. Defining the bindings for a network adapter allows you to configure both protocol preferences and select which protocols are available for server and client services. In Figure 13.2, a computer with both TCP/IP and

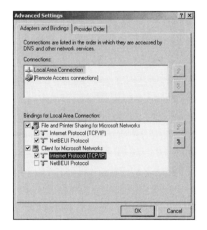

FIGURE 13.2
Connections and bindings can be prioritized for a computer.

NetBEUI installed is shown. The File and Printer Sharing for
Microsoft Networks (known as the Server service) is configured to
use both TCP/IP and NetBEUI. Connection attempts will first
attempt connection using TCP/IP and then NetBEUI. The Client
for Microsoft Networks (the Workstation service) is configured to
attempt connections using only TCP/IP. The NetBEUI protocol has
been disabled for the Workstation service.

The Provider Order tab allows you to set preferred order for
accessing network resources when multiple network providers are
installed. For example, if clients for both Microsoft Windows and
Novell NetWare are installed, you can order the network providers
so that connection attempts use Microsoft Windows methods and
then attempt to connect using the NetWare client if the connection
attempt fails using the Microsoft Windows client.

The Windows Optional Networking Components Wizard

The Windows Optional Networking Components Wizard can be
used to install management and monitoring tools (such as the
Network Monitor), network services (such as DHCP and DNS),
and other file and print services (such as File and Print Services for
Macintosh and Print Services for UNIX).

To install these services, invoke the wizard by choosing the
Advanced, Optional Networking Components command from
within the Network and Dial-Up Connections dialog box. When
you're prompted for the components to install, select the ones you
want and continue with the installation. Most of the components
you install here will require configuration after installation is
complete.

FIGURE 13.3
Connection properties can be used to add new
clients, protocols, and network services.

The Connection Properties Dialog Box

The Connection Properties dialog box allows you to install and configure new protocols, clients, and network services (see Figure 13.3) .

You can access the Connection Properties by right-clicking a connection and selecting Properties from the menu that appears.

From that point, you can choose to add new clients, protocols, and services by clicking the Install button and then following the instructions for each.

In addition, when you select a component, you can also configure its properties by clicking the Properties button.

INSTALLING AND CONFIGURING NWLINK AND NETBEUI PROTOCOLS

Install, configure, and troubleshoot network protocols.

A *network protocol* is a collection of rules and procedures governing communication among the computers on a network. In a sense, a protocol is a language your computer uses when speaking to other computers. If two computers don't use the same protocols, they cannot communicate. Three protocols are used for communication in a Windows 2000 network in which interoperability with other network types is not an issue:

- ◆ NWLink
- ◆ NetBEUI
- ◆ TCP/IP

Other protocols are used on Windows 2000. However, these are installed when there is a need for interoperability with other network types (such as AppleTalk, for example).

Installing and Maintaining the NWLink Protocol

One of the protocols used in Windows 2000 networks is the NWLink IPX/SPX/NetBIOS Compatible Transport Protocol, NWLink for short. This protocol is Microsoft's emulation of Novell's IPX/SPX protocol and was developed to enable interconnectivity between Microsoft and NetWare networks.

NWLink is routable, meaning that it can be transferred from a local network to a remote one through a router. NWLink configures its own routing tables, which makes it nice for small networks; however, it is not practical for large WANs, such as the Internet, and cannot be used to connect directly to the Internet.

NWLink has the following benefits:

◆ NWLink enables communications with NetWare servers.

◆ NWLink allows multisegment networks to communicate with less configuration required than TCP/IP.

Installing NWLink

The NWLink protocol is installed via the properties for a network connection. From the Properties dialog box, you can choose to install a new component; in this case, you would install the NWLink IPX/SPX/NetBIOS Compatible Transport Protocol.

Configuring NWLink

As discussed in a previous chapter, the key configuration options for NWLink are the external network number and the frame type definitions. A network connection must use the same external network number and frame type as other IPX/SPX hosts. If the same settings are not used, communications between the Windows 2000 Server using NWLink and the other hosts will fail. For a full discussion, see the section "Installing and Configuring the NWLink Protocol" in Chapter 9, "Installing, Configuring, and Troubleshooting Access to Resources."

Troubleshooting NWLink

Although NWLink is primarily self-configuring, certain things that might go wrong can be repaired. This includes ensuring that NWLink is bound to the desired network connections and that the NWLink is configured to use the correct external network number and/or frame type.

Bindings can be verified by checking the Advanced Settings for a network connection to ensure that NWLink is enabled for the network connection. External network numbers and/or frame types can

be verified using the IPXROUTE CONFIG command-line utility.
When executed from a Windows 2000 command prompt, this utility identifies the connection names, the external network number,
the node number (a unique identifier for the local machine obtained
from the hardware address of the network adapter), and the
frame type.

When you enter the `IPXROUTE CONFIG` command, you see information similar to this:

```
NWLink IPX Routing and Source Routing Control Program v2.00

Num   Name                    Network    Node          Frame
============================================================
1.    IpxLoopbackAdapter      1234cdef   000000000002  [802.2]
2.    Local Area Connection 2 00000000   0050dab5c056  [802.2]
3.    NDISWANIPX              00000000   D86720524153  [EthII]
```

In this case, the connection to the LAN is represented by the name
`Local Area Connection 2`. For the Local Area Connection 2 network connection to function correctly, the external network number
for all other IPX/SPX hosts on the local network must be using
external network ID `00000000` and be using the `802.2` frame type. I
n some cases, you may have to configure multiple frame types f
or a single network segment. The manual configuration of networks
and frame types was discussed in Chapter 9 in the section "Interoperation with Novell NetWare."

Installing and Maintaining the NetBEUI Protocol

NetBEUI is a nonroutable network transport suite for use in small,
single-segment networks consisting of 50 or fewer computers. In the
Microsoft networking world, NetBEUI was the primary protocol for
Windows 3.11 (Windows for Workgroups).

NetBEUI is easy to use because it is self-configuring. There is nothing to do except install it. It has limitations; network communication is done primarily by broadcast (rather than directed), for example, and as a result, the larger the network, the more cumbersome network traffic becomes.

NetBEUI may be used in a Windows 2000 network where Windows 3.11 clients still exist and the 32-bit TCP/IP protocol has not been installed. However, in situations such as that, you should investigate the practicality of upgrading the Windows 3.11 clients to Windows 98 or Windows 2000 Professional.

Installing NetBEUI

NetBEUI can be installed through the properties of the connection over which you want to communicate with NetBEUI.

ON THE CD

Step by Step 13.1, "Installing the NetBEUI Protocol," illustrates how to install the NetBEUI protocol. See the file **Chapter13-01StepbyStep.pdf** in the CD's **Chapter13\StepbyStep** directory.

Troubleshooting NetBEUI

Because NetBEUI is such a simple protocol with no manual configuration, very few things can go wrong with communication over NetBEUI. If you encounter a problem with NetBEUI-based communication, you should check three things:

◆ Check the network infrastructure, including network cards, cables, and drivers (through the Device Manager).

◆ Check computer names to ensure that there are no duplicates on your network. The computer name (called the NetBIOS name) is located in the System Properties dialog box for your computer.

◆ Check network bindings to verify that the protocol is being used with the desired network adapters (see the section "Configuring a Connection in Windows 2000" earlier in this chapter for information on configuring bindings).

Step by Step 13.2 demonstrates how to view and modify a computer's NetBIOS name if a duplicate computer NetBIOS name exists on the network.

ON THE CD

Step by Step 13.2, "Viewing and Modifying a Computer's NetBIOS Name," demonstrates how to view and modify a computer's NetBIOS name if a duplicate computer NetBIOS name exists on the network. See the file **Chapter13-02StepbyStep.pdf** in the CD's **Chapter13\StepbyStep** directory.

INSTALLING, CONFIGURING, AND MAINTAINING THE TCP/IP PROTOCOL SUITE

Transmission Control Protocol/Internet Protocol (TCP/IP) is commonly used because it is the protocol that defines Internet connectivity and is scalable to accommodate even the largest Wide Area Network design.

TCP/IP is a suite of protocols designed to ensure the most flexible network communication. Some components of the TCP/IP suite are designed purely for communication, others for ensuring proper information delivery, and others for troubleshooting. For simplicity, the protocol suite will often be referred to as the TCP/IP protocol, but you need to realize that it is much more than a single transport mechanism.

This section will deal with TCP/IP, its configuration, and the tools in Windows 2000 for implementing it. Because the concepts and tools behind TCP/IP are extensive, this section addresses only those features that directly pertain to understanding the basic functions of TCP/IP communication. This section covers the following TCP/IP topics:

- ◆ TCP/IP addresses and subnets
- ◆ TCP/IP name resolution theory

◆ Manual TCP/IP configuration

◆ Automatic TCP/IP configuration using DHCP

◆ Implementing DNS for name resolution

◆ Implementing WINS for name resolution

TCP/IP Addresses and Subnets

> **NOTE**
>
> **Ipv6** There is an evolving standard, Ipv6, which will greatly expand this configuration, but that is not the version of TCP/IP implemented in Windows 2000.

Current TCP/IP addresses (Internet Protocol version 4.0) are defined by four octets separated by decimals (for example, 204.219.197.223). These octets are displayed as decimal numbers between 0 and 255. Each octet is really a binary number of 8 digits that ranges between 00000000 and 11111111 (0 to 255). On the public Internet, each TCP/IP address uniquely identifies a specific computer, so no duplicate addresses are given out.

A TCP/IP address is divided into two parts: the network address and the host address. The TCP/IP address is like a phone number. The area code represents the region (or network) where a phone number is located, and the actual phone number represents the unique phone (host) within the area code.

The network address is always the high-order end of the address (some set of numbers beginning from the left side), and the host address is always the low-order end of the address (the rest of the numbers up to the end of the right side). The *subnet mask* is used to define which portion of a TCP/IP address refers to the network and which portion of a TCP/IP address refers to the host. The combination of the subnet mask and the TCP/IP address defines where information should be delivered.

Because subnet theory can be very complex, let me give you some quick examples. Groups of TCP/IP addresses are defined by their class. Three classes are commonly used worldwide: classes A, B, and C. In class A addresses, the subnet mask indicates that the first octet defines the network and the last three define hosts. In class B addresses, the subnet mask indicates that the first two octets represent the network and the last two represent the host address. In class C addresses, the subnet mask indicates that the first three octets represent the network address and the last octet represents the host address.

As you may have already figured out, the fewer octets that are available for host addresses, the fewer host addresses a particular network can have. Class C "streets" are short, consisting of a maximum of 254 addresses (0 and 255 cannot be used as a host address for technical reasons). Class B networks are midsized, consisting of a maximum of 65,534 host addresses. Class A networks are very large, consisting of up to 16,777,214 host addresses.

The following is an example of a typical class C address with a subnet:

```
207.219.193.233
255.255.255.0
```

In this subnet mask, the first three 255s indicate that 207.219.193 is the network address and 233 is the host address. Class B addresses have a subnet mask of 255.255.0.0, and class A addresses have a subnet mask of 255.0.0.0 by default.

Subnet masks are necessary in TCP/IP addressing because TCP/IP is a routed protocol. This means that not every address is directly accessible by your computer. A target TCP/IP address is compared to the client computer's assigned subnet mask. If the source and destination hosts share the same network portion of the TCP/IP address, the two hosts are on the same network segment and can communicate directly with each other. If the network portion of the address is different for the source and destination host, all traffic between the two hosts must be passed through a router when communicating. A router, in essence, is a hardware device that is responsible for directing network traffic from one network (subnet) to another. A router is configured with a set of network addresses and told where to direct network traffic that is destined for any of the networks the router knows about.

If information really does need to travel through a router out to reach a separate network, a third piece of information must be supplied in the configuration: the default gateway. That is generally the address of the router that directs information out of your LAN to the outside world.

TCP/IP, ARP, and Address Resolution

In a TCP/IP network, communication between computers does not actually happen based on the TCP/IP address. There is an identifier even more fundamental to network communication than the TCP/IP address: the Media Access Control (MAC) address. An adapter's MAC address is universally unique and is assigned to the network card when it is manufactured. When communication occurs between two TCP/IP-based computers, some background communication must occur to determine which MAC address is associated with the destination TCP/IP address. This communication happens via the Address Resolution Protocol (ARP) .

When a computer resolves another machine's TCP/IP address to a MAC address, it is stored for between 2 and 10 minutes (depending on how many subsequent times it is used) in a local ARP cache. Because of this cache, if the same machine is contacted again within a short period of time, the MAC address does not have to be resolved by way of a network broadcast.

The MAC address of another machine (or even the local machine) can be determined using ARP and the ARP cache. Step by Step 13.3 shows you how to use ARP to determine what is in the cache.

ON THE CD

Step by Step 13.3, "Investigating the Contents of the Local ARP Cache," shows you how to use ARP to determine what is in the cache. See the file **Chapter13-03StepbyStep.pdf** in the CD's **Chapter13\StepbyStep** directory.

TCP/IP and Name Resolution

As has been mentioned, TCP/IP identifies computers using a numeric address, which is fine for computers. However, people generally find numeric addresses nonintuitive. Instead, people prefer to identify servers by way of names.

As a result, people have found it convenient to give computers names. Two types of names are commonly given to computers: NetBIOS names (commonly referred to as the "computer name") and hostnames (the name associated with TCP/IP configuration). If names are to be used, some way to map a specific name to a specific TCP/IP address is required.

There are five common ways to resolve names of servers to their TCP/IP addresses: DNS, WINS, HOSTS files, LMHOSTS files, and network broadcast.

DNS (which is used to resolve hostnames) and WINS (which is used to resolve NetBIOS names) are discussed briefly here and more fully in the section titled "Installing and Configuring Network Services," later in this chapter.

Name Resolution Using DNS

DNS is unquestionably the most widely used name resolution mechanism on the planet, primarily because it is the resolution method used on the Internet. If you type www.microsoft.com, somehow your browser knows how to get to the Microsoft Web site— and this is a result of DNS. The power of the resolution capabilities of DNS is that many DNS servers (rather than a single one) are responsible for resolving names. Each Internet domain must have at least two DNS servers that are responsible for resolving the names of computers (hosts) within that domain. If there is more than one DNS machine for an Internet domain, one of them is designated the Start of Authority (SOA). The SOA machine is the definitive expert on the domain, meaning that if you want to find a specific machine in a domain and the SOA for that domain does not know what you are looking for, the answer cannot be found using DNS.

If a client is using TCP/IP and is configured to use DNS to resolve hostnames, it is configured with a primary DNS server to query should a name need to be resolved. If you consider that there are tens of thousands of Internet domains representing millions of individual hosts, it is obvious that each DNS server cannot know

about all the other hosts worldwide. Each DNS server knows about
a certain set of hosts (the ones in its domain), and it knows about
certain root DNS servers. The DNS structure of Internet names is
set up in a tree. For example, the host www.IKTHUSE.com falls into a
DNS structure (see Figure 13.4). As the figure shows, starting from
the root (the "dot" server), each level has progressively more nodes in
it (all the nodes are not shown, even in the second level). To get to
www.IKTHUSE.com, you travel from the root (.) to com to IKTHUSE,
where www is a host in the ikthuse.com domain.

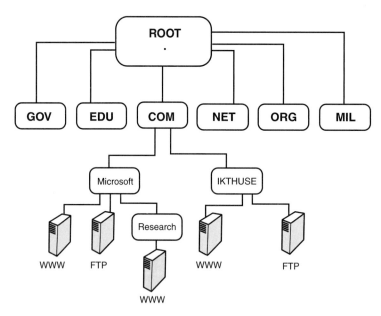

FIGURE 13.4
This is a small part of the global DNS hierarchy.

If your computer queried its DNS to find out about
www.IKTHUSE.com, it would come up empty-handed if it had to rely
on its own local information to resolve that name (a recursive
query). Instead, an iterative query is initiated. The iteration goes as
follows. Your client queries its designated DNS server. If that server
cannot resolve the name, it queries a root DNS server. The root
knows about only those name spaces that are directly below it. In
effect, the root server returns back to your DNS with the message,
"I can't find it, but I know where COM is." At that point, your
DNS server is given the name of the nearest COM server. Your
DNS server queries the COM server for the hostname, and gets the
response, "I can't find it, but I know where IKTHUSE is." Your
DNS then queries the server that is the SOA for IKTHUSE, and it
returns the TCP/IP address 24.66.33.130 as a resolution for
www.IKTHUSE.com.

The strength of DNS is that the hierarchical structure ensures quick
resolution of names and ensures that the amount of information
actually known by any one server is kept to a minimum.

There are three major drawbacks to the traditional implementation
of DNS name resolution. First, it is complex to set up. To get it
working, you must configure one or more DNS servers (depending
on the size of your implementation). Second, it has been, to this
point, a manually configured set of mappings. That means new
hosts must be put into the DNS database as they are configured, or
there will be no name resolution for those hostnames. Third, the
DNS structure on a server is held in a text file that can be deleted or
modified by anyone with sufficient access to it.

The implementation of DNS under Windows 2000 has solutions
for all three of these problems. First, DNS is essential to the configuration of a Windows 2000 domain. Because DNS is used almost
exclusively for name resolution under Windows 2000, it is a requirement for the configuration of Active Directory. Although this does
not actually make the configuration of DNS any simpler, the complexity is coupled with other configuration and research you are
doing to set up Active Directory, so it is not an isolated task.

Second, a new DNS standard allows for automatic configuration of DNS records. DNS clients can automatically update the DNS resource records using *dynamic DNS updates*.

Finally, the problem of security is alleviated somewhat through the use of Active Directory–integrated zones. When DNS is integrated into the Active Directory, each resource record is protected by a Discretionary Access Control List (DACL) to ensure that resource records are not overwritten.

Name Resolution Using WINS

NetBIOS is a TCP/IP interface that operates at the Application layer of the OSI model. It was designed to provide a naming strategy for small networks. It consists of a flat namespace (names can be used only once in an organization) of up to 16 character names for devices.

Until Windows 2000, NetBIOS was required for networking with Windows operating systems. In a pure Windows 2000 network, NetBIOS is no longer required; however, in a network with a mixture of clients, support is still necessary.

Like the hostnames used in DNS, NetBIOS names need to be resolved to TCP/IP addresses if TCP/IP-based communication is to work. Microsoft implemented WINS, a variation on the standard TCP/IP NetBIOS name server standard, to allow the automated resolution of NetBIOS names on TCP/IP networks.

In a simple WINS implementation, a single WINS server is installed. This WINS server has a database that is dynamically populated with the mapping of NetBIOS names with TCP/IP addresses as clients announce their presence on the network. To increase the efficiency of the WINS registration process, each WINS client has the TCP/IP address of its registration server configured into its TCP/IP properties. When a client is started, that client registers its name, function, and TCP/IP address with the WINS server.

When a client wants to locate another computer using its NetBIOS name, a request is made to its WINS server for the TCP/IP address corresponding to the name. If the WINS server has a mapping, the address is returned; if not, the resolution fails and the client may have to try another method (depending on how it was configured to resolve NetBIOS names) .

To ensure that the WINS database is efficient and that names of NetBIOS computers that are no longer present on the network do not persist in the database, when a client machine is shut down, it sends a message to its WINS server telling the server to remove its name from the WINS database. In addition, to ensure that WINS entries are removed even if clients are not shut down properly, the WINS server places a time limit (Time-to-Live, or TTL) on each record that is created when the client registers. By default, this limit is six days. When the client registers itself, the WINS server sends back a message indicating the TTL of the registration. At half of the TTL, the client sends a renewal notice to the WINS server to indicate that it is still present on the network, and the client is again issued a six-day TTL on its registration. If the WINS server does not try to contact the client to ensure that the registration is renewed, the client's entry is removed from the WINS database when the TTL expires.

Clients can be configured to use WINS in different ways to resolve NetBIOS names. As you will see when configuring DHCP (see the section "Installing and Configuring DHCP" to follow), a WINS client is given a node type to indicate what kind of NetBIOS name resolution will occur. These types always differentiate between a client using WINS to resolve NetBIOS names and using broadcast (simply calling out on the network to see if a client with a particular name responds). A client can be configured with one of four node types:

◆ **B-node (broadcast).** Uses only broadcast to resolve NetBIOS names. Clients configured with b-node will never use WINS.

◆ **P-node (peer-to-peer).** Uses only WINS for NetBIOS name resolution. It will never use broadcast, even if the WINS server cannot resolve the name.

◆ **M-node (mixed).** Uses a combination of broadcast and WINS. Clients configured to use m-node first use broadcast (b-node) to resolve; if that is unsuccessful, they query the configured WINS server (p-node) .

◆ **H-node (hybrid).** Uses a combination of broadcast and WINS. Clients configured to use h-node first query the WINS server (p-node); if that is unsuccessful, they try broadcast (b-node) to resolve.

By default, Windows 2000 clients are configured to use b-node. However, if a client's TCP/IP configuration is changed to include the address of a WINS server, it changes to h-node.

Name Resolution Using HOSTS and LMHOSTS Files

Although DNS and WINS are both excellent ways of configuring for host and NetBIOS name resolution, there are cases where it would be impractical or impossible to configure DNS and WINS servers to provide name resolution for all TCP/IP names. In these cases, you can configure files on local computers to do name resolution. The HOSTS file can be configured to resolve hostnames. The HOSTS file can be the sole method of hostname resolution, or it can be a supplement to the DNS database for names that are not, or cannot, be configured there.

On the other hand, if resolution of NetBIOS names is required and there is no WINS server available, an LMHOSTS file can be configured to replace or supplement WINS.

On a Windows 2000 computer, both files are created and stored in the \WINNT\SYSTEM32\DRIVERS\ETC folder. To aid you in creating these files, there are samples of both in that folder under the names HOSTS and LMHOSTS.SAM. You can use these as templates for creating your own files, but the .SAM extension must be removed from the LMHOSTS.SAM file before it will function.

The HOSTS file has entries that map TCP/IP addresses to hostnames. In the case of the HOSTS file provided, one mapping is already present, the one mapping 127.0.0.1 with the name localhost. Other entries can be configured simply by creating

new lines with the TCP/IP address followed by a space and the hostname (which can be a single name or an Internet hostname, such as
www.microsoft.com).

The LMHOSTS file is configured in much the same way the
HOSTS file is, but is used for NetBIOS name resolution. The sample file provided (LMHOSTS.SAM) outlines the configuration specifications for file entries. At its most basic, an LMHOSTS entry
consists of a TCP/IP address followed by at least one space and a
computer name (of up to 15 characters). There is, however, one
additional setting that is worth mentioning: the #PRE designator.
The #PRE option preloads a NetBIOS name into the NetBIOS
cache for speedier NetBIOS name resolution.

Integration of Name Resolution Methods

Because of the variety of name resolution methods, you may find
that more than one is suitable in your organization. For example, if
your Windows 2000 network contains Windows 9x or Windows
NT clients, you will have to retain support for NetBIOS name resolution as well as the default DNS used by Windows 2000. When a
hostname is being resolved, the following order is used in resolution:

1. Check to see whether the name being referenced is the hostname of the local machine.

2. Check to see whether the name being referenced is in the local
   HOSTS file.

3. Check with the configured DNS server to see whether it can
   resolve the name.

4. Check the local NetBIOS name cache for the name.

5. Check the configured WINS servers for the name.

6. Broadcast on the local LAN for the name.

7. Check the local LMHOSTS file for a match.

8. Return with a failure message.

These steps are tried in order. If any of them successfully resolves the
name, the resolution process ends, and network operation continues.

When a NetBIOS name is being resolved (such as when a NET command is issued at a command prompt), the following order is used in resolution:

1. Check to see whether the name being referenced is in the local NetBIOS name cache of the local machine.

2. Check the configured WINS servers for the name.

3. Broadcast on the local LAN for the name.

4. Check the local LMHOSTS file for a match.

5. Check the local HOSTS file for a match.

6. Check with the configured DNS server to see whether it can resolve the name

7. Return with a failure message.

As with hostname resolution, these steps are followed in order until the name is resolved or the failure message is generated.

Installing TCP/IP

TCP/IP is the default protocol installed when you install Windows 2000 Server. If the Windows 2000 Server is an upgrade from a previous version of Windows NT or TCP/IP has been removed, you may have to install TCP/IP on a Windows 2000 Server.

Protocols are installed from the properties of the connection over which they are to be used to communicate. Step by Step 13.4 leads you through the process of installing the TCP/IP protocol suite.

ON THE CD

Step by Step 13.4, "Installing the TCP/IP Protocol Suite," leads you through the process of installing the TCP/IP protocol suite. See the file **Chapter13-04StepbyStep.pdf** in the CD's **Chapter13\ StepbyStep** directory.

Configuring TCP/IP

The only required information for TCP/IP is the IP address and subnet mask. However, a default gateway is an additional requirement for those networks that use a router. Even though those three settings are the only required ones, other settings make working with a TCP/IP network user-friendlier. These include the DNS server and/or the WINS server a client will use.

Configuration of TCP/IP can be done in three ways:

◆ Manually

◆ Automatically via DHCP

◆ Automatically via system configuration

Manual configuration is the most labor-intensive configuration method; it is also the most prone to misconfiguration. Manually configuring a TCP/IP address requires that you open the properties of the TCP/IP protocol on each machine and type in the appropriate TCP/IP address, subnet mask, default gateway, and any other configuration that you require. To configure the TCP/IP properties on a computer, you have to be in the Administrators local group. Step by Step 13.5 demonstrates how to manually configure TCP/IP.

ON THE CD

Step by Step 13.5, "Manually Configuring TCP/IP," demonstrates how to manually configure TCP/IP. See the file **Chapter13-05StepbyStep.pdf** in the CD's **Chapter13\StepbyStep** directory.

Manual configuration can lead to duplicate addresses being assigned on your network. Duplicate addresses are problematic because the destination for network transmissions is ambiguous. As a result, the possibility exists for one machine to get information that is destined for another.

Despite the problems that are associated with manual configuration, many large companies and agencies still use it. Assigning TCP/IP addresses manually increases security. Many government agencies use manual configuration, because automatic configuration means that anyone who enters a location and can plug a laptop into the LAN will get a TCP/IP address and can begin the process of hacking into servers. In addition, although manual configuration introduces administrative effort, it also eliminates the need for computers to give out addresses. This is especially important for networks with many subnets and few hosts in each, because a configuration server is required to be locally available on each subnet.

On the other hand, automatic configuration has many advantages and should be used in all but special circumstances. The basis of automatic configuration is DHCP, which can be set up on a Windows 2000 Server. A DHCP server has a pool of IP addresses and is preconfigured with other TCP/IP parameters, such as a ubnet mask, default gateway, and name resolution servers.

When the TCP/IP protocol is set to get its configuration from a DHCP server, two types of address request situations are possible. You might obtain a TCP/IP address when none exists already, or you might renew an existing TCP/IP address lease.

In the first situation, the client machine does not already have a TCP/IP address, and without one, it cannot communicate on the network using TCP/IP. The following steps are taken to obtain an address:

1. The client broadcasts a message using the DHCP protocol to the entire LAN to which it is connected, asking for an address from any DHCP server that can provide one.

2. All DHCP servers that are on the LAN receive the request and, if they have an address available, they broadcast a message back onto the network, informing the machine that requested the address that there is one available. This message is directed back to the client using the hardware (MAC) address that it provided with its request. At this point, the DHCP servers responding have tentatively reserved the address being offered so that no other machine can grab it in the meantime.

3. The client receives the addresses offered. It sends a message back to each DHCP server that responded. To the first one it sends back a request for the address. To the others, it sends back a message that it does not need the addresses offered.

4. The DHCP server whose address was accepted makes a permanent entry in its database pairing the TCP/IP address it gave out with the hardware address of the machine that accepted it. All other DHCP servers remove the tentative reservation for the addresses they offered so that those addresses can be offered again.

5. The client receives the acknowledgment from the DHCP server whose address it accepted, and it begins to use the TCP/IP address configuration that was sent out (at least for the duration of the lease). The client can now communicate using TCP/IP.

Addresses given out by a DHCP server always have a lifetime associated with them referred to as the *lease duration*. In an attempt to continue to use the address, the client periodically tries to renew the address.

There are two instances in which a client will try to renew a lease. The first comes whenever a client computer is rebooted, and the second occurs when the current lease has reached 50% of its life. In both cases, the DHCP server that issued the TCP/IP address is contacted directly, and the address is requested. Unless the server is unavailable, the address will generally be renewed. There are a few instances when a lease may not be renewed. For example, a lease will not be renewed if the client has been shut off for a period of time during which the lease expired. At that point, the address may have been given to another client. The lease will also not be renewed if the address requested is now in a part of the address range that is excluded from being given out after the initial offering. In all of these cases, the client must begin the lease discovery process again as though it were getting an address for the first time. Step by Step 13.6 outlines the process for configuring a client to use DHCP to configure TCP/IP.

ON THE CD

Step by Step 13.6, "Automatically Configuring TCP/IP Using DHCP," outlines the process for configuring a client to use DHCP to configure TCP/IP. See the file **Chapter13-06StepbyStep.pdf** in the CD's **Chapter13\StepbyStep** directory.

The final method for obtaining an address is to get one automatically when no DHCP server is available. This may occur when clients have inadvertently been set to obtain an address automatically but no DHCP server exists. It may also happen when all the TCP/IP addresses in the address pool to be given out by a DHCP server have been allocated to other clients.

If a client is configured to obtain an address automatically but a DHCP server cannot be contacted, it automatically configures its own TCP/IP address from the class B address reserved for general internal use: 169.254.x.x. Correspondingly, it configures itself with a subnet mask of 255.255.0.0 (the appropriate one for a class B address). The Internet community has reserved this set of addresses for internal use only.

To ensure that the address a client has autoconfigured is not being used by another client, the client sends out a network message (called a *gratuitous ARP*). You will recall that ARP is a tool used to resolve hardware addresses from TCP/IP addresses. The ARP sent here attempts to locate the network adapter with which a specific TCP/IP address is associated. The ARP is gratuitous, because the client has no desire to resolve the address, but only to determine whether the address is in use. If no reply is received, the client knows that the address is not being used and it configures itself.

Troubleshooting TCP/IP

TCP/IP configuration can be complex. Proper communication depends on the address and subnet mask being configured properly and on the default gateway being configured properly if information is ever to be sent to other networks. In addition, proper communication also depends on the proper configuration of every machine you are trying to communicate with.

Three tools are specifically designed for troubleshooting the following:

- ◆ IPCONFIG
- ◆ PING
- ◆ TRACERT

IPCONFIG

IPCONFIG is used for two things: to determine the current
TCP/IP configuration for the local computer, and to manually
release and renew DHCP addresses.

To obtain a summary of the current TCP/IP configuration of the
local machine, you can go to a command prompt and type
IPCONFIG. You should see something like the following listing:

```
Windows 2000 IP Configuration

Ethernet adapter Local Area Connection:

        Connection-specific DNS Suffix. . : ikthuse.com
        IP Address. . . . . . . . . . . : 179.254.0.21
        Subnet Mask . . . . . . . . . . : 255.255.0.0
        Default Gateway . . . . . . . . : 179.254.0.1
```

This configuration indicates that my TCP/IP address is
179.254.0.21, my subnet mask is 255.255.0.0, and my default gateway is 179.254.0.1.

To obtain detailed information about the current TCP/IP configuration, type IPCONFIG /all. You should see something like the following listing:

```
Windows 2000 IP Configuration

        Host Name . . . . . . . . . . . : win2000s
        Primary DNS Suffix  . . . . . . : ikthuse.com
        Node Type . . . . . . . . . . . : Hybrid
        IP Routing Enabled. . . . . . . : No
        WINS Proxy Enabled. . . . . . . : No
        DNS Suffix Search List. . . . . : ikthuse.com

Ethernet adapter Local Area Connection:

        Connection-specific DNS Suffix. . : ikthuse.com
        Description . . . . . . . . . . : 3Com EtherLink XL
➡10/100 PCI NIC (3C905-TX)
        Physical Address. . . . . . . . : 00-60-97-D5-22-CA
        DHCP Enabled. . . . . . . . . . : Yes
        Autoconfiguration Enabled . . . : Yes
        IP Address. . . . . . . . . . . : 179.254.0.21
        Subnet Mask . . . . . . . . . . : 255.255.0.0
        Default Gateway . . . . . . . . : 179.254.0.1
        DHCP Server . . . . . . . . . . : 179.254.0.1
        DNS Servers . . . . . . . . . . : 179.254.0.1
        Primary WINS Server . . . . . . : 179.254.0.1
        Lease Obtained. . . . . . . . . : Monday, December
➡27, 1999 11:55:57 AM
        Lease Expires . . . . . . . . . : Tuesday, January
➡04, 2000 11:55:57 AM
```

IPCONFIG is useful for troubleshooting because it not only allows you to see what your configuration is, it helps you determine whether you have a TCP/IP address at all. If communication with other computers fails, your first action should be to check your TCP/IP configuration using IPCONFIG. If the TCP/IP address is 0.0.0.0, you do not have an address. If your TCP/IP address begins with 169.254, you have a problem with your DHCP process because your client is not receiving addresses from your DHCP server.

IPCONFIG can also be used to force the DHCP server to renew your lease. At a command prompt, enter IPCONFIG /release to release your current address or enter IPCONFIG /renew to renew your address.

PING

The PING command is also useful for troubleshooting. Whereas IPCONFIG tells you what your TCP/IP configuration is, PING tells you whether you can communicate with other computers using TCP/IP. The syntax of the PING command is PING *x.x.x.x*, where *x.x.x.x* is the address of the host for which you want to test connectivity. A result of unknown host or host unreachable is a sign of a connectivity problem at your end, the remote end, or somewhere between.

The following steps outline how to perform the standard connectivity test with PING:

1. PING the address 127.0.0.1. This is called the *loopback address*, and a response indicates that TCP/IP has been installed correctly on your computer.

2. PING the address of one of the adapters on the local computer. A response from this address indicates that the IP address is configured correctly.

3. PING the address of the default gateway (your router). A response from this address indicates that your interface to the outside world is reachable from your location.

4. PING the address of a remote host (something on the other side of the router). A response from this address indicates that the connection between your router's external interface and the next machine in the chain is functioning properly.

By following these steps, you can determine where the breakdown in communication is. If there is a problem at any point, you know where to go to determine what the problem is.

TRACERT

The third troubleshooting tool is TRACERT. It is used to determine what route is being taken from one host to another. It is helpful when you have already established that there is a connectivity problem with that host (as determined by a PING test). The problem with PING is that it is an all-or-nothing proposition: When the echo request leaves your router, there is no way of telling where the problem is. On the other hand, TRACERT tells you what links can be successfully established and where communication is breaking down. This lets you know if the problem lies with your ISP, the remote host's ISP, or something between, and you can determine whether you can take any course of action or whether you simply have to wait for connectivity to be reestablished.

The syntax for TRACERT is TRACERT *ipaddress* or TRACERT *name*.

INSTALLING AND CONFIGURING NETWORK SERVICES

Install and configure network services.

Windows 2000 network services provide support for optional functions that assist in the administration and management of the network. As such, many services are optional. This section discusses three network services you might install on a Windows 2000 Server: DHCP, DNS, and WINS.

Installing and Configuring DHCP

When it comes to configuring TCP/IP on the clients in your organization, installing and configuring a DHCP server is arguably the most important administrative task you will perform.

> **NOTE**
>
> **Verify that Servers Have Static TCP/IP Addresses** Although Windows 2000 Server allows you to install DHCP and WINS on a computer that gets its address from a DHCP server, this may result in unstable performance (which you will be informed of if you try it). Before you install any of these services, you should make sure your server has a statically assigned TCP/IP address.

Notwithstanding the special cases in which DHCP is not recommended, DHCP is an essential part of administering a TCP/IP-based network.

The job of the DHCP server is threefold:

◆ It maintains pools of IP addresses to give out to clients. Each pool has preconfigured options to assign to clients.

◆ It responds to client requests and sends address configuration.

◆ It updates the DNS server with the hostnames and IP addresses of clients when they get leases.

After you have configured the address pool and the desired additional TCP/IP information, the DHCP server does its work independent of you. It needs very little maintenance and very little ongoing configuration. Therefore, it's essential that the service is installed properly and configured properly. Everything else that happens is based on client request.

DHCP configuration begins with installing the service on your Windows 2000 Server. Step by Step 13.7 walks you through the installation process.

ON THE CD

Step by Step 13.7, "Installing DHCP on a Windows 2000 Server," shows how to install the DHCP service on your Windows 2000 Server. See the file **Chapter13-07StepbyStep.pdf** in the CD's **Chapter13\StepbyStep** directory.

After you install DHCP on your server, it needs to be configured. The first step in DHCP configuration is to define a pool of IP addresses for DHCP clients. When defining a the pool of IP addresses (known as a scope), you also define the subnet mask that the DHCP clients will use with their assigned IP address, any excluded IP addresses for the scope, and the length of time a DHCP address lease will be valid. Step by Step 13.8 shows how to configure the DHCP scope on a Windows 2000 Server.

ON THE CD

Step by Step 13.8, "Configuring a DHCP Scope on a Windows 2000 Server," shows how to configure the DHCP scope on a Windows 2000 Server. See the file **Chapter13-08StepbyStep.pdf** in the CD's **Chapter13\StepbyStep** directory.

If your DHCP server is a member server in a Windows 2000 domain, it must be authorized in the Active Directory before it can assign addresses. This prevents *rogue* DHCP servers from assigning incorrect or duplicate IP addresses to DHCP clients. Step by Step 13.9 shows how to authorize a DHCP server in the Active Directory.

ON THE CD

Step by Step 13.9, "Authorizing a DHCP Server in the Active Directory," shows how to authorize a DHCP server in the Active Directory. See the file **Chapter13-09StepbyStep.pdf** in the CD's **Chapter13\StepbyStep** directory.

When a DHCP server is authorized, it is a good practice to configure the DHCP server properties. A DHCP server's properties are accessed by right-clicking on the DHCP server in the DHCP MMC console and choosing Properties from the menu that appears. The properties that can be configured include

◆ **Enabling DHCP logging.** This feature is enabled by default and creates a daily log file stored in the Audit Path as defined on the Advanced property page.

◆ **Enabling DNS updates for DHCP clients.** DHCP can be configured to perform dynamic DNS updates on behalf of DHCP clients. If the DHCP server is configured to perform dynamic DNS updates for DHCP clients, the DHCP server can be configured to negotiate with the DHCP client or to always perform the dynamic DNS update. In addition, the DHCP server can be configured to perform updates for non–Windows 2000 clients that do not support dynamic DNS updates (see Figure 13.5).

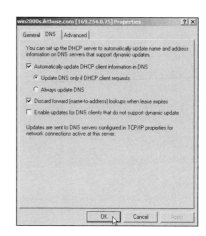

FIGURE 13.5
The DHCP server can be configured to update (and delete) DNS records for DHCP clients when addresses are allocated to or unallocated from them.

◆ **Enabling DNS resource record scavenging.** The DHCP server can be configured to remove DNS records for DHCP clients when the lease expires or the DHCP client shuts down properly.

◆ **Enabling conflict detection attempts.** This setting defines how many times the DHCP server pings the network for a response to an address that it is about to allocate to a client. If a response is detected, the DHCP server knows that another client is using the address and tries to allocate another.

In addition to the IP address and subnet mask defined in a DHCP scope, a DHCP server can be configured to assign additional TCP/IP configuration information to DHCP clients. Configuration properties can be set by the DHCP server for a specific scope. If DHCP configuration settings conflict at the server level and at a specific scope level, the settings defined for a scope will always take precedence.

To configure the server TCP/IP options, right-click Server Options in the details pane and select Configure Options from the menu that appears (see Figure 13.6).

Although there are a number of options, most of them define DHCP options that are not applicable to Microsoft clients. The following properties are applicable to all Microsoft clients:

◆ Router

◆ DNS Server

◆ DNS Domain Name

◆ WINS Server

◆ NetBIOS Node Type

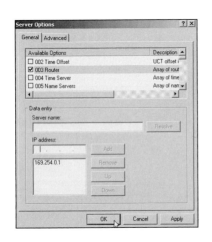

FIGURE 13.6
Server TCP/IP options set default options for the properties selected and configured.

In addition, Windows 2000 DHCP clients also accept configuration of Perform Router Discovery and Static Route. All other configuration settings will be ignored by Microsoft clients.

In addition to the options for the DHCP server in general, you can also set options for the specific scope(s) you have configured, which override settings configured in the server scope. To set these, right-click Scope Options and choose Configure Options from the menu that appears.

A final alternative for dynamic TCP/IP configuration is to configure reservations for specific computers based on the MAC address of tier network adapter. This has the effect of creating a static configuration without actually having to modify the TCP/IP properties on the client. Address reservations are useful in a number of situations. For example, if you have a network printer that obtains its TCP/IP address via DHCP but must always have the same address, you can use a reservation. In addition, if you want to explicitly set the TCP/IP address of a machine because it has a particular service installed but you want it to benefit from the other configuration parameters given out by the DHCP server, you could also use a reservation.

When you have a TCP/IP address and the MAC address of the computer for which you want to create a reservation, you can create an address reservation by following Step by Step 13.10.

NOTE

Obtaining the MAC Address The MAC address for a network adapter can be obtained using the `IPCONFIG /all` command at a command prompt. The line with the label *Physical Address* displays the MAC address in the format *00-60-97-D5-22-CA*. When you receive the MAC address for a DHCP reservation, you remove the hyphens.

ON THE CD

Step by Step 13.10, "Configuring an Address Reservation," lets you create an address reservation when you have a TCP/IP address and the MAC address of the computer. See the file **Chapter13-10StepbyStep.pdf** in the CD's **Chapter13\StepbyStep** directory.

Installing and Configuring DNS

As discussed in the earlier section "Name Resolution Using DNS," the Active Directory uses the DNS service as its primary locator service. For security and reliability, DNS is usually configured on a domain controller. Although the most secure version of a DNS server requires a domain controller, DNS can also be implemented on a Windows 2000 Server.

DNS servers are installed as one of three types: a primary name server, a secondary name server, or a caching-only server. A primary name server is responsible for one zone and obtains its configuration from a local DNS file. A secondary name server obtains its configuration information from another name server using a process called *zone transfer*. A caching-only server does not have a DNS file locally and is responsible only for resolving names and caching that information locally.

To configure a Windows 2000 Server as a primary DNS server, you first must install DNS. This is outlined in Step by Step 13.11.

ON THE CD

Step by Step 13.11, "Installing DNS on a Windows 2000 Server," is used to install DNS on a Windows 2000 Server. See the file **Chapter13-11StepbyStep.pdf** in the CD's **Chapter13\StepbyStep** directory.

After the DNS service has been installed on your server, you can configure it. The basic configuration involves setting up the DNS server as a primary server and configuring a domain name for which it is the SOA. In addition, it involves configuring a forward lookup zone and a reverse lookup zone. A *forward lookup zone* is one that maps a hostname to a TCP/IP address. A *reverse lookup zone* is one that maps a TCP/IP address to a hostname.

Step by Step 13.12 demonstrates how to configure a Windows 2000 Server as a primary name server.

ON THE CD

Step by Step 13.12, "Configuring a Server as a First Network DNS on a Windows 2000 Server," demonstrates how to configure a Windows 2000 Server as a primary name server. See the file **Chapter13-12StepbyStep.pdf** in the CD's **Chapter13\StepbyStep** directory.

Although many of the DNS records on your name server are automatically configured, there are still times when you have to manually configure resource records. For example, you might need to configure resolution for hosts that run other operating systems or configure advanced DNS resource records, such as a Mail Exchanger (MX) record used to find a mail server. In these cases, you want to manually create records.

Step by Step 13.13 shows you how to create a variety of records. A host record (A) is the mapping of a hostname to a TCP/IP address. An alias record (CNAME) is the mapping of one hostname (the alias) to another hostname for which there is already a host record. A Mail Exchanger (MX) record is a record that defines the location of a mail server in this domain.

ON THE CD

Step by Step 13.13, "Manually Adding a New Record to a DNS Server," shows you how to create a variety of records to add to a DNS Server. See the file **Chapter13-13StepbyStep.pdf** in the CD's **Chapter13\StepbyStep** directory.

Installing and Configuring WINS

As explained in the earlier section "Name Resolution Using WINS," WINS is used to resolve NetBIOS names to TCP/IP addresses. In a Windows 2000 environment, WINS is used when clients and software require NetBIOS name resolution. In the most straightforward case, WINS is very easy to configure. You simply install the service and configure the clients to use the WINS server, and it begins to work. The best way to configure the clients is by creating a WINS entry in the DHCP configuration.

Step by Step 13.14 shows you how to install WINS on a Windows 2000 Server.

ON THE CD

Step by Step 13.14, "Installing WINS on a Windows 2000 Server," shows you how to install WINS on a Windows 2000 Server. See the file **Chapter13-14StepbyStep.pdf** in the CD's **Chapter13\StepbyStep** directory.

INSTALLING, CONFIGURING, AND TROUBLESHOOTING SHARED ACCESS

Install, configure, and troubleshoot shared access.

Many offices have a greater need for Internet access than they have connections. A home-based office might have a single Internet connection and two or three computers on a LAN. In other cases, perhaps two or three Internet connections are available in an office, but there are 10 machines on the company LAN. In both cases, Connection Sharing can be used to provide access to everyone who needs it.

Connection Sharing provides access from one network to another through a single (or multiple) point(s) of contact. Connection Sharing always involves a computer with two network cards, one to communicate with the internal network and the other to communicate with the Internet. In the simplest case, a computer is configured for Connection Sharing, and all the other network infrastructure changes are made automatically. In cases that are more complex, a number of Internet addresses are made available through a special protocol called network address translation (NAT).

Shared Access Using Connection Sharing

Figure 13.7 shows a typical small office configuration. A single computer might be connected to the Internet using either a dial-up line or a dedicated line. By default, if a second computer is then added to the equation with a LAN connection between it and the first, the second computer can connect to the first computer, but not to the Internet.

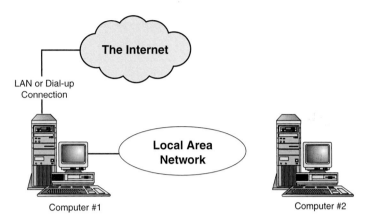

Computer #1

Computer #2

FIGURE 13.7
A shared connection allows one computer to access the Internet through the connection on another.

In this scenario, the solution is as simple as enabling automatic TCP/IP configuration on the second machine and enabling Connection Sharing on the first machine's Internet connection (LAN or dial-up).

When you enable Connection Sharing on the Internet connection, some configuration changes are made on your network. First, the TCP/IP address associated with the shared connection is changed to 192.168.0.1. Second, the computer with Connection Sharing enabled becomes the *de facto* DHCP server for all other computers on the network, providing them with TCP/IP addresses in the network 192.168.x.x.

Step by Step 13.15 demonstrates how to enable shared Internet access using Connection Sharing.

ON THE CD

Step by Step 13.15, "Enabling Shared Access via Connection Sharing," demonstrates how to enable shared Internet access using Connection Sharing. See the file **Chapter13-15StepbyStep.pdf** in the CD's **Chapter13\StepbyStep** directory.

Shared Access Using the NAT Routing Protocol

The NAT protocol allows for the situation where a number of TCP/IP addresses are available, but there are not enough for all the clients who need addresses. Only a single special configuration is required of clients who use a NAT server to connect to the Internet: the clients must set their default gateway to the address of the NAT server.

Installing Shared Access Using NAT

For the NAT protocol to function, you must first enable sharing using NAT on a server. Step by Step 13.16 shows you how to do just that.

ON THE CD

Step by Step 13.16, "Enabling Sharing Using NAT on a Member Server," enables sharing using NAT on a server. See the file **Chapter13-16StepbyStep.pdf** in the CD's **Chapter13\StepbyStep** directory.

After you enable the sharing, your NAT server is essentially ready to begin processing Internet access requests from clients. However, some configuration may be required for your specific situation. The next section talks about that.

Configuring Shared Access Using NAT

In simple scenarios, NAT configuration is complete as soon as it is installed. However, if the simplest situation was all you wanted, it would be more efficient to configure shared access by using Connection Sharing, because it is easier to set up.

NAT differs from Connection Sharing in that it is configurable. You can configure the internal addresses to be given out automatically. You can also configure more than one external address to use for communication (in the case where two or more addresses are provided by your ISP). In addition, you can also configure logging and statistical collection to define an ongoing log of NAT protocol translation.

Shared access using NAT is configured through the Routing and Remote Access console. From that console, you can configure a number of routing tasks, including RAS, which will be discussed in the next section.

In the Routing and Remote Access manager, you can configure the properties of the NAT protocol in general, as well as the properties of the connection that you are using to access the public network you are connecting to.

The NAT protocol can be configured with the following properties:

◆ **Logging.** You can define the level of activity logging that will be written to the System log in the Event Viewer.

◆ **Translation intervals.** You can define the time that NAT retains an address and port mapping between a private (internal) address and a public (Internet) address. The timeout values defined ensure that communication is complete before a mapping is removed from the NAT table. The default values are 1440 minutes (24 hours) for TCP and 1 minute for UDP. It is not recommended that you change these values unless performance is suffering.

NOTE

You Can See the Current Mappings
You can see the current mappings for the NAT server by right-clicking the connection name in the details pane and choosing Show Mappings from the menu that appears.

◆ **Reserved ports for applications.** If an application uses a specific port for communications, NAT can reserve these ports so that they are not used in normal NAT port translations. It also ensures that the NAT server knows what to do with the transmissions.

◆ **An address pool.** The NAT server can operate as a DHCP server for assigning internal IP addresses. Like DHCP, you can configure a pool of addresses and a subnet mask to be given out. By using the Exclude button, you can configure addresses in the pool that should be excluded because they are statically assigned. This option can be disabled if a DHCP server exists on the internal network.

◆ **DNS Request Forwarding.** The NAT server can be configured to forward DNS name resolution requests to a public DNS server. You can also indicate whether this resolution request is allowed to initiate a dial-up to the Internet through a demand-dial interface.

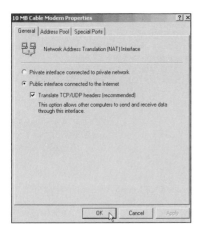

FIGURE 13.8

For NAT to work, one connection must be
connected to the public network.

ON THE CD

Step by Step 13.17, "Opening the NAT Properties," shows you how
to open the NAT properties. See the file **Chapter13-
17StepbyStep.pdf** in the CD's **Chapter13\StepbyStep** directory.

The second step of configuring NAT is to configure the properties of
the external network interface on the NAT server. The following
properties can be defined for the external interface:

◆ The external interface must be configured as the public interface and TCP and UDP headers will be translated (see Figure
13.8). The configuration wizard sets this option automatically
when you install NAT. This must stay as it's configured for
NAT to work.

◆ If your ISP has allocated multiple IP addresses to you, you can
configure these additional addresses by creating an address
pool. In this way, you can have network traffic translated to
two or more addresses instead of just one.

◆ If you have internal servers that must be accessed from the
Internet, you can create mappings that allow connections to an
external IP address to be passed to a server on the private network. This also requires restricting the mappings to only
defined ports. For example, if you were passing connections to
a Telnet server, you would enable only connections to port 23
using TCP to be passed to the Telnet server. All others would
be discarded.

Troubleshooting Shared Access Using NAT

The proper functioning of shared access using NAT depends on
a number of factors, all of which have been discussed here. If a
client fails to connect to an external server, you need to check the
following:

◆ There must be connectivity at the client; TCP/IP should be
configured properly.

◆ There must be connectivity at the NAT server, both on the
private network and the public network.

◆ The TCP/IP addresses for all the private computers must match the TCP/IP address for the private connection on the NAT server.

◆ Address translation must be enabled for the connection to the public network.

◆ If addresses are being assigned to private clients by the NAT server, there cannot be another DHCP server on the private LAN also giving out addresses in the same range unless it is configured to exclude addresses given out by the NAT server.

◆ If the NAT server is not enabled for DNS, it must be configured to forward DNS requests from the private clients to a public DNS server.

◆ If the public connection on the NAT server is dial-up, a demand-dial interface must be configured for it.

◆ If clients are connecting to application servers on the public network, they might need special ports configured on the NAT connection.

INSTALLING, CONFIGURING, AND TROUBLESHOOTING REMOTE ACCESS

Configure, monitor, and troubleshoot remote access.

- **Configure inbound connections.**
- **Create a remote access policy.**
- **Configure a remote access profile.**

Remote access allows clients to connect to the corporate network via a remote access server and thereby access resources on the corporate network. The components of a remote access system are

◆ A remote access server

◆ A remote access client

◆ A remote access policy

The remote access server is responsible for accepting (or denying) an access request from a client and then directing that client to appropriate network resources as required. The remote access client is responsible for initiating a connection through an approved media (telephone, ISDN, and so on) to the remote access server and providing appropriate credentials to identify the remote access user. Finally, the remote access policy defines valid users and the appropriate resources for them to access. All three of these must be functioning properly for remote access to work properly.

A Windows 2000 member server can supply two types of remote access connectivity: dial-up networking (DUN) and virtual private networking (VPN). Both provide access to remote systems. However, their configurations are quite different. Dial-up networking is configured over a private communication link, such as a telephone line, whereas virtual private networking is configured as a secured transmission over an already established communication link, such as an Internet connection or a LAN.

Both remote access types require a server to receive and process requests, and both create a connection to a network that is the same in functionality (but usually not in speed) as though the user were physically connected to the LAN. This section discusses the configuration of remote access via dial-up networking, and the next section discusses VPNs.

Dial-up networking is based on a dial-up connection. As such, it supports connections over hardware, such as packet switching networks (the phone line), IDSN, and X.25. In addition, for data transfers between computers in close physical proximity, you can use direct cable connections between parallel or serial ports (LPT or COM).

Two communication protocols are currently being used to facilitate dial-up networking: Point-to-Point Protocol (PPP) and Serial Line Interface Protocol (SLIP). PPP is a more robust protocol and has largely superseded SLIP. However, some dial-up servers still use SLIP technology (mainly UNIX machines). SLIP has not been supported by Windows Servers since NT 3.51; therefore, SLIP clients cannot connect to Windows 2000 remote access servers.

PPP provides a variety of features in dial-up networking. It allows for the transmission of TCP/IP, IPX, NetBEUI, AppleTalk, and other protocols via the dial-up connection. In addition, it also supports the dynamic allocation of TCP/IP addresses to clients at connect time (much like DHCP). PPP also supports secured transmission, although usually it is not required, because the communication mechanisms are, by their nature, private.

Configuring Inbound Connections

The configuration of a remote access server requires two things: enabling of the Routing and Remote Access Service (RRAS) and configuration of at least one hardware device to accept incoming calls.

The Routing and Remote Access Service is installed by default when you install Windows 2000 Server. However, it must be manually enabled. Step by Step 13.18 shows how to enable RRAS if it is not already enabled.

ON THE CD

Step by Step 13.18, "Enabling the Routing and Remote Access Service (RRAS)," shows how to enable RRAS if it is not already enabled. See the file **Chapter13-18StepbyStep.pdf** in the CD's **Chapter13\StepbyStep** directory.

If RRAS has already been enabled, the remote access portion can be disabled. If it is, your server will not accept any incoming dial-up networking connections. To enable the remote access feature of the server, follow Step by Step 13.19.

ON THE CD

Step by Step 13.19, "Enabling the Remote Access on Your Server," describes how to enable the remote access feature of the server. See the file **Chapter13-19StepbyStep.pdf** in the CD's **Chapter13\StepbyStep** directory.

When RRAS has been started, you need to have a dial-in device configured. This could be a modem, an ISDN adapter, an X.25 connection, or a serial or parallel cable connected to a COM or LPT port. If you have a modem installed in your Windows 2000 Server, it should have been detected by the Plug and Play manager and automatically configured. If it wasn't, you have to install it manually. Step by Step 13.20 describes how to manually install a modem.

ON THE CD

Step by Step 13.20, "Manually Installing a Modem," describes how to manually install a modem. See the file **Chapter13-20StepbyStep.pdf** in the CD's **Chapter13\StepbyStep** directory.

All modem devices are automatically enabled for incoming traffic when RRAS is enabled. Any modems installed after RRAS is enabled are also automatically configured for RRAS. However, you may want to enable or disable one or more of these devices. In the RRAS Manager, these devices are listed as ports, and you can configure the properties of each of the ports to allow or disallow routing or remote access.

Step by Step 13.21 shows how to enable a port for remote access.

ON THE CD

Step by Step 13.21, "Enabling a Port for Remote Access," shows how to enable a port for remote access. See the file **Chapter13-21StepbyStep.pdf** in the CD's **Chapter13\StepbyStep** directory.

Configuring the Server for Security and Network Access

When enabled, the server can be configured to fit the authentication, security, and logging needs of your organization. You can configure what protocols will be allowed to pass from the client, as well as how much of the network a remote user will be allowed to access. Both are configured from the server properties.

Within a server's property pages, you can configure whether the local server will handle authentication requests or whether the authentication requests will be passed to a Remote Authentication Dial-In User Service (RADIUS) server for approval or rejection (see Figure 13.9).

Because authentication requires the passing of name and password information over a possibly insecure line, a variety of encryption schemes are available. The server and client will negotiate for the least common denominator between them and use that method to encrypt the password data being transmitted. If a client cannot provide the authentication method demanded by the server, the client will not be able to authenticate and will generally not be able to connect to the remote network. The following remote access authentication methods are available:

- ◆ **Extensible Authentication Protocol (EAP)** is an authentication method that leaves the forms of available authentication open-ended. Under EAP, the server and client negotiate the actual authentication used. This authentication may use smart cards or other authentication types. This authentication method can incorporate secondary checks, such as prompting the user for a PIN number to go with whatever authentication has been provided.

- ◆ **Microsoft Challenge Handshake Authentication Protocol version 2 (MS-CHAP v2)** allows challenge-response authentication based on a two-way encryption algorithm and the username/password combination provided. MS-CHAP v2 eliminates some of the security holes in the original MS-CHAP authentication method. However, when used with dial-up networking, it is available to only Windows 2000, Windows NT 4.0, and Windows 98 clients.

- ◆ **Challenge Handshake Authentication Protocol (CHAP)** method allows encrypted authentication with non-Microsoft clients. This ensures that encrypted authentication can happen even with non-Microsoft dial-up clients. CHAP authentication relies on the MD5 hashing scheme and the storage of user passwords in a reversibly encrypted form in the Active Directory.

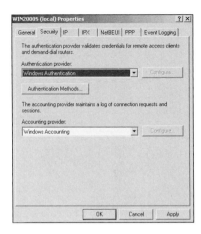

FIGURE 13.9
You can configure so that either Windows 2000 or a RADIUS server should provide authentication and/or accounting services.

> NOTE
>
> **Windows 2000 Can Function as a RADIUS Server** Windows 2000 has the capability of functioning as a RADIUS server. This implementation is referred to as the Internet Authentication Services (IAS) and allows for the centralization of many remote access management functions in an enterprise or multiple enterprise environment.

◆ **Shiva Password Authentication Protocol (SPAP)** is an encryption mechanism employed by Shiva. This method is more secure than sending passwords as clear text (no encryption), but not as secure as MS-CHAP or CHAP. Although the password is encrypted under this method, the same password is always encrypted the same way. This is a security risk because the password packets that are sent could be re-sent by a hacker to provide the appropriately encrypted password.

◆ **Password Authentication Protocol (PAP)** is the least secure method of authentication available in dial-up access, because passwords are sent as plain text without any sort of encryption. This method should be left available only if authentication is required and the client has no way of providing encryption.

In addition to the authentication provider, you can also configure an accounting provider for remote access sessions. This can be either a RADIUS server or the remote access server. If you configure Windows accounting, a record of connection requests and sessions is logged using the logging settings defined in the Routing and Remote Access manager.

If your server is running the TCP/IP protocol, you have the option of making this protocol available for remote access communication. To do that, you must select Allow IP-Based Remote Access and Demand-Dial Connections. When TCP/IP is enabled for remote access, you have the choice of restricting access to just the dial-up server, or allowing DUN clients to access the entire network. This is done by either selecting or deselecting the Enabling IP Routing option.

When a user connects to your network using DUN and TCP/IP, his or her modem effectively becomes a network card. As such, that interface needs a TCP/IP address to communicate using the TCP/IP protocol. If a DHCP server is available to the remote access server, you could choose to assign addresses from the DHCP scope. If you do not have a DHCP server available or if you do not want to use addresses from your LAN scope, you can give out addresses configured on this property page.

If your server is running the NWLink protocol, you have the option of making the IPX protocol available for remote access communication. To do that, you must select Allow IPX-Based Remote Access and Demand-Dial Connections. If you enable IPX, you have the option of defining the scope of network access using this protocol. As with TCP/IP, you can either restrict access to the dial-up server or allow access to the entire network.

If your server is running the NetBEUI protocol, you have the option of making that protocol available for remote access communication. To do that, you must select Allow NetBEUI-Based Remote Access Clients to Access. Then you must choose either This Computer Only or The Entire Network to define the scope of network access.

On the PPP property page, you can configure the remote access server to use PPP advanced properties (see Figure 13.10). Multilink provides increased transmission bandwidth by combining multiple physical links into one virtual link. By configuring both the server and the client with multilink, you can turn two 56KB connections into a single 112KB connection. This requires two phone lines and modems to be available on both the server and the client side.

An enhancement to Windows 2000 is the addition of the Bandwidth Allocation Protocol (BAP) and Bandwidth Allocation Control Protocol (BACP) to dynamically allocate lines to a connection as required.

Finally, you can configure software compression of data sent over the dial-up connection.

Step by Step 13.22 shows how to modify the properties of the RRAS server.

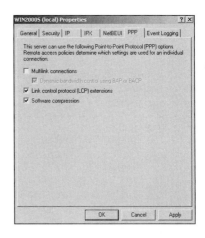

FIGURE 13.10
Multilink allows you to expand the incoming bandwidth that's available by combining two or more physical connections into a single virtual connection.

ON THE CD

Step by Step 13.22, "Modifying Remote Access Server Properties," shows how to modify the properties of the RRAS server. See the file **Chapter13-22StepbyStep.pdf** in the CD's **Chapter13\ StepbyStep** directory.

Configuring User Accounts for Remote Access

Although remote access is automatically available after you have enabled the Routing and Remote Access Service, all clients are, by default, denied the ability to access the network using remote access.

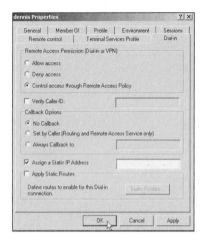

FIGURE 13.11
The user's properties must be configured to allow remote access.

> **WARNING**
>
> **One Remote Access Policy Must Exist**   For any user in your organization to connect using remote access, at least one remote access policy must exist. If no remote access policies exist, all users will be denied remote access regardless of the settings in their account properties.

Because in the average organization it is likely that only a small fraction of the network user community uses remote access, this is a reasonable policy.

Included in the dial-in properties for a user's account is the capability of using remote access to get to the network (see Figure 13.11).

You can choose to allow access, deny access, or grant access based on remote access policy. This allows all connection requests to be granted or denied based on a centralized policy that defines allowed connection requests.

In addition to enabling or disabling remote access for a user, you can configure a number of other properties for remote access users:

◆ You can enable Verify Caller-ID, where the remote access server checks the caller's phone number against a preconfigured phone number to ensure that the call originates at the approved source phone number.

◆ You can set Callback Options. Callback can be set so that the dial-up server terminates an incoming call and then calls the dialer back at either a user-entered phone number or at a preset phone number.

◆ You can preset an IP address for a remote access user by selecting the Assign a Static IP Address option and entering a predetermined TCP/IP address. This setting overrides any automatic IP address configuration.

◆ You can define the dial-up user's routing table by selecting Apply Static Routes and adding any required routing information.

To set these properties on the local account for a server, open the Computer Management console, open the users list, and edit the user properties on the Dial-In property page. To set these properties on an Active Directory account, open the Active Directory Users and Computers console, open the users list, and edit the user properties on the Dial-In property page.

Creating a Remote Access Policy

Remote access policy is a set of rules that define the ability of a user or group of users to connect to a server by way of remote access. Within remote access policy, you can define conditions that must be met for a connection to be granted. For example, you can create a remote access policy that allows access only during business hours. If you have more than one remote access policy, each is designated with a number. The lower the number, the sooner it is evaluated. If a user is granted access based on one policy and denied access based on another, and the granting policy has a lower number, the user gets access. If it has a higher number, the user is denied access.

An initial remote access policy is created by default. This policy grants deny access to all users by default. Do not delete this policy. If you have no policies at all, no one gets access by remote access regardless of the account properties, so be sure to override the policy. If you want your access policy to be more complex, you can modify the default policy to put rules in place, and/or you can add more policies to control users or groups based on certain rules.

Step by Step 13.23 shows you how to create a remote access policy.

ON THE CD

Step by Step 13.23, "Creating a Remote Access Policy," shows you how to create a remote access policy. See the file **Chapter13-23StepbyStep.pdf** in the CD's **Chapter13\StepbyStep** directory.

Configuring a Remote Access Profile

If remote access policies are the rules by which users are explicitly granted or denied remote access, remote access profiles define what the nature of the access is to be.

Remote access profiles are always associated with specific policies. A user is granted remote access restricted by the definition in the policy. This may include placing a time limit on the connection or

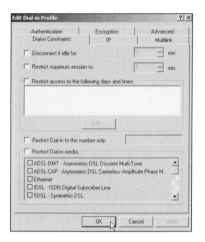

FIGURE 13.12
The dial-in constraints are restrictions placed on a client to whom the profile is applied.

restricting the connection to a certain media type. Even if the user has been granted explicit access through account properties, a profile belonging to a policy that would have applied to the user is still applied.

You can create profiles at the same time that you create a policy (see step 8 of Step by Step 13.23), or you can create and modify profiles afterward (see Figure 13.12).

Regardless, configuring the properties for a profile consists of defining the following:

◆ **Dial-in constraints.** You can configure so that connections are automatically disconnected after a certain length of idle time takes place. You can restrict connections to specific days of the week or hours of the day. You can also configure a specific number to dial from. Finally, you can even go so far as to restrict access from a specific media type, such as Ethernet or ISDN.

◆ **IP properties.** You can configure where IP address assignments take place (client-requested or server-assigned). In addition, you define packet filters that restrict specific IP protocols that can be used between a remote client and the remote access server.

◆ **Multilink settings.** You can allow the server properties to define multilink, disable multilink, or limit the number of ports multilink functions over. In addition, you can configure the BAP settings to drop multilink connections based on bandwidth usage.

◆ **Authentication methods.** You can restrict what authentication methods are allowed when connecting to a remote access server. The settings defined in a remote access profile override any settings defined in server properties.

◆ **Encryption settings.** You can define the levels of encryption for remote access connections to be either No Encryption, Basic or Strong Encryption. You can enable any combination of encryption levels.

Step by Step 13.24 shows how to edit a remote access profile for a remote access policy.

ON THE CD

Step by Step 13.24, "Editing a Remote Access Profile for a Remote Access Policy," shows how to edit a remote access profile for a remote access policy. See the file **Chapter13-24StepbyStep.pdf** in the CD's **Chapter13\StepbyStep** directory.

Install, configure, and troubleshoot a virtual private network (VPN).

The idea of the virtual private network (VPN) is that a secure tunnel is established between one point and the next. This tunnel could be established through a dial-up connection, through an Internet connection established via an ISP, or on a local LAN. A point-to-point connection already exists before the tunnel can be established. This tunnel can be established using a secure protocol that encapsulates encrypted data within it. Regardless of the data being sent, the communication is secure, because even if the tunneling packets are intercepted, they cannot be compromised as they are encrypted.

Two tunneling protocols are available under Windows 2000 Remote Access Services: Point-to-Point Tunneling Protocol (PPTP) and Layer Two Tunneling Protocol (L2TP).

PPTP uses TCP/IP as a means of transporting encrypted packets containing the real network communication. PPTP encrypts all data using Microsoft Point-to-Point Encryption (MPPE) as it is transmitted across an existing TCP/IP network.

L2TP is a new tunneling protocol. L2TP does not have a built-in encryption algorithm, as in PPTP. Instead, L2TP relies on IPSec (Internet Protocol Security), to provide encryption of data within the L2TP tunnel. Table 13.1 compares the two protocols.

TABLE 13.1	
PPTP/L2TP COMPARISON	
PPTP	*L2TP*
Transit network must be TCP/IP	Transit Network can be TCP/IP, Frame Relay, X.25, or ATM
No header compression	Header compression for reduced overhead
No tunnel authentication	Tunnel authentication for increased security
Inherent encryption	No inherent encryption; requires IPSec for encryption

When Routing and Remote Access is enabled, five PPTP and five L2TP ports are created automatically. If you need more, you can easily create them by adjusting a property for each in the Ports properties. Step by Step 13.25 shows you how to create additional PPTP and L2TP ports.

ON THE CD

Step by Step 13.25, "Creating PPTP and L2TP Ports," shows you how to create additional PPTP and L2TP ports. See the file **Chapter13-25StepbyStep.pdf** in the CD's **Chapter13\StepbyStep** directory.

As has already been mentioned, VPN connections can be established via two transport mechanisms: through a direct LAN/WAN connection (such as the Internet) or via a dial-up connection to the remote access server. Both pose problems in terms of control of the security being used.

The solution to both these problems rests in a remote access policy defining traffic of type PPTP and the filtering (and disposal) of non-PPTP or L2TP protocols from the remote access server. By creating a policy demanding a tunneling protocol, you ensure that all remote access traffic will be encrypted.

Configuring a Remote Access Server for PPTP-Only Communication

To configure a RRAS server to allow only PPTP communication, you have to set some filters. PPTP communicates on TCP port 1723. In addition, it uses a special protocol called the Generic Routing Encapsulation (GRE) protocol, which is assigned the protocol ID 47. Both of these are present during communication using PPTP. If you want to eliminate all other traffic, you simply need to configure the RRAS server to drop all communication that does not connect to TCP port 1723 and protocol 47. That procedure is outlined in Step by Step 13.26.

ON THE CD

Step by Step 13.26, "Configuring a PPTP Remote Access Server," shows how to configure the RRAS server to drop all communication that does not connect to TCP port 1723 and protocol 47. See the file **Chapter13-26StepbyStep.pdf** in the CD's **Chapter13\ StepbyStep** directory.

Configuring a Remote Access Server for L2TP-Only Communication

Configuring a server for L2TP communication is a little more complex than configuring for PPTP. This is because the tunnel itself is not secure. As a result, you have to add IPSec encryption to the transmission to ensure security. The encryption protocol supplied with Windows 2000 is IPSec.

INSTALLING, CONFIGURING, AND TROUBLESHOOTING TERMINAL SERVICES

Install, configure, monitor, and troubleshoot Terminal Services:

- **Remotely administer servers by using Terminal Services.**
- **Configure Terminal Services for application sharing.**
- **Configure applications for use with Terminal Services.**

Terminal Services is a session hosting service that allows a Windows 2000 Server to provide environment resources (memory, processor, and hard drive) so that a client needs to provide only minimal memory and processor resources. The end result is that both thin clients (such as Windows CE machines) and fat clients (any PC running the Terminal Services Client) will be able to use a Windows 2000 environment with little loss of performance over a Pentium machine with 64MB of RAM running the same applications.

This capability allows legacy hardware to be redeployed, reducing the amount spent on hardware upgrades for old machines. It also means that legacy operating systems can continue to be used while, at the same time, taking advantage of 32-bit Windows 2000 applications. In addition, control can be exercised over what software can be installed by clients and what applications can be run. Finally, through the Terminal Services administrator, you can take remote control of client sessions, which makes help desk functions much easier.

The disadvantage of using Terminal Services is that it uses server memory and sometimes increases network traffic. Because all the processing is happening on the server side, all that happens on the client is input from the keyboard and mouse and display of screen information. That means all keyboard and mouse commands have to be sent over the network to the server, and all display information must be sent to the client over the network. However, network bandwidth utilization should be monitored. In addition, memory needs to be increased in any server that is running Terminal Services to allow multiple sessions.

Terminal Services Hardware and Software

A Terminal server implementation consists of two environments: the server environment and the client environment. The server environment is where the client session is hosted, and it must be robust enough to provide services to as many concurrent users as is permitted without loss of performance in other areas on the server. As a result, hardware requirements need to be carefully considered, and hardware may need to be upgraded before and during your Terminal server implementation.

The Terminal Services Server

The Terminal server requires a Windows 2000 Server to host it. It is recommended that the server be a member server in a domain rather than a domain controller (a server that authenticates domain logon) because Terminal Services may degrade the server's functions in other areas. Furthermore, if your implementation is large, you might need several Terminal servers to service all your clients.

The primary hardware components to be managed in a Terminal server environment are memory and processor power. Of course, the minimum memory requirements for Windows 2000 must be met (64MB). In addition, it is recommended that 4–8MB of RAM for every anticipated concurrent user must be included.

Like memory, processor requirements scale linearly as the number of users increase. As a result, it is recommended that when you first implement Terminal server, you use a server that is capable of being expanded to multiple processors in case additional processing power is required down the line.

Microsoft divides users into three categories:

◆ Task-based (those users who run a single data entry application)

◆ Typical (those users who run one or two simultaneous applications but whose data entry requirements are low; they may run a word processor and a browser)

◆ Advanced (those users whose requirements are heavy, running three or more simultaneous applications and/or doing large queries on databases).

The number of users that can be supported on any given server depends on the kinds of users being supported.

Based on data published by Microsoft, Table 13.2 provides a sample of Terminal server users supported on given server hardware platforms.

TABLE 13.2

AVERAGE NUMBER OF USERS SUPPORTED ON SELECT SERVER PLATFORMS

Server Configuration	Task-Based	Typical	Advanced
Single processor, Pentium Pro, 200MHz, 128MB RAM	25	15	8
Dual processor, Pentium Pro, 200MHz, 256MB RAM	50	30	15
Quad processor, Pentium Pro, 200MHz, 512MB RAM	100	60	30

In addition to memory and processor power, fast hard drives are recommended, as is a network infrastructure tuned for maximum throughput.

The Terminal Services Client

Because Terminal Services runs almost exclusively on the server, the client can be much less powerful than would be necessary if the client were hosting applications itself. That fact is one of the benefits of using Terminal Services. In fact, Terminal Services allows a wide variety of clients to support Windows 2000 applications, as shown in the following list:

◆ Windows 2000 (all types)

◆ Windows NT (all types and versions running on Intel or Alpha processors)

◆ Windows 9x

◆ Windows for Workgroups (3.11)

◆ Windows CE clients

◆ Windows-based terminals ("thin clients")

To operate, all that is required is that certain minimum hardware specifications be met and that the Terminal Services Client be installed on the computer. After that, when a session is opened, the user executes in a Windows 2000 window and is able to work as though his or her local operating system as if it were Windows 2000.

Table 13.3 lists the Windows operating systems on which Terminal Services clients operate and their minimum hardware requirements.

TABLE 13.3

MINIMUM HARDWARE REQUIREMENTS BY OPERATING SYSTEM

Operating System	RAM	Processor	Video Card
Windows 2000	32MB	Pentium	VGA
Windows NT	16MB	486	VGA
Windows 98	16MB	486	VGA
Windows 95	16MB	386	VGA
Windows 3.11	16MB	386	VGA
Windows CE	Any	Any	Any

One more hardware requirement needs to be mentioned. Certain applications that are hosted from the Terminal server may require special input devices (such as barcode readers) to function properly. Because all input comes from the client, two criteria must be met. First, the device must be installed on the client computer. Second, the device must operate as a keyboard-input device for its data to be recognized by the Terminal Services server.

Hosted Terminal Services Applications

Any applications that are to be run by the Terminal Services Client must be Windows 2000–compliant. If an application will not run under Windows 2000, a Terminal Services Client cannot use it. Although it is theoretically possible to run DOS, Windows 16-bit, and Windows 32-bit applications under Terminal Services, for best performance, Windows 32-bit applications are recommended.

Installing the Terminal Services Server

When you install Terminal Services, you have three options in terms of the software to be installed. Of course, the Terminal Services server must be installed. In addition, you can install the Terminal Services Client creator, used for creating client installation disks (which are not required if you are going to install the client software over the network). Finally, you can install the Terminal Services License Manager. You are required to install this software once for each enterprise in which applications are to run from Terminal Services Clients.

During the installation process, you will be prompted for the kind of application your Terminal Services installation will have. You have two choices: remote administration and application server. Remote administration is used when the purpose for installing Terminal Services is to be able to open server consoles from remote machines to administer the server. You are limited to two simultaneous connections in this configuration.

Application server mode is used when the primary reason for installing Terminal Services is to host client sessions executing applications. In this case, the hardware requirements will be greater, but so will the administration. In addition to installing the applications for execution by the clients, you also have to administer licensing the clients.

Terminal Services licensing is not part of the license that you buy with the operating system your clients are running. As a result, you are required to install the Terminal Services License Manager on at least one computer in your company. When a client connects to a Terminal Server for the first time, it obtains and stores locally a license from the License Manager. On subsequent occasions, the local license is presented to the Terminal Server for validation. A Terminal Server allows unlicensed clients to connect for 90 days, at which time it requires a License Manager with valid licenses to function.

The License Manager can be installed on a member server but, to work for all the users in your domain, it must be installed on a domain controller. Therefore, it is recommended that the License Manager always be installed on a domain controller.

Step by Step 13.27 shows you how to install Terminal Services to facilitate remote server administration.

ON THE CD

Step by Step 13.27, "Installing Terminal Services for Remote Server Administration," shows you how to install Terminal Services to facilitate remote server administration. See the file **Chapter13-27StepbyStep.pdf** in the CD's **Chapter13\StepbyStep** directory.

Step by Step 13.28 shows you how to install Terminal Services to facilitate the running of applications.

ON THE CD

Step by Step 13.28, "Installing Terminal Services for Application Server Operation," shows you how to install Terminal Services to facilitate the running of applications. See the file **Chapter13-28StepbyStep.pdf** in the CD's **Chapter13\StepbyStep** directory.

If you need to reconfigure your server from one mode to the other (from Administration to Application or vice versa), you can do so through the Add/Remove Programs applet in the Control Panel. Step by Step 13.29 illustrates this process.

ON THE CD

Step by Step 13.29, "Switching Between Server Modes," shows how to reconfigure your server from one mode to the other (from Administration to Application or vice versa). See the file **Chapter13-29StepbyStep.pdf** in the CD's **Chapter13\StepbyStep** directory.

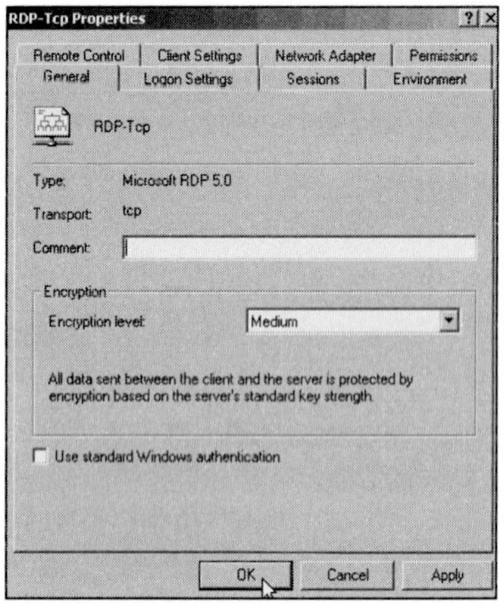

FIGURE 13.13
Client-server encryption defines the times at
which encryption is applied to communication
and how strong it is.

> **NOTE**
>
> **Where Is High Encryption Available?**
> High encryption is available in all
> countries except those that support
> state-sponsored terrorism. At time of
> printing, this list included Cuba, Iran,
> Iraq, Libya, North Korea, Syria, Sudan,
> Serbia and Taliban-controlled areas of
> Afghanistan.

Configuring Terminal Services Server

Configuration of the Terminal Services server is done in two separate
areas. First, the server itself is configured. Then users are configured
for Terminal Services sessions.

Terminal Services Server Configuration

The Terminal Services Configuration Manager allows you to set
defaults for the operation of the Terminal server. From the manager,
you can configure the settings for the Terminal server connection,
Remote Desktop Protocol-Transmission Control Protocol (RDP-
Tcp), and the settings for the Terminal server itself.

All communications between Terminal Services Clients and a
Windows 2000 Terminal server use RDP-Tcp. The following properties for RDP-Tcp can be configured:

◆ **Encryption level.** The connection between the Terminal
Services Client and the Terminal server can be set to either
Low (data is encrypted as it is sent from the client to the
server), Medium (data is encrypted in both directions between
the client and the server, using 40-bit or 56-bit encryption),
or High (data is encrypted in both directions between the
client and the server, using 128-bit encryption), as shown in
Figure 13.13.

◆ **Logon name.** You can have users provide their own logon credentials, or you can provide a single account that all users connect to the server with. If a single account is configured, you
must also configure the password that will be used for the preconfigured account.

◆ **Timeout and reconnection settings.** You can set limits for
active sessions and for idle sessions. The Active Session Limit
defines how long an active session can remain active. When
the session limit is reached, you can define whether the session
is terminated (all applications are closed) or disconnected (the
link to the client is terminated but any running applications
remain active on the Terminal server. The Idle Session Limit
defines how long a session can remain idle before the session is
either terminated or disconnected.

◆ **Initial program.** You can configure an initial program to run when a client is connected and whether wallpaper should be displayed. These settings will override any settings configured within the user property settings.

◆ **User shell.** You can define the shell that the user will use for the Terminal Services session. The default is the Windows Explorer, but it can be changed to any application. Most commonly, this is set to the single application that is being used by Terminal Services Clients.

◆ **Remote control settings.** You can set whether network administrators or help desk personnel can take control of a Terminal Services Client's desktop. When activated, it allows a remote administrator to connect to an active session and transmit mouse and keyboard commands. You can choose to not allow remote control, to allow remote control if the user gives an administrator permission, to allow remote control at any time, or to use the settings defined in individual user properties (see Figure 13.14).

◆ **Printing options.** You can choose to disable Windows printer mapping (preventing users from creating mappings to network printers), to disable the client LPT port mapping (preventing users from using local printers attached to their parallel ports), or to disable the client COM port mapping (preventing users from using local printers attached to their serial ports).

◆ **Maximum sessions.** You can configure the maximum number of simultaneous connections supported by the Terminal server. If multiple adapters exist on the Terminal server, you can also choose which network adapters support Terminal sessions.

◆ **Approved users.** You can configure which users or groups are allowed access to the Terminal server and their access level. Access levels can be set to Full Control (assigned to the System account and Administrators group), User access, or Guest access.

NOTE **Distinguishing Between Terminal Server Sessions** An active session is one in which the client is working and keyboard or mouse information is being transferred to the server. An idle session is one in which no keyboard or mouse information is being transferred to the server. A disconnected session is one in which a user has exited the client software but has not logged off. The user can return to this session later as long as it is not terminated. Disconnected sessions take up resources on the server and, if the number of sessions is limited, may prevent other users from connecting. Terminated sessions are not sessions at all, but are the absence of a session and the release of system resources formerly dedicated to a session.

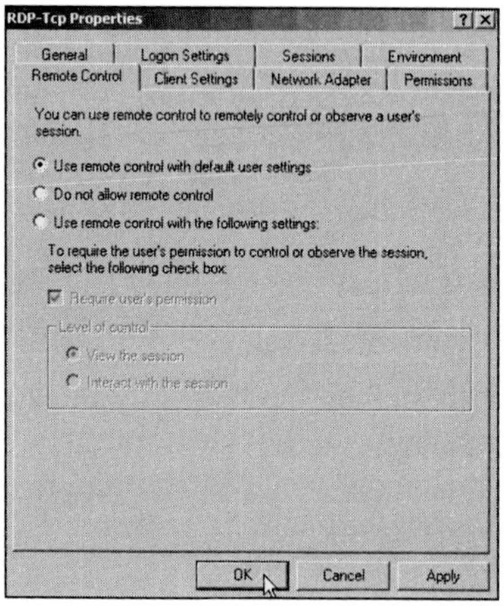

FIGURE 13.14
Configure the ability for administrators to watch or control client sessions.

Terminal Services User Account Configuration

The installation of Terminal Services server on a Windows 2000 Server makes fundamental changes to the properties of the user accounts. These changes not only extend to the local accounts, but if the server is a member server in a domain, they also extend to the properties of the domain accounts.

The extension of the user properties takes the form of four property pages that allow configuration of Terminal Services access:

◆ Terminal Services Profile

◆ Remote Control

◆ Sessions

◆ Environment

The Terminal Services Profile property page allows the configuration of a special profile for use when connecting to a Terminal server, a home directory for use when connecting to a Terminal server, and a check box that enables a user as a potential Terminal Services Client.

The Remote Control property page enables you to set specific remote control properties for the user account. If you have not configured these properties to be overridden in the connection properties for the server, they take effect when a user connects to the Terminal server.

The Sessions property page enables you to set session-specific time and disconnection options. If you have not configured these properties to be overridden in the connection properties for the server, they take effect when a user connects to the Terminal server.

The Environment property page enables you to set the startup environment for the user. If you have not configured these properties to be overridden in the connection properties for the server, they take effect when a user connects to the Terminal server.

Installing Terminal Services Client

To access the Terminal Services server from a user workstation, the Terminal Services Client must be installed. The installation files can be distributed either on a floppy disk set (for 16-bit or 32-bit Intel) or via a network share (for any of the platforms).

When you install Terminal Services on a Windows 2000 Server, a folder is installed into the system root folder (WINNT) that contains the installation files for 16-bit Intel, 32-bit Intel, and 32-bit Alpha clients. In addition, within the selection to install Terminal Services is the option to install the Client Creator Files that installs the program to create setup disks.

To enable installation of the Terminal Services Client over the network, share the appropriate client installation files from the path \WINNT\System32\clients\tsclient. Also, ensure that at least Read access is configured for all users who need to install the client.

Step by Step 13.30 describes how to create a Client Installation Disk Set. Step by Step 13.31 describes how to install a Terminal Services Client using that disk set.

ON THE CD

Step by Step 13.30, "Creating a Client Installation Disk Set," describes how to create a Client Installation Disk Set. See the file **Chapter13-30StepbyStep.pdf** in the CD's **Chapter13\StepbyStep** directory.

Step by Step 13.31, "Installing the Terminal Services Client," describes how to install a Terminal Services Client using that disk set. See the file **Chapter13-31StepbyStep.pdf** in the CD's **Chapter13\StepbyStep** directory.

Connecting Using the Terminal Services Client

After the server has been configured and the client has been installed on a workstation, connecting to a Terminal server is quite simple.

Step by Step 13.32 shows how to connect to a Terminal server using the Terminal Services Client.

ON THE CD

Step by Step 13.32, "Connecting Using the Terminal Services Client," shows how to connect to a Terminal server using the Terminal Services Client. See the file **Chapter13-32StepbyStep.pdf** in the CD's **Chapter13\StepbyStep** directory.

Locally Administering a Terminal Services Client

Although connecting to a Terminal server is straightforward, a tool exists to make the connection process even simpler: the Client Connection Manager. Using this tool, you can preconfigure connection settings and then invoke certain connections simply by choosing a menu option.

Step by Step 13.33 shows how to create a connection using the Client Connection Manager.

ON THE CD

Step by Step 13.33, "Creating Connections Using Client Connection Manager," shows how to create a connection using the Client Connection Manager. See the file **Chapter13-33StepbyStep.pdf** in the CD's **Chapter13\StepbyStep** directory.

Remotely Administering Servers Using Terminal Services

If you install Terminal Services on your servers only to facilitate remote administration, you should implement certain performance and security optimizations. Change the following settings on the properties page of the RDP-Tcp Connection:

◆ **Sessions\End a Disconnected Session.** Change to 1 minute to ensure that memory and resources are freed as soon as possible.

◆ **Sessions\Idle Session Limit.** Change to 5 minutes to ensure that sessions are ended promptly and you do not attempt to exceed the maximum number of sessions (2) by leaving a session running accidentally.

◆ **Environment\Disable Wallpaper.** Enable this option to ensure that unnecessary network traffic is not produced.

◆ **General\Encryption Level.** Change to High to ensure that maximum encryption is configured for administration.

◆ **Permissions.** Restrict access to only System and Administrators to reduce the possibility that unauthorized users get administrative access.

◆ **Network Adapter\Maximum Connections.** Set this to a low number to minimize security breaches.

◆ **Client Settings.** Disable Windows Printer Mapping, LPT Port Mapping, and Clipboard Mapping to reduce the possibility that confidential information is left on the client after the session is complete.

Configuring Terminal Services for Application Sharing

For a Terminal server to host applications for Terminal Services Clients, two things must be done. First, the Terminal server must be put into Application server mode. Second, a License Manager must be configured in your domain or enterprise within 90 days after installation of the application server.

Step by Step 13.34 shows you how to install the Terminal Services License Manager.

ON THE CD

Step by Step 13.34, "Installing Terminal Services License Manager," shows you how to install the Terminal Services License Manager. See the file **Chapter13-34StepbyStep.pdf** in the CD's **Chapter13\StepbyStep** directory.

Configuring Applications for Use with Terminal Services

Applications must be configured properly to work for all clients as though they were being executed on their local machines. You first need to ensure that they are installed using the right method. Then you may have to execute a script after installation to ensure that the applications have been tuned for Terminal Services execution.

Installing Applications on a Terminal Server

Any application that is installed on a Terminal server could be available to all users on that server. You must ensure that they are available, including shortcuts in the Start menu to invoke them. In addition, you must ensure that when each new user uses the application, he starts with his own settings, which are maintained independent of everyone else's.

The tool for doing this is the `change user` command. When invoked at a command line with the `/install` switch, it puts the system into a "watch" mode that tracks the initial settings for an application and records them. If you install an application in this mode, all pertinent data can be recorded and made available to all users. To complete the process, you then must invoke the `change user /execute` command, which takes you out of the watching mode.

This may seem like a complex process to go through every time you install an application. To make the process easier, it is done automatically for you when you install applications as an administrator through a Client Services session.

Step by Step 13.35 demonstrates how to install an application through a Terminal Services Client session.

ON THE CD

Step by Step 13.35, "Installing Applications Through a Terminal Services Client Session," demonstrates how to install an application through a Terminal Services Client session. See the file **Chapter13-35StepbyStep.pdf** in the CD's **Chapter13\StepbyStep** directory.

Occasionally, an application cannot be installed through Add/Remove Programs. For example, when you are browsing with Internet Explorer, you are frequently prompted to install plug-in software. To ensure that the settings are recorded properly for Terminal Services Clients, before proceeding with the installation, switch to a command prompt and run `change user/install`. When the installation is complete, run `change user/execute`.

Using Application Compatibility Scripts to Fine-Tune Application Execution

Microsoft has provided Application Compatibility Scripts for common applications to fine-tune the installations for use with Terminal Services. These scripts will modify settings to ensure that applications are set for optimal execution under Terminal Services.

The Application Compatibility Scripts are available in the path `WINNT\Application Compatibility Scripts\Install`.

Step by Step 13.36 outlines the process for running Application Compatibility Scripts.

ON THE CD

Step by Step 13.36, "Running Application Compatibility Scripts," outlines the process for running Application Compatibility Scripts. See the file **Chapter13-36StepbyStep.pdf** in the CD's **Chapter13\StepbyStep** directory.

NOTE

Not All Application Scripts Are Provided   Although a number of application compatibility scripts are provided by Microsoft, not all applications have scripts. Many popular Microsoft applications and some applications by other vendors are provided. At this point, for example, Office 2000 is notably absent. In fact, it will not install under Terminal server at all unless you install the Terminal Services components available in the Office 2000 Resource Kit. For more specific information on Office 2000 in a Terminal Services environment, go to `http://www.Microsoft.com/office/ork/2000/two/30t3.htm`.

CASE STUDY: IN YOUR TOWN INC.

ESSENCE OF THE CASE

This case requires that the following results be satisfied:

▶ Allow Isaiah to connect to head office servers to do administration when he is on the road.

▶ Secure the communications between his laptop and servers while administration is going on.

SCENARIO

Isaiah is the network administrator for In Your Town Inc. (IYT), a national company with 30 regional offices in the United States and Canada. Although IYT has a number of national locations, it has very few employees and a small IT staff (Isaiah and two technical assistants), which works out of the head office in New Orleans, Louisiana. As a result, Isaiah finds himself traveling a great deal to service servers in different locations (there is at least one Windows 2000 Server in each regional office). When he is on the road, Isaiah would like to be able to administer the Windows 2000 Servers at the head office from his laptop.

Not only does Isaiah want to be able to do simple administration (such as creating new users and checking printer queues), he also wants to be able to start and stop services, start Performance Monitors, observe running tasks, and restart servers that may have problems.

Because security is an issue with IYT, a firewall is configured to protect the head office servers. In addition, any communication between Isaiah's laptop and the head office servers must be done over some kind of secured connection.

You have been called in to analyze this situation and make recommendations.

ANALYSIS

Windows 2000 Server has features that will allow Isaiah to satisfy both his accessibility and his security issues. First, he can install the Terminal Services component of Windows 2000 Server and configure it to operate in

CASE STUDY: IN YOUR TOWN INC.

Administration mode. This, coupled with the installation of the Terminal Services Client on his laptop, will enable him to connect remotely to a local session on each server. This feature will work as long as he is inside the firewall. However, on the road, the firewall will prevent direct access to his servers from his laptop. That can be overcome by installing the RRAS services on a server inside the firewall (or by configuring a new server to be a RRAS server). Finally, for Isaiah to connect to the RRAS server, he needs to do three things: configure the RRAS server to accept VPN connections (PPTP), configure his laptop to connect to the RRAS server to establish VPN sessions, and open port 1723 in the firewall to allow the VPN traffic to pass through.

Using this configuration, Isaiah will be able to use any Internet connection to establish a VPN connection, through his firewall to his RRAS server at his head office. Having established that connection, he can then use the Terminal Services Client to establish a session with any of his servers, and he will be able to perform secure administration of his servers.

The following table summarizes the solution.

OVERVIEW OF THE REQUIREMENTS AND SOLUTIONS IN THIS CASE STUDY

Requirement	Solution Provided By
Access to server sessions	Installing Terminal Services on servers in Administration mode; installing Terminal Services Client on roaming laptop
Secure connection to network	Configuring a RRAS his server to accept PPTP connections via a VPN connection and placing this server inside the firewall
Secure connection through the firewall	Opening port 1723 in the firewall to allow PPTP traffic to pass

---

CHAPTER SUMMARY

KEY TERMS

- Connection
- Binding
- Protocol
- TCP/IP
- NWLink
- NetBEUI
- Subnet mask
- DHCP
- DHCP lease
- IPCONFIG
- TRACERT
- PING
- Scope
- Dynamic DNS
- WINS
- Connection Sharing
- NAT
- Demand Dial Interface
- Remote access server
- Dial-Up Networking
- RADIUS server
- EAP
- MS-CHAP v2
- Multilink
- BAP/BACP

Summarized briefly, this chapter covered the following main points:

◆ **Configuring the infrastructure for network communications on a Windows 2000 Server.** This includes network adapters and drivers, network protocols, and network connections.

◆ **Installing and configuring network services.** This includes DHCP (for automatic configuration of TCP/IP on clients) and WINS (for NetBIOS address resolution).

CHAPTER SUMMARY

◆ **Installing and configuring the Routing and Remote Access Services.** This includes shared Internet connections, dial-up networking, and virtual private networking.

◆ **Installing and configuring Terminal Services.** This includes installing Terminal Services to provide remote server administration as well as application hosting. It also includes configuring Terminal Services Clients.

- Remote access policy
- Remote access profile
- Virtual private networking
- PPTP
- L2TP
- IP filter
- Terminal Services
- Remote Administration mode
- Application Server mode
- Remote control
- Terminal Services profile
- Terminal Services License Manager
- Application Compatibility Script

APPLY YOUR KNOWLEDGE

Review Questions

1. What service is available to automatically configure TCP/IP addresses on client machines? What are some advantages to using this kind of configuration over manual configuration?

2. What are the two main reasons for using the NWLink protocol?

3. What two mechanisms are available for sharing a single connection to the Internet among a number of client machines on a LAN? What are the main differences between the two?

4. Before connecting to a RRAS server over a VPN, what must already be established from the client to that server?

5. What two protocols are available under Windows 2000 for use with VPNs? How do their security mechanisms differ?

6. What are the two modes in which Terminal Services can run on a Windows 2000 Server? What are the licensing requirements of each?

7. What Windows operating systems can support the Terminal Services client, and what is the minimum hardware required?

Answers to Review Questions

1. The service available to automatically configure TCP/IP addresses on client machines is called DHCP. DHCP has many advantages over manual configuration. Some of them include removal of the tedium of manually configuring clients with TCP/IP addresses, capability of automatically configuring a wide variety of TCP/IP-based

properties (including name resolution servers), and the capability of reducing TCP/IP conflicts on your network by keeping track of addresses allocated and by doing PING tests prior to allocating addresses. For more information, see the sections "Installing, Configuring, and Maintaining the TCP/IP Protocol Suite" and "Installing and Configuring DHCP."

2. The two main reasons for using NWLink are to allow communication with NetWare servers using only IPX/SPX and to increase security on Windows 2000 networks. Many NetWare servers are still configured to use only IPX/SPX and, therefore, interoperability with them requires a common protocol; NWLink is Microsoft's implementation of the IPX/SPX protocol. Security on Windows 2000 networks can be enhanced by replacing TCP/IP with NWLink. Because NWLink is routable, it can be used in WAN implementations. As long as there is no need for access to the Internet, NWLink can safely be used and will eliminate TCP/IP-based attacks on your network. For more information, see the section "Installing and Maintaining the NWLink Protocol."

3. The two mechanisms available for sharing a single connection to the Internet among a number of client machines are Connection Sharing and NAT. The main differences are ease of configuration and flexibility. Connection Sharing can be configured simply by selecting a check box, whereas NAT requires that you configure RRAS. On the other hand, NAT is much more flexible, allowing a greater array of control mechanisms for incoming and outgoing information, as well as the ability to provide more than one address in a pool to share amongst

APPLY YOUR KNOWLEDGE

internal clients. For more information, see the section "Installing, Configuring, and Troubleshooting Shared Access."

4. To establish a VPN connection, you must already have a connection to the RRAS server established. This could be in the form of a direct connection via the Internet or via a dial-up connection. Because a VPN uses a tunneling protocol, the tunnel must have been established first. For more information, see the section "Installing, Configuring, and Troubleshooting Remote Access."

5. Two tunneling protocols are available for use with VPNs: PPTP and L2TP. These protocols differ in their security mechanisms. PPTP has built-in encryption, whereas L2TP requires a secondary encryption mechanism (such as IPSec). For more information, see the section "Installing, Configuring, and Troubleshooting Remote Access."

6. Terminal Services run in two server modes: Administration and Application. In Administration mode, a maximum of two connections can be established for the purposes of administering a server. These connections do not require client licenses. In Application mode, 90 days' grace is given from the point when

Terminal Services is placed into that mode. After that, licenses must be purchased from Microsoft and managed by the Terminal Services License Manager. These licenses are separate from client access licenses for regular connections to a server. For more information, see the section "Configuring Terminal Services for Application Sharing."

7. The following Windows operating systems can support Terminal Services clients: Windows 3.11, Windows 95, Windows 98, Windows NT 4.0, and Windows 2000. The minimum hardware is supported under Windows 3.11. It consists of a 386 processor, 16MB of RAM, and a VGA video card. For more information, see the section "Terminal Services Hardware and Software."

ON THE CD

This book's companion CD contains specially designed supplemental material to help you understand how well you know the concepts and skills you learned in this chapter. You'll find related exercises and exam questions and answers. See the file **Chapter13ApplyYourKnowledge.pdf** in the CD's **Chapter13\ApplyYourKnowledge** directory.

Suggested Readings and Resources

1. Microsoft Windows 2000 Server Resource Kit: *Microsoft Windows 2000 Server Internetworking Guide.* Microsoft Press, 2000.

   - Chapter 2: Routing and Remote Access Service
   - Chapter 3: Unicast IP Routing
   - Chapter 7: Remote Access Server
   - Chapter 8: Internet Authentication Service
   - Chapter 9: Virtual Private Networking
   - Chapter 16: NetBEUI

2. Microsoft Windows 2000 Server Resource Kit: *Microsoft Windows 2000 Server Deployment Planning* Guide. Microsoft Press, 2000.

   - Chapter 7: Determining Network Connectivity Strategies
   - Chapter 11: Planning Distributed Security
   - Chapter 16: Deploying Terminal Services
   - Chapter 17: Determining Windows 2000 Network Security Strategies

3. Microsoft Windows 2000 Server Resource Kit: *TCP/IP Core Networking Guide.* Microsoft Press, 2000.

   - Part 1 (Chapters 1–3): Windows 2000 TCP/IP
   - Chapter 4: Dynamic Host Configuration Protocol
   - Chapter 7: Windows Internet Name Service
   - Chapter 8: Internet Protocol Security

4. *Microsoft Windows 2000 Professional Resource Kit* Microsoft Press, 2000.

   - Chapter 13: Security
   - Chapter 21: Local and Remote Network Connections
   - Chapter 22: TCP/IP in Windows 2000 Professional
   - Chapter 23: Windows 2000 Professional on Microsoft Networks
   - Chapter 24: Interoperability with NetWare

5. Microsoft Official Curriculum course 1560: *Updating Support Skills from Microsoft Windows NT 4.0 to Microsoft Window 2000.*

   - Module 10: Installing and Configuring Terminal Services
   - Module 11: Configuring Remote Access
   - Module 12: Securing Windows 2000
   - Module 13: Supporting DHCP and WINS

6. Microsoft Official Curriculum course 1562: *Designing a Microsoft Windows 2000 Networking Services Infrastructure.*

   - Module 3: Designing an Automated IP Configuration Service Using DHCP
   - Module 5: Designing a NetBIOS Name Resolution Service Using WINS
   - Module 6: Designing Internet Connectivity Using Network Address Translation
   - Module 9: Designing Remote User Connectivity
   - Module 10: Designing a Remote Access Solution Using RADIUS

Suggested Readings and Resources

7. Microsoft Official Curriculum course 2152: *Supporting Microsoft Windows 2000 Professional.*

   - Module 14: Configuring Windows 2000 for Mobile Computing
   - Module 15: Installing and Configuring Terminal Services

8. Microsoft Official Curriculum course 2153: *Supporting a Microsoft Windows 2000 Network Infrastructure.*

   - Module 2: Automating Internet Protocol (IP) Address Assignment
   - Module 4: Implementing Name Resolution Using WINS
   - Module 5: Configuring Network Traffic Security and Cross-Platform Authentication

   - Module 6: Configuring remote Access to a Network
   - Module 7: Supporting Remote Access to a Network
   - Module 8: Extending Remote Access Capabilities Using RADIUS
   - Module 13: Integrating Windows 2000 Network Services
   - Module 14: Managing a Windows 2000 Network

9. Web Sites

   - www.microsoft.com/windows2000
   - www.microsoft.com/train_cert

This chapter helps you prepare for the "Implementing, Monitoring, and Troubleshooting Security" section of the exam.

Microsoft provides the following objectives for the "Implementing, Monitoring, and Troubleshooting Security" unit:

Encrypt data on a hard disk by using Encrypting File System (EFS).

▶ This objective is necessary because someone certified in the use of Windows 2000 Server technology must understand how to locally encrypt hard drive data for maximum security against data loss from people with malicious intent.

Implement, configure, manage, and troubleshoot policies in a Windows 2000 environment.

- **Implement, configure, manage, and troubleshoot local policy in a Windows 2000 environment.**

- **Implement, configure, manage, and troubleshoot system policy in a Windows 2000 environment.**

▶ This objective is necessary because someone certified in the use of Windows 2000 Server technology must understand how local and system policies are implemented on a Windows 2000 member server and how they affect user and server function.

CHAPTER 14

Implementing, Monitoring, and Troubleshooting Security

Implement, configure, manage, and troubleshoot auditing.

▶ This objective is necessary because someone certified in the use of Windows 2000 Server technology must understand how to implement auditing for tracking resource access and failed access.

Implement, configure, manage, and troubleshoot local accounts.

▶ This objective is necessary because someone certified in the use of Windows 2000 Server technology must understand how to create and manage local accounts.

Implement, configure, manage, and troubleshoot account policy.

▶ This objective is necessary because someone certified in the use of Windows 2000 Server technology must understand how local account policy can be configured and how it affects functionality.

Implement, configure, manage, and troubleshoot security by using the Security Configuration Toolset.

▶ This objective is necessary because someone certified in the use of Windows 2000 Server technology must understand how to efficiently analyze and configure servers using the tools available in the Security Configuration Toolset.

STUDY STRATEGIES

▶ On the exam, you can expect that the new features implemented in Windows 2000 Server will be points of examination. For this chapter, that includes the Encrypting File System (EFS) and the Security Configuration Toolset (SCTS). Of course, this is not to say that the other parts of the chapter will not be tested, but you can be sure that EFS and SCTS will be.

▶ As it pertains to local accounts, you need to be familiar with the concept of the security identifier (SID) and how it uniquely identifies an account. You also need to understand the implications of deleting an account.

▶ Be sure you understand the elements of local password policy and local lockout policy. Remember that domain policy overrides these policies if they are set locally.

▶ Understand auditing as it pertains to both the exercise of rights and the access of resources relative to local and system policies. Know, for example, that file auditing requires that NTFS be implemented first.

▶ You must understand what EFS is, as well as the role of the EFS recovery agent. Be sure to understand that EFS does not prevent deletion of files, just the reading of files.

▶ You might be tested on the Security Configuration Toolset. Be sure you know how to create the consoles for managing these tools. In addition, know how to create and use templates and configuration databases.

▶ Preparation for questions based on this chapter involves being familiar with the material here and, as usual, doing the labs and walking through the Step by Steps.

▶ As has been mentioned in other chapters, nothing prepares you better than experience working with Windows 2000 Servers. Try out as many as possible of these concepts with real machines before you attempt the exam.

INTRODUCTION

Security is a major concern in any network environment. Much of any company's critical, confidential, and proprietary data is stored on servers somewhere. As a result, the ability to control access to this data is of paramount importance. Threats against data exist both externally and internally. This chapter deals with the central security mechanism in Windows 2000—the user account. From there, this chapter moves to policies you can put into place to restrict what people can do with certain accounts.

Most security configuration in a Windows 2000 environment is configured using Active Directory. Because this book deals with only Windows 2000 standalone servers, it does not talk directly about Active Directory. Where discussions of Active Directory are required to explain concepts in this chapter, it will be covered. However, material here will stay away from Active Directory whenever possible.

IMPLEMENTING, CONFIGURING, MANAGING, AND TROUBLESHOOTING LOCAL ACCOUNTS

Implement, configure, manage, and troubleshoot local accounts.

In a Windows 2000 network environment, every user must authenticate with a directory service to get access to network resources. Authentication is no more complex than providing a username the computer recognizes and a password that identifies you as being authorized to act as a certain person. Both these things rely on the presence of user accounts.

The two kinds of user accounts in Windows 2000 are domain accounts and local accounts. Domain accounts are held in the Active Directory. These accounts are available for logon from any computer that is a member of a domain.

Local accounts are held in the security database of a member or standalone server. (The difference between the two is that a member server is part of a domain, and a standalone server is part of a workgroup.) Local accounts are managed at a local computer using the Computer Management console and are recognized only by the local computer.

To allow a user to log into the server with a local account, you first need to create it. Step by Step 14.1 outlines that procedure.

ON THE CD

Step by Step 14.1, "Creating a Local Account on a Windows 2000 Member Server," walks you through creating a local account. See the file **Chapter14-01StepbyStep.pdf** in the CD's **Chapter14\StepbyStep** directory.

After an account has been created, you eventually need to manage it. Account management includes renaming, changing account properties, resetting passwords, and deleting accounts.

Renaming an Account

When an account is created, it is assigned a security identifier (SID). This SID is unique; no two accounts have the same one. Regardless of what you call yourself or how you change your name, you are still identified as the same person by this number. When you give an account access to a particular resource, it is really the SID that is put into the Discretionary Access Control List (DACL), despite the fact that you use the account name. This is why you can rename accounts without having to re-grant access to resources. Step by Step 14.2 walks you through the process of renaming a local account.

ON THE CD

Step by Step 14.2, "Renaming a Local Account on a Windows 2000 Member Server," shows you how to rename a local account. See the file **Chapter14-02StepbyStep.pdf** in the CD's **Chapter14\ StepbyStep** directory.

FIGURE 14.1

Changing account properties.

Changing Account Properties

An administrator or member of the Power Users group can change user account properties using the Computer Management console (see Figure 14.1).

By default, four property sheets are associated with each account:

◆ **General.** This property sheet allows you to change the full name and description of the user account. In addition, the user account's password can be set to be changed at next logon, set to not allow changes by the user, or set to never expire. Finally, you can disable an account or unlock an account that has been locked due to too many failed logons within a short time frame.

◆ **Member Of.** This property sheet allows you to select which groups the user account is a member of. By placing users into groups, you can make security administration easier, because any security authorization or restriction you place on a group will automatically be placed on all its members.

◆ **Profile.** This property sheet allows you to configure profile paths, logon scripts, and a home directory for the user account. These can be set locally on a computer or by using a Universal Naming Convention (UNC) path; the profile path or home directory can be configured to roam with the user account as it logs on from different computers.

◆ **Dial-In.** This property sheet allows you to configure dial-in ability and dial-in properties for the user account, including whether the account is allowed to dial-in, callback security, and user-based routing information.

Step by Step 14.3 shows you how to configure local account properties.

ON THE CD

Step by Step 14.3, "Configuring Account Properties," covers setting up local account properties. See the file **Chapter14-03StepbyStep.pdf** in the CD's **Chapter14\StepbyStep** directory.

Resetting User Account Passwords

Occasionally a user will forget his or her account password. When that happens, the user becomes locked out of network access until the password is reset. An administrator can replace the current password with a new one. If a user calls requesting that you find out the password or calls to tell you that he or she cannot remember an account password, follow Step by Step 14.4 to reset the password.

ON THE CD

Step by Step 14.4, "Resetting an Account Password," shows you how to reset a password. See the file **Chapter14-04StepbyStep.pdf** in the CD's **Chapter14\StepbyStep** directory.

Deleting a User Account

Deleting a user account is a simple process. However, it is one that you should consider carefully before you do it. If you delete the user account, that user is removed from all the groups and the DACLs for all resources. That means that if a new employee is hired or an employee returns from a leave, you have to create a new account and repopulate groups and DACLs with the new user's name.

A better solution is to disable the user account while it's not needed. Then, when a new person is hired, you can simply rename and reconfigure the account and then reenable it. This would be the same for someone on a leave of absence. The only difference is that the account does not need to be renamed. This ensures that the new user continues to have the same access rights as the old user.

However, sometimes you really do need to delete an account. If you've thought it through and you're sure you want to delete a user account, follow the process described in Step by Step 14.5.

ON THE CD

Step by Step 14.5, "Deleting a User Account," covers deletion of a user account. See the file **Chapter14-05StepbyStep.pdf** in the CD's **Chapter14\StepbyStep** directory.

WINDOWS 2000 SERVERS AND POLICIES

Policies in Windows 2000 define rules about how some aspect of user configuration or interaction works. The policies that are discussed in the next few sections define rules and parameters by which security is implemented in Windows 2000, specifically Windows 2000 member servers.

Two levels of policies are applied to Windows 2000 member servers: local policies of the server and Group Policies of the domain. Becoming a member server in a domain means that a server must obey the rules of the domain. As a result, the domain rules take precedence in cases where local policies for the server and the Group Policy conflict.

For most policy settings, when you view them, you see two sets of values for the configuration: the local setting and the effective setting (see Figure 14.2). In this book, you are introduced to the local setting because the Active Directory and Group Policy are beyond the scope of the exam. However, you must note that when you set local policy on the server, the effective policy will not change unless the Group Policy is undefined. In that case, the local policy setting is the effective setting.

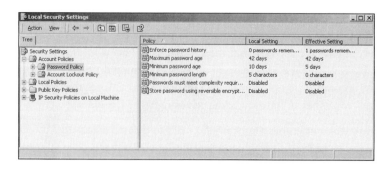

FIGURE 14.2
On a member server, the local properties are not always the effective ones.

For all the figures shown in the policy sections to follow, Group Policy settings are disabled. As a result, the effective policy will always appear as the local policy. This is generally not the case in real life, but it makes the policy settings less confusing while you are learning.

IMPLEMENTING, CONFIGURING, MANAGING, AND TROUBLESHOOTING ACCOUNT POLICY

Implement, configure, manage, and troubleshoot account policy.

In Windows 2000 Servers, account policy defines two separate policy areas: password policy and account lockout policy. *Password policy* defines how many characters passwords have to be, password aging, and other related settings. *Account lockout policies* define at what point an account is locked after too many failed password attempts, how long the lockout lasts, and when the counter is reset.

Implementing Local Password Policy

Local password policy allows you to ensure that users adhere to the password requirements for your organization. When implementing password policy, the user community must be educated to the security requirements in your organization and the possibility of external vandals breaking into their systems. If the people acknowledge the need, it becomes their need and makes the requirement much easier for them to handle.

A Windows 2000 password policy consists of six settings:

◆ **Password history.** This policy maintains a running list of the passwords that have been set for a particular account. The setting consists of a counter that's set between 0 and 24. This defines the number of unique passwords in Windows 2000 users must use before they can reuse a previous password.

If, for example, the history is set to 3 and the history records passwords of apple, orange, and banana, those three words cannot be used until they are not in the history. If the same user changes the password to cucumber, apple will be forgotten and can be used again. The reason for using a password history setting is to keep users from switching back and forth between two passwords when they are required to change them.

◆ **Maximum age.** This setting allows an administrator to exercise control over how long a user keeps the same password. Before the password expires, the user will be warned; if it does expire, the user will not be allowed to log on until the password is changed.

◆ **Minimum age.** This setting defines the minimum length of time a password must be in place before a user can change it. Although on the surface it looks as though this property contradicts the maximum age, they actually go together with the password history to form a complete package. This prevents a user from attempting to immediately change their password back to their previous password when requested to change their password.

◆ **Minimum length.** This setting allows an administrator to define the minimum length for an account password to a value between 0 and 14 characters. If the value is 0, an account password is optional.

◆ **Complexity.** Enabling this setting requires all passwords to be at least six characters long, regardless of the minimum length defined in the policy, and not contain the user's username or any single name portion of the full name. In addition, the password must contain characters from at least three of the following four character groups:

  • English uppercase characters (A, B, C...)

  • English lowercase characters (a, b, c...)

  • Arabic numerals (0, 1, 2...)

  • Nonalphanumeric characters, such as punctuation and other symbols (!, @, $, and so on)

◆ **Reverse encryption storage.** This setting is required for digest authentication for Web Servers. It stores the passwords, using a reversible encryption scheme that can be provided during the authentication process. This is considered a security risk by some network administrators.

Step by Steps 14.6 and 14.7 show how to configure local password and domain password policies, respectively.

ON THE CD

Step by Step 14.6, "Configuring Local Password Policy," covers configuration of local password policies. See the file **Chapter14-06StepbyStep.pdf** in the CD's **Chapter14\StepbyStep** directory.

Step by Step 14.7, "Configuring Domain Password Policy," covers configuration of domain password policies. See the file **Chapter14-07StepbyStep.pdf** in the CD's **Chapter14\StepbyStep** directory.

Implementing Local Account Lockout Policy

Account lockout policy allows administrators to ensure that they have control over how many times a user can enter an incorrect password and what happens at the point when they think that an attempt to crack the network is occurring. You can control how many bad passwords can be entered before the account is locked. You can control how long the counter tracking incorrect lockouts stays active. You can also control how long an account is locked before a user can access it again.

A Windows 2000 account lockout policy consists of three settings:

◆ **Account Lockout Duration.** This setting allows you to define the length of time an account will remain locked out before it is released. This number can be set from 0 to 99999 minutes; 0 represents an infinite time, which requires an administrator to manually unlock the account. When an account is locked, it can be unlocked from the General property sheet of the Properties dialog box for the user account.

◆ **Account Lockout Threshold.** This setting allows you to define the number of incorrect password attempts that will cause the account to be locked out from the network (unavailable to the user). This number can be set from 0 to 999, where 0 represents an infinite number of attempts. The higher the security you want in your organization, the smaller this number should be.

◆ **Reset Account Lockout Counter After.** This setting allows you to define the length of time Windows 2000 remembers failed logon attempts before resetting the counter to 0. This number can be set from 1 to 99999 minutes. The implication of this setting is that after users have typed a password incorrectly a couple of times, they can wait a predefined length of time and try again, knowing that the previous two attempts will not be held against them. Regardless of this setting, a correct logon password resets the counter to 0.

Step by Steps 14.8 and 14.9 (respectively) demonstrate how to configure lockout policy locally and in a domain.

ON THE CD

Step by Step 14.8, "Configuring Local Account Lockout Policy," covers configuration of local lockout policy. See the file **Chapter14-08StepbyStep.pdf** in the CD's **Chapter14\StepbyStep** directory.

Step by Step 14.9, "Configuring Domain Account Lockout Policy," covers configuration of domain lockout policy. See the file **Chapter14-09StepbyStep.pdf** in the CD's **Chapter14\StepbyStep** directory.

Troubleshooting Account Policy

Most troubleshooting in the realm of account policies involves understanding the implications of the different settings and how they interact with one another. One of the biggest sources of trouble with account policy is the interaction of complexity requirements with the other account policy and account lockout settings. Be sure that users understand the requirements for passwords under an enforced complexity policy. This prevents confusion when passwords are rejected for not conforming to the rules.

IMPLEMENTING, CONFIGURING, MANAGING, AND TROUBLESHOOTING LOCAL POLICY AND GROUP POLICIES

Implement, configure, manage, and troubleshoot policies in a Windows 2000 environment.

Local and Group Policies on a Windows 2000 member server allow you to control the environment a user is allowed to operate in. Profiles record what a user *has* done and how the desktop has been configured, but these policies define what a user *can* do. Policies may control user rights to log on to a server locally or to shut a server down. Policies may control whether the Run command is found in the start menu and what wallpaper is present on the desktop.

As with other policies, because a member server is part of a domain, the local policy settings are subject to the Group Policy settings and, as a result, effective settings might not be those that were configured locally.

Configuring Local Policies on a Windows 2000 Member Server

Local policies on a Windows 2000 member server define three areas of configurations:

◆ Audit Policy

◆ User Rights Assignment

◆ Security Options

Implementing Audit Policy

Audit policy allows the tracking of various resource access rights exercised on your server, based on either successes or failures. Before any auditing can occur on a Windows 2000 Server, the audit policy must be adjusted to allow auditing in that area. Figure 14.3 shows events marked for auditing.

Configuring a particular event or access to be audited is, for the most part, as simple as opening the entry and selecting Success and/or Failure. Success auditing tracks every time a specific event occurs successfully (for example, every time anyone successfully logs on to the server). Failure auditing tracks only those events that did not happen because the users did not have sufficient rights or permissions to do what they tried to do (for example, every time someone tries to access a folder for which NTFS security settings disallow access to that user).

One audit setting, Audit Object Access, requires more configuration than simply enabling success or failure. Object access applies to printers, files, and folders. For access to specific objects to be audited, the object has to be enabled for auditing as well as the general policy of audit access. This is touched on again in the section "Implementing, Configuring, Managing, and Troubleshooting Auditing," later in this chapter.

Step by Steps 14.10 and 14.11 walk you through setting up local audit and domain audit policies, respectively.

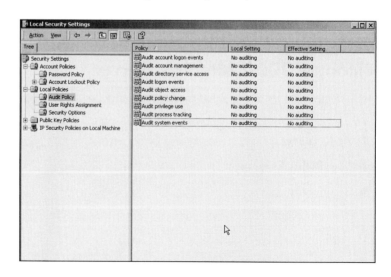

FIGURE 14.3
You can audit a variety of event types, which is configured by the audit policy.

ON THE CD

Step by Step 14.10, "Configuring Local Audit Policy," shows you how to set up local audit policies. See the file **Chapter14-10StepbyStep.pdf** in the CD's **Chapter14\StepbyStep** directory.

Step by Step 14.11, "Configuring Centralized Audit Policy," shows you how to set up a centralized audit policy. See the file **Chapter14-11StepbyStep.pdf** in the CD's **Chapter14\StepbyStep** directory.

Implementing User Rights Assignment

Assigning user rights allows the administrator to control who is allowed to do special tasks or have special privileges on the server. Most tasks a user would want to undertake are covered under the User Rights Assignment policy. This policy covers all the administrative tasks and some of the mundane tasks that might be carried out on a server.

Unlike the other policies you have seen so far, the assignment of a user right is based on inclusion in the list of SIDs that have been assigned that user right.

This list contains some of the user rights that you might find helpful:

- ◆ **Access This Computer from the Network.** Defines users' ability to log on and access resources from the network. By default, everyone has this right.

- ◆ **Back Up Files and Directories.** Defines who can perform backups on the computer. This right allows the specified users to bypass local security to place files onto backup tape.

- ◆ **Log On Locally.** Defines which user accounts will be allowed to authenticate locally at a Windows 2000 standalone server. Although the default setting is to allow Everyone to log on locally, to increase security, you might want to remove the Users group from this list.

- ◆ **Restore Files and Directories.** Defines who can restore information to the server from a backup.

◆ **Take Ownership of Files or Other Objects.** Defines who can take ownership of any files or objects on the server. By default, all people in the local Administrators group have this right.

Step by Steps 14.12 and 14.13 define the procedures for configuring a local user right and a domain user right, respectively.

ON THE CD

Step by Step 14.12, "Configuring a Local User Right," presents you with an example of how to configure a local user right. See the file **Chapter14-12StepbyStep.pdf** in the CD's **Chapter14\StepbyStep** directory.

Step by Step 14.13, "Configuring Centralized User Rights," walks you through configuring a domain user right. See the file **Chapter14-13StepbyStep.pdf** in the CD's **Chapter14\StepbyStep** directory.

Implementing Security Options

Security options define the basic and complex security settings that can be configured on a systemwide basis. These options create a number of security restrictions or perform system tasks to ensure a secure environment. These options are settings-oriented, generally not pointed toward specific users. Where they are, lists of users are provided as the properties for the option.

This list contains security options that you might find helpful:

◆ **Clear Virtual Memory Pagefile When System Shuts Down.** Ensures that when a server is shut down, the page file is deleted. This prevents the page file from being examined after a reboot.

◆ **Do Not Display Last User Name in Logon Screen.** Defines whether the username of the last person to log onto a Windows 2000 machine is displayed for logon convenience. Enabling this option ensures the User Name field always comes up blank.

◆ **Message Text for Users Attempting to Log On.** Defines the text of a special security dialog box that appears just before the Logon dialog box. This text box is used to make it clear to users who owns the system, who is welcome, and who is not welcome. For example, you might configure a message such as this: `Network access is restricted to Company XYZ Inc. employees only!`.

Step by Steps 14.14 and 14.15 show you how to configure a local security option and a domain user right, respectively.

ON THE CD

Step by Step 14.14, "Configuring a Security Option," walks you through setting up a local security option. See the file **Chapter14-14StepbyStep.pdf** in the CD's **Chapter14\StepbyStep** directory.

Step by Step 14.15, "Configuring Centralized Security Options," covers setting up centralized security options through the domain. See the file **Chapter14-15StepbyStep.pdf** in the CD's **Chapter14\StepbyStep** directory.

Configuring Local Policy on a Windows 2000 Member Server

Windows 2000 allows tuning system configuration settings through the Group Policy Editor snap-in. In a domain environment, the Group Policy Editor allows computer and user settings to be configured for a Group Policy Container (sites, domains, and organization units). On a member server, the Group Policy Editor can be focused on the Local Computer object to configure the local policy for the computer and user of the computer.

To edit the local policy of a computer, you must create a console that has the Group Policy snap-in loaded. You can do this by creating a new console or by adding the Group Policy to one that already exists. Step by Step 14.16 describes how to add the snap-in.

ON THE CD

Step by Step 14.16, "Creating a Group Policy Console," shows you how to add the snap-in for the Group Policy console. See the file **Chapter14-16StepbyStep.pdf** in the CD's **Chapter14\StepbyStep** directory.

After you create the console following Step by Step 14.16, you can access it by choosing Start, Programs, Administrative Tools, Local Policy.

As you can see in Figure 14.4, the Group Policy console consists of two main sections: the computer configuration and the user configuration.

An administrator can manage specific Registry settings by configuring Administrative templates for computer configuration (when the Registry settings are applied to the HKEY_LOCAL_MACHINE Registry key) or for user configuration (when the Registry settings are applied to the HKEY_CURRENT_USER key).

FIGURE 14.4

The Local Computer Policy console allows configuration of the various security Administrative Templates for the computer and users.

Administrative Templates in Computer Configuration

Administrative Templates for computer configuration are divided into four sections:

◆ **Windows Components.** Allows you to define settings for the configuration and operation of NetMeeting, Internet Explorer, Task Scheduler, and Windows Installer.

◆ **System.** Allows you to configure logon, disk quotas, DNS client configuration, Group Policy configuration, and Windows File protection.

◆ **Network.** Allows you to configure network operations in areas pertaining to offline files and network and dialup connections.

◆ **Printers.** Allows you to configure computer properties pertaining to printers and printing.

Administrative Templates in User Configuration

The settings defined in the Administration Templates for users are applied to every user who logs on to the member server. These settings primarily have the effect of removing icons and tools from sight or from access (for example, you can disable access to the Control Panel):

◆ **Windows Components.** Allows you to set configuration settings for such components as NetMeeting, Internet Explorer, Windows Explorer, Microsoft Management Console, Task Scheduler, and Windows Installer.

◆ **Start Menu & Taskbar.** Allows you to define what components show and do not show on the Start menu and what kinds of functions can be performed from the Start menu.

◆ **Desktop.** Allows you to customize the desktop including what icons will be displayed.

◆ **Control Panel.** Allows you to define what components (if any) of the Control Panel are accessible and what options function.

◆ **Network.** Allows you to configure network operations in areas pertaining to offline files and network and dialup connections.

◆ **System.** Allows you to define how the system looks to the user, including using a custom shell replacing Explorer and how logon/logoff functions.

Modifying the System Policy

When you modify the Administrative Templates in the Group Policy console, two files are created. A file called NTUSER.POL is created in the profile location for the current user. In addition, a file called REGISTRY.POL is created in the path `\WINNT\System32\ GroupPolicy\User`.

ON THE CD

Step by Step 14.17, "Modifying System Policy," addresses changing the System Policy. See the file **Chapter14-17StepbyStep.pdf** in the CD's **Chapter14\StepbyStep** directory.

IMPLEMENTING, CONFIGURING, MANAGING, AND TROUBLESHOOTING AUDITING

Implement, configure, manage, and troubleshoot auditing.

Auditing is the process by which you track access to system resources. The access that you track may be general (such as logging on) or specific (such as access to a specific file), and it may be successful access or unsuccessful access.

Auditing is done mainly when you are concerned about people trying to access specific resources that they are not supposed to access. However, it is sometimes necessary to check resource usage and to track that usage.

Step by Step 14.17 describes how to change the System Policy.

Auditing and the Audit Policy

Configuring auditing begins with an audit policy. That policy will encompass all the facets of system use that you want to track. The method for setting up an audit policy was discussed in this chapter in the section "Implementing Audit Policy." Let's look more closely at the kinds of events you can audit and what configuration settings are required to audit (specifically as it relates to object access).

Table 14.1 lists Audit Policy settings and what activities are included in each audit policy.

When you have decided which area you want to audit, you must determine whether you are interested in successes or failures. You should audit successes when you are interested in knowing each time a resource (such as a specific financial report) is accessed. You should audit failures if you are interested in knowing every time someone tried to access a resource but failed because of insufficient rights. This could be used to determine whether someone is trying to hack into your system by manually (or automatically) trying to guess an account password.

TABLE 14.1

AUDIT POLICIES

Audit Policy	Encompasses
Account Logon	Requests made to validate user accounts.
Account Management	Modification of a user account or group. This includes adding and deleting accounts and changing passwords or other account properties.
Directory Service Access	Access to Active Directory objects. This does not apply to audit policy on member servers.
Logon	The actual logging on or off of a user.
Object Access	User gained access to a file, folder, or printer to perform any action (read, write, delete, manage, and so on).
Policy Change	Modification to any of the security policy properties, user rights, or audit policies.
Privilege Use	The exercise of any user right (such as changing system time or shutting down a server).
Process Tracking	Actions performed by a program. This is generally of interest only to programmers who want to track certain events that their programs are causing.
System	Server was started or stopped, or the Security log filled up and entries have been discarded.

Most audit configurations are as simple as enabling success or failure auditing. The exception is the auditing of object access. Object access is a finely tunable audit event. When the audit policy is in place, you must configure the individual objects (files, folders, printers) for the kind of events you are looking for and the people you want to watch. Finally, to add one more variable, you can audit only file objects on NTFS volumes.

Step by Step 14.18 describes how to configure file resource auditing.

ON THE CD

Step by Step 14.18, "Configuring File Resource Auditing," covers configuration of file resource auditing. See the file **Chapter14-18StepbyStep.pdf** in the CD's **Chapter14\StepbyStep** directory.

When you have an audit policy in place, you need to check on the logged events occasionally. It is a good idea to regularly do this, because you cannot know what is happening unless you take time to look at the logs.

Auditing and the Security Log

Audit events are written into the Security log on the local machine. This Security log can be accessed from the Event Viewer, which is a part of the Administrative Tools. An administrator can configure the following settings for the Security log:

◆ Set the default size for the Security log. The more you audit, the larger the Security log should be set.

◆ Configure what to do when the log fills up. Your choices are to overwrite old events, to overwrite old events only if they are beyond a certain age, or to never overwrite old events. In a high-security environment, you might want to enable the security policy item that shuts down the server when the security log is full (this prevents anyone from accessing anything if it cannot be tracked).

◆ Archive log entries at any time so you can have a permanent record of all log entries made throughout history.

Step by Steps 14.19 and 14.20 show how to configure the Security log properties and how to archive log entries, respectively.

ON THE CD

Step by Step 14.19, "Configuring Security Log Properties," walks you through setting up the Security log properties. See the file **Chapter14-19StepbyStep.pdf** in the CD's **Chapter14\StepbyStep** directory.

Step by Step 14.20, "Archiving Log Entries," walks you through archiving log entries. See the file **Chapter14-20StepbyStep.pdf** in the CD's **Chapter14\StepbyStep** directory.

Depending on what event you audit, the Security log can contain numerous events. To find specific events, you can implement filters. You can choose to see only certain event types; in the case of security, you can see either successes or failures. You can also choose to filter out events that fall outside of a particular time range. Step by Step 14.21 shows you how to view and filter events in the log.

ON THE CD

Step by Step 14.21, "Viewing and Filtering Security Log Entries," covers viewing and filtering events in the log. See the file **Chapter14-21StepbyStep.pdf** in the CD's **Chapter14\StepbyStep** directory.

Troubleshooting Auditing

Problems with auditing usually occur for one of three reasons:

◆ You are collecting too much data.

◆ You are collecting too little data.

◆ You are not collecting the right data.

To get auditing configured right, you have to begin with a goal. The goal should never be to collect information; information gathering is only a tool that helps you reach your goal. If, for example, your goal is to investigate how many attempts are made to hack into your server at night, you will want to audit failed logon attempts and then filter the results to show only those that occurred during certain hours.

Troubleshooting auditing always comes down to your understanding what the policies are and then applying what you know about them to the goal you want auditing to help you reach.

ENCRYPTING DATA USING ENCRYPTING FILE SYSTEM

Encrypt data on a hard disk by using Encrypting File System (EFS).

One of the issues with NTFS file security on Windows 2000 volumes is that it is dependent on the drive being in the computer on which the files were created. You can gain access to NTFS files if you can steal the hard drive out of the computer, because, by putting the drive into another computer, the local administrator can take ownership of the files and access the data.

Local encryption has long been available through third-party software as a way of ensuring that only the user who encrypted them can access the files. The Encrypting File System (EFS) is built into NTFS version 5, so no add-ons are required. In addition, when it is in place, encryption and decryption of data happens transparently to the user.

Although encryption is extremely useful for locally securing data, it comes with a price. Encrypted data cannot be used on file systems except NTFS version 5; this means that it cannot be applied to FAT and FAT32 partitions. In addition, encrypted files are secure only on the hard drive; if you access an encrypted file over the network, the network transmission of the data is not secure unless you also use network encryption such as IPSec. Finally, encryption is not compatible with compression; if you encrypt a compressed file, the compression will be removed.

Although encryption secures data from being accessed, that does not eliminate the need for NTFS security. Encryption prevents a file's contents from being viewed or modified; however, it does not prevent the file from being deleted. To ensure the best security, make sure that both encryption and NTFS security are applied.

The following principles apply to the encryption attribute:

◆ You can designate a folder as being encrypted by setting its Encryption attribute; however, the folder is not actually encrypted, only its contents are.

◆ If a folder is encrypted, all new content created in, copied into, or moved into the folder is also automatically encrypted.

◆ If a file is encrypted and is copied or moved into an unencrypted folder, the Encryption attribute is retained unless the folder is located on a non-NTFS partition—in which case, the encryption is removed.

◆ When a file is encrypted, the file can be decrypted only by the user who encrypted the file and by a designated recovery agent. (For more information on how EFS works, please see the section titled "Understanding EFS Encryption," which follows.°

Step by Step 14.22 outlines how to encrypt a file or folder.

ON THE CD

Step by Step 14.22, "Encrypting a File or Folder," shows you how to encrypt a file or folder. See the file **Chapter14-22StepbyStep.pdf** in the CD's **Chapter14\StepbyStep** directory.

For your convenience, Windows 2000 also offers a command-line utility that encrypts files and folders with your encryption key called CIPHER.EXE. For most applications, you will find it more convenient to use the GUI to encrypt. However, some useful features are found only in the command-line version. For example, cipher allows you to encrypt only those files with the .DOC extension. CIPHER also allows you to force encryption of files that

Windows 2000 thinks are encrypted but have not been because an error prevented them from being encrypted completely. For example, if the power failed during encryption, a file's encryption attribute might have been set before the file actually got encrypted.

The basic syntax of the CIPHER program is as follows:

```
CIPHER [/e or /d] [/s:dir] [/i] [/f] [/q] [filename(s)]
```

Table 14.2 lists the parameters you can set when performing encryption using the CIPHER program.

TABLE 14.2

CIPHER PARAMETERS

Parameter	Function
none	Displays the encryption state of the current folder.
/e	Encrypts the specified folder or file.
/d	Decrypts the specified folder or file.
/s:dir	Applies the encryption or decryption to the folder specified by dir. If dir is missing, it applies to the current folder. This applies to all files and subfolders as well.
/I	Ignores any errors during encryption (by default, an error causes encryption to fail).
/f	Forces encryption or decryption, even if the attributes indicate that the objects to be acted on are already in that state. (This allows the repair of objects for which the Encryption attribute is incorrectly set because of system error during the last encryption or decryption attempt.)
/q	Does not report detailed progress information.
/filename	Indicates the file or folder to encrypt. Many files or folders can be listed with spaces between them, and wildcard characters (* and ?) can be used. If you use wildcards, no folder in the tree will have its Encryption attribute set unless it conforms to the wildcard format.

Understanding EFS Encryption

The EFS encryption process takes place using the following steps (see Figure 14.5) :

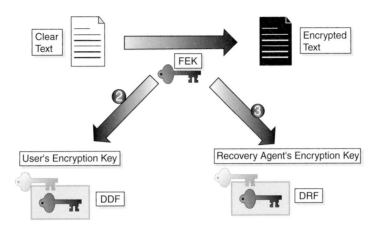

FIGURE 14.5
The EFS encryption process.

1. EFS encryption encrypts the data file using a file encryption key (FEK).

2. The FEK is stored in a header attached to the encrypted data file known as the data decryption field (DDF). The DDF is encrypted so that only the user that encrypted the file can decrypt the FEK. After the user has decrypted the FEK, he or she can decrypt the data file using the FEK.

3. The FEK is also stored in a second header known as the data recovery field (DRF). The DRF is encrypted so that only the designated recovery agent can decrypt the FEK. After the recovery agent has decrypted the FEK, he or she can decrypt the data file using the FEK.

Implementing an EFS Recovery Policy and Recovering Encrypted Files

With encryption-based security comes a large inherent weakness: If a user's account is deleted, the ability to decrypt data can be lost if a recovery agent is not defined. Therefore, it is imperative that before encryption starts to be used in your organization, a recovery policy is put into place. Such a policy designates someone as a recovery agent and allows that account to decrypt any encrypted data.

When a Windows 2000 Server is installed, a default recovery policy is put into place. In fact, without such a policy, encryption is not available on the machine at all. This policy consists of the designation of the local administrator as the recovery agent. This user is capable of recovering files encrypted by any user on the local machine.

To recover a file that has been encrypted with an encryption key that is no longer available, that file must be sent to the recovery agent, who is authorized to decrypt any file. When it is decrypted, the file can then be sent back to the original location.

USING THE SECURITY CONFIGURATION TOOLSET

Implement, configure, manage, and troubleshoot security by using the Security Configuration Toolset.

Security is an integral part of Windows 2000 Server. Hardly an area in the administrative structure is not impacted by security in some way. The Security Configuration Toolset is an integrated tool for analyzing and configuring your servers and workstations. It allows you to create baselines that can be used as the basis for configuring other servers and workstations. Finally, it allows you to analyze security configuration against those baselines and to ultimately use the defined baselines.

All the security tools discussed in this chapter (and more) are configurable using the Security Configuration Toolset. This includes analysis and settings for the following security areas:

- ◆ Account policies
- ◆ Local policies
- ◆ Event log
- ◆ Restricted (system) groups
- ◆ System services
- ◆ Registry
- ◆ The file system

Using the Security Configuration Toolset is straightforward. After you start it, you can load a predefined security template. This security template can be either a default security template shipped with Windows 2000 or one that you've created specifically for the servers, workstations, or domain controllers in your environment.

The template file defines the recommended security settings in a number of areas for computers in specific roles with specific security requirements (generally, security is defined as basic, secure, and high secure). These INF files can be used to check your Windows 2000 machines against the recommended setups, and then, if wanted, configure the settings on your machines to conform to the settings. Deploying security templates ensures that all your domain controllers, servers, and workstations are configured with the same settings without having to configure each computer individually.

When you install Windows 2000, a number of security templates are installed in the `\WINNT\Security\Templates` folder. Some of those templates are described in Table 14.3.

TABLE 14.3

PREDEFINED SECURITY TEMPLATES

Template Filename	*Description*
BASICDC.INF	A basic security domain controller. Specifies default security settings for all security areas, with the exception of user rights and group memberships. Designed for low-to-medium security environments.
SECUREDC.INF	A secure domain controller. Beginning from default settings, this increases security settings for account policy, auditing, and registry keys. This template assumes that BASICDC.INF was installed before it.
HISECDC.INF	A high-security domain controller. This assumes a network environment containing only Windows 2000 Servers and workstations, because the security precludes communication with any other machines. This template defines security for network communications that are digitally signed and encrypted. This template assumes that BASICDC.INF was installed before it.
BASICSV.INF	A basic security Windows 2000 Server (non–domain controller). Same as BASICDC.INF, only for standalone or member servers.
BASICWK.INF	A basic security Windows 2000 Professional client. Same as BASICDC.INF, only for workstations.
SECUREWS.INF	A secure Windows 2000 Professional client. Same as SECUREDC.INF, only designed for workstations.
HISECWS.INF	A high-security Windows 2000 Professional client. Same as HISECDC.INF, only designed for workstations.

Creating the Security Configuration Toolset Console

To access the Security Configuration Toolset, you first have to create a Microsoft Management Console that includes the Security Configuration and Analysis snap-in. Setting up the console is illustrated in Step by Step 14.23.

ON THE CD

Step by Step 14.23, "Creating the Security Configuration Toolset Console," covers setting up the console. See the file **Chapter14-23StepbyStep.pdf** in the CD's **Chapter14\StepbyStep** directory.

After you create the console as described in Step by Step 14.23, you can access it by choosing Start, Programs, Administrative Tools, Security Configuration and Analysis.

Analyzing Your Server

Analyzing a server begins with a configuration database, which you create by applying one or more security templates to a blank configuration. This database can be saved and used to analyze the server again and again. In addition, you can export its settings to create a new template you can then use to create databases for the analysis of other servers.

When a database is first created, a security template must be imported into it. At that point, additional security templates can be merged until the configuration database is complete.

Step by Step 14.24 shows how to create and configure a configuration database.

ON THE CD

Step by Step 14.24, "Creating and Configuring a Configuration Database," covers creating and configuring a configuration database. See the file **Chapter14-24StepbyStep.pdf** in the CD's **Chapter14\StepbyStep** directory.

After you create the configuration database, you are ready to analyze the local computer with it. Step by Step 14.25 describes this process.

ON THE CD

Step by Step 14.25, "Analyzing a Server with a Configuration Database," illustrates analysis of a server. See the file **Chapter14-25StepbyStep.pdf** in the CD's **Chapter14\StepbyStep** directory.

When the analysis is complete, you can examine the results in the GUI interface by expanding the security sections and comparing the Database Setting with the Computer Setting for the same policy entries. An icon is displayed next to each property to help you. An icon with a green check mark means there is a setting in the database, and it is the same as the computer setting. A red circle with an X in it indicates there is a setting in the database, and it is not the same as the computer setting (see Figure 14.6). An icon with neither a check mark nor an X indicates the setting is not defined in the database or on the server.

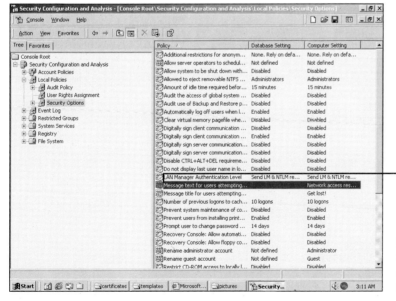

— Red Circle with a white X

FIGURE 14.6
Red circle with a white X
A red circle with a white X in it indicates a contradiction in settings.

If, after the analysis, you decide that a database entry should be changed, you can change it by double-clicking the entry and filling in the value you want. As the notes on the dialog boxes indicate, this changes only the database and not the system configuration.

Creating a New Security Template

There are two ways to create a new security template. Either you can modify an existing security template using the Security Templates snap-in, or you can export a current database's settings to a security template file. Step by Step 14.26 shows how to modify an existing Security Template using the Security Templates snap-in.

ON THE CD

Step by Step 14.26, "Modifying an Existing Template," covers modifying a security template using the Security Templates snap-in. See the file **Chapter14-26StepbyStep.pdf** in the CD's **Chapter14\StepbyStep** directory.

On the other hand, if your configuration includes a number of security templates and some manual modifications, you are well advised to configure a database and then export it. This process is illustrated in Step by Step 14.27.

ON THE CD

Step by Step 14.27, "Exporting a Database Configuration to a Template," covers the process of exporting a database to a template. See the file **Chapter14-27StepbyStep.pdf** in the CD's **Chapter14\StepbyStep** directory.

Configuring a Server Using a Configuration Database

With a configuration database that has been created for your server, you can easily configure your server to conform to the database. This ensures that the server meets the minimum security standards for your organization. In addition, by leaving server-unique settings undefined in the database, you can allow some flexibility on the part of individual administrators for special properties.

Step by Step 14.28 demonstrates how to export a configuration database to a security template.

ON THE CD

Step by Step 14.28, "Exporting a Configuration Database to a Template," illustrates how to export a configuration database to a security template. See the file **Chapter14-28StepbyStep.pdf** in the CD's **Chapter14\StepbyStep** directory.

CASE STUDY: PAYROLL IS US

ESSENCE OF THE CASE

This case requires that the following results be satisfied:

▶ Force users to change passwords more frequently.

▶ Adjust other password options as necessary.

▶ Determine who is accessing critical files.

▶ Determine who is printing critical files and when.

SCENARIO

Matthew is the network administrator for Payroll Is Us (PIU), a North American payroll company specializing in custom payroll solutions for companies with 1,000 or more employees. Security is a major issue at PIU—physical security, that is. The company has locks on the doors and uses guards with guns and armor-plated trucks. However, to this point, their network security has been rather lax. A survey of the 500 employees indicates that many have not changed their password since the day they were hired, and many have the password "password," which is the default for new accounts. Even the Administrator password for the domain is easy to remember (and guess): "payroll."

What has really brought this issue to a head is the apparent leak of confidential information from the company's databases and from people's network shares. Confidential memos are being referred to in the newspaper, and PIU's clients are getting calls from businesses that seem to know how many employees they have and what those employees' salaries are (more than a little disconcerting for the clients and the management of PIU). They think that access to this data is coming primarily from people on the outside hacking into the corporate network using passwords that have been guessed.

Your job is to tighten security. At this point, the security needs to focus on passwords and auditing, but you will be given more latitude to make further changes if you prove to be successful at this task.

CASE STUDY: PAYROLL IS US

ANALYSIS

Through the judicious use of policies, Matthew can attain all the stated goals. He can begin by applying account policy. In this way, he can control how many characters passwords must contain, how often passwords need to be changed, how long they must be in place before they can be changed again, and how many passwords are remembered to prevent duplicates too often. In addition, he can also put lockout policies in place to prevent brute-force attacks on the logon process (creating programs to send random passwords at the logon to attempt to guess the password)—or at the very least, to prevent those attacks from succeeding. These account policies might eliminate the current visible problems.

To satisfy the requirements of determining who is accessing and printing critical files, Matthew can implement an audit policy. This allows him to determine what level of auditing he wants (whether to watch for reads or writes or changes) and which files to audit. Of course, for these audits to work, he must make sure all the hard drives are converted to NTFS. He can also apply auditing to printers to determine who is using them and when and what is being printed when they are being used. The System log can then be monitored periodically to determine who is accessing resources.

The following table summarizes Matthew's solution.

OVERVIEW OF THE REQUIREMENTS AND SOLUTIONS IN THIS CASE STUDY

Requirement	Solution Provided By
Force users to change passwords.	Implement account policies to force passwords to be changed frequently.
Implement other password controls.	Implement account policies to save history, control password age, and configure lockout policies.
Determine who is accessing files.	Configure audit policies on critical files to watch for access.
Monitor printing of critical files.	Configure audit policies on printers.

CHAPTER SUMMARY

KEY TERMS

- Local account
- Security identifier (SID)
- Local password policy
- Password history
- Password age
- Account lockout
- Audit policy
- User rights
- System policy
- Configuration templates
- Security log
- Encrypting File System (EFS)
- File Encryption Key (FEK)
- Data Decryption Field (DDF)
- Data Recovery Field (DRF)
- Security Configuration Toolset
- Security template
- Security configuration database

Summarized briefly, this chapter covered the following main points.

◆ **Creating and managing local accounts.** This includes creating, renaming, configuring, and deleting local user accounts.

◆ **Establishing and maintaining account policy.** This includes configuring password length, history, age, and complexity and using reversible encryption. This also includes configuring lockout polices for accounts and recovering locked out accounts.

◆ **Configuring local and group policies.** This includes configuring audit policy and user rights and configuring and using computer and user security templates.

◆ **Configuring and managing auditing.** This includes creating and activating an audit log and investigating the Security log.

◆ **Encrypting data using the Encrypting File System.** This includes implementing EFS locally and recognizing the implications of doing so.

◆ **Using the Security Configuration Toolset.** This includes creating the Security Configuration Toolset console, implementing server configuration analysis, creating and modifying security templates, and setting up server configuration using configuration databases.

APPLY YOUR KNOWLEDGE

Review Questions

1. How are accounts identified internally by Windows 2000, and what is the implication of deleting an account?

2. When a Windows 2000 Server is part of a domain, what is the interaction between domain policy and local policy?

3. What criteria apply to an account password when complexity rules are enforced?

4. Logically, what is the rationale for denying most users in your organization the right to log onto a server locally?

5. To audit access to a specific file on a Windows 2000 Server, what three administrative tasks must first be done?

6. To ensure that all files encrypted by EFS on a Windows 2000 computer can be accessed by at least one person, a recovery agent must be designated. Who is the default recovery agent on a Windows 2000 Server?

7. What steps are required for automating the configuration of a Windows 2000 Server to a specific security specification, using the Security Configuration Tool Set?

Answers to Review Questions

1. Accounts are identified internally using a security identifier (SID). These SIDs are assigned object access and user rights. Because the SID and not the username is effectively given access to resources, if an account is deleted, that SID ceases to exist, and object access is effectively terminated for that user. If a user account is created with the same username, the SID will be different, so that account will not have the same access to the resources, and all DACLs and rights must be reassigned. For more information, see the section "Implementing, Configuring, Managing, and Troubleshooting Local Accounts."

2. When a Windows 2000 Server is part of a domain, the domain policy settings (when configured) become the effective policy settings. When a policy setting is not configured at the domain level, the local policy becomes the effective policy setting. For more information, see the section "Windows 2000 Member Servers and Policies."

3. Enforcing complexity rules ensures that passwords must conform to three of the following four criteria: lowercase characters, uppercase characters, numbers, and symbolic characters. In addition, these passwords must be at least six characters long and cannot contain any parts of the username. For more information, see the section "Implementing Local Password Policy."

4. Denying local logon access to servers is recommended because it reduces the local access a user has to a server. Local access is always a potential security problem because it allows access to files on FAT and FAT32 partitions and also allows a user to bypass any share permissions that have been established. Removing local logon also means that users will not be tempted to use the server as a workstation. For more information, see the section "Configuring Local Policies on a Windows 2000 Member Server."

APPLY YOUR KNOWLEDGE

5. To audit access to file resources, three things must be done. First, the partition on which the files are located must be (or must be converted to) NTFS. Second, local (or domain) policy must be set to enable auditing of object access. Third, each file resource must have its audit settings configured for the type of access to be audited. For more information, see the section "Implementing, Configuring, Managing, and Troubleshooting Auditing."

6. The default EFS recovery agent on a Windows 2000 Server is the local administrator. This person has the ability to decrypt any file encrypted using EFS on that server. For more information, see the section "Encrypting Data Using Encrypting File System."

7. Before you can automate the configuration of a Windows 2000 computer, you must take the following steps. First, if required, create and configure a custom configuration template. Second, create a configuration database using a predefined or a custom configuration template. Third, configure the server using the configuration database. For more information, see the section "Using the Security Configuration Toolset."

ON THE CD

This book's companion CD contains specially designed supplemental material to help you understand how well you know the concepts and skills you learned in this chapter. You'll find related exercises, review questions and answers, and exam questions and answers. See the file **Chapter14ApplyYourKnowledge.pdf** in the CD's **Chapter14\ApplyYourKnowledge** directory.

Suggested Readings and Resources

1. Microsoft Windows 2000 Server Resource Kit: *Microsoft Windows 2000 Server Deployment Planning* Guide. Microsoft Press, 2000.

   - Chapter 11: Planning Distributed Security

2. Microsoft Windows 2000 Server Resource Kit: *Microsoft Windows 2000 Server Distributed Systems Guide.* Microsoft Press, 2000.

   - Chapter 15: Encrypting File System
   - Chapter 22: Group Policy

3. *Microsoft Windows 2000 Professional Resource Kit.* Microsoft Press, 2000.

   - Chapter 7: Introduction to Configuration and Management
   - Chapter 13: Security
   - Chapter 23: Windows 2000 Professional on Microsoft Networks
   - Chapter 24: Interoperability with NetWare

4. Microsoft Official Curriculum course 1556: *Administrating Microsoft Windows 2000.*

   - Module 2: Setting Up User Accounts
   - Module 5: Administering User Accounts
   - Module 7: Managing Data Storage

5. Microsoft Official Curriculum course 1557: *Installing and Configuring Microsoft Windows 2000.*

   - Module 10: Configuring File Resources

6. Microsoft Official Curriculum course 1558: *Advanced Administration for Microsoft Windows 2000.*

   - Module 8: Implementing Security in a Windows 2000 Network

7. Microsoft Official Curriculum course 1560: *Updating Support Skills from Microsoft Windows NT 4.0 to Microsoft Window 2000.*

   - Module 12: Securing Windows 2000

8. Microsoft Official Curriculum course 2152: *Supporting Microsoft Windows 2000 Professional.*

   - Module 4: Creating and Managing User Accounts
   - Module 10: Implementing Windows 2000 Security

9. Web Sites

   - www.microsoft.com/windows2000
   - www.microsoft.com/train_cert

IMPLEMENTING AND ADMINISTERING A MICROSOFT WINDOWS 2000 NETWORK INFRASTRUCTURE

This chapter discusses network infrastructure with Domain Name System (DNS). DNS is the forerunner of many of the name resolution and directory services available today. We cover the "Installing, Configuring, Managing, Monitoring, and Troubleshooting DNS in a Windows 2000 Network Infrastructure" objectives for this exam. One of the most important services in a Transmission Control Protocol/Internet Protocol (TCP/IP) infrastructure—particularly one running Active Directory—is DNS. In this chapter, we examine all the facets of running the DNS server in a Windows 2000 network.

Microsoft defines the "Installing, Configuring, Managing, Monitoring, and Troubleshooting DNS in a Windows 2000 Network Infrastructure" objectives as:

Install, configure, and troubleshoot DNS.

- **Install the DNS service.**
- **Configure a root name server.**
- **Configure zones.**
- **Configure a caching-only server.**
- **Configure a DNS client computer.**
- **Configure zones for dynamic updates.**
- **Test the DNS server service.**
- **Implement a delegated zone for DNS.**
- **Manually create DNS resource records.**

▶ One of your first tasks when getting ready to deploy a production Windows 2000 network environment is to ensure that DNS is installed and configured correctly. DNS is the foundation that Active Directory relies on, and you need to have a thorough understanding not only of the Windows 2000 DNS server, but also how DNS itself functions. The objectives for this chapter are to see that you can install DNS, configure it for use in an Active Directory network, and test it to make sure it is functioning.

CHAPTER 15

Installing, Configuring, Managing, Monitoring, and Troubleshooting DNS in a Windows 2000 Network Infrastructure

Manage and monitor DNS.

▶ Your ability to maintain the DNS server after it is installed, configured, and authorized is the final objective. Managing DNS server services and monitoring the DNS server's activities is critical to the ongoing administration of a Windows 2000 network, particularly a network that relies on Active Directory.

▶ DNS provides the name-resolution backbone for the Internet today, and with the introduction of Active Directory, it is now the backbone of Microsoft's name resolution as well. It is very important you understand where DNS came from, how it works, and the enhancements Microsoft made to DNS for Active Directory.

▶ Part of the power of the Microsoft DNS service is its integration with DHCP through Dynamic DNS (DDNS). Make sure you understand the relationship between the two and how DDNS works.

▶ Microsoft's Windows 2000 DNS service supports a variety of zone types and DNS server types. Be sure you understand what they are, how they work, and when you might use them in a production environment.

▶ Because of Microsoft's emphasis on practical exam questions, be sure to review closely the Step by Steps and the exercises that are referenced throughout the chapter.

INTRODUCING THE DOMAIN NAME SYSTEM (DNS)

If you have ever connected to a Web site by name, you have used the DNS. DNS is used on the Internet for resolving fully qualified domain names (FQDN) to their actual IP addresses. What DNS does is put a user-friendly face on that obscure numeric address. With DNS, you can tell a friend to go to www.newriders.com on the Internet rather than 205.133.113.87. DNS translates the FQDN, www.newriders.com, to the IP address 205.133.113.87. It's like a big phone book. You put in a name and it gives you the correct number. Fortunately for those of us with a limited ability to memorize strings of numbers, the Internet community recognized the benefits of a name resolution system as a critical part of the infrastructure that would make up the original Internet architecture. Thus, DNS was born.

History of DNS

DNS is a hierarchical database containing names and addresses for IP networks and hosts and is used almost universally to provide name resolution. This statement is now even more accurate because Microsoft is embracing DNS as its name resolution method for Windows 2000, in favor of the less accepted Windows Internet Naming System (WINS). But, before we tackle the Domain Name System in a Windows 2000 network, we should cover a little of the history and makeup of DNS in general.

Back in the early days of the Internet, when it was known as the Advanced Research Products Agency Network (ARPAnet) and the number of hosts on the network was less than 100, there used to be a master list of names and IP addresses called the HOSTS.TXT file. It was maintained by the Stanford Research Institute's Network Information Center (known as the SRI-NIC at the time), and it worked very well as long as the number of hosts was low and changes were infrequent. Everyone using the network would periodically download a copy of this file, and they would have a local table of names and addresses to connect to computers by name. Windows 2000 still has this functionality, although it is seldom used in conjunction with the Internet any longer. This method of name resolution was great for a while, but as the number of computers grew, this solution ran into a few issues, including the following:

◆ **Traffic.** As more and more people tried to access this file, the load on the SRI network and servers was becoming excessive.

◆ **Consistency.** As the number of hosts and the number of changes grew larger and larger, propagation of the HOSTS.TXT file became nearly impossible. As the file propagated to the most distant servers, new servers would have already been added to the network, rendering the file just distributed obsolete.

◆ **Flat-file limitations.** The HOSTS.TXT file was a flat file, so every name had to be unique. No hierarchical capabilities were built in to the naming structure. As a result, coming up with unique names that were also intuitive was becoming more and more difficult.

The network needed a better answer than a text file for name resolution. In 1984, in Request for Comments (RFCs) 882 and 883, Paul Mockapetris provided that better answer by introducing the Domain Name System. These first RFCs have since been superceded by RFCs 1034 and 1035, the current DNS specification.

DNS is a distributed database allowing local control of DNS for smaller segments of the namespace, while maintaining a logical architecture to provide the local information throughout the network. Each piece of the DNS database resides on a server known as a *name server*. The architecture of DNS is designed so there can be multiple name servers for redundancy, and caching of names to the local server is supported, further enhancing DNS's robustness. In addition, with parts of the overall namespace placed on separate computers, the data storage and query loads are distributed through thousands of DNS servers over the Internet. The hierarchical nature of DNS is designed in such a way that every computer on or off the Internet can be named as part of the DNS namespace.

To effectively install, configure, and support the Windows 2000 DNS server, you must have an understanding of the underlying architecture of today's DNS. Instead of having you read the RFCs (although you are encouraged to do so to improve your further understanding of DNS), we discuss the DNS namespace architecture and how individual DNS servers support their portions of the overall namespace. We then move on to the specifics of the Windows 2000 DNS server operation.

DNS Domains Defined

As we've discussed, you probably have already used DNS, whether you were familiar with the underlying mechanism or not. Domain names are easy. Names, such as www.microsoft.com, www.newriders.com, or even www.mcse.com, are all easy to comprehend. However, this simplicity comes at a price. The DNS namespace is complex. DNS names are created as part of a hierarchical database that functions much like the directories in a file system. Hierarchies are powerful database structures because they can store tremendous amounts of data while making it easy to search for specific bits of information. Before examining the specifics of the DNS namespace hierarchy, let's review some rules about hierarchies in general.

Hierarchies

Before we get into the details of a hierarchy, you should be familiar with the following terms:

◆ **Tree.** A type of data structure wherein each element is attached to one or more elements directly beneath it. In the case of DNS, this structure is often called an inverted tree because it is generally drawn with the root at the top of the tree.

◆ **Top-level domain (TLD).** Refers to the suffix attached to an Internet domain name. A limited number of predefined suffixes exist, the most popular being COM, EDU, GOV, MIL, NET, and ORG.

◆ **Node.** A point where two or more lines in the tree intersect. In the case of DNS, a node can represent a TLD, a subdomain, or an actual network node (host).

◆ **FQDN.** A domain name that includes all domains between the host and the root of DNS is an FQDN. For example, `www.microsoft.com` is an FDQN.

◆ **Leaf.** An item at the very bottom of a hierarchical tree structure that does not contain any other objects.

◆ **Zone.** A DNS zone is a logical grouping of hostnames within DNS. For example, `newriders.com` is considered the forward lookup zone for New Riders. It is where the information about the New Riders host is contained within DNS.

In DNS, the hierarchy starts with a root container, called the *root domain*. The root domain does not have a name, so it is typically represented by a single period (see Figure 15.1). Directly below the root domain are the TLDs. Lower-level domains are second-level, third-level, and so on. Every domain name has a suffix that indicates which TLD domain it belongs to. Only a limited number of such domains exist. For example:

◆ **COM.** Originally, the COM domain was supposed to contain commercial entities, but COM has become the overwhelming favorite TLD, and everyone wants his or her personal subdomains to be in COM. Crowding in COM is the main impetus behind the definition of new TLDs.

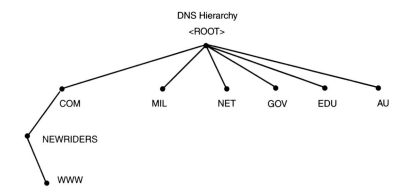

FIGURE 15.1

This portion of the DNS hierarchy shows the location of *www.newriders.com* in the DNS database in relation to the rest of the DNS database.

◆ **ORG.** This domain is supposed to accommodate organizations that are noncommercial in nature. Although many noncommercial organizations have registered in the COM domain, most have respected the intent of this domain. ORG is a good place for nonprofit organizations, professional groups, churches, and other such organizations.

◆ **EDU.** This domain was originally supposed to embrace all types of educational institutions, but it began to fill up quickly as schools gained access to the Internet. Now it is primarily reserved for higher education institutions. Primary and secondary schools are supposed to register in their state domains, which are subdomains of their country domains.

◆ **GOV.** This domain contains agencies of the United States federal government apart from the military, which have the MIL domain.

◆ **NET.** This domain supports Internet Service Providers and Internet administrative computers.

◆ **Country.** Each country is assigned a unique TLD. Some common examples include the following:

  • **CA.** Canada

  • **AU.** Australia

  • **TO.** Tonga

◆ **CC.** This new domain was created for the same purpose as the COM domain. It is intended to extend the number of names available for commercial endeavors.

A shortage of domain names at the top level has caused the Internet Ad Hoc Committee (IAHC) to propose six new TLDs, which could be implemented sometime in the year 2000:

◆ **STORE.** Domain name for merchants.

◆ **WEB.** Domains focused on Web activities.

◆ **ARTS.** Arts and cultural entities.

◆ **REC.** Recreation and entertainment entities.

◆ **INFO.** Information services.

◆ **NOM.** Domains registered to individuals.

The creation of these new TLDs is expected to alleviate the gold rush-like fervor associated with "good" domain names. Unfortunately, the various groups ultimately in charge of implementing the new domains have been dragging their feet. Everyone wants to control the process, but they cannot seem to agree on whose plan will ultimately be implemented.

As we have discussed, DNS is used to translate a hostname to an IP address. The DNS name typically looks something like this:

```
isaac.widgets.urwrite.net
```

This is known as the host's FQDN because it lists the host's precise location in the DNS hierarchy. The DNS name in the example represents the host ISAAC in the subdomain WIDGETS (this is frequently a department or division in a company), which is in the subdomain URWRITE (this is frequently the name of the company or organization that has registered the domain), which is in the top-level domain of .NET.

> **EXAM TIP**
>
> **Know About FQDN**   For the exam, make certain you have a good understanding of what an FQDN is and how it is represented.

When an organization wants to establish a domain name on the Internet, the domain name must be registered with one of the authorized registration authorities. One that many people are familiar with is Network Solutions, formerly the InterNIC. You can research new domain names and access registration forms at `http://www.networksolutions.com`. You also can contact your Internet Service Provider (ISP) for assistance. To register a domain, you need at least two name servers. Two types of name servers are defined within the DNS specifications. They are the following:

◆ **Primary Master.** This server obtains the information on the zones it is authoritative over (resolves names for) from files on the host it runs on. This is also the server where you make additions, modifications, and deletions to the DNS zone.

Know the Difference Between the Primary and the Secondary Domains   The major difference is that a secondary domain holds a read-only version of the DNS database.

The Role of a Domain   If you ever anticipate connecting your network to the Internet, your first installation of DNS is an excellent time to do a little preparation. More important, after Active Directory has been installed, the underlying DNS domain cannot be changed without removing and reinstalling Active Directory and losing all your users and permissions.

◆ **Secondary Master.** This server gets its zone information from the primary or secondary master name server that is authoritative for that domain. When a secondary server starts, it contacts the name server it receives updates from and gets the latest copy of the zone data.

After you have identified the two (or more) name servers, you are ready to register your domain. To register a domain name at Network Solutions, follow Step by Step 15.1.

ON THE CD

Step by Step 15.1, "Registering a DNS Domain," demonstrates how to register a domain name at Network Solutions. See the file **Chapter15-01StepbyStep.pdf** in the CD's **Chapter15\StepbyStep** directory.

After you have registered a domain on the Internet, the next step is to understand how DNS works. In other words, after you enter the name, how does it get translated to an IP address?

The DNS name server resolves a name to an IP address using the following process:

1. The client computer makes a request to the local DNS server. This generally occurs when an application tries to make a connection using a hostname, such as when you enter www.newriders.com into your Web browser.

2. The DNS server looks in a local memory cache for names it has recently resolved. If the name is found in the local cache, the name server returns the IP address the client computer requires. Most DNS servers cache both local and remote domain names in the memory, so even a DNS request for a host on your local network may be in cache.

3. The name server looks in the DNS server's host tables to see if there is a static entry (or in the case of DDNS, a dynamic entry) for the hostname to an IP address lookup. If an entry exists, the DNS server forwards the IP address to the client computer.

4. If the request has not been resolved, the name server refers the request to a root name server. Root name servers support the root of the namespace hierarchy. At present, ten computers support the root domain.

5. The root name server refers the request to a name server for the first-level domain in the hostname. In other words, if you have requested a host address for the newriders.com domain, the root name server forwards the request to the newriders.com DNS server. The first-level domain name server refers the request to a name server for the second-level domain in the hostname, and so on, until a name server is encountered that can resolve the complete hostname.

6. The first name server that can resolve the hostname to an IP address reports the IP address to the client computer.

To ensure this process works in your environment, you need to perform two tasks. First, make sure your network has at least one, and preferably more, DNS name servers. These name servers can include your Windows 2000 Server DNS server, older Microsoft DNS servers, third party (UNIX, Linux, OS/2, and so on) DNS servers, or even name servers provided by your ISP. Second, make sure your client computers are all configured to use these servers for DNS lookups.

Reverse Lookups

We have discussed how to get the most common form of DNS lookups, also known as forward lookups, in which you enter a name and the DNS server returns the IP address. Another kind of lookup is a reverse lookup, which works very much as its name implies. You query the DNS server with an IP address, and it returns the DNS name for that host. This can be very useful if you are trying to keep track of network usage, trying to track down a host that is causing issues on the network, or trying to verify the identity of a host. If your host doesn't have an entry in a reverse lookup table, you cannot download the software. We discuss the different record types in the "DNS Record Types" section of this chapter, but it is important to know that reverse lookup tables use Pointer (PTR) records to resolve IP addresses to names. A PTR record is a pointer to a location (an FQDN) in the DNS domain.

> **EXAM TIP**
>
> **Understand the Function of the Reverse Lookup Table** Reverse lookup tables represent an excellent topic for exam questions because they are less frequently used, and as a result, are less understood when compared to the forward lookup table.

IN THE FIELD

SPAM EMAILS AND REVERSE LOOKUPS

You may discover the need for a reverse lookup when sending Internet email. One of the latest weapons in the anti-SPAM wars is the use of reverse lookups to verify the validity of the domain from which an email originates. After the mail server receives an email, it checks to see if it is from a valid domain and rejects it if it is not. Many SPAM writers use fictitious domains as part of their attempt to hide their real identities. Therefore, if you are setting up DNS on the Internet, be sure to include a reverse zone for your mail servers.

The naming convention for a reverse lookup zone is

```
<Reverse order of network octets of an IP address>.
➥in-addr.arpa
```

Thus, the reverse table for the IP network 205.133.113.87 is 113.133.205.in-addr.arpa.

It is important to be aware that the Active Directory Installation Wizard does not automatically add a reverse lookup zone and PTR resource records. You need to do that manually because it is possible that another server may control the reverse lookup zone. You may want to add one if this is not the case. Although a reverse lookup zone is not necessary for Active Directory to work, it is useful for the reasons listed previously.

DNS Record Types

Before we continue the discussion of DNS, you should take a quick look at the different types of records you can create in a DNS domain. Table 15.1 lists the record types supported by the Windows 2000 DNS—and their meanings.

DNS Naming Conventions

Before we move on to the installation portion of this chapter, we need to quickly review the parameters for creating a DNS name. Table 15.2 shows the restrictions for creating a DNS name and an FQDN.

Now let's look at installing the Windows 2000 DNS server service.

NOTE

The Windows 2000 DNS Server Service Supports Additional Standards Microsoft has included support for RFCs 2181 and 2044, which support UTF-8 character encoding. UTF-8 supports characters from a variety of foreign languages that may not be supported by non-Windows 2000 versions of DNS.

TABLE 15.1

DNS RECORD TYPES

Record Type and RFC	Value and Meaning
AFSDB (RFC 1183)	Andrew File System database server record. Indicates the location of either an AFS volume location server or a Distributed Computing Environment (DCE) server.
CNAME (RFC 1035)	One of the original record types, a CNAME indicates an alias domain name for a name already specified as another resource type in this zone. CNAME is the acronym for canonical name.
ATMA	ATM address—maps a DNS name to an ATM address.
A (RFC 1035)	A host address record—maps a DNS name to an IP (version 4) address.
AAAA (RFC 1886)	Similar to the A record, the AAAA record is a host address for IPv6 hosts. It is used to map a DNS name to an IP (version 6) address.
ISDN (RFC 1183)	An Integrated Services Digital Network (ISDN) maps a DNS name to an ISDN telephone number.
MX (RFC 1035)	A mail exchanger record is used to provide message routing to a specific mail exchange host for a specific DNS name.
MG (RFC 1035)	A mail group record is used to add mailbox (MB) records as members of a domain mailing group.
MB (RFC 1035)	A mailbox record maps a specified domain mailbox name to the host that hosts the mailbox.
MINFO (RFC 1035)	Mailbox or mailing list information specifies a domain mailbox name to contact. It can also can specify a mailbox for error messages.
PTR (RFC 1035)	A pointer record points to a location in the domain. This is typically used for reverse lookups or IP address to DNS name lookups.
MR (RFC 1035)	A renamed mailbox record is used to specify a domain mailbox (MB) that is the proper rename of an existing mailbox (MB) record.
RP (RFC 1183)	A responsible person record specifies the domain mailbox for a responsible person for which text (TXT) records exist.
TXT (RFC 1035)	A text record is used to hold a string of characters that serve as descriptive text to be associated with a specific DNS name.
RT (RFC 1183)	A route through record provides an intermediate-route-through binding for internal hosts that do not have their own direct wide area network (WAN) address.
SRV (RFC 2782)	A service record enables administrators to use several servers for a single DNS domain, to easily move a TCP/IP service from host to host, and to designate primary and backup service hosts.
WKS (RFC 1035)	A well-known service record is used to describe well-known TCP/IP services supported by a particular protocol (that is, TCP or User Datagram Protocol (UDP)) on a specific IP address.
X25 (RFC 1183)	An X.25 record is used to map a DNS name to a Public Switched Data Network (PSTN) address.

TABLE 15.2

DNS NAME RESTRICTIONS

Restriction	Standard DNS (Including Windows NT 4.0)	DNS in Windows 2000
Characters	Supports RFC 1123, which permits A to Z, a to z, 0 to 9, and the hyphen (-).	Several different configurations are possible; RFC 1123 standard, as well as support for RFCs 2181, and the character set specified in RFC 2044 (UTP-8).
FQDN length	63 bytes per label and 255 bytes for an FQDN.	Domain controllers are limited to 155 bytes for an FQDN.

Installing, Configuring, and Troubleshooting DNS

Install, configure, and troubleshoot DNS.

Now that you have an general understanding of how DNS works, we can look at installing the Windows 2000 DNS server service. One of the first questions that needs to be answered is, "Do we need to upgrade to Windows 2000 DNS?" The answer is yes and no.

If you don't want to take advantage of all the benefits of a Windows 2000 network and Active Directory, you don't need to upgrade. If you happen to be running a version of DNS that supports RFC 2136 (covering dynamic update of DNS resource records) and RFC 2782 (support of SRV resource records), you can run your existing DNS and take advantage of Windows 2000's features. If your current DNS server does not support RFC 2136 and RFC 2782, why should you upgrade? The Windows 2000 DNS contains a number of significant improvements over standard DNS (including Windows NT's implementation), including the following:

◆ **Notification-driven zone transfers.** The standard model for DNS updates requires secondary name servers to periodically poll the master server for table updates. Under Windows 2000's DNS, the master server can notify the secondary DNS servers when an update has occurred. This immediate notification is not only more efficient than the older methods, but it also allows for much faster distribution of changes because updates are no longer dependent on polling intervals.

> **EXAM TIP**
> **Be Familiar with the Advantages of the Windows 2000 Dynamic DNS (DDNS) Over More Traditional Servers** Because Active Directory is based entirely on DNS, this is important for the success of Active Directory—which makes it a good topic for exam questions.

◆ **Integrated zone tables.** With the Windows 2000 DNS server service, you can integrate DNS into Active Directory. Resource records are then stored in Active Directory and can be updated by any domain controller running DNS. This integration is a proprietary feature of the Windows 2000 DNS, but it can yield a much more secure, robust, and fault-tolerant implementation than standard DNS.

◆ **Incremental zone transfers.** The standard model for DNS zone transfers is to transfer the entire zone whenever an update is made. Transferring entire zones is very inefficient. Windows 2000 DNS allows secondary servers to request incremental updates, which contain changes only since the last transfer.

◆ **Secure DNS updates.** Windows 2000 DNS updates can be restricted to authorized secondaries.

◆ **DNS/DHCP integration.** The power of DDNS is the integration of DHCP with the DNS table. Any Windows 2000 DHCP client computer is automatically added to the DNS table at the time its IP address is issued.

Now that you have the justification, let's install the Windows 2000 DNS server service.

Installing the DNS Server Service

One of the major improvements in Windows 2000 is the capability to install services in various ways. In fact, there are several ways to install the DNS server service. The first way to install the Windows 2000 DNS server service is shown in Step by Step 15.2.

ON THE CD

Step by Step 15.2, "Installing the DNS Server Service," shows you one of the methods for installing the Windows 2000 DNS server service. See the file **Chapter15-02StepbyStep.pdf** in the CD's **Chapter15\StepbyStep** directory.

The second way to install the Windows 2000 DNS server service is shown in Step by Step 15.3.

ON THE CD

Step by Step 15.3, "Using an Alternative Method to Install the Windows 2000 DNS Server," shows you an alternative method for installing the Windows 2000 DNS server service. See the file **Chapter15-03StepbyStep.pdf** in the CD's **Chapter15\StepbyStep** directory.

After DNS is installed, you need to configure the first DNS zone, as discussed in the following section.

Configuring a Primary Name Server

Let's discuss what Microsoft means when they ask you to configure a primary name server. The primary name server of a domain is the name server that is acting as the Start of Authority (SOA) for that zone. The SOA record is the first in the database, and it has the following format:

```
IN SOA <source host> <contact email> <serial number>
<refresh time> <retry time>
[ccc]<expiration time> <time to live>
```

- **Source host.** The DNS server that maintains the write-enabled version of the file.

- **Contact email.** The Internet email address for the person responsible for this domain's database file.

- **Serial number.** This is important. The serial number acts as the version number for the database file and should increase each time the database file is changed. The file with the highest serial number takes precedence during zone transfers.

- **Refresh time.** This number reflects the elapsed time (in seconds) that a secondary server waits between checks with its master server to see whether the database file has changed and if a zone transfer should be requested. It is set at 15 minutes by default, but it can be increased in an environment where DNS does not change often.

> **NOTE**
>
> **Don't Use a Standard Email Address for the SOA** One very important fact about the contact email in the SOA is that it does not use the standard Internet email format. Instead, you replace the "@" symbol in the email name with a "."; therefore, admin@microsoft.com should be admin.microsoft.com in the zone file.

◆ **Retry time.** This number reflects the elapsed time (in seconds) that a secondary server waits before retrying a failed zone transfer. The default for Windows 2000 is 10 minutes, and it can be increased or decreased as needed for your environment.

◆ **Expiration time.** This number reflects the elapsed time (in seconds) that a secondary server keeps trying to download a zone. After this time limit expires, the old zone information is discarded—one day by default. It, too, can be modified as needed. You may want to increase this number for areas with intermittent connectivity where outages are common. DNS across a virtual private network (VPN) is one example.

◆ **Time to live (TTL).** This number reflects the elapsed time (in seconds) that a DNS server is allowed to cache any resource records from the database file.

The SOA indicates the primary server for the zone.

Configuring Zones

DNS configuration is handled through a snap-in for the Microsoft Management Console. This may be found in the Administrative Tools program folder, under the entry DNS. It becomes available after DNS is installed. Although it is possible to manually configure the text files DNS creates, the DNS console makes it much easier to manage your DNS namespace configuration. When you first install your DNS server, you need to configure it with its first zones. We will look at how to do this using the wizard and then take a look at how to do this if you need to add additional zones down the road.

Before we jump into the configuration of DNS zones, we need to take a moment to discuss the types of zone storage used in DNS.

◆ **Active Directory-Integrated.** This zone option stores all DNS information in Active Directory. If your entire domain infrastructure is run on a Windows 2000 platform, this is a good selection, as it is the most secure option for maintaining DNS tables. All your DNS information is stored in Active Directory, and all your updates pass as Active Directory updates. Unlike the text file method used by most DNS implementations, DNS tables stored in Active Directory cannot be read by a text editor, such as Notepad.

> **EXAM TIP**
>
> **The Most Secure Implementation of DNS Is Active Directory-Integrated** Active Directory is more secure than a flat file, and updates and zone transfers occur as part of Active Directory replication activities, which are encrypted.

◆ **Standard Primary.** This zone option stores the information in a text file, like most non-Windows 2000 DNS servers.

◆ **Standard Secondary.** This option creates a read-only copy of an existing zone. The master copy (read/write version) is stored on a primary server and is generally used to provide redundancy or load balancing of DNS on a network.

To configure the zones on your DNS server for the first time, perform Step by Step 15.4.

ON THE CD

Step by Step 15.4, "Configuring Zones for the First Time," walks you through the process of configuring zones on your DNS server for the first time. See the file **Chapter15-04StepbyStep.pdf** in the CD's **Chapter15\StepbyStep** directory.

> **EXAM TIP**
>
> **DNS Names Used with Active Directory Cannot Be Changed** In choosing a domain name to use when installing DNS, it is a good idea to register with the appropriate domain-name registration agency and use that registered name, even if your internal network is isolated (not connected to the Internet) because the DNS name used with Active Directory cannot be changed. That the DNS name used with the Active Directory Services cannot be changed would make an excellent exam question.

Now you have created a zone using the Configure the DNS Server Wizard. Next, you need to know how to create a new zone using the DNS console application.

To create a Standard Primary Forward Lookup zone on your DNS server, use Step by Step 15.5. To create a Reverse Lookup zone, follow Step by Step 15.6.

ON THE CD

Step by Step 15.5, "Creating a Standard Primary Forward Lookup Zone," demonstrates how to create a Standard Primary Forward Lookup zone on your DNS server. See the file **Chapter15-05StepbyStep.pdf** in the CD's **Chapter15\StepbyStep** directory.

Step by Step 15.6, "Creating a Reverse Lookup Zone," illustrates how to create a Reverse Lookup zone. See the file **Chapter15-06StepbyStep.pdf** in the CD's **Chapter15\StepbyStep** directory.

After reading this far, you should have a good understanding of how zones are created. Now let's take a look at setting up a caching-only server.

Configuring a Caching-Only Server

Caching-only servers are used to speed up client computer DNS queries by gathering a large number of cached records based on client computer DNS queries. A caching-only server does not have a copy of the zone table and therefore cannot respond to queries against the zone—unless they are already cached. A caching server is not authoritative on any zone.

ON THE CD

Step by Step 15.7, "Creating a Caching-Only DNS Server," shows you how to create a Caching-Only DNS server. See the file **Chapter15-07StepbyStep.pdf** in the CD's **Chapter15\StepbyStep** directory.

> **NOTE**
>
> **Room for Cached Information**   All the cache entries on a caching-only server are stored in random-access memory (RAM). You want to be sure that your caching server has plenty of RAM; otherwise, it will not be effective.
>
> To configure a caching-only server, install DNS as described previously in the installing DNS procedure and then perform Step by Step 15.7.

Configuring a DNS Client Computer

After you have installed and configured the DNS server portion of Windows 2000 DNS, you should take a look at how to install DNS on a Windows 2000 client computer. The key is to keep in mind that DNS is installed in two places.

First, DNS is configured as part of the TCP/IP interface. The second place DNS must be installed is under Windows 2000 in the System Properties. The DNS information configured under System Properties is used as the DNS suffix for building FQDNs (similar to the suffix information configured under TCP/IP properties on other Windows operating systems). It also is used as part of the process for registering the computer in DDNS, which is new with Windows 2000. Step by Step 15.8 shows you how to configure DNS client settings in TCP/IP properties.

> **ON THE CD**
>
> Step by Step 15.8, "Configuring a DNS Client Computer," guides you through the process of configuring a DNS client computer. See the file **Chapter15-08 StepbyStep.pdf** in the CD's **Chapter15\ StepbyStep** directory.

A number of advanced TCP/IP options can be configured in conjunction with the DNS client computer. They include the following:

◆ DNS server addresses (in order of use)

◆ Parameters for resolving unqualified domain names— options include the following:

- **Append Primary and Connection Specific DNS Suffixes.** This option appends the domain suffixes configured in the System Properties to any unqualified domain names sent for resolution.

- **Append Parent Suffixes of the Primary DNS Suffix.** This option adds not only the specified domain suffixes but also the suffixes of any parent domains to any unqualified domain names sent for resolution.

- **Append These DNS Suffixes (in order).** This option enables you to specify which DNS suffixes should be appended to any unqualified domain names sent for resolution.

- **DNS Suffix for this Connection.** This option enables you to configure a specific DNS suffix for this connection in the list of Network and Dial-up Connections. You can specify different suffixes in case you have multiple local area network (LAN) adapters loaded or you want to use different suffixes between LAN and dial-up connections.

- **Register this Connection's Addresses in DNS.** This is how you configure the computer to take advantage of DDNS.

- **Use this Connection's DNS Suffix in DNS Registration.** This option enables you to use the DNS suffix specified with this connection as part of the information used when the host is registered with DDNS.

To modify the DNS settings in the System Properties, use Step by
Step 15.9.

ON THE CD

Step by Step 15.9, "Modifying the DNS Settings for Active
Directory Integration," demonstrates how to modify the
DNS settings for Active Directory integration. See the file
Chapter15-09StepbyStep.pdf in the CD's **Chapter15\StepbyStep**
directory.

After you complete the configuration of your Windows 2000 DNS
client computer, configure the zones for dynamic updates. This is
discussed in the following section.

Configuring Zones for Dynamic Updates

One of the major advantages to running a Windows 2000 network
is the capability to use DDNS. You can configure a zone for
dynamic updates.

To configure your DNS zone for dynamic updates, follow Step by
Step 15.10.

ON THE CD

Step by Step 15.10, "Configuring Your Zone for Dynamic Updates,"
illustrates how to configure your DNS zone for dynamic updates.
See the file **Chapter15-10StepbyStep.pdf** in the CD's **Chapter15**
StepbyStep directory.

Before we move on to testing the DNS server service, we should
briefly discuss what DDNS is.

DDNS is specified in RFC 2136—Dynamic Updates in the
Domain Name System (DNS UPDATE). It is the foundation of a
successful Active Directory Service implementation. As we have
discussed, DNS is used to resolve a name to an IP address, or vice
versa, using a defined hierarchical naming structure to ensure
uniformity. DDNS takes that architecture to the next level.

This section describes the Windows 2000 implementation of dynamic update.

In Windows 2000, client computers can send dynamic updates for three types of network adapters: DHCP adapters, statically configured adapters, and remote access adapters. We examined these configurations in the "Configuring a DNS Client Computer" section earlier in the chapter.

What DDNS does is integrates DHCP and DNS, as described in RFC 2136. Every time a computer requests a new address or renews its address, the computer sends an option 81 and FQDN to the DHCP server and requests that the DHCP server register an entry in the reverse lookup DNS zone on its behalf. The DHCP client computer also requests an entry in the forward lookup zone on its own behalf. The end result is that every DHCP client computer has an entry in the DNS zones, both forward and reverse. This information can be used by other Windows 2000 computers in place of WINS for identifying the names and IP addresses of other hosts.

By default, the dynamic update client computer dynamically registers its A resource records whenever any of the following events occur:

- ◆ The TCP/IP configuration is changed.
- ◆ The DHCP address is renewed, or a new lease is obtained.
- ◆ A Plug and Play event occurs.
- ◆ An IP address is added or removed from the computer when the user changes or adds an IP address for a static adapter.

By default, the dynamic update client computer automatically de-registers name-to-IP address mappings whenever the DHCP lease expires.

You can force a re-registration by using the command-line tool, Ipconfig. For Windows 2000-based client computers, type the following at the command prompt:

```
ipconfig /registerdns
```

NOTE

Option 81 Is FQDN   Option 81 (also known as the FQDN option) allows the client computer to send its FQDN to the DHCP server when it requests an IP address.

Now let's take a quick look at the dynamic update process and see how a Windows 2000 host gets dynamically registered with DNS. A dynamic update occurs in the following manner:

1. The DNS client computer queries its local name server to find the primary name server and the zone that is authoritative for the name it is updating. The local name server performs the standard name resolution process to discover the primary name server and returns the name of the authoritative server and zone.

2. The client computer sends a dynamic update request to the primary server. The authoritative server then performs the update and replies to the client computer regarding the result of the dynamic update.

Now that DNS is installed and configured, let's look at how to test DNS.

Testing the DNS Server Service

How can you test to make sure DNS is working? Several applications enable you to perform these tests, which we discuss in order of complexity.

The first application for testing DNS is the PING.EXE utility. What PING enables you to do is send an Internet Control Message Protocol (ICMP) packet to a TCP/IP host. By using the correct flag, PING also can perform name resolution as part of its testing procedure. The correct format for this command is the following:

```
PING <destination address>
```

A sample PING session might look like this:

```
ping -a www.newriders.com
Pinging scone.donet.com [205.133.113.87] with 32 bytes of
data:
Reply from 205.133.113.87: bytes=32 time=47ms TTL=241
Reply from 205.133.113.87: bytes=32 time=60ms TTL=242
Reply from 205.133.113.87: bytes=32 time=40ms TTL=242
Reply from 205.133.113.87: bytes=32 time=37ms TTL=242
Ping statistics for 205.133.113.87:
Packets: Sent = 4, Received = 4, Lost = 0 (0% loss),
Approximate round trip times in milli-seconds:
Minimum = 37ms, Maximum =  60ms, Average =  46ms
```

A number of other switches can be used with the PING utility. They
are as follows:

◆ **-t.** Ping the specified host until stopped. If you want to view
the statistics and then continue, type `Control+Break`. To end
the pinging, type `Control+C`.

◆ **-n count.** Ping the specified host "n" times.

◆ **-l size.** Ping the specified host with packets of l size.

◆ **-f.** Set the Don't Fragment flag in the packet.

◆ **-i TTL.** Set the TTL to `i`. TTL is the equivalent of router
hops.

◆ **-v TOS.** Set the type of service used.

◆ **-r count.** Record route for count hops.

◆ **-s count.** Timestamp for count hops.

◆ **-j host-list.** Loose source route along host list. This is not a
frequently used flag because source routing is seldom used.

◆ **-k host list.** Strict source route along host list—used very
seldom.

◆ **-w timeout.** Timeout in milliseconds to wait for each reply.

NOTE

An Alias for Another Server's FQDN
If you are familiar with the Internet's
server-hosting architecture, you may
surmise that this means the server
www.newriders.com is hosted by a
third-party company with the domain
of donet.com.

From this sample, you can see several things. First, because your
ping returned the IP address of 205.133.113.87, you know that
DNS is functional. Second, because this also returned the alternate
hostname of scone.donet.com, you can see that www.newriders.com is
a DNS alias, or CNAME for another server's FQDN.

The rest of the information has to do with network latency and has
little application for this chapter.

The next utility to look at is NSLOOKUP.EXE. NSLOOKUP is
a standard command-line tool provided in most DNS server
implementations, including Windows 2000. NSLOOKUP offers
the capability to perform query testing of DNS servers and obtain
detailed responses at the command prompt. This information can
be useful for diagnosing and solving name resolution problems,
for verifying that resource records are added or updated correctly

in a zone, and for debugging other server-related problems. NSLOOKUP can be used by going to a DOS prompt and typing NSLOOKUP and pressing Enter. It can be run with the following options:

◆ **NAME.** Print info about the host/domain NAME using default server.

◆ **NAME1 NAME2.** Same as the preceding, but use NAME2 as server.

◆ **help or ?.** Print info on common commands.

◆ **set OPTION.** Set an option.

- **all.** Print options, current server and host.

- **[no]debug.** Print debugging information.

- **[no]d2.** Print exhaustive debugging information.

- **[no]defname.** Append domain name to each query.

- **[no]recurse.** Ask for recursive answer to query.

- **[no]search.** Use domain search list.

- **[no]vc.** Always use a virtual circuit.

- **domain=NAME.** Set default domain name to NAME.

- **srchlist=N1[/N2/.../N6].** Sets the domain name (N1) to append to a hostname during searches and additional domain names (n1, n2, ...) that can also be appended as DNS suffixes.

- **root=NAME.** Set root server to NAME.

- **retry=X.** Set number of retries to X.

- **timeout=X.** Set initial timeout interval to X seconds.

- **type=X.** Set query type (for example, A, ANY, CNAME, MX, NS, PTR, SOA, SRV).

- **querytype=X.** Same as type.

- **class=X.** Set query class—for example, IN (Internet), ANY.

- **[no]msxfr.** Use MS fast zone transfer.

- **ixfrver=X.** Current version to use in Incremental Transfer (IXFR) transfer request.

◆ **server NAME.** Set default server to NAME, using current default server.

◆ **lserver NAME.** Set default server to NAME, using initial server.

◆ **finger [USER].** Finger the optional NAME at the current default host.

◆ **root.** Set current default server to the root.

◆ **ls [opt] DOMAIN [> FILE].** List addresses in DOMAIN (optional: output to FILE).

- **-a.** List canonical names and aliases.

- **-d.** List all records.

- **-t TYPE.** List records of the given type (for example, A, CNAME, MX, NS, PTR, and so on).

◆ **view FILE.** Sort an 'ls' output file and view it with pg.

◆ **exit.** Exit the program.

If you are not familiar with NSLOOKUP, these options are probably as clear as mud. The best way to get a thorough understanding of the NSLOOKUP options and flags is to try them out. For a simple test of a DNS using NSLOOKUP, select a hostname you know is in DNS and type in the following:

```
nslookup kubla.urwrite.net
```

This command returns the following:

```
Server:  kubla.urwrite.net
Address:  10.225.10.190
Name:  kubla.urwrite.net
Address:  10.225.10.190
```

In this example, you used the name of the DNS server for the test, but you can use any host in the DNS table. The first name and address returned are the name and address for the DNS server you

are querying. If this server does not have a PTR record in a reverse
lookup zone, the server name is returned with a message that says:

```
*** Can't find server name for address (the address
[ccc]of the configured DNS server): Nonexistent domain
*** Default servers are unavailable
```

This does not mean anything is malfunctioning. If you still get
name resolution in the Name/Address section of the response, your
DNS server is working.

Another method for testing the DNS server service is to use the
monitoring capabilities built in to the DNS console application.
To set up testing and monitoring for the DNS server, use Step by
Step 15.11.

ON THE CD

Step by Step 15.11, "Testing the DNS Service," shows you how to
set up testing and monitoring for the DNS server. See the file
Chapter15-11StepbyStep.pdf in the CD's **Chapter15\StepbyStep**
directory.

The test we just discussed enables you to perform two types of
queries. Before we move on, we should discuss exactly what those
queries are and how they work, as follows:

◆ **Simple (iterative) query.** A simple (or iterative) query is one
in which the name server provides the best response based on
what that server knows from local zone files or from caching.
If a name server doesn't have any information to answer the
query, it simply sends a negative response.

◆ **Recursive query.** A recursive query forces a DNS server to
respond to a request with either a failure or a successful
response. With a recursive query, the DNS server must contact
any other DNS servers it needs to resolve the request, which is
a much more resource-intensive mechanism.

If the test fails, you see an error message in the DNS console
application, and an alert icon appears on the DNS server.

Implementing a Delegated Zone for DNS

The next thing to discuss is how to create a delegated zone for your DNS. Delegating a domain means that DNS queries on the existing domain are referred to the name server in the delegated domain for resolution. You can delegate only down the hierarchy, so the delegated domain must be a subdomain of the domain doing the delegation. That may be a little confusing, but the configuration procedure should make it a little more clear.

To create a delegated zone, use Step by Step 15.12.

ON THE CD

Step by Step 15.12, "Creating a Delegated Zone," demonstrates how to create a delegated zone. See the file **Chapter15-12StepbyStep.pdf** in the CD's **Chapter15\StepbyStep** directory.

Creating DNS Resource Records Manually

We've spent most of the chapter looking at the dynamic methods for creating entries in the DNS table. Now let's look at how to manually create an entry. You might use this for non-Windows 2000 hosts, table entry types that are not supported by DDNS, or for hosts you just want to configure with a static entry. When you manually create a DNS entry, you have four options for what type of entry to create:

- **New Host.** This creates an A record.
- **New Alias.** This creates a CNAME record.
- **New Mail Exchanger.** This creates an MX record.
- **Other New Records.** This allows you to select the other record types.

The process of creating a new host record is outlined in Step by Step 15.13.

ON THE CD

Step by Step 15.13, "Manually Creating a DNS Entry," shows you
how to create a new host record. See the file **Chapter15-
13StepbyStep.pdf** in the CD's **Chapter15\StepbyStep** directory.

After you install, configure, and create entries for zones, you then
need to manage and monitor your DNS server.

MANAGING AND MONITORING DNS

Manage and monitor DNS.

We have looked at installing and configuring the Windows 2000
DNS server service. Next, we need to look at managing and
monitoring the server once it is running. If your job is typical
of most, you will spend a great deal more time managing DNS
servers than installing them.

Although the DNS server doesn't include any specific monitoring
capabilities, you should be aware of a number of additional options
as you manage your DNS server over the long term. One utility that
is very useful for managing your DNS server is the DNS snap-in to
the Microsoft Management Console (MMC) console, which is listed
as DNS in the Administrative Tools menu.

For a closer look at the capabilities of the DNS console, open the
DNS console application. Select the DNS server and click the
Action menu to see the available actions:

◆ **Set Aging/Scavenging for All Zones.** Opens the Server
Aging/Scavenging Properties dialog box.

◆ **Scavenge Stale Resource Records Manually.** All removal of
older DNS resource records is performed by an administrator,
rather than automatically.

◆ **All Tasks.** Includes starting, stopping, pausing, resuming, and
restarting the DNS server service.

◆ **Delete.** Deletes the DNS server.

◆ **Refresh.** Causes all the displayed information to be refreshed with a current status.

◆ **Export List.** Exports the information from the DNS server to a tab- or comma-delimited text or Unicode text file.

◆ **Properties.** Opens the Properties dialog box for the selected DNS server.

The following sections take a closer look at several of these actions.

Setting Aging/Scavenging for All Zones

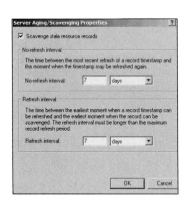

FIGURE 15.2
Setting the record scavenging parameters correctly can improve server performance and reduce problems.

When you choose Action, Set Aging/Scavenging for All Zones, you can use the Server Aging/Scavenging Properties dialog box (see Figure 15.2) to set three options:

◆ **Scavenge Stale Resource Records.** Allows the server to remove stale resource records. With DDNS updates enabled, records are automatically added to the zone when computers come onto the network. In some cases, these records are not automatically deleted. For example, if a computer is disconnected from the network, its associated resource record might not be deleted. To keep your zone table clean of inaccurate records, you should enable this option.

◆ **No-Refresh Interval.** Controls the time between the most recent refresh of a record's time stamp and when the time stamp can be refreshed again. In a very dynamic network where computers come on and leave frequently, you might want to lower the 7-day default.

◆ **Refresh Interval.** Sets the time between the earliest moment that a record time stamp can be refreshed and the earliest moment a record can be scavenged.

Scavenging Stale Resource Records Manually

The Scavenge Stale Resource Records Manually option scavenges old resource records. When you choose this command, the Update Server Data Files option writes any changes to the table that are in RAM to the server's hard drive.

Setting Properties

When you choose Action, Properties, the Properties dialog box opens (see Figure 15.3). As shown in the figure, the Properties dialog box gives you access to a number of tabs that allow you to configure the DNS server.

The Interfaces page enables you to select which interfaces the DNS service will operate on if multiple interfaces exist on the DNS server. You can choose to enable all interfaces or individually list the interfaces on which you will implement the DNS service.

The Forwarders page enables you to configure a list of forwarders for the server to use. A forwarder is like a shortcut to domain resolution. Ordinarily, when a DNS server receives a request for a zone that it is not authoritative on, it forwards the request to the root server for the domain and then walks the tree until it either times out or receives a resolution. By using a forwarder, you are betting that it has already cached the response to the DNS request and can respond much faster.

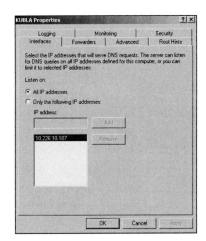

FIGURE 15.3
The DNS Properties page can be used to configure the DNS server's behavior.

The Advanced page enables you to configure the following advanced options:

◆ **Disable Recursion.** Allows the DNS server to make iterative queries and refer the client computer to the address of a DNS server that might have the answer. If recursion is enabled, the DNS server is forced to resolve the request itself. Iterative queries require much less overhead on the server.

◆ **BIND Secondaries.** Enables support for the BIND version of DNS.

Know When to Use Round Robin DNS For the exam, you should be aware that round robin DNS is also known as "Poor Man's Load Balancing." Round robin enables you to use DNS to help spread the load on a group of servers by tying multiple IP addresses to a single DNS record. Each time a resolution is requested, DNS returns the "next" record in the list of addresses.

◆ **Fail on Load If Bad Zone Data.** Prevents the server from loading if there is corrupt data in the zone file.

◆ **Enable Round Robin.** Allows a pooling of servers in a DNS entry so that the response to a query for the hostname can be any of a group of addresses.

◆ **Enable Netmask Ordering.** Enabled by default; specifies that the DNS server resolves the query with the address closest to the requesting client computer's IP address and is listed first in the response. If both round robin and netmask ordering are enabled, netmask ordering is attempted first.

◆ **Secure Cache Against Pollution.** Helps ensure that bad entries are not loaded into the server's DNS cache.

◆ **Name Checking.** Allows you to specify the types of names the server accepts as part of its DNS table.

◆ **Load Zone Data on Startup.** Allows you to specify from where DNS loads its initial table when the service starts. The most secure option is From Active Directory and Registry.

◆ **Enable Automatic Scavenging of Stale Records.** Gives you the capability to automate the scavenging of stale records and also to specify the scavenging period.

Do Not Memorize All the Counters Microsoft does not expect you to memorize all these counters. You should, however, be familiar with the different types and know how to use the Performance console.

From the Root Hints page, you can configure other DNS servers on the network for the forwarding of DNS requests where appropriate.

From the Logging page, you can configure server logging. You can specify which logging options by selecting the option to enable it. The log file can be found at *SystemRoot*\system32\dns\dns.log. *SystemRoot* is usually your Windows system file directory.

The Monitoring page automates the testing of the DNS server service, and from the Security page you configure the rights to the DNS service.

The VIP Counters Are AXFR and IXFR Two types of counters that are especially important are the AXFR and IXFR counters. Remember that AXFR counters are used in conjunction with full zone transfers, whereas IXFR counters are used in conjunction with incremental zone transfers.

Now that you have looked at the options for managing the DNS server, let's take a look at some of the ways to monitor the service. Before we do this, however, we should discuss *what* you can monitor.

The following groups of counters are available for the DNS object. Because of the large number of counters, we discuss here the types of counters instead:

◆ **AXFR Counters.** These counters are associated with the full zone transfer requests received by the master DNS server. This group includes Requests Received, Requests Sent, Response Received, Success Received, and Success Sent.

◆ **Caching Memory.** This counter tracks the amount of memory used by the DNS server.

◆ **Database Node Memory.** This counter tracks the amount of database node memory used by the DNS server.

◆ **Dynamic Update.** These counters are associated with the dynamic updating of DNS. This group includes NoOperation, NoOperation/sec, Queued, Received, Received/sec, Rejected, Timeouts, Written to Database, and Written to Database/sec.

◆ **IXFR Counters.** These counters are associated with the incremental zone transfer requests received by the master DNS server. This group includes Requests Received, Requests Sent, Response Received, Success Received, Success Sent, TCP Success Received, and UDP Success Received.

◆ **Notify Received/Sent.** These counters track the notifications sent and received by the secondary DNS server.

◆ **Record Flow Memory.** This counter tracks the amount of record flow memory used by the DNS server.

◆ **Recursive.** The recursive counters are associated with the recursive queries the DNS server must make. This group includes Queries, Queries/sec, Query Failure, Query Failure/sec, Send TimeOuts, and TimeOut/sec.

◆ **Secure Update.** The secure update group of counters is associated with the number of secure updates sent and received. The group includes Failure, Received, and Received/sec.

◆ **TCP/UDP.** These counters track the respective TCP and UDP queries and responses. These groups include Message Memory, Query Received, Query Received/sec, Response Sent, and Response Sent/sec.

◆ **Total.** This group of counters totals the respective categories of requests and responses. This group includes Query Received, Query Received/sec, Response Sent, and Response Sent/sec.

◆ **WINS.** Because DNS under Windows 2000 can be used for WINS lookups, the DNS counters include the following WINS-specific counters: Lookup Received, Lookup Received/sec, Response Sent, Response Sent/sec, Reverse Lookup Received, Reverse Lookup Received/sec, Reverse Response Sent, and Reverse Response Sent/sec.

◆ **Zone Transfer.** The zone transfer counters are associated with the process of transferring copies of the DNS table between DNS servers. This group includes Failure, Request Received, SOA Request Sent, and Success.

To configure DNS performance monitoring, follow Step by Step 15.14.

ON THE CD

Step by Step 15.14, "Configure DNS Performance Monitoring," walks you through the process of configuring DNS performance monitoring. See the file **Chapter15-14StepbyStep.pdf** in the CD's **Chapter15\StepbyStep** directory.

You've looked at the management options available in the DNS console application, and you've taken a look at how to monitor the performance of the different DNS counters using the Performance console. At this point you should have a good understanding of the Windows 2000 DNS server service and DNS in general. Now let's see how well you can apply your skills in a practical situation.

CASE STUDY: IMPLEMENTING DNS IN A COMPLEX ENVIRONMENT

ESSENCE OF THE CASE

The essence of the case is as follows:

▶ Your company is about to migrate to a pure Windows 2000 environment.

▶ Your company is actually made up of three companies, each needing to maintain local control of its DNS.

▶ Users for each company need to be able to resolve addresses for the other companies' hosts as quickly as possible.

▶ Corporate headquarters needs to resolve addresses for each of the companies but does not need to maintain a DNS domain.

SCENARIO

You are the network administrator for NR Widgets Inc., a multinational conglomerate, and you are based in the conglomerate's corporate headquarters. NR Widgets Inc. is made up of three companies: NR Manufacturing, NR Consulting, and NR Telecommunications. Each company has its own IT department and maintains its own network infrastructure. Each company also has its own DNS domain.

You have been asked to prepare the network for a complete Windows 2000 rollout, both client computers and servers, with the goal being a pure Windows 2000 network. The first thing on your list is to implement a Windows 2000-capable DNS infrastructure. What is the best way to do this to accomplish the following:

◆ Each IT department keeps control of its own domain.

◆ Each company's users have the fastest possible resolution for other company's hosts.

◆ The users in the headquarters facility need fast DNS resolution for each of the company's hosts.

◆ Because the headquarters is a not a computing center, you do not need to maintain any master DNS servers.

What should you do?

continues

CASE STUDY: IMPLEMENTING DNS IN A COMPLEX ENVIRONMENT

continued

ANALYSIS

First, you need to roll out Windows 2000 DNS servers. In reality, you also should have completed an Active Directory Services design, but you are concerned just with DNS services at this time. You should roll out the servers in the following manner:

◆ First, each company gets the primary master DNS server for its own DNS domain, which gives it control of the domain. For redundancy, each company also should have a secondary master server.

◆ To allow each company to quickly resolve addresses for the other companies, each of the primary master DNS servers are also secondary master servers for the other companies. This enables users to do local lookups.

◆ Corporate headquarters needs a caching-only server configured to receive cache updates from the other DNS servers on the network. An alternate possibility is to set up a DNS server to act as a secondary master to the three company domains.

◆ Finally, all DNS servers should be set to accept dynamic updates—a requirement in a pure Windows 2000 environment.

This case study should have been fairly easy if you read the chapter carefully. Of course, after the DNS servers are set up and running, you also would set up some of the monitoring we discussed at the end of the chapter.

CHAPTER SUMMARY

Let's recap what we've discussed in this chapter. We have discussed all the key components of using a Windows 2000 DNS server in a Windows 2000 environment, beginning with the history and function of DNS.

We discussed reverse lookups, where an IP address can be resolved to a hostname and the different types of records. We also looked at the naming conventions for both standard DNS and the DNS service included with Windows 2000.

Next, we discussed installing and configuring the Windows 2000 DNS service. This involved all the major configuration activities from the initial installation to the manual creation of DNS records. We also covered configuring a DNS client computer and configuring a zone for dynamic updates.

We wrapped up the chapter with a discussion of managing and monitoring the DNS service. Now let's take a look at some exercises and questions.

KEY TERMS

- Caching
- Caching-only server
- Domain
- Domain Name System (DNS)
- Dynamic Host Control Protocol (DHCP)
- DNS server
- DNS client computer
- Exclusion
- Forward lookup
- Reverse lookup
- Record types
- Lease
- Primary master
- Request for Comments (RFC)
- Secondary master
- Start of Authority (SOA)
- Suffix
- Tree
- Top-level domain (TLD)
- Node
- Fully qualified domain name (FQDN)
- Leaf
- Hierarchy
- Transmission Control Protocol/ Internet Protocol (TCP/IP)
- Zone

APPLY YOUR KNOWLEDGE

Review Questions

1. You are the network administrator for Exponent
   Mathematicians, and you have been asked
   to implement DNS for a pure Windows
   environment, taking full advantage of the
   benefits of Windows 2000. How should you
   do this and why?

2. You are the administrator of the Get Stuffed
   Taxidermists chain DNS server. You are getting
   complaints from several field locations that it
   takes a long time to resolve Internet addresses. All
   the sites complaining are across slow WAN links.
   What should you do?

3. You are the Windows 2000 administrator for
   Bug-B-Gone Exterminators. Your intranet is
   broken up into several DNS zones, each
   maintained by their respective departments.
   You are getting complaints from several field
   locations that it takes a long time to resolve
   internal addresses. All the sites complaining are
   across slow WAN links. What should you do?

4. You're the administrator of Little Faith
   Enterprise's Windows 2000 DNS server. You
   have an end user who is trying to download the
   128-bit version of the Windows 2000 Service
   Pack 1. Microsoft's Web site keeps denying him
   access, saying that his domain cannot be resolved.
   What can you do to fix this?

5. You're the LAN administrator for Think About
   IT Consulting Services. You are running a
   Windows NT 4 domain architecture and have
   just implemented your first Windows 2000 client

computers. You have configured the client
computers to perform dynamic updates to DNS,
but they are not appearing in the table. Why not,
and what should you do to fix the problem?

Answers to Review Questions

1. Placement of the DNS servers is very dependent
   on the network infrastructure of the company,
   but you need a Windows 2000 DNS service.
   Windows NT 4 DNS does not support the
   DDNS, and although other DNS servers support
   DDNS, the requirement for a pure Windows
   environment leaves them out. Although there
   may be benefits to some of the other platforms, a
   single platform solution is not uncommon in
   environments where the administrators are most
   familiar with Windows NT. See the section titled
   "Configuring Zones for Dynamic Updates" in
   this chapter.

2. Place a secondary master DNS server at each of
   the complaining sites. This gives them local DNS
   resolution and a local cache of commonly visited
   Internet addresses. See the section titled
   "Installing, Configuring, and Troubleshooting
   DNS."

3. Place a caching-only DNS server at each of the
   complaining sites and configure them to pull the
   cache information from the other DNS servers
   on the network. See the section titled
   "Configuring a Caching-Only Server."

APPLY YOUR KNOWLEDGE

4. Make sure the user has an entry in your reverse lookup table. Microsoft's site is trying to verify his location based on your domain and needs to be able to do a reverse lookup. If you do not have a reverse lookup zone, you need to create one. See the section titled "Reverse Lookups."

5. Windows NT 4's DNS server does not support DDNS updates. You need to upgrade to Windows 2000 DNS or migrate to a third-party DNS that supports dynamic updates. See the section titled "Configuring Zones for Dynamic Updates."

ON THE CD

This book's companion CD contains specially designed supplemental material, related exercises and exam questions and answers, to help you measure how well you have grasped the concepts and skills you learned in this chapter. See the file **Chapter15ApplyYourKnowledge.pdf** in the CD's **Chapter15\ApplyYourKnowledge** directory.

Suggested Readings and Resources

1. Albitz, Paul, and Cricket Liu. *DNS and Bind.* Sebastopol, CA: O'Reilly and Associates, Inc., 1998.

2. Branley, Edward. *Sams Teach Yourself DNS/Bind in 24 Hours.* Indianapolis, IN: Sams Publishing, 2000.

3. Komar, Brian. *Sams Teach Yourself TCP/IP Network Administration.* Indianapolis, IN: Sams Publishing, 1998.

4. Ruth, Andy. *Concise Guide to Windows 2000 DNS.* Indianapolis, IN: Que Corporation, 2000.

5. Siyan, Karanjit S. *Windows NT TCP/IP.* Indianapolis, IN: New Riders Publishing, 1998.

One of the most important services for successfully implementing Active Directory Services is DHCP. In this chapter, we will examine all the facets of running the DHCP service in a Windows 2000 network.

Microsoft defines the "Installing, Configuring, Managing, Monitoring, and Troubleshooting DHCP in a Windows 2000 Network Infrastructure" objectives as the following:

Install, configure, and troubleshoot DHCP. Tasks include the following:

- **Install the DHCP server service.**

- **Create and manage DHCP scopes, superscopes, and multicast scopes.**

- **Configure DHCP for DNS integration.**

- **Authorize a DHCP server in Active Directory.**

▶ One of the first tasks when getting ready to deploy a production in the Windows 2000 network environment is to ensure that DHCP is installed and configured correctly. DHCP is tightly integrated with DNS and Active Directory Services. This objective expects you to be able to install DHCP and configure it for use in an Active Directory Services network.

Manage and monitor DHCP.

▶ The final objective requires that you be able to maintain your DHCP server after it is installed, configured, and authorized. The capability to manage DHCP services and monitor the DHCP server's activities is critical to the ongoing administration of a Windows 2000 network.

CHAPTER 16

Installing, Configuring, Managing, Monitoring, and Troubleshooting DHCP in a Windows 2000 Network Infrastructure

Study Strategies

▶ DHCP is a service that has been used in TCP/IP-based networks for quite a while. Microsoft has extended the functionality of DHCP as part of its Windows 2000 operating system. Be sure you understand where DHCP came from, how it works, and what enhancements Microsoft's Windows 2000 DHCP server service adds to the protocol.

▶ DHCP is used not only to dynamically allocate IP addresses, but also plays a critical part in registering hosts in Active Directory. Be sure you understand the roles DHCP plays in a Windows 2000 network.

▶ Microsoft's Windows 2000 DHCP server service supports several types of scopes. Be sure you understand the types, how each works, and when you would use each in a production environment.

INTRODUCTION

This chapter covers many facets of DHCP. It begins with a discussion of the nature of the protocol itself. Then installation, configuration, and troubleshooting of DHCP are covered. Finally, maintenance and management of the DHCP service are included in this chapter.

UNDERSTANDING DYNAMIC HOST CONFIGURATION PROTOCOL

The *TCP/IP protocol* is the de facto standard for computer networking and appears to have no challengers in the networking protocol arena. If you are going to be working with Windows 2000, you can expect to be working with TCP/IP. One of the keys to successfully working with the TCP/IP protocol is to have an understanding of the concept of a TCP/IP address. The designers of the TCP/IP protocol wanted an identification scheme that was independent of any one computer or network equipment design; thus, they established a scheme of IP addresses.

If you've ever surfed the World Wide Web, you have almost certainly seen IP addresses, numbers such as 192.168.144.77. As you administer TCP/IP on your network, a considerable part of your time will be devoted to IP address assignment, because IP addresses don't just happen. They have to be entered manually into the configuration of each TCP/IP computer on your network. When a computer is added to your network, it needs an IP address. When a computer moves, it probably needs a new IP address. If you are just starting out with managing a large TCP/IP network, you may find the notion of managing all those addresses a bit daunting. Change the IP address of a DNS server, and you have to reconfigure every client computer. Move a client computer to a new subnet, and you have to update its IP address.

If you manually manage your IP addresses, almost any change to the network will require a visit to one or more computers to update the TCP/IP configuration. This is not a happy prospect. Fortunately, the people who brought us DNS to replace the HOSTS.TXT file also came up with a solution to this dilemma.

EXAM TIP

Don't Sweat the RFCs for DHCP
Although Microsoft has been known to be very detailed in its exam questions, it will not expect you to be able to recite the RFCs for each of the protocols or services in Windows 2000.

NOTE

RFCs Are Notes About the Internet
Request For Comment documents are used to make notes about the Internet and Internet technologies. If an RFC can garner enough interest, it may eventually become a standard. Topics of RFCs range from the File Transfer Protocol (originally RFC 114, but updated by RFC 141, RFC 171, and RFC 172) to the Hitchhikers Guide to the Internet (RFC 1118). Steve Crocker posted the first RFC in 1969, and the topic was host software. You can find listings of all the RFCs at a number of Internet sites. One place is
`http://www.rfc-editor.org/`.

The *Dynamic Host Configuration Protocol* (DHCP) was the Internet community's answer to dynamically distributing IP addresses. DHCP is open and standards based, as defined by the Internet Engineering Task Force's (IETF) Requests For Comments (RFCs) 2131 and 2132. (The *IETF* is the main standards organization for the Internet.)

Typically, IP addresses are registered with the IANA (Internet Assigned Numbers Authority) so that IP addresses used on the Internet can be tracked. In some cases, a network will not be connected to the Internet and will not need to use registered addresses. In other cases, the network is connected to the Internet with special hardware and software that can be configured to allow the network to use unregistered addresses in conjunction with address translations. Windows 2000 includes this capability, and it is discussed in detail in Chapter 21, "Installing, Configuring, and Troubleshooting Network Address Translation (NAT)."

Quite often, network administrators use unregistered addresses on their internal network to ensure that there are addresses for all users. This model works great as long as the network is never tied directly to the Internet. However, with the shortage of Class A and Class B (and even Class C) IP addresses, there are some environments that use small pools of registered addresses to service larger numbers of DHCP clients—the idea being that not every client computer would need access simultaneously. These environments require aggressive leasing policies to ensure that everyone can get an address.

In addition to IP addresses, DHCP can also provides several additional IP options including gateway addresses, DNS server addresses, and WINS server addresses—in essence, everything the client computer needs to participate in the network. This lets all available IP addresses be stored in a central database along with associated configuration information, such as the subnet mask, gateways, and addresses of DNS servers.

The DHCP Protocol

It's great to say that DHCP provides the mechanism for dynamically distributing IP addresses on a network, but it is a bit more complicated than that. Here's how a client computer gets an address:

1. The client computer broadcasts a DHCPDiscover message that is forwarded to the DHCP server(s) on the network. The address of the DHCP server(s) is configured on the router, if necessary. Forwarding is done using a process called a BOOTP Forwarder. We will discuss this in more detail in the next section, "The BOOTP Protocol."

2. Each DHCP server that receives the discover message responds with a DHCP Offer message that includes an IP address that is appropriate for the subnet where the client computer is attached. The DHCP server determines the appropriate address by looking at the source subnet for the broadcast DHCPDiscover message. This message is also a broadcast message. The client identifies that the message is intended for that specific computer based on the MAC address included in the DHCP message.

3. The client computer considers the Offer message and selects one (usually the first offer it receives). It broadcasts a request to use that address with the IP address of the DHCP server that originated the offer included in the request.

4. The DHCP server acknowledges the request and grants the client computer a lease to use the address. This is sent again using a broadcast message that includes the MAC address of the client computer.

5. The client computer uses the IP address to bind to the network. If the IP address is associated with any configuration parameters, the parameters are incorporated into the client computer's TCP/IP configuration.

The first step of this process indicates that DHCP clients request their addresses using broadcast messages. If you are familiar with routing, particularly TCP/IP routing, you are probably familiar with the fact that one of the benefits of routing is that the router segregates broadcast domains. In other words, broadcasts do not generally cross routers. Does that mean that DHCP works only on the local segment and you need 50 DHCP servers for your 50 subnets? Not if you configure your routers to forward all BOOTP protocol messages (as defined in RFC 1542). *BOOTP* is the precursor to DHCP and was the first protocol used to assign IP addresses dynamically. The protocol was especially designed to pass across a router, and it continues to be used to allow DHCP broadcasts to propagate across routers. Thanks to BOOTP relaying, a DHCP server can service clients on any number of subnets, and you can do something else with 48 of those DHCP servers you were planning on buying.

The BOOTP Protocol

Before we get into installing the DHCP service in Windows 2000, a brief discussion about the BOOTP protocol is a good idea. A number of DHCP's features had their beginnings in BOOTP. The BOOTP (Bootstrap Protocol) protocol was originally designed in 1985 by Bill Croft and John Gilmore to automate the configuration of network devices. To use BOOTP, the network administrator must create a table with a list of client computers, their IP addresses, and network configurations. When a client computer comes onto the network, it broadcasts a request that the BOOTP server receives. The BOOTP server looks up the client computer in the table and responds with the configuration information stored in the table, which allows the client computer to communicate on the network.

The BOOTP protocol works pretty well and was used extensively in the early 90s in conjunction with diskless workstations. A BOOTP chip was a common option on a network interface card, and many networks thrived on BOOTP. The downside of BOOTP is that it provides only the configuration information entered in the table. The administrator still needs to configure the table. The limitations of BOOTP effectively prevented any automation of these tasks; thus, it was eventually replaced with DHCP. BOOTP and DHCP packets look virtually identical, and DHCP even takes advantage of the BOOTP Forwarder functionality of many routers and switches. DHCP added the automation features BOOTP was lacking.

INSTALLING, CONFIGURING, AND TROUBLESHOOTING DHCP

The first thing many managers ask when presented with a request to install Windows 2000 DHCP is, "Can't we just use our existing DHCP?" The answer to this question is both yes and no. If you are maintaining a legacy domain and WINS-style network, Windows 2000 can receive DHCP information from any DHCP server that Windows NT worked with. However, if you want to take advantage of the features of Active Directory Services, you will need the Windows 2000 DHCP service.

The first thing we need to discuss when working with the Windows 2000 DHCP service is how to install the service.

Installing the DHCP Server Service

Install the DHCP server service.

One of the features that is going to make Windows 2000 very popular with system administrators is its extensive use of configuration wizards. Most of the server configuration tasks have been bundled into the Configure Your Server application, allowing you to start a wizard for the most common configuration activities. We will try to highlight this new feature of Windows 2000 as much as possible because it is a major enhancement to the operating system and could prove to be fertile ground for exam questions.

When you install Windows 2000 Server, you have the ability to install DHCP as one of the optional services. For the purposes of the exam, we will be looking at installing DHCP on a server that is already installed but that does not have DHCP loaded.

DHCP is installed as a Windows 2000 Server networking service. To install the DHCP server service, follow Step by Step 16.1.

ON THE CD

Step by Step 16.1, "Using the Configure Your Server Application to Install the DHCP Server Service," walks you through DHCP server service installation. See the file **Chapter16-01StepbyStep.pdf** in the CD's **Chapter16\StepbyStep** directory.

As we discussed, DHCP service can be installed in multiple ways. DHCP can also be installed using the Control Panel, as show in Step by Step 16.2.

> **NOTE**
>
> **A DHCP Server Cannot Also Be a DHCP Client** If you currently have your server configured as a DHCP client, the DHCP installation will recommend that you enter a static IP address for your server.

> **EXAM TIP**
>
> **Windows 2000 Offers Many Ways to Complete Common Tasks** Having multiple ways to complete common configuration tasks should make administering a Windows 2000 network much easier for system administrators, but it will undoubtedly make the exams more challenging, because you will probably need to know all the different methods of completing common tasks.

ON THE CD

Step by Step 16.2, "Using the Control Panel to Install DHCP," walks you through a DHCP installation via the Control Panel. See the file **Chapter16-02StepbyStep.pdf** in the CD's **Chapter16\StepbyStep** directory.

Now that you have seen two of the methods for installing DHCP, let's discuss how to configure DHCP. One of the important things you need to understand before you delve into the configuration of your newly installed DHCP server is the concept of scopes, including scopes, superscopes, and multicast scopes.

Understanding DHCP Scopes

NOTE **You Need at Least One Scope** After installing the DHCP service, you must define at least one scope on the server. Otherwise, the service will not respond to DHCP requests.

A *scope* is a range of IP addresses that are available for dynamic assignment to hosts on a given subnet. The scope for a particular subnet is determined by the network address of the broadcast DHCP request. In addition to address information, a scope can include a set of configuration parameters to be assigned to client computers when the address is assigned. This list includes DNS servers, WINS server, gateway and subnet masks, NetBIOS scope ID, IP routing, and WINS Proxy information. To find this information, go to the command prompt, type ipconfig /all, and press Enter.

You should make the scope as large as you can. Later in the scope-creation process, you have the ability to exclude addresses, and you can also define reservations for particular addresses that do exist within the scope.

Understanding DHCP Superscopes

The next type of scope was introduced to the Windows NT product family with Service Pack 2 for Windows NT 4. What a *superscope* allows you to do is support a supernetted or multinetted network with a Windows 2000 DHCP Server. A *supernetted* network is a network that has multiple network addresses or subnets running on the same segment. You commonly see this configuration in network environments with more than 254 hosts on a subnet, or in an environment in which certain hosts need to be isolated from the rest of the logical network for security or routing reasons. Superscopes will support a local multinet or a multinet that is located across a router configured to use the BOOTP Forwarder service. We discuss creating a superscope in the section "Creating a Superscope."

Understanding Multicasting and Multicast Scopes

Before we discuss the multicast scopes, we need to look at what multicasting is. *Multicasting* is the act of transmitting a message to a select group of recipients. This is in contrast to the concept of a *broadcast* in which traffic is sent to every host on the network, or a *unicast* in which the connection is a one-to-one relationship, and there is only one recipient of the data.

Here's an example, using an email message. If you send an email message to your manager, it is an example of a unicast message. If you send an email message to every user on the system, it is a broadcast. Send an email message to a mailing list, and you have sent a multicast message, which falls between the definitions of the previous two. Teleconferencing and videoconferencing use the concept of multicasting, as does broadcast audio, in which the connection is a one to a selected group. At this time, only a few applications take advantage of this feature, but with the growing popularity of multicast applications, you may see more in the future.

We should discuss a few terms before discussing the Windows 2000 multicast capabilities:

◆ **Multicast DHCP (MDHCP).** An extension to the DHCP protocol standard that supports dynamic assignment and configuration of IP multicast addresses on TCP/IP-based networks.

◆ **Multicast forwarding table.** The table used by an IP router to forward IP multicast traffic. An entry in the IP multicast forwarding table consists of the multicast group address, the source IP address, a list of interfaces to which the traffic is forwarded (next hop interfaces), and the single interface on which the traffic must be received to be forwarded (the previous hop interface).

◆ **Multicast group.** A group of member TCP/IP hosts configured to listen and receive datagrams sent to a specified destination IP address. The destination address for the group is a shared IP address in the Class D address range (224.0.0.0 to 239.255.255.255).

◆ **Multicast scope.** A range of IP multicast addresses in the range of 239.0.0.0 to 239.255.255.255. Multicast addresses in this range can be prevented from propagating in either direction (send or receive) through the use of scope-based multicast boundaries.

A new feature for Windows 2000's DHCP service is the concept of a *multicast scope.* The Microsoft DHCP server has been extended to allow the assignment of multicast addresses in addition to unicast (single computer) addresses. A proposed IETF standard—RFC 2730, Multicast Address Dynamic Client Allocation Protocol (MADCAP—defines multicast address allocation. The proposed standard would allow administrators to dynamically allocate multicast addresses to be assigned in the same fashion as unicast addresses. The Windows 2000 DHCP multicasting capability also supports dynamic membership. *Dynamic membership* allows individual computers to join or leave the multicast group at any time. This is similar to registering to receive an Internet broadcast or joining and leaving an email mailing list. Group membership is not limited by size, and computers are not restricted to membership in any single group.

Now the question is, "How do client computers join and leave a multicast group?" The answer is the Multicast Address Dynamic Client Allocation Protocol (MADCAP) protocol and the MADCAP API. MADCAP assists in simplifying and automating configuration of multicast groups on your network, but it is not required for the operation of multicast groups or for the DHCP service. Multicast scopes provide only address configuration and do not support or use other DHCP-assignable options. MADCAP address configuration for client computers should be done independently of how the client computers are configured to receive their primary IP address. Computers that use either static or dynamic configuration through a DHCP server can also be MADCAP clients.

EXAM TIP

Use Class D IP Addresses for the Multicast Scope Remember that along with your primary IP address, you receive your multicast address, and it is for multicasts only and uses the Class D IP addresses specified in the multicast scope. They are not used for regular network traffic, such as Web traffic or other IP-based applications.

Creating a Scope on Your DHCP Server

Now that you are familiar with the different types of scopes, let's look at creating one. To create a DHCP scope, follow Step by Step 16.3.

ON THE CD

Step by Step 16.3, "Creating a DHCP Scope," walks you through the process of DHCP scope creation. See the file **Chapter16-03StepbyStep.pdf** in the CD's **Chapter16\StepbyStep** directory.

You have successfully created a scope for your DHCP server. For it to go into production, it needs to be authorized in Active Directory. If you have been following Microsoft's objectives closely, you will notice that we are about to go out of order. That's because in the real world you would want to bring up the server and test it before creating additional scopes and/or superscopes.

Authorizing a DHCP Server in Active Directory

For security reasons, a new Windows 2000 DHCP server must be authorized in Active Directory before it can assign IP addresses. This prevents unauthorized Windows 2000 DHCP servers from running on your network. One of the nastier things someone wanting to disrupt your network can do is to put up a "rogue" DHCP server and have it issue addresses that conflict with infrastructure devices. The nice thing about this feature is if you are running Windows 2000 client computers and they are using Active Directory, they will not accept DHCP addresses from an unauthorized server. To authorize a DHCP server in Active Directory, follow Step by Step 16.4.

ON THE CD

Step by Step 16.4, "Authorizing a DHCP Server," walks you through DHCP server authorization. See the file **Chapter16-04StepbyStep.pdf** in the CD's **Chapter16\StepbyStep** directory.

WARNING

Exclude Routers from DHCP Scopes When you are configuring the gateway address for your DHCP scope, you have an excellent opportunity to ensure that your routers are excluded from your DHCP scope. You do not want to find out the hard way—when a client computer is issued the router's address and all traffic off the network stops abruptly because of an address conflict.

EXAM TIP

When to Use the New Multicast Scope Option The Action menu is used to create a new scope and a new multicast scope as two different tasks. If you get a question on the exam regarding the procedure for creating a multicast scope, remember that you need to select New Multicast Scope.

EXAM TIP

DHCP Clients Automatically Attempt to Extend Leases For the exam, you should be aware of how DHCP leases work. Any DHCP client that had been assigned an address will automatically try to extend the lease when half the time of the lease has passed. If it is unable to do so, it will continue to try to do so for the duration of the lease.

Only Windows 2000 DHCP server can be authorized in Active Directory. There is still a possibility of Windows NT DHCP server or third-party DHCP servers existing on the network and assigning duplicate or incorrect IP addresses.

All Scopes in Superscopes Must Be Active   You can select only active scopes for the superscope, so be sure that all the scopes you want to include are active before you begin setting up the super-scope.

You have now installed, configured, and authorized a Windows 2000 DHCP server. Before you look at configuring your DHCP server for DNS integration, let's take a quick look at setting up a superscope.

Creating a Superscope

We've discussed how to create your first scope and how to authorize your DHCP server in the Active Directory. Now we need to look at creating a superscope. Remember that a *superscope* is a grouping of scopes that are used to support multinetted IP subnets on the same physical network. To create a superscope, you must create more than one scope on your DHCP server. If you need to review how to do this, refer to the section "Creating a Scope on Your DHCP Server." When you have multiple scopes on the DHCP server, you can create a superscope.

The best reason to use superscopes is to make the scopes in a multi-netted environment easier to support. If you have an environment with a lot of multinetting, it can get very confusing identifying which scope goes with which network. However, if you create a superscope named 4thFloor, for example, and you add all the multi-netted addresses on the fourth floor to it, you'll know where to go when you need to modify or add a scope, or when there are issues related to it. You can also get statistics for all the scopes within the superscope from the superscope statistics. Step by Step 16.5 outlines the steps involved in creating a superscope.

ON THE CD

Step by Step 16.5, "Creating a Superscope," walks you through the process for superscope creation. See the file **Chapter16-05StepbyStep.pdf** in the CD's **Chapter16\StepbyStep** directory.

You have now created a superscope, which will allow you to manage multiple scopes on the same physical network.

Creating a Multicast Superscope

Now let's discuss creating a multicast scope. To create a multicast scope, use Step by Step 16.6.

ON THE CD

Step by Step 16.6, "Creating a Multicast Scope," guides you through the process for multicast scope creation. See the file **Chapter16-06StepbyStep.pdf** in the CD's **Chapter16\StepbyStep** directory.

Now let's look at integrating DHCP into DNS.

Configuring DHCP for DNS Integration

One of the keys to effectively implementing an Active Directory environment is the capability for Windows 2000 workstations using DHCP to be automatically registered in DNS. Three settings can be set for DNS integration. They are

◆ **Automatically Update DHCP Client Information in DNS.** This is enabled by default, and, if selected, the DHCP server registers the DHCP client for both forward (A-type records) and reverse lookups (PTR-type records) in DNS only when requested to by the client computer. These settings are usually adequate for a pure, Windows 2000 environment because a Windows 2000 client computer updates DNS directly. If you have older Microsoft or non-Microsoft client computers on your network, you may want to change this to Always Update DNS. If the Always Update DNS option is selected, the DHCP server always registers the DHCP client for both the forward (A-type records) and reverse lookups (PTR-type records) with DNS.

◆ **Discard Forward (Name-to-Address) Lookups When Lease Expires.** This is also enabled by default and means that after the lease for an IP address expires (is no longer in use by the client computer), DHCP sends a request to the DNS server to discard the registered DNS records.

◆ **Enable Updates for DNS Clients That Do Not Support Dynamic Update.** This is another parameter you may want to enable if you are using Active Directory in a mixed client computer environment.

Where do you configure the DNS server(s) to update? You don't. The DHCP server automatically updates any DNS server configured as part of the server's TCP/IP network properties. It is important to be sure that your primary DNS server is configured as one of the DNS servers, because any updates sent to it will be propagated to the rest of the DNS servers for that domain.

However, the DNS server in question must support dynamic updates, discussed in Chapter 15, "Installing, Configuring, Managing, Monitoring, and Troubleshooting DNS in a Windows 2000 Network Infrastructure." The Windows 2000 DNS server supports these updates, as do a number of other DNS servers.

To configure this capability, you must perform Step by Step 16.7.

ON THE CD

Step by Step 16.7, "Configuring DHCP for DNS Integration," walks you through DHCP/DNS integration configuration. See the file **Chapter16-07StepbyStep.pdf** in the CD's **Chapter16\StepbyStep** directory.

EXAM TIP

DHCP and DNS   It is important to remember that Windows 2000 client computers update the A records in DNS without any assistance from the DHCP server. The only client computers that DHCP updates A records for are non-Windows 2000 client computers.

That takes care of the mechanics of integrating DHCP into your DNS environment. We should also discuss how the DHCP server actually makes the updates to DNS. At the writing of this book, this is still a draft standard. (The text of the proposed standard at the time of this writing can be found at `http://www.ietf.cnri.reston.va.us/internet-drafts/draft-ietf-dhc-dhcp-dns-11.txt`. This draft expired in April 2000.) This IETF draft specifies how a DHCP server may register and update pointer (PTR) and address (A) resource records on behalf of its DHCP-enabled clients. It also specifies how to assign an additional DHCP option code (option code 81) that enables the return of a client's fully qualified domain name (FQDN) to the DHCP server. (PTR and A records, as well as FDQN, are discussed in Chapter 15.)

The capability to register both A- and PTR- type records lets a
DHCP server register non-Windows 2000 client computers in
DNS, as you just learned. The DHCP server can differentiate
between Windows 2000 Professional and other client computers.

MANAGING AND MONITORING DHCP

Manage and monitor DHCP.

We have looked at installing and configuring the Windows 2000
DHCP service. The final piece of the DHCP puzzle is managing
and monitoring the server after it is installed and configured. The
Windows 2000 DHCP server bundles enhanced monitoring and
statistical reporting for precisely that purpose.

The DHCP manager has several additional features, found on the
Action menu. The Display Statistics command opens the Server
Statistics window shown in Figure 16.1. This screen displays the
following statistics:

◆ **Start Time.** The date and time the service was started.

◆ **Up Time.** The total up time for the DHCP service. If you
restart the service, this number resets to 0, even if the
Windows 2000 server has not been restarted.

◆ **Discovers.** The number of DHCPDiscover packets the server
has received.

◆ **Offers.** The number of DHCPOffer packets the server has
sent.

◆ **Requests.** The number of DHCPRequest packets the server
has received.

◆ **Acks.** The number of DHCP Acknowledgement packets the
server has sent.

◆ **Nacks.** The number of DHCP Negative Acknowledgement
packets the server has sent.

◆ **Declines.** The number of DHCPDecline packets the server
has received.

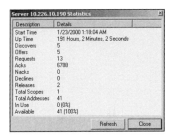

FIGURE 16.1
The Server Statistics screen gives you an
excellent snapshot of the server's activities.

◆ **Releases.** The number of DHCPRelease messages the server has received.

◆ **Total Scopes.** The total number of scopes active on the server.

◆ **Total Addresses.** The total number of addresses configured for leases. This number includes the number of addresses for all the active scopes on the server.

◆ **In Use.** The number of addresses presently leased to DHCP client computers.

◆ **Available.** The number of addresses available for lease for the Total Address pool.

FIGURE 16.2
If you are experiencing what appears to be DHCP database corruption issues, this is the place to check the database consistency.

The Reconcile All Scopes command allows you to compare the information contained in the DHCP database with the information stored in the Registry. Use this option only when you are having issues with the DHCP server and need to verify the configured addresses. Clicking the Verify button shown in Figure 16.2 checks the consistency of the database and returns any errors it finds.

The Unauthorize command removes the DHCP server from the list of authorized DHCP servers in Active Directory. You will be warned before the removal occurs (see Figure 16.3).

Define User Classes, Define Vendor Classes, and Set Predefined Options are advanced concepts that are beyond the scope of this exam. You will probably not use them in the context of a standard DHCP installation, but you should be aware of what user classes and vendor classes are for the exam:

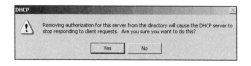

FIGURE 16.3
Only unauthorize a DHCP server when you are sure you will need it to respond to DHCP requests.

◆ **User Classes.** User classes are generally created for administrative purposes, and are similar to user groups. They can be used to identify all the DHCP clients in a specific department or location. User classes are used to assign DHCP options to groups of DHCP clients.

◆ **Vendor Classes.** Vendor classes are generally used to provide vendor-specific DHCP enhancements. For example, the Windows 2000 DHCP service has the capability to disable NetBIOS over TCP/IP on its DHCP clients.

The All Tasks selection allows you to perform the following tasks for your DHCP server:

◆ **Start.** Starts the DHCP service. Available only if the service is stopped or paused.

◆ **Stop.** Stops the DHCP service. Available when the service is running or paused. This option causes the server statistics to be reset.

◆ **Pause.** Pauses the DHCP service. This option does not reset the statistics.

◆ **Resume.** Resumes the DHCP service when paused. This option is available only when the service is paused.

◆ **Restart.** This option restarts the DHCP service, resetting the server statistics in the process. This option is available unless the server is stopped.

The next three commands are common ones. Delete deletes the DHCP server. Refresh causes all the displayed information to be refreshed with a current status. Export List allows you to export the information from the DHCP server to a tab- or comma-delimited text or Unicode text file.

The final command is Properties, which opens the Properties dialog box for the selected DHCP server. The Properties dialog box opens to the General tab, which allows you to configure the following options (see Figure 16.4):

◆ **Automatically Update Statistics Every.** This option allows you to set the automatic refresh of the statistics, as well as the interval at which they are refreshed.

◆ **Enable DHCP Audit Logging.** This option allows you to log all the DHCP activity to a file, which can be viewed in the system log, using Event Viewer. This is an excellent option to select if you are troubleshooting a DHCP issue and want to see what activity is taking place on the server. Figure 16.5 shows a sample of the system log with DHCP messages in it. You can also see these messages in the DHCP Audit Log, located at `C:\systemroot\System32\dhcp`.

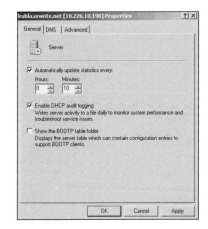

FIGURE 16.4

The General tab allows you to configure the statistics, logging, and BOOTP configuration information for your DHCP server.

FIGURE 16.5
The system Log can be viewed using the Event Viewer. Every DHCP action is logged in the system log when the Enable DHCP Audit Logging option is selected.

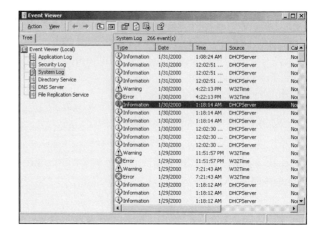

◆ **Show the BOOTP table folder.** This option deals with BOOTP backward compatibility and allows you to view the table where the BOOTP configuration entries are contained. This table appears in the Tree window of the DHCP manager (see Figure 16.6) and allows you to configure a BOOTP image file, which can be loaded to a BOOTP client from either a full server path or a TFTP file server.

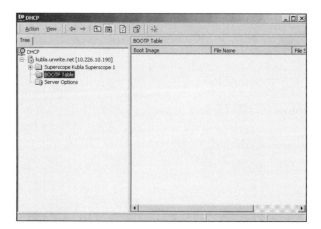

FIGURE 16.6
Use the BOOTP option only for legacy BOOTP clients. These clients are becoming more and more rare and are used in few corporate environments.

The DNS tab of the Properties dialog box was discussed in detail in the "Configuring DHCP for DNS Integration" section earlier in the chapter. Use the Advanced tab for the following configuration options (see in Figure 16.7):

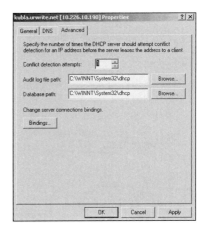

◆ **Conflict Detection Attempts.** This option will cause the DHCP server to check for conflicting IP addresses on the network before issuing an address. Although this sounds like a great way to make sure there are no address conflicts, this can add significant overhead to the server and should be used only while troubleshooting address conflict issues. By default, this is set to 0.

◆ **Audit Log File Path.** If DHCP Audit Logging is enabled, the log file is located in the `C:\<%system_root%>\System32\dhcp` directory. You can modify the default from this tab.

FIGURE 16.7
The Advanced options shouldn't be modified without a thorough understanding of the options and the ramifications of the change.

◆ **Database Path.** This option allows you to specify the location of the DHCP database. By default, it is in `C:\<%system_root%>\System32\dhcp`.

◆ **Change Server Connection Bindings.** This option allows you to view the connections the DHCP server is providing addresses through. If you have multiple connections to your DHCP server, you may want to configure DHCP for only selected interfaces. Click the Bindings button to view this screen (see Figure 16.8).

Now that you have looked at the options for managing the DHCP server, let's take a look at some of the ways to monitor the service. First, you need to be familiar with the counters that can be measured for DHCP:

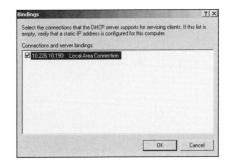

FIGURE 16.8
The Bindings section allows you to configure the interfaces that will be used to respond to DHCP requests.

◆ **Packets Received/Sec.** The number of message packets received per second by the DHCP server. A large number indicates a large number of DHCP message traffic to the server. These include requests for addresses, renewal requests, and releases.

◆ **Duplicates Dropped/Sec.** The number of duplicate packets per second dropped by the DHCP server. Duplicate packets on a network are never a good sign, and in this case, it indicates that DHCP clients are timing out before the server can respond. Client computers timing out too fast or the server not responding fast enough can cause this.

EXAM TIP

Know the Types of DHCP Statistics   Although you don't need to memorize these counters for the exam, you should at least be familiar with the types of statistics that can be gathered for DHCP.

♦ **Packets Expired/Sec.** The number of packets per second that expire and are dropped by the DHCP server. A packet remaining in the server's internal message queue for too long causes this. A large number here indicates that the server is either taking too long to process some packets, causing other packets to wait in queue, or the traffic on the network is too high for the DHCP server to handle.

♦ **Milliseconds Per Packet (Avg).** The average time, in milliseconds, the DHCP server takes to process each packet it receives. A sudden increase in this counter could indicate a disk issue or an increased load on the server.

♦ **Active Queue Length.** The current length of the internal message queue of the DHCP server. This number represents the number of unprocessed messages received by the server. A large number here could indicate an unusually high amount of network traffic or a high load on the server.

♦ **Conflict Check Queue Length.** The current length of the conflict check queue for the DHCP server. Before a Windows 2000 DHCP server will issue an address, it checks to see if any IP address conflicts exist. A large value here could indicate heavy lease traffic at the server.

♦ **Discovers/Sec.** The number of DHCPDiscover messages received per second by the server. A sudden increase in this counter could indicate that a large number of client computers are attempting to initialize and obtain an IP address lease from the server at the same time.

♦ **Offers/Sec.** The number of DHCPOffer messages sent per second by the DHCP server to client computers. A sudden increase in this value could indicate heavy traffic or a heavy load on the server.

♦ **Requests/Sec.** The number of DHCPRequest messages received per second by the DHCP server from client computers. An increase in this number indicates that a large number of client computers are probably trying to renew their leases with the DHCP server. This could be because of a short lease time configuration, or a number of new computers could be entering the network.

◆ **Informs/Sec.** The number of DHCPInform messages received per second by the DHCP server. This is part of the Dynamic DNS integration, and an unusual increase in this number could indicate a large number of addresses being issued.

◆ **Acks/Sec.** The number of DHCPAck messages sent per second by the DHCP server to client computers. An increase in this number indicates that a large number of client computers are probably trying to renew their leases with the DHCP server. This could be because of a short lease time configuration, or a number of new computers could be entering the network.

◆ **Nacks/Sec.** The number of DHCP negative acknowledgment messages sent per second by the DHCP server to client computers. This indicates the server is unable to fulfill the DHCP request. A very high value for this counter could indicate a network issue or misconfiguration of client computers or the server. Keep an eye out for a deactivated scope as a possible culprit.

◆ **Declines/Sec.** The number of DHCPDecline messages received per second by the DHCP server from client computers. You will see this number rise when client computers start having address conflict issues. This could indicate a network issue, computers with static addresses that are also part of a scope, or potentially a "rogue" DHCP server on the network.

◆ **Releases/Sec.** The number of DHCPRelease messages received per second by the DHCP server from client computers. A DHCPRelease message is sent only when the client computer manually releases an address, such as when the ipconfig /release command or the Release All button in the winipcfg utility is used at the client computer. Because most users do not manually release their addresses, this number should be low in all but the most unusual network environment.

To configure DHCP Performance monitoring, follow Step by Step 16.8.

EXAM TIP

What Can You Do to Resolve Conflict Issues? When you start seeing a high number of declines per second, you may want to enable conflict detection on the DHCP server. This will cause the server to look for conflicts before issuing an address, and it should take care of the conflict issues until you can find the problem. This should be used only until the issue is addressed. Forcing the DHCP server to detect conflicts every time it issues an address adds a lot of overhead to the server and the DHCP service and should be avoided on a long-term basis. After you have resolved the issue, be sure to turn this feature off.

ON THE CD

Step by Step 16.8, "Monitoring DHCP Performance," walks you through DHCP performance monitoring. See the file **Chapter16-08StepbyStep.pdf** in the CD's **Chapter16\StepbyStep** directory.

You've looked at the management options available in the DHCP manager application, and you've taken a look at how to monitor the performance of the different DHCP counters using the Performance utility. One other feature of the DHCP service should be discussed—Simple Network Management Protocol (SNMP).

The Simple Network Management Protocol (SNMP) and Management Information Bases (MIBs) form an industry standard set of management protocols for managing complex networks. First developed in the early 1980s, SNMP works by sending messages, called to different parts of a network. SNMP-compliant devices store statistical data about themselves in MIBs and return this data to the SNMP-compliant managers.

The DHCP manager now supports SNMP and MIBs, which allows the DHCP server to report statistics and send alerts to any of a number of management platforms, including HP OpenView, Seagate Nerve Center, and even Novell's ManageWise product. This allows administrators to monitor DHCP information, including the following:

◆ The number of available addresses

◆ The number of used addresses

◆ The number of leases being processed per second

◆ The number of messages and offers processed

◆ The number of Requests, Acknowledgements, Declines, Negative Status Acknowledgment messages (Nacks), and Releases received

◆ The total number of scopes and addresses on the server, the number used, and the number available

If you would like to know more about SNMP and MIBS, check out
A Practical Guide to SNMPv3 and Network Management, by David
Zeltserman (Prentice Hall).

At this point, you should have a good understanding of the
Windows 2000 DHCP service. Next, you'll see how to apply it
in a practical situation.

CASE STUDY: IMPLEMENTING DHCP IN A COMPLEX ENVIRONMENT

ESSENCE OF THE CASE

The essence of the case is as follows:

▶ Your company is about to migrate to a pure Windows 2000 environment.

▶ Your company has three networks, two with users and one as a backbone. The Sales network has approximately 400 users; the Engineering network has 75 users.

▶ The three networks are connected by two routers—Router A and Router B.

▶ The Sales network has plenty of addresses because of the multinetted network. The Engineering network does not have enough addresses for its network, but the engineers are able to work because they work in shifts.

SCENARIO

You are the network administrator for NR Widgets Inc., a computer manufacturing company. NR Widgets Inc. is just about to migrate to a pure Windows 2000 environment. You have two user networks (see Figure 16.9)—Sales and Engineering, and a corporate backbone network. The Sales network has more than 400 users and is multinetted to provide an adequate number of addresses for everyone. The Engineering network has only 75 users, but the network also contains a number of printers, plotters, and test equipment, so that there are only 40 addresses for the users. The users work three shifts in Engineering, with 25 engineers working each shift.

Today, all the hosts use static addresses, which works okay for the Sales network, but it means that to avoid IP address resolution issues, the engineers have to be careful about which computers are left connected to the network. Yesterday your manager suggested, "While you're migrating to Windows 2000, why don't you fix the IP address problems on the network?"

continues

CASE STUDY: IMPLEMENTING DHCP IN A COMPLEX ENVIRONMENT

continued

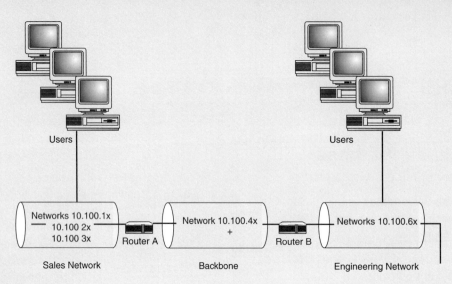

FIGURE 16.9
Case Study network diagram.

Keeping in mind that the boss's "suggestions" usually mean "Have it done by the end of the week," what should you do?

ANALYSIS

This situation provides an excellent opportunity to deploy the Windows 2000 DHCP service as part of the Windows 2000 rollout. To make it work, you need to make sure you do the following:

- Allocate the server resources to support at least one DHCP server. To avoid as much traffic traversing the router as possible, you should plan on placing the server on the network that will be generating the most

DHCP requests. Because 400 users are on the Sales network, at first glance you may think that is where all the requests will be coming from. Think again. Because there are plenty of addresses for the Sales network, you can configure exceptionally long lease times, so the number of requests after the initial lease will be pretty low. On the Engineering network, however, users will be requesting a new address every time they power up the computer, because of the limited number of addresses.

- After you have identified the server and placed it on the network, you will need to install and configure DHCP. After the service is installed, you will need to authorize the server in the Active Directory.

CASE STUDY: IMPLEMENTING DHCP IN A COMPLEX ENVIRONMENT

- When you create your scopes, you should create a single scope for the Engineering network and a superscope for the Sales network. The superscope allows you to combine multiple scopes (the Sales network has three network addresses) for easier management. The lease for each of the scopes within the superscope should be at least 30 days, to ensure that a limited amount of lease traffic traverses the routers. The lease for the Engineering network should be 8 hours so that addresses are available for the incoming shift as the previous shift leaves for home.

- Finally, you need to be sure that the BOOTP Forwarder service is running on the routers and is configured to point to the appropriate DHCP server for forwarding DHCP traffic.

This should have been a fairly easy case study if you read the chapter carefully. Of course, after the DHCP server is set up and running, you would also want to set up some of the monitoring discussed at the end of the chapter.

CHAPTER SUMMARY

KEY TERMS

- Address pool
- Domain Name System (DNS)
- Dynamic Host Control Protocol (DHCP)
- DHCP server
- DHCP client
- Exclusion
- Lease
- Management Information Bases (MIB)
- Reservation
- Scope
- Simple Network Management Protocol (SNMP)
- Superscope
- Transmission Control Protocol/Internet Protocol (TCP/IP)
- Request For Comment (RFC)
- BOOTP protocol
- Multicast scope
- Registered IP address
- Supernetted network
- Unicast addresses

Let's recap what was discussed in this chapter. We have discussed all the key components of using a Windows 2000 DHCP Server in a Windows 2000 environment. We first discussed what DHCP was and where it came from. We covered the different types of scopes in detail, and then we went through the steps of installing DHCP, creating the first scope, and then authorizing the server in Active Directory. That is enough to give you a working DHCP server.

From there, we discussed creating superscopes and multicast scopes, integrating DNS and DHCP, and we finished the chapter with a discussion of the different methods for monitoring and managing DHCP.

APPLY YOUR KNOWLEDGE

Review Questions

1. You are the network administrator for Exponent Mathematicians, and you have been asked to implement DHCP on a multinetted network segment. What should you do to ensure that this is successful?

2. You are the administrator of the Get Bux pawnshop chain's DHCP server. You are getting complaints from users that they keep getting address conflict messages when they turn on their computers. What DHCP counter might help you identify the issue?

3. You are the Windows 2000 Administrator for Fly Away Travel. When administering Fly Away's DHCP server, you notice that the number of DHCP requests is very high for the number of users on the network. Where is the first place you should look for a server-related issue?

4. You're the administrator of Little Faith Enterprise's Windows 2000 DHCP Server. You notice that the DHCP server is running sluggishly during peak hours. While checking the Performance utility, you notice the DHCP Conflict Check Queue Length is very high. What could be causing this issue?

5. You're the administrator of Little Faith Enterprise's Windows 2000 DHCP Server, and you have just installed the DHCP service and created your first scope using the Scope Wizard. You are trying to provide DHCP addresses to a group of users that are two router hops away. What do you still need to do?

Answers to Review Questions

1. To successfully implement DHCP in a multinetted environment, you should consider using a superscope to ease the management of the scopes for each of the multinetted networks. For more information, see the section "Installing, Configuring, and Troubleshooting DHCP."

2. In the Performance utility, check the Declines/Sec counter for the DHCP object. The number of DHCPDecline messages received per second by the DHCP server from client computers can be used to see if the DHCP client computer has declined the IP address issued by the server. You will see this number rise when client computers start having address conflict issues. This could indicate a network issue, computers with static addresses that are also part of a scope, or potentially a "rogue" DHCP server on the network. For more information, see the section "Managing and Monitoring DHCP."

3. Check the length of the DHCP lease. If the lease has been set to a very short duration, client computers would need to request addresses frequently. For more information, see the section "Installing, Configuring, and Troubleshooting DHCP."

4. There are either a lot of DHCP requests occurring during peak hours, or the Conflict Detection Attempts parameter is set too high. If this is enabled, Windows 2000 DHCP server will issue an address, and it will check to see if any IP address conflicts exist. This can put a lot of additional overhead on the server and drive up the DHCP Conflict Check Queue Length. For more information, see the section "Managing and Monitoring DHCP."

APPLY YOUR KNOWLEDGE

5. First, you need to activate the DHCP server in Active Directory. It will not be able to provide addresses until that occurs. You also need to configure the BOOTP Forwarder on any routers between the DHCP server and the client workstations so that the routers know where to forward DHCP messages. For more information, see the section "Installing, Configuring, and Troubleshooting DHCP."

ON THE CD

This book's companion CD contains specially designed supplemental material to help you understand how well you know the concepts and skills you learned in this chapter. You'll find related exercises and exam questions and answers. See the file **Chapter16ApplyYourKnowledge.pdf** in the CD's **Chapter16ApplyYourKnowledge** directory.

Suggested Readings and Resources

1. Droms, Dr. Ralph, and Ted Lemon. *The DHCP Handbook: Understanding, Deploying, and Managing Automated Configuration Services.* Indianapolis, IN: Macmillan Technical Publishing, 1999.

2. Siyan, Karanjit S. *Windows NT TCP/IP.* Indianapolis, IN: New Riders Publishing, 1998.

3. Kercheval, Berry. *DHCP: A Guide to Dynamic TCP/IP Network Configuration.* Upper Saddle River, NJ: Prentice Hall Computer Books, 1998.

If you have ever used a modem to connect your Windows computer to another server or network, you have used *remote access*. With Windows 2000, Microsoft has introduced many new remote access capabilities to its operating system. This chapter covers the "Configuring, Managing, Monitoring, and Troubleshooting Remote Access in a Windows 2000 Network Infrastructure" objectives for this exam.

Microsoft defines the "Configuring, Managing, Monitoring, and Troubleshooting Remote Access in a Windows 2000 Network Infrastructure" objectives as:

Configure and troubleshoot remote access.

- **Configure inbound connections.**

- **Create a remote access policy.**

- **Configure a remote access profile.**

- **Configure a virtual private network (VPN).**

- **Configure multilink connections.**

- **Configure Routing and Remote Access for Dynamic Host Configuration Protocol (DHCP) Integration.**

▶ Windows servers have always functioned as remote access servers, and with Windows 2000, Microsoft enhances remote access capabilities. This objective helps you understand how to configure the different remote access features included with Windows 2000 Server.

Manage and monitor remote access.

▶ If you are going to use your Windows 2000 Server for remote access, you need to know how to manage and monitor it.

CHAPTER 17

Configuring, Managing, Monitoring, and Troubleshooting Remote Access in a Windows 2000 Network Infrastructure

Configure remote access security.

- **Configure authentication protocols.**

- **Configure encryption protocols.**

- **Create a remote access policy.**

▶ Security is becoming more important in today's computing environment. This objective tests your understanding of the security capabilities of Windows 2000 Server and remote access.

▶ Make certain you have a thorough understanding of the security capabilities of all the different remote access mechanisms.

▶ Review the different types of encryption available for authenticating and securing your information through remote access.

▶ Pay close attention to the capabilities of remote access policies. Windows 2000 includes a number of policy-based management capabilities, and understanding the policies associated with remote access is important for this exam.

▶ Complete the exercises at the end of the chapter. Microsoft is striving to make certification exams more rigorous. Familiarity not only with the theory, but also with the hands-on portion of the configuration and troubleshooting of remote access is important for this exam.

CONFIGURING AND TROUBLESHOOTING REMOTE ACCESS

Configure and troubleshoot remote access.

Before we begin discussing how to configure remote access with Windows 2000 Server, we should take a minute to review exactly what remote access is under Windows 2000.

The Routing and Remote Access Service is installed automatically with the operating system, and also bundles a number of features that used to be distributed through other services under Windows NT. The following is a list of items included in Routing and Remote Access Service:

◆ Full integration with the Windows 2000 operating system.

◆ Consistent management interface for all routing-based activities, including remote access, VPN, and Internet Protocol (IP) and IPX routing.

◆ Fewer reboots. If you worked with earlier versions of Windows, you are familiar with the "change any network configuration and reboot the machine" method of managing Windows networking. With Windows 2000, the number of times you need to reboot the server is dramatically lessened.

◆ Additional VPN services and simplified VPN management. The VPN interfaces (PPTP and L2TP) are installed and configured by default, requiring no additional configuration.

◆ Network Address Translation has been added, as has Internet Connection Sharing.

◆ Additional authentication mechanisms have been added to Routing and Remote Access, including MS-CHAP v2, Remote Authentication Dial-in User Service (RADIUS), and Extensible Authentication Protocol (EAP) (for smart card and certificate support).

One other key point to remember when discussing Microsoft's Routing and Remote Access Service and remote access capabilities is that in previous incarnations, the term Remote Access Service (RAS) was used interchangeably to refer to the dial-in connections as well as the service that ran the dial-up server. With the new Routing and Remote Access Service, Microsoft is striving to clarify its use of terminology. So in Windows 2000 vernacular, Routing and Remote Access refers only to the Routing and Remote Access application. The server is called either a dial-in or dial-up server, or in the case of VPN, a VPN server. The client computers are called dial-in or dial-up clients.

It is important to keep in mind that Microsoft's Routing and Remote Access Service considers all connections to be local area network (LAN) connections. What this means from a functionality perspective is that all the services available via LAN connection are also available via modem connection.

Understanding Remote Access Protocols

Microsoft's Routing and Remote Access Service supports two data link control protocols for asynchronous connections:

◆ **Serial Line Interface Protocol (SLIP).** Supported for legacy applications and is almost never used due to security issues, such as clear-text authentication. SLIP can only be used on dial-up client computers, and no support for accepting SLIP dial-up connections exists.

◆ **Point-to-Point Protocol (PPP).** PPP is the protocol most use when connecting via modem. PPP can automatically establish and re-establish connections, use error correction, and support multiple protocols. The Windows 2000 implementation for PPP is fully RFC 1661 "Point-to-Point Protocol" compliant.

Windows 2000 can connect to any other RFC 1661-compliant dial-up server and can accept connections from any compliant client computers. The real strength of this protocol is the support for multiple network protocols, such as IPX, IP, and AppleTalk. SLIP was restricted to only IP. PPP uses a number of authentication protocols, as discussed later in the chapter.

We discuss many of these features as we move through this chapter. For now, let's take a look at the simplest use for the Routing and Remote Access Service.

Configuring Inbound Connections

If your company has mobile users, it is certain you have dealt with requests for access to the network, such as access to mail or the company intranet or even to file shares or applications. Windows 2000 permits inbound connections via attached modems as part of Routing and Remote Access.

IN THE FIELD

ISSUES TO CONSIDER IN CONFIGURING SYSTEMS FOR MOBILE USERS

If you deploy Windows 2000 as your remote access solution for mobile users, you need to keep a couple of things in mind. First, because any server has only a limited number of communication ports, you probably need a multiport modem card. Various manufacturers offer these types of products, but be sure to check the Microsoft Hardware Compatibility List before making any purchases.

Also, avoid installing this capability on any domain controllers or application servers. Although the overhead associated with supporting dial-up users is fairly low, the security ramifications of connecting a modem or modems to a production application server, or even worse—a domain controller—are significant. You should try to avoid that architecture if at all possible.

In the latest version of Routing and Remote Access, Microsoft has added some new features as part of the management. One of the features that has the most impact on the discussion of remote access is the addition of remote access policies. Remote access policies are a radical departure from the Windows NT 3.5x and 4 models, in which user authorization was based on a simple Grant Dial-In Permission to User option in User Manager or the Remote Access Admin console. Callback options were also configured on a per-user basis. In Windows 2000, authorization is granted based on the dial-in properties of a user account and remote access policies.

Remote access policies are a set of conditions and connection settings that give network administrators more flexibility in authorizing connection attempts. The Windows 2000 Routing and Remote Access Service uses remote access policies to determine whether to accept or reject connection attempts. With remote access policies, you can grant remote access by individual user account or through the configuration of specific remote access policies. We look at setting up a policy in the "Creating a Remote Access Policy" section later in the chapter.

Windows 2000 uses the following three types of policies to control remote access:

- **Local Internet Authentication Services policies.** These local policies are derived from RADIUS and can be used to define access permissions based on a number of client attributes.

- **Central Internet Authentication Services policies.** A dial-up server can be configured to use a central IAS RADIUS server to provide its policies. This allows multiple Routing and Remote Access dial-up servers to use the same policies without requiring manual replication of policies and settings.

- **Group Policies.** More in line with the older versions of remote access; access can be controlled by Group Policies.

> **EXAM TIP**
>
> **Know Where Remote Access Group Policies Are Stored**
> Remote Access Group Policies are stored in the file system in the default `WINNT\SYSVOL\SYSVOL\ <domain name>` directory.

Now let's look at how to configure a Windows 2000 Server to support an inbound connection.

ON THE CD

Step by Step 17.1, "Configuring Remote Access Inbound Connections," guides you through the process of configuring remote access inbound connections. See the file **Chapter17-01StepbyStep.pdf** in the CDs **Chapter17\StepbyStep** directory.

Now that you have a dial-up connection, let's explore creating a remote access policy to define what can be done with the new connections.

Creating a Remote Access Policy

A remote access policy is a set of actions that can be applied to a group of dial-up users that meet a specified set of requirements. Microsoft uses the example of email rules to illustrate this point. In many email packages, you can configure a rule that allows you to delete all messages from a specific user or group of users. A remote access policy is similar in that you can specify actions based on a number of criteria.

ON THE CD

Step by Step 17.2, "Creating a Remote Access Policy," illustrates how to create a remote access policy. See the file **Chapter17-02StepbyStep.pdf** in the CD's **Chapter17\StepbyStep** directory.

Configuring a Remote Access Profile

After creating a remote access policy, the next phase of the process is configuring a remote access profile. To learn how to do this, follow Step by Step 17.3.

ON THE CD

Step by Step 17.3, "Configuring a Remote Access Profile," shows you how to configure a remote access profile. See the file **Chapter17-03StepbyStep.pdf** in the CD's **Chapter17\StepbyStep** directory.

The following is a list of some of the parameters you can configure within a remote access profile:

◆ **Dial-in Constraints.** You can configure restrictions on the dial-in users (see Figure 17.1), including the idle disconnect timer, the maximum length of the session, the time and day access is permitted, the dial-in number allowed, and the dial-in media allowed.

◆ **IP.** You can set an IP Address Assignment Policy, if necessary (see Figure 17.2). The following are three possible settings for the IP Address Assignment Policy:

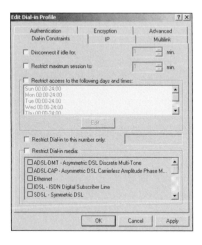

FIGURE 17.1
Dial-in constraints include settings for disconnect intervals, time of day, phone number, and media restrictions.

- **Server Must Supply an IP Address.** For this setting to work, the server must have a DHCP range configured for remote access. The client computer cannot connect without requesting an address.

- **Client May Request an IP Address.** This setting leaves the determination on whether to use a DHCP address to the client computer. If the client computer has a statically configured address, it still can connect.

- **Server Settings Define Policy.** This setting defers the decision on IP address policy to the Routing and Remote Access Server's Global Policy.

You can also apply IP Packet Filters from the IP tab. Packet filters can be configured for traffic sent to the client computer or traffic received from the client computer. These filters are applied by the network and can be used to filter a variety of IP-based protocols, including Any, Other, Internet Control Message Protocol (ICMP), User Datagram Protocol (UDP), Transmission Control Protocol (TCP), and TCP [established].

❖ **Multilink.** You can configure Windows 2000's capability to aggregate multiple analog phone lines connected to multiple modems to provide greater bandwidth. From the Multilink Settings section, you can configure the following (see Figure 17.3) :

- **Default to Server Settings.** Defers the configuration to the Routing and Remote Access global settings.

- **Disable Multilink (Restrict Client to a Single Port).** This configuration restricts dial-up clients from gaining access to multilink capabilities.

- **Allow Multilink.** This configuration allows a client computer to connect using multiple ports, and you can configure the number of ports they can use.

The Bandwidth Allocation Protocol (BAP) can be used to configure when to drop one of the multilink lines, based on usage. If the usage drops below a configurable amount of bandwidth (50% is the default) for a specified amount of time (2 minutes is the default), one of the multilink lines is dropped. You can also enable the Require BAP for Dynamic Multilink Requests.

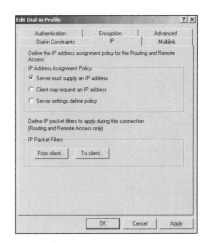

FIGURE 17.2
IP settings include IP Address Assignment Policy and Packet Filter definitions.

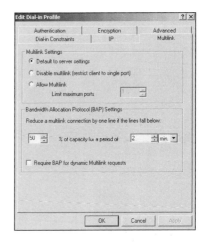

FIGURE 17.3
The multilink capabilities of Windows 2000 allow you to maximize bandwidth across multiple analog phone systems.

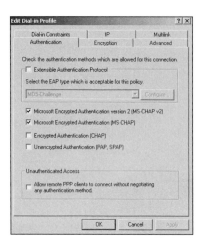

FIGURE 17.4
To take advantage of the multilink capabilities
of Windows 2000, enable it for the appropriate
group.

◆ **Authentication.** You can configure the authentication methods supported by Windows 2000 (See Figure 17.4). The protocols supported for authentication are covered later in this chapter in the section titled "Configuring Authentication Protocols."

◆ **Encryption.** You can set the level of encryption required with Routing and Remote Access authentication. You can set it to No Encryption, Basic, Strong, or allow any combination of the three (see Figure 17.5).

◆ **Advanced.** You can set RADIUS attributes and any additional attributes on the Advanced tab (see Figure 17.6).

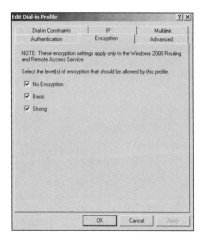

FIGURE 17.5
Routing and Remote Access supports three
levels of encryption.

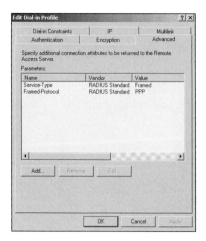

FIGURE 17.6
If you need to configure RADIUS attributes, do
so on the Advanced tab.

IN THE FIELD

PUTTING RADIUS TO WORK

If you have worked in a large remote access environment, you might have run across RADIUS already. But for those of you who haven't, we discuss it a bit here. RADIUS is an authentication and accounting system used by many Internet Service Providers (ISPs) and enterprise networks. When you dial in to the ISP, you must enter your username and password. This information is passed to a RADIUS server, which checks that the information is correct and then authorizes access to the ISP system. Though not an official standard, the RADIUS specification is maintained by a working group of the Internet Engineering Task Force (IETF).

Another place you see RADIUS used is in leveraging account information in a Windows 2000 domain. The built-in RADIUS server can be used not only to authenticate Routing and Remote Access client computers, but it can also be used by third-party dial-in servers as an authentication method. In fact, some ISPs authenticate users for an enterprise account by passing RADIUS authentication requests to a local RADIUS server, allowing the company to control who gets access to the Internet.

Configuring a Virtual Private Network (VPN)

Several different VPN solutions are available: Firewall vendors have VPN components within their firewall platform, router vendors also have VPN services bundled with the router OS, and some solutions run on a network operating system, such as the VPN bundled with Windows 2000. For the sake of our discussion, a VPN is a private network constructed using a public network (such as the Internet) to connect its nodes.

The first thing you need to be aware of when discussing the Windows 2000 VPN is the encryption protocols available. Windows 2000 has two main encryption protocols that are used in the VPN. They include the following:

◆ **Point-to-Point Tunneling Protocol (PPTP).** PPTP is Microsoft's legacy protocol for supporting VPNs. Developed jointly by Microsoft Corporation, U.S. Robotics, and several remote access vendor companies, known collectively as the PPTP Forum, PPTP encountered some security issues in its original form. It has been revised by Microsoft but has never been widely accepted by the security community. Although still supported on a variety of vendors' VPN servers, PPTP is rapidly being overtaken by the more widely adopted IPSec protocol.

◆ **IP Security Protocol (IPSec).** IPSec is a suite of cryptography-based protection services and security protocols that are used for the first standards-based VPN protocol. In Windows 2000, IPSec is used to provide machine-level authentication, as well as data encryption, for Layer 2 Tunneling Protocol (L2TP)-based VPN connections. Unlike some other IPSec-based VPNs, Microsoft's implementation uses the L2TP protocol for transporting the usernames, passwords, and data whereas IPSec is used to negotiate the secure connection between a computer and its remote tunnel server.

Table 17.1 shows the differences that exist between L2TP/IPSec and PPTP.

TABLE 17.1

THE DIFFERENCES BETWEEN L2TP/IPSEC AND PPTP

L2TP/IPSec	PPTP
Standards-based	Microsoft proprietary
Windows, Linux, Macintosh, Solaris, and other platforms	Windows OS and Linux platforms
DES/3DES encryption	Microsoft proprietary encryption
Requires only that the tunnel media provide packet-oriented, point-to-point connectivity	Requires an IP-based transit internetwork
Supports header compression	No header compression

ON THE CD

Step by Step 17.4, "Configuring a Virtual Private Network," demonstrates how to configure a virtual private network. See the file **Chapter17-04StepbyStep.pdf** in the CD's **Chapter17\StepbyStep** directory.

IN THE FIELD

YOUR VPN IS ONLY AS GOOD AS YOUR INTERNET CONNECTION

Although VPNs are used frequently to replace more traditional remote access methods, such as dial-in, people overlook a couple of things when putting together a VPN. First, the assumption is that a VPN is faster than dialing a remote access server, which is not necessarily true. Bottleneck conditions at your ISP connection, congestion issues on the Internet, or even server capacity issues on the VPN server itself can hinder the speed of the VPN connection. Make sure you set realistic expectations for your users regarding the capabilities of your new VPN. Second, just putting up a VPN does not mean that all your remote access problems are solved. You'll find that a host of new issues can quickly arise. How end users get access to the Internet, the size and capacity of the VPN server, even the available Internet bandwidth can place a quick bottleneck on the performance of your VPN.

Configuring Multilink Connections

Windows 2000 includes the capability of aggregating multiple modem lines to form a single, higher-bandwidth connection to a remote access server, which was first introduced as part of Windows 98. This connection is usually to an ISP, but it could also be to another Windows 2000 Server, perhaps at a different location. As part of this capability, you can leverage the BAP, a PPP control protocol used to dynamically add or remove additional links to a multilink connection.

> **NOTE**
>
> **Before You Begin Configuring Multilink** If you want to configure multilink, a couple of prerequisites must be met. First, you must have at least two modems installed on the system. Second, you need to have an incoming remote access connection created.

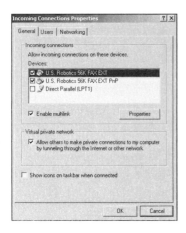

FIGURE 17.7
The Incoming Connections Properties dialog box is where you can configure all the parameters for dialing in, including the multilink configuration.

To set up a multilink connection, you simply need to open the Network and Dial-up Connections window, right-click the Incoming Connections icon, select Properties (see Figure 17.7), and then select Enable Multilink.

If a user dials in with two modems, the server aggregates the connections and allows the user to use the additional bandwidth as needed.

Configuring Routing and Remote Access for DHCP Integration

If you have users who are connecting to your Routing and Remote Access Server, you probably want to dynamically assign them a TCP/IP address on the network. The best way to do this is with DHCP, which must be configured.

DHCP and the Routing and Remote Access Service have an important relationship that you need to understand. When the remote access server is configured to use DHCP, the Routing and Remote Access Server uses the DHCP client component to obtain 10 IP addresses from a DHCP server. This could be on the network or on the same server as the Routing and Remote Access Server. The remote access server uses the first IP address obtained from DHCP for the RAS interface, and subsequent addresses are allocated to TCP/IP-based remote access client computers as they connect. IP addresses are freed because remote access client computers that are disconnecting are reused. When all 10 addresses have been allocated, the process starts again with the DHCP client computer requesting an additional 10 addresses.

ON THE CD

Step by Step 17.5, "Configure Routing and Remote Access for DHCP Integration," shows you how to configure Routing and Remote Access for DHCP integration. See the file **Chapter17-05StepbyStep.pdf** in the CD's **Chapter17\StepbyStep** directory.

MANAGING AND MONITORING REMOTE ACCESS

Manage and monitor remote access.

Now you have a functional Routing and Remote Access Server up and running. How do you manage and monitor it? Let's start by taking a look at the kinds of information the Performance console can provide. It is generally the best tool for monitoring specifics about Windows 2000 services. The Performance console offers the following counters for the RAS object:

EXAM TIP

Don't Memorize All the Counters
Just be familiar with the general categories and how to use the Performance console.

◆ **Alignment Errors.** The size of the packet received is different from the size expected.

◆ **Buffer Overrun Errors.** The software is unable to handle the rate that data is being received.

◆ **Bytes Received.** Total amount of bytes received by the service.

◆ **Bytes Received/Sec.** Number of bytes received by the service in a second.

◆ **Bytes Transmitted.** Total amount of bytes transmitted by the service.

◆ **Bytes Transmitted/Sec.** Number of bytes transmitted by the service in a second.

◆ **CRC Errors.** A received frame contains erroneous data, and the packet did not pass the Cyclic Redundancy Check (CRC).

◆ **Frames Received.** Total number of frames received by the service.

◆ **Frames Received/Sec.** Number of frames received by the service per second.

◆ **Frames Transmitted.** Total number of frames transmitted by the service.

◆ **Frames Transmitted/Sec.** Number of frames transmitted by the service per second.

◆ **Percent Compression In.** Tells how well inbound traffic is being compressed.

> **What Are We Measuring—Aggregate or Port Level?**   The Performance console allows you to monitor these counters on either a port–by–port or an entire server level. Select RAS Ports to look at a single port or RAS Total to see the statistics for the entire server.

◆ **Percent Compression Out.** Tells how well outbound traffic is being compressed.

◆ **Errors—Serial Overrun Errors, Timeout Errors, Total Errors, and Total Errors/Sec.** These objects handle all the error information for the Routing and Remote Access Service.

Now that we have looked at the counters for the service, let's examine some of the ways to monitor the service. To configure Routing and Remote Access Performance monitoring, follow Step by Step 17.6.

ON THE CD

Step by Step 17.6, "Monitor Routing and Remote Access," illustrates the process for configuring Routing and Remote Access Performance monitoring. See the file **Chapter17-06StepbyStep.pdf** in the CD's **Chapter17\StepbyStep** directory.

If you want to view statistics on a VPN connection, use Step by Step 17.7.

ON THE CD

Step by Step 17.7, "Checking the Status of a Port," shows you how to view statistics on a VPN connection. See the file **Chapter17-07StepbyStep.pdf** in the CD's **Chapter17\StepbyStep** directory.

CONFIGURING REMOTE ACCESS SECURITY

The name of this section is a bit of a misnomer. Most of what we have discussed in this chapter so far has to do with remote access security, but Microsoft has used the term Remote Access Security for one specific group of settings. To configure this group of settings, follow Step by Step 17.8.

Configure remote access security.

Step by Step 17.8, "Configuring Remote Access Security," demonstrates how to configure remote access security. See the file **Chapter17-08StepbyStep.pdf** in the CD's **Chapter17\StepbyStep** directory.

Now that you have learned how to complete the RADIUS and Windows authentication, let's look at Windows 2000 authentication protocols.

Configuring Authentication Protocols

Windows 2000 supports a number of authentication protocols; therefore, almost any connection configuration is supported. The protocols include the following:

◆ **Extensible Authentication Protocol (EAP).** EAP-TLS is an extension to the PPP. EAP provides a standard mechanism for support of additional authentication methods within PPP, such as smart cards, one-time passwords, and certificates. EAP is critical for securing Windows 2000 VPNs because it offers stronger authentication methods (such as X.509 certificates) rather than relying on the user ID and password schemes traditionally used.

◆ **Challenge Handshake Authentication Protocol (CHAP).** CHAP negotiates an encrypted authentication using Message Digest 5 (MD5), an industry-standard hashing scheme. CHAP uses challenge-response with one-way MD5 hashing on the response. This allows you to authenticate to the server without actually sending your password over the network. Because MD5 is an industry standard authentication method, it allows Windows 2000 to securely connect to almost all third-party PPP servers.

◆ **Microsoft-Created Challenge Handshake Authentication Protocol (MS-CHAP).** Microsoft created MS-CHAP, an extension of CHAP, to authenticate remote Windows workstations, increasing the protocol's functionality by integrating the encryption and hashing algorithms used on Windows networks. Like CHAP, MS-CHAP uses a challenge-response mechanism with one-way encryption. Although MS-CHAP is consistent with standard CHAP as much as possible, the MS-CHAP response packet is in a format specifically designed for computers running a Windows operating system. A new version of the Microsoft Challenge Handshake Authentication Protocol (MS-CHAP v2) is also available. This new protocol provides mutual authentication, stronger initial data-encryption keys, and different encryption keys for sending and receiving.

◆ **SPAP.** Shiva Password Authentication Protocol (SPAP) is used specifically to allow Shiva client computers to connect to a Windows 2000 Server and to allow Windows 2000 client computers to connect to Shiva servers.

◆ **PAP.** Password Authentication Protocol (PAP) uses unencrypted (plain text) passwords for authenticating users and is considered the least secure authentication protocol available. PAP is usually used as a last resort. You might need to use this protocol when you are connecting to a non-Windows-based server.

To configure these protocols, follow Step by Step 17.9.

ON THE CD

Step by Step 17.9, "Configuring Authentication Protocols," guides you through the process of configuring authentication protocols. See the file **Chapter17-09StepbyStep.pdf** in the CD's **Chapter17\StepbyStep** directory.

Configuring Encryption Protocols

The first thing to be aware of when discussing the encryption protocols available with Windows 2000 is that two main encryption protocols are used in a Windows 2000 VPN. We discussed PPTP and IPSec earlier in the chapter, but a couple of encryption protocols are used in conjunction with IPSec that we need to cover.

Under the Microsoft model, IPSec encryption does not rely on any authentication methods for its initial encryption keys. The encryption method is determined by the IPSec Security Association (SA). An SA is a combination of a destination address, a security protocol, and a unique identification value, called a Security Parameters Index (SPI). The available encryption methods for IPSec include the following:

◆ **Data Encryption Standard (DES).** DES uses a 56-bit encryption key. This is considered adequate encryption for business use, and this level of encryption has been broken using specialized hardware.

◆ **Triple DES (3DES).** Like DES, 3DES uses a 56-bit key. But as the name implies, it encrypts the data using three 56-bit encryption keys. This is considered a 168-bit encryption key ($3 \times 56 = 168$) and is used in high-security environments. Until recently, the U.S. government tightly controlled the export of applications using 3DES encryption. Although these restrictions have been relaxed, at the time of this printing, exporting 3DES applications still requires government approval.

DES and 3DES are available for remote access in Windows 2000. Windows 2000 does use other encryption methods, but they are not applicable to remote access. To configure these protocols, follow the instructions in Step by Step 17.10.

ON THE CD

Step by Step 17.10, "Configuring Encryption Protocols," shows you how to configure encryption protocols. See the file **Chapter17-10StepbyStep.pdf** in the CD's **Chapter17\StepbyStep** directory.

CASE STUDY: IMPLEMENTING ROUTING AND REMOTE ACCESS IN A COMPLEX ENVIRONMENT

ESSENCE OF THE CASE

The essence of the case is as follows:

▶ The management of your company is reluctant to make a major investment in toll charges for a dial-based remote access solution.

▶ Your company has three main populations of users, each with different remote access requirements.

▶ Each team has the requisite level of security.

SCENARIO

You are the network administrator for NR Widgets Inc., a multinational conglomerate, and you are based in the conglomerate's corporate headquarters. NR Widgets Inc. has a mobile population of about 200 people who need access to the network for submitting expense reports.

Approximately 100 of the users live and work within your local area code, and the rest are scattered throughout the country. Your management does not want to pay for long-distance calls for remote access.

The mobile users consist of three groups. The first group is the highly technical telecommuters, who need access to everything. They are also very security conscious and want to be certain their information is as secure as possible. The second group is the local users who need access but are not overly concerned about the security of the connection. The third group consists of about 35 users who work from home and have high-speed Internet connections.

What is the best course of action to take so that the following is accomplished?

- Each group has access to the network.

- Each group of users has the information security it needs.

- Long-distance or toll-free numbers are not allowed.

CASE STUDY: IMPLEMENTING ROUTING AND REMOTE ACCESS IN A COMPLEX ENVIRONMENT

ANALYSIS

As you have discovered in this chapter, you can meet these requirements by installing the Windows 2000 Routing and Remote Access Service, but a bit more is required than simply running the Configuration Wizard. First you need to take a close look at each user population. The technical telecommuters, who have access to confidential information, need to have a configuration that leverages the robust security and encryption mechanisms of the Windows 2000 Routing and Remote Access Service. You may need their remote access profiles configured to use callback security, and they also may need to use smart cards for authentication. For the second group of users, you probably need to limit their access to sensitive information on the network, since they are using a less secure, more user-friendly authentication policy. Finally, while it is easy to configure a network—an Internet-based VPN, for example—you still need to make some decisions. You need to determine the amount of bandwidth to the Internet necessary to support these users, and you need to consider where the server should be placed. Should it be behind a firewall or directly on the Internet? You need to consider which VPN protocol is best-suited for your environment. You may even find that your remote users who are not in the local area code want to utilize a local ISP in conjunction with the VPN solution, allowing you to further save on toll charges. All this is dependent, of course, on the environment and the circumstances and requires effective planning. You need to install the following to implement the solutions you choose:

- One server must run Windows 2000 Server and the Routing and Remote Access Service.

- The server needs to have modems installed and configured for dial-in users.

- Users who do not have the ability to dial the server locally need to leverage the Windows 2000 VPN service; therefore, the server needs an Internet connection.

- The server needs remote access profiles configured to control the session security for each group.

Let's do a quick chapter recap.

CHAPTER SUMMARY

KEY TERMS

- Virtual private network (VPN)
- Modem
- Multilink
- Encryption
- Dynamic Host Control Protocol (DHCP)
- Authentication
- Remote Access Service (RAS)
- Callback

In this chapter we covered in detail how to use the Windows 2000 Routing and Remote Access Service to provide remote access services. We started the chapter discussing how to configure Routing and Remote Access to support inbound connections, DHCP, VPNs, multilink connections, and we also discussed the creation and use of a remote access policy. We examined how to use and configure a remote access profile as well.

We then discussed monitoring and managing the Routing and Remote Access Service and wrapped up the chapter by discussing the different security aspects of the service, including remote access security configuration, authentication protocols, and encryption.

ON THE CD

This book's companion CD contains specially designed supplemental material that will help you assess how well you absorbed the concepts and skills you learned in this chapter. You'll find related exercises and exam questions and answers. See the file **Chapter17ApplyYourKnowledge.pdf** in the CD's **Chapter17\ ApplyYourKnowledge** directory.

Suggested Readings and Resources

1. Boswell, William. *Inside Windows 2000 Server.* Indianapolis, IN: New Riders Publishing, 2000.

2. Siyan, Karanjit S. *Windows NT TCP/IP.* Indianapolis, IN: New Riders Publishing, 1998.

Install, configure, and troubleshoot network protocols.

- **Install and configure TCP/IP.**
- **Install the NWLink protocol.**
- **Configure network bindings.**

▶ A Windows 2000 Server obviously requires connectivity with other computers and devices on a network to be effective. You need to be knowledgeable in the fundamentals of TCP/IP and NWLink for this exam. In addition, a complete understanding of network bindings is essential. Network bindings are a method of "linking" a protocol to a network card or service in a particular, defined order.

Configure TCP/IP packet filters.

▶ As a Windows 2000 administrator, you want control of how packets are allowed to enter and leave your network. Proper network design coupled with TCP/IP packet filters will ensure a good foundation for network security.

Configure and troubleshoot network protocol security.

▶ As networks become more sophisticated, more connected to the outside world, and reliant on the WAN connectivity, more back doors are created and, therefore, more doors to lock. This chapter examines how Windows 2000 provides basic protocol security and how you can implement and troubleshoot your security plan.

Manage and monitor network traffic.

▶ Windows 2000 includes some tools to monitor, manage, and troubleshoot network traffic. For this exam, you need a working knowledge of these tools. We will examine the productivity of these tools and how you can implement plans to reduce overall network traffic while increasing reliability.

CHAPTER 18

Installing, Configuring, Managing, Monitoring, and Troubleshooting Network Protocols in a Windows 2000 Network Infrastructure

Configure and troubleshoot IPSec.

- **Enable IPSec.**

- **Configure IPSec for transport mode.**

- **Configure IPSec for tunnel mode.**

- **Customize IPSec policies and rules.**

- **Manage and monitor IPSec.**

▶ As a Windows 2000 administrator, you should be familiar with IPSec (Internet Protocol Security) to secure data from network to network. We will examine, configure, and troubleshoot IPSec for different network environments. You need a firm understanding of IPSec policies and rules, configuring IPSec transport and tunneling modes, and monitoring IPSec.

STUDY STRATEGIES

▶ Windows 2000 networking encompasses many areas. As you study network protocol security, break down the issue modularly. Examine and learn a chunk at a time, and then begin to combine those chunks to fit into different network solutions. The Step by Steps on the accompanying CD not only offer you the essential hands-on experience, but they also offer a second learning channel.

▶ Make sure that you understand the basics of TCP/IP. Windows 2000 is very reliant on TCP/IP; no doubt, this exam will focus heavily on the more complex issues of TCP/IP and how it works with Windows 2000. Take some time to review the basics of IP and then build from there.

▶ The Step by Steps throughout this book provide plenty of directions and exercises, but go beyond these examples and create some of your own. If you can, experiment with each of the objectives to see how they work and why you would use each one.

INTRODUCTION

The way you design your network should take into account the geographical locations of your servers, the topology of your network (including Ethernet, token ring, Fiber Distributed Data Interface (FDDI), and so on), and, of course, the protocols your network will use to communicate with servers, workstations, and printers. In this chapter, we discuss the TCP/IP and NWLink (IPX/SPX-compatible) protocols.

TCP/IP is becoming the protocol of choice as our networks grow and interact with other networks around the world. NWLink is a necessity when you migrate legacy NetWare Servers to or integrate them with Windows 2000.

As our network grows, we must also examine the security measures and threats that protocols allow. This chapter focuses on protocol security, management, and monitoring.

INSTALLING, CONFIGURING, AND TROUBLESHOOTING NETWORK PROTOCOLS

First, let's examine the security measurements needed for TCP/IP and NWLink in a Windows 2000 environment. To get started, we need a brief understanding of these protocols and how to install and configure them with Windows 2000.

Understanding TCP/IP

Install and Configure TCP/IP

What is *TCP/IP*? TCP/IP is a suite of protocols that allows host, networks, and operating systems to communicate with each other. As you may know, TCP/IP was originally intended for the Department of Defense to allow its mainframes and servers to communicate with each other locally and remotely.

As mentioned in Chapter 15, "Installing, Configuring, Managing, Monitoring, and Troubleshooting DNS in a Windows 2000 Network Infrastructure," TCP/IP actually evolved from a network created by a vast research agency—the Advanced Research Projects Agency, or ARPA, which performed advanced technical research for the Department of Defense (DOD). This collection of networks, called ARPAnet, connected research centers, such as universities, to each other and with DOD sites such as the Pentagon.

ARPAnet ran on top of the original routing protocol, Network Core Protocol, or NCP. NCP was composed of the TCP and IP protocols. They are actually two separate components, which we will examine in a moment.

The basic design on TCP/IP is simple, fault tolerant, routable, and vendor neutral.

Originally, TCP/IP was used to connect the mainframes. However, the '80s saw the evolution of UNIX and personal computers. UNIX led the way in integrating TCP/IP to connect these PCs. The Macintosh world used the AppleTalk protocol, and much of the Windows world stuck with either NetBEUI or NWLink IPX/SPX-compatible for connectivity with NetWare.

And then this thing called the World Wide Web happened; everyone needed TCP/IP and needed it right away.

Mechanics of IP

IP allows data to travel from one computer to another, either on a local network or through a router to a remote network. How does this work?

If you have eight computers in Chicago connected on the same Ethernet network, you have a LAN. There's no routing and no need for it. In an Ethernet network, each computer receives every packet, regardless of whether the packet is intended for it or not. Recall that it's the physical address (Media Access Control or MAC address) of the network card that determines whether the packet is to be accepted or discarded.

When Computer A needs to send a packet to Computer B on the same Ethernet network via TCP/IP, the packets don't have to pass through a router. What has to happen, however, is that Computer A needs to know the IP address of Computer B. Then, IP resolves that IP address to the MAC address of the network adapter card in Computer B. That MAC address is in the header of the packets sent out onto the network, and only Computer B will accept those headers because only Computer B has that exact MAC address on its network card.

But what about when Computer A in Chicago needs to talk to Computer Z in Atlanta (see Figure 18.1)? Now we have a WAN, so we need a router. A router is a device that routes packets from network to network to network and eventually to the host. Now when Computer A needs to chat with Computer Z, the packets are forwarded onto the router because the destination is not on the local network.

The router then forwards the packet, based on its routing table, to the next router, and onward until eventually the packet ends up at the final network and onto the target computer.

IP Addresses

For routing to happen, a network design must be based on specific rules. The first rule of TCP/IP is that you use a valid IP address. An *IP address* is a series of numbers that represents your computer—for example, 131.108.116.55. Each of the numbers in this IP address is an octet, made up of 8 bits; the whole IP address is 32 bits.

If you were to look at 131.108.116.55 in binary, as the computer sees it, you would see 10000011 01101100 01110100 00110111. IP addresses are typically displayed in decimal format. Each host that requires connectivity on a TCP/IP network requires its own unique IP address.

IP addresses are organized by classes: Class A, B, and C. Table 18.1 defines the range and amount of hosts included with each network.

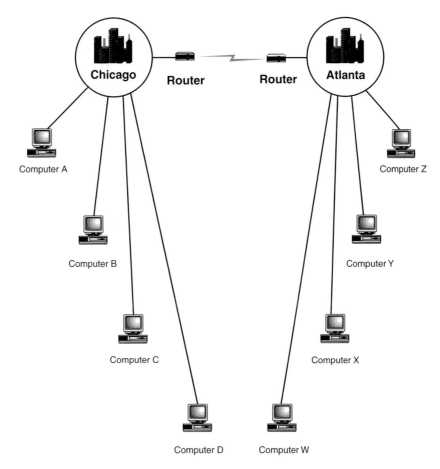

FIGURE 18.1
A wide area network with computers located in Chicago and Atlanta connected via routers.

TABLE 18.1

DETAILS OF IP ADDRESSES

Class	From (First Octet)	To (First Octet)	Number of Net IDs	Number of Host IDs
A	1	126	126	16,777,214
B	128	191	16,384	65,534
C	192	223	2,097,152	254

Subnets and Subnet Masks

If we assume that an IP address identifies your computer, it's fair to say that a subnet identifies where your computer is. The component of an IP address that determines whether packets are to be sent locally or through a router is the subnet mask. The subnet mask tells the protocol whether the local host and the destination host are on the same subnet.

Basically, when the subnet bits match, the host and destination host are on the same subnet and no routing is needed. When the subnet bits don't match, the destination host is on a remote network and the packets are sent to the router.

Default Gateway

A default gateway is the IP address of the router that the packets from a host should use to leave this subnet. The typical process of how a packet leaves a host and gets to a destination is as follows:

1. Computer A resolves Computer Z to an IP address.

2. The IP address of Computer Z is determined to be local or remote.

3. If the address is remote, Computer A sends the packets to the default gateway's MAC address.

4. The default gateway then forwards the packets onto the next router according to its routing table.

5. If Computer Z's IP address is on the same subnet, the IP address of Computer Z is resolved to the MAC address through ARP.

6. Computer A and Computer Z communicate, and there is no need for routing.

This section briefly explained the basics of TCP/IP, its evolution, mechanics, and components. Now you can install TCP/IP.

Installing TCP/IP

Install, configure, and troubleshoot network protocols.

To begin using TCP/IP on your network, you need a list of valid IP licenses, the IP address of your default gateway (router), and the subnet mask for your network. More than likely, your Windows 2000 computer already has TCP/IP installed as its default protocol. Step by Step 18.1 walks you through the process of adding TCP/IP, in case you chose not to install it during Windows 2000 installation.

ON THE CD

Step by Step 18.1, "Adding TCP/IP," walks you through the process of adding TCP/IP in case you chose not to install it during Windows 2000 installation. See the file **Chapter18-01StepbyStep.pdf** in the CD's **Chapter18\StepbyStep** directory.

Configuring TCP/IP

After you have installed the TCP/IP protocol, you will need to configure the protocol with the necessary TCP/IP configuration information. There are two ways to configure an IP address for a Windows 2000 computer. The first is through DHCP (Dynamic Host Configuration Protocol). A DHCP server maintains a database, also known as a scope, of valid IP addresses for a subnet. When a computer configured for DHCP requires an IP address, the computer searches the network for a DHCP server. The DHCP server or servers respond with a valid IP address for the subnet the host is located on.

Using DHCP has many advantages, including the following:

◆ Centralized management of IP address allocation.

◆ Changes made at the server rather than on each computer.

◆ Resolves conflicts of IP addresses.

◆ Resolves problems when hosts move from subnet to subnet.

◆ Saves time from visiting each computer to set the IP properties.

The second choice, which is waning in popularity, is to manually set the IP address on each computer. Although this option may not be popular for workstations, it may be realistic for servers. For services that manipulate TCP/IP, such as WINS, DNS, DHCP, and others, it is recommended that the server has a static IP address.

Step by Step 18.2 guides you through the process of using DHCP on this host or assigning a manual IP address.

ON THE CD

Step by Step 18.2, "Configuring TCP/IP," guides you through the process of using DHCP. See the file **Chapter18-02StepbyStep.pdf** in the CD's **Chapter18\StepbyStep** directory.

After you have added and configured TCP/IP, you may still have to set some additional settings on the protocol. On the TCP/IP Properties dialog box, you can access these settings through the Advanced tab. The following is a listing and explanation of these additional settings:

◆ **IP Settings.** This tab reveals the currently configured IP address assigned to the network card. Also, it allows you to include additional IP addresses to a network card and to specify additional default gateways.

◆ **DNS.** This tab reveals the DNS servers used to resolve fully qualified domain names (FQDNs) and hostnames. In addition, you can specify that Windows 2000 should search for hostnames within this domain first. To connect to a computer whose FQDN is server5.publishing.Midwest.newriders.com, for example, you enter http://server5 rather than the entire FQDN. You can also specify that Windows 2000 search other specified domains for computer names.

◆ **WINS.** Windows Internet Naming Service (WINS) is a service that resolves NetBIOS names to IP addresses. If you're using WINS (and you probably will be if your network includes operating systems such as Windows 98, Windows 95, and possibly Windows NT 4), you need to enter the IP address of the WINS server.

◆ **Options.** The Options tab allows you to access IP Security settings and the TCP/IP filtering settings. These settings are covered in more detail later in this chapter.

Installing the NWLink Protocol

NWLink is Microsoft's 32-bit implementation of IPX/SPX (Internet Packet Exchange/Sequenced Packet Exchange). NWLink, like its Novell counterpart, is a routable, reliable protocol. Older versions of NetWare, such as NetWare 3.*x*, were reliant on IPX/SPX, but newer versions of NetWare can use TCP/IP.

Before installing NWLink on your Windows 2000 computers, you need to gather some information. Following are some common questions you need to answer before installing NWLink:

◆ Will you be migrating your NetWare server to Windows 2000? Or will you be integrating NetWare and Windows 2000?

◆ What version of NetWare are you integrating with Windows 2000? Can that version use TCP/IP in lieu of IPX/SPX?

◆ What is the internal network number for your NetWare server(s) that is being integrated?

◆ What is the frame type in place with your NetWare servers?

The actual process of adding NWLink is fairly straight-forward. When you have the answers to the preceding questions, you are ready to add the protocol and begin the conversion from NetWare or the integration with NetWare. Step by Step 18.3 guides you through the installation process.

ON THE CD

Step by Step 18.3, "Adding NWLink to Windows 2000," guides you through the installation process of NWLink. See the file **Chapter18-03StepbyStep.pdf** in the CD's **Chapter18\StepbyStep** directory.

Configuring NWLink

After adding NWLink, you can configure the protocol with the necessary information to lay the foundation to communicate with NetWare servers and client computers. Remember, this is only the protocol to connect to NetWare servers; typically, additional software, such as Client Services for NetWare (CSNW), Gateway Services for NetWare (GSNW), or File and Print Services for NetWare (FPNW) are required to complete connectivity with NetWare servers and client computers.

CSNW allows a Windows 2000 client computer to connect to NetWare server shares. GSNW allows Windows 2000 Servers to connect to NetWare shares and then act as a gateway by providing Windows network shares linking to the NetWare share points. FPNW allows Windows 2000 Servers to provide network share points that can be accessed by NetWare clients.

ON THE CD

Step by Step 18.4, "Configuring the NWLink Protocol," shows you how to configure NWLink. See the file **Chapter18-04StepbyStep.pdf** in the CD's **Chapter18\StepbyStep** directory.

Configuring Network Bindings

> **EXAM TIP**
>
> **Know Network Bindings** On the exam, you will be tested on your knowledge of what network bindings are and how to configure and edit them.

Network bindings are configurations indicating which protocol Windows 2000 will use first on a network connection for a network service. For example, if your network is locally configured to connect both to NetWare servers via IPX/SPX and to Microsoft networks via TCP/IP, you can specify which protocol should be referenced, or used, first when attempting to connect to resources.

In dealing with network bindings in the past, a specific protocol was associated with a network card. Although that description still holds some truth, Windows 2000 has added a layer of functionality: allowing you to first determine the provider order.

A provider is the component that allows you to connect to network resources. The default provider in Windows 2000 is the Microsoft Windows Network. As you include additional providers, such as GSNW, you need to determine which provider should be used first.

Network providers are not the only components involved in bindings. You also get to choose print providers. Like its counterpart, a print provider helps you get to a different type of resource—a printer.

To set up a binding, position the provider you use most often, (for example, the Microsoft Windows Network) first in the list of providers, followed by FPNW. Position TCP/IP as the first in the list of protocols and NWLink as the second. You establish these priorities by modifying the bindings order.

Changing the bindings sounds easy, but it does take a little planning. As your network grows, you will probably find that you add more and more services; when adding these services, you are also automatically binding the installed protocols to each service. Most likely, your binding order will change as your network changes.

Why should you even worry about bindings? A simple, tiny change in the configuration of your bindings can make a great impact on the performance of your server-to-server and server-to-client relationships. Later in this chapter, you examine networks and how to monitor the impact that a change in the bindings order has had on your overall network performance.

Step by Step 18.5 walks you through the actions required to configure network and print providers. This example presumes that you have a second provider, such as GSNW, installed.

ON THE CD

Step by Step 18.5, "Arranging the Provider Order," walks you through the actions required to configure network and printer providers. See the file **Chapter18-05StepbyStep.pdf** in the CD's **Chapter18\StepbyStep** directory.

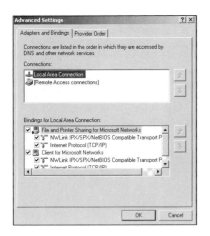

FIGURE 18.2
Bindings are a way of associating a protocol with a network card, service, and connection.

You can also arrange the order of the protocols on the installed services. What you are actually doing here is telling Windows 2000 which protocol to expect to use first. This improves performance—the service will connect and be connected to faster. Figure 18.2 shows the binding order of a typical Windows 2000 Server.

WORKING WITH TCP/IP PACKET FILTERS

Configure TCP/IP packet filters.

Now that you know how to add and configure protocols, arrange the bindings for your connection's services, and prioritize providers, let's look at controlling TCP/IP packets. This section guides you through defining and modifying packet filters.

Windows 2000 allows you to control the type of TCP/IP information that is sent to your computer. You can configure a universal rule for the type of data that reaches all network cards in your server, or you can configure each card individually.

TCP provides guaranteed packet delivery. Table 18.2 lists some common TCP ports that you can allow or deny access to.

TABLE 18.2

COMMON TCP PORT NUMBERS

TCP Port Number	Description
20	FTP Server data channel
21	FTP Server control channel
23	Telnet
80	Web Server – specifically HTTP
139	NetBIOS Session service

UDP does not provide guaranteed packet delivery; instead, it makes a best-effort attempt for delivery. Table 18.3 lists some common UDP ports that you can allow or deny access to.

TABLE 18.3

COMMON UDP PORT NUMBERS

UDP Port Number	Description
53	DNS name queries
69	Trivial File Transfer Protocol
137	NetBIOS Name Server (NBNS)
161	SNMP
520	Routing Information Protocol (RIP)

IP is composed of different protocols. Table 18.4 lists common IP protocol numbers to which you can allow or deny access.

TABLE 18.4

COMMON IP PROTOCOL NUMBERS

Protocol Number	Protocol
1	ICMP Internet Control Message
2	IGMP Internet Group Management
3	GGP Gateway-to-Gateway
4	IP in IP (encapsulation)
5	ST Stream
6	TCP Transmission Control
7	CBT
8	EGP Exterior Gateway Protocol
47	Generic Routing Encapsulation
50	IPSec Authentication Headers (AH)
51	IPSec Encapsulating Security Payloads (ESP)

TCP/IP packet filtering allows you to determine the type of TCP ports that can be accessed, the UDP ports that are accessed, and more directly, which IP protocols can access this computer. For example, you can filter port 80, which is used by the HTTP protocol. By filtering this port, you deny access to all Web servers.

To create a TCP/IP packet filter, assign the appropriate port or IP protocol number in the Advanced properties of TCP/IP. Step by Step 18.6 guides you through the process of creating an IP packet filter.

ON THE CD

Step by Step 18.6, "Establishing IP Filtering," guides you through the process of creating an IP packet filter. See the file **Chapter18-06StepbyStep.pdf** in the CD's **Chapter18\StepbyStep** directory.

After you have established a packet filter, you may find it necessary to revise the existing filter. To change a filter, open the TCP/IP Properties and choose Advanced. On the Options tab, make changes as needed. Approve your changes to enforce the setting.

CONFIGURING AND TROUBLESHOOTING NETWORK PROTOCOL SECURITY

Configure and troubleshoot network protocol security.

As networks grow and interact with other networks, data becomes more vulnerable to attack, interception, and eavesdropping. You must secure your networks to secure your data. This section looks at configuring and troubleshooting your protocols, including the following topics:

◆ Network data security

◆ Using security hosts

◆ Understanding Kerberos

◆ VPNs and tunneling security features

Network Data Security

Windows 2000 has many facets of network protocol security. The most well-known is the IPSec. We will examine IPSec in detail in a moment. For now, know that IPSec is used to secure IP packets transmitted between hosts on a LAN or WAN environment. IPSec provides private communications over the Internet.

The Windows 2000 Router Service provides data security in both LAN and WAN environments. You need to implement Virtual Private Networks where you see the router service and security working in tandem, which we will discuss in more detail later. VPNs and the router service are grounded on either Point-to-Point Tunneling Protocol (PPTP) or Layer Two Tunneling Protocol (L2TP).

A proxy server, although not a standard component of Windows 2000, is a valuable feature to secure client computers on a network. A proxy server accepts outbound network requests and completes the request as a "proxy" for the originating host. Typically, a proxy server acts as a firewall defense to block incoming packets from ever reaching the internal network.

Security Hosts

Security hosts are intermediary devices between remote dial-up client computers and your network. These devices intercept the dial-up request and require additional information to access and be authenticated on your network. You can use two types of security hosts with Windows 2000:

◆ **Authentication at the time of the call.** These intermediary devices typically require an additional piece of information to access the server. A prime example is a security manager and security card. The security manager is the software located at the dial-up server. The security card is a business card-sized device and looks like a pocket calculator. The security card has an LCD display that changes numbers every minute or so. The numbers in the display are in sync with the security manager software. When users call in to the server, they must provide the number on the security card before they enter their Windows 2000 credentials.

◆ **Authentication in tandem with the logon process.** These components can be hardware and/or software based. A common example is the RADIUS server, which authenticates client computers on behalf of Routing and Remote Access.

Other examples include software programs that could communicate and verify remote smart cards to allow the users to provide network credentials.

Kerberos V5 Authentication

Kerberos V5 is the default authentication protocol used within a Windows 2000 domain. You don't have to do anything to implement Kerberos—it's already there. Kerberos authenticates Windows 2000 client computers logging in to a Windows 2000 domain and is the foundation of Windows 2000 network security.

Windows 2000 is not the first operating system to use Kerberos. It was developed by MIT in the '80s. Different operating systems using Kerberos can be configured to interact with one another to access objects in the Active Directory.

A user must complete several steps to log in to a Windows 2000 domain and access network resources. The steps are as follows:

1. A user enters a valid username and password. A Key Distribution Center (KDC) approves the logon request.

2. At logon, the KDC generates a ticket, which will allow the user to request network services. This ticket is called a ticket-granting ticket, or TGT.

3. The client computer presents the TGT to the ticket-granting service (TGS) The ticket-granting service issues a service ticket to the requestor.

4. The user attempts to access a resource or, more specifically, a network service. The service ticket allows the client computer to have a level of access to the network service by providing the user's identification to the service.

Windows 2000 Domain Controllers

Every domain controller, which authenticates users, also serves as a KDC. As client computers log on to the domain, they are assigned their ticket-granting ticket.

Recall that in Windows 2000, DNS is used to locate the nearest domain controller for the client computer. Should the nearest domain controller be unavailable, DNS will look up the next available domain controller, or KDC, for authentication of the user account.

Kerberos V5 Interoperability

As mentioned earlier, Microsoft Windows 2000 is not the first OS to use Kerberos. Because other operating systems already use this authentication protocol, you can configure your domains to interact with these systems so that client computers using other operating systems (such as UNIX), with Kerberos-based security, may access resources on Windows 2000 servers.

Windows 2000 supports two types of interoperability, as follows:

◆ A trust relationship between a Windows 2000 domain and a MIT-based realm.

◆ UNIX workstations and servers can have accounts within the Active Directory and will obtain authentication from the KDC.

Virtual Private Networks

A Virtual Private Network (VPN) consists of two or more locations linked via a shared or public network, such as the Internet. Through a VPN, users can connect to remote servers and resources as if the resources were on a LAN. The following process creates a VPN connection:

1. Data is encapsulated. The header provides routing information to the destination network or host ID.

2. The data travels through the public network to the remote host. These packets are encrypted.

3. As packets reach the destination, the packets are de-encrypted and the information is read as if the packet came through a secure, private network.

Windows 2000 supports two types of VPNs:

◆ Point-to-Point Tunneling Protocol (PPTP). This protocol uses PPP authentication and Microsoft Point-to-Point Encryption (MPPE) for data.

◆ Layer Two Tunneling Protocol (L2TP) with IPSec. This protocol uses L2TP to authenticate the user account and IPSec Encapsulating Security Payloads (ESP) to encrypt the L2TP tunnel.

The L2TP allows you to access your Windows 2000 domain over the Internet as if the entire routable path were on a private network. L2TP is an industry-standard protocol that has similar features to PPTP.

A primary difference between PPTP and L2TP is that PPTP will not support tunneling over X.25, frame relay, or ATM networks. It is designed for Internet tunneling only.

As with PPTP, L2TP encapsulates packets and then sends them on to the remote network. This feature allows client computers and servers to use protocols independent of TCP/IP. This capability is useful should an application require a specific protocol to operate properly, such as Appletalk 6.07. L2TP also provides support for header compression and tunnel authentication, whereas PPTP does not.

PPT uses PPP encryption for authentication, whereas L2TP uses the IPSec encryption standard. L2TP combined with IPSec ensures a secure transfer of data between two host IDs. The IPSec encryption standard is discussed later.

MANAGING AND MONITORING TRAFFIC

As a network administrator, you will find that network traffic can directly influence your productivity and design of a network. You will want to implement a solid plan to monitor existing traffic and then deduce how to manage that traffic. Your constant battle will be that when you add new services, you lose a percentage of bandwidth. Through planning, tweaking, and design, you can keep those lost percentages small. This section covers the following:

◆ Network traffic basics

◆ Network Monitor

◆ Configuring Network Monitor

◆ How to reduce network traffic

Understanding Network Traffic and the Network Monitor

Network traffic is any activity to and from a host on your network. Any packet that leaves a network card is contributing to network traffic. The more hosts you have on a network, the more services you add to a network, and the more network you fail to segment properly, the more network traffic you will have.

Why is the issue of network traffic so important? A crowded network, like rush-hour traffic, clogs the speed of the network, causes the network to become a bottleneck, and ultimately, can cause your network to fail.

As a rule, the more network services, shares, and resources you add to a network, the more network traffic you are generating. Think of this situation: you have 100 Windows 2000 Professional workstations and four Windows 2000 Servers in a domain. You added DHCP, WINS, DNS, GSNW, TCP/IP, NetBEUI, AppleTalk, and NWLink on every server. This contributes to network traffic in a major way—especially if your only client computers are Windows 2000 Workstations running TCP/IP. This is definitely a time when less is more.

Windows 2000 has lots of tools and third-party add-ons to monitor your network's activity. However, one tool is more powerful than any piece of software: your brain! Plan your networks before you implement them, and you will be happier in the long run. Following are a few tips for designing a network with traffic in mind:

◆ Less is more.

◆ Get rid of unneeded protocols.

◆ Get rid of unneeded services.

◆ Don't be afraid to segment your network. The more users you have in an environment the more chatter—and contention—you will experience.

◆ Use Network Monitor to create a baseline of network activity. Use this baseline to compare how your network is evolving.

WARNING

Limited Network Monitor
Windows 2000 includes a limited version of Network Monitor. This limited version of Network Monitor captures only frames between the host and other computers. The full version of Network Monitor, included with SMS, can capture frames sent to and from all computers in a network segment.

Installing Network Monitor

You will use Network Monitor to capture packets on your network. From these packets you can troubleshoot network problems, discern how busy a network load is, and predict how your network will grow.

Network Monitor comprises two primary components:

◆ **Network Monitor.** Network Monitor is the tool you use to capture packets sent to and from this server. This version of Network Monitor records only packets sent to and from this server and the LAN.

◆ **Network Monitor Driver.** The Network Monitor Driver is installed automatically when you install Network Monitor on a server. However, you may want to install just the Network Monitor Driver for remote computers to be monitored through the full version of Network Monitor included with SMS.

Network Monitor is not installed by default, but it is easy enough to add. Step by Step 18.7 walks you through the steps to add this software.

ON THE CD

Step by Step 18.7, "Adding Network Monitor," shows you how to add Network Monitor. See the file **Chapter18-07StepbyStep.pdf** in the CD's **Chapter18\StepbyStep** directory.

Installing the Network Monitor Driver

If you are using the SMS Network Monitor from another computer on this network, you need to add the Network Monitor Driver. Step by Step 18.8 guides you through the process of adding only the driver.

ON THE CD

Step by Step 18.8, "Adding the Network Monitor Driver," shows you how to add the Network Monitor Driver. See the file **Chapter18-08StepbyStep.pdf** in the CD's **Chapter18\StepbyStep** directory.

Using Network Monitor to Capture Data

Network Monitor, shown in Figure 18.3, captures frames, or packets, to and from the local computer and the network. This section walks you through the process of using Network Monitor and creating a simple capture. Later, we will go into greater detail on creating a capture filter through Network Monitor.

FIGURE 18.3
Network Monitor has four window panes that
report information.

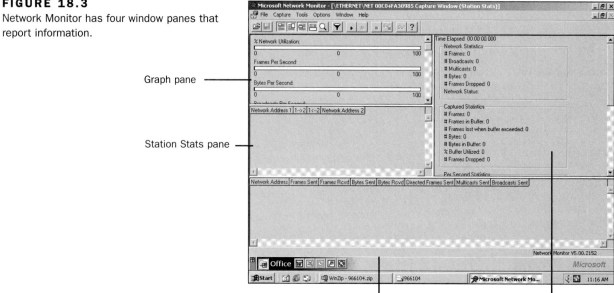

Graph pane

Station Stats pane

Total Stats pane   Session Stats pane

Four panes with Network Monitor report information about your
current activity, or captured file:

◆ The Graph pane reports back percentages of activity in a bar
chart format.

◆ The Session Stats pane reports back individual statistics of
client-to-server activity during the capture of live activity.

◆ The Station Stats pane reports information on each workstation's activity on a network. Keep in mind that this is actually
activity between that workstation and this server with this
version of Network Monitor.

◆ The Total Stats pane reports the totals of the stats for all the
other panes.

ON THE CD

Step by Step 18.9, "Creating a Network Capture," details how to
capture network traffic. See the file **Chapter18-09StepbyStep.pdf** in
the CD's **Chapter18\StepbyStep** directory.

Interpreting Captured Data

Interpreting captured data depends on the type of server you work with. What is this server's role in the domain? Is it a domain controller? An application server? A file server? Each of these roles will have different traffic patterns. What we need to get is an accurate picture of the activity for this server as a filter.

Filters allow us to strip away packets that may not be relevant to the server, capture, or type of packets we are looking for. Within Network Monitor, choose Filter from the Capture menu. The Capture menu dialog box will allow you to do the following:

- **Specify capture filter protocols.** You can designate which protocols you would like displayed in your capture. Complete the SAP/ETYPE= field by designating the protocol(s) you would like displayed.

- **Specify address pairs.** This option allows you to pick up to three pairs of addresses that have sent and received packets from each other.

- **Specify frame data patterns to capture.** This setting includes many options to build your own variables to display the captured data. You can display frames that contain a designated pattern.

Before you implement changes to your network, always create a baseline. A *baseline* is a snapshot of how your network is operating under normal conditions.

After creating the baseline, make the desired changes and run the test again. After running the test, ask yourself the following questions:

- Did the changes help or hinder performance?

- If the changes hindered performance, have I configured all the options for this change properly? For example, have I configured bindings again?

◆ Has one area of network performance improved, such as logon times, but other areas of network performance worsened, such as communication between domain controllers?

◆ Is this network capacity more than 75%? If so, should I add a switch or router to break up the network?

After you have added and configured the changes to your network, create another baseline as a snapshot of how the system is after these changes. During the next few days, weeks, and months, periodically run the same test again and compare these results to this baseline. This will help you predict how your network will be growing and what resources are eating your bandwidth.

CONFIGURING AND TROUBLESHOOTING IPSEC

IPSec provides data integrity between two host IDs. The data and identity is safe and kept from being changed or read by other users through intermediary software. In this section, you learn about enabling IPSec and working with the two modes: transport and tunnel.

IPSec provides security for computers, data, and users. The major benefits and features of IPSec are as follows:

◆ IPSec on Windows 2000 can use Kerberos V5, public-key certificates, or a preshared secret.

◆ IPSec mutually authenticates computers prior to any data being exchanged.

◆ IPSec establishes a security association (SA) between the two host computers involved in the data transfer. An SA is the collection of a policy and keys, which define the rules for security settings.

◆ IPSec encrypts data using Data Encryption Standard (DES), Triple DES (3DES), or 40-bit DES.

◆ IPSec is invisible to users. IPSec operates at the network level of the OSI model; therefore, it is invisible to users and applications.

An understanding of the following features, however, will help you troubleshoot problems that may arise in connectivity:

◆ IPSec policies are part of the local (and/or) group policies within Active Directory. This built-in feature allows changes and management to be centralized. Settings for IPSec are enforced on the computer as the policy is enforced.

◆ The Internet Security Association and Key Management Protocol (ISAKMP) monitors the negotiations between the hosts and provides the keys to use with security algorithms.

◆ The installed IPSec driver secures traffic between the two hosts.

Enabling IPSec Through a Policy

Before enabling IPSec on your local computer or domain, you'll want to configure IPSec through policies. Policies allow you to quickly and easily configure IPSec. Follow Step by Step 18.10 to create an IPSec policy.

ON THE CD

Step by Step 18.10, "Creating an IPSec Policy," shows you how to create an IPSec policy. See the file **Chapter18-10StepbyStep.pdf** in the CD's **Chapter18\StepbyStep** directory.

Configuring IPSec for Transport Mode

When transferring data over the wire, you must have IPSec enabled, as in Step by Step 18.11, to ensure that the data is encrypted.

If you are using Encrypting File System (EFS), be aware that the encrypted data is not encrypted when transferred over the wire. IPSec must be used to ensure that data transferred over the network is encrypted.

Configuring IPSec for Tunnel Mode

Tunneling is the process of encapsulating packets inside of other packets for secure, private transmissions on LANs and WANs. As the packet travels from network to network, the encapsulated packet is hidden within the outer packet. This outer packet delivers itself to the destination network where it is stripped away; the original packet is then unencapsulated and sent to the host ID.

The tunnel is the path that the packets take from host ID to destination host ID. To the user, this is all transparent and just another way to get from "my computer to his computer" on the network. Behind the scenes, of course, it's a bit more involved.

L2TP and IPSec

L2TP, similar to PPTP, allows other protocols besides TCP/IP to be encapsulated and then sent over an IP network. Thus, protocols such as IPX and NetBEUI can actually be sent to different networks via the Internet. However, what of the security and integrity of the encapsulated data within the L2TP packets?

When using L2TP to transfer data, IPSec is used to secure the tunnel. L2TP encapsulates the packet in a PPP frame. The PPP frame is then added to a UDP-type frame assigned to port 1701. UDP, being part of the TCP/IP suite, qualifies for IPSec to secure the contents; thus, the contents of L2TP are secure regardless of the originating protocol and/or data type.

IPSec Tunneling

What if your other networks, routers in the mix, or the target operating system cannot support L2TP? You have to use straight IPSec tunneling. IPSec tunneling is supported only in gateway-to-gateway tunnel mode.

CASE STUDY: MORGAN ENTERPRISES

ESSENCE OF THE CASE

The essential elements in this case are as follows:

▶ Install the appropriate protocol for the environment.

▶ Configure a method for securing the data between the sites on their network.

▶ Configure a way for the NetWare servers to remain active in this domain.

▶ Configure a method for secure authentication of dial-up clients.

SCENARIO

Morgan Enterprises is a conglomerate of companies consisting of publications, commercial printers, investment companies, insurance brokerages, and distribution centers. The conglomerate already has a plan in place to flatten the domains and make one domain through Windows 2000. The system administrators are somewhat concerned, however, because they have never connected all the networks to each other in Windows NT 4. They need a protocol for connectivity, but the data must remain secure and reliable.

Many sales people from all divisions travel with laptops and need to dial in to the office and access resources. The authentication between the dial-up client computers and the server must be secured to prevent unauthorized users from entering the network.

In addition, two NetWare 3 servers are in the Texas office that must remain available to users from the Dallas office.

All client computers will be using Windows 2000 Professional, and all servers, except the NetWare servers, will be using Windows 2000 Advanced Server.

ANALYSIS

The first step is to install a reliable, routable protocol for Morgan Enterprises. At first glance, IPX may be tempting because it is routable, it can be secured over the Internet, and it is needed by the

continues

CASE STUDY: MORGAN ENTERPRISES

users in Dallas for connectivity to the NetWare servers. However, a network of this magnitude in a Windows 2000 environment is more suited for TCP/IP.

To secure the data between sites, IPSec should be implemented. The protocol L2TP will be used to compress and encrypt the data between the sites, using the Internet as the backbone.

In the Dallas office, you can use NWLink for the servers that need to connect to the NetWare servers. The recommendation is that Morgan

Enterprises upgrade these servers to Windows 2000—or use a connection tool such as GSNW at the very least.

Finally, for the dial-up client computers, implement a security host, such as the security card that has a changing number in sync with the software on the server. As users dial in to the server, they will be required to enter the number on the security card before being able to provide their Windows 2000 authentication information.

CHAPTER SUMMARY

To have a secure, reliable, routable network, effective planning should be the first thing you implement.

Within Windows 2000, TCP/IP is installed by default. We've seen that so many features of Windows 2000 rely on TCP/IP. TCP/IP requires a valid IP address, subnet mask, default gateway, and DNS servers. This information may be entered manually at each client computer and server, or, preferably, through DHCP. DHCP assigns the host an IP address as it is needed by the client computer.

WINS, Windows Internet Naming Service, resolves NetBIOS names, such as Computer5, to an IP address. You can access the WINS properties through the Advanced tab of TCP/IP Properties.

When integrating with NetWare, you need information about the network number and frame type that the NetWare servers will require.

Network Bindings are a way of ordering network providers, protocols, and connections in the order in which they will most likely be used by the OS.

Kerberos V5 Authentication is the protocol Windows 2000 uses by default. No configuration is required to use this security protocol with Windows 2000. Computers in a trusted MIT-realm can be allowed to access resources in the local Kerberos (Windows 2000) domain.

VPNs are a way of connecting networks while, most likely, using the existing structure of the Internet as their backbone. IPSec can be coupled with VPNs to ensure quality and guarantee delivery of packets.

As a network grows, so does the amount of traffic created. Administrators need to monitor this traffic through Network Monitor. Network Monitor allows you to capture real-time activity, create filters on the type of protocols you would like to view, and then save that information to a file. Keep in mind that the Network Monitor included with Windows 2000 is not the full Network Monitor. The full Network Monitor is included with SMS.

KEY TERMS

- TCP/IP
- IP address
- Subnet mask
- DNS server
- NWLink
- Frame type
- Network binding
- Provider connections
- TCP/IP filter
- Kerberos V5
- L2TP
- Network Monitor
- Baseline
- IPSec
- Tunneling

APPLY YOUR KNOWLEDGE

Review Questions

1. What are three requirements for a valid IP address in a Windows 2000 environment?

2. How does TCP/IP know if the packets are local to this network or need to be forwarded to another network?

3. Why should a company choose to use DHCP over manually assigning IP addresses?

4. Why is it important to have a DNS server's IP address for a client computer in a Windows 2000 network?

5. What is NWLink used for?

6. Why is a matching frame type important for NWLink?

7. Why should a network administrator be concerned about bindings?

8. What must an administrator do to enable Kerberos Authentication in a Windows 2000 domain?

9. What is a VPN?

10. What is a baseline, and why is it important to create one?

11. Why is IPSec so important in a routed environment?

12. What is tunneling?

Answers to Review Questions

1. IP address, subnet mask, and default gateway.

2. The subnet mask defines the network ID portion of the IP address. If the destination of the packet has a different network ID, it is forwarded to the gateway.

3. DHCP allows the dynamic assignment of IP addresses and provides greater flexibility in address management. For example, a client computer using DHCP does not have a hard-coded IP address and so can be moved to another network without having to modify the TCP/IP configuration.

4. A DNS server provides the capability of resolving hostnames to IP addresses. Without a DNS server, you would need to know the actual IP address of the target computer. Also, with Windows 2000 Active Directory and DHCP, DNS can be dynamically updated.

5. NWLink is the IPX/SPX compatible protocol used to communicate to NetWare servers.

6. NWLink must use a matching frame type to communicate with NetWare servers. If NWLink is configured with an incorrect frame type for the IPX network it is trying to access, it will not be able to communicate.

7. A network administrator should review what bindings are installed and modify the order in which the bindings are accessed so that the most frequently used one is accessed first. For example, if you primarily communicate with a NetWare network and only rarely access the Internet, you would want to move the NWLink protocol above the Internet Protocol.

8. Nothing. Kerberos is implemented automatically with Windows 2000.

9. A virtual private network (VPN) consists of two or more locations linked via a shared or public network, such as the Internet.

APPLY YOUR KNOWLEDGE

10. A baseline is a set of performance readings taken at a specific time and used to reference future readings to identify changes in performance.

11. IPSec provides data integrity between two host IDs. The data and identity is safe and kept from being changed or read by other users through intermediary software.

12. Tunneling is the process of encapsulating packets inside other packets for secure, private transmissions on LANs and WANs.

ON THE CD

This book's companion CD contains specially designed supplemental material to help you understand how well you know the concepts and skills you learned in this chapter. You'll find related exercises and exam questions and answers. See the file **Chapter18ApplyYourKnowledge.pdf** in the CD's **Chapter18\ApplyYourKnowledge** directory.

Suggested Readings and Resources

1. Minasi, Mark, Christa Anderson, Brian M. Smith, and Doug Toombs. *Mastering Windows 2000 Server.* Alameda, CA. Sybex Press, 2000.

2. Morimoto, Rand. *Windows 2000 Design and Migration.*

3. Shields, Paul, Ralph Crump, and Martin Weiss. *Windows 2000 Server System Administration Handbook.* Rockland, MA. Syngress Media, 1999.

4. Komar, Brian. *Sams Teach Yourself TCP/IP Network Administration in 21 Days.* Sams Publishing, 1998.

5. www.isi.edu

You may be aware that if you implement Active Directory with the required DNS infrastructure, you can do away with your legacy WINS (Windows Internet Naming Service) servers. However, because most environments require support for legacy servers, domains, and applications, it is important that Windows 2000 supports WINS and that administrators understand how to install, maintain, and troubleshoot a Windows 2000 WINS implementation.

Microsoft defines the "Installing, Configuring, Managing, Monitoring, and Troubleshooting WINS in a Windows 2000 Network Infrastructure" objectives as the following:

Install, configure, and troubleshoot WINS.

▶ As with any of the Windows 2000 services, it is critical that you understand how to install, configure, and troubleshoot WINS. Although WINS is not strictly required by Windows 2000, having been replaced by DNS and Active Directory, WINS is an absolute requirement in mixed environments that contain Windows NT Servers and workstations. WINS is the foundation that the legacy domain infrastructure relies on in an IP environment. You need to have a thorough understanding not only of the Windows 2000 WINS service, but also how WINS itself functions. This objective expects you to be able to install WINS, configure it for use in conjunction with legacy hosts, and be able to determine the issue if it is not working.

Configure WINS replication.

▶ One of the key features of WINS is the WINS database that can be replicated between WINS servers. In a distributed Windows 2000 and Windows NT domain environment, this capability is critical for providing WINS resolution for all IP segments. You need to understand how WINS replication works and how to install the service.

CHAPTER 19

Installing, Configuring, Managing, Monitoring, and Troubleshooting WINS in a Windows 2000 Network Infrastructure

Configure NetBIOS name resolution.

▶ The key to legacy Microsoft networking is the use of NetBIOS name resolution for locating hosts and services on the network. For this objective, you need to understand how NetBIOS name resolution works, as well as how to configure it on a Windows 2000 Server.

Manage and monitor WINS.

▶ The final objective requires that you be able to manage and monitor the WINS service. As with any other service provided by Windows 2000, you absolutely must be able to maintain WINS after installation. The majority of work on any Windows 2000 implementation will be the long-term mainte-nance of the server and services, particularly given the number of installation and configuration wiz-ards included with Windows 2000.

▶ Be sure that you have a thorough understanding of the WINS service and NetBIOS name resolution. Although this is a legacy Microsoft protocol, it will still be required in most environments, and Microsoft wants to be absolutely sure you understand how it works.

▶ Review the use of the monitoring tools and the different parameters of WINS that can be monitored. In its exams, Microsoft has focused a great deal of attention on the monitoring and troubleshooting of the different services, including the WINS service.

▶ Be sure to complete the exercises at the end of the chapter and on the CD. As Microsoft strives to make its exams more rigorous, a familiarity with not only the theory, but also the hands-on portion of installation, configuration, and troubleshooting of the WINS service will be important.

INSTALLING, CONFIGURING, AND TROUBLESHOOTING WINS

Install, configure, and troubleshoot WINS.

If you are at all familiar with Windows NT 4 networks, you are undoubtedly familiar with the intricacies of a WINS infrastructure. You may also be wondering why Microsoft didn't get rid of WINS with Windows 2000. Well, the good news is that with Windows 2000, WINS is only for backward compatibility. Windows 2000 Server running in native mode does not use WINS at all. The Active Directory and Domain Name Service (DNS) are used to provide the functionality of WINS—resolving names into addresses.

Until your network is 100% Windows 2000, you will still need WINS to provide backward compatibility for legacy Windows operating systems and NetBIOS-based applications.

Introduction to WINS

In the Internet-centric environment that most companies are designing and maintaining, Transmission Control Protocol/Internet Protocol (TCP/IP) has become the ubiquitous networking protocol.

Microsoft originally used NetBEUI as its default protocol for networking. NetBEUI was a pretty good protocol for small networks; it required no configuration and didn't require complex addressing as TCP/IP does. However, NetBEUI does not support routing and does not perform well in large environments. Microsoft needed to add TCP/IP support.

When Microsoft began to add TCP/IP support to its LAN Server products, the company ran into a little problem. The naming system used on Microsoft networks at that time would not function on routed TCP/IP networks. Microsoft LAN Manager computers used the computer's NetBIOS names for identification. Although this makes maintaining the network very simple for an administrator, because servers are automatically advertised on the network by name, this naming system was a problem with the TCP/IP protocol.

NetBIOS has a design limitation that shows up in routed networks. NetBIOS relies heavily on broadcast messages to advertise servers and their shared resources. Broadcast messages are messages that are received by every computer on a network segment, rather than by a specific computer. To confine the impact of broadcast messages on a TCP/IP network, IP routers will not forward broadcast messages. To function in a TCP/IP environment, Microsoft's TCP/IP implementation had to find a way to make NetBIOS naming work in a standard TCP/IP network where broadcast packets are not routed between network segments.

IN THE FIELD

THE NWLINK PROTOCOL

Most of the Windows 2000 documentation and most of the chapters in this book discuss the TCP/IP protocol and TCP/IP services. However, it is important to recall that a significant population of companies still run Windows operating systems in conjunction with a Novell NetWare server.

The NWLink protocol was originally written to allow Windows to communicate using the IPX/SPX protocol used by Novell NetWare servers, back in the days when Novell was the dominant Intel-based network operating system. Although Novell has also embraced TCP/IP as its primary protocol, you still stand a pretty good chance of running into IPX, and you may find that you need to run the NWLink protocol. So be sure you understand all the TCP/IP information contained in this chapter and in this book, but don't be surprised if you find yourself loading NWLink on your Windows 2000 Server one of these days.

Microsoft's first solution, introduced in its older LAN Manager server, was to use a LAN Manager HOSTS (LMHOSTS) file on each computer on the network. Similar to the HOSTS file used before DNS was available, an LMHOSTS consists of records matching NetBIOS names to IP addresses. When a computer couldn't find a particular NetBIOS computer on the local network, it consulted its LMHOSTS file to see whether the computer could be found elsewhere.

An LMHOSTS file is a text file that must be edited manually. After creating a master LMHOSTS file, an administrator must copy the file to every computer on the network. Every time a computer was installed or removed, the master LMHOSTS file had to be updated and redistributed.

Microsoft also needed a dynamic name service that would keep itself current on computers on the network—a name service that could work in routed TCP/IP environments. Microsoft's answer was the Windows Internet Name Service (WINS). Four elements can be found in a WINS network:

◆ **WINS servers.** When WINS client computers enter the network, they contact a designated WINS server using a directed message. The client computer registers its NetBIOS names with the WINS server and uses the WINS server to resolve NetBIOS names to IP addresses.

◆ **WINS client computers.** WINS client computers use directed messages to communicate with WINS servers and are typically configured to use a combination of directed and broadcast messages. Windows 2000, Windows NT, Windows 95 and 98, and Windows for Workgroups computers can be WINS client computers.

◆ **Non-WINS client computers.** Older Microsoft network client computers that can't be configured to use WINS can still benefit from WINS. Their broadcast messages are intercepted by WINS proxy computers that act as intermediaries between the non-WINS client computers and WINS servers. MS-DOS and Windows 3.1 client computers function as non-WINS clients.

◆ **WINS proxies.** Windows NT, Windows 95 and 98, and Windows for Workgroups client computers can function as WINS proxies. They intercept NetBIOS broadcasts on their local subnet and communicate with a WINS server on behalf of the non-WINS client computer.

As you'll learn in the section "Configuring WINS Replication," later in this chapter, WINS servers can replicate their databases so that each WINS server can provide name resolution for the entire network. When possible, it is desirable to have at least two WINS servers. This lets name resolution take place when one name server is down. It also lets administrators distribute WINS activity across multiple servers to balance the processing loads. WINS server addresses are one of the configuration settings that can be issues with DHCP.

Installing WINS

As discussed in earlier chapters, Windows 2000 allows you to perform tasks, such as installing services, in a number of ways. This section covers two of the more common methods for installing WINS. Finding the method you are most comfortable with and sticking to it consistently is generally the best method for working with the operating system.

To install the Windows 2000 WINS service, follow the steps in Step by Step 19.1.

NOTE

DHCP and the WINS Service If a Windows 2000 Server is hosting both of the WINS services, it should have a static IP address. If you are installing the WINS service on a server with a DHCP-assigned IP address, you will be offered the chance to change the IP address to a static IP address.

ON THE CD

Step by Step 19.1, "Using the Network and Dial-Up Connections Properties to Install the Windows Internet Naming Service," walks you through installing the WINS service. See the file **Chapter19-01StepbyStep.pdf** in the CD's **Chapter19\StepbyStep** directory.

Keep in mind that you still need to configure your client computers to use the new WINS server. Step by Step 19.2 shows you an alternative way to install the WINS service.

ON THE CD

Step by Step 19.2, "Using the Add/Remove Programs Applet to Install the Windows Internet Naming Service," walks you through starting a networked installation. See the file **Chapter19-02StepbyStep.pdf** in the CD's **Chapter19\StepbyStep** directory.

Configuring WINS

A number of properties can be configured in the Windows Internet Naming Service. They can be accessed by opening the WINS console (Start, Programs, Administrative Tools, WINS) and selecting the server you want to configure (see Figure 19.1). Right-click the server and select Properties. The sections that follow describe the property options.

General Settings

The General tab (shown in Figure 19.2) is used to configure statistics and backups. You can use this tab to configure the automatic update of WINS statistics and the interval that they update from this tab. You also can configure the default backup path for the WINS database, and you can enable the automatic back up of the database when the server is shut down.

> **NOTE**
>
> **To Back Up or Not to Back Up?** You should always configure the default database path and the automatic back up of the database on shutdown to removable media whenever possible. This configuration ensures the maximum fault tolerance for the WINS database in case the server hosting the WINS service fails.

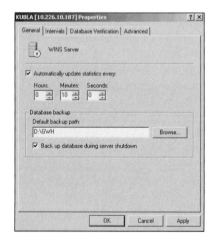

FIGURE 19.2
The General tab is used for configuring statistics and backups for the WINS database.

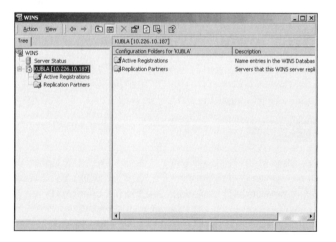

FIGURE 19.1
The WINS manager is used for all configurations for the WINS service.

Intervals Settings

The Intervals tab (shown in Figure 19.3) is used to set the WINS
database records renewal, deletion, and verification intervals. You
can set the following intervals:

◆ **Renew Interval.** Determines the frequency of record renewal.
The default is six days and is good for all but the most
dynamic environments. If you have a very dynamic environment with computers entering and exiting the network frequently, you may want to reduce this interval.

◆ **Extinction Interval.** Determines the length of time before a
record is considered extinct and is removed from the database.
Again, in all but the most dynamic environments, the four-day
default is usually adequate.

◆ **Extinction Timeout.** Determines the length of time a record
is checked before it is declared extinct. When this occurs, the
record is deleted after the Extinction Interval is met.

◆ **Verification Interval.** Determines the frequency that database
records are verified for accuracy.

FIGURE 19.3

In most networks, the default intervals
are usually adequate for a stable WINS
environment.

Database Verification Settings

The Database Verification tab (shown in Figure 19.4) allows you to
configure the parameters associated with the WINS database. You
can enable database verification for a specific interval. The default
interval is 24 hours; thus, if enabled, the database consistency will be
verified once a day. You also specify the time to begin the consistency check, the number of database records to check for each
period, as well as the source to verify the database against. You can
verify database consistency against owner servers (these are the
servers that the WINS record originally created) or randomly
selected partner servers.

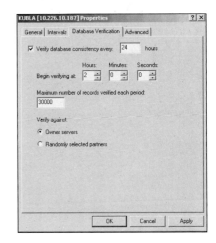

FIGURE 19.4

Ensuring the consistency of the WINS database
is critical to a stable WINS environment.

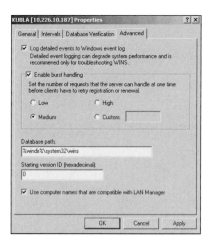

FIGURE 19.5
The Advanced tab functions as the catchall for the remaining WINS parameters and contains some important parameters for troubleshooting and load regulating.

Advanced Settings

The Advanced tab (shown in Figure 19.5) is used to configure the remaining WINS parameters, including the following:

◆ **Logging.** You can enable detailed event logging for troubleshooting WINS when there are problems.

◆ **Burst Handling.** You can configure the load that can be put on the server by specifying the number of WINS requests that the server will accept before returning a retry message. This can be set to Low, Medium, High, or Custom, which allows you to specify a number of connections.

◆ **Database Path.** If you have fault-tolerant drives in your server, make sure that the WINS database path is set to store the database on the fault-tolerant drives.

◆ **Database Version Number.** You should not need to modify this parameter, but the starting version number is used for consistency purposes. By giving each version of the database an incrementing version number, Windows 2000 is able to compare two WINS databases and tell which is the most recent. DNS uses a similar mechanism for synchronizing its tables.

◆ **LAN Manager Compatibility.** You can also set WINS to use LAN Manager–compatible computer names so that any legacy LAN Manager installations can still use WINS for name resolution.

That covers the configuration of a WINS server. Let's look at configuring WINS replication between two WINS servers.

Configuring WINS Replication

Configure WINS replication.

In most environments that rely on WINS for name resolution for legacy systems, it is important to ensure that more than one WINS server exists to provide redundancy and availability. To ensure that each server has a current copy of the database, it is important to configure replication between your WINS servers. Let's take a quick look at the different types of replication you can configure for the WINS service:

◆ **Pull replication.** In pull replication, your server pulls the database from the replication partner. A pull replication is time-based and occurs at the time you have configured. You can decide whether to establish a persistent connection for replication, and you can set the start time and interval for replication.

◆ **Push replication.** In push replication, your server signals for a pull replication partner to pull at a specified time or interval. A push replication is event-driven, and the number of database updates determines when the event occurs. You can decide whether to use a persistent connection for push activities, and you can set the number of changes in version ID before replication.

◆ **Replication partner type.** The partner type can be push, pull or push/pull, depending on your requirements. (In push/pull replication, database replication can occur using either method: push or pull.)

> **EXAM TIP**
>
> **WINS Replication** One new feature of the Windows 2000 WINS servers is the capability of maintaining a persistent connection with one or more of the replication partners, enabling real-time replication. Because this is one of the new features of the WINS service, you will probably find it on the test.

To configure WINS replication, follow Step by Step 19.3.

ON THE CD

Step by Step 19.3, "Configuring WINS Replication," walks you through setting up WINS replication. See the file **Chapter19-03StepbyStep.pdf** in the CD's **Chapter19\StepbyStep** directory.

Global replication properties can also be set for WINS replication. To review the global replication properties, open the WINS manager application as described in Step by Step 19.3 and select the Replication Partners folder in the left pane. Right-click and select Properties from the Context menu. This opens the Replication Partners Properties. This opens to the General tab. Replication partners configurations can be set on the following tabs:

◆ **General.** The General tab allows you to restrict replication to replication partners and configure the server to allow the overwriting of static mappings on the server.

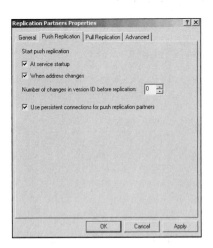

FIGURE 19.6
The Push Replication tab allows you to set the thresholds for triggering a push replication.

◆ **Push Replication.** As you can see in Figure 19.6, you can use this tab to establish whether replication will start at system startup. You also can use this tab to configure the number of changes required to trigger the push replication and whether to use persistent connections for the push replication.

◆ **Pull Replication.** As you can see in Figure 19.7, you can use this tab to establish whether pull replication starts at system startup, when the replication should start, the interval between replications, the number of retries, and whether to use persistent connections.

◆ **Advanced.** The tab shown in Figure 19.8 allows you to block servers from being able to replicate, as well as to configure the autodiscovery and autoconfiguration of WINS partners. Because this uses multicasts (or multicasting) to find and configure the servers, enable this for small networks only.

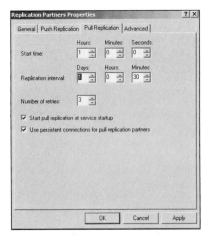

FIGURE 19.7
The Pull Replication tab allows you to configure the timing for a pull replication.

FIGURE 19.8
The Advanced tab allows you to set up your WINS server for a small network, as well as to block WINS servers from replicating.

You have now successfully configured all the possible Windows replication partner parameters. Let's take a quick look at identifying WINS issues.

TROUBLESHOOTING WINS ISSUES

The majority of WINS issues you will encounter will be related to connectivity, so the first thing we need to take a look at is testing TCP/IP connectivity. The first application for testing IP connectivity is the PING.EXE utility. PING allows you to send an Internet Control Message Protocol (ICMP) to a TCP/IP host. By using the correct flag, PING can also perform name resolution as part of its testing procedure. The correct format for this command is

```
PING <destination address>
```

A sample PING session might look like this:

```
ping -a wins1.newriders.com
Pinging wins1.newriders.com [205.123.113.87] with 32 bytes
➥of data:
Reply from 205.123.113.87: bytes=32 time=47ms TTL=241
Reply from 205.123.113.87: bytes=32 time=60ms TTL=242
Reply from 205.123.113.87: bytes=32 time=40ms TTL=242
Reply from 205.123.113.87: bytes=32 time=37ms TTL=242
Ping statistics for 205.123.113.87:
Packets: Sent = 4, Received = 4, Lost = 0 (0% loss),
Approximate round trip times in milliseconds:
Minimum = 37ms, Maximum = 60ms, Average = 46ms
```

Because the number of sent packets equals the number of receive packets, the connection between the workstation and the WINS server is good. If you do not get any packets returned, you should investigate the network issues further.

The next piece of the WINS puzzle is the client computer WINS configuration. To see whether the WINS configuration of your Windows 2000 client computers is correct, follow Step by Step 19.4.

ON THE CD

Step by Step 19.4, "Checking the WINS Settings in a Client Computer," covers WINS configuration of Windows 2000 client computers. See the file **Chapter19-04StepbyStep.pdf** in the CD's **Chapter19\StepbyStep** directory.

NOTE

What's Multicasting? Multicasting is the act of transmitting a message to a select group of recipients. This is in contrast to the concept of a broadcast, where traffic is sent to every host on the network, or a unicast, where the connection is a one-to-one relationship and there is only one recipient of the data. Teleconferencing and videoconferencing use the concept of multicasting, as does broadcast audio, where the connection is one to a selected group. At this time, only a few applications take advantage of this feature, but with the growing popularity of multicast applications, you may see more multicast applications in the future.

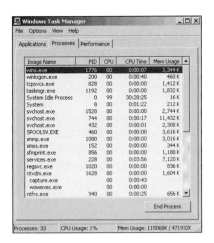

FIGURE 19.9
Task Manager is one of the fastest ways to verify that a service is running.

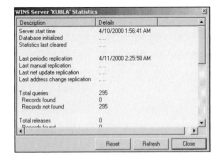

FIGURE 19.10
The WINS Server Statistics provide an excellent snapshot of the WINS service.

The final piece of the WINS puzzle is verifying that the server is functioning:

◆ **Is the WINS service running?** You can determine this by opening the Task Manager (press Ctrl+Alt+Del and select Task Manager), and on the Processes tab (see Figure 19.9), verify that the WINS service (WINS.EXE) is running. If the service is not running, you can restart the WINS service in the Computer Management MMC snap-in.

◆ **Is the WINS service responding to requests?** The best way to discover this is to check the server statistics. To check the server statistics, right-click the server in the WINS manager and select WINS Server Statistics (see Figure 19.10). If you check these statistics over a 15-minute period of time and they don't increment, you probably have a WINS issue somewhere.

We have covered the basic steps in troubleshooting WINS. As with any equipment-down situation, your steps may vary. Every situation is unique and may require unique troubleshooting steps.

CONFIGURING NETBIOS NAME RESOLUTION

Configure NetBIOS name resolution.

Microsoft TCP/IP uses NetBIOS over TCP/IP (NetBT) as specified in RFCs 1001 and 1002 to support the NetBIOS client and server programs in the LAN and WAN environments. Before we look at the specifics of NetBIOS name resolution, let's briefly review how computers communicate on the network. This helps in understanding how the different NetBIOS modes work and why some are preferable to others.

Computers can use two ways to communicate on a network:

◆ Through broadcast messages, which every computer receives

◆ Through directed messages, which are sent to a specific computer

When possible, it is preferable to communicate through directed messages. This cuts down on the amount of network traffic and ensures that only the affected hosts receive the message. This also ensures that the messages will cross any intermediate routers. So, Microsoft needed to make sure that WINS communicated primarily with directed messages. The company accomplished this by allowing several types of NetBIOS naming methods. These naming methods are commonly called *node types*. A *node* is a device on a network. Every computer on a Microsoft computer is configured as one of four node types. The node type determines whether the computer will learn names through broadcast messages, directed messages, or some combination of broadcast and directed messages. Before you can work with WINS, you need to know what the node types are and when they are used:

◆ **B-node (broadcast node).** Relies exclusively on broadcast messages and is the oldest NetBIOS name resolution mode. A host needing to resolve a name request sends a message to every host within earshot, requesting the address associated with a hostname. B-node has two shortcomings: broadcast traffic is undesirable and becomes a significant user of network bandwidths, and TCP/IP routers don't forward broadcast messages, which restricts b-node operation to a single network segment.

◆ **P-node (point-to-point node).** Relies on WINS servers for NetBIOS name resolution. Client computers register themselves with a WINS server when they come on the network. They then contact the WINS server with NetBIOS name resolution requests. WINS servers communicate using directed messages, which can cross routers, so p-node can operate on large networks. Unfortunately, if the WINS server is unavailable or if a node isn't configured to contact a WINS server, p-node name resolution fails.

◆ **M-node (modified node).** A mixed mode that first attempts to resolve NetBIOS names using the b-node mechanism. If that fails, an attempt is made to use p-node name resolution. M-node was the first hybrid mode put into operation, but it has the disadvantage of favoring b-node operation, which is associated with high levels of broadcast traffic.

◆ **H-node (hybrid node).** A hybrid mode that favors the use of WINS for NetBIOS name resolution. When a computer needs to resolve a NetBIOS name, it first attempts to use p-node resolution to resolve a name via WINS. Only if WINS resolution fails does the host resort to b-node to resolve the name via broadcasts. Because it typically results in the best network utilization, h-node is the default mode of operation for Microsoft TCP/IP client computers configured to use WINS for name resolution.

IN THE FIELD

THE METHOD WINS USES TO RESOLVE A NAME

The time may come when you need to understand exactly how WINS resolves a name. (Because h-node is not only the default but is also the recommended configuration, we will restrict our discussion to the h-node name resolution.) When a WINS client computer configured for hybrid mode needs to resolve a hostname, it goes through the following series of steps:

1. Checks its NetBIOS name cache. If the name is found, returns it.

2. Queries the WINS server. If the name is found, returns it.

3. Issues a broadcast to find the host on the local network. If the name is found, returns it.

4. Looks for the LMHOSTS file to check for an entry. If the name is found, returns it.

5. Look for the host file to check for an entry. If the name is found, returns it.

6. Queries the DNS server for the entry. If the name is found, returns it.

7. If all these methods fail, the WINS client computer issues an error message saying that it cannot communicate with the host.

To see which node type is configured on a Windows 2000 computer, follow Step by Step 19.5.

ON THE CD

Step by Step 19.5, "Identifying the NetBIOS Node Type," walks you through a check of the node type that is configured on a Windows 2000 computer. See the file **Chapter19-05StepbyStep.pdf** in the CD's **Chapter19\StepbyStep** directory.

Let's wrap up the chapter by looking at the best way to manage and monitor WINS and manage your new WINS server.

MANAGING AND MONITORING WINS

Manage and monitor WINS.

We have looked at installing and configuring the Windows 2000 WINS Server service. Next, we need to look at managing and monitoring the server now that it is running. If your job is typical of most, you spend a great deal more time managing WINS servers than installing them.

Although the WINS server includes limited monitoring capabilities, you do have access to the WINS statistics referenced in the section "Troubleshooting WINS Issues," earlier in the chapter. To get the server statistics, just open WINS manager and right-click the server in question. From the Context menu, select Display Server Statistics, and a snapshot of the server statistics is displayed (see Figure 19.11).

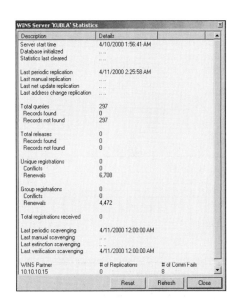

FIGURE 19.11
The WINS Server Statistics provide a good snapshot of WINS activity.

The WINS manager application has additional capabilities. From the open WINS manager application, you can select the WINS server and then use the Action menu to access these available actions:

◆ The Display Server Statistics option displays statistics discussed in a preceding section.

◆ The Scavenge Database option allows you to manually clean unused entries from the WINS database.

◆ The Verify Database Consistency option causes the server to go out to the network hosts and verify the entries in the WINS database. This process can be very processor- and network-intensive.

◆ The Verify Version ID Consistency option forces the WINS server to go to all the other WINS servers on the network and has them check the database version numbers to ensure that they are consistent. As with verifying the WINS data, this process is network- and processor-intensive.

◆ The Start Push Replication option manually performs a push replication.

◆ The Start Pull Replication option manually performs a pull replication.

◆ The Back Up Database option allows you to make a backup copy of the WINS database. Always make sure you have a copy of this database, just in case. If you specify the backup directory, the server automatically backs up the database every 24 hours.

◆ The Restore the Database option allows you to restore a backup copy of the database.

◆ The Tasks option leads to a menu consisting of the following commands:

• **Start.** Starts the WINS Server service. This option is available only if the service is stopped or paused.

• **Stop.** Stops the WINS Server service. Available when the service is running or paused. This option causes the server statistics to be reset.

- **Pause.** Pauses the WINS Server service. This option does not reset the statistics.

- **Resume.** Resumes the WINS Server service when paused. This option is available only when the service is paused.

- **Restart.** Restarts the WINS Server service. This option is available unless the server is stopped.

◆ The Delete option deletes a WINS server from the WINS manager.

◆ The Refresh option causes all the displayed information to be refreshed with a current status.

◆ The Export List option allows you to export the information from the DNS server to a tab- or comma-delimited text or Unicode text file.

◆ The Properties option opens the server properties, as discussed in a preceding section.

The Windows 2000 WINS service also includes some new functionality for managing the WINS database. If you open the WINS manager and click Active Registrations, you see a list of all the dynamically added entries in the WINS database. Although this is useful, it would be nice to be able to search for a specific entry, or even to filter on specific record types. The good news is that you can. If you right-click the Active Registration folder and select Find by Name or Find by Owner, you can search the WINS database for specific entries. And under Find by Owner, you can even filter what WINS record types should be shown. If you are working in a large environment (500 computers or greater), you will find these capabilities invaluable, because computers can often enter 10 to 12 entries each into the WINS database.

Windows 2000's WINS service also allows you to delete not only static records, but also dynamic records. This is a major improvement that was first introduced in Windows NT with Service Pack 4.

Now that you have looked at the options for managing the WINS server, let's take a look at some of the ways to monitor the service. Before you get into the Step by Step, you should look at what counters you can use to monitor WINS. The WINS object has the following counters associated with it.

◆ **Failed Queries/Sec.** Gives you the number of failed WINS queries per second. If this number is very high or suddenly spikes, you may have an issue with WINS resolution.

◆ **Failed Releases/Sec.** Gives you the number of failed WINS released per second. If this number is very high or suddenly spikes, you may have an issue with WINS resolution.

◆ **Group Conflicts/Sec.** The rate at which group registrations by the WINS server resulted in conflicts with the database.

◆ **Group Registrations/Sec.** The rate at which group registrations are being received.

◆ **Group Renewals/Sec.** The rate at which group registrations are being received.

◆ **Queries/Sec.** The rate at which queries are being received.

◆ **Releases/Sec.** The rate at which releases are being received.

◆ **Successful Queries/Sec.** The number of successful queries per second. This is useful if you are trending your WINS usage.

◆ **Successful Releases/Sec.** The number of successful releases per second. This is useful if you are trending your WINS usage.

◆ **Total Number of Conflicts/Sec.** This is the sum of the unique and group conflicts per second.

◆ **Total Number of Registrations/Sec.** This is the sum of the unique and group registrations per second.

◆ **Total Number of Renewals/Sec.** This is the sum of the unique and group renewals per second.

◆ **Unique Conflicts/Sec.** The rate at which unique registrations/renewals caused conflicts with the database.

◆ **Unique Registrations/Sec.** The rate at which unique registrations are received by the server.

◆ **Unique Renewals/Sec.** The rate at which unique renewals are received by the server.

To configure WINS performance monitoring, work through Step by Step 19.6.

ON THE CD

Step by Step 19.6, "Monitoring WINS Performance," covers configuration of WINS performance monitoring. See the file **Chapter19-06StepbyStep.pdf** in the CD's **Chapter19\StepbyStep** directory.

We've looked at the management options available in the WINS manager application, and we've taken a look at how to monitor the performance of the different WINS counters using the Performance console. At this point you should have a good understanding of the Windows 2000 WINS Server service and WINS in general. Now let's see how you do applying it in a practical situation.

CASE STUDY: CONFIGURING NETWORK ADDRESS TRANSLATION IN A 100-USER NETWORK

ESSENCE OF THE CASE

The essence of the case is as follows:

▶ You have a five-site network, each site with its own IP subnet.

▶ You need a centralized NetBIOS name resolution service to allow users to resolve names.

▶ You want to deploy this to all users, and it must resolve for all Microsoft servers.

SCENARIO

You are the network administrator for LFE Incorporated. LFE Inc. is a lawn furniture manufacturing company. You have a five-site network, and each site has its own IP subnet. You are presently running a lot of Windows NT Workstations and Servers and are in the process of upgrading to Windows 2000 Servers right now.

You have been using LMHOSTS files for NetBIOS name resolution thus far, but you would like to move to a centralized name resolution solution as part of the Windows 2000 migration, to support legacy applications. You need to make sure name resolution is available for all computers on all subnets, and that they resolve all hosts on the network.

What do you need to do?

continues

CASE STUDY: CONFIGURING NETWORK ADDRESS TRANSLATION IN A 100-USER NETWORK

continued

ANALYSIS

This is an excellent example of a small Microsoft network desperately in need of a WINS infrastructure. A good WINS design requires that there be a WINS server at each location for both local and remote resolution. To make it work, you need to make sure you do the following:

- Install the Windows 2000 WINS service on at least one Windows 2000 Server in each location.

- Configure the WINS servers as replication partners and make sure they replicate their databases appropriately.

- Configure each of the client computers to use WINS resolution with the local WINS server as the primary server.

- If you are using DHCP, make sure to update the DHCP setting to reflect the new WINS servers.

If you are migrating to a Windows 2000 network and you do not have a WINS infrastructure for your existing Microsoft client computers, this might be a good model to deploy for interim support until you have completed your Windows 2000 migration.

CHAPTER SUMMARY

KEY TERMS

- Domain Name System (DNS)
- Dynamic Host Control Protocol (DHCP)
- Windows Internet Naming Service (WINS)
- Replication partner
- Transmission Control Protocol/Internet Protocol (TCP/IP)
- Request For Comment (RFC) documents
- NetBIOS
- Push replication
- Pull replication
- Push/pull replication
- Active Directory
- NWLink protocol for IPX
- LAN Manager HOSTS (LMHOSTS)
- Internet Control Message Protocol (ICMP)
- H-node
- B-node
- P-node
- M-node

Let's recap what we've looked at in this chapter. We started with a discussion of what WINS is and what services it provides. In a Windows 2000 environment, it provides name resolution for non–Windows 2000 client computers.

Then we moved on to the installation, configuration, and troubleshooting of WINS. The installation is wizard-driven, and configuration consists mainly of setting parameters for your environment. You also explored the different areas to check if you are having issues with WINS.

This chapter discussed configuring NetBIOS and configuring WINS replication partners. We wrapped up the chapter with a discussion of the different mechanisms available for managing and monitoring your WINS servers.

In the next chapter, you look at installing, configuring, managing, monitoring, and troubleshooting IP routing in a Windows 2000 network infrastructure.

APPLY YOUR KNOWLEDGE

Review Questions

1. You are the network administrator for a small company with several sites, each with host computers. You are in the process of migrating to Windows 2000, but you want to be sure that all your legacy Windows NT 4 computers can browse the network. What should you do?

2. You have successfully deployed WINS in your environment, and it is working. Your users can browse the network. How does the WINS database get populated to make this possible?

3. After the WINS is fully implemented and the database is populated, how are entries deleted from the database?

4. What is the major difference between push replication and pull replication?

5. You're the administrator of Little Faith Enterprise's Windows 2000 Server, and you are considering setting up WINS. You feel you need a better understanding of how NetBIOS works and how the different node types work. What are the four NetBIOS node types, and how do they work?

Answers to Review Questions

1. You need to deploy WINS in your environment. Depending on your environment, you may be able to deploy redundant WINS servers in your central site, or you may need to deploy WINS servers to each location. In either event, you need to configure replication between the servers. For more information, see the section "Installing WINS."

2. The WINS database is populated by the WINS client computer. When the WINS client computer comes on the network, it registers its name and address with the WINS server automatically. After the client computer is registered, it receives a time to live for its registration. For more information, see the section "Configuring WINS."

3. Two automated mechanisms exist for removing entries. When a client computer shuts down gracefully, it will send a release request to the WINS server. The entries are also removed when the time to live for that client computer's registration expires. For more information, see the section "Configuring WINS Replication."

4. The main difference between push and pull replication (besides the direction the database is replicated) is the trigger for the event. In the case of a push replication, the trigger is event-based. When a specified number of changes are made to the database, the replication is triggered. A pull replication is triggered by the time configured for the replication. This is user-configured. For more information, see the section "Configuring WINS Replication."

5. There are four node types, and the main difference between the types is the method each uses for name resolution (broadcast versus direct connection):

    • B-node (broadcast node), which relies exclusively on broadcast messages and is the oldest NetBIOS name resolution mode. A host needing to resolve a name request sends a message to every host within earshot, requesting the address associated with a hostname. B-node has two shortcomings:

APPLY YOUR KNOWLEDGE

broadcast traffic is undesirable and becomes a significant user of network bandwidths, and TCP/IP routers don't forward broadcast messages, which restricts B-node operation to a single network segment.

- P-node (point-to-point node) relies on WINS servers for NetBIOS name resolution. Client computers register themselves with a WINS server when they come on the network. They then contact the WINS server with NetBIOS name resolution requests. WINS servers communicate using directed messages, which can cross routers, so p-node can operate on large networks. Unfortunately, if the WINS server is unavailable or if a node isn't configured to contact a WINS server, p-node name resolution fails.

- M-node (modified node) is a hybrid mode that first attempts to resolve NetBIOS names using the b-node mechanism. If that fails, an attempt is made to use p-node name resolution. M-node was the first hybrid mode put into operation, but it has the disadvantage of favoring b-node operation, which is associated with high levels of broadcast traffic.

- H-node (hybrid node) is also a hybrid mode that favors the use of WINS for NetBIOS name resolution. When a computer needs to resolve a NetBIOS name, it first attempts to use p-node resolution to resolve a name via WINS. Only if WINS resolution fails does the host resort to b-node to resolve the name via broadcasts. Because it typically results in the best network utilization, h-node is the default mode of operation for Microsoft TCP/IPs configured to use WINS for name resolution. Microsoft recommends leaving TCP/IP client computers in the default h-node configuration. For more information, see the section "Configuring NetBIOS Name Resolution."

ON THE CD

This book's companion CD contains specially designed supplemental material to help you understand how well you know the concepts and skills you learned in this chapter. You'll find related exercises and exam questions and answers. See the file **Chapter19ApplyYourKnowledge.pdf** in the CD's **Chapter19\ApplyYourKnowledge** directory.

Suggested Readings and Resources

1. Boswell, William. *Inside Windows 2000 Server.* Indianapolis, IN: New Riders Publishing, 2000.

2. Heywood, Drew. *Networking with Microsoft TCP/IP, Third Edition.* Indianapolis, IN: New Riders Publishing, 1998.

3. Komar, Brian. *Sams Teach Yourself TCP/IP Network Administration.* Indianapolis, IN: Sams Publishing, 1998.

4. Microsoft Corporation. *Microsoft Windows 2000 Server Resource Kit.* Redmond, WA: Microsoft Press, 2000.

This chapter helps you prepare for the Network Infrastructure portion of the Accelerated exam by covering the following objectives:

Install, configure, and troubleshoot IP routing protocols.

- **Update a Windows 2000-based routing table by means of static routes.**

- **Implement demand-dial routing.**

▶ To understand how to install, configure, and troubleshoot IP routing protocols, it is necessary to have an understanding of how they function. The procedures for properly configuring and implementing the protocols can then be understood.

▶ Network environments that try to minimize communication costs between remote locations and a central office can make use of demand-dial routing. This feature of Windows 2000 also provides the capability to build fault tolerance into a network design.

▶ In some types of network environments, it is easier to implement routing by manually configuring the routing tables than incurring the overhead of a dynamic routing protocol. To do this, the network administrator needs to be familiar with the ROUTE command.

Manage and monitor IP routing.

- **Manage and monitor border routing.**

- **Manage and monitor internal routing.**

- **Manage and monitor IP routing protocols.**

▶ One of the tasks in implementing computer software and hardware is that of managing and monitoring its ongoing operation and trouble-shooting issues that may arise. To help with this task, it is necessary to understand how to use the tools to monitor its operation and manage changes in the configuration.

CHAPTER 20

Installing, Configuring, Managing, Monitoring, and Troubleshooting IP Routing in a Windows 2000 Network Infrastructure

▶ On the exam, you can expect a number of questions related to routing protocols and their operation. Many of these will be in scenario format, in which the implementation of a particular protocol will be based on a network topology design. Therefore, you need to have a strong understanding of the way the protocol works in small, medium, and large network designs and to understand where each protocol best fits within these network scenarios. After you have a solid understanding of the theory presented here, you should try to gain some practical experience by using Windows 2000 Advanced Server as much as possible. Implement the various protocols to see how they work and how they are configured within a network environment.

▶ You also should expect scenario questions on implementing and configuring a demand-dial routing environment. Expect to have answers for where a demand-dial routing solution is best used and the special considerations that are required when implementing the various routing protocols over this type of configuration.

INSTALLING, CONFIGURING, AND TROUBLESHOOTING IP ROUTING PROTOCOLS: THE THEORY

Install, configure, and troubleshoot IP routing protocols.

This chapter's main purpose is to explain how the routing protocols within Windows 2000 work and how to implement and configure them. The underlying theory of routing is discussed so that you receive a firm foundation for the later discussion on routing protocols, such as OSPF and RIP.

The chapter also explains demand-dial routing, including how demand-dial routing works and the special considerations that must be taken into account when implementing a demand-dial routing configuration into your network environment. Step by Steps for implementing, managing, and monitoring a demand-dial configuration are included.

Finally, this chapter gives a brief overview of some of the problems you may encounter within a routing environment, and it discusses tools that can be used to help diagnose problems and issues.

Introduction to IP Routing

Routing is the process of forwarding a packet based on the destination IP address. Routing occurs at a sending Transmission Control Protocol/Internet Protocol (TCP/IP) host, which is known as host routing, and at an IP router, known as router routing. In both cases, a decision has to be made about where the packet is to be forwarded.

To make these decisions, the IP layer consults a routing table stored in memory. Routing table entries are created by default when TCP/IP initializes and additional entries are added either manually by a system administrator or automatically through communication with routers.

Host Routing

For a host to communicate with a destination computer, it must first identify where that host exists. If the user enters a logical name rather than an IP address, the sending host uses an address resolution mechanism such as the Domain Name System (DNS) or Windows Internet Naming System (WINS) to obtain the address.

After the hostname is resolved to an IP address, the sending host must then determine whether it can communicate directly with the destination or if it needs to forward data to a router to send on its behalf. To determine this, the sending host compares the network address of the source with the network address of the destination. If the two network addresses are the same, the sending host knows the destination is on the same segment and addresses the packet to the destination's physical address.

If the two network addresses do not match, the host must forward the message on to a router so it can try to send the packet to the destination on the sending host's behalf. Based on the destination address, the router then uses its routing table to determine the best interface to send the packet out on to reach its destination. Each router along the path repeats this process until the destination host finally receives the packet. If routers determine that the destination host is unreachable, a destination unreachable packet is sent back to the host.

For the host to send the packet to its destination via the router, it must first determine the address of the router to which to send the packet. This can be accomplished using one of the following processes:

◆ The default gateway address is determined, and the local Address Resolution Protocol (ARP) cache is queried to identify the physical address to be used to reach the desired router.

◆ An Internet Control Message Protocol (ICMP) redirect message is sent by an IP router to the sending host, informing it of a better route to a destination host. The better route becomes a host route in the routing table.

◆ A TCP/IP host can "listen" to the routing protocol traffic used by routers. This is known as eavesdropping or wiretapping. Eavesdropping hosts have the same routing information as the routers. Windows 2000 implements eavesdropping through a feature called silent Routing Information Protocol (RIP).

The process for enabling RIP listening is outlined in Step by Step 20.1.

ON THE CD

Step by Step 20.1, "Enabling RIP 'Listening' on a Windows 2000 Professional Workstation," walks you through setting up RIP listening. See the file **Chapter20-01StepbyStep.pdf** in the CD's **Chapter20\StepbyStep** directory.

Router Routing

When a router receives a packet that must be forwarded to a destination host, the router must either deliver it to the destination host or to another router that can, in turn, continue the process of forwarding it to the destination host. To determine whether to forward to a host or to forward to a router, the router examines the destination network address and determines whether or not it is directly attached to that network. If so, the router forwards the packet to the destination host on that network.

If the router is not directly attached to the destination network, it uses the information in its routing tables to choose the best interface on which to forward the packet out. It does this by addressing the packet to the physical address of another router along the path to the destination host that is connected to a network segment that the current router is connected to. The decision as to which router to forward the packet to is determined by a number of variables about each of the network paths to the destination host, including the number of hops, the cost of each hop, and so on.

Windows 2000 Advanced Server provides router routing using Routing and Remote Access Services (RRAS). To enable RRAS within Windows 2000 Advanced Server, complete Step by Step 20.2.

ON THE CD

Step by Step 20.2, "Enabling Routing and Remote Access Services," covers Routing and Remote Access Services. See the file **Chapter20-02StepbyStep.pdf** in the CD's **Chapter20\ StepbyStep** directory.

The Routing Process

When a packet is received by a router or is forwarded by a host, they both must make decisions about how to send the packet. To do this, the router and host consult a database of information known as the routing table. This database is stored in random access memory (RAM) so that the lookup process is optimized. As the packet is forwarded through various routers toward its destination, each router makes a decision as to how to proceed by consulting its routing table. When a destination host replies to a packet, it is possible that the same path may not be used to reach the original sender. This depends on the metrics of each path along the route.

The information in the routing table can be generated in one of two ways. The first method is to manually configure the routing table with the routes for each destination network. This is known as *static routing*. Static routing is more suited to small environments where the amount of information to configure is small, and the overhead of generating the routing information is unacceptable. Static routers do not scale well to large or dynamically changing internetworks because of their manual administration.

The second method for generating routing table information is to make use of a *dynamic routing protocol*. A dynamic routing protocol consists of routing tables that are built and maintained automatically through an ongoing communication between routers. Periodically, or on demand, messages are exchanged between routers to update information kept in their routing tables. Dynamic routers generally require little maintenance after they have been configured, which allows them to be used in much larger environments where it would not be practical to use static routers. Two dynamic routing protocols that are provided with Windows 2000 are

◆ Routing Information Protocol (RIP)

◆ Open Shortest Path First (OSPF)

Dynamic routers can detect information from other routers, making dynamic routing fault tolerant. If a router or link goes down, the routers sense the change in the internetwork topology through the expiration of the route information in the routing table. The router can then rebuild its links based on the new network topology and forward the routing information to other routers—so that all the routers on the internetwork become aware of the new internetwork topology. This capability is not available with static routers.

IN THE FIELD

DISCERNING WHEN A ROUTER IS DOWN

Suppose you have a network that has three routers: router 1 connects to router 2 over Network A, and router 2 connects to router 3 over Network B (see Figure 20.1). If router 1 goes down, router 2 is unable to reach router 1 over Network A, as indicated by the route in its routing table. After a period of time, router 2 expires the route information in its routing table and requests an update, at which time it determines that it can no longer reach router 1. This is then reflected in its routing tables. Router 2 eventually broadcasts its routing information to router 3, at which time router 3 updates its tables with the information that router 1 is not available.

To add the RIP protocol in Routing and Remote Access, follow Step by Step 20.3.

ON THE CD

Step by Step 20.3, "Adding the Routing Information Protocol (RIP)," shows you how to add the RIP protocol. See the file **Chapter20-03StepbyStep.pdf** in the CD's **Chapter20\StepbyStep** directory.

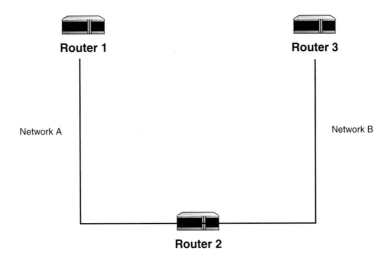

FIGURE 20.1
This diagram shows the networks and routers involved in discerning when a router is down.

The capability to scale and recover from internetwork faults makes dynamic routing, rather than static routing, the better choice for medium, large, and very large internetworks.

Routing Technology

Routing protocols are based either on a distance-vector or link-state technology. The main differences between distance-vector and link-state routing protocols are the following:

◆ **What routing information is exchanged.** When a link or router fails, the internetwork must reconfigure itself to reflect the new topology. Information in routing tables must then be updated.

◆ **How the information is exchanged.** The time it takes for the internetwork to reconverge is known as the convergence time, which varies based on the routing protocol and the type of failure (downed link or downed router).

◆ **How quickly the internetwork can recover from a downed link or a downed router.** How quickly it can recover is determined by the type of fault, how it is sensed, and how the routing information is propagated through the internetwork.

Distance-Vector Routing

Distance-vector routing is the oldest and most common routing algorithm. Distance-vector routers build their routing information tables based on information received from other routers. The routers pass this information to other routers on each of their attached segments.

Routing information is generally exchanged when routers are started, when routes change, and at regular intervals. Upon receipt of new routing information, routers update their routing information tables and broadcast the new routing information onto all attached networks. If, however, a router cannot communicate at all (that is, the router is not available), a route-aging algorithm must come into play to remove the route information from a router's tables.

One of the negative attributes of distance-vector-based routing is slow convergence. In using distance-vector-based routing methods, each router receives route change information, updates its tables, calculates the hop counts to existing routes, and broadcasts new routing information.

The count-to-infinity problem is one of the major disadvantages of distance-vector routing. This condition is caused when a router (or a link to a router) becomes unavailable. The convergence time is slow; therefore, incorrect routing information can propagate through the system.

IN THE FIELD

THE EXCHANGE OF INFORMATION

Suppose you have two routers: 1 and 2 (see Figure 20.2). Router 1's connection to Network A has been destroyed. Router 1 knows it cannot reach Network A itself, but router 2 advertises that Network A is two hops away. Router 1 then assumes that it is now three hops from Network A, and router 2 is the way to access Network A. Router 2, however, still believes that router 1 is the way to Network A, and it resets its routing information tables to reflect that Network A is now four hops away, using router 1 as the best route. Again, router 2 broadcasts this information, and router 1 resets its tables again to reflect that it is now five hops away, using router 2 as the best way to Network A.

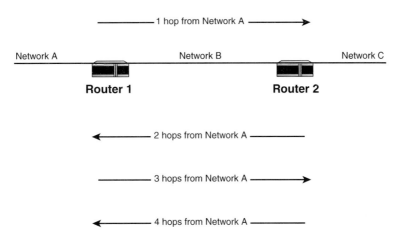

FIGURE 20.2
This diagram shows the way the routers calculate the hops in transferring data.

The routers continue to reset their routing information tables and increase the hop count value until "infinity" is reached. Infinity usually means the maximum number of hop counts a routing protocol can accept before a routing information packet is discarded.

Routing protocols can take various steps to avoid the count-to-infinity problem. Three avoidance mechanisms that can be implemented are

◆ **Split horizon.** This mechanism relies on not sending routing information back in the direction from which it was received. Basically, the router says, "I learned about network *xx* from you, so you can't get to network *xx* through me." Split horizon eliminates count-to-infinity and routing loops during convergence in single-path internetworks and reduces the chances of count to infinity in multipath internetworks.

◆ **Split horizon with poison reverse.** This mechanism differs from split horizon in that it announces all networks. However, those networks learned in a given direction are announced with a hop count of 16, indicating that the network is unreachable. In a single-path internetwork, split horizon with poison reverse has no benefit beyond split horizon. However, in a multipath internetwork, split horizon with poison reverse greatly reduces count-to-infinity and routing loops. Count to infinity can still occur in a multipath internetwork because routes to networks can be learned from multiple sources.

◆ **Triggered updates.** This mechanism allows a router to announce changes in metric values almost immediately, instead of waiting for the next periodic announcement. The trigger is a change to a metric in an entry in the routing table. For example, networks that become unavailable can be announced with a hop count of 16 through a triggered update. If triggered updates were sent by all routers immediately, each triggered update could cause a cascade of broadcast traffic across the IP internetwork. Triggered updates improve the convergence time of RIP internetworks but at the expense of additional broadcast traffic as the triggered updates are propagated.

Other disadvantages of distance-vector routing are slow convergence and high overhead. In distance-vector routing, when a change is made, the changes must be propagated to each router. This propagation causes all routing tables affected by this change to be recalculated. Distance-vector routing can converge very slowly after a change in topology occurs. In addition, having a large number of routes within the network can lead to very large routing tables, which requires additional resources on each router and can cause significant traffic on the network during routing information updates.

The advantages of distance-vector routing are that it requires low maintenance and is easy to configure, making it popular in small network environments.

Link-State Routing

As previously discussed, distance-vector-based routing protocols periodically broadcast route information to each other, whether or not the information has changed. Link-state-routing protocols, on the other hand, exchange information only about the specific routes that have changed.

Routers using link-state routing protocols learn about their network environment by "meeting" their neighboring routers. This is done through a "hello" packet. The network information is then sent to each of the neighboring routers using a link-state advertisement (LSA). The neighboring routers copy the contents of the packet and forward the LSA to each attached network, except for the one the LSA was received on. This is known as *flooding*.

Routers using a link-state routing protocol build a tree, or "map," of shortest paths with itself as the root. The tree is based on all the LSAs seen and contains the route to each destination in the network. Figure 20.3 depicts a network that is using a link-state routing protocol.

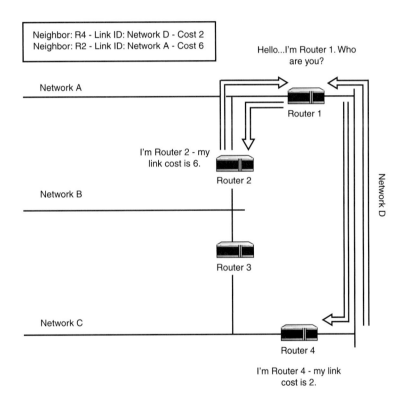

FIGURE 20.3
The network in this diagram uses link-state communication.

Router 1 transmits a "hello" packet to learn about its neighboring routers. Each neighbor replies with information regarding the link it is attached to and the route cost. Router 1 builds its routing database directly from the information received in response to the "hello" packets.

The next step in link-state routing is to transmit LSAs to its neighbors. The LSAs that are transmitted contain information about router 1's neighbors and their associated costs. This packet is copied by each neighbor, and the LSA is forwarded to each of their neighbors. Because the routers maintain the original advertisement, whenever another router needs LSA information, it requests a copy of the original from its neighbor. Because the advertisement is never altered by a router, it is considered to be first-hand information.

Because LSAs contain information only about the neighbors of a particular router, this leads to smaller routing tables. In addition, because link-state information is not exchanged after the network has converged, it does not have the high traffic impact on the network that distance-vector routing does, making it more efficient.

The disadvantages of link–state-based protocols are that they are more complex to understand and configure than distance-vector protocols.

Routing Networks

Many organizations today cannot tolerate downtime in their networks. To meet service-level agreements, information technology professionals must find ways of building redundancy or fault tolerance into their network designs. Traditional single-path designs, in which a single path exists between any two networks in the internetwork, simplify the routing tables and the packet flow paths; however, they do not provide any redundancy. A dynamic router might sense a fault, but the networks across the failure are unreachable for the duration of the fault. A downed link or a downed router must be brought back up before packets can be delivered successfully across the downed link or router.

In a multipath routing infrastructure, multiple paths exist between networks within the internetwork. Multipath internetworks provide redundancy when dynamic routing is used, and some routing protocols, such as OSPF, can balance the load of network traffic across multiple paths with the same metric value. Multipath internetworks, however, can be more complex to configure and can have a higher probability of routing loops during convergence when using distance-vector–based routing protocols.

In small networks, information about each network ID is maintained in the routing table. This allows every host to connect to every other host on the network by referring to the network on which the host is located. The routers within such a network maintain information about every route to a particular network ID so that routing of network/host address pairs can be accomplished. Each network is not classified into smaller networks using net/subnet information, only network and host information. This type of network has a flat routing infrastructure.

This type of infrastructure does not scale to very large networks. One such large network is the Internet. The Internet has evolved into a collection of Internet Service Providers (ISPs). ISPs are interconnected among themselves to provide Internet-wide connectivity among all their subscribers.

Initially, IP routing on the Internet was designed using a flat model approach consisting of network/host address information. Each host on the Internet is represented by an address that identifies both the network that the host is located on, as well as the address of the individual host. Routing entries for each network address are maintained within a routing table and are used to route information between hosts.

As the Internet grew, address utilization became inefficient, and routing suffered scalability issues. Considering there are 2,097,152 Class C networks, a routing table entry for each network would result in large and inefficient routing tables.

To accommodate scalability issues, routing between multiple, interconnected providers who each may have a significant number of networks, subnets, and hosts, the IP routing architecture modeled each Internet provider as a collection of interconnected autonomous systems (AS). Routing within each AS is provided by means of intradomain (interior) routing protocols such as RIP, OSPF, or Interior Gateway Protocol (IGP). Routing among ASs is provided by means of interdomain (exterior) routing protocols, such as External

Gateway Protocol (EGP) and Border Gateway Protocol (BGP). Interdomain (exterior) routing protocols summarize IP routes and help to remove the scalability issues that IGPs can have.

Autonomous systems may be further divided into routing domains (also known as regions or areas) that define a hierarchy within the AS. This type of network infrastructure is called a hierarchical internetwork. The network IDs in a hierarchical internetwork have a network/subnet/sub-subnet structure. A routing table entry for the highest level (the network) is also the route used for the subnets and sub-subnets of the network. When routing between routing domains, groups of network IDs can be represented as a single routing table entry through route summarization.

Hierarchical routing infrastructures simplify routing tables and lower the amount of routing information that is exchanged, but they require more planning.

INSTALLING, CONFIGURING, AND TROUBLESHOOTING IP ROUTING PROTOCOLS: THE PRACTICE

Up to this point, the chapter has discussed the theory behind different routing protocols, how they work, and some of the mechanisms that are used to resolve issues that arise regarding the different types of routing protocols. Next, this discussion focuses on the actual routing protocols, beginning with the RIP, followed by the OSPF protocol.

Working with RIP

The RIP is a distance-vector protocol that uses hop count as its metric for measuring the number of routers that must be crossed to reach the desired network. RIP is widely used for routing traffic in the global Internet and is an IGP, which means that it performs routing within a single AS. There are two versions of RIP, and are defined as follows.

RIP Version 1

In RIP Version 1 (v1), all route announcements are addressed to the IP subnet, and a Media Access Control (MAC)-level broadcast is initiated. As a result, non-RIP hosts and RIP hosts alike receive RIP announcements. Large and very large RIP internetworks can receive a significant amount of broadcast traffic on each subnet.

To configure RIP on an RRAS, follow Step by Step 20.4.

ON THE CD

Step by Step 20.4, "Configuring RIP on Windows 2000," covers configuration of RIP on a Routing and Remote Access Server. See the file **Chapter20-04StepbyStep.pdf** in the CD's **Chapter20\StepbyStep** directory.

While the RIP produces additional broadcast traffic, the broadcast nature of RIP v1 enables the use of silent RIP. A silent RIP router processes RIP announcements but does not announce its own routes. Silent RIP could be enabled on nonrouter hosts to produce a routing table with as much detail as the RIP routers. With more detailed routes in the routing table, a silent RIP host can make better routing decisions. To enable silent RIP on your router, complete Step by Step 20.5.

ON THE CD

Step by Step 20.5, "Enabling Silent RIP on Windows 2000," walks you through the process of enabling silent RIP on a router. See the file **Chapter20-05StepbyStep.pdf** in the CD's **Chapter20\StepbyStep** directory.

RIP v1 was designed for class-based IP internetworks in which the network ID can be determined from the values of the first 3 bits of the IP address in the RIP route. Because the subnet mask is not included or announced with the route, the RIP router must determine the network ID based on a limited set of information. For each route in an RIP v1 message, the RIP v1 router performs the following process:

◆ If the network ID fits the address classes (Class A, Class B, or Class C), the default class-based subnet mask is assumed.

◆ If the network ID does not fit the address class and the network ID fits the subnet mask of the interface on which it is received, the subnet mask of the interface on which it was received is assumed. If the network ID does not fit the subnet mask of the interface on which it is received, the network ID is assumed to be a host route with the subnet mask 255.255.255.255.

As a result of the assumptions listed previously, supernetted routes might be interpreted as a single network ID rather than as the range of network IDs they are designed to represent, and subnet routes advertised outside of the network ID being subnetted might be interpreted as host routes.

As a mechanism for supporting subnetted environments, RIP v1 routers do not advertise the subnets of a subnetted class-based network ID outside the subnetted region of the IP internetwork. However, because only the class-based network ID is being advertised outside the subnetted environment, subnets of a network ID in an RIP v1 environment must be contiguous. If subnets of an IP network ID are noncontiguous, known as disjointed subnets, the class-based network ID is announced by separate RIP v1 routers in different parts of the internetwork. As a result, IP traffic can be forwarded to the wrong network.

Finally, RIP v1 does not provide any protection from a rogue RIP router starting up on a network and announcing false or inaccurate routes. RIP v1 announcements are processed regardless of their source.

RIP Version 2

RIP Version 2 (v2) seeks to address some of the problems associated with RIP v1. The design goals of RIP v2 were to minimize broadcast traffic, use variable-length subnetting to conserve IP addresses, and secure routing environments from misconfigured or malicious routers. To help resolve these issues, the following key features were added:

◆ Instead of broadcasting RIP announcements, RIP v2 supports sending RIP announcements to the IP multicast address of 224.0.0.9. Non-RIP nodes are not disturbed by RIP router-announcement traffic. The disadvantage of this new feature is that silent RIP nodes also must be listening for multicast traffic sent to 224.0.0.9. If you are using silent RIP, verify that your silent RIP nodes can listen for multicasted RIP v2 announcements before deploying multicast RIP v2. The use of multicasted announcements is optional. The broadcasting of RIP v2 announcements is supported.

◆ RIP v2 announcements send the subnet mask along with the network ID. RIP v2 can be used in subnetted, supernetted, and variable-length subnet mask environments. Subnets of a network ID do not have to be contiguous (they can be disjointed subnets).

◆ RIP v2 supports the use of authentication mechanisms to verify the origin of incoming RIP announcements. Simple password authentication was defined in Request for Comments (RFC) 1723, but newer authentication mechanisms, such as Message Digest 5 (MD5), are available.

RIP Updates

RIP sends routing update messages at regular intervals and when the network topology changes. When a router receives a routing update that includes changes to an entry, it updates its routing table to reflect the new route. The metric value for the path is increased by one, and the sender is indicated as to the next hop. RIP routers maintain only the best route, the route with the lowest metric value, to a destination. After updating its routing table, the router immediately begins transmitting routing updates to inform other network routers of the change.

If the RIP router is storing a complete list of all the networks and all the possible ways to reach each network, the routing table can have hundreds or even thousands of entries in a large IP internetwork with multiple paths. Because only 25 routes can be sent in a single RIP packet, large routing tables have to be sent as multiple RIP packets.

RIP routers advertise the contents of their routing tables every 30 seconds on all attached networks through an IP subnet and a MAC-level broadcast. Large IP internetworks carry the broadcast RIP overhead of large routing tables. This can be especially problematic on wide-area network (WAN) links in which significant portions of the WAN-link bandwidth are devoted to the RIP passing traffic. As a result, RIP-based routing does not scale well to large internetworks or WAN implementations.

RIP Routing Metric

RIP uses a single routing metric (hop count) to measure the distance between the source and a destination network. Each hop in a path from source to destination is assigned a hop count value, which is typically 1. When a router receives a routing update that contains a new or changed destination network entry, the router adds one to the metric value indicated in the update and enters the network in the routing table. The IP address of the sender is used as the next hop.

RIP prevents routing loops from continuing indefinitely by implementing a limit on the number of hops allowed in a path from the source to a destination. The maximum number of hops in a path is 15; therefore, the number of routers between any two hosts is limited to 15. If a router receives a routing update that contains a new or a changed entry, and if increasing the metric value by one causes the metric to be infinity (that is, 16), the network destination is considered unreachable.

Open Shortest Path First (OSPF)

OSPF is a link-state routing protocol. It functions by sending LSAs to all other routers within the same hierarchical area. Don't worry if you don't understand what is meant by *hierarchical area*. This is discussed in a later section. LSAs for routers consist of a router, its attached networks, and their configured costs. As OSPF routers accumulate link-state information into a database called the link-state database, they use the Shortest Path First (SPF) algorithm to calculate the shortest path to each node. OSPF has the following features:

◆ OSPF has better convergence than RIP because routing changes are propagated instantaneously, not periodically.

◆ OSPF calculated routes are always loop free.

◆ OSPF sends updates only when routing changes instead of sending routing updates periodically. This ensures better use of bandwidth.

◆ OSPF allows for logical definition of networks where routers can be divided into areas. This provides a mechanism for aggregating routes and cutting down on the unnecessary propagation of subnet information.

◆ OSPF was designed to advertise the subnet mask with the network and supports variable-length subnet masks (VLSM), disjointed subnets, and supernetting.

◆ OSPF allows routing authentication using different methods of password authentication.

◆ Routes outside of the OSPF AS are advertised within the AS so that OSPF routers can calculate the least cost route to external networks. This keeps track of external routes injected by exterior protocols.

To configure OSPF on a Routing and Remote Access server, proceed with Step by Step 20.6

ON THE CD

Step by Step 20.6, "Installing and Configuring OSPF on Windows 2000," walks you through configuration of OSPF on a Routing and Remote Access server. See the file **Chapter20-06StepbyStep.pdf** in the CD's **Chapter20\StepbyStep** directory.

Routing Hierarchies

Unlike RIP, OSPF can operate within a hierarchy. The basic structure to this hierarchy includes areas, ASs, and the backbone. The largest entity within the hierarchy is the AS. An AS is a collection of networks under common administration, sharing a

---

NOTE

Subnetting and Supernetting. Variable-length subnetting is a technique of allocating subnetted network IDs that use subnet masks of different sizes. However, all subnetted network IDs are unique and can be distinguished from each other by their corresponding subnet mask.

Supernetting is the process of linking pieces of the Class C address space. Supernetting can be used to consolidate several Class C network addresses into one logical network. To use supernetting, the IP network addresses that are to be combined must share the same high order bits, and the subnet mask is shortened to take bits away from the network portion of the address and add them to the host portion.

Disjointed subnets are subnets of an IP Network ID that are noncontiguous.

common routing strategy. Each AS can be further divided into areas linked by an OSPF backbone, which, in itself, is also an area.

Areas

Each network area of an AS is identified by an area ID. This identifier has no relation to an IP address or IP network ID and are not used to reflect routing data. However, if all the networks within an area correspond to a single subnetted network ID, the area ID can be set to reflect the network ID for administrative convenience. For example, if an area contains all the subnets of the IP network 10.1.0.0, the area ID can be set to 10.1.0.0. The purpose of defining areas within an AS are to reduce the size of a topological database.

To keep the size of topological databases for each router to a minimum, LSAs for an area's networks and routers are flooded within the area but not to routers outside of the area. Each area becomes its own link-state domain with its own topological database.

Routers with multiple interfaces can participate in multiple areas. These routers, which are called area border routers (ABRs), maintain separate topological databases for each area. The routing tables within border routers are a combination of the routing table entries of all the SPF trees for each topological database, as well as static routes, SNMP configured routes, and routes learned from other routing protocols. To reduce the number of entries in the routing table, the networks inside of the area can be advertised outside the area using summary route advertisements. By keeping area topologies separate, OSPF passes less routing traffic than it would if the AS were not partitioned.

The OSPF Backbone

An OSPF backbone is responsible for distributing routing information between areas, and there is at least one backbone per OSPF internetwork. A backbone has a reserved area ID of 0.0.0.0. It consists of all ABRs, networks not in any one area, and their attached routers. The backbone has to be at the center of all areas within the AS. That is, all areas have to be physically connected to the backbone. The reasoning behind this is that OSPF expects all areas to inject routing information into the backbone and, in turn, the backbone disseminates that information into other areas. Figure 20.4 shows an example of an internetwork with several areas and a backbone.

NOTE **Topological Databases** A topological database is essentially an overall picture of networks in relationship to routers. It contains the collection of LSAs received from all routers in the same area. In a very large AS with a large number of networks, each OSPF router must keep the LSA of every other router in its topological database. The SPF calculation of a large topological database can require a substantial amount of processing and can result in very large routing tables. To prevent this, an AS is further divided into areas.

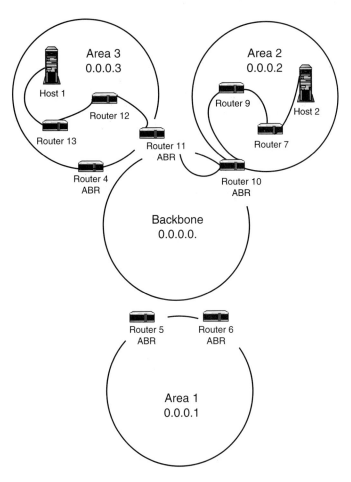

FIGURE 20.4
This OSPF network has several areas
and a backbone.

In this example, Routers 4, 5, 6, 10, and 11 make up the backbone.
If Host 1 in Area 3 wants to send a packet to Host 2 in Area 2, the
packet is sent to Router 13, which forwards the packet to Router 12,
which sends the packet to Router 11. Router 11 forwards the packet
along the backbone to ABR Router 10, which sends the packet
through two intra-area routers (Router 9 and Router 7) to be
forwarded to Host 2.

Because the backbone itself is an OSPF area, all backbone routers can use the same procedures and algorithms to maintain routing information within the backbone that any area router would. This allows backbone routers not only to route host traffic between areas but also to disseminate summary routes within areas to other routers on the backbone that can then propagate the information within their own areas to area routers. This ensures that any host within an area can reach any host in another area. To minimize the size of routing tables, OSPF ensures that the backbone topology is invisible to all intra-area routers in the same way that individual area topologies are invisible to the backbone.

In rare cases it is possible that a new area is introduced to the AS that cannot have direct physical access to the backbone. In this instance, it is necessary to configure a connection of the new area to the backbone through a connection called a *virtual link*, which provides the disconnected area a logical path to the backbone. The virtual link has to be established between two ABRs that have a common area, with one ABR connected to the backbone. Virtual links are configured over a non-backbone area known as a transit area. Figure 20.5 provides an example of an OSPF network with a virtual link.

Step by Step 20.7 shows you how to configure a virtual link within RRAS.

ON THE CD

Step by Step 20.7, "Configuring a Virtual Routing Link for Windows 2000," covers configuration of a virtual link within RRAS. See the file **Chapter20-07StepbyStep.pdf** in the CD's **Chapter20\ StepbyStep** directory.

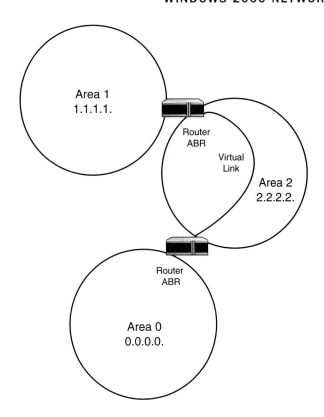

FIGURE 20.5
This OSPF network has a virtual link,
which is configured over a transit area.

Area Routing

Area partitioning creates two types of OSPF routing, intra-area and
inter-area, depending on whether the source and destination are in
the same or in different areas.

◆ Intra-area routing occurs when the source and destination are
in the same area. With intra-area routing, the source routes the
packet to its default gateway (an internal area router). The
internal area router then makes use of the explicit routes
(as calculated by the SPF algorithm) maintained in the area
routers and routes the packet through the appropriate interface
to the destination internal area router. The destination internal
area router then forwards the packet to the destination host.

◆ Inter-area routing occurs when the source and destination are in different areas. When routing between areas, the source routes the packet to its default gateway (an internal area router), and the area router then forwards the packet to an ABR using the shortest path. The ABR then forwards the packets through backbone routers using the shortest path to the ABR for the destination host. The ABR for the destination host then forwards the packets through internal area routers using the shortest path until the packets reach their destination.

Step by Step 20.8 shows you how to create additional OSPF areas.

> **ON THE CD**
>
> Step by Step 20.8, "Creating an OSPF Area with Windows 2000 Routing and Remote Access," walks you through the creation of additional OSPF areas. See the file **Chapter20-08StepbyStep.pdf** in the CD's **Chapter20\StepbyStep** directory.

Autonomous System Routing

Routing does not occur only within areas using OSPF. When internetworks are connected to other internetworks that are under different administrative control, routing must be established. This type of routing between ASs is established using external routes. AS border routers running OSPF learn about exterior routes through other routing protocols, such as Interior Gateway Routing Protocol (IGRP), RIP, or BGP. AS border routers are similar to ABRs, except that they route between different ASs.

By default, AS border routers advertise all external routes within its AS. This allows all areas and networks within areas to reach destination networks that may lie outside the AS. As a network manager, you may find it necessary to restrict the external routes that are advertised within the AS. Using Windows 2000 RRAS, you can configure the AS border router to accept or ignore the routes of certain external sources, such as routing protocols (RIP v2) or other sources (static routes or Simple Network Management Protocol [SNMP]). You also can configure the AS border router to accept or discard specific routes by configuring one or multiple (Destination, Network Mask) pairs. To enable AS border routing, perform Step by Step 20.9.

ON THE CD

Step by Step 20.9, "Configuring Autonomous System Border Routing in Windows 2000 Routing and Remote Access," shows you how to enable system border routing. See the file **Chapter20-09StepbyStep.pdf** in the CD's **Chapter20\StepbyStep** directory.

As a network manager, you want to tune your routing protocols for the best efficiency you can obtain. If external routes are allowed to be flooded into areas within your AS, this consumes routing resources. To avoid using additional resources on your routers, you can configure area border routers to advertise a default route into the area. The default route is then flooded to all routers within the area. This default route is then used by all routers within the area for any destination addresses not reachable within the AS. Areas configured with a default route are known as stub areas.

OSPF Operation

The SPF routing algorithm is the basis for OSPF operations. When an SPF router is powered up, it initializes its routing protocol data structures and then waits for indications from lower-layer protocols that its interfaces are functional.

After a router is assured that its interfaces are functioning, it uses the OSPF Hello protocol to acquire neighbors. Neighbors are routers with interfaces to a common network. The router sends hello packets to its neighbors and receives their hello packets. In addition to helping acquire neighbors, hello packets also act as keep-alives to let routers know that other routers are still functional.

Designated Routers

On multiaccess networks (networks supporting more than two routers), the Hello protocol elects a designated router and a backup designated router. Because the designated router is adjacent to all other routers, it acts as a hub for the distribution of link-state information, maintaining the synchronization of the topological database and for controlling adjacencies between routers within the network.

As an example of why a designated router is required, consider a broadcast network with six OSPF routers. Without controlling the adjacency behavior, each router could establish an adjacency with each of the other routers, for a total of 15 adjacency relationships. On a broadcast network with n routers, a total of $n*(n-1)/2$ adjacencies would be formed. This can result in unneeded flooding traffic as routers attempt to synchronize with all their adjacent routers. Designated routers allow a reduction in network traffic and in the size of the topological database.

The designated router is elected via the Hello protocol. Hello packets are exchanged via IP multicast packets on each segment. The router with the highest OSPF priority on a segment becomes the designated router for that segment. In the case of a tie, the router with the highest router ID wins. The default for the interface OSPF priority is 1. A Router Priority of 0 means that the router does not become a designated router.

In addition to electing a designated router, a backup designated router also is elected for each multiaccess network to prevent the loss in connectivity associated with the loss of a designated router. Like the designated router, the backup designated router is adjacent to all routers on the network. When the designated router fails, the backup designated router immediately becomes the designated router by sending LSAs to all its adjacent routers, announcing its new role. There is a very short period of time when transit traffic could be impaired as the backup designated router takes over the role of the designated router.

Like the designated router, the backup designated router is elected by the exchange of hello packets. Each hello packet contains a field for the backup designated router of the network. If the backup designated router is not specified, the router with the highest router priority that is not already the designated router becomes the backup designated router. If multiple routers are with the highest router priority, the router with the highest router ID is elected the backup designated router.

Adjacencies

When the topological databases of two neighboring routers are synchronized, the routers are said to be adjacent. On multiaccess networks, the designated router determines which routers should become adjacent. Topological databases are synchronized between pairs of adjacent routers. Adjacencies control the distribution of routing protocol packets. These packets are sent and received only on adjacencies.

Adjacencies are first developed when an OSPF router initializes; it sends out a periodic OSPF hello packet. The OSPF hello packet contains configuration information such as the router's Router ID and the list of neighboring routers for which the router has received a hello packet. Initially, the neighbor list in the OSPF hello packet does not contain any neighbors.

The initializing OSPF router also listens for neighboring routers' hello packets. From the incoming hello packets, the initializing router determines the specific router or routers with which an adjacency is to be established. Adjacencies are formed with the designated router and backup designated router, which are identified in the incoming hello packets. Designated routers and backup designated routers are discussed in more detail later in this chapter.

To begin the adjacency, the routers forming the adjacency describe the contents of their topological databases through a sequence of database description packets. This is known as the database exchange process, during which the two neighboring routers form a master/slave relationship. The contents of each router's topological database is acknowledged by its neighboring router.

Each router compares its LSAs with the LSAs of its neighbor and notes which LSAs need to be requested from the neighbor to synchronize the topological database. The missing or more recent LSAs are then requested through link-state request packets. Link-state update packets are sent in response to the link-state request packets, and their receipt is acknowledged. When all link-state requests of both routers have been satisfied, the topological databases of the neighboring routers are fully synchronized, and an adjacency is formed.

After the adjacency has formed, each neighboring router sends a periodic hello packet to inform its neighbor that the router is still active on the network. The lack of hello packets from a neighbor is used to detect a downed router.

If an event occurs such as a downed link or router or the addition of a new network that changes the topological database of one router, the topological database of adjacent routers are no longer synchronized. The router whose topological database has changed sends link-state update packets to its adjacent neighbor, and the receipt of the link-state update packets is acknowledged. After the exchange the topological databases of the adjacent routers are again synchronized.

Demand-Dial Routing

In some network environments, a network manager might require that redundancy be built in to the network design so that if the permanent network connection between sites goes down, an alternate route via a demand-dial link is in place to provide a backup route. In other locations a permanent connection is required, but the cost of establishing the connection or the technologies available to implement the connection may be limited. In such cases, a technology called demand-dial routing can be put in place that allows packets to be routed across a dial-up link.

A demand-dial network consists of a calling router and an answering router. Both the calling and receiving routers have RRAS installed. To enable demand-dial routing on an existing RRAS server, complete Step by Step 20.10.

ON THE CD

Step by Step 20.10, "Enabling Demand-Dial Routing," walks you through the setup of demand-dial routing on an existing RRAS server. See the file **Chapter20-10StepbyStep.pdf** in the CD's **Chapter20\StepbyStep** directory.

When a calling router receives a packet over the network, the router determines the best route to forward the packet. If the route chosen is a demand-dial route, a connection is initiated with the other side. The type of connection that is established is a PPP connection that is initiated over either a physical connection such as an analog or Integrated Services Digital Network (ISDN) line or over a logical connection known as a tunnel. The tunnels are established using either Point-to-Point Tunneling Protocol (PPTP) or Layer 2 Tunneling Protocol (L2TP).

After the demand-dial router determines that a connection needs to be established, the demand-dial router determines whether or not one currently exists. If the status is connected, the packet is forwarded to the destination host. If no connection is in place, the calling router must establish a connection.

To establish a connection from the calling router to the answering router, the calling router checks the dial-out hours and demand-dial filters configured on the interface. If dial-out hours or demand-dial filters prohibit establishing a connection, the connection attempt fails, and the host that originated the packets is notified that the destination host is unreachable. If after checking, the connection can proceed, the router retrieves the configuration of the demand-dial interface and then, based on the configuration, a connection is established with the answering router. The demand-dial router must accommodate several types of connections. These include the following:

◆ **Modem or ISDN connection.** With this type of configuration, the configured phone number is dialed.

◆ **Virtual Private Network connection.** With this type of configuration, the configured host or IP address is used to establish either a PPTP or Internet Protocol Security (IPSec) connection.

◆ **Direct serial or direct parallel port connection.** With this type of configuration, a direct connection is made between the calling router and the answering router over the serial port or parallel port.

After the connection has been made, it is then necessary for the calling router to negotiate a Point-to-Point Protocol (PPP) connection with the answering router. Part of the negotiation is to send the credentials of the calling router. The answering router then checks the credentials against a local accounts database and/or remote policies or forwards the connection attributes to a RADIUS server where the credentials are checked.

In addition to authenticating the user's credentials, PPP negotiates parameters for the connection, such as the IP addresses of both routers, the name servers to be used, and any static routes that may have been put in place by the user.

Finally, the answering router looks up the user that is initiating the connection for a matching interface. If a matching demand-dial interface is located, the connection state is changed to a connected state, and the routing connection is established. If a matching interface is not found, the calling entity is then identified as a remote access client computer, and a routing connection cannot be established.

Types of Demand-Dial Connections

Two types of connections are available with demand-dial routing: demand connection and persistent connection. An on-demand connection is initiated when a packet is received by the calling router. When the calling router receives information for the answering router, it initiates the connection. After the information has been transmitted to the answering router and the connection has remained idle for a period of time, the connection is dropped. You can configure the demand-dial timeout on the Options tab of the Demand-Dial Interface Properties.

In a demand-dial environment, one or both routers can be configured to initiate the connection. If only one router is configured to initiate the connection, this is known as a one-way connection. If both routers are configured to initiate connections, this is known as a two-way connection.

In a one-way initiated connection, the calling router is configured with a username that is used to connect to the answering router. Associated with this user account are static routes that define which packets are to be routed to the other side. When the connection is initiated and the username is authenticated by the answering router, the static routes associated with the username are added to the routing table of the answering router.

A two-way initiated connection is very similar to a one-way initiated connection, except that both routers must now be configured with the necessary information to allow each to establish the connection.

In addition, the calling and answering routers must both be configured.

In both a one-way initiated connection and a two-way initiated connection, the router initiating the call must be configured with a username that matches the demand-dial interface on the answering router.

An on-demand connection can introduce problems for time-sensitive applications because the application must be able to tolerate a delay while the calling router initiates the connection with the answering router, and the static routes configured on both routers are propagated throughout the internetworks on both sides. The length of this delay varies for the type of physical or logical connection being established.

The second type of connection available within a demand-dial routing environment is a persistent connection. With this type of connection, there is no delay while the calling router initiates a connection with the answering router, which is available on a permanent basis. This type of connection is generally found in WAN environments where the connection is over a leased line, an X.25 connection or ISDN connection. With a persistent connection, if the connection is lost, the calling router can be configured to reestablish the connection automatically.

The choice of connection provides insight into the type of routing that should be configured over the connection. If the connection is persistent, one of the dynamic routing protocols, such as RIP or OSPF, may be used with special configuration to take into consideration the use of a demand-dial connection.

In an on-demand connection scenario, the choice of a dynamic routing protocol may not be the most appropriate. Dynamic protocols need to periodically exchange information between routers to keep their routing tables up to date. This is a function of dynamic routing protocols. This requirement to periodically exchange information with other routers in the environment can cause a connection to be made each time the update process takes place, or in some cases, it can keep the connection up permanently depending on how often the update process takes place. This may not be what is desired, however, in an environment where you are trying to minimize costs.

In an on-demand connection, the preferred way of enabling routing is to use either static routes or autostatic updates.

An autostatic update is a request from a router for all known routes or services from the router on the other side of the connection. After the request is received, the router adds the requested routes to its routing table. An autostatic update is a one-time, one-way exchange of routing information. Autostatic updates do not occur automatically on initiation of a demand-dial connection. Rather, the autostatic update must be manually initiated, or a schedule must be put in place to update routes. After the routes have been sent, the two routers do not exchange routing information updates unless a manual request to update is made or a scheduled request occurs, depending on how autostatic updates are configured within your environment. Autostatic updates are useful for environments where you require routes to be added once across a connection, but there are too many to make adding them using static routes practical.

Configuring static routes within a demand-dial network is different from configuring static routes using the ROUTE command. Step by Step 20.11 outlines how to configure static routes for a demand-dial interface.

One consideration when configuring static routes is to consider the default IP route (0.0.0.0) carefully. The default IP route is used to specify what should be done with network traffic when none of the existing routes provide a path for it. If no route exists, the router forwards the traffic through the default route.

This is fine for Internet traffic, because the probability is that the destination address is a host on the Internet. Within an intranet, this may not be the case, which can have an impact on a demand-dial router. For instance, if the default route is specified through the demand-dial router, every time an invalid address is specified, it is routed through the demand-dial router. This initiates a connection, and the traffic is forwarded, only to determine that the host does not exist on the other side. Therefore, you have incurred a cost for routing traffic to an unreachable host.

In this type of situation, you want to ensure that your demand-dial router is configured with routes specific to the destination network and that do not specify the demand-dial router as the default route.

Demand-Dial Security

Security concerns for most companies is a byproduct of today's interconnected world. As companies have become connected to the Internet, they have needed to take measures to ensure their networks are protected against malicious attacks and unauthorized access. Demand-dial security provides a number of security features to ensure that the appropriate calling router is initiating the connection and that the proper answering router is answering the connection. These features include the following:

◆ Remote access permission

◆ Authentication

◆ Encryption

◆ Callback

◆ Caller ID

◆ Remote access account lockout

In a demand-dial routing environment, the primary mechanism for enabling security between a calling router and an answering router is to associate a user account with the router that is initiating the connection. This provides the answering router with a mechanism to ensure that the router initiating the connection is authorized and has the appropriate permissions to access the router via a remote dial-in connection. To enable an account with the appropriate permissions, an administrator can either explicitly enable the account through the Dial-in Properties tab of the user account within either Computer Management or Active Directory Users and Computer, or the account can have permissions enabled for it by being associated with a remote access policy configured within a RADIUS/Internet Authentication service server.

In addition to ensuring the account has appropriate permissions, the answering router must authenticate the user account to ensure that the initiator can verify authenticity. This authentication can occur in one direction from the calling router to the answering router or in both directions. If the authentication is one-way, it does not protect against masquerading routers.

Windows 2000 includes support for PPP authentication at both the end-user level and the computer level. The protocols supported are the following:

◆ Password Authentication Protocol (PAP)

◆ Shiva Password Authentication Protocol (SPAP)

◆ Challenge Handshake Authentication Protocol (CHAP)

◆ Microsoft Challenge Handshake Authentication Protocol version 1 (MS-CHAP v1)

◆ Microsoft Challenge Handshake Authentication Protocol version 2 (MS-CHAP v2)

◆ Extensible Authentication Protocol-MD 5 CHAP (EAP-MD5)

Each of these protocols provides a set of rules for ensuring that the end users are actually who they claim to be.

Each of the preceding protocols involve the transfer of a username, a domain name, and a password so they can be authenticated. If passing credential information for authentication is not preferred, authentication can occur using certificates that represent the end user or the computer initiating the connection. Certificate-based authentication is provided through the following mechanisms:

◆ **Extensible Authentication Protocol-Transport Layer Security (EAP-TLS).** Using this protocol, the answering router authenticates by sending its certificate to the calling router, where it can be verified.

◆ **If IPSec is used for a L2TP over an IPSec demand-dial connection, no user authentication can be done.** Instead, two computers must authenticate themselves to each other. This type of computer-level authentication is performed through the exchange of certificates (also known as machine certificates) during the establishment of the IPSec security association.

After the connection has been authenticated, it still might be necessary to further secure the connection. To prevent unauthorized access to information being transferred over the connection, one of the encryption technologies available to demand-dial routing can be used. Two types of encryption are

◆ Microsoft Point–to-Point Encryption protocol (MPPE)

◆ IPSec

Each of these types of encryption schemes can be used to ensure that unauthorized access to information is not obtained while it is being transferred over the connection.

Callback is a feature that is available to the network manager to further secure the connection between the calling router and the answering router. With callback, the calling router makes the initial connection to the answering server. The answering server is then configured to call the calling router back at a predefined number.

Another security feature that the network manager can use is caller ID. This feature allows the answering router to ensure that the incoming call is coming from a specified phone number. This feature requires significant configuration with respect to other security features. With caller ID, the caller's phone line, the phone system, the remote access server's phone line, and the Windows 2000 driver for the dial-up equipment must all be configured to support caller ID.

A final security feature available in a demand-dial routing environment is remote access account lockout. This feature works similarly to user account lockout. That is, the network manager specifies as part of the configuration the number of times a remote access authentication fails against a valid user account before the user is denied remote access. This type of feature is useful against malicious attacks that involve a dictionary attack. A *dictionary attack* is a brute force type of attack that has the attacker repeatedly trying the connection with username/password combinations until the proper username/password pair is guessed.

MANAGING AND MONITORING IP ROUTING

Manage and monitor IP routing.

Up to this point, this chapter has discussed the theory behind routing protocols and further explored the individual routing protocols. This section focuses on some of the other tools that can be used within a network environment to help configure routing and to troubleshoot routing issues. The section finishes with a discussion of some troubleshooting options for each of the routing protocols.

Using the ROUTE Command to Configure Static Routes

The ROUTE command is used primarily to configure static routes within a network. It also can be used to troubleshoot by listing all the routes that the computer knows about.

The syntax of the ROUTE command is as follows:

```
route [-f] [-p] [command [destination] [mask subnetmask]
[gateway] [metric costmetric]]
```

The –f parameter is used to clear the routing tables of all entries. The –p parameter is used to make the route persistent. When a route is added to the router, the entry, by default, is not kept across reboots of the system. The –p parameter ensures that the entry is maintained in the routing table across reboots of the system.

The following commands are used to specify what can be done with the ROUTE command:

- ◆ **Print.** Prints the existing entries in the routing table.

- ◆ **Add.** Adds a new route to the routing table.

- ◆ **Delete.** Deletes an existing route from the routing table.

- ◆ **Change.** Modifies an existing route in the routing table.

The destination parameter specifies the destination you want to reach. The destination parameter can contain the following:

- ◆ Host address
- ◆ Subnet address

◆ Network address

◆ Default gateway

The mask parameter defines what portion of the destination address must match for that route to be used. When the mask is written in binary, a 1 is significant (must match), and a 0 need not match. For example, a 255.255.255.255 mask is used for a host entry. The mask of all 255s (all 1s) means that for this route to be used, the destination address of the packet to be routed must exactly match the network address. For another example, the network address 157.57.8.0 has a netmask of 255.255.248.0. This netmask means the first two octets must match exactly, the first 5 bits of the third octet must match (248=11111000), and the last octet does not matter. Thus, any address of 157.57 and the third octet of 8 through 15 (15=00001111) uses this route.

The gateway parameter specifies where the packet needs to be sent. This can be the local network card or a router on the local subnet.

The metric parameter specifies a cost that is to be associated with that route, which is used in the decision on how packets should be routed. Packets are routed through the route that has the lowest cost.

Step by Step 20.11 shows you how to configure a static route for the network 199.199.42.0.

ON THE CD

Step by Step 20.11, "Adding a Static Route to Windows 2000," covers configuration of a static route. See the file **Chapter20-11StepbyStep.pdf** in the CD's **Chapter20\StepbyStep** directory.

Using Network Monitor

Network Monitor is a tool for capturing network traffic. It can be used to diagnose problems when two computers do not communicate or when a computer has trouble functioning within a network environment. For instance, a computer may have issues resolving names or finding a path to another computer (routing issues).

Network Monitor can be configured to capture network traffic in several ways. It can be configured to capture all network traffic that it receives, configured to respond to events on the network, or configured to monitor only a subset of the traffic (for instance, a particular protocol such as HTTP traffic only). After the network data has been captured, Network Monitor analyzes the data and translates it into its logical frame structure to make the protocol information readable to the person capturing the information. Each frame contains the following:

◆ The source address of the computer that is sending the frame

◆ The destination address of the computer that received the frame

◆ Headers from each protocol used to send the frame

◆ The data or a portion of the information being sent

After the data has been translated, the information is presented through the graphical display provided by Network Monitor. Figure 20.6 shows an example of what the data looks like after it has been captured. Chapter 18, "Installing, Configuring, Managing, Monitoring, and Troubleshooting Network Chapter Protocols in a Windows 2000 Network Infrastructure," discusses using Network Monitor to monitor network traffic.

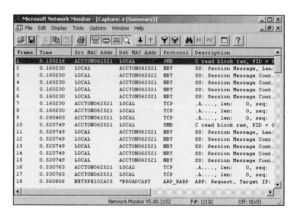

FIGURE 20.6

Use Network Monitor to capture data on network traffic.

Managing and Monitoring IP Routing Protocols

As a network administrator, you have the task of configuring and installing RRAS. After these services are configured and installed, you are then responsible for managing additional changes to the existing configuration, monitoring the installed configuration for problems, and troubleshooting problems when they arise. This chapter provides an overview of some of the things to do to accomplish these tasks.

RRAS Operation

After you have installed RRAS, you can perform several tasks to manage its ongoing operation. Some of the items that must be managed and monitored include the following:

◆ Administering a remote router.

◆ Checking the status of existing interfaces.

◆ Viewing existing routing tables and verifying that routes are being received from routing protocols.

◆ Determining the status of the RRAS and resetting the services, if required.

In a number of organizations today, users are distributed throughout various locations. The information services department is often centralized to minimize costs, which presents an issue for managing remote installations. With RRAS, it is possible to remotely manage RRAS routers from a central location

After you can manage the local server and remote servers, you can use this tool to quickly determine whether the existing interfaces are active. In addition to monitoring the event logs for possible messages indicating a problem, you also can check the individual interfaces to observe their operational states.

You may have determined that the interfaces for a particular server are operational. But it's still possible that the existing interfaces are not receiving routes to update the server's routing tables. You, as an administrator, would like to determine whether the router is indeed receiving updates. Again, the management tool provided with

Windows 2000 Advanced Server enables you to do this. To view the routing tables of a particular protocol, within the Routing and Remote Access tool, select and expand the server and IP Routing, and then select Static Routes. Right-click Static Routes and select the Show IP Routing Table option. You can then verify that the router is receiving updates to its routing table from other routers within the network.

Finally, you may want to check the overall status of the services to determine if they are running. If they are not running, then you would need to start them by choosing Computer Management, selecting Services and Applications, and then selecting Services. In the Details pane for Routing and Remote Access, verify that the Status column displays Started. If the service is not started, right-click Routing and Remote Access, and then click Start. If the router does not start, check the system event log for error messages.

Troubleshooting RIP Environments

After RIP is configured within your environment, you may be called on from time to time to troubleshoot issues that arise with routing. Although every problem is unique, the following outlines some of the items that may help when you're responding to issues within a RIP environment:

◆ Routing tables have improper routing information within a mixed RIP v1 and 2 network. RIP v2 routers are configured to multicast announcements. Multicast announcements are never received by RIP v1 routers.

◆ If you have a mixed environment of RIP v1 and RIP v2, ensure that the routers configured with RIP v2 are using broadcast rather than multicast.

◆ Silent RIP hosts are not receiving routes. RIP v2 routers are configured to multicast announcements. Multicast announcements are never received by silent RIP hosts.

If silent RIP hosts on a network are not receiving routes from the local RIP router, verify the version of RIP supported by the silent RIP hosts. If it is the listening service in Windows NT 4 Service Pack 4 or Windows 2000, you must configure the RIP routers for RIP v1 or RIP v2 broadcasting.

◆ RIP routers are not being updated properly with valid routes.
You are deploying variable-length subnetting, disjointed
subnets, or supernetting in a RIP v1 or mixed RIP v1 and RIP
v2 environment.

◆ Do not deploy variable length subnetting, disjointed subnets,
or supernetting in a RIP v1 or mixed RIP v1 and RIP v2
environment because it is not supported.

◆ RIP routers are not being updated properly with valid routes.
You are using autostatic RIP and you did not do an initial
manual update.

◆ When you use autostatic RIP on a demand-dial interface, the
first time you make a connection, you must manually update
routes.

◆ You also must update routes manually on the router for the
corresponding interface. The routes then appear in the IP
routing table.

◆ Host or default routes are not being propagated. RIP by
default is not configured to propagate host or default routes. If
these need to be propagated, change the default settings on the
Advanced tab of the properties of a RIP interface.

These are only some of the issues that can arise within a RIP
environment. For further troubleshooting information, refer to
Microsoft Technet or the Windows 2000 Advanced Server
documentation.

Troubleshooting OSPF Environments

OSPF is a more complex protocol than RIP, and the risk of
experiencing difficulties is greater due to this complexity. Because
OSPF is also more hierarchical than other protocols, which provides
the opportunity to help troubleshoot issues that may arise. It then
becomes easier to isolate issues to a particular area or the
interconnectivity between areas. Considerations include the
following:

◆ **OSPF adjacency is not forming between two neighbors.**
OSPF is not enabled on the interface. Verify that OSPF is
enabled on the interface on the network segment where an

adjacency should form. By default, when you add an interface to the OSPF routing protocol, OSPF is disabled for the interface and must be manually enabled.

◆ **OSPF adjacency is not forming between two neighbors.** PING the neighboring router to ensure basic IP and network connectivity. Use the TRACERT command to trace the route to the neighboring router. There should not be any routers between the neighboring routers.

◆ **A virtual link is not forming between two areas.** This can indicate mismatched configuration of the password, hello interval, or dead interval. Verify that the virtual link neighbor routers are configured for the same password, hello interval, and dead interval.

◆ **A virtual link is not forming between two areas.** Virtual link neighbors are configured for the incorrect transit-area ID. Verify that both virtual link neighbors are configured for the same correct transit-area ID.

◆ **Routing tables are not being updated with OSPF routes or improper OSPF routes.** Not receiving summarized routes. If you are not receiving summarized OSPF routes for an area, verify that the ABRs for the area are configured with the proper (Destination, Network mask) pairs summarizing that area's routes.

◆ **Routing tables are not being updated with OSPF routes or improper OSPF routes.** Verify that all ABRs are either physically connected to the backbone or logically connected to the backbone by using a virtual link.

These are only some of the issues that can arise within an OSPF environment. For further troubleshooting information, refer to Microsoft Technet or the Windows 2000 Advanced Server documentation.

CASE STUDY: SMALL OFFICE WITH A DEDICATED CONNECTION TO THE INTERNET

ESSENCE OF THE CASE

The following points summarize the essence of the case study:

► There must be a dedicated connection to the Internet.

► The network may expand in the future, and this must be done with minimum configuration.

► Only one segment is on the network.

► The connection must be online at all times.

SCENARIO

You are the administrator of a small office. You have been asked by the company owner to configure a connection to the Internet. You want to configure a dedicated connection that will enable you to assign a TCP/IP address to all the workstations that will identify it on the Internet. You currently have only one segment on your company network with approximately 50 work-stations. Your connection must be online at all times, and you would like to minimize the management that is necessary on your part. You believe that your network will grow within the next year, and you would like to ensure that this can be done with minimum configuration.

ANALYSIS

When configuring a small office network, you can connect the office to the Internet in several ways. For instance, a small office network can be connected to the Internet via a demand-dial connection, or a router can be configured with Network Address Translation. However, based on the requirements of the scenario, the most appropriate solution is to implement a dedicated connection. Because the network manager would like to minimize the required configuration, configuration based on either static routes or RIP should be provided. OSPF in this type of scenario is much too complex a solution. To determine whether to use static routes or RIP, you must look closely at the requirements. Because the network may expand in the future and this must be done with a minimum of configuration, it is best to pursue a dynamic routing protocol that can adapt to a change in the network topology. This would imply RIP over static routing.

CHAPTER SUMMARY

KEY TERMS

- Routing Information Protocol (RIP)
- Open Shortest Path First (OSPF)
- Distance vector
- Link state
- Split horizon
- Split horizon with poison reverse
- Adjacency
- Area
- Autonomous system
- Interior Gateway Protocol (IGP)
- Exterior Gateway Protocol (EGP)

This chapter focused on routing. It covered the underlying fundamentals of routing and covered such topics as distance-vector routing and link-state routing. In addition, how a host determines whether it should deliver a packet directly to the end host or via a router was touched on. The chapter also discussed some of the problems of each type of routing and solutions to those problems, such as split horizon, split horizon with poison reverse, and triggered updates.

The next topic discussed was the Routing Information Protocol (RIP). Both Version 1 and Version 2 of RIP were discussed, along with specific features such as silent RIP. Features of the RIP protocol were related back to the fundamental discussion of routing covered earlier in the chapter, such as distance vector and split horizon. A discussion of how RIP functions within a network environment was provided along with a Step by Step for implementing RIP using the RRAS features of Windows 2000 Advanced Server.

The second routing protocol to be discussed was the OSPF protocol. The features of OSPF and how they differ from RIP were presented. The discussion then looked at the components and processes that make up the OSPF routing protocol. A discussion of how OSPF functions within a network environment was provided along with a Step by Step for implementing OSPF using the RRAS features of Windows 2000 Advanced Server.

Demand-dial routing provides a facility for connecting remote locations into corporate networks or for providing redundancy when building fault-tolerant networks. The chapter began with a discussion of how demand-dial routing works and then provided insight into some of the routing issues that you must consider when implementing a demand-dial solution. Security is a issue that every network manager must consider in any solution. As such, a discussion of the security features available for demand-dial routing was provided.

CHAPTER SUMMARY

Lastly, an overview of some of the tools for working with routing and diagnosing problems with routing was presented. A discussion of the ROUTE command and an overview of network monitor was provided, which are the tools that can help you diagnose problems. In addition to an overview of the tools used, a brief discussion of problems that may arise with the different protocols and what can be done to resolve these problems was supplied. By no means are they comprehensive, but they do provide insight into some of the different things to check should problems arise.

APPLY YOUR KNOWLEDGE

Review Questions

1. What is a topological database?

2. Provide one reason why link-state protocols are more efficient than distance-vector algorithms?

3. What is split horizon?

4. If you use autostatic updates, what must you do the first time you connect to a remote router?

5. Which parameter of the ROUTE command clears all existing routing table entries?

6. What is the ID reserved for the OSPF backbone?

7. What is one of the major problems of distance-vector routing?

8. What is an autonomous system (AS)?

Answers to Review Questions

1. A topological database is essentially an overall picture of networks in relationship to routers. The topological database contains the collection of LSAs received from all routers in the same area. In a very large AS with a large number of networks, each OSPF router must keep the LSA of every other router in its topological database. Each router in a large OSPF AS has a large topological database. The SPF calculation of a large topological database can require a substantial amount of processing and can result in very large routing tables. To prevent this, ASs are further divided into areas. See the section "Open Shortest Path First (OSPF)."

2. A link-state routing protocol is generally more efficient than a distance-vector protocol. Because LSAs contain only information about the neighbors of a particular router, this leads to smaller routing tables. For large networks, LSAs contain only neighbor information, and therefore the impact on the network is much less than on a network using a distance-vector routing protocol. With a distance-vector routing protocol, all the routes in a routing table are propagated resulting in a greater usage of bandwidth than in link-state protocols. In addition, because link-state information is not exchanged after the network has converged, it does not have the impact on the network that distance-vector routing does. Distance-vector routing, by default, broadcasts its information on a periodic basis whether required or not. See the section "Routing Technology."

3. Split horizon is a mechanism that prevents routing information from being sent back in the direction it was received from. Basically, the router says, "I learned about network xx from you, so you can't get to network xx through me." Split horizon eliminates count-to-infinity and routing loops during convergence in single-path internetworks and reduces the chances of count-to-infinity in multipath internetworks. See the section "Routing Technology."

4. Autostatic updates do not occur automatically on initiation of a demand-dial connection. Rather, the autostatic update must be manually initiated or a schedule must be put in place to update routes. After the routes have been sent, the two

APPLY YOUR KNOWLEDGE

routers do not exchange updates of routing information unless a manual request to update is made or a scheduled request occurs, depending on how autostatic updates are configured within your environment. Therefore, the first time a connection is made, an autostatic update must be manually initiated to configure the router with proper routes to the destination network. See the section "Demand-Dial Routing."

5. The –f parameter is used to clear the routing tables of all entries. See the section "Using the ROUTE Command to Configure Static Routes."

6. An OSPF backbone has a reserved area ID of 0.0.0.0. An OSPF backbone is responsible for distributing routing information between areas. At least one backbone per OSPF internetwork exists. It consists of all ABRs, networks not in any one area, and their attached routers. The backbone has to be at the center of all areas within the AS. That is, all areas have to be physically connected to the backbone. The reasoning behind this is that OSPF expects all areas to inject routing information into the backbone and in turn, the backbone disseminates that information into other areas. See the section "Open Shortest Path First (OSPF)."

7. The count-to-infinity problem is one of the major disadvantages of distance-vector routing. This condition is caused when a router (or link to a router) becomes unavailable. The convergence time is slow and, therefore, incorrect routing information is propagated through the system. See the section "Routing Technology."

8. An autonomous system is a collection of networks under common administration, sharing a common routing strategy. Each AS can be further divided into areas with areas being linked by a OSPF backbone, which is also itself an area. See the section "Open Shortest Path First (OSPF)."

Suggested Readings and Resources

1. Marcus, Scott J. *Designing Wide Area Networks and Internetworks: A Practical Guide.* Upper Saddle River, NJ: Addison Wesley, 1999.

2. Microsoft Corporation Staff. *Microsoft Windows NT 4.0 Network Administration Training Kit.* Redmond, WA: Microsoft Press, 1998.

3. Thomas, Thomas M. *OSPF Network Design Solutions.* Indianapolis, IN: Macmillan Technical Publishing, 1998.

4. Komar, Brian A. *Sams Teach Yourself TCP/IP Network Administration in 21 Days.* Sams Publishing, 1998.

With the release of the Windows 2000 operating system, Microsoft included the Internet Connection Sharing (ICS) and Network Address Translation (NAT) features as part of the Network and Dial-up Connections. This feature enables you to use your Windows 2000 Server to connect your office network to the Internet. ICS provides a simple configuration for NAT, IP address allocation, and name resolution services.

Microsoft defines the "Installing, Configuring, and Troubleshooting Network Address Translation (NAT)" objectives as follows:

Install Internet Connection Sharing.

▶ Internet Connection Sharing provides an automated method for configuring Demand-Dial Routing, Network Address Translation, DHCP, and a DNS Proxy service to an ISP's DNS server. Because it is well suited for small offices, Microsoft expects you to know how to install this service.

Install NAT.

▶ Network Address Translation (NAT) is used in conjunction with an Internet connection and is for offices that want to use the security and address-preservation features of NAT. Microsoft expects you to understand the installation process for NAT.

Configure NAT properties.

▶ After NAT is installed, you need to understand the properties associated with it. Understanding NAT properties is critical not only to the functioning of NAT, but also to the security of your network. Improper configuration could potentially result in security holes. Microsoft expects you to have a thorough understanding of these properties for this objective.

CHAPTER 21

Installing, Configuring, and Troubleshooting Network Address Translation (NAT)

Configure NAT interfaces.

▶ The final objective requires you to be able to configure the interface within NAT. Much like the properties discussed in the previous objective, understanding how to configure the interfaces is critical not only to the functioning of NAT, but also to the security of your network. Improper configuration could potentially result in security holes. Microsoft expects you to have a thorough understanding of the interface configuration for this objective.

▶ Internet Connection Sharing provides a wizard-driven mechanism for configuring all the services you need to connect a small office to the Internet. Be sure you understand the features of this service, as well as how it differs from manually configuring NAT.

▶ Make sure you understand the function of NAT and how to properly configure both the interfaces and properties. Although installing NAT is relatively easy, Microsoft recognizes that the configuration is the key to NAT.

▶ Review the TCP/IP section of Chapter 18, "Installing, Configuring, Managing, Monitoring, and Troubleshooting Network Protocols in a Windows 2000 Network Infrastructure," to be sure you are familiar with how TCP/IP works. Understanding TCP/IP is critical to understanding how NAT works.

INSTALLING INTERNET CONNECTION SHARING

Install Internet Connection Sharing.

In the first section of this chapter, the Internet Connection Sharing (ICS) services are discussed. The ICS services provide an automated demand-dial installation process for the following services:

◆ Network Address Translation (NAT)

◆ Dynamic Host Control Protocol (DHCP)

◆ DNS Proxy

These services make ICS a great solution for a small office looking for a quick and easy way to connect to the Internet via dial-up.

ICS has a few features that are not available in the NAT implementation. These features include the following:

◆ **H.323 proxy.** This feature permits users to make and receive Microsoft NetMeeting calls.

◆ **Lightweight Directory Access Protocol (LDAP) proxy.** The ability to proxy LDAP requests enables users to register with an Internet Locater Service (ILS) server as part of a NetMeeting directory.

◆ **Directplay proxy.** This allows users to play Directplay games across the NAT router. This feature is more suited for home use than for a small office; it is also offered in the Windows 98 version of ICS.

Now you know what ICS does for you. Before you jump right into installing ICS, however, you should learn what this automated process is going to install and configure. Keep in mind that a server running ICS must have a LAN and a modem connection. Otherwise, you cannot install the service. ICS does the following at installation:

◆ ICS sets the IP address of the LAN interface to 192.168.0.1, a private IP address. Because you are working with the internal interface for the ICS server (that is, the internal NIC in the Windows 2000 Server), it is set to a private address for security reasons. You can reset this address, although it is a good idea to use a private network address on the internal network whenever possible. Private addresses cannot be routed over the Internet, so using them adds an additional layer of security.

◆ The WAN interface (usually a modem) is set to be a Demand-Dial Router pointed at the Internet service provider (ISP).

◆ A DNS Proxy service is installed to provide DNS services to the office. This service passes client DNS requests to the DNS server configured in the ICS server's DHCP settings.

◆ The AutoDHCP service is installed. This service provides a subset of the services included with a full DHCP installation, but AutoDHCP is configured to issue addresses on the new 198.168.0.0/24 network.

> **EXAM TIP**
>
> **The DDL That Controls DNS Proxy and AutoDHCP Service** The dynamic link library used to control both the DNS Proxy and the AutoDHCP service is IPNATHLPR. DLL.

> **EXAM TIP**
>
> **The AutoDHCP Service Uses a Private Network** Although it is unlikely that Microsoft will expect you to memorize the exact network that the AutoDHCP service uses, you should be aware that it is a private network.

Step by Step 21.1 outlines the process of installing ICS.

ON THE CD

Step by Step 21.1, "Installing the Internet Connection Sharing Service," outlines the process of installing ICS. See the file **Chapter21-01StepbyStep.pdf** in the CD's **Chapter21\StepbyStep** directory.

IN THE FIELD

HOW DO YOU DETERMINE THE PORT NUMBER AN APPLICATION USES?

If you are working with ICS, you have the ports of common applications predefined in the application. These are shown in Table 21.1.

continues

continued

TABLE 21.1

PREDEFINED PORTS OF COMMON APPLICATIONS

Application	Port
FTP Server Data	20
FTP Server Control	21
Internet Mail Access Protocol Version 4 (IMAP4)	143
Internet Mail Server (SMTP)	25
Post-Office Protocol Version 3 (POP3)	110
Telnet Server	23
HTTP	80

This is great if you want to use one of the predefined applications. But what do you do if you have a different application that you want to enable? How can you find the port you need? There are four methods generally used.

First, check the product documentation and Help files. If you are using an application commonly used on the Internet, the vendor generally documents the port you need to have open to use the application. If you cannot find the information in the product documentation, you can look on the Internet, or more specifically the Internet Assigned Numbers Authority (http://www.iana.net). This authority provides registration services for vendors who want to reserve a TCP/IP port for their application. If you cannot find your application listed, there's a good chance the vendor is using an unregistered port.

The next step in tracking down the port is network analysis. You can use network analysis tools to analyze the traffic the application uses. If you are running the application on a Windows 2000 Server, you can use the Network Monitor tool included with the operating system to provide this information.

When all else fails, find a comfortable chair and a speakerphone and call the vendor. You may have to wait on hold for a while, but the vendor can almost always tell you what port its application uses.

That is about all there is to the ICS service. It is an easy, quick service perfect for a small office environment. Now let's see what to do if you are in a larger environment or need more flexibility in your connection.

INSTALLING NAT

Install NAT.

Suppose you have a larger network than the one described in the ICS section, but you still want to use Windows 2000 to connect to the Internet. You will find the Network Address Translation capabilities of Windows 2000 very useful. But just in case you are not familiar with NAT, take a quick look at how NAT works and what it does before you jump right into installing it.

Network Address Translation does pretty much what the name describes. It takes an IP address entering on one interface of the Windows 2000 Server and translates it to a different address exiting a different (usually the Internet-connected) interface. For example, suppose that your PC has an IP address of `10.10.10.10`. This is an address in the reserved network of `10.0.0.0`, which is not routable on the Internet. You want to be able to connect to the Internet, so you need to have an Internet-routable (registered) IP address. A server running NAT takes each packet from your workstation, strips the `10.10.10.10` source address from it, and resends the packet with a registered address in the source IP address field. The original address and the registered address are stored in a table so that the server knows what translation was used. The packet is routed to the appropriate destination. If the destination responds with a packet, the NAT server looks up the address in its NAT table and reverses the original process, placing `10.10.10.10` into the destination address and resending the packet.

There are basically two reasons for doing this:

◆ **Security.** If you are connecting your network to the Internet, you really don't want uninvited users connecting to your private hosts. By translating the addresses of those hosts, you provide a level of security for that host.

> **EXAM TIP**
>
> **Know NAT** For the exam, you need to understand what NAT is and how it works. The key features are the replacing of the "internal" addresses and the NAT table for maintaining the translation.

NOTE

I Wish There Were an RFC for This
You're in luck. The RFC defining the private addresses usually used in conjunction with NAT is RFC 1918. It sets aside the address ranges `10.0.0.0` to `10.255.255.255`, `172.16.0.0` to `172.31.255.255`, and `192.168.0.0` to `192.168.255.255`. RFC 1631 defines the method for Network Address Translation.

◆ **IP Address Conservation.** As hard as it is to believe, the Internet is running out of addresses. In the mid-1990s, some enterprising people recognized that this problem was coming and came up with NAT as a mechanism for conserving addresses. Although clearly a stop-gap mechanism until the next version of IP is widely adopted, NAT allows a company to use private addresses on its internal network and translate those addresses to a single address or to multiple registered addresses. This many-to-few address-conservation mechanism has contributed in large part to the Internet's capability of continuing to grow.

NAT can handle the address translation in two ways. If the translating device has only a single registered IP address available, it translates the source address in the IP packet to the registered address and then sets the source port to a random port number.

For example, if the NAT device handles a request for an HTTP connection, it connects to the server on port 80, but listens for the response on the random port it assigned during the translation. It substitutes its address in the source address field and the random port number in place of the client's original source port. It then uses this information to create an address mapping in the NAT table that tells it where to send the HTTP responses.

If you have multiple registered IP addresses, the NAT device performs a one-to-one translation of the address and skips any port translations.

One final point before we look at the installation: Like the ICS service, NAT is a two-way street. You can configure NAT not only for outbound private-to-public translations, but also for public-to-private translations for inbound requests. If you want to put a Web server on your internal network, NAT allows you to do that.

Follow Step by Step 21.2 to install NAT.

ON THE CD

Step by Step 21.2, "Installing Network Address Translation," shows you how to install NAT. See the file **Chapter21-02StepbyStep.pdf** in the CD's **Chapter21\StepbyStep** directory.

Now that you have installed NAT, take a look at how to configure it.

CONFIGURING NAT PROPERTIES

Configure NAT properties.

A number of properties can be configured in conjunction with Network Address Translation. They can all be accessed by opening the Routing and Remote Access window, right-clicking the Network Address Translation icon, and selecting Properties from the context menu. You will see the following tabs: General, Translation, Address Assignment, and Name Resolution.

The General tab, shown in Figure 21.1, is used to configure event logging. Any logging enabled in this section appears in the System Event Log. You can configure event logging for the following levels:

◆ **Log errors only.** Logging errors is a useful setting when you want to restrict your logging to critical messages. In a busy environment, it is frequently difficult to review logs filled with warnings that are not in fact real issues. By keeping the logging to errors only, you increase the chances that you will see serious errors in the log.

◆ **Log errors and warnings.** The default setting, logging errors and warnings, is a good idea in smaller networks. If you find that the warnings are filling the log, it may be time to log only errors.

◆ **Log the maximum amount of information.** When you first set up your Network Address Translation, you may want to log the maximum amount of information to get a good understanding of what is going on with NAT. Keep in mind that the information logged at this level is extremely detailed and sometimes decipherable only by Microsoft support. It's great to use if you are troubleshooting an issue with Microsoft; otherwise, this is probably not a setting you need to use.

◆ **Disable event logging.** Unless you are extremely resource-bound on this server, you should never disable logging.

The Translation tab shown in Figure 21.2 is used to set the timeout values for the translations. You also have the ability to add inbound applications exactly the way you could in ICS. In fact, any applications configured in ICS (if you were to switch to NAT) are automatically added to the NAT translations.

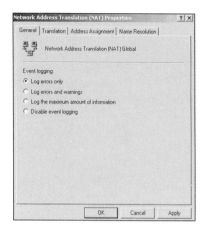

FIGURE 21.1
If you want to configure logging for the NAT protocol, do it from the General screen.

EXAM TIP

Use the Event Viewer to Check Out Logging Events Remember that any logging events are logged in the System Event Log and can be viewed with the Event Viewer. Microsoft considers the capability of logging errors and warnings to be very important, and you need to know where to find the information so that you can answer any logging questions surrounding NAT.

NOTE

To Log or Not to Log? Keep in mind that logging uses resources. Only enable the Log the Maximum Amount of Information option when troubleshooting NAT configuration, because this option will rapidly fill the System Log. Otherwise, you may want to restrict your logging to errors and warnings, the default setting.

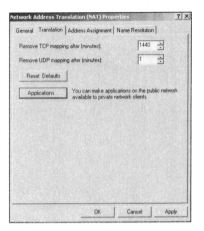

FIGURE 21.2
Use the Translation tab to set the timeouts and to add inbound application translations for the NAT protocol.

WHAT SETTINGS WORK BEST IN REAL LIFE?

As a general rule (and this is true with many Microsoft applications), the defaults usually work for your network. Where you might want to reset these timeout values is in the case of a special application that requires higher timeouts to function. For example, if you had a UDP-based application that needed to maintain connections for a long period of time, you might want to set the UDP mapping timer to 60. However, I am not aware of any UDP-based applications that have that requirement, because of the connectionless nature of UDP.

In the TCP field, you might want to lower the TCP mapping timer if you have a large number of users connecting across the server for limited periods of time, and if you are resource-constrained. Making this parameter shorter causes resources to become available more quickly. Remember that if you are using this for NAT, you probably don't want to be resource-constrained. You should consider an upgrade if the situation is that severe.

> **EXAM TIP**
>
> **Use the NAT DHCP Service to Enable the Clients** If you are planning to use NAT, the easiest way to enable the clients is through the NAT DHCP service. This configures the clients with the correct information to use the NAT gateway when they are assigned their IP address via DHCP. If you are using the NAT DHCP, you do not need the Windows 2000 DHCP service.

The Address Assignment tab allows you to configure the private IP addresses and configure the DHCP service used in conjunction with NAT (see Figure 21.3). To enable the NAT DHCP, just check the box marked Automatically assign IP addresses by using DHCP. This DHCP service can be used in place of the Windows 2000 DHCP service discussed in Chapter 16, "Installing, Configuring, Managing, Monitoring, and Troubleshooting DHCP in a Windows 2000 Network Infrastructure." If you are using the Windows 2000 DHCP service, do not select the NAT DHCP option.

The Name Resolution tab (see Figure 21.4) is used to configure DNS for the NAT protocol. From this tab you can configure who should receive DNS resolution services and how to handle resolution of nonlocal names. You can even configure the server to automatically dial the Internet if it needs to resolve a name.

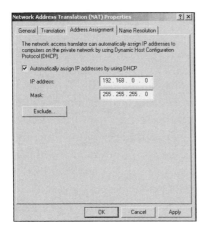

FIGURE 21.3
The Address Assignment tab allows you to configure the DHCP service for the NAT protocol.

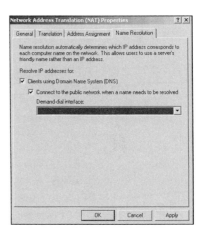

FIGURE 21.4
Use the Name Resolution tab to set the DNS resolution parameters for the NAT protocol.

You should have noticed that although ICS and NAT are different services, the capabilities are largely the same. The configuration does differ fairly significantly, however. To recap, both ICS and the NAT service provide Network Address Translation (NAT), Dynamic Host Control Protocol (DHCP), and DNS Proxy capabilities. ICS automates the installation and configuration of these services, whereas the NAT interface requires some configuration by the administrator. In addition, ICS supports features not included in NAT, such as H.323 Proxy, Lightweight Directory Access Protocol (LDAP) Proxy, and Directplay Proxy.

Now let's look at the final part of configuring NAT—configuring the interfaces.

EXAM TIP

You Can Configure NAT Properties to Dial an ISP for DNS Resolution
For the exam, you should be aware that you can configure NAT Properties to dial an ISP for DNS resolution if necessary. Just select the Resolve IP addresses for Clients using Domain Name System (DNS) and then select Connect to the Public Network When a Name Needs to Be Resolved. In the Demand-Dial Interface pull-down box, select your ISP connection. This works only if you have a dial-up ISP configured on the system.

CONFIGURING NAT INTERFACES

Configure NAT interfaces.

So far in this chapter, you have installed NAT and configured the properties. You haven't configured the interface that NAT will run through. A NAT interface defines the connection properties for the Network Address Translation. This can be either the private interface, connected to the internal (private) network, or the public interface, connected to the Internet. Because your NAT server will most likely be bridging your private network and the Internet, you need to set up an internal and an external NAT interface.

To configure an interface for NAT, follow Step by Step 21.3.

> **ON THE CD**
>
> Step by Step 21.3, "Configuring a NAT Interface," demonstrates how to configure a NAT interface. See the file **Chapter21-03StepbyStep.pdf** in the CD's **Chapter21\StepbyStep** directory.

That completes the installation, configuration, and interfaces for the Network Address Translation protocol. Let's use the following case study to see how well you can apply what you've learned.

EXAM TIP

Know the Difference Between the Public and Private Interfaces Be sure to know the difference between the public and private interfaces for the exam. The public interface is your connection to the Internet, and the private interface is your internal network. All interface configuration occurs on the public interface.

EXAM TIP

Remember Where the Mappings Are Located Because being able to monitor these mappings is one of the key components to supporting a NAT installation, you might see a question on the exam concerning the mappings.

EXAM TIP

Know the Differences Between NAT and ICS Capabilities Distinguishing between the two is excellent exam question material.

CASE STUDY: CONFIGURING NETWORK ADDRESS TRANSLATION IN A 100-USER NETWORK

ESSENCE OF THE CASE

The essence of the case is as follows:

▶ Your company is implementing an Internet connection using a T1 and Windows 2000 Server. The T1 will connect to the server using a LAN interface.

▶ You need to connect 100 users to the Internet for Web browsing.

▶ You need to set up a Web server on the internal network, but it needs to be accessible from the Internet for customers.

▶ You have no existing DNS or DHCP services on the network.

SCENARIO

You are the security administrator for LFE Incorporated. LFE Inc. is a lawn furniture manufacturing company. You have just decided to get your first connection to the Internet. You are going to go all out and get a T1 connection that will be up all the time. This will connect to your Windows 2000 Server, providing routing services as an Ethernet connection. The T1 will be used for Web browsing by the 100 employees, and your manager has also asked you to bring up a Web server on the internal network so that customers can look at your lawn furniture.

At this time, you have not implemented any DNS or DHCP services on the network. Everyone uses static IP addresses and connects to other hosts by addresses. You planned ahead and are using 10.0.1.x addresses for all your machines.

What do you need to do?

ANALYSIS

This situation provides an excellent opportunity to deploy the Windows 2000 NAT protocol as part of the Windows 2000 Routing and Remote Access Service. Because of the size of the network and the fact that you will not be using a demand-dial connection to the Internet, the Internet Connection Sharing service is not an option. To make the Network Address Translation protocol work, you need to make sure you do the following:

continues

CASE STUDY: CONFIGURING NETWORK ADDRESS TRANSLATION IN A 100-USER NETWORK

continued

- Install the NAT protocol using the Routing and Remote Access manager.

- Add the internal and external interfaces. Be careful not to confuse the two interfaces.

- Configure the DHCP properties to reflect the 10.0.1.x network addressing. You should also be sure to exclude any hosts that will retain a static address, such as servers and printers.

- Convert your users to DHCP. Not only will it make managing the IP addresses easier, but it will also provide the client configuration information needed to use the NAT gateway to the Internet.

- Configure the DNS service to connect to the Internet to provide name resolution. Your users need to be able to resolve names so that they can surf the Internet effectively.

- Finally, you need to go to the Translation tab of the Network Address Translation (NAT) Properties and configure the translation for the Web server. You will use port 80 for HTTP and will need the internal address of the server to complete the configuration.

This is a particularly good case study if you are working on a smaller company, because more companies are using Network Address Translation capabilities to connect to the Internet. Although the basic mechanism is the same no matter what device you use to provide the translation, the interface provided by Windows 2000 is very clean and easy to configure and use.

CHAPTER SUMMARY

Let's recap what you learned in this chapter. You started by looking at the Internet Connection Sharing service, which is an automated installation for a suite of services designed to get a small office up and connected to the Internet quickly.

Then you moved on to the manually installed and configured Network Address Translation protocol. You learned about installing, configuring, and adding interfaces for NAT.

In the next chapter, you look at "Installing, Configuring, Managing, Monitoring, and Troubleshooting Certificate Services," the final chapter in this section.

KEY TERMS

- Domain Name System (DNS)
- Dynamic Host Control Protocol (DHCP)
- Network Address Translation (NAT)
- Internet Connection Sharing (ICS)
- Routing and Remote Access
- Transmission Control Protocol/Internet Protocol (TCP/IP)
- Request For Comment (RFC) documents
- Registered IP address
- Private IP address
- Internet service provider (ISP)

APPLY YOUR KNOWLEDGE

Review Questions

1. You are the network administrator for a small company that wants to connect to the Internet for the first time. The company has 12 employees and you don't have a lot of experience with Windows 2000 or routing. What should you do to ensure that you connect to the Internet successfully?

2. The network in the previous question has grown to 50 users, and management wants to upgrade to a DSL connection. You have configured several dozen custom applications, both inbound and outbound, as part of ICS. What should you do to accommodate the DSL connections and the applications you've configured?

3. You are the Windows 2000 administrator for Fly Away Travel. Your boss has asked you to explain the difference between the NAT protocol and the ICS services. Other than manual versus automated features, what does ICS support that NAT does not?

4. That was a good start, but now she wants to know what services are included as part of ICS.

5. You're the administrator of Little Faith Enterprise's Windows 2000 Server and you are considering setting up NAT. Why would you want to set up NAT?

Answers to Review Questions

1. You should implement Internet Connection Sharing in conjunction with a dial-up ISP connection. ICS is easy to install and maintain, and it bundles the services you need to make this connection work. See "Installing Internet Connection Sharing."

2. You should just migrate to the Network Address Translation protocol. This accommodates the DSL connection without a problem (although you need to manually configure both the internal and external interfaces), and the applications you configured still appear in the NAT list of custom applications. See "Configuring NAT Interfaces."

3. ICS supports the following standards: H.323 Proxy, LDAP Proxy, and Directplay Proxy. See "Installing Internet Connection Sharing."

4. ICS installs a DNS and DHCP service. It also sets the IP address of the LAN interface to `192.168.0.1` and sets the WAN interface to be a Demand-Dial Router pointed at the ISP. See "Installing Internet Connection Sharing."

5. Two reasons exist for using NAT. First, it provides a level of security for your network when it is connected to the Internet. Not only does NAT hide your internal addresses, but it also restricts the services that can access the internal network. You also need to conserve public IP addresses. Unless you are fortunate and have enough registered addresses for your users, you need NAT. See "Configuring NAT Properties."

ON THE CD

This book's companion CD contains specially designed supplemental material to help you understand how well you know the concepts and skills you learned in this chapter. You'll find related exercises and exam questions and answers. See the file **Chapter21ApplyYourKnowledge.pdf** in the CD's **Chapter21\ApplyYourKnowledge** directory.

Suggested Readings and Resources

1. Atkins, Derek. *Internet Security: Professional Reference*. Indianapolis: New Riders Publishing, 1997.

2. Boswell, William. *Inside Windows 2000 Server*. Indianapolis: New Riders Publishing, 2000.

This chapter details the Microsoft-specified objectives for the Certificate Services section of the 70-240 Exam objectives. The exam objectives for Certificate Services are as follows:

Install and configure Certification Authority.

▶ Windows 2000 includes Certificate Services for intranet and Internet security. This chapter examines the planning and implementation of Certification Authority.

Issue and revoke certificates.

▶ As part of a successful implementation of Certificate Services, you need to set guidelines for issuing and revoking certificates. In this chapter, you learn how to implement and explore these guidelines.

Remove the Encrypting File Systems (EFS) recovery keys.

▶ Part of Certificate Services is the implementation of EFS. In this chapter, you examine the attributes of EFS and how the recovery keys work in tandem with Certification Authority.

CHAPTER *22*

Installing, Configuring, Managing, Monitoring, and Troubleshooting Certificate Services

▶ Certificates are a new feature for Windows 2000. To fully prepare for the exam objectives, you need a working knowledge of what certificates are, where they are derived from, and how they are configured.

▶ Complete the Step by Steps on the accompanying CD. Hands-on experience intensifies your study process. Be familiar with CA and the fundamentals of why an entity would want to use certificates.

▶ Invest time in experimenting with Certification Authority and EFS. This book covers all the exam objective details, but it's up to you to take the information presented here and transform it to knowledge.

INTRODUCTION

As you may realize, networks today keep growing and intermingling with other networks. This growth presents a challenge, because it increases network exposure to less–than–honest users. What makes it possible for all these networks to be vulnerable to attack? They share a common protocol.

The common protocol used in the exchange of data is TCP/IP. Data sent via TCP/IP is broken up and sent over various routes to the final destination. Because of the design of TCP/IP, data can be intercepted easily without the sender or the receiver knowing that the data may have been intercepted. Certainly, as data passes through networks around the globe, it is susceptible to interception or forgery, and users are often the recipients of data whose content may jeopardize their own data.

We need a way to protect our outgoing data and ensure that our incoming data has not been compromised. Enter certificates. This chapter introduces the fundamentals of certificates and then discusses installing and configuring Certification Authority Services.

Looking at Public Key Infrastructure (PKI)

To combat the openness of TCP/IP without losing the functionality of the protocol, Public Key Infrastructure (PKI) has been developed in tandem with TCP/IP as a means of offering security for data sent between hosts—on an intranet or on the Internet.

Using encryption, network administrators and security experts can ensure that the data is read only by the intended recipient, and that data received has not been tampered with. The analogy of physical signature and envelopes sealed with wax is an excellent parallel to how PKI is used today. In lieu of your "John Hancock" and sealing wax, you use a digital signature.

A digital signature ensures that the message is from the source it says it's from and that the message hasn't been digitally "steamed open." In addition to digital signatures, you can implement digital identifications—thus, the digital certificate.

Certificates

What exactly is a digital certificate? Essentially, it's the electronic version of your password or employee identification. It proves that you are the person you say you are. This certificate is what ultimately allows you to access resources and data.

Certificates are issued not only to individuals, but also to organizations, businesses, routers, and other entities as a way of controlling and securing data. A digital certificate contains the following information:

◆ The user's name

◆ The user's public key

◆ Serial number

◆ Expiration date

◆ Information on the certificate itself

◆ Information on the organization (called a Certification Authority) that issued the certificate

When transferring secure data, an electronic seal is inserted into the data through cryptography. When the recipient opens the data, the electronic seal is verified to exist, and that the data has not been tampered with is also verified. In addition, the recipient can be assured that the sender of the data is accurate.

Traditionally, when you want to send encrypted data to other users, you use your key to encrypt and secure the data. When the recipients want to open the encrypted data, they use their copy of the key to unlock the data. Should others without the key intercept the packets, they will not be able to decrypt the information. This method of security is not really all that secure. The problem is that when unauthorized users gain access to the key, they gain access to the data—not unlike discovering your house keys in the outside lock of your door.

Digital certificates, however, use a slightly different method of locking and unlocking the data. With digital certificates, you no longer have to make copies of keys for others to unlock your data. Digital certificates use a private key to lock the data and then a different key, the public key, to unlock the data. No longer is the same key used to lock and unlock data.

> **EXAM TIP**
>
> **Distributing Public Keys** Be sure that any exam solution includes the encryption of public keys when they are distributed to a recipient.

With this two-key technology, your key remains private. No one but the rightful owner should ever have access to it. However, by means of the digital certificate, you can disperse the public key to the person who needs it.

Certification Authorities

All certificates are issued by a Certification Authority (CA), such as VeriSign. The Certification Authority verifies that the owner of the certificate is the person the owner claims to be. A Certification Authority is a trusted third party that is responsible for physically verifying the legitimacy of the identity of an individual or organization before issuing a digital certificate. A Certification Authority is also responsible for issuing certificates, revoking certificates, and publishing a list of revoked certificates.

With Windows 2000, you can use a third-party Certification Authority, or you can create your own Certification Authority through Microsoft's Windows 2000 Certificate Services, which offers these types of CAs: Enterprise Root CA, Enterprise Subordinate CA, Standalone Root CA, and Standalone Subordinate CA. You take a closer look at these types of CAs throughout this chapter.

> **NOTE**
>
> **Choosing the Right CA** When you have to determine the correct type of CA to use, always determine which users will require certificates. If users outside your company require access using certificates, you most likely need the services of a third-party CA.

If you elect to create an internal Certification Authority for your organization, you'll want to establish some rules and guidelines to verify that users are employees. You can use social security numbers, employee badges, or an even more secure method—smart cards, which are physical, portable devices that allow users to log in and access and send data, such as email and data on a network.

Windows 2000 Enterprise Certification Authority

A Windows 2000 Enterprise Certification Authority provides certificates for the internal security of an entire organization, whereas an external Certification Authority provides security for external security needs. Microsoft provides support for both, and you may mix and match as your business needs see fit.

In a Windows 2000 environment, if users request a certificate, the Windows 2000 user account acts as the credential for the users because they are logged on and recognized in the Active Directory.

A Windows 2000 Enterprise Certification Authority has five characteristics:

◆ The Certification Authority server may run on any Windows 2000 Server. Plan for activity, network load, and physical placement of the server for best implementation.

◆ Because the Certification Authority name is integrated into the certificates it assigns, the name of the server should be determined before implementing Certification Authority services.

◆ The Enterprise Certification Authority is integrated into the Active Directory.

◆ When you've installed an Enterprise Certification Authority, a policy module is created. An administrator may edit the policy.

◆ Because the Certification Authority is crucial for the successful implementation of the PKI, it must have a fault-tolerance scheme and a schedule of regular secure backups.

> **EXAM TIP**
>
> **Choosing an Enterprise CA** If an exam question discusses the use of templates or the fact that the user's account will determine whether they should receive a certificate, the CA type will always be an Enterprise CA.

Standalone Certification Authorities

Another type of CA that Windows 2000 allows you to install is a Standalone CA. The Standalone CA doesn't require the interaction of an Active Directory, but it can use one if it's available.

A Standalone CA is useful in issuing certificates and digital signatures and supports secure email (S/MIME) and SSL (Secure Sockets Layer) or TLS (Transport Layer Security).

A typical Standalone CA has these characteristics:

◆ It doesn't require Active Directory interaction.

◆ It can be used with extranets.

◆ It doesn't verify the requests for certificates. (All requests are pending until an administrator approves them.)

◆ Users requesting a certificate from a Standalone CA must supply all user account information. This is not required within an Enterprise CA because the user is recognized by the logon account in the Active Directory.

◆ No certificate templates are used.

◆ Windows 2000 logon credential certificates are not stored on smart cards. Other certificates can be, however.

◆ An administrator must distribute the Standalone CA certificate to the Trusted Root Certificate Store.

If an Active Directory exists and a Standalone CA can access it, additional options are available:

◆ If a domain administrator with Write access to the Active Directory installs the Standalone CA, the standalone is added to the Trusted Root Certification Authorities Certificate Store. In this situation, make certain that the default action of pending requests isn't changed to allow the Standalone CA to automatically approve all requests for certificates. Do not change the default action of pending certificate requests on a Standalone CA.

◆ If a domain administrator group member of the parent domain (or an administrator with Write access to the Active Directory) installs the Standalone CA, the Standalone CA publishes the certificate and the Certificate Revocation list to the Active Directory.

Planning to Install a Certificate Authority

After you've decided that you'd like to install a CA, some planning must take place. Before your installation of the CA, you need to have a plan that addresses these questions:

◆ Who will manage the security?

◆ Will administrative duties be delegated?

◆ How will the CA be monitored? Who will monitor it?

◆ What kind of auditing should be in place for the CA?

◆ Where will the CA be located?

After you've answered these questions and have documented your answers to formulate a plan, you're ready to move into the final stages of planning.

Planning the Public Key Infrastructure

When you are preparing to install a CA, you should start by planning how to configure your PKI. As we've discussed, certificates and CAs are a means to prove an identity. But what if a user discovers Bob's password and logs on to the domain as Bob? As far the system is concerned, the unauthorized user must be Bob because, after all, it is Bob's username and password.

The most popular solution to securing a network is, of course, physical security. Next is the implementation of a strong policy: strong passwords that change frequently. Finally, another secure choice is the implementation of smart cards, because they allow users to carry their digital credentials with them from home to office to anywhere they need to go.

Windows 2000's group policy can allow you to publish and revoke certificates directly to user accounts. This feature can allow you to change a user's digital information and enforce it for accessing and retrieving data. Finally, your PKI scheme should include measures for your enterprise to secure email using S/MIME and SSL and/or TLS.

Planning the CA Hierarchies

Windows 2000 PKI allows for and encourages a dispersed hierarchy of CAs. Building a tree of CAs allows scalability with other organizations, internal and external resources, and compatibility with third-party CA implementations.

Ideally, an enterprise would have one Certification Authority; this is not usually a reality, however. Each CA hierarchy begins with the Root CA, and multiple CAs branch from this Root CA in a parent-child relationship. The child CAs are certified by the parent CA all the way back to the Root CA. The parent CAs bind a Certification Authority public key to the child CA's identity.

In this parent-child relationship, child CAs are trusted by the parent. That parent is, in turn, trusted by its parent CA, all the way back to the originating Root CA. Also in this model, when an organization trusts a CA by adding its certificate in the Trusted Root Certification Authorities Certificate Store, the organization therefore trusts every Subordinate CA in the hierarchy. Should a Subordinate CA have its certificate revoked by the issuing CA, the revoked CA is no longer trustworthy.

Hierarchies serve many purposes. Some of the reasons for creating a Certification Authority hierarchy include the following:

♦ **Varying usages.** Certificates can be issued for a number of purposes, such as secure email, SSL, and TSL. Different CAs can be responsible for different areas of security.

♦ **Politics.** A hierarchy allows various departments within an enterprise to use unique policies.

♦ **Geography.** In a WAN environment, a different CA may be needed in each physical location to save on network resources.

♦ **Security.** The Root CA requires a very secure environment with fault-tolerant devices. Subordinate CAs do not require the same amount and type of security as the root.

♦ **Revoking.** Most organizations need to have the capability of revoking individual CAs rather than being forced to revoke an entire enterprise.

As you're planning your hierarchy, remember that a Root CA is a CA from which all Subordinate CAs branch. This CA should be the most secure and should probably be taken offline after the installation to ensure the security of the originating certificate and keys.

Renewing Certification Authorities

When a Root or Subordinate CA issues a certificate, the certificate includes a validity period. A validity period is the length of time the certificate is good for—not unlike a digital expiration date.

At the end of the validity period, the certificate is disabled, assuming that the certificate has not been revoked prior to this expiration date. When the certificate expires, a new certification must be renewed.

In a parent-child relationship between CAs, the parent CA issues a certificate as part of the relationship to designate the child CA. Just like the certificate to a client, the certificate to a Subordinate CA includes a validity period.

When the validity period expires for a CA, its own certificate must be renewed before it can grant any certification requests from client computers. When organizing your PKI, take into account the time a certification in a parent-child relationship should last.

As a safety and security measure, the program is set up so that a CA cannot issue certificates to requestors that will last beyond its own certificate's expiration date. This is handy because it ensures, for example, that a CA scheduled to expire this October cannot issue a certificate that may expire later than October.

Even the Root CA's own certificate eventually expires. Because of this, certificates that it issues to subordinates will be staggered from its own expiration date. In other words, when the Root CA expires, all Subordinate CAs also will have expired. No Subordinate CAs are valid beyond the date of the originating CA.

INSTALLING THE CERTIFICATION AUTHORITY

Install and configure Certification Authority.

When you understand Certificate Services and have a plan for installing the service and a plan for renewing certificates for users, servers, and CAs, you are ready to install a Certification Authority.

You can choose from four options for installing a CA:

- ◆ **After Windows 2000 has been installed.** Use Add/Remove Programs in Control Panel to add the Certificate Services to the current installation.

- ◆ **As part of the Windows 2000 installation.** During the installation of Windows 2000, you can choose from the optional components. After Windows 2000 is installed, you complete the installation of the service according to your PKI plans.

◆ **Upgrading from Certificate Server 1.0.** When you install Windows 2000 on a server that is running Certificate Server 1.0, the Windows 2000 installation program automatically upgrades the service.

◆ **Through an unattended installation.** If you are using an unattended installation to install Windows 2000, you can include the installation of a CA through the Setup file.

Whichever method you choose to install Certificate Services, you're required to supply the following information:

◆ **Certification Authority type.** What type of CA will this be?

- **Enterprise Root CA.** The Enterprise Root CA is the root of all CAs in your hierarchy. Typically, only one exists per enterprise. Requires Active Directory. Intermediate Subordinate CAs branch off this server. This can only be a parent.

- **Enterprise Subordinate CA.** A Subordinate CA must obtain its certificate from a CA higher in the hierarchy. Requires Active Directory. This is the child of another CA. It is possible that this CA could also be a parent to another CA.

- **Standalone Root CA.** A Standalone Root CA is like an Enterprise Root CA, except that it does not require Active Directory but can use it if it exists. Often this CA is offline to protect the validity of the originating certificates and keys.

- **Standalone Subordinate CA.** This CA does not require Active Directory but may use it if Active Directory is available to it. The Subordinate CA must obtain its certificate from another CA. This is the child in the relationship but may become a parent if it supplies a certificate to another CA.

◆ **Advanced options.** If you enable advanced options during the install of your CA, you have to provide the following:

- **The cryptographic service provider (CSP).** To generate the public and private keys.

- **Key length.** The longer the key, the more secure the key.

- **Hash algorithm.** A computation to produce a hash value of some piece of data. The default is SHA-1, which is a 160-bit hash value.

◆ **CA name.** You can use just about any character you want. The name you assign the CA will also be the CN (common name) of the CA's distinguished name in Active Directory.

◆ **Organization.** The name of your organization as it is known throughout its community.

◆ **Organizational unit.** The division this CA manages.

◆ **Locality.** The city where the CA is physically located.

◆ **State or province.** The state or province where the CA is physically located.

◆ **Country.** The X.500 two-character code for your country.

◆ **Location of the database.** By default, it's stored in `\systemroot\system32\certlog`.

◆ **Shared folder.** You can create a shared folder for Certification Authorities information if the CA is not participating in an Active Directory (such as a standalone server).

Installing and Configuring an Enterprise Subordinate CA

After you've installed a Root CA, you'll most likely want to install additional CAs, the Subordinate CAs. The relationship between the Root CA and each immediate Subordinate CA is parent-child. The child CA can then form a relationship to another CA and become the parent in that relationship. There can be a long line of chains of parent-child CAs, or these can branch out to cover different organizational units, divisions, geographical locations, and so on.

To install and configure an Enterprise Subordinate CA, follow Step by Step 22.1.

ON THE CD

Step by Step 22.1, "Installing and Configuring a Certification Authority," shows you how to install and configure an Enterprise Subordinate Certificate Authority. See the file **Chapter22-01StepbyStep.pdf** in the CD's **Chapter22\StepbyStep** directory.

Installing and Configuring a Standalone Root CA

Installing a Standalone CA server is very similar to installing an Enterprise CA server. The main difference in installing a standalone server is that you do not need to request a certificate from an existing CA server, because a Standalone CA server generates its own originating certificate.

Upgrading Certificate Server 1.0

When you upgrade to Windows 2000 from a Windows NT 4 Server that is also running Certificate Server 1.0, Windows 2000 automatically upgrades Certificate Server 1.0 with the CA services.

When Certificate Server 1.0 is using its own policy before the upgrade, Windows 2000 allows the server to continue to its policy instead of the default policy included with Windows 2000's Certificate Services. This original policy is referred to as a *legacy policy module*.

When the Certificate Server 1.0 is using the default policy included with that software, Windows 2000 upgrades the policy to the default security policy it uses for certification services.

Remember that Certificate Server 1.0 is not automatically upgraded as part of the installation. The new certification services are installed, but the configuration is blank. You have to finish the configuration. To import the old database into the upgraded CA, follow Step by Step 22.2.

ON THE CD

Step by Step 22.2, "Importing an Old Database into the Newly Upgraded CA," guides you though the process of how to import an old database into an upgraded CA. See the file **Chapter22-02StepbyStep.pdf** in the CD's **Chapter22\StepbyStep** directory.

Renewing Certificates for Certification Authorities

Part of your role is to renew the certificates for each type of CA in your environment. The Root CA is the most important CA in the hierarchy. Often, for security, it's in a physically secure environment with hardware fault-tolerance, and possibly is even offline to prevent any tampering. Because of the demands placed on a Root CA, plan to configure the Root CA's certificate so that it doesn't expire for a long time.

IN THE FIELD

THE KEY TO SECURITY

When creating the Root CA, you also need to ensure a long lifetime for the public and private key of this CA by using a long key length as a deterrent for hackers who make brute force attacks. The longer the key, the longer you may use the private and public keys with confidence that the keys have not been compromised.

Microsoft recommends creating a 4096-bit RSA key during Certification Service Setup. A brute force attack against a key of this size may last for 15–20 years. In addition, the 4096-bit key could be configured during Setup to expire in five years. When the CA needs to be renewed, technology may have surpassed the 4096-bit key length and a different algorithm could be used.

Follow Step by Step 22.3 to renew a Root Certification Authority.

ON THE CD

Step by Step 22.3, "Renewing a Root Certification Authority,"
explains how to renew a Root Certification Authority. See the file
Chapter22-03StepbyStep.pdf in the CD's **Chapter22\StepbyStep**
directory.

Microsoft recommends issuing Subordinate CAs a new certificate 6
to 12 months before their certificates are actually scheduled to
expire. Within your hierarchy, you may have created Intermediate
CAs that do not issue certificates to users but only to other subordinates below them. This delegation of certificate issuance is acceptable because these Intermediary CAs are the only CAs that would
communicate with the Root CAs.

The planning involved, however, is when will the certificates issued
by the Root CA expire on these Intermediary CAs? Recall that the
Root CA staggers the validity date for its subordinates. An
Intermediary Subordinate, then, will also stagger its issuance of certificate validity. The guideline is that you must monitor when certificates are due to expire and from that allow plenty of time (6 to 12
months) to create and issue a new certificate to all subordinates.

When you choose to renew a CA certificate from a subordinate,
keep in mind that the expiration date on a Subordinate CA is
slightly shorter than the expiration date on a parent CA. In other
words, renew the parent CA's certificate before renewing the child
CA's certificate. Otherwise, you'll renew a new certificate but the
expiration date will be influenced by the expiration date on the
parent CA.

ISSUING AND REVOKING CERTIFICATES

Issue and revoke certificates.

Before a CA can issue a certificate, a request must be made.
Requests for certificates can be made from users, computers, or
even services—such as other CAs.

Based on how the CAs are installed and configured, requests for certificates can happen automatically. An example of this is using a smart card to log on to a domain. As part of the smart card logon, a certificate request can be issued automatically.

Using the Certificates Snap-In

With the Certificates snap-in, users can use the Certificate Request Wizard to request a new certificate from the Windows 2000 Enterprise CA.

As an administrator, you can add the snap-in to your MMC and manage your user account, the computer account, and local services. As a regular user, you can manage only your own user account certificates.

To add the Certificate snap-in to the MMC, use Step by Step 22.4.

ON THE CD

Step by Step 22.4, "Starting the Certificate Snap-in," shows you how to add the Certificate snap-in to the MMC. See the file **Chapter22-04StepbyStep.pdf** in the CD's **Chapter22\StepbyStep** directory.

When you've added the Certificates snap-in, you can query the CA for a certificate. Within the Certificate console, select the Certification Authority from which you will be requesting the certificate.

You also need to choose the appropriate certificate template for the new certificate. A certificate template is a predefined set of rules for the certificate to be issued. Through the Advanced Options, you can choose CSP for the keys to be assigned from the CA.

Using the Windows 2000 Certificate Services Web Page

The second way a certificate can be requested is through the Windows 2000 Certificate Servers Web pages. During the installation of a CA, Web pages are installed on the corresponding IIS. By default, users can access these pages through `http://servername/certsrv`.

To request certificates from a standalone server, you must use the Windows 2000 Certification Services Web page, because standalone servers are not reliant on Active Directory to disperse their certificates. In addition, if you do not mark your keys as exportable, you have to use these Web pages to export the keys; the Certificate Request Wizard does not offer that option.

Processing Requests

So what happens when the requests issued by any method arrive at the CA?

The request immediately processes whether the CA is an Enterprise Certification Authority. The results of the processed request are either failed or granted. When a certificate is granted, it is issued to the requestor and a prompt to install the certificate is issued.

If, however, your request has been issued to a standalone server, the standalone server marks all certificate requests as pending by default. They remain in pending mode until an administrator approves or denies the request.

Checking on Pending Requests

When you've submitted a request to a standalone server, the request is marked as pending. A CA administrator must either approve or deny the issuing of the certificate to reset the certificate's pending status. To check the status of the pending request, follow Step by Step 22.5 using Internet Explorer.

EXAM TIP

Pending Certificates Existing Only on a Standalone CA   If an exam question references the verification of pending certificate requests, the CA in question is a Standalone CA. An Enterprise CA verifies the request against Active Directory and immediately approves or rejects the request.

ON THE CD

Step by Step 22.5, "Checking on a Pending Certificate Request," walks you through the process of checking the status of pending certificate requests. See the file **Chapter22-05StepbyStep.pdf** in the CD's **Chapter22\StepbyStep** directory.

Mapping Certificates to User Accounts

Thus far, you've looked at the request for a certificate and the response of a CA. But what about preparing the certificates and then mapping them out to users? You can do that, too.

With the standard (without the use of a smart card) logon to a Windows 2000 domain, logon requests are forwarded to a domain controller. The user's valid logon ID and password are verified, and then the user is allowed to log on.

This model of a client/server relationship through a named pipe is reliable and guarantees user authentication. What if your networks continue to grow and intermingle with other networks and eventually your database contains, or needs to contain, millions of user accounts? A new solution is required: a mapped certificate to a user account.

A mapped certificate to a user's account replaces the need for a centralized database of usernames and passwords at logon time. In its place, a public key is mapped to each user account so that at logon time the certificate can be examined to verify or deny the user logon.

The user presents the system its certificate, and then the system examines the key and determines which user account should be allowed to log on.

Mapping is accomplished either through Active Directory or through IIS. One certificate is typically mapped to only one user account; this is called *one-to–one mapping*. You can choose, however, to map many certificates to one user account; this is called *many-to–one mapping*.

User Principal Name Mapping

Through Active Directory, the user's principal name is matched with the certificate from the Enterprise CA. As part of the creation of certification on an Enterprise CA, users' principal names are included in the certificate.

EXAM TIP

Choosing Where to Map Accounts
If the account mapping is localized to a single IIS server, perform the mapping within IIS. If the mapping must be shared between applications, or between servers, the best choice is to perform the mapping in Active Directory.

One-to–One Mapping

One-to–one mapping, as the name implies, is a single certificate mapped to a single user account. An example of implementing one-to–one mapping is through an extranet. If your company created a Web site that allows sales reps to update and submit sales reports, check on commissions, status of orders, and other related sales information, you would no doubt want the site secure.

By issuing your users certificates mapped to Windows 2000 accounts, the users can access the site over the Internet, supply their credentials, and then access the information on the page as if they were on the LAN in your office.

Many-to–One Mapping

A bit more rare, but occasionally needed, is many-to–one mapping. As its names implies, this option allows you to map many certificates from different CAs to one individual Windows 2000 account.

Viewing an Issued Certificate

After a certificate has been issued, you can then view the information that has been included in the certificate. To view the information about a certificate, open the appropriate MMC, choose Certificates, Logical Store, Certificates, and double-click the certificate in the details pane. The dialog box that opens displays pages that provide the following information:

- ◆ An overview of certificates
- ◆ Uses of the certificate
- ◆ To whom the certificate was issued
- ◆ Validity period of the issued certificate
- ◆ Trusted Root CA
- ◆ Subordinate CA certificate
- ◆ Status of trust
- ◆ Certification status
- ◆ Version of the certificate

◆ Serial number

◆ Algorithm

◆ Issuer

◆ Subject—that is, the name of the CA (or individual issuing the certificate)

◆ Public key

◆ Thumbprint algorithm

◆ Thumbprint

◆ Friendly name

◆ Enhance Key Usage option, which defines how this certificate may be used

Revoking Issued Certificates

Sometimes you'll find it necessary to revoke an issued certificate. Reasons include, but are not limited to, the following:

◆ A user with an issued certificate leaves the entity.

◆ A user with an issued certificate can no longer be trusted by the entity.

◆ Suspicion arises that a user's private key has become jeopardized.

◆ A user obtains the certificate when he or she does not have rights to it.

When you revoke an issued certification, the certificate is added, and then published, to the certificate revocation list (CRL). Like a commercial CA, these CRLs are available for client computers to access so that they can verify valid certificates.

Revoking an Issued Certificate

You can use the Certificates snap-in to revoke certifications. This activity should be performed as soon as the certificate becomes suspect. After the certificate has been revoked, it's scheduled to be published on the CRL. To revoke a certificate, follow Step by Step 22.6.

> **ON THE CD**
>
> Step by Step 22.6, "Revoking a Certificate," demonstrates how to revoke a certificate. See the file **Chapter22-06StepbyStep.pdf** in the CD's **Chapter22\StepbyStep** directory.

Working with the Revocation List

After you've revoked a certificate, the certificate is slated to be published in the CRL. As an administrator, you can set the timings for publishing the CRL or choose to force an early publication date.

Each certificate has CRL distribution points included within itself as a way to update the system if the certificate is deleted. The distribution points are actually pointers to where the CRL can be retrieved. By default, the CRL file is located on the issuing CA's `systemroot\system32\certsrv\certenroll`.

You can set the timings for how often the CRL is published by selecting Revoked Certificates in the Console tree, choosing Action, Properties, and providing the required information. To manually publish a CRL, choose Action, All Tasks, Publish, and then confirm that you want to overwrite the previous CRL.

USING THE ENCRYPTING FILE SYSTEM (EFS) RECOVERY KEYS

Remove the Encrypting File System (EFS) recovery keys.

Microsoft Windows 2000 includes a new Encrypted File System (EFS). EFS is built on the same security principles that are involved in certificates. EFS works by encrypting data files on a computer's hard drive using EFS keys, much the same way information is encrypted using certificates. The EFS keys can then be stored on media separate from the computer.

EFS is an ideal data security tool, especially for laptop users. For example, an employee leaves on a business trip with a laptop containing company secrets. You may think that you are safe because the company secrets are encrypted. But what if the laptop is stolen and the thief is able to guess the logon name and password? What if the smart card was in the briefcase along with the laptop?

Exporting EFS Keys

To protect your data from theft, you can remove the EFS keys from all vulnerable computers and store the keys on the network, a floppy, or some other type of media.

By removing the EFS keys, you prevent an intruder from gaining access to the data simply by logging on to the computer. The keys for the data are stored elsewhere. Again, think physical security. Where will you keep these floppies?

To remove the EFS keys, follow Step by Step 22.7.

WARNING	**Password Alert** Choose your password for all EFS operations wisely. If you forget this password, your data will be inaccessible.

ON THE CD

Step by Step 22.7, "Exporting the EFS Keys," illustrates how to remove EFS keys. See the file **Chapter22-07StepbyStep.pdf** in the CD's **Chapter22\StepbyStep** directory.

Restoring EFS Keys

After you've exported the EFS keys and made backups of them, you need to import the keys back into the system when you want to access files using EFS. The importing process is very similar to exporting, as you can see in Step by Step 8.8.

ON THE CD

Step by Step 22.8, "Importing EFS Keys," walks you through the process of importing EFS keys. See the file **Chapter22-08StepbyStep.pdf** in the CD's **Chapter22\StepbyStep** directory.

CASE STUDY: ROCKWELL FINANCIAL SERVICES

ESSENCE OF THE CASE

The essential elements in this case are

▶ Rockwell wants to upload sensitive data over the Internet.

▶ Rockwell wants to allow clients to securely access their own data over the Web.

▶ Rockwell wants secure data from start to finish.

SCENARIO

Rockwell Financial Services is a company that deals in all aspects of financial management and investments. It has agents throughout North America that represent various firms for insurance and investments.

These agents use Windows 2000 Professional on their laptops. From the client's site, agents use the laptop to enter the investment information, and then they commute back to their respective networks and transfer the data to their local SQL Server, which is then transferred to a centralized SQL Server in Chicago.

The company realizes the need for the security of this data, and this is why the agents currently must return to the office to transfer their information. However, the agents are complaining that they are losing valuable time that could be used to visit other clients, and in some cases, sales are lost because the market may fluctuate and opportunities are missed.

Rockwell Financial Services would like to implement a plan that would allow its agents to use the Internet to connect to the central SQL Server and upload the data through a Web interface—while securing data. In addition, the company would like to offer services to its clients that would allow its clients to access their account information online.

ANALYSIS

Rockwell Financial should install Certificate Services. A hierarchy of Certification Authorities could start in the central office of Chicago and

CASE STUDY: ROCKWELL FINANCIAL SERVICES

then be dispersed to a child CA in each geographical location.

Sales reps would be issued a certificate from the local CA. A Web presence with a sales front and a SQL interface would be created that would support secure uploads of clients' data over the Internet. In addition, a plan could be developed

to secure any data saved on the laptops by the sales reps through smart cards or through EFS implementation.

A Web presence would be created for clients accessing their personal data. A certificate would be issued by a CA that would verify that the clients have access to only their data.

CHAPTER SUMMARY

Certificate mechanisms are used for ensuring that data is secure between users, computers, and services. Certificates may be issued through a third-party CA, such as VeriSign, or through Microsoft's CA Services.

A CA scheme needs to be developed to determine the number of CAs to be created, the location of CAs, and the role of each CA. An Enterprise Root CA is the foundation of a typical CA schema. The Enterprise Root CA issues certificates to Intermediary CAs. The Intermediary CAs then issue certificates to Subordinate CAs.

As servers and services are removed from the network, and more likely, users leave the company, it becomes necessary, for security, to revoke certificates.

The EFS is a component that allows your data to be kept secure, especially on a laptop, should the physical security of the computer become jeopardized. By encrypting the data on the laptop and then removing the public and private keys, the data is secure if the computer is vandalized or stolen. To access the data, the private key is required.

KEY TERMS

- Certificate
- Certification Authority
- Standalone Certification Authorities
- Validity period
- Enterprise Root CA
- Intermediate CA
- User Principal Name mapping
- One-to–one mapping
- Many-to–one mapping
- Revoked certificate
- Revocation list
- EFS

APPLY YOUR KNOWLEDGE

Review Questions

1. What is a certificate?

2. What is a Certification Authority?

3. What is an Enterprise Certification Authority?

4. What is the role of an Intermediary CA?

5. Why would an organization have a Standalone Certification Authority?

6. Why would an issued certificate need to be revoked?

7. Why would a CA need to renew its certificate?

8. How are certificate requests handled at a Standalone CA server?

9. What is many–to–one mapping?

10. How can EFS be effective when planning for the worst, such as on a lost or stolen laptop?

Answers to Review Questions

1. A certificate is a component that allows you to send and receive secure data over a network. It assures the recipient that you are the person you claim to be, and it assures the sender that the data will reach the recipient without being jeopardized. For more information, see the section titled "Certificates."

2. A Certification Authority (CA) is an entity that is responsible for verifying the credentials of a certificate requestor before giving the requestor a certificate. You may use a third-party CA or use Microsoft's Certificate Services. For more information, see the section titled "Certification Authorities."

3. An Enterprise Certification Authority is the Root Certification Authority in an organization. Typically, as additional CAs are added they are issued certificates from the Root CA. For more information, see the section titled "Windows 2000 Enterprise Certification Authority."

4. An Intermediary CA is responsible for issuing certificates to child CAs. The Enterprise Root CA issues a certificate to the Intermediary CA. The Intermediary CA then issues certificates to all child CAs rather than the Root CA issuing the certificates directly. For more information, see the section titled "Certification Authorities."

5. A Standalone CA is an excellent choice when Active Directory is not present or when you want to manually approve certificate requests. For more information, see the section titled "Standalone Certification Authorities."

6. An issued certificate would be revoked for a number of reasons: the user has left the organization, the keys may have been jeopardized, or a certification was assigned under false pretenses. For more information, see the section titled "Revoking Issued Certificates."

7. When a CA is created, it is assigned a certificate. This certificate, like all certificates, is set to expire. When a certificate has or is about to expire, an administrator can choose to renew the certificate. For more information, see the section titled "Renewing Certificates for Certification Authorities."

8. Standalone CAs mark all requests as pending. An administrator must manually approve or deny each certificate request. For more information, see the section titled "Standalone Certification Authorities."

APPLY YOUR KNOWLEDGE

9. Many–to–one mapping is the process of assigning multiple certificates to one Windows 2000 user account. For more information, see the section titled "Issuing and Revoking Certificates."

10. When using EFS on a laptop, to be most secure you need to export the private keys and delete the local keys. This secures the data should the laptop be lost or stolen. For more information, see the section titled "Exporting EFS Keys."

ON THE CD

This book's companion CD contains specially designed supplemental material to help you understand how well you know the concepts and skills you learned in this chapter. You'll find related exercises and exam questions and answers. See the file **Chapter22ApplyYourKnowledge.pdf** in the CD's **Chapter22\ApplyYourKnowledge** directory.

Suggested Readings and Resources

1. Komar, Brian. *Sams Teach Yourself TCP/IP Network Administration in 21 Days.* Indianapolis: Sams Publishing, 1998.

2. Marcus, Scott J. *Designing Wide Area Networks and Internetworks: A Practical Guide.* Upper Saddle River, NJ: Addison Wesley, 1999.

3. Thomas, Thomas M. *OSPF Network Design Solutions.* Indianapolis: Macmillan Technical Publishing, 1998.

IMPLEMENTING AND ADMINISTERING A MICROSOFT WINDOWS 2000 DIRECTORY SERVICES INFRASTRUCTURE

This chapter looks at the DNS server that comes with Windows 2000 as it relates to the Active Directory. Although it concentrates on how to integrate with Active Directory, the chapter starts with a brief discussion of the basics of Domain Name System (DNS). After that, a discussion of the installation is presented along with a look at the roles of a DNS server. After these basics are covered, the chapter turns to how it works with Active Directory.

The following objectives from the exam are covered in this chapter:

Install, configure, and troubleshoot DNS for Active Directory.

- **Integrate Active Directory DNS zones with non-Active Directory DNS zones.**

- **Configure zones for dynamic updates.**

▶ This objective is included to make sure that you are able to work with DNS both for Active Directory and for other types of computers on your network. Also, one of the important changes in DNS for Windows 2000 is the capability to deal with dynamic updates. This is important for Active Directory so that it can register various services with the DNS server to enable clients to find LDAP servers and domain controllers.

Manage, monitor, and troubleshoot DNS.

- **Manage replication of DNS data.**

▶ In managing replication of DNS, you need to understand the difference between zone transfers for standard zones and Active Directory replication of Active Directory–integrated zones.

CHAPTER 23

Configuring DNS for Active Directory

▶ The DNS component of the Active Directory implementation exam is likely to be fairly small. You primarily need to concentrate on the following points:

- Creating DNS forward and reverse lookup zones.

- Configuring DNS zones to accept dynamic updates.

- Configuring secondary zone files.

- Integrating Active Directory–integrated zones with other DNS servers.

- Configuring a zone as Active Directory integrated.

INTRODUCTION

Probably the most important aspect of Active Directory is that it is hierarchical. This enables Active Directory to use the concept of namespace, allowing an almost infinite number of objects to be stored and represented. The hierarchical aspect of Active Directory enables an organization to have a single root, or main, domain and then break it down into more and more precise sections.

INTRODUCTION TO DNS

Given that DNS provides the hierarchy for Active Directory, you need to fully understand how the system works and how to implement it in Windows 2000. The next few sections serve as a basic discussion of DNS including a look at fully qualified domain names (FQDNs) and how they are resolved.

DNS is made up of three parts:

◆ **Name servers.** These are the servers that provide address and other information about the computers you find on the Internet or intranet.

◆ **Resolvers.** A resolver is a small piece of code built in to the operating system or into a particular package that requests the IP address for a hostname from the name server.

◆ **Namespace.** Just like the organizational chart that starts at the top and breaks down, the namespace starts at a root and breaks down into domains, the hierarchy of your enterprise. On the Internet, the namespace includes a root domain and all the domains that exist below it.

Understanding Fully Qualified Domain Names

DNS namespace covers every computer directly connected to the Internet, a maximum of 3,720,314,628, and many others that are behind firewalls, all of which could have more than one name.

Although the sheer number of hosts to which you can possibly connect is staggering, you can do it with ease if you know the name of the system. Obviously, this would be impossible if all the listings were on a single, large computer on the Internet. The network load on this single computer would make searching impossible. Just like a company organizes departments into sections, the name servers on the Internet must break down the domain names into manageable chunks that can be delegated to other systems.

Consider the FQDN `www.newriders.com`. From this name, we can determine the servers that are involved with managing this name. You read an FQDN from left to right, with the specific server to which you connect on the left and the root domain for the Internet on the right. Each part of the name is separated by a period (.), and there is a trailing period that represents the root domain, which is not normally entered.

To take this further, you might break newriders down by different divisions or by geographic location. Then you might have `www.shipping.newriders.com` and `www.production.newriders.com`.

Levels in an FQDN

These parts of the FQDN represent different levels in the name space hierarchy. The example, `www.newriders.com.`, tells us that from the root domain there is a com domain, in the com domain there is a newriders domain, and in that domain there is a server called www.

Part of Name	Represents	Level
Trailing period (.)	Root domain	Root
com	Com domain	Top level
newriders	Newriders domain	Second level
www	Server name or alias	-

Various bodies on the Internet manage the root- and top-level domains. There is only one root domain, and this acts as the starting point for all names; it represents the starting point for the Internet namespace.

There are many top-level domains, the most familiar being .com, .gov, .edu, and .net, with more being added. In some countries, the top-level domain based on the country code, such as .ca or .au, can be obtained as well.

The second level is where the hierarchy flattens out considerably. This is where companies, organizations, or individuals can start to register their names. In the previous example, newriders would have registered with the com domain. It is critical to register with the domain above you, the parent domain; otherwise, the resolution process discussed in the following "Resolving an FQDN" section will not work.

When you register your name, you are responsible for providing name resolutions for that part of the namespace. Therefore, you need to create one or more DNS name servers. If you are registering a domain on the Internet, you are generally required to provide the IP addresses of two name servers that will be used to resolve your domain structure. The theory behind this is that at least one will always be available. After the server is created, you can add entries for your domain in a zone file.

Understanding Zones

Any server you want to be resolved from the Internet needs to have an entry in a zone file. A name server is authoritative for a zone if it hosts the zone file used to resolve DNS queries for that zone. This can be somewhat confusing because many people draw a parallel at this point between a zone and a domain. In most cases, this is not a problem because the two are the same. However, in some cases, an organization might decide to take the namespace it controls and further break it down.

For example, you work at newriders.com and want to separate the book publishing from the electronic publishing. You could create a subdomain called "electronic" to separate that business from the other. You would then have the main domain called newriders.com and a subdomain called electronic.newriders.com. These could now be separate zone files, or they could be in the same zone file. If they are on the same server, they will be in the same zone file.

If they are on separate servers, they are definitely two separate zones. In this case, you need to add Name Server (NS) records in the newriders.com zone that point at the name servers for electronic. newriders.com. This is the delegation process, the same process that happens on the Internet name servers when you register your domain; they add the name server records for your subdomain. These name server records are required to allow the process of name resolution to happen.

Resolving an FQDN

When you enter an address to browse, your operating system uses the resolver previously mentioned. The resolver queries your config- ured DNS server for the IP address of the name you entered. If the local DNS server has a zone file (is authoritative) for the zone you are querying, it returns the information to you from this file.

Unless you only browse for servers within your organization's namespace, the local DNS server will not be authoritative for the requested domain. This means that the server must now go out and find the address you are requesting. It does this by querying other DNS servers in the hierarchy for their best answer to the question, starting with the root and working down until it finds the server that is authoritative for the domain you are seeking.

For example, if you enter `http://www.newriders.com` into a browser, the browser needs to look this up using a resolver. It first queries the local DNS server. If this server cannot answer the query, the DNS server checks the root-level server. The root-level server does not know the full path but does know where the com domain is located. Because this is all the root domain knows about your request, it will return the address of one or more com domain (COM-DOM) servers.

Your local DNS server queries one of the com domain servers for the address you entered. Again, that server doesn't know where the host is but does know where the newriders.com domain is (NEWRIDERS-DOM). It will, therefore, return the NS records for the domain.

Your local DNS server queries the name servers for NEWRIDERS-DOM, which hopefully returns the IP address for the server www. This means that your server now knows the address and can return

NOTE

DNS Can Also Use Forwarders Many companies will configure their DNS servers to forward any requests that cannot be resolved by the local DNS server to their ISP's DNS server. The ISP's DNS server will either resolve the request, forward the request to yet another DNS server, or check the root-level servers.

the address to the resolver on your system. The resolver on your system lets the browser know so it can open the page from the other company's Web server. This whole process is shown in Figure 23.1.

As you might have noticed, there are actually two types of queries in this discussion:

◆ **Recursive.** The query from your system to the local DNS server is the recursive query. Recursive queries require that the remote server return an authoritative answer or a "not found" message.

◆ **Iterative.** The other queries that came from your DNS server and queried the other DNS servers on the Internet are iterative. Several iterative queries (iterations) can be sent to locate an authoritative answer; each requests the best answer the other server can give.

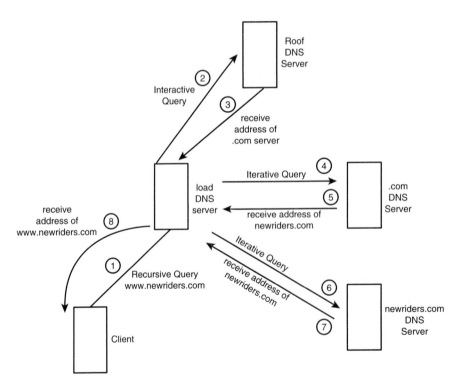

FIGURE 23.1

The steps in resolving a DNS query.

The answers are cached on the local server for a period of time specified by the remote server, known as the *Time-to-Live* (TTL). As a result, your next query to http://www.newriders.com will be answered from the cache on your local DNS server.

INSTALLING DNS

You need to have a working DNS server before you can install Active Directory. Normally, Windows 2000 is installed as a server and then the DNS server service is configured; after that is done, you can install the Active Directory.

This part of the chapter assumes that you can install Windows 2000 and concentrates on installation and configuration of the DNS server.

Prerequisites

Before you can install the DNS server, you need to have a working Windows 2000 Server or Windows 2000 Advanced Server. The system must be configured with TCP/IP and have disk space to hold the records that will be installed.

Although it is not required, you should confirm the computer name before you proceed. This ensures that the correct information can be verified when DNS is installed. To confirm the computer name, follow the steps outlined in Step by Step 23.1.

NOTE

> **Autoconfiguration** With final release, you do not have to configure the DNS server beforehand. The Active Directory Installation Wizard autoconfigures the DNS service on the domain controller. It configures only the forward lookup zone and configures the zone as an Active Directory–integrated zone using secure updates.

ON THE CD

Step by Step 23.1, "Verifying Your Computer Name," walks you through confirming the computer name. See the file **Chapter23-01StepbyStep.pdf** in the CD's **Chapter23\StepbyStep** directory.

The Process

The process is simple, as Step by Step 23.2 demonstrates.

ON THE CD

Step by Step 23.2, "Installing the DNS Service," walks you through the installation process. See the file **Chapter23-02StepbyStep.pdf** in the CD's **Chapter23\StepbyStep** directory.

Next, you need to create the reverse and forward lookup zones for your network, and then you can install Active Directory. Forward lookups resolve a name to an IP address and reverse lookups enable you to find the name of a host from its IP address.

ROLES FOR DNS SERVERS

Now that the DNS server is installed, you need to decide what role the DNS server will play in your organizational scheme. The role of the server depends on the zone files it has; because a server could have many different zone files, it can fill different roles. The main roles you will configure include

- ◆ **Cache only.** This is the simplest type of server to configure because all you have to do is install the DNS server service. After this is done, other computers can point at this server to provide name resolution for names on the Internet or intranet. Because there are no zone files on this type of server, it will always have to find the resolution on other servers. Because it will cache these, this type of server is known as a cache only server. In addition, the server can be configured to use a forwarder; your local server can recursively ask another DNS server to resolve the name.

- ◆ **Primary.** A primary, actually in this version a standard primary, is the server that maintains the original zone file. Windows 2000 DNS server can host multiple primary zones. The information for a primary zone is kept in the Registry. It is also kept in a file located in `c:\winnt\system32\dns` for default installations. There are two types of primary zones you'll deal with: forward and reverse. Forward lookup zones resolve an FQDN or hostname to an IP address, as you saw earlier. The reverse zone resolves IP addresses to FQDNs.

◆ **Secondary.** A secondary server stores a read-only copy of the zone data file. The secondary server copies the zone file from another server. This could be the primary server or another secondary server. In this case, the secondary is also a master server.

Step by Step 23.3 describes the process of setting up a secondary server.

ON THE CD

Step by Step 23.3, "Configuring a Secondary Server," walks you through the process of setting up a secondary server. See the file **Chapter23-03StepbyStep.pdf** in the CD's **Chapter23\StepbyStep** directory.

No matter which role the DNS server is playing, the DNS server stores a combination of forward and reverse lookup zones.

Forward Lookup Zones

The process for creating a standard forward lookup zone is described in Step by Step 23.4.

ON THE CD

Step by Step 23.4, "Creating a Forward Lookup Zone," shows you how to create a standard forward lookup zone. See the file **Chapter23-04StepbyStep.pdf** in the CD's **Chapter23\StepbyStep** directory.

As you can see, configuring a forward lookup zone is very simple. After this is done, you will configure additional properties of the zone. Then you will configure secondary servers.

Configuring Forward Lookup Zones

Now that you have created the zone you will use, you should configure the zone. This is simply a matter of configuring the options you want to use and possibly adding some hostnames.

In general, configuring the zone is a simple matter; the steps in Step by Step 23.5 will get you into the property sheets for the zones.

ON THE CD

Step by Step 23.5, "Configuring a Forward Lookup Zone," shows you how to set up a forward lookup zone. See the file **Chapter23-05StepbyStep.pdf** in the CD's **Chapter23\StepbyStep** directory.

When you are configuring a primary zone, the following series of options are available.

General

The General tab (see Figure 23.2) enables you to configure some of the basic information about the zone. The options available include

◆ **Status.** This tells you the current status of the zone and enables you to pause a zone or to start a paused zone.

◆ **Type.** This enables you to change the type of zone between primary, secondary, and Active Directory integrated. This can be used to change the server role in a case a primary server goes offline. It can also be used if you want to later change a server that was used during installation to an Active Directory–integrated server.

◆ **Zone File Name.** This enables you to change the name that stores the zone file information without data lose. You should note that the zone information is actually in the Registry, and the file is updated occasionally for compatibility with BIND secondary servers. You can force an update by choosing Update Server Data Files from the context menu.

◆ **Allow Dynamic Updates?** This is a new feature that works with DHCP to enable the client or the DHCP server to update the DNS zone dynamically. This is discussed further in the section "Integrating DNS and Active Directory."

FIGURE 23.2
The General tab for a forward lookup zone.

◆ **Aging.** Because systems can register themselves, you will occasionally end up with records that are no longer valid from a computer that is removed or perhaps a laptop for a user who visits the office. Aging enables you to configure whether the system will verify and occasionally delete records that are dynamically created. If you click the Aging button, there are three options you can set:

• **Scavenge Stale Resource Records.** This check box enables or disables scavenging, the process that removes old dynamic resource records if the system has not reregistered its name. This can be configured at the server level or the zone level.

• **No-Refresh Interval.** This is the period of time that a record is assumed to be okay. The client system will keep the record for at least this period of time.

• **Refresh Interval.** This is the period of time that the client system has to refresh its record after the no-refresh interval has expired.

Start of Authority

The *Start of Authority* (SOA) record (see Figure 23.3) is used to find the server that has authority for a domain. The tab enables you to configure the normal DNS parameters that are part of the SOA record. These options include the following:

◆ **Serial Number.** This is the serial number for the zone file. This will change incrementally each time the file is changed. Secondary servers will compare their version number to that of the primary and will copy (AXFR) the file if they are different. You can set this number to a higher value to force a change to be copied to a secondary server. A Windows 2000 Server can also use an incremental zone transfer (IXFR), which only transfers the changes since the previous version number, reducing the amount of information being transferred.

◆ **Primary Server.** This is the name of the primary server. This server has the read/write version of the zone file.

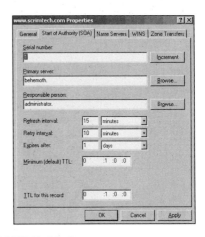

FIGURE 23.3
The SOA tab for a forward lookup zone.

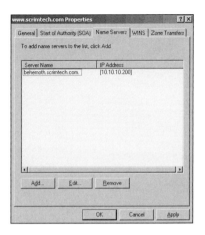

FIGURE 23.4
On this tab, you can add, edit, or remove name servers for your domain.

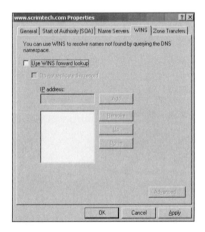

FIGURE 23.5
The WINS tab in a forward lookup zone.

◆ **Responsible Person.** This is the email address of the person in charge of the zone. The @ sign in the address is replaced by a period so the record can be correctly stored in the zone file. This is because the @ sign in a zone file means "this zone."

◆ **Refresh Interval.** This value sets how often secondary servers will attempt to contact the primary to verify the version number and transfer the zone if required.

◆ **Retry Interval.** If a secondary server cannot connect to the primary server at the refresh interval, it will retry the attempt at this interval.

◆ **Expires After.** This is the period after which a secondary server will stop resolving an address for a zone file it could not verify.

◆ **Minimum (default) TTL.** This setting is passed to other servers during name resolution and tells them how long they can cache the entry.

◆ **TTL for this Record.** You can change which server is the primary server at any time. This is because an expiration time was added to the SOA record. The servers will check to see whether they are still the primary when this TTL expires.

Name Servers

The Name Servers tab (see Figure 23.4) lists the name servers in this zone. Listing a server here creates an NS record for the zone. These should match the servers registered with the domain one level up; the domain one level up will return these records when another server queries for your domain.

WINS

If you need to support older Windows clients, you might configure the WINS tab (see Figure 23.5.) This provides the server with the IP address of one or more WINS servers that it can query if it doesn't have the name you are looking up. The DNS server queries for the hostname on the WINS server and can then append the zone file name to create the FQDN.

The options on this tab include

◆ **Use WINS Forward Lookup.** This option enables or disables this functionality.

◆ **Do Not Replicate This Record.** If this is not checked, the WINS record will not be included in zone transfers to configured secondary DNS servers. This should be selected if some of the secondary servers are non-Microsoft servers and do not support WINS resource records.

◆ **IP Address.** This is where you can add, remove, or order the IP address(es) of the WINS server you want to use.

◆ **Advanced.** This opens another dialog box with the following options.

  • **Cache Time-Out.** When an address is resolved using the WINS server, this setting controls how long the DNS server keeps the entry in cache.

  • **Lookup Time-Out.** This determines how long the DNS server waits for the WINS server to respond before giving up.

Zone Transfers

The last tab in the forward lookup zone configuration is the Zone Transfers tab (see Figure 23.6). This tab configures how zone transfers, copying the zone from a primary server to a secondary, take place. You can configure this at the server with the primary zone file or at a server with a secondary file. At the secondary server, this affects other secondary servers that get their copy of the zone file from it. In this role, it is a master server.

The options available include

◆ **Allow Zone Transfers.** This enables you to disable the capability to transfer the zone. You will almost always have this enabled.

◆ **To Any Server.** This enables your zone to be transferred to any server that requests it. This should be avoided because it could give hackers information about your environment that could be used to help them break in.

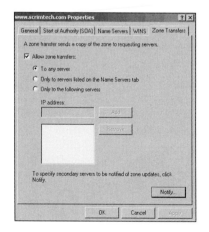

FIGURE 23.6
The Zone Transfers tab for a forward lookup zone.

◆ **Only to Servers Listed on the Name Servers Tab.** This option is the most likely to be used because it will ensure that all secondary servers can retrieve a copy of the zone information.

◆ **Only to the Following Servers.** In some cases, you will need to control where servers get their copy of the zone file. This is true if you are creating a multitiered DNS architecture, which you might do if your network includes slow links.

◆ **Notify.** This button opens a dialog box that enables you to control which servers will be notified when the zone information changes. The options available are

  • **Automatically Notify.** Turn this feature on or off. Turning this feature on could increase the bandwidth usage; however, it will ensure that the secondary servers are kept up-to-date.

  • **Servers Listed on the Name Servers Tab.** This setting automatically notifies all the servers listed in the Named Servers tab.

  • **The Following Servers.** This enables you to control which servers are notified.

Reverse Lookup Zones

One of the many confusing subjects is how a reverse lookup zone works. You should know that forward lookups resolve names moving from right to left, from the root domain to the top level to the second level. Looking at an IP address, you might notice it is the other way around. That is, the last number is changed for each host instead of the first octet. Therefore, the same process works, except it would need to go backward or from left to right.

If you wanted the DNS server to work in reverse, you would essentially have to rewrite the resolvers and the name servers. Because there are many thousands of them already out there, this would be far too large a task. So if you cannot reverse the process, reverse the data. Take the numbers of the address and reverse them. Now, instead of looking up 152.124.25.14, your resolver will look up 14.25.124.152 reading from right to left, just like it does with an FQDN.

After you have created the reverse lookup zone, the DNS snap-in will update it as you change the forward lookup zones. Therefore, the first zone you should configure is the reverse lookup zone. Step by Step 23.6 covers creating a reverse lookup zone.

ON THE CD

Step by Step 23.6, "Creating a Reverse Lookup Zone Name," walks you through the creation of such a zone. See the file **Chapter23-06StepbyStep.pdf** in the CD's **Chapter23\StepbyStep** directory.

After this is configured, you can configure the forward lookup zone. There are additional properties you can configure for the zone; however, some of these depend on the information in the forward zone. This is covered in the following section.

Configuring a Reverse Lookup Zone

Configuring a reverse lookup zone is almost identical to configuring a forward lookup zone. The only difference is the size of the tabs and the WINS-R tab.

WINS-R

Because this is the only tab that is different, it is the only one included here (see Figure 23.7). This WINS-R record will point at the forward zone file; the name of that zone will be appended to records returned in reverse queries.

The options available are

◆ **Use WINS-R Lookup.** This enables or disables the use of a WINS server for reverse lookups.

◆ **Do Not Replicate This Record.** This prevents the WINS-R record from being replicated to other DNS servers. This should be used if there are local WINS servers where the other DNS servers are located.

◆ **Domain to Append to Returned Name.** This option sets the domain portion of the FQDN that will be returned.

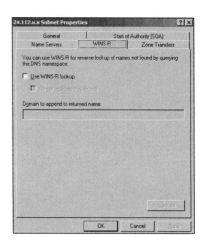

FIGURE 23.7
The WINS-R tab, which only requires that you enter the forward lookup zone.

◆ **Advanced.** This opens the Advanced Options tab. There are three options available on that tab:

- **Cache Time-Out.** This is how long the name will be cached on the DNS server.

- **Lookup Time-Out.** This is how long the DNS server will wait, assuming that the WINS server is not available.

- **Submit DNS Name as NetBIOS Scope.** This appends the DNS domain name entered in the Domain to Append to Returned Name field as the NetBIOS scope in the query to the WINS server.

INTEGRATING DNS AND ACTIVE DIRECTORY

After you have the DNS server installed and configured, you can perform the last few steps to prepare to install Active Directory. You now should have created the reverse and forward lookup zones for your Active Directory structure and configured the zones to allow updates.

There are a couple different ways that the Active Directory zone can be integrated with your organization. These integration methods should be chosen by the people who planned the Active Directory structure. The three common methods include the following:

◆ Use the same domain internally and externally. (For example, just use the DNS name you registered with the InterNIC, such as MCP.com.)

◆ Use a subdomain of the external domain. (For example, create a subdomain from your public domain for Active Directory, such as AD.MCP.com.)

◆ Use a separate domain internally. (For example, use a different name internally, such as MCP.local. Because you are not registering with the InterNIC, any top-level domain can be used. Microsoft recommends .local.)

Whichever way you have decided to integrate the public and private networks, you should configure the reverse and forward lookup zones first.

Configuring Active Directory Integration

You need to configure the zones you use for Active Directory as Active Directory–integrated zones. This is a simple process done on a domain controller running DNS that involves the steps shown in Step by Step 23.7.

ON THE CD

Step by Step 23.7, "Configuring a Zone as Active Directory–Integrated," addresses the need to configure the zones you use for Active Directory as Active Directory–integrated. See the file **Chapter23-07StepbyStep.pdf** in the CD's **Chapter23\StepbyStep** directory.

Remember that if you are going to create an Active Directory–integrated zone, you must use a domain controller as the DNS server.

Allowing Updates

Install, configure, and troubleshoot DNS for Active Directory

- **Configure zones for dynamic updates.**

This is an important issue because the domain controllers need to create several records so users can find them. These include service records, A or host records, and PTR or reverse lookup records. You need to configure all the zones used in Active Directory to allow updates so that the servers and the clients can update their own records. This is done on the General tab of the zone properties.

For a standard zone, you have the choices of Yes or No. Yes allows updates and No does not allow updating. If the type of zone is Active Directory integrated, you will also have the option of allowing Only Secure Updates. When the zone is integrated with Active Directory, the zone information is moved into the Active Directory; therefore, you can apply permissions. If Only Secure Updates is selected, only computers with computer accounts in the forest where the DNS server is located will be able to register a computer.

The Update Process

The update process can be initialized either from the client or from the Dynamic Host Configuration Protocol (DHCP) server. If the client knows about dynamic DNS (for example, Windows 2000), it will perform the update. Otherwise, you will need to configure the DHCP server to process updates.

Windows 2000 clients will, by default, update the information on the DNS server. There are several instances that cause the client to update the information on the DNS server:

◆ A change to one or more local IP addresses.

◆ The IP address leased from the DHCP server is refreshed or changed, either as a matter of course or by a user issuing the IPCONFIG /RENEW command.

◆ A user at the system forces the update using IPCONFIG /REGISTERDNS.

◆ The system or, in some cases, a service restarts.

◆ The computer name is changed.

◆ Updates are sent by Windows 2000 clients every 24 hours.

In any of these cases, the system will need to update the information. The update process follows these steps:

1. The DHCP client sends a SOA query for the domain name with which it is registered. This query is used to find a server where the update can be processed.

2. An authoritative server responds to the query with the address for the primary server, the one with the primary zone file. In the case of an Active Directory–integrated zone, any DNS server can perform the update because the information is stored as part of Active Directory.

3. The client attempts to contact the server to perform the update. If the update fails, the client queries for the NS records for the domain. The client then queries the first name server for a SOA record and tries the server listed in this record.

4. The client then sends the update. The server attempts to process the update. It first needs to make sure that updates are allowed, and if the server is Active Directory integrated, it also checks whether the computer performing the update has the necessary permissions to perform the update.

Changes in Zones Used for Active Directory

There are several important things that take place in DNS when you are working with Active Directory. Some of these changes only take place in Active Directory–integrated zones, while others are made as requirements of Windows 2000. This section looks at those changes, including the following:

◆ In Active Directory–integrated zones, any domain controller running DNS can accept dynamic registrations.

◆ The Netlogon service registers with the DNS server(s) so that users can locate the services.

◆ You can apply security to DNS updates.

◆ Zone information becomes part of the Active Directory and is replicated using AD replication.

The Netlogon service registers additional names for a domain controller; these names enable the users to locate Lightweight Directory Access Protocol (LDAP) servers. This, in turn, enables users to search for logon servers or for other objects in the Active Directory.

The entries that the Netlogon service registers are stored in a file on the domain controller in `c:\winnt\system32\config`, by default, in a file named NETLOGON.DNS. The file contains entries to register the server services including LDAP, Kerberos, and the Global Catalog service. The contents look like the following:

```
mydom.local. 600 IN A 10.10.10.200
_ldap._tcp.mydom.local. 600 IN SRV 0 100 389
comp.mydom.local.
_ldap._tcp.pdc._msdcs.mydom.local. 600 IN SRV 0 100 389
comp.mydom.local.
_ldap._tcp.gc._msdcs.mydom.local. 600 IN SRV 0 100 3268
comp.mydom.local.
_ldap._tcp.a3c99adb-f3fe-4a88-8ea8-
7fc4945be8d6.domains._msdcs.mydom.local. 600 IN SRV 0 100
389 comp.mydom.local.
gc._msdcs.mydom.local. 600 IN A 10.10.10.200
2b8e8e62-6f26-4d89-ab0e-29ce9cec8458._msdcs.mydom.local.
600 IN CNAME comp.mydom.local.
_kerberos._tcp.dc._msdcs.mydom.local. 600 IN SRV 0 100 88
comp.mydom.local.
_ldap._tcp.dc._msdcs.mydom.local. 600 IN SRV 0 100 389
comp.mydom.local.
_kerberos._tcp.mydom.local. 600 IN SRV 0 100 88
comp.mydom.local.
_gc._tcp.mydom.local. 600 IN SRV 0 100 3268
comp.mydom.local.
_kerberos._udp.mydom.local. 600 IN SRV 0 100 88
comp.mydom.local.
_kpasswd._tcp.mydom.local. 600 IN SRV 0 100 464
comp.mydom.local.
_kpasswd._udp.mydom.local. 600 IN SRV 0 100 464
comp.mydom.local.
_ldap._tcp.Default-First-Site-Name._sites.mydom.local. 600
IN SRV 0 100 389 comp.mydom.local.
_ldap._tcp.Default-First-Site-
Name._sites.gc._msdcs.mydom.local. 600 IN SRV 0 100 3268
comp.mydom.local.
_kerberos._tcp.Default-First-Site-
Name._sites.dc._msdcs.mydom.local. 600 IN SRV 0 100 88
comp.mydom.local.
_ldap._tcp.Default-First-Site-
Name._sites.dc._msdcs.mydom.local. 600 IN SRV 0 100 389
comp.mydom.local.
_kerberos._tcp.Default-First-Site-Name._sites.mydom.local.
600 IN SRV 0 100 88 comp.mydom.local.
_gc._tcp.Default-First-Site-Name._sites.mydom.local. 600 IN
SRV 0 100 3268 comp.mydom.local.
```

Each line of the file registers a different service with the DNS server. The format for the lines is

```
service.protocol.name ttl class SRV preference weight port
target
```

The first part, `service.protocol.name`, lets the DNS server know what service is being registered and which transport protocol it will use. The choices of transport protocol are limited to either TCP or UDP. The `ttl` is the Time-to-Live. This is the length of time that the clients will be able to cache this entry. The class is always set to `IN`, which indicates that this is an Internet entry, followed by `SRV`, which tells the DNS server this is a service locator record.

When several servers provide the same service, the preference value indicates which record(s) should be returned first when a query is sent for that service with lower values first. If more than one server is at the same preference, the weight is used to determine which server to try first. The port identifies which port the service is on. This information is passed to the client so that nonstandard ports can be used. Finally, the target is added as either an IP address or a hostname.

For the moment, it is not important what specific entries are registered. At this point, you only need to know that the file exists and that it is used to register network services.

The other changes all affect Active Directory–integrated zones. These changes come about because the entries are now part of the Active Directory. The entries will be treated as objects in the Active Directory and therefore can have security applied to them. This allows for secure updates. This also means that the updates can be performed on any DNS server that handles this zone because Active Directory uses multimaster replication.

TRANSFERRING ZONE INFORMATION

Manage, monitor, and troubleshoot DNS.

- **Manage replication of DNS data.**

Whether your zone is integrated or not, you need to replicate the zone amongst the DNS servers. The next couple sections cover how this is done.

In the Standard Environment

When you are configuring zone transfers in the standard DNS environment, you simply create a secondary server. You configure another DNS server to copy the zone file from the primary server or another secondary server. The zone transfer uses the parameters defined in the SOA record for the zone.

To configure a DNS server to act as a secondary server for an existing zone, you need to perform the steps outlined in Step by Step 23.8.

ON THE CD

Step by Step 23.8, "Configuring a Secondary Server," covers setting up a secondary server when you are dealing with an existing zone. See the file **Chapter23-08StepbyStep.pdf** in the CD's **Chapter23\StepbyStep** directory.

After this is configured, the zone information is transferred according to the information you configured in the SOA record or if you specifically force a transfer. There are actually two types of transfers that can take place: full and incremental.

During the initial replication for the zone file, a full (AFXR) zone transfer takes place. If, however, both the primary server and the secondary server support incremental (IFXR) zone transfers, subsequent transfers will only need to transfer records that have changed.

The incremental zone transfer uses the serial number of the zone file to track changes. When a secondary requests the IXFR, the serial numbers are compared. If they are the same, no zone transfer is performed. If they are different, the primary DNS server sends the changes that have occurred since the last zone transfer to the secondary server. It determines which records by comparing the serial number that the secondary has in the SOA resource record with the serial number that the secondary DNS server has in its version of the SOA resource record. All resource records that have been added or modified between the two serial numbers are transferred to the secondary zone.

In the Active Directory Environment

During the discussion of the Active Directory–integrated zone, you might have noticed that the servers were no longer primary or secondary but just integrated. This is because the information is loaded from Active Directory. Active Directory handles the replication. Instead of performing zone transfers, the DNS servers poll Active Directory for updates every 15 minutes; this is set in the zone properties.

This is why all the domain controllers in an Active Directory–integrated zone that run DNS can accept updates. They have a write-enabled copy of the zone.

You should be aware that the zone data is stored within the domain where the DNS servers are located. The problem with this is that data in Active Directory–integrated zones can only be replicated within a single domain using Active Directory replication. You can, therefore, only configure one domain to use Active Directory–integrated zones. All other domains need to use secondary DNS servers to the Active Directory–integrated zone.

In a Mixed Environment

Install, configure, and troubleshoot DNS for Active Directory.

- **Integrate Active Directory DNS zones with non-Active Directory DNS zones.**

Many networks throughout the world run with many different operating systems. This creates a situation where a Microsoft DNS server must communicate and share DNS data with non-Microsoft systems.

Microsoft has spent considerable effort ensuring that their DNS server is RFC compliant. This means that a Microsoft DNS server should be able to work with all other types of DNS servers on the market that also comply with the same RFCs. Primarily, these are Berkeley Internet Name Domain (BIND) systems.

These servers can act as if they are secondary servers to the Active Directory–integrated servers. When transfers are made between two DNS servers running on Windows 2000 servers, the information

> **NOTE**
>
> **BIND Versions** Turning off compression is only required for BIND version 4.9.4 or earlier. This is not likely to be a requirement because you need BIND 4.9.6 as a minimum to support SRV resource records and 8.1.2 for full dynamic update compatibility with Windows 2000.

that is transferred is compressed. This causes a transfer to a non-Windows 2000 server to fail. This option can be turned off in the DNS snap-in using Step by Step 23.9.

ON THE CD

Step by Step 23.9, "Configuring Windows 2000 DNS for Old BIND Secondary Servers," covers configuration for old BIND secondary servers. See the file **Chapter23-09StepbyStep.pdf** in the CD's **Chapter23\StepbyStep** directory.

Even if this option is set correctly, there might be problems if the server receiving the records is not able to understand some of the records. For example, if the server does not support SRV records, these records could show up incorrectly or could cause the transfer to fail.

TROUBLESHOOTING DNS

Because the DNS service is required for Active Directory to function, you need to know how to troubleshoot. Several tools, in addition to the DNS snap-in, can be used to troubleshoot DNS problems. The following sections look at these tools.

Cannot Create Dynamic Entries

There are a couple fairly simple items you should check when you are troubleshooting a DNS server problem if you cannot create your dynamic entries on the server. These items are presented in the following sections.

Security

The first thing you should check is whether the computer is allowed to add entries dynamically to the DNS server. This is controlled under the zone properties on the Security tab.

The key settings to look for here are the Authenticated Users and Everyone. The Authenticated Users should be allowed to create child objects. This might sound strange because the user will log on long after the computer starts. Remember that computers also have accounts and are considered to be part of Authenticated Users; it is the computer account that will be used to update the information. The Everyone group should have permissions to Read so that users will be able to query the DNS server.

Wrong DNS Server

You should check the DNS configuration to make sure that the client is pointing at a DNS server that supports dynamic updates or is a secondary server to one that does. You should also make sure that the domain name entered is correct and that it matches a domain on the server with which you are attempting to register.

DNS Snap-in

The DNS snap-in provides a basic testing tool for the DNS service as well as the capability to enable logging. These options can be found by opening the server properties in the DNS Manger. Two tabs can be of use when trying to troubleshoot a DNS problem: Logging and Monitoring.

Logging

On the Logging tab, you can turn on logging options that enable you to log the activity of the DNS server. There are several different items that you log:

- ◆ **Query.** This logs queries received by the server.
- ◆ **Notify.** This logs notifications that the server receives from other DNS servers.
- ◆ **Update.** This logs the dynamic update requests received from clients.
- ◆ **Questions.** This logs the information portion of the standard query packets sent to the server.

◆ **Answers.** This option logs the information portion of the standard response packets returned by the server.

◆ **Send.** This logs the number of iterative queries sent by the server.

◆ **Receive.** This logs the number of iterative queries received by the server.

◆ **UDP.** This logs the number of requests received using the User Datagram Protocol (UDP).

◆ **TCP.** This logs the number of requests received using the Transmission Control Protocol (TCP).

◆ **Full Packets.** This logs the number of full packets sent or received by the server.

◆ **Write Through.** This logs the number of records written by the DNS server to the zone file.

The log files can be found in the `c:\winnt\system32\dns` directory by default. This allows you to see what the service is or is not doing with the requests it receives.

Monitoring

The Monitoring tab enables you to test the DNS server to make sure that it is able to function correctly. You can select the test type, simple or recursive, and then can either choose the Test Now button or choose to have the test performed on an ongoing basis.

Using NSLOOKUP

The NSLOOKUP command is actually a fairly complex command that has both a command line and an interactive interface. For the purposes of quick testing, it is sufficient to understand the command line. There are two main types of queries you will send using the NSLOOKUP command: forward and reverse queries.

Most of the time, you will send a basic forward lookup query in which you will attempt to resolve a name from a client to ensure that the DNS server is able to find the client. There are a couple results to the basic query:

◆ The host is found, but you receive timeout errors. This is common if the reverse lookup zone doesn't have an entry for the DNS server or if there is no reverse lookup zone at all.

◆ The host is resolved with the full FQDN but not with the name alone. This is normally a result of an incorrect configuration on the client. Make sure the DNS setting includes the correct domain name information.

The basic query sent to the DNS server cyclops.scrimtech.com looks like this:

```
C:\>nslookup behemoth.scrimtech.local
Server:  cyclops.scrimtech.com
Address:  24.142.192.45

Name:    behemoth.scrimtech.local
Addresses:  10.10.10.200, 24.112.93.248
```

The other type of query is the reverse query. This can be helpful if you cannot find a host that you know exists. By querying the IP address of the known host, you will be able to tell what name is being associated with the host, as in the following example:

```
C:\>nslookup 207.236.145.38
Server:  cyclops.scrimtech.com
Address:  24.142.192.45

Name:    virgile.hq.newroma.com
Address:  207.236.145.38
```

Using IPCONFIG

The IPCONFIG command has been revamped from NT 4.0 to include three new switches that affect the interaction with DNS. These switches, as well as /ALL, can be useful when you are attempting to troubleshoot DNS problems.

◆ **/ALL.** This provides you with information about the configuration of each network connection on your computer including the DNS server used by each of the cards.

◆ **/FLUSHDNS.** This clears all the cached information you have received from the DNS servers. You can try this to force the station to reread the information from the DNS server.

◆ **/REGISTERDNS.** This renews any DHCP leases you currently have and also reregisters all the dynamic entries you have created on the DNS server.

◆ **/DISPLAYDNS.** This shows the entries currently in cache from the DNS server. This enables you to ensure that the DNS server is providing the correct information.

Starting and Stopping Netlogon

If you remember the review of the NETLOGON.DNS file in the section "Changes in Zones Used for Active Directory," there are many entries added dynamically to the DNS server by the Netlogon service. You can quickly reregister this information by stopping and starting the Netlogon service.

CASE STUDY: IMPLEMENTING DNS FOR SUNSHINE BREWING

ESSENCE OF THE CASE

As you look at the problems involved, you will see a few key issues. The following are the main issues:

▶ There are some locations that have slow links.

▶ The locations of the laptop computers used by the Executive and Sales users move and change IP addresses.

▶ There are five domains for which you need to provide resolution.

▶ Resolution for external addresses needs to be provided.

▶ The server addresses tend to remain static.

SCENARIO

In this chapter, you learned about DNS and how it is used in the Windows 2000 Active Directory. Now that you have some knowledge on the subject, it is time to see how it can be applied to a real-world situation. In this case study, you will see how DNS will be configured in the SunShine Brewing company.

Before you can install Active Directory, before you create your first user, you need to make sure that you have a working DNS structure. As you will recall from the case study in Chapter 1, "Installing Windows 2000 Professional," the network designers have broken the organization down into what will become five different domains. You now need to consider the practical side of the design and look at how you will ensure that name resolution can take place across all the domains and all the locations that make up SunShine Brewing.

CASE STUDY: IMPLEMENTING DNS FOR SUNSHINE BREWING

ESSENCE OF THE CASE

▶ Some of the systems on the network are UNIX-based and will not be Active Directory clients.

▶ Some of the internal applications are Web-based, and you need to be able to advertise these in DNS.

▶ You want computers to be dynamically registered.

▶ You need to support SRV records.

▶ You need to control the replication.

ANALYSIS

The best choice in this case is an Active Directory–integrated zone for the root domain. The other domains will be child domains of this domain.

It is obvious that you need to create a domain that Active Directory can use. In this case, Windows 2000 DNS servers that are also domain controllers handle the DNS. The first server is installed, and DNS is loaded on the server. That server also will be the first server installed on your tree. After you install Active Directory, you convert the zone to Active Directory integrated and ensure that DNS is installed on all the domain controllers for the root domain.

This requires that you install a domain controller for the root domain in every location. On the upside, however, is the fact that an Active Directory–integrated domain uses multiple master replication. This means a user that dials into the Victoria office registers with the domain name server in that office rather than trying to register with the one in Ottawa. Further, you can control replication using the same site links that are created to control all the other forms of replication.

Because the only addresses that change tend to be those of the laptop users, the fact that replication is not happening instantly shouldn't cause any problem. If you configure the zone with a longer refresh interval, you might find the laptop users are on and off again before their entries have to be replicated anyway.

continues

CASE STUDY: IMPLEMENTING DNS FOR SUNSHINE BREWING

continued

Because you can add other records to an Active Directory–integrated zone, the requirements of the UNIX servers and the Web-based network applications are handled.

All that remains is to handle the resolution of the external addresses. This can be handled simply by configuring the DNS server to forward the requests through the firewall to a caching only server or to an ISP's DNS server external to your network. This means that the domain controller running the Active Directory–integrated zone is not exposed but is still able to resolve external addresses.

CHAPTER SUMMARY

KEY TERMS

- Active Directory integrated
- Caching server
- Dynamic Host Configuration Protocol
- Dynamic updates
- Forward lookup
- Fully qualified domain name (FQDN)
- Iterative query
- LDAP
- Master server
- Name server
- Namespace
- Netlogon
- Notification
- NSLOOKUP
- Primary server
- Recursive query
- Resolver
- Reverse lookup
- Scavenging
- Secondary server
- Service records (SRV)
- Start of Authority (SOA)
- Time-to-Live
- Windows Internet Naming System
- Zone
- Zone transfer

Although by no means a full discussion of the DNS service that is part of Windows 2000, this chapter has presented the key information you need to know to make the DNS service work with Active Directory. The key points you need to know as you move on to the installation of Active Directory include

◆ For Active Directory to function, the DNS server must support SRV records and should support dynamic updates.

◆ When a zone is integrated with Active Directory, the zone information is stored in Active Directory, which will then handle security and replication.

◆ Several tools can be used to help troubleshoot DNS including the DNS snap-in, IPCONFIG, and NSLOOKUP.

APPLY YOUR KNOWLEDGE

Review Questions

1. How are dynamic entries created on the DNS server?

2. What is the filename of the file containing the entries that the Netlogon service will register?

3. What are the two types of transfers that can take place between DNS servers configured with standard zones?

4. How are DNS entries replicated in the Active Directory–integrated mode?

5. What type of record must a DNS server support if it will be used by Active Directory?

6. What is the difference between a master server and primary server?

Answers to Review Questions

1. Dynamic updates can be made on the DNS server either by a client capable of performing the update or by the DHCP server that provided the client with the address. See the section "The Update Process."

2. The Netlogon service on each domain controller will create a series of entries in the DNS server that will enable the clients to locate the services it provides on the network. These entries are stored in a file called NETLOGON.DNS that is located in the `systemroot\system32\dns directory`. See the section "Integrating DNS and Active Directory."

3. In Windows 2000, the DNS server supports both normal or full transfers (AFXR) as well as incremental transfers (IFXR) based on the serial number of the zone file located on the servers. See the section "Transferring Zone Information."

4. If a zone is configured as Active Directory integrated, replication will be handled by Active Directory, which defaults to every 5 minutes within a site and is controlled by the site links between sites. The DNS server(s) will poll every 15 minutes by default for updates to the information. See the section "Transferring Zone Information."

5. For a DNS server to work with Active Directory, it must support SRV, service locator, records. In addition, it should, but does not need to, support dynamic updates. See the section "Integrating DNS and Active Directory."

6. The primary server contains the original, write-enabled zone file. This file is copied to secondary servers throughout an enterprise. In some cases, a secondary server will get its copy of the zone file from another secondary, which then becomes its master server. See the section "Transferring Zone Information."

ON THE CD

This book's companion CD contains specially designed supplemental material to help you understand how well you know the concepts and skills you learned in this chapter. You'll find related exercises and exam questions and answers. See the file **Chapter23ApplyYourKnowledge.pdf** in the CD's **Chapter23\ApplyYourKnowledge** directory.

Suggested Readings and Resources

1. *Windows 2000 Server Resource Kit TCP/IP Core Networking Guide.* Microsoft, 2000.

2. *Windows 2000 Domain Name System Overview.* White paper. Microsoft, 2000.

3. Scrimger, Rob and Kelli Adams. *MCSE Training Guide: TCP/IP 2nd Edition.* New Riders Publishing, 1999.

4. Komar, Brian. *Sams Teach Yourself TCP/IP Network Administration in 21 Days.* Sams Publishing, 1998.

The first part of this chapter concentrates on the logical structure of Active Directory. The last part of the chapter shows you how to create a root domain.

Install, configure, and troubleshoot the components of Active Directory.

- **Install Active Directory.**

- **Verify Active Directory installation.**

- **Create sites.**

- **Create subnets.**

- **Create connection objects.**

- **Create site links.**

- **Create site link bridges.**

- **Move server objects between sites.**

- **Create global catalog servers.**

▶ This objective is included primarily to make sure you can install Active Directory and verify that it is installed. This objective also is included to ensure that you can configure a domain to match the physical network. You should know the requirements for installation, primarily the DNS server requirements. You should also understand the changes made to the system due to the installation.

The domain configuration aspect of this objective requires that you know how to set up Active Directory based on the network. This includes creating sites, which are collections of subnets, and then making sure replication is possible using site links and site link bridges. You also need to know how to create a connection object. Using connection objects, you can override the system-generated connections. Finally, you need to know how to create a global catalog server.

CHAPTER 24

Building Your Active Directory Structure

Manage and troubleshoot Active Directory replication.

- **Manage intrasite replication.**

- **Manage intersite replication.**

▶ This objective is included to ensure that you are familiar with the replication process and are able to recognize and resolve replication issues. An important aspect of managing and troubleshooting Active Directory replication includes understanding the Knowledge Consistency Checker (KCC) and how it works with site links to build the replication topology.

STUDY STRATEGIES

▶ This chapter covers three main topics: logical structure, physical structure, and replication. You should understand how these work together to move information around an Active Directory network. Most notably, you should pay attention to the following:

- The installation of domain controllers and their differences, depending on where they are logically located
- The creation and use of sites and site links
- The role and function of the Knowledge Consistency Checker (KCC)
- The ways in which replication takes place and how replication works
- How to use global catalog servers and where they should be placed

INTRODUCTION

In this chapter, you look at how to roll out the domain controllers and how to configure replication between these domain controllers. Keeping your organization running smoothly requires the replication of information about both the structure of and the objects in Active Directory.

UNDERSTANDING ACTIVE DIRECTORY'S LOGICAL STRUCTURE

The discussion begins with a look at domains and the purpose of domains, which are the building blocks of the logical structure. Then the discussion turns to the ways in which you can tie domains together into trees and, eventually, how trees can expand to make a forest.

Domains

The basic unit of Active Directory is the domain. By breaking your enterprise into different domains, you can achieve several benefits:

♦ Domains enable you to organize objects within a single department or a single location. Within the domain, all information about the objects is available.

♦ Domains act as a security boundary; domain administrators can have complete control over all the resources within the domain.

♦ Domain objects can be made available to other domains, and each object can be published in Active Directory.

♦ Domain names follow the DNS naming structure. This permits an infinite number of child domains.

♦ Domains enable you to control replication; objects stored in the domain are fully replicated only to other domain controllers in the domain.

There are two ways to create Active Directory domains: by upgrading a Windows NT 4.0 domain or by installing a Windows 2000 Server and then promoting it to be a domain controller.

After you have created a root domain, you can then move on to create trees. A *tree* always starts with the root domain, but then can branch out to include other domains. This provides you with the first level of hierarchies within Active Directory.

Trees and Forests

To tie the domains together, you need to organize them into a logical structure known as a *forest*.

The DNS hierarchy is used in Windows 2000 to tie the various domains together and to create the domain tree. If you start with a domain such as Widgets.com, for example, you could create a single domain, that contains all the objects in your enterprise. However, this might not be practical if your organization has offices in two major geographical areas and each area works independently from the other. In this case, you might opt to create separate domains that could be independently managed. In Figure 24.1, you will notice that there is a Widgets.com, an East.Widgets.com, and a West.Widgets.com. In this case, the top domain is a pointer to one or the other of the lower-level domains.

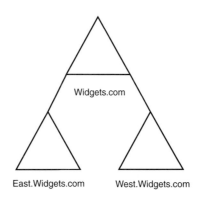

FIGURE 24.1
A sample domain tree for Widgets.com broken down using geography.

If you broke down the organization along the lines of an organizational chart, the tree might look more like Figure 24.2. In this figure, there is a domain for sales and marketing, a domain for logistics, and a domain for research and development. The administration and other support roles, in this case, are in the top-level domain.

There are some cases, however, in which a domain tree will not work. In cases where different parts of the organization need to have separate public identities, you cannot use the same structure if the internal naming is to mirror the external nature. In a case such as this, you might have more than one tree. However, it is still important to keep the three common elements: shared schema, shared configuration, and the global catalog. To do this, one of the domains becomes the root of the enterprise. The other domains are members of the same forest even though their names look different. In Figure 24.3, stuff.com has been added. Convention dictates that the line joining the new tree to the forest is drawn to the top of the root to show that it is not just a child domain.

From here, you could add children to stuff.com (see Figure 24.4).

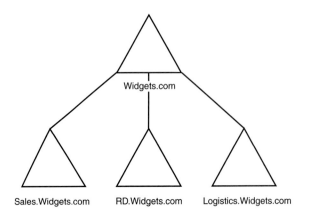

FIGURE 24.2

A sample domain tree for Widgets.com broken down by function.

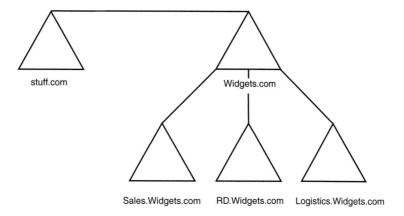

FIGURE 24.3
A sample domain forest.

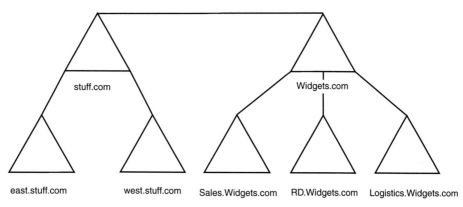

FIGURE 24.4
An expanded domain forest.

After you have installed the first domain controller for the first domain, you can begin to build the hierarchy by using DCPROMO to create other domain controllers. During the promotion, you have the option of creating new domain controllers in the existing domain, a new controller for a new child domain, or a new root controller for a new tree in the forest.

The combination of trees and forests provides you absolute flexibility in the design of your domain structure and, therefore, in the design of your Active Directory.

Organizational Units

A new feature of Windows 2000 gives you the ability to delegate control of part of a domain to a user or a group of users. This is achieved through the use of organizational units. An organizational unit is a container within Active Directory that you create. After you create the container, you can move computers, users, and other objects into the container.

After this is accomplished, you could delegate control of those objects in the container to a set of users or groups. As a domain administrator, you would still have control, but the people you delegate can also control these objects. This enables you to create workgroup administrators who can handle a limited section of your domain.

Figure 24.5 shows an example of how the Widgets.com network can fit in a single domain while still providing local administrators to deal with a group of users and computers.

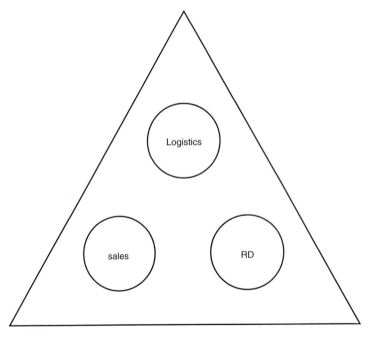

FIGURE 24.5
The Widgets.com network designed using organizational units.

You can even create organizational units within another organizational unit. This enables you to create a hierarchy of organizational units within a domain.

You need to decide for your organization whether you should use domains or organizational units to manage users, computers, and the other objects in Active Directory. The following guidelines should be used to decide whether to use domains or organizational units:

◆ Use domains if the organization is one in which different users and resources are managed by completely different sets of administrators or in cases where different areas of the organization have dissimilar account policy settings.

◆ Use domains for a network in which parts of the network are separated by a slow link. This can also be accomplished using sites, which you see later in the section "Working in the Physical Network."

◆ Use organizational units to mimic the structure of your organization.

◆ Use organizational units to delegate administrative control over smaller groups of users, groups, and other objects.

◆ Use organizational units if this particular part of your company is likely to change later.

As you can see, the logical structure of Active Directory is used to build a hierarchy that enables you to organize users within any size of organization. Using domains, you can create security and replication boundaries, and then using organizational units, you can further divide domains into manageable sections.

INSTALLING THE FIRST DOMAIN

Install, configure, and troubleshoot the components of Active Directory.

• **Install Active Directory.**

Now that you are familiar with the logical structure of Active Directory, it is time to look at the installation of Active Directory.

The installation is a simple process. Before beginning installation, however, you will want to have planned the structure of your enterprise.

Prerequisites

As you have probably guessed, a number of necessary items and tasks need to be completed before you install Active Directory. The following is a list of the key items that need to be in place:

◆ You need to have a Windows 2000 Server installed and running.

◆ You should have a DNS server installed with a forward lookup zone configured. The DNS server must support SRV (service) records and should allow dynamic updates and standard zones incremental transfers.

◆ You need to be sure that the correct DNS server is selected for the computer you are making a domain controller and that the name of the computer is correct. The computer also needs to have TCP/IP installed and correctly functioning.

◆ You need to be sure that you have an NTFS partition on the computer you are making into a domain controller. You also need to have enough space for the directory (1GB is recommended).

◆ You need to be sure that the system time zone is correct. You also need to be sure that the correct time is set on the system.

In addition to the physical systems in place to install the domain controller, you need to know the name of the domain controller to install. You also need to know the domain name for the domain you are creating.

> **N O T E**
>
> **Do You Need to Preconfigure the DNS Server?** Technically, the answer is no. You can choose to have the DCPROMO utility configure the current server to be the DNS server. The only issue is that you may already have a DNS infrastructure that you want to use.

Naming Your Domain

There are several different ways you can decide to name the domain. The three main choices are as follows:

◆ Use your organization's current Internet domain name. This means that your internal and external identities would be the same, and the risk is that your Active Directory structure could be exposed to the public Internet.

◆ Use a subdomain under your existing Internet domain. In other words, create something like AD.Widgets.com as the starting point for the Active Directory. This makes it easier to separate the public and private structure. However, this approach adds complexity to the naming system.

◆ Use a totally separate name internally. This means you can keep the public and private parts of the network completely separate. Microsoft suggests that you can use .local if you plan to separate the internal and external naming of the organization. You might use Widgets.com for the Internet and Widgets.local for the Active Directory.

The domain name, of course, should be decided before you begin to perform the installations. Naming domains probably will require a lot of discussion. Assuming you have all the required information and the prerequisites are met, it is time to install Active Directory.

The Installation Process

The installation of Active Directory is accomplished by using the Active Directory Installation Wizard or DCPROMO command. This Wizard asks you all the necessary questions to determine the configuration of the new domain controller. The installation of the root domain is very straightforward, and the complete process is outlined in Step by Step 24.1.

ON THE CD

Step by Step 24.1, "Installing Active Directory," shows the installation of the root domain. See the file **Chapter24-01StepbyStep.pdf** in the CD's **Chapter24\StepbyStep** directory.

At this point, Active Directory is installed. After the system has restarted, you might want to verify the installation.

Verifying the Installation

Install, configure, and troubleshoot the components of Active Directory.

- **Verify Active Directory installation.**

After the installation of Active Directory, you should verify that the installation worked and that the system is running correctly. This ensures that the other servers you add to the domain and the other domains you add to the tree will install correctly.

It is a fairly simple matter to verify that Active Directory is installed on the computer. All you need to do is verify that the following options are now in the Administrative Tools folder on the Start menu:

◆ **Active Directory Users and Computer.** This is used to manage users and computers as well as organizational units within your domain.

◆ **Active Directory Domains and Trusts.** This is used to manage domains and trust relationships between domains.

◆ **Active Directory Sites and Services.** This is used to configure sites, subnets, and replication between sites.

You can also use Step by Step 24.2 to verify that Active Directory is installed.

ON THE CD

Step by Step 24.2, "Verifying that Active Directory Is Installed," verifies that Active Directory is installed. See the file **Chapter24-02StepbyStep.pdf** in the CD's **Chapter24\StepbyStep** directory.

Getting the first domain controller installed and running correctly is critical, because all the other installations need to communicate with this system as they proceed.

NOTE

Verify the DNS Server   When the new domain controller has rebooted, it is always a good idea to verify that the DNS server has recorded the new SRV resource records registered by the domain controller. If the SRV resource records do not appear, you can force their registration by stopping and starting the NETLOGON service.

WARNING

SRV Resource Records Are Required   You cannot install any additional domain controllers into the domain until the SRV resource records exist in DNS. The SRV resource records are used to locate an existing domain controller in the domain.

OTHER INSTALLATIONS

Now that you have a working domain controller, you will want to add at least one other domain controller for redundancy. In most cases, you will add several more domain controllers to a domain. In addition, you need to be able to add other domains to your domain tree or more trees to the forest. This section looks at these types of installations.

Adding a Domain Controller

To provide redundancy and load balancing, you need to add more domain controllers to the domains you create. The process for adding a domain controller is straightforward. You begin with a computer with Windows 2000 Server and then perform Step by Step 24.3.

ON THE CD

Step by Step 24.3, "Adding a Domain Controller to an Existing Domain," adds a domain controller. See the file **Chapter24-03StepbyStep.pdf** in the CD's **Chapter24\StepbyStep** directory.

You should now be able to add a domain controller to an existing domain. Using multiple domain controllers is important for redundancy and for load balancing.

Adding a Child Domain

As you build the Active Directory structure for your organization, you may need to add child domains. The process is more like creating a new domain than adding a domain controller. Step by Step 24.4 describes the process.

ON THE CD

Step by Step 24.4, "Adding a Child Domain to a Domain Tree," adds child domains. See the file **Chapter24-04StepbyStep.pdf** in the CD's **Chapter24\StepbyStep** directory.

Remember that child domains act as boundaries for replication and security. Child domains become part of the same name space. In some cases, this isn't what you require, and you need to create a new tree making a forest.

Creating a Forest

Creating a forest is the final setup to explore. Your internal organization will probably use one naming scheme, so creating a forest is not a common event. In any case, the process is almost identical to that of adding a child domain. Step by Step 24.5 helps you create a forest.

ON THE CD

Step by Step 24.5, "Adding a Root Server in a Forest," helps you create a forest. See the file **Chapter24-05StepbyStep.pdf** in the CD's **Chapter24\StepbyStep** directory.

If you put hundreds of domain controllers in a single domain, perhaps in different locations, you will still have a replication problem. This problem is addressed by using sites that enable you to further control replication. This requires addressing the physical network.

WORKING IN THE PHYSICAL NETWORK

The physical parts of Active Directory—sites and subnets—are used to control replication. By creating sites and later site links, you are able to determine at what times replication can occur and how often during that period it will happen.

One of the main supporting components of Active Directory is the TCP/IP protocol. TCP/IP enables you to break your enterprise into sites and to control replication between sites.

The following are the properties you can set on each tab:

◆ **Site.** Enter a description for the site on this tab.

◆ **Location.** Enter a location for the site.

◆ **Object.** Enables you to see the full name of the object and other details, such as when it was created. There is nothing you can edit on this tab.

◆ **Security.** Enables you to set the security for the object in Active Directory. The default security enables Administrators to manage the site and enables others to read the information.

◆ **Group Policy.** Enables you to assign Group Policies to the site and create and modify the policies.

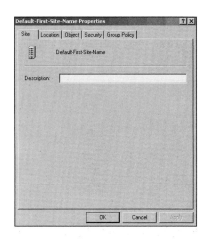

FIGURE 24.6
The site Properties dialog box.

Working with Subnets

Install, configure, and troubleshoot the components of Active Directory.

• **Create subnets.**

Now that you can create and delete sites, you need to be able to populate the sites. This is a matter of deciding which subnets should be in a site and creating them in Active Directory. Decisions about which subnets to include depend on the network design and how you actually control the location of objects in Active Directory.

When you add a new TCP/IP subnet to your network, you should immediately create a new subnet in Active Directory Sites and Services. Adding a subnet is very simple, as you will see in Step by Step 24.9.

ON THE CD

Step by Step 24.9, "Creating a Subnet in Active Directory," adds a subnet. See the file **Chapter24-09StepbyStep.pdf** in the CD's **Chapter24\StepbyStep** directory.

Deleting a subnet is as simple as adding a subnet. Follow Step by Step 24.10 to delete a subnet.

Likewise, when a subnet has been removed from the network, there is no longer a need for the subnet to be referenced in Active Directory Sites and Services.

ON THE CD

Step by Step 24.10, "Deleting a Subnet," show how to delete a subnet. See the file **Chapter24-10StepbyStep.pdf** in the CD's **Chapter24\StepbyStep** directory.

Although you can delete subnets, it is far more common to move a subnet to a different site. This happens as the network changes and the distribution of users and servers changes.

The steps for moving a subnet are, again, very simple, as shown in Step by Step 24.11.

ON THE CD

Step by Step 24.11, "Moving a Subnet to Another Site," show how to move a subnet. See the file **Chapter24-11StepbyStep.pdf** in the CD's **Chapter24\StepbyStep** directory.

In most cases, even moving subnets is a rare occurrence. Moving subnets happens only when the physical network is reorganized.

As you can see, there are other tabs in this dialog box. The following list describes the other options you can set on each tab:

- ◆ **Subnet.** Enables you to enter a description for the subnet and move it to another site.

- ◆ **Location.** Enables you to enter a location for the subnet.

- ◆ **Object.** Enables you to see the full name of the object and other details, such as when it was created.

- ◆ **Security.** Enables you to set the security for the object in Active Directory. The default security enables Administrators to manage the site and enables others to read the information.

REPLICATING ACTIVE DIRECTORY INFORMATION

Replication is the process of reading information from one system and copying it to another system. In Windows 2000, replication is a very important element. Updates to Active Directory can occur at any domain controller in the domain.

In addition to the multiple master replication model for the domain objects, there is additional information that needs to be replicated throughout the organization. The following is a list of the information that needs to be replicated:

◆ **Schema information.** The schema defines all attributes and classes that exist in Active Directory. Within a forest, there exists a single schema that is replicated to all domain controllers in the forest.

◆ **Configuration information.** The configuration container includes the overall design of the entire enterprise. It includes the domains, their names, and where they fit into the hierarchy. It also includes other information, such as the replication topology. This information is used by all the domain controllers and therefore is replicated to all domain controllers.

◆ **Domain data.** This is the information you store about the objects making up your domain. All the information is replicated within a domain by the domain controllers. The global catalog servers throughout the enterprise replicate a subset of the information.

As you can see, there are two levels of replication. There is the replication within a domain and the replication for the enterprise.

Global catalog servers require that replication include all objects in the forest, although only a partial list of attributes is replicated for objects from other domains in the forest. At least one global catalog server is required in the enterprise. There should also be one global catalog server for each domain and for each site in the enterprise.

Now that you know what is replicated, we will look at how replication works.

How Replication Works

Replication is based on the Update Sequence Number (USN) in Active Directory. The USN tracks, for each domain controller, the number of changes it has made to its version of the directory. As a change is made, the current USN is assigned to the object, and the USN for the domain controller is incremented.

Each domain controller keeps track of its own USN and the USNs for its replication partners. Periodically (every five minutes by default), the server checks for changes on its replication partners. Requesting any changes since the last known USN for the partner accomplishes this check. The partner can then send all the changes since the USN number.

A domain controller could be offline for a period of time, and after it comes back, be able to get back up-to-date quickly.

There is a danger here. Assume a domain controller receives an update. It makes the change and then updates its USN. The domain controller that made the change originally now requests the USN for the server that got the change. Its USN is updated, so the change is requested. The system that originated the change now has its own change back. If the system made the change and updated its USN, this whole cycle repeats ad infinitum.

To avoid this scenario, Active Directory tracks the number of originating writes that have occurred for each attribute. The number of times a user changed the value, rather than the number of times it was changed using replication, is tracked. In the preceding case, the first system in which the change was made finds that it has the correct originating write value and will not make the change.

There is also the possibility that two different users could be changing the same attribute of the same object at the same time on two different controllers. When these changes both start to replicate, a conflict will be detected. Windows 2000 will choose the change with the newer timestamp (the more recent change) to resolve the conflict. If the two changes were made at the same millisecond, the change with the higher Globally Unique Identifier (GUID) wins.

Now that you have seen the theory of replication, it is time to see how the replication is configured within a site and between sites.

Replication Within a Site

Manage and troubleshoot Active Directory replication.

- **Manage intrasite replication.**

Although there is little you need to do with intrasite replication, it is important for you to understand how it works and the components involved. This serves as a basis for intersite replication.

Replication within a site is handled by Active Directory. There is no need for you to take any action. The KCC evaluates the domain controllers in the site and automatically creates a replication topology. In general, the KCC configures connections so that each domain controller replicates with at least two other domain controllers.

The KCC automatically adjusts the replication topology as the network conditions change. As domain controllers are added or removed, the KCC continues to make sure that each domain controller replicates with at least two others. Within a site, replication does not use compression, and in some cases (such as a password change), the replication is completed on an immediate basis.

Replication within a site is quite easy to work with; there is nothing to do. The KCC does most of the work for you by creating the correct connection objects to link all your servers together.

Connection Objects

Install, configure, and troubleshoot the components of Active Directory.

- **Create connection objects.**

Connection objects serve as the backbone for replication; they define network paths through which replication can occur. You need to know what these are and how they are defined; you should also be able to define them yourself.

The KCC essentially manages the replication within a site by creating connection objects between the various domain controllers in the site. The KCC also creates connection objects between sites where required.

A connection represents a permanent or temporary network path that can be used for replication. Normally, you do not create the connection objects within a site yourself. It is assumed that all the paths between servers are of equal speed, so the KCC should be able to handle creating the connection objects.

You can create connections within a site. You can also edit the connections created by the KCC; however, you should be careful when doing this. In the case of a connection that you create, the connection is never evaluated by the KCC and is never deleted until you do so. This could cause problems if your network changes and you neglect to remove the connection you created. In cases in which you edit the connection that the KCC makes, the changes you make will be lost when the KCC next updates the connections.

The main reason you might want to create a connection object is to specify the bridgehead servers that will be used to link to sites. The bridgehead servers will be the main method of replication across a site link. To create a connection object, follow Step by Step 24.12.

ON THE CD

Step by Step 24.12, "Creating a Connection Object Manually," shows how to create a connection object. See the file **Chapter24-12StepbyStep.pdf** in the CD's **Chapter24\StepbyStep** directory.

Replication Between Sites

Manage and troubleshoot Active Directory replication.

• **Manage intersite replication.**

The capability to manage intersite replication is critical for administrators on Windows 2000 networks. Without this capability, the replication would easily saturate some WAN connections and make Windows 2000 Active Directory unmanageable.

Within a site, Active Directory assumes a high-speed connection and, to save processing time, does not compress the data. Between-site bandwidth is assumed to be lower. Therefore, Active Directory compresses the data being transferred between sites.

Active Directory also enables the replication between the sites to be scheduled so that it happens only during scheduled hours. During those hours, you still have the option of changing the interval of the replication. Before you can set this up, you need to move a domain controller to another site. Then you need to create a connection between that domain controller and one in another site.

Because replication takes place between domain controllers, you need to add domain controllers to the site to which they physically belong. Clients within a site also look for a domain controller in the site to log on to, and by moving a domain controller to the site, you decrease the logon times, increasing satisfaction with the network.

Moving Domain Controllers

Install, configure, and troubleshoot the components of Active Directory.

- **Move server objects between sites.**

The capability to control replication and to ensure that users are able to log on within a reasonable amount of time requires that you be able to locate domain controllers near the users. This requires that you occasionally move a domain controller between sites.

The purposes of a site are to help manage the replication between domain controllers and to manage replication across slow network links. In addition to creating the site and adding subnets to that site, you need to move domain controllers into the site.

To move a domain controller, follow Step by Step 24.13.

ON THE CD

Step by Step 24.13, " Moving a Domain Controller," show how to move a domain controller. See the file **Chapter24-13StepbyStep. pdf** in the CD's **Chapter24\StepbyStep** directory.

Now that you have moved the domain controllers to different sites, you need to create a site link between the sites. This provides the path through which replication to this site takes place.

Connecting Sites

Install, configure, and troubleshoot the components of Active Directory.

- **Create site links**

The key to controlling replication is to create sites. Sites enable you to create site links that enable you to control when a link exists and how often replication can take place while the link is available. Multiple site links can be used to create different replication schedules at different times or to provide redundant links with higher costs.

Now that you have moved the domain controllers to different sites, you need to create a site link between the sites. This provides the path through which replication to this site takes place.

By creating and configuring site links, you provide the KCC with information about what connection objects to create to replicate directory data. Site links indicate where connection objects should be created. Connection objects use the network to exchange directory information.

Follow Step by Step 24.14 to create a site link.

ON THE CD

Step by Step 24.14, "Creating a Site Link," show how to creates a site link. See the file **Chapter24-14StepbyStep.pdf** in the CD's **Chapter24\StepbyStep** directory.

When creating site links, you have the option of using either IP or SMTP as the transport protocol for the site link:

- ◆ **SMTP replication.** SMTP can be used only for replication between different domains. If a single domain encompasses multiple sites, domain replication cannot use SMTP.

   SMTP is asynchronous, meaning it typically ignores all schedules. Beware if you choose to use SMTP over site links; you must install and configure an enterprise Certification Authority (CA). The CA signs SMTP messages that are exchanged between domain controllers, ensuring the authenticity of directory updates.

◆ **IP replication.** IP replication uses Remote Procedure Calls (RPC) for replication. This is the same for both intersite and intrasite replication.

After the site link is created, you can go back and set the other properties of the site link. You do this by locating the site link in the IP or SMTP folder and then bringing up the properties of the link.

The General tab on the properties sheet sets the properties for the site link. There are also Object and Security tabs, which are the same as the tabs previously discussed. These are the items you can configure:

◆ **Description.** This is a description of the link for your information.

◆ **Site in this Site Link.** This area can be used to add domain controllers to and remove them from a site link.

◆ **Cost.** This is a relative value, and it is used by Active Directory to decide what route to use when replicating information. The cheapest available route is used based on the overall cost.

◆ **Replicate Every.** This is the interval at which replication takes place over this link.

◆ **Change Schedule.** This button enables you to change when the site link is available for replication. Replication during the period that the link is available occurs at a frequency determined by the interval.

Bridgehead Servers

A bridgehead server is the main server used for intersite replication. You can configure a bridgehead server for each site you create for each of the intersite replication protocols. This enables you to control which server in a site is used to replicate information to other servers. Step by Step 24.15 walks you through the configuration of a bridgehead server.

ON THE CD

Step by Step 24.15, "Configuring a Server as a Bridgehead Server," walks you through the configuration of a bridgehead server. See the file **Chapter24-15StepbyStep.pdf** in the CD's **Chapter24\ StepbyStep** directory.

The capability to configure a server as a bridgehead server gives you greater control over the resources used for replication between two sites or in cases such as a site link bridge between multiple sites.

Site Link Bridges

Install, configure, and troubleshoot the components of Active Directory.

- **Create site link bridges.**

In many cases, you do not need to deal with site link bridges. By default, all site links are automatically bridged, a property known as *transitive site links*. In some cases, you will want to control through which sites data can flow. In these cases, you need to create site link bridges.

By default, all the site links you create are bridged. This bridging enables all the sites to communicate with each other. If this is not physically possible because of the structure of your network, you need to disable the automatic bridging and create the appropriate site link bridges.

For example, consider Figure 24.7. You see three sites (1, 2, and 3) directly connected to each other. In this case, automatic bridging works fine. However, Site 4 is connected using a low-speed connection, so you would not want it to replicate with all the other sites. In this case, you would want Site 4 to replicate only with Site 1.

To resolve this replication problem, you turn off automatic bridging. Then create a site link containing the three sites that are directly connected. Create a second site link between Site 1 and Site 4. Then create a site link bridge that gives Active Directory a way to get information from Sites 2 and 3 to Site 4 through Site 1 and vice versa.

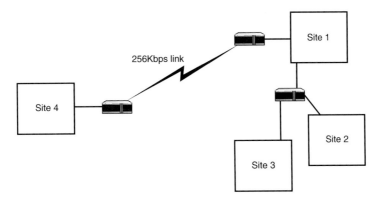

To disable the automatic bridging, follow Step by Step 24.16.

ON THE CD

Step by Step 24.16, "Disabling Transitive Site Links (Automatic Bridging)," show how to disable the automatic bridging. See the file **Chapter24-16StepbyStep.pdf** in the CD's **Chapter24\StepbyStep** directory.

On the General tab, notice that there is also an option to ignore all schedules. This option is used only to force changes to flow through, whether or not replication was currently scheduled.

After you ensure that transitive site links exist—in other words, that automatic bridging is off—you need to create the site link bridge (or bridges) as shown in Step by Step 24.17.

ON THE CD

Step by Step 24.17, "Creating a Site Link Bridge," demonstrates hot to create the site link bridge. See the file **Chapter24-17StepbyStep.pdf** in the CD's **Chapter24\StepbyStep** directory.

Global Catalog Servers

Install, configure, and troubleshoot the components of Active Directory.

- **Create global catalog servers**

Global catalog servers provide you the ability to query objects on a forestwide level. The global catalog contains a partial set of attributes for all objects within the forest. When a query is made against the entire forest, the query is directed to a global catalog server.

You should locate a global catalog server at each site defined in Active Directory. This ensures that a global catalog server on the local network handles requests made to a global catalog server, such as universal group membership. Step by Step 24.18 shows you how to make a domain controller a global catalog server.

ON THE CD

Step by Step 24.18, "Configuring a Server as a Global Catalog Server," shows you how to make a domain controller a global catalog server. See the file **Chapter24-18StepbyStep.pdf** in the CD's **Chapter24\StepbyStep** directory.

One of the key jobs of an administrator is to keep the directory information up-to-date and to ensure that all the domain controllers have the correct information. Replication makes this possible. You need to understand this for both the exam and real life.

CASE STUDY: INSTALLING AND CONFIGURING ACTIVE DIRECTORY

ESSENCE OF THE CASE

There are a few points that you need to consider as you look at this case:

▶ Some of the physical locations have a link to only one other location. Some form of backup link is needed.

▶ Some of the locations are large and probably need multiple controllers. These locations might require multiple sites.

▶ To ensure that locating objects around the world is possible and that users can log on from anywhere, global catalog servers are required at each site.

▶ Because the domains are divided by function instead of geography, each location requires at least one domain controller for each domain.

▶ The overall size of any domain is comparatively small. Combined with low turnover and infrequent password changes, there should be minimal replication.

▶ Because there are domain controllers from each domain local to the location, users are able to make changes that are reflected at their locality, meaning replication does not have to happen immediately.

SCENARIO

In this chapter, you have looked at the physical and logical configuration of Active Directory. In addition, you have seen how to install the domain controller and child domains and how to install another tree in the forest.

The other major topic discussed was replication. You should now understand the three partitions of Active Directory: schema, configuration, and domain. You should also understand how these partitions would be replicated.

Recall from the previous case studies that SunShine Brewing is located in 15 cities around the world, with some of those locations having multiple sites. You might also recall that the domain structure is to follow reporting lines instead of geography because of the different needs of the users around the world.

Now it is time to implement this in the real world and to look at the concerns and issues that will be faced.

The scenario is very simple. You need to install an Active Directory tree that spans the globe. In addition, you need to ensure that replication is able to keep all the domains in all the locations up-to-date without saturating the bandwidth between any of the locations.

With these facts in mind and considering the general purpose of the network, the following analysis presents a solution for this scenario.

continues

CASE STUDY: INSTALLING AND CONFIGURING ACTIVE DIRECTORY

continued

ANALYSIS

In looking at this scenario, there are a couple of factors driving the analysis. First, you need to ensure reliable replication. The replication, however, does not need to be any faster than the time it takes a user to physically move between two offices.

This being said, the shorter distances, such as Victoria to Los Angeles, or Ottawa to New York, or Paris to London, take over an hour in the air. This means you should aim for replication every three hours between the main sites and longer between the other sites, such as between Cape Town and Buenos Aries.

The other consideration with respect to replication is that not all the locations have a back link to another location and could become isolated if the main link goes down. To ensure that replication can continue in these cases, secondary sites links need to be configured between locations using the Internet and a virtual private network or SMTP as the intersite transport.

SMTP is a choice because the certificate server is able to create a certificate for you, but that handles only the replication. Because you also want to be able to move other traffic if the main link goes, a VPN makes more sense.

This leaves intersite replication within a location. This can be handled simply by having all the sites within a location use the same site link. Therefore, there is a site link per location. The replication within the site takes place using the defaults. In each location, one site is created to link the locations, and these sites are also part of a site link to at least one other site using the network and two more sites either using the network or a VPN connection. If site links are configured that use VPNs, the cost is set to double the value of the highest network-connected site link.

To control the replication, three hours is used as the interval for sites connected via T1 during the day. Another site link is created for each site that replicates once every hour overnight. The timing for other types of connections is based on the timing for T1 connections.

CHAPTER SUMMARY

This chapter provided opportunities for hands-on work with Active Directory. As you can see, the structure of Active Directory is basically organized into two parts: the logical and the physical designs. The logical design consists of organizational units that break down the administration of domains, domains that make up the root and branches of a tree, and trees that make up forests.

There is also the physical design that takes the enterprise and breaks this down into high-speed networks. On the physical side, there are multiple sites that make up the network and a Knowledge Consistency Checker (KCC) that tracks all the site links building the connections forming the replication topology. You have the option of creating your own connections and of modifying the replication topology using your own site link bridges. All these things are put into place to ensure your ability to replicate all the objects in your domain.

In addition, you need to create global catalog servers, typically one per site and one per domain. These global catalog servers replicate the enterprisewide information, such as the global catalog (a list of the objects from all domains with a subset of the attributes), the schema, and the configuration information.

KEY TERMS

- Child domain
- Configuration partition
- Connection objects
- DCPROMO
- Domain partition
- Forest
- Knowledge Consistency Checker
- Originating write
- Remote Procedure Call
- Schema partition
- Simple Mail Transfer Protocol
- Site
- Site link bridges
- Site links
- Subnet
- Tree
- Update Sequence Number

APPLY YOUR KNOWLEDGE

Review Questions

1. What are two main reasons for creating a domain?

2. What is the purpose of an organizational unit?

3. What is the difference between a site link and a site link bridge?

4. When would you create an Active Directory connection?

5. What is the definition of a site?

6. What is the difference between a forest and a tree?

7. What type of server is used to replicate the schema for an enterprise?

8. What options can you set on a site link to control replication?

9. If you create site link bridges manually, what must you do to make sure your site link bridges are used?

10. What can you do to force replication across all site links to take place?

Answers to Review Questions

1. Domains create a replication and a security boundary within your organization. Users who are members of the Enterprise Administrators security group have the ability to control all domains. However, users who are members of the Domain Admins security group have control over only their own domain. See the section "Understanding Active Directory's Logical Structure."

2. An organizational unit can be used to delegate control of a selected group of computers, users, and other objects within a domain to a user or group. This effectively creates an Administrator-type account with a limited scope. Organizational units can also be used to apply group policies. See the section "Organizational Units."

3. A site link is used to describe a network path that exists directly between two sites, whereas a site link bridge describes a path between two sites that uses a third site to which both of the sites have a site link. See the section "Replication Between Sites."

4. Normally, you don't need to create Active Directory connections. The exception is a case in which the Knowledge Consistency Checker will not be able to correctly find the connection between two servers. Connections represent a direct network path between two servers. See the section "Connection Objects."

5. A site is best defined as one or more IP subnets interconnected using a high-speed (above T1) network. See the section "Working with Sites."

6. A tree is a structure that starts at a root domain containing only direct descendants. All the domains share a common name space. A forest enables you to create the same type of structure; however, there is more than one name space. See the section "Trees and Forests."

7. Whereas the domain controllers for a domain are responsible for the replication of objects that belong to the domain, the global catalog servers replicate the information about the enterprise, including a list of all objects, the schema, and configuration information. See the section "Global Catalog Servers."

APPLY YOUR KNOWLEDGE

8. The options you can set on a site link include the scheduled periods during which the site link is available and the interval (frequency) at which the controllers check for updates. See the section "Replication Between Sites."

9. By default, all site links are bridged. This means that all the sites can be reached through any combination of site links. If you are going to manage this manually, you need to disable the automatic site link bridging in the IP or SMTP properties. See the section "Replication Between Sites."

10. Site links are available only during scheduled times. If you need to force them all to be available, you need to select the Ignore All Schedules option in the IP or SMTP properties. See the section "Replication Between Sites."

ON THE CD

This book's companion CD contains specially designed supplemental material to help you understand how well you know the concepts and skills you learned in this chapter. You'll find related exercises and exam questions and answers. See the file **Chapter24ApplyYourKnowledge.pdf** in the CD's **Chapter24\ApplyYourKnowledge** directory.

Suggested Readings and Resources

1. *Windows 2000 Server Resource Kit. Deployment Planning Guide.* Microsoft, 2000.

2. Archer, Scott. *MCSE Training Guide: Windows 2000 Directory Services Design.* Indianapolis: New Riders Publishing, 2000.

This chapter helps prepare you for the Microsoft exam by covering the "Manage Active Directory objects" objective and parts of the "Install, configure, and troubleshoot the components of Active Directory objective."

Manage Active Directory objects.

- **Move Active Directory objects.**

- **Publish resources in Active Directory.**

- **Locate objects in Active Directory.**

- **Create and manage accounts manually or by scripting.**

- **Control access to Active Directory objects.**

- **Delegate administrative control of objects in Active Directory.**

▶ One of the key changes in the directory services from Windows NT 4.0 is the capability to set permissions on objects in Active Directory. You must be able to set the permissions and understand the implications of setting objectives.

Active Directory also has the capability to list printers and shares on the network. As with adding users and computers, you need to be able to add these objects by publishing them to Active Directory.

In addition to adding users, computers, shares, and printers, you also need to know how to find these objects both from the administrator's point of view and the user's perspective.

Active Directory includes the capability to delegate the administration of parts of the directory to other users or groups. Your ability to perform the steps required to delegate administrative tasks will be tested.

You must be able to move users within a domain, between OUs, and between domains. This is also new to Active Directory; in NT 4.0 you had to delete and re-create the object to move it.

CHAPTER 25

Administering Active Directory Services

Install, configure, and troubleshoot the components of Active Directory.

- **Implement an organizational unit (OU) structure.**

▶ Organizational units in Active Directory are intended to take the place of resource domains. This objective is included, along with the delegation objective, to ensure that you can work effectively with OUs.

STUDY STRATEGIES

This chapter deals with a lot of different topics, all related to the basic functions of an administrator. You may have already performed these functions. Keep this in mind as you read through the chapter. In particular, you should pay attention to the following:

▶ Note the management of objects, including their creation, modification, movement, and deletion.

▶ Although it's not an exam topic, you should understand both how groups work and the AGLP (that is, **A**ccounts are grouped in **G**lobal groups that belong to domain **L**ocal groups that have **P**ermissions).

▶ Understand what a universal group does.

▶ Pay attention to the descriptions of the tabs used for searches.

▶ Make note of how to use organizational units.

▶ Review the options for sharing directories and how the share gets into Active Directory. This should include printers.

INTRODUCTION

This chapter takes a look at some of the key components of network administration and how to perform the required functions. This includes adding user and computer accounts, managing groups of users and computers, locating objects in Active Directory, delegating administration, moving objects, creating shares and printers, and troubleshooting Active Directory.

PERFORMING BASIC ADMINISTRATION

Manage Active Directory objects.

- **Create and manage accounts manually or by scripting.**

User and computer accounts provide the following capabilities on a Windows 2000 network:

- ◆ Authenticate the identity of the user or computer
- ◆ Authorize or deny access to domain resources
- ◆ Administer other security principals
- ◆ Audit actions performed using the user or computer account

Because users need to have a computer to log on to, it makes sense to start this discussion by looking at computer accounts.

Computer Accounts

In Windows 2000, the management of computer accounts has been expanded so that computer accounts can be managed almost like a user account. Any computer running Windows 2000 or Windows NT 4.0 can join the domain and, therefore, will be authenticated when the computer starts up.

By having the computer authenticated on start up, the network can audit activity from the computer and can manage the computer from a central location. This is only possible for Windows 2000 and Windows NT 4.0 computers. Windows 95 and Windows 98 do not have the advanced security features of the other operating systems—although they can be used as workstations, they cannot be managed.

Managing Computers

The main tool used to manage computers on a network is the Active Directory Users and Computers snap-in. This tool enables you to add, delete, move, and manage the computer accounts. By default, only the group Domain Admins has permission to add and manage computers for a domain.

You can perform several different actions on a computer. Let's start by seeing how to add a computer. This can be done either from the computer itself (see Step by Step 25.1) or from the Active Directory Users and Computers snap-in.

ON THE CD

Step by Step 25.1, "Adding a Computer to a Domain from the Computer," shows you how to add a computer to a domain. See the file **Chapter25-01StepbyStep.pdf** in the CD's **Chapter25\ StepbyStep** directory.

You can easily add a computer to the domain as you are installing the system.

You can also create the computer account before you install the computer. In this case, the person performing the installation does not need to be a member of the Domain Admins group because he or she doesn't need to create the computer account in the domain. Follow Step by Step 25.2 to add a computer account to the domain before the computer is added.

ON THE CD

Step by Step 25.2, "Adding a Computer Account," adds a computer account to the domain before the computer is added. See the file **Chapter25-02StepbyStep.pdf** in the CD's **Chapter25\StepbyStep** directory.

After you have added the computer account to Active Directory, you might want to set the computer account properties. Several items can be set, and some are for information only. To change the properties of computer accounts, follow Step by Step 25.3.

ON THE CD

Step by Step 25.3, "Modifying Computer Account Properties," sets the computer account properties. See the file **Chapter25-03StepbyStep.pdf** in the CD's **Chapter25\StepbyStep** directory.

The first two Step by Steps showed you how to create the computer account, and this one showed you how to set the properties for the computer accounts. Many different properties can be set for a computer.

The following list explains the options you can set on each of the tabs in the Properties dialog box.

- ◆ **General.** This option is used to view the computer name, the DNS name, and the role of the computer. You can add a description. You also can set the computer as trust computer for delegation. This enables the local system account on the computer to request services from another system on the network.

- ◆ **Operating System.** This option shows the name of the operating system running on the computer, including the name, version, and service pack.

- ◆ **Member Of.** This option enables you to control the group membership of the computer. To add a computer to a group, choose Add and select the group from the list that appears.

- ◆ **Location.** This option enables you to enter a location for the computer.

- ◆ **Managed By.** This option enables you to set the user account or group account that will manage the computer. If you have entered the contact information for the user, it will appear here.

- ◆ **Object.** This option displays the object's full name, creation data, and update information.

◆ **Security.** This option enables you to set the security on the object. This does not set the security on the computer but on the object in Active Directory.

Occasionally, you will have to remove a computer from Active Directory. You might remove a computer when it joins a different domain or if the computer is being removed from the network. Follow Step by Step 25.4 to delete a computer account.

ON THE CD

Step by Step 25.4, "Deleting a Computer Account," illustrates how to delete a computer account. See the file **Chapter25-04StepbyStep.pdf** in the CD's **Chapter25\StepbyStep** directory.

Deleting a computer account, like deleting any other object, removes the object and the security identifier (SID) for the object. Creating a new object of the same name creates a different SID and, therefore, a different object.

The main reason for creating computer accounts in Active Directory is to manage the computers on your network. This includes putting them into groups and controlling their properties using group policies, but it can also include working with the Computer Management snap-in, as shown in Step by Step 25.5.

ON THE CD

Step by Step 25.5, "Managing a Computer," demonstrates how to manage the computers on your network. See the file **Chapter25-05StepbyStep.pdf** in the CD's **Chapter25\StepbyStep** directory.

The Computer Management snap-in enables you to manage all aspects of the computer, and it gives you critical information for troubleshooting from a central location on the network.

Occasionally, computers will crash. When this happens, you might have to reload or even rebuild the computer.

In Windows 2000, computers can be members of groups, they can be assigned managers, and they can have group policies that apply to them. If the SID changes, then all of these would need to be reset.

To save you from doing that, you can reset the computer account. This breaks the computer connection with the domain and enables you to add the computer back in without having to reset security information. Step by Step 25.6 walks you through resetting a computer account.

ON THE CD

Step by Step 25.6, "Resetting a Computer Account," walks you through resetting a computer account. See the file **Chapter25-06StepbyStep.pdf** in the CD's **Chapter25\StepbyStep** directory.

Along the same vein, you might also need to suspend a computer's account for a period of time. For example, you should disable the computer account if you send a computer out for service so that the computer cannot be used to break into your network. Follow Step by Step 25.7 to learn how to disable a computer account.

ON THE CD

Step by Step 25.7, "Disabling a Computer Account," shows you how to disable a computer account. See the file **Chapter25-07StepbyStep.pdf** in the CD's **Chapter25\StepbyStep** directory.

The computer, once disabled, will not be able to reconnect to the network until the account is enabled again.

Of course, if you disable a computer account, you need to be able to enable the account when the computer is available again. Follow Step by Step 25.8 to learn how to enable a computer account.

ON THE CD

Step by Step 25.8, "Enabling a Computer Account," shows you how to enable a computer account. See the file **Chapter25-08StepbyStep.pdf** in the CD's **Chapter25\StepbyStep** directory.

User Accounts

A user account enables a user to log on to computers and domains with an identity that can be authenticated and authorized for access to domain resources. Every user needs his or her own user account and password.

Windows 2000 provides two predefined user accounts that you can use to log on to a computer running Windows 2000. These predefined accounts are the Guest and Administrator accounts.

Generally, the Guest account is disabled within a domain except in cases in which security is not a concern. The Administrator account is the account you will use to create and manage all aspects of Active Directory.

Managing Users

Probably the most obvious place to start looking at the management of user accounts is with the creation of user accounts. Follow Step by Step 25.9 to add a user account.

ON THE CD

Step by Step 25.9, "Adding a User Account," explains how to add a user account. See the file **Chapter25-09StepbyStep.pdf** in the CD's **Chapter25\StepbyStep** directory.

As you probably guessed, after you have completed creating a user account, there are several additional options that can be configured for the newly created user account. To access these options, you must edit the account in Active Directory Users and Computers. Step by Step 25.10 shows you how to edit the properties of user accounts.

ON THE CD

Step by Step 25.10, "Modifying User Account Properties," shows you how to edit the properties. See the file **Chapter25-10StepbyStep.pdf** in the CD's **Chapter25\StepbyStep** directory.

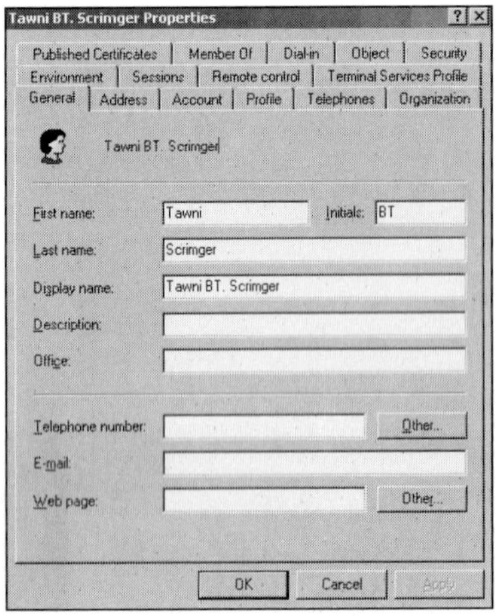

FIGURE 25.1
The General tab of the user Properties
dialog box.

> **NOTE**
>
> **The %USERNAME% Variable** The
> %USERNAME% variable can be used
> to create a directory with the same
> name as the user's pre-Windows
> 2000 logon name. This can be used
> for the profile path (for example,
> \\server\share\%USERNAME%) or
> for the home folder.

The following properties can be set for a user account (see
Figure 25.1):

◆ **General.** This property enables you to set general user properties. These include the first name, initials, last name, display
name, description, office number, telephone number, email
address, and Web page URL.

◆ **Address.** This property provides the user's mailing address.
This is comprised of the street, P.O. Box, city, state/province,
Zip/postal code, and country.

◆ **Account.** This property enables you to control account settings for the user account. These include the user logon name,
down-level logon name, logon hours, workstation restrictions,
account lockout status, an account expiration date, and
account options. The account options include forcing a user
to change their password, disabling a user from changing the
password, setting no expiration on a user's password, and storing the password in reversible encryption. They also include
disabling the account, requiring a smart card for logon,
enabling delegation options for the account, and setting
encryption and authentication options for the account.

◆ **Profile.** This property sets the user's home directory, logon
script, and the location for the user profile.

◆ **Telephones.** This property is used to track the various phone
numbers that a user may have including office, home, fax, and
mobile phone numbers.

◆ **Organization.** This property is used to enter information
about a user's role within the organization. This can include
title, department, company, manager, and any direct reports
that are managed by the user account.

◆ **Published Certificates.** This property enables you to control
the certificates available for the user. These are X.509 certificates that can be used for Internet authentication and that are
also used by the Encrypting File System.

◆ **Member Of.** This property manages which groups a user
belongs to and which group is the user's primary group. The
user's primary group applies only to users who log on to the
network from a Macintosh or to users who run POSIX

applications. Unless you are using these services, there is no need to change the primary group from Domain Users, which is the default value.

◆ **Dial-in.** This property sets the user's dial-in options. These include granting dial-in access, verifying the phone number used by the caller by using caller ID, setting callback options (no callback, callback phone number set by the user, or callback only to a pre-assigned phone number), and setting the static IP address or static IP routing settings.

◆ **Object.** This property enables you to view advanced information on the user account. This includes the full name of the object, when the object was created, when the object was updated, and the update sequence number.

◆ **Security.** This property enables you to set security on the Active Directory object.

◆ **Environment.** This property is used to set options that control the user's environment when he or she uses Terminal Server. This includes the shell program and whether the client can access local devices when connected to a Terminal Services session.

◆ **Sessions.** This property is used to configure session timeout and reconnection settings. This includes setting limits on how long a disconnected session can remain active before being disconnected, setting active and idle session limits, and setting the option that determines whether an existing session can be reconnected from any workstation or only from the originating workstation.

◆ **Remote Control.** This property enables you to set the options for taking control of the user session. This includes setting the option that determines if remote control is allowed, setting the option that determines if user permissions are required for remote control to take place, and setting what the level of interaction that is allowed from a remote management station.

◆ **Terminal Services Profile.** This property enables you to set the option that determines whether or not the user account is enabled for Terminal Services usage. If enabled, you can set an alternate user profile location and home directory for Terminal Services sessions.

NOTE

Terminal Service-Related Tabs The final four tabs deal with configuration settings for Terminal Server. These tabs only apply if you have Terminal Server installed.

EXAM TIP

User Account Options For the exam, you will not have to know which tab is used to set each and every option. Just be aware of the types of options that can be set on a per-account basis.

Other User Management Functions

In addition to adding an account, there are several other functions you might have to perform on user accounts. This section looks at how to perform some of these functions.

At times, you will need to delete a user account. Remember, after a user account has been deleted, all permissions and memberships associated with that user account are deleted. The SID for each account is unique; therefore, a new user account with the same name as a previously deleted user account does not automatically assume the permissions and memberships of the previously deleted account. To delete a user account, follow the steps in Step by Step 25.11.

ON THE CD

Step by Step 25.11, "Deleting a User Account," explains how to delete a user account. See the file **Chapter25-11StepbyStep.pdf** in the CD's **Chapter25\StepbyStep** directory.

Occasionally, you will need to rename a user account. This might happen when a new employee is replacing an employee that has left the organization or if one of your users changes his or her name for legal reasons. To rename a user account, follow Step by Step 25.12.

ON THE CD

Step by Step 25.12, "Renaming a User Account," explains how to rename a user account. See the file **Chapter25-12StepbyStep.pdf** in the CD's **Chapter25\StepbyStep** directory.

There are also times when you need to disable a user account. Disabling user accounts is a good practice when a user leaves the organization or is going to be gone for an extended period of time. In the case of a user who leaves, you can later rename the account if a replacement is hired.

You can also create disabled user accounts with common group memberships. Disabled user accounts can be used as account templates to simplify user account creation. Follow the steps in Step by Step 25.13 to learn how to disable a user account.

ON THE CD

Step by Step 25.13, "Disabling a User Account," demonstrates how to disable a user account. See the file **Chapter25-13StepbyStep.pdf** in the CD's **Chapter25\StepbyStep** directory.

Obviously, at some point you will delete the account or re-enable the account. Disabled accounts have an X in a red circle on their icon in Active Directory Users and Computers. Follow Step by Step 25.14 to learn how to enable a disabled user account.

ON THE CD

Step by Step 25.14, "Enabling a Disabled User Account," shows how to enable a disabled user account. See the file **Chapter25-14StepbyStep.pdf** in the CD's **Chapter25\StepbyStep** directory.

Another function you will need to perform, probably more often than other functions, is resetting a user's password because he or she forgot it. Always make sure that you are talking to the user who is requesting a new password. Resetting a user password is presented in Step by Step 25.15.

WARNING

Service Account Password Any service authenticated with a user account must be reset if the password for the service's user account is changed.

ON THE CD

Step by Step 25.15, "Resetting a User Password," resets a user password. See the file **Chapter25-15StepbyStep.pdf** in the CD's **Chapter25\StepbyStep** directory.

Using Templates

You can use template accounts to create a shell that can be copied to create new user accounts. This is done by creating a user account and setting the groups and other options for the account. Then, when you need another account for a section, you have a template that you can copy. You can also edit the details of the template to personalize the account. Using templates and copying them to create new user accounts saves you a great deal of time versus creating each user account manually. Copying a user account is demonstrated in Step by Step 25.16.

ON THE CD

Step by Step 25.16, "Copying a User Account," shows you how to create a user's account. See the file **Chapter25-16StepbyStep.pdf** in the CD's **Chapter25\StepbyStep** directory.

The process is, as you saw, twofold. First, create a user account with the basic information, which is disabled; then, copy it as required.

There are other ways you can create and manage objects in Active Directory, and you should be aware of them.

OTHER TOOLS FOR MANAGING OBJECTS

In addition to what you have already seen, there are some tools you should be aware of for both the exam and for real-life experience. This includes the directory exchange utilities, LDIFDE and CSVDE, and the ADSI interface. These tools and how they can be used is the focus of this section.

Directory Exchange Utilities

The two directory exchange utilities enable you to import users and other directory objects including attributes and classes. They have been included to both give you a way of dealing with a large number of updates simultaneously, and so that you don't have to spend a week implementing the changes to create a program for a "one-off" job.

Using LDIFDE

The LDAP Data Interchange Format (LDIF) Directory Exchange (LDIFDE) utility can be used to import data to or export data from Active Directory. Because the LDIF standard is an industry standard for importing or modifying LDAP directories, the LDIFDE utility can be used to perform these functions in Windows 2000. This command is run from the command line, and the operation is controlled partially by the options selected and partially by the information in the file.

The command line looks like the following:

```
LDIFDE -i -f -s -c -v -t -d -r -p -l -o -m -n -j -g -k -a
➥-b -? -u
```

-i sets the command to import mode. The default is export mode, which requires no switch.

-f *filename* provides the utility with the name of the file to import from or export to.

-s *servername* tells the command on which domain controller to perform the operation. If this is not given, a domain controller from the domain the user is currently logged on to will be used.

-c *distinguishedname distinguishedname* tells the command to replace every occurrence of the first distinguished name with the second name listed.

-v tells the command to use verbose mode, which returns more information.

-t *portnumber* allows an alternate port to be set for the LDAP server, rather than the default port 389. For example, the port number for the global catalog is 3268.

-d *distinguishedname* specifies the starting point for an export. The root of the current domain is used if this is not included.

-r *LDAPfilter* enables you to filter which records are to be exported using an LDAP property as criteria.

-p *LDAPsearchscope* enables you to specify the scope of the LDAP search. The options are base, one-level, or the entire subtree.

-l *LDAPattributelist* sets the list of LDAP attributes you want to export. The default is all attributes.

-o *attributelist* enables you to omit specific attributes from an export. This way, you can create a LDAP file that is importable to another LDAP-compliant system that does not support so many attributes.

-m tells the command to exclude Active Directory–specific information in the export file. This is used if you are planning to import the same list back in after making changes.

-n tells the command not to export binary values. By default, these values are exported.

-j *filepath* sets the path for the log file generated during an export.

-g turns off paged searches during an export.

-k *action* enables you to set the action that should be taken if there is an error.

-a *distinguishedname password* tells the command what username and password to send to the LDAP server for authentication. For password, you can enter an asterisk (*) and receive a prompt for the password, which will be hidden.

-b *username domain password* enables you to use the standard logon information rather than a distinguished name. For password, you can enter an "*" and receive a prompt for the password, which will be hidden.

-? provides you with online help.

-u tells the command that the file you are using should be Unicode.

As you can see, there are a number of options. Most of them, however, are used in the export function. For the exam, you should be familiar with basic import and export functionality.

The file you will be working with is a text file, and you will be able to edit it as such. The following is a sample of the file:

```
dn: CN=Scrim,CN=Users,DC=ScrimTech, DC=com
changetype: add
cn: Scrim
description: Rob Scrimger
objectClass: user
sAMAccountName: Scrim
```

You can create this file, or it can be created if you export the directory by the LDIFDE command. In either case, you can edit the file until the information is correct, and then you import it using the following syntax:

```
ldifde -i -f import.ldf
```

As you can see, the LDIFDE utility is a quick way to get a list of users from Active Directory, or to import a list from another source into Active Directory, or even to export a list of attributes to modify

and then re-import afterward. The utility works exclusively with
LDIF files, though, and you may have to use CSVDE if your file is
a comma-separated file.

Using CSVDE

The other tool available is the CSVDE, which works with comma-
separated value files. This type of file is useful if you are working
with programs, such as Excel, to clean up files that should be
imported or exported.

This command is very similar to the LDIFDE command; the most
notable difference is that it can only be used to add records to Active
Directory. It cannot modify them. The file is also simpler in that it
consists of a header row of attribute names and a number of records
with those attributes, one per line similar to the following list:

```
dn,cn,firstName,surname,description,objectClass,
➥sAMAccountname
"cn=Heidi Hagan,cn=Users,dc=ScrimTech,dc=com",Heidi
Hagan,Heidi,Hagan,VP - Research,user,HHagan
"cn=Wayne Cassidy,cn=Users,dc=ScrimTech,dc=com",Wayne
Cassidy,Wayne,Cassidy,Manager,user,WCassidy
```

If you look closely, you will notice that there is no changetype
included in the file. This is why you cannot perform modifications.
The command line is almost identical to LDIFDE, and the options
present have the same meaning as they did for LDIFDE, as shown
in the following:

```
CSVDE -i -f -s -c -v -t -d -r -p -l -o -m -n -e -j -g -k -a
➥-b -? -u
```

Although they are slightly different, both LDIFDE and CSVDE are
able to move information into or out of Active Directory. You also
will want to address Active Directory programmatically. To do this,
you need to use the ADSI.

Scripting Using the ADSI

As you can see, it is easy enough to create and import a list of users
into Active Directory. Because the classes and attributes and their
definitions are also part of Active Directory, it is also possible to add
these with the utilities you have just seen. However, there are going
to be times when you will want to work interactively with Active

Directory. The best way to do this is to work with the Active Directory Service Interface (ADSI).

This interface can be used from various languages including the Windows scripting host to interact with Active Directory. ADSI conforms to the Component Object Model and supports standard COM features.

A full discussion of creating ADSI scripts is best left for discussions on programming, which is well outside the scope of this text. For our purposes, you should be aware that ADSI exists and works with any language including the Windows scripting host. To give you an idea of how simple the interface is, the following example is included:

```
Dim objDomain
Dim objUser

Set
objDomain=GetObject("LDAP://OU=Users,DC=ScrimTech,DC=com")
Set objUser = objDomain.Create("user","cn=Dave Shapton")
objUser.Put "samAccountName","DShapton"
objUser.Put "givenName","Dave"
objUser.Put "sn","Shapton"
objUser.Put "userPrincipalName","DShapton@ScrimTech.com"
objUser.SetInfo
MsgBox "User created " & objUser.Name
Set objDomain = Nothing
MsgBox "Finished"
WScript.Quit
```

> **EXAM TIP**
>
> **Know When to Use ADSI**   ADSI scripting is a very powerful tool in Windows 2000. Any time that you want to add several users or edit the same properties for multiple user accounts simultaneously, ADSI scripting is the best solution.

In this case, the first two lines are creating placeholders for the objects that will be created. Next, the connection is made to the LDAP server using the LDAP:// component. A user object is then created with the new name. Next, various attributes are set. Then, the information is saved. A dialog box tells you that the user was created, and the program ends.

Again, it is a simple program, but it begins to show you what is possible.

GROUPS IN WINDOWS 2000

Obviously, you don't want to have to manage 70,000 users one at a time. You need to be able to group together users and computers so that you can work with many users or computers at the same time.

As you start to learn about groups in Windows 2000, it is worth looking back over all the information you are able to store about users. One of the intents of Windows 2000 is to bring together directory services from the network side and from the email side. A large part of the information you can store for users is information that normally, until now, you would have stored in the email system.

This becomes even more evident as you start to look at groups. There are two main types of groups you are going to be able to create in the Windows 2000 directory services:

◆ **Distribution groups.** These groups are generally collections of users, such as email distribution lists, and cannot be used in discretionary access control lists to set security on an object.

◆ **Security groups.** These groups can be used to group together users or to assign permissions to objects on the network or in Active Directory. These groups can also be used for email.

Although the distribution group is a valid object in the Windows 2000 Active Directory, the rest of this discussion concentrates on security groups. The following section examines the main functions of groups, domain modes, strategies for using groups, built-in and predefined groups, predefined global groups, special identities, and the management of groups.

There are two main functions that a group in the Windows 2000 Active Directory takes on—groups are used to gather user accounts into a single entity to simplify the administration of users, and groups assign permissions to objects and resources. The difference in function is in the scope of the group, as noted in the following:

◆ **Global.** Global groups typically are used to gather user accounts together and should normally not be given permissions. The users gain permissions from adding the global group to a local group that has permissions. Global groups can contain users from the local domain only. They are available in the domain in which they are created and in other domains in the tree or forest.

◆ **Local.** Local groups are used to gather permission to perform functions within a domain. The local group in a Windows NT domain is available only on the computer on which it is created. In Windows 2000, the local group is available on all systems in the domain that run Windows 2000 and are referred to as domain local groups.

◆ **Universal.** Universal groups combine the capabilities of the global and local groups. They can contain users and groups from any domain in the tree or forest and can be assigned rights to resources or objects in any domain. This group removes the boundaries of domains from management. It increases the amount of replication required between global catalog servers because the membership of universal groups is stored in the global catalog. These groups are only available in native mode.

Domain Modes

The actual use and scope of the groups depend on the mode in which you are running the domain. There are two domain modes in which you can run a Windows 2000 domain as noted in the following:

◆ **Mixed mode.** In this mode, you can use both Windows NT and Windows 2000 domain controllers in the same domain. This is the default domain mode, and it provides you with the functionality needed during the upgrade process.

◆ **Native mode.** In this mode, you can take advantage of several group enhancements including the capability to work with universal groups.

Windows 2000 native mode is only available for domains that have no Windows NT 4.0 backup domain controllers. If you have upgraded all the domain controllers that you plan to and have removed all Windows NT domain controllers, you can upgrade to native mode. Changing domain modes is addressed in Step by Step 25.17.

> **ON THE CD**
>
> Step by Step 25.17, "Changing Domain Modes," shows you how to change domain modes. See the file **Chapter25-17StepbyStep.pdf** in the CD's **Chapter25\StepbyStep** directory.

Table 25.1 summarizes the effect of domain modes on groups.

You need to plan for the use of groups. The following section covers strategies for using groups.

TABLE 25.1

EFFECT OF DOMAIN MODES ON GROUPS

Type of group	Function	Mixed Mode	Native Mode
Universal	What can be included as members	Not available	Accounts, global groups, and universal groups from any domain
	What it can be a member of	Not available	Can be put into other groups in any domain
	What it is used for	Not available	Can be assigned permissions in any domain
	Can be converted to other types	Not available	Not available
Global	What can be included as members	Accounts from the same domain	Accounts and other global groups from the same domain
	What it can be a member of	Local groups in any domain	Can be put into other groups in any domain
	What it is used for	Can be assigned permissions in any domain	Can be assigned permissions in any domain
	Can be converted to other types	Not available	Can be converted to universal scope as long as it is not a member of any other group having global scope
Domain local	What can be included as members	Accounts and global groups from any domain	Accounts, global groups, and universal groups from any domain as well as domain local groups from the same domain
	What it can be a member of	Not available	Can be put into other domain local groups in the same domain
	What it is used for	Can be assigned permissions in the local domain	Can be assigned permissions only in the same domain
	Can be converted to other types	Not available	Can be converted to universal scope as long as it does not have as its member another group having domain local scope

Strategies for Using Groups

Planning how you are going to use groups before deploying Windows 2000 will save you a lot of work trying to retrofit groups into your network. The first step in planning your groups, as you might guess, is to determine the domain mode you will be using. Local, global, and universal groups offer the administrator varying levels of control.

Using Domain Local Groups

Normally, you use domain local groups to assign permissions. By using a domain local group to hold the permissions, you are able to use global groups and universal groups from any domain to add users to the permissions.

For example, you have a printer and allow accountants in your domain to use it. You could take a global group that has the accountants in it and add it to a local group with permissions on the printer. If you later need to add an accounting group from another domain, you can simply add the global group. Or, if you needed to switch the permissions to another printer, you can just give the local group permissions on that printer.

Using local groups enables you to work with multiple global groups that need access to multiple local resources through a single entity.

Using Global Groups

Global groups should normally be used to gather users from a domain into a collective entity that can be used in the local domain or any other domain in the tree or forest. Because groups with global scope are not replicated outside of their own domain, accounts in a group that have global scope can be changed frequently without generating replication traffic to the global catalog.

Using Universal Groups

Use groups with universal scope to consolidate groups that span domains. To do this, add the accounts to groups with global scope and nest these groups within groups with universal scope. Using this strategy, any membership changes in the groups with global scope do not affect the groups with universal scope.

This is important because any changes to universal group membership cause the entire membership of the group to be replicated to every global catalog in the forest.

When working with groups, it is important to remember that global groups are used to gather users, and local groups are used to assign permissions. The addition of a global group to a local group is what gives the users rights. Universal groups enable you to gather global groups and add them to multiple local groups across domains.

In addition to the groups you will create, there are several built-in groups you can use to manage your network.

Built-in and Predefined Groups

During the installation of the domain, several groups are created by default. These groups represent various roles users will take on your network, and they are included to help you set up the management of you network. The groups appear either in the Built-in folder for local groups or in the Users folder for global groups.

Built-in Local Groups

The groups placed in the Built-in folder for Active Directory Users and Computers include the following:

- ◆ Account Operators
- ◆ Administrators
- ◆ Backup Operators
- ◆ Guests
- ◆ Print Operators
- ◆ Replicator
- ◆ Server Operators
- ◆ Users
- ◆ Power Users (found on Professional and standalone servers only)

These groups have domain local scope and are primarily used to assign permissions to users who have an administrative role in that domain. Table 25.2 shows the default rights for each of these groups as well as the general rights for all users, which is a special group called Everyone.

In addition to the local groups that are added, several other predefined groups are global in scope.

Predefined Global Groups

The predefined groups placed in the Users folder for Active Directory Users and Computers are as follows:

- ◆ Cert Publishers
- ◆ Domain Admins
- ◆ Domain Computers
- ◆ Domain Controllers
- ◆ Domain Guests
- ◆ Domain Users
- ◆ Enterprise Admins
- ◆ Group Policy Admins
- ◆ Schema Admins

These groups enable you to collect different types of users and link them to the built-in local groups. By default, all users are members of the Domain Users groups, and all computers are added to Domain Computers. These groups can be used to manage the bulk of the users and computers on your network. By default, the Domain Users group in a domain is a member of the Users group in the same domain.

The Domain Admins group is used for the administrators of the domain. The Domain Admins group is a member of the local Administrators group. You should only add users to this group if they need to have full administrator privileges within the domain.

The built-in and predefined groups can be used to manage most of your network. These groups, in conjunction with the groups you will create, make management simple and easy.

TABLE 25.2

RIGHTS ASSIGNED TO THE BUILT-IN ADMINISTRATION GROUPS

User Right	Allows	Groups Assigned This Right by Default
Access this computer from the network	Connect to the computer over the network	Administrators, Everyone, Power Users
Back up files and file folders	Back up files and folders regardless of file and folder permissions	Administrators, Backup Operators
Bypass traverse checking	Move through a folder in which a user has no permissions to enable him or her to get a subfolder	Everyone
Change the system time	Set the time for the computer	Administrators, Power Users
Create a pagefile	This right has no effect	Administrators
Debug programs	Debug various low-level objects such as threads	Administrators
Force shutdown from a remote system	Shut down a remote computer	Administrators
Increase scheduling priority	Increase the processing priority of a process	Administrators, Power Users
Load and unload device drivers	Install and remove device drivers	Administrators
Log on locally	Log on at the physical computer	Administrators, Backup Operators, Everyone, Guests, Power Users, and Users
Manage auditing and the security log	Configure auditing, and view and clear the security log (members of the Administrators group can always view and clear the security log)	Administrators
Modify firmware environment variables	Modify system environment variables stored in nonvolatile RAM on computers that support this type of configuration	Administrators
Profile a single process	Perform performance sampling on a process	Administrators, Power Users
Profile system performance	Perform profiling performance sampling on the computer	Administrators
Restore files and file folders	Restore backed-up files and folders regardless of file and folder permissions	Administrators, Backup Operators
Shut down the system	Shut down the computer	Administrators, Backup Operators, Everyone, Power Users, and Users
Take ownership of files or other objects	Take ownership of files, folders, printers, and other objects on (or attached to) the computer	Administrators

Special Identities

There are three special groups to which users can belong. Users become members of these groups not by you adding them to the group, but by the actions they take themselves. These groups are as follows:

- ◆ **Everyone.** This group represents all current users of a system whether they connect across the network or log on locally.

- ◆ **Network.** This group includes any user who utilizes a resource across the network.

- ◆ **Interactive.** This group is for users who are physically at the computer.

Although the special identities can be assigned rights and permissions to resources, you cannot modify or view the memberships of these special identities. You do not see them when you administer groups, and you cannot place the special identities into groups. Group scopes do not apply to special identities. Users are automatically assigned to these special identities whenever they log on or access a particular resource.

Managing Groups

Now that you have seen some of the theory behind groups, it is time to see how administrators work with groups. This section shows you how to add, edit, and delete groups, and how to add and remove members. Use Step by Step 25.18 to learn how to add a group.

ON THE CD

Step by Step 25.18, "Adding a Group," shows you how to add a group. See the file **Chapter25-18StepbyStep.pdf** in the CD's **Chapter25\StepbyStep** directory.

Recall that you add global groups to gather users you want to manage as a single entity. Local groups are created to gather rights. You should always check to see if an existing group meets your needs because this reduces the overall number of groups and, in general, reduces the permissions checking.

As with the user options, there are more options you can set. To edit these options, you need to edit the group properties. Use Step by Step 25.19 to learn how to modify group properties.

ON THE CD

Step by Step 25.19, "Modifying Group Properties," demonstrates how to modify group properties. See the file **Chapter25-19StepbyStep.pdf** in the CD's **Chapter25\StepbyStep** directory.

Although you can change all the properties of groups, you normally just change the membership of groups. This enables you to add or remove users from the group. You might also change the manager of a group if the management is being delegated.

There are six tabs you use to configure groups. The following is a list of the tabs and what you can configure on each of the tabs.

◆ **General.** This tab enables you to change the down-level name of the group. You can also add a description and an email address, change the scope and type of group, and add notes.

◆ **Members.** This tab enables you to add or remove members of the group.

◆ **Member Of.** The Member Of tab enables you to add the group to or remove the group from other groups.

◆ **Managed By.** This tab enables you to set the user who is the manager for the group.

◆ **Object.** This tab tells you the name, creation, update dates, and update sequence number for the object.

◆ **Security.** This tab enables you to set security on the object in Active Directory.

There will be times when you want to delete a group. Remember, though, that just like a user, a unique SID represents a group. When you delete the group, you are deleting the SID. Creating a new

group with exactly the same name does not provide the rights and
permissions that were assigned to the group without you assigning
them again. Use Step by Step 25.20 to learn how to delete a group.

ON THE CD

Step by Step 25.20, "Deleting a Group," explains how to delete a
group. See the file **Chapter25-20StepbyStep.pdf** in the CD's
Chapter25\StepbyStep directory.

When you finish using a group and are sure no one else is using it,
you should delete it to make sure that there are no stray permissions
on the group. This also removes the object from Active Directory.

Remember that you can either open the group properties to add the
user or open the user properties to add the user to a group. You can
also use these to see what groups a user belongs to or which users are
members of a group.

As with all network operating systems, groups are a key management
tool. They enable you to manage a large number of users quickly
and easily. Although groups are not officially part of the exam, questions about them have appeared in some cases. Make sure that you
understand both the types of groups (security and distribution) and
the scope of groups (global, universal, and local).

LOCATING OBJECTS IN DIRECTORY SERVICES

Manage Active Directory objects.

- **Locate objects in Active Directory.**

As the number of objects you store in Active Directory increases,
you obviously need some method of finding the objects so that
you can work with them. In addition, there would be little point in
configuring Active Directory to create a list of all the objects across
your enterprise if the users were not able to locate the objects. In this
section, you will see how to locate objects in Active Directory from
both the administrative interface and the user interface.

Finding Objects in the Management Interface

When you are working with the users and computers that make up your network, you need to be able to find the object you want to manage. This can be done using either the Find command located in the context menu for the domain or the Find icon on the tool bar. Step by Step 25.21 walks you through using the Find command to locate an object.

ON THE CD

Step by Step 25.21, "Locating an Object Using the Find Command," walks you through using the Find command to locate an object. See the file **Chapter25-21StepbyStep.pdf** in the CD's **Chapter25\StepbyStep** directory.

After you have found the object or objects for which you were looking, you can select them and use the right-click button of your mouse to bring up the context menu. This gives you the same options as locating the object manually and then right-clicking it.

Advanced Search

By performing an Advanced Search, or using Custom Search, you can be more specific about the objects you are trying to find. The objects you can search for appear along with a list of their attributes. Use Step by Step 25.22 to explore the Advanced Search options.

ON THE CD

Step by Step 25.22, "Advanced Searches," explores the Advanced Search options. See the file **Chapter25-22StepbyStep.pdf** in the CD's **Chapter25\StepbyStep** directory.

Being able to use the Advanced Search functions enables you to find the objects you need quicker, and an Advanced Search reduces the number of objects that appear in the results window. The Advanced Search also enables you to access characteristics to find groups of objects with a common setting.

Finding Objects as a User

Users also need to be able to search for objects in Active Directory. The users can easily find either printers or people using the Search tools on the Start menu. Step by Step 25.23 walks you through a search for a printer.

ON THE CD

Step by Step 25.23, "Searching for a Printer as a User," walks you through a search for a printer. See the file **Chapter25-23StepbyStep.pdf** in the CD's **Chapter25\StepbyStep** directory.

When the user finds a printer, he or she can right-click the printer and choose Connect to use the printer. Finding people is similar to finding printers. Step by Step 25.24 walks you through finding people with Active Directory.

ON THE CD

Step by Step 25.24, "Finding People Using Active Directory," walks you through finding people with Active Directory. See the file **Chapter25-24StepbyStep.pdf** in the CD's **Chapter25\StepbyStep** directory.

You might be wondering about the security if just anybody can find objects on your network. This is not a concern because the objects are all protected by a Discretionary Access Control List.

At this point, you have seen how to work with user and computer accounts and how to manage them using groups. You also know how to find the objects in Active Directory. The next section discusses organizational units, which you can use to delegate control of some of the objects to other users or groups.

CREATING AN ORGANIZATIONAL UNIT

Install, configure, and troubleshoot the components of Active Directory.

- **Implement an organizational unit (OU) structure.**

As your network begins to grow, you will find that you have a large number of users to organize. You will also find that you will need to separate the users so you can manage groups of users together. Ideally, you want to be able to delegate the control of groups of users to others on the network.

Organizational units enable you to logically organize the users, computers, and other resources in your network. Using organizational units enables you to maintain centralized control of the network. It also enables you to group users and computers for the delegation of control and for the application of group policies.

WHERE TO CREATE OUS

The choice between domains or organizational units is part of the network's design. Typically, domains act as replication and security boundaries. If these are not created, your logical division in the network will be done using OUs (see Step by Step 25.25).

ON THE CD

Step by Step 25.25, "Creating an Organizational Unit," demonstrates how to create OUs. See the file **Chapter25-25StepbyStep.pdf** in the CD's **Chapter25\StepbyStep** directory.

After you have created an OU, you can move users and computers into the OU or you can just create them in the OU. In addition, you can create other objects in the OU such as groups, printers, shared folders, and other organizational units.

Recall that the main reason for creating an OU is to enable you to delegate authority for the OU to another user or group. This is done by setting permissions on the OU so that a user or group can have control.

PERMISSIONS IN ACTIVE DIRECTORY SERVICES

Manage Active Directory objects.

- **Control access to Active Directory objects.**

Every object in Active Directory has a *security ID* (SID)—a unique number identifying the object. When a user logs on to Windows 2000, the system generates an access token, which is attached to the user's initial process (Explorer) by default. The access token is made up of the SID of the user and the SID of any security groups to which the user belongs, along with other information.

The access token is then attached to each process the user launches. It is used to compare object permissions to determine whether the user has access to the object. In Windows 2000, this includes access to the object in Active Directory.

Each object has a security descriptor, which includes the SID of the owner, the SID of the principal group of the owner, and a Discretionary Access Control List (DACL), along with a System Access Control List (SACL). The SID of the owner is used to give the owner access to change permissions. The SID of the group is used for group access from POSIX applications and from Services for Macintosh. The SACL sets audit settings for the object.

The DACL is filled with access control entries. An access control entry (ACE) contains a SID, the type of access the entry represents, and whether the access is granted or denied. When object access is attempted (you try to read an object's attributes, for example), the access token for your session is read, and each SID is compared with the first ACE. If this gives one of the SIDs in your access token permission, that's it. You have access. On the other hand, if this denies you the access you need, that's also it—you are denied access. Denies are always listed first. If your access is not resolved on the first ACE, then the next one is checked and so on until you either have the rights you require or you are denied access.

By setting the permission on objects, you can set the actions people can perform on the objects. This is how you can allow other users or groups in the network to manage parts of your organization.

Object-Level Permissions

Before you can set or even see the object-level permissions, you need to be able to see the advanced settings for the objects in the Active Directory. This can be turned on under the View option in the menu. If you click View, you will see the Advanced Features option. If there is a check mark next to an option, it is turned on. Otherwise, the option is inactive. The option acts as a toggle; if you choose it when it is off, it will turn on, and vice versa.

With the Advanced Features turned on, you can view and set object-level permissions. You do not normally do this; rather, you create an OU and then delegate control of the OU to a user or group. If you do want to view and set object-level permissions from the Advanced Features option, Step by Step 25.26 covers the procedure.

ON THE CD

Step by Step 25.26, "Setting Permissions on an Object," shows how to create an OU and then delegate control of the OU to a user or group. See the file **Chapter25-26StepbyStep.pdf** in the CD's **Chapter25\StepbyStep** directory.

There are five different permissions you can set. These permissions are fairly straightforward. The following list reviews them:

◆ **Full Control.** This permission enables the user or group to perform any action on the object within Active Directory. Full Control encompasses all the permissions that follow.

◆ **Read.** The Read permission enables a user to read the object and the properties associated with the object. This is the default permission for everyone so that everyone can find the object when searching Active Directory.

◆ **Write.** This permission enables the user to change the properties of the object.

◆ **Create All Child Objects.** This permission enables a user or group with permissions to create objects within the container, such as users, computers, or organizational units.

◆ **Delete All Child Objects.** This permission enables a user to delete the child objects from a container object, such as an OU, even if the user did not create the object.

On the Permissions tab for all objects, you will notice that there is also an Advanced button. This button enables you to get into greater specificity with permissions, as well as configure the auditing allowing you to take ownership of the object. Step by Step 25.27 walks you through setting advanced permissions.

> **ON THE CD**
>
> Step by Step 25.27, "Setting Advanced Permissions," walks you through setting advanced permissions. See the file **Chapter25-27StepbyStep.pdf** in the CD's **Chapter25\StepbyStep** directory.

Normally, you do not set the advanced permissions yourself. Advanced permissions are set through the Delegation of Control Wizard. You can also use the procedure shown in Step by Step 25.27 to check the permissions, which is common.

A large number of permissions can be set; these are presented in the following list. Note that these are more for your information than for the exam itself.

Permissions you can set on an object include the following:

♦ **Full Control.** This permission gives the user or group full control of the object. It is included here so that you can control the scope to which it is applied.

♦ **List Contents.** This permission enables a user or group to list the contents of a container object only.

♦ **Read All Properties.** This permission enables a user or group to read all the properties of an object.

♦ **Write All Properties.** This permission enables a user or group to write to all the properties of an object.

♦ **Delete.** This permission gives the user or group permission to delete the object.

♦ **Delete Subtree.** This permission enables the user or group to delete the object and all objects it contains.

♦ **Read Permissions.** This permission allows the user or group to read the permissions on the object.

- ◆ **Modify Permissions.** This permission allows the user or group to modify the permissions on the object.

- ◆ **Modify Owner.** This permission allows the user or group to take ownership of the object.

- ◆ **All Validated Writes.** This permission enables the user or group to perform any write operation on the object.

- ◆ **All Extended Rights.** This permission gives the user or group access to the extended rights on the object.

- ◆ **Create/Delete All Child Objects.** This permission grants the user or group the ability to create child objects, and, with the Delete permission, delete all child objects including those belonging to others.

- ◆ **Create/Delete Named Objects.** This allows the user or group to create or delete only the class of object named in the ACE. For example, this is how you can delegate control of computers within an OU.

On the Properties tab, you can selectively give or deny a user the capability to read and write the properties of the object. Consider carefully whether or not to use these settings. These settings force Active Directory to check permissions on a column-by-column basis.

The options for the scope break down in a manner similar to the properties. The permissions can be set to affect the current object only, the current object and its children, only the children, or a specific type of object.

Permissions you set on an object can actually affect other objects, too.

Permissions Inheritance

The objects created in a container inherit permissions set on container objects in Active Directory.

This means that, if you set permissions on an OU and then create another OU within it, the permissions that are set on the top-level OU flow down to the lower-level OU and onto the objects created within it.

Although this is the default behavior, it is not always the desired behavior. For this reason, you have the option of blocking the inheritance of permissions. This is done on the Security tab. Step by Step 25.28 explores blocking inherited permissions.

ON THE CD

Step by Step 25.28, "Blocking Permissions Inheritance," explores blocking inherited permissions. See the file **Chapter25-28StepbyStep.pdf** in the CD's **Chapter25\StepbyStep** directory.

Know How Permissions Work   You will never get a question on the exam that is simply about permissions. Permissions will play a big part of most questions in some shape or form. Knowing how permissions are inherited will help you determine whether a solution is valid.

EXAM TIP

Permissions are not inherited again unless you recheck the box. This is true even if you move the object to another container.

In most cases, you won't set these permissions directly; you will delegate control of an organizational unit that contains the objects.

Delegating Administrative Control

Manage Active Directory objects.

- **Delegate administrative control of objects in Active Directory.**

Combining the use of organizational units and permissions provides you with the capability to delegate the management of portions of Active Directory to other users. This means you can create an organizational unit and give a user or group the rights they need to manage that OU, effectively creating a workgroup or local administrator within a single domain.

Applying the required full control permissions using the Security tab can delegate control; however, you should use the Delegation of Control Wizard. This wizard enables you to completely delegate control or to delegate only partial control of an OU, as you will learn in Step by Step 25.29.

ON THE CD

Step by Step 25.29, "Delegating Control with the Wizard," shows you how to completely delegate control or to delegate only partial control of an OU. See the file **Chapter25-29StepbyStep.pdf** in the CD's **Chapter25\StepbyStep** directory.

The main reason for creating organizational units is so that you can delegate control. The delegation adds the required permissions. This can be run more than once and adds more permissions as required.

Understanding the permissions you can set on objects is important because permissions control the actions of the users, and, in some cases, the administrators. It is the permissions that make delegation of control and secure dynamic updates possible. You also need to be able to set permissions on printers and shared folders.

MANAGING SHARES

A *share* is a part of your disk that you allow people to access resources across the network. The point at which you create the share and all the directories below it is accessible through the share. This is the primary method for allowing your users to access data on servers.

Obviously, sharing directories is not part of managing Active Directory. This section is included to make sure you have the basics and can understand the publishing of shares in Active Directory and the permissions you can set.

When you share a directory, you create a name representing the directory on the network, which users can access using a Uniform Naming Convention (UNC) name. Creating a share is a simple process you can accomplish in several different ways. Step by Step 25.30 walks you through creating a share from the command line.

ON THE CD

Step by Step 25.30, "Creating a Share from the Command Line," walks you through creating a share from the command line. See the file **Chapter25-30StepbyStep.pdf** in the CD's **Chapter25\ StepbyStep** directory.

Although you will not normally use the command line to create a share, you need to know how to do this so that you can create scripts to automate some of your administrative functions. This is also very useful if you take advantage of the Telnet service included in Windows 2000. It can also be used to obtain a list of the directories you have shared and their names. Step by Step 25.31 helps you learn how to retrieve a list of shares.

ON THE CD

Step by Step 25.31, "Retrieving a List of Shares at the Command Line," helps you learn how to retrieve a list of shares. See the file **Chapter25-31StepbyStep.pdf** in the CD's **Chapter25\StepbyStep** directory.

In most cases, you create shares from your computer using Explorer, the Computer Management snap-in, or the Active Directory Users and Computers snap-in. This uses the graphical user interface to create the share. Step by Step 25.32 shows you how to create shares using the Explorer.

ON THE CD

Step by Step 25.32, "Sharing a Directory Using the Explorer," shows you how to create shares using the Explorer. See the file **Chapter25-32StepbyStep.pdf** in the CD's **Chapter25\StepbyStep** directory.

You can also create a share using the Computer Management snap-in. To get to the Computer Management snap-in, you can either open Computer Management from the Administrative Tools menu, or you can open Active Directory Users and Computers. Then, you can right-click the computer where you want to create the share, and choose Manage from the context menu. Step by Step 25.33 walks you through using the Computer Management snap-in to create a share.

ON THE CD

Step by Step 25.33, "Creating a Share in Computer Management," walks you through using the Computer Management snap-in to create a share. See the file **Chapter25-33StepbyStep.pdf** in the CD's **Chapter25\StepbyStep** directory.

Sharing a folder is a very basic operation on the network, and it is one you will do many times. However you decide to share files, you need to set permissions on the shares.

Share Permissions

When you create a share, the information in the share is exposed to the network. You need to set the permissions for the users that will access the share to ensure that only the users who are supposed to use the share are doing so. The effective permissions for a share are a combination of the share permissions and the NTFS permissions if the share is on an NTFS drive.

Normally, you set the share permissions to be more liberal than the NTFS permissions, because the same share permissions are used for the shared directory and all subdirectories. The permissions through the share are compared to the NTFS permissions, and the more restrictive permissions are applied.

If a user is given control of a file through NTFS, but only Read permissions to the share, the Read permissions are most restrictive, and the user cannot exercise the rights he or she has been given. On the other hand, if the user has Full Control through the share and Full Control only on the one file, but nothing on the other files, he or she will be able to work with that one file. The permissions of the share and file combine and are equal, so that the user can access the file. The Control permission with No permission combines to give the users no permissions on the other files in the directory.

The standard share permissions let the user perform different functions. There are three permissions you can either give or deny users—Read, Change, and Full Control. Step by Step 25.34 walks you through setting shared folder permissions.

ON THE CD

Step by Step 25.34, "Setting Shared Folder Permissions," walks you through setting shared folder permissions. See the file **Chapter34-34StepbyStep.pdf** in the CD's **Chapter34\StepbyStep** directory.

NOTE **Denying Permissions** Microsoft suggests that you use the Deny permission sparingly. Deny overrides all other permissions, even if a user has Full Control. Depending on where the Deny permission is set, it could be hard to track down. Remember that if you do not give a user permissions, the user does not have them. If you are careful about the permissions you give, you should not have to use Deny.

In addition to setting the share permissions, you should also set the NTFS permissions. This is done in a similar manner by right-clicking in Explorer the file or folder on which you want to set permissions and then by choosing Properties. From there, you can choose the Security tab and set NTFS permissions.

Publishing a Share

Manage Active Directory objects.

- **Publish resources in Active Directory.**

By publishing a share, users can find the share in Active Directory. Publishing a share is a simple process done in Active Directory Users and Computers. This is demonstrated in Step by Step 25.35.

ON THE CD

Step by Step 25.35, "Publishing a Share in Active Directory," shows how to publish a share. See the file **Chapter25-35StepbyStep.pdf** in the CD's **Chapter25\StepbyStep** directory.

The inclusion of a share within Active Directory makes it easier for the user to locate shares. Many users do not understand the meaning of UNC names, and this is a means to make it easier to find the share that is needed.

Just as you can publish folders, you can also publish printers to make them easier to find.

PUBLISHING PRINTERS

Manage Active Directory objects.

- **Publish resources in Active Directory.**

Publishing printers makes them available to Active Directory, which means that users can search for them and then attach them as required. In Windows 2000, you can do this on the Sharing tab of the printer's Properties sheet by clicking List in Active Directory.

If the printer is not connected to a Windows 2000 computer, you need to add it in Active Directory Users and Computers. This is demonstrated in Step by Step 25.36.

ON THE CD

Step by Step 25.36, "Publishing a non-Windows 2000 Printer in Active Directory," adds a non-Windows 2000 printer. See the file **Chapter25-36StepbyStep.pdf** in the CD's **Chapter25\StepbyStep** directory.

This makes the printer an object that users can then search for in Active Directory. Although this section is brief, printers are one of the objects added to Active Directory by default, and you need to know how to add them. In addition, you need to know how to move them.

MOVING OBJECTS WITHIN THE DIRECTORY

Manage Active Directory objects.

- **Move Active Directory objects.**

As time goes by, you will be adding organizational units and rearranging users. This happens as companies reorganize or as employees change jobs within an organization. The process for moving objects in Active Directory is a very simple one if you are moving users between organizational units. If you need to move a user to a different domain, you need to use the MoveTree utility or the Active Directory Migration Tool. Step by Step 25.37 walks you through the process of moving an object between OUs.

ON THE CD

Step by Step 25.37, "Moving an Object Between Organizational Units," shows you how to move an object between OUs. See the file **Chapter25-37StepbyStep.pdf** in the CD's **Chapter25\StepbyStep** directory.

Being able to move objects enables you to deal with the organizational changes that occur over time. This capability used to require third-party utilities. Having the capability to move objects built in to Active Directory Users and Computers should make the life of administrators easier.

> **EXAM TIP**
>
> **Do Not Spend Much Time Studying MoveTree and ADMT**   Moving objects between domains is beyond the scope of the exam. Moving objects between domains requires writing the previous SID for the object into another attribute known as the SIDHistory. Both the MoveTree utility and the Active Directory Migration Tool (ADMT) provide the capability to move objects between domains.

CASE STUDY: ADMINISTERING ACTIVE DIRECTORY

ESSENCE OF THE CASE

We want to look at the creation of the organizational units and the placement of servers. There is little that you really need to consider as long as you keep a few basic points in mind, as noted in the following:

▶ Each site requires at least one global catalog server and should have at least one domain controller from each domain.

▶ There are five domains based on the user's function in the organization rather than his or her location.

▶ The sites were created for the different locations, and the sites have been configured to replicate so that information should not be more than three hours out-of-date at any major location.

▶ There are 15 sites, four of which are major offices and the other 11 of which are minor offices.

Again, this is a fairly straightforward example in which you need to make sure that there is a global catalog server in each site and in which you need to create organizational units.

SCENARIO

This chapter has presented a great deal of information. Most of it does not affect the design of the network directly but rather affects the policies that need to be followed on the network. There need to be policies about the creation and use of the types of groups and about the addition of objects to Active Directory.

Policies also need to be developed to deal with the delegation of control of organizational units and what that control will entail. Further, SunShine Brewing should set standards for different levels of security on documents and should determine the permissions and auditing requirements for these documents.

This case study looks at the creation of organizational units and at the placement of global catalog servers. By ensuring that the sites are in place as discussed in the preceding chapter, and by ensuring the correct placement of servers and the creation of appropriate organizational units, we can facilitate whatever policy is created.

ANALYSIS

The organizational units will be, perhaps, a little numerous; however, because they exist only as objects within Active Directory, this is not a problem. For each of the domains, you will end up having a separate organizational unit for each location.

CASE STUDY: ADMINISTERING ACTIVE DIRECTORY

This will enable you to manage all the users of one type at the domain level or to manage all the users of one type at the same location—the OU level. This will make the application of site-level Group Policy more difficult because you will need to define it in one domain and link to it from the other domains. This means that site-level policies should be defined in the root domain, which will need to have at least one domain controller in each location.

As for the global catalog servers, in this case, we will look at configuring the bridgehead servers for the site links to act as the global catalog servers.

CHAPTER SUMMARY

This chapter looked at the basic administration of Active Directory. You have seen how to create objects of different types, move the objects, and set permissions on the objects. You have also seen how to create organizational units and how to delegate control of those organizational units to other users and groups.

KEY TERMS

- Distribution group
- Domain local group
- Global group
- Inheritance
- Local group
- Mixed mode
- MoveTree
- Native mode
- Object-level permissions
- Rights
- Security group
- Security principal
- Universal group

APPLY YOUR KNOWLEDGE

Review Questions

1. What is the main purpose of organizational units?

2. What protocol is used to search Active Directory?

3. What is the purpose of groups?

4. What is the greatest number of levels you should nest in OUs?

5. What is the effect of delegating control of an organizational unit?

6. If you set permissions on an organizational unit, what happens to the permissions of the object in the OU?

7. What do you need to do to publish a printer in Active Directory?

8. If you move an object within a domain, what tool should you use?

9. If you move an object to another domain, what happens to the permissions on the object if you have cleared the Inherit Permissions check box?

10. What does the Advanced tab on the Search screen let you do?

Answers to Review Questions

1. The main purpose of an organizational unit is to enable you to delegate the control of a set of users, computers, and other objects in Active Directory. This is done either by manually setting permissions on the organizational unit or by using the Delegation of Control Wizard. For more information, see the section "Creating an Organizational Unit."

2. Although you don't see it called LDAP, the protocol used to search Active Directory is Lightweight Directory Access Protocol, which was originally defined in the X.500 specifications. For more information, see the section "Locating Objects in Directory Services."

3. The purpose of groups is to collect users or rights. Global groups are used to gather users into a manageable unit and to make this group available in the local domain and all the other domains. The local group typically is used to gather the rights you want to assign. Users acquire the rights when you add the global group to the local group. Universal groups act as a bridge between global and local groups that can span many domains. For more information, see the section "Groups in Windows 2000."

4. Microsoft recommends that you do not nest organizational units beyond three layers. This is primarily because each OU level, in addition to the domain and site to which a user belongs, can have group policies assigned to it. The loading of more than five Group Policy documents would cause the logon process to become unreasonably slow. For more information, see the section "Creating an Organizational Unit."

5. When you delegate control of an organizational unit, you are really setting the permissions on the OU and the objects in the OU so that the delegate can control whatever the permissions allow. For more information, see the section "Delegating Administrative Control."

6. When you set permissions on an OU, the objects in the OU inherit the changes you make. This is the normal behavior and can be overridden by blocking inheritance. For more information, see the section "Permissions Inheritance."

APPLY YOUR KNOWLEDGE

7. If the printer is on a Windows 2000 computer, all you need do is share the printer and check the List in Directory box. This is checked by default. For more information, see the section "Publishing Printers." If the printer is not on a Windows 2000 computer, then its path (UNC) is entered.

8. Moving an object within a domain can be done using the Move command on the context menu for the object. If you need to move the object between domains, you need to use MoveTree. For more information, see the section "Moving Objects Within the Directory."

9. The permissions will stay the same. The permissions on an object on which you have cleared the inheritance will stay the same whether or not the object is moved. For more information, see the section "Moving Objects Within the Directory."

10. The Advanced tab enables you to specify, in detail, what you are looking for by giving you a list of the objects for which you can search and the attributes that are available to search. For more information, see the section "Advanced Search."

ON THE CD

This book's companion CD contains specially designed supplemental material to help you understand how well you know the concepts and skills you learned in this chapter. You'll find related exercises and exam questions and answers. See the file **Chapter25ApplyYourKnowledge.pdf** in the CD's **Chapter25\ApplyYourKnowledge** directory.

Suggested Readings and Resources

1. *Microsoft Windows 2000 Server Manual.* Microsoft Press, 2000.

2. Microsoft Windows 2000 Resource Kit. *Deployment Planning Guide.* Microsoft Press, 2000.

This chapter covers some of the objectives and subobjectives from the units on "Installing, Configuring, and Troubleshooting Active Directory" and "Managing, Monitoring, and Optimizing the Components of Active Directory." Other objectives and subobjectives from these units are covered in other chapters.

Install, configure, and troubleshoot the components of Active Directory.

- **Transfer operations master roles.**

▶ This objective is included because of the importance of the operations masters. You need to understand what the various operations masters do and the effects of them being online. In addition, you should be able to transfer the operations master roles whether or not the previous master is available.

Back up and restore Active Directory.

- **Perform an authoritative restore of Active Directory.**

- **Recover from a system failure.**

▶ Backup and recovery are important aspects of managing a network. This includes backing up and recovering the directory services. This objective is included to make sure you are able to perform a normal recovery either by installing a replacement controller or by restoring from backup. In addition, you need to fully understand what an authoritative restore is and when you need to use it.

CHAPTER 26

Managing Servers

Manage Active Directory performance.

- **Monitor, maintain, and troubleshoot domain controller performance.**
- **Monitor, maintain, and troubleshoot Active Directory components.**

▶ This objective is included primarily to make sure you know how to monitor and maintain the Active Directory database. You need to know what tools are available and what tools you should use.

STUDY STRATEGIES

This chapter looks at the general administration of servers. The discussion begins with a look at the roles a server can take on for the network. Then, there is a discussion of the backup and recovery of servers, focusing on the three ways you can recover a domain controller. The remainder of the chapter looks at monitoring and maintaining servers on the network. As you read through the chapter, pay particular attention to the following points:

▶ You need to know the five operations master roles.

▶ You should note which roles are domain level and which are enterprise level.

▶ You should know how to transfer seize the roles.

▶ You should know which servers can be reinstated if the role is seized.

▶ You should know the standard backup and restore options when using the Microsoft Backup program.

▶ You need to know the three ways to restore a domain controller and when you should use each.

▶ You should be familiar with the options available on NTDSUTIL.

▶ You should know what tools are available to monitor a server or the network and when they can be used.

INTRODUCTION

One of the most common jobs a network administrator faces is managing servers. As you move into Windows 2000, there are no longer primary domain controllers, backup domain controllers, and member servers. However, there are several special types of servers of which you need to be aware and be able to manage, including the schema master, the domain-naming master, the PDC emulator, the RID master, and the infrastructure master.

Essentially, in addition to the tasks you learned about in Chapter 25, "Administering Active Directory Services," you need to be able to monitor your servers. You must perform backups and restores. You will also transfer the key server roles from one server to another.

SERVER ROLES

Install, configure, and troubleshoot the components of Active Directory.

- **Transfer operations master roles.**

The operations masters are critical to the operation of the network, and you need to make sure they are available when necessary. Some of these roles can be offline for a time without effect, while others have a dramatic impact if they are offline for even a short time.

In the next few sections, you will learn about each of the operations master roles. From there, the discussion will look at the placement of the roles and how to transfer the roles. Then, you will learn how to seize a role from a server that has crashed. Finally, there will be a look at the Global Catalog server.

Operations Masters

In Active Directory, changes to user accounts, computer accounts, shares, and so on can be made on any domain controller. This provides a great deal of flexibility. Some changes, however, should be made only in one place (changing the schema, for example).

Active Directory gets around this limitation by using a group of servers called operations masters. These servers are responsible for a role within the enterprise or within each domain. If a server is being brought down for service or crashes, you need to understand and be able to transfer the following five operations masters:

◆ **Schema master.** There is only one schema master for the entire enterprise. The schema master has the original version of the schema and is the only place where the schema can be changed.

◆ **Domain-naming master.** The server performing this role is responsible for the addition and removal of domains within the entire enterprise; therefore, there is only one in the enterprise. This server ensures the uniqueness of the domain name and makes sure that it fits within the enterprise name space. The information about the logical structure of the Active Directory name space is used in managing the trust relationship between the domains.

◆ **Relative ID (RID) master.** Every object created on a domain controller has a security ID (SID). In Active Directory, this is a combination of the domain's security ID plus a unique ID within the domain. The RID master is responsible for creating the second part of the SID; it generates a series of them for each domain controller and gives these identifiers to the controllers. Because the entire SID is only unique in the domain, it is considered a *relatively unique ID*. Obviously, there must be a RID master for each domain.

◆ **PDC emulator.** To support down-level clients, one of the domain controllers in a domain takes on the role of primary domain controller (PDC) emulator. This domain controller is responsible for replicating the Active Directory domain with the NT 4.0 backup domain controllers (BDCs). If your domain is in native mode, the PDC emulator receives preferential replication of password changes. If a down-level client attempts to log on and is serviced by another controller that has not received the update, that controller forwards the logon request to the PDC emulator.

> **EXAM TIP**
>
> **Enterprise Versus Domain Roles**
> Only two of the operations masters, the schema master and the domain-naming master, are enterprise roles in the forest. There can only be one of each of these operations masters in the entire forest.

◆ **Infrastructure master.** This server maintains the user-to-group mappings for its domain. As users are renamed or moved to a different container, the infrastructure master updates the references and replicates them to the other domain controllers. Each infrastructure master handles the accounts within its own domain, even for groups from other domains.

Each of these roles needs to be managed to make sure that it is available to the other systems on the network and to make sure that there is recoverability in case of a system crash. This involves planning the correct locations for these servers.

Planning Operations Master Locations

When you start to install your domain structure by installing your first domain controller, you are setting the location for all the roles previously mentioned. As the enterprise grows and you add child domains, the first domain controller you install in each of the domains is the domain operations master (RID, PDC emulator, and infrastructure) for that domain.

Generally, this works fine for a small domain located within a single building or for a forest that has few domains with few controllers. As you start to move beyond these basics, you might consider moving some of the domain operations masters. Planning the operations masters in a domain is discussed first in the next section, followed by a discussion of planning the operations masters in a forest.

Planning the Operations Masters in a Domain

In a domain with only one domain controller, that controller handles all the operations master roles. Because you are normally going to have multiple domain controllers, you have some choice as to which controllers to use for the various operations master roles. Generally, this should be one of the more powerful systems on the network. In addition, you can specify a standby operations master; this system should have a good connection to the operations master.

Usually, you keep the operations master roles together on the same server so that you don't have to keep track of the different roles.

However, if you have a large number of changes to groups, a large number of down-level clients, or you are constantly adding users and computers, you might consider separating the roles. Normally, you separate the roles by moving the PDC emulator to another system. If you do this, make sure that the system to which you move the role has good network connectivity with the standby operations master.

Planning the Operations Masters in a Forest

There is no advantage to separating the schema master and the domain-naming master. These are both operations that are performed only on occasion. The server that houses these roles should be near the stations used for administration. Other than this logistical concern, there is little need to change their location.

Now that you have seen how to plan for the location of the operations masters, you also need to know how to transfer these roles.

Setting Operations Master Roles

Transferring a master role moves the role from one server to another when both of the servers are available. The steps are similar for each of the roles you might have to move, as you will see in the next few sections.

Transferring the Schema Master Role

The schema master is one of the enterprise-level roles, and it only causes you problems when an administrator or a software installation attempts to modify the schema. Ensure that the schema master is available on the network whenever you install Active Directory-integrated software that performs schema modifications. Remember that the schema operations master role can only be transferred using the Active Directory Schema, MMC console, or using NTDSUTIL.

To transfer the schema master role, follow Step by Step 26.1.

ON THE CD

Step by Step 26.1, "Transferring the Schema Master Role," shows you how to transfer the schema master role. See the file **Chapter26-01StepbyStep.pdf** in the CD's **Chapter26\StepbyStep** directory.

Transferring the Domain-Naming Master Role

Make sure that the domain-naming master, like the schema master, is on a subnet that contains another domain controller so that all changes are quickly replicated to the second controller. Typically, you have the schema master and the domain-naming master on the same controller with another controller located on the same subnet for backup purposes.

The domain-naming master should also be configured as a Global Catalog server to ensure that the domain controller has knowledge of all domains and objects in the forest.

Use the procedure in Step by Step 26.2 to change the location of the domain-naming master role.

ON THE CD

Step by Step 26.2, "Changing the Location of the Domain-Naming Master Role," demonstrates how to change the location of the domain-naming master role. See the file **Chapter26-02StepbyStep.pdf** in the CD's **Chapter26\StepbyStep** directory.

Transferring the Domain-Level Master Roles

The operations masters at the domain level are typically on a single controller with another controller on the same subnet for backup purposes. You might occasionally have to move these roles to perform maintenance on the controller or if the server is about to crash. Step by Step 26.3 describes how to move one or all of the domain-level master roles.

Step by Step 26.3, "Transferring Domain-Level Single-Operations Masters," demonstrates how to change the location of the domain-naming master role. See the file **Chapter26-03StepbyStep.pdf** in the CD's **Chapter26\StepbyStep** directory.

As you can see, it is easy to move the operations master roles if the systems are both online. If this is not the case, you need to consider which master has failed and how long the system will be down. In some cases, you might have to seize the role.

Recovering from a Master Failure

As in Windows NT 4.0, if a system crashes, you need to take some action to correct the problem. In this case, you seize the role from the system that previously had it and give it to the standby system. This is a drastic step in some cases because the entire network could become corrupted if you were to return the original master to service at a later time. If you can, always transfer an operations master role rather than seizing the role. A seizure should be used only as a last resort. To seize a server role, follow the steps shown in Step by Step 26.4.

Step by Step 26.4, "Seizing a Single-Operations Master," illustrates how to seize a server role. See the file **Chapter26-04StepbyStep.pdf** in the CD's **Chapter26\StepbyStep** directory.

The complete session could look like the following screen dump.

```
C:\>ntdsutil
ntdsutil: roles
fsmo maintenance: connections
server connections: connect to server behemoth
Binding to behemoth ...
Connected to behemoth using credentials of locally logged
on user
server connections: quit
fsmo maintenance: seize PDC
Attempting safe transfer of PDC FSMO before seizure.
FSMO transferred successfully - seizure not required.
Server "behemoth" knows about 5 roles
```

EXAM TIP

Only Seize a Role When All Else Fails Seizing a role should be the method of last resort because this can cause problems on the network. When presented the option on the exam, you should always select transferring the role if the previous role holder can be restarted on the network.

```
Schema - CN=NTDS
Settings,CN=BEHEMOTH,CN=Servers,CN=HeadOffice,CN=Sites,CN=Co
nfiguration,DC=SunShineBrewing,DC=com
Domain - CN=NTDS
Settings,CN=BEHEMOTH,CN=Servers,CN=HeadOffice,CN=Sites,CN=Co
nfiguration,DC=SunShineBrewing,DC=com
PDC - CN=NTDS
Settings,CN=BEHEMOTH,CN=Servers,CN=HeadOffice,CN=Sites,CN=Co
nfiguration,DC=SunShineBrewing,DC=com
RID - CN=NTDS
Settings,CN=BEHEMOTH,CN=Servers,CN=HeadOffice,CN=Sites,CN=Co
nfiguration,DC=SunShineBrewing,DC=com
Infrastructure - CN=NTDS
Settings,CN=BEHEMOTH,CN=Servers,CN=HeadOffice,CN=Sites,
CN=Configuration,DC=SunShineBrewing,DC=com
fsmo maintenance: quit
ntdsutil: quit
Disconnecting from behemoth ...
```

Global Catalog Servers

In addition to the roles you already have seen, there is another role that a server can play within your enterprise: the role of Global Catalog server. The Global Catalog server keeps a listing of all information about objects in its domain, plus all the objects located in the other domains throughout the enterprise, but only a subset of the other domain object's properties.

The global catalog is used to contain some enterprise-wide information, such as the membership of universal groups. The other main function of the global catalog is to enable users and other processes to search the entire enterprise for objects that are required.

The first domain controller in the forest is the Global Catalog server by default. You can add more Global Catalog servers if you want or drop existing ones. However, there must always be at least one Global Catalog server per forest. To configure a domain controller as a Global Catalog server, follow the steps shown in Step by Step 26.5.

ON THE CD

Step by Step 26.5, "Configuring a Domain Controller to Host the Global Catalog," teaches you how to configure a domain controller as a Global Catalog server. See the file **Chapter26-05StepbyStep.pdf** in the CD's **Chapter26\StepbyStep** directory.

BACKING UP AND RESTORING SERVERS

System backup is critical in every production environment. There are always going to be problems requiring you to recover information that was accidentally lost or destroyed due to a system failure of some kind.

The version of Backup that ships with Windows 2000 is a drastic improvement over the previous versions. The most notable improvement is that you can now use media other than tape when performing backups. The Backup program enables you to perform the following:

◆ Back up selected files and folders.

◆ Restore backed-up files to the same or a different disk.

◆ Create an Emergency Repair Disk (ERD).

◆ Make a copy of remote storage data and data in mounted drives.

◆ Make a copy of the system state data including the Registry, the Active Directory database, and the certificate service database.

◆ Schedule backups to automate the process.

In the next few sections, you will learn about the Backup utility and how to use it to back up and restore a Windows 2000 Server.

Backup Types

As a rule, your first decision concerns the type and frequency of the backups you will perform as well as what you will back up. The Backup utility in Windows 2000 enables you to back up File Allocation Table (FAT) or NT File System (NTFS) partitions local to the system you are using to run the backup software. The Backup utility also enables you to back up FAT or NTFS partitions to which you are connected across the network.

There are five different types of backup you can perform to prevent data loss. These can be used alone or in combination. The following list describes the five types of backups you can perform.

◆ **Copy.** This type of backup simply takes the files you select and copies them to the backup media. The archive attribute is not changed during this type of backup. This is useful when you need to perform a quick backup before installing new software because it does not interfere with full or incremental backups.

◆ **Daily.** This backup method uses the date attribute of a file to copy any files that have changed during the day the backup is performed. This type of backup doesn't change the archive attribute either and, therefore, does not affect other types of backups. This is a quick method of grabbing the changes that take place during the day, and it can be used in conjunction with other types of backups to recover to the minute.

◆ **Differential.** During a differential backup, all the files where the archive attribute is set are backed up. The attribute, however, is not reset. This means that you can fully back up a system and then perform differential after differential. When restoring, you only need to restore the full backup and the last differential. The downside is that the size of the backup increases greatly over time.

◆ **Incremental.** This backs up all the files that have changed since the last full or incremental backup. It backs up the files and then resets the archive attribute to indicate the file has been backed up. With this type of backup, you would need to restore a full backup and then each incremental in sequence from that point forward.

◆ **Normal.** This is the full backup, and it simply copies all the selected files and clears the archive attribute as it is backed up. To effectively work with any other type of backup, you need to have first done a normal backup that can serve as a baseline.

Normally, you choose to work either with normal and incremental backups or with normal and differential. In either method, you perform a full backup weekly and then the differential or incremental daily. Using incremental backups reduces the amount of space required to hold the backups and the amount of time required to perform the daily backups. However, the recovery process takes longer. Using differential takes more backup space and more time, but the recovery time is reduced because only the normal and the last differential need to be restored.

Permissions Required for Backups

Obviously, if just anyone could go through and perform a backup, users could easily grab data off a system. By restoring that data somewhere else, users could access information they should not have. Therefore, you need to have the correct permissions to perform a backup.

To perform a backup, you generally need to be a member of the Backup Operators, Server Operators, or Administrators group. You need to be in one of these groups for the local system and for any system you are backing up remotely. This enables you to back up data that is not your own.

There are a couple precautions you might want to take when performing backups to make sure they don't become a security risk. One option you have during backup is to Allow Only the Owner and the Administrator Access to the Backup Data. This option prevents a person who accesses the tape, or another backup device, from restoring the files. Further, you can change User Rights so that Backup Operators can only back up data and not restore it.

> **WARNING**
>
> **Using Read Permissions**
> Remember that any user with read or higher permissions is able to copy (and therefore read) information.

Backing Up System State Data

The system state data is special data you need to plan to back up. This data cannot be backed up from across the network. It must be backed up from the local system. The system state data can include the following:

◆ The Registry

◆ The COM+ class registration database

◆ The boot files including the system files

◆ The certificate services database

◆ The Active Directory service database

◆ The *system volume* (Sysvol)

◆ The cluster service information

Not all these components are applicable to all configurations of Windows 2000. However, if you configure the backup system to back up system state data, the preceding items that are present will be backed up. You do not have the choice to back up individual pieces of the system state data; due to the interaction between the components, backup is an all or nothing deal.

When restoring system state data, you need to start the system in a special mode known as directory services restore mode. This is one of the choices from the F8 menu. You do have the choice to restore the system state data to an alternate location. This, however, only restores the Registry files, system volume information, cluster service database, and the system boot files. The other information is not restored because the COM+ registration database is built as components are installed, and they typically need to be reinstalled if the source files are in different locations. The certificate information also needs to be rebuilt because the certificate server needs to be reinstalled and will, therefore, have a new signing key.

The Active Directory database does not need to be restored. It is assumed that you will have more domain controllers and that, so they will be able to restore the information through the process of replication.

This can lead to a problem if part of your Active Directory is lost by accident. For example, if an organizational unit were accidentally deleted, restoring it from a backup would not restore the organizational until (OU). To restore a deleted object from Active Directory, you need to perform an authoritative restore.

Authoritative Restores

In cases such as a deleted OU, you could force a full restore to the normal location. This will restore the Active Directory database. The problem is that the original update sequence numbers (USN) will be restored with the object (every change to an object updates the sequence number, and the highest number is considered the most recent state). This means that the USN of the deleted object that is still in Active Directory will be higher than the one of the restored object, forcing the object to be deleted again.

If the OU were restored, during the next replication, the update sequence numbers would tell the local system that the OU had been deleted. Therefore, the OU would be deleted again and would not be replicated to the other domain controllers. To get around this problem, you use NTDSUTIL to perform an authoritative restore.

The process is straightforward in that you still perform the restore process. However, before you restart the server, you run NTDSU-TIL to tag the part of the Active Directory you are trying to recover. The process simply sets the update sequence number to a higher number. When you start the server and replication begins, the number on the copy you have is higher and is replicated to the other domain controllers.

Remember that if you are simply trying to recover a broken computer you need to perform a regular restore. This type of restore replaces the information, and then the replication process brings the system back up-to-date. If you restore to an alternate location, only part of the system state data is recovered, and the replication again brings the system up-to-date.

You need to perform an authoritative restore only if part of the Active Directory database is lost.

Performing Backups

Now that the theory is covered, it is time to look at how to perform backup and restore operations in detail. As you might guess, this section concentrates on using the Backup utility that comes with Windows 2000.

The Backup program that comes with Windows 2000 enables you to back up to tape or to a file. When you use a file, you need to give the location and a name for the file. The default extension of BKF (backup file) is optional; however, it is best to use defaults so that other users are aware of the file type. The file can be located on any fixed or removable media on the system or a share on a remote computer. If you use a tape, it must be local to your system.

The basic steps involved in a backup are as follows:

1. Using the tree view in the Backup program, select the files and folders you want to back up.

2. Choose the backup media you are using: either a file or a tape. Identify the file or tape you will use.

3. Choose the options you want, such as the type of backup you want to perform and whether you want to log the backup. You can also select whether to back up data from mounted drives, to specify files types not to backup, and whether to verify the backup.

4. Set any Advanced options and select the schedule for the backup.

You can also use the wizard incorporated to configure the backup.

Using the Backup Wizard

When backing up your network using Windows 2000 Backup, you can either manually configure the backup or use the Windows 2000 Backup Wizard.

Step by Step 26.6 walks you through the process of using the Backup Wizard to configure a backup.

ON THE CD

Step by Step 26.6, "Performing a Backup Using the Backup Wizard," guides you through the process of performing a backup using the Backup Wizard. See the file **Chapter26-06StepbyStep.pdf** in the CD's **Chapter26\StepbyStep** directory.

NOTE — Editing Scheduled Tasks To edit a scheduled task, open Start, Programs, Accessories, System Tools, Scheduled Tasks, and double-click the task.

Within the Backup Wizard, you can choose to schedule the backup process to take place at regular intervals. If you choose to set a schedule, multitudes of options are available including the capability to have multiple schedules. Step by Step 26.7 walks you through the scheduling of a backup.

ON THE CD

Step by Step 26.7, "Scheduling a Backup," walks you through the scheduling of a backup. See the file **Chapter26-07StepbyStep.pdf** in the CD's **Chapter26\StepbyStep** directory.

Performing a Non-Authoritative Restore

Being able to restore the information on a domain controller, or any other server, is important. This section looks at the basic restore. The next section looks at an authoritative restore.

The basics of restoring information to the server are fairly simple, as shown in Step by Step 26.8.

ON THE CD

Step by Step 26.8, "Performing a Basic Restore," illustrates the basics of restoring information to the server. See the file **Chapter26-08StepbyStep.pdf** in the CD's **Chapter26\StepbyStep** directory.

WARNING

Restoring to FAT If the information was backed up from an NTFS partition under Windows 2000, the data should be restored to the same partition. Several features of the NTFS are backed up including the permissions, encryption settings, and remote storage information, and they cannot be restored if the target drive is FAT. Some, but not all, of these features can be restored to an NTFS partition under NT 4.0.

Restoring a Domain Controller—Non-Authoritative

Back up and restore Active Directory.

- **Recover from a system failure.**

There are a couple ways you can restore a domain controller. You can allow replication to restore the Active Directory data to its current state on the network. This means you will be completely up-to-date. You can also restore the system state information from a backup.

Before you can perform either of the restores, you need to correct the problem with the system or reinstall the computer. If you need to rebuild the computer, you should make sure that the number and size of the disk volumes and their format are the same.

Restoring Using Replication

The easiest way to restore a domain controller is to use replication. This is normally done when you have to rebuild the computer due to a hardware problem or complete corruption of the operating system. This procedure works only if the system is not currently a domain controller (that is, the computer is freshly installed, and you have not run dcpromo). Any extra services that were running on the system need to be reinstalled and configured; otherwise, the entire configuration will be lost.

The process is very simple and relatively quick. Step by Step 26.9 walks you through the process of restoring a domain controller using replication.

ON THE CD

Step by Step 26.9, "Restoring a Domain Controller Using Replication," teaches you how to restore a domain controller using replication. See the file **Chapter26-09StepbyStep.pdf** in the CD's **Chapter26\StepbyStep** directory.

This process creates a working domain controller with all the current Active Directory information. Even if you plan to fully restore a system that is dead, you normally reinstall the computer and should follow this procedure to start the process.

Restoring from a Backup

If the domain controller had other services configured on it, you need to restore the entire domain controller. You need to back up the files and system state data before you begin this process.

Before you can restore system state data, you need to restart the computer and enter the Directory Services Restore mode. To do this, follow Step by Step 26.10.

ON THE CD

Step by Step 26.10, "Starting Your Computer in Directory Services Restore Mode," explains how to start your computer in Directory Services Restore mode. See the file **Chapter26-10StepbyStep.pdf** in the CD's **Chapter26\StepbyStep** directory.

After your system is in the correct mode, you can use the Restore program to restore the system state data and any other data you require such as the files required for services. To restore system state data, follow Step by Step 26.11.

ON THE CD

Step by Step 26.11, "Restoring System State Data," walks you through the process of restoring system state data. See the file **Chapter26-11StepbyStep.pdf** in the CD's **Chapter26\StepbyStep** directory.

After you restart, the system should be back to normal except that it might be out-of-date. This should clear up in short order, though, as replication brings in changes from all the other domain controllers in the domain.

This, of course, raises a question: What if you are restoring the Active Directory to restore one or more objects that had been deleted? Unfortunately, this type of restore will not work because it replicates with the other domain controllers and makes the local copy of Active Directory like every other copy. To restore a deleted object, you must perform an authoritative restore.

Performing an Authoritative Restore

Back up and restore Active Directory.

- **Perform an authoritative restore of Active Directory.**

Normally, when you restore a domain controller from backup, the information restored is exactly what was on the system. In most cases, this is exactly what you want to happen. However, if you are trying to undo the deletion of an Active Directory object, this won't work.

The attribute update sequence number for the object being restored is lower than the last update sequence number on the version of the object in the Active Directory of the other domain controllers. This means that when replication starts the other domain controllers, having a higher update sequence number on the object forces the local controller to delete this object. To prevent this, you need to

Restoring Domain Controllers
Whether you are performing an
authoritative or non-authoritative
restore, you must restart the computer in Active Directory Restore
mode. The Active Directory database cannot be online during a
restoration process.

perform an authoritative restore. An authoritative restore follows
exactly the same steps outlined in Step by Step 26.11, with the
addition of one other step before you restart the computer. This
additional step comes between the previous steps 7 and 8. The
purpose of this step is to increase the attribute update sequence
number to force the other servers to accept this as the newest
update to the object.

Step by Step 26.12 walks you through an authoritative restore.

ON THE CD

Step by Step 26.12, "Updating the USN to Undelete an Object,"
shows you how to update the USN to undelete an object. See the
file **Chapter26-12StepbyStep.pdf** in the CD's
Chapter26\StepbyStep directory.

The whole process looks like the following listing:

```
C:\>ntdsutil
ntdsutil: authoritative restore
authoritative restore: restore subtree
cn=testit,dc=sunshinebrewing,dc=com
Opening DIT database... Done.
The current time is 03-10-00 15:00.52.
Most recent database update occurred at 03-10-00 13:51.56.
Increasing attribute version numbers by 10000.
Counting records that need updating...
Records found: 0000000018
Done.

Found 18 records to update.
Updating records...
Records remaining: 0000000000
Done.

Successfully updated 18 records.
Authoritative Restore completed successfully.
authoritative restore: quit
ntdsutil: quit

C:\>
```

Hopefully, you will not have to perform authoritative restores too
often. However, as you can see, they are not overly difficult.

OTHER ADMINISTRATIVE FUNCTIONS

Manage Active Directory performance.

- **Monitor, maintain, and troubleshoot domain controller performance.**

- **Monitor, maintain, and troubleshoot Active Directory components.**

In addition to being able to handle problems that can arise from time to time, you should also know how to monitor your servers, including your domain controllers. Monitoring your domain controllers enables you to keep them performing at their optimum level.

This section looks at monitoring in general and at the tools available to help with monitoring. Various problems you might have with domain controllers and how to fix them are also addressed.

The NTDSUTIL Command

One of the key utilities for managing Active Directory is NTDSUTIL. This is a command-line utility that performs several different functions. These functions include the following:

- **Authoritative Restore.** As you have already seen, the authoritative restore can be used to force an object to be recovered. Restoring the object from a backup and then updating the update sequence number on the object does this.

- **Domain Management.** This option enables you to precreate objects in Active Directory, such as child domains, so that the user physically installing the system does not need to have Enterprise Administrator privileges.

- **File.** This option enables you to manage NTDS.DIT and related directory service database files. To manage these files, you need to start the computer in directory services restore mode so the files are not open.

- **IPDeny List.** This enables you to create a list of IP addresses from which the server will reject LDAP queries. This setting affects the default LDAP policy and, as such, affects all domain controllers that do not have a specific LDAP policy.

◆ **LDAP Policies.** To ensure that domain controllers continue to work properly, you might need to specify limits for a number of LDAP operations. This option enables you to set those limits.

◆ **Metadata Cleanup.** In a case in which a domain controller has failed or a domain has been removed without using DCPROMO, there will still be information about the domain or server in the configuration data. This utility enables you to clean up these orphaned records.

◆ **Roles.** As you have seen, there are five operations master roles. These roles need to be available for certain functions on the network to take place. This command enables you to transfer or seize the operations master roles.

◆ **Security Account Management.** This option enables you to find and clean up duplicate SIDs when there has been a problem with the RID master and there is a possibility of duplicate SIDs on the network.

◆ **Semantic Database Analysis.** The FILES command deals with the files that make up Active Directory. The semantic database analysis can be used to find problems with the linkages between logical structures. For example, it might find an orphaned user that is part of an OU that no longer exists. These inconsistencies should show up in the lost and found container as well.

EXAM TIP

The NTDSUTIL Command For the exam, you will not need to know the syntax of the NTDSUTIL command. Just be aware of the common functions that can be performed using the NTDSUTIL command.

The utility is very easy to use but does not provide a GUI interface. However, several of these functions might need to be performed at the recovery console, which is command line, so this utility will remain in place.

In addition to the NTDSUTIL used to examine and manage the Active Directory, there are also several utilities that can be used to monitor domain controllers and the network.

Monitoring a Domain Controller

Several tools can be used to monitor the systems on your network. The following sections examine the Task Manager, Event Viewer, Network Monitor, and Performance tools. Each of the tools has a particular use. Generally, you need to use more than one tool to find and resolve a problem.

Some of the tools are used more than others; most notably, the Task Manager can quickly determine whether more complete monitoring is required. This tool will be examined first.

Task Manager

One of fastest and easiest ways to check your system performance is to use the Task Manager. This tool was primarily meant for you to be able to start, stop, and view the tasks running on your system. In fact, however, Task Manager is also very useful as a troubleshooting tool.

To access the Task Manager, you can do any of the following:

◆ Press Ctrl+Shift+Esc.

◆ Right-click the taskbar and choose Task Manager.

◆ Press Ctrl+Alt+Del and click the Task Manager button.

After the Task Manager has started, you will notice that it has three different tabs: Applications, Processes, and Performance (see Figure 26.1).

Each of the tabs in the Task Manager shows you different information. The Applications tab tells you which applications are loaded and which of them are running. This is where you can end a task that is hung or frozen by selecting the application and clicking the End Task button. The New Task button can be used to start a new application.

The Processes tab enables you to see all the processes running on the system, including the applications and the services that make up Windows 2000. By default, you see the following columns in the Task Manager Processes tab.

◆ **Image Name.** This is the name of the process currently running. This enables multiple instances of the same program to run at the same time under different image names.

◆ **PID.** This is the process ID, which is used by the system to track the processes running within the Windows 2000 Kernel.

FIGURE 26.1
The Task Manager with Applications tab selected.

◆ **CPU.** This is the current percentage of the CPU time being used by the process. This is a quick way to tell which process is hogging the CPU. If you click a column label, such as CPU, it sorts the list by that column.

◆ **CPU Time.** This is the amount of time a process has spent actually executing.

◆ **Mem Usage.** This is the amount of memory the application is using on the system. This is another good counter if you need to quickly find out why you don't have enough memory or why you are experiencing excessive swapping to disk.

In addition to these counters, a number of other counters can be added. To add a counter, use the steps in Step by Step 26.13.

ON THE CD

Step by Step 26.13, "Adding Columns in the Task Manager," illustrates how to add columns in the Task Manager. See the file **Chapter26-13StepbyStep.pdf** in the CD's **Chapter26\StepbyStep** directory.

There are numerous columns you can add. If you are not sure about the meaning of a column, you can use the Help item on the menu to get details.

The last tab is a quick overview of the performance. This is not meant to be the sole source of performance information; rather, it is a quick look at the status of the system at the current moment. There are six main sections to this tab. These are broken down in the following list.

◆ **CPU Usage.** This shows the current CPU usage and graphs the usage for the last minute or so, depending on the update frequency you chose. Two options under the View item on the menu affect this area. CPU History refers to the graph where you can choose to have one graph per CPU or one total graph. The other option, Show Kernel Times, adds a second line in red to the graph showing kernel mode time. This is a quick check on the CPU for the system. If the processor(s) is (are) constantly over 80%, you should look at the Processes tab to see what service is having a problem. If no single process is overloaded, you should consider a system upgrade.

◆ **Mem Usage.** This shows the amount of memory currently in use. This can be a quick guide as to whether a system is overloaded. If the amount of memory in use is greater than that physically in the system, you need more memory.

◆ **Totals.** This section tells you the total number of handles, threads, and processes.

◆ **Physical Memory (KB).** This is the amount of physical memory in the system with a breakdown of the amount available and the amount used for system cache. Ideally, available memory should never drop below 4,096KB. Generally, the more memory available the better. However, if you find you have more than 65,536KB free, you probably have too much memory in the system, or some services didn't start.

◆ **Commit Charge (KB).** This is the total amount of memory committed to all the applications running on the system including both the physical RAM and the paging files. The Total is the amount currently committed. If this value is more than the total physical RAM, you should consider more memory for the system. The Limit is the amount of RAM and paging file space available. The Peak is the highest amount of memory committed since the system was last restarted.

◆ **Kernel Memory (KB).** This is the memory allocated to kernel functions, such as the server service and the RPC subsystem. The Total amount changes as the demands on the system increase. The Paged amount is the amount of memory that could be paged to disk, if required. The Nonpaged memory is the core of the operating system and varies depending on the drivers installed. If you notice that this amount increases slowly but steadily on a system, you probably have a memory leak. A memory leak occurs when a driver or other program allocates and uses memory but then does not free the memory correctly. Eventually, this causes your system to need to be restarted. You should remove the drivers, one at a time, until you see the leak stop. At that point, you should find a newer version of the driver.

Event Viewer

Windows 2000 can start even if there are problems with some services or devices. Although it is frustrating to sit there waiting for the service or device to fail so that the boot can continue, Windows 2000 does enable you to get into the system and fix the problem. After the system has started, you should look in the Event Viewer to determine the cause of the problem.

Parts of the Event Log

Like all the administrative tools in Windows 2000, the Event Viewer is a snap-in to the MMC. This has enabled Microsoft, and will enable other manufacturers, to add its logs to the event viewer. The six most common logs you will see are listed here for your reference:

◆ **Applications Log.** Any application written to Microsoft standards has the capability to record information in the applications log. This log often tells you why Exchange Server is not working or why the SQL server couldn't start.

◆ **Security Log.** Events that deal with the security of the system are tracked in this log. The information that is logged depends on the settings you select in the Group Policies. Remember, however, that excessive auditing is likely to affect system performance.

◆ **System Log.** All the device drivers and services, as well as other system-related components, record their errors in the system log. This is the log to look at when you get the At Least One Driver or Service Has Failed to Start message when you start Windows 2000.

◆ **Directory Service.** This is the log that tracks events related to the Active Directory database and its replication.

◆ **DNS Server.** This log tracks events that affect the DNS server. If you are having problems resolving network names or logging on, you should check this log.

◆ **File Replication Service.** This is the service that manages the replication of the files in the Sysvol. If you find that Group Policies or other information contained in the Sysvol directory fail to get to all the domain controllers, you should check this log.

A good habit to get into is checking the event logs on a regular basis. Event logs can often tell you what problems occurred that you weren't aware of and can indicate which errors might occur in the future.

Configuring the Event Logs

The event logs store a good deal of information. The more services and applications on a system and the more auditing you require, the larger the amount of information you receive. To prevent the event logs from filling up, which can cause other problems, you should configure the logs to the size you think will be required. This ensures that the log information will be there when you need it. Step by Step 26.14 shows you how to configure the event log settings.

ON THE CD

Step by Step 26.14, "Configuring Event Log Settings," demonstrates how to configure event log settings. See the file **Chapter26-14StepbyStep.pdf** in the CD's **Chapter26\StepbyStep** directory.

Because the event logs are recorded separately at each of the computers in your network, you need to set these options for each computer in your network. This can be done either by going to each system or by connecting to them over the network.

Connecting to a Remote System

You can view and configure the logs on a remote system by using your Event Viewer to connect to the event logs on the remote system. This is done using the steps shown in Step by Step 26.15.

ON THE CD

Step by Step 26.15, "Viewing the Event Log on a Remote Server," illustrates how to view event logs on a remote server. See the file **Chapter26-15StepbyStep.pdf** in the CD's **Chapter26\StepbyStep** directory.

Viewing event logs on a remote server enables you to check the status for remote systems without having to visit the system physically. This can be very useful if your clients are running Windows 2000 Professional because you can troubleshoot problems remotely using the event log.

Using the Event Log

The event log records all the activity on a system. Errors, along with the normal activity of a system, are recorded. Each type of event recorded in the event log is marked by an icon, which makes it easier to find problems. There are five icons you will see.

 Information. This is not a critical event but just an occurrence that took place. An informational message can be useful when you are making sure processes are running correctly.

 Warning. This is a warning that something didn't work correctly. The error didn't stop the process; however, you should check the process. There is some kind of problem.

 Error. This is a critical error and indicates that the process was not able to continue because of the error. Some processes continue to retry forever, filling the log with these critical errors.

 Failure. This indicates that someone was trying to perform an action for which he or she was not given permissions. This only occurs in the security log and should be checked.

 Success. This indicates that an action was attempted and the user had the correct permissions to perform the action. This is generally a good sign. However, you can use this information to track down people who have managed to break in to your system.

In most cases, you can ignore the informational messages. The key issues are the Failure audits in the security log. These should be checked immediately because they indicate that someone is attempting to do something for which they have not been granted permission.

In the other logs, you need to look at both the Warnings and the Errors. Normally, people start at the top of the log and move down when they first start to work with the event logs. The trick, however, is to find out where the errors start and then work up the log. When looking at the event log, the key is to find the event that was recorded when the computer most recently rebooted. Then, look sequentially from that point to determine what errors have occurred since the reboot occurred. This enables you to see the progression of the problem.

When you find the first or earliest event in the sequence that led to the failure, you should view the details of the event.

Viewing Event Details

Viewing the event details gives you more information about the event and sometimes even some useable data. All you need to do to view an event is double-click it (see Figure 26.2).

The Event Properties dialog box is divided into four main sections. The information at the top identifies the error and its source. There are three buttons that enable you to move about in the event log. The dialog box also contains the event Description and Data sections.

The section contains the following pieces of information:

- ◆ **Date.** The date of the event.

- ◆ **Time.** The time the event occurred.

- ◆ **Type.** The type of error (for example, Information, Warning, or Error).

- ◆ **User.** The name of the user causing the error or running the process that caused the error.

- ◆ **Computer.** The name of the computer where the event occurred.

- ◆ **Source.** The process, a program or service, that reported the event.

- ◆ **Category.** Some services have several components to them, and this helps identify which part of the service had the problem.

- ◆ **Event ID.** The number you look up in TechNet. This is the internal number from the service that describes this event.

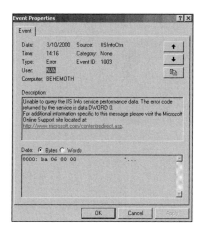

FIGURE 26.2
The details of an event.

The buttons that enable you to move about in the event log include an up arrow. This enables you to move up the event log, or forward in time, by default. This option is good for following the sequence of events. The down arrow does the opposite. The other button enables you to copy the event to the clipboard, so you can paste it into another application, such as email.

The description is supposed to help you understand what the error is, and Microsoft has come a long way in making these useful in Windows 2000. Occasionally, you still need to refer to other sources, such as TechNet for the Microsoft Web site, for the more cryptic messages.

The data is occasionally useful and can be displayed either as bytes or as words. Displaying it as bytes is best because this gives you readable characters on the right side. Displaying the message as words (16 bits of data makes a word) rarely ever gives you any useful information.

The process of going through the entire event log can take some time. To cut down the time required, you can filter the information listed in the log.

Filtering

There can be thousands of events listed in the event logs. To simplify the job of finding the problem, you can filter the log. Follow the steps shown in Step by Step 26.16 to filter a log.

ON THE CD

Step by Step 26.16, "Filtering an Event Log," walks you through the process of filtering an event log. See the file **Chapter26-16StepbyStep.pdf** in the CDs **Chapter26\StepbyStep** directory.

Filtering is one way to change the view of the events in the log. Other view options also are available, as discussed in the following section.

View Options

In addition to filtering the events, you can also use the View item from the Context menu to affect how the information is listed (see Figure 26.3).

NOTE

Finding Details on Event Log Messages Windows 2000 now ships with a database of error IDs that are found in the event viewer. This database is installed with the Windows 2000 support tools (located on the Windows 2000 CD in the \support\tools\support.cab file). After the support tools are installed, select Error and Event Messages from the Support Tools in the Start menu.

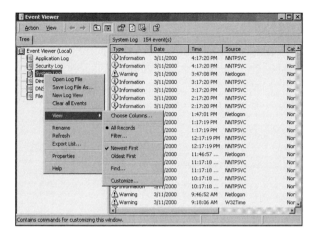

FIGURE 26.3
The View menu within the Context menu. You
need to click the log first to set the focus and
then right-click.

The following options are available:

◆ **Choose Columns.** This enables you to choose which columns
you see in the detail pane. By default, all the columns
are shown.

◆ **All Records.** This turns off a filter if one is applied.

◆ **Filter.** This is another way to get to the data filtering settings.

◆ **Newest First.** This lists the records from newest to oldest.

◆ **Oldest First.** This is the opposite of Newest First. Records are
listed from oldest to newest.

◆ **Find.** This brings up a dialog box similar to the Filter dialog
box. The difference is Find takes you to the next record, up or
down, matching your entry.

◆ **Customize.** This enables you to customize your view of the
Microsoft Management Console.

Now that you have seen most of the options that enable you to
customize the view of the event logs, this section concludes with a
quick look at saving and loading the log files.

Archiving Logs

In some cases, you might want to archive the event logs to review
them at a later time. You might want to pass them through a custom
application to look for problems. Saving and loading an event log is
done from the Context menu, as shown in Step by Step 26.17.

ON THE CD

Step by Step 26.17, "Saving and Retrieving Event Log Information," teaches you how to save and load an event log. See the file **Chapter26-17StepbyStep.pdf** in the CD's **Chapter26\StepbyStep** directory.

You can keep track of the events from a system over a period of time and review them at a later date.

Network Monitor

Although a full discussion of the Network Monitor would be interesting, it is outside the scope of this book. You are strongly encouraged to delve into the Network Monitor, however, so you can understand how to troubleshoot not only the local system but also the network to which it is attached.

As you prepare for the 70-240 exam, you need to know the function of the Network Monitor.

When a packet is sent on a broadcast-based network, such as Ethernet or Token Ring, the packet is received at every card on the subnet. Normally, the packet is evaluated, and the destination address is checked to see if it is a full broadcast or is intended for the local machine. If the packet is not destined to one of these addresses, it is discarded.

Network Monitor tells the card to enter promiscuous mode. The card begins grabbing all the packets on the network and storing them for analysis (see Figure 26.4).

The Network Monitor summarizes the data and reports the various protocols on the network. It can also enable you to actually see the traffic in a useful format (see Figure 26.5) in which it has interpreted all the codes from the network into understandable terms.

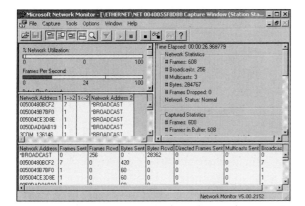

FIGURE 26.4
The Network Monitor capturing data.

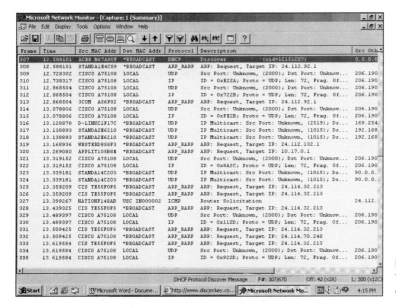

FIGURE 26.5
The view of the data that crossed the network
while the capture ran.

You can even zoom in on the information and look at the different layers (see Figure 26.6).

The Network Monitor enables you to see the information floating around on your network. This can be useful if you are having problems finding computers. You can see what the DNS query is and where it is going. If you can't authenticate, you can look at the session and authentication handshake. These are just two examples of what you can look for when using Network Monitor.

The Network Monitor enables you to see what is happening on the network. This might not help if the problem is the computer you are trying the fix. Therefore, Microsoft included the Performance tool, the other key diagnostic tool included in Windows 2000.

Performance

A full discussion of the Performance tool falls well outside the scope of this book. As you prepare for the 70-240 exam, however, you need to know the purpose and use of the Performance tool.

There are two parts to the Performance tool. There is the System Monitor, which enables you to graphically view the current activity or logged activity on a server. This enables you to see trends over a period of time and can give you up-to-the-minute information about your system.

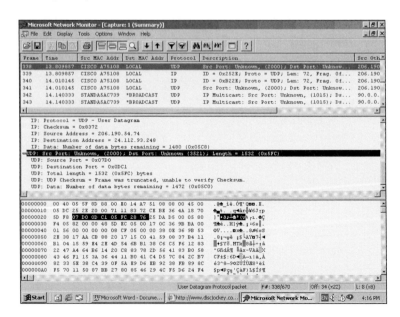

FIGURE 26.6
Looking at a packet of data in detail.

The other portion of the Performance tool is Performance Logs and Alerts, which enables you to create log files of the activity on a server or to configure alerts that will fire when certain thresholds are reached. You can use these tools to help you in several different tasks as noted in the following:

◆ Profile the services running on a computer to let you know how many users it supports and what resources are left for other services. This can be used to optimize the services used on domain controllers.

◆ Create a baseline of the performance of a system using Performance. That way, when you make changes in an attempt to increase the performance, you can compare current performance with baseline performance to judge the net effect.

◆ Maintain the level of service by monitoring the performance and tuning the system by adding or removing resources as the usage on the system changes.

You can draw a parallel here between the Network Monitor and Performance. What Network Monitor does for you on the network, Performance does for you on the computer.

Objects

Performance works by reading various performance counters. All the Microsoft services have built-in counters that Performance reads. The values that are read can be graphed, logged, or checked against an alert.

The source of the counter, the service that the counter is built in to, is known from the Performance point-of-view as a Performance object. For example, the processor is a Performance object exposed by the kernel, and server is a Performance object exposed by the Server service.

Each object has different counters you can read. There are some counters that most objects have, such as the % Processor Time. There are also counters specific to the object. For example, the Processor object has an Interrupts/Sec counter, and the Server object has a Logon/Sec counter.

In addition to choosing the object and the counter for the object, you can choose which instance of the object you want to examine. This is required because you can have more than one instance of an object available. For example, you could run two copies of the same program, or more likely, you could have two or more physical disks in a computer.

As mentioned previously, the Performance tool is broken down into two main pieces: the System Monitor and the Performance Logs and Alerts. The System Monitor is where you do the analysis and look at the data that the computer is generating or that you captured previously.

System Monitor

System Monitor is used to analyze the data you collect. The information for the System Monitor can come from the live system or can be read from a log file. From the live system, you can select any available object to monitor and can add whatever counters you want for the instance you want to examine.

In addition, you can specify the update frequency when looking at live data or the time window you want to view for recorded logs.

Another part of the Performance tool is its capability to log the counters on the system so you can look at them later in the System Monitor. It can also be used to set up alerts that fire when certain counters for a specific instance of a performance object fall below or rise above a given value.

Performance Logs and Alerts

Performance logs record the same information that you graph in the System Monitor. In fact, the data is viewed using that tool. Counter logs can be created to record any of the objects and counters available and can be scheduled to start and stop recording at given times. You also need to specify an update frequency for the log files.

There is also a Trace log you can create. This log tracks information about the starting and stopping of processes, or threads, or tracks disk I/O.

WARNING

Update Frequency Using a small update frequency—that is, many updates—affects system performance and causes the log to grow quickly, possibly filling the disk.

Alerts are the other part of Performance. Alerts enable you to configure a threshold value for a counter and have the system take an action when the value is exceeded (above or below). The specified action can be to send a network alert, start a counter log, or run a program.

Performance is the tool you use to determine the number of users a server can handle or to determine the source of a performance bottleneck.

You have now reviewed the main tools used for monitoring a domain controller or aspects of a domain controller. Several other tools are used to look at specific parts of Windows 2000 and Active Directory.

Other Troubleshooting Tools

In addition to the tools previously discussed, several other tools are part of the Resource Kit. The setup for these tools is found in the \SUPPORT\TOOLS folder on the Windows 2000 CD. Not all of the tools are related to Active Directory, but you should be aware of the following ones:

◆ **ACLDiag.** This utility enables you to determine whether a user has been given access to a directory object. It can also be used to reset access control lists to their default state.

◆ **ADSIEdit.** This MMC snap-in enables you to view all objects in the directory and to modify the objects or set access control lists on them.

◆ **DNSCMD.** This utility checks the dynamic registration of DNS resource records.

◆ **DOMMAP.** This utility checks the replication topology and domain relationships.

◆ **DSACLS.** This enables you to check and edit the access control list on directory objects.

◆ **DSAStat.** This compares the information on domain controllers, looking for differences.

◆ **ESEUtil.** This utility works on the extensible storage engine and can repair, check, compact, move, and dump database files. The NTDSUtil calls these functions to perform various tasks.

◆ **NETDOM5.** This utility handles the batch management of trusts, joining computers to domains and verifying trusts and secure channels.

◆ **NETTest.** This utility can check end-to-end network connectivity as well as distributed services functions.

◆ **NLTest.** This program makes sure the locator service and secure channel are functioning.

◆ **NTDSUtil.** In addition to managing operations masters and allowing authoritative restores, this utility manages the database files using ESEUtil and lists site, domain, and server information.

◆ **REPAdmin.** This checks replication consistency between replication partners, monitors replication status, displays replication metadata, and forces replication events and knowledge consistency checker recalculation.

◆ **REPLMon.** This program displays replication topology, monitors replication status, and can force replication events and knowledge consistency checker recalculation.

◆ **SDCheck.** This tool enables an administrator to determine whether access control lists are being correctly inherited and whether access control list changes are being replicated from one domain controller to another.

◆ **SIDWalker.** This utility enables you to set the ACL on objects owned by accounts that have been moved, deleted, or orphaned.

EXAM TIP

Know the Tools That Are Available to You   These tools can be used after you determine where the problem lies to pinpoint the problem and to help you fix it. You should be familiar with the name and purpose of each of these tools for the exam. If you have time, you should also try each of the tools to have a feel for them.

The monitoring of servers is important for being able to fix problems before they occur. The tools you have just seen all have a place and time when they should be employed, and you should make sure you understand the use for each.

CASE STUDY: MONITORING AND MANAGING ACTIVE DIRECTORY

ESSENCE OF THE CASE

Looking back at the SunShine Brewing company, you will remember that there are a number of locations you need to deal with and five different domains that span all the locations. This makes the recovery more difficult because you need to be able to recover any domain from any location. Some of the other factors to consider are listed here.

▶ There are few changes to Active Directory, and although users might move from location to location, they will typically stay in the same line of work and therefore the same domain.

▶ You will need to have a Global Catalog server per site. There will be a large number of sites.

▶ For recoverability, you will control the operations masters in Ottawa.

▶ You will schedule all backups to happen automatically.

With this in mind, there isn't a lot that requires analysis in this case.

SCENARIO

This case study deals with preparing for recovery. This is something that should be planned well in advance and should include where to get parts or other servers. You should also plan for locating servers in case the computer room is not available. Your plan should also deal with emergency power.

This case, however, deals specifically with the placement of servers and how the backup strategy will be planned.

ANALYSIS

To facilitate the operations master, a pair of domain controllers will be located in Ottawa, and a connection object will be created between them to make sure they are replication partners. One of these servers will be configured as the schema and domain-naming master, and the other will be just a domain controller. For the domain-level operations masters, a similar pairing will be created in the Ottawa office for each of the domains.

In the Ottawa office, backups will be taken weekly with a differential taken each night for the servers configured as the operations master and backup. These backups will be kept for four weeks and then rotated back through the backups. There will also be monthly, quarterly, and yearly backups. The monthly backups will be kept on site until the next monthly backup, at which time they will be stored off site for 15 years.

CHAPTER SUMMARY

KEY TERMS

- Authoritative restore
- Backup
- Event Viewer
- Global Catalog server
- Infrastructure master
- Network Monitor
- NTDSUTIL
- Operations master
- PDC emulator
- Performance
- Restore
- RID master
- Single master
- System state data
- Task Manager

This chapter looked at server roles, including the two enterprise roles: schema master and domain-naming master. It also looked at the three master roles found in each domain: the PDC emulator, the RID master, and the infrastructure master. You saw what purpose each role served and how to move the role to another server or seize the role when the server crash is unrecoverable.

Next, you looked at the backup and restore options available in Windows 2000. The basics of backups—the different types and their uses—were discussed, and the Backup program was introduced. The restore process for servers that had other services was examined. You also learned how to reinstall basic servers. The discussion then covered the authoritative restore process and the requirements associated with this process.

Finally, you were introduced to some of the monitoring/troubleshooting tools available. These tools take a lot of practice, and you should work with them for a period of time before attempting the exam.

APPLY YOUR KNOWLEDGE

Review Questions

1. What is the role of domain-naming master?

2. What must you restore before restoring an incremental backup?

3. You need to determine the number of users that a new type of server can handle. Which tool should you use?

4. What are the two components that make up the SID of an object in Active Directory?

5. What utility do you use to grab the schema master role if it has failed?

6. You have a server that cannot find other servers on the network. What tool can you use to determine what queries it is sending?

7. You have had to seize the schema master role. What precaution should you take with the server it has replaced?

8. When you start your computer, you get a message indicating that a service or device failed to start. What should you do to determine the cause of the problem?

9. You need to restore an organizational unit that was accidentally deleted. What must you do?

10. If you need to seize a role, what should you consider when choosing the server on which to place the role?

Answers to Review Questions

1. The domain-naming master is responsible for the addition and removal of domains within the entire enterprise. Therefore, there is only one in the enterprise. This server ensures the uniqueness of the domain name and that it fits within the enterprise name space. See the section "Server Roles."

2. To restore an incremental backup, you first need to restore the last full backup before the incremental. You also need to restore all the incremental backups that were performed in order. See the section "Backup Types."

3. In this case, you should use the Performance tool. This will enable you to profile the services that the server will run so you can determine what size load each service will place on the server. This information will enable you to estimate the number of users that the server can handle. See the section "Monitoring a Domain Controller."

4. The SID of an object is made up of the domain SID followed by a relative identifier supplied to the domain controller in batches from the RID master. See the section "Server Roles."

5. If you need to seize a role, you should use NTD-SUTIL. This tool forcibly takes the role, even if the original server is not available. In most cases, you should make sure the previous server is never returned to service because this would place two of the same operations masters on the network. See the section "Recovering from a Master Failure."

APPLY YOUR KNOWLEDGE

6. In this case, you would use the Network Monitor to enable you to see the actual queries being sent and the responses, if any, from the other servers. See the section "Monitoring a Domain Controller."

7. After seizing the schema master role, you must make sure the previous server is never returned to the network because this would place two schema masters on the same network. See the section "Recovering from a Master Failure."

8. Whenever you get this message, the first place you should look is the Event Viewer. The event log should contain details about the error that occurred during startup. Remember to find a time before the error occurred and work your way forward in time. See the section "Monitoring a Domain Controller."

9. If you need to restore an Active Directory object that has been deleted, you need to perform an authoritative restore. This increases the change number on the object to one sufficiently high enough to force the object to replicate back to the other servers. See the section "Performing an Authoritative Restore."

10. The best server is a server that is on the same subnet as the previous server. This way, you can be assured that the server had the most up-to-date information possible. Failing this, you should check the Sites and Services to determine the replication partners for the server and then choose one of these. See the section "Recovering from a Master Failure."

ON THE CD

This book's companion CD contains specially designed supplemental material to help you understand how well you know the concepts and skills you learned in this chapter. You'll find related exercises and exam questions and answers. See the file **Chapter26ApplyYourKnowledge.pdf** in the CD's **Chapter26\ApplyYourKnowledge** directory.

Suggested Readings and Resources

1. Microsoft Windows 2000 Server Resource Kit. *Microsoft Windows 2000 Server Operations Guide.* Microsoft Press, 2000.

2. Microsoft Windows 2000 Server Resource Kit. *Microsoft Windows 2000 Server Deployment Planning Guide.* Microsoft Press, 2000.

This chapter covers some of the objectives and subobjectives from the unit "Installing, Configuring, Managing, Monitoring, Optimizing, and Trouble-shooting Change and Configuration Management." The other objectives and subobjectives are covered in other chapters.

Implement and troubleshoot Group Policy:

- **Modify Group Policy inheritance.**

- **Create a Group Policy object (GPO).**

- **Link an existing GPO.**

- **Filter Group Policy settings by associating security groups to GPOs.**

- **Delegate administrative control of Group Policy.**

- **Modify Group Policy.**

▶ Group Policy is one of the key features of Windows 2000. This feature enables you to control user and computer environments. The purpose of this objective is to help you become comfortable with the process of adding Group Policy to an Active Directory container, linking existing Group Policies to an Active Directory container, and deleting Group Policy objects (GPOs). You will also be tested on the inheritance of Group Policy between different Active Directory containers: sites, domains, and organizational units. Configuring security of Group Policy objects, including delegating administration of a Group Policy to other users, will also be tested.

C H A P T E R 27

Using Group Policy to Manage Users

Manage and troubleshoot user environments by using Group Policy.

- **Control user environments by using administrative templates.**

- **Assign script policies to users and computers.**

▶ The purpose of this objective is to help you become familiar with the process of creating and modifying Group Policy to manage user environments. This can be done in one of two ways: using administrative templates or using scripts.

Administrative templates modify Registry settings for either or both the user and computer onto which the user is logging. You will be tested on the options available to manage what the user is able to do and when to use computer settings or user settings within the administrative templates.

In some cases, scripts might be necessary to provide more control over a user environment beyond that which is available through administrative templates. You will be tested on how to create scripts, how scripts are processed, as well as what types of scripts are possible.

Manage network configuration using Group Policy.

▶ The purpose of this objective is to make sure you are familiar with network elements that can be controlled using Group Policy. This includes redirection of certain folders, settings for how Remote Access System (RAS) and network connections work, and whether users are able to make changes to network settings.

► When preparing for the Group Policy elements of the Implementing and Administering a Microsoft Windows 2000 Directory Services Infrastructure exam, the best way to become proficient in the topic is to make use of it. In other words, it is imperative that you follow the Step by Steps and exercises in this chapter to understand how Group Policy functions and what kind of things it can be used to control. A thorough understanding of Group Policy inheritance,
filtering, and the options surrounding these two areas is also required. You will be tested on your knowledge of not only how to configure Group Policy but of how it works. The exam and review questions at the end of this chapter and on the accompanying CD will also help you understand more about how it works.

► Because Group Policy is such a large topic in the Windows 2000 world, it has been broken down into three chapters in this section of the book. A good understanding of what can be accomplished with Group Policy in all its areas (administrative templates, security settings, software deployment, and desktop configuration) is also recommended. For this reason, you should be comfortable with the information presented in this chapter as well as the next two chapters.

INTRODUCTION

One of the most powerful tools within the Windows 2000 Active Directory construct is the capability of using Group Policy to provide centralized control over users, groups, and computers within a large enterprise. Group Policy enables the administrator of a very large network to control what occurs on a user's desktop even if the user is many miles away.

INTRODUCTION TO GROUP POLICY

A challenge facing any administrator of a Windows 2000 network is how to make sure users' desktops and other settings conform to corporate standards. This is especially true of large organizations with many users and even several sites in different and disparate locations. Group Policy is able to ensure that administration of these settings can be controlled centrally and to ensure that the settings apply to all users who require them, regardless of the user's location.

With Group Policy, an administrator can define the state of a user's work environment once. Windows 2000 Active Directory continually enforces these settings no matter which machine the individual uses or where he or she might happen to be. With Group Policy, an administrator is able to do the following:

◆ Enforce centralized control of user and computer settings at the site and domain level or, optionally, provide the ability for local administrators to incorporate local settings at the organizational unit (OU) level.

◆ Provide a desktop environment that enables users to perform their duties while ensuring that critical applications cannot be modified or removed.

◆ Control what a desktop looks like and how a computer behaves, including which software is or can be installed.

◆ Ensure that corporate policies, including business rules and security requirements, are enforced.

Group Policy is an Active Directory object. It can be used to enforce the previously mentioned settings on any Windows 2000 client computer. These clients include Windows 2000 Professional, Windows 2000 Server, Windows 2000 Advanced Server, and Windows 2000 Data Center Server.

GROUP POLICY COMPONENTS

Group Policy is an object within Active Directory. It is commonly referred to as a Group Policy object (GPO). The GPO includes settings that enable you to control many different aspects of the computing environment. It is an object within Active Directory and can be associated with different Active Directory containers (sites, domains, and OUs). Because GPOs can be associated with different Active Directory containers, they can be used to enforce organizationwide (site and domain) or department-level (OU) rules.

Group Policy objects are actually composed of two parts: the Group Policy container (GPC) and the Group Policy Template (GPT).

The GPC (see Figure 27.1) is an Active Directory object that includes GPO attributes and version information. Each GPO is represented by a Globally Unique Identifier (GUID). The GUID is a 128-bit number that uniquely identifies the GPO within the forest, domain tree, and domain. The GUID cannot be changed or removed by the user and is automatically maintained by Active Directory. Version information is also attached to the GPO and is tracked within Active Directory. This information is attached to the GPC and is shared by domain controllers. Each domain controller uses the information contained within Active Directory and the GPC to make sure it is running the most recent version of a GPO. If it does not have the most recent version, replication occurs, transferring the most recent version from another domain controller. Step by Step 27.1 shows you how this is done.

> **NOTE**
>
> **Group Policy on Older Windows Clients**   Group Policy can be used to enforce settings only on Windows 2000 clients. Windows NT 3.51 or Windows NT 4.0 clients must use System Policies to enforce user and computer settings within the NT domain structure. The same also holds true for Windows 95 and Windows 98 clients.

> **NOTE**
>
> **Preconfigured GPOs**   When you install Active Directory and create the first domain controller in the first domain in the first forest, Windows 2000 Active Directory creates two Group Policy objects automatically: the Default Domain Policy and the Default Domain Controller Policy. If you want to have a default set of values in GPOs for all users and computers in the domain, you modify the Default Domain Policy. Similarly, if you want all domain controllers in all domains to start with the same settings, you modify the Default Domain Controller Policy on that first domain controller. As you will find out later, domain administrators within the subdomains can modify these after the fact.

FIGURE 27.1

The Group Policy container within Active Directory Users and Computers.

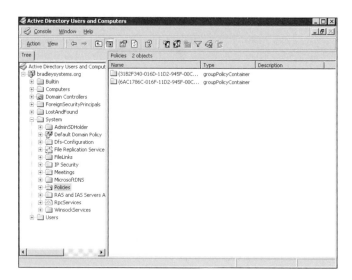

ON THE CD

Step by Step 27.1, "Viewing Group Policy GUIDs," demonstrates the process for viewing Group Policy GUIDs. See the file **Chapter27-01StepbyStep.pdf** in the CD's **Chapter27\StepbyStep** directory.

> **EXAM TIP**
>
> **Know Where Group Policy Is Stored**   Remember when taking the exam that the actual Group Policy information is stored in the SYSVOL shared folder. The Group Policy that is applied to a computer or user is determined by querying Active Directory, but the actual Group Policy is read from the SYSVOL share.

The GPT is a set of folders and subfolders in the SYSVOL share on Windows 2000 domain controllers. Each GPO created always results in the creation of a folder hierarchy, which contains the physical files and settings required by the GPO. These include administrative templates, security settings, scripts, software installation information, and folder redirection settings. Windows 2000 clients connect to the SYSVOL shared folder to obtain these settings and apply what is contained within them.

Each GPT folder is named the same as the GUID of the GPO, which is also the same GUID used to identify it in the GPC. In this way, if you rename a GPO after creating it, the unique identifier used by Active Directory (the GUID) and the corresponding GPT structure, as well as the GPC, do not change. Figure 27.2 shows the structure of a sample GPT in the SYSVOL share of a domain controller.

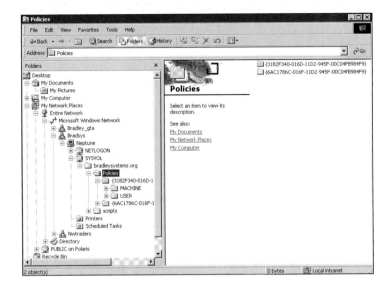

FIGURE 27.2
The Group Policy Template folder hierarchy within the SYSVOL share of a Windows 2000 domain controller.

GROUP POLICY SCOPE

Group Policy has particular sets of rules it follows when applied to users and computers. One set of these rules deals with what happens at each Active Directory container where Group Policy exists (inheritance), while another deals with how settings from multiple GPOs are combined to provide an effective policy application. Finally, a third set of rules deals with how GPOs are processed within the same Active Directory container. All these areas are addressed in this section.

Each GPO can be linked to one or more containers within Active Directory because GPOs are composed of a separate Group Policy container. You can create a single Group Policy object with a predefined collection of settings to be applied. This GPO can then be selectively linked to only the Sales and Marketing organizational units within the Corporate domain, while other organizational units such as R&D and Tech Support might not have these GPOs linked to them. In this way, GPOs make sure only certain users and computers have these settings enforced and others do not. The benefit derived is that it is unnecessary to create separate GPOs to enforce the same settings for several parts of your company. One GPO can be used for more than one organizational component within Active Directory.

Administrators can also link more than one GPO to the same Active Directory container. For example, instead of putting both user desktop settings and software installation information into one GPO, an administrator might decide to have a separate GPO for each item. In this way, any changes to the desktop, which are made through the GPO, do not cause the software installation GPO to be unnecessarily replicated. This makes administration easier and can have a beneficial impact on performance. When a user logs on or a computer is started, the appropriate GPOs are applied if configured for that container.

Group Policy Inheritance

When processing Group Policies, a clear inheritance hierarchy is followed (see Figure 27.3): x, then y, and then z. This means that if similar settings exist at different levels, the order in which the GPOs are applied determines which setting is the final one applied to the computer or user. In this way, it is possible for an administrator at an OU level to overwrite a setting defined at the domain or site level. As you will see later in this chapter, it is also possible for a higher-level (domain or enterprise) administrator to override this capability.

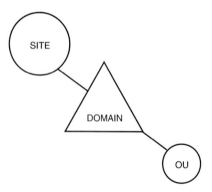

FIGURE 27.3
Group Policy inheritance during processing.

The first GPOs to be processed are those for the Active Directory site where the user's computer is physically located. The computer and user settings for the site are processed and applied to the Registry. Because the site represents a physical location and because a single site can actually have more than one domain, it is important to start with the Group Policy that usually takes into account language and other regional differences.

The next GPOs to be processed are those for a domain. Each user, group, and computer is always associated with a domain. Domainwide policies affect all users and are primarily used to enforce domainwide security restrictions or general business rules and settings that need to be in place. As with the application of GPOs to sites, computer and user settings defined within the policy are applied to the Registry.

The last GPOs to be processed are those for the OU in which the user or computer is located within Active Directory. Active Directory enables a domain or enterprise administrator to further subdivide the users and computers within a domain into administrative units called OUs, so this policy should apply to the smallest number of objects and should make sure a very specific set of rules is also enforced.

Group Policy Processing

As previously mentioned, GPOs can be linked to a site, domain, or OU within Active Directory. More than one GPO can be linked to the same container, and they will all be processed together depending on the security and other settings configured.

When a user logs on to a Windows 2000 computer, any GPOs that have been associated with the site, domain, or OU to which the user belongs and that have been configured to run for that user, or the group of which that user is a member, will be applied. This means that two users logging on to the same computer at different times might have completely different environments as a result of the policy settings applied to each. Further, after a user logs on to a computer, Windows 2000 also processes any logon scripts that have been configured to run for him or her or for a group of which he or she is a member.

NOTE

Local Group Policy Object Each computer running Windows 2000 also has a local GPO. In this way, it is possible to configure settings that apply only to this one computer and are not replicated to other Windows 2000 machines. When Active Directory is used, these settings can be overwritten by policies defined at the site, domain, or OU level. These settings have the lowest priority. In a non–Active Directory environment, as in a workgroup setting with no Windows 2000 domain controllers, these GPOs are the only ones that can be applied and thereby increase in importance.

NOTE

System Policy Processing In environments in which both Windows 2000 clients and Windows 95/98 or Windows NT 4.0 clients exist, you might still need to keep System Policies around to enforce desktop and other settings. When a Windows 95/98 or Windows NT 4.0 client is used to log on to the network, it still processes System Policy, not Group Policy.

If Windows NT 4.0 domain controllers exist on the domain, they also supply System Policy to users when they log on to the domain. This can change the configuration of client computers, even Windows 2000 clients, based on the policy settings. It is recommended that domain controllers be upgraded to Windows 2000 as quickly as possible.

Administrators can change what is contained in GPOs over time, and some of these settings might need to be applied within a very short time. This is why Windows 2000 provides for an automatic refresh of Group Policy while systems are running and users are still logged on. This ensures that Group Policy is consistently applied to all users and computers, even if the user never logs off or if the computer is never turned off.

Domain controllers within Windows 2000 Active Directory refresh or reapply GPOs every five minutes. Windows 2000 member servers, considered clients in the processing of Group Policy, refresh Group Policy every 90 minutes, plus or minus a 30-minute stagger factor. This ensures that all the domain controllers and the servers to which users will be connecting have an up-to-date copy of any Group Policy.

Windows 2000 clients also refresh GPOs but only every 90 minutes, plus or minus 30 minutes. The refresh internal itself is staggered among Windows 2000 client computers to ensure that network bandwidth does not get saturated because of GPO refresh.

The default refresh rate for a GPO can be changed within the GPO template. This means that if the preceding default settings are too frequent, you can reduce the frequency of GPO refresh or vice versa. Caution should be used when changing the refresh rate. Changing the refresh rate can result in a long lag time between a change to a GPO and its application on a client computer. Changing the refresh rate can cause network problems if the refresh internal is shortened because all clients need to communicate more frequently with domain controllers to see if a refresh is required.

One of the major changes in Windows 2000 is the capability of having Group Policy settings inherited at different levels of Active Directory (site, domain, or OU). Having GPO settings automatically reapplied to all domain controllers, member servers, and Windows 2000 clients to ensure an up-to-date list of settings is a key benefit. The combination of Group Policy inheritance (the order in which GPOs are evaluated) and processing (how GPOs are processed within the same container and on the network) is a very important point of discussion and is covered next.

> **NOTE**
>
> **Refresh Rules** Software installation, offline files, and folder redirection settings, which can be configured in Group Policy, do not follow the refresh rules. These GPO settings are applied only when a computer starts up or a user logs on.

Combining Group Policies

Implement and troubleshoot Group Policy.

• **Modify Group Policy inheritance.**

It is possible to create more than one policy at the site, domain, or OU level with different or similar settings. Therefore, it is important to understand exactly what will happen if GPOs are combined and what the net effect of all the GPOs will be as a result.

When a computer starts up and a user logs on, the domain controller figures out which GPOs need to be applied for both the computer and the user. In doing so, the domain controller processes the GPOs for the computer first and then for the user and forwards to the client a list of GPOs to be applied. The client then connects to the SYSVOL folder of the domain controller, locates the GPT of the first GPO provided by the domain controller, and applies the Group Policy settings. This process is repeated for all GPOs that the domain controller specified to the client.

The process proceeds according to the Group Policy inheritance rules previously discussed (site, then domain, and finally OU). If at any level of this processing, multiple GPOs apply to the computer and/or user at the same level (site, domain, or OU), they are processed, bottom to top, in the order in which they appear in the Group Policy tab of the container to which they are linked. In the example shown in Figure 27.4, if both GPOs are applied to the same user or computer, the Password Policy would be applied first and then the Default Domain Policy. If any settings in the Password Policy (see Figure 27.5 for an example of password settings) also existed in the Default Domain Policy, the setting in the Default Domain Policy would take precedence.

Connecting to the GPO   Because site, domain, and OU policies may all be processed, the client computer actually connect to more than one domain controller. As a rule, the client must connect to a domain controller in the domain where the GPO was created. For domain GPOs and OU GPOs, this always is the domain in which the user logging on is defined; for sites, it is the domain in which the GPO was defined.

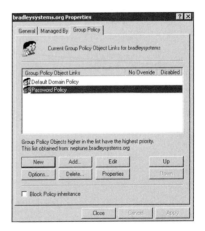

FIGURE 27.4
Multiple GPOs can be linked to the same Active Directory container. Processing is bottom to top.

FIGURE 27.5
Password Policy settings for complexity and password length.

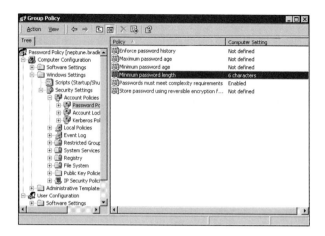

Group Policy Processing Rules

As previously mentioned, a series of rules are followed by Windows 2000 when applying Group Policy. Some of these already have been discussed, but it is beneficial to have the rules presented together:

◆ All Group Policy settings apply unless a conflict is encountered. This means the effective policy settings applied to a user or computer are the sum total of all site, domain, and OU GPOs that have been specified for the user and computer.

◆ A conflict may occur and is defined as the same setting being defined at more than one level or in more than one GPO at the same level. When a conflict is encountered, the rules of policy inheritance are followed until it is resolved.

◆ Policy inheritance follows the path of site, then domain, and finally OU.

◆ If more than one GPO is linked to the same Active Directory container, GPOs are processed from the bottom to the top as they are listed in the Group Policy tab for the container.

◆ The last setting processed always applies. This means that when settings from different GPOs in the inheritance hierarchy conflict, the one that applies is the setting specified in the last container.

◆ When settings from GPOs linked to the same Active Directory container conflict, the GPO at the top of the list is the one that applies.

◆ If a setting is specified for a user as well as a computer at the same GPO level, the computer setting always applies when it conflicts with a user setting. In other words, at the same GPO level, computer settings take precedence over user settings.

CREATING AND MANAGING GROUP POLICY

Implement and troubleshoot Group Policy.

• **Create a Group Policy object (GPO).**

• **Link an existing GPO.**

You can create GPOs in a site, domain, or OU if you have administrative rights for the container in which you want to create the policy. Step by Step 27.2 shows you how to create a Group Policy for the domain.

ON THE CD

Step by Step 27.2, "Creating a Group Policy for the Domain," illustrates how to create a Group Policy for the domain. See the file **Chapter27-02StepbyStep.pdf** in the CD's **Chapter27\StepbyStep** directory.

Creating a GPO is a very straightforward process. Managing it after the fact is quite easy as well. The hard part is determining which settings to apply within the GPO and which users and computers should have the policy enforced. These are discussed later when you are introduced to administrative templates as well as in Chapter 28, "Software Distribution Using Group Policy," and Chapter 29, "Managing Security Using Group Policy."

GROUP POLICY SECURITY

Implement and troubleshoot Group Policy.

- **Filter Group Policy settings by associating security groups to GPOs.**

- **Delegate administrative control of Group Policy.**

One of the best features of Group Policy in Windows 2000 is the capability of determining which users and computers a GPO applies to as well as which users are allowed to administer the policy. Through the selective use of permissions and security, the administrator has the ability to provide very precise access to and application of any GPO created.

When setting permissions for Group Policy, the administrator is able to configure two things:

◆ To whom the policy will apply

◆ Which users will be permitted to make changes to the policy, as well as its inheritance

Configuring Group Policy Security

In configuring Group Policy security, you should be concerned with a number of areas. First, you need to set permissions on Group Policy to determine to which users and computers the GPO will apply. You also need to specify permissions to enable other users to modify the policy. If you want to be very precise, you can configure advanced permissions for the GPO; this gives you extremely fine control of which privileges will be given to whom.

Setting Permissions to Use the Policy

Setting permissions is the initial stage in configuring Group Policy security. By default, Group Policy is applied to members of the Authenticated Users system group. If you do not want this to be the case and want to restrict the application of Group Policy to a specific set of users, computers, or groups, you would assign permissions explicitly. Step by Step 27.3 walks you through setting permissions.

ON THE CD

Step by Step 27.3, "Setting Permissions to Use a GPO," teaches you how to set permission to use a GPO. See the file **Chapter27-03StepbyStep.pdf** in the CD's **Chapter27\StepbyStep** directory.

Setting Permissions to Manage the Policy

In larger enterprise environments, administration of a Windows 2000 Active Directory structure could be quite decentralized. At the same level in the Active Directory hierarchy, there might be many different administrators all with a specific set of tasks to perform. Group Policy encompasses many areas related to computer configuration and user environment settings. For this reason, it might be beneficial to have other individuals responsible for modifying GPO settings.

As an administrator, you can grant the ability to change and update settings of GPOs that have been created to other users who do not actually have administrative privileges on the container to which the GPO has been linked. For users to make changes to GPO settings, they need two permissions: Read, to be able to see the current settings and Write, to change them. Only users who are members of the Domain Admins or Enterprise Admins security group are able to grant the Write permission to other users, regardless of who owns the GPO.

To set permissions for a user to manage a Group Policy, perform Step by Step 27.4.

ON THE CD

Step by Step 27.4, "Setting Permissions to Manage a GPO," guides you through the process of setting permissions to manage a GPO. See the file **Chapter27-04StepbyStep.pdf** in the CD's **Chapter27\StepbyStep** directory.

In most cases, when setting permissions for the application and modification of Group Policy, you make use of the default, combined permissions previously outlined. With these, you can set to which users, computers, and groups the policy will be applied as

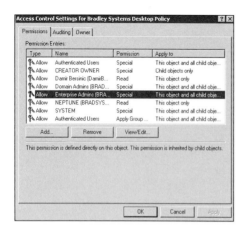

FIGURE 27.6
The Access Control Settings dialog box for Group Policy can be opened by clicking Advanced in the Group Policy Properties Security tab.

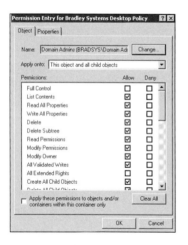

FIGURE 27.7
This detailed permission view in the Permission Entry dialog box is presented by clicking View/Edit in the Access Control Settings dialog box.

well as who has control over making changes to the policy. If you need more specific control over permissions, you can make use of the advanced permissions available.

Advanced Group Policy Permissions

Windows 2000 Active Directory provides for a vast number of permissions that can be applied or denied to a user, group, or computer. These are normally hidden from view to simplify the assignment of permissions, but they are available should you desire to change them.

Clicking the Advanced button in the Security tab of the Group Policy Properties dialog box opens the dialog box shown in Figure 27.6. From here you are able to view and modify the current permissions, view and modify auditing, and view and change the owner of the GPO on which you are focused.

In the Permissions tab of the Access Control Settings dialog box, you can now see the type of permission (Allow or Deny). You can see the names of users, groups, or computers to which the permission applies (Name). The name of the permission is displayed. Permissions might be Special, which means you need to select View/Edit to see more, or Apply Group Policy. You can also see to what these settings apply: the object and all child objects, just this object, or only child objects. In the Permissions tab, you also can Add, Remove, and View/Edit the specific permissions that have been applied.

Selecting an existing user or group to whom permission has been applied and then clicking View/Edit presents you with a dialog box similar to the one shown in Figure 27.7. The specific permissions included within the simplified selection shown in the Security tab of the GPO Properties dialog box are shown. As you can see, the permissions of Write, Read, Create All Child Objects, and Remove Child Objects allowed to Domain Admins on the Security tab actually break out into a much larger group of more specific permissions. These include Read All Properties, List Contents, Read Permissions, and Write Permissions, to name a few. These, and many others, are the permissions presented in the Object tab of the Permission Entry dialog box. Permissions that apply only to the properties of the GPO are available in the Properties tab, as shown in Figure 27.8.

On either tab, you also will notice a few other items. First, the Name field provides you with the user, group, or computer to which these permissions apply, making sure you are aware for what or whom you are currently setting permissions. The Change button beside the Name field enables you to change to whom these permissions apply.

The Apply Onto list box enables you to specify at which level these permissions should apply: this object only, this object and all its children, its children only, computers only, groups only, sites, or users. By selectively applying GPO permissions to only certain Active Directory objects, you can further narrow the scope of the policy and provide excellent control over the application of GPOs within your enterprise.

The main part of the dialog box shows all the permissions that can be applied and those that have been allowed or denied to the named object indicated. You are able to check and uncheck permissions until you achieve the combination desired.

At the bottom of the dialog box, a couple of other options also are available. To clear all the permissions that appear onscreen, instead of removing them one by one, you can select the Clear All button. This enables you to start fresh and apply only the permissions you require. It is usually a good idea to take note of what permissions existed before clearing them in case you want to get back to a known state.

The Apply These Permissions to Objects and/or Containers Within This Container Only check box is at the bottom of the screen. This limits the propagation of permissions to this level only and does not apply them to all lower levels. This is not that much of a concern for GPOs.

By using permissions, the administrator can control to whom the policy will apply as well as who has the privilege to create or modify the policy settings. In this way, you are able to ensure that certain policies apply to a particular group of users or computers and that other policies do not.

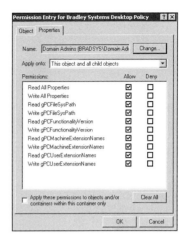

FIGURE 27.8

Permissions that can be applied to the properties of a GPO are shown in the Properties tab of the Permission Entry dialog box.

Group Policy Inheritance

In some cases, simply setting permissions to a GPO might not be enough. You might want to block GPOs from being applied to a part of Active Directory or force corporate standards to make sure they are adhered to by all parts of an organization. Finally, you might want to have a GPO apply only to certain users or computers and not to others. These three elements are called blocking, forcing, and filtering Group Policy and are discussed next.

Although not specifically an aspect of security, one very important element in determining how Group Policy is implemented is Group Policy inheritance. By using one or more of the methods of blocking, forcing, and filtering, you are able to fine-tune the application of Group Policy within your organization.

Using these same methods, you can force certain settings on all users (forcing), prevent higher-level policies from applying to a lower level such as an OU (blocking), or set permissions to make sure a policy applies only to the users it should (filtering). These methods are examined in the following sections.

Blocking Group Policy Inheritance

An administrator at the OU or domain level might not want to have higher-level GPOs apply to his or her specific OU. Essentially, blocking is beneficial when you need a specific set of GPO settings applied, and the inheritance of higher-level settings might be problematic because of regional differences or OU-specific characteristics. Blocking is most useful when an administrator for a container, such as an OU, needs to have total control over all characteristics of that container including GPOs.

When deciding whether to use blocking, it is important to be aware of two rules. First, when you decide to block policy inheritance, you are doing it for all GPOs higher up in the inheritance hierarchy. You cannot selectively decide which GPOs are blocked. It is an all-or-nothing proposition.

The second rule to consider when deciding whether to use blocking is that higher-level administrators might not want certain GPOs blocked. In this case, they might force the application of a GPO, whether or not you decide to block inheritance. This is to ensure that vital corporate settings exist everywhere.

To block Group Policy inheritance, perform Step by Step 27.5.

ON THE CD

Step by Step 27.5, "Blocking Group Policy Inheritance," walks you through the process of blocking Group Policy inheritance. See the file **Chapter27-05StepbyStep.pdf** in the CD's **Chapter27\StepbyStep** directory.

Setting a GPO to block policy inheritance is quite easy, but you must be aware of the consequences. After GPO settings are blocked at a particular Active Directory container, typically an OU, no higher-level settings will be applied to the container. This means that if you want the behavior provided by the policies you just blocked, you need to create a GPO with the same settings.

Forcing Group Policy Settings

As a domain- or site-level administrator, you are responsible for a large number of users and computers within the organization. Lower-level administrators might be delegated administrative rights for their subdomain or OU. You want to be certain that several important settings, dictated by business policies, are not modified by lower-level administrators. These business policies might specify that a corporate logo must be used as desktop wallpaper by all users or that antivirus software must be installed on all machines. You create one or more GPOs with these corporate requirements configured and now need to ensure that they are applied across the entire enterprise. Group Policy enables you to do this by forcing these GPOs and their settings to all lower levels, whether or not GPO inheritance has been blocked.

When deciding whether to force a GPO to lower levels, always make sure this is the best way of accomplishing your goals. When a GPO is forced, its settings override all lower-level settings, whether or not they have been changed at the lower-level container.

When deciding whether to force GPO settings on lower levels of the hierarchy, ask yourself two questions: "Do all containers below this level *have to* have these settings?" and "Should lower-level administrators be able to change these settings?" If the answer to the first question is "Yes," you might want to consider forcing the GPO. If the answer to the second question is "Yes," you might want to reconsider forcing the GPO. When the answer to the first is "Yes" and the answer to the second is "No," forcing the GPO is the best route so far.

To force GPO settings to be applied at all lower levels, follow Step by Step 27.6.

ON THE CD

Step by Step 27.6, "Forcing Group Policy Inheritance," demonstrates how to force GPO settings to be applied at all lower levels. See the file **Chapter27-06StepbyStep.pdf** in the CD's **Chapter27\StepbyStep** directory.

Once again, it is important to reiterate that choosing to force GPO settings by selecting No Override in the Options dialog box forces the settings at that level to all lower-level Active Directory containers, whether or not these same settings have been changed at the lower level.

Filtering Group Policy

So far, you have seen how to block all GPOs from applying to a lower-level container and how to force GPO settings to all lower-level containers. However, you might want to have certain GPOs apply to some users, groups, or computers but not to others. The process used to selectively apply GPO settings is called *filtering*.

Filtering Group Policy means applying permissions on the GPO so it excludes certain users, security groups, or computers.

GPOs linked to Active Directory containers were discussed previously. When a GPO is linked to an Active Directory container, by default the Authenticated Users security group, which includes all users and computers, is granted the Read and Apply Group Policy permission. This means that, by default, GPO settings apply to everyone and everything unless other permissions are specified, including Administrators. To filter Group Policy settings, perform Step by Step 27.7.

ON THE CD

Step by Step 27.7, "Filtering Group Policy,"" illustrates how to filter Group Policy settings. See the file **Chapter27-07StepbyStep.pdf** in the CD's **Chapter27\StepbyStep** directory.

As you have learned, Group Policy inheritance can be blocked, forced, and filtered. Blocking policy inheritance means that GPO settings from higher-level Active Directory containers (sites and domains, typically) are not applied to lower-level Active Directory containers (OUs). Forcing GPO settings is the opposite of blocking—ensuring that settings in a GPO created at a higher-level Active Directory container apply to all lower-level Active Directory containers, regardless of whether GPO inheritance has been blocked. Filtering is the careful application of permissions to ensure that GPO settings apply only to the users and/or computers to which the Apply Group Policy permission has been granted.

All this is well and good, but what can you control using Group Policy? The next section discusses some of the reasons you would use Group Policy and how user and computer environments can be controlled using GPOs through administrative templates. Chapters 28 and 29 provide more detail about other aspects of Group Policy.

MANAGING USER ENVIRONMENTS USING GROUP POLICY

Manage and troubleshoot user environments by using Group Policy:

- **Control user environments by using administrative templates.**
- **Assign script policies to users and computers.**

One of the challenges faced by administrators of Windows 2000, or any other network, is to make sure users have access to the resources required to do their jobs. The ideal end result should be a lessening of the workload for administrators and properly configured environments for users.

Windows 2000 Group Policy enables the administrator, through the use of administrative templates and scripts, to configure user and computer environments once and then have these settings automatically applied to all users and computers requiring these settings. Administrative templates are changes made to the Registry, and scripts are batch files, executable programs, or Windows Scripting Host files (such as VBScript or JavaScript). Changes made to GPOs within a container (for example, an OU) are automatically applied to all users and computers within that container, assuming permissions have been so configured. This means that any new user or computer added at the same container (for example, OU) level take on the settings specified without any additional configuration required on behalf of the administrator.

In managing user environments through the use of administrative templates and scripts, GPOs can be configured that enable you to

◆ Guarantee that all users have a standard corporate desktop. The idea is to guarantee that most of what users need to have configured on their desktops and what they need to do their job is configured for them. They do not need to make changes to their settings to perform their designated function but can if they want to step outside the norm.

◆ Restrict users from accessing certain programs or parts of the operating system. Generally, the goal of restricting user access is twofold. Preventing users from damaging their systems and minimizing any potential impact their actions might have on support costs to the organization is part of the goal. Providing users with all the requisite tools to do their jobs is the other part of the goal.

◆ Guarantee that users always have the desktop settings, network and printer connections, and programs they need to do their job, no matter what machine they use to connect to the network.

◆ Configure and restrict the use of certain Windows 2000 components, such as Internet Explorer, Windows Explorer, and Microsoft Management Console. As an administrator, you can prevent users from executing certain Windows components through GPOs.

◆ Maintain a clean computer and desktop. One of the nice features of using GPOs to manage user environments is the capability of removing one user's settings from the desktop before another logs on. When a user logs off or restarts the machine, administrative templates can remove any desktop settings configured for that user from the computer and present a clean desktop and configuration for the next user logging on.

Administrative Template Settings

Manage and troubleshoot user environments by using Group Policy:

- **Control user environments by using administrative templates.**

When editing a GPO to configure or modify settings, you are presented with a Microsoft Management Console with the Group Policy snap-in similar to Figure 27.9. As is evident in the figure, administrative templates can apply to both the computer configuration and the user configuration of the Group Policy. Although many settings apply to both, a few are specific to either the computer or the user.

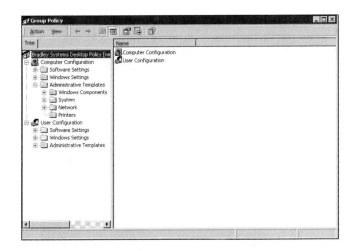

FIGURE 27.9
Some administrative templates apply to either the computer configuration or the user configuration of Group Policy.

The following types of administrative template settings exist in Group Policy:

◆ **Windows Components.** With this setting for both computers and users, you are able to configure the behavior of parts of Windows 2000, including Internet Explorer, Microsoft NetMeeting, Windows Explorer, Windows Installer, Task Scheduler, and the Microsoft Management Console. The types of things that can be configured include whether the program can be launched, which portions of the program can be used, and how the program behaves when launched.

◆ **System.** This setting for both computers and users configures how parts of Windows 2000 operate, including what happens at logon or logoff, DNS client suffix configuration, whether disk quotas are enforced, Group Policy characteristics (such as refresh internal), and Windows File Protection.

◆ **Network.** This setting for both computers and users configures attributes of network connections, such as whether RAS support is available for either dial-out or dial-in; whether modifications to network properties can be made; offline file configuration, including whether the user can make use of offline files; and how and when synchronization takes place.

◆ **Printer.** This computer setting allows printer configuration, including whether the printers can be published in Active Directory, whether the publishing is automatic, whether Web-based printing is permitted, and other settings, such as computer location, the polling frequency for printers, and others.

◆ **Start Menu & Taskbar.** This user setting configures the Start menu and taskbar settings, such as restricting portions of the Start menu (the Search command or Run command), display of common program groups, and display of the Windows Update option.

◆ **Desktop.** This user setting configures desktop settings. These include whether to enable Active Desktop, permit or prohibit a user from making changes to desktop settings, specify a desktop wallpaper for the user, hide My Network Places icon from the user, save settings upon exit, and many others.

◆ **Control Panel.** This user setting allows restrictions to be enabled for the Control Panel. These restrictions include which Control Panel applets are available to the user; whether the user is able to run Add/Delete Programs to install and/or remove software; where the software can be installed from (CD, Web, network); control over Display properties, including the ability to add a screen saver, modify settings, enable or disable changing the wallpaper, and more; the addition, deletion, and modification of printers; and whether a specific language will be used by all users to whom the GPO applies.

The next sections examine the administrative template settings that affect the user.

Administrative Template Settings That Affect the User

As previously indicated, administrative template settings that affect users can be broken down into six categories: Windows Components, Start Menu & Taskbar, Desktop, Control Panel, Network, and System. Each of these enables an administrator to lock down certain aspects of a user's experience. In the following sections, each of these categories is examined.

Administrative Template Windows Components Settings for Users

Windows components administrative template settings enable you to configure the behavior and capabilities of six components of the Windows 2000 operating system: Microsoft NetMeeting, Internet Explorer, Windows Explorer, Microsoft Management Console, Task Scheduler, and Windows Installer.

Microsoft NetMeeting

Using the template for Microsoft NetMeeting, you can specify settings, such as whether the whiteboard feature is enabled and whether the user is allowed to enter chat mode. You also have three additional folders with more settings that deal with configuration: Application Sharing, Audio & Video, and the NetMeeting Options Page.

In Application Sharing, you can set whether the user can share an application during a NetMeeting session, enable others to take control of the application, or enable sharing of the desktop.

When configuring Audio & Video, you can determine the amount of bandwidth a NetMeeting session is allowed to consume as well as whether video and audio can be used and their characteristics.

The Options Page settings enable you to specify what will be visible and modifiable by the users when they select options for NetMeeting.

Internet Explorer

Windows 2000 Group Policy enables you to be very precise about how Internet Explorer (IE) will behave for a user and how the user is able to configure IE. The settings that can be specified have to do with Internet Control Panel. You can configure a number of general Internet Explorer settings, such as whether the user has the option to manage digital certificates, language settings, color settings, whether the user can customize the search page, and others. In addition, a number of other elements of IE can be set using Group Policy, including the following:

◆ **Internet Control Panel.** Which pages are available when users select Tools, Preferences in IE.

◆ **Offline pages.** The configuration of channels and subscriptions and the frequency of updates.

◆ **Browser menus.** The characteristics of the menus available and which options should be included. For example, disabling the source menu option to view the HTML source for a page.

◆ **Toolbars.** The configuration of toolbar buttons and whether they can be modified by the user.

◆ **Persistence behavior.** Limits the amount of disk space used for caching for different types of IE zones.

◆ **Administrator-approved controls.** Which controls and components the user is able to make use of (for example, Media Player or Shockwave).

Windows Explorer

As an administrator, you also are able to configure the characteristics of Windows Explorer for the user through Group Policy administrative templates. This enables you to specify whether the user is able to see other computers on the network by enabling or disabling Entire Network and Computers Near Me in Windows Explorer. You can also specify whether a user is allowed to have the option to map network drives from within Windows Explorer. Other characteristics that can be set include the appearance of Windows Explorer, whether recent files are tracked and available to the user, and the behavior of shortcuts when a user is roaming.

Microsoft Management Console

One of the nice features of administrative templates for configuring user settings, as it applies to administering Windows 2000, is the ability of a domain administrator to delegate authority but also lock down which Microsoft Management Console (MMC) features are available to the junior administrators. A senior administrator can specify whether a junior administrator or any other user is able to modify the MMC consoles. You can also specify whether a junior administrator can make use of all or a subset of the MMC snap-ins available or can make changes to aspects of Group Policy that might have been configured.

Task Scheduler

Windows 2000 provides for a Task Scheduler. This feature is much improved as compared to the AT scheduler in Windows NT. You can set the behavior of the Task Scheduler for a user including whether he or she is able to delete tasks, create new tasks, or even run tasks. In this way, you can prevent unwanted jobs from running when they shouldn't or from running at all.

Windows Installer

Windows Installer template settings are extremely useful in preventing users from installing software they should not have on their machines. Using Windows Installer settings for the user, you can configure the media search order for files to be installed. You can disable the capability of installing software from removable media. You can also specify whether, during installation, the install program should run with administrative privileges.

Administrative Template Start Menu & Taskbar Settings for the User

Start Menu & Taskbar settings that can be configured for the user with administrative templates determine how the Windows Start menu appears as well as its functionality. You are able to specify whether the user has a Run command on his or her Start menu, allowing him or her to launch any program. Disabling the Run command prevents the user from running any program except those for which shortcuts already exist, although other methods (such as the command prompt or double-clicking a file in Windows Explorer) can still allow a user to launch a program. It also enables you to specify whether the Search, Help, Favorites, and Documents menus are available from the Start menu. You can also include or remove the common program groups, the user program groups, or both/neither from the list of programs, thereby further limiting what programs the user is able to run.

Administrative Template Desktop Settings for the User

Desktop settings that can be specified for the user with administrative templates include Active Directory and Active Desktop settings as well as some general desktop configurations. Some of the general settings that can be configured include whether My Documents appears on the desktop and/or the Start menu. You also can determine whether changes to the desktop are saved when the user logs off. This template enables you to choose whether Internet Explorer, My Network Places, or even any icons appear on the desktop. This template also enables you to determine whether the user can make changes to the location of the taskbar.

For Active Desktop, Group Policy administrative templates enable you to set whether Active Desktop is used, the wallpaper that will be used, and whether that wallpaper is a bitmap (BMP) file or another type, such as a JPEG or GIF. You also can configure whether the user is allowed to make changes to the desktop, including adding, deleting, modifying, and even closing items. A comprehensive Prohibit Changes setting can also be specified to prohibit changes of any kind.

Only a few settings can be specified for the user for Active Directory. The settings available deal with the depth of Active Directory searches (the number of objects returned in a single search) and enabling you to configure whether the user can filter those searches. These settings are intended for use in large organizations with tens of thousands of users and many more computers. These settings primarily ensure that a search through Active Directory does not take up a lot of time or consume a great deal of network bandwidth or domain controller resources.

Desktop settings that can be specified for the user with administrative templates enable the administrator to predetermine elements of the desktop, such as the wallpaper to be displayed, the redirection of key folders to a network drive for backup, and others. They are used to ensure that all desktops conform to corporate policies.

Administrative Template Control Panel Settings for the User

One of the areas of greatest potential concern to an administrator is the user changing his or her configuration without being fully aware of the consequences of the changes.

In administrative templates user settings that relate to Control Panel, you can configure four main items: Add/Remove Programs, Display, Printers, and Regional Options (as well as some general settings). The most useful of these general settings is the capability of disabling Control Panel. This is useful for a many users who do not need to make any changes to their systems or who are allowed to run only a corporate-standard desktop. If you would like to permit users to make use of some of the applets in Control Panel, you are able to specify which ones to show or hide. This regulates the amount of potential damage users can inflict upon their systems.

As previously mentioned, you can configure administrative template user settings relating to the Control Panel:

◆ **Add/Remove Programs.** You can configure whether a user can make use of this applet. Further, if you decide to allow the user to run the Add/Remove Programs applet, you can specify whether the user is able to add, change, or remove programs. You can specify whether the user can add programs from a CD, floppy, the network, or from Microsoft (Windows

Update capability). You also can allow or prevent a user from installing Windows Components, such as games or other parts of the operating system, which can be specified during the installation process of Windows 2000.

◆ **Display.** As an administrator, you can specify whether users can make any changes to their display settings and, if so, what these can include. Changes you might specify include such items as the display background or screen saver. You can specify password protection of the screen saver when enabled. This is useful to provide a minimal level of security when users walk away from their desks. You can also control the ability of the user to change resolution and number of colors.

◆ **Printers.** You can set whether a user can add or remove printers through the Printer applet in the Control Panel or by going to Settings, Printers from the Start menu. You can also specify where the user can search for printers that he or she might be allowed to add (a Web site, Active Directory, or the network).

◆ **Regional Options.** Regional Options can be either allowed or disallowed. This enables you to configure whether users can change the language and other territory- or region-specific characteristics of their machines. These characteristics include the date/time format, currency, and numeric format, such as decimal and thousand separators.

In specifying Control Panel settings, the administrator is able to preconfigure with Group Policy which options in Control Panel are available to users to make changes to their computers and which are locked down. This ensures that users do not, through their own actions, cause their computers to stop functioning, thereby requiring support personnel to be dispatched.

Administrative Template Network Settings for the User

With Network settings for the user through Group Policy administrative templates, you are able to specify the behavior of Offline Files and Network and Dial-Up Connections (see Figure 27.10).

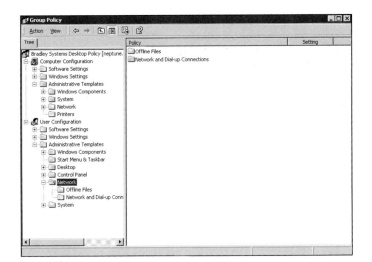

FIGURE 27.10
Administrative templates network settings that can be configured for the user.

Offline Files Network Settings

One of the nice features of Windows 2000, especially for individuals who travel a fair bit and make use of a notebook computer to connect to the office network, is the ability to configure certain network folders to be available offline. Administrative templates enable you to configure how offline files behave for the user. You are able to specify whether this feature is turned off completely. You can control which folders users can make available offline and whether they can configure this themselves. You can specify the frequency of reminders about synchronization and offline file availability. Administrative templates enable you to determine what happens when a server becomes available (that is, whether cache copies of files should be used or the files should become unavailable). You also determine whether the Make Available Offline menu option is even shown for network file resources.

Dial-Up Connections

The other part of Network settings that can be configured for the user has to do with the behavior of dial-up connections and network configuration. Through these policy settings, you can specify whether a user can add or remove dial-up connections for themselves or all users. You can specify whether users can connect and disconnect using RAS or the network, can rename RAS connections, or can modify TCP/IP settings.

Administrative Template System Settings for the User

The last set of configuration items that can be specified through administrative templates for the user deals with system behavior. This includes some general settings, as well as two particular categories of system settings: Logon/Logoff and Group Policy.

General Settings

In the general portion of System settings, you can specify whether a welcome screen is displayed to the user at logon. You also can control whether the user is able to use Registry editing tools. You can lock down the applications that the user is able to run. You can disable Autoplay for CDs inserted into the CD-ROM drive. You also can disable the command prompt. These are probably the most restrictive settings that can be applied to a user and have the greatest immediate impact of what is permitted or denied for the user.

Logon/Logoff Settings

When dealing with Logon/Logoff settings for a user, you can set the behavior of logon and logoff script execution. For example, you can determine whether these scripts are visible or run asynchronously. You govern the ability of a user to change his or her password or even to log off. You can limit the size of the user's profile, remove certain folders from the profile, and outline what programs run or are not run at logon.

Group Policy

The Group Policy portion of the System settings of the administrative template for a user enables you to set which domain controllers are used to download the GPTs from a domain controller. You can determine how frequently the computer refreshes any policy from a domain controller. You also can determine whether administrative template (ADM) files should be automatically updated.

The Usefulness of Administrative Template Settings for the User

Now that you have seen some of the things that can be set for the user when using administrative templates, it might be worthwhile to review what types of control this provides the administrator.

NOTE

Disable the Use of Registry Editing Tools It is strongly recommended that you disable the use of Registry editing tools for the majority of your users. The Registry stores critical system settings and application information that is needed by Windows 2000 and to run most Windows 2000 applications. A modification of the Registry by a user is an immediate action that cannot be rolled back unless the user remembers the changes he or she made during the modification.

Using administrative templates to control user settings, the
administrator is able to

◆ **Lock down user desktops.** Through proper configuration of
Windows Components, Desktop, and Start Menu & Taskbar
settings, you can control the appearance and capabilities of the
desktop that a user can use.

◆ **Lock down user access to resources.** By making use of settings for Windows Components, Desktop, and Start Menu &
Taskbar, you also can limit the user to a specific set of network
folders, printers, and local resources. These are in addition
to—and not a replacement for—proper NTFS and share
permissions for these resources.

◆ **Lock down user access to administrative tools and
applications.** Through specification of Windows Components,
Desktop, Start Menu & Taskbar, and System settings, you can
prevent users from making use of administrative tools, such
as Control Panel, MMC, Registry editing tools, and other
applications that might cause their configuration to become
unusable.

Administrative Template Settings That Affect the Computer

As previously mentioned, administrative templates apply to both
the user and the computer. The number of areas in which you can
configure administrative template settings for the computer is fewer
than for the user (see Figure 27.11). You can configure four areas
instead of six, and the number of settings available is also fewer. This
is primarily because any setting configured for the computer applies
to all users on that particular machine. Any user logging on to a
machine for which computer settings have been configured through
administrative templates has those settings applied. The settings that
can be configured for the computer include Windows Components,
System, Network, and Printer settings.

NOTE

**Administrative Templates in
Computer and User Portions of Group
Policy** Any administrative template
setting existing in both the computer
portion and the user portion of Group
Policy always has the computer setting applied. This is because a user
can log on to several machines and
have the same GPO settings applied
no matter where he or she logs on,
but a computer can exist only once,
and its configuration must be
protected at the expense of user
preferences.

FIGURE 27.11
Administrative templates settings that can be configured for the computer.

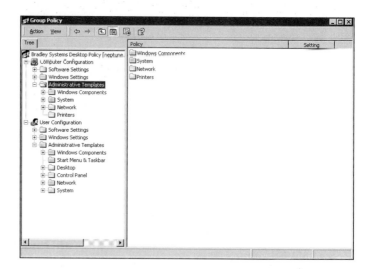

Generally, the number of items that can be configured for the computer using administrative templates is far fewer than the number of items to be configured for the user with the same portion of the administrative template. This is because many of the settings are changes that need to be made to the user portion of the Registry (HKEY_CURRENT_USER) instead of the computer portion (HKEY_LOCAL_MACHINE). It only makes sense that more changes need to be made to the user portion for application and other configuration settings than to the computer portion. The computer portion deals with the characteristics of the machine for all users (that is, a minimal required configuration), and the user portion deals with individual preferences, of which there might be many.

Administrative Template Windows Components Settings for the Computer

In the Windows Components portion of the administrative template for the computer, you are presented with four areas of Windows 2000 for which you can configure settings: NetMeeting, Internet Explorer, Task Scheduler, and Windows Installer. These all were also found in the user portion of the GPO, though the user portion also included MMC and Windows Explorer.

NetMeeting

In the NetMeeting folder, only one setting can be configured for the computer: whether to allow remote desktop sharing. This is unlike the many settings available for the user. Remote desktop sharing is the capability of the desktop to be controlled remotely through NetMeeting. You configure this for the computer so that no one can access and take control of the computer remotely, a potential security risk.

Internet Explorer

Using the computer settings related to Internet Explorer, you can lock down proxy settings as well as security policies for all users on the computer. You also have the option to remove the Internet Explorer splash screen on the invocation of Internet Explorer. You can control whether IE checks for updates to itself or automatically installs any missing components because of a single user's interaction with a site requiring a component not currently installed.

Task Scheduler

The Task Scheduler settings that can be configured for the computer are almost identical to those for the user. As previously mentioned, the computer setting always wins in the event of a conflict, so this is the preferred location for any setting that should apply to all users. These settings include whether any user on the computer can create or delete a task and whether the task's property pages are visible.

Windows Installer

In configuring settings for Windows Installer at the computer level, you have the ability to control whether Windows Installer can be used to install applications on Windows 2000 computers and how those installs behave when interacting with the user. These interaction settings include such options as whether the user has control over installs. Another option is whether a user is able to perform certain additional tasks, such as browse the media or patch the application while his or her permissions are elevated as a result of the install of an application taking place. You also can control elevating the user's privileges during the install and whether to log the install.

Administrative Template System Settings for the Computer

On the System side, administrative template settings that can be configured at the computer level (see Figure 27.12) deal with five areas: Logon, Disk Quotas, DNS Client, Group Policy, and Windows File Protection. Some general settings also can be configured that pertain to the computer as a whole. These include whether certain options appear on the Start menu if the user is logging on to Windows 2000 through a Terminal Services connection. The appearance of status messages to the user during boot, logon, logoff, or shutdown can be configured with this template. Finally, you can control which programs to run at startup.

Logon

During logon, Windows 2000 goes through a number of phases, and some of these require user interaction. The Logon portion of the System administrative template of the GPO enables you to specify what happens when some of these conditions are encountered. Here, you can set how startup scripts are run for the computer. This is different from logon scripts for the user, which are set in the user portion of this GPO. You can specify whether roaming profiles are deleted after a user logs off. You can force the download of a user profile even if logon is taking place over a slow network connection, such as a modem dial-in. You can specify timeout settings for dialog boxes and profile downloads.

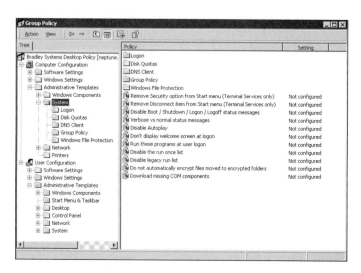

FIGURE 27.12
Administrative templates system settings that can be configured for the computer.

Disk Quotas

The Disk Quotas folder of the System settings portion of the computer administrative template lets you enable or disable disk quotas for a machine. Disk quotas are used to limit the amount of disk space that any one user can occupy on a machine. Enabling disk quotas in the template provides the possibility of setting them at the file system level; disabling them in the policy turns off quota enforcement whether or not they are configured at the file system level. You also can specify what happens when a user exceeds his or her quota. You can establish the default quota limit. Finally, this portion of the template enables you to determine whether to log, in the Windows 2000 event log, when a user reaches a warning or maximum quota level.

DNS Client

There is only one setting for the computer in the DNS Client portion of the administrative template; this setting is the Primary Domain Name System (DNS) Suffix. This setting enables you to specify what should be appended to the name of the machine to create a Fully Qualified Domain Name (FQDN) for the host. This is required for Active Directory functionality and hostname resolution. Setting the suffix here prevents all users, including administrators, from changing it in the TCP/IP Properties dialog box for the computer's network configuration.

Group Policy

Similar to the Group Policy portion of the user administrative template, the computer settings for Group Policy within the System folder of the administrative template is used to govern what happens during GPO processing for the computer. This also controls the frequency of refreshes for both domain controllers and other types of Windows 2000 computers. You also are able to specify which portions of the GPO are processed for the computer, including scripts, software installation policy, encrypting file System Policy, and disk quota policy.

Windows File Protection

Windows File Protection (WFP) is the capability of Windows 2000 computers to automatically replace critical system files when they have been overwritten by other applications such as an installer program for a piece of software. The WFP portion of the computer administrative template enables you to specify the frequency of scans by WFP. These scans determine whether any files need to be restored to their original state. You can determine the location of the WFP cache in case you want to move it from the default. You can determine whether a limit should be placed on the cache. The cache is used to store copies of Windows 2000 files that may be replaced by other programs, so they can be more easily restored without requiring you to insert a CD containing the original files. You also can determine whether the file scan progress window is hidden as the scans take place.

Administrative Template Network Settings for the Computer

Manage network configuration by using Group Policy.

Like the user portion of the Network settings for the administrative template, the computer portion (see Figure 27.13) enables you to configure Offline File settings as well as Network and Dial-Up Connections configuration.

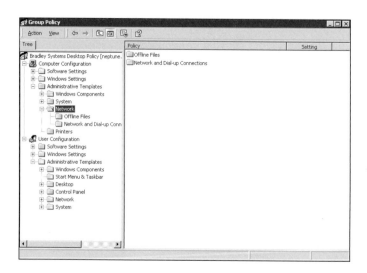

FIGURE 27.13
Administrative templates network settings that can be configured for the computer.

Offline Files

The Offline Files settings that can be configured from the computer portion of the administrative template are almost identical to the user settings. Here you also find such options as whether to show the Make Files Available Offline option for a folder and balloon reminder settings. There also are other computer-level settings. These settings include your ability to configure whether offline files are supported on this machine. You can determine whether local copies of offline files should be erased from the hard drive after a user logs off. You also can determine the logging level for offline file events and the default cache size. In other words, settings that can impact many users and reduce disk space are available only on the computer portion of the administrative template.

Network and Dial-Up Connections

The only setting that can be specified in the Network and Dial-Up Connections folder of the Network portion of the computer administrative template is whether to allow configuration of connection sharing on the computer. Connection sharing is a feature of Windows 2000 that enables users to configure their system as a gateway to the Internet for a small network of 2 to 10 users.

Administrative Template Printers Settings for the Computer

The Printers portion of the computer administrative template (see Figure 27.14) enables you to specify whether printers defined on the computer can be published in Active Directory. You also can determine whether Web-based printing, a new Windows 2000 feature, should be allowed. This portion of the template enables you to specify whether printers on the computer are announced for browsing on the network. You can determine whether printers should be pruned and the pruning characteristics. Pruning is a feature of Windows 2000 domain controllers that automatically removes printers from Active Directory if they become unavailable and republishes them if they come back to life.

FIGURE 27.14
Administrative templates printer settings
that can be configured for the computer.

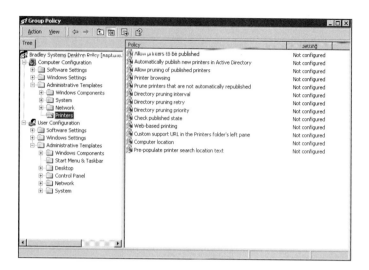

Modifying Administrative Template Settings

Although much time has been spent outlining just what kind of settings can be applied to the user, the computer, or both, how to actually implement an administrative template setting has not yet been mentioned.

Specifying Group Policy settings using administrative templates is quite simple (see Step by Step 27.8). Pick the setting you want to enable or disable and click the appropriate button, and Group Policy is specified. The hardest part is determining which setting should be enabled or disabled, and it might require many hours of discussion to arrive at a cohesive policy. However, in some cases, administrative templates do not provide the functionality needed to properly configure a user's or computer's environment. For these eventualities, Microsoft Windows 2000 enables you to create scripts and have them enforced using Group Policy.

ON THE CD

Step by Step 27.8, "Configuring an Administrative Template Setting in Group Policy," provides you with the necessary information to modify an administrative template. See the file **Chapter27-08StepbyStep.pdf** in the CD's **Chapter27\StepbyStep** directory.

Configuring and Using Scripts in Group Policy

In this section, you learn about scripts and how they are processed on Windows 2000 computers. You are then shown how to attach a script to a GPO for the computer portion of the GPO (startup and shutdown scripts) or the user portion of the GPO (logon and logoff scripts).

The options available with administrative templates might not be sufficient to provide the complete environment needed by a user to perform his or her job. Examples of this include the automatic creation of certain shortcuts on the desktop or the establishment of printer and network shared folder connections at the time a user logs on. To have these changes take place automatically when a computer starts up or a user logs on, you can make use of Group Policy scripts.

Group Policy enables you to configure scripts that run when a machine starts up or shuts down. You can configure scripts that run when a user logs on or logs off to implement changes to the environment for all or a single user. You can also configure scripts to clean up any modifications made by others before the next user logs on or the system restarts. Scripts can be batch files (BAT or CMD), executable programs (EXE), or Windows Script Host scripts (VBScript or Jscript). Generally, you make use of scripts when you want to implement a Group Policy and when the requirement cannot be met by any administrative template setting. You can set up a script to perform that task to achieve the desired result. With support for VBScript and Windows Script Host (WSH) in Windows 2000, scripts can be created to accomplish virtually any task.

Group Policy Script Processing Order

The order of execution of Group Policy scripts is quite specific, as is the application of any Group Policy setting. Similarly, if there is a conflict between different scripts, the setting found in the last script processed always prevails. This is significant because it is a slight departure from the application of administrative template settings.

When you specify an administrative template setting for both the user and the computer, the computer setting always takes precedence. Suppose that in the System folder of the administrative template for the computer, you configure Autoplay to be disabled, but you enable the same setting for the user. In this case, Autoplay remains disabled because the computer setting indicated it should be disabled.

When scripts are configured, they can be run at computer startup, user logon, user logoff, and computer shutdown. Each of these is a very distinct event, and scripts are processed when the event occurs. Because scripts are simply batch files, executable files, or Windows scripting host (VBScript of JScript) scripts, they do not have any way to really check for the previous state and then determine that settings specified within the script should not be applied. The assumption is that all the settings should be applied no matter what. This blanket desire to apply all the settings specified in the script makes it possible for a setting configured in the user logon script to override one configured in the computer startup script. This is the way it is intended to work, and you, as the administrator, need to be aware of this.

The actual processing order of scripts is as follows:

1. When a user starts a computer and logs on, two scripts run: startup scripts and logon scripts. Startup scripts run in sequential order (synchronously). Each script must complete or time out before the next one starts. Scripts run in the background and are not visible to the user. The order of execution of startup scripts is specified in the Startup Properties dialog box shown in Figure 27.15. It is found under Computer Configuration, Windows Settings, Scripts, Startup in the Group Policy Editor.

   Logon scripts run after the startup scripts and are run asynchronously with the possibility of more than one script executing at the same time. If conflicting settings appear in two or more logon scripts, the last setting to execute is the one that applies. This means it might not always be possible to predict what the end result of logon script execution will be if the same setting is applied in more than one script. As a general rule of thumb, do not apply the same setting in several scripts.

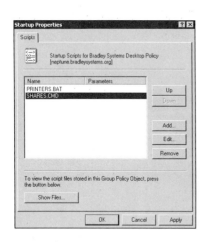

FIGURE 27.15
Startup script order of execution can be set in the Startup Properties dialog box under Windows Setting, Scripts, Startup in the Group Policy Editor.

2. When a user logs off, logoff scripts run.

3. When a user shuts down or restarts the computer as part of the logoff process, shutdown scripts run.

Once again, it is important to note that startup scripts run at the time the computer starts, and logon scripts run when a user logs on. Similarly, logoff scripts run when a user logs off the computer, and shutdown scripts run when the computer is shut down. As previously mentioned, startup scripts run in the order specified in Group Policy, and logon scripts run in no particular order. If you have the same setting applied in more than one logon script, there is no way to predict the exact end result of the scripts.

Implementing Scripts Using Group Policy

Perhaps the hardest part of implementing scripts in Windows 2000 is their creation. This can be done using Notepad or any other editor, and it needs to take place prior to associating the script with the computer or user configuration of Group Policy (see Step by Step 27.9). As previously mentioned, scripts can be BAT or CMD files, executable programs, or Windows Script Host files.

After you have created a script to be used to configure either a computer at startup or shutdown or a user environment at logon or logoff, you need to do two things. You must copy the file to a shared location where it can be downloaded and run. This is typically in a folder within the GPO structure located on the SYSVOL shared folder on a domain controller. You must also associate the script with a GPO.

ON THE CD

Step by Step 27.9, "Implementing Scripts to be Used in Group Policy," guides you through copying the file and associating it with a GPO. See the file **Chapter27-09StepbyStep.pdf** in the CD's **Chapter27\StepbyStep** directory.

In terms of configuring and using scripts, the most important elements to keep in mind are that you need to determine what types of scripts are available (logon, logoff, startup, or shutdown)

NOTE **Default Timeout Value** The default timeout value for script processing is 10 minutes. This means that if a script has not completed processing in 10 minutes, it is assumed to have timed out, and the next script starts. If your scripts are complex and require more than 10 minutes to run, you can change the default timeout value by modifying the setting found at Computer Configuration, Administrative Templates, System, Logon, Maximum Wait Time for Group Policy Scripts. The setting applies to all scripts: startup, shutdown, logon, and logoff.

NOTE **BAT Files and CMD Files** Although you can create and execute both batch (BAT) files and command (CMD) files in Windows 2000, they execute quite differently. Batch files execute within an NT Virtual Machine (NTVDM) and are designed to be compatible with DOS and MS Windows 3.x/95/98. They are inherently 16-bit, and if the BAT file hangs, it might cause the entire NTVDM to hang (if it is being shared with other applications). CMD files are 32-bit and execute in their own memory space using the CMD.EXE command interpreter. Any problem with a CMD file does not affect the execution of other programs because it is an isolated process.

and why these scripts are necessary. Scripts are not shipped with Windows 2000 by default, so any you need must be created manually.

Scripts can be attached to GPOs and assigned to users and computers. Obviously, startup and shutdown scripts are assigned to computers. These scripts execute sequentially, and if settings within scripts conflict, the last setting processed is the one applied. Logon and logoff scripts apply only to users and are processed in no particular order (asynchronously), so conflicting settings might cause unpredictable behavior.

Scripts should always be stored in the SYSVOL folder on a domain controller under the GUID of the GPO where they are used (as part of the Group Policy Template). They need to be copied there manually by the administrator.

In addition to Scripts and administrative templates, order settings can also be configured using Group Policy. These are summarized in the next section. Software settings and security settings are discussed in other chapters.

Other Settings Configurable Using Group Policy

In addition to administrative templates and Scripts, a number of other settings are configurable through Group Policy. Several of these, including Software Installation, Security Settings, and Remote Installation Services, are covered in other chapters. Figure 27.16 shows the other Windows Settings that can be configured. You will notice that the other settings for the computer (Software Settings and Security Settings) are covered in the chapters that follow. The next sections take a look at the settings that won't be covered later, including Internet Explorer Maintenance and Folder Redirection.

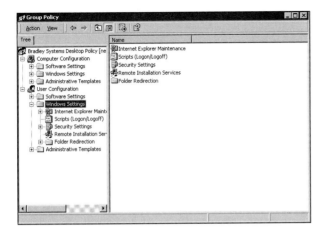

FIGURE 27.16
Other Windows settings for the Computer
Configuration and the User Configuration that
can be specified using Group Policy.

Internet Explorer Maintenance Settings for the User

Windows 2000 Group Policy enables the administrator to preconfigure several Internet Explorer settings outside of GPO administrative templates. These include the Browser User Interface,
Connection settings, several preconfigured URLs, IE Security settings, and programs invoked automatically by IE.

Browser User Interface

The Browser User Interface settings available for you to specify for
the user include the Browser Title configuration, which includes the
title appearing on the toolbar as well as a background bitmap for the
toolbar. Animated Bitmaps settings enable you to customize the animated bitmap that appears in the upper-right corner of the browser
as it waits for all data to be transferred from a Web site. You also can
specify a Custom Logo that will appear in the upper-right corner of
the browser window after a Web page has been fully transferred.
Finally, you can configure additional Browser Toolbar Buttons for
the user or can remove the current toolbar buttons and replace them
with a new set you have created.

Connection Settings

To make sure Internet Explorer works properly for the user, Group
Policy enables you to preset connection information. The user never
receives the dreaded error message telling him or her that it was not
possible to connect to a site. The configuration options that can be

specified include the capability of replacing a user's Connection settings with a customized set of options. You can determine whether proxy server settings are automatically detected. You can manually set up a proxy server configuration and impose it upon the user. Finally, you also are allowed to specify the User Agent String, the identification information transmitted by the browser when it connects to a Web site.

Preconfigured URL Settings

The URL settings portion of Internet Explorer Maintenance enables you to make sure certain sites appear in the list of Favorites and Links for the user. You also have the option to remove existing Favorites that the user might have added or just replace those created by the administrator. This option enables you to update an older set of Favorites and Links with a more up-to-date version. Important URLs can also be specified; they include the home page for the user, the default search page, and a URL for online support. Finally, you also can preset channels to which the user will subscribe.

IE Security Zones

As an administrator, you might want to impose control over how Internet Explorer Security Zones are configured, as well as whether Authenticode support should be enabled within Internet Explorer. Both of these can be specified through the Security option of Internet Explorer Maintenance.

Preset Programs

Finally, the administrator also is able to preset the programs that will be started when the user decides to read Usenet newsgroups, retrieve and send Internet email, receive a call via the Internet, enter and retrieve appointments, edit a Web page, and look up contacts. These can be preconfigured to make sure a corporate standard is maintained by all—or a specific group of—users.

Specifying Folder Redirection Settings for the User

Folder Redirection, configurable through Group Policy (see Figure 27.17), is the selective placement of folders that all users use on different volumes of local computers or on shared network volumes where they can be backed up. Unlike Windows NT 4.0, which provided this capability through roaming profiles, Windows 2000

Group Policy enables an administrator to selectively place a folder on one location while another folder, which is also part of the standard user profile, is kept local. Furthermore, the folders that are redirected are not copied to the local machine, thereby saving disk space.

An example of this could be the My Documents folder that is often used to store an individual's current word processor, spreadsheet program, and other files. To make sure these files are backed up, the administrator might decide to redirect them to a network share on a hard drive that is backed up nightly. Other folders, such as Desktop shortcuts, the Start menu configuration, or the Application Data folder may remain on the local drive.

To redirect a folder to a location other than the default, select which folder you want to redirect, right-click the name, and select Properties. A dialog box such as that shown in Figure 27.18 displays, enabling you to decide how to redirect the folder. You can redirect the folder to a common location for all users (Basic), redirect the folder to a different location for a user based on his or her group membership (Advanced), or leave the current settings intact.

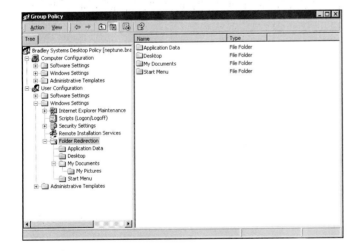

FIGURE 27.17
Folder Redirection settings that can be configured for the user through Group Policy.

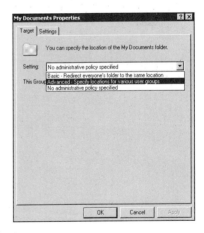

FIGURE 27.18
Folder redirection properties enable you to redirect folders for all users or selectively by group membership.

If you decide to redirect all users' folders to the same location, you can further configure the behavior of the folder. This configuration includes whether to move the current contents of the folder to the new location. You also have the option to grant only the user permissions to the redirected folder; this prevents others from seeing the contents of the folder when they should not have access. You can specify what will happen when the folder redirection policy is removed, as well as other settings based on which folder you are redirecting.

Microsoft stated that one of the design goals of Windows 2000 was to reduce the total cost of ownership (TCO) of Windows 2000–based computers. With the combination of Active Directory and Group Policy, this goal has been largely achieved. Group Policy enables the administrator to configure user and computer settings at the site, domain, or OU level and to selectively apply these settings to users and computers. In configuring user and computer environments, the administrator can use administrative templates to specify settings. Administrative templates modify the Registry entries on the target computer for either the user or the computer. In situations in which administrative templates might not provide sufficient functionality, you are able to use scripts to configure other elements of the user and computer environment.

Naturally, proper planning is required to make sure the behavior received is the one expected and desired. Sometimes, despite the best planning, implementation might not always work as expected, so troubleshooting is required.

TROUBLESHOOTING GROUP POLICY

In some cases, it might be necessary to determine exactly what is happening with Group Policy, because the configuration settings you've specified do not appear to be taking effect on users' computers. Windows 2000 provides for the capability of auditing Group Policy processing. The audit enables you to determine exactly what is occurring and thereby help resolve the problem.

Group Policy Implementation Considerations

One of the best ways to ensure that Group Policy functions properly is to adhere to some of the recommendations from Microsoft regarding its proper implementation. These recommendations, summarized in the following list, should serve as a guideline to be used in your own environments when implementing Group Policy.

◆ **Minimize the number of GPOs you create.** Even though it is possible to create and enforce Group Policy at the site, domain, and OU level, this could be too much of a good thing. The ideal number of GPOs is the smallest number possible to accomplish any business requirement. If you do not need site-level GPOs, don't create them. You will probably want to implement one domain-level GPO, but you need to determine whether a second or a third would be beneficial. Create OU-level GPOs only if the OU has a very specific set of characteristics that are not shared by the rest of the users and computers on the domain. Minimalism creates fewer GPOs; fewer GPOs have a decreased potential to cause problems. Furthermore, the more GPOs that need to be processed when a user logs on, the longer the logon process will take.

◆ **Configure user-level settings rather than computer-level settings to control desktops.** Computer-level GPO settings apply only to a machine and affect the users logged on to that particular computer. User-level settings apply to the user, no matter which computer he or she uses to log on and connect to the network. Because the scope of user-level settings is potentially greater, they provide a better mechanism to control the user environment.

◆ **Use security group membership to filter the application of Group Policy.** By default, GPOs are enforced for members of the Authenticated Users group, which includes Administrators, Domain Admins, and Enterprise Admins. If certain GPOs should not be enforced for other users, place those users in

a security group (preferably at the same level as the GPO
from which you intend to filter them) and check the Deny
permission box for Apply Group Policy to make sure GPO is
not applied. Users who do not have an Access Control Entry
(ACE) indicating that a particular GPO should be applied to
them have faster logons because GPO processing is bypassed
for them.

◆ **Disable parts of a Group Policy that are not being
enforced.** If you decide to configure only the user portion of a
GPO and leave the computer portion intact, configure the
options for the Group Policy so that the Computer
Configuration settings are not downloaded and processed.
This also improves the speed of GPO processing and results in
considerable time saved during user logon.

◆ **After making a change to a GPO, log on as an affected
user and test to make sure what should happen is, indeed,
taking place.** The worst thing that an administrator can do
with Group Policy is assume it will work. Just remember what
you were taught about the word "assume." All settings and
scripts should be fully tested before the policy is implemented.
Through filtering, you can make sure only the test users are
affected by the policy until it is ready to be released throughout the rest of the organization.

◆ **Perhaps this really should be the first point: Planning the
implementation of Group Policy is paramount.** You should
always ask yourself what it is you are trying to accomplish, and
why and what is the best way to get there? Group Policy could
be the right answer. If so, plan its introduction and configuration very carefully and, as previously mentioned, test it as well.
There is nothing worse for job security than an unplanned,
and premature implementation of a feature with
widespread impact.

◆ **Limit the use of blocking and forcing, and (to a lesser extent) filtering of GPOs.** Blocking, forcing, and filtering could make it more difficult to determine where a problem actually originates and might also result in unpredictable behavior (unless carefully planned).

◆ **Do not delegate administrative control over GPOs to others unless you need to do so.** Too many cooks in the kitchen usually spoil the broth (or result in a very strange set of toppings for pizza). As an administrator, you should enjoy holding control, not giving it away. However, if you are the administrator of a large multinational conglomerate, you have to give some control away, so be flexible.

As previously indicated, the cardinal principle to be followed when planning and implementing Group Policy is KIS—keep it simple. Do not try to do too much with a single policy. At the same time, don't have so many policies that processing takes a long time. Keep common settings at the domain level and specific ones at the OU level. Don't have a GPO at each OU level (have one only where needed), and let policies flow through inheritance.

If this still does not work, you might have a simple common problem that can be easily solved.

Common Group Policy Problems

Despite the best planning, and even though you have followed all the recommendations laid out in the preceding list, it might still be possible for things to go awry. Some common problems and their solutions are presented in the following table:

Problem	*Cause*	*Solution*
Group Policy is not being applied to users and computers in a site, domain, or OU.	The most likely cause is that GPO inheritance has been blocked. A second possible reason for this behavior is that the GPO has been filtered to exclude the users and computers.	Configure No Override for the GPO to prevent lower-level administrators from blocking GPO settings.
	When multiple GPOs are applied (site-, domain-, and OU-level), it is possible that settings at a higher-level (such as domain) GPO have been overwritten by a lower-level (such as OU) GPO.	Verify GPO security settings to make sure filtering has not been applied too broadly.
Group Policy is not being enforced for a security group in an OU to which it is linked.	Group Policy can be linked to sites, domains, or OUs. Because a GPO can be linked to an OU does not mean it will be applied to security groups in the OU. The determination of which security groups have the GPO applied is made by the permissions configured for the GPO.	Grant the security group Read and Apply Group Policy permissions.
An administrator cannot open a GPO to edit it.	Any user who needs to modify a GPO needs to have Full Control privileges for the GPO. If an administrator is unable to view the GPO settings and/or modify them, he or she most likely does not have sufficient permissions.	Grant the user or security group the Full Control permission for the GPO.
Attempting to edit a GPO returns a Failed to Open the Group Policy Object error.	This problem usually occurs when network problems exist. These could include physical problems with the network, the server being down, or most likely, DNS configuration.	Verify that a domain controller is available. Verify that the network is not experiencing problems. Verify DNS configuration and availability.

Most problems that occur as a result of Group Policy processing can easily be solved if you apply a logical approach to the problem-solving process. First, verify that domain controllers are around and that they contain the Group Policy Templates in question. Second, walk through what should happen and the permissions assigned to the policy. Most problems either are permission-related, or the GPO is not at the right level.

If more extensive checking of how GPOs are processed is required, you can always configure auditing.

Auditing Group Policy

In situations in which the problems you are experiencing are not easily classified and you have faithfully followed the recommended procedures for implementing Group Policy, Microsoft Windows 2000 provides the capability of configuring auditing Group Policy execution and modification.

To configure auditing for a GPO, follow the steps outlined in Step by Step 27.10.

ON THE CD

Step by Step 27.10, "Configuring Auditing for Group Policy," shows you how to configure auditing for GPO. See the file **Chapter27-10StepbyStep.pdf** in the CD's **Chapter27\StepbyStep** directory.

After you have configured auditing, you can view the results of auditing by opening Event Viewer and selecting the Security Log. This should provide you with information about GPO processing. This also tells you with which users and computers GPO processing is encountering problems.

When troubleshooting Group Policy, first determine what is going wrong and for whom. Check GPO processing in terms of permissions for the GPO as well as inheritance and blocking. In situations in which the problem encountered is hard to track down, you can configure auditing to log success and/or failure events of GPO processing, which can be used to step through what is happening and, hopefully, determine the cause of the problem.

CASE STUDY: USING GROUP POLICIES TO CONFIGURE USER AND COMPUTERS SETTINGS AT SUNSHINE BREWING

You have received the following specific requests:

▶ The CEO has decided that all users should have a common desktop background wallpaper, the company logo, so that visitors to any SunShine Brewing location will always be able to see the corporate identity displayed. Currently, users throughout the company can choose their own background.

▶ Sales managers in each office want to constantly remind the sales team of the current promotion by having it displayed on their desktop at all times.

▶ Users at corporate headquarters have been complaining that when they want to take documents on shared folders on servers home to work on them, they have to keep remembering to copy them to the local disk on the notebook. Sometimes they forget, and they have to drive back to the office to get the files. They would like files they are working on to be automatically copied to the hard disk of their notebook computer and then copied back to the network when they log on.

▶ The help desk staff at headquarters has developed a Web site that provides answers to many common user questions. They would like this site to be automatically added as a Favorite in all instances of Internet Explorer used within the company. Because IE5 is the corporate standard, this would ensure that any user in the company could go to the help desk site to have his

SCENARIO

In this chapter, you were introduced to Group Policy and how it can be used to manage user and computer environments. SunShine Brewing has a large international implementation that can be helped by using Group Policy to configure user and computer settings throughout the enterprise.

The implementation of Active Directory sites, OUs, and domains at SunShine Brewing has successfully taken place, as has the migration of user desktop and notebook computers to Windows 2000 Professional. The key-user computers now all operate on the Windows 2000 platform. You, as the key administrator at SunShine Brewing, now find yourself receiving requests from junior administrators at the different sites, as well as management, to have specific settings applied to these environments.

You have been asked to come up with a plan that satisfies these requirements in the shortest possible time as well as ensuring that any changes to these settings can be made easily and applied to the user or computer without manual intervention.

The CIO and CEO want these requests implemented unless the operating system does not support them.

ANALYSIS

As you can see, the requests range from companywide requirements to specific elements that deal with only a part of the organization. Your solution needs to incorporate all these elements while also being easy to administer. The best

CASE STUDY: USING GROUP POLICIES TO CONFIGURE USER AND COMPUTERS SETTINGS AT SUNSHINE BREWING

or her questions answered instead of calling the help desk first. This would save time and resources for the help desk.

▶ Users are complaining that when they want to find a printer close to them, they have to scroll down a long list when they use the Windows 2000 search feature to locate a printer. They want a list of printers near them displayed by default instead of all printers.

▶ The Admin heads in each office are finding that their staff spends a lot of time running games and other applications during office hours. They want the ability to restrict these users to only the accounting program, email, office suites, and Internet Explorer.

▶ All users, with the exception of IT and R&D, should be able to run only Add/Remove Programs and Display applets in Control Panel.

▶ Administrators for each department should be able to configure department-level settings, which might not have been identified yet.

solution for these requirements is to make use of Windows 2000 Group Policy, using administrative templates and Windows Settings configuration settings in the GPO.

The first requirement (common background wallpaper featuring the corporate logo) can be satisfied by creating a Group Policy at the domain level that includes the wallpaper to be used. You specify the location of the wallpaper on a network share that is replicated to other servers through a fault-tolerant DFS link. This could be part of the Default Domain Policy GPO installed by Windows 2000 Active Directory.

The requirement for sales users to have a background wallpaper that reflects the current promotion can be handled by creating a GPO at the site level that specifies the wallpaper containing the current promotion. Because you do not want this wallpaper to be modified by the domain-level policy, you configure No Override for the site policy to make sure the setting is not changed. Further, to ensure that the GPO applies only to sales users in the site, you filter the GPO so that its settings are applied only to members of the Sales security group.

To provide users not connected to the network with access to their files, or if the server hosting the files goes down, you configure support for Offline Files using a GPO at the corporate HQ site in Ottawa and, using the GPO, specify which shared folders have Offline Files turned on automatically. This way, users can work with

continues

CASE STUDY: USING GROUP POLICIES TO CONFIGURE USER AND COMPUTERS SETTINGS AT SUNSHINE BREWING

continued

their files while away from the office and, as long as they open a file before leaving, have it copied to their machine.

To assist the help desk staff in making sure all users have a Favorites link in IE to the help desk Web site, create a GPO at the domain level with No Override that adds the URL for the Web site to the users' list of Favorites. This way, the shortcut is always available to the user.

Searches in Active Directory default to the Entire Directory. To change the default search location for printers, create a GPO at the domain level that enables filtering of Active Directory searches by enabling the setting in administrative templates, Desktop, Active Directory. In this way, searches for printer objects default to only those printers physically close to the user's location.

To ensure that Admin users are able to run only specified applications, create a GPO at the Admin OU and specify which applications can be run by users. Any applications other than those appearing on the list will not be available to users.

To ensure that all users can run only Add/Remove Programs and Display in Control Panel, restrict the list of applets that can be run to these two. To ensure that this policy does not apply to R&D and IT staff, filter the Group Policy by making sure the Apply Group Policy check box for these security groups is not checked.

Finally, to enable administrators at the OU level or site level to create new policies, delegate administrative control to these containers and grant necessary privileges, such as Create Group Policy Container Object.

As you can see, using Group Policy can solve many complex requirements including those that might appear to be conflicting.

CHAPTER SUMMARY

In this chapter, you were introduced to Group Policy and how it can be used to enforce a consistent configuration at the site, domain, and/or OU level. Group Policy is a very powerful feature of Windows 2000 and is a tremendous improvement over System Policy, which was available in Windows 95/98 and Windows NT.

By configuring Group Policy, you are able to specify how a computer is configured and whether users can make changes to certain computer configurations. You can lock down the desktop and other characteristics of a user's environment, no matter where he or she logs on to the domain from: his or her usual workstation, a remote machine through dial-up, another node in the same location, or a computer halfway around the world.

Group Policy is composed of two parts: a Group Policy container (GPC) and a Group Policy Template (GPT). GPCs are Active Directory objects linked to a site, domain, or OU. GPTs are physical files, including administrative templates and scripts, which are stored within the Policies container for the SYSVOL share on domain controllers. Each GPT is stored in a folder with the same name as the GUID of the GPO for which it is a template.

Group Policy settings specified at a higher level, such as a domain or a site, are automatically inherited by all lower-level Active Directory objects, such as OUs. A local administrator responsible for a subdomain or OU can block policy inheritance from higher levels, such as a site, thereby ensuring that only his or her GPOs are processed. However, higher-level administrators have the option to override the blocking of GPO application at lower levels, thereby forcing GPO settings even if they are blocked at a lower level.

The order of Group Policy processing is always site, domain, and then OU. Because it is possible to have OUs within OUs, it is possible for many GPOs to be processed when a user logs on or a computer starts up. It is recommended that fewer rather than more GPOs be created to provide acceptable logon performance.

KEY TERMS

- Administrative templates
- Blocking policy inheritance
- Folder redirection
- Forcing Group Policy
- GPO inheritance
- GPO scope
- Group Policy Container
- Group Policy filtering
- Group Policy Object
- Group Policy precedence
- Group Policy Template
- GUID
- Logon/logoff scripts
- No Override
- Registry
- Startup/shutdown scripts

CHAPTER SUMMARY

Group Policy can be filtered to ensure that it is processed only by the users for whom it is intended. In this way, it is possible to selectively implement Group Policy for a security group, computer, or user. To ensure that proper application of Group Policy is taking place, the administrator is able to configure auditing for GPO processing and view the results in the Event Viewer. This is also a good troubleshooting tool when needed.

GPO settings can be applied through administrative templates or scripts. Administrative templates and scripts can be configured for both the computer and the user. If a conflict exists in the application of an administrative template setting between a user and a computer, computer settings always override user settings. For scripts, the last script to execute is the one whose settings are applied, regardless of whether the script is a user logon script or a system startup script.

In situations in which a GPO has been linked to an Active Directory container and the GPO contains only computer configuration settings, the administrator is able to speed up processing by setting a GPO option to process only the computer settings and not to bother downloading the user settings on GPO application. The converse is also true and helps provide better performance in situations in which many scripts might need to be processed.

APPLY YOUR KNOWLEDGE	

Review Questions

1. What is the difference between a Group Policy container (GPC) and a Group Policy Template (GPT)?

2. If you want to make sure a GPO for a site is applied to all users and computers in the site, what do you need to do?

3. To which users and computers do GPO settings apply by default?

4. What is the difference between administrative templates and scripts?

5. What types of scripts are supported by Windows 2000 Group Policy?

6. What are the benefits that Group Policy provides to administrators?

7. You want to make sure all users in the domain have the same background wallpaper on their desktops: a corporate logo. The director of sales also wants to have a quarterly promo as the background for the sales staff members who are part of the Sales security group. How do you accomplish both goals?

8. If a computer setting in a GPO disables AutoPlay and a user setting in the same GPO enables AutoPlay, will AutoPlay be disabled or enabled?

9. What does the term forcing Group Policy mean?

10. What permissions are required if you want to grant a user administrative control of a GPO? Where do the permissions need to be set to enable the users to create additional GPOs in the same container?

11. If all Group Policies you have configured deal with only the user portion of the GPO, how can you improve performance of GPO processing?

Answers to Review Questions

1. A GPO consists of two parts: a Group Policy container (GPC) and a Group Policy Template (GPT). The GPC is an Active Directory object that contains GPO attributes and version information. Domain controllers use the GPC to determine whether they have the most recent version of the GPO. The GPT is a folder hierarchy in the shared SYSVOL folder on domain controllers. The GPT contains all the GPO settings, including administrative templates, scripts, software installation, folder redirection, and security settings for the GPO. See "Introduction to Group Policy" and "Group Policy Components."

2. To make sure a GPO for a site is applied to all users and computers in the site, you select the No Override option for the GPO. This forces the GPO settings to be applied to all subsequent levels of the hierarchy, including domains and OUs because GPOs for a site are processed first. See "Group Policy Security," "Group Policy Inheritance," and "Forcing Group Policy Settings."

3. GPO settings apply to members of the Authenticated Users group by default. At this level, all users who log on to the domain, as well as all computers that log on to the domain when started, have GPO settings applied to them. See "Group Policy Security" and "Configuring Group Policy Security."

APPLY YOUR KNOWLEDGE

4. Administrative templates settings within GPOs make modifications to the Registry in either the HKEY_LOCAL_MACHINE Registry hive (if you modify the Computer Configuration of the administrative template) or the HKEY_CURRENT_USER Registry hive (if you modify the User Configuration of the administrative template). Scripts can be used to perform any task and to modify any setting, including Registry settings, because they are either a BAT or CMD file, a VBScript or Jscript script processed by Windows Script Host, or an executable (EXE) file. See "Managing User Environments Using Group Policy."

5. Windows 2000 Group Policy supports four types of scripts. For the computer, startup and shutdown scripts are available. For the user, logon and logoff scripts can be configured. See "Managing User Environments Using Group Policy" and "Configuring and Using Scripts in Group Policy."

6. Group Policy enables the administrator to set centralized and/or decentralized policies that provide control over computer and user environments. GPOs enable the administrator to make sure users have the application and requisite environmental settings to perform their jobs. They enable the administrator to have control over user and computer environments whether they are located in the next room or halfway around the world. Because GPO administration can be delegated to others, it enables a corporate administrator to make sure the local requirements are incorporated into any centralized administration of desktops that is desired. Finally, GPOs enable

the administrator to make sure corporate policies and business rules can be enforced throughout the enterprise. See "Introduction to Group Policy" and "Group Policy Scope."

7. To make sure all users in the domain have the corporate logo as the background wallpaper on their desktop, you create a GPO at the domain level and configure the wallpaper settings in the User Configuration portion of the administrative templates settings of the GPO. You also make sure the Domain Users security group has been assigned the Read and Apply Group Policy permissions on the GPO.

   To ensure that members of the sales department have a quarterly promo as the background wallpaper on the desktop, you create a GPO at the domain level and configure the wallpaper settings in the User Configuration portion of the administrative templates settings of the GPO. You also make sure the Sales security group has been assigned the Read and Apply Group Policy permission on the GPO. To not have this GPO applied to any other users in the domain, you also remove the Domain Users security group from the list of users and groups assigned permissions on the GPO.

   Next, to ensure that the sales users do not receive the background wallpaper that all other users are getting, you filter the domain users Group Policy, add the Sales security group to the list of groups assigned permissions on the domain users GPO, and uncheck the Apply Group Policy permission so that the policy is not enforced for the Sales security group.

APPLY YOUR KNOWLEDGE

Finally, to ensure that these settings are not tampered with by lower-level administrators, you set the No Override option for both GPOs. See "Managing User Environments Using Group Policy" and "Group Policy Scope."

8. AutoPlay will be disabled. Computer settings take precedence over user settings; hence, the computer setting of disable AutoPlay wins out. See "Group Policy Scope" and "Group Policy Processing."

9. *Forcing Group Policy* means you have configured the No Override option for the GPO. The end result is that the settings in the GPO with the No Override option set cannot be modified by lower-level GPOs even if the administrator at that lower level (domain or OU) has blocked policy inheritance. See "Group Policy Security."

10. For users to be able to modify an existing GPO, they need to be assigned both Read and Write permissions on the GPO. If you want them to create additional GPO objects within the same container, they need to be granted permissions on the container in which the GPO is defined. Specifically, they would require the Create group Policy Container Objects and Delete group Policy Container Objects permissions on the Active Directory container. Granting them Read and Write permissions also works, but it might provide them with more privileges than you want. See "Group Policy Security," "Configuring Group Policy Security," and "Setting Permissions to Manage the Policy."

11. To improve performance of policy processing if only the user portion of the GPO is specified for your policy, you can check the Disable Computer Configuration settings on the General tab of the GPO Properties dialog box. This tells all computers applying the policy to download only the user configuration settings and not waste time downloading the computer portion, because it is not used. See "Troubleshooting Group Policy."

ON THE CD

This book's companion CD contains specially designed supplemental material to help you judge how well you understand the concepts and skills you learned in this chapter. You'll find related exercises and exam questions and answers. See the file **Chapter27ApplyYourKnowledge.pdf** in the CD's **Chapter27\ApplyYourKnowledge** directory.

Suggested Readings and Resources

1. Hill, Tim. *Windows 2000 Windows Script Host.* Macmillan Technical Publishing, 1999.

2. Microsoft Windows 2000 Resource Kit. *Deployment Planning Guide.* Microsoft Press, 2000.

3. Web sites

   Using Group Policy Scenarios from Microsoft's Web site at `http://www.microsoft.com/windows2000/library/howitworks/management/grouppolicy.asp`

   Introduction to Windows 2000 Group Policy from Microsoft's Web site at `http://www.microsoft.com/windows2000/library/howitworks/management/grouppolicyintro.asp`

   Windows 2000 Simplifies Top 15 Administrative Tasks from Microsoft's Web site at `http://www.microsoft.com/windows2000/library/howitworks/management/adminsave.asp`

   Windows Script Host: A Universal Scripting Host for Scripting Languages from Microsoft's Web site at `http://www.microsoft.com/windows2000/library/howitworks/management/winscrwp.asp`

   Windows 2000 Desktop Management Overview from Microsoft's Web site at `http://www.microsoft.com/windows2000/library/howitworks/management/ccmintro.asp`

   Step-by-Step Guide to Understanding the Group Policy Feature Set from Microsoft's Web site at `http://www.microsoft.com/windows2000/library/planning/management/groupsteps.asp`

   Step-by-Step Guide to User Data and User Settings from Microsoft's Web site at `http://www.microsoft.com/windows2000/library/planning/management/userdata.asp`

   Manage Change with the Windows 2000 Platform from Microsoft's Web site at `http://www.microsoft.com/windows2000/guide/server/solutions/managechange.asp`

   Group Policy Simplifies Administration from Microsoft's Web site at `http://www.microsoft.com/windows2000/guide/server/solutions/gpsimplifies.asp`

This chapter covers an objective from the unit, "Installing, Configuring, Managing, Monitoring, Optimizing, and Troubleshooting Change and Configuration Management." Additional objectives and subobjectives from this unit are covered in other chapters. The exam objective addressed by this chapter follows.

Maintain and troubleshoot software by using Group Policy.

- **Deploy software by using Group Policy.**

- **Maintain software by using Group Policy.**

- **Configure deployment options.**

- **Troubleshoot common problems that occur during software deployment.**

▶ The deployment of software in any organization can be a daunting task. Windows 2000 Active Directory provides a method that can make the job easier: Group Policy. You will be tested on your understanding of software deployment within the Group Policy context. For the exam you need to have a thorough comprehension of the two deployment methods available for Group Policy—assigning and publishing. Software can be assigned to computers or users and published to users only. Questions regarding the upgrade and removal of software, as well as the different ways these two tasks can be performed, also are included on the test.

CHAPTER 28

Software Distribution Using Group Policy

▶ In preparing for the Microsoft exam, it is strongly recommended that you perform all the Step by Steps as well as the exercises for this chapter on the accompanying CD.

▶ An understanding of the different options available when deploying software, Windows Installer, Group Policy, and ZAP files is required. Test yourself with the review questions and the sample exam questions in this chapter.

▶ Be familiar with the features and rules surrounding Group Policy, specifically inheritance, filtering, and precedence.

▶ As the old saying goes, "Practice makes perfect." Practicing using Group Policy, creating software packages, deploying them, upgrading them, and removing them will help hold you in good stead to deal with the issues presented on the exam.

INTRODUCTION

In the preceding chapter, you were introduced to Windows 2000 Group Policy and how it can be used to configure a computer and user environments. Group Policy also has a number of additional capabilities, making it an indispensable tool for the Windows 2000 network administrator. One of these is the capability to distribute software applications to the users who require them or for the purpose of enforcing a corporate standard. This feature also enables you to upgrade software after a new release comes out or forcibly remove software from the user's computer should the organization no longer desire to use the software.

THE SOFTWARE DISTRIBUTION LIFE CYCLE

When deploying software in an enterprise or in a central location, as can be done with Group Policy, you typically go through four stages:

◆ **Preparation.** The preparation stage deals with all the elements that need to be in place prior to software deployment. These elements include creating a Windows Installer Package for deployment, creating a network share folder to hold the software to be installed, and copying the files for the software application to be deployed to the network shared folder. In some cases software might not come in a format that can be used by the Windows Installer component of Windows 2000. You might need to use a third-party tool to create the package or, as an alternative, to create a ZAP file to install the software application. All these elements are dealt with in the "Preparing Software for Deployment Using Group Policy" section of this chapter.

◆ **Deployment.** The deployment stage is when you actually get the software out to the user and/or computer. At this stage, you create a Group Policy Object (GPO), automating the installation of the software and linking it to the appropriate Active Directory container (site, domain, or organizational unit). You must decide whether the software is to be published or assigned, whether it should be deployed for the computer or the user, and how much interaction the user has during the installation process. This, in many ways, is the easiest part of software deployment. The hard work was done in the preparation stage. If software has been properly configured, this process should run well. The different ways to deploy software and the creation of a GPO are covered in the "Software Deployment Using Group Policy" section of this chapter.

◆ **Maintenance.** As you are probably already well aware, nothing stays static in this industry. Software is no exception. Over time, you might need to configure and deploy an upgrade to some of the software on users' machines. Other times, software that has been deployed might need to be redeployed, or patches or a service pack might need to be applied to bring software up to the most current incarnation and/or to repair any deficiencies that might exist. The "Maintaining Software Packages Using Group Policy" section discusses how to upgrade software in the field and the upgrade options available.

◆ **Removal.** Sometimes, software loses its usefulness and might need to be removed. How many of your users still need Microsoft Word 2.0 on their machines? The "Removing a Package" section deals with the issues surrounding the removal of software, forced or unforced, from users' desktops.

Each of these stages is characterized by a distinct series of steps that need to take place before the next deployment phase commences.

PREPARING SOFTWARE FOR DEPLOYMENT USING GROUP POLICY

Before you can make use of the features of Group Policy that make deploying software such an easy task, preparation must be done to ensure that the software to be deployed is in a format that can be used by Windows 2000 Group Policy. Next, a software distribution share must be created on a server from which the software is installed, and the necessary files must be copied to that location. You are then ready to create the GPO to deploy the software.

Packaging Software for Deployment

As previously mentioned, the first step in deploying software using Group Policy is to package the software in a format that Windows Installer can use to automate the distribution process. If the software you are deploying is a newer application that has been certified to work with Windows 2000 (for example, Microsoft Office 2000), you might not have all that much work to do. Newer applications most likely come in a format that can be used by Windows Installer. However, if your application is older (such as Microsoft Office 97), you might need to perform some additional tasks to make sure the automated installation proceeds as it should. You also might need to repackage the application in a format compatible with Windows Installer or create a text file (that is, a ZAP file) to tell Windows Installer how to install the application.

Windows Installer Technology

First introduced on a large scale with Microsoft Office 2000, Windows Installer is the technology that enables Group Policy to deploy and manage software. It consists of two main components:

- Windows Installer Service
- Windows Installer Package

The Windows Installer Service runs on all Windows 2000 machines and facilitates the automated installation and deployment of software. It also provides the capability to automatically repair or modify existing applications when files are overwritten or removed. Thus, it ensures that the software is properly installed and stays in working order. You can use the Windows Installer Service to install an application directly from a CD-ROM, through Group Policy, or via other distribution media.

NOTE

Windows Installer on NT 4.0
Windows Installer also is installed on Windows NT 4.0 or Windows 9x when you install Microsoft Office 2000 or any application that makes use of it. It can be incorporated into the Setup program of an application by the developer. It is installed on the target machine when the Setup program is launched, if it is not found.

Windows NT 4.0 does not support Windows 2000 Group Policy and therefore cannot make use of the software deployment features of Group Policy. Both support of Group Policy and support of the Windows Installer Service are required on the target desktop to make use of Group Policy to automate software deployment.

EXAM TIP

Software Deployment and Windows 2000   You can only deploy software to Windows 2000 computers using Group Policy. Remember that only Windows 2000 computers can have Group Policy applied. If a scenario includes Windows NT 4.0 or Windows 9x computers, you must use products such as SMS to deploy applications.

The Windows Installer Package contains all the necessary information that the Windows Installer Service needs to install or remove an application. This includes the files required by the software, as well as registry and INI file changes that need to be made. It also includes any additional support files that are required, summary information on the package and the application that can be shown to the user, and a reference to the location of the product files. The majority of this information is contained in a single file with an .MSI extension, which is the package file itself. As previously mentioned, the full package to be installed also may include other supplementary files.

Windows Installer provides the administrator, as well as the end user, with the following three major benefits over what has existed previously:

◆ **Resilient software.** With the Windows Installer Service, should a critical file for an application be accidentally deleted or modified in any way (for example, virus on the system), the Windows Installer Service connects to the software distribution share and replaces the file with a known good copy.

◆ **Clean removal.** One of the many problems that exist with past Windows software is that removing one piece of software may actually remove a file needed by another piece. Windows Installer runs as a service on each Windows 2000 computer and keeps track of which files are needed by which applications. This ensures that any shared critical files are not removed and that files no longer needed are removed. It does this for all applications in which it was used to perform the installation.

◆ **Elevated security.** In many situations, software applications require that the user performing the installation have administrative rights and permissions on the machine where the application is being installed. Automating the installation of these packages presented a challenge prior to Windows Installer. Because Windows Installer runs as a service under the LocalSystem account by default, it already has elevated privileges on the system. Applications that require the capability to make changes to the machine component of Windows

2000 can do so during the installation process while still not allowing the user to have administrative privileges. In this way, applications can be deployed that make changes to critical operating system settings (for example, registering DLLs and COM objects or changing the HKEY_LOCAL_MACHINE registry hive) without giving the end user the same capability.

Windows Installer is a component that can provide many benefits to the administrator in automating software deployment. The Windows Installer Service is required to perform automated installation, upgrades, and removal of software using Group Policy. Windows Installer Package files are the preferred method of having software prepared for automated deployment.

What if you do not have a package for the software to be deployed? In Windows 2000, you can still configure software to be deployed even if you do not have a ready-made Windows Installer Package file. There are two ways to do this: You can create a ZAP file to tell Windows Installer how to install the application, or you can create a Windows Installer Package using a third-party tool. Let's look at both of these methods, starting with the ZAP file.

Creating a ZAP File to Deploy Software with Group Policy

In some cases, it might be necessary to deploy software on older Windows 2000 computers. The software might have been developed in-house or simply do not follow the Windows Installer conventions Microsoft has outlined. As the number of the applications far outstrips the number that actually use the Windows Installer Package format, Microsoft has provided a way to deploy these software packages as well: the ZAP file format.

The ZAP file is a plain text file created with any text editor that specifies a number of things about the software to be installed. The ZAP file might contain the application name, the name of the setup program, and any parameters to be used for setup as well as any file extensions to be associated with the application and technical support Web site. Not all of this information needs to be included in the ZAP file, only the application name (FriendlyName) and the setup executable filename (SetupCommand). The sample ZAP file in the following code block shows a simple set of tags that can be used.

```
[Application]
FriendlyName = Microsoft Office 97
SetupCommand = setup.exe /unattend
DisplayVersion = 8.0
Publisher = Microsoft Corporation
URL = http://www.microsoft.com/office

[Ext]
DOC=
DOT=
XLS=
PPT=
RTF=
```

ZAP File Sections

The ZAP file is made up of two sections, as shown in the preceding code block: the Application section and the Ext or Extensions section. The Application section outlines information about the software package and how to install it. The Ext or Extensions section specifies which file extensions should be associated with the application in Active Directory.

The Application section has a number of tags that can be applied. These include the following:

◆ **FriendlyName.** Identifies the name displayed to the user and administrator when the application is installed and in the Add/Remove Programs applet in Control Panel. This is a required tag.

◆ **SetupCommand.** Identifies the name of the executable program used to install the application. This could be an EXE file or a BAT or CMD file, as long as it performs the necessary steps to install the application. The filename specified should be relative to the physical location of the ZAP file containing it. For example, the ZAP file and the SETUP.EXE are both in a folder called Office97 on the network distribution share. You only need to configure the tag to read SetupCommand=setup.exe /unattend with no pathname preceding the filename. If, on the other hand, the ZAP file is in the software distribution shared folder and the setup program is in a subfolder called Office97, then the tag should include the pathname, as in SetupCommand=Office97\setup.exe /unattend. This is also a required tag.

◆ **DisplayVersion.** Identifies the version number of the application. This number appears in Add/Remove Programs and in the Software Installation portion of Group Policy and identifies the different versions of an application that might have similar names.

◆ **Publisher.** Lists the name of the company or individual who publishes the software application. The publisher of the application also appears in Add/Remove Programs and in the Software Installation portion of Group Policy.

◆ **URL.** Lists the URL containing additional information about the application and/or technical support details. The URL also appears in Add/Remove Programs and the Software Installation portion of Group Policy.

A ZAP file needs to contain only the Application section and the FriendlyName and SetupCommand tags. All other portions, including the Ext section, are optional.

The Ext, or Extensions, section of the ZAP file is used to associate the application with a file extension in Windows 2000 Active Directory. Windows 2000 uses the Ext section to determine which application should be installed when a user decides to open, or double-click, an operating system file. If the file's extension does not match a list of applications on the computer that can be used to open the file, the Setup program for the application that defined a particular extension as belonging to or supported by itself is called. The Setup program then installs the application, enabling the user to view the file.

To add the Ext section to the ZAP file, simply type the Ext heading on a line by itself. On lines below it, specify the extensions to be associated with the application without the leading period.

ZAP File Limitations

ZAP files do have some limitations and are not as good as Windows Installer Packages. It should be noted that the preferred method of installing any piece of software is to create a Windows Installer Package using a third-party tool. With packages, all options are available. Applications deployed using ZAP files have the following limitations:

◆ ZAP files cannot be assigned to users, only published. This prevents mandatory installation of a software package. Only voluntary installations can be performed with ZAP files.

◆ ZAP files are not self-repairing. Windows Installer does not track what was installed by the application's setup program when using a ZAP file and, therefore, cannot tell whether the application is damaged.

◆ ZAP files usually require user intervention to be installed and invoke the install program for the application. Unless the software package has a fully unattended mode, and this mode has been properly configured, the user has to provide some information for the install to complete.

◆ ZAP files cannot be installed using elevated privileges; only Windows Installer Packages can. ZAP files are installed using the security context of the currently logged on user and may fail if the user has insufficient rights.

<table>
<tr><td>EXAM TIP</td><td>**Know the Limitations of ZAP Files** You will probably see questions on the exam that test you on whether you can use ZAP files in a specific scenario. Remember that ZAP files cannot be assigned and that they are not self-repairing.</td></tr>
</table>

After reading this far, you are likely asking yourself when you should use a ZAP file. The answer is hardly ever. ZAP files are perfectly acceptable tools to use to publish software not required for a specific machine—optional software. Examples of applications that can be safely deployed using ZAP files include WinZip32 or file decompressors, Adobe Acrobat Reader, and utilities. These applications are useful, though not required, on a user's machine, and the user often has the choice of whether or not to install the product.

ZAP files should not be used to deploy a critical line of business applications or any pieces of software that all users require and that need to be maintained at a consistent level for all users at all times. If an application you need to deploy fits into one of these categories but does not have a Windows Installer Package available, you can create a Windows Installer Package for the application using a third-party tool.

Creating a Windows Installer Package Using Third-Party Tools

In some cases, you might need to repackage an application so it can be deployed using Windows Installer. As previously shown, it is often preferable to create a Windows Installer Package to deploy an application than to use a ZAP file to perform the same task.

NOTE

Location of WinINSTALL LE
Microsoft, on the Windows 2000 installation CD-ROM, provides a third-party application called WinINSTALL LE by Veritas Software to repackage an application. The program can be found in the VALUEADD\3RDPARTY\ MGMT\WINSTLE folder on any of the Windows 2000 versions (Professional, Server, and Advanced Server) and is, itself, a Microsoft Windows Installer Package file.

Packages offer a bit more flexibility for deployment and are also self-repairing, a feature that gives you peace of mind and cuts down your workload.

The process of repacking an application and creating a Windows Installer Package to be used to deploy a piece of software involves several steps and, preferably, two computers. It is performed using WinINSTALL LE, which is shipped with Windows 2000, or any other third-party program that supports the creation of packages such as InstallShield and others. Using WinINSTALL LE shall be assumed for the rest of this section.

The steps involved in repackaging an application include preparing a reference computer, preparing a network installation shared folder, installing Veritas WinINSTALL LE, and taking a before image of the system configuration.

1. First, to install the application you want to repackage, you must prepare the machine for installation. The reference computer should have only Windows 2000 on it and no other software. Other software installed on the machine might cause parts of the application to be repackaged to *not* install, which might provide incorrect information to WinINSTALL LE during the repackaging process.

2. Prepare a network installation shared folder to store the Windows Installer Packages and their supporting files. Users connect to this shared folder to install the application. The shared folder name also is specified in the Group Policy Software Installation section so that Windows Installer knows where to find it when Group Policy assigns or publishes the application to the user or computer.

3. The next step is to install Veritas WinINSTALL LE on a second Windows 2000 machine. You should not install WinINSTALL LE on the same machine you are using as a reference computer because this might contaminate the clean environment you have configured. Always install WinINSTALL LE on a second Windows 2000 machine.

ON THE CD

Step by Step 28.1, "Installing and Configuring WinINSTALL LE," shows you how to install and configure WinINSTALL LE. See the file **Chapter28-01StepbyStep.pdf** in the CD's **Chapter28\StepbyStep** directory.

4. After installing WinINSTALL LE and sharing the WINSTALL folder, you are ready for the first major step in repackaging an application. You are ready to take the before image of the reference computer.

   Taking the before image involves using the WinINSTALL Discover program to take a snapshot of the system configuration of your reference computer before the software is installed. To take the before snapshot, perform the steps shown in Step by Step 28.2.

ON THE CD

Step by Step 28.2, "Taking a Before Image of the Reference Computer," shows you how to take a "before" snapshot of your reference computer. See the file **Chapter28-02StepbyStep.pdf** in the CD's **Chapter28\StepbyStep** directory.

5. Now that you have taken the before image of the reference computer, and the setup program has been launched for the application you want to repackage, you simply go through the normal application configuration as if you were installing it on any machine. You should choose the settings that make sense for all users who should have this package installed. If this requires you to create additional desktop icons as shortcuts, do this as well. If the install program calls for reboots, perform them. In other words, go through the same process you would use to set up the application.

6. After the application has been configured, you need to take an after image of the reference computer. This is scanned for differences, and the Discover Wizard determines the necessary contents of the package. Connect the reference computer to the WINSTALL share and launch the Discover Wizard again to start the process of creating an after image. Step by Step 28.3 guides you through the process.

ON THE CD

Step by Step 28.3, "Taking an After Image of the Reference Computer," shows you how to take an "after" snapshot of your reference computer. See the file **Chapter28-03StepbyStep.pdf** in the CD's **Chapter28\StepbyStep** directory.

7. You have now successfully repackaged an application. You should, at this point, copy the package file to the software distribution share you created earlier so it can be made available for installation.

When copying packages to the software distribution point, keep the following in mind:

◆ Create individual folders for each package on the software distribution share. In other words, put each package and all its associated files in a separate folder on the software distribution share. This makes it easy to maintain the packages and reduces any potential problems associated with figuring out which files belong with which packages.

◆ Make the software distribution share a hidden share so users won't be able to see it when browsing the network or searching Active Directory. This ensures that software can still be deployed and that users won't be installing the package just because they found it on the network.

◆ Use Distributed File System (DFS) to provide a single logical share point for all applications, even if the files are physically located on a different machine. DFS also enables you to configure replicas of shared folders on multiple machines, thereby ensuring that software can be installed even if a single machine is down.

If you want to make further modifications to the package, you might want to do so prior to copying it to the software distribution share. This ensures that no users install the application before it is ready. You can make these modifications later if the application only is installed using Group Policy.

Modifying a Windows Installer Package File Using Third-Party Tools

After you have created a package for the software you are deploying to users and computers using Group Policy, you might want to modify the contents of the package. This can be done using a third-party tool such as Veritas WinINSTALL LE, found on the Windows 2000 CD-ROM. Modifying a package can include adding desktop shortcuts to start the application, providing technical support Web site addresses and names, adding more files to the package, or removing some that might not be required. A great many options are available.

To modify a package, start the Veritas Software Console for WinINSTALL LE and open the package to make the necessary changes as outlined in Step by Step 28.4.

ON THE CD

Step by Step 28.4, "Modifying an Application Package Using WinINSTALL LE Software Console," demonstrates how to modify an application package. See the file **Chapter28-04StepbyStep.pdf** in the CD's **Chapter28\StepbyStep** directory.

SOFTWARE DEPLOYMENT USING GROUP POLICY

Manage and troubleshoot software by using Group Policy.

- **Deploy software by using Group Policy.**

Now that you've repackaged the software to be deployed, created software distribution share points, and applied permissions to the shares, you are ready to configure Group Policy to deploy the

---

EXAM TIP

Know the Difference between Publishing and Assigning Software Expect questions regarding when you would assign and when you would publish software. Only *assigning* software is used when you want mandatory deployment of a software package.

software. In doing so, you have the option to assign a package
to a user or computer or to publish a package to a user.

Publishing Software

Publishing of software enables users to install the software, and
they can initiate the installation of the software package in one of
the following two ways:

◆ **Using Add/Remove Programs from within Control Panel.**
When users select Add/Remove Programs in Control Panel,
they are presented with a list of software available based on
their group membership and the Group Policy created by the
administrator. They then can select the software to install, and
Windows Installer installs the application for them.

◆ **Using file or document activation.** File or document activation is the automatic invocation of the installation of a software package when users double-click a document whose
file extension matches the file extensions configured for the
application. By double-clicking the file and not having the
software application already installed on the hard disk, they
have signaled to Windows Installer that they want to install
the program configured to read and interpret a file whose
extension matches the one on which they have double-clicked.

Publishing of software is useful when you want to give the user a
choice of which software products to install. Publishing is also useful
when you want to ensure that users can view documents, but not all
users need to have support to view all document types. Publishing
software enables you to give the user more choice and is, therefore,
only useful for non-critical applications.

Assigning Software to Users and Computers

Software can be assigned either to users or computers, which
ensures that the software is always available.

Assigning software to users enables the software to be advertised on the user's desktop. This means icons for the application are available even though the application is not currently installed. Double-clicking the software icon, or a file extension associated with the software applications, causes the installation to take place automatically. If the user never double-clicks the software icon or a file with the software extension associated with the package, the software is not installed, thus saving disk space, network bandwidth, and administrative load.

Assigning software to computers ensures that the software is installed when the computer is turned on and connects to the network. The next time the computer processes its Group Policy settings, it finds that software has been assigned to it, and the software is automatically installed. Any software assigned to a computer is available to all users on the computer.

Software that must be installed in all cases should be assigned to a computer. Software needed by all users that is not required to be on the machine initially can be assigned to the user or group and can be installed when required. Either method ensures that the software is available when required.

Deploying Software Using Group Policy

To publish or assign software, you make use of Group Policy. Determining which method to use to deploy the software occurs when the software application is associated with the GPO.

To deploy software using Group Policy, follow Step by Step 28.5.

ON THE CD

Step by Step 28.5, "Deploying Software Using Group Policy," illustrates how to deploy software using Group Policy. See the file **Chapter28-05StepbyStep.pdf** in the CD's **Chapter28\StepbyStep** directory.

Package Deployment Options

Manage and troubleshoot software by using Group Policy.

- **Configure deployment options.**

After you have deployed a package, you can configure some of its options, which changes its behavior and enables you to set additional options. You do this by right-clicking the Software Installation object in the Software Settings folder of the Group Policy where you configured the package.

The Software Installation Properties dialog box, as shown in Figure 28.1, enables you to configure general settings for all packages within the scope of that container. These settings include the default installation location for packages, and the default type of installation for new packages (Publish, Assign, Advanced Published or Assigned, or Present the Dialog Box Shown Earlier). You can determine the amount of user interaction possible during package installation (Basic interaction, which is not much, or Maximum). You have the option to specify whether a package is uninstalled if it falls outside the scope of the GPO. You also can configure file extension preferences and software categories, which is discussed later.

If you right-click a package and select Properties, you can input general information about the package including the manufacturer, platform, support URL, and contact information.

The Deployment tab enables you to change the deployment information for this package. You can change the Deployment type from Published to Assigned and vice versa. The Deployment options portion of this tab determines what happens when deployment takes place, including auto-installing the application when activated through file extension. If you uncheck this box, the file extensions associated with this package are not published, and document invocation cannot take place. You also can uninstall the application if the GPO no longer applies to the user (that is, he or she moved to another OU within the Active Directory hierarchy). You also have the option to not advertise the package in Add/Remove Programs, so a user does not know that the package exists to install it.

The Installation user interface options enable you to specify how much user interaction is available to the user during installation. The default setting, Basic, simply lets the user watch as the application is

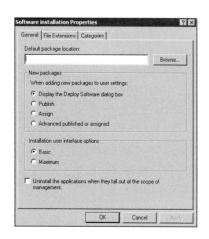

FIGURE 28.1
The Software Installation Properties dialog box in Group Policy Editor.

NOTE

Advanced Published or Assigned
The Advanced published or assigned option shown when you add a package is not a special type of option for the package. Stating that you want to use this option simply means the properties for the package are displayed to you, thereby enabling you to configure other options on the package. It is the same as right-clicking the package after assigning or publishing it and selecting Properties.

installed with default configuration settings. The Maximum setting prompts the user to enter values during installation.

You have now added the package to a Group Policy so it can be deployed to users or computers. You have configured the package's deployment options and have outlined how it is presented to the user. You also have determined whether the package needs to be installed on all computers, in which case you configured the package in the Computer Configuration portion of Group Policy, or whether it is assigned or published to users. In addition, over time you might need to modify these options or even upgrade packages. The issue of maintaining software packages is presented next.

MAINTAINING SOFTWARE PACKAGES USING GROUP POLICY

Manage and troubleshoot software by using Group Policy.

- **Maintain software by using Group Policy.**

The only constant in this industry is change, and invariably at some point after deploying your package using Group Policy, you most likely will have to provide an update to keep the software applications on user machines current. This section shows you how to configure an upgrade for a package using Group Policy and how to provide both mandatory and optional upgrades. Finally, you learn how to remove software that is no longer needed by the organization or whose licenses have expired.

Upgrading a Package

In Microsoft Windows 2000 Group Policy, upgrades to existing packages can be one of two types: mandatory or optional.

Mandatory upgrades are those that must be installed where the previous version of the software exists. For example, you repackaged Microsoft Office 2000 and then received notification that the version on users' desktops is not the most recent one. You decide to upgrade all users to the most recent version of Office 2000 to correct any deficiencies in the software. To do so, you configure the upgrade to be mandatory. The upgrade package is automatically installed on users' machines the next time the user logs on (if the package was assigned to the user or was published), or the machine is restarted (if the software was assigned to the computer). Mandatory upgrades are an ideal way to make sure all users have the most recent version of critical business applications installed.

Optional upgrades enable the user to continue to use the older version of the software or, optionally, to upgrade to the most recent version. Optional upgrades provide users with a message indicating that a newer version is available and asking if they would like to upgrade at that time. If the user agrees to the upgrade, the new version of the software is installed, and the old version is replaced. If the user does not agree to the upgrade, he or she continues to work with the older version of the software. The user continues to be prompted to install the new version. You also can configure a "drop-dead date" by which users must install the upgrade, or it is installed on their machine whether they like it or not. To perform either type of upgrade, follow Step by Step 28.6.

ON THE CD

Step by Step 28.6, "Upgrading Software Using Group Policy," helps you perform upgrades using Group Policy. See the file **Chapter28-06StepbyStep.pdf** in the CD's **Chapter28\StepbyStep** directory.

Configuring upgrades to packages is quite simple except for making sure the upgrade is in the proper format (that is, an MSI file). You can configure the upgrade to be mandatory or optional.

Redeploying Software

In some situations, instead of upgrading a package, you might simply want to reinstall it on all users' machines. This method is known as redeploying, the reinstallation of an existing package. This method is preferable if you modified a package without changing its name, added shortcuts, changed registry settings, or in any other way changed an existing package. To ensure that all users have the updated software, you might want to redeploy the package.

You also might create a new package (MSI) file with the exact same name as the existing package and put it in the same location as the original package. By using this method, you can incorporate more widespread changes to the software than by simply modifying an existing package. As long as the version and package name are identical, it is considered to be the same software. You then can redeploy the package as needed.

To redeploy a package, after making your modification, perform the steps shown in Step by Step 28.7.

ON THE CD

Step by Step 28.7, "Redeploying a Package Using Group Policy," demonstrates how to redeploy packages using Group Policy. See the file **Chapter28-07StepbyStep.pdf** in the CD's **Chapter28\ StepbyStep** directory.

You should remember, however, that redeploying a package causes it to be reinstalled on all client machines, which can use up large amounts of network bandwidth.

Removing a Package

After you have deployed software using Group Policy, you also have the option to have Group Policy automate the removal of the software for you. In this way, applications that are no longer needed or software that is out-of-date can be removed from users' computers without a great deal of manual intervention on your part.

The removal options available in Group Policy also can be used in the case of an optional upgrade. In this situation, users have some time to upgrade to a new version. After a reasonable amount of time has lapsed, you can decide to remove the old version of the application from their machines.

Software can be removed by using one of the following two options:

◆ **Mandatory or forced removal.** The software is removed from the user's computer whether or not he or she still requires it. This is selected by specifying the Immediately Uninstall

Software From Users and Computers option when configuring removal of a package for the GPO. The software is removed prior to the presentation of the user's desktop and is transparent to the user—if it was assigned to the user. If the package was assigned to the computer, it is removed the next time the computer restarts. If an upgrade of the software exists, the user can install the upgraded version to continue to have the functionality of the software; if not, the software becomes unavailable.

◆ **Optional removal.** This enables the user to continue to use the software and is selected when you specify the Allow Users to Continue to Use the Software but Prevent New Installations option when configuring removal. The software does not appear in the list of applications under Add/Remove Programs in Control Panel but does remain installed. After the user manually removes the software through Add/Remove Programs on his or her computer, he or she no longer can install it.

To configure removal of a package, perform the steps shown in Step by Step 28.8.

ON THE CD

Step by Step 28.8, "Removing a Package Using Group Policy," illustrates how to remove packages using Group Policy. See the file **Chapter28-08StepbyStep.pdf** in the CD's **Chapter28\StepbyStep** directory.

MANAGING SOFTWARE DEPLOYMENT

The process of deploying software in large organizations might require that additional tasks be performed to make the deployment process more friendly, by recognizing geographic and language differences. Deployment can be designed to help users select which software to install by creating software categories for similar packages. It also can be designed to automatically initiate the installation when a particular file is invoked by the user. The deployment process itself can encounter problems, and the administrator needs to be aware of how to correct some of the common problems encountered in software deployment. Repackaging applications also can present problems during deployment, and an administrator should be familiar with these issues as well.

Configuring Package Modifications

Windows 2000 Group Policy allows the use of software modification, or *transform (MST) files*, to deploy several configurations of the same application. Transform files have an MST extension and are associated with an existing package. In combination with several GPOs, MST files are used to change the behavior of a package when it is deployed in different regions.

For example, your organization, with offices in the United States, Canada, England, and France, wants to deploy Microsoft Office 2000 worldwide. However, users in Paris and Quebec need to receive French dictionaries, as well as English, when Office 2000 is installed. To solve this problem, you create one package file for Office 2000. To deal with the different dictionaries that need to be supported, you create MST files for each dictionary. You then create a separate GPO for the Parisian site to include the Office 2000 package as well as the French dictionary MST file. For Quebec, you could use the same or another GPO to roll out the French dictionary also. For Canada, the United States, and England, you might create one or more GPOs that would include the English dictionary MST file.

To add modifications to a software package, perform the steps in Step by Step 28.9.

ON THE CD

Step by Step 28.9, "Modifying a Package with an MST File," guides you through the process of adding modifications to packages with an MST file. See the file **Chapter28-09StepbyStep.pdf** in the CD's **Chapter28\StepbyStep** directory.

NOTE

Transform (MST) Files An MST file modifies what is installed on a user's computer based on the GPO used to deploy the software. After the software has been installed on a user's machine, it cannot be modified using an MST file. Only prior to the installation taking place on a computer can the transform file have any effect. For example, 20 users have already installed application X, and you decide to specify a modification using an MST file of application X. Any users who already have application X installed cannot have the modification deployed to them. Only users who do not have application X installed get the software modification specified in the MST file. To apply an MST file to all users (old and new), you also need to redeploy the package.

NOTE

Where the MST File Is Generated The MST is generated either using a deployment product such as WinInstaller or within the actual application. For example, Office 2000 can generate an MST file using the Office 2000 Customization Wizard.

Using software modifications within the scope of software deployment in a GPO enables you to modify the settings for a deployed application package. This is a good way to have the same package deployed to different users or computers without having to repackage the software for each specific configuration. MST files enable you to store only the specific changes to be applied against a package and to have those deployed with a specific GPO.

Creating Software Categories

In large organizations, or even in smaller ones in which many different software applications are in use, it might be beneficial to create software categories to make it easier for users to install the package they want. Creating software categories changes the display in Add/Remove Programs in Control Panel (see Figure 28.2) and enables the user to locate the software type he or she needs.

A single application can appear in more than one category. For example, Microsoft Office 2000 can be placed in the Office Packages category as well as in Word Processors, Spreadsheets, and Presentation Software, because it includes all of these. Specifying a category for a particular package only makes it easier for the user to find the application. It does not, in any way, change the behavior of the Group Policy in which the package is configured for deployment. Furthermore, if you add new categories or if you decide to start using categories, you can modify the software category under which a package should be listed at any time.

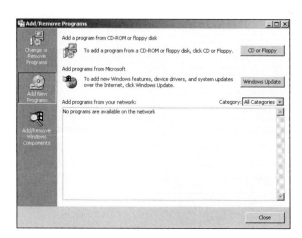

FIGURE 28.2
Add/Remove Programs in Control Panel lists packages available on the network in categories.

One very important point that needs to be conveyed is that software categories function on a domain-wide basis and when configured in any GPO on the domain, are available throughout the domain. You cannot have one set of categories in the Sales OU, for example, and another set in the Development OU of the same domain. All categories in all OUs are available throughout the domain. However, you can have a different set of categories in different domains.

To create software categories, follow the steps in Step by Step 28.10.

ON THE CD

Step by Step 28.10, "Creating Software Categories for the Domain," shows you how to create software categories for a domain. See the file **Chapter28-10StepbyStep.pdf** in the CD's **Chapter28\StepbyStep** directory.

After you have created the categories, they can be used to categorize existing packages or new ones you have configured for deployment. To assign a software category to a package, follow the steps in Step by Step 28.11.

ON THE CD

Step by Step 28.11, "Assigning a Software Package to a Category," teaches you how to assign software packages to a category. See the file **Chapter28-11StepbyStep.pdf** in the CD's **Chapter28\StepbyStep** directory.

As you have seen, creating categories for software is easy. It is of great benefit to organizations that want to publish many applications using Group Policy, and it makes it easier for users to find the applications they want to install. Administrators categorize the packages available, and then users can use these categories to browse what is available. As noted, the same package can exist in multiple categories.

But what if users do not have access to Add/Remove Programs in Control Panel?

Associating File Extensions with Applications

Windows 2000 Active Directory provides great new functionality when deploying software applications using Group Policy. When you obtain a package (MSI) file or after you repackage an application using third-party products such as Veritas WinINSTALL LE, you might find that the package publishes file extensions supported by the software.

For example, Adobe Acrobat 4 is used to open files with a PDF extension. It can be set such that an automatic installation of the software application is performed whenever a user double-clicks a PDF file to open it, and the software is not yet installed on the machine.

The list of file extensions and applications (packages) that support these extensions is published and tracked by Windows 2000 Active Directory. The mapping of file extension to software package is kept domain-wide, but the determination of which software package is installed when a user attempts to open a file of a particular extension can be configured at an OU or other level. This means users in one particular branch of Active Directory (the Sales OU, for example) can install one application when they activate a document by double-clicking it, while users in another OU (the Development OU) can have a different application installed.

If multiple applications are defined for opening a single extension type, you can configure the priority of the application by adjusting the GPO used to deploy software in a specific OU.

Filename extension priorities are configured on a per-GPO basis. You configure the priority of a particular application to be installed through document activation within the GPO, and it only affects users that have the GPO applied to them. Other users are not affected by the priority established in a GPO and might, in fact, install different applications for the same file extension.

To modify and configure filename extension priorities, perform the steps in Step by Step 28.12.

NOTE

Windows 2000 Only   File-extension priority only applies to packages deployed using Windows 2000 Group Policy. It does not apply to software deployed using any other method.

ON THE CD

Step by Step 28.12, "Configuring File Extension Priority for a GPO," illustrates how to modify and configure filename extension priorities. See the file **Chapter28-12StepbyStep.pdf** in the CD's **Chapter28\StepbyStep** directory.

If you're wondering how the file extension got associated with a particular package, think back to the "Packaging Software for Deployment" section of this chapter. If you recall, when repackaging an application, you are able to specify with which file extensions that application should be associated. In the same vein, when a software developer creates a package used to install their software, they also associate certain file extensions with their application. In this way, users are able to make use of the application as intended.

Whichever way is used to associate an extension with an application, this association is published within Active Directory and is maintained on each client machine. This is so the files can be opened, and the users are not left in the situation in which they have files that cannot be used.

Troubleshooting Software Deployment

Maintain and troubleshoot software by using Group Policy.

- **Troubleshoot common problems that occur during software deployment.**

After you have configured software deployment, especially if you have a large organization with many GPOs to deploy software, occasions might occur when the deployment is not working exactly as you would expect. Listed next are some of the more common problems and their causes:

◆ **Application cannot be installed.** The most likely cause of this problem is that the user cannot reach the network share where the application package is located. Verify that the share is available and that the user has permissions to access the package files. The permissions required are Read on the share and Read and Execute at the NTFS level on the volume where the package files are located.

◆ **Applications do not appear as expected on the user's desktop.** The most likely cause of this problem is in the way the application was deployed. If the application was assigned to the user, the shortcuts for the application should appear on the user's desktop. If they do not, log in as the user and check to see if the application is listed under Add/Remove Programs in Control Panel. If it is, then the application was published, not assigned, and must be installed manually or have the installation begin through document activation. If the application is not listed in Add/Remove Programs and no shortcuts appear on the desktop, it might be that the application was never deployed or was deployed in another OU.

◆ **Deployed applications do not work properly after installation.** In some cases in which applications are repackaged using a third-party packaging program such as Veritas WinINSTALL LE, the process might not have taken place properly. If during repackaging the setup program of the application did not install certain files on the reference computer's hard drive, for example, these files will not be in the package file created and will need to exist on the user's hard drive. To correct the problem, repackage the application or add the necessary files to the package.

◆ **Package installation removes other files.** This is also a repackaging problem. When an application is repackaged, the period between the before and after snapshot can cause other changes on the system if other programs are launched. This can cause the final package, after the after snapshot is created, to include instructions to remove files from the hard drive. If this is the case, when the package is deployed, it causes those same files to be removed from the user's computer and might cause other software to stop functioning. To solve this problem, modify the package to remove any reference to file deletion or repackage the software to make sure it is correctly configured.

◆ **Applications are not deployed as expected or are not deployed at all.** The most likely cause of this is Group Policy conflicts. GPOs can be created at different levels of Active Directory, and these same GPOs can have application deployment configured within them. It is possible that a setting in one GPO associated with an Active Directory container might conflict with a setting in another GPO in a lower-level Active Directory container. Furthermore, because software can be assigned to both computers and users, computer settings can override user settings depending on the Active Directory level at which they are applied. It is always a good idea to check the inheritance of GPOs within the Active Directory structure.

As you see, many of the common problems associated with software deployment deal with either improper repackaging or Group Policy issues. Understanding how GPOs work in general (whether or not you are using GPOs for software deployment) is critical. Testing software deployment on a few machines before rolling it out on a large scale reduces the chances of experiencing a large-scale problem.

CASE STUDY: USING GROUP POLICY TO DEPLOY SOFTWARE APPLICATIONS AT SUNSHINE BREWING

ESSENCE OF THE CASE

SunShine Brewing has purchased a new enterprise resource planning (ERP) application that needs to be deployed to all executives and administrative users. Sales people need to have the Customer Relationship Management (CRM) component of the application installed on their computers as well because they use the intelligence of the system to process orders, profile customers, and check on the status of client orders and other elements. Furthermore, Microsoft Office 2000 has been purchased as the corporate office suite standard, and it needs to be installed on all users' desktops. Because the company operates in a multinational environment, specific settings for Office 2000, such as dictionary components used for spell checking, need to conform to local requirements.

SCENARIO

In this chapter, you were shown how Group Policy is used to deploy software packages across the enterprise or to a specific set of users. You also were introduced to methods that can be used to upgrade packages that have been deployed, and you learned how to repackage software that does not come in a format compatible with Windows Installer. Here you determine how this can be used to solve a specific problem at SunShine Brewing.

ANALYSIS

Although the initial challenge presented by the scope of this software deployment might seem somewhat daunting, using Group Policy to perform the deployment easily solves this problem.

continues

CASE STUDY: USING GROUP POLICY TO DEPLOY SOFTWARE APPLICATIONS AT SUNSHINE BREWING

continued

It also has been decided that Windows Installer Package files for utility software, including WinZIP, Adobe Acrobat Reader, and RealAudio Player, which have been acquired from your software supplier, will be available for users as an optional installation. If the users attempt to open a file type supported by the utility, they should be asked whether they want to install the package.

Historically, large-scale deployments of software of this nature have been handled by the IT staff with the help of co-op or summer students who perform the bulk of the grunt work. After calculating the budget for using this approach, the figure presented to the CEO was rejected, and the IT department has been told to perform the deployment using existing resources within a three-month period. As the champion of Windows 2000 in the organization, you have been told to make sure this can be done or face the consequences.

After looking at the requirements, you decide to contact the ERP vendor to see if the software has any specific installation capabilities that could assist in a deployment of this scale. The third-party vendor of the ERP application has stated that an installation program must be run on each client computer even though the end result is always the same, assuming the same components are installed. A Windows Installer Package does not exist for the ERP system, nor does the vendor plan to offer one without SunShine Brewing paying a hefty price. (They admit they have not tried it and would be starting from scratch.)

On the ERP side, you would require at least two different software configurations: one for the sales personnel who will have a subset of the ERP package (the CRM component only) and the other for all admin users who will have the entire ERP client software installed on their desktops. Because the ERP vendor does not have the application in a Windows Installer Package format and because this would not help you with the sales requirement, you first need to create two Windows Installer Packages with the correct configuration.

To create the Windows Installer Package for the admin users, you would start with a clean Windows 2000 Professional computer and use Veritas WinInstall LE (or another third-party product) to create a before snapshot of the computer. You would then install and configure the ERP application, as it should exist on all admin users' machines. During this period, you would create any shortcuts and configure any software settings, as they require. After configuring the ERP software as needed, you would use the Discover Wizard of Veritas WinInstall LE (or the third-party tool) to create the package file with the correct configuration.

To create a Windows Installer Package file for the sales users, you would perform similar steps as for the admin package creation but only include those components of the application required by sales CRM. At this point, you would have two Windows Installer Packages that you would place on a network share in their own separate folders. You also would place Microsoft Office 2000 on the same share point in its own folder.

CASE STUDY: USING GROUP POLICY TO DEPLOY SOFTWARE APPLICATIONS AT SUNSHINE BREWING

To deploy the software, you would need to create three GPOs: one for the Admin OU for the ERP package, a second for the Sales OU for the CRM component of the ERP package, and a third for Microsoft Office 2000. The Microsoft Office 2000 GPO would be created at each site and would include MST files that would modify the package to include local settings.

You would apply the ERP package GPO to Authenticated Users in the Admin OU, the CRM package to Authenticated Users in the Sales OU,

and Microsoft Office 2000 to Authenticated Users at the site level with No Override to make sure all users get Microsoft Office 2000.

For the utility software, you would publish all the packages to Authenticated Users using a GPO at the domain level and would enable document activation on each package.

CHAPTER SUMMARY

In this chapter, you learned how to use Group Policy to deploy software applications within your enterprise. Software to be deployed using Group Policy must be in a format compatible with Windows Installer. These formats include Windows Installer Package (MSI) files and ZAP files, which the Windows Installer service can parse to start the software installation process.

Software can be delivered to users through Group Policy either by assigning or by publishing. Assigning a software package to a computer automatically installs that package. Assigning a software package to a user automatically places icons on the desktop. When a package is assigned to a user, the software installation process is triggered when the user clicks an icon or a document whose file extension matches one associated with the package.

Publishing software makes the application available to the user but does not immediately install the software. The software is installed either through Control Panel Add/Remove Programs or by document activation. Document activation involves an attempt by the user to open a file with an extension associated with a particular package. Windows 2000 checks to see if an application is available to open the file on the user's machine. If not, Active Directory is

KEY TERMS

- Assigning software
- Forced (mandatory) package removal
- GPO scope
- Group Policy filtering
- Group Policy inheritance
- Group Policy Object (GPO)
- Group Policy precedence
- Mandatory upgrade
- Optional removal
- Optional upgrade
- Package modifications
- Publishing software
- Redeployment

CHAPTER SUMMARY

KEY TERMS

- Repackaging an application
- Repackaging software
- Software categories
- Transform (MST) files
- Windows Installer
- Windows Installer Service
- ZAP file

checked for a list of applications and their priority. After the list is reviewed, Group Policy is used to trigger Windows Installer to install the application.

Only Windows Installer Package files can be either assigned or published to users. These files contain the information necessary to install the application without user intervention. ZAP files can only be published and require the user to perform the normal install process for the software application. For this reason, third-party tools are available to repackage an application that is not provided in a Windows Installer Package file format. One such tool included on the Windows 2000 CD-ROM is Veritas WinINSTALL LE.

Administrators can use MST files to deploy the same software package with different options to different OUs within the enterprise. MST files also modify an existing package to meet specific requirements such as language or geographic location. Administrators also can categorize software applications to make it easier for users to select which software to install through Add/Remove Programs in Control Panel.

After some time, it might be necessary for users to receive a newer version of an application or to remove applications that are no longer required. The administrator can designate a software package as either a required or an optional upgrade for an existing application. Required upgrades are installed without the user having a choice in the decision; optional upgrades enable the user to decide whether he or she wants to upgrade to the most recent version. Software removal also can be forced or optional. Forced removal requires the software package be removed from the user's machine. An optional removal enables the user to continue to use the application after it has been designated for removal. Even though the user might decide to leave the package on the system, after he or she removes the application, it no longer is available for installation because it no longer is being published in Active Directory.

CHAPTER SUMMARY

Most problems regarding the deployment of software using Group Policy result from network errors, such as not being able to reach the software distribution point or trouble with the application of Group Policy itself. When deciding the nature of a problem, you must adhere to all the rules governing policy inheritance, filtering, and other elements outlined in Chapter 27, "Using Group Policy to Manage Users." Deployment is an extremely useful aspect of Group Policy, and it does not change the way Group Policy works in general.

APPLY YOUR KNOWLEDGE

Review Questions

1. How must software be configured for it to be deployed using Group Policy?

2. You need to make sure that all users in your organization have Microsoft Outlook 2000 installed as their email client. How would you accomplish this?

3. Users in your office in Germany are complaining that they do not have Microsoft Outlook 2000 prompts and other information in German. How would you correct this problem?

4. If a software application is not shipped as a Windows Installer Package file, what alternatives are available for deploying it using Group Policy?

5. If your organization has many software packages deployed, how can you make it easier for users to find the application they want?

6. When would you assign an application to a computer rather than a user?

7. What software deployment options are not available when using ZAP files?

8. How would you add a support telephone number and Web site location to an existing MSI file?

9. Why would a software package remove files from the user's machine when it is deployed?

10. How could you be sure that users would still be able to use an application after it has been removed from the GPO?

Answers to Review Questions

1. Software must be in the form of a Windows Installer Package file, or you must create a ZAP file if you want to deploy the software using Group Policy.

   The MSI file is in native Windows Installer format and contains the files, registry settings, and shortcuts that make up an application, as well as information on where these elements should be installed.

   A ZAP file is a text file that specifies information on the program to be invoked to install the application including any parameters, as well as file extensions, that should be associated with the application. See the section "Preparing Software for Deployment Using Group Policy."

2. Configure a GPO at the domain level and create the Microsoft Outlook 2000 package in the Users Configuration container of the GPO. Assign, rather than publish, the application to make sure it is installed on all users' desktops. See the section "Software Deployment Using Group Policy."

3. Create a GPO at the German users' OU in Active Directory and assign the package to it. Configure an MST file with the German language characteristics required and associate it with the package. This ensures that Microsoft Outlook 2000 is still installed (it is assigned), but the language requirements of the German users also are taken into consideration through the MST file. See the section "Managing Software Deployment."

APPLY YOUR KNOWLEDGE

4. You can create a ZAP file to install the application and then publish the software product in Group Policy. You also can repackage the application using a third-party repackaging tool such as Veritas WinINSTALL LE, which creates a Windows Installer Package file, providing you with greater flexibility in deployment. See the section "Preparing Software for Deployment Using Group Policy."

5. Create software categories that are available domain-wide. Then modify your packages in the various GPOs and assign them to one or more categories. In this way, when a user wants to install an application that has been published, he or she can view the list of all software or only the categories in which he or she is interested when using Add/Remove Programs in Control Panel. See the section "Managing Software Deployment."

6. You would assign an application to a computer rather than a user when the application's availability is required for all users on one or more machines. In this way, users always have critical software available. See the section "Software Deployment Using Group Policy."

7. When using ZAP files, you cannot assign the package to computers or users; you can only publish them. This is because a ZAP file simply tells Windows Installer what program to invoke to start the installation process. Windows Installer has no control over what actually occurs during the application installation and, therefore, cannot control it, and packages cannot be assigned because this would require Windows Installer to automate the installation of a software application. See the section "Preparing Software for Deployment Using Group Policy."

8. To add a support telephone number and Web site location to an existing MSI file, you would modify the MSI file using a third-party repackaging product such as Veritas WinINSTALL LE. See the section "Windows Installer Technology."

9. A software package can remove files from a user's machine when it is deployed if it was repackaged and, during the repackaging, files were removed. Because repackaging takes a before and after snapshot of the user's computer to determine what has changed during the software installation process, any files that were removed or modified either by the product's setup program or the user is incorporated in the package. If the administrator did not carefully examine the resulting package file created and correct any items that should not be passed on to users' machines, it is possible for a repackaged application to make unwanted changes to a user's system. To correct this problem, either modify the package or repackage the application. See the section "Troubleshooting Software Deployment."

10. To ensure that users can still use an application after it has been removed from a GPO, make the package removal optional. If the removal is optional, users can still make use of the application until they themselves decide to remove it, after which time the application is no longer available. See the section "Maintaining Software Packages Using Group Policy."

APPLY YOUR KNOWLEDGE

ON THE CD

This book's companion CD contains specially designed supplemental material to help you determine how well you understand the concepts and can use the skills you learned in this chapter. You'll find related exercises and exam questions and answers. See the file **Chapter28ApplyYourKnowledge.pdf** in the CD's **Chapter28\ApplyYourKnowledge** directory.

Suggested Readings and Resources

1. *Microsoft Windows 2000 Resource Kit. Deployment Planning Guide.* Microsoft Press, 2000.

2. *Automated Deployment Options: An Overview White Paper* on Microsoft's Web site at http://www.microsoft.com/windows2000/library/planning/client/deployops.asp.

3. *Software Installation and Maintenance* on Microsoft's Web site at http://www.microsoft.com/windows2000/library/operations/management/siamwp.asp.

4. *Automating the Deployment of Windows 2000 Professional and Office 2000* on Microsoft's Web site at http://www.microsoft.com/windows2000/library/planning/incremental/sysprep.asp.

5. *Desktop Deployment Solutions from Third-Party Companies* on Microsoft's Web site at http://www.microsoft.com/windows2000/guide/server/partners/DesktopSolutions.asp.

6. *Software Deployment Using Windows 2000 and Systems Management Server 2.0* on Microsoft's Web site at http://www.microsoft.com/windows2000/library/planning/management/smsintell.asp.

7. *Windows Installer* on Microsoft's Web site at http://www.microsoft.com/windows2000/library/howitworks/management/installer.asp.

The following objectives from the "Configuring, Managing, Monitoring, and Troubleshooting Active Directory Security Solutions" section of the exam are addressed by this chapter:

Configure and troubleshoot security in a directory services infrastructure.

- **Apply security policies by using Group Policy.**

- **Create, analyze, and modify security configurations by using Security Configuration and Analysis and Security Templates.**

- **Implement an audit policy.**

▶ Microsoft wants to make sure you are familiar with the process of modifying security settings using Group Policy security templates. Knowing what security elements can be configured and applied, where they apply (user or computer), and the end result of a security policy are also tested. You need to know the capabilities and features of the Security Configuration and Analysis MMC snap-in and how it can be used to apply and verify your security policies.

Monitor and analyze security events.

▶ Microsoft also tests your ability to track security policy settings through auditing and your ability to set an audit policy to determine the actual outcome of that security policy. You need to know where to locate security event information and how to analyze the details to determine the cause of a security breach.

CHAPTER 29

Managing Security Using Group Policy

STUDY STRATEGIES

▶ The best way to prepare for this portion of the exam is to use the appropriate tools mentioned in this chapter. Using Security Configuration and Analysis to analyze security on a computer interactively and to create a template provides you with critical hands-on experience that will aid you in answering questions dealing with these tools. Also, exporting security settings through Security Configuration and Analysis should be attempted.

▶ You should configure SECEDIT.EXE through Task Scheduler to analyze security settings on one or more computers, and then review the database information that is created.

▶ You should be familiar with the options available in security templates and configure one or more Group Policy objects to test these settings.

▶ Understanding what happens and knowing the options available in configuring an audit policy are also tested; thus, you should configure one or more audit settings as well as use Windows Explorer to enable file and object access.

▶ Finally, being able to answer the review and exam questions in this chapter, and being able to work through the exercises and Step by Steps on the accompanying CD will assist you in preparing for the exam. As always, working through the practice exam in the book and on the CD will also help.

INTRODUCTION

In this chapter, you find out what security settings are configurable through Windows 2000. Information on security settings that can be configured for the computer, as well as for the user, is presented. The functionality and usefulness of security settings is examined. A discussion on the use and types of security templates available, as well as how security templates can be created, is presented. You are also introduced to the Security Templates snap-in for Microsoft Management Console (MMC) and how to make use of it to create and modify security settings in templates.

Next, you will be shown how to analyze and configure security settings for a computer using Security Configuration and Analysis, another MMC snap-in. The creation of security templates using Security Configuration and Analysis is also shown. A discussion of the benefits and limitations of using this MMC snap-in is included. Using Group Policy to apply security settings to a number of computers is outlined.

After configuring these security settings using Group Policy, you can use auditing to ensure that the settings are being applied as necessary.

SECURITY SETTINGS AVAILABLE IN WINDOWS 2000 GROUP POLICY

Configure and troubleshoot security in a directory services infrastructure.

- **Apply security policies by using Group Policy.**

As you have seen in the two preceding chapters, Group Policy can be used to apply both computer and group settings. This remains true for applying security policy. However, because the more important element in security is to make sure access to resources is restricted to only those individuals who should have it, Group Policy in the security context is overwhelmingly slanted toward the computer side.

The settings that can be configured in Group Policy for the computer (see Figure 29.1) are as follows:

◆ **Account Policies.** This setting enables you to specify password and account lockout policy settings. Password policy settings include the password age, the number of passwords that will be remembered to prevent password reuse, the minimum password length, and password complexity. Account lockout policy settings include the duration of account lockout, the number of incorrect log on attempts before invoking lockout, and the account lockout interval.

◆ **Local Policies.** This setting enables you to configure local computer settings for auditing, user rights assignment, and specific computer security options.

◆ **Event Log.** The Event Log setting enables the configuration of log file sizes for the system, security, and application logs. Settings also include whether logs should be overwritten after their maximum size is reached, and restrictions on who is allowed to read the log files.

◆ **Restricted Groups.** This setting enables you to manage which users can be members of certain security groups and to configure in which other groups these groups can also be members.

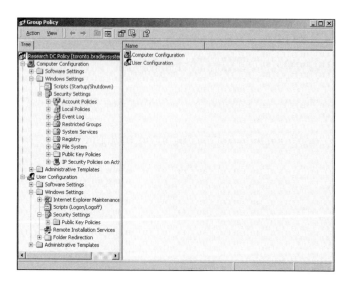

FIGURE 29.1
Group Policy security configuration options.

◆ **System Services.** This setting enables the administrator to specify how services and devices will be started on the computer.

◆ **Registry.** The Registry setting enables you to define permissions for specific keys in the computer's registry.

◆ **File System.** Through this security setting, you are able to specify file system security settings for folders and files on NTFS partitions, and you are able to ensure that they will apply when the policy is in effect.

◆ **Public Key Policies.** This setting enables you to set Encrypting File System (EFS) recovery agents. You can also import certificate files from root certification authorities that will be trusted by Windows 2000, configure trust settings for authorities and certificates they have issued, and specify automatic certificate request settings.

◆ **IP Security Polices on Active Directory.** This setting enables you to configure how clients, servers, and domain controllers communicate and what level of IP security is requested, required, or declined.

On the User Configuration side, only one area of configuration exists within Group Policy—Public Key Policies.

Public key policies that can be configured have only a single area— enterprise trusts. This enables the administrator to specify for the user which root Certification Authorities (CAs) will be trusted, and it ensures that no other CAs are allowed by the user.

IMPLEMENTING SECURITY POLICIES

Configure and troubleshoot security in a directory services infrastructure.

- **Create, analyze, and modify security configurations by using Security Configuration and Analysis and Security Templates.**

In Windows 2000, there are two main ways to implement security policies—using security templates or using Group Policy. The difference is not that great. Templates make it easier to reapply similar settings to many systems. A selection of settings also can be saved using a text file and then reapplied in different areas if necessary.

Security Templates in Windows 2000

A *security template* is a text file with an INF extension This file includes security settings that can be applied to a single computer using the Security Configuration and Analysis MMC snap-in. These settings can be imported into Group Policy and applied at the site, domain, or OU level. Security templates are a preconfigured list of settings and might include one or more of the sections previously described.

Microsoft Windows 2000 ships with a number of preconfigured security templates designed to be used in domain controllers, servers, and workstations. Security templates are stored in the WINNT\ Security\Templates folder on Windows 2000 computers. The four levels of security templates are as follows:

◆ **Basic.** Basic templates are the default security level of Windows 2000. They provide a high degree of application functionality but prevent basic security problems, such as users configuring blank passwords or reusing the same passwords over and over again. Microsoft ships default, basic templates for domain controllers (basicdc), servers (basicsv), and workstations (basicwk).

◆ **Compatible.** Compatible templates provide more security, such as restricted access to certain parts of the Registry, but still ensure that business applications run as required. By default, Windows 2000 includes only one compatible template for workstations (compatws).

◆ **Secure.** Secure templates lean toward tighter security rather than compatibility for business application functionality. This means that business applications are not guaranteed to function in a secure environment, because they might attempt to make use of portions of the operating system that have been secured. Secure templates are included for domain controllers (securedc) and workstations (securews).

◆ **High.** High templates enforce the maximum-security settings in Windows 2000 and do not guarantee that line-of-business applications will work. They are not normally used in a Windows 2000 environment because they might break too many applications, but they are useful in the development of high-security Windows 2000 applications. High-security templates include the signing of IP packets between server and workstation, lockout and disconnection of users, protection of Registry and file system components, and many other settings. Windows 2000 ships with high-security templates for domain controllers (hisecdc) and workstations (hisecws).

In addition to the four basic template settings, Microsoft Windows 2000 also ships with other templates used for specific tasks. These are all variations of the four basic levels. These additional templates are listed here:

◆ **DC security.** This template includes the default security settings applied on all domain controllers. It includes file system and Registry protection to ensure that domain controllers function properly. DC security template is automatically configured and installed on all domain controllers in the domain and is part of the Default Domain Controller policy in the Domain Controller container in Active Directory.

◆ **notssid.** The notssid template removes the Terminal Server SID from the Windows 2000 Server computer. Users have their access to the Terminal Server defined by their SID and group memberships, not the Terminal Server account SID.

◆ **ocfiless/ocfilesw.** The ocfiless security template is used to provide additional file security on Windows 2000 Server machines. The files included on the policy may not be installed, which can be problematic because the policy removes permissions to install the files for most users including the Administrator and System. ocfiless is intended for servers and ocfilesw is intended for work-stations.

◆ **Setup security.** This template is the default, and includes out-of-the-box settings applied to Windows 2000 Professional and Windows 2000 Server computers.

Creating and Modifying Security Templates

The creation and modification of security templates in Windows 2000 is performed using the Security Templates MMC snap-in. This snap-in is not preconfigured in any MMC console available in either Administrative Tools or Control Panel. To open Microsoft Management Console (MMC) and add the Security Templates snap-in to the console, follow Step by Step 29.1.

ON THE CD

Step by Step 29.1, "Configuring MMC with the Security Templates Snap-in," shows you how to open Microsoft Management Console and add the Security Templates snap-in to the console. See the file **Chapter29-01StepbyStep.pdf** in the CD's **Chapter29\StepbyStep** directory.

NOTE

Using an Existing Security Template Instead of creating a security template from scratch, you can take an existing security template and use it to create a new template. To do this, right-click the template you want to copy, and select Save As. In the Save As dialog box, enter a filename for the copy of the template you want to create.

A main advantage of copying a security template is that you can make modifications to include more settings. If most of the settings you want to enforce already exist in the template you are copying, it won't take as long to add all the changes as it would to add them from scratch.

After you have configured an MMC console, you can use and reuse it to create and modify security templates. Now, you are ready to create a template. To create a security template, perform the steps in Step by Step 29.2.

ON THE CD

Step by Step 29.2, "Creating a Security Template Using the Security Templates MMC Snap-in," teaches you how to create a security template. See the file **Chapter29-02StepbyStep.pdf** in the CD's **Chapter29\StepbyStep** directory.

After you have created the security template, you need to modify its settings to make sure the security policy reflects the behavior you want. To modify a security template, follow the steps presented in Step by Step 29.3.

ON THE CD

Step by Step 29.3, "Modifying Security Template Settings Using the Security Templates MMC Snap-in," modifies a security template. See the file **Chapter29-03StepbyStep.pdf** in the CD's **Chapter29\StepbyStep** directory.

Although not yet stated, you can also delete security templates that are no longer useful. This can be done by deleting the file directly from the folder in which it resides (C:\WINNT\Security\Templates, for example) or by using the Security Templates MMC snap-in.

Using Security Configuration and Analysis

Another tool that can be used to configure security settings on a computer is the Security Configuration and Analysis snap-in for MMC. The Security Templates snap-in was used to configure settings, which will later be imported into Group Policy. Security Configuration and Analysis is primarily designed to analyze local system security settings and apply security templates to the local computer. It can also be used to retrieve the local computer security configuration and to create a security template that will reflect the computer's settings.

In analyzing your system's security settings, Security Configuration and Analysis can be used to import a security template. This will be compared with the local machine's security configuration. The results of the analysis can be stored in a database, which enables the administrator to track changes in security settings over time. The default extension for the database file is SDB, and one SDB file is created by default when you install Windows 2000, although you cannot access it directly.

In configuring system security, Security Configuration and Analysis can be used to import security template settings and then apply them directly on the local computer. Unlike Group Policy, Security Configuration and Analysis cannot be used to apply the template settings to more than one computer at a time. If you need to do this, you should import a security template into Group Policy in the Active Directory container where the machines are located.

To open Microsoft Management Console and add the Security Configuration and Analysis snap-in to the console, follow the steps presented in Step by Step 29.4.

NOTE

Analyzing Many Computers   In situations in which frequent analysis of a large number of computers is required, Windows 2000 provides a command-line utility called SECEDIT. This utility can be passed the database filename, log location, and other parameters specified within Security Configuration and Analysis. The utility performs the security analysis as you did with the MMC, but you still need to use the Security Configuration and Analysis snap-in to view the results of the analysis.

The command-line SECEDIT.EXE utility can be of value in environments in which scheduling the analysis to occur at off-peak hours is useful. In fact, it is primarily intended to be used through the Task Scheduler and not from the command prompt. Administrators can configure a central location for database files for many computers, and they can also have the results placed there. Following the overnight analysis, the administrator can review each of the database's contents using the Security Configuration and Analysis snap-in to determine whether problems exist.

ON THE CD

Step by Step 29.4, "Configuring MMC with the Security Configuration and Analysis Snap-In," shows you how to open Microsoft Management Console (MMC) and add the Security Configuration and Analysis snap-in to the console. See the file **Chapter29-04StepbyStep.pdf** in the CD's **Chapter29\StepbyStep** directory.

A database to hold the security settings must be created when using the Security Configuration and Analysis snap-in. You can then use this database to perform analysis of your settings against a security template, as well as use it to store your current configuration.

To create a database to be used to analyze your computer against a template, follow the steps shown in Step by Step 29.5.

ON THE CD

Step by Step 29.5, "Configuring a Database for Analyzing Your Computer in Security Configuration and Analysis," shows you how to create a database to be used to analyze your computer against a template. See the file **Chapter29-05StepbyStep.pdf** in the CD's **Chapter29\StepbyStep** directory.

Analyzing Your Computer Using Security Configuration and Analysis

Analyzing a computer's security settings means comparing the current configuration of the computer to the desired configuration as stored in a security template. The tool used is the Security Configuration and Analysis MMC snap-in. You can compare security settings against a template to make sure the computer's settings are in compliance with a corporate security policy or to determine whether the settings have changed since the last time you performed the analysis.

To analyze a computer's security, perform the steps included in Step by Step 29.6.

ON THE CD

Step by Step 29.6, "Analyzing a Computer's Security Configuration Using Security Configuration and Analysis," shows you how to analyze a computer's security. See the file **Chapter29-06StepbyStep.pdf** in the CD's **Chapter29\StepbyStep** directory.

Configuring a Computer with Security Settings

Using Security Configuration and Analysis, you can take the results of an analysis and determine whether template settings are properly configured. Through Security Configuration and Analysis, you can also apply security templates settings to the local computer. To do this, perform the steps in Step by Step 29.7.

ON THE CD

Step by Step 29.7, "Configuring a Computer with Security Settings Using Security Configuration and Analysis," teaches you how to apply security template settings to the local computer. See the file **Chapter29-07StepbyStep.pdf** in the CD's **Chapter29\StepbyStep** directory.

Exporting Security Settings into a Template File

One of the other features of Security Configuration and Analysis is the capability to export current settings presented within the console into a security template file. In this way, you can take the configuration of an existing system and export it to a template that can be imported into other systems or applied using Group Policy.

To export a security configuration into a security template using Security Configuration and Analysis, follow Step by Step 29.8.

ON THE CD

Step by Step 29.8, "Exporting Security Settings and Creating a
Security Template Using Security Configuration and Analysis,"
shows you how to export a security configuration into a security
template using Security Configuration and Analysis. See the file
Chapter29-08StepbyStep.pdf in the CD's **Chapter29\StepbyStep**
directory.

Using Group Policy to Apply Security Settings

As you have seen in previous chapters, *Group Policy* is an Active
Directory object that can be used to apply a large number of configuration settings to a collection of objects located within an Active
Directory container, such as an OU, domain, or site. Just as you can
use Group Policy to simultaneously apply Administrative Template
settings or software deployment to a number of computers within an
Active Directory container, the same holds true for security settings.

When applying security settings to computers using Group Policy,
you still make use of templates. Group Policy has default templates
that have no preconfigured settings and are modified manually. It is
a better approach to create a template file, and then import it into
Group Policy to make sure that all settings required to conform to a
corporate security policy are properly defined. This also enables the
administrator to create and test security settings outside of Group
Policy before rolling them out to a large number of computers on
the domain, OU, or site level.

To apply security policies for an Active Directory container using
Group Policy, you import one or more of the security templates into
security settings into a Group Policy object. Importing a security
template into a Group Policy object ensures that all members of the
container automatically have the settings applied when the Group
Policy propagates.

To apply security settings using Group Policy, and to import a
security template into a GPO, follow the steps presented in
Step by Step 29.9.

ON THE CD

Step by Step 29.9, "Propagating Security Template Settings Using Group Policy," shows how to apply security settings using Group Policy, and it shows how to import a security template into a GPO. See the file **Chapter29-09StepbyStep.pdf** in the CD's **Chapter29\ StepbyStep** directory.

As the discussion indicates, importing security templates and applying them in a GPO is quite straightforward. The settings included in the template are now applied to all computers and/or users within the scope of the GPO. You can use the Security Configuration and Analysis MMC snap-in to verify settings on individual computers.

Windows 2000 provides the administrator with a great deal of flexibility in implementing a security policy for both users and computers. As you have seen, security templates enable you to configure the settings that should be in place for a computer or user. Security Configuration and Analysis enables you to compare the currently running settings to those in a template, enabling you to compare the current security settings against those that should be in place (that is, those in the security template). To implement the same security settings on a number of different computers or for a number of users, you can make use of Group Policy to assign those settings at the site, domain, or OU level.

> **EXAM TIP**
>
> **Know When to Use the Tools** For the exam, be sure you know that the Security Templates snap-in is used to configure templates, while Security Configuration and Analysis is used to import or export the templates. Security Configuration and Analysis is also used to configure a computer using a template.

CONFIGURING AND IMPLEMENTING AN AUDIT POLICY

Configure and troubleshoot security in a directory services infrastructure.

- **Implement an audit policy.**

As you have seen, you can configure a security policy either in Security Configuration and Analysis or by using Group Policy. One very important element that must be considered is tracking security-related events to determine whether your settings are effective and to thus prevent unauthorized access to resources.

Security auditing policy is a portion of security policy that enables you to configure which security-related events to monitor or have the potential to monitor. By monitoring these security-related system events, you are able to detect attempts by intruders to compromise data on the system or to gain access to resources that they should not be able to reach.

When you perform auditing, you are tracking user and operating system activities, or events on a computer. This information is stored in the security log of Event Viewer. Each entry, or record, in the security log consists of the action performed, the user who performed the action, and whether the action was successful.

The events to be audited are configured in an audit policy, which is a component of security policy. As mentioned, an audit policy can be configured within the Security Settings of Group Policy or by using Security Configuration and Analysis to configure which events to monitor on a single computer. The events that can be monitored and may be part of the audit policy are quite diverse. The following events can be tracked for success or failure:

◆ **Account logon.** This takes place on a domain controller when a domain controller is receiving a request to validate a user account. This type of event takes place when a user attempts to log on to a computer and specifies a domain-level logon account. It should be noted that computers, as well as users, can request account logon.

◆ **Account management.** An account management event occurs when an administrator creates, changes, or deletes a user account or group.

◆ **Directory services access.** This tracks user access to a specific Active Directory object. Enabling this audit event in Windows 2000 does not automatically turn on tracking of access to all Active Directory objects. You must specify which users and groups should have access to a specific Active Directory container tracked by modifying entries in the Auditing tab of the Advanced Security settings for an Active Directory object.

◆ **Logon.** This is triggered when a user logs on to or logs off of a local computer. It can also be used to track network access to a computer, because connecting through the network to a machine requires the user to log on to establish the connection.

◆ **Object access.** Object access is used to track a user attempting to gain access to a file or folder on an NTFS partition or to a printer. Enabling the object access event, such as directory service access, does not turn it on automatically for the computer; rather, it turns on the possibility of auditing for files and printers on the machine. To specify which files, folders, and printers will be audited, you would modify the security settings of the object for which you want to track access.

◆ **Policy change.** This tracks the success or failure on attempts to change user security options such as password policy, user rights assignment, account lockout settings, or audit policies.

◆ **Privilege use.** This tracks the use of certain privileges and user rights by an individual. These include taking ownership of a file or folder, changing the system time, loading and unloading device drivers, and modifying quotas.

◆ **Process tracking.** This is used to track the execution of processes on the system. This includes invoking and stopping an application as well as the other programs an application itself opened.

◆ **System.** This deals with the user shutting down or restarting the computer. Other events include anything that would affect the security elements of Windows 2000, such as clearing out the security log in Event Viewer, or other security-related settings on the computer.

It is possible to track almost any action taken on a system, should one desire to do so. Generally, however, too much auditing is not recommended. Auditing can severely impact the performance of the target system. On the other hand, although no auditing is great for performance, it provides no information on any attempts to gain access to resources by intruders. The ideal amount of auditing is the fine line between performance and security and is different for each organization. Planning is the key.

Planning an Audit Policy

When deciding whether to implement an audit policy and to what extent, planning is the most important aspect of the decision. The general rule of thumb is to audit only those events that make sense in your environment.

When planning an audit policy, consider the following guidelines:

- **Determine which computers should have auditing configured.** Auditing can be turned on or off for individual computers; therefore, you should determine which ones should have the success or failure of user actions tracked. For example, file servers and domain controllers, which contain sensitive or critical data, are good candidates for auditing. However, users' desktop computers, except in very high-security environments such as national security agencies, the military, or certain parts of financial institutions, should probably not be audited.

- **Determine the types of events to audit for each computer.** Some computers should have certain types of events audited that might not apply to other computers. For example, domain controllers are great candidates for the auditing of account logon, account management, and directory service access events. Windows 2000 Servers are more likely to have file and folder access, as well as Privilege use events, tracked. All computers may be good candidates for System and Logon events tracking.

- **Do you need to track successful access to or use of a resource, failure to do so, or both?** Obviously, tracking both successful access and failure provides more data, but will this data be useful information or just make it more difficult to locate attempts to bypass security settings on the computer? Success and failure together can be used for resource planning, while failure alone can alert you to possible breaches of security.

◆ **Determine for which objects and users you want to track events.** As previously outlined, some events, such as object (file, folder, and printer) access and directory service access, need to be configured for the object in question as well as the users whose access you want to monitor. Tracking success and failure by the Everyone system group includes all users, but might, once again, provide too much data and not much useful information. You need to decide which users and for which objects you want to monitor access.

◆ **Determine whether you need to track usage trends over time.** If you decide to track usage trends over time, you are required to archive security logs on a regular basis and maintain them for longer periods of time. Factors involved include how long to keep the logs, where to keep them, whether they should be rolled up periodically to track trends, and how this should be done.

◆ **Review the logs frequently and regularly.** Configuring an audit policy and never looking at the security logs is about as useful as winning the lottery, but failing to cash in the winning ticket. In making sure everything is running as it should be, administrators need to check the logs on a regular basis (daily is good) and be on the lookout for any events that should not be there.

Setting Up an Audit Policy

In setting up an audit policy, you can use one of two tools, depending on the scope of the policy. To configure an audit policy for a single computer, you can make use of the Security Configuration and Analysis snap-in on the local machine where the policy is to be implemented. However, doing so only ensures that the audit policy affects that one machine and might not provide as much value as having similar settings applied to a whole range of machines.

To configure an audit policy for several machines at once, you can make use of Group Policy. To set an audit policy using Group Policy, follow the steps outlined in Step by Step 29.10.

> **ON THE CD**
>
> Step by Step 29.10, "Configuring an Audit Policy Using Group Policy," shows you how to configure an audit policy for several machines at once. See the file **Chapter29-10StepbyStep.pdf** in the CD's **Chapter29\StepbyStep** directory.

As you can see, setting up auditing is quite simple. Remember, however, that for object access and directory service access, you still need to configure which objects (files, folders, or printers) or Active Directory containers you want to monitor access to and by whom.

Auditing Access to Resources

After you have configured the audit policy to audit object access or Directory Service access, you need to perform additional steps and perform more planning to ensure that events on key resources are monitored. These resources include file system objects, printer objects, and Active Directory objects.

Auditing Access to File System Objects

When you configure auditing on file system files and folders, you are doing so for files and folders on NTFS file systems only. Auditing of files on FAT or FAT32 file systems is not available; these file systems do not provide any type of security, which is required for auditing.

When you specify auditing on file system objects, keep the following in mind:

◆ Audit failure events for Read operations on critical or sensitive files to determine which users are attempting to gain access to files for which they have no permissions.

◆ Audit success and failure for Delete operations on confidential or archival files to monitor which users might be attempting malicious activities and to track which files were deleted by which users.

◆ Audit success and failure operations for Change Permissions and Take Ownership permission usage for confidential and personal files of users. These events might indicate that someone is trying to change security settings on files to which he does not have access so that he can gain access to data to which he does not currently have the rights. This also records an Administrator taking ownership of a user's file or modifying permissions on a file so that he or she can gain access. Even though Administrators might be able to cover their tracks a little better than most, the event is still recorded in the log.

◆ Audit success and failure of all events performed by members of the Guests group. This should be done on the folders to which guests should not have access. You can verify that no attempts by unauthorized users took place, and, if they did, when they occurred so that you can locate a pattern.

◆ Audit file and folder access (both success and failure) on all computers containing shared data that should normally be secured. This way, shared folder activities can be tracked to make sure no unwanted attempts to breach security were made.

To specify auditing on a particular file or folder on an NTFS partition, after enabling Object Access Auditing (Success and Failure), perform the steps detailed in Step by Step 29.11.

> **EXAM TIP**
>
> **File Auditing** Remember that file auditing can only take place on an NTFS volume. There is no auditing capability if the files are stored on a FAT volume.

ON THE CD

Step by Step 29.11, "Configuring Auditing on Files and Folders," specifies auditing on a particular file or folder on an NTFS partition. See the file **Chapter29-11StepbyStep.pdf** in the CD's **Chapter29\ StepbyStep** directory.

Auditing Access to Printer Objects

You can configure auditing on printer objects to track usage as well as to determine whether attempts to make use of sensitive printers (for example, MICR printers that can be used to create checks) are taking place. Although most printers do not require auditing, those that are specialized or expensive to run, such as high-end color laser printers, might require some auditing.

When auditing printers, use these guidelines:

◆ Audit failure events for Print operations on sensitive printers
such as those used to print or encode sensitive company documents or preprinted forms. For example, a record store using
printers to create gift certificates might want to limit access to
the printer that has the gift certificate stock in it.

◆ Audit failure and success for Print operations on expensive
printers so that you can track usage and possibly use this
information to charge back costs to a department or user.

◆ Audit success and failure events for use of Full Control
permissions on all printers to track administrative changes to
the printer. This includes updating the printer driver as well as
creating and removing shares.

◆ Audit success events on Delete permissions on commonly
used printers so that purging of documents can be seen as
an administrative correction rather than a printer failure.

◆ Audit success and failure events on Change Permissions and
Take Ownership permissions on sensitive printers to have a
record of who was assigned or removed from the access control
list for the printer. In this way, you can determine whether an
administrator might have inadvertently given permissions to a
user who should not have them and who can track security
breaches.

To specify auditing on a printer, after enabling Object Access
Auditing (Success and Failure), perform the steps shown in Step
by Step 29.12.

ON THE CD

Step by Step 29.12, "Configuring Auditing on Printers," specifies
auditing on a printer. See the file **Chapter29-12StepbyStep.pdf** in
the CD's **Chapter29\StepbyStep** directory.

It is a good idea to audit access to very specific or critical printers
(such as check-printing printers or expensive color printers), but it is
not a good idea to audit basic printers used by everyone or those on
a user's desk.

Auditing Access to Active Directory Objects

When you configure auditing on Active Directory objects, you are able to track changes, or even simply read access, to a component of Active Directory. The objects that can be tracked are virtually everything in Active Directory.

When auditing Active Directory object access, be sure to audit both the success and failure for critical objects, such as user accounts and any groups whose membership is sensitive. You should do this for all administrative users and especially for those to whom you might have delegated control of an Active Directory object. This enables you to determine whether any of the individuals entrusted with maintaining parts of your network infrastructure are attempting to gain more access than they have been assigned.

To audit Active Directory object access, set the audit policy to track directory service access and use. Enable auditing of the object by using the appropriate MMC console, such as Active Directory Users and Computers, Active Directory Sites and Services, or Active Directory Domains and Trusts. For example, to enable auditing for the Users container in Active Directory, perform the steps described in Step by Step 29.13.

. ON THE CD

Step by Step 29.13, "Configuring Auditing on Active Directory Objects," shows how to enable auditing for the Users container in Active Directory. See the file **Chapter29-13StepbyStep.pdf** in the CD's **Chapter29\StepbyStep** directory.

One of the features of Windows 2000 for administrators is the flexibility and control provided by Active Directory. However, ensuring that only those individuals who need it have access to a particular part of Active Directory is critical to ensuring that it operates properly. Configuring of auditing for access to Active Directory objects, as shown in Step by Step 29.13, enables you to track improper attempts at access.

Reviewing and Monitoring Security Events

Monitor and analyze security events.

After configuring an audit policy, it is of no use to simply let it run without checking to see if there are any events of concern. The whole point of auditing actions is to be able to review and analyze them later; not doing so makes auditing pointless and a waste of resources.

The tool you use to view security records is Event Viewer. Audit entries are stored in the security log in Event Viewer in chronological order. Events are always stored in the machine local to where the event occurred, except for Account Logon events, which are stored in the security event log of the domain controller that processed the request.

To view the security event log of a computer, you can use the Computer Management MMC console from Administrative Tools, or you can use the Event Viewer MMC console directly. For example, to view the security event log on your domain controller, follow the steps described in Step by Step 29.14.

ON THE CD

Step by Step 29.14, "Reviewing Auditing Events Using Event Viewer," shows you how to view the security event log on your domain controller. See the file **Chapter29-14StepbyStep.pdf** in the CD's **Chapter29\StepbyStep** directory.

Using Event Viewer to review any audit events that have occurred on a computer is the only way an administrator can tell whether the security settings implemented through Group Policy or Security Configuration and Analysis are working. By enabling auditing on those parts of Windows 2000 that have been configured through security templates, you are able to track any unauthorized attempts and determine who is trying to gain access to your network or computer. Furthermore, enabling auditing to track the success of an action also enables you to have a log of activity on parts of the system, such as files or printers, as well as Windows 2000 components, such as Active Directory.

CASE STUDY: USING GROUP POLICY TO ENFORCE SECURITY REQUIREMENTS AT SUNSHINE BREWING

ESSENCE OF THE CASE

The CEO of SunShine Brewing has just returned from a conference on business in the twenty-first century. While being wowed by the possibilities of e-commerce and its offerings, he was also introduced to the problem of ensuring safe transmission of data and protecting internal corporate assets from internal tampering. He has called you into his office to outline his concerns and to ask for your input on how to protect the network from external and internal tampering, as well as how to track what is taking place on the network.

Specifically, he is concerned about the following:

▶ He wants to track any unauthorized attempts to access servers on the intranet and extranet. He would like to know where these attempts are coming from and when they are coming, as well as which user accounts are being used to attempt to gain access.

▶ He wants to have a historical record of all security-related events on all key servers in the organization, whether used for internal use only or for external access as well.

▶ He wants to make sure users have to log on to their workstations with a password, and he wants to make sure passwords are not reused over and over again. Users should have to change their password periodically (such as every month) and should not be able to reuse them for a year.

SCENARIO

Ensuring that proper security policies are applied uniformly across an enterprise, or a portion thereof, is critical to the safe transmission and access of data. Being able to track who is attempting to use a resource without authorization, as well as having a method of verifying that the guardians of these policies are not abusing their position, is something that can be enforced using Security Templates in Group Policy. In this case study, you will see how Group Policy can be used to solve a specific problem at SunShine Brewing.

ANALYSIS

The security requirements outlined by the CEO of SunShine can all be accomplished through the use of Group Policy security settings. Because these can be applied at different levels of Active Directory and through Group Policy filtering to specific machines on the enterprise network, you feel confident.

Your first recommendation should be to create a domain audit policy that enables auditing of failure of account logon, and to create logon events to track which user accounts are being used to attempt unauthorized access to key servers. This policy would be applied to a specific list of computers. This list could be kept in a global security group maintained by an administrator and with the GPO filtered to be applied to that security group only. In this way, other noncritical servers would not have their logon events audited. The Group Policy should have the No Override option enabled.

continues

CASE STUDY: USING GROUP POLICY TO ENFORCE SECURITY REQUIREMENTS AT SUNSHINE BREWING

continued

▶ For critical corporate servers, such as the main R&D server, accounting, customer service, and any machines where sensitive data is stored, the list of users who can administer these machines should be centrally controlled. The list of these servers will change from time to time, so that it should be easy to modify the list of users.

▶ Any attempt to log on to the domain with a user account that fails three times within 30 minutes should lock the user out. Only administrators should be allowed to unlock the user account.

▶ Users in the R&D department will require smart cards to access their computers, and any removal of a smart card from the machine should log the user off immediately.

▶ The Telnet service on all critical servers should always be disabled, and the list of users who can log on locally to these servers needs to be centrally controlled.

The CEO outlines the preceding and asks whether this can be accomplished with minimal overhead. You reply, "Absolutely." He gives you a week to come up with a plan and submit it to him.

To maintain a historical record of security events, you can configure the event log settings using the security policy for those key servers, to never overwrite the security log. You would naturally increase the log size using the GPO to a size (100MB or so) that would enable you to capture many events for those intervals between the clearing of the log file. You would also restrict guest access to the security log using the same policy, and, for maximum security, configure the settings so that the computer shuts down if the security log fills up. The GPO should be configured with No Override at the domain level.

Because the list of administrators for key corporate servers needs to be centrally controlled, you could create another GPO that would use the Restricted Groups portion of the security settings to add users to the SecureServerAdmins security group you create through the GPO. This GPO would also be applied to a list of specific servers and would be filtered so that it does not restrict administration of other servers in the organization. The GPO should be created at the domain level and be configured with No Override.

For password enforcement, create another domain-level policy with the appropriate settings (maximum password age of 30 days and remember 12 passwords, for example). The policy should also have a minimum password age of at least 1 day to prevent users from changing their passwords in less than 12 days back to the original. Password length, although not specified, should be set to at least one character (although

CASE STUDY: USING GROUP POLICY TO ENFORCE SECURITY REQUIREMENTS AT SUNSHINE BREWING

five or six might be a better length), so that users are required to have a password. This policy could also hold the account lockout settings of no more than three attempts within 30 minutes. The GPOs should also be configured with No Override so that they are uniformly enforced throughout the company. They should be filtered to include all users.

It is possible to disable the Telnet service through the System Services portion of security settings. The policy should also be created at the domain level, and it should be filtered to those servers considered critical.

Finally, to ensure that when an R&D user removes his or her smart card from the computer he or she is immediately logged off, configure the smart card removal behavior in the security options of local policies in a GPO at the R&D OU level. This automatically logs the user off when the card is removed.

Because you have implemented all these security requirements through GPOs, they can easily be administered centrally and will be applied throughout the domain, or at the OU level, as needed.

CHAPTER SUMMARY

KEY TERMS

- Active Directory
- Audit policy
- Auditing
- Blocking policy inheritance
- Disk quotas
- GPO inheritance
- GPO scope
- Group Policy filtering
- Registry
- Security Configuration and Analysis
- Security template

In this chapter, you learned how to create a security policy and how to monitor the effectiveness of that security policy using auditing. It should be noted that auditing itself is a component of security policy and should be considered for use while you are planning your security policy as a whole. (How would you know if your security policy works otherwise?)

In setting up a security policy, you can use one of two tools—the Security Configuration and Analysis MMC snap-in or Group Policy within Active Directory. Security Configuration and Analysis enables you to configure the security policy for the local computer. It also enables you to retrieve current security settings for the computer and compare them against a security template containing a preconfigured collection of security settings. In this way, you are able to compare your computer's current security configuration settings with the list of desired ones contained in the template. You can also export your current security settings on the computer to a template using Security Configuration and Analysis. Finally, you can import a security template into Security Configuration and Analysis and then apply its settings against your computer to enable a local policy.

To apply a security policy against several computers at the same time, you can make use of Group Policy. It should be noted once again that computers can be members of security groups in Windows 2000, and the easiest way to apply the same settings to a number of computers is to add them to a security group. Like other Group Policy settings, once configured, a security policy applies to all machines within the scope of the Group Policy. In this way, you can apply the same security configuration at the same time to computers with sensitive information and be sure that the security configuration will take effect. When using Group Policy to apply and configure a security policy, you also import security templates and modify them as required. The template settings are applied to all machines within the scope of the policy. When using Group Policy to enforce a security policy, the same rules regarding Group Policy inheritance and filtering still apply.

Chapter Summary

Security templates are text files with preset security configuration information that can be imported into Security Configuration and Analysis and/or Group Policy. Windows 2000 ships with a number of default security templates providing preconfigured settings at various security levels from none to highly secure. When choosing a template, consider whether you need the level of protection provided and why you are making use of the protection. Security should only be as tight as required—no more, no less.

To determine whether your security configuration is working or if unauthorized access is being attempted on key resources, you can configure an audit policy. An *audit policy* is a subset of security policy and is configured using the same tools. The types of events that can be audited include file and folder access, logon and logoff activity, and use of privileges. When configuring auditing, it might be necessary to be more precise than simply configuring the audit policy using Group Policy or Security Configuration and Analysis. You might actually have to modify object permissions to further refine your audit policy. This is required for files and folders, printers, and Active Directory objects, because turning auditing on for everything would present too high a level of overhead. When configuring auditing for these objects, or in general, audit only as much as is required so as not to introduce too high an overhead on the system.

APPLY YOUR KNOWLEDGE

Review Questions

1. You want to ensure that only users of the MAN-AGERS security group are able to access files and folders on a server called CORPSECURE. You have not yet created the MANAGERS security group. The list of users who will be members of the managers group needs to be protected at all times, and the assignment of users to this group cannot be delegated to others. How can you accomplish this?

2. You suspect that co-op students hired by the software development department have been trying to gain access to the CORPSECURE server from the network. How can you determine whether this is the case?

3. Your company has just installed a new $35,000 color printer whose use should be limited to only the graphic arts department. You want to track any attempts to use this printer by others as well as which users in the graphic arts department who make the greatest use of the printer. How would you accomplish this?

4. For what can you use Security Configuration and Analysis?

5. You want to ensure that all communication between Windows 2000 member servers in your finance department is encrypted. You also want to ensure that client computers in the finance department communicate with the payroll server in a secure manner. How would you accomplish this?

6. You need to configure the same audit policy for three Windows 2000 Server computers in the development department. You also want to enforce the same audit policy for a Windows

2000 member server in the quality assurance department. How can you accomplish this?

7. What is the default extension of the database files created by Security Configuration and Analysis?

8. You want to ensure that all users in your Windows 2000 domain change their passwords every 30 days. Members of the Sales Clerks OU do not need to change their passwords because they are assigned passwords by the IS department. How would you satisfy these requirements?

Answers to Review Questions

1. The best way to accomplish your desired goals is to create a security policy on CORPSECURE with Restricted Groups settings to include the MANAGERS group. Assign users to the MAN-AGERS group through the security policy only, thereby not allowing other users to be added except through the policy. Assign the MAN-AGERS group the Access This Computer from the Network user right, and remove it from the group Everyone and the group Authorized Users. See "Implementing Security Policies" for more information.

2. To determine whether co-op students are attempting to gain access to the CORPSECURE server, create an audit policy configured to audit privilege use for the Everyone group (because it could be some other users) and failure to use the privilege in question (Access This Computer from the Network). For more information, see "Configuring and Implementing an Audit Policy."

APPLY YOUR KNOWLEDGE

3. Enable object access auditing on the Windows 2000 computer where the printer is defined. Assign appropriate permissions to the shared printer to ensure that only members of the graphic arts department have access to it. Configure auditing on the printer for Failure to Print and Read for the Everyone group and Success and Failure for members of the graphic arts department. The former enables you to track unauthorized attempts to access the printer. The latter tracks printer usage within the graphic arts department. For more information, see "Configuring and Implementing an Audit Policy."

4. Security Configuration and Analysis can be used to analyze system security by creating a security database and comparing the settings to a security template. It can also be used to configure system security by applying template settings to the computer. Finally, it can be used to create new templates for the current computer configuration or to merge existing settings with a template to create a new security template. See "Implementing Security Policies."

5. You would first create two security groups: one for all the member servers in the finance department and another for the client computers in the finance department. Next you would create an OU for the finance department, if an OU for the finance department did not already exist, and place the computers in the OU as well as the security groups. You would then create a GPO at the Finance OU level with the required settings and assign the GPO to the two security groups. See "Implementing Security Policies."

6. The best way to accomplish your goals is to create a GPO at the Development OU level. Configure a Security template with the appropriate settings and import the template into the GPO. Then assign the GPO to the computers in the Development OU. This assigns the template settings to the development department computers. To have the same settings on the computer in quality assurance, you would use Security Configuration and Analysis on the quality assurance computer to import the template and configure the settings on the quality assurance computer. See "Implementing Security Policies."

7. The default extension for the security database files created by Security Configuration and Analysis is SDB. See "Implementing Security Policies."

8. To force all users in the domain to change their passwords every 30 days, you would create a GPO at the domain level with the appropriate password policy settings. You would assign this GPO to the Authenticated Users group. To not have the policy apply to the sales clerks, you would create a security group and place all users who are sales clerks in the security group. You would then Deny the Apply Group Policy permission to the sales clerks security group. See "Implementing Security Policies."

APPLY YOUR KNOWLEDGE

ON THE CD

This book's companion CD contains specially designed supplemental material to help you understand how well you know the concepts and skills you learned in this chapter. You'll find related exercises and exam questions and answers. See the file **Chapter29ApplyYourKnowledge.pdf** in the CD's **Chapter 29\ApplyYourKnowledge** directory.

Suggested Readings and Resources

1. Windows 2000 Resource Kit. *Deployment Planning Guide.* Microsoft Press, 2000.

2. *Security Configuration Toolset* on Microsoft's Web site at `http://www.microsoft.com/ windows2000/library/howitworks/security/ sctoolset.asp`.

3. *Securing Windows 2000 Network Resources* on Microsoft's Web site at `http://www.microsoft. com/windows2000/library/planning/ incremental/securenetworkresources.asp`.

4. *Step-by-Step Guide to Using the Security Configuration Toolset* on Microsoft's Web site at `http://www.microsoft.com/windows2000/ library/planning/incremental/ securenetworkresources.asp`.

5. *Step-by-Step Guide to Configuring Enterprise Security Policies* on Microsoft's Web site at `http://www.microsoft.com/windows2000/ library/planning/security/entsecsteps.asp`.

6. *Default Access Control Settings* on Microsoft's Web site at `http://www.microsoft.com/ windows2000/library/planning/security/ secdefs.asp`.

7. *Secure Networking Using Windows 2000 Distributed Security Services* on Microsoft's Web site at `http://www.microsoft.com/ windows2000/library/howitworks/security/ distsecservices.asp`.

This chapter covers the two objectives from the unit "Installing, Configuring, Managing, Monitoring, Optimizing, and Troubleshooting Change and Configuration Management" that are concerned with Remote Installation Services.

Deploy Windows 2000 by using Remote Installation Services (RIS).

- **Install an image on a RIS client computer.**

- **Create a RIS boot disk.**

- **Configure remote installation options.**

- **Troubleshoot RIS problems.**

- **Manage images for performing remote installations.**

▶ The purpose of this objective is to make sure you know how to install and configure Remote Installation Services on a Windows 2000 member server computer. This includes making sure you have the prerequisites for both the RIS server and the client, being able to create CD-based and RIPrep images, knowing how to create a RIS boot disk and when to use one, and using RIS to deploy Windows 2000.

Configure RIS security.

- **Authorize a RIS server.**

- **Grant computer account creation rights.**

- **Prestage RIS client computers for added security and load balancing.**

▶ In testing you on deploying Windows 2000 using RIS, Microsoft wants to make sure you are completely familiar with the security aspects of RIS. This includes knowing how to authorize a RIS server to respond to client requests. It also includes knowing how and when to delegate the creation of computer accounts to other users in the organization, and finally, knowing how to ensure that only those computers whose identification is known are allowed to deploy Windows 2000 using RIS (that is, prestaging a client computer).

CHAPTER 30

Deploying Windows 2000 Using Remote Installation Services

STUDY STRATEGIES

▶ The best way to prepare for the Remote Installation Services portion of the exam is to fully understand the requirements for both the RIS server and clients. Working through the exercises in this chapter and having two computers available will help you prepare for the exam because you will be able to configure a RIS server and use RIS to deploy Windows 2000 Professional on the second computer.

▶ You should also practice prestaging a client as well as authorizing a RIS server in Active Directory. Knowing how to configure client-machine naming and how to authorize users to create computer accounts in the domain is also required. Generally, this can be accomplished by working through the Step by Steps included on the accompanying CD as well as the exercises.

▶ Being able to answer the review questions and the exam questions will help in your preparation for the exam. What can go wrong with a RIS deployment should be understood as well, because Microsoft tends to ask you questions on this topic.

▶ Once again, the best way to prepare for this portion of the exam is to work with the product and perform a rollout of at least one machine using RIS.

INTRODUCTION

As you have seen, after you have configured Active Directory using Group Policy, you have a lot of features you can make use of—including Group Policy—to control the user environment, deploy software and updates to users and computers, and configure and monitor security settings. However, you still need to install Windows 2000 Professional, or other Windows 2000 variants, on computers to be able to use these features.

When installing Windows 2000 on client computers, you have several methods available to you. First, you can install Windows 2000 by using the CD-ROM and configuring all settings manually for each machine, which is quite time consuming and requires a lot of user interaction to be performed properly.

Another method that can be used is to create an unattended installation file, and then to automate the installation—either from a network share or using the CD-ROM—so that less user interaction is required.

A third method is to create an image of a Windows 2000 reference computer using a third-party imaging product, such as Symantec Ghost or PowerQuest Disk Image Pro, and then copy the image to other machines with the exact same hardware abstraction layer (HAL) characteristics. This process is quite quick and can also be a viable solution.

A fourth method is to make use of the new Windows 2000 feature called Remote Installation Service (RIS), which enables the automated installation of Windows 2000 Professional on client machines from a network share. It also provides additional security and other features, which might make it the right choice for a deployment in many organizations.

OVERVIEW OF REMOTE INSTALLATION SERVICES

Deploy Windows 2000 by using Remote Installation Services (RIS).

Remote Installation Services (RIS) is a Windows 2000 component that enables automatic installation of Windows 2000 Professional on client computers. Computers connect to the RIS server during the initial boot phase and start the installation of Windows 2000 Professional remotely. The installation of Windows 2000 Professional can make use of either the Windows 2000 Professional installation files found on the CD-ROM or a RIPrep image containing the operating system as well as the configuration of other applications. The image files are stored on the RIS server and are downloaded at boot time to the client machine to start the installation.

The remote installation process relies upon a number of key technologies in both the server and client machines. On the server side, RIS requires the following:

◆ An NTFS partition containing the images of Windows 2000 Professional that will be installed on client computers.

◆ Images to be used to perform the installation of Windows 2000 Professional on client computers. Images can be the Windows 2000 Professional installation files found on the CD-ROM or Remote Installation Preparation (RIPrep) images. RIPrep images represent a fully configured computer, including additional application software, desktop settings, and network connections, and they represent an easy way to quickly install the same configuration on several computers.

◆ The Remote Installation Service, which listens for and responds to client requests to install Windows 2000 Professional on a client computer. Remote Installation Service makes use of three other Windows 2000 networking components, which must be installed and running on the RIS server. These networking components are listed in the following:

> **NOTE**
>
> **Windows 2000 Professional Only**
> Remote Installation Services in Windows 2000 only supports the installation of Windows 2000 Professional client software through RIS.

- Boot Information Negotiation Layer (BINL), which responds to client requests and helps service client computers.

- Single Instance Store (SIS), which helps minimize disk space used by RIS images by replacing duplicate copies of files on the disk with a link to the common store location for those files shared by multiple images.

- Trivial File Transfer Protocol (TFTP), which is used to download the images to the client computers and start the installation of Windows 2000 Professional.

◆ The Dynamic Host Configuration Protocol (DHCP) service installed, activated, and authorized on a Windows 2000 Server, Advanced Server, or Data Center Server computer to respond to client requests for an IP address. Clients are assigned a DHCP address to use when connecting to the RIS server to start the install.

◆ Windows 2000 Active Directory to be installed and configured with at least one Windows 2000 domain. RIS requires Active Directory to install and manage its configuration and locate computer accounts allowed to use RIS to install Windows 2000 Professional.

◆ Domain Name Service (DNS) to locate Active Directory services within the domain.

On the client side, to perform an installation of Windows 2000 Professional using RIS, the client must have a network card or computer conforming to a particular set of specifications. The client-side requirements include:

◆ **A Pentium 166 or higher CPU-based computer.** This meets the minimum specifications required for the Windows 2000 Professional operating system.

◆ **A hard disk with at least 1GB of free space configured as a primary partition.** A 2GB hard disk is preferred to allow for application installation.

◆ **64MB of RAM required; 128MB recommended.** The more memory on the computer, the better the performance of Windows 2000 Professional.

◆ **A 10Mbps network adapter; 100Mbps recommended.** The network adapter must conform to the Pre-Boot Execution Environment (PXE) specification version 0.99c or later or be a PCI-based network adapter supported by a RIS boot disk.

◆ The BIOS (Basic Input/Output System) of the client computer must be configured to boot from the network card if using a PXE-compliant card. If you are using a RIPrep image, the client computer must be configured to boot from the floppy.

> **NOTE**
>
> **PCMCIA/PC Card Not Supported**
> PC Card or PCMCIA network cards found in notebook computers are not supported by RIS. This means it is not possible to use RIS to roll out a large-scale notebook deployment except by using a docking station with a RIS-compliant network card installed.

The Process of Installing Windows 2000 Professional Using RIS

Deploy Windows 2000 by using Remote Installation Services (RIS).

• **Install an image on a RIS client computer.**

The actual process of performing an installation of Windows 2000 Professional after configuring a RIS server and creating an image takes place as follows:

1. During the boot process, using either a PXE-compliant network card or the RIS boot disk, the user presses F12. This initiates the process of configuring the computer using RIS.

2. The client computer sends out a DHCP Discover packet to locate a DHCP server and request an IP address. The packet also includes the globally unique identifier (GUID) for the computer as well as a request to be serviced by a RIS server. The GUID is an important element, as you will soon see.

3. The DHCP server assigns the client an IP address so it can communicate on the network.

4. The client computer is directed to and connects to a RIS server.

5. The RIS server checks Active Directory to see whether the client computer has been prestaged (that is, preconfigured to receive a specific list of images for a particular RIS server in the enterprise). If the client computer's GUID exists in Active Directory, then the computer is considered prestaged.

6. If the client computer is prestaged, the RIS server directs the client to contact its designated RIS server as specified in Active Directory, and then it provides a username and password to log on.

   If the computer is not prestaged, the RIS server that the user contacted prompts the user to provide his or her username and password to log on.

7. After the user logs on to the RIS server, the user is presented with a list of available images to choose to install and is required to select one.

8. After selecting an image, the installation process begins to configure the computer with Windows 2000 Professional.

The configuration and use of Remote Installation Services is a four-step process:

1. The installation of Remote Installation Services.

2. The configuration of the RIS server and the starting of the RIS, including creating the necessary images to be used to install Windows 2000 Professional.

3. The authorization of the RIS server in DHCP Manager so that clients getting a DHCP address can also make a request to use a RIS server during the initial boot-up process.

4. The granting of the right to create computer accounts in the domain to users who will be using RIS to install Windows 2000 on their computer and adding the computers to the domain .

Installing and Configuring a RIS Server

The process of installing Remote Installation Services is actually quite straightforward. First, you need to make sure the requisite hardware and software requirements are met, and then you can add Remote Installation Services to a Windows 2000 Server that is a member of your domain. You can have more than one RIS server in a domain, but only one will ever be used to install the operating system to a machine at one time.

Remote Installation Services Prerequisites

Prior to installing Windows 2000 Remote Installation Services, you need to ensure that your server meets the requirements for RIS. These include the hardware requirements for the server computer itself, as well as other Windows 2000 components needed by Remote Installation Services.

Server Hardware Requirements

The hardware needed to run Remote Installation Services includes the following:

◆ **A Pentium 166 or higher CPU.** A Pentium II 300 or better is recommended.

◆ **A 10Mbps network adapter (for example, 10BASE-T).** A 100Mbps network adapter (for example, 100BASE-TX) is recommended.

◆ **256MB of RAM minimum, although a 128MB RAM configuration is supported.** Additional memory is required if you plan to run DHCP, DNS, or other services on the same server as RIS.

◆ **2GB of hard disk space minimum (4GB recommended) split into two partitions on the hard disk.** One partition is used to store the RIS images and must use NTFS; the other is used for the Windows 2000 Server operating system. It is recommended that all partitions be NTFS. The RIS image partition must have sufficient space to hold all images that will be available on the server.

◆ **A VGA video card with 800×600 resolution.**

◆ **A mouse and keyboard.**

◆ **A CD-ROM drive.** This is recommended so you can copy the
Windows 2000 Professional CD contents to the image location if using CD-based images.

RIS Software Requirements

Remote Installation Services requires that additional services are
available on your LAN. You can install these services on the same
server as Remote Installation Services or, for better performance, on
another Windows 2000 Server or Advanced Server computer.

The services that Remote Installation Services requires include:

◆ **Domain Name System (DNS).** DNS is required to locate
objects in Active Directory. Any DNS server that can be used
with Active Directory will work. The RIS computer needs to
be configured with the IP address of the DNS server.

◆ **Active Directory.** RIS requires Active Directory to locate computer accounts and to manage the RIS configuration. RIS will
not work if it is not in an Active Directory environment.

◆ **DHCP Service.** RIS uses DHCP to assign IP addresses to
client machines. DHCP servers authorize RIS server machines
and forward the client's request to connect to a RIS server to
the one it knows about or the one to which the client has been
prestaged.

Setting Up a RIS Server

To set up a RIS server, you perform four tasks:

1. Install Remote Installation Services on the Windows 2000
   Server computer. You can install RIS during the installation of
   Windows 2000 Server or afterward.

2. Configure the RIS server and start it by using the Remote
   Installation Services Setup Wizard. This step also requires you
   to create an initial image and requires that you have the source
   files for Windows 2000 Professional available.

3. Authorize the RIS server in Active Directory by using DHCP Manager. Upon doing so, the RIS server is able to respond to client requests to start a remote install.

4. Grant the rights to create computer accounts on the domain to users who will be performing remote installations using RIS.

Installing RIS on a Windows 2000 Server Computer

If you did not select RIS to be installed during your Windows 2000 Server installation, you can always install it after the fact by using Add/Remove Programs from Control Panel or by using the Configure Your Server Wizard. You need to have the Windows 2000 Server CD-ROM available or a path to the source files on your network.

To install Remote Installation Services, follow Step by Step 30.1.

ON THE CD

Step by Step 30.1, "Installing RIS Using the Configure Your Server Wizard," shows you how to install Remote Installation Services. See the file **Chapter30-01StepbyStep.pdf** in the CD's **Chapter30\StepbyStep** directory.

Configuring Remote Installation Services

After installing Remote Installation Services on a Windows 2000 Server computer, you need to configure it to make it usable. Configuration consists of specifying the folder on an NTFS partition that will be used to store RIS images as well as configuring initial settings for how the RIS server will respond to client requests. You also need to provide the location of the Windows 2000 Professional source files that will be copied to the RIS folder and used to create the initial CD-based image.

You can configure RIS by running the Remote Installation Services Setup Wizard by using the risetup.exe utility, as shown in Step by Step 30.2.

N O T E

There Are Other Ways to Install RIS RIS can also be installed through the Configure Your Server Wizard if RIS is installed as part of a server's initial setup or by adding the Remote Installation Service from the Add/Remove Windows Components option in the Add/Remove Windows Programs applet in Control Panel.

ON THE CD

Step by Step 30.2, "Configuring RIS Using the Remote Installation Services Setup Wizard," configures RIS by running the Remote Installation Services Setup Wizard by using the risetup.exe utility. See the file **Chapter30-02StepbyStep.pdf** in the CD's **Chapter30\StepbyStep** directory.

By running the Remote Installation Services Setup Wizard, you have created the initial configuration of RIS. You now need to authorize the RIS server and can add additional images and further refine the installation.

Authorizing the RIS Server

Configure RIS security.

- **Authorize a RIS server.**

After you have configured RIS on a computer, you must authorize the RIS server in Active Directory. If your RIS is also the DHCP server and the DHCP server has been authorized in Active Directory, this step has already been completed.

To authorize your RIS server, you use the DHCP console. The DHCP console is available only if you have DHCP installed on a server or if you have the Administration Pack loaded. The Administration Pack is loaded by double-clicking \winnt\system32\Adminpak.msi on your machine.

After installing Administrative Tools, to authorize your server, follow Step by Step 30.3.

ON THE CD

Step by Step 30.3, "Authorizing the RIS Server in Active Directory," demonstrates how to authorize your server. See the file **Chapter30-03StepbyStep.pdf** in the CD's **Chapter30\StepbyStep** directory.

Granting the Right to Create a Computer Account in the Domain

Configure RIS Security.

- **Grant computer account creation rights.**

For users to be able to make use of RIS and install an operating system image on their computer, they need to be able to create computer accounts in the domain. This privilege is normally limited to administrators because it affects the domain structure within Active Directory. When using RIS, however, it is necessary that this permission be granted to those users performing the operating system installation.

It is a good idea to create a security group within Active Directory, add the users who will be using RIS to install Windows 2000 Professional to the group, and then grant the right to the group.

To grant the right to create computer accounts in the domain to a security group, follow Step by Step 30.4.

ON THE CD

Step by Step 30.4, "Granting the Create Computer Account in the Domain Right to Users," shows how to grant the right to create computer accounts in the domain to a security group. See the file **Chapter30-04StepbyStep.pdf** in the CD's **Chapter30\StepbyStep** directory.

At this point, you have performed all the necessary tasks for other users to use Remote Installation Services to install a default configuration of Windows 2000 Professional on client computers and to have those computers join the domain.

CREATING REMOTE INSTALLATION SERVICES IMAGES

Deploy Windows 2000 by using Remote Installation Services (RIS).

- **Manage images for performing remote installations.**

As mentioned previously in this chapter, Remote Installation Services supports two different image types—CD-based images and RIPrep images.

CD-based images are images of the Windows 2000 Professional operating system and its default settings that are configured using an answer file. The answer file is created manually or by using Windows Setup Manager. Remote Installation Services, when configured, installs a default CD-based image. You can configure others as well.

A *RIPrep image* is an image of Windows 2000 Professional preconfigured on a reference or source computer; it can include the operating system as well as additional applications. When a RIPrep image is deployed, a copy of the reference computer is made on a target machine by using Remote Installation Services. You create a RIPrep image by using the Remote Installation Preparation Wizard, which is included with Windows 2000 Server, Advanced Server, or Data Center Server.

Creating a CD-Based Image for Remote Installation Services

As you already have seen, Remote Installation Services installs a default CD-based image when you configure RIS. This image is a copy of the Windows 2000 Professional installation files from the CD-ROM and a standard answer file called Ristandard.sif. You can modify the default answer file (also known as a setup information file, or SIF) using Windows Setup Manager, or you can create additional answer files using the same tool.

Installing Windows Setup Manager

Windows Setup Manager is part of the Windows 2000 Resource Kit and can be found in the SUPPORT\TOOLS folder of the Windows 2000 CD-ROM. To install Windows Setup Manager on your computer (if it is not already installed), use Step by Step 30.5.

ON THE CD

Step by Step 30.5, "Installing Windows Setup Manager," installs Windows Setup Manager on your computer if it is not already installed. See the file **Chapter30-05StepbyStep.pdf** in the CD's **Chapter30\StepbyStep** directory.

Using Windows Setup Manager to Create an Unattended Installation File

After you have installed Windows Setup Manager, you can use it to configure an unattended installation file for a CD-based image that you will use to install Windows 2000 Professional using Remote Installation Services. In creating an unattended installation or SIF file with Windows Setup Manager, you are preconfiguring the settings that will be used on the target computer when Windows 2000 Professional is deployed using RIS.

To create and configure an unattended installation file using Windows Setup Manager, use Step by Step 30.6.

ON THE CD

Step by Step 30.6, "Configuring an Unattended Installation File for RIS Using Windows Setup Manager," shows you how to create and configure an unattended installation file using Windows Setup Manager. See the file **Chapter30-06StepbyStep.pdf** in the CD's **Chapter30\StepbyStep** directory.

NOTE — **Modifying the Answer File** The document UNATTEND.DOC, located in DEPLOY.CAB on the Windows 2000 CD-ROM in the SUPPORT\TOOLS folder, provides information on answer file sections and tags. This file should be reviewed prior to making any manual changes to answer files.

After creating the answer file, you might want to modify the file to include additional changes. For example, you might not want to install games on the client computers in a business environment. To modify the answer file, use Notepad and make the necessary changes.

Associating an Answer File with a CD-Based Image

After creating the SIF file to be configured to use Remote Installation Services to perform the installation of Windows 2000 Professional, it is necessary to associate this answer file with a CD-based image.

It is possible to associate several answer files with the same CD-based image because the files used to install Windows 2000 Professional on a computer are the same for a given CPU family (for example, Intel processors). You would have more than one CD-based image if a locale-specific version of Windows 2000 Professional needs to be used (for example, Canadian French).

To associate an answer file with a CD-based image, follow Step by Step 30.7.

ON THE CD

Step by Step 30.7, "Associating an Answer File with a CD-Based Image," shows you how to associate an answer file with a CD-based image. See the file **Chapter30-07StepbyStep.pdf** in the CD's **Chapter30\StepbyStep** directory.

Restricting Images Through Permissions

After an image is created and an answer file is associated with the image, it is available to all users who can connect to the RIS server. You can restrict which users are able to use certain images when installing a computer.

Assigning NTFS permissions to the SIF file on the hard drive restricts access to images. Typically, you would create a security group and add users who will be performing installs of a particular image to the group. You would then assign permissions to the group so its members have access to the image, while other users and groups do not.

Step by Step 30.8 shows you how to assign permissions to the SIF file you just associated with an image.

ON THE CD

Step by Step 30.8, "Assigning Permissions to Images," shows you how to assign permissions to the SIF file you just associated with an image. See the file **Chapter30-08StepbyStep.pdf** in the CD's **Chapter30\StepbyStep** directory.

Creating a RIPrep Image for Remote Installation Services

An alternative to CD-based images with Remote Installation Services is to use a Remote Installation Preparation (RIPrep) image. RIPrep images enable you to deploy not only Windows 2000 Professional, but also a preconfigured computer installation including other applications and other PC settings. Furthermore, RIPrep images are a compressed form of the operating system and applications copied onto computers by RIS; therefore, they allow a quick installation of all required components for a user's desktop.

Determining whether to use a CD-based image or a RIPrep image depends on a number of factors including frequency of changes. If the standard user desktop configuration changes frequently, a RIPrep image would have to be updated and installed on a RIS server whenever a change took place. This would require the preparation of a source computer with the new settings whenever the configuration changed. Doing this might require more work than using a CD-based image and installing the software manually or through Group Policy. However, if the standard applications used in the organization are not updated too frequently (such as every three months or even less frequently), RIPrep could provide an easy way to deploy fully configured desktops. Any minor changes to the computer configuration and application settings can be deployed using Group Policy or through SMS or some other method.

When creating a RIPrep image to be used to install Windows 2000 Professional and applications, you need two computers, as noted in the following:

CD-Based Image Needed   To install a RIPrep image on a RIS server and have that image available for installation on other machines, the RIS server must already contain a CD-based image. This should not normally be a problem because the configuration of RIS creates a default CD-based image.

◆ **Source computer.** The source computer is the one onto which you will install Windows 2000 Professional and all applications. The source computer is the basis for the creation of the RIPrep image using a tool provided with Remote Installation Services.

◆ **RIS server.** A RIS server is the one onto which the RIPrep image will be copied and from which it will be available to be installed onto other machines to clone the source computer applications and settings.

Configuring the Source Computer

The first thing you need to do to create a RIPrep image is to configure the source computer with the same configuration and applications that will be deployed on the additional workstations. This involves five tasks, as follows:

1. Install Windows 2000 Professional on the source machine.

2. Configure Windows 2000 components and settings as required for the source and all target machines. This can include desktop settings and TCP/IP configuration options, such as DHCP assigned IP addresses.

3. Install and configure the applications required for this desktop configuration. In installing the applications, use the normal setup programs or Windows Installer packages to copy the necessary files, and then add any additional items—such as desktop shortcuts, menu items, or company templates—onto the hard drive of the source computer.

4. Test the operating system and applications to make sure everything works as expected. Test the source installation to be sure all the applications and the operating system work as required on the target computers after being deployed using RIS.

5. Copy the Administrator profile of the source computer to the default User profile. This is required because all the configuration and installation of applications on the source machine are typically performed while logged on as Administrator. For these same settings to be available to the user of the target computer after the image is deployed, you need to have it configured as the default User profile.

Step by Step 30.9 leads you through the process of copying the Administrator profile to the default User profile.

ON THE CD

Step by Step 30.9, "Copying the Administrator Profile to the Default User Profile on the Source Machine," leads you through the process of copying the Administrator profile to the default User profile. See the file **Chapter30-09StepbyStep.pdf** in the CD's **Chapter30\StepbyStep** directory.

Creating the RIPrep Image and Copying It to a RIS Server

The final step in making the RIPrep image available to users is to use a tool to image the source computer and copy the image to the RIS server. To do this, you run the Remote Installation Preparation Wizard across the network on the source computer itself. A RIS server must be available, and it must be configured with a CD-based image of the same CPU family as the source computer for this step to work.

The Remote Installation Preparation Wizard does the following:

◆ It configures the source computer to a generic state by removing all unique settings, such as a security identifier (SID) for the machine, the name of the computer, and any registry settings that need to be unique on each target computer.

◆ It creates a RIPrep image with the computer settings and copies the image to the RIS server you specify.

◆ It creates an answer (SIF) file and associates the answer file with the RIPrep image.

NOTE

Manual Load Balancing of RIPrep Images   The Remote Installation Preparation Wizard creates and installs the RIPrep image of the source computer on only one RIS server. To make the RIPrep image available on other RIS servers, copy the image to other RIS servers, and users can deploy it.

To create a RIPrep image and install it on a RIS server by running the Remote Installation Preparation Wizard, follow Step by Step 30.10.

ON THE CD

Step by Step 30.10, "Using the Remote Installation Preparation Wizard to Create a RIPrep Image on a RIS Server," creates a RIPrep image and installs it on a RIS server by running the Remote Installation Preparation Wizard. See the file **Chapter30-10StepbyStep.pdf** in the CD's **Chapter30\StepbyStep** directory.

PERFORMING A REMOTE INSTALLATION

After the RIPrep image is installed on the RIS server, you are ready to enable users to install a Windows 2000 Professional image on a target computer. As always, when deploying a new technology, it is a good idea to test each configuration thoroughly before a large-scale deployment.

Configuring Server Installation Options

Deploy Windows 2000 by using Remote Installation Services (RIS).

- **Configure remote installation options.**

Before enabling clients to make use of RIS, you might want to configure options on the RIS server to set how computer account names are generated. You can also specify the directory service context in Active Directory where the computer account will be created. Invoking the Properties dialog box for the RIS server in Active Directory Users and Computers, as outlined in Step by Step 30.11, does this.

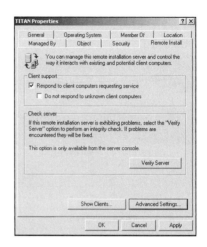

FIGURE 30.1
Make sure to check the Respond to Client Computers Requesting Service check box on the Remote Install tab of the RIS server.

Step by Step 30.11, "Configuring Client Computer-Naming Options and Directory Context," specifies the directory service context in Active Directory where the computer account will be created. See the file **Chapter30-11StepbyStep.pdf** in the CD's **Chapter30\StepbyStep** directory.

Do not forget to check the Respond to Client Computers Requesting Service check box on the RIS server computer Remote Install tab of the Properties dialog box (see Figure 30.1); otherwise, clients are not able to connect to the RIS server and be given a list of images to install.

Configuring Client Installation Options

Deploy Windows 2000 by using Remote Installation Services (RIS).

• **Install an image on a RIS client computer.**

During the installation of Windows 2000 Professional from a RIS server, you might want to give certain users performing the installation the capability to specify settings or to force the installation to operate completely without user interaction. The characteristics of the installation are specified in a Group Policy Object (GPO) assigned to the user performing the installation.

To configure client installation options in Group Policy for users performing the install, follow Step by Step 30.12.

Step by Step 30.12, "Configuring Client Installation Options Using Group Policy," shows you how to configure client installation options in Group Policy for users performing the install. See the file **Chapter30-12StepbyStep.pdf** in the CD's **Chapter30\StepbyStep** directory.

Group Policy, once again, is a powerful tool in specifying the behavior of Windows 2000 services—RIS in this case. Group Policy can be used to make sure corporate policies on the deployment of Windows 2000 using RIS are adhered to.

Client Computer Requirements

The first step in deploying Windows 2000 Professional on a computer using Remote Installation Services is to make sure the computer meets the hardware requirements for Windows 2000 Professional as well as RIS, as outlined earlier in this chapter. Installing Windows 2000 using RIS does not change the requirements for the operating system, only the method used to install the operating system on a machine.

If your target computer meets the hardware requirements, you are now ready to deploy Windows 2000 Professional to the machine using RIS.

Using RIS to Install an Image on a Computer with a PXE-Compliant Network Card

To install Windows 2000 Professional on a computer with a PXE-enabled network card, make sure the computer is configured to boot from the network card. To verify this, during the computer's Power-On Self Test (POST), press the key combination that enables you to enter BIOS setup and verify that the first boot device is the network card.

After making sure the network card is the first boot device, restart the computer. When the network card indicates that it is trying to boot from the network, press F12. After the client computer establishes a connection with a RIS server (and after it has been assigned an IP address by a DHCP server and referred to a RIS server), the user is prompted to enter F12 again to download the Client Installation Wizard.

After the Client Installation Wizard has been downloaded, the user is prompted to log on to the domain. If the logon is successful, the user is provided with a list of options, as follows:

◆ **Automatic Setup.** Users are allowed to choose which image to install, and if the user has permission to access the image, the one chosen is installed on the client computer without user intervention. If only a single image is available, the installation of that image starts automatically.

◆ **Custom Setup.** Users will be able to override the computer name and Active Directory container in which the computer will be stored. This option works only if the user has not been denied Custom Setup permissions in Group Policy.

◆ **Restart Setup.** Users can restart a failed attempt to install the image on the computer. This option restarts the entire installation process from the beginning but does not prompt the user to provide options that were already registered during the initial installation attempt.

◆ **Maintenance and Troubleshooting.** The user can use third-party maintenance tools to perform troubleshooting on the target computer.

After you have made your selection, the installation process commences. If you selected a custom setup, you are prompted for the name to be used for the computer and the location of the Active Directory container in which to create the computer account.

> NOTE
>
> **Multilingual Deployment**   The menu presented to the user when he presses F12 is based on the contents of a file called WELCOME.OSC located in the OSChooser folder in the RIS shared folder on the RIS server. By default, this file is in English and assumes that all user prompts are in English. Microsoft provides a sample file called MULTILNG.OSC in the same location that shows you how to make your prompts and user interaction with RIS multilingual.

Using RIS to Install an Image on a Computer Using a RIS Boot Disk

Deploy Windows 2000 by using Remote Installation Services (RIS).

• **Create a RIS boot disk.**

In situations in which the network card on a machine is not PXE-compliant, you are still able to use RIS to deploy a Windows 2000 Professional image on a target machine. If the target machine has a

PCI network card supported by the RIS boot disk, you can create the disk and have it emulate the PXE environment by following Step by Step 30.13.

ON THE CD

Step by Step 30.13, "Creating a RIS Boot Disk," shows you how to create a RIS boot disk. See the file **Chapter30-13StepbyStep.pdf** in the CD's **Chapter30\StepbyStep** directory.

After you have created the RIS boot disk, make sure the floppy drive is the default boot device on the target computer, insert the RIS boot disk in the floppy drive, and power on the machine. Similar to a PXE-compliant network boot, when the boot process starts, press F12 when prompted to do so. The rest of the steps to deploy a Windows 2000 Professional image using RIS are the same as a PXE-compliant network card boot (shown in Step by Step 30.12).

Prestaging Client Computers

Configure RIS security.

- **Prestage RIS client computers for added security and load balancing.**

By default, after a RIS server is installed, unless you specifically indicated that the RIS server should only respond to requests from known computers, the RIS server responds to requests from any client machine given an IP address through DHCP and requests the location of a RIS server in the DHCP Discover packet. Clearly, this presents a potential security hole and might allow the installation of a Windows 2000 Professional image by any user with a valid domain account that has permissions to the answer file.

To restrict the computers to which a RIS server responds, you need to prestage the client computers so that their identity will be known to the RIS server. Prestaging a client computer also designates which RIS server is used by the client to provide a list of images and to act as the source of the deployment image.

To prestage a client computer, you need to know the globally unique identifier (GUID) of the client computer, and then create the computer account in the domain before the RIS install takes place. The GUID of a client computer is provided by the manufacturer as part of the PXE specification and is commonly found on a label either inside or outside the computer case or might also commonly be found by looking at the BIOS settings. The GUID is always 32 characters long and has the following format:

{*dddddddd-dddd-dddd-dddd-dddddddddddd*}

where *d* is a hexadecimal value.

If your client computer does not have a PXE-enabled network card and you are using a RIS boot disk to deploy the Windows 2000 Professional image on the client computer, you can still prestage the computer. The GUID of a computer starting with a RIS boot disk is the MAC address of the network card padded with leading zeros to make sure the entire string is 32 characters long. For example:

{*00000000-0000-0000-0000-00104BF91001*}

After you have determined the GUID of the client machine, you can prestage the client computer using Active Directory Users and Computers. To prestage a client computer, follow Step by Step 30.14.

ON THE CD

Step by Step 30.14, "Prestaging a Client Computer with a Known GUID," shows you how to prestage the client computer using Active Directory Users and Computers. See the file **Chapter30-14StepbyStep.pdf** in the CD's **Chapter30\StepbyStep** directory.

In some situations, especially on older computers, the GUID might not be known, such as when you are using a RIS boot disk and the MAC address of the network card cannot be easily found. To prestage a computer for which the GUID is not known, follow Step by Step 30.15.

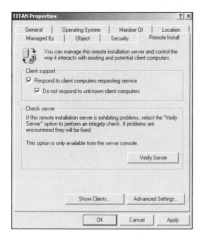

FIGURE 30.2
To make sure the RIS server only responds to requests from prestaged clients, select the Do Not Respond to Unknown Client Computers check box on the Remote Install tab for the RIS server.

ON THE CD

Step by Step 30.15, "Prestaging a Client Computer with an Unknown GUID," shows you how to prestage a computer for which the GUID is not known. See the file **Chapter30-15StepbyStep.pdf** in the CD's **Chapter30\StepbyStep** directory.

At this time, the RIS client has been prestaged and can receive an image from any RIS server. If you want to assign the client computer to a specific RIS server, do so in the Properties dialog box of the RIS client computer in Active Directory Users and Computers.

A final task you might want to complete is to configure the RIS server to respond only to requests from clients that have been prestaged. This is accomplished by selecting the Do Not Respond to Unknown Client Computers check box in the Remote Install Properties tab for the RIS server, as shown in Figure 30.2.

TROUBLESHOOTING REMOTE INSTALLATION SERVICES

Deploy Windows 2000 by using Remote Installation Services (RIS).

- **Troubleshoot RIS problems.**

Even though we all try to make sure problems do not occur, sometimes things go wrong despite our best efforts. Common problems that can occur with Remote Installation Services include those listed in the following:

◆ **Client computers do not obtain an IP address.** This scenario usually occurs when a Windows 2000 DHCP server is not available. Verify that the DHCP is running, that the DHCP scope is activated, and that IP addresses are available in the DHCP scope. If the client is on a different subnet than the DHCP server, ensure that a DHCP Relay Agent is available to forward DHCP requests to the DHCP server.

◆ **The DHCP server does not provide access to the RIS server.** RIS requires that the DHCP server be authorized in Active Directory. This requires that the DHCP server be a Windows 2000 DHCP server. Alternative DHCP servers, such as the Windows NT 4.0 DHCP server, cannot be used.

◆ **Clients are assigned an IP address but do not display the BINL message indicating a connection to the RIS server.** This occurs when the RIS server is either not online or has not been authorized in Active Directory. Either turn on the RIS server or authorize the RIS server in the DHCP console.

◆ **Client computers cannot start the download of an image.** This is a symptom of a hung NetPC Boot Service Manager (BINLSVC) on the RIS server. To correct the problem, restart the NetPC Boot Service Manager Service on the RIS server.

◆ **Clients using the RIS boot disk cannot connect to the RIS server.** This usually happens when the RIS book disk does not support the network card used by the computer. If this is the case, you must replace the adapter with a compatible network adapter.

◆ **Pressing F12 initiates a remote boot, but the client cannot connect to the RIS server.** This happens when the PXE-based network card has a boot ROM earlier than version .99C. You must replace the network card or upgrade the boot ROM to fix this problem. This can also occur when the RIS server is unavailable.

◆ **The expected installation options are not available.** This can occur when multiple Group Policy objects are applied to a computer and a higher-level GPO is overridden by a lower-level GPO. In this scenario, verify all GPOs that are applied to the computer.

As you have seen, the majority of problems with RIS deal with necessary supporting servers not being available or client components not working quite right. As always, careful planning of all aspects of RIS, as well as the Group Policy elements that affect it, will ensure a robust and problem-free installation (for the most part).

CASE STUDY: USING REMOTE INSTALLATION SERVICES TO DEPLOY WINDOWS 2000 PROFESSIONAL TO NEW DESKTOP COMPUTERS AT SUNSHINE BREWING

ESSENCE OF THE CASE

A number of the desktops at SunShine Brewing are starting to become outdated, and it has been decided that a capital acquisition strategy will be implemented to replace these aging machines. The number of new desktops to be purchased is estimated at 2,500, with about 500 of these machines used to replace R&D desktops, 235 for the executives, 500 for IT, and the remainder for admin. Sales recently received a new group of notebooks, so no new machines are needed for them. All machines are Pentium III 650MHz and on the Windows 2000 Hardware Compatibility List. Each of the machines has at least 256MB of memory and a 12GB hard disk. The new computers all have Intel Pro/100+ PCI 100BASE-TX network cards, which have a PXE boot ROM at version .99c or later.

The R&D machines should only include the base Windows 2000 Professional operating system because additional applications to be installed by R&D are specialized. Common corporate applications, such as Office 2000, will be deployed after the machines are configured with Windows 2000 Professional using Group Policy. The names of R&D machines should be prestaged in the R&D OU to make sure only the machines targeted for R&D will be created and assigned the inherited permissions of the OU.

SCENARIO

Deployment of Windows 2000 Professional on new desktop computers, either by itself or with additional applications, can be a time-consuming process. In this chapter, you were introduced to Remote Installation Services and how it can speed up the process of operating system deployment as well as, through the use of RIPrep images, additional applications. You will see how this can be applied to solve a problem at SunShine Brewing.

ANALYSIS

The simple solution for this problem is the Remote Installation Services component of Windows 2000. Because all new computers have a PXE-enabled network card of the appropriate version and all components of the machines are on the HCL, you do not need to worry about strange problems during the deployment (unless they're hardware-related).

To make sure the deployment succeeds, perform the following:

- Install and configure a RIS server at each site.

- Load an initial CD-based image of Windows 2000 Professional on each RIS server during the configuration and call it Standard Windows 2000 Professional Install.

- Authorize each RIS server in Active Directory.

- Make sure a DHCP server exists at each location and is authorized in Active

CASE STUDY: USING REMOTE INSTALLATION SERVICES TO DEPLOY WINDOWS 2000 PROFESSIONAL TO NEW DESKTOP COMPUTERS AT SUNSHINE BREWING

Executives' machines should include Office 2000 Professional and the reporting software for the ERP package. Other applications that need to be installed will be handled manually or via Group Policy. The machines should be prestaged.

The IT machines also should only contain Windows 2000 Professional and the Administrative Tools for Active Directory, as well as the Windows 2000 Resource Kit.

Admin machines should mimic their current desktop configuration and do not need to be prestaged.

The deployment of all machines, with the exception of R&D, will be performed by IT staff at the various locations using an over-the-network install. You want to make sure the wide area network is not used to transfer the files needed for the OS installation (that is, each site should have its own server to act as a source for the operating system deployment).

Directory.

- Create a RIPrep image of a typical executive's machine (including the additional applications) and copy it to each RIS servers where executive machines will be located.

- Use Active Directory Users and Computers to prestage the executives' machines with the GUID of the machine.

- Create a RIPrep image for the Admin users by creating an image of a typical admin machine as it currently exists. Place the image of all RIS servers in all sites where admin machines will be created.

- Create a RIPrep image with the configuration of the IT users and place the image in all sites where IT staff is located.

- Grant the R&D security group permissions to create computer accounts in the R&D OU and have them prestage the computers.

- Boot each machine from the network card and select the appropriate image to install.

Using the preceding list of steps and configuration settings will enable you to deploy Windows 2000 Professional and all the necessary applications to each class of user computer as necessary.

CHAPTER SUMMARY

KEY TERMS

- Active Directory
- Answer file
- Authorizing a RIS server
- Dynamic Host Configuration Protocol (DHCP)
- Domain Name System (DNS) server
- Globally unique identifier (GUID)
- Media Access Layer (MAC) address
- Prestaging
- Pre-boot execution environment (PXE)
- RBFG.EXE (Remote Boot Disk Generator)
- Remote Installation Preparation (RIPrep)
- Remote Installation Services (RIS)
- RIS boot disk
- RIS image
- Remote Installation Services Installation and Configuration Wizard (RISETUP)
- Setup Manager
- Single Instance Store (SIS) service
- SYSPREP utility
- Trivial File Transfer Protocol (TFTP)

Remote Installation Services (RIS) is a component of the IntelliMirror technology of Windows 2000 that enables you to deploy Windows 2000 Professional images during the boot phase on a client computer.

RIS supports clients meeting the NetPC specification, which requires a PXE-enabled network card with a PXE-boot ROM that is version .99c or later. Client computers that do not have a PXE-enabled network card can still be deployed using RIS by creating a RIS boot disk with a supported network card.

On the server side, RIS needs to be installed on a Windows 2000 Server, Advanced Server, or Data Center Server computer. The RIS Server depends on other Windows 2000 technologies including Active Directory, DNS, and DHCP. A RIS server must be authorized in Active Directory for it to be able to provide images to clients who want to install Windows 2000 Professional.

When you install RIS, all the necessary files required by RIS are installed; however, you must also configure the RIS server. Configuring the RIS server creates an initial CD-based image on the server and starts all the required services for RIS including Trivial File Transfer Protocol (TFTP), Single Instance Store (SIS), and the Boot Service Manager Service (BINLSVC).

Images used to deploy Windows 2000 Professional using RIS can be CD-based images or Remote Installation Preparation (RIPrep) images. CD-based images are a copy of the files needed for installation of Windows 2000 Professional, and they provide the same process as an unattended installation using the Windows 2000 Professional CD. RIPrep images enable you to configure Windows 2000 Professional as well as other applications on a source computer, create an image on a RIS shared folder that contains the entire computer configuration, and then deploy it to target machines. RIPrep images provide the fastest deployment of both the operating system and applications.

CHAPTER SUMMARY

A single RIS server is able to hold several images. Images must be stored on a separate partition formatted with NTFS, although storing images on a separate physical disk is recommended for performance reasons. You might also have several RIS servers on the same network. It is a good idea to copy the common images to more than one server for load balancing.

Client computers might be prestaged, which requires that you know the GUID of the client computer. Prestaging involves creating the client computer in the proper Active Directory container in Active Directory Users and Computers. The GUID can be found in the BIOS of the computer or on a label provided by the vendor. Computers for whom a RIS boot disk is needed can also be prestaged by using the MAC address of the network card and padding it with leading zeros so that it matches the same format as a GUID.

Assigning permissions to the answer (SIF) file used by a particular image enables you to restrict who is able to install a particular image. Users installing Windows 2000 Professional on a computer that has not been prestaged must have the Create Computer Object privilege within the container where the computer account will be created. The container where the computer account will be created can be configured on the advanced properties of the RIS server in Active Directory Users and Computers, as can the naming format used to create the computer accounts.

APPLY YOUR KNOWLEDGE

Review Questions

1. What types of images can be deployed using Remote Installation Services?

2. What permission must a user have before he can use Remote Installation Services to configure a client computer?

3. What advantages does prestaging clients provide the Administrator?

4. By default, which RIS server responds to a client request to install an operating system on the client computer?

5. You need to name client computers based on the MAC address of the network adapter preceded by PC-. How can this be accomplished?

6. You need to make sure network shared printers are also installed on a client computer deployed using RIS. How can you accomplish this?

7. You want to deploy Windows 2000 Professional on new computers that will be used in your accounting department. Management has decided that games should not be installed on any computer in the organization. How can you configure RIS to not install games on these new machines?

8. Your company just purchased 100 new notebook computers for your sales staff. You want to simplify the deployment of Windows 2000 Professional with Microsoft Office 2000 and several proprietary applications developed by your in-house programmers on these notebook computers. How will RIS help you to simplify the deployment?

9. What key needs to be pressed on a client computer to start the deployment of Windows 2000 Professional?

10. When configuring Remote Installation Services, what actions does the Remote Installation Setup Wizard perform?

Answers to Review Questions

1. You can deploy CD-based and RIPrep images using Remote Installation Services. At least one CD-based image needs to be on the RIS server before a RIPrep image can be placed on the server. For more information, see "Overview of Remote Installation Services."

2. The user must have the Create Computer Object permission in the Active Directory container where the computer account will be created. If the user performing the installation does not have this permission, the installation fails. For more information, see "Performing a Remote Installation" and "Installing and Configuring a RIS Server."

3. Prestaging client computers enables the administrator to create the client computer in Active Directory before the deployment, and specify which RIS server will be used as a source for the images presented to the user performing the deployment. Prestaging clients, along with a RIS server configuration that only allows the RIS server to respond to known clients, will ensure that RIS can't be used to deploy Windows 2000 Professional on machines that should not have it installed. For more information, see "Performing a Remote Installation."

APPLY YOUR KNOWLEDGE

4. The RIS server that responds to service a client request is the one that has been configured to do so. If the client is prestaged and configured to receive an image from a specific RIS server, that RIS server responds. If the client has not been prestaged, any server that is allowed to respond to unknown client requests will respond and start the installation after a user successfully logs on. In the latter case, it most likely will be the server nearest to the client and least busy; however, this cannot always be predicted, which is why prestaging is recommended. For more information, see "Installing and Configuring a RIS Server."

5. To name clients with the MAC address of the network card preceded by "PC-", you would configure custom client naming options in the RIS server's Remote-Installation-Services Properties dialog box in Active Directory Users and Computers. The string you would enter to allow this naming is PC-%MAC%. For more information, see "Performing a Remote Installation."

6. To ensure that network printers are also installed when an operating system is deployed using RIS, create a new answer file that includes the network printers in the settings. Associate it with an existing CD-based image, or modify the existing answer file to include the printers using the Setup Manager Wizard or Notepad. For more information, see "Creating Remote Installation Services Images."

7. To make sure games are not installed on the new machines that will be deployed using RIS, manually modify the answer file for the image to be

deployed on the machines and modify the Component section to not include games as follows:

```
[Components]
    freecell=off
    minesweeper=off
    pinball=off
    solitaire=off
```

For more information, see "Creating Remote Installation Services Images."

8. This is a tough question to answer. If the notebook computers have a PC Card or PCMCIA network adapter, you cannot use RIS to deploy a RIPrep image including both the operating system and Office 2000. However, if the notebook computers have docking stations with a PCI-based network card with a PXE boot ROM or if the network card is on the supported list for a RIS boot disk, you could use RIS to deploy the RIPrep image. For more information, see "Performing a Remote Installation."

9. You need to press F12 when booting a client computer to connect to the RIS server and initiate a RIS deployment of Windows 2000 Professional on the computer. For more information, see "Performing a Remote Installation."

10. When configuring RIS, the Remote Installation Setup Wizard creates the RIS shared folder, copies files needed by RIS, copies the Windows 2000 Professional files to the image folder, creates an answer file for the image, configures RIS, updates the registry, creates a Single Instance Store (SIS) volume, and starts the RIS services. For more information, see "Installing and Configuring a RIS Server."

APPLY YOUR KNOWLEDGE

ON THE CD

This book's companion CD contains specially designed supplemental material to help you understand how well you know the concepts and skills you learned in this chapter. You'll find related exercises and exam questions and answers. See the file **Chapter30ApplyYourKnowledge.pdf** in the CD's **Professional\ApplyYourKnowledge** directory.

Suggested Readings and Resources

1. Microsoft Windows 2000 Resource Kit. *The Deployment Planning Guide.* Microsoft Press, 2000.

2. *Automated Deployment Options: An Overview White Paper* on Microsoft's Web site at `http://www.microsoft.com/windows2000/library/planning/client/deployops.asp`.

3. *Windows 2000 Professional Automated Deployment Options: An Introduction* on Microsoft's Web site at `http://www.microsoft.com/windows2000/library/planning/client/autodeploy.asp`.

4. *Automating the Deployment of Windows 2000 Professional and Office 2000* on Microsoft's Web site at `http://www.microsoft.com/windows2000/library/planning/incremental/sysprep.asp`.

5. *Desktop Deployment Solutions from Third-Party Companies* on Microsoft's Web site at `http://www.microsoft.com/windows2000/guide/server/partners/DesktopSolutions.asp`.

PART V

APPENDICES

What's on the CD-ROM

This appendix is a brief rundown of what you'll find on the CD-ROM that comes with this book. For a more detailed description of the newly developed *ExamGear, Training Guide Edition* exam simulation software, see Appendix B, "Using the *ExamGear, Training Guide Edition* Software." All items on the CD-ROM are easily accessible from the simple interface. In addition to *ExamGear, Training Guide Edition,* the CD-ROM includes the electronic version of this book in Portable Document Format (PDF), as well as a document that shows you where each objective is covered in the Training Guide. In addition, the CD also contains PDFs of Step by Steps and Apply Your Knowledge sections for each chapter of the book. Several utility and application programs are also included on the CD.

EXAMGEAR, TRAINING GUIDE EDITION

ExamGear is an exam environment developed exclusively for New Riders Publishing. It is, we believe, the best exam software available. In addition to providing a means of evaluating your knowledge of the *Training Guide* material, *ExamGear, Training Guide Edition* features several innovations that help you improve your mastery of the subject matter.

For example, the practice tests allow you to check your score by exam area or category to determine which topics you need to study more. In another mode, *ExamGear, Training Guide Edition* allows you to obtain immediate feedback on your responses in the form of explanations for the correct and incorrect answers.

Although *ExamGear, Training Guide Edition* exhibits most of the full functionality of the retail version of *ExamGear,* including the exam format and all question types, this special version is written to the Training Guide content. It is designed to aid you in assessing how well you understand the *Training Guide* material and enable you to experience most of the question formats you will see on the actual exam. It is not as complete a simulation of the exam as the full *ExamGear* retail product. It also does not include some of the features of the full retail product, such as access to the mentored discussion groups. However, it serves as an excellent method for assessing your knowledge of the Training Guide content and gives you the experience of taking an electronic exam.

Again, for a more complete description of *ExamGear, Training Guide Edition* features, see Appendix B, "Using the *ExamGear, Training Guide Edition* Software."

EXCLUSIVE ELECTRONIC VERSION OF TEXT

The CD-ROM also contains the electronic version of this book in PDF. The electronic version comes complete with all figures as they appear in the book. You will find that the search capabilities of the reader come in handy for study and review purposes.

COPYRIGHT INFORMATION AND DISCLAIMER

New Riders Publishing's *ExamGear* **test simulator**: Copyright 2000 New Riders Publishing. All rights reserved. Made in U.S.A.

Using the ExamGear, Training Guide Edition Software

This training guide includes a special version of *ExamGear*—a revolutionary new test engine that is designed to give you the best in certification exam preparation. *ExamGear* offers sample and practice exams for many of today's most in-demand technical certifications. This special Training Guide edition is included with this book as a tool to utilize in assessing your knowledge of the Training Guide material while also providing you with the experience of taking an electronic exam.

In the rest of this appendix, we describe in detail what *ExamGear, Training Guide Edition* is, how it works, and what it can do to help you prepare for the exam. Note that although the Training Guide edition includes nearly all the test simulation functions of the complete, retail version, the questions focus on the Training Guide content rather than on simulating the actual Microsoft exam. Also, this version does not offer the same degree of online support that the full product does.

EXAM SIMULATION

One of the main functions of *ExamGear, Training Guide Edition* is exam simulation. To prepare you to take the actual vendor certification exam, the Training Guide edition of this test engine is designed to offer the most effective exam simulation available.

Question Quality

The questions provided in the *ExamGear, Training Guide Edition* simulations are written to high standards of technical accuracy. The questions tap the content of the Training Guide chapters and help you review and assess your knowledge before you take the actual exam.

Interface Design

The *ExamGear, Training Guide Edition* exam simulation interface provides you with the experience of taking an electronic exam. This enables you to effectively prepare for taking the actual exam by making the test experience a familiar one. Using the test simulation can help eliminate the sense of surprise or anxiety that you might experience in the testing center, because you will already be acquainted with computerized testing.

STUDY TOOLS

ExamGear provides you with several learning tools to help prepare you for the actual certification exam.

Effective Learning Environment

The *ExamGear, Training Guide Edition* interface provides a learning environment that not only tests you through the computer, but also teaches the material you need to know to pass the certification exam. Each question comes with a detailed explanation of the correct answer and provides reasons why the other options were incorrect. This information helps to reinforce the knowledge you have already and also provides practical information you can use on the job.

Automatic Progress Tracking

ExamGear, Training Guide Edition automatically tracks your progress as you work through the test questions. From the Item Review tab (discussed in detail later in this appendix), you can see at a glance how well you are scoring by objective, by unit, or on a question-by-question basis (see Figure B.1). You can also configure *ExamGear* to drill you on the skills you need to work on most.

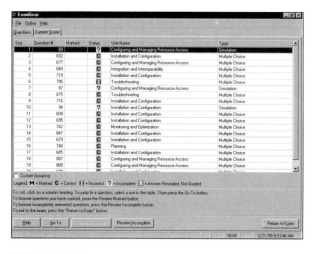

FIGURE B.1
Item review.

HOW EXAMGEAR, TRAINING GUIDE EDITION WORKS

ExamGear comprises two main elements: the interface and the database. The *interface* is the part of the program that you use to study and to run practice tests. The *database* stores all the question-and-answer data.

Interface

The *ExamGear, Training Guide Edition* interface is designed to be easy to use and provides the most effective study method available. The interface enables you to select from the following modes:

◆ **Study Mode.** In this mode, you can select the number of questions you want to see and the time you want to allow for the test. You can select questions from all the chapters or from specific chapters. This enables you to reinforce your knowledge in a specific area or strengthen your knowledge in areas pertaining to a specific objective. During the exam, you can display the correct answer to each question along with an explanation of why it is correct.

◆ **Practice Exam.** In this mode, you take an exam that is designed to simulate the actual certification exam. Questions are selected from all test-objective groups. The number of questions selected and the time allowed are set to match those parameters of the actual certification exam.

◆ **Adaptive Exam.** In this mode, you take an exam simulation using the adaptive testing technique. Questions are taken from all test-objective groups. The questions are presented in a way that ensures your mastery of all the test objectives. After you have a passing score or if you reach a point where it is statistically impossible for you to pass, the exam is ended. This method provides a rapid assessment of your readiness for the actual exam.

Database

The *ExamGear, Training Guide Edition* database stores a group of test questions along with answers and explanations. At least three databases are included for each Training Guide edition product. One includes the questions from the ends of the chapters. Another includes the questions from the Assessment Exam. The third is a database of new questions that have not appeared in the book. Additional exam databases may also be available for purchase online and are simple to download. Look ahead to the section "Obtaining Updates" in this appendix to find out how to download and activate additional databases.

INSTALLING AND REGISTERING EXAMGEAR, TRAINING GUIDE EDITION

This section provides instructions for *ExamGear, Training Guide Edition* installation and describes the process and benefits of registering your Training Guide edition product.

Requirements

ExamGear requires a computer with the following:

◆ Microsoft Windows 95, Windows 98, Windows NT 4.0, or Windows 2000.

A Pentium or later processor is recommended.

◆ Microsoft's Internet Explorer 4.01 or later version.

Internet Explorer 4.01 (or a later version) must be installed. (Even if you use a different browser, you still need to have Internet Explorer 4.01 or later installed.)

◆ A minimum of 16MB of RAM.

As with any Windows application, the more memory, the better your performance.

◆ A connection to the Internet.

An Internet connection is not required for the software to work, but it is required for online registration, product updates, downloading bonus question sets, and for unlocking other exams. These processes are described in more detail later.

Installing ExamGear, Training Guide Edition

Install *ExamGear, Training Guide Edition* by running the setup program that you found on the *ExamGear, Training Guide Edition* CD. Follow these instructions to install the Training Guide edition on your computer:

1. Insert the CD in your CD-ROM drive. The Autorun feature of Windows should launch the software. If you have Autorun disabled, click Start, and choose Run. Go to the root directory of the CD and choose START.EXE. Click Open and OK.

2. Click the button in the circle, and you see the welcome screen. From here you can install *ExamGear*. Click the ExamGear button to begin installation.

3. The Installation Wizard appears onscreen and prompts you with instructions to complete the installation. Select a directory on which to install *ExamGear, Training Guide Edition* (the Installation Wizard defaults to `C:\Program Files\ExamGear`).

4. The Installation Wizard copies the *ExamGear, Training Guide Edition* files to your hard drive, adds ExamGear, Training Guide Edition to your Program menu, adds values to your Registry, and installs test engine's DLLs to the appropriate system folders. To ensure that the process was successful, the Setup program finishes by running *ExamGear, Training Guide Edition*.

5. The Installation Wizard logs the installation process and stores this information in a file named `INSTALL.LOG`. This log file is used by the uninstall process in the event that you choose to remove *ExamGear, Training Guide Edition* from your computer. Because the *ExamGear* installation adds Registry keys and DLL files to your computer, it is important to uninstall the program appropriately (see the section "Removing *ExamGear, Training Guide Edition* from Your Computer").

Registering ExamGear, Training Guide Edition

The Product Registration Wizard appears when *ExamGear, Training Guide Edition* is started for the first time, and *ExamGear* checks at startup to see whether you are registered. If you are not registered, the main menu is hidden, and a Product Registration Wizard appears. Remember that your computer must have an Internet connection to complete the Product Registration Wizard.

The first page of the Product Registration Wizard details the benefits of registration; however, you can always elect not to register. The Show This Message at Startup Until I Register option enables you to decide whether the registration screen should appear every time *ExamGear, Training Guide Edition* is started. If you click the Cancel button, you return to the main menu. You can register at any time by selecting Online, Registration from the main menu.

The registration process is composed of a simple form for entering your personal information, including your name and address. You are asked for your level of experience with the product you are testing on and whether you purchased *ExamGear, Training Guide Edition* from a retail store or over the Internet. The information will be used by our software designers and marketing department to provide us with feedback about the usability and usefulness of this product. It takes only a few seconds to fill out and transmit the registration data. A confirmation dialog box appears when registration is complete.

After you have registered and transmitted this information to New Riders, the registration option is removed from the pull-down menus.

Registration Benefits

Remember that registration allows you access to download updates from our FTP site using *ExamGear, Training Guide Edition* (see the later section "Obtaining Updates").

Removing ExamGear, Training Guide Edition from Your Computer

In the event that you elect to remove the *ExamGear, Training Guide Edition* product from your computer, an uninstall process has been included to ensure that it is removed from your system safely and completely. Follow these instructions to remove *ExamGear* from your computer:

1. Click Start, Settings, Control Panel.

2. Double-click the Add/Remove Programs icon.

3. You are presented with a list of software that is installed on your computer. Select ExamGear, Training Guide Edition from the list and click the Add/Remove button. The *ExamGear, Training Guide Edition* software is then removed from your computer.

It is important that the INSTALL.LOG file be present in the directory where you have installed *ExamGear, Training Guide Edition* should you ever choose to uninstall the product. Do not delete this file. The INSTALL.LOG file is used by the uninstall process to safely remove the files and Registry settings that were added to your computer by the installation process.

Using ExamGear, Training Guide Edition

ExamGear is designed to be user friendly and very intuitive, eliminating the need for you to learn some confusing piece of software just to practice answering questions. Because the software has a smooth learning curve, your time is maximized because you start practicing almost immediately.

General Description of How the Software Works

ExamGear has three modes of operation: Study Mode, Practice Exam, and Adaptive Exam (see Figure B.2).

All three sections have the same easy-to-use interface. Using Study Mode, you can hone your knowledge as well as your test-taking abilities through the use of the Show Answers option. While you are taking the test, you can expose the answers along with a brief description of why the given answers are right or wrong. This gives you the ability to better understand the material presented.

The Practice Exam section has many of the same options as Study Mode, but you cannot reveal the answers. This way, you have a more traditional testing environment with which to practice.

The Adaptive Exam questions continuously monitor your expertise in each tested topic area. If you reach a point at which you either pass or fail, the software ends the examination. As in the Practice Exam, you cannot reveal the answers.

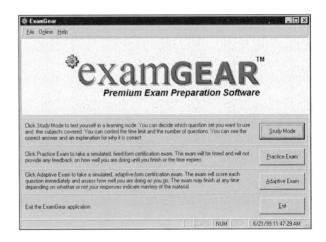

FIGURE B.2
The opening screen offers three testing modes.

Menu Options

The *ExamGear, Training Guide Edition* interface has an easy-to-use menu that provides the following options:

Menu	Command	Description
File	Print	Prints the current screen.
	Print Setup	Allows you to select the printer.
	Exit ExamGear	Exits the program.
Online	Registration	Starts the Registration Wizard and allows you to register online. This menu option is removed after you have successfully registered the product.
	Check for Product Updates	Downloads product catalog for Web-based updates.
	Web Browser	Opens the Web browser. It appears like this on the main menu, but more options appear after the browser is opened.
Help	Contents	Opens *ExamGear, Training Guide Edition*'s help file.
	About	Displays information about *ExamGear, Training Guide Edition*, including serial number, registered owner, and so on.

File

The File menu allows you to exit the program and configure print options.

Online

In the Online menu, you can register *ExamGear, Training Guide Edition*, check for product updates (update the *ExamGear* executable as well as check for free, updated question sets), and surf Web pages. The Online menu is always available, except when you are taking a test.

Registration

Registration is free and allows you access updates. Registration is the first task that *ExamGear, Training Guide Edition* asks you to perform. You will not have access to the free product updates if you do not register.

Check for Product Updates

This option takes you to *ExamGear, Training Guide Edition*'s Web site, where you can update the software. Registration is required for this option to be available. You must also be connected to the Internet to use this option. The *ExamGear* Web site lists the options that have been made available since your version of *ExamGear* was installed on your computer.

Web Browser

This option provides a convenient way to start your Web browser and connect to the New Riders Web site while you are working in *ExamGear, Training Guide Edition*. Click the Exit button to leave the Web browser and return to the *ExamGear* interface.

Help

As it suggests, this menu option gives you access to *ExamGear's* help system. It also provides important information like your serial number, software version, and so on.

Starting a Study Mode Session

Study Mode enables you to control the test in ways that actual certification exams do not allow:

- ◆ You can set your own time limits.

- ◆ You can concentrate on selected skill areas (units).

- ◆ You can reveal answers or have each response graded immediately with feedback.

◆ You can restrict the questions you see again to those missed or those answered correctly a given number of times.

◆ You can control the order in which questions are presented—random order or in order by skill area (unit).

To begin testing in Study Mode, click the Study Mode button from the main Interface screen. You are presented with the Study Mode configuration page (see Figure B.3).

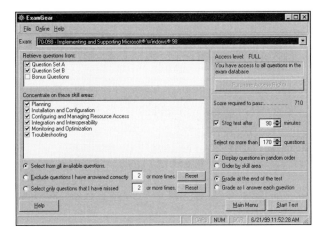

FIGURE B.3
The Study Mode configuration page.

At the top of the Study Mode configuration screen, you see the Exam drop-down list. This list shows the activated exam that you have purchased with your *ExamGear, Training Guide Edition* product, as well as any other exams you may have downloaded or any Preview exams that were shipped with your version of *ExamGear*. Select the exam with which you want to practice from the drop-down list.

Below the Exam drop-down list, you see the questions that are available for the selected exam. Each exam has at least one question set. You can select the individual

question set or any combination of the question sets if there is more than one available for the selected exam.

Below the Question Set list is a list of skill areas or chapter on which you can concentrate. These skill areas or chapters reflect the units of exam objectives defined by Microsoft for the exam. Within each skill area you will find several exam objectives. You can select a single skill area or chapter to focus on, or you can select any combination of the available skill areas/chapters to customize the exam to your individual needs.

In addition to specifying which question sets and skill areas you want to test yourself on, you can also define which questions are included in the test based on your previous progress working with the test. *ExamGear, Training Guide Edition* automatically tracks your progress with the available questions. When configuring the Study Mode options, you can opt to view all the questions available within the question sets and skill areas you have selected, or you can limit the questions presented. Choose from the following options:

◆ **Select from All Available Questions.** This option causes *ExamGear, Training Guide Edition* to present all available questions from the selected question sets and skill areas.

◆ **Exclude Questions I Have Answered Correctly *X* or More Times.** *ExamGear* offers you the option to exclude questions that you have previously answered correctly. You can specify how many times you want to answer a question correctly before *ExamGear* considers you to have mastered it (the default is two times).

◆ **Select Only Questions That I Have Missed *X* or More Times.** This option configures *ExamGear, Training Guide Edition* to drill you only on questions that you have missed repeatedly. You may specify how many times you must miss a question before *ExamGear* determines that you have not mastered it (the default is two times).

At any time, you can reset *ExamGear, Training Guide Edition*'s tracking information by clicking the Reset button for the feature you want to clear.

At the top-right side of the Study Mode configuration sheet, you can see your access level to the question sets for the selected exam. Access levels are either Full or Preview. For a detailed explanation of each of these access levels, see the section "Obtaining Updates" in this appendix.

Under your access level, you see the score required to pass the selected exam. Below the required score, you can select whether the test will be timed and how much time will be allowed to complete the exam. Select the Stop Test After 90 Minutes check box to set a time limit for the exam. Enter the number of minutes you want to allow for the test (the default is 90 minutes). Deselecting this check box allows you to take an exam with no time limit.

You can also configure the number of questions included in the exam. The default number of questions changes with the specific exam you have selected. Enter the number of questions you want to include in the exam in the Select No More than *X* Questions option.

You can configure the order in which *ExamGear, Training Guide Edition* presents the exam questions. Select from the following options:

◆ **Display Questions in Random Order.** This option is the default option. When selected, it causes *ExamGear, Training Guide Edition* to present the questions in random order throughout the exam.

◆ **Order by Skill Area.** This option causes *ExamGear* to group the questions presented in the exam by skill area. All questions for each selected skill area are presented in succession. The test progresses from one selected skill area to the next, until all the questions from each selected skill area have been presented.

ExamGear offers two options for scoring your exams. Select one of the following options:

◆ **Grade at the End of the Test.** This option configures *ExamGear, Training Guide Edition* to score your test after you have been presented with all the selected exam questions. You can reveal correct answers to a question, but if you do, that question is not scored.

◆ **Grade as I Answer Each Question.** This option configures *ExamGear* to grade each question as you answer it, providing you with instant feedback as you take the test. All questions are scored unless you click the Show Answer button before completing the question.

You can return to the *ExamGear, Training Guide Edition* main startup screen from the Study Mode configuration screen by clicking the Main Menu button. If you need assistance configuring the Study Mode exam options, click the Help button for configuration instructions.

When you have finished configuring all the exam options, click the Start Test button to begin the exam.

Starting Practice Exams and Adaptive Exams

This section describes practice exams and adaptive exams, defines the differences between these exam options and the Study Mode option, and provides instructions for starting them.

Differences Between the Practice and Adaptive Exams and Study Modes

Question screens in the practice and adaptive exams are identical to those found in Study Mode, except that the

Show Answer, Grade Answer, and Item Review buttons are not available while you are in the process of taking a practice or adaptive exam. The practice exam provides you with a report screen at the end of the exam. The adaptive exam gives you a brief message indicating whether you've passed or failed the exam.

When taking a practice exam, the Item Review screen is not available until you have answered all the questions. This is consistent with the behavior of most vendors' current certification exams. In Study Mode, Item Review is available at any time.

When the exam timer expires, or if you click the End Exam button, the Examination Score Report screen comes up.

Starting an Exam

From the *ExamGear, Training Guide Edition* main menu screen, select the type of exam you want to run. Click the Practice Exam or Adaptive Exam button to begin the corresponding exam type.

What Is an Adaptive Exam?

To make the certification testing process more efficient and valid and therefore make the certification itself more valuable, some vendors in the industry are using a testing technique called *adaptive testing*. In an adaptive exam, the exam "adapts" to your abilities by varying the difficulty level of the questions presented to you.

The first question in an adaptive exam is typically an easy one. If you answer it correctly, you are presented with a slightly more difficult question. If you answer that question correctly, the next question you see is even more difficult. If you answer the question incorrectly, however, the exam "adapts" to your skill level by presenting you with another question of equal or lesser difficulty on the same subject. If you answer that question correctly, the test begins to increase the difficulty level again. You must correctly answer several questions at a predetermined difficulty level to pass the exam. After you have done this successfully, the exam is ended and scored. If you do not reach the required level of difficulty within a predetermined time (typically 30 minutes), the exam is ended and scored.

Why Do Vendors Use Adaptive Exams?

Many vendors who offer technical certifications have adopted the adaptive testing technique. They have found that it is an effective way to measure a candidate's mastery of the test material in as little time as necessary. This reduces the scheduling demands on the test taker and allows the testing center to offer more tests per test station than they could with longer, more traditional exams. In addition, test security is greater, and this increases the validity of the exam process.

Studying for Adaptive Exams

Studying for adaptive exams is no different from studying for traditional exams. You should make sure that you have thoroughly covered all the material for each of the test objectives specified by the certification exam vendor. As with any other exam, when you take an adaptive exam, either you know the material or you don't. If you are well prepared, you will be able to pass the exam. *ExamGear, Training Guide Edition* allows you to familiarize yourself with the adaptive exam testing technique. This will help eliminate any anxiety you might experience from this testing technique and allow you to focus on learning the actual exam material.

ExamGear's Adaptive Exam

The method used to score the adaptive exam requires a large pool of questions. For this reason, you cannot use this exam in Preview mode. The adaptive exam is presented in much the same way as the practice exam. When you click the Start Test button, you begin answering questions. The adaptive exam does not allow item review, and it does not allow you to mark questions to skip and answer later. You must answer each question when it is presented.

Assumptions

This section describes the assumptions made when designing the behavior of the *ExamGear, Training Guide Edition* adaptive exam.

◆ You fail the test if you fail any chapter or unit, earn a failing overall score, or reach a threshold at which it is statistically impossible for you to pass the exam.

◆ You can fail or pass a test without cycling through all the questions.

◆ The overall score for the adaptive exam is Pass or Fail. However, to evaluate user responses dynamically, percentage scores are recorded for units and the overall score.

Algorithm Assumptions

This section describes the assumptions used in designing the *ExamGear, Training Guide Edition* Adaptive Exam scoring algorithm.

Unit Scores

You fail a unit (and the exam) if any unit score falls below 66%.

Overall Scores

To pass the exam, you must pass all units and achieve an overall score of 86% or higher.

You fail if the overall score percentage is less than or equal to 85% or if any unit score is less than 66%.

Inconclusive Scores

If your overall score is between 67% and 85%, it is considered to be *inconclusive*. Additional questions will be asked until you pass or fail or until it becomes statistically impossible to pass without asking more than the maximum number of questions allowed.

Question Types and How to Answer Them

Because certification exams from different vendors vary, you will face many types of questions on any given exam. *ExamGear, Training Guide Edition* presents you with different question types to allow you to become familiar with the various ways an actual exam may test your knowledge. The Solution Architectures exam, in particular, offers a unique exam format and utilizes question types other than multiple choice. This version of *ExamGear* includes cases—extensive problem descriptions running several pages in length, followed by a number of questions specific to that case. Microsoft refers to these case/question collections as *testlets*. This version of *ExamGear, Training Guide Edition* also includes regular questions that are not attached to a case study. We include these question types to make taking the actual exam easier because you will already be familiar with the steps required to answer each question type. This section describes each of the question types presented by *ExamGear* and provides instructions for answering each type.

Multiple Choice

Most of the questions you see on a certification exam are multiple choice (see Figure B.4). This question type asks you to select an answer from the list provided. Sometimes you must select only one answer, often indicated by answers preceded by option buttons (round selection buttons). At other times, multiple correct answers are possible, indicated by check boxes preceding the possible answer combinations.

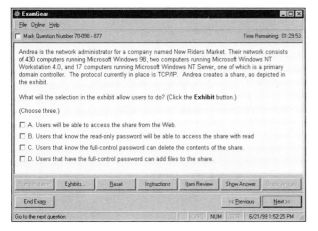

FIGURE B.4
A typical multiple-choice question.

You can use three methods to select an answer:

◆ Click the option button or check box next to the answer. If more than one correct answer to a question is possible, the answers will have check boxes next to them. If only one correct answer to a question is possible, each answer will have an option button next to it. *ExamGear, Training Guide Edition* prompts you with the number of answers you must select.

◆ Click the text of the answer.

◆ Press the alphabetic key that corresponds to the answer.

You can use any one of three methods to clear an option button:

◆ Click another option button.

◆ Click the text of another answer.

◆ Press the alphabetic key that corresponds to another answer.

You can use any one of three methods to clear a check box:

◆ Click the check box next to the selected answer.

◆ Click the text of the selected answer.

◆ Press the alphabetic key that corresponds to the selected answer.

To clear all answers, click the Reset button.

Remember that some of the questions have multiple answers that are correct. Do not let this throw you off. The *multiple correct* questions do not have one answer that is more correct than another. In the *single correct* format, only one answer is correct. *ExamGear, Training Guide Edition* prompts you with the number of answers you must select.

Drag and Drop

One form of drag-and-drop question is called a *Drop and Connect* question. These questions present you with a number of objects and connectors. The question prompts you to create relationships between the objects by using the connectors. The gray squares on the left side of the question window are the objects you can select. The connectors are listed on the right side of the question window in the Connectors box. An example is shown in Figure B.5.

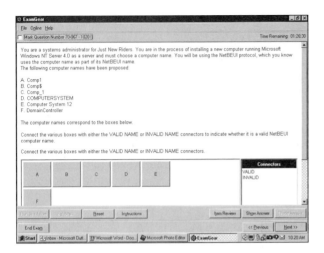

FIGURE B.5
A typical Drop and Connect question.

FIGURE B.6
The error message.

To select an object, click it with the mouse. When an object is selected, it changes color from a gray box to a white box. To drag an object, select it by clicking it with the left mouse button and holding the left mouse button down. You can move (or drag) the object to another area on the screen by moving the mouse while holding the left mouse button down.

To create a relationship between two objects, take the following actions:

1. Select an object and drag it to an available area on the screen.

2. Select another object and drag it to a location near where you dragged the first object.

3. Select the connector that you want to place between the two objects. The relationship should now appear complete. Note that to create a relationship, you must have two objects selected. If you try to select a connector without first selecting two objects, you are presented with an error message like that illustrated in Figure C.6.

Initially, the direction of the relationship established by the connector is from the first object selected to the second object selected. To change the direction of the connector, right-click the connector and choose Reverse Connection.

You can use either of two methods to remove the connector:

◆ Right-click the text of the connector that you want to remove, and then choose Delete.

◆ Select the text of the connector that you want to remove, and then press the Delete key.

To remove from the screen all the relationships you have created, click the Reset button.

Keep in mind that connectors can be used multiple times. If you move connected objects, it will not change the relationship between the objects; to remove the relationship between objects, you must remove the connector that joins them. When *ExamGear, Training Guide Edition* scores a drag-and-drop question, only objects with connectors to other objects are scored.

Another form of drag-and-drop question is called the *Select and Place* question. Instead of creating a diagram as you do with the Drop and Connect question, you are asked a question about a diagram. You then drag and drop labels onto the diagram in order to correctly answer the question.

Ordered-List Questions

In the *ordered-list* question type (see Figure B.7), you are presented with a number of items and are asked to perform two tasks:

1. Build an answer list from items on the list of choices.

2. Put the items in a particular order.

FIGURE B.7
A typical ordered-list question.

You can use any one of the following three methods to add an item to the answer list:

◆ Drag the item from the list of choices on the right side of the screen to the answer list on the left side of the screen.

◆ From the available items on the right side of the screen, double-click the item you want to add.

◆ From the available items on the right side of the screen, select the item you want to add; then click the Move button.

To remove an item from the answer list, you can use any one of the following four methods:

◆ Drag the item you want to remove from the answer list on the left side of the screen back to the list of choices on the right side of the screen.

◆ On the left side of the screen, double-click the item you want to remove from the answer list.

◆ On the left side of the screen, select the item you want to remove from the answer list, and then click the Remove button.

◆ On the left side of the screen, select the item you want to remove from the answer list, and then press the Delete key.

To remove all items from the answer list, click the Reset button.

If you need to change the order of the items in the answer list, you can do so using either of the following two methods:

◆ Drag each item to the appropriate location in the answer list.

◆ In the answer list, select the item that you want to move, and then click the up or down arrow button to move the item.

Keep in mind that items in the list can be selected twice. You may find that an ordered-list question will ask you to list in the correct order the steps required to perform a certain task. Certain steps may need to be performed more than once during the process. Don't think that after you have selected a list item, it is no longer available. If you need to select a list item more than once, you can simply select that item at each appropriate place as you construct your list.

Ordered-Tree Questions

The *ordered-tree* question type (see Figure B.8) presents you with a number of items and prompts you to create a tree structure from those items. The tree structure includes two or three levels of nodes.

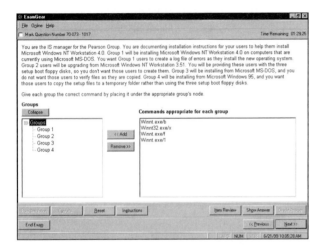

FIGURE B.8
A typical ordered-tree question.

An item in the list of choices can be added only to the appropriate node level. If you attempt to add one of the list choices to an inappropriate node level, you are presented with the error message shown in Figure B.9.

FIGURE B.9
The Invalid Destination Node error message.

Like the ordered-list question, realize that any item in the list can be selected twice. If you need to select a list item more than once, you can simply select that item for the appropriate node as you construct your tree.

Also realize that not every tree question actually requires order to the lists under each node. Think of them as simply tree questions rather than ordered-tree questions. Such questions are just asking you to categorize hierarchically. Order is not an issue.

You can use either of the following two methods to add an item to the tree:

◆ Drag the item from the list of choices on the right side of the screen to the appropriate node of the tree on the left side of the screen.

◆ Select the appropriate node of the tree on the left side of the screen. Select the appropriate item from the list of choices on the right side of the screen. Click the Add button.

You can use either of the following two methods to remove an item from the tree:

◆ Drag an item from the tree to the list of choices.

◆ Select the item and click the Remove button.

To remove from the tree structure all the items you have added, click the Reset button.

Simulations

Simulation questions (see Figure B.10) require you to actually perform a task.

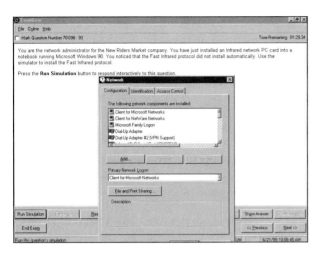

FIGURE B.10
A typical simulation question.

The main screen describes a situation and prompts you to provide a solution. When you are ready to proceed, you click the Run Simulation button in the lower-left corner. A screen or window appears on which you perform the solution. This window simulates the actual software that you would use to perform the required task in the real world. When a task requires several steps to complete, the simulator displays all the necessary screens to allow you to complete the task. When you have provided your answer by completing all the steps necessary to perform the required task, you can click the OK button to proceed to the next question.

You can return to any simulation to modify your answer. Your actions in the simulation are recorded, and the simulation appears exactly as you left it.

Simulation questions can be reset to their original state by clicking the Reset button.

Hot Spot Questions

Hot spot questions (see Figure B.11) ask you to correctly identify an item by clicking an area of the graphic or diagram displayed. To respond to the question, position the mouse cursor over a graphic. Then press the right mouse button to indicate your selection. To select another area on the graphic, you do not need to deselect the first one. Just click another region in the image.

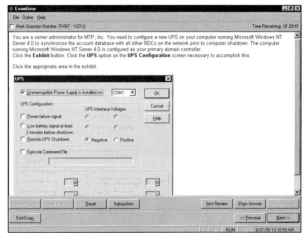

FIGURE B.11
A typical hot spot question.

Standard ExamGear, Training Guide Edition Options

Regardless of question type, a consistent set of clickable buttons enables you to navigate and interact with questions. The following list describes the function of each of the buttons you may see. Depending on the question type, some of the buttons will be grayed out and will be inaccessible. Buttons that are appropriate to the question type are active.

◆ **Run Simulation.** This button is enabled if the question supports a simulation. Clicking this button begins the simulation process.

◆ **Exhibits.** This button is enabled if exhibits are provided to support the question. An *exhibit* is an image, video, sound, or text file that provides supplemental information needed to answer the question. If a question has more than one exhibit, a dialog box appears, listing exhibits by name. If only one exhibit exists, the file is opened immediately when you click the Exhibits button.

◆ **Reset.** This button clears any selections you have made and returns the question window to the state in which it appeared when it was first displayed.

◆ **Instructions.** This button displays instructions for interacting with the current question type.

◆ **Item Review.** This button leaves the question window and opens the Item Review screen. For a detailed explanation of the Item Review screen, see the "Item Review" section later in this appendix.

◆ **Show Answer.** This option displays the correct answer with an explanation of why it is correct. If you choose this option, the current question will not be scored.

◆ **Grade Answer.** If Grade at the End of the Test is selected as a configuration option, this button is disabled. It is enabled when Grade as I Answer Each Question is selected as a configuration option. Clicking this button grades the current question immediately. An explanation of the correct answer is provided, just as if the Show Answer button were pressed. The question is graded, however.

◆ **End Exam.** This button ends the exam and displays the Examination Score Report screen.

◆ **<< Previous.** This button displays the previous question on the exam.

◆ **Next >>.** This button displays the next question on the exam.

◆ **<< Previous Marked.** This button is displayed if you have opted to review questions that you have marked using using the Item Review screen. This button displays the previous marked question. Marking questions is discussed in more detail later in this appendix.

◆ **<< Previous Incomplete.** This button is displayed if you have opted to review questions that you have not answered using the Item Review screen. This button displays the previous unanswered question.

◆ **Next Marked >>.** This button is displayed if you have opted to review questions that you have marked using the Item Review screen. This button displays the next marked question. Marking questions is discussed in more detail later in this appendix.

◆ **Next Incomplete>>.** This button is displayed if you have opted to review questions, using the Item Review screen, that you have not answered. This button displays the next unanswered question.

Mark Question and Time Remaining

ExamGear provides you with two methods to aid in dealing with the time limit of the testing process. If you find that you need to skip a question or if you want to check the time remaining to complete the test, use one of the options discussed in the following sections.

Mark Question

Check this box to mark a question so that you can return to it later using the Item Review feature. The adaptive exam does not allow questions to be marked because it does not support item review.

Time Remaining

If the test is timed, the Time Remaining indicator is enabled. It counts down minutes remaining to complete the test. The adaptive exam does not offer this feature because it is not timed.

Item Review

The Item Review screen allows you to jump to any question. *ExamGear, Training Guide Edition* considers an *incomplete* question to be any unanswered question or any multiple-choice question for which the total number of required responses has not been selected. For example, if the question prompts for three answers and you selected only A and C, *ExamGear* considers the question to be incomplete.

The Item Review screen enables you to review the exam questions in different ways. You can enter one of two *browse sequences* (series of similar records): Browse Marked Questions or Browse Incomplete Questions. You can also create a custom grouping of the exam questions for review based on a number of criteria.

When using Item Review, if Show Answer was selected for a question while you were taking the exam, the question is grayed out in item review. The question can be answered again if you use the Reset button to reset the question status.

The Item Review screen contains two tabs. The Questions tab lists questions and question information in columns. The Current Score tab provides your exam score information, presented as a percentage for each unit and as a bar graph for your overall score.

The Item Review Questions Tab

The Questions tab on the Item Review screen (see Figure B.12) presents the exam questions and question information in a table. You can select any row you want by clicking in the grid. The Go To button is enabled whenever a row is selected. Clicking the Go To button displays the question on the selected row. You can also display a question by double-clicking that row.

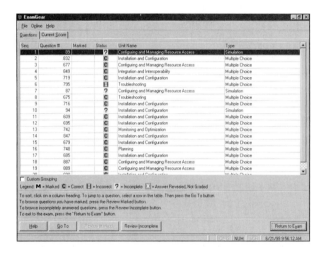

FIGURE B.12
The Questions tab on the Item Review screen.

Columns

The Questions tab contains the following six columns of information:

◆ **Seq.** Indicates the sequence number of the question as it was displayed in the exam.

◆ **Question Number.** Displays the question's identification number for easy reference.

◆ **Marked.** Indicates a question that you have marked using the Mark Question check box.

◆ **Status.** The status can be M for Marked, ? for Incomplete, C for Correct, I for Incorrect, or X for Answer Shown.

◆ **Unit Name.** The unit associated with each question.

◆ **Type.** The question type, which can be Multiple Choice, Drag and Drop, Simulation, Hot Spot, Ordered List, or Ordered Tree.

To resize a column, place the mouse pointer over the vertical line between column headings. When the mouse pointer changes to a set of right and left arrows, you can drag the column border to the left or right to make the column more or less wide. Simply click with the left mouse button and hold that button down while you move the column border in the desired direction.

The Item Review screen enables you to sort the questions on any of the column headings. Initially, the list of questions is sorted in descending order on the sequence number column. To sort on a different column heading, click that heading. You will see an arrow appear on the column heading indicating the direction of the sort (ascending or descending). To change the direction of the sort, click the column heading again.

The Item Review screen also allows you to create a *custom grouping*. This feature enables you to sort the questions based on any combination of criteria you prefer. For instance, you might want to review the question items sorted first by whether they were marked, then by the unit name, then by sequence number. The Custom Grouping feature allows you to do this. Start by checking the Custom Grouping check box (see Figure B.13). When you do so, the entire questions table shifts down a bit onscreen, and a message appear at the top of the table that reads Drag a column header here to group by that column.

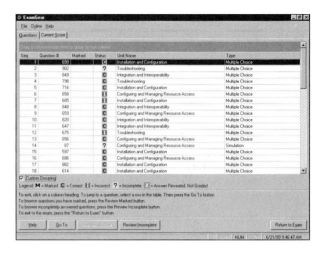

FIGURE B.13
The Custom Grouping check box allows you to create your own question sort order.

Simply click the column heading you want with the left mouse button, hold that button down, and move the mouse into the area directly above the questions table (the custom grouping area). Release the left mouse button to drop the column heading into the custom grouping area. To accomplish the custom grouping previously described, first check the Custom Grouping check box. Then drag the Marked column heading into the custom grouping area above the question table. Next, drag the Unit Name column heading into the custom grouping area. You will see the two column headings joined together by a line that indicates the order of the custom grouping. Finally, drag the Seq column heading into the custom grouping area. This heading will be joined to the Unit Name heading by another line indicating the direction of the custom grouping.

Notice that each column heading in the custom grouping area has an arrow indicating the direction in which items are sorted under that column heading. You can reverse the direction of the sort on an individual column-heading basis using these arrows. Click the column heading in the custom grouping area to change the direction of the sort for that column heading only. For example, using the custom grouping created previously, you can display the question list sorted first in descending order by whether the question was marked, in descending order by unit name, and then in ascending order by sequence number.

The custom grouping feature of the Item Review screen gives you enormous flexibility in how you choose to review the exam questions. To remove a custom grouping and return the Item Review display to its default setting (sorted in descending order by sequence number), simply uncheck the Custom Grouping check box.

The Current Score Tab

The Current Score tab of the Item Review screen (see Figure B.14) provides a real-time snapshot of your score. The top half of the screen is an expandable grid. When the grid is collapsed, scores are displayed for each unit. Units can be expanded to show percentage scores for objectives and subobjectives. Information about your exam progress is presented in the following columns:

◆ **Unit Name.** This column shows the unit name for each objective group.

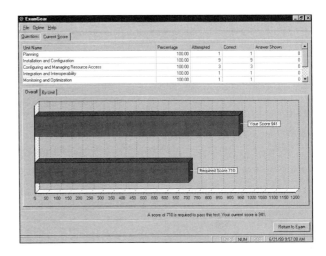

FIGURE B.14
The Current Score tab on the item review screen.

◆ **Percentage.** This column shows the percentage of questions for each objective group that you answered correctly.

◆ **Attempted.** This column lists the number of questions you answered either completely or partially for each objective group.

◆ **Correct.** This column lists the actual number of questions you answered correctly for each objective group.

◆ **Answer Shown.** This column lists the number of questions for each objective group that you chose to display the answer to using the Show Answer button.

The columns in the scoring table are resized and sorted in the same way as those in the questions table on the Item Review Questions tab. Refer to the earlier section "The Item Review Questions Tab" for more details.

A graphical overview of the score is presented below the grid. The graph depicts two red bars: The top bar represents your current exam score, and the bottom bar represents the required passing score. To the right of the bars in the graph is a legend that lists the required score and your score. Below the bar graph is a statement that describes the required passing score and your current score.

In addition, the information can be presented on an overall basis or by exam unit. The Overall tab shows the overall score. The By Unit tab shows the score by unit.

Clicking the End Exam button terminates the exam and passes control to the Examination Score Report screen.

The Return to Exam button returns to the exam at the question from which the Item Review button was clicked.

Review Marked Items

The Item Review screen allows you to enter a browse sequence for marked questions. When you click the Review Marked button, questions that you have previously marked using the Mark Question check box are presented for your review. While browsing the marked questions, you will see the following changes to the buttons available:

◆ The caption of the Next button becomes Next Marked.

◆ The caption of the Previous button becomes Previous Marked.

Review Incomplete

The Item Review screen allows you to enter a browse sequence for incomplete questions. When you click the Review Incomplete button, the questions you did not answer or did not completely answer are displayed for your review. While browsing the incomplete questions, you will see the following changes to the buttons:

◆ The caption of the Next button becomes Next Incomplete.

◆ The caption of the Previous button becomes Previous Incomplete.

Examination Score Report Screen

The Examination Score Report screen (see Figure B.15) appears when the Study Mode, Practice Exam, or Adaptive Exam ends—as the result of timer expiration, completion of all questions, or your decision to terminate early.

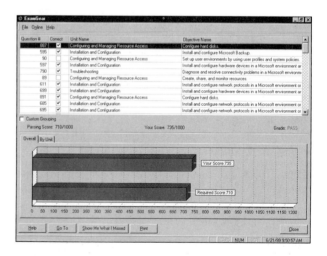

FIGURE B.15
The Examination Score Report screen.

This screen provides you with a graphical display of your test score, along with a tabular breakdown of scores by unit. The graphical display at the top of the screen compares your overall score with the score required to pass the exam. Buttons below the graphical display allow you to open the Show Me What I Missed browse sequence, print the screen, or return to the main menu.

Show Me What I Missed Browse Sequence

The Show Me What I Missed browse sequence is invoked by clicking the Show Me What I Missed button from the Examination Score Report or from the configuration screen of an adaptive exam.

Note that the window caption is modified to indicate that you are in the Show Me What I Missed browse sequence mode. Question IDs and position within the browse sequence appear at the top of the screen, in place of the Mark Question and Time Remaining indicators. Main window contents vary, depending on the question type. The following list describes the buttons available within the Show Me What I Missed browse sequence and the functions they perform:

◆ **Return to Score Report.** Returns control to the Examination Score Report screen. In the case of an adaptive exam, this button's caption is Exit, and control returns to the adaptive exam configuration screen.

◆ **Run Simulation.** Opens a simulation in Grade mode, causing the simulation to open displaying your response and the correct answer. If the current question does not offer a simulation, this button is disabled.

◆ **Exhibits.** Opens the Exhibits window. This button is enabled if one or more exhibits are available for the question.

◆ **Instructions.** Shows how to answer the current question type.

◆ **Print.** Prints the current screen.

◆ **Previous or Next.** Displays missed questions.

Checking the Web Site

To check the New Riders Home Page or the *ExamGear, Training Guide Edition* Home Page for updates or other product information, choose the desired Web site from the Web Sites option of the Online menu. You must be connected to the Internet to reach these Web sites. When you select a Web site, the Internet Explorer browser opens inside the *ExamGear, Training Guide Edition* window and displays the Web site.

OBTAINING UPDATES

The procedures for obtaining updates are outlined in this section.

The Catalog Web Site for Updates

Selecting the Check for Product Updates option from the Online menu shows you the full range of products you can either download for free or purchase. You can download additional items only if you have registered the software.

Product Updates Dialog Box

This dialog box appears when you select Check for Product Updates from the Online menu. *ExamGear, Training Guide Edition* checks for product updates from the New Riders Internet site and displays a list of products available for download. Some items, such as *ExamGear* program updates or bonus question sets for exam databases you have activated, are available for download free of charge.

Types of Updates

Several types of updates may be available for download, including various free updates and additional items available for purchase.

Free Program Updates

Free program updates include changes to the *ExamGear, Training Guide Edition* executables and runtime libraries (DLLs). When any of these items are downloaded, *ExamGear* automatically installs the upgrades. *ExamGear, Training Guide Edition* will be reopened after the installation is complete.

Free Database Updates

Free database updates include updates to the exam or exams that you have registered. Exam updates are contained in compressed, encrypted files and include exam databases, simulations, and exhibits. *ExamGear, Training Guide Edition* automatically decompresses these files to their proper location and updates the *ExamGear* software to record version changes and import new question sets.

CONTACTING NEW RIDERS PUBLISHING

At New Riders, we strive to meet and exceed the needs of our customers. We have developed *ExamGear, Training Guide Edition* to surpass the demands and expectations of network professionals seeking technical certifications, and we think it shows. What do you think?

If you need to contact New Riders regarding any aspect of the *ExamGear, Training Guide Edition* product line, feel free to do so. We look forward to hearing from you. Contact us at the following address or phone number:

New Riders Publishing
201 West 103rd Street
Indianapolis, IN 46290
800-545-5914

You can also reach us on the World Wide Web:

> http://www.newriders.com

Technical Support

Technical support is available at the following phone number during the hours specified:

317-581-3833

Monday through Friday, 10:00 a.m.–3:00 p.m. Central Standard Time.

Customer Service

If you have a damaged product and need a replacement or refund, please call the following phone number:

800-858-7674

Product Updates

Product updates can be obtained by choosing *ExamGear, Training Guide Edition*'s Online pull-down menu and selecting Products Updates. You'll be taken to a private Web site with full details.

Product Suggestions and Comments

We value your input! Please email your suggestions and comments to the following address:

`nrfeedback@newriders.com`

LICENSE AGREEMENT

YOU SHOULD CAREFULLY READ THE FOLLOWING TERMS AND CONDITIONS BEFORE BREAKING THE SEAL ON THE PACKAGE. AMONG OTHER THINGS, THIS AGREEMENT LICENSES THE ENCLOSED SOFTWARE TO YOU AND CONTAINS WARRANTY AND LIABILITY DISCLAIMERS. BY BREAKING THE SEAL ON THE PACKAGE, YOU ARE ACCEPTING AND AGREEING TO THE TERMS AND CONDITIONS OF THIS AGREEMENT. IF YOU DO NOT AGREE TO THE TERMS OF THIS AGREEMENT, DO NOT BREAK THE SEAL. YOU SHOULD PROMPTLY RETURN THE PACKAGE UNOPENED.

LICENSE

Subject to the provisions contained herein, New Riders Publishing (NRP) hereby grants to you a nonexclusive, nontransferable license to use the object-code version of the computer software product (Software) contained in the package on a single computer of the type identified on the package.

SOFTWARE AND DOCUMENTATION

NRP shall furnish the Software to you on media in machine-readable object-code form and may also provide the standard documentation (Documentation) containing instructions for operation and use of the Software.

LICENSE TERM AND CHARGES

The term of this license commences upon delivery of the Software to you and is perpetual unless earlier terminated upon default or as otherwise set forth herein.

TITLE

Title, ownership right, and intellectual property rights in and to the Software and Documentation shall remain in NRP and/or in suppliers to NRP of programs contained in the Software. The Software is provided for your own internal use under this license. This license does not include the right to sublicense and is personal to you and therefore may not be assigned (by operation of law or otherwise) or transferred without the prior written consent of NRP. You acknowledge that the Software in source code form remains a confidential trade secret of NRP and/or its suppliers and therefore you agree not to attempt to decipher or decompile, modify, disassemble, reverse engineer, or prepare derivative works of the Software or develop source code for the Software or knowingly allow others to do so. Further, you may not copy the Documentation or other written materials accompanying the Software.

UPDATES

This license does not grant you any right, license, or interest in and to any improvements, modifications, enhancements, or updates to the Software and Documentation. Updates, if available, may be obtained by you at NRP's then-current standard pricing, terms, and conditions.

LIMITED WARRANTY AND DISCLAIMER

NRP warrants that the media containing the Software, if provided by NRP, is free from defects in material and workmanship under normal use for a period of sixty (60) days from the date you purchased a license to it.

THIS IS A LIMITED WARRANTY AND IT IS THE ONLY WARRANTY MADE BY NRP. THE SOFTWARE IS PROVIDED "AS IS" AND NRP SPECIFICALLY DISCLAIMS ALL WARRANTIES OF ANY KIND, EITHER EXPRESS OR IMPLIED, INCLUDING, BUT NOT LIMITED TO, THE IMPLIED WARRANTY OF MERCHANTABILITY AND FITNESS FOR A PARTICULAR PURPOSE. FURTHER, COMPANY DOES NOT WARRANT, GUARANTEE, OR MAKE ANY REPRESENTA-TIONS REGARDING THE USE, OR THE RESULTS OF THE USE, OF THE SOFTWARE IN TERMS OR CORRECTNESS, ACCURACY, RELIABILITY, CURRENTNESS, OR OTHERWISE AND DOES NOT WARRANT THAT THE OPERATION OF ANY SOFTWARE WILL BE UNINTERRUPTED OR ERROR FREE. NRP EXPRESSLY DISCLAIMS ANY WARRANTIES NOT STATED HEREIN. NO ORAL OR WRITTEN INFORMATION OR ADVICE GIVEN BY NRP, OR ANY NRP DEALER, AGENT, EMPLOYEE, OR OTHERS SHALL CREATE,

MODIFY, OR EXTEND A WARRANTY OR IN ANY WAY INCREASE THE SCOPE OF THE FOREGOING WARRANTY, AND NEITHER SUBLICENSEE OR PURCHASER MAY RELY ON ANY SUCH INFORMATION OR ADVICE. If the media is subjected to accident, abuse, or improper use, or if you violate the terms of this Agreement, then this warranty shall immediately be terminated. This warranty shall not apply if the Software is used on or in conjunction with hardware or programs other than the unmodified version of hardware and programs with which the Software was designed to be used as described in the Documentation.

LIMITATION OF LIABILITY

Your sole and exclusive remedies for any damage or loss in any way connected with the Software are set forth below.

UNDER NO CIRCUMSTANCES AND UNDER NO LEGAL THEORY, TORT, CONTRACT, OR OTHERWISE, SHALL NRP BE LIABLE TO YOU OR ANY OTHER PERSON FOR ANY INDIRECT, SPECIAL, INCIDENTAL, OR CONSEQUENTIAL DAMAGES OF ANY CHARACTER INCLUDING, WITHOUT LIMITATION, DAMAGES FOR LOSS OF GOODWILL, LOSS OF PROFIT, WORK STOPPAGE, COMPUTER FAILURE OR MALFUNCTION, OR ANY AND ALL OTHER COMMERCIAL DAMAGES OR LOSSES, OR FOR ANY OTHER DAMAGES EVEN IF NRP SHALL HAVE BEEN INFORMED OF THE POSSIBILITY OF SUCH DAMAGES, OR FOR ANY CLAIM BY ANOTHER PARTY. NRP'S THIRD-PARTY PROGRAM SUPPLIERS MAKE NO WARRANTY, AND HAVE NO LIABILITY WHATSOEVER, TO YOU. NRP's sole and exclusive obligation and liability and your exclusive remedy shall be: Upon NRP's election, (i) the replacement of our defective media; or (ii) the repair or correction of your defective media if NRP is able, so that it will conform to the above warranty; or (iii) if NRP is unable to replace or repair, you may terminate this license by returning the Software. Only if you inform NRP of your problem during the applicable warranty period will NRP be obligated to honor this warranty. SOME STATES OR JURISDICTIONS DO NOT ALLOW THE EXCLUSION OF IMPLIED WARRANTIES OR LIMITATION OR EXCLUSION OF CONSE-QUENTIAL DAMAGES, SO THE PRECEDING LIMITATIONS OR EXCLUSIONS MAY NOT APPLY TO YOU. THIS WARRANTY GIVES YOU SPECIFIC LEGAL RIGHTS AND YOU MAY ALSO HAVE OTHER RIGHTS THAT VARY BY STATE OR JURISDICTION.

MISCELLANEOUS

If any provision of the Agreement is held to be ineffective, unenforceable, or illegal under certain circumstances for any reason, such decision shall not affect the validity or enforceability (i) of such provision under other circumstances or (ii) of the remaining provisions hereof under all circumstances, and such provision shall be reformed to and only to the extent necessary to make it effective, enforceable, and legal under such circumstances. All headings are solely for convenience and shall not be considered in interpreting this Agreement. This Agreement shall be governed by and construed under New York law as such law applies to agreements between New York residents entered into and to be performed entirely within New York, except as required by U.S. Government rules and regulations to be governed by Federal law.

YOU ACKNOWLEDGE THAT YOU HAVE READ THIS AGREEMENT, UNDERSTAND IT, AND AGREE TO BE BOUND BY ITS TERMS AND CONDITIONS. YOU FURTHER AGREE THAT IT IS THE COMPLETE AND EXCLUSIVE STATE-MENT OF THE AGREEMENT BETWEEN US THAT SUPERSEDES ANY PROPOSAL OR PRIOR AGREEMENT, ORAL OR WRITTEN, AND ANY OTHER COMMUNICATIONS BETWEEN US RELATING TO THE SUBJECT MATTER OF THIS AGREEMENT.

U.S. GOVERNMENT RESTRICTED RIGHTS

Use, duplication, or disclosure by the Government is subject to restrictions set forth in subparagraphs (a) through (d) of the Commercial Computer-Restricted Rights clause at FAR 52.227-19 when applicable, or in subparagraph (c) (1) (ii) of the Rights in Technical Data and Computer Software clause at DFARS 252.227-7013, and in similar clauses in the NASA FAR Supplement.

Index

G

S

U

Additional Tools for Certification Preparation

Taking the author-driven, no-nonsense approach that we pioneered with our *Landmark* books, New Riders proudly offers something unique for Windows 2000 administrators—an interesting and discriminating book on Windows 2000 Server, written by someone in the trenches who can anticipate your situation and provide answers you can trust.

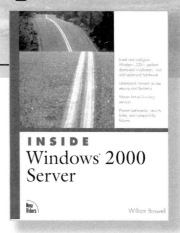

INSIDE
Windows 2000
Server

William Boswell

ISBN: 1-56205-929-7

Windows 2000
ESSENTIAL
REFERENCE

Includes coverage of Server, Workstation, and Professional

Steven Tate, et al.

Architected to be the most navigable, useful, and value-packed reference for Windows 2000, this book uses a creative "telescoping" design that you can adapt to your style of learning. It's a concise, focused, and quick reference for Windows 2000, providing the kind of practical advice, tips, procedures, and additional resources that every administrator will need.

ISBN: 0-7357-0869-X

Understanding the Network is just one of several new titles from New Riders' acclaimed *Landmark* series. This book addresses the audience in practical terminology, and describes the most essential information and tools required to build high-availability networks in a step-by-step implementation format. Each chapter could be read as a standalone, but the book builds progressively toward a summary of the essential concepts needed to put together a wide area network.

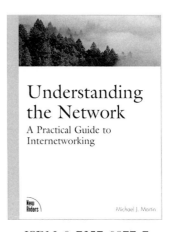

Understanding
the Network
A Practical Guide to
Internetworking

Michael J. Martin

ISBN: 0-7357-0977-7

New Riders
Windows 2000 Resources

Advice and Experience for the Windows 2000 Networker

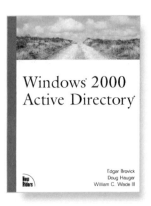

LANDMARK SERIES

We know how important it is to have access to detailed, solution-oriented information on core technologies. *Landmark* books contain the essential information you need to solve technical problems. Written by experts and subjected to rigorous peer and technical reviews, our *Landmark* books are hard-core resources for practitioners like you.

ESSENTIAL REFERENCE SERIES

The *Essential Reference* series from New Riders provides answers when you know what you want to do but need to know how to do it. Each title skips extraneous material and assumes a strong base of knowledge. These are indispensable books for the practitioner who wants to find specific features of a technology quickly and efficiently. Avoiding fluff and basic material, these books present solutions in an innovative, clean format—and at a great value.

CIRCLE SERIES

The *Circle Series* is a set of reference guides that meet the needs of the growing community of advanced, technical-level networkers who must architect, develop, and administer Windows NT/2000 systems. These books provide network designers and programmers with detailed, proven solutions to their problems.

The Road to MCSE Windows 2000

The new Microsoft Windows 2000 track is designed for information technology professionals working in a typically complex computing environment of medium to large organizations. A Windows 2000 MCSE candidate should have at least one year of experience implementing and administering a network operating system.

MCSEs in the Windows 2000 track are required to pass **five core exams and two elective exams** that provide a valid and reliable measure of technical proficiency and expertise.

See below for the exam information and the relevant New Riders title that covers that exam.

Core Exams

MCSE Candidates (Who Have Not Already Passed Windows NT 4.0 Exams) t Take All 4 of the Following Core Exams:

n 70-210: Installing, Configuring Administering Microsoft dows 2000 Professional

n 70-215: Installing, Configuring Administering Microsoft dows 2000 Server

m 70-216: Implementing Administering a Microsoft dows 2000 Network astructure

m 70-217: Implementing Administering a Microsoft dows 2000 Directory ices Infrastructure

ISBN 0-7357-0965-3

ISBN 0-7357-0968-8

ISBN 0-7357-0966-1

ISBN 0-7357-0976-9

or

MCPs Who Have Passed 3 Windows NT 4.0 Exams (Exams 70-067, 70-068, and 70-073) Instead of the 4 Core Exams at Left, May Take:

Exam 70-240: Microsoft Windows 2000 Accelerated Exam for MCPs Certified on Microsoft Windows NT 4.0.

(This accelerated, intensive exam, which will be available until September, 2001, covers the core competencies of exams 70-210, 70-215, 70-216, and 70-217.)

ISBN 0-7357-0979-3

MCSE Training Guide: Core Exams (Bundle)

ISBN 0-7357-0976-9

PLUS - All Candidates - 1 of the Following Core Elective Exams Required:

am 70-219: Designing a Microsoft Windows 2000 Directory vices Infrastructure

am 70-220: Designing Security for a Microsoft Windows 2000 Network

am 70-221: Designing a Microsoft Windows 2000 work Infrastructure

ISBN 0-7357-0983-1

ISBN 0-7357-0984-X

ISBN 0-7357-0982-3

LUS - All Candidates - 2 of the Following Elective Exams Required:

y current MCSE electives (visit www.microsoft.com for a list of current electives)

ected third-party certifications that focus on interoperability will be accepted as an alternative to one tive exam. Please watch for more information on the third-party certifications that will be acceptable.)

am 70-219: Designing a Microsoft Windows 2000 Directory Services Infrastructure

am 70-220: Designing Security for a Microsoft Windows 2000 Network

am 70-221: Designing a Microsoft Windows 2000 Network Infrastructure

am 70-222: Upgrading from Microsoft Windows NT 4.0 to Microsoft Windows 2000

re exams that can also be used as elective exams may only be counted once toward a certification; that is, if a candidate receives lit for an exam as a core in one track, that candidate will not receive credit for that same exam as an elective in that same track.

ISBN 0-7357-0983-1

ISBN 0-7357-0984-X

ISBN 0-7357-0982-3

Books for Networking Professionals

Windows NT/2000 Titles

Windows 2000 TCP/IP

Windows 2000 TCP/IP
By Karanjit Siyan, Ph.D.
2nd Edition
900 pages, $39.99
ISBN: 0-7357-0992-0
Available August 2000

Windows 2000 TCP/IP cuts through the complexities and provides the most informative and complex reference book on Windows 2000-based TCP/IP topics. The book is a tutorial-reference hybrid, focusing on how Microsoft TCP/IP works, using hands-on tutorials and practical examples. Concepts essential to TCP/IP administration are explained thoroughly, and are then related to the practical use of Microsoft TCP/IP in a serious networking environment.

Windows 2000 DNS

Windows 2000 DNS
By Roger Abell, Herman Knief, Andrew Daniels, and Jeffrey Graham
2nd Edition
450 pages, $39.99
ISBN: 0-7357-0973-4

The Domain Name System is a directory of registered computer names and IP addresses that can be instantly located. Without proper design and administration of DNS, computers wouldn't be able to locate each other on the network, and applications like email and Web browsing wouldn't be feasible. Administrators need this information to make their networks work. *Windows 2000 DNS* provides a technical overview of DNS and WINS, and how to design and administer them for optimal performance in a Windows 2000 environment.

Windows 2000 Registry

Windows 2000 Registry
By Sandra Osborrne
2nd Edition
550 pages, $34.99
ISBN: 0-7357-0944-0
Available August 2000

Windows 2000 Registry is a powerful tool for accomplishing many important administration tasks, but little information is available on registry settings and how they can be edited to accomplish these tasks. This title offers unique insight into using registry settings to software or configure client systems in a Windows 2000 environment. The approach of the book is that of revealing the GUI through the registry, allowing system administrators to edit the registry settings to efficiently accomplish critical tasks such as configuration, installation, and management.

Windows 2000 Server
PROFESSIONAL REFERENCE

Windows 2000 Server Professional Reference
By Karanjit Siyan, Ph.D.
3rd Edition
1800 pages, $75.00
ISBN: 0-7357-0952-1

Windows 2000 Server Professional Reference is the benchmark of references available for Windows 2000. Although other titles take you through the setup and implementation phase of the product, no other book provides the user with detailed answers to day-to-day administration problems and tasks. Real-world implementations are key to help administrators discover the most viable solutions for their particular environments. Solid content shows administrators how to manage, troubleshoot, and fix problems that are specific to heterogeneous Windows networks, as well as Internet features and functionality.

Windows 2000 Professional

By Jerry Honeycutt
350 pages, $34.99 US
ISBN: 0-7357-0950-5

Windows 2000 Professional explores the power available to the Windows workstation user on the corporate network and Internet. The book is aimed directly at the power user who values the security, stability, and networking capabilities of NT alongside the ease and familiarity of the Windows 95/98 user interface. This book covers both user and administration topics, with a dose of networking content added for connectivity.

Windows NT Power Toolkit

By Stu Sjouwerman and Ed Tittel
1st Edition
800 pages, $49.99
ISBN: 0-7357-0922-X

This book covers the analysis, tuning, optimization, automation, enhancement, maintenance, and troubleshooting of Windows NT Server 4.0 and Windows NT Workstation 4.0. In most cases, the two operating systems overlap completely. Where the two systems diverge, each platform is covered separately. This advanced title comprises a task-oriented treatment of the Windows NT 4.0 environment. By concentrating on the use of operating system tools and utilities, resource kit elements, and selected third-

party tuning, analysis, optimization, and productivity tools, this book will show you how to carry out everyday and advanced tasks.

Windows 2000 User Management

By Lori Sanders
300 pages, $34.99
ISBN: 1-56205-886-X

With the dawn of Windows 2000, it has become even more difficult to draw a clear line between managing the user and managing the user's environment and desktop. This book, written by a noted trainer and consultant, provides comprehensive, practical advice to managing users and their desktop environments with Windows 2000.

Windows 2000 Deployment & Desktop Management

By Jeffrey A. Ferris, MCSE
1st Edition
400 pages, $34.99
ISBN: 0-7357-0975-0

More than a simple overview of new features and tools, *Windows 2000 Deployment & Desktop Management* is a thorough reference to deploying Windows 2000 Professional to corporate workstations. Incorporating real-world advice and detailed excercises, this book is a one-stop resource for any system administrator, integrator, engineer, or other IT professional.

Planning for Windows 2000

By Eric K. Cone, Jon Boggs, and Sergio Perez
1st Edition
400 pages, $29.99
ISBN: 0-7357-0048-6

Windows 2000 is poised to be one of the largest and most important software releases of the next decade, and you are charged with planning, testing, and deploying it in your enterprise. Are you ready? With this book, you will be. *Planning for Windows 2000* lets you know what the upgrade hurdles will be, informs you of how to clear them, guides you through effective Active Directory design, and presents you with detailed rollout procedures. Eric K. Cone, Jon Boggs, and Sergio Perez give you the benefit of their extensive experiences as Windows 2000 Rapid Deployment Program members by sharing problems and solutions they've encountered on the job.

Inside Windows 2000 Server

By William Boswell
2nd Edition
1533 pages, $49.99
ISBN: 1-56205-929-7

Finally, a totally new edition of New Riders' best-selling *Inside Windows NT Server 4.* Taking the author-driven, no-nonsense approach pioneered with the *Landmark* books, New Riders proudly offers something unique for Windows 2000 administrators—an interesting, discriminating book on Windows 2000 Server written by someone who can anticipate your situation and give you workarounds that won't leave a system unstable or sluggish.

BackOffice Titles

Implementing Exchange Server

By Doug Hauger, Marywynne Leon, and William C. Wade III
1st Edition
400 pages, $29.99
ISBN: 1-56205-931-9

If you're interested in connectivity and maintenance issues for Exchange Server, this book is for you. Exchange's power lies in its capability to be connected to multiple email subsystems to create a "universal email backbone." It's not unusual to have several different and complex systems all connected via email gateways, including Lotus Notes or cc:Mail, Microsoft Mail, legacy mainframe systems, and Internet mail. This book covers all of the problems and issues associated with getting an integrated system running smoothly, and it addresses troubleshooting and diagnosis of email problems with an eye toward prevention and best practices.

Exchange System Administration

By Janice Rice Howd
1st Edition
300 pages, $34.99
ISBN: 0-7357-0081-8

Your Exchange server is installed and connected—now what? Email administration is one of the most critical networking jobs, and Exchange can be particularly troublesome in large, heterogeneous environments. Janice Howd, a noted consultant and teacher with more than a decade of email administration experience, has put together this advanced, concise handbook for daily, periodic, and emergency administration. With in-depth coverage of topics like managing disk resources, replication, and disaster recovery, this is the one reference every Exchange administrator needs.

SQL Server System Administration

By Sean Baird,
Chris Miller, et al.
1st Edition
352 pages, $29.99
ISBN: 1-56205-955-6

How often does your SQL Server go down during the day when everyone wants to access the data? Do you spend most of your time being a "report monkey" for your coworkers and bosses? *SQL Server System Administration* helps you keep data consistently available to your users. This book omits introductory information. The authors don't spend time explaining queries and how they work. Instead, they focus on the information you can't get anywhere else, like how to choose the correct replication topology and achieve high availability of information.

Internet Information Services Administration

By Kelli Adam
1st Edition,
200 pages, $29.99
ISBN: 0-7357-0022-2

Are the new Internet technologies in Internet Information Services giving you headaches? Does protecting security on the Web take up all of your time? Then this is the book for you. With hands-on configuration training, advanced study of the new protocols, the most recent version of IIS, and detailed instructions on authenticating users with the new Certificate Server and implementing and managing the new e-commerce features, *Internet Information Services Administration* gives you the real-life solutions you need. This definitive resource prepares you for upgrading to Windows 2000 by giving you detailed advice on working with Microsoft Management Console, which was first used by IIS.

SMS 2 Administration

By Michael Lubanski
and Darshan Doshi
1st Edition
350 pages, $39.99
ISBN: 0-7357-0082-6

Microsoft's new version of its Systems Management Server (SMS) is starting to turn heads. Although complex, it allows administrators to lower their total cost of ownership and more efficiently manage clients, applications, and support operations. If your organization is using or implementing SMS, you'll need some expert advice. Michael Lubanski and Darshan Doshi can help you get the most bang for your buck with insight, expert tips, and real-world examples. Michael and Darshan are consultants specializing in SMS and have worked with Microsoft on one of the most complex SMS rollouts in the world, involving 32 countries, 15 languages, and thousands of clients.

SQL Server Essential Reference

By Sharon Dooley
1st Edition
500 pages, $35.00 US
ISBN: 0-7357-0864-9

SQL Server Essential Reference is a comprehensive reference of advanced how-tos and techniques for SQL Server 7 administrators. This book provides solid grounding in fundamental SQL Server 7 administrative tasks to help you tame your SQL Server environment. With coverage ranging from installation, monitoring, troubleshooting security, and backup and recovery plans, this book breaks down SQL Server into its key conceptual areas and functions. This easy-to-use reference is a must-have for any SQL Server administrator.

UNIX/Linux Titles

Solaris Essential Reference
By John P. Mulligan
1st Edition
300 pages, $24.95
ISBN: 0-7357-0023-0

Looking for the fastest and easiest way to find the Solaris command you need? Need a few pointers on shell scripting? How about advanced administration tips and sound, practical expertise on security issues? Are you looking for trustworthy information about available third-party software packages that will enhance your operating system? Author John Mulligan—creator of the popular "Unofficial Guide to The Solaris™ Operating Environment" Web site (sun.icsnet.com)—delivers all that and more in one attractive, easy-to-use reference book. With clear and concise instructions on how to perform important administration and management tasks, and key information on powerful commands and advanced topics, *Solaris Essential Reference* is the book you need when you know what you want to do and only need to know how.

Linux System Administration
By M. Carling,
Stephen Degler,
and James Dennis
1st Edition
450 pages, $29.99
ISBN: 1-56205-934-3

As an administrator, you probably feel that most of your time and energy is spent in endless firefighting. If your network has become a fragile quilt of temporary patches and work-arounds, this book is for you. Have you had trouble sending or receiving email lately? Are you looking for a way to keep your network running smoothly with enhanced performance? Are your users always hankering for more storage, services, and speed? *Linux System Administration* advises you on the many intricacies of maintaining a secure, stable system. In this definitive work, the authors address all the issues related to system administration, from adding users and managing file permissions, to Internet services and Web hosting, to recovery planning and security. This book fulfills the need for expert advice that will ensure a trouble-free Linux environment.

GTK+/Gnome Application Development
By Havoc Pennington
1st Edition
492 pages, $39.99
ISBN: 0-7357-0078-8

This title is for the reader who is conversant with the C programming language and UNIX/Linux development. It provides detailed and solution-oriented information designed to meet the needs of programmers and application developers using the GTK+/Gnome libraries. Coverage complements existing GTK+/Gnome documentation, going into more depth on pivotal issues such as uncovering the GTK+ object system, working with the event loop, managing the Gdk substrate, writing custom widgets, and mastering GnomeCanvas.

Developing Linux Applications with GTK+ and GDK
By Eric Harlow
1st Edition
490 pages, $34.99
ISBN: 0-7357-0021-4

We all know that Linux is one of the most powerful and solid operating systems in existence. And as the success of Linux grows, there is an increasing interest in developing applications with graphical user interfaces that take advantage of the power of Linux. In this book, software developer Eric Harlow gives you an indispensable development handbook focusing on the GTK+ toolkit. More than an overview of the elements of application or GUI design, this is a hands-on book that delves into the technology. With in-depth material on the various GUI programming tools and loads of examples, this book's unique focus will give you the information you need to design and launch professional-quality applications.

Linux Essential Reference
By Ed Petron
1st Edition
350 pages, $24.95
ISBN: 0-7357-0852-5

This book is all about getting things done as quickly and efficiently as possible by providing a structured organization for the plethora of available Linux information. We can sum it up in one word—value. This book has it all: concise instructions on how to perform key administration tasks, advanced information on configuration, shell scripting, hardware management, systems management, data tasks, automation, and tons of other useful information. This book truly provides groundbreaking information for the growing community of advanced Linux professionals.

Lotus Notes and Domino Titles

Domino System Administration
By Rob Kirkland, CLP, CLI
1st Edition
850 pages, $49.99
ISBN: 1-56205-948-3

Your boss has just announced that you will be upgrading to the newest version of Notes and Domino when it ships. How are you supposed to get this new system installed, configured, and rolled out to all of your end users? You understand how Lotus Notes works—you've been administering it for years. What you need is a concise, practical explanation of the new features and how to make some of the advanced stuff work smoothly by someone like you, who has worked with the product for years and understands what you need to know. *Domino System Administration* is the answer—the first book on Domino that attacks the technology at the professional level with practical, hands-on assistance to get Domino running in your organization.

Lotus Notes & Domino Essential Reference

By Tim Bankes, CLP
and Dave Hatter, CLP, MCP
1st Edition
650 pages, $45.00
ISBN: 0-7357-0007-9

You're in a bind because you've been asked to design and program a new database in Notes for an important client who will keep track of and itemize myriad inventory and shipping data. The client wants a user-friendly interface that won't sacrifice speed or functionality. You are experienced (and could develop this application in your sleep), but feel you need something to facilitate your creative and technical abilities—something to perfect your programming skills. The answer is waiting for you: *Lotus Notes & Domino Essential Reference*. It's compact and simply designed. It's loaded with information. All of the objects, classes, functions, and methods are listed. It shows you the object hierarchy and the relationship between each one. It's perfect for you. Problem solved.

Networking Titles

Network Intrusion Detection: An Analyst's Handbook

By Stephen Northcutt
1st Edition
267 pages, $39.99
ISBN: 0-7357-0868-1

Get answers and solutions from someone who has been in the trenches. The author, Stephen Northcutt, original developer of the Shadow intrusion detection system and former director of the United States Navy's Information System Security Office at the Naval Security Warfare Center, gives his expertise to intrusion detection specialists, security analysts, and consultants responsible for setting up and maintaining an effective defense against network security attacks.

Understanding Data Communications, Sixth Edition

By Gilbert Held
Sixth Edition
600 pages, $39.99
ISBN: 0-7357-0036-2

Updated from the highly successful fifth edition, this book explains how data communications systems and their various hardware and software components work. More than an entry-level book, it approaches the material in textbook format, addressing the complex issues involved in internetworking today. A great reference book for the experienced networking professional that is written by the noted networking authority, Gilbert Held.

Other Books By New Riders

Microsoft Technologies

ADMINISTRATION

Inside Windows 2000 Server
1-56205-929-7 • $49.99 US / $74.95 CAN
Windows 2000 Essential Reference
0-7357-0869-X • $35.00 US / $52.95 CAN
Windows 2000 Active Directory
0-7357-0870-3 • $29.99 US / $44.95 CAN
Windows 2000 Routing and Remote Access
Service
0-7357-0951-3 • $34.99 US / $52.95 CAN
Windows 2000 Deployment & Desktop
Management
0-7357-0975-0 • $34.99 US / $52.95 CAN
Windows 2000 DNS
0-7357-0973-4 • $39.99 US / $59.95 CAN
Windows 2000 User Management
1-56205-886-X • $34.99 US / $52.95 CAN
Windows 2000 Professional
0-7357-0950-5 • $34.99 US / $52.95 CAN
Planning for Windows 2000
0-7357-0048-6 • $29.99 US / $44.95 CAN
Windows 2000 Server Professional Reference
0-7357-0952-1 • $75.00 US / $111.95 CAN
Windows 2000 Security
0-7357-0991-2 • $39.99 US / $59.95 CAN
Available September 2000
Windows 2000 TCP/IP
0-7357-0992-0 • $39.99 US / $59.95 CAN
Available August 2000
Windows 2000 Registry
0-7357-0944-0 • $34.99 US / $52.95 CAN
Available August 2000
Windows 2000 Terminal Services and Citrix
MetaFrame
0-7357-1005-8 • $39.99 US / $59.95 CAN
Available October 2000
Windows NT/2000 Network Security
1-57870-253-4 • $45.00 US / $67.95 CAN
Available August 2000
Windows NT/2000 Thin Client Solutions
1-57870-239-9 • $45.00 US / $67.95 CAN
Windows 2000 Virtual Private Networking
1-57870-246-1 • $45.00 US / $67.95 CAN
Available September 2000
Windows 2000 Active Directory Design &
Migration
1-57870-242-9 • $45.00 US / $67.95 CAN
Available September 2000
Windows 2000 and Mainframe Integration
1-57870-200-3 • $40.00 US / $59.95 CAN
Windows 2000 Server: Planning and Migration
1-57870-023-X • $40.00 US / $59.95 CAN
Windows 2000 Quality of Service
1-57870-115-5 • $45.00 US / $67.95 CAN
Windows NT Power Toolkit
0-7357-0922-X • $49.99 US / $74.95 CAN
Windows NT Terminal Server and Citrix
MetaFrame
1-56205-944-0 • $29.99 US / $44.95 CAN
Windows NT Performance: Monitoring,
Benchmarking, and Tuning
1-56205-942-4 • $29.99 US / $44.95 CAN

Windows NT Registry: A Settings Reference
1-56205-941-6 • $29.99 US / $44.95 CAN
Windows NT Domain Architecture
1-57870-112-0 • $38.00 US / $56.95 CAN

SYSTEMS PROGRAMMING

Windows NT/2000 Native API Reference
1-57870-199-6 • $50.00 US / $74.95 CAN
Windows NT Device Driver Development
1-57870-058-2 • $50.00 US / $74.95 CAN
DCE/RPC over SMB: Samba and Windows NT
Domain Internals
1-57870-150-3 • $45.00 US / $67.95 CAN

APPLICATION PROGRAMMING

Delphi COM Programming
1-57870-221-6 • $45.00 US / $67.95 CAN
Windows NT Applications: Measuring and
Optimizing Performance
1-57870-176-7 • $40.00 US / $59.95 CAN
Applying COM+
ISBN 0-7357-0978-5 • $49.99 US / $74.95 CAN
Available August 2000

WEB PROGRAMMING

Exchange & Outlook: Constructing Collaborative
Solutions
ISBN 1-57870-252-6 • $40.00 US / $59.95 CAN

SCRIPTING

Windows Script Host
1-57870-139-2 • $35.00 US / $52.95 CAN
Windows NT Shell Scripting
1-57870-047-7 • $32.00 US / $45.95 CAN
Windows NT Win32 Perl Programming:
The Standard Extensions
1-57870-067-1 • $40.00 US / $59.95 CAN
Windows NT/2000 ADSI Scripting for System
Administration
1-57870-219-4 • $45.00 US / $67.95 CAN
Windows NT Automated Deployment and
Customization
1-57870-045-0 • $32.00 US / $45.95 CAN

BACK OFFICE

SMS 2 Administration
0-7357-0082-6 • $39.99 US / $59.95 CAN
Internet Information Services Administration
0-7357-0022-2 • $29.99 US / $44.95 CAN
SQL Server System Administration
1-56205-955-6 • $29.99 US / $44.95 CAN
SQL Server Essential Reference
0-7357-0864-9 • $35.00 US / $52.95 CAN

Open Source

MySQL
0-7357-0921-1 • $49.99 US / $74.95 CAN
Web Application Development with PHP
0-7357-0997-1 • $45.00 US / $67.95 CAN
Available June 2000
PHP Functions Essential Reference
0-7357-0970-X • $35.00 US / $52.95 CAN
Available August 2000

Python Essential Reference
0-7357-0901-7 • $34.95 US / $52.95 CAN
Autoconf, Automake, and Libtool
1-57870-190-2 • $35.00 US / $52.95 CAN
Available August 2000

Linux/Unix

ADMINISTRATION

Linux System Administration
1-56205-934-3 • $29.99 US / $44.95 CAN
Linux Firewalls
0-7357-0900-9 • $39.99 US / $59.95 CAN
Linux Essential Reference
0-7357-0852-5 • $24.95 US / $37.95 CAN
UnixWare 7 System Administration
1-57870-080-9 • $40.00 US / $59.99 CAN

DEVELOPMENT

Developing Linux Applications with GTK+ and
GDK
0-7357-0021-4 • $34.99 US / $52.95 CAN
GTK+/Gnome Application Development
0-7357-0078-8 • $39.99 US / $59.95 CAN
KDE Application Development
1-57870-201-1 • $39.99 US / $59.95 CAN

GIMP

Grokking the GIMP
0-7357-0924-6 • $39.99 US / $59.95 CAN
GIMP Essential Reference
0-7357-0911-4 • $24.95 US / $37.95 CAN

SOLARIS

Solaris Advanced System Administrator's Guide,
Second Edition
1-57870-039-6 • $39.99 US / $59.95 CAN
Solaris System Administrator's Guide, Second
Edition
1-57870-040-X • $34.99 US / $52.95 CAN
Solaris Essential Reference
0-7357-0023-0 • $24.95 US / $37.95 CAN

Networking

STANDARDS & PROTOCOLS

Cisco Router Configuration & Troubleshooting,
Second Edition
0-7357-0999-8 • $34.99 US / $52.95 CAN
Understanding Directory Services
0-7357-0910-6 • $39.99 US / $59.95 CAN
Understanding the Network: A Practical Guide to
Internetworking
0-7357-0977-7 • $39.99 US / $59.95 CAN
Understanding Data Communications, Sixth
Edition
0-7357-0036-2 • $39.99 US / $59.95 CAN
LDAP: Programming Directory Enabled
Applications
1-57870-000-0 • $44.99 US / $67.95 CAN

Gigabit Ethernet Networking
1-57870-062-0 • $50.00 US / $74.95 CAN
Supporting Service Level Agreements
on IP Networks
1-57870-146-5 • $50.00 US / $74.95 CAN
Directory Enabled Networks
1-57870-140-6 • $50.00 US / $74.95 CAN
Differentiated Services for the Internet
1-57870-132-5 • $50.00 US / $74.95 CAN
Quality of Service on IP Networks
1-57870-189-9 • $50.00 US / $74.95 CAN
Designing Addressing Architectures for
Routing and Switching
1-57870-059-0 • $45.00 US / $69.95 CAN
Understanding & Deploying LDAP Directory
Services
1-57870-070-1 • $50.00 US / $74.95 CAN
Switched, Fast and Gigabit Ethernet, Third
Edition
1-57870-073-6 • $50.00 US / $74.95 CAN
Wireless LANs: Implementing Interoperable
Networks
1-57870-081-7 • $40.00 US / $59.95 CAN
Wide Area High Speed Networks
1-57870-114-7 • $50.00 US / $74.95 CAN
The DHCP Handbook
1-57870-137-6 • $55.00 US / $81.95 CAN
Designing Routing and Switching Architectures for
Enterprise Networks
1-57870-060-4 • $55.00 US / $81.95 CAN
Local Area High Speed Networks
1-57870-113-9 • $50.00 US / $74.95 CAN
Available June 2000
Network Performance Baselining
1-57870-240-2 • $50.00 US / $74.95 CAN
Economics of Electronic Commerce
1-57870-014-0 • $49.99 US / $74.95 CAN

SECURITY

Intrusion Detection
1-57870-185-6 • $50.00 US / $74.95 CAN
Understanding Public-Key Infrastructure
1-57870-166-X • $50.00 US / $74.95 CAN
Network Intrusion Detection: An Analyst's
Handbook
0-7357-0868-1 • $39.99 US / $59.95 CAN
Linux Firewalls
0-7357-0900-9 • $39.99 US / $59.95 CAN

LOTUS NOTES/DOMINO

Domino System Administration
1-56205-948-3 • $49.99 US / $74.95 CAN
Lotus Notes & Domino Essential Reference
0-7357-0007-9 • $45.00 US / $67.95 CAN

Software Architecture & Engineering

Designing for the User with OVID
1-57870-101-5 • $40.00 US / $59.95 CAN
Designing Flexible Object-Oriented Systems with
UML
1-57870-098-1 • $40.00 US / $59.95 CAN

Constructing Superior Software
1-57870-147-3 • $40.00 US / $59.95 CAN
A UML Pattern Language
1-57870-118-X • $45.00 US / $67.95 CAN

Professional Certification

TRAINING GUIDES

MCSE Training Guide: Networking Essentials,
2nd Ed.
156205919X • $49.99 US / $74.95 CAN
MCSE Training Guide: Windows NT Server 4,
2nd Ed.
1562059165 • $49.99 US / $74.95 CAN
MCSE Training Guide: Windows NT
Workstation 4, 2nd Ed.
1562059181 • $49.99 US / $74.95 CAN
MCSE Training Guide: Windows NT Server 4
Enterprise, 2nd Ed.
1562059173 • $49.99 US / $74.95 CAN
MCSE Training Guide: Core Exams Bundle, 2nd
Ed.
1562059262 • $149.99 US / $223.95 CAN
MCSE Training Guide: TCP/IP, 2nd Ed.
1562059203 • $49.99 US / $74.95 CAN
MCSE Training Guide: IIS 4, 2nd Ed.
0735708657 • $49.99 US / $74.95 CAN
MCSE Training Guide: SQL Server 7
Administration
0735700036 • $49.99 US / $74.95 CAN
MCSE Training Guide: SQL Server 7
Database Design
0735700044 • $49.99 US / $74.95 CAN
CLP Training Guide: Lotus Notes 4
0789715058 • $59.99 US / $84.95 CAN
MCSD Training Guide: Visual Basic 6 Exams
0735700028 • $69.99 US / $104.95 CAN
MCSD Training Guide: Solution Architectures
0735700265 • $49.99 US / $74.95 CAN
MCSD Training Guide: 4-in-1 Bundle
0735709122 • $149.99 US / $223.95 CAN
CCNA Training Guide
0735700516 • $49.99 US / $74.95 CAN
A+ Certification Training Guide, 2nd Ed.
0735709076 • $49.99 US / $74.95 CAN
Network+ Certification Guide
073570077X • $49.99 US / $74.95 CAN
Solaris 2.6 Administrator Certification Training
Guide, Part I
157870085X • $40.00 US / $59.95 CAN
Solaris 2.6 Administrator Certification Training
Guide, Part II
1578700868 • $40.00 US / $59.95 CAN
MCSE Training Guide: Windows 2000
Professional
0735709653 • $49.99 US / $74.95 CAN •
MCSE Training Guide: Windows 2000 Server
0735709688 • $49.99 US / $74.95 CAN •
MCSE Training Guide: Windows 2000 Network
Infrastructure
0735709661 • $49.99 US / $74.95 CAN
MCSE Training Guide: Windows 2000 Network
Security Design
073570984X • $49.99 US / $74.95 CAN

MCSE Training Guide: Windows 2000 Network
Infrastructure Design
0735709823 • $49.99 US / $74.95 CAN
MCSE Training Guide: Windows 2000 Directory
Svcs. Infrastructure
0735709769 • $49.99 US / $74.95 CAN
MCSE Training Guide: Windows 2000 Directory
Services Design
0735709831 • $49.99 US / $74.95 CAN
MCSE Training Guide: Windows 2000
Accelerated Exam
0735709793 • $59.99 US / $89.95 CAN
MCSE Training Guide: Windows 2000 Core
Exams Bundle
0735709882 • $149.99 US / $223.95 CAN

HOW TO CONTACT US

IF YOU NEED THE LATEST UPDATES ON A TITLE THAT YOU'VE PURCHASED:

1) Visit our Web site at www.newriders.com.

2) Enter the book ISBN number, which is located on the back cover in the bottom right-hand corner, in the site search box on the left navigation bar.

3) Select your book title from the list of search results. On the book page, you'll find available updates and downloads for your title.

IF YOU ARE HAVING TECHNICAL PROBLEMS WITH THE BOOK OR THE CD THAT IS INCLUDED:

1) Check the book's information page on our Web site according to the instructions listed above, or

2) Email us at nrfeedback@newriders.com, or

3) Fax us at 317-581-4663 ATTN: Tech Support.

IF YOU HAVE COMMENTS ABOUT ANY OF OUR CERTIFICATION PRODUCTS THAT ARE NON-SUPPORT RELATED:

1) Email us at nrfeedback@newriders.com, or

2) Write to us at New Riders, 201 W. 103rd St., Indianapolis, IN 46290-1097, or

3) Fax us at 317-581-4663.

IF YOU ARE OUTSIDE THE UNITED STATES AND NEED TO FIND A DISTRIBUTOR IN YOUR AREA:

Please contact our international department at international@mcp.com.

IF YOU ARE INTERESTED IN BEING AN AUTHOR OR TECHNICAL REVIEWER:

Email us at opportunities@newriders.com. Include your name, email address, phone number, and area of technical expertise.

IF YOU WANT TO PREVIEW ANY OF OUR CERTIFICATION BOOKS FOR CLASSROOM USE:

Email us at nrmedia@newriders.com. Your message should include your name, title, training company or school, department, address, phone number, office days/hours, text in use, and enrollment. Send these details along with your request for desk/examination copies and/or additional information.

IF YOU ARE A MEMBER OF THE PRESS AND WOULD LIKE TO REVIEW ONE OF OUR BOOKS:

Email us at nrmedia@newriders.com. Your message should include your name, title, publication or Web site you work for, mailing address, and email address.

Fold here and tape to mail

New Riders Publishing
201 W. 103rd St.
Indianapolis, IN 46290

By opening this package, you are bound by the following agreement: